Marketing text in the world?

Answer:
Experience. Leadership. Innovation.

Marketing
The Core

4/e

Roger A. Kerin
Southern Methodist University

Steven W. Hartley
University of Denver

William Rudelius
University of Minnesota

McGraw-Hill
Irwin

McGraw-Hill Irwin

MARKETING: THE CORE

Published by McGraw-Hill/Irwin, a business unit of The McGraw-Hill Companies, Inc., 1221 Avenue of the Americas, New York, NY, 10020. Copyright © 2011, 2009, 2007, 2004 by The McGraw-Hill Companies, Inc. All rights reserved. No part of this publication may be reproduced or distributed in any form or by any means, or stored in a database or retrieval system, without the prior written consent of The McGraw-Hill Companies, Inc., including, but not limited to, in any network or other electronic storage or transmission, or broadcast for distance learning.

Some ancillaries, including electronic and print components, may not be available to customers outside the United States.

This book is printed on acid-free paper.

1 2 3 4 5 6 7 8 9 0 DOW/DOW 1 0 9 8 7 6 5 4 3 2 1 0

ISBN   978-0-07-811206-5
MHID   0-07-811206-0

Vice president and editor-in-chief: *Brent Gordon*
Editorial director: *Paul Ducham*
Publisher: *Doug Hughes*
Director of development: *Ann Torbert*
Developmental editor: *Gina Huck Siegert*
Editorial coordinator: *Sean M. Pankuch*
Vice president and director of marketing: *Robin J. Zwettler*
Marketing director: *Amee Mosley*
Marketing manager: *Katie Mergen*
Vice president of editing, design, and production: *Sesha Bolisetty*
Lead project manager: *Christine A. Vaughan*
Senior buyer: *Carol A. Bielski*
Lead designer: *Matthew Baldwin*
Senior photo research coordinator: *Jeremy Cheshareck*
Photo researcher: *Mike Hruby*
Media project manager: *Joyce J. Chappetto*
Cover image: *© Getty Images*
Typeface: *10.5/12 Times Roman*
Compositor: *Lachina Publishing Services*
Printer: *R. R. Donnelley*

Library of Congress Cataloging-in-Publication Data

Kerin, Roger A.
   Marketing : the core / Roger A. Kerin, Steven W. Hartley, William Rudelius. -- 4th ed.
    p. cm.
   Includes index.
   ISBN-13: 978-0-07-811206-5 (alk. paper)
   ISBN-10: 0-07-811206-0 (alk. paper)
   1. Marketing. I. Hartley, Steven William. II. Rudelius, William. III. Title.
HF5415.K452 2011
658.8--dc22

                2010030951

www.mhhe.com

A MESSAGE FROM THE AUTHORS

Who could have anticipated the incredible changes the past several years have brought to business and marketing? Every aspect of our business lives—from the economy, to government's role, to consumers' attitudes and lifestyles—has changed recently. While many of the changes have been disruptive, they create a unique challenge and opportunity for our discipline.

Just as business and marketing are ever-changing, so too are the vehicles we use to educate about them. With the introduction of *Connect Marketing* to the Kerin/Hartley/Rudelius text package, comes the addition of the newest member of our team, Erin Steffes. Erin will serve as digital coauthor, overseeing and leading the development of exciting, new application-based technology to meet students where they are today.

Marketing, more than any other discipline, is a field that embraces the changes and facilitates the development of new products, services, and ideas to respond to the new environment and improve our marketplace. You've certainly noticed the new focus on issues such as global economic growth, regulation, consumer spending, and employment. The future promises to bring many additional issues to our attention and to be an extraordinarily exciting time for marketing students. Welcome to what will surely be viewed as one of our most dramatic periods of business history. We are excited to be part of the educational journey you are undertaking!

You'll soon discover that your past experiences as a consumer provide you with a rich source of important information that will become part of your business perspective. As a student of marketing you will learn how the dynamic changes taking place in the world change business practices. In the future, as a marketing manager, you will use your experiences and knowledge to become a true business professional. This text is our effort to help you begin the transition. We appreciate the opportunity to share our own managerial and educational expertise with you. From our perspective, your career starts here.

This edition of *Marketing: The Core* represents a milestone for us for several reasons. First, it is the 4th edition—an important achievement, but more importantly, it is an indication of the need for keeping up with the changes in business and marketing. Second, it is the result of more than 25 years of writing—we began writing in 1983! Finally, this edition represents our most advanced offering as an educational resource. We are committed to (1) building on our past experiences as authors, (2) continuing our leadership role in bringing new topics and perspectives to the classroom, and (3) focusing on pedagogical innovation that truly responds to new teaching and learning styles. We believe our efforts have created the most comprehensive, up-to-date, engaging, and technically advanced textbook available today. We hope you'll agree.

As you begin reading *Marketing: The Core* you will find that it uses an active-learning approach to bring marketing theories and concepts to life. Each chapter offers a balance of traditional and contemporary perspectives presented in an easy-to-read style using familiar examples of companies, products and services, and business strategies. This approach has been a "perfect match" for today's practical, visual, connected learners. The response from students and instructors has been extraordinary. *Marketing: The Core*, and its translations into many other languages, is now the No. 1 marketing text in the world! Our 4th edition strives to continue this tradition of success.

Thank you for the opportunity to share our passion for marketing with you. We hope we succeed in making your studies fun and interesting and that they will become the foundation of an enlightened and productive career!

Roger A. Kerin
Steven W. Hartley
William Rudelius

Preface

Marketing: The Core utilizes a unique, innovative, and effective pedagogical approach developed by the authors through the integration of their combined classroom, college, and university experiences. The elements of this approach have been the foundation for each edition of *Marketing: The Core* and serve as the core of the text and its supplements as they evolve and adapt to changes in student learning styles, the growth of the marketing discipline, and the development of new instructional technologies. The distinctive features of the approach are illustrated below:

High Engagement Style
Easy-to-read, high-involvement, interactive writing style that engages students through active learning techniques.

Rigorous Framework
A pedagogy based on the use of Learning Objectives, Learning Reviews, Learning Objectives Reviews, and supportive student supplements.

Personalized Marketing
A vivid and accurate description of businesses, marketing professionals, and entrepreneurs—through cases, exercises, and testimonials—that allows students to personalize marketing and identify possible career interests.

**Marketing:
The Core, 4/e**
*Pedagogical
Approach*

Traditional and Contemporary Coverage
Comprehensive and integrated coverage of traditional and contemporary concepts.

Marketing Decision Making
The use of extended examples, cases, and videos involving people making marketing decisions.

Integrated Technology
The use of powerful technical resources and learning solutions.

The goal of the 4th edition of *Marketing: The Core* is to create an exceptional experience for today's students and instructors of marketing. The development of *Marketing: The Core* was based on a rigorous process of assessment, and the outcome of the process is a text and package of learning tools that are based on *experience*, *leadership*, and *innovation* in marketing education.

EXPERIENCE

The authors bring extraordinary experience to the development of their text. For example, they have benefited from the feedback of many users of previous editions of *Marketing: The Core*, and its hardcover version—a group that now exceeds more than 1 million students! In addition, the authors are experienced instructors who, in their combined careers, have taught more than 50,000 students, using many teaching styles, tools, and technologies. Finally, as researchers and consultants, the authors have worked with many of the world's leading marketing companies.

How has their experience shaped the 4th edition?

- With the development of **Connect Marketing:**

  Connect Marketing is a comprehensive online resource that enables students to learn faster, study more efficiently, and increase knowledge retention. It contains powerful features that allow assignment management and includes a library and a study center.

- By integrating assessment tools that allow instructors to meet *AACSB assurance-of-learning requirements*:

Each chapter begins with learning objectives, includes in-chapter learning reviews, and ends with learning objective summaries. In addition, the *Marketing: The Core*, 4/e, Test Bank includes learning objective, AACSB learning standards, and Bloom's Taxonomy designations for each question. The combination of the objectives, standards, and taxonomy designation with the specific questions provides an important tool for meeting AACSB assurance-of-learning requirements.

- With the most comprehensive package of *teaching and learning resources*:

The resources that accompany *Marketing: The Core*, 4/e, are a comprehensive and integrated package of tools designed to ensure the highest level of learning for all students and assist in making an instructor's life easier in the process. The resources range from a package of exciting videos, to online quizzes, to comprehensive PowerPoint slides, to the one-of-a-kind *Instructor's Survival Kit*, to an *Instructor's Manual*, to a world-class visually enhanced test bank.

LEADERSHIP

- The first text to integrate new content areas such as ethics, technology, interactive marketing, and marketing dashboards and metrics.

- The first custom-made videos to accompany a marketing text.

- The first teaching package to utilize active learning approaches in the text and the instructor resources.

These are just a few examples that illustrate how the Kerin author team has played a leadership role in the development and delivery of marketing pedagogy. This book is recognized as the market leader in the United States and Canada, and it continues to introduce new, leading-edge principles and practices to students and instructors around the world. How does *Marketing: The Core*, 4/e, continue this tradition of leadership?

- By focusing on ***marketplace diversity:***

  A diverse mix of buyers and sellers populates today's dynamic marketplace. Students will find that successful marketers are not limited to any particular culture, nationality, race, ethnic group, or gender. Rather, like the consumers they serve, marketers mirror society, both domestically and globally. This diversity in today's marketplace is reflected in examples throughout the text.

- By emphasizing the feature *Using Marketing Dashboards:*

The use of marketing dashboards among marketing professionals is popular today. Marketing dashboards graphically portray the metrics that marketers use to track and analyze marketing phenomena and performance. Students will find commonly used measures applied by successful marketers throughout the text and be exposed to their calculation, interpretation, and application.

Using Marketing Dashboards

Which States Are Underperforming?

In 2008, you started your own company to sell a nutritious, high-energy snack you developed. It is now January 2010. As a marketer, you ask yourself, "How well is my business growing?"

Your Challenge The snack is sold in all 50 states. Your goal is 10 percent annual growth. To begin 2010, you want to quickly solve any sales problems that occurred during 2009. You know that states whose sales are stagnant or in decline are offset by those with greater than 10 percent growth.

Studying a table of the sales and percent change versus a year ago in each of the 50 states would work, but it would be very time consuming. A good graphic is better. You choose the following marketing metric, where "sales" is measured in units:

Annual % sales change

$$= \frac{(2009\ \text{Sales} - 2008\ \text{Sales}) \times 100}{2008\ \text{Sales}}$$

You want to act quickly to improve sales. In your map growth that is greater than 10 percent is GREEN, 0 to 10 percent growth is ORANGE, and decline is RED. Notice that you (1) picked a metric and (2) made your own rules that GREEN is good, ORANGE is bad, and RED is very bad.

Your Findings You see that sales growth in the northeastern states is weaker than the 10 percent target, and sales are actually declining in many of the states.

Your Action Marketing is often about grappling with sales shortfalls. You'll need to start by trying to identify and correct the problems in the largest volume states that are underperforming—in this case, in the northeastern United States.

You'll want to do marketing research to see if the problem starts with (1) an external factor, like changing consumer tastes, or (2) an internal factor, like a breakdown in your distribution system.

Annual Percentage Change in Unit Volume, by State

THE NEW-PRODUCT PROCESS

LO6

Finding ways to stimulate American innovation and provide jobs is a vital concern to federal and state governments, business firms, and citizens alike.[18] Organizations conduct global searches to find the scientists and engineers that can achieve the creative breakthroughs needed for new high-tech products. For example, Chinese, Indian, Russian, and other immigrant engineers represent half the total number of engineers in California's Silicon Valley.[19]

To develop new products efficiently, companies such as General Electric and 3M use a specific sequence of steps to make their products ready for market. Figure 10–5 shows the **new-product process**, the seven stages an organization goes through to identify business opportunities and convert them into salable products or services.

new-product process
The seven stages an organization goes through to identify business opportunities and convert them into salable products or services.

Stage 1: New-Product Strategy Development

For companies, *new-product strategy development* is the stage of the new-product process that defines the role for a new product in terms of the firm's overall objectives. During this stage, the firm uses both a SWOT analysis (Chapter 2) and environmental scanning (Chapter 3) to assess its strengths and weaknesses relative to the trends it identifies as opportunities or threats. The outcome not only defines the vital "protocol" for each new-product idea but also identifies the strategic role it might serve in the firm's business portfolio.

New-product development in services, such as buying a stock or airline ticket or watching a Major League Baseball game, is often difficult. Why? Because services

INNOVATION

What if your research showed that many students in your introductory marketing course don't attempt to read and understand the tables and charts in the textbook? What could you do to increase their interest and involvement? Read on for the answer.

To secure the position of *Marketing: The Core 4/e* in the marketplace, the Kerin author team consistently creates innovative pedagogical tools that encourage interaction and match students' learning styles. How did they accomplish this in the 4th edition?

- With the creation of **Lecture Capture** and **eBook**.

  Instructors can now help students focus on in-class discussions rather than note-taking by using **Connect Marketing**'s Lecture Capture to record and distribute lectures and PowerPoint presentations. In addition, the use of eBook provides students with access to the text anytime and anywhere!

- With the increased emphasis on **visually enhanced test questions.**

The *Marketing: The Core*, 4/e, Test Bank has been updated to include the latest concepts and ideas from the textbook. When research by the Kerin author team revealed many students were skipping the tables and charts in the chapter, they decided to do something about it. The visually enhanced test bank includes key tables, charts, ads, and photos from the textbook to emphasize their importance and to reward students who study these key elements.

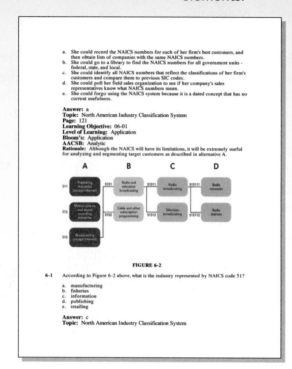

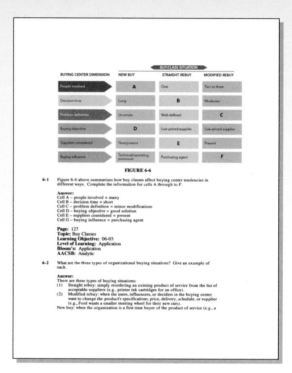

- Through the *Instructor's Survival Kit:*

This supplement is exactly what it says it is: an instructor's guide to surviving in today's classroom. Instructors create interaction by breaking the classroom into teams that analyze marketing problems presented through in-class activities. Students who are kinesthetic (tactile) learners especially appreciate the hands-on product samples, brochures, and props that are tied to specific In-Class Activities (ICAs) that are intended to build on the idea of "cooperative learning."

New and Revised Content

New Coverage of Customer Relationships, Customer Value, and Social Entrepreneurship. The efforts of 3M inventor David Windorski to create customer value with the new 3M Post-it® Flag Highlighter are described in the opening example of Chapter 1 and in the end-of-chapter video case. New examples such as Hot Pockets Sideshots and AT&T's CruiseCast have been added, and a description of new social entrepreneurship activities is included in the section on social responsibility.

New Coverage and Examples of Organizational Strategies. Netflix's changing business models are discussed in Chapter 2. In addition, updated examples of the application of the Boston Consulting Group growth-share matrix to four strategic business units at Kodak are included in the section on business portfolio analysis. Chapter 2 also has an updated introduction to the Using Marketing Dashboards box.

Introduction of the GPS Revolution and New Trends in Marketing. The many new location-aware services and applications that are part of the GPS revolution are described in the opening example of Chapter 3. Recent trends related to authenticity, sustainability, shift to a service economy, mobile marketing, customer-generated content, and regulation related to privacy and customer engagement have been added. Discussions of multicultural advertising, cloud computing, wireless power transmission, software pricing, and the *Internet Tax Freedom Act* are also included.

Integration of "Triple Bottom Line," "Greenwashing," and New Examples of Ethics and Social Responsibility in Marketing. The three concepts of social responsibility presented in Chapter 4 now include a discussion of the balance between people, planet, and profits—the triple bottom line. In addition, the discussion of consumer ethics includes "greenwashing," or the confusion caused by some environmental claims. New examples such as the global ethics program at UPS are also included.

New Examples of Consumer Behavior Concepts. The Chapter 5 discussion of alternative evaluation is now based on information about smart phones such as Apple, BlackBerry, and Motorola. Other new examples include Hershey's Extra Dark Chocolate advertising, which links the product to improved blood pressure; Unilever's advertising, which features an endorsement from cardiologists to reduce perceived risk; and Oscar Mayer's efforts to change attitudes toward its beef bologna product.

Updated Coverage of Sustainable Procurement. The description of JCPenney's paper procurement process has been expanded to include the growing importance of environmental programs in addition to price, quality, capacity, and other traditional factors. Chapter 6 also includes new coverage of Starbucks's sustainable procurement program, which rewards its coffee bean suppliers for ecologically sound growing practices and invests in the farming communities where the coffee is produced.

New Emphasis on Growth in Emerging Economies. Chapter 7 includes a new chapter opening example featuring Dell's global initiative to begin sales and distribution of low-cost personal computers in Asia, Africa, and Latin America. The section on customs now includes a description of how Siemens AG paid an $800 million fine for alleged bribes of government officials.

New Coverage of Neuromarketing, Buy•ology, and Measuring Social Networks. A new section on neuromarketing, which uses brain scans to record responses to marketing actions, has been added to Chapter 8. A new Marketing Matters box discusses Martin Lindstrom's book, *Buy•ology*, and its conclusions about logos, product placement, advertising with sex appeals, and warning labels on cigarettes. Chapter 8 also now includes a new section on data mining on social networks such as Facebook, LinkedIn, and Twitter.

Updated Coverage of Zappos and Wendy's Segmentation Examples, and Expanded Discussion of Perceptual Maps. The Chapter 9 opening example about Zappos.com has been updated to include the addition of clothes, accessories, and electronics to its original segmentation strategy. The chapter also includes coverage of Wendy's new segmentation strategy to include 25- to 49-year-old customers. Finally, the discussion of perceptual maps and the repositioning of chocolate milk has been expanded.

Introduction of Open Innovation, Crowdsourcing, and Industrial Design. The idea generation section of the chapter now covers two methods of using outside sources of new-product ideas—called open innovation and crowdsourcing. In addition, new coverage of industrial design at IDEO, Apple, and Google has been added.

Updated Product Management and Branding Examples. Gatorade's new labels, such as "Bring It" on Gatorade Fierce and "Be Tough" on Gatorade X-Factor, are discussed in the updated opening example for Chapter 11. Ralph Lauren's sunglasses licensing agreement with Luxottica is now included in the Brand Equity section. The section titled "Managing the Marketing of Services" has been updated to utilize the "Eight Ps of Services Marketing" framework. The framework includes product (service), price, place, promotion, people, physical environment, process, and productivity.

New Pricing Examples. Chapter 12 now opens with a description of Vizio's use of pricing to help it become the fastest growing HDTV company in the United States. In addition, the factors that increase or decrease the final price of an offering are illustrated in Chapter 12 with a new example—the Tesla Roadster Sport. The example includes incentives, allowances, and extra fees in the price equation.

Channel Management and Supply Chain Update. The opening example for Chapter 13 describes how Callaway Golf added an online channel and still maintains its traditional retail partnerships with Golf Galaxy, Dick's Sporting Goods, and PGA Tour Superstores. Chapter 13 also describes the trend toward selective distribution for products such as Dell computers.

Introduction of Cyber Monday and Other Retailing Trends. The growing importance of online retailing and the recognition of the Monday after Thanksgiving as "Cyber Monday" are now presented in Chapter 14. New discussions of environmentally friendly retailing, the use of self-service kiosks as a method of making customers co-creators of value, electronic payment options, and "green" mailing and digital catalogs have also been added.

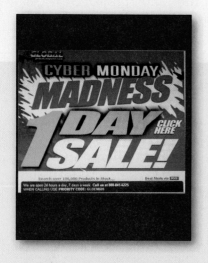

Introduction of the "Age of Engage" in Integrated Marketing Communications. Chapter 15 discusses how consumers increasingly use interactive technologies to stay connected and be engaged with a shopping experience. New forms of integrated marketing communications, including online social viewing rooms for television programs, "fan pages" on Facebook and MySpace, and product integration with video games, have been added to the chapter discussion. New company examples include Gap's iPhone applications, and Columbia Pictures's integrated campaign for the movie *Angels and Demons*. A new Making Responsible Decisions box discusses efforts by direct marketers to "go green" by using recycled paper, removing unresponsive people from mailing lists, and installing "green" printers.

New Advertising and Sales Promotion Examples and Content. Discussion of the trend toward three-dimensional advertising has been added to Chapter 16. Examples of the first 3-D advertisements on the Super Bowl and future applications on digital billboards, video games, and outdoor laser productions are also discussed. Other examples of new forms of advertising include Porsche's "Can You Afford a Porsche?" mobile campaign, Geico's viral video campaign featuring the Geico gecko, Microsoft's "I'm a PC" campaign, and Barack Obama's use of infomercials. Media changes such as the growth of satellite radio, magazines based on user-generated content, the decline of newspaper circulation, the migration of yellow pages users to the Web, the incredible growth of search advertising, and the conversion of outdoor advertising to digital billboards have been added. New examples of sales promotions include Cream of Wheat's online advertising to identify consumers for a coupon offer, Doritos "Crash the Super Bowl" contest asking people to create their own 30-second ad, and *American Idol's* sweepstakes to win a trip to the season finale.

Updated Description of Salesperson Qualifications. An updated description of salesperson qualifications has been added to Chapter 17. In addition, the methods of evaluating prospective salespeople are discussed.

New and Updated Examples of Interactive Marketing. Chapter 18 includes an updated description of Seven Cycles's use of its interactive, multilanguage Web site to become the world's largest custom bicycle frame builder. Trends in online shopping, total online retail sales, and sales by product category through 2012 are also presented. New examples such as customized M&Ms and online shoe sales at Zappos.com have been added to the chapter.

New and Updated Career Information. Appendix B, "Planning a Career in Marketing," has been updated to include new salary information, job descriptions, résumé preparation, job search techniques, and interview skills.

Organization

The 4th edition of **Marketing: The Core** is divided into four parts. Part 1, **"Initiating the Marketing Process,"** looks first at what marketing is and how it creates customer value and customer relationships (Chapter 1). Then Chapter 2 provides an overview of the strategic marketing process that occurs in an organization—which provides a framework for the text. Appendix A provides a sample marketing plan as a reference for students. Chapter 3 analyzes the five major environmental forces in our changing marketing environment, while Chapter 4 provides a framework for including ethical and social responsibility considerations in marketing decisions.

Part 2, **"Understanding Buyers and Markets,"** first describes, in Chapter 5, how individual consumers reach buying decisions. Next, Chapter 6 looks at organizational buyers and markets and how they make purchase decisions. And finally, in Chapter 7, the dynamics of world trade and the influence of cultural diversity on global marketing practices are explored.

In Part 3, **"Targeting Marketing Opportunities,"** Chapter 8 discusses the marketing research function and how information about prospective consumers is linked to marketing strategy and decisions, and sales forecasting. The process of segmenting, targeting markets, and positioning products appears in Chapter 9.

Part 4, **"Satisfying Marketing Opportunities,"** covers the marketing mix elements. The product element is divided into the natural chronological sequence of first developing new products and services (Chapter 10) and then managing the existing products, services, and brands (Chapter 11). In Chapter 12, pricing is covered in terms of the way organizations set prices. Two chapters address the place (distribution) aspects of marketing: "Managing Marketing Channels and Supply Chains" (Chapter 13), and "Retailing and Wholesaling" (Chapter 14). Chapter 15 discusses integrated marketing communications and direct marketing, topics that have grown in importance in the marketing discipline recently. The primary forms of mass market communication—advertising, sales promotion, and public relations—are covered in Chapter 16. Personal selling and sales management are covered in Chapter 17. Chapter 18 describes how interactive and multichannel marketing influences customer value and the customer experience through context, content, community, customization, connectivity, and commerce.

The book closes with Appendix B, "Planning a Career in Marketing," which discusses marketing jobs and how to get them. Other useful supplemental sections include a detailed Glossary, Learning Review Answers, and three indexes (name, company/product, and subject).

Engaging Features

Chapter-opening vignettes introduce students to chapter concepts by using an exciting company as an example. Students are immediately engaged while learning about real-world companies. Chapter 10 discusses *Bloomberg BusinessWeek*'s most innovative company in 2009, Apple.

Marketing Matters boxes highlight real-world examples of customer value creation and delivery and entrepreneurship, giving students further insight into the practical world of marketing.

Marketing Matters >>>>>> customer value

Feature Bloat: Geek Squad to the Rescue!

Adding more features to a product to satisfy more consumers seems like a no-brainer strategy.

Feature Bloat

In fact, most marketing research with potential buyers of a product done *before* they buy shows they say they do want more features in the product. It's when the new product gets home that the "feature bloat" problems occur—often overwhelming the consumer with mind-boggling complexity.

Computers pose a special problem for homeowners because there's no in-house technical assistance like that existing in large organizations. Also, to drive down prices of home computers, usually little customer support service is available. Ever call the manufacturer's toll-free "help" line? One survey showed that 29 percent of the help-line callers wound up swearing at the customer service representative and 21 percent just screamed.

The Geek Squad to the Rescue

Computer feature bloat has given rise to what TV's *60 Minutes* says is "the multibillion-dollar service industry popu-

More than a decade ago he turned his geekiness into the Geek Squad—a group of technically savvy people who can fix almost any computer problem. "There's usually some frantic customer at the door pointing to some device in the corner that will not obey," Stephens explains.

"The biggest complaint about tech support people is rude, egotistical behavior," says Stephens. So he launched the Geek Squad to show some friendly humility by having team members work their wizardry while:

1. Showing genuine concern to customers.
2. Dressing in geeky white shirts, black clip-on ties, and white socks, a "uniform" borrowed from NASA engineers.
3. Driving to customer homes or offices in black-and-white VW "geekmobiles."

Do customers appreciate the 6,000-person Geek Squad, now owned by Best Buy? Robert Stephen explaining, "People will say, 'They saved my data.'" This includes countless college ing on their papers or theses with data lo

Making Responsible Decisions boxes focus on social responsibility, sustainability, and ethics. These boxes provide exciting, current examples of how companies approach these subjects in their marketing strategy.

Making Responsible Decisions >>>>>> ethics

Flexible Pricing—Is There Race and Gender Discrimination in Bargaining for a New Car?

What do 60 percent of prospective buyers dread when looking for a new car? That's right! They dread negotiating the price. Price bargaining demonstrates a shortcoming of flexible pricing when purchasing a new car: the potential for minority price discrimination.

A National Bureau of Economic Research study of 750,000 car purchases indicated that African Americans, Hispanics, and women, on average, paid roughly $423, $483, and $105 more, respectively, for a new car in the $21,000 range than the typical purchaser. Smaller price premiums remained after adjusting for income, education, and other factors that may affect price negotiations.

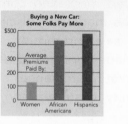

Buying a New Car: Some Folks Pay More

building your marketing plan

To do a consumer analysis for the product—the good, service, or idea—in your marketing plan:

1. Identify the consumers who are most likely to buy your product—the primary target market—in terms of (*a*) their demographic characteristics and (*b*) any other kind of characteristics you believe are important.

2. Describe (*a*) the main points of difference of your product for this group and (*b*) what problem these characteristics help solve for the consumer, in terms of the

first stage in the consumer purchase decision process in Figure 5–1.

3. Identify the one or two key influences for each of the four outside boxes in Figure 5–4: (*a*) marketing mix, (*b*) psychological, (*c*) sociocultural, and (*d*) situational influences.

This consumer analysis will provide the foundation for the marketing mix actions you develop later in your plan.

Building Your Marketing Plan is an end-of-chapter feature that requires students to go through the practical application of creating their own marketing plan.

INSTRUCTOR RESOURCES

Element*	Online Learning Center www.mhhe.com/kerin	Instructor's Resource CD (IRCD)	Other
Using Marketing Dashboards Video	X	X	
Instructor's Manual (IM)	X	X	
Visually Enhanced Test Bank	X	X	
PowerPoint Presentations	X (basic)	X (enhanced)	
Video Cases			Video DVD
Instructor's Survival Kit (ISK)			Stand-alone kit
Instructor Newsletter			e-mail
Connect Marketing			online

*All instructor resources are compatible with any online platform—including Blackboard Learn and eCollege.

- **Using Marketing Dashboards Video:**

  Marketing dashboards are being used among marketing professionals to graphically portray the measures used to track and analyze marketing performance. The key feature in *Marketing: The Core*, 4/e, Using Marketing Dashboards, is a way to bring this concept home to your students. Watch this video and even share it with your class for more information on how dashboards are being used today.

- **Instructor's Manual:**

  The Instructor's Manual (IM) to accompany *Marketing: The Core*, 4/e, is an all-inclusive resource designed to make an instructor's preparation for teaching much easier. The *Instructor's Manual* includes detailed lecture notes from which an instructor can construct a custom lecture.

- **Visually Enhanced Test Bank:**

  We offer more than 5,000 test questions categorized by topic and level of learning (knowledge, comprehension, or application) and correlated to both the Learning Objectives and Bloom's Level of Learning to assist instructors in developing their exams. There are also a number of visually enhanced questions in the test bank that include images and figures from the book itself to ensure student learning and preparation.

- **Test Bank Online:**

  A comprehensive bank of test questions is provided within a computerized test bank powered by McGraw-Hill's flexible digital Web-based testing software program EZ Test Online (www.eztestonline.com). EZ Test Online allows you to create paper and online tests or quizzes in this easy-to-use program.

  Imagine being able to create and access your test or quiz anywhere, at any time, without installing the testing software. Now, with EZ Test Online, instructors can select questions from multiple McGraw-Hill test banks or author their own, and then either print the test for paper distribution or deliver it online.

- **Test Creation**

  - Author/edit questions online using different question type templates.
  - Create printed tests or deliver online to get instant scoring and feedback.
  - Create question pools to offer multiple versions online—great for practice.
  - Export your tests for use in WebCT, Blackboard Learn, and PageOut.
  - Compatible with EZ Test Desktop tests you've already created.
  - Sharing tests with colleagues, adjuncts, and TAs is easy.

- **Online Test Management**

  - Set availability dates and time limits for your quiz or test.
  - Control how your test will be presented.
  - Assign points by question or question type with drop-down menu.
  - Provide immediate feedback to students or delay until all finish the test.
  - Create practice tests online to enable student mastery.
  - Upload your roster to enable student self-registration.

- **Online Scoring and Reporting**

  - Automated scoring for most of EZ Test's numerous question types.
  - Allows manual scoring for essay and other open response questions.
  - Manual re-scoring and feedback is also available.
  - EZ Test's grade book is designed to easily export to your grade book.
  - View basic statistical reports.

- **Support and Help**

  - User's Guide and built-in page specific help.
  - Flash tutorials for getting started on the support site.
  - Support Web site: www.mhhe.com/eztest.
  - Product specialist available at 1-800-331-5094.
  - Online Training: http://auth.mhhe.com/mpss/workshops/.

PowerPoint Presentations:

The PowerPoint Presentations feature slides that can be used and personalized by instructors to help present concepts to students efficiently. The Online Learning Center contains a basic version of the media-enhanced PowerPoint Presentations that are found on the IRCD. The media-enhanced version has video and commercials embedded in the presentations and makes for an engaging and interesting classroom lecture. A third—narrated—version is also available.

New and Revised Video Cases:

A unique series of 18 contemporary marketing video cases is available on DVD. Each video case corresponds with chapter-specific topics and the end-of-chapter case in the text. The video cases feature a variety of organizations and provide balanced coverage of services, consumer products, small businesses, *Fortune* 500 firms, and business-to-business examples. The 4th edition package includes new videos about Google, Under Armour, Pizza Hut, Activeion, and Prince tennis rackets.

Instructor's Survival Kit (ISK):

The Instructor's Survival Kit contains product samples for use in the classroom to illustrate marketing concepts and encourage student involvement and learning, often with teams working on a task for 5 to 30 minutes in class. Today's students are more likely to learn and be motivated by active participative experiences than by classic classroom lecture and discussion. *Marketing: The Core* utilizes product samples from both large and small firms that will interest today's students. When appropriate, sample print and TV ads are included among our PowerPoint Presentations.

Instructor Newsletter:

The Instructor Newsletter has been developed for adopters of *Marketing: The Core*. This newsletter is devoted to providing innovative resources to help improve student learning, offer timely marketing examples, and make class preparation easier. The newsletter includes links to video clips from *Fox Business* and other sources, synopses of articles with in-class discussion questions, teaching tips, and discussion of pedagogical features of *Marketing: The Core*. The newsletter will be offered eight times during the academic year and is available through e-mail and on our Web site, www.mhhe.com/kerin.

Less Managing. More Teaching. Greater Learning.

McGraw-Hill *Connect Marketing* is an online assignment and assessment solution that connects students with the tools and resources they'll need to achieve success.

McGraw-Hill *Connect Marketing* helps prepare students for their future by enabling faster learning, more efficient studying, and higher retention of knowledge.

McGraw-Hill *Connect Marketing* Features

Connect Marketing offers a number of powerful tools and features to make managing assignments easier, so faculty can spend more time teaching. With *Connect Marketing*, students can engage with their coursework anytime and anywhere, making the learning process more accessible and efficient. *Connect Marketing* offers you the features described below.

Simple Assignment Management

With *Connect Marketing*, creating assignments is easier than ever, so you can spend more time teaching and less time managing. The assignment management function enables you to:

- Create and deliver assignments easily with selectable end-of-chapter questions and test bank items.
- Streamline lesson planning, student progress reporting, and assignment grading to make classroom management more efficient than ever.
- Go paperless with the eBook and online submission and grading of student assignments.

Smart Grading

When it comes to studying, time is precious. *Connect Marketing* helps students learn more efficiently by providing feedback and practice material when they need it, where they need it. When it comes to teaching, your time also is precious. The grading function enables you to:

- Have assignments scored automatically, giving students immediate feedback on their work and side-by-side comparisons with correct answers.
- Access and review each response; manually change grades or leave comments for students to review.
- Reinforce classroom concepts with practice tests and instant quizzes.

Instructor Library

The *Connect Marketing* Instructor Library is your repository for additional resources to improve student engagement in and out of class. You can select and use any asset that enhances your lecture. The *Connect Marketing* Instructor Library includes:

- *eBook*
- *PowerPoint Presentations*
- *Video Cases*
- *Instructor's Manual*
- *Instructor's Survival Kit and In-Class Activities Guide CD*

Student Study Center

The *Connect Marketing* Student Study Center is the place for students to access additional resources. The Student Study Center:

- Offers students quick access to lectures, practice materials, eBooks, and more.
- Provides instant practice material and study questions, easily accessible on the go.
- Gives students access to the Personalized Learning Plan.

Student Progress Tracking

Connect Marketing keeps instructors informed about how each student, section, and class is performing, allowing for more productive use of lecture and office hours. The progress-tracking function enables you to:

- View scored work immediately and track individual or group performance with assignment and grade reports.
- Access an instant view of student or class performance relative to learning objectives.
- Collect data and generate reports required by many accreditation organizations, such as AACSB.

McGraw-Hill *Connect Plus Marketing*

McGraw-Hill reinvents the textbook learning experience for the modern student with *Connect Plus Marketing*. A seamless integration of an eBook and *Connect Marketing*, *Connect Plus Marketing* provides all of the *Connect Marketing* features plus the following:

- An integrated eBook, allowing for anytime, anywhere access to the textbook.

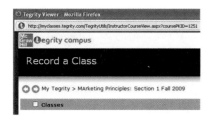

Lecture Capture

Increase the attention paid to lecture discussion by decreasing the attention paid to note taking. For an additional charge, Lecture Capture offers new ways for students to focus on the in-class discussion, knowing they can revisit important topics later. Lecture Capture enables you to:

- Record and distribute your lecture with the click of a button.
- Record and index PowerPoint Presentations and anything shown on your computer so it is easily searchable, frame by frame.
- Offer access to lectures anytime and anywhere by computer, iPod, or mobile device.
- Increase intent listening and class participation by easing students' concerns about note-taking. Lecture Capture will make it more likely you will see students' faces, not the tops of their heads.

- Dynamic links between the problems or questions you assign to your students and the location in the eBook where that problem or question is covered.
- A powerful search function to pinpoint and connect key concepts in a snap.

In short, *Connect Marketing* offers you and your students powerful tools and features that optimize your time and energies, enabling you to focus on course content, teaching, and student learning. *Connect Marketing* also offers a wealth of content resources for both instructors and students. This state-of-the-art, thoroughly tested system supports you in preparing students for the world that awaits. For more information about Connect, go to **www.mcgrawhillconnect.com**, or contact your local McGraw-Hill sales representative.

Tegrity Campus: Lectures 24/7

Tegrity Campus is a service that makes class time available 24/7 by automatically capturing every lecture in a searchable format for students to review when they study and complete assignments. With a simple one-click start-and-stop process, you capture all computer screens and corresponding audio. Students can replay any part of any class with easy-to-use browser-based viewing on a PC or Mac.

Educators know that the more students can see, hear, and experience class resources, the better they learn. In fact, studies prove it. With Tegrity Campus, students quickly recall key moments by using Tegrity Campus's unique search feature. This search helps students efficiently find what they need, when they need it, across an entire semester of class recordings. Help turn all your students' study time into learning moments immediately supported by your lecture.

To learn more about Tegrity watch a two-minute Flash demo at **http://tegritycampus.mhhe.com**.

Assurance of Learning Ready

Many educational institutions today are focused on the notion of *Assurance of Learning*, an important element of some accreditation standards. *Marketing: The Core* is designed specifically to support your assurance of learning initiatives with a simple, yet powerful solution.

Each test bank question for *Marketing: The Core, 4/e* maps to a specific chapter learning outcome/objective listed in the text. You can use our test bank software, EZ Test and EZ Test Online, or *Connect Marketing* to easily query for learning outcomes/objectives that directly relate to the learning objectives for your course. You can then use the reporting features of EZ Test to aggregate student results in a similar fashion, making the collection and presentation of assurance-of-learning data simple and easy.

AACSB Statement

The McGraw-Hill Companies is a proud corporate member of AACSB International. Understanding the importance and value of AACSB accreditation, *Marketing: The Core*, 4/e, recognizes the curricula guidelines detailed in the AACSB standards for business accreditation by connecting selected questions in the test bank to the six general knowledge and skill guidelines in the AACSB standards.

The statements contained in *Marketing: The Core*, 4/e, are provided only as a guide for the users of this textbook. The AACSB leaves content coverage and assessment within the purview of individual schools, the mission of the school, and the faculty. While *Marketing: The Core*, 4/e, and the teaching package make no claim of any specific AACSB qualification or evaluation, we have labeled selected questions according to the six general knowledge and skills areas.

McGraw-Hill Customer Care Contact Information

At McGraw-Hill, we understand that getting the most from new technology can be challenging. That's why our services don't stop after you purchase our products. You can e-mail our product specialists 24 hours a day to get product-training online. Or you can search our knowledge bank of Frequently Asked Questions on our support Web site. For Customer Support, call **800-331-5094**, e-mail **hmsupport@ mcgraw-hill.com,** or visit **www.mhhe.com/support.** One of our technical support analysts will be able to assist you in a timely fashion.

Acknowledgments

To ensure continuous improvement of our textbook and supplements we have utilized an extensive review and development process for each of our past editions. Building on that history, the *Marketing: The Core*, 4th edition, development process included several phases of evaluation and a variety of stakeholder audiences (students, instructors, etc.).

Reviewers who were vital in the changes that were made to this edition include:

Wendi Achey
Northampton Community College

Praveen Aggarwal
University of Minnesota—Duluth

Harry Christopher Anicich
California State University—Fullerton

April Atwood
University of Washington

Timothy W. Aurand
Northern Illinois University

Leta Beard
University of Washington

Christopher P. Blocker
Baylor University

Elten Briggs
University of Texas—Arlington

Glen H. Brodowsky
California State University—San Marcos

Kendrick W. Brunson
Liberty University

Mary Conran
Temple University

Jane Cromartie
University of New Orleans

Richard M. Dailey
University of Texas—Arlington

Clay Daughtrey
Metropolitan State College

Shanmugasundaram Doraiswamy
Northeastern Illinois University

Darrin C. Duber-Smith
Metropolitan State College

Phyllis Fein
SUNY Westchester Community College

Tracy Fulce
Oakton Community College

Roland Gau
Tulane University

Kimberly D. Grantham
University of Georgia

Donna M. Hope
Nassau Community College

Jianfeng Jiang
Northeastern Illinois University

Ann T. Kuzma
Minnesota State University—Mankato

Jane Lang
East Carolina University

Yong Liu
University of Arizona

Ritu Lohtia
Georgia State University

Harold W. Lucius
Rowan University

Sanjay S. Mehta
Sam Houston State University

James A. Muncy
Valdosta State University

Linda Pettijohn
Missouri State University

Robert Pitts
College of Charleston

Timothy H. Reisenwitz
Valdosta State University

William Rice
California State University—Fullerton

Bruce Robertson
San Francisco State University

Robert Rouwenhorst
University of Iowa

Philip Shum
William Paterson University

Rob Simon
University of Nebraska—Lincoln

Julie Sneath
University of South Alabama

Sushila Umashankar
University of Arizona

Bronis J. Verhage
Georgia State University

Joann Wayman
Columbia College

Letty Workman
Utah Valley University

James E. Zemanek, Jr.
East Carolina University

The preceding section demonstrates the amount of feedback and developmental input that went into this project, and we are deeply grateful to the numerous people who have shared their ideas with us. Reviewing a book or supplement takes an incredible amount of energy and attention. We are glad so many of our colleagues took the time to do it. Their comments have inspired us to do our best.

Reviewers who contributed to the first three editions of this book include:

Nadia J. Abgrab
Kerri Acheson
Roy Adler
Christie Amato
Linda Anglin
Ismet Anitsal
William D. Ash

Corinne Asher
Gerard Athaide
Andy Aylesworth
Patricia Baconride
Ainsworth Bailey
Siva Balasubramanian
A. Diane Barlar

James H. Barnes
Karen Becker-Olsen
Frederick J. Beier
Thom J. Belich
Joseph Belonax
Jill Bernaciak
Thomas M. Bertsch

Parimal Bhagat
Carol Bienstock
Kevin W. Bittle
Brian Bittner
Chris Black
Jeff Blodgett
Nancy Bloom

Charles Bodkin

Larry Borgen

Koren Borges

Nancy Boykin

Thomas Brashear

Martin Bressler

Bruce Brown

William Brown

William G. Browne

Judy Bulin

David J. Burns

Alan Bush

John Buzza

Stephen Calcich

Nate Calloway

William J. Carner

Larry Carter

Gerald O. Cavallo

Carmina Cavazos

S. Tamer Cavusgil

Bruce Chadbourne

S. Choi Chan

Joel Chilsen

Sang Choe

Kay Chomic

Melissa Clark

Alfred Cole

Deb Coleman

Mark Collins

Howard Combs

Clare Comm

Clark Compton

Cristanna Cook

Sherry Cook

John Coppelt

John Cox

Scott Cragin

Donna Crane

Ken Crocker

Joe Cronin

Linda Crosby

James Cross

Lowell E. Crow

Brent Cunningham

John H. Cunningham

Bill Curtis

Bob Dahlstrom

Dan Darrow

Neel Das

Hugh Daubek

Martin Decatur

Francis DeFea

Joseph Defilippe

Linda M. Delene

Tino DeMarco

Jobie Devinney-Walsh

Alan Dick

Irene Dickey

Paul Dion

William B. Dodds

James H. Donnelly

Michael Dore

Michael Drafke

Lawrence Duke

Bob Dwyer

Eddie V. Easley

Eric Ecklund

Roger W. Egerton

Steven Engel

Barbara Evans

Ken Fairweather

Bagher Fardanesh

Larry Feick

Lori Feldman

Kevin Feldt

Karen Flaherty

Theresa Flaherty

Elizabeth R. Flynn

Leisa Flynn

Charles Ford

Renee Foster

Judy Foxman

Donald Fuller

Stan Garfunkel

Stephen Garrott

Glen Gelderloos

Susan Geringer

David Gerth

James Ginther

Susan Godar

Dan Goebel

Marc Goldberg

Leslie A. Goldgehn

Kenneth Goodenday

Robert Gorman

Darrell Goudge

James Gould

Kimberly Grantham

Nancy Grassilli

Barnett Greenberg

James L. Grimm

Pamela Grimm

Pola B. Gupta

Amy Handlin

Richard Hansen

Donald V. Harper

Dotty Harpool

Lynn Harris

Robert C. Harris

Ernan Haruvy

Santhi Harvey

Ron Hasty

James A. Henley, Jr.

Ken Herbst

Jonathan Hibbard

Richard M. Hill

Nathan Himelstein

Donald Hoffer

Al Holden

Fred Honerkamp

Kristine Hovsepian

Jarrett Hudnal

Mike Hyman

Rajesh Iyer

Donald R. Jackson

Kenneth Jameson

David Jamison

Deb Jansky

James C. Johnson

Wesley Johnston

Keith Jones

Robert Jones

Mary Joyce

Jacqueline Karen

Janice Karlen

Sudhir Karunakaran

Rajiv Kashyap

Herbert Katzenstein

Philip Kearney

George Kelley

Katie Kemp

Ram Kesaran

Roy Klages

John Kohn

Douglas Kornemann

Kathleen Krentler

Terry Kroeten

Anand Kuman

Nanda Kumar

Michelle Kunz

Ann Kuzma

John Kuzma

Priscilla LaBarbera

Duncan G. LaBay

Christine Lai

Jay Lambe

Tim Landry

Jane Lang

Irene Lange

Richard Lapidus

Donald Larson

Ron Larson

Ed Laube

J. Ford Laumer

Debra Laverie

Marilyn Lavin

Gary Law

Robert Lawson

Wilton Lelund

Karen LeMasters

Richard C. Leventhal

Leonard Lindenmuth

Natasha Lindsey

Ann Little

Eldon L. Little

Yunchuan Liu

James Lollar

Paul Londrigan

Lynn Loudenback

Ann Lucht

Harold Lucius

Mike Luckett

Robert Luke

Michael R. Luthy

Richard J. Lutz

Marton L. Macchiete

Rhonda Mack

Patricia Manninen

Kenneth Maricle

Tom Marshall

Elena Martinez

James Maskulka

Carolyn Massiah

Tamara Masters

Charla Mathwick

Michael Mayo

James McAlexander

Peter J. McClure

Phyllis McGinnis

Jim McHugh

Gary F. McKinnon

Ed McLaughlin

Jo Ann McManamy

Kristy McManus

Bob McMillen

Samuel E. McNeely

Lee Meadow

James Meszaros

George Miaoulis

Ronald Michaels

Herbert A. Miller

Stephen W. Miller

Soon Hong Min

Theodore Mitchell

Steven Moff

Kim Montney

Rex Moody

Melissa Moore

Linda Morable

Fred Morgan

Gordon Mosley
William Motz
Rene Mueller
Donald F. Mulvihill
James Munch
James A. Muncy
Jeanne Munger
Linda Munilla
Bill Murphy
Brian Murray
Janet Murray
Keith Murray
Joseph Myslivec
Sunder Narayanan
Nancy Nentl
Bob Newberry
Eric Newman
Donald G. Norris
Carl Obermiller
Dave Olson
Lois Olson
James Olver
Ben Oumlil
Notis Pagiavlas
Allan Palmer
Dennis Pappas
June E. Parr
Philip Parron
David Terry Paul
Richard Penn
John Penrose
William Pertula
Michael Peters
Susan Peterson
Renee Pfeifer-Luckett
Bruce Pilling
William S. Piper
Stephen Pirog
Gary Poorman
Vonda Powell
Carmen Powers
Joe Puzi
Edna Ragins
Priyali Rajagopal
Daniel Rajaratnam
James P. Rakowski
Rosemary Ramsey
Barbar Ribbens
Cathie Rich-Duval
Joe Ricks
Heikki Rinne
Linda Rochford
William Rodgers
Christopher Roe
Jean Romeo

Teri Root
Tom Rossi
Vicki Rostedt
Heidi Rottier
Larry Rottmeyer
Robert W. Ruekert
Maria Sanella
Charles Schewe
Starr F. Schlobohm
Roberta Schultz
Lisa M. Sciulli
Stan Scott
Eberhard Seheuling
Harold S. Sekiguchi
Doris M. Shaw
Eric Shaw
Ken Shaw
Dan Sherrel
Philip Shum
Susan Sieloff
Bob E. Smiley
Allen Smith
David Smith
Kimberly D. Smith
Ruth Ann Smith
Sandra Smith
Norman Smothers
James V. Spiers
Craig Stacey
Miriam B. Stamps
Cheryl Stansfield
Joe Stasio
Tom Stevenson
Kathleen Stuenkel
Scott Swan
Rick Sweeney
Michael Swenson
Robert Swerdlow
Vincent P Taiani
Clint Tankersley
Ruth Taylor
Andrew Thacker
Tom Thompson
Scott Thorne
Dan Toy
Fred Trawick
Thomas L. Trittipo
Gary Tucker
Ottilia Voegtli
Jeff von Freymann
Gerald Waddle
Randall E. Wade
Blaise Waguespack, Jr.
Harlan Wallingford
Mark Weber

Don Weinrauch
Robert S. Welsh
Ron Weston
Michelle Wetherbee
Sheila Wexler
Max White
Alan Whitebread
James Wilkins
Erin Wilkinson
Janice Williams
Kaylene Williams
Robert Williams
Jerrry W. Wilson
Joseph Wisenblit
Robert Witherspoon
Kim Wong
Van R. Wood
Wendy Wood
Lauren Wright
William R. Wynd
Donna Yancey
Poh-Lin Yeoh
Mark Young
Sandra Young
Gail M. Zank
Jim Zemanek
Leon Zurawicki

Thanks are also due to many faculty members who contributed to the text chapters and cases. They include Linda Rochford of the University of Minnesota—Duluth; Kevin Upton of the University of Minnesota—Twin Cities; Nancy Nentl of Metropolitan State University; David Brennan of the University of St. Thomas; and Leigh McAlister of the University of Texas at Austin. Michael Vessey provided cases, research assistance, many special images, and led our efforts on the Instructor's Manual, In-Class Activities, and Instructor's Survival Kit. Rick Armstrong of Armstrong Photography, Nick Kaufman and Michelle Morgan of NKP Media, Bruce McLean of World Class Communication Technologies, Paul Fagan of Fagan Productions, Dan Hundley and George Heck of Token Media, Martin Walter of White Room Digital, Scott Bolin of Bolin Marketing, and Dan Stephenson of the Philadelphia Phillies produced the videos. Margaret Edmunds of Electronic Office was responsible for the revision of the test bank.

Many businesspeople also provided substantial assistance by making available information that appears in the text, videos, and supplements—much of it for the first time in college materials. Thanks are due to David Ford and Don Rylander of Ford Consulting Group; Mark Rehborg of Tony's Pizza; Vivian Callaway, Sandy Proctor, and Anna Stoesz of General Mills; David Windorski of 3M; Nicholas Skally, Linda Glassel, and Tyler Herring of Prince Sports; David Montgomery, David Buck, and Bonnie Clark of the Philadelphia Phillies; Todd Schaeffer, Amber Arnseth, and Chris Deets of Activeion Cleaning Solutions; Ian Wolfman of imc^2; Brian Niccol of Pizza Hut; Stan Jacot of ConAgra Snack Foods; Sandra Smith of Smith Communications; Erin Patton of the MasterMind Group, LLC; Kim Nagele of JCPenney, Inc.; Charles Besio of the Sewell Automotive Group, Inc.; Kate Hodebeck of Cadbury Schweppes America's Beverages, Inc.; Beverly Roberts of U.S. Census Bureau; Jennifer Gebert of Ghirardelli Chocolate Company; Michael Kuhl of 3M Sports and Leisure; Barbara Davis of Ken Davis Products, Inc.; Kerry Barnett of Valassis Communications; and Leslie Herman and Jeff Gerst of Bolin Marketing working with Carma Laboratories (Carmex). We also acknowledge the special help of a team that worked with us on the Fallon Worldwide In-Class Activity: Fred Senn, Bruce Blister, Kevin Flat, Ginny Grossman, Kim Knutson, Julie Smith, Erin Taut, and Rob White.

Staff support from the Southern Methodist University, the University of Denver, and the University of Minnesota was essential. We gratefully acknowledge the help of Wanda Hanson, Jeanne Milazzo, and Gloria Valdez for their many contributions.

Checking countless details related to layout, graphics, clear writing, and last-minute changes to ensure timely examples is essential for a sound and accurate textbook. This also involves coordinating activities of authors, designers, editors, compositors, and production specialists. Christine Vaughan of McGraw-Hill/Irwin's production staff and editorial consultant Gina Huck Siegert of Imaginative Solutions, Inc., provided the necessary oversight and hand-holding for us, while retaining a refreshing sense of humor, often under tight deadlines. Thank you again.

Finally, we acknowledge the professional efforts of the McGraw-Hill/Irwin staff. Completion of our book and its many supplements required the attention and commitment of many editorial, production, marketing, and research personnel. Our Burr Ridge–based team included Paul Ducham, Doug Hughes, Sankha Basu, Sean Pankuch, Melissa Hernandez, Carol Bielski, Matthew Baldwin, Jeremy Cheshareck, Sue Lombardi, Katie Mergen, and many others. In addition we relied on Michael Hruby for constant attention regarding photo elements of the text. Handling the countless details of our text, supplement, and support technologies has become an incredibly complex challenge. We thank all these people for their efforts!

Roger A. Kerin
Steven W. Hartley
William Rudelius

BRIEF CONTENTS

Part 1   Initiating the Marketing Process
              1 Creating Customer Relationships and Value through Marketing   2
              2 Developing Successful Marketing and Organizational Strategies   20
                 APPENDIX A   Building an Effective Marketing Plan   44
              3 Scanning the Marketing Environment   58
              4 Ethical and Social Responsibility in Marketing   78

Part 2   Understanding Buyers and Markets
              5 Understanding Consumer Behavior   94
              6 Understanding Organizations as Customers   118
              7 Understanding and Reaching Global Consumers and Markets   136

Part 3   Targeting Marketing Opportunities
              8 Marketing Research: From Customer Insights to Actions   160
              9 Market Segmentation, Targeting, and Positioning   186

Part 4   Satisfying Marketing Opportunities
              10 Developing New Products and Services   208
              11 Managing Successful Products, Services, and Brands   232
              12 Pricing Products and Services   260
              13 Managing Marketing Channels and Supply Chains   286
              14 Retailing and Wholesaling   310
              15 Integrated Marketing Communications and Direct Marketing   332
              16 Advertising, Sales Promotion, and Public Relations   356
              17 Personal Selling and Sales Management   380
              18 Implementing Interactive and Multichannel Marketing   402

                 APPENDIX B   Planning a Career in Marketing   424

Glossary   434
Learning Review Answers   440
Chapter Notes   447
Credits   469
Name Index   471
Company/Product Index   477
Subject Index   483

DETAILED CONTENTS

Part 1   Initiating the Marketing Process

1   CREATING CUSTOMER RELATIONSHIPS AND VALUE THROUGH MARKETING   2

Researching How College Students Study to Launch a New Product at 3M   3

What Is Marketing?   4

    Marketing and Your Career   4

    Marketing Matters: Payoff for the Joys (!) and Sleepless Nights (?) of Starting Your Own Small Business: YouTube!!!!   5

    Marketing: Delivering Benefits to the Organization, Its Stakeholders, and Society   5

    The Diverse Factors Influencing Marketing Activities   6

How Marketing Discovers and Satisfies Consumer Needs   7

    Discovering Consumer Needs   7

    The Challenge: Meeting Consumer Needs with New Products   7

    Satisfying Consumer Needs   9

The Marketing Program: How Customer Relationships Are Built   10

    Customer Value and Customer Relationships   10

    Relationship Marketing and the Marketing Program   11

    3M's Strategy and Marketing Program to Help Students Study   12

How Marketing Became So Important   14

    Evolution of the Market Orientation   14

    Ethics and Social Responsibility: Balancing Interests of Groups   14

    The Breadth and Depth of Marketing   15

Learning Objectives Review   16

Focusing on Key Terms   17

Applying Marketing Knowledge   17

Building Your Marketing Plan   18

Video Case 1: 3M's Post-it® Flag Highlighter: Extending the Concept!   18

2   DEVELOPING SUCCESSFUL MARKETING AND ORGANIZATIONAL STRATEGIES   20

Be an Entrepreneur: Get an "A" in a Correspondence Course in Ice Cream Making!   21

Today's Organizations   22

    Kinds of Organizations   22

What Is Strategy? *22*
Structure of Today's Organizations *22*

**Making Responsible Decisions: The Global Dilemma:
How to Achieve Sustainable Development 23**

Strategy in Visionary Organizations *24*
Organizational Foundation: Why Does It Exist? *24*
Organizational Direction: What Will It Do? *26*
Organizational Strategies: How Will It Do It? *27*
Tracking Strategic Performance with Marketing
Dashboards *27*

**Using Marketing Dashboards: How Well Is Ben & Jerry's
Doing? 29**

Setting Strategic Directions *29*
A Look Around: Where Are We Now? *29*
Growth Strategies: Where Do We Want to Go? *31*
The Strategic Marketing Process *34*
The Planning Phase of the Strategic Marketing Process *34*
The Implementation Phase of the Strategic Marketing
Process *37*
The Evaluation Phase of the Strategic Marketing Process *38*

Learning Objectives Review 40
Focusing on Key Terms 41
Applying Marketing Knowledge 41
Building Your Marketing Plan 41

*Video Case 2: General Mills Warm Delights™: Indulgent,
Delicious, and Gooey! 42*

Appendix A   Building an Effective Marketing Plan 44

3   SCANNING THE MARKETING ENVIRONMENT 58

Where in the World Are You? In the Middle of the GPS
Revolution! *59*
Environmental Scanning *60*
An Environmental Scan of Today's Marketplace *60*
Social Forces *60*
Demographics *60*

**Making Responsible Decisions: Millennials Are Making a
Difference—through Environmental Sustainability! 63**

Culture *64*
Economic Forces *65*
Macroeconomic Conditions *65*
Consumer Income *66*
Technological Forces *67*
Technology of Tomorrow *67*
Technology's Impact on Customer Value *68*

Electronic Business Technologies   *69*

Competitive Forces   *69*

Alternative Forms of Competition   *69*

Small Businesses as Competitors   *70*

Regulatory Forces   *70*

Protecting Competition   *70*

Product-Related Legislation   *70*

Pricing-Related Legislation   *72*

Distribution-Related Legislation   *72*

Marketing Matters: The Web Allows New Uses and Misuses of Trademarks   73

Advertising- and Promotion-Related Legislation   *73*

Control through Self-Regulation   *73*

Learning Objectives Review   74

Focusing on Key Terms   75

Applying Marketing Knowledge   75

Building Your Marketing Plan   75

Video Case 3: Geek Squad: A New Business for a New Environment   75

4   ETHICAL AND SOCIAL RESPONSIBILITY IN MARKETING   78

Responsibility Matters at Anheuser-Busch   *79*

Nature and Significance of Marketing Ethics   *80*

Ethical/Legal Framework in Marketing   *80*

Current Perceptions of Ethical Behavior   *80*

Understanding Ethical Marketing Behavior   *81*

Societal Culture and Norms   *81*

Business Culture and Industry Practices   *82*

Corporate Culture and Expectations   *83*

Making Responsible Decisions: Corporate Conscience in the Cola War   84

Your Personal Moral Philosophy and Ethical Behavior   *85*

Understanding Social Responsibility in Marketing   *86*

Three Concepts of Social Responsibility   *86*

Marketing Matters: Will Consumers Switch Brands for a Cause? Yes, If . . .   88

The Social Audit and Sustainable Development: Doing Well by Doing Good   *88*

Turning the Table: Consumer Ethics and Social Responsibility   *89*

Learning Objectives Review   90

Focusing on Key Terms   91

Applying Marketing Knowledge   91

Building Your Marketing Plan   91

Video Case 4: Starbucks Corporation: Serving More Than Coffee 91

Part 2   Understanding Buyers and Markets

5   **UNDERSTANDING CONSUMER BEHAVIOR**   94

Enlightened Carmakers Know What Custom(h)ers Value   *95*
Consumer Purchase Decision Process and Experience   *96*
    Problem Recognition: Perceiving a Need   *96*
    Information Search: Seeking Value   *96*
    Alternative Evaluation: Assessing Value   *97*
    Purchase Decision: Buying Value   *98*
    Postpurchase Behavior: Value in Consumption or Use   *98*

    Marketing Matters: The Value of a Satisfied Customer to the Company   99

    Consumer Involvement and Problem-Solving Variations   *99*
    Situational Influences   *101*
Psychological Influences on Consumer Behavior   *102*
    Motivation and Personality   *102*
    Perception   *103*

    Making Responsible Decisions: The Ethics of Subliminal Messages   104

    Learning   *104*
    Values, Beliefs, and Attitudes   *106*
    Consumer Lifestyle   *107*
Sociocultural Influences on Consumer Behavior   *108*
    Personal Influence   *108*

    Marketing Matters: BzzAgent—The Buzz Experience   109

    Reference Groups   *110*
    Family Influence   *110*
    Culture and Subculture   *112*

Learning Objectives Review   115
Focusing on Key Terms   115
Applying Marketing Knowledge   115
Building Your Marketing Plan   116

Video Case 5: Best Buy: Using Customer Centricity to Connect with Consumers   116

6   **UNDERSTANDING ORGANIZATIONS AS CUSTOMERS**   118

Buying Is Marketing, Too! Purchasing Publication Paper at JCPenney   *119*
The Nature and Size of Organizational Markets   *120*
    Industrial Markets   *120*

Reseller Markets *121*
Government Markets *121*
Measuring Domestic and Global Industrial, Reseller, and
Government Markets *121*
Characteristics of Organizational Buying *122*
Demand Characteristics *122*
Size of the Order or Purchase *122*
Number of Potential Buyers *123*
Organizational Buying Objectives *123*
Organizational Buying Criteria *124*
Buyer–Seller Relationships and Supply Partnerships *124*

**Marketing Matters: Harley-Davidson's Supplier
Collaboration Creates Customer Value . . . and a Great
Ride 125**

**Making Responsible Decisions: Sustainable Procurement
for Sustainable Growth 126**

The Organizational Buying Process and the
Buying Center *126*
Stages in the Organizational Buying Process *126*
The Buying Center: A Cross-Functional Group *126*
Online Buying in Organizational Markets *129*
Prominence of Online Buying in Organizational Markets *129*
E-Marketplaces: Virtual Organizational Markets *129*

**Marketing Matters: eBay Means Business for
Entrepreneurs 130**

Online Auctions in Organizational Markets *131*

Learning Objectives Review 132
Focusing on Key Terms 132
Applying Marketing Knowledge 133
Building Your Marketing Plan 133

Video Case 6: Lands' End: Where Buyers Rule 133

7 **UNDERSTANDING AND REACHING GLOBAL
CONSUMERS AND MARKETS 136**

Dell's Quest for Growth in Emerging Economies *137*
Dynamics of World Trade *138*
Decline of Economic Protectionism *138*
Rise of Economic Integration 138
A New Reality: Global Competition among Global Companies
for Global Consumers *140*

**Marketing Matters: The Global Teenager—A Market
of 2 Billion Voracious Consumers with $200 Billion to
Spend 142**

Emergence of a Networked Global Marketspace *143*

A Global Environmental Scan   144
    Cultural Diversity   *144*
    Economic Considerations   *147*
    Political-Regulatory Climate   *148*
Comparing Global Market-Entry Strategies   149

Marketing Matters: Creative Cosmetics and Creative Export Marketing in Japan   150

    Exporting   *150*
    Licensing   *151*
    Joint Venture   *151*
    Direct Investment   *152*
Crafting a Worldwide Marketing Program   152
    Product and Promotion Strategies   *153*
    Distribution Strategy   *154*
    Pricing Strategy   *155*

Learning Objectives Review   156
Focusing on Key Terms   156
Applying Marketing Knowledge   156
Building Your Marketing Plan   157

Video Case 7: CNS Breathe Right Strips: Going Global   157

Part 3

Targeting Marketing Opportunities

8 MARKETING RESEARCH: FROM CUSTOMER INSIGHTS TO ACTIONS   160

Test Screenings: How Listening to Consumers Reduces Movie Risks   161

The Role of Marketing Research   162
    What Is Marketing Research?   *162*
    The Challenges in Doing Good Marketing Research   *162*
    Five-Step Marketing Research Approach   *163*
Step 1: Define the Problem   163
    Set the Research Objectives   *163*
    Identify Possible Marketing Actions   *163*
Step 2: Develop the Research Plan   164
    Specify Constraints   *164*
    Identify Data Needed for Marketing Actions   *164*
    Determine How to Collect Data   *165*
Step 3: Collect Relevant Information   166
    Secondary Data: Internal   *166*
    Secondary Data: External   *166*
    Advantages and Disadvantages of Secondary Data   *167*

Marketing Matters: Online Databases and Internet Resources Useful to Marketers   168

Primary Data: Watching People   *168*
Primary Data: Asking People   *170*

Marketing Matters: Buy•ology: How "Neuromarketing" Is Trying to Understand Consumers   171

Primary Data: Other Sources   *175*
Advantages and Disadvantages of Primary Data   *177*
Step 4: Develop Findings   **178**
Analyze the Data   *178*
Present the Findings   *178*
Step 5: Take Marketing Actions   **180**
Make Action Recommendations   *180*
Implement the Action Recommendations   *180*
Evaluate the Results   *180*
Sales Forecasting Techniques   **181**
Judgments of the Decision Maker   *181*
Surveys of Knowledgeable Groups   *181*
Statistical Methods   *181*

Learning Objectives Review   **182**
Focusing on Key Terms   **183**
Applying Marketing Knowledge   **183**
Building Your Marketing Plan   **184**

Video Case 8: Ford Consulting Group, Inc.: From Data to Actions   *184*

9   **MARKET SEGMENTATION, TARGETING, AND POSITIONING**   **186**

Zappos.com: Delivering "WOW" through Market Segmentation and Service   **187**
Why Segment Markets?   **188**
What Market Segmentation Means   *188*
When and How to Segment Markets   *189*
Steps in Segmenting and Targeting Markets   **191**
Step 1: Group Potential Buyers into Segments   *192*

Marketing Matters: What "Flock" Do You Belong to?   193

Step 2: Group Products to Be Sold into Categories   *196*
Step 3: Develop a Market-Product Grid and Estimate the Size of Markets   *197*
Step 4: Select Target Markets   *198*
Step 5: Take Marketing Actions to Reach Target Markets   *199*

Marketing Matters: Apple's Segmentation Strategy— Camp Runamok No Longer   201

Market-Product Synergies: A Balancing Act   *201*

Positioning the Product *202*
    Two Approaches to Product Positioning *202*
    Writing a Positioning Statement *203*
    Product Positioning Using Perceptual Maps *203*
    A Perceptual Map to Reposition Chocolate Milk for Adults *203*

Learning Objectives Review *204*
Focusing on Key Terms *205*
Applying Marketing Knowledge *205*
Building Your Marketing Plan *205*

Video Case 9: Prince Sports, Inc.: Tennis Racquets for Every Segment *205*

Part 4   Satisfying Marketing Opportunities

10 DEVELOPING NEW PRODUCTS AND SERVICES *208*

Apple's New-Product Innovation Machine *209*
What Are Products and Services? *210*
    A Look at Goods, Services, and Ideas *210*
    Classifying Products *210*
    Product Items, Product Lines, and Product Mixes *212*
    Classifying Services *212*
    The Uniqueness of Services *213*
    The Goods–Services Continuum *214*

    Marketing Matters: Feature Bloat: Geek Squad to the Rescue! **215**

New Products and Why They Succeed or Fail *215*
    What Is a New Product? *215*

    Why Products and Services Succeed or Fail *217*

    How Marketing Dashboards Can Reduce New-Product Failures *219*

    Using Marketing Dashboards: Which States Are Underperforming? **220**

The New-Product Process *220*
    Stage 1: New-Product Strategy Development *220*
    Stage 2: Idea Generation *221*

    Marketing Matters: IDEO—the Innovation Lab Superstar in Designing New Products **223**

    Stage 3: Screening and Evaluation *224*
    Stage 4: Business Analysis *224*
    Stage 5: Development *225*
    Stage 6: Market Testing *225*

    Marketing Matters: Marissa Mayer: The Talent behind Google's Familiar White Home Page **226**

Stage 7: Commercialization   *227*

Learning Objectives Review   228
Focusing on Key Terms   229
Applying Marketing Knowledge   229
Building Your Marketing Plan   229

*Video Case 10: Activeion Cleaning Solutions: Marketing a
High-Tech Cleaning Gadget   230*

**11 MANAGING SUCCESSFUL PRODUCTS, SERVICES,
AND BRANDS   232**

Gatorade: Quenching the Active Thirst within You   **233**
Charting the Product Life Cycle   **234**
    Introduction Stage   *234*
    Growth Stage   *236*
    Maturity Stage   *237*

    **Marketing Matters: Will E-mail Spell Extinction for Fax
    Machines?   238**

    Decline Stage   *238*
    Three Aspects of the Product Life Cycle   *239*
Managing the Product Life Cycle   **241**
    Role of a Product Manager   *241*
    Modifying the Product   *241*

    **Using Marketing Dashboards: Knowing Your CDI and
    BDI   242**

    Modifying the Market   *243*
    Repositioning the Product   *243*
Branding and Brand Management   **244**

    **Making Responsible Decisions: Consumer Economics of
    Downsizing—Get Less, Pay More   245**

    Brand Personality and Brand Equity   *245*
    Picking a Good Brand Name   *248*
    Different Branding Strategies   *248*
Packaging and Labeling Products   **250**

    **Marketing Matters: Creating Customer Value through
    Packaging—Pez Heads Dispense More Than Candy   251**

    Creating Customer Value and Competitive Advantage through
    Packaging and Labeling   *251*
    Packaging and Labeling Challenges and Responses   *253*
Managing the Marketing of Services   **253**
    Product (Service)   *254*
    Productivity   *254*
    Price   *254*
    Place (Distribution)   *254*

Promotion   255
People   255
Physical Environment   255
Process   256

Learning Objectives Review   256
Focusing on Key Terms   257
Applying Marketing Knowledge   257
Building Your Marketing Plan   257

*Video Case 11: Philadelphia Phillies, Inc.: Sports
Marketing 101   257*

12 PRICING PRODUCTS AND SERVICES   260

Vizio, Inc.—Where Vision Meets Value™ in HDTV   261
Nature and Importance of Price   262
   What Is a Price?   262
   Price as an Indicator of Value   263
   Price in the Marketing Mix   263
General Pricing Approaches   264
   Demand-Oriented Pricing Approaches   264

   **Marketing Matters: Energizer's Lesson in Price
   Perception—Value Lies in the Eye of the Beholder   265**

   Cost-Oriented Pricing Approaches   266
   Profit-Oriented Pricing Approaches   267
   Competition-Oriented Pricing Approaches   268

   **Using Marketing Dashboards: Are Cracker Jack Prices
   Above, At, or Below the Market?   269**

Estimating Demand and Revenue   270
   Fundamentals of Estimating Demand   270
   Fundamentals of Estimating Revenue   272
Determining Cost, Volume, and Profit Relationships   272
   The Importance of Controlling Costs   273
   Break-Even Analysis   273
Pricing Objectives and Constraints   275
   Identifying Pricing Objectives   275
   Identifying Pricing Constraints   276
Setting a Final Price   278
   Step 1: Select an Approximate Price Level   278
   Step 2: Set the List or Quoted Price   278

   **Making Responsible Decisions: Flexible Pricing—Is There
   Race and Gender Discrimination in Bargaining for a New
   Car?   279**

   Step 3: Make Special Adjustments to the List or Quoted
   Price   279

Learning Objectives Review   281
Focusing on Key Terms   282

Applying Marketing Knowledge 282
Building Your Marketing Plan 283

Video Case 12: Washburn Guitars: Using Break-Even Points to Make Pricing Decisions 283

13 MANAGING MARKETING CHANNELS AND SUPPLY CHAINS *286*

Callaway Golf: Designing and Delivering the Goods for Great Golf *287*

Nature and Importance of Marketing Channels *288*
    What Is a Marketing Channel of Distribution? *288*
    Value Is Created by Intermediaries *288*

Channel Structure and Organization *290*
    Marketing Channels for Consumer Products and Services *290*
    Marketing Channels for Business Products and Services *291*
    Electronic Marketing Channels *292*
    Direct and Multichannel Marketing *293*
    Dual Distribution and Strategic Channel Alliances *293*
    Vertical Marketing Systems *293*

Marketing Matters: Nestlé and General Mills—Cereal Partners Worldwide 294

Marketing Channel Choice and Management *296*
    Factors Affecting Channel Choice and Management *296*
    Managing Channel Relationships: Conflict and Cooperation *298*

Using Marketing Dashboards: Channel Sales and Profit at Charlesburg Furniture 299

Logistics and Supply Chain Management *301*
    Supply Chains versus Marketing Channels *301*
    Sourcing, Assembling, and Delivering a New Car: The Automotive Supply Chain *301*
    Supply Chain Management and Marketing Strategy *302*

Marketing Matters: IBM's Integrated Supply Chain— Delivering a Total Solution for Its Customers 303

Two Concepts of Logistics Management in a Supply Chain *304*
    Total Logistics Cost Concept *305*
    Customer Service Concept *305*

Learning Objectives Review 306
Focusing on Key Terms 307
Applying Marketing Knowledge 307
Building Your Marketing Plan 307

Video Case 13: ACT II Microwave Popcorn: The Surprising Channel 307

14 RETAILING AND WHOLESALING *310*

84 Million Consumers Were Shopping Online on Cyber
Monday. Were You One of Them? *311*
The Value of Retailing *312*
    Consumer Utilities Offered by Retailing *312*
    The Global Economic Impact of Retailing *313*
Classifying Retail Outlets *313*

    ***Making Responsible Decisions: Environmentally Friendly
    Retailing Takes Off!* 314**

    Form of Ownership *314*
    Level of Service *315*
    Type of Merchandise Line *316*
Nonstore Retailing *317*
    Automatic Vending *317*
    Direct Mail and Catalogs *318*
    Television Home Shopping *318*
    Online Retailing *319*
    Telemarketing *320*
    Direct Selling *320*
Retailing Strategy *321*
    Retail Pricing *321*
    Store Location *322*
    Retail Communication *323*
    Merchandise *323*

    ***Using Marketing Dashboards: Why Apple Stores May Be
    the Best in the United States!* 324**

The Changing Nature of Retailing *325*
    The Wheel of Retailing *325*
    The Retail Life Cycle *326*
Wholesaling *326*
    Merchant Wholesalers *327*
    Agents and Brokers *328*
    Manufacturer's Branches and Offices *328*

Learning Objectives Review *329*
Focusing on Key Terms *329*
Applying Marketing Knowledge *329*
Building Your Marketing Plan *330*

*Video Case 14: Mall of America: Shopping and a Whole Lot
More* *330*

**15 INTEGRATED MARKETING COMMUNICATIONS AND
DIRECT MARKETING** *332*

Integrated Marketing Communications Ushers in the 'Age of
Engage' *333*
The Communication Process *334*
    Encoding and Decoding *335*
    Feedback *336*

Noise   *336*
The Promotional Elements   **336**
 Advertising   *336*
 Personal Selling   *337*
 Public Relations   *338*
 Sales Promotion   *339*
 Direct Marketing   *339*
Integrated Marketing Communications—Developing the Promotional Mix   **340**
 The Target Audience   *340*
 The Product Life Cycle   *340*

***Marketing Matters: Mobile Marketing Reaches Generation Y, 32/7!*   341**

 Channel Strategies   *342*
Developing an IMC Program   **343**
 Identifying the Target Audience   *343*
 Specifying Promotion Objectives   *344*
 Setting the Promotion Budget   *344*

***Using Marketing Dashboards: How Much Should You Spend on IMC?*   345**

 Selecting the Right Promotional Tools   *345*
 Designing the Promotion   *346*
 Scheduling the Promotion   *346*
Executing and Assessing the Promotion Program   **346**
Direct Marketing   **348**
 The Growth of Direct Marketing   *348*
 The Value of Direct Marketing   *348*
 Technological, Global, and Ethical Issues in Direct Marketing   *349*

***Making Responsible Decisions: Can Direct Marketing "Go Green"?*   350**

Learning Objectives Review   350
Focusing on Key Terms   351
Applying Marketing Knowledge   351
Building Your Marketing Plan   352

Video Case 15: Under Armour: Using IMC to Create a Brand for This Generation's Athletes   352

16 ADVERTISING, SALES PROMOTION, AND PUBLIC RELATIONS   356

Advertising Moves to a New Dimension: The Third Dimension   357
Types of Advertisements   358
 Product Advertisements   *358*
 Institutional Advertisements   *359*

Developing the Advertising Program   *359*
　　Identifying the Target Audience   *359*
　　Specifying Advertising Objectives   *360*
　　Setting the Advertising Budget   *360*
　　Designing the Advertisement   *360*
　　Selecting the Right Media   *362*

　　Using Marketing Dashboards: What Is the Best Way to Reach 1,000 Customers?   363

　　Different Media Alternatives   *363*

　　Making Responsible Decisions: Who Is Responsible for Click Fraud?   367

　　Scheduling the Advertising   *367*
Executing the Advertising Program   **368**
　　Pretesting the Advertising   *368*
　　Carrying Out the Advertising Program   *369*
Assessing the Advertising Program   **369**
　　Posttesting the Advertising   *369*
Sales Promotion   **370**
　　Consumer-Oriented Sales Promotions   *370*
　　Trade-Oriented Sales Promotions   *373*
Public Relations   **375**

Learning Objectives Review   **375**
Focusing on Key Terms   **376**
Applying Marketing Knowledge   **376**
Building Your Marketing Plan   **377**

Video Case 16: Google, Inc.: The Right Ads at the Right Time   377

17 PERSONAL SELLING AND SALES MANAGEMENT   *380*

Xerox Succeeds by Doing What's Right for the Customer   **381**
Scope and Significance of Personal Selling and Sales Management   **382**
　　Nature of Personal Selling and Sales Management   *382*
　　Selling Happens Almost Everywhere   *382*
　　Personal Selling in Marketing   *382*
　　Creating Customer Solutions and Value through Salespeople: Relationship Selling   *382*
The Many Forms of Personal Selling   **384**
　　Order-Taking Salespeople   *384*
　　Order-Getting Salespeople   *385*
The Personal Selling Process: Building Relationships   **386**
　　Prospecting: Identifying and Qualifying Prospective Customers   *386*
　　Preapproach: Preparing for the Sales Call   *387*
　　Approach: Making the First Impression   *388*
　　Presentation: Tailoring a Solution for a Customer's Needs   *388*

Marketing Matters: Imagine This . . . Putting the Customer into Customer Solutions! 390

Close: Asking for the Customer's Order or Business *390*
Follow-Up: Solidifying the Relationship *391*
The Sales Management Process 391
Sales Plan Formulation: Setting Direction *391*

Marketing Matters: Creating and Sustaining Customer Value through Cross-Functional Team Selling 393

Sales Plan Implementation: Putting the Plan into Action *394*
Salesforce Evaluation: Measuring Results *396*
Salesforce Automation and Customer Relationship Management *396*

Using Marketing Dashboards: Tracking Salesperson Performance at Moore Chemical & Sanitation Supply, Inc. 397

Learning Objectives Review 398
Focusing on Key Terms 399
Applying Marketing Knowledge 399
Building Your Marketing Plan 399

Video Case 17: Xerox: Building Customer Relationships through Personal Selling 399

18 IMPLEMENTING INTERACTIVE AND MULTICHANNEL MARKETING 402

Seven Cycles. One Bike. Yours. 403
Creating Customer Value, Relationships, and Experiences in Marketspace 404
Customer Value Creation in Marketspace *404*
Interactivity, Individuality, and Customer Relationships in Marketspace *405*
Creating an Online Customer Experience *407*
Online Consumer Behavior and Marketing Practice in Marketspace 409
Who Is the Online Consumer? *409*

Using Marketing Dashboards: Sizing Up Site Stickiness at Sewell Automotive Companies 410

What Online Consumers Buy *410*

Marketing Matters: Meet Today's Internet Mom—All 38 Million! 411

Why Consumers Shop and Buy Online *411*
When and Where Online Consumers Shop and Buy *415*
Cross-Channel Shoppers and Multichannel Marketing 415
Who Is the Cross-Channel Shopper? *415*

Making Responsible Decisions: Let the E-Buyer Beware 416

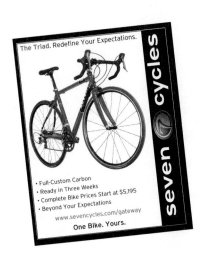

Implementing Multichannel Marketing   *416*

Learning Objectives Review   419
Focusing on Key Terms   419
Applying Marketing Knowledge   **419**
Building Your Marketing Plan   420

Video Case 18: Pizza Hut and imc²: Becoming a Multichannel Marketer   *420*

Appendix B   Planning a Career in Marketing   424

Glossary   *434*
Learning Review Answers   *440*
Chapter Notes   *447*
Credits   *469*
Name Index   *471*
Company/Product Index   *477*
Subject Index   *483*

Marketing

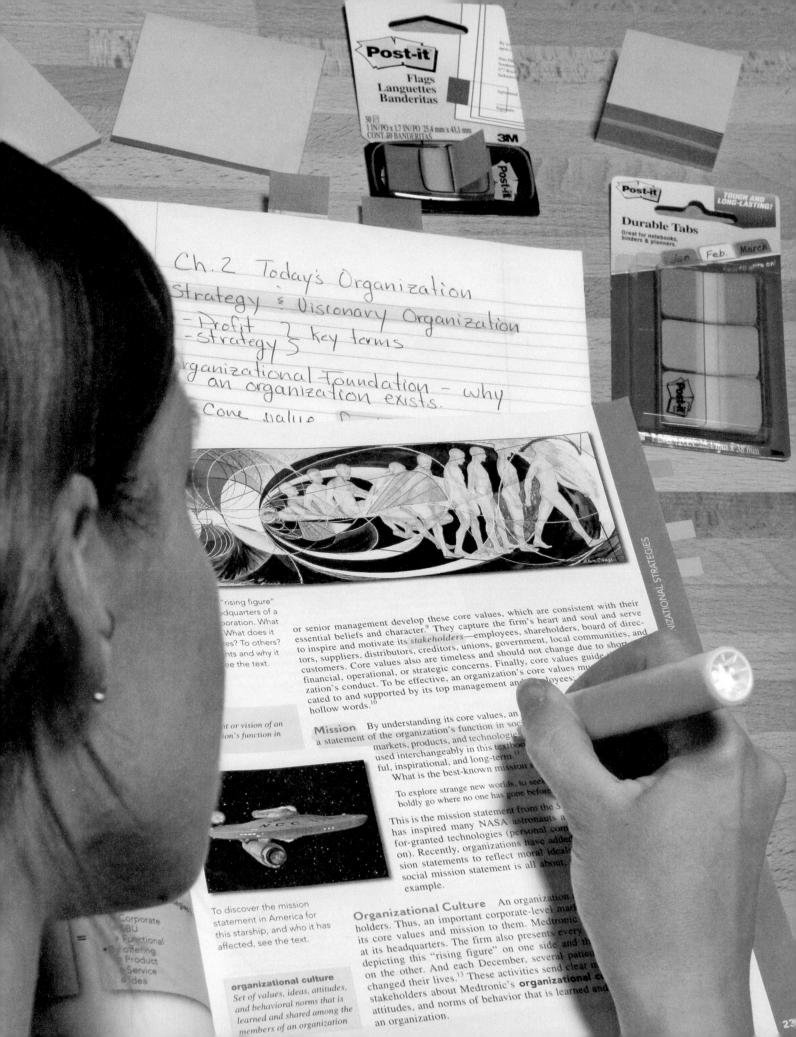

1

Creating Customer Relationships and Value through Marketing

LEARNING OBJECTIVES

After reading this chapter you should be able to:

LO1 Define marketing and identify the diverse factors influencing marketing activities.

LO2 Explain how marketing discovers and satisfies consumer needs.

LO3 Distinguish between marketing mix factors and environmental forces.

LO4 Explain how organizations build strong customer relationships and customer value through marketing.

LO5 Describe how today's customer relationship era differs from prior eras.

RESEARCHING HOW COLLEGE STUDENTS STUDY TO LAUNCH A NEW PRODUCT AT 3M

David Windorski, a 3M inventor, faced a curious challenge—understanding how college students study!

Specifically, how do they read their textbooks, take class notes, and prepare for exams? After finding the answers, he needed to convert this knowledge into a product that actually helps students improve their studying. Finally, Windorski and 3M had to manufacture and market this product using 3M's world-class adhesive technology.

Sound simple? Perhaps. But David Windorski invested several years of his life conducting marketing research on students' study behavior, developing product ideas, and then creating an actual product students could use.[1] This process of discovering and satisfying consumer needs is the essence of how organizations such as 3M create genuine customer value through effective marketing. David Windorski's invention got a personal testimonial from host Oprah Winfrey on her 2008 TV show. More on this later.[2]

Discovering Student Study Needs

As an inventor of Post-it® brand products, David Windorski's main job is to design new products. He gets creative "thinking time" under 3M's "15% Rule," during which inventors can use up to 15 percent of their time to do initially unfunded research that might lead to marketable 3M products. Windorski and a team of four college students observed and questioned dozens of students about how they used their textbooks, took notes, wrote term papers, and reviewed for exams.

Windorski describes what college students told him: "It's natural behavior to highlight a passage and then mark the page with a Post-it® Note or Post-it® Flag of some kind. So it's reasonable to put Post-it® products together with a highlighter to have two functions in one."

Satisfying Student Study Needs

In designing a marketable product for students, Windorski used a lot of creativity, hard work, and attention to countless details. Windorski used wood blocks and modeling clay to mock up a number of nonworking models that showed him how the product would feel.

His search for the 2-in-1 highlighter plus Post-it® Flags produced working models that students could actually use to give him feedback. Windorski had taken some giant steps in trying not only to discover students' needs for his product but also to satisfy those needs with a practical, useful product. Later in the chapter we'll see what products resulted from his innovative thinking and the initial marketing plan that 3M used to launch his products.

3M's Post-it® Notes or Post-it® Flags

Felt tip highlighters

3M product that will combine Post-it® Notes or Post-it® Flags and Highlighters

For the creative way a student project helped lead to a new product for college students using 3M's technology, see the text.

WHAT IS MARKETING?

To understand how three 20-somethings launched YouTube, see the text and Marketing Matters box.

The good news is that you are already a marketing expert! You perform many marketing activities and make marketing-related decisions every day. For example, would you sell more Panasonic Viera 50-inch 3D HDTVs at $2,499 or $999 each? You answered $999, right? So your experience in shopping gives you some expertise in marketing. As a consumer, you've been involved in thousands of marketing decisions, but mostly on the buying and not the selling side. But to test your expertise, answer the "marketing expert" questions posed in Figure 1–1. You'll find the answers within the next several pages.

The bad news is, good marketing isn't always easy. That's why every year thousands of new products fail in the marketplace and then quietly slide into oblivion. Examples of new products that vary from spectacular successes to dismal failures appear in the next few pages.

Marketing and Your Career

Marketing affects all individuals, all organizations, all industries, and all countries. This book seeks to teach you marketing concepts, often by having you actually "do marketing"—by putting you in the shoes of a marketing manager facing actual marketing decisions. The book also shows marketing's many applications and how it affects our lives. This knowledge should make you a better consumer, enable you to be a more informed citizen, and help you in your career planning.

Perhaps your future will involve doing sales and marketing for a large organization. Working for a well-known company—Apple, General Electric, Target, or

FIGURE 1–1
The see-if-you're-really-a-marketing-expert test.

Answer the questions below. The correct answers are given later in the chapter.

1. True or false. You can now buy a satellite TV receiver for your minivan or sport utility vehicle (SUV) so that backseat passengers can watch high-definition television (HDTV) programs.

2. True or false. The 60-year lifetime value of a loyal Kleenex customer is $994.

3. To be socially responsible, 3M puts what recycled material into its very successful ScotchBrite® Never Rust™ soap pads? (*a*) aluminum cans, (*b*) steel-belted tires, (*c*) plastic bottles, (*d*) computer screens.

Marketing Matters > > > > > entrepreneurship

Payoff for the Joys (!) and Sleepless Nights (?) of Starting Your Own Small Business: YouTube!!!!

What happens when you drop Mentos into a bottle of Diet Coke?

Don't know the answer?

Then you're not a serious YouTube viewer! If you need an answer, ask the student sitting next to you in class. But don't try it in your room.

In one 12-month period, a single Web site—YouTube .com—revolutionized the Internet's world of videos and was named *Time* magazine's Invention of the Year for 2006. YouTube's numbers are astounding: In early 2010, five years after its launch, YouTube's Web site has exceeded 2 billion views per day.

The minds behind YouTube are three 20-somethings: Steve Chen, Chad Hurley, and Jawed Karim. Even the three entrepreneurs are astounded at their success. *Time* says the reason for YouTube's success is its rare combination of being both "edgy and easy" for users.

The three men met at PayPal, now the Internet's leading online payment service. Then they left PayPal and worked together on a new concept—a Web site where anyone could upload content that others could view. That was radical because until then only those who owned the Web site could provide the content.

Google bought YouTube in October 2006 for $1.65 billion, only 21 months after its founding. Hurley (standing) and Chen (sitting) in the left photo are now Google employees. They face issues such as making YouTube.com profitable through its advertising and avoiding potential lawsuits resulting from uploaded content that is copyrighted. Karim (in the right photo) left the company and is doing graduate work in computer science at Stanford University.

Where will this end? Go to YouTube.com and see for yourself!

---

eBay—can be personally satisfying and financially rewarding, and you may gain special respect from your friends.

Small businesses also offer marketing careers. Small businesses are the source of the majority of new U.S. jobs. So you might become your own boss by being an entrepreneur and starting your own business. The Marketing Matters box describes the revolutionary impact that three entrepreneurs in their 20s have had on the Internet—and perhaps on how you spend some of your free time.[3] The three entrepreneurs—Steve Chen, Chad Hurley, and Jawed Karim—founded YouTube, which has achieved tremendous Internet success and is now part of Google. Not every Internet start-up connects with the millions of viewers YouTube reaches each month. In fact, more than half of new businesses fail within five years of their launch.

Marketing: Delivering Benefits to the Organization, Its Stakeholders, and Society

marketing
The activity for creating and delivering offerings that benefit the organization, its stakeholders, and society.

The American Marketing Association represents marketing professionals. Combining its 2004 and 2007 definitions, "**marketing** is the activity for creating, communicating, delivering, and exchanging offerings that benefit the organization, its stakeholders and society at large."[4] This definition shows marketing is far more than simply advertising or personal selling. It stresses the need to deliver genuine benefits in the offerings of goods, services, and ideas marketed to customers. Also, note that the organization doing the marketing, the stakeholders affected (such as customers, employees, suppliers, and shareholders), and society should all benefit.

To serve both buyers and sellers, marketing seeks (1) to discover the needs and wants of prospective customers and (2) to satisfy them. These prospective customers include both individuals, buying for themselves and their households, and organizations that buy for their own use (such as manufacturers) or for resale (such as wholesalers and retailers). The key to achieving these two objectives is the idea of **exchange**, which is the trade of things of value between buyer and seller so that each is better off after the trade.[5]

The Diverse Factors Influencing Marketing Activities

Although an organization's marketing activity focuses on assessing and satisfying consumer needs, countless other people, groups, and forces interact to shape the nature of its activities (see Figure 1–2). Foremost is the organization itself, whose mission and objectives determine what business it is in and what goals it seeks. Within the organization, management is responsible for establishing these goals. The marketing department works closely with a network of other departments and employees to help provide the customer-satisfying products required for the organization to survive and prosper.

Figure 1–2 also shows the key people, groups, and forces outside the organization that influence its marketing activities. The marketing department is responsible for facilitating relationships, partnerships, and alliances with the organization's customers, its shareholders (or often representatives of groups served by a nonprofit organization), its suppliers, and other organizations. Environmental forces involving social, economic, technological, competitive, and regulatory considerations also shape an organization's marketing activities. Finally, an organization's marketing decisions are affected by and, in turn, often have an important impact on society as a whole.

The organization must strike a balance among the sometimes differing interests of these individuals and groups. For example, it is not possible to simultaneously provide the lowest-priced and highest-quality products to customers and pay the highest prices to suppliers, the highest wages to employees, and the maximum dividends to shareholders.

FIGURE 1–2

A marketing department relates to many people, organizations, and forces. Note that the marketing department both *shapes* and *is shaped by* its relationship with these internal and external groups.

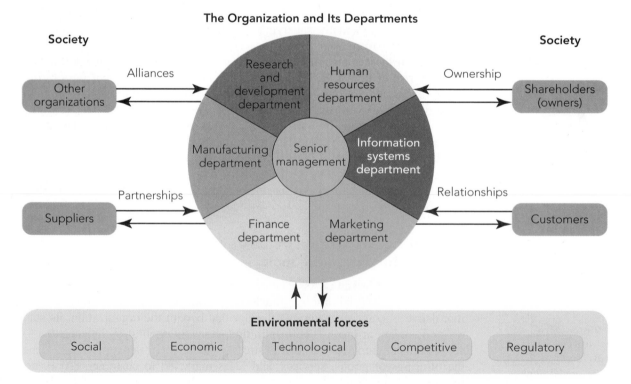

HOW MARKETING DISCOVERS AND SATISFIES CONSUMER NEEDS

LO2

The importance of discovering and satisfying consumer needs is so critical to understanding marketing that we look at each of these two steps in detail next.

For these four products, identify (1) what benefits the product provides buyers and (2) what factors might doom the product in the marketplace. Answers are discussed in the text.

Vanilla-mint-flavored toothpaste in an aerosol container

Microwavable mini-cheeseburger sensations

TV service in backseats of cars, minivans, and SUVs

A diet cola with ginseng and extra caffeine

Discovering Consumer Needs

The first objective in marketing is discovering the needs of prospective customers. But these prospective customers may not always know or be able to describe what they need and want. When Apple built its first Apple II personal computer and started a new industry, consumers didn't really know what the benefits would be. So they had to be educated about how to use personal computers. In contrast, Bell, a U.S. bicycle helmet maker, listened to its customers, collected hundreds of their ideas, and put several into its new products.[6] This is where effective marketing research, the topic of Chapter 8, can help.

The Challenge: Meeting Consumer Needs with New Products

New-product experts generally estimate that up to 94 percent of the more than 33,000 new consumable products (food, beverage, health, beauty, and other household and pet products) introduced in the United States annually "don't succeed in the long run."[7] Robert M. McMath, who has studied more than 100,000 of these new-product launches, has two key suggestions: (1) focus on what the customer benefit is, and (2) learn from the past.[8]

The solution to preventing such product failures seems embarrassingly obvious. First, find out what consumers need and want. Second, produce what they need and want, and don't produce what they don't need and want. The four products shown on page 7 illustrate just how difficult it is to achieve new-product success, a topic covered in more detail in Chapter 10.

Without reading further, think about the potential benefits to customers and possible "showstoppers"—factors that might doom the product—for each of the four products pictured. Some of the products may come out of your past, and others may be on your horizon. Here's a quick analysis of the four products, some with comments adapted from McMath:

- *Dr. Care Toothpaste.* After extensive research, Dr. Care family toothpaste in its aerosol container was introduced more than two decades ago. The vanilla-mint-flavored product's benefits were advertised as being easy to use and sanitary. Pretend for a minute that you are five years old and left alone in the bathroom to brush your teeth using your Dr. Care toothpaste. Hmm! Apparently, surprised parents were not enthusiastic about the bathroom wall paintings sprayed by their future Rembrandts—a showstopper that doomed this creative product.[9]

- *Hot Pockets.* Introduced in 1983, these convenient meat and cheese microwavable sandwiches are a favorite brand among students. More than 80 varieties have been introduced, from Hot Pockets Pizza Snacks to Hot Pockets Subs and now Hot Pockets Sideshots—a mini-cheeseburger that first appeared in 2009. A none-too-serious potential showstopper: Excessive ice crystals can form on the product due to variations in freezer temperatures; if this happens and the sandwich is thawed and refrozen before being microwaved, it may not taste as good.[10]

- *AT&T CruiseCast.* In early 2009, AT&T and RaySat Broadcasting launched the AT&T CruiseCast service that enables families and commuters in the backseat of cars, minivans, and SUVs to watch over 20 channels (Disney Channel, CNBC, Nickelodeon, etc.) of satellite high-definition TV anywhere in the United States (question 1, Figure 1–1). The antenna/receiver is mounted on the roof of the vehicle and incorporates technology that overcomes line-of-sight obstacles, such as overpasses, tunnels, and so on. Potential showstopper: the initial cost of $1,299 for the antenna and $28 per month for the somewhat limited programming.[11]

- *Pepsi Max.* In early 2009, PepsiCo launched Pepsi Max. "This is the first diet cola for men" 25 and older who haven't liked the taste of other diet colas, according to the humorous "I'm Good" ad that ran during Super Bowl XLIII (2009). Pepsi Max is rebranded Diet Pepsi Max, a reformulated soft drink from Britain that was introduced to the United States in 2007 as the "Invigorating Zero-Calorie Cola." Pepsi Max has ginseng and extra caffeine to differentiate it from Diet Pepsi. One potential showstopper: women may not consume a soft drink specifically targeted at men.[12]

Firms spend billions of dollars annually on marketing and technical research that significantly reduces, but doesn't eliminate, new-product failure. So meeting the changing needs of consumers is a continuing challenge for firms around the world.

Consumer Needs and Consumer Wants Should marketing try to satisfy consumer needs or consumer wants? Marketing tries to do both. Heated debates rage over this question, fueled by the definitions of needs and wants and the amount of freedom given to prospective customers to make their own buying decisions.

A *need* occurs when a person feels deprived of basic necessities such as food, clothing, and shelter. A *want* is a need that is shaped by a person's knowledge, culture, and personality. So if you feel hungry, you have developed a basic need and desire to eat something. Let's say you then want to eat an apple or a candy bar because, based on your past experience, you know these will satisfy your hunger need. Effective marketing, in the form of creating an awareness of good products at convenient locations, can clearly shape a person's wants.

Certainly, marketing tries to influence what we buy. A question then arises: At what point do we want government and society to step in to protect consumers? Most consumers would say they want government to protect us from harmful drugs and unsafe cars but not from candy bars and soft drinks. To protect college students, should government restrict their use of credit cards?[13] Such questions have no clear-cut answers, which is why legal and social issues are central to marketing. Because even psychologists and economists still debate the exact meanings of *need* and *want*, we shall use the terms interchangeably throughout the book.

As shown in the left side of Figure 1–3, discovering needs involves looking carefully at prospective customers, whether they are children buying M&Ms candy, college students buying highlighters, or firms buying Xerox photocopying machines. A principal activity of a firm's marketing department is to scrutinize its consumers to understand what they need and want and the forces that shape those needs and wants.

market
People with both the desire and the ability to buy a specific offering.

What a Market Is   Potential consumers make up a **market**, which is people with both the desire and the ability to buy a specific offering. All markets ultimately are people. Even when we say a firm bought a Xerox copier, we mean one or several people in the firm decided to buy it. People who are aware of their unmet needs may have the desire to buy the product, but that alone isn't sufficient. People must also have the ability to buy, such as the authority, time, and money. People may even "buy" an idea that results in an action, such as having their blood pressure checked annually or turning down their thermostat to save energy.

target market
One or more specific groups of potential consumers toward which an organization directs its marketing program.

Satisfying Consumer Needs

Marketing doesn't stop with the discovery of consumer needs. Because the organization obviously can't satisfy all consumer needs, it must concentrate its efforts on certain needs of a specific group of potential consumers. This is the **target market**—one or

FIGURE 1–3
Marketing seeks first to discover consumer needs through extensive research. It then seeks to satisfy those needs by successfully implementing a marketing program possessing the right combination of the marketing mix—the four Ps.

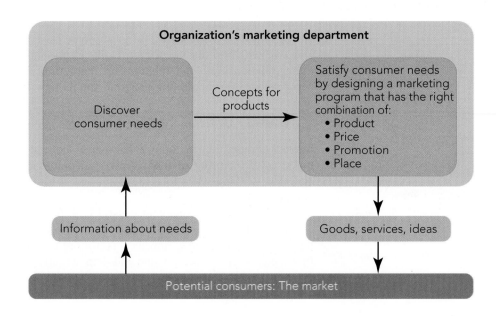

Organization's marketing department

Discover consumer needs

Concepts for products →

Satisfy consumer needs by designing a marketing program that has the right combination of:
• Product
• Price
• Promotion
• Place

↑ Information about needs   Goods, services, ideas ↓

Potential consumers: The market

more specific groups of potential consumers toward which an organization directs its marketing program.

The Four Ps: Controllable Marketing Mix Factors   Having selected its target market consumers, the firm must take steps to satisfy their needs, as shown in the right side of Figure 1–3. Someone in the organization's marketing department, often the marketing manager, must develop a complete marketing program to reach consumers by using a combination of four tools, often called "the four Ps"—a useful shorthand reference to them first published by Professor E. Jerome McCarthy:[14]

- *Product.* A good, service, or idea to satisfy the consumer's needs.
- *Price.* What is exchanged for the product.
- *Promotion.* A means of communication between the seller and buyer.
- *Place.* A means of getting the product to the consumer.

We'll define each of the four Ps more carefully later in the book, but for now it's important to remember that they are the elements of the **marketing mix**. These four elements are the controllable factors—product, price, promotion, and place—that can be used by the marketing manager to solve a marketing problem. For example, when a company puts a product on sale, it is changing one element of the marketing mix—namely, the price. The marketing mix elements are called *controllable factors* because they are under the control of the marketing department in an organization.

The Uncontrollable, Environmental Forces   While marketers can control their marketing mix factors, there are other forces that are mostly beyond their control (see Figure 1–2). These are the **environmental forces** in a marketing decision, those involving social, economic, technological, competitive, and regulatory forces. Examples are what consumers themselves want and need, changing technology, the state of the economy in terms of whether it is expanding or contracting, actions that competitors take, and government restrictions. Covered in detail in Chapter 3, these five forces may serve as accelerators or brakes on marketing, sometimes expanding an organization's marketing opportunities while at other times restricting them.

marketing mix
The controllable factors—product, price, promotion, and place—that the marketing manager can use to solve a marketing problem.

environmental forces
The uncontrollable social, economic, technological, competitive, and regulatory forces that affect the results of a marketing decision.

THE MARKETING PROGRAM: HOW CUSTOMER RELATIONSHIPS ARE BUILT

An organization's marketing program connects it with its customers. To clarify this link, we will first discuss the critically important concepts of customer value, customer relationships, and relationship marketing. Then we will illustrate these concepts using 3M's marketing program for its new Post-it® products for students.

Customer Value and Customer Relationships

Intense competition in today's fast-paced domestic and global markets has caused massive restructuring of many American industries and businesses. American managers are seeking ways to achieve success in this new, more intense level of global competition.

This has prompted many successful U.S. firms to focus on "customer value." That firms gain loyal customers by providing unique value is the essence of successful marketing. What is new, however, is a more careful attempt at understanding how a firm's customers perceive value and then actually creating and delivering that value.[15] For our purposes, **customer value** is the unique combination of benefits received by

customer value
Buyers' benefits, including quality, convenience, on-time delivery, and before- and after-sale service at a specific price.

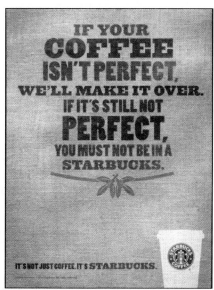

Southwest Airlines, Starbucks, and Home Depot provide customer value using three very different approaches. For their strategies, see the text.

targeted buyers that includes quality, convenience, on-time delivery, and both before-sale and after-sale service at a specific price. Loyal, satisfied customers are likely to repurchase more over time.[16] Firms now actually try to place a dollar value on the purchases of loyal, satisfied customers during their lifetimes. For example, loyal Kleenex customers average 6.7 boxes a year, about $994 over 60 years in today's dollars (question 2, Figure 1–1).[17]

Research suggests that firms cannot succeed by being all things to all people. Instead, firms must find ways to build long-term customer relationships to provide unique value that they alone can deliver to targeted markets. Many successful firms have chosen to deliver outstanding customer value with one of three value strategies: best price, best product, or best service.[18]

Companies such as Walmart, Southwest Airlines, and Costco have all been successful offering consumers the best price. Other companies, such as Starbucks, Nike, and Johnson & Johnson, claim to provide the best products on the market. Finally, companies such as Marriott, Lands' End, and Home Depot deliver value by providing exceptional service.

Relationship Marketing and the Marketing Program

A firm achieves meaningful customer relationships by creating connections with its customers through careful coordination of the product, its price, the way it's promoted, and how it's placed.

Relationship Marketing: Easy to Understand, Hard to Do   The hallmark of developing and maintaining effective customer relationships is today called **relationship marketing**, which links the organization to its individual customers, employees, suppliers, and other partners for their mutual long-term benefit. In terms of selling a product, relationship marketing involves a personal, ongoing relationship between the organization and its individual customers that begins before and continues after the sale.[19]

Huge manufacturers find this rigorous standard of relationship marketing difficult to achieve. Today's information technology, along with cutting-edge manufacturing and marketing processes, have led to tailoring goods or services to the tastes of individual customers in high volumes at a relatively low cost. So you can place an Internet order for all the components of an Apple computer and have it delivered in four or five days—in a configuration tailored to your unique wants. But with today's Internet purchases, you will probably have difficulty achieving

relationship marketing
Linking the organization to its individual customers, employees, suppliers, and other partners for their mutual long-term benefit.

the same personal, tender-loving-care connection that you once had with your own local computer store, bookstore, or other retailer.[20]

The Marketing Program   Effective relationship marketing strategies help marketing managers discover what prospective customers need. They must translate this information into some concepts for products the firm might develop (see Figure 1–3). These concepts must then be converted into a tangible **marketing program**—a plan that integrates the marketing mix to provide a good, service, or idea to prospective buyers. These prospects then react to the offering favorably (by buying) or unfavorably (by not buying), and the process is repeated. As shown in Figure 1–3, in an effective organization this process is continuous: Consumer needs trigger product concepts that are translated into actual products that stimulate further discovery of consumer needs.

> **marketing program**
> *A plan that integrates the marketing mix to provide a good, service, or idea to prospective buyers.*

---

learning review

3. An organization can't satisfy the needs of all consumers, so it must focus on one or more subgroups, which are its _____.

4. What are the four marketing mix elements that make up the organization's marketing program?

5. What are environmental forces?

3M's initial product line of Post-it® Flag Highlighters and Post-it® Flag Pens includes variations in color and line widths.

3M's Strategy and Marketing Program to Help Students Study

To see some specifics of an actual marketing program, let's return to our earlier example of 3M inventor David Windorski and his search for a way to help college students in their studying.

Moving from Ideas to a Marketable Highlighter Product   After working on 15 or 20 wood and clay models, Windorski concluded he had to build a highlighter product that would dispense Post-it® Flags because the Post-it® Notes were simply too large to put inside the barrel of a highlighter.

Hundreds of the initial highlighter prototypes with Post-it® Flags inside were produced and given to students—and also office workers—to get their reactions. This research showed users wanted a convenient, reliable cover to protect the Post-it® Flags in the highlighter. So Windorski's rotating cover for the Post-it® Flags was born.

Extending the Product Line   David Windorski also considered other related products. Many people in offices need immediate access to Post-it® Flags while writing with pens. Marketing research among office workers refined the design and showed the existence of a sizable market for a Post-it® Flag Pen.

A Marketing Program for the Post-it® Flag Highlighter and Pen After several years of research, development, and production engineering, 3M introduced its new products. Figure 1–4 outlines the strategies for each of the four marketing mix elements in 3M's program to market its Post-it® Flag Highlighters and Post-it® Flag Pens. Although similar, we can compare the marketing program for each of the two products:

- *Post-it® Flag Highlighter.* The target market is mainly college students, so 3M's initial challenge was to build student awareness of a product that they didn't know existed. The company used a mix of print ads in college newspapers and

MARKETING MIX ELEMENT	COLLEGE STUDENT SEGMENT	OFFICE WORKER SEGMENT	RATIONALE FOR MARKETING PROGRAM ACTIVITY
Product strategy	Offer Post-it® Flag Highlighter to help college students in their studying	Offer Post-it® Flag Pen to help office workers in their day-to-day work activities	Listen carefully to the needs and wants of potential customer segments to use 3M technology to introduce a useful, innovative product
Price strategy	Seek retail price of about $3.99 to $4.99 for a single Post-it® Flag Highlighter or $5.99 to $7.99 for a three-pack	Seek retail price of about $3.99 to $4.99 for a single Post-it® Flag Pen; wholesale prices are less	Set prices that provide genuine value to the customer segment that is targeted
Promotion strategy	Run limited promotion with a TV ad and some ads in college newspapers and then rely on student word-of-mouth messages	Run limited promotion among distributors to get them to stock the product	Increase awareness of potential users who have never heard of this new, innovative 3M product
Place strategy	Distribute Post-it® Flag Highlighters through college bookstores, office supply stores, and mass merchandisers	Distribute Post-it® Flag Pens through office wholesalers and retailers and mass merchandisers	Make it easy for prospective buyers to buy at convenient retail outlets (both products) or to get at work (Post-it® Flag Pens only)

FIGURE 1–4
Marketing programs for the launch of two Post-it® brand products targeted at two customer market segments.

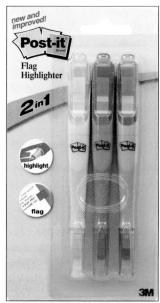

The second generation of Post-it® Flag Highlighters

a TV ad and then relied on word-of-mouth advertising—students telling their friends how great the product is. Gaining distribution in college bookstores and having attractive packaging was also critical. Plus, 3M charged a price to distributors that it hoped would give a reasonable bookstore price to students and an acceptable profit to distributors and 3M.

- *Post-it® Flag Pen.* The primary target market is people working in offices. But some students are potential customers, so 3M gained distribution in some college bookstores of Post-it® Flag Pens, too. But the Post-it® Flag Pens are mainly business products—bought by the purchasing department in an organization and stocked as office supplies for employees to use. So the marketing program in Figure 1–4 reflects the different distribution or "place" strategies for the two products.

How well did these new 3M products do in the marketplace? They have done so well that 3M bestowed a prestigious award on David Windorski and his team. Their success has also led Windorski to design a second generation of Post-it® Flag Highlighters and Pens *without* the rotating cover to make it easier to insert replacement flags. The new tapered design is also easier for students to hold and use. Note how prominently the "2-in-1" benefit is displayed on the packaging in the photo of the new, second-generation Post-it® Flag Highlighters.

In what must be the answer to every almost inventor's dream, Oprah Winfrey flew David Windorski to Chicago to appear on her TV show and thank him in person. She told Windorski and her audience that the Post-it® Flag Highlighter is changing the way she does things at home and at work—especially in going through potential books she might recommend for her book club. "David, I know you never thought this would happen when you were in your 3M lab . . . but I want you to take a bow before America for the invention of this . . . (highlighter). It's the most incredible invention," she said.[21]

HOW MARKETING BECAME SO IMPORTANT

To understand why marketing is a driving force in the modern global economy, let us look at (1) the evolution of the market orientation, (2) ethics and social responsibility in marketing, and (3) the breadth and depth of marketing activities.

Evolution of the Market Orientation

Many American manufacturers have experienced four distinct stages in the life of their firms.[22] The first stage, the *production era,* covers the early years of the United States up until the 1920s. Goods were scarce and buyers were willing to accept virtually any goods that were available and make do with them.[23] In the *sales era* from the 1920s to the 1960s, manufacturers found they could produce more goods than buyers could consume. Competition grew. Firms hired more salespeople to find new buyers. This sales era continued into the 1960s for many American firms.

marketing concept
The idea that an organization should strive to satisfy the needs of consumers while also trying to achieve the organization's goals.

In the 1960s, marketing became the motivating force among many American firms and the *marketing concept era* dawned. The **marketing concept** is the idea that an organization should (1) strive to satisfy the needs of consumers (2) while also trying to achieve the organization's goals. General Electric probably launched the marketing concept and its focus on consumers when its 1952 annual report stated: "The concept introduces . . . marketing . . . at the beginning rather than the end of the production cycle and integrates marketing into each phase of the business."[24]

market orientation
Focusing organizational efforts to collect and use information about customers' needs to create customer value.

Firms such as General Electric and Marriott have achieved great success by putting huge effort into implementing the marketing concept, giving their firms what has been called a *market orientation.* An organization that has a **market orientation** focuses its efforts on (1) continuously collecting information about customers' needs, (2) sharing this information across departments, and (3) using it to create customer value.[25] The result is today's *customer relationship era,* in which firms seek continuously to satisfy the high expectations of customers.

This focus on customers has led to *customer relationship management (CRM),* the process of identifying prospective buyers, understanding them intimately, and developing favorable long-term perceptions of the organization and its offerings so that buyers will choose them in the marketplace.[26] This requires the commitment of managers and employees throughout the organization.[27]

The foundation of customer relationship management is really *customer experience,* which is the internal response that customers have to all aspects of an organization and its offering. This internal response includes both the direct and indirect contacts of the customer with the company. Direct contacts include the customer's contacts with the seller through buying, using, and obtaining service. Indirect contacts most often involve unplanned "touches" with the company through word-of-mouth comments from other customers, reviewers, and news reports.[28]

Ethics and Social Responsibility: Balancing Interests of Groups

Today, the standards of marketing practice have shifted from an emphasis on producers' interests to consumers' interests. Organizations increasingly consider the social and environmental consequences of their actions for all parties.

Ethics   Many marketing issues are not specifically addressed by existing laws and regulations. Should information about a firm's customers be sold to other organizations? Should consumers be on their own to assess the safety of a product? These questions raise difficult ethical issues. Many companies, industries, and professional associations have developed codes of ethics to assist managers.

societal marketing concept

The view that organizations should satisfy the needs of consumers in a way that also provides for society's well-being.

Social Responsibility   While many ethical issues involve only the buyer and seller, others involve society as a whole. A manufacturer dumping toxic wastes into streams has an impact on the environment and society. This example illustrates the issue of social responsibility, the idea that individuals and organizations are accountable to a larger society. The well-being of society at large should be recognized in an organization's marketing decisions. In fact, some marketing experts stress the **societal marketing concept**, the view that an organization should discover and satisfy the needs of its consumers in a way that also provides for society's well-being.[29] For example, Scotchbrite® Never Rust™ soap pads from 3M—which are made from recycled plastic bottles—are more expensive than competitors' products (SOS and Brillo) but superior because they don't rust or scratch (question 3, Figure 1–1).

As another example of societal marketing, consider Bridging, a not-for-profit organization that has found a way to connect those who have too much "stuff" lying around their house or room with others who have a need for those items. Bridging matches people's gifts of surplus things such as dishes and furniture with other people's needs. Bridging is an example of today's *social entrepreneurship*, innovative activities that help solve the practical needs of society.[30]

The Breadth and Depth of Marketing

Marketing today affects every person and organization. To understand this, let's analyze (1) who markets, (2) what is marketed, (3) who buys and uses what is marketed, (4) who benefits from these marketing activities, and (5) how they benefit.

Who Markets?   Every organization markets. It's obvious that business firms involved in manufacturing (Heinz), retailing (Target), and providing services (Marriott) market their offerings. And nonprofit organizations such as your local hospital, your college, places (cities, states, countries), and even special causes (Race for the Cure) also engage in marketing. Finally, individuals such as political candidates often use marketing to gain voter attention and preference.[31]

What Is Marketed?   Goods, services, and even ideas are marketed. *Goods* are physical objects such as iron ore, apples, or a computer. *Services* are intangible items such as airline trips, financial advice, or telephone calls. *Ideas* are intangible concepts and thoughts about products, actions, or causes.

Financial pressures have caused art museums to innovate to market their unique services—the viewing of artworks by visitors—to increase revenues. This often involves levels of rare creativity unthinkable several decades ago. For example, the search for new revenues spurred the Dallas Museum of Art to stay open for 100 consecutive hours to celebrate its centennial.[32]

France's Louvre, home to the Mona Lisa painting and Winged Victory of Samothrace statue, has launched exotic fund-raising dinners and partnerships with museums around the world.[33] To reach potential future visitors, Russia's 1,000-room State Hermitage Museum has partnered with IBM to let you take a "virtual tour" of its exhibits. To be a "virtual tourist," go to www.hermitagemuseum.org, and click on the "Virtual Visit" link.

Ideas are most often marketed by nonprofit organizations or the government. For example, your local library may market the idea of developing improved reading

France's Louvre and Russia's State Hermitage Museum are using creative marketing efforts to generate new revenues and attract first-time visitors.

skills, and the Nature Conservancy markets the cause of protecting the environment. Charities market the idea that it's worthwhile for you to donate your time or money.

ultimate consumers
The people who use the goods and services purchased for a household.

organizational buyers
Manufacturers, wholesalers, retailers, and government agencies that buy goods and services for their own use or for resale.

Who Buys and Uses What Is Marketed? Both individuals and organizations buy and use goods and services that are marketed. **Ultimate consumers** are the people—whether 80 years or eight months old—who use the goods and services purchased for a household. In contrast, **organizational buyers** are those manufacturers, wholesalers, retailers, and government agencies that buy goods and services for their own use or for resale. Although the terms *consumers, buyers,* and *customers* are sometimes used for both ultimate consumers and organizations, there is no consistency on this. In this book you will be able to tell from the example whether the buyers are ultimate consumers, organizations, or both.

Who Benefits? In our free-enterprise society there are three specific groups that benefit from effective marketing: consumers who buy, organizations that sell, and society as a whole. True competition between products and services in the marketplace ensures that consumers can find value from the best products, the lowest prices, or exceptional service. Providing choices leads to the consumer satisfaction and quality of life that we have come to expect from our economic system.

Organizations that provide need-satisfying products with effective marketing programs—for example, Target, IBM, and Avon—have blossomed. But competition creates problems for ineffective competitors, such as eToys and the hundreds of other dot-com businesses that have failed in the last few years.

Finally, effective marketing benefits society.[34] It enhances competition, which, in turn, both improves the quality of products and services and lowers their prices. This makes countries more competitive in world markets and provides jobs and a higher standard of living for their citizens.

utility
The benefits or customer value received by users of the product.

How Do Consumers Benefit? Marketing creates **utility**, the benefits or customer value received by users of the product. This utility is the result of the marketing exchange process and the way society benefits from marketing. There are four different utilities: form, place, time, and possession. The production of the good or service constitutes *form utility. Place utility* means having the offering available where consumers need it, whereas *time utility* means having it available when needed. *Possession utility* is the value of making an item easy to purchase through the provision of credit cards or financial arrangements. Marketing creates its utilities by bridging space (place utility) and hours (time utility) to provide products (form utility) for consumers to own and use (possession utility).

---

learning review

6. What are the two key characteristics of the marketing concept?

7. What is the difference between ultimate consumers and organizational buyers?

LEARNING OBJECTIVES REVIEW

LO1 *Define marketing and identify the diverse factors influencing marketing activities.*
Marketing is an organizational function and a set of processes for creating, communicating, and delivering value to customers

and for managing customer relationships in ways that benefit the organization and its stakeholders. This definition relates to two primary goals of marketing: (*a*) discovering the needs of prospective customers and (*b*) satisfying them. Achieving these two goals also involves the four marketing mix factors largely controlled by the organization and the five environmental forces that are generally outside its control.

LO2 *Explain how marketing discovers and satisfies consumer needs.*

The first objective in marketing is discovering the needs and wants of consumers who are prospective buyers and customers. This is not easy because consumers may not always know or be able to describe what they need and want. A need occurs when a person feels deprived of basic necessities such as food, clothing, and shelter. A want is a need that is shaped by a person's knowledge, culture, and personality. Effective marketing can clearly shape a person's wants and tries to influence what a person buys. The second objective in marketing is satisfying the needs of targeted consumers. Because an organization obviously can't satisfy all consumer needs, it must concentrate its efforts on certain needs of a specific group of potential consumers or target market—one or more specific groups of potential consumers toward which an organization directs its marketing program. Having selected its target market consumers, the organization then takes action to satisfy their needs by developing a unique marketing program to reach them.

LO3 *Distinguish between marketing mix factors and environmental forces.*

Four elements in a marketing program designed to satisfy customer needs are product, price, promotion, and place. These elements, called the marketing mix, or the four Ps, are controllable variables because they are under the general control of the marketing department. Environmental forces, also called uncontrollable variables, are largely beyond the organization's control. These include social, economic, technological, competitive, and regulatory forces.

LO4 *Explain how organizations build strong customer relationships and customer value through marketing.*

The essence of successful marketing is to provide sufficient value to gain loyal, long-term customers. Customer value is the unique combination of benefits received by targeted buyers that usually includes quality, price, convenience, on-time delivery, and both before-sale and after-sale service at a specific price. Marketers do this by using one of three value strategies: best price, best product, or best service.

LO5 *Describe how today's customer relationship era differs from prior eras.*

U.S. business history is divided into four overlapping periods: the production era, the sales era, the marketing concept era, and the current customer relationship era. The production era covers the period to the 1920s when buyers were willing to accept virtually any goods that were available. The central notion was that products would sell themselves. The sales era lasted from the 1920s to the 1960s. Manufacturers found they could produce more goods than buyers could consume, and competition grew, so the solution was to hire more salespeople to find new buyers. In the late 1960s, the marketing concept era dawned when organizations adopted a strong market orientation and integrated marketing into each phase of their business. In today's customer relationship era that started in the 1980s, organizations seek continuously to satisfy the high expectations of customers—an aggressive extension of the marketing concept era.

FOCUSING ON KEY TERMS

customer value p. 10
environmental forces p. 10
exchange p. 6
market p. 9
market orientation p. 14

marketing p. 5
marketing concept p. 14
marketing mix p. 10
marketing program p. 12
organizational buyers p. 16

relationship marketing p. 11
societal marketing concept p. 15
target market p. 9
ultimate consumers p. 16
utility p. 16

APPLYING MARKETING KNOWLEDGE

1 What consumer wants (or benefits) are met by the following products or services? (*a*) Carnation Instant Breakfast, (*b*) Adidas running shoes, (*c*) Hertz Rent-A-Car, and (*d*) television home shopping programs.

2 Each of the four products, services, or programs in question 1 has substitutes. Respective examples are (*a*) a ham and egg breakfast, (*b*) regular tennis shoes, (*c*) taking a bus, and (*d*) a department store. What consumer benefits might these substitutes have in each case that some consumers might value more highly than those mentioned in question 1?

3 What are the characteristics (e.g., age, income, education) of the target market customers for the following products or services? (*a*) *National Geographic* magazine, (*b*) *Wired* magazine, (*c*) New York Giants football team, and (*d*) the U.S. Open tennis tournament.

4 A college in a metropolitan area wishes to increase its evening-school offerings of business-related courses such as marketing, accounting, finance, and management. Who are the target market customers (students) for these courses?

5 What actions involving the four marketing mix elements might be used to reach the target market in question 4?

6 What environmental forces (uncontrollable variables) must the college in question 4 consider in designing its marketing program?

7 Does a firm have the right to "create" wants and try to persuade consumers to buy goods and services they didn't know about earlier? What are examples of "good" and "bad" want creation? Who should decide what is good and bad?

If your instructor assigns a marketing plan for your class, don't make a face and complain about the work—for two special reasons. First, you will get insights into trying to actually "do marketing" that often go beyond what you can get by simply reading the textbook. Second, thousands of graduating students every year get their first job by showing prospective employers a "portfolio" of samples of their written work from college—often a marketing plan if they have one. This can work for you.

This "Building Your Marketing Plan" section at the end of each chapter suggests ways to improve and focus your marketing plan. You will use the sample marketing plan in Appendix A (following Chapter 2) as a guide, and this section after each chapter will help you apply those Appendix A ideas to your own marketing plan.

The first step in writing a good marketing plan is to have a business or product that enthuses you and for which you can get detailed information, so you can avoid glittering generalities. We offer these additional bits of advice in selecting a topic:

- *Do* pick a topic that has personal interest for you— a family business, a business or product you or a friend might want to launch, or a student organization needing marketing help.
- *Do not* pick a topic that is so large it can't be covered adequately or so abstract it will lack specifics.

1 Now to get you started on your marketing plan, list four or five possible topics and compare these with the criteria your instructor suggests and those shown above. Think hard, because your decision will be with you all term and may influence the quality of the resulting marketing plan you show to a prospective employer.

2 When you have selected your marketing plan topic, whether the plan is for an actual business, a possible business, or a student organization, write the "company description" in your plan, as shown in Appendix A.

"I didn't go out to students and ask, 'What are your needs, or what are your wants?' " 3M inventor David Windorski explains to a class of college students. "And even if I did ask, they probably wouldn't say, 'Put flags inside a highlighter.'"

So Windorski turned the classic textbook approach to marketing on its head.

That classic approach—as you saw earlier in Chapter 1—says to start with needs and wants of potential customers and then develop the product. But sometimes new-product development runs in the opposite direction: Start with a new product idea—such as personal computers— and then see if there is a market. This is really what Windorski did, using a lot of marketing research along the way after he developed the concept of the Post-it® Flag Highlighter.

EARLY MARKETING RESEARCH

During this new-product development process, Windorski and 3M did a lot of marketing research on students. For example, students were asked to dump the contents of their backpacks on the table and to explain what they carried around and then to react to some early highlighter models. Also, several times six or seven students were interviewed together and observed by 3M researchers from behind a one-way mirror—the focus group technique discussed in Chapter 8. Other students were interviewed individually.

Windorski's early models were nonworking clay ones like he is holding in the photo on the next page. These nonworking models told him how the innovative highlighters would feel to students eventually using the real ones. When early working models of the Post-it® Flag Highlighter finally existed, several hundred were produced and given to students to use for a month. Their reactions were captured on a questionnaire.

THE NEW-PRODUCT LAUNCH

After the initial marketing research and dozens of technical tests in 3M laboratories, David Windorski's new 3M highlighter product was ready to be manufactured and marketed.

Here's a snapshot of the pre-launch issues that were solved before the product could be introduced:

- *Technical issues.* Can we generate a computer-aided database for injection molded parts? What tolerances do we need? The 3M highlighter is really a technological marvel. For the parts on the highlighter to work, tolerances must be several thousandths of an inch—less than the thickness of a piece of paper.
- *Manufacturing issues.* Where should the product be manufactured? Because 3M chose a company outside the United States, precise translations of critical technical specifications were needed. Windorski spent time in the factory working with engineers and manufacturing specialists there to ensure that 3M's precise production standards would be achieved.

- *Product issues.* What should the brand name be for the new highlighter product? Marketing research and many meetings gave the answer: "The Post-it® Flag Highlighter." How many to a package? What color(s)? What should the packaging look like in order to (1) display the product well at retail and (2) communicate its points of difference effectively?
- *Price issues.* With many competing highlighters, what should the price be for 3M's premium highlighter that will provide 3M adequate profit? Should the suggested retail price be the same in college bookstores, mass merchandisers (Walmart, Target), and office supply stores (Office Max, Office Depot)?
- *Promotion issues.* How can 3M tell students the product exists? Might office workers want it and use it? Should there be print ads, TV ads, and point-of-sale displays explaining the product?
- *Place (distribution) issues.* With the limited shelf space in college bookstores and other outlets, how can 3M persuade retailers to stock its new product?

THE MARKETING PROGRAM TODAY AND TOMORROW

The highlighter turned out to be more popular than 3M expected. The company often hears from end users how much they like the product.

So what can 3M do for an encore to build on the product's initial success? This involves taking great care to introduce product extensions to attract new customers while still retaining its solid foundation of loyal existing customers. Also, 3M's products have to appeal not only to the ultimate consumers but also to retailers who want new items to display in high-traffic areas.

Product and packaging decisions for the Post-it® Flag Highlighter reflect this innovative focus. In terms of product extensions, David Windorski designed new Post-it® Flag Highlighters and Pens that are easier to hold and that have the flags permanently accessible without twisting (see photo on page 13). As to packaging, it's critical that it (1) communicate the 2-products-in-1 idea, (2) be attractive, and (3) achieve both goals with the fewest words.

At 3M, promotion budgets are limited because it relies heavily on its technology for a competitive advantage. This also applies to the Post-it® Flag Highlighter. So you probably have never seen a print or TV ad for it. Yet potential student buyers, the product's main target market, must be made aware that it exists. So 3M searches continually for simple, effective promotions to alert students about this product.

Great technology is meaningless unless the product is available where potential buyers can purchase it. Unlike college bookstores that exist largely to serve students, mass merchandisers and office supply stores track, measure, and seek to maximize the profit of every square foot of selling space. So 3M must convince these retail chains that selling space devoted to its highlighter line will be more profitable than stocking competing products. The challenge for 3M: finding ways to make the Post-it® Flag Highlighter prominent on shelves of college bookstores and retail chains.

If the Post-it® Flag Highlighter is doing well in the United States, why not try to sell it around the world? But even here 3M faces critical questions: Which countries will be the best markets? What highlighter colors and packaging works best in each country? How do we physically get the product to these markets in a timely and cost-efficient basis?

Questions

1 *(a)* How did 3M's David Windorski get ideas from college students to help him in designing the final commercial version of the Post-it® Flag Highlighter? *(b)* How were these ideas important to the success of the product?

2 What *(a)* special advantages and *(b)* potential problems did 3M have in introducing a new highlighter-with-flags product for college students?

3 Visit your college bookstore before you answer. *(a)* Where would you display the Post-it® Flag Highlighter in a college bookstore, and *(b)* how can the display increase student awareness of the product?

4 In what ways might 3M try to promote its Post-it® Flag Highlighter and make students more aware of the product?

5 What are *(a)* the special opportunities and *(b)* potential challenges for 3M in taking its Post-it® Flag Highlighter into international markets? *(c)* On which countries should 3M focus its marketing efforts?

Ben & Jerry's Mission

Ben & Jerry's is founded on & dedicated to a sustainable corporate concept of linked prosperity. Our mission consists of 3 interrelated parts:

SOCIAL mission

To operate the Company in a way that actively recognizes the central role that business plays in society by initiating innovative ways to improve the quality of life locally, nationally and internationally.

PRODUCT mission

To make, distribute and sell the finest quality all natural ice cream and euphoric concoctions with a continued commitment to incorporating wholesome, natural ingredients and promoting business practices that respect the Earth and the Environment.

ECONOMIC mission

To operate the Company on a sustainable financial basis of profitable growth, increasing value for our stakeholders and expanding opportunities for development and career growth for our employees.

Underlying the Mission

is the determination to seek new & creative ways of addressing all 3 parts, while holding a deep respect for individuals inside & outside the company, & for the communities of which they are a part.

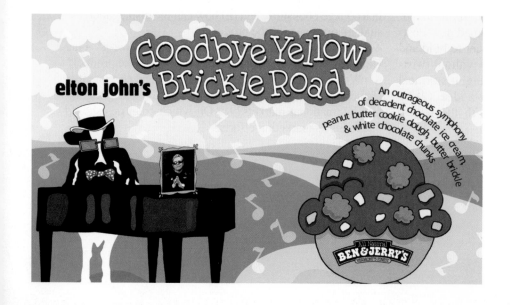

2

Developing Successful Marketing and Organizational Strategies

LEARNING OBJECTIVES

After reading this chapter you should be able to:

LO1 Describe two kinds of organizations and the three levels of strategy in them.

LO2 Describe how core values, mission, organizational culture, business, and goals are important to organizations.

LO3 Explain why managers use marketing dashboards and marketing metrics.

LO4 Discuss how an organization assesses where it is now and where it seeks to be.

LO5 Explain the three steps of the planning phase of the strategic marketing process.

LO6 Describe the elements of the implementation and evaluation phases of the strategic marketing process.

BE AN ENTREPRENEUR: GET AN "A" IN A CORRESPONDENCE COURSE IN ICE CREAM MAKING!

Here's what the two founding entrepreneurs who aced their $5 college correspondence course in ice cream making are doing in their organization today:

- They buy their milk and cream from one dairy cooperative whose members guarantee the supplies are bovine growth-hormone free.

- Their PartnerShop, Scoopers Making Change, and Cones 2 Career programs help nonprofit organizations give jobs to at-risk youth.

- The summer 2009 limited edition "Goodbye Yellow Brickle Road" ice cream is a partnership with Sir Elton John to help his worldwide AIDS Foundation. The name is a play on one of his most popular song titles. The flavor is "an outrageous symphony of decadent chocolate ice cream, peanut butter cookie dough, butterbrickle and white chocolate chunks." Will it reappear in 2011?

- They are developing a "Cleaner Greener Freezer" for Ben & Jerry's U.S. retail locations, an innovative freezer that uses an eco-friendly refrigerant to save the ozone layer and reduce greenhouse gases.

This creative, funky business is Ben & Jerry's Homemade Holdings, Inc., which links its mission statement to social causes designed to improve humanity, as shown on the opposite page.

Their business started in 1978 when long-time friends Ben Cohen and Jerry Greenfield headed north to Vermont to start an ice cream parlor in a renovated gas station. Buoyed with enthusiasm, $12,000 in borrowed and saved money, and ideas from a $5 Penn State correspondence course in ice cream making, Ben and Jerry were off and scooping.[1] Today, Ben & Jerry's is owned by Unilever, which is the market leader in the global ice cream industry—one that is expected to reach $54 billion by 2013.[2] While customers love Cherry Garcia and the company's other rich premium ice cream flavors, many buy its products to support Ben & Jerry's social mission.

Chapter 2 describes how organizations such as Ben & Jerry's, Medtronic, and Kodak set goals to give an overall direction that is linked to their organizational and marketing strategies. The marketing department of an organization converts these strategies into plans that must be implemented. The results are then evaluated to assess the degree to which they accomplish the organization's goals, consistent with its core values and mission.

TODAY'S ORGANIZATIONS

In studying today's visionary organizations, it is important to recognize (1) the kinds of organizations that exist, (2) what strategy is, and (3) how this strategy relates to the three levels of structure found in many large organizations.

Kinds of Organizations

An *organization* is a legal entity that consists of people who share a common mission. This motivates them to develop *offerings* (products, services, or ideas) that create value for both the organization and its customers by satisfying their needs and wants.[3] Today's organizations can be divided into business firms and nonprofit organizations.

A *business firm* is a privately owned organization such as Google or Nike that serves its customers to earn a profit so that it can survive.[4] **Profit** is the money left after a business firm's total expenses are subtracted from its total revenues and is the reward for the risk it undertakes in marketing its offerings.

In contrast, a *nonprofit organization* is a nongovernmental organization that serves its customers but does not have profit as an organizational goal. Instead, its goals may be operational efficiency or client satisfaction. Regardless, it also must receive sufficient funds above its expenses to continue operations. Nature Conservancy, with its focus on protecting the environment, is an example of a nonprofit organization. Both business firms and nonprofit organizations increasingly seek to achieve sustainable development, as described in the Making Responsible Decisions box.[5] For simplicity in the rest of the book, the terms *firm, company, corporation,* and *organization* are used interchangeably to cover both business and nonprofit operations.

Organizations that develop similar offerings create an *industry*, such as the computer industry or the automobile industry.[6] As a result, organizations make strategic decisions that reflect the dynamics of the industry to create a compelling and sustainable advantage for their offerings relative to those of competitors to achieve a superior level of performance.[7] The foundation of much of an organization's marketing strategy is having a clear understanding of the industry within which it competes.

What Is Strategy?

An organization has limited human, financial, technological, and other resources available to produce and market its offerings—it can't be all things to all people! Every organization must develop strategies to help focus and direct its efforts to accomplish its goals. However, the definition of strategy has been the subject of debate among management and marketing theorists.[8] For our purpose, **strategy** is an organization's long-term course of action designed to deliver a unique customer experience while achieving its goals.[9] All organizations set a strategic direction. And marketing helps both set this direction and also move the organization there.

Structure of Today's Organizations

Large organizations are extremely complex. They usually consist of three organizational levels whose strategies are linked to marketing, as shown in Figure 2–1.

profit
The reward to a business firm for the risk it undertakes in marketing its offerings.

strategy
An organization's long-term course of action that delivers a unique customer experience while achieving its goals.

Business firms such as Google shown here and nonprofit organizations use strategies and organizational structures to achieve their goals.

The Global Dilemma: How to Achieve Sustainable Development

Corporate executives and world leaders are increasingly asked to address the issue of "sustainable development." This term was formally defined in a 1987 United Nations report as meeting present needs "without compromising the ability of future generations to meet their own needs."

With more than half of the households in many developing nations below the poverty level, should the immediate goal be a cleaner environment or more food, clothing, housing, and consumer goods for its citizens? What should the heads of these governments do? What should business firms and nonprofit organizations trying to enter these developing nations do? What will be the impact on future generations?

The 3M Company has developed an innovative program called Pollution Prevention Pays (3P) to reduce harmful environmental impacts, while making a profit doing so. The company estimates that the 3P program in the last quarter century has cut its pollution by 1.6 billion pounds while saving almost $900 million in raw materials and avoiding fines.

Should the environment or economic growth come first? What are the societal trade-offs?

Corporate Level The *corporate level* is where top management directs overall strategy for the entire organization. "Top management" usually means the board of directors and senior management officers with a variety of skills and experiences that are invaluable in establishing overall strategy.

The president or chief executive officer (CEO) is the highest ranking officer in the organization and is usually a member of its board of directors. This person must possess leadership skills and expertise ranging from overseeing the organization's daily operations to spearheading strategy planning efforts that may determine its very survival.

In recent years many large firms have changed the title of the head of marketing from vice president of marketing to chief marketing officer (CMO). These CMOs have an increasingly important role in top management because of their ability to think strategically. Most bring multi-industry backgrounds, cross-functional management expertise, analytical skills, and intuitive marketing insights to their job.[10]

FIGURE 2–1
The board of directors oversees the three levels of strategy in organizations: corporate, business unit, and functional.

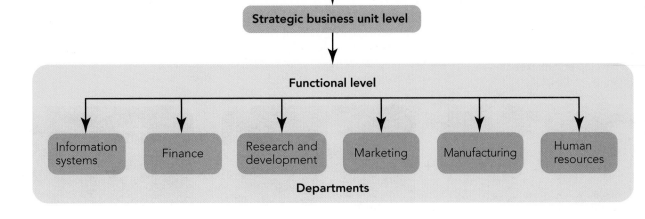

Strategic Business Unit Level   Some multimarket, multiproduct firms, such as General Electric or Johnson & Johnson, manage a portfolio or group of businesses.[11] Each group is a *strategic business unit (SBU),* which is a subsidiary, division, or unit of an organization that markets a set of related offerings to a clearly defined group of customers. At the *strategic business unit level*, managers set a more specific strategic direction for their businesses to exploit value-creating opportunities. For less complex firms with a single business focus, such as Ben & Jerry's, the corporate and business unit levels may merge.

Functional Level   Each strategic business unit has a *functional level*, where groups of specialists actually create value for the organization. The term *department* generally refers to these specialized functions such as marketing and finance (see Figure 2–1). At the functional level, the organization's strategic direction becomes its most specific and focused. Just as there is a hierarchy of levels within an organization, there is a hierarchy of strategic directions set by managers at each level.

A key role of the marketing department is to look outward, keeping the organization focused on creating value both for it and for customers. This is accomplished by listening to customers, developing and producing offerings, and implementing marketing program activities.

When developing marketing programs for new offerings or for improving existing ones, an organization's senior management may form *cross-functional teams.* These consist of a small number of people from different departments who are mutually accountable to accomplish a task or a common set of performance goals. Sometimes these teams will have representatives from outside the organization, such as suppliers or customers, to assist them.

---

learning review

1. What is the difference between a business firm and a nonprofit organization?

2. What are examples of a functional level in an organization?

STRATEGY IN VISIONARY ORGANIZATIONS

LO2

To be successful, today's organizations must be forward looking. They must both anticipate future events and respond quickly and effectively. A visionary organization must specify its foundation (why does it exist?), set a direction (what will it do?), and formulate strategies (how will it do it?) as shown in Figure 2–2.[12]

Organizational Foundation: Why Does It Exist?

An organization's foundation is its philosophical reason for being—why it exists. Successful visionary organizations use this foundation to guide and inspire their employees through three elements: core values, mission, and organizational culture.

FIGURE 2–2
Today's visionary organization uses key elements to (1) establish a foundation and (2) set a direction using (3) strategies that enable it to develop and market its offerings successfully.

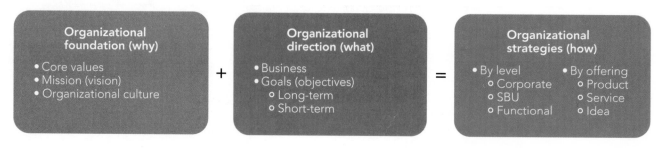

Organizational foundation (why)		Organizational direction (what)		Organizational strategies (how)	
• Core values	+	• Business	=	• By level	• By offering
• Mission (vision)		• Goals (objectives)		○ Corporate	○ Product
• Organizational culture		○ Long-term		○ SBU	○ Service
		○ Short-term		○ Functional	○ Idea

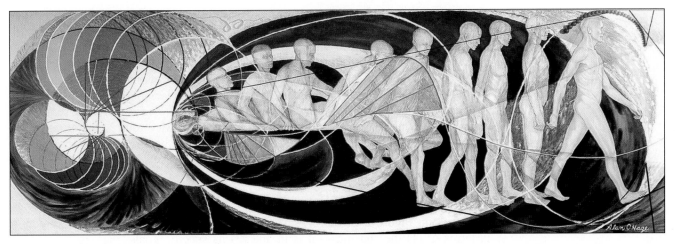

People see this "rising figure" mural in the headquarters of a world-class corporation. What does it signify? What does it say to employees? To others? For some insights and why it is important, see the text.

core values
The fundamental, passionate, and enduring principles that guide an organization.

mission
A statement or vision of an organization's function in society.

Core Values An organization's **core values** are the fundamental, passionate, and enduring principles that guide its conduct over time.[13] A firm's founders or senior management develop these core values, which are consistent with their essential beliefs and character.[14] They capture the firm's heart and soul and serve to inspire and motivate its *stakeholders*—employees, shareholders, board of directors, suppliers, distributors, creditors, unions, government, local communities, and customers. Core values also are timeless and should not change due to short-term financial, operational, or marketing concerns. Finally, core values guide the organization's conduct. To be effective, an organization's core values must be communicated to and supported by its top management and employees; if not, they are just hollow words.[15]

Mission By understanding its core values, an organization can take steps to define its **mission**, a statement of the organization's function in society that often identifies its customers, markets, products, and technologies. Often used interchangeably with *vision*, a *mission statement* should be clear, concise, meaningful, inspirational, and long-term.[16]

Medtronic is a world leader in producing heart pacemakers and other electrical stimulation devices to treat diabetes, Parkinson's disease, and chronic back pain.[17] Earl Bakken, its founder, wrote this mission statement for Medtronic when it was launched a half century ago (and which today remains virtually unchanged):

> To contribute to human welfare by application of biomedical engineering in the research, design, manufacture, and sale of instruments or appliances that alleviate pain, restore health, and extend life.

Similar inspiration and focus appear in the mission statements of both business firms and nonprofit organizations:

- Southwest Airlines: To be dedicated "to the highest quality of Customer Service delivered with a sense of warmth, friendliness, individual pride, and Company Spirit."
- American Red Cross: "To provide relief to victims of disaster and help prevent, prepare for, and respond to emergencies."

Each statement exhibits the qualities of a good mission: a clear, challenging, and compelling picture of an envisioned future.

Recently, many organizations have added a social element to their mission statements to reflect an ideal that is morally right and worthwhile. This is what Ben & Jerry's social mission statement shows in the chapter opening. Stakeholders, particularly customers, employees, and now society, are asking organizations to be exceptional citizens by providing long-term value while solving society's problems.[18]

Organizational Culture An organization must connect with all of its stakeholders. Thus, an important corporate-level marketing function is communicating its core values and mission to them. Medtronic has a "rising figure" wall mural at its headquarters. The firm also presents every new employee with a medallion depicting this "rising figure" on one side and the company's mission statement on the other. And each December, several patients describe to a large employee holiday celebration how Medtronic devices have changed their lives.[19] These activities send clear messages to employees and other stakeholders about Medtronic's **organizational culture**, the set of values, ideas, attitudes, and norms of behavior that is learned and shared among the members of an organization.

organizational culture
The set of values, ideas, attitudes, and behavioral norms that is learned and shared among the members of an organization.

Organizational Direction: What Will It Do?

As shown in Figure 2–2, the organization's foundation enables it to set a direction in terms of (1) the "business" it is in and (2) its specific goals.

Business A **business** describes the clear, broad, underlying industry or market sector of an organization's offering. To help define its business, an organization looks at the set of organizations that sell similar offerings—those that are in direct competition with each other—such as "the ice cream business." The organization can then begin to answer the questions, "What do we do?" or "What business are we in?"

business
The underlying industry or market sector of an organization's offering.

In his famous "Marketing Myopia" article, Theodore Levitt argues that senior managers of 20th century American railroads defined their business too narrowly, proclaiming, "We are in the railroad business!" This myopic focus caused these firms to lose sight of who their customers were and what they needed. Thus, railroads only saw other railroads as direct competitors and failed to develop strategies to compete with airlines, barges, pipelines, and trucks—firms whose offerings carry both goods and people. As a result, many railroads merged or went bankrupt. Railroads would have fared better if they had realized they were in "the transportation business."[20]

With today's increased global competition and worldwide financial crises, many organizations are rethinking their *business model*, the strategies an organization develops to provide value to the customers it serves. Technological innovation is often the trigger for this business model change. American newspapers are looking for a new business model as former subscribers get their news online and buy cars from Craigslist Inc. rather than using newspaper want ads.[21] Bookstore retailer Barnes & Noble, too, is rethinking its business model as e-book readers like Amazon's Kindle and Apple's iPad are projected to capture over 20 percent of book sales by 2013.[22]

In the first half of the 20th century, what "business" did railroad executives believe they were in? The text reveals their disastrous error.

Netflix founder Reed Hastings got the idea for his unique business model in 1997 when he was charged a late fee of $40 for a VHS tape of *Apollo 13*. "So I started to investigate the idea of how to create a movie-rental business by mail," he told a *Fortune* magazine interviewer.[23] His business model has gone from (1) a mail movie-rental business to (2) a mail subscription service to (3) letting subscribers watch downloaded movies on their own TV. So a Netflix "any movie, any time" business model is just around the corner.

goals (objectives)
Targets of performance to be achieved, often by a specific time.

Goals **Goals** or **objectives** (terms used interchangeably in the textbook) are statements of an accomplishment of a task to be achieved, often by a specific time. For example, Netflix might set a goal of being the top provider of online movies by 2012. Goals convert an organization's mission and business into long- and short-term performance targets to measure how well it is doing (see Figure 2–2).

Business firms can pursue several different types of goals:

- *Profit.* Most firms seek to maximize profits—to get as high a financial return on their investments (ROI) as possible.

market share
Ratio of a firm's sales to the total sales of all firms in the industry.

- *Sales* (dollars or units). If profits are acceptable, a firm may elect to maintain or increase its sales even though profits may not be maximized.
- *Market share.* **Market share** is the ratio of sales revenue of the firm to the total sales revenue of all firms in the industry, including the firm itself. A firm may choose to maintain or increase its market share, sometimes at the expense of greater profits if industry status or prestige is at stake.
- *Quality.* A firm may offer the highest quality, as Medtronic does with its implantable medical devices.
- *Customer satisfaction.* Customers are the reason the organization exists, so their perceptions and actions are of vital importance. Satisfaction can be measured with surveys or by the number of customer complaints an organization receives.
- *Employee welfare.* A firm may recognize the critical importance of its employees by stating its goal of providing them with good employment opportunities and working conditions.
- *Social responsibility.* Firms may seek to balance the conflicting goals of stakeholders to promote their overall welfare, even at the expense of profits.

Nonprofit organizations (such as museums and hospitals) also have goals, such as to serve consumers as efficiently as possible. Similarly, government agencies set goals that seek to serve the public good.

Organizational Strategies: How Will It Do It?

As shown in Figure 2–2, the organizational foundation sets the "why" of organizations and the organizational direction sets the "what." To convert these into actual results, the organizational strategies are concerned with the "how." These organizational strategies vary in at least two ways, depending on (1) a strategy's level in the organization and (2) the offerings an organization provides to its customers.

Variation by Level   Moving from the corporate to the strategic business unit to the functional level involves creating increasingly detailed strategies and plans. For example, at the corporate level, top managers may struggle with writing a meaningful mission statement; while at the functional level, the issue may involve whether Joan or Adam makes the sales call tomorrow.

Variation by Offering   Organizational strategies also vary by the organization's offering. The strategy will be far different when marketing a very tangible physical product (a Medtronic heart pacemaker), a service (a Southwest Airlines flight), or an idea (a donation to the American Red Cross).

The remainder of Chapter 2 covers many aspects of developing these organizational strategies.

---

learning review

3. What is the meaning of an organization's mission?

4. What is the difference between an organization's business and its goals?

LO3

Tracking Strategic Performance with Marketing Dashboards

Although marketing managers can set strategic directions for their organizations, how do they know if they are making progress in getting there? One answer is to measure performance by using marketing dashboards.

marketing dashboard
The visual computer display of essential marketing information.

Car Dashboards and Marketing Dashboards   A **marketing dashboard** is the visual computer display of the essential information related to achieving a marketing objective.[24] Often, it is a computer-based display with real-time information and active hyperlinks to provide further detail. An example is when a chief marketing officer (CMO) wants to see daily what the effect of a new TV advertising campaign is on a product's sales in order to allocate marketing resources effectively.[25]

The idea of a marketing dashboard really comes from the display of information found on a car's dashboard. On a car's dashboard we glance at the fuel gauge and take action when our gas is getting low. With a marketing dashboard, a marketing manager glances at a graph or table and makes a decision whether to take action or to analyze the problem further.[26]

Dashboards, Metrics, and Plans The marketing dashboard of Oracle, a large software firm, appears in Figure 2–3. It shows graphic displays of key performance measures of a product category such as sales versus cost of sales.[27] Each variable in a marketing dashboard is a **marketing metric**, which is a measure of the quantitative value or trend of a marketing activity or result.[28] The choice of which marketing metrics to display is critical for a busy marketing manager, who can be overwhelmed with too much or inappropriate information.[29]

Dashboard designers take great care to show graphs and tables in easy-to-understand formats to enable clear interpretation at a glance.[30] The Oracle marketing dashboard in Figure 2–3 presents several marketing metrics on the computer screen. The three-step "challenge-findings-action" format in the Using Marketing Dashboards box for Ben & Jerry's is the one used throughout the textbook. This format stresses the importance of using marketing dashboards and the metrics contained within them to produce effective marketing strategy and program actions. The Ben & Jerry's dashboard shows that both its dollar sales and dollar market share grew from 2010 to 2011.

Most organizations tie the marketing metrics they track in their marketing dashboards to the quantitative objectives established in their **marketing plan**, which is a road map for the marketing activities of an organization for a specified future time period, such as one year or five years. The planning phase of the strategic marketing process (discussed later in this chapter) usually results in a marketing plan that sets the direction for the marketing activities of an organization.

Appendix A at the end of this chapter provides guidelines for writing a marketing plan and also presents a sample marketing plan for Paradise Kitchens® Inc., a firm

marketing metric
A measure of the value or trend of a marketing activity or result.

marketing plan
A road map for the marketing activities of an organization for a specified future time period.

FIGURE 2–3
An effective marketing dashboard, like this one from Oracle, helps managers assess a business situation at a glance.

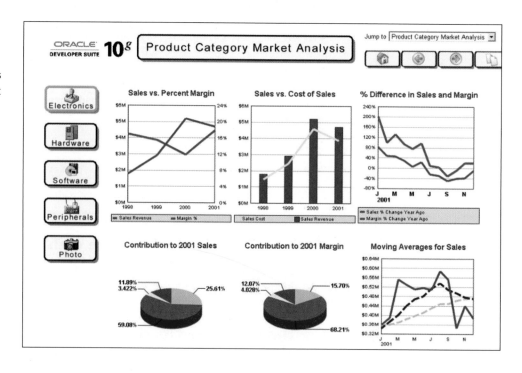

Using Marketing Dashboards

How Well Is Ben & Jerry's Doing?

As the marketing manager for Ben & Jerry's, you have been asked to provide a snapshot of the firm's total super-premium ice cream product line performance for the United States. You choose the following marketing metrics: dollar sales and dollar market share.

Your Challenge SymphonyIRI Group provides scanner data from grocery stores and other retailers. It has just sent you a report showing that the total ice cream sales for 2011 were $25 billion. Of that total, 5 percent or $1.25 billion (0.05 × $25 billion) comprises the super-premium category—the segment of the market that Ben & Jerry's competes in. Internal company data show you that Ben & Jerry's sold 50 million units at an average price of $5.00 per unit in 2011.

Your Findings The metrics you chose (dollar sales and dollar market share) are goals that firms such as Ben & Jerry's use to measure performance. They can be calculated for 2011 using simple formulas and displayed on the Ben & Jerry's marketing dashboard as follows:

Dollar sales ($) = Average price × Quantity sold
= $5.00 × 50 million units
= $250 million

$$\text{Dollar market share (\%)} = \frac{\text{Ben \& Jerry's sales (\$)}}{\text{Total industry sales (\$)}}$$

$$= \frac{\$250 \text{ million}}{\$1.25 \text{ billion}}$$

= 0.20 or 20%

Your dashboard displays show that from 2010 to 2011 dollar

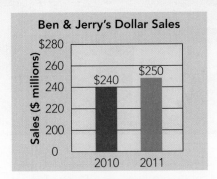

Ben & Jerry's Dollar Sales

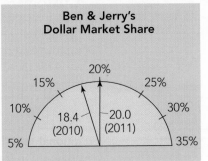

Ben & Jerry's Dollar Market Share

sales increased from $240 million to $250 million and that dollar market share grew from 18.4 to 20.0 percent.

Your Action The results need to be compared with the goals established for these metrics. In addition, they should be compared with previous years' results to see if the trends are increasing, flat, or decreasing. NOTE: Marketers also find it useful to calculate market share based on the number of units sold, if data are available.

that produces and distributes a line of spicy chili under the Howlin' Coyote® brand name. Appendix A also links each section of the marketing plan to the relevant textbook chapter to assist students who are writing marketing plans.

SETTING STRATEGIC DIRECTIONS

To set a strategic direction, an organization needs to answer two difficult questions: (1) Where are we now? and (2) Where do we want to go?

A Look Around: Where Are We Now?

Asking an organization where it is at the present time involves identifying its competencies, customers, and competitors.

Lands' End's unconditional guarantee for its products highlights its focus on customers.

Competencies Senior managers must ask the question: What do we do best? The answer involves an assessment of the organization's core *competencies*, which are its special capabilities—the skills, technologies, and resources—that distinguish it from other organizations and provide customer value. Exploiting these competencies can lead to success.[31] Medtronic's competencies include world-class technology, training, and service that respond to life-threatening medical needs. *Bloomberg Businessweek* magazine calls Medtronic "the standard setter for quality."[32] Competencies should be distinctive enough to provide a *competitive advantage*, a unique strength relative to competitors that provides superior returns, often based on quality, time, cost, or innovation.[33]

Customers Ben & Jerry's customers are ice cream and frozen yogurt eaters who have different preferences (form, flavor, health, and convenience). Medtronic's customers are cardiologists and heart surgeons who serve patients. Lands' End communicates a remarkable commitment about its customer experience and product quality with these unconditional words:

Guaranteed. Period.®

The Lands' End Web site points out that this guarantee has always been an unconditional one. It reads: "If you're not satisfied with any item, simply return it to us at any time for an exchange or refund of its purchase price." But to get the message across more clearly to its customers, it created the two-word guarantee. The point is that Lands' End's strategy must provide genuine value to customers to ensure that they have a satisfying experience.[34]

Competitors In today's global competition, the distinctions among competitors are increasingly blurred. Lands' End started as a catalog retailer. But today, Lands' End competes with not only other clothing catalog retailers but also traditional department stores, mass merchandisers, and specialty shops. Even well-known clothing brands such as Liz Claiborne now have their own chain stores. Although only some of the clothing in any of these stores directly competes with Lands' End offerings, all these retailers have Web sites to sell their offerings over the Internet. This means there's a lot of competition out there.

Kodak today must make a series of difficult marketing decisions. From what you know about cameras and photos, assess Kodak's sales opportunities for the four products shown here. For some possible answers and a way to show these opportunities graphically, see the text and Figure 2–4.

Kodak digital cameras

Kodak digital picture frames

Kodak ink-jet printers and cartridges to print photos at home

Kodak film

Growth Strategies: Where Do We Want to Go?

Knowing where the organization is at the present time enables managers to set a direction for the firm and allocate resources to move in that direction. Two techniques to aid managers with these decisions are (1) business portfolio analysis and (2) diversification analysis strategies.

Business Portfolio Analysis   The Boston Consulting Group (BCG), a nationally known management consulting firm, has developed **business portfolio analysis**. It is a technique that managers use to quantify performance measures and growth targets to analyze their firms' strategic business units (SBUs) as though they were a collection of separate investments.[35] The purpose of the tool is to determine the appeal of each SBU or offering and then determine the amount of cash each should receive. More than 75 percent of the largest U.S. firms have used this analytical tool.

The BCG business portfolio analysis requires an organization to locate the position of each of its SBUs on a growth-share matrix (see Figure 2–4 on the next page). The vertical axis is the *market growth rate*, which is the annual rate of growth of the SBU's industry. The horizontal axis is the *relative market share*, defined as the sales of the SBU divided by the sales of the largest firm in the industry. A relative market share of $10\times$ (at the left end of the scale) means that the SBU has 10 times the share of its largest competitor, whereas a share of $0.1\times$ (at the right end of the scale) means it has only 10 percent of the share of its largest competitor.

The BCG has given specific names and descriptions to the four resulting quadrants in its growth-share matrix based on the amount of cash they generate for or require from the organization:

- *Cash cows* are SBUs that generate large amounts of cash, far more than they can invest profitably in themselves. They have dominant shares of slow-growth markets and provide cash to cover the organization's overhead and to invest in other SBUs.
- *Stars* are SBUs with a high share of high-growth markets that may need extra cash to finance their own rapid future growth. When their growth slows, they are likely to become cash cows.
- *Question marks* are SBUs with a low share of high-growth markets. They require large injections of cash just to maintain their market share, much less increase it. The name implies management's dilemma for these SBUs: choosing the right ones to invest in and phasing out the rest.
- *Dogs* are SBUs with low shares of slow-growth markets. Although they may generate enough cash to sustain themselves, they do not hold the promise of ever becoming real winners for the organization. Dropping SBUs that are dogs may be required, except when relationships with other SBUs, competitive considerations, or potential strategic alliances exist.[36]

An organization's SBUs often start as question marks and go counterclockwise around Figure 2–4 to become stars, then cash cows, and finally dogs. Because an organization has limited influence on the market growth rate, its main alternative is to try to change its relative market share. To do this, management decides what future role each SBU should have and either injects or removes cash from it.

Kodak provides an example of how new technology and changing consumer tastes can force a company to convert a crisis into potential long-run opportunities.[37] Until 2000, Kodak relied on its film for the bulk of its revenues and profits because of the billions of photos taken every year. The company made money on repeat business from traditional film sales and *not* on camera purchases. The appearance of digital cameras changed Kodak's business forever as film sales began to evaporate.

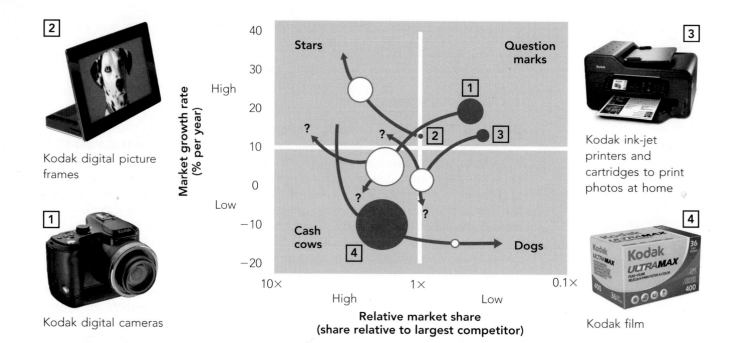

Kodak digital picture frames

Kodak digital cameras

Kodak ink-jet printers and cartridges to print photos at home

Kodak film

FIGURE 2–4

Boston Consulting Group business portfolio analysis for Kodak's consumer-related SBUs as they appeared in 2003 (solid red circles) and might appear in 2012 (white circles).

Four Kodak SBUs (see the solid red circles in Figure 2–4) are shown as they may have appeared in 2003 and can serve as an example of BCG analysis. The area of each solid red circle in Figure 2–4 is roughly proportional to the SBU's 2003 sales revenue. In a more complete analysis, Kodak's other SBUs would be included. This example also shows the agonizing strategic decisions that executives must make in an industry facing profound change—the situation Kodak confronted due to the arrival of digital technology.

The success of Kodak's new digital strategy and its product lines shown in Figure 2–4 depends on how millions of consumers (1) take photos and convert them into printed or online images in the coming years and (2) continue to be affected by the global economic recession. Here is a snapshot of where sales revenues were for four Kodak consumer product lines in 2003 (the solid red circles) and where they now appear to be headed in 2012 (the white circles).

1. *Kodak digital cameras.* In 2008, about 80 percent of U.S. consumers owned a digital camera because it is now easier to use than a film camera, is cheaper, and allows images to be uploaded and shared online. But Kodak's digital camera sales may flatten due to high household penetration, the economic downturn, and increased competition. Kodak remains No. 3 in market share behind Canon and Sony. Today more women are buying digital cameras because they are small and light. Bottom line: Kodak expects this SBU to continue to be a *cash cow*, with its new digital camera models generating mainly replacement sales.[38]

2. *Kodak digital picture frames.* In 2007, Kodak introduced a line of digital picture frames that allowed consumers to upload, store, and view digital images. In 2009, Kodak expanded its line with more than 11 items ranging in price from $60 to $180. And in 2009, it introduced the $999 OLED (organic light-emitting diode) digital picture frame that features a high-resolution flat-panel display to present extremely sharp photo images. Global demand has exploded, and today Kodak is the market leader—clearly a *star*. By 2013, sales could approach 50 million units.[39]

3. *Kodak ink-jet printers and cartridges to print photos at home.* In 2008, the ink-jet printer market dramatically changed as consumers shifted from single-purpose to multifunction machines designed to print photos, make copies, scan images, and send faxes. Today Kodak now offers only multifunction models. Moreover, Kodak's high-quality ink cartridges make photos at half the cost of Hewlett-Packard's (HP) printers. The result: In two short years, Kodak has sold over 1 million printers. Consumers buy an average of

How can Ben & Jerry's develop new products and social responsibility programs that contribute to its mission? The text describes how the strategic marketing process and its SWOT analysis can help.

diversification analysis
A technique a firm uses to search for growth opportunities from among current and new products and markets.

eight ink cartridges a year. Because HP is the entrenched 300-pound gorilla in this market, the future of this *question mark* could evolve into a *star* if Kodak is able to double or triple unit sales. Or this SBU may turn into a *dog* because online printing and sharing have taken off and may soon reach $1 billion.[40]

4. *Kodak film.* An $8 billion *cash cow* in 2003, Kodak film sales were the company's biggest single source of revenue. Now in a free fall because of digital cameras, Kodak film sales dropped to $500 million in 2009, moving it from being a *cash cow* to a potential *dog*. Kodak stopped producing its Kodachrome slides in late 2009. Experts believe film sales will almost evaporate by 2012.[41]

The primary strength of business portfolio analysis lies in forcing a firm to place each of its SBUs in the growth-share matrix, which in turn suggests which SBUs will be cash producers and cash users in the future. Weaknesses of this analysis arise from the difficulty in (1) getting the needed information and (2) incorporating competitive data into business portfolio analysis.[42]

Diversification Analysis **Diversification analysis** is a technique that helps a firm search for growth opportunities from among current and new markets as well as current and new products.[43] For any market, there is both a current product (what the firm now sells) and a new product (what the firm might sell in the future). And for any product there is both a current market (the firm's existing customers) and a new market (the firm's potential customers). As Ben & Jerry's seeks to increase sales revenues, it considers all four market-product strategies shown in Figure 2–5:

- *Market penetration* is a marketing strategy to increase sales of current products in current markets, such as Ben & Jerry's current ice cream products to U.S. consumers. There is no change in either the basic product line or the markets served. Increased sales are generated by selling either more ice cream (through better promotion or distribution) *or* the same amount of ice cream at a higher price to its current customers.
- *Market development* is a marketing strategy to sell current products to new markets. For Ben & Jerry's, Brazil is an attractive new market. There is good news and bad news for this strategy: As household incomes of Brazilians increase, consumers can buy more ice cream; however, the Ben & Jerry's brand may be unknown to Brazilian consumers.
- *Product development* is a marketing strategy of selling new products to current markets. Ben & Jerry's could leverage its brand by selling children's clothing in the United States. This strategy is risky because Americans may not see the company's expertise in ice cream extending to children's clothing.
- *Diversification* is a marketing strategy of developing new products and selling them in new markets. This is a potentially high-risk strategy for Ben & Jerry's if it decides to try to sell Ben & Jerry's branded clothing in Brazil. Why? Because the firm has neither previous production nor marketing experience on which to draw in marketing clothing to Brazilian consumers.

FIGURE 2–5
Four market-product strategies: alternative ways to expand sales revenues for Ben & Jerry's using diversification analysis.

MARKETS	PRODUCTS	
	Current	**New**
Current	**Market penetration** Selling more Ben & Jerry's super-premium ice cream to Americans	**Product development** Selling a new product such as children's clothing under the Ben & Jerry's brand to Americans
New	**Market development** Selling Ben & Jerry's super-premium ice cream to Brazilians for the first time	**Diversification** Selling a new product such as children's clothing under the Ben & Jerry's brand to Brazilians for the first time

5. What is the difference between a marketing dashboard and a marketing metric?

6. What is business portfolio analysis?

7. Explain the four market-product strategies in diversification analysis.

THE STRATEGIC MARKETING PROCESS

LO5

strategic marketing process
An approach whereby an organization allocates its marketing mix resources to reach its target markets.

situation analysis
Taking stock of where a firm or product has been recently, where it is now, and where it is headed.

After an organization assesses where it is and where it wants to go, other questions emerge, such as:

1. How do we allocate our resources to get where we want to go?
2. How do we convert our plans into actions?
3. How do results compare with our plans, and do deviations require new plans?

To answer these questions, an organization uses the **strategic marketing process**, whereby an organization allocates its marketing mix resources to reach its target markets. This process is divided into three phases: planning, implementation, and evaluation, as shown in Figure 2–6.

The Planning Phase of the Strategic Marketing Process

Figure 2–6 shows the three steps in the planning phase of the strategic marketing process: (1) situation (SWOT) analysis, (2) market-product focus and goal setting, and (3) the marketing program.

Step 1: Situation (SWOT) Analysis The essence of **situation analysis** is taking stock of where the firm or product has been recently, where it is now, and where it is headed in terms of the organization's marketing plans and the external forces and trends affecting it. The situation (SWOT) analysis box in Figure 2–6 is the first of the three steps in the planning phase. An effective summary of a situation

FIGURE 2–6
The strategic marketing process has three vital phases: planning, implementation, and evaluation. The figure also shows where these phases are discussed in the text.

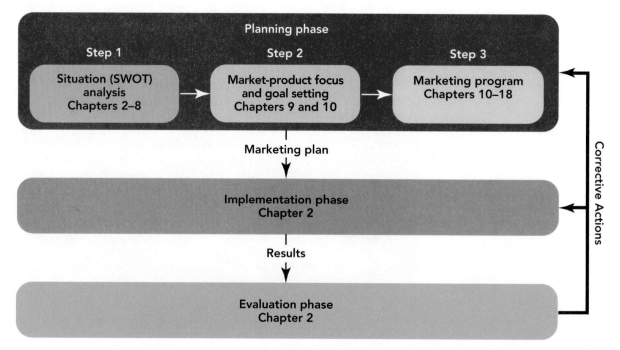

FIGURE 2–7
Ben & Jerry's: a SWOT
analysis to keep it growing.
The picture painted in this
SWOT analysis is the basis for
management actions.

LOCATION OF FACTOR	TYPE OF FACTOR	
	Favorable	Unfavorable
Internal	**Strengths** • Prestigious, well-known brand name among U.S. consumers • Complements Unilever's other ice cream brands • Recognized for its social mission, values, and actions	**Weaknesses** • B&J's social responsibility actions could reduce focus • Experienced managers needed to help growth • Modest sales growth and profits in recent years
External	**Opportunities** • Growing demand for quality ice cream in overseas markets • Increasing U.S. demand for 100-calorie novelties such as cones and bars • Many U.S. firms successfully use product and brand extensions	**Threats** • B&J customers read nutritional labels and are concerned with sugary and fatty desserts • Competes with General Mills and Nestlé brands • Increasing competition in international markets

SWOT analysis

An acronym describing an organization's appraisal of its internal strengths and weaknesses and its external opportunities and threats.

analysis is a **SWOT analysis**, an acronym describing an organization's appraisal of its internal **S**trengths and **W**eaknesses and its external **O**pportunities and **T**hreats.

The SWOT analysis is based on an exhaustive study of four areas that form the foundation upon which the firm builds its marketing program:

- Identify trends in the organization's industry.
- Analyze the organization's competitors.
- Assess the organization itself.
- Research the organization's present and prospective customers.

Assume you are responsible for doing the SWOT analysis for Unilever, Ben & Jerry's parent company shown in Figure 2–7. Note that the SWOT table has four cells formed by the combination of internal versus external factors (the rows) and favorable versus unfavorable factors (the columns) that identify Ben & Jerry's strengths, weaknesses, opportunities, and threats.

The task is to translate the results of the SWOT analysis into specific actions that will help the firm grow. The ultimate goal is to identify the *critical* strategy-related factors that impact the firm and then build on vital strengths, correct glaring weaknesses, exploit significant opportunities, and avoid disaster-laden threats.

The Ben & Jerry's SWOT analysis in Figure 2–7 can be the basis for these kinds of specific actions. An action in each of the four cells might be:

- *Build on a strength.* Find specific efficiencies in distribution with Unilever's existing ice cream brands.
- *Correct a weakness.* Recruit experienced managers from other consumer product firms to help stimulate growth.
- *Exploit an opportunity.* Develop new product lines of low-fat, low-carb frozen yogurts and sorbets to respond to consumer health concerns.[44]
- *Avoid a disaster-laden threat.* Focus on less risky international markets, such as Canada and Mexico.

Step 2: Market-Product Focus and Goal Setting Determining which products will be directed toward which customers (step 2 of the planning phase in Figure 2–6) is essential for developing an effective marketing program (step 3). This decision is often based on **market segmentation**, which involves aggregating prospective buyers into groups, or segments, that (1) have common needs and (2) will respond similarly to a marketing action. This enables an organization to identify the segments on which it will focus its efforts—its target market segments—and develop specific marketing programs to reach them.

market segmentation

The sorting of potential buyers into groups that have common needs and will respond similarly to a marketing action.

As always, understanding the customer is essential. In the case of Medtronic, executives researched a potential new market in Asia by talking extensively with doctors in India and China. They learned that these doctors saw some of the current state-of-the-art features of heart pacemakers as less essential and too expensive. Instead, they wanted an affordable pacemaker that was reliable and easy to implant. This information led Medtronic to develop and market a new product, the Champion heart pacemaker, directed at the needs of these Asian market segments.

Goal setting involves setting measurable marketing objectives to be achieved. For example, the goal may be to introduce a new product, such as Medtronic's Champion pacemaker in Asia or Toyota's launch of its Prius hybrid car in the United States.

Let's examine Medtronic's five-year plan to reach the "affordable and reliable" segment of the pacemaker market that results in its marketing program shown in Figure 2-8:[45]

- *Set marketing and product goals.* The chances of new-product success are increased by specifying both market and product goals. Based on their market research showing the need for a reliable yet affordable pacemaker, Medtronic executives set the following as their goal: Market such a pacemaker in the next three years that could be manufactured in China for the Asian market.
- *Select target markets.* The Champion pacemaker will be targeted at cardiologists and medical clinics performing heart surgery in India, China, and other Asian countries.
- *Find points of difference.* **Points of difference** are those characteristics of a product that make it superior to competitive substitutes. Just as a competitive advantage is a unique strength of an entire organization compared to its competitors, points of difference are unique characteristics of one of its products that make it superior to competitive products it faces in the marketplace. For the Champion pacemaker, the key points of difference are *not* the state-of-the-art features that drive up costs and are important to only a minority of patients. Instead, they are high quality, long life, reliability, ease of use, and low cost.
- *Position the product.* The pacemaker will be "positioned" in cardiologists' and patients' minds as a medical device that is high quality and reliable with a long, nine-year life. The name Champion was selected after testing acceptable names among doctors in India, China, Pakistan, Singapore, and Malaysia. So step 2 in the planning phase of the strategic marketing process is the foundation for step 3 developing the marketing program.

points of difference
Those characteristics of a product that make it superior to competitive substitutes.

FIGURE 2–8
The 4 Ps elements of the marketing mix must be blended to produce a cohesive marketing program.

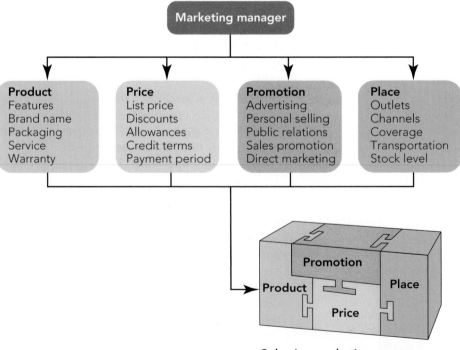

Cohesive marketing program

Step 3: Marketing Program Activities in step 2 tell the marketing manager which customers to target and which customer needs the firm's product offerings can satisfy—the *who* and *what* aspects of the strategic marketing process. The *how* aspect—step 3 in the planning phase—involves developing the program's marketing mix (the 4 Ps) and its budget. Figure 2–8 shows that each marketing mix element is combined to provide a cohesive marketing program. The five-year marketing plan of Medtronic's Champion pacemaker includes these marketing mix activities:

The Champion: Medtronic's high-quality, long-life, low-cost heart pacemaker for Asian market segments.

- *Product strategy.* Offer a Champion brand heart pacemaker with features needed by Asian patients.
- *Price strategy.* Manufacture the Champion to control costs so that it can be priced below $1,000 (in U.S. dollars)—an affordable price for Asian markets.
- *Promotion strategy.* Feature demonstrations at cardiologist and medical conventions across Asia to introduce the Champion and highlight the device's features and application.
- *Place (distribution) strategy.* Search out, utilize, and train reputable medical device distributors across Asia to call on cardiologists and medical clinics.

Putting this marketing program into effect requires that the firm commit time and money to it in the form of a sales forecast (see Chapter 8) and budget that must be approved by top management.

learning review

8. What are the three steps of the planning phase of the strategic marketing process?

9. What are points of difference and why are they important?

The Implementation Phase of the Strategic Marketing Process

LO6

As shown in Figure 2–6, the result of the tens or hundreds of hours spent in the planning phase of the strategic marketing process is the firm's marketing plan. Implementation, the second phase of the strategic marketing process, involves carrying out the marketing plan that emerges from the planning phase. If the firm cannot put the marketing plan into effect—in the implementation phase—the planning phase was a waste of time.

There are four components of the implementation phase: (1) obtaining resources, (2) designing the marketing organization, (3) developing planning schedules, and (4) actually executing the marketing program designed in the planning phase. Kodak provides a case example.

Kodak's new Zi6 pocket video camera can upload its videos to YouTube.

Obtaining Resources In 2003, Kodak announced a bold plan to reenergize the film marketer for the new age of digital cameras and prints. Kodak needed huge sums of cash to implement the plan. So by early 2009, it had sold or transformed several of its SBUs that provided over $300 million to develop and market new products, such as the exciting Zi6 pocket video camera, which takes HD quality videos that can be uploaded to YouTube.[46]

Designing the Marketing Organization A marketing program needs a marketing organization to implement it. Figure 2–9 on the next page shows the organization chart of a typical manufacturing firm, giving some details of the marketing department's structure. Four managers of marketing activities are shown to report to the vice president of marketing. Several regional sales managers and an international sales manager may report to the manager of sales. The product or brand managers and their subordinates help plan, implement, and evaluate the marketing plans for their offerings. However, the entire marketing organization is responsible for converting these marketing plans into reality as part of the corporate marketing team.

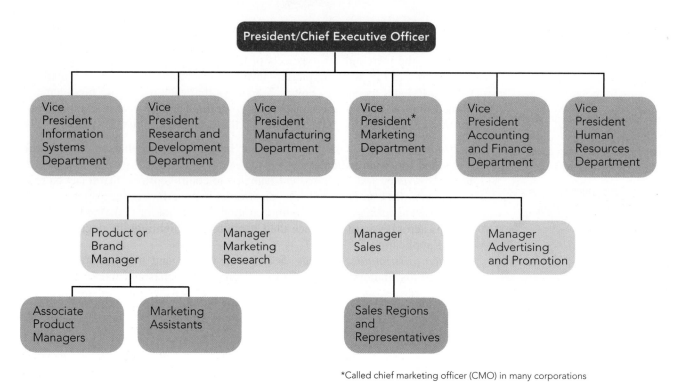

*Called chief marketing officer (CMO) in many corporations

FIGURE 2–9
Organization of a typical manufacturing firm, showing a breakdown of the marketing department.

Developing Planning Schedules To implement marketing plans, members of the marketing department hold meetings to identify the tasks that need to be done, the time to allocate to each one, the people responsible, and the deadlines for their accomplishment. In most cases, each team member works on different parts of the plan.

Executing the Marketing Program Marketing plans are meaningless pieces of paper without effective execution of those plans. Effective execution requires attention to detail for both marketing strategies and marketing tactics. A **marketing strategy** is the means by which a marketing goal is to be achieved, usually characterized by a specified target market and a marketing program to reach it. The term implies both the end sought (target market) and the means to achieve it (marketing program). At this marketing strategy level, Kodak will seek to increase sales of digital cameras, ink-jet printers, and digital picture frames.

To implement a marketing program successfully, hundreds of detailed decisions are often required. These decisions, called **marketing tactics**, are detailed day-to-day operational decisions essential to the overall success of marketing strategies. At Kodak, writing ads and setting prices for its new lines of digital cameras are examples of marketing tactics.

marketing strategy
The means by which a marketing goal is to be achieved.

marketing tactics
Detailed day-to-day operational decisions essential to the overall success of marketing strategies.

The Evaluation Phase of the Strategic Marketing Process

The evaluation phase of the strategic marketing process seeks to keep the marketing program moving in the direction set for it (see Figure 2–6). Accomplishing this requires the marketing manager to (1) compare the results of the marketing program with the goals in the written plans to identify deviations and (2) act on these deviations—correcting negative deviations and exploiting positive ones.

To help fill in its planning gap, Kodak is pursuing opportunities for sales of digital cameras in France.

Comparing Results with Plans to Identify Deviations

Suppose you are on a Kodak task force in 2003 responsible for making plans through 2012. You observe that Kodak's sales revenues from 1998 through 2003, or line AB in Figure 2–10, exhibit a very flat trend. Extending the 1998–2003 trend to 2012 along line BC shows very flat sales revenues, a totally unacceptable, no-growth strategy.

Kodak's growth target of 5 to 6 percent annually, the line BD in Figure 2–10, would give sales revenues of $16 billion in 2006 and $24 billion in 2012. This reveals a wedge-shaped shaded gap in the figure. Planners call this the *planning gap*, the difference between the projection of the path to reach a new goal (line BD) and the projection of the path of the results of a plan already in place (line BC). The ultimate purpose of the firm's marketing program is to "fill in" this planning gap—in the case of your Kodak task force, to move its future sales revenue line from the no-growth line BC up to the challenging target of line BD. But poor performance can result in actual sales revenues being far less than the targeted levels, the actual situation faced by Kodak in 2009 (line BE), where sales were about $8 billion. This is the essence of evaluation: comparing actual results with goals set.

In this example, the Kodak task force in 2003 used trend extrapolation to project the historic trend through 2012. But as shown by the discrepancy between line BC (the trend extrapolation) and line BE (Kodak's actual annual sales revenues), serious forecasting problems can occur. In this case, Kodak failed to anticipate the drastic effect that digital technology would have on sales of its film and film cameras. This challenge for Kodak highlights the difficulties in making long-range projections in industries in which technology is changing rapidly.

Acting on Deviations When evaluation shows that actual performance has failed to meet expectations, managers need to take corrective actions. In response to the negative and positive deviations from targets, your Kodak task force might consider the following in 2011:[47]

- *Exploiting a positive deviation.* If Kodak's innovative digital cameras sell better than expected, Kodak might try to move quickly to offer these to international customers—such as those in France.
- *Correcting a negative deviation.* However, if Panasonic is able to surpass Kodak in global market share of digital cameras, Kodak may need to reduce prices.

FIGURE 2–10

The evaluation phase of the strategic marketing process requires that the organization compare actual results with goals to identify and act on deviations to fill in its "planning gap." The text describes how Kodak hopes to fill in its planning gap by 2012.

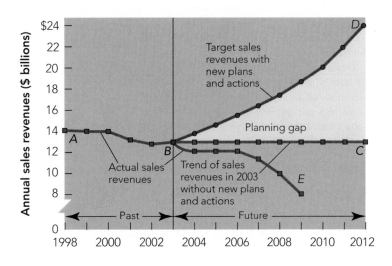

Kodak also might (1) develop more feature-laden digital cameras using its proprietary sensor technologies that improve image (picture) quality to (2) launch a new aggressive global marketing program that integrates its digital camera images into its Kodak digital picture frame.

learning review

10. What is the implementation phase of the strategic marketing process?

11. How do the goals set for a marketing program in the planning phase relate to the evaluation phase of the strategic marketing process?

LEARNING OBJECTIVES REVIEW

LO1 *Describe two kinds of organizations and the three levels of strategy in them.*
An organization is a legal entity of people who share a common mission. There are two kinds. One is a business firm that is a privately owned organization that serves its customers to earn a profit so that it can survive. The other is a nonprofit, nongovernmental organization that serves its customers but does not have profit as a goal. Most large business firms and nonprofit organizations are divided into three levels of strategy: (*a*) the corporate level, where top management directs overall strategy for the entire organization; (*b*) the strategic business unit level, where managers set a more specific strategic direction for their businesses to set value-creating opportunities; and (*c*) the functional level, where groups of specialists actually create value for the organization.

LO2 *Describe how core values, mission, organizational culture, business, and goals are important to organizations.*
Organizations exist to accomplish something for someone. To give organizations direction and focus, they continuously assess their core values, mission, organizational culture, business, and goals. Today's organizations specify their foundation, set a direction, and formulate strategies—the "why," "what," and "how" factors, respectively. Core values are the organization's fundamental, passionate, and enduring principles that guide its conduct over time—what Enron forgot when it lost sight of its responsibilities to its stakeholders. The organization's mission is a statement of its function in society, often identifying its customers, markets, products, and technologies. Organizational culture is a set of values, ideas, attitudes, and norms of behavior that is learned and shared among the members of an organization. To answer the question, "What business are we in?" an organization defines its "business"—the clear, broad, underlying industry category or market sector of its offering. Finally, the organization's goals (or objectives) are statements of an accomplishment of a task to be achieved, often by a specific time.

LO3 *Explain why managers use marketing dashboards and marketing metrics.*
Marketing managers use marketing dashboards to visually display on a single computer screen the essential information to make a decision to take an action or further analyze a problem. This information consists of key performance measures of a product category, such as sales or market share, and is known as a marketing metric, which is a measure of the quantitative value or trend of a marketing activity or result. Most organizations tie their marketing metrics to the quantitative objectives established in their marketing plan, which is a road map for the marketing activities of an organization for a specified future time period, such as one year or five years.

LO4 *Discuss how an organization assesses where it is now and where it seeks to be.*
Managers of an organization ask two key questions to set a strategic direction. The first question, "Where are we now?" requires an organization to (*a*) reevaluate its competencies to ensure that its special capabilities still provide a competitive advantage; (*b*) assess its present and prospective customers to ensure they have a satisfying customer experience—the central goal of marketing today; and (*c*) analyze its current and potential competitors from a global perspective to determine whether it needs to redefine its business.

The second question, "Where do we want to go?" requires an organization to set a specific direction and allocate resources to move it in that direction. Business portfolio and diversification analyses help an organization do this. Managers use business portfolio analysis to assess the organization's strategic business units (SBUs), product lines, or individual products as though they were a collection of separate investments (cash cows, stars, question marks, and dogs) to determine the amount of cash each should receive. Diversification analysis is a tool that helps managers use one or a combination of four strategies to increase revenues: market penetration (selling more of an existing product to existing markets); market development (selling an existing product to new markets); product development (selling a new product to existing markets); and diversification (selling new products to new markets).

LO5 *Explain the three steps of the planning phase of the strategic marketing process.*
An organization uses the strategic marketing process to allocate its marketing mix resources to reach its target markets.

This process is divided into three phases: planning, implementation, and evaluation. The planning phase consists of (*a*) a situation (SWOT) analysis, which involves taking stock of where the firm or product has been recently, where it is now, and where it is headed. This assessment focuses on the organization's internal factors (strengths and weaknesses) and the external forces and trends affecting it (opportunities and threats); (*b*) a market-product focus through market segmentation—grouping buyers into segments with common needs and similar responses to marketing programs—and goal setting, which in part requires creating points of difference—those characteristics of a product that make it superior to competitive substitutes; and (*c*) a marketing program that specifies the budget and activities (marketing strategies and tactics) for each marketing mix element.

LO6 *Describe the elements of the implementation and evaluation phases of the strategic marketing process.*
The implementation phase of the strategic marketing process carries out the marketing plan that emerges from the planning phase. It has four key elements: (*a*) obtaining resources;

(*b*) designing the marketing organization to perform product management, marketing research, sales, and advertising and promotion activities; (*c*) developing schedules to identify the tasks that need to be done, the time that is allocated to each one, the people responsible for each task, and the deadlines for each task's accomplishment; and (*d*) executing the marketing strategies, which are the means by which marketing goals are to be achieved, and their associated marketing tactics, which are the detailed day-to-day operational decisions essential to the overall success of a firm's marketing strategies. These are the marketing program actions a firm takes to achieve the goals set forth in its marketing plan.

The evaluation phase of the strategic marketing process seeks to keep the marketing program moving in the direction that was established in the marketing plan. This requires the marketing manager to compare the results from the marketing program with the marketing plan's goals to (*a*) identify deviations or "planning gaps" and (*b*) take corrective actions to exploit positive deviations or correct negative ones.

FOCUSING ON KEY TERMS

business p. 26
business portfolio analysis p. 31
core values p. 25
diversification analysis p. 33
goals p. 26
market segmentation p. 35
market share p. 27

marketing dashboard p. 27
marketing metric p. 28
marketing plan p. 28
marketing strategy p. 38
marketing tactics p. 38
mission p. 25
objectives p. 26

organizational culture p. 26
points of difference p. 36
profit p. 22
situation analysis p. 34
strategic marketing process p. 34
strategy p. 22
SWOT analysis p. 35

APPLYING MARKETING KNOWLEDGE

1 (*a*) Using Medtronic as an example, explain how a mission statement gives it a strategic direction. (*b*) Create a mission statement for your own career.

2 What competencies best describe (*a*) your college or university and (*b*) your favorite restaurant?

3 Why does a product often start as a question mark and then move counterclockwise around the BCG's growth-share matrix shown in Figure 2–4?

4 Select one strength, one weakness, one opportunity, and one threat from the Ben & Jerry's SWOT analysis

shown in Figure 2–7. Suggest an action that a marketing manager there might take to address each factor.

5 What is the main result of each of the three phases of the strategic marketing process? (*a*) planning, (*b*) implementation, and (*c*) evaluation.

6 The goal-setting step in the planning phase of the strategic marketing process sets quantified objectives for use in the evaluation phase. What does a manager do if measured results fail to meet objectives? Exceed objectives?

building your marketing plan

1 Read Appendix A, "Building an Effective Marketing Plan." Then write a 600-word executive summary for the Paradise Kitchens marketing plan using the numbered headings shown in the plan. When you have completed the draft of your own marketing plan, write a 600-word executive summary to go in the front of your own marketing plan.

2 Using Chapter 2 and Appendix A as guides, focus your marketing plan by (*a*) writing your mission statement in 25 words or less, (*b*) listing three nonfinancial goals and three financial goals, (*c*) writing your competitive advantage in 35 words or less, and (*d*) doing a SWOT analysis table.

3 Draw a simple organization chart for your organization.

Vivian Milroy Callaway (photo), vice president for the Center for Learning and Experimentation at General Mills, retells the story for the "indulgent, delicious, and gooey" Warm Delights™. She summarizes, "When you want something that is truly innovative, you have to look at the rules you have been assuming in your category and break them all!"

The creators of Betty Crocker Warm Delights stress that if the marketing decisions had been based on the history of the cake category, a smaller, struggling business would have resulted. The team challenged the assumptions of accumulated cake category business experience. Today Warm Delights is a roaring success.

PLANNING PHASE: INNOVATION, BUT A SHRINKING MARKET

"In the typical grocery store, the baking mix aisle is a quiet place," says Callaway. Shelves sigh with flavors, types, and brands. Prices are low, but there is little consumer traffic. Cake continues to be a tradition for birthdays and social occasions. But consumer demand still declines. The percentage of U.S. households that buy at least one baking mix in a year is shrinking.

Today, a promoted price of 89 cents to make a 9×12 inch cake is common. Many choices, but little differentiation, gradually falling sales, and low uniform prices are the hallmarks of a mature category. But it's not that consumers don't buy cake-like treats. In fact, indulgent treats are growing. The premium prices for ice cream ($3.00 a pint) and chocolate ($3.00 a bar) are not slowing consumer purchases.

The Betty Crocker marketing team challenged the food scientists at General Mills to create a great tasting, easy to prepare, single-serve cake treat. The goal: Make it indulgent, delicious, and gooey. The team focused the scientists on a product that would have:

- Consistent great taste.
- Quick preparation.
- A single portion.
- No cleanup.

The food scientists delivered the prototype! Now, the marketing team began hammering out the four Ps. They started with a descriptive name "Betty Crocker Dessert Bowls" and a plan to shelve it in the "quiet" cake aisle. This practical approach would meet the consumer need for a "small, fast, microwave cake" for dessert. Several marketing challenges emerged:

- *The comparison problem.* The easy shelf price comparison to 9×12 inch cakes selling for 89 cents would make it harder to price Dessert Bowls at $2.00.
- *The communication problem.* The product message "a small, faster-to-make cake" wasn't compelling. For example, after-school snacks should be fast and small, but "dessert" sounds too indulgent.
- *The quiet aisle problem.* The cake-aisle shopper is probably not browsing for a cake innovation.
- *The dessert problem.* Consumers' on-the-go, calorie conscious meal plans don't generally include a planned dessert.
- *The microwave problem.* Consumers might not believe it tastes good.

In sum, the small, fast-cake product didn't resonate with a compelling consumer need. But it would be a safe bet because the Dessert Bowl positioning fit nicely with the family-friendly Betty Crocker brand.

IMPLEMENTATION PHASE: LEAVING THE SECURITY OF FAMILY BEHIND

The consumer insights team really enjoyed the hot, gooey cake product. But they feared that it would languish in the cake aisle under the Dessert Bowl name since this didn't capture the essence of what the food delivered. They explored who the indulgent treat customers really are. The data revealed that the heaviest buyers of premium treats are women without children. This focused the team on a target consumer: "What does she want?" They asked an ad agency and consultants to come up with a name that would appeal to "her." Several independently suggested "Warm Delights," which became the brand name.

Targeting the on-the-go women who want a small, personal treat had marketing advantages:

- The $2.00 Warm Delights price compared favorably to the price of many single-serve indulgent treats.
- The product's message of "warm, convenient, delightful" is compelling.
- On-the-go women's meal plans do include the occasional delicious treat.

One major problem remained: The cake-aisle shopper is probably not browsing for an indulgent, single-serve treat.

The marketing team solved this shelving issue by using advertising and product displays outside the cake aisle. This would raise women's awareness of Warm Delights. Television advertising and in-store display programs are costly, so Warm Delights sales would have to be strong to pay back the investment.

Vivian Callaway and the team turned to market research to fine-tune the plan. The research put Warm Delights (and Dessert Bowls) on the shelf in real (different) stores to study sales. A few key findings emerged. First, the name "Warm Delights" beat "Dessert Bowls." Second, the Warm Delights with nuts simply wasn't easy to prepare, so nuts were removed. Third, the packaging with a disposable bowl beat the typical cake-mix packaging involving using your own bowl.

Another result of obtaining this consumer feedback was that many buyers said they wanted a smaller size of Warm Delights. So Callaway and her team introduced Warm Delights Minis—a smaller, 150-calorie version (photo) of the regular, 370-calorie Warm Delights.

An interesting postscript to the team's brand name research: A competitor apparently liked not only the idea of a quick, gooey, microwavable dessert but also the "Dessert Bowls" name! You may now see this competitive product on your supermarket's shelves.

EVALUATION PHASE: TURNING THE PLAN INTO ACTION!

The marketing plan isn't action. Sales for "Warm Delights" required the marketing team to (1) get the retailers to stock the product, preferably somewhere other than the cake aisle, and (2) appeal to consumers enough to have them purchase, like, and repurchase the product.

The initial acceptance of a product by retailers is important. But each store manager must experience good sales of Warm Delights to be motivated to keep its shelves restocked with the product. Also, the Warm Delights team must monitor the display activity in the store. Are the displays fully stocked at all times? Do the sales increase when a display is present?

Other key questions: Did the customer buy one or two Warm Delights? Did the customer return for a second purchase a few weeks later? The syndicated services that sell household panel purchase data provide the answers. The Warm Delights team evaluates these reports to see if the number of people who try the product matches with expectations and how the repeat purchases occur.

For ongoing feedback, calls by Warm Delights consumers to the free consumer information line are monitored. This is a great source of real-time feedback. If a pattern emerges and these calls are mostly about the same problem, that is bad. However, when consumers call to say "thank you" or "it's great," that is good. This is an informal quick way to identify if the product is on track.

GOOD MARKETING MAKES A DIFFERENCE

The team took personal and business risks by choosing a Warm Delights plan over the more conservative Dessert Bowl plan. Today, General Mills has loyal Warm Delights consumers who are open to trying new flavors, new sizes, and new forms. If you were a consultant to the Warm Delights team, what would you do to grow this brand?

Questions

1 What is the competitive set of desserts in which Warm Delights is located?

2 (*a*) Who is the target market? (*b*) What is the point of difference in regard to the positioning for Warm Delights? (*c*) What are the potential opportunities and hindrances of the target market and positioning?

3 (*a*) What marketing research did Vivian Callaway execute? (*b*) What were the critical questions that she sought research and expert advice to get answers to? (*c*) How did this affect the product's marketing mix price, promotion, packaging, and distribution decisions?

4 (*a*) What initial promotional plan directed to consumers in the target market did Callaway use? (*b*) Why did this make sense to Callaway and her team when Warm Delights was launched?

5 If you were a consultant to Vivian Callaway, what product changes would you recommend to increase sales of Warm Delights?

A BUILDING AN EFFECTIVE MARKETING PLAN

"New ideas are a dime a dozen," observes Arthur R. Kydd, "and so are new products and new technologies." Kydd should know. As chief executive officer of St. Croix Venture Partners, he and his firm have provided the seed money and venture capital to launch more than 60 start-up firms in the last 25 years. Today, those firms have more than 5,000 employees. Kydd explains:

> I get 200 to 300 marketing and business plans a year to look at, and St. Croix provides start-up financing for only two or three. What sets a potentially successful idea, product, or technology apart from all the rest is markets and marketing. If you have a real product with a distinctive point of difference that satisfies the needs of customers, you may have a winner. And you get a real feel for this in a well-written marketing or business plan.[1]

This appendix (1) describes what marketing and business plans are, including the purposes and guidelines in writing effective plans, and (2) provides a sample marketing plan.

MARKETING PLANS AND BUSINESS PLANS

After explaining the meanings, purposes, and audiences of marketing plans and business plans, this section describes some writing guidelines for them and what external funders often look for in successful plans.

Meanings, Purposes, and Audiences

A marketing plan is a road map for the marketing activities of an organization for a specified future time period, such as one year or five years.[2] No single "generic" marketing plan applies to all organizations and all situations. Rather, the specific format for a marketing plan for an organization depends on the following:

- *The target audience and purpose.* Elements included in a particular marketing plan depend heavily on (1) who the audience is and (2) what its purpose is. A marketing plan for an internal audience seeks to point the direction for future marketing activities and is sent to all individuals in the organization who must imple-

ment the plan or who will be affected by it. If the plan is directed to an external audience, such as friends, banks, venture capitalists, or potential investors for the purpose of raising capital, it has the additional function of being an important sales document. In this case, it contains elements such as the strategic plan/ focus, organization, structure, and biographies of key personnel that would rarely appear in an internal marketing plan. Also, the financial information is far more detailed when the plan is used to raise outside capital. The elements of a marketing plan for each of these two audiences are compared in Figure A–1.

- *The kind and complexity of the organization.* A small neighborhood restaurant has a somewhat different marketing plan than Medtronic, which serves international markets. The restaurant's plan would be relatively simple and directed at serving customers in a local market. In Medtronic's case, because there is a hierarchy of marketing plans, various levels of detail would be used—such as the entire organization, the strategic business unit, or the product/product line.

- *The industry.* Both the restaurant serving a local market and Medtronic, selling heart pacemakers globally, analyze competition. However, their geographic thrusts are far different, as are the complexities of their offerings and, hence, the time periods likely to be covered by their plans. A one-year marketing plan may be adequate for the restaurant, but Medtronic may need a five-year planning horizon because product-development cycles for complex, new medical devices may be three or four years.

In contrast to a marketing plan, a **business plan** is a road map for the entire organization for a specified future period of time, such as one year or five years.[3] A key difference between a marketing plan and a business plan is that the business plan contains details on the research and development (R&D)/operations/manufacturing activities of the organization. Even for a manufacturing business, the marketing plan is probably 60 or 70 percent of the entire business plan. For firms like a small restaurant or an auto repair shop, their marketing and business plans

Element of the plan	Marketing plan		Business plan	
	For internal audience (to direct the firm)	For external audience (to raise capital)	For internal audience (to direct the firm)	For external audience (to raise capital)
1. Executive summary	✓	✓	✓	✓
2. Description of company		✓		✓
3. Strategic plan/focus		✓		✓
4. Situation analysis	✓	✓	✓	✓
5. Market-product focus	✓	✓	✓	✓
6. Marketing program strategy and tactics	✓	✓	✓	✓
7. R&D and operations program			✓	✓
8. Financial projections	✓	✓	✓	✓
9. Organization structure		✓		✓
10. Implementation plan	✓	✓	✓	✓
11. Evaluation and control	✓		✓	
Appendix A: Biographies of key personnel		✓		✓
Appendix B, etc.: Details on other topics	✓	✓	✓	✓

FIGURE A–1
Elements in typical marketing and business plans targeted at different audiences.

are virtually identical. The elements of a business plan typically targeted at internal and external audiences appear in the two right-hand columns in Figure A–1.

The Most-Asked Questions by Outside Audiences

Lenders and prospective investors reading a business or marketing plan that is used to seek new capital are probably the toughest audiences to satisfy. Their most-asked questions include the following:

1. Is the business or marketing idea valid?
2. Is there something unique or distinctive about the product or service that separates it from substitutes and competitors?
3. Is there a clear market for the product or service?
4. Are the financial projections realistic and healthy?
5. Are the key management and technical personnel capable, and do they have a track record in the industry in which they must compete?
6. Does the plan clearly describe how those providing capital will get their money back and make a profit?

Rhonda Abrams, author of *The Successful Business Plan*, observes, "Although you may spend five months preparing your plan, the cold, hard fact is that an investor or lender can dismiss it in less than five minutes."[4] While her comments apply to plans seeking to raise capital, the first five questions listed above apply equally well to plans for internal audiences.

Writing and Style Suggestions

There are no magic one-size-fits-all guidelines for writing successful marketing and business plans. Still, the following writing and style guidelines generally apply:[5]

- Use a direct, professional writing style. Use appropriate business terms without jargon. Present and future tenses with active voice ("I will write an effective marketing plan") are generally better than past tense and passive voice ("An effective marketing plan was written by me").
- Be positive and specific to convey potential success. At the same time, avoid superlatives ("terrific," "wonderful"). Specifics are better than glittering generalities.

- Use numbers for impact, justifying projections with reasonable quantitative assumptions, where possible.
- Use bullet points for succinctness and emphasis. As with the list you are reading, bullets enable key points to be highlighted effectively.
- Use A-level (the first level) and B-level (the second level) headings under the numbered section headings to help readers make easy transitions from one topic to another. This also forces the writer to organize the plan more carefully. Use these headings liberally, at least one every 200 to 300 words.
- Use visuals where appropriate. Photos, illustrations, graphs, and charts enable massive amounts of information to be presented succinctly.
- Shoot for a plan 15 to 35 pages in length, not including financial projections and appendixes. An uncomplicated small business may require only 15 pages, while a high-technology start-up may require more than 35 pages.
- Use care in layout, design, and presentation. Laser printers give a more professional look than ink-jet printers do. Use 11- or 12-point type (you are now reading 10.5-point type) in the text. Use a serif type (with "feet," like that you are reading now) in the text because it is easier to read, and sans serif (without "feet") in graphs and charts like Figure A–1. A bound report with a nice cover and a clear title page adds professionalism.

These guidelines are used, where possible, in the sample marketing plan that follows.

SAMPLE FIVE-YEAR MARKETING PLAN FOR PARADISE KITCHENS,® INC.

To help interpret the marketing plan for Paradise Kitchens, Inc., that follows, we will describe the company and suggest some guidelines in interpreting the plan.

Background on Paradise Kitchens, Inc.

With a degree in chemical engineering, Randall F. Peters spent 15 years working for General Foods and Pillsbury with a number of diverse responsibilities: plant operations, R&D, restaurant operations, and new business development. His wife, Leah, with degrees in both molecular cellular biology and food science, held various Pillsbury executive positions in new category development, packaged goods, and restaurant R&D. In the company's start-up years, Paradise Kitchens survived on the savings of Randy and Leah, the cofounders. With their backgrounds, they decided Randy should serve as president and CEO of Paradise Kitchens, and Leah should focus on R&D and corporate strategy.

Interpreting the Marketing Plan

The marketing plan on the next pages, based on an actual Paradise Kitchens plan, is directed at an external audience (see Figure A–1). To protect proprietary information about the company, some details and dates have been altered, but the basic logic of the plan has been kept.

Notes in the margins next to the Paradise Kitchens plan fall into two categories:

1. *Substantive notes* are in blue boxes. These notes elaborate on the significance of an element in the marketing plan and are keyed to chapter references in this textbook.
2. *Writing style, format, and layout notes* are in red boxes and explain the editorial or visual rationale for the element.

A word of encouragement: Writing an effective marketing plan is hard but also challenging and satisfying work. Dozens of the authors' students have used effective marketing plans they wrote for class in their interviewing portfolio to show prospective employers what they could do and to help them get their first job.

The Table of Contents provides quick access to the topics in the plan, usually organized by section and subsection headings.

Seen by many experts as the single most important element in the plan, the two-page Executive Summary "sells" the plan to readers through its clarity and brevity. For space reasons, it is not shown here, but the Building Your Marketing Plan exercise at the end of Chapter 2 asks the reader to write an Executive Summary for this plan.

The Company Description highlights the recent history and recent successes of the organization.

The Strategic Focus and Plan sets the strategic direction for the entire organization, a direction with which proposed actions of the marketing plan must be consistent. This section is not included in all marketing plans. See Chapter 2.

The qualitative Mission statement focuses the activities of Paradise Kitchens for the stakeholder groups to be served. See Chapter 2.

FIVE-YEAR MARKETING PLAN
Paradise Kitchens,® Inc.

Table of Contents

1. Executive Summary

2. Company Description

Paradise Kitchens®, Inc., was started by cofounders Randall F. Peters and Leah E. Peters to develop and market Howlin' Coyote® Chili, a unique line of single serve and microwavable Southwestern/Mexican style frozen chili products. The Howlin' Coyote line of chili was first introduced into the Minneapolis–St. Paul market and expanded to Denver two years later and Phoenix two years after that.

To the Company's knowledge, Howlin' Coyote is the only premium-quality, authentic Southwestern/Mexican style, frozen chili sold in U.S. grocery stores. Its high quality has gained fast, widespread acceptance in these markets. In fact, same-store sales doubled in the last year for which data are available. The Company believes the Howlin' Coyote brand can be extended to other categories of Southwestern/Mexican food products, such as tacos, enchiladas, and burritos.

Paradise Kitchens believes its high-quality, high-price strategy has proven successful. This marketing plan outlines how the Company will extend its geographic coverage from 3 markets to 20 markets by the year 2016.

3. Strategic Focus and Plan

This section covers three aspects of corporate strategy that influence the marketing plan: (1) the mission, (2) goals, and (3) core competency/sustainable competitive advantage of Paradise Kitchens.

Mission
The mission of Paradise Kitchens is to market lines of high-quality Southwestern/ Mexican food products at premium prices that satisfy consumers in this fast-growing food segment while providing challenging career opportunities for employees and above-average returns to stockholders.

<u>Goals</u>

For the coming five years Paradise Kitchens seeks to achieve the following goals:

- Nonfinancial goals
  1. To retain its present image as the highest-quality line of Southwestern/ Mexican products in the food categories in which it competes.
  2. To enter 17 new metropolitan markets.
  3. To achieve national distribution in two convenience store or supermarket chains by 2012 and five by 2013.
  4. To add a new product line every third year.
  5. To be among the top five chili lines—regardless of packaging (frozen or canned)—in one-third of the metro markets in which it competes by 2013 and two-thirds by 2015.
- Financial goals
  1. To obtain a real (inflation-adjusted) growth in earnings per share of 8 percent per year over time.
  2. To obtain a return on equity of at least 20 percent.
  3. To have a public stock offering by the year 2013.

<u>Core Competency and Sustainable Competitive Advantage</u>

In terms of core competency, Paradise Kitchens seeks to achieve a unique ability to (1) provide distinctive, high-quality chilies and related products using Southwestern/Mexican recipes that appeal to and excite contemporary tastes for these products and (2) deliver these products to the customer's table using effective manufacturing and distribution systems that maintain the Company's quality standards.

To translate these core competencies into a sustainable competitive advantage, the Company will work closely with key suppliers and distributors to build the relationships and alliances necessary to satisfy the high taste standards of our customers.

To help achieve national distribution through chains, Paradise Kitchens introduced this point-of-purchase ad that adheres statically to the glass door of the freezer case.

To improve readability, each numbered section usually starts on a new page. (This is not done in this plan to save space.)

The Situation Analysis is a snapshot to answer the question, "Where are we now?" See Chapter 2.

The SWOT analysis identifies strengths, weaknesses, opportunities, and threats to provide a solid foundation as a springboard to identify subsequent actions in the marketing plan. See Chapter 2.

Each long table, graph, or photo is given a figure number and title. It then appears as soon as possible after the first reference in the text, accommodating necessary page breaks. This also avoids breaking long tables like this one in the middle. Short tables or graphs are often inserted in the text without figure numbers because they don't cause serious problems with page breaks.

Effective tables seek to summarize a large amount of information in a short amount of space.

4. Situation Analysis

This situation analysis starts with a snapshot of the current environment in which Paradise Kitchens finds itself by providing a brief SWOT (strengths, weaknesses, opportunities, threats) analysis. After this overview, the analysis probes ever-finer levels of detail: industry, competitors, company, and consumers.

SWOT Analysis

Figure 1 shows the internal and external factors affecting the market opportunities for Paradise Kitchens. Stated briefly, this SWOT analysis highlights the great strides taken by the company since its products first appeared on grocers' shelves.

Figure 1.   SWOT Analysis for Paradise Kitchens

Internal Factors	Strengths	Weaknesses
Management	Experienced and entrepreneurial management and board	Small size can restrict options
Offerings	Unique, high-quality, high-price products	Many lower-quality, lower-price competitors
Marketing	Distribution in three markets with excellent acceptance	No national awareness or distribution; restricted shelf space in the freezer section
Personnel	Good workforce, though small; little turnover	Big gap if key employee leaves
Finance	Excellent growth in sales revenues	Limited resources may restrict growth opportunities when compared to giant competitors
Manufacturing	Sole supplier ensures high quality	Lack economies of scale of huge competitors
R&D	Continuing efforts to ensure quality in delivered products	Lack of canning and microwavable food processing expertise

External Factors	Opportunities	Threats
Consumer/Social	Upscale market, likely to be stable; Southwestern/Mexican food category is fast-growing segment due to growth in Hispanic American population and desire for spicier foods	Premium price may limit access to mass markets; consumers value a strong brand name
Competitive	Distinctive name and packaging in its markets	Not patentable; competitors can attempt to duplicate product; others better able to pay slotting fees
Technological	Technical breakthroughs enable smaller food producers to achieve many economies available to large competitors	Competitors have gained economies in canning and microwavable food processing
Economic	Consumer income is high; convenience important to U.S. households	More households "eating out," and bringing prepared take-out into home
Legal/Regulatory	High U.S. Food & Drug Administration standards eliminate fly-by-night competitors	Mergers among large competitors being approved by government

The text discussion of Figure 1 (the SWOT Analysis table) elaborates on its more important elements. This "walks" the reader through the information from the vantage point of the plan's writer.

The Industry Analysis section provides the backdrop for the subsequent, more detailed analysis of competition, the company, and the company's customers. Without an in-depth understanding of the industry, the remaining analysis may be misdirected. See Chapter 2.

Sales of Mexican entrees are significant and provide a variety of future opportunities for Paradise Kitchens.

Even though relatively brief, this in-depth treatment of sales of Mexican foods in the United States demonstrates to the plan's readers the company's understanding of the industry in which it competes.

The Competitor Analysis demonstrates that the company has a realistic understanding of its major chili competitors and their marketing strategies. Again, a realistic assessment gives confidence that subsequent marketing actions in the plan rest on a solid foundation. See Chapters 2, 3, 8, and 9.

In the Company's favor internally are its strengths of an experienced management team and board of directors, excellent acceptance of its lines in the three metropolitan markets in which it competes, and a strong manufacturing and distribution system to serve these limited markets. Favorable external factors (opportunities) include the increasing appeal of Southwestern/Mexican foods, the strength of the upscale market for the Company's products, and food-processing technological breakthroughs that make it easier for smaller food producers to compete.

Among unfavorable factors, the main weakness is the limited size of Paradise Kitchens relative to its competitors in terms of the depth of the management team, available financial resources, and national awareness and distribution of product lines. Threats include the danger that the Company's premium prices may limit access to mass markets and competition from the "eating-out" and "take-out" markets.

Industry Analysis: Trends in Frozen and Mexican Foods

Frozen Foods. According to *Grocery Headquarters*, consumers are flocking to the frozen food section of grocery retailers. The reasons: hectic lifestyles demanding increased convenience and an abundance of new, tastier, and nutritious products.[6] By 2007, the latest year for which data are available, total sales of frozen food in supermarkets, drugstores, and mass merchandisers, such as Target and Costco (excluding Walmart) reached $29 billion. Prepared frozen meals, which are defined as meals or entrees that are frozen and require minimal preparation, accounted for $8.1 billion, or 26 percent of the total frozen food market.

Sales of Mexican entrees totaled $506 million in 2007.[7] Heavy consumers of frozen meals, those who eat five or more meals every two weeks, tend to be kids, teens, and adults 35–44 years old.[8]

Mexican Foods. Currently, Mexican foods such as burritos, enchiladas, and tacos are used in two-thirds of American households. These trends reflect a generally more favorable attitude on the part of all Americans toward spicy foods that include red chili peppers. The growing Hispanic population in the United States, about 48 million and almost $978 billion in purchasing power in 2009, partly explains the increasing demand for Mexican food. This Hispanic purchasing power is projected to be over $1.3 trillion in 2014.[9]

Competitor Analysis: The Chili Market

The chili market represents over $500 million in annual sales. On average, consumers buy five to six servings annually, according to the NPD Group. The products fall primarily into two groups: canned chili (75 percent of sales) and dry chili (25 percent of sales).

Bluntly put, the major disadvantage of the segment's dominant product, canned chili, is that it does not taste very good. A taste test described in an issue of *Consumer Reports* magazine ranked 26 canned chili products "poor" to "fair" in overall sensory quality. The study concluded, "Chili doesn't have to be hot to be good. But really good chili, hot or mild, doesn't come out of a can."

Company Analysis

The husband-and-wife team that cofounded Paradise Kitchens, Inc., has 44 years of experience between them in the food-processing business. Both have played key roles in the management of the Pillsbury Company. They are being advised by a highly seasoned group of business professionals, who have extensive understanding of the requirements for new-product development.

The Company now uses a single outside producer with which it works closely to maintain the consistently high quality required in its products. The greater volume has increased production efficiencies, resulting in a steady decrease in the cost of goods sold.

Customer Analysis

In terms of customer analysis, this section describes (1) the characteristics of customers expected to buy Howlin' Coyote products and (2) health and nutrition concerns of Americans today.

Customer Characteristics. Demographically, chili products in general are purchased by consumers representing a broad range of socioeconomic backgrounds. Howlin' Coyote chili is purchased chiefly by consumers who have achieved higher levels of education and whose income is $50,000 and higher. These consumers represent 50 percent of canned and dry mix chili users.

The household buying Howlin' Coyote has one to three people in it. Among married couples, Howlin' Coyote is predominantly bought by households in which both spouses work. While women are a majority of the buyers, single men represent a significant segment.

Because the chili offers a quick way to make a tasty meal, the product's biggest users tend to be those most pressed for time. Howlin' Coyote's premium pricing also means that its purchasers are skewed toward the higher end of the income range. Buyers range in age from 25 to 54 and often live in the western United States, where spicy foods are more readily eaten.

The five Howlin' Coyote entrees offer a quick, tasty meal with high-quality ingredients.

Health and Nutrition Concerns. Coverage of food issues in the U.S. media is often erratic and occasionally alarmist. Because Americans are concerned about their diets, studies from organizations of widely varying credibility frequently receive significant attention from the major news organizations. For instance, a study of fat levels of movie popcorn was reported in all the major media. Similarly, studies on the healthfulness of Mexican food have received prominent play in print and broadcast reports. The high caloric levels of much Mexican and Southwestern-style food have been widely reported and often exaggerated. Some Mexican frozen-food competitors, such as Don Miguel, Mission Foods, Ruiz Foods, and Jose Ole, plan to offer or have recently offered more "carb-friendly" and "fat-friendly" products in response to this concern.

Howlin' Coyote is already lower in calories, fat, and sodium than its competitors, and those qualities are not currently being stressed in its promotions. Instead, in the space and time available for promotions, Howlin' Coyote's taste, convenience, and flexibility are stressed.

5. Market-Product Focus

This section describes the five-year marketing and product objectives for Paradise Kitchens and the target markets, points of difference, and positioning of its lines of Howlin' Coyote chilies.

Marketing and Product Objectives

Howlin' Coyote's marketing intent is to take full advantage of its brand potential while building a base from which other revenue sources can be mined—both in and out of the retail grocery business. These are detailed in four areas below:

- Current markets. Current markets will be grown by expanding brand and flavor distribution at the retail level. In addition, same-store sales will be grown by increasing consumer awareness and repeat purchases, thereby leading to the more efficient broker/warehouse distribution channel.

- New markets. By the end of Year 5, the chili, salsa, burrito, and enchilada business will be expanded to a total of 20 metropolitan areas, which represent 53 percent of the 38 major U.S. metropolitan markets. This will represent 70 percent of U.S. food store sales.

- Food service. Food service sales will include chili products and smothering sauces. Sales are expected to reach $693,000 by the end of Year 3 and $1.5 million by the end of Year 5.

- New products. Howlin' Coyote's brand presence will be expanded at the retail

A heading should be spaced closer to the text that follows (and that it describes) than the preceding section to avoid confusion for the reader. This rule is not followed for the Target Markets heading, which now unfortunately appears to "float" between the preceding and following paragraphs.

This section identifies the specific niches or target markets toward which the company's products are directed. When appropriate and when space permits, this section often includes a market-product grid. See Chapter 9.

An organization cannot grow by offering only "me-too products." The greatest single factor in a new product's failure is the lack of significant "points of difference" that set it apart from competitors' substitutes. This section makes these points of difference explicit. See Chapter 10.

A positioning strategy helps communicate the company's unique points of difference of its products to prospective customers in a simple, clear way. This section describes this positioning. See Chapters 9 and 10.

level through the addition of new products in the frozen-foods section. This will be accomplished through new-product concept screening in Year 1 to identify new potential products. These products will be brought to market in Years 2 and 3.

Target Markets

The primary target market for Howlin' Coyote products is households with one to three people, where often both adults work, with individual income typically above $50,000 per year. These households contain more experienced, adventurous consumers of Southwestern/Mexican food and want premium quality products.

To help buyers see the many different uses for Howlin' Coyote chili, recipes are even printed on the *inside* of the packages.

Points of Difference

The "points of difference"—characteristics that make Howlin' Coyote chilies unique relative to competitors—fall into three important areas:

- Unique taste and convenience. No known competitor offers a high-quality, "authentic" frozen chili in a range of flavors. And no existing chili has the same combination of quick preparation and home-style taste that Howlin' Coyote does.
- Taste trends. The American palate is increasingly intrigued by hot spices. In response to this trend, Howlin' Coyote brands offer more "kick" than most other prepared chilies.
- Premium packaging. Howlin' Coyote's packaging graphics convey the unique, high-quality product contained inside and the product's nontraditional positioning.

Positioning

In the past chili products have been either convenient or tasty, but not both. Howlin' Coyote pairs these two desirable characteristics to obtain a positioning in consumers' minds as very high-quality "authentic Southwestern/Mexican tasting" chilies that can be prepared easily and quickly.

6. Marketing Program

The four marketing mix elements of the Howlin' Coyote chili marketing program are detailed below. Note that "chile" is the vegetable and "chili" is the dish.

Product Strategy

After first summarizing the product line, the approach to product quality and packaging is covered.

Product Line. Howlin' Coyote chili, retailing for $3.99 for an 11-ounce serving, is available in five flavors. The five are Green Chile Chili, Red Chile Chili, Beef and Black Bean Chili, Chicken Chunk Chili, and Mean Bean Chili.

Unique Product Quality. The flavoring systems of the Howlin' Coyote chilies are proprietary. The products' tastiness is due to extra care lavished upon the ingredients during production. The ingredients used are of unusually high quality. Meats are low-fat cuts and are fresh, not frozen, to preserve cell structure and moistness. Chilies are fire-roasted for fresher taste. Tomatoes and vegetables are select quality. No preservatives or artificial flavors are used.

Packaging. Reflecting the "cutting edge" marketing strategy of its producers, Howlin' Coyote bucks conventional wisdom in packaging. It avoids placing predictable photographs of the product on its containers. Instead, Howlin' Coyote's package shows a Southwestern motif that communicates the product's out-of-the-ordinary positioning.

The Southwestern motif makes Howlin' Coyote's packages stand out in a supermarket's freezer case.

Price Strategy

Howlin' Coyote Chili is, at $3.99 for an 11-ounce package, priced comparably to the other frozen offerings and higher than the canned and dried chili varieties. However, the significant taste advantages it has over canned chilies and the convenience advantages over dried chilies justify this pricing strategy.

Promotion Strategy

Key promotion programs feature in-store demonstrations, recipes, and cents-off coupons.

In-Store Demonstrations. In-store demonstrations enable consumers to try Howlin' Coyote products and discover their unique qualities. Demos will be conducted regularly in all markets to increase awareness and trial purchases.

Recipes. Because the products' flexibility of use is a key selling point, recipes are offered to consumers to stimulate use. The recipes are given at all in-store demonstrations, on the back of packages, through a mail-in recipe book offer, and in coupons sent by direct-mail or freestanding inserts.

Cents-Off Coupons. To generate trial and repeat-purchase of Howlin' Coyote products, coupons are distributed in four ways:

- In Sunday newspaper inserts. These inserts are widely read and help generate awareness.

- In-pack coupons. Each box of Howlin' Coyote chili will contain coupons for $1 off two more packages of the chili. These coupons will be included for the first three months the product is shipped to a new market. Doing so encourages repeat purchases by new users.

- Direct-mail chili coupons. Those households that fit the Howlin' Coyote demographics described previously will be mailed coupons.

- In-store demonstrations. Coupons will be passed out at in-store demonstrations to give an additional incentive to purchase.

Sunday newspaper inserts encourage consumer trial and provide recipes to show how Howlin' Coyote chili can be used in summer meals.

Place (Distribution) Strategy

Howlin' Coyote is distributed in its present markets through a food distributor. The distributor buys the product, warehouses it, and then resells and delivers it to grocery retailers on a store-by-store basis. As sales grow, we will shift to a more efficient system using a broker who sells the products to retail chains and grocery wholesalers.

7. Financial Data and Projections

Past Sales Revenues

Historically, Howlin' Coyote has had a steady increase in sales revenues since its introduction in 2003. In 2007, sales jumped spectacularly, due largely to new promotion strategies. Sales have continued to rise, but at a less dramatic rate. Sales revenues appear in Figure 2.

<u>Five-Year Projections</u>

Five-year financial projections for Paradise Kitchens appear below. These projections reflect the continuing growth in number of cases sold (with eight packages of Howlin' Coyote chili per case).

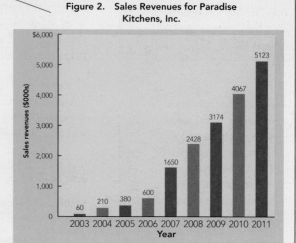

Figure 2.   Sales Revenues for Paradise Kitchens, Inc.

| | | | | Projections | | |
Financial Element	Units	Actual 2011	Year 1 2012	Year 2 2013	Year 3 2014	Year 4 2015	Year 5 2016
Cases sold	1,000	353	684	889	1,249	1,499	1,799
Net sales	$1,000	5,123	9,913	12,884	18,111	21,733	26,080
Gross profit	$1,000	2,545	4,820	6,527	8,831	10,597	12,717
Operating profit (loss)	$1,000	339	985	2,906	2,805	3,366	4,039

8. Organization

Paradise Kitchens' present organization appears in Figure 3. It shows the four people reporting to the President. Below this level are both the full-time and part-time employees of the Company.

Figure 3.   The Paradise Kitchens Organization

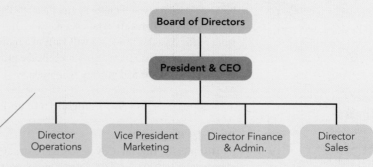

The Implementation Plan shows how the company will turn plans into results. Charts are often used to set deadlines and assign responsibilities for the many tactical marketing decisions needed to enter a new market.

The essence of Evaluation is comparing actual sales with the targeted values set in the plan and taking appropriate actions. Note that the section briefly describes a contingency plan for alternative actions, depending on how successful the entry into a new market turns out to be.

Various appendixes may appear at the end of the plan, depending on the purpose and audience for them. For example, résumés of key personnel or detailed financial spreadsheets often appear in appendixes. For space reasons these are not shown here.

At present Paradise Kitchens operates with full-time employees in only essential positions. It now augments its full-time staff with key advisors, consultants, and subcontractors. As the firm grows, people with special expertise will be added to the staff.

9. Implementation Plan

Introducing Howlin' Coyote chilies to 17 new metropolitan markets is a complex task and requires that creative promotional activities gain consumer awareness and initial trial. Counting the three existing metropolitan markets in which Paradise Kitchens competes, by 2016 it will be in 20 metropolitan markets or 53 percent of the top 38 U.S. metropolitan markets. The anticipated rollout schedule to enter these metropolitan markets appears in Figure 4.

Figure 4. Rollout Schedule to Enter New U.S. Markets

Year	New Markets Added Each Year	Cumulative Markets	Cumulative Percentage of 38 Major U.S. Markets
Today (2011)	2	5	16
Year 1 (2012)	3	8	21
Year 2 (2013)	4	12	29
Year 3 (2014)	2	14	37
Year 4 (2015)	3	17	45
Year 5 (2016)	3	20	53

The diverse regional tastes in chili will be monitored carefully to assess whether minor modifications may be required in the chili recipes. As the rollout to new metropolitan areas continues, Paradise Kitchens will assess manufacturing and distribution trade-offs. This is important in determining whether to start new production with selected high-quality regional contract packers.

10. Evaluation

Monthly sales targets in cases have been set for Howlin' Coyote chili for each metropolitan area. Actual case sales will be compared with these targets and tactical marketing programs modified to reflect the unique sets of factors in each metropolitan area.

Appendix A. Biographical Sketches of Key Personnel

Appendix B. Detailed Financial Projections

3

Scanning the Marketing Environment

LEARNING OBJECTIVES

After reading this chapter you should be able to:

LO1 Explain how environmental scanning provides information about social, economic, technological, competitive, and regulatory forces.

LO2 Describe how social forces such as demographics and culture can have an impact on marketing strategy.

LO3 Discuss how economic forces such as macroeconomic conditions and consumer income affect marketing.

LO4 Describe how technological changes can affect marketing.

LO5 Discuss the forms of competition that exist in a market.

LO6 Explain the major legislation that ensures competition and regulates the elements of the marketing mix.

WHERE IN THE WORLD ARE YOU? IN THE MIDDLE OF THE GPS REVOLUTION!

You may have heard the old saying that the three most important things for many businesses are location, location, and location. Today, the GPS revolution is making the entire marketplace completely location-based for consumers and marketers. If you have a cell phone, use MapQuest, or drive a car with a navigation system, you are already part of the revolution!

The global positioning system (GPS) that is driving the revolution utilizes a grid of 32 satellites in space to triangulate the location, speed, direction, and time of any GPS receiver on the ground. Navigation and map services have quickly become popular with consumers. Many car models, for example, include navigation systems that show the vehicle's location on a detailed map. Other recent uses include a tracking device for athletes who want to monitor the distance and speed of their workouts. In Sydney, Australia, public buses are linked to traffic lights by GPS devices so they can maintain an on-time schedule.

The future will have many more new and exciting location-aware services and applications, many of which are designed for the 444 million cell phones with GPS capability expected to be in use by 2011. JOYity will allow you to play "tag" with strangers—just get within 80 feet of the subject the game assigns to you. Other applications will soon allow you to find nearby restaurants and gas stations. Manufacturers and retailers will also benefit from location-based marketing by using GPS devices to track cargo location and delivery times.

How did the GPS revolution happen? The marketing environment changed! First, technologies such as GPS satellites, Wi-Fi nodes, and cellular signal towers were developed and became readily available. Second, the regulatory environment changed to make cell phone frequencies and former military technologies available for commercial use. Third, competitive forces by companies such as Garmin, TomTom, Apple, Google, and Nokia quickly created many new products and services. Finally consumers changed. They are becoming "geo-enthusiasts" that use information about their location to be more social and to enhance their use of Web sites such as Flickr, Twitter, Tumblr, and blogs. The GPS revolution means that consumers will always know exactly where they are![1]

Many businesses operate in environments where important forces change. Anticipating and responding to changes often means the difference between marketing success and failure. This chapter describes how the marketing environment has changed in the past and how it is likely to change in the future.

ENVIRONMENTAL SCANNING

LO1

environmental scanning
The process of acquiring information on events outside the organization to identify and interpret potential trends.

social forces
The demographic characteristics of the population and its values.

demographics
Description of a population according to characteristics such as age, gender, ethnicity, income, and occupation.

Changes in the marketing environment are a source of opportunities and threats to be managed. The process of continually acquiring information on events occurring outside the organization to identify and interpret potential trends is called **environmental scanning**. Environmental trends typically arise from five sources: social, economic, technological, competitive, and regulatory forces. As shown in Figure 3–1 and described later in this chapter, these forces affect the marketing activities of a firm in numerous ways.

An Environmental Scan of Today's Marketplace

What trends might affect marketing in the future? A firm conducting an environmental scan of the marketplace might uncover key trends such as those listed in Figure 3–2 for each of the five environmental forces.[2] Although the list of trends is far from complete, it reveals the breadth of an environmental scan—from the growing concern for environmental impact and sustainability, to the increasing government ownership of large businesses, to the greater concern for privacy and personal information collection. These trends affect consumers and the businesses and organizations that serve them. Trends such as these are described in the following discussions of the five environmental forces.

SOCIAL FORCES

LO2

The **social forces** of the environment include the demographic characteristics of the population and its values. Changes in these forces can have a dramatic impact on marketing strategy.

Demographics

FIGURE 3–1
Environmental forces affect the organization, as well as its suppliers and customers.

Describing a population according to selected characteristics such as age, gender, ethnicity, income, and occupation is referred to as **demographics**. Several organizations such as the Population Reference Bureau and the United Nations monitor the

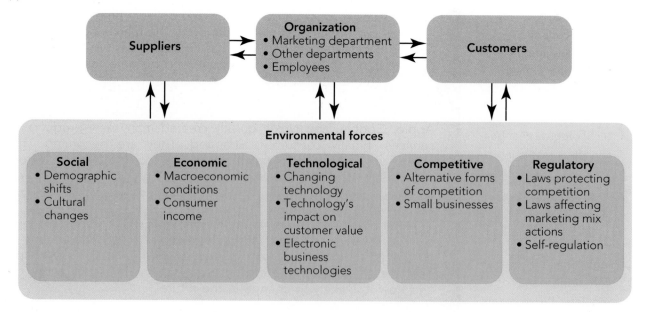

ENVIRONMENTAL FORCE	TREND IDENTIFIED BY AN ENVIRONMENTAL SCAN
Social	• Shifting of social networks and social media to mainstream forms of communication for consumers • Increasing expectation for authentic and experiential relationships with companies and brands • Growing concern for environmental impact and sustainability
Economic	• Continued shift to a service economy, including service components of goods • Growing importance of China, India, and Africa in the world economy • Increasing government ownership and management of large businesses and key industries
Technological	• Greater interest in mobile marketing • Shift from analog to digital technologies in telephone, cable, and Internet industries • Growing impact of biomimicry, or the emulation of nature, on innovation
Competitive	• Continued outsoucing of routine business processes and decision-making functions • Growing difficulty recruiting talent from abroad due to increasingly restrictive immigration rules • Dramatic increase in customer-generated content about competitive options
Regulatory	• Growing interest in revising federal and state consumer credit regulations • Greater concern for privacy and personal information collection • New regulations related to customer engagement methods such as e-mail solicitation, promotions, and contests

FIGURE 3–2

An environmental scan of today's marketplace shows the many important trends that influence marketing.

world population profile, while many other organizations such as the U.S. Census Bureau provide information about the American population.

The World Population at a Glance   The most recent estimates indicate there are 6.8 billion people in the world today, and the population is likely to grow to 9.35 billion by 2050. While this growth has led to the term *population explosion*, the increases have not occurred worldwide; they are primarily in the developing countries of Africa, Asia, and Latin America. In fact, India is predicted to have the world's largest population in 2050 with 1.75 billion people, and China will be a close second with 1.44 billion people.[3]

Another important global trend is the shifting age structure of the world population. The number of people 60 and older is expected to more than triple in the coming decades and reach 2 billion by 2050. Again, the magnitude of this trend varies by region, and developed countries such as the United States are expected to face the highest growth rates of the elderly age group. Global income levels and living standards have also been increasing, although the averages across countries are very different. Per capita income, for example, ranges from $64,320 in Luxembourg, to $36,220 in Canada, to $870 in Ethiopia.

For marketers, global trends such as these have many implications. Obviously, the relative size of countries such as India and China will mean they represent huge markets for many product categories. Elderly populations in developed countries are likely to save less and begin spending their funds on health care, travel, and other retirement-related products and services. Economic progress in developing countries will lead to growth in entrepreneurship, new markets for infrastructure related to manufacturing, communication, and distribution, and the growth of exports.[4]

The U.S. Population   Studies of the demographic characteristics of the U.S. population suggest several important trends. Generally, the population is becoming larger, older, and more diverse. In 2010, the U.S. population was estimated to be 310 million people. If current trends in life expectancy, birthrates, and immigration continue, by 2030 the U.S. population will exceed 373 million people. This growth suggests that niche markets based on age, life stage, family structure, geographic location, and ethnicity will become increasingly important. The global trend toward an older population is particularly true in the United States. Today, there are approximately 40 million people 65 and older. By 2030, this age group will include more than 72 million people, or almost 20 percent of the population. You may have noticed companies trying to attract older consumers. Mobile phone manufacturer Samsung, for example, recently introduced the Jitterbug with large easy-to-read buttons for seniors. Finally, the term *minority* as it is currently used is likely to become obsolete as the size of most ethnic groups will double during the next two decades.[5]

Generational Cohorts A major reason for the graying of America is that the 76 million **baby boomers**—the generation of children born between 1946 and 1964—are growing older. Baby boomers are retiring at a rate of 10,000 every 24 hours, and they will all be 65 or older by 2030. Their participation in the workforce has made them the wealthiest generation in U.S. history, with an estimated $1 trillion in annual buying power. While boomers represent a diverse group in terms of their age and life stages, one commonality is their interest in health, wellness, and appearance. Companies that target boomers will need to respond to their interests in fitness, retirement housing, financial planning, and personal appearance. Olay, for example, offers anti-aging and restoration products for this age group.[6]

The baby boom cohort is followed by **Generation X**, which includes the 15 percent of the population born between 1965 and 1976. This period is also known as the *baby bust*, because the number of children born each year was declining. Generation X consumers are self-reliant, supportive of racial and ethnic diversity, and better educated than any previous generation. They are not prone to extravagance and are likely to pursue lifestyles that are a blend of caution, pragmatism, and traditionalism. In terms of net worth, Generation X is the first generation to have less than the previous generation. As baby boomers move toward retirement, however, Generation X is becoming a dominant force in many markets. Generation X, for example, is replacing baby boomers as the largest segment of business travelers. In response, hotel companies are creating new concepts that appeal to the younger market. Surveys of Generation X travelers indicate they want casual, tech-friendly

---

baby boomers
The generation of children born between 1946 and 1964.

Generation X
Members of the U.S. population born between 1965 and 1976.

Which generational cohorts are these three advertisers trying to reach?

Making Responsible Decisions > > > > sustainability

Millennials Are Making a Difference— through Environmental Sustainability!

Millennials, also known as Generation Y, are determined to make a difference in the world and, by doing so, make the world a better place. They are idealistic and eager to get started, particularly when it comes to environmental sustainability, which millennials believe is part of what it means to be socially responsible. The group includes students in college and graduate school, and many early career employees. In different ways each group is making its voice heard.

There are approximately 17 million undergraduate millennials who expect sustainable campus communities that include LEED (Leadership in Energy and Environmental Design)-certified housing, campus transit systems, and recycling programs. Graduate students are looking for programs with sustainability electives, case studies, and potential for involvement with organizations such as Net Impact, a nonprofit for students who want to "use business to improve the world." Early career

employees want "green" jobs such as social responsibility officer, environmental consultant, or sustainability database specialist at companies that are eco-conscious and advocate good citizenry.

Sara Hochman is a typical example. She was interested in environmental issues in college, and her first job was as an environmental consultant. To make a bigger impact on her clients, she decided she "needed to beef up my business skills," so she enrolled in graduate school at the University of Chicago where she could take an elective on renewable energy and join the Energy Club.

Have you made similar choices or decisions based on your interest and concern about sustainability? What will the world look like after the millennials have made their changes? It is difficult to predict. As experts Peter Leyden and Ruy Teixeira advise, however, we should "Hang on for the ride!"

---

lodging with 24-hour access to food and drinks, so Hyatt Corporation is building 400 new Hyatt Place all-suite hotels featuring free wireless Internet, flat-panel high-definition televisions, a 24-hour guest kitchen, a fitness center, and remote printing.[7]

The generational cohort labeled **Generation Y** includes the 72 million Americans born between 1977 and 1994. This was a period of increasing births, which resulted from baby boomers having children, and it is often referred to as the *echo-boom* or *baby boomlet*. Generation Y exerts influence on music, sports, computers, video games, and especially cell phones. Generation Y views wireless communication as a lifeline to friends and family and was the first to use Web-enabled mobile phones to stream video, send and receive text messages, play games, and access e-mail. They are strong-willed, passionate about the environment, and optimistic. This is also a group that is attracted to purposeful work where they have control. The Making Responsible Decisions box describes how Generation Y's interest in sustainability is influencing colleges, graduate schools, and employers. The term *millennials* is also used, with inconsistent definitions, to refer to younger members of Generation Y and sometimes to Americans born since 1994.[8]

Because the members of each generation are distinctive in their attitudes and consumer behavior, marketers have been studying the many groups or cohorts that make up the marketplace and have developed *generational marketing* programs for them.

Population Shifts A major regional shift in the U.S. population toward southern and western states is under way. From 2007 to 2008, the populations of Utah,

> **Generation Y**
> *The 72 million Americans born between 1977 and 1994.*

Arizona, Texas, North Carolina, and Colorado grew at the fastest rates in the nation. Nearly a century ago each of the top 10 most populous cities in the United States was within 500 miles of the Canadian border. Today, seven of the top 10 are in states that border Mexico. Last year, Texas gained more people than any other state—its population increased by almost 500,000![9]

To assist marketers in gathering data on the population, the Census Bureau has developed a classification system to describe the varying locations of the population. The system consists of two types of *statistical areas*:

- A *metropolitan statistical area* has at least one urbanized area of 50,000 or more people and adjacent territory that has a high degree of social and economic integration.
- A *micropolitan statistical area* has at least one urban cluster of at least 10,000 but less than 50,000 people and adjacent territory that has a high degree of social and economic integration.

If a metropolitan statistical area contains a population of 2.5 million or more, it may be subdivided into smaller areas called *metropolitan divisions*. In addition, adjacent metropolitan statistical areas and micropolitan statistical areas may be grouped into *combined statistical areas*.[10]

There are currently 363 metropolitan statistical areas, which include 83 percent of the population, and 577 micropolitan areas, which include 10 percent of the population.

Racial and Ethnic Diversity A notable trend is the changing racial and ethnic composition of the U.S. population. Approximately one in four U.S. residents is an African American, American Indian, Asian, Pacific Islander, or a representative of another racial or ethnic group. Diversity is further evident in the variety of peoples that make up these groups. For example, Asians consist of Asian Indians, Chinese, Filipinos, Japanese, Koreans, and Vietnamese. For the first time, the 2000 Census allowed respondents to choose more than one of the six race options, and more than 4 million reported more than one race. Hispanics, who may be from any race, currently make up 15 percent of the U.S. population and are represented by Mexicans, Puerto Ricans, Cubans, and others of Central and South American ancestry. While the United States is becoming more diverse, Figure 3–3 suggests that the minority racial and ethnic groups tend to be concentrated in geographic regions.[11]

While the growing size of these groups has been identified through new Census data, their economic impact on the marketplace is also very noticeable. By 2012, Hispanics, African Americans, and Asian Americans will spend $1.20 trillion, $1.13 trillion, and $670 billion each year, respectively. To adapt to this new marketplace, many companies are developing **multicultural marketing** programs, which are combinations of the marketing mix that reflect the unique attitudes, ancestry, communication preferences, and lifestyles of different races. Because businesses must now market their products to a consumer base with many racial and ethnic identities, in-depth marketing research that allows an accurate understanding of each culture is essential.[12]

multicultural marketing
Marketing programs that reflect unique aspects of different races.

Culture

A second social force, **culture**, incorporates the set of values, ideas, and attitudes that is learned and shared among the members of a group. Because many of the elements of culture influence consumer buying patterns, monitoring national and global cultural trends is important for marketing. Cross-cultural analysis needed for global marketing is discussed in Chapter 7.

Culture also includes values, which vary with age but tend to be very similar for men and women. All age groups, for example, rank "protecting the family" and "honesty" as the most important values. Consumers under 20 years old rank "friendship"

culture
The set of values, ideas, and attitudes that is learned and shared among the members of a group.

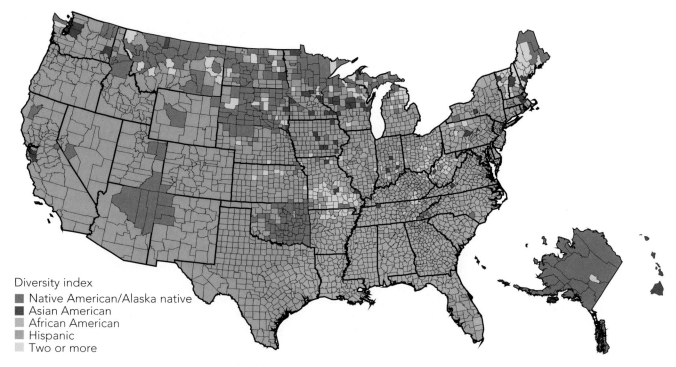

Diversity index
- ■ Native American/Alaska native
- ■ Asian American
- ■ African American
- ■ Hispanic
- ▦ Two or more

FIGURE 3–3
Racial and ethnic groups (excluding Caucasians) are concentrated in geographic regions of the United States.

third, while the 20-to-29 and 30-to-39 age groups rank "self-esteem" and "health and fitness" as their third most important values, respectively.

An increasingly important value for consumers is sustainability and preserving the environment. Concern for the environment is one reason consumers are buying hybrid gas-electric automobiles such as the Toyota Prius and energy-efficient lightbulbs such as General Electric's Energy Smart™ fluorescent bulbs. Companies are also changing their business practices to respond to trends in consumer values. Walmart has set ambitious goals to cut energy use, switch to renewable power, and reduce packaging on the products it carries. Recent research also indicates that consumers around the world are committed to brands with a strong link to social action. For example, Brita's "Filter for Good" campaign asks consumers to take a pledge to reduce their plastic bottle waste.[13]

---

learning review

1. Describe three generational cohorts.

2. Why are many companies developing multicultural marketing programs?

3. How are important values such as sustainability reflected in the marketplace today?

ECONOMIC FORCES

LO3

The second component of the environmental scan, the **economy**, pertains to the income, expenditures, and resources that affect the cost of running a business and household. We'll consider two aspects of these economic forces: a macroeconomic view of the marketplace and a microeconomic perspective of consumer income.

Macroeconomic Conditions

Of particular concern at the macroeconomic level is the inflationary or recessionary state of the economy, whether actual or perceived by consumers or businesses. In an

economy
Pertains to the income and resources that affect the cost of running a business or household.

inflationary economy, the cost to produce and buy products and services escalates as prices increase. From a marketing standpoint, if prices rise faster than consumer incomes, the number of items consumers can buy decreases. This relationship is evident in the cost of a college education. The National Center for Public Policy and Higher Education reports that since 1980 college tuition and fees have increased 440 percent while family income has risen less than 150 percent.[14]

Whereas inflation is a period of price increases, recession is a time of slow economic activity. Businesses decrease production, unemployment rises, and many consumers have less money to spend. The U.S. economy experienced recessions from 1973–75, 1981–82, 1990–91, as well as in 2001 and 2008.[15]

Consumer Income

The microeconomic trends in terms of consumer income are also important issues for marketers. Having a product that meets the needs of consumers may be of little value if they are unable to purchase it. A consumer's ability to buy is related to income, which consists of gross, disposable, and discretionary components.

Gross Income　The total amount of money made in one year by a person, household, or family unit is referred to as *gross income* (or "money income" at the Census Bureau). While the typical U.S. household earned only about $8,700 of income in 1970, it earned about $50,303 in 2008. When gross income is adjusted for inflation, however, income of that typical U.S. household was relatively stable. In fact, inflation-adjusted income has only varied between $41,995 and $52,587 since 1968. Figure 3–4 shows the distribution of annual income among U.S. households.[16] Are you from a typical household?

Disposable Income　The second income component, *disposable income*, is the money a consumer has left after paying taxes to use for necessities such as food, housing, clothing, and transportation. Thus, if taxes rise or fall faster than income, consumers are likely to have more or less disposable income. Similarly, dramatic changes in prices of products can require spending adjustments. In recent years, for example, as the price of gasoline increased and declined dramatically, consumers found themselves adjusting their spending in other categories. In addition, the decline in home prices has had a psychological impact on consumers who tend to spend more when they feel their net worth is rising and postpone purchases when it declines. During a recessionary period, spending, debt, and use of credit are all expected to decline.[17]

Discretionary Income　The third component of income is *discretionary income*, the money that remains after paying for taxes and necessities. Discretionary income is used for luxury items such as a Regent cruise. An obvious problem in defining

FIGURE 3–4

U.S. households have a large range of gross incomes. See the text for descriptions of gross, disposable, and discretionary incomes.

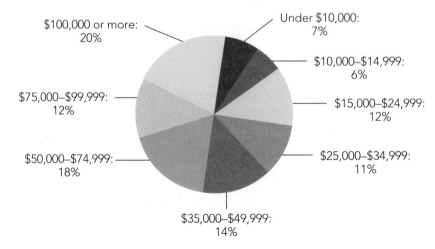

$100,000 or more: 20%

Under $10,000: 7%

$10,000–$14,999: 6%

$15,000–$24,999: 12%

$25,000–$34,999: 11%

$35,000–$49,999: 14%

$50,000–$74,999: 18%

$75,000–$99,999: 12%

As consumers' discretionary income increases, so does the opportunity to indulge in the luxurious leisure travel marketed by Regent.

discretionary versus disposable income is determining what is a luxury and what is a necessity.

The Department of Labor monitors consumer expenditures through its annual Consumer Expenditure Survey. In 2007, consumers spent about 12 percent of their income on food, 34 percent on housing, and 4 percent on clothes. While an additional 24 percent is often spent on transportation, health care, and insurance, the remainder is generally viewed as discretionary. The percentage of income spent on food and housing typically declines as income increases, which can provide an increase in discretionary income. Discretionary expenditures also can be increased by reducing savings. Since the 1990s, the Bureau of Labor Statistics has observed a decline in the savings rate. After reaching a level of approximately zero, the savings rate began to increase in 2008 when consumers saved their economic stimulus package checks.[18]

TECHNOLOGICAL FORCES

technology
Inventions from applied science or engineering research.

Our society is in a period of dramatic technological change. **Technology**, the third environmental force, refers to inventions or innovations from applied science or engineering research. Each new wave of technological innovation can replace existing products and companies. See if you recognize the items pictured on the next page. What products might they replace?

Technology of Tomorrow

Technological change is the result of research, so it is difficult to predict. Some of the most dramatic technological changes occurring now, however, include the following:

- Cloud computing will allow businesses and consumers to access software applications directly from third parties over the Internet and "pay as they go."
- Researchers are developing a wireless power process to transmit power to electrical products without interconnecting wires.
- Advances in nanotechnology, the science of unimaginably small electronics, will lead to smaller microprocessors, efficient fuel cells, and cancer-detection sensors.

Technological change leads to new products. What products might be replaced by these innovations?

- Biotechnology and agricultural genome research is being used to develop genetically modified crops to create enough food for a growing world population.

Some of these trends in technology are already seen in today's marketplace. Google, for example, has developed a cloud computing collection of software including e-mail and word processing called Google Apps. A new company called Powercast is manufacturing holiday lights that run on wireless power, and MIT has developed "WiTricity," which can power a TV from across a room. Nanotechnology is used in the Samsung flash memory chips that are part of the iPod nano. Other technologies such as 3D TV, online meeting services, and customized music services are likely to replace or become substitutes for existing products and services such as plasma screen televisions, business travel, and radio.[19]

Technology's Impact on Customer Value

Advances in technology have important effects on marketing. First, the cost of technology is plummeting, causing the customer value assessment of technology-based products to focus on other dimensions such as quality, service, and relationships. *PC Magazine* publishes an article titled, "The Best Free Software," each year to tell readers about companies that give their software away, with the expectation that advertising or upgrade purchases will generate revenue. A similar approach is used by many U.S. cellular telephone vendors, who charge little for the telephone if the purchase leads to a long-term telephone service contract.[20]

Technology also provides value through the development of new products. Recent examples that have generated extraordinary consumer interest include Nintendo's Wii, Activision's *Guitar Hero* series, and Apple's iPhone. A new version of Amazon's electronic book reader, Kindle, also received attention from many consumers. The new product provides a high-resolution display, holds as many as 1,500 books, and offers a "text-to-speech" feature that allows readers to listen to books. Other new products likely to be available soon include injectable health monitors that will send glucose, oxygen, and other clinical information to a wristwatch-like monitor, LED lights that look like traditional fluorescent light bulbs, and Bluetooth-enabled speakers and video cameras.[21]

Electronic Business Technologies

marketspace
An information- and communication-based electronic exchange environment occupied by digitized offerings.

The transformative power of technology may be best illustrated by the rapid growth of the **marketspace**, an information- and communication-based electronic exchange environment mostly occupied by sophisticated computer and telecommunication technologies and digitized offerings. Any activity that uses some form of electronic communication in the inventory, exchange, advertisement, distribution, and payment of goods and services is often called *electronic commerce*. Network technologies are now used for everything from filing expense reports, to monitoring daily sales, to sharing information with employees, to communicating instantly with suppliers.

Many companies have adapted Internet-based technology internally to support their electronic business strategies. An *intranet*, for example, is an Internet-based network used within the boundaries of an organization. It is a private network that may or may not be connected to the public Internet. *Extranets*, which use Internet-based technologies, permit communication between a company and its suppliers, distributors, and other partners (such as advertising agencies).

COMPETITIVE FORCES

competition
Alternative firms that could provide a product to satisfy a specific market's needs.

The fourth component of the environmental scan, **competition**, refers to the alternative firms that could provide a product to satisfy a specific market's needs. There are various forms of competition, and each company must consider its present and potential competitors in designing its marketing strategy.

Alternative Forms of Competition

LO5

Four basic forms of competition form a continuum from pure competition to monopolistic competition to oligopoly to pure monopoly.

At one end of the continuum is *pure competition*, in which there are many sellers and they each have a similar product. Companies that deal in commodities common to agribusiness (for example, wheat, rice, and grain) often are in a pure competition position in which distribution (in the sense of shipping products) is important but other elements of marketing have little impact.

In the second point on the continuum, *monopolistic competition*, many sellers compete with substitutable products within a price range. For example, if the price of coffee rises too much, consumers may switch to tea. Coupons or sales are frequently used marketing tactics.

Oligopoly, a common industry structure, occurs when a few companies control the majority of industry sales. The wireless telephone industry, for example, is dominated by Verizon, AT&T, Sprint, and T-Mobile, which have 92, 87, 48, and 34 million subscribers, respectively. Similarly, the entertainment industry in the United States is dominated by Viacom, Disney, and Time Warner, and the major firms in the U.S. defense contractor industry are Boeing, Northrup Grumman, and Lockheed Martin. Critics of oligopolies suggest that because there are few sellers, price competition among firms is not desirable because it leads to reduced profits for all producers.[22]

The final point on the continuum, *pure monopoly*, occurs when only one firm sells the product. Monopolies are common for producers of goods considered essential to a community: water, electricity, and cable service. Typically, marketing plays a small role in a monopolistic setting because it is regulated by the state or federal government. Government control usually seeks to ensure price protection for the buyer. Concern that Microsoft's 86 percent share of the PC operating system market is a monopoly has led to lawsuits and consent decrees from the U.S. Justice Department and fines and ongoing investigations from the European Union.[23]

Small Businesses as Competitors

While large companies provide familiar examples of the forms and components of competition, small companies make up the majority of the competitive landscape for most businesses. Consider that there are approximately 29 million small businesses in the United States, which employ half of all private sector employees. In addition, small businesses generate 60 to 80 percent of all new jobs annually and 50 percent of the gross domestic product (GDP). Research has shown a strong correlation between national economic growth and the level of new small business activity in the previous years.[24]

learning review

4. What is the difference between a consumer's disposable and discretionary income?

5. How does technology impact customer value?

6. In pure competition there are _____ sellers.

REGULATORY FORCES

LO6

regulation
Restrictions that state and federal laws place on business.

For any organization, the marketing and broader business decisions are constrained, directed, and influenced by regulatory forces. **Regulation** consists of restrictions that state and federal laws place on a business with regard to the conduct of its activities. Regulation exists to protect companies as well as consumers. Much of the regulation from the federal and state levels is the result of an active political process and has been passed to ensure competition and fair business practices. For consumers, the focus of legislation is to protect them from unfair trade practices and ensure their safety.

Protecting Competition

Major federal legislation has been passed to encourage competition, which is deemed desirable because it permits the consumer to determine which competitor will succeed and which will fail. The first such law was the *Sherman Antitrust Act* (1890). Lobbying by farmers in the Midwest against fixed railroad shipping prices led to the passage of this act, which forbids (1) contracts, combinations, or conspiracies in restraint of trade and (2) actual monopolies or attempts to monopolize any part of trade or commerce. Because of vague wording and government inactivity, however, there was only one successful case against a company in the nine years after the act became law, and the Sherman Act was supplemented with the *Clayton Act* (1914). This act forbids certain actions that are likely to lessen competition, although no actual harm has yet occurred.

In the 1930s, the federal government had to act again to ensure fair competition. During that time, large chain stores appeared, such as the Great Atlantic & Pacific Tea Company (A&P). Small businesses were threatened, and they lobbied for the *Robinson-Patman Act* (1936). This act makes it unlawful to discriminate by charging different prices to different purchasers of the same product, where the effect may substantially lessen competition or help to create a monopoly.

Product-Related Legislation

Various federal laws in existence specifically address the product component of the marketing mix. Some are aimed at protecting the company, some at protecting the consumer, and at least one at protecting both.

A company can protect its competitive position in new and novel products under the patent law, which gives inventors the right to exclude others from making, using, or selling products that infringe upon the patented invention. The federal copyright law is another way for a company to protect its competitive position in a product. The copyright law gives the author of a literary, dramatic, musical, or artistic work the exclusive right to print, perform, or otherwise copy that work. Copyright is secured automatically when the work is created. However, the published work should bear an appropriate copyright notice, including the copyright symbol and the first year of publication. In addition, the published work should include the name of the copyright owner and be registered under the federal copyright law. Digital technology has necessitated additional copyright legislation, called the *Digital Millennium Copyright Act* (1998), to improve the protection of copyrighted digital products. In addition, producers of DVD movies, music recordings, and software want protection from devices designed to circumvent antipiracy elements of their products.[25]

There are many consumer-oriented federal laws regarding products. The various laws include more than 30 amendments and separate laws relating to food, drugs, and cosmetics, such as the *Infant Formula Act* (1980), the *Nutritional Labeling and Education Act* (1990), new labeling requirements for dietary supplements (1997), and proposed labeling guidelines for trans fats (2006).[26] Various other consumer protection laws have a broader scope, such as the *Fair Packaging and Labeling Act* (1966), the *Child Protection Act* (1966), and the *Consumer Product Safety Act* (1972), which established the Consumer Product Safety Commission to monitor product safety and establish uniform product safety standards. Many of these laws came about because of **consumerism**, a grassroots movement started in the 1960s to increase the influence, power, and rights of consumers in dealing with institutions. This movement continues and is reflected in growing consumer demands for ecologically safe products and ethical and socially responsible business practices. One hotly debated issue concerns liability for environmental abuse.

Trademarks are intended to protect both the firm selling a trademarked product and the consumer buying it. A Senate report states:

> The purposes underlying any trademark statute [are] twofold. One is to protect the public so that it may be confident that, in purchasing a product bearing a particular trademark which it favorably knows, it will get the product which it asks for and wants to get. Secondly, where the owner of a trademark has spent energy, time, and money in presenting to the public the product, he is protected in this investment from misappropriation in pirates and cheats.

This statement was made in connection with another product-related law, the *Lanham Act* (1946), which provides for registration of a company's trademarks.

consumerism

A movement started to increase the influence, power, and rights of consumers in dealing with institutions.

These products are identified by protected trademarks. Are any of these trademarks in danger of becoming generic?

Historically, the first user of a trademark in commerce had the exclusive right to use that particular word, name, or symbol in its business. Registration under the Lanham Act provides important advantages to a trademark owner that has used the trademark in interstate or foreign commerce, but it does not confer ownership. A company can lose its trademark if it becomes generic, which means that it has primarily come to be merely a common descriptive word for the product. Coca-Cola, Whopper, and Xerox are registered trademarks, and competitors cannot use these names. Aspirin and escalator are former trademarks that are now generic terms in the United States and can be used by anyone.

In 1988, the *Trademark Law Revision Act* resulted in a major change to the Lanham Act, allowing a company to secure rights to a name before actual use by declaring an intent to use the name.[27] In 2003, the United States agreed to participate in the *Madrid Protocol,* which is a treaty that facilitates the protection of U.S. trademark rights throughout the world.[28] See the Marketing Matters box to learn how the Internet and technology have led to a use (or misuse) of trademarks called doppelgangers.[29]

One of the most recent changes in trademark law is the U.S. Supreme Court's ruling that companies may obtain trademarks for colors associated with their products. Over time, consumers may begin to associate a particular color with a specific brand. Examples of products that may benefit from the new law include NutraSweet's sugar substitute in pastel blue packages and Owens-Corning Fiberglas Corporation's pink insulation.[30] Another recent addition to trademark law is the *Federal Dilution Act* (1995), which is used to prevent someone from using a trademark on a noncompeting product (e.g., "Cadillac" brushes).[31]

Pricing-Related Legislation

The pricing component of the marketing mix is the focus of regulation from two perspectives: price fixing and price discounting. Although the Sherman Act did not outlaw price fixing, the courts view this behavior as *per se illegal* (*per se* means "through or of itself"), which means the courts see price fixing itself as illegal.

Certain forms of price discounting are allowed. Quantity discounts are acceptable; that is, buyers can be charged different prices for a product provided there are differences in manufacturing or delivery costs. Promotional allowances or services may be given to buyers on an equal basis proportionate to volume purchased. Also, a firm can meet a competitor's price "in good faith." Legal and regulatory aspects of pricing are covered in more detail in Chapter 12.

Distribution-Related Legislation

The government has four concerns with regard to distribution—earlier referred to as "place" actions in the marketing mix—and the maintenance of competition. The first, *exclusive dealing,* is an arrangement a manufacturer makes with a reseller to handle only its products and not those of competitors. This practice is illegal under the Clayton Act only when it substantially lessens competition.

Requirement contracts require a buyer to purchase all or part of its needs for a product from one seller for a time period. These contracts are not always illegal but depend on the court's interpretation of their impact on distribution.

Exclusive territorial distributorships are a third distribution issue often under regulatory scrutiny. In this situation, a manufacturer grants a distributor the sole rights to sell a product in a specific geographical area. The courts have found few violations with these arrangements.

The fourth distribution strategy is a *tying arrangement,* whereby a seller requires the purchaser of one product to also buy another item in the line. These contracts may be illegal when the seller has such economic power in the tying product that the seller can restrain trade in the tied product.

Marketing Matters > > > > > > > > technology

The Web Allows New Uses and Misuses of Trademarks

Have you seen an ad or a logo that looked like a familiar brand but was slightly different? Some examples you might be familiar with include a commercial for Chevy Tahoe saying "global warming is here," and Starbucks logos that read "Evil Empire" or "Frankenbucks Coffee." These parodies—sometimes called doppelgangers—are a growing form of citizen protest called culture jamming. The purpose of culture jamming ranges from offering an alternative, often creative, perspective to undermining the integrity of existing brand marketing. Digital technologies make this possible. Image and video editing software makes changes easy, and Web sites such as YouTube and Adbusters offer outlets for these activities.

Companies currently have different responses to doppelgangers. Some companies ignore them, others try to monitor the parodies for insight about consumer perceptions of the company, and others fight back. Starbucks, for example, has used cease and desist letters, injunctions, and trademark infringement litigation to try to stop the creation and distribution of doppelgangers. Jeben Berg, YouTube's creative strategist, however, argues that culture jamming is important because it is "so disruptive that it forces you to look." Obviously culture jamming and doppelgangers are just two of many possible uses of new technologies. What will be next?

Companies must meet certain requirements before they can display this logo on their Web sites.

Advertising- and Promotion-Related Legislation

Promotion and advertising are aspects of marketing closely monitored by the Federal Trade Commission (FTC), which was established by the *FTC Act of 1914*. The FTC has been concerned with deceptive or misleading advertising and unfair business practices and has the power to (1) issue cease and desist orders and (2) order corrective advertising. In issuing a *cease and desist order*, the FTC orders a company to stop practices the commission considers unfair. With *corrective advertising*, the FTC can require a company to spend money on advertising to correct previous misleading ads. The enforcement powers of the FTC are so significant that often just an indication of concern from the commission can cause companies to revise their promotion.

Other laws have been introduced to regulate promotion practices. The *Deceptive Mail Prevention and Enforcement Act* (1999), for example, provides specifications for direct-mail sweepstakes, such as the requirement that the statement "No purchase is necessary to enter" is displayed in the mailing, in the rules, and on the entry form. Similarly, the *Telephone Consumer Protection Act* (1991) provides requirements for telemarketing promotions, including fax promotions. Telemarketing is also subject to a law that created the *National Do Not Call Registry*, which is a list of consumer phone numbers of people who do not want to receive unsolicited telemarketing calls. Finally, new laws such as the *Children's Online Privacy Protection Act* (1998), the *European Union Data Protection Act* (1998), and the *Controlling the Assault of Non-Solicited Pornography and Marketing (CAN-SPAM) Act* (2004) are designed to restrict information collection and unsolicited e-mail promotions, and specify simple opt-out procedures on the Internet. A related Internet issue, taxation, has generated an ongoing debate and temporary laws such as the *Internet Tax Freedom Act* (2007).[32]

Control through Self-Regulation

self-regulation
An alternative to government control, whereby an industry attempts to police itself.

The government has provided much legislation to create a competitive business climate and protect the consumer. An alternative to government control is **self-regulation**, whereby an industry attempts to police itself. The major television networks, for example, have used self-regulation to set their own guidelines for TV ads for children's toys. These guidelines have generally worked well. There are two problems with self-regulation, however: noncompliance by members and enforcement. In addition, if attempts at self-regulation are too strong, they may violate the Robinson-Patman Act. The best-known self-regulatory group is the Better Business Bureau (BBB). This agency is a voluntary alliance of companies whose goal is to help maintain fair practices. Although the BBB has no legal power, it does try to use "moral suasion" to get members to comply with its standards. The BBB recently developed a reliability assurance program, called BBB Online, to provide objective consumer protection for Internet shoppers. Before they display the BBB Online logo on their Web site, participating companies must be members of their local Better Business Bureau, have been in business for at least one year, agree to participate in BBB's advertising self-regulation program, abide by the BBB Code of Business Practices, and work with the BBB to resolve consumer disputes that arise over goods or services promoted or advertised on their site.[33]

learning review

7. The _____ Act was punitive toward monopolies, whereas the _____ Act was preventive.

8. Describe some of the recent changes in trademark law.

9. How does the Better Business Bureau encourage companies to follow its standards for commerce?

LEARNING OBJECTIVES REVIEW

LO1 *Explain how environmental scanning provides information about social, economic, technological, competitive, and regulatory forces.*
Many businesses operate in environments where important forces change. Environmental scanning is the process of acquiring information about these changes to allow marketers to identify and interpret trends. There are five environmental forces businesses must monitor: social, economic, technological, competitive, and regulatory. By identifying trends related to each of these forces, businesses can develop and maintain successful marketing programs. Several trends that most businesses are monitoring include the increasing diversity of the U.S. population, the growing economic impact of China and India, and the dramatic growth of customer-generated content.

LO2 *Describe how social forces such as demographics and culture can have an impact on marketing strategy.*
Demographic information describes the world population; the U.S. population; the generational cohorts such as baby boomers, Generation X, and Generation Y; the structure of the American household; the geographic shifts of the population; and the racial and ethnic diversity of the population that has led to multicultural marketing programs. Cultural factors include the trend toward fewer differences in male and female consumer behavior and the impact of values such as "health and fitness" on consumer preferences.

LO3 *Discuss how economic forces such as macroeconomic conditions and consumer income affect marketing.*
Economic forces include the strong relationship between consumers' expectations about the economy and their spend-

ing. Gross income has remained stable for more than 30 years although the rate of saving has been declining.

LO4 *Describe how technological changes can affect marketing.*
Technological innovations can replace existing products and services. Changes in technology can also have an impact on customer value by reducing the cost of products, improving the quality of products, and providing new products that were not previously feasible. Electronic commerce is transforming how companies do business.

LO5 *Discuss the forms of competition that exist in a market and key components of competition.*
There are four forms of competition: pure competition, monopolistic competition, oligopoly, and monopoly. While large companies are often used as examples of marketplace competitors, there are 29 million small businesses in the United States. These small businesses have a significant impact on the economy.

LO6 *Explain the major legislation that ensures competition and regulates the elements of the marketing mix.*
Regulation exists to protect companies and consumers. Legislation that ensures a competitive marketplace includes the Sherman Antitrust Act. Product-related legislation includes copyright and trademark laws that protect companies and packaging and labeling laws that protect consumers. Pricing- and distribution-related laws are designed to create a competitive marketplace with fair prices and availability. Regulation related to promotion and advertising reduces deceptive practices and provides enforcement through the Federal Trade Commission. Self-regulation through organizations such as the Better Business Bureau provides an alternative to federal and state regulation.

FOCUSING ON KEY TERMS

baby boomers p. 62
competition p. 69
consumerism p. 71
culture p. 64
demographics p. 60

economy p. 65
environmental scanning p. 60
Generation X p. 62
Generation Y p. 63
marketspace p. 69

multicultural marketing p. 64
regulation p. 70
self-regulation p. 73
social forces p. 60
technology p. 67

APPLYING MARKETING KNOWLEDGE

1 For many years Gerber has manufactured baby food in small, single-serving sized containers. In conducting an environmental scan, identify three trends or factors that might significantly affect this company's future business, and then propose how Gerber might respond to these changes.

2 Describe the new features you would add to an automobile designed for consumers in the 55+ age group. In what magazines would you advertise to appeal to this target market?

3 New technologies are continuously improving and replacing existing products. Although technological change is often difficult to predict, suggest how the following companies and products might be affected by the Internet and digital technologies: (*a*) Kodak cameras and film, (*b*) American Airlines, and (*c*) the Metropolitan Museum of Art.

4 In recent years in the brewing industry, a couple of large firms that have historically had most of the beer sales (Anheuser-Busch and Miller) have faced competition from many small "micro" brands. In terms of the continuum of competition, how would you explain this change?

5 Why would Xerox be concerned about its name becoming generic?

6 Develop a "Code of Business Practices" for a new online vitamin store. Does your code address advertising? Privacy? Use by children? Why is self-regulation important?

building your marketing plan

Your marketing plan will include a situation analysis based on internal and external factors that are likely to affect your marketing program.

1 To summarize information about external factors, create a table similar to Figure 3–2 and identify three trends related to each of the five forces (social, economic, technological, competitive, and regulatory) that relate to your product or service.

2 When your table is completed, describe how each of the trends represents an opportunity or a threat for your business.

video case 3   Geek Squad: A New Business for a New Environment

"As long as there's innovation there is going to be new kinds of chaos," explains Robert Stephens, founder of the technology support company Geek Squad. The chaos Stephens is referring to is the difficulty we have all experienced trying to keep up with the many changes in our environment, particularly those related to computers, technology, software, communication, and entertainment. Generally, consumers have found it difficult to install, operate, and use many of the electronic products available today. "It takes time to read the manuals," Stephens says. "I'm going to save you that time because I stay home on Saturday nights and read them for you!"

THE COMPANY

The Geek Squad story begins when Stephens, a native of Chicago, passed up an Art Institute scholarship to pursue a degree in computer science. While Stephens was a computer science student he took a job fixing computers for a research laboratory, and he also started consulting. He could repair televisions, computers, and a variety of other items, although he decided to focus on computers. His experiences as a consultant led him to realize that most people needed help with technology and that they saw value in a service whose employees would show up at a specified time, be friendly, use understandable language, and solve the problem. So, with just $200, Stephens formed Geek Squad in 1994.

Geek Squad set out to provide timely and effective help with all computing needs regardless of the make, model, or place of purchase. Geek Squad employees were called "agents" and wore uniforms consisting of black pants or skirts, black shoes, white shirts, black clip-on ties, a badge, and a black jacket with a Geek Squad logo to create a "humble" attitude that was not threatening to customers. Agents drove black-and-white Volkswagen Beetles, or Geekmobiles, with a logo on the door, and

charged fixed prices for services, regardless of how much time was required to provide the service. The "house call" services ranged from installing networks, to debugging a computer, to setting up an entertainment system, and cost from $100 to $300. "We're like 'Dragnet'; we show up at people's homes and help," Stephens says. "We're also like *Ghostbusters* and there's a pseudogovernment feel to it like *Men in Black*."

In 2002, Geek Squad was purchased by leading consumer electronics retailer Best Buy for about $3 million. Best Buy had observed very high return rates for most of its complex products. Shoppers would be excited about new products, purchase them and take them home, get frustrated trying to make them actually work, and then return them to the store demanding a refund. In fact, Best Buy research revealed that consumers were beginning to see service as a critical element of the purchase. The partnership was an excellent match. Best Buy consumers welcomed the help. Stephens became Geek Squad's chief inspector and a Best Buy vice president and began putting a Geek Squad "precinct" in every Best Buy store, creating some stand-alone

Geek Squad Stores, and providing 24-hour telephone support. There are now more than 24,000 agents in the United States, Puerto Rico, Canada, the United Kingdom, and China, and return rates have declined by 25 to 35 percent. Geek Squad customer materials now suggest that the service is "Saving the World One Computer at a Time. 24 Hours a Day. Your Place or Ours!"

THE CHANGING ENVIRONMENT

Many changes in the environment occurred to create the need for Geek Squad's services. Future changes are also likely to change the way Geek Squad operates. An environmental scan helps explain the changes.

The most obvious changes may be related to technology. Wireless broadband technology, high-definition televisions, products with Internet interfaces, and a general trend toward computers, phones, entertainment systems, and even appliances being interconnected are just a few examples of new products and applications for consumers to learn about. There are also technology-related problems such as viruses, spyware, lost data, and "crashed" or inoperable computers. New technologies have also created a demand for new types of maintenance such as password management, operating system updates, disk cleanup, and "defragging."

Another environmental change that contributes to the popularity of Geek Squad is the change in social factors such as demographics and culture. In the past many electronics manufacturers and retailers focused primarily on men. Women, however, are becoming increasingly interested in personal computing and home entertainment, and, according to the Consumer Electronics Association, are likely to outspend men in the near future. Best Buy's consumer research indicates that women expect personal service during the purchase and installation after the purchase—exactly the service Geek Squad is designed to provide. Our culture is also embracing the Geek Squad concept. If you follow television programming you may have noticed the series *Chuck* where one of the characters works for the "Nerd Herd" at "Buy More" and drives a car like a Geekmobile on service calls!

Competition, economics, and the regulatory environment have also had a big influence on Geek Squad. As discount stores such as Walmart and PC makers such as

Dell began to compete with Best Buy, new services such as in-home installation were needed to create value for customers. Now, just as changes in competition created an opportunity for Geek Squad, it is also leading to another level of competition as Dell has introduced its own computer support service, Dell-On-Call, and cable companies are offering their own services. The economic situation for electronics continues to improve as prices decline and the median income in the United States, particularly for women, is increasing. In 2009, consumers purchased 30 million high-definition televisions, but household penetration is still below 40 percent. Finally, the regulatory environment continues to change with respect to electronic transfer of copyrighted materials such as music and movies and software. Geek Squad must monitor the changes to ensure that its services comply with relevant laws.

Best Buy has created partnerships with home builders to wire new houses with high-speed cables and networking equipment that Geek Squad agents can use to create ideal computer and entertainment systems. Geek Squad is also using new technology to improve. Agents now use a smart phone to access updated schedules, log in their hours, and run diagnostics tests on clients' equipment. Finally, to attract the best possible employees, Geek Squad and Best Buy are trying a "results-only work environment" that has no fixed schedules and no mandatory meetings. By encouraging employees to make their own work-life decisions, the Geek Squad hopes to keep morale and productivity high.

Other changes and opportunities are certain to appear soon. Despite the success of the Geek Squad, and the potential for additional growth, however, Robert Stephens is modest and claims, "Geeks may inherit the Earth, but they have no desire to rule it!"

THE FUTURE FOR GEEK SQUAD

The combination of many positive environmental factors helps explain the extraordinary success of Geek Squad. Today, it repairs more than 3,000 PCs a day and generates more than $1 billion in revenue. Because Geek Squad services have a high-profit margin they contribute to the overall performance of Best Buy, and they help generate traffic in the store and create store loyalty. To continue to grow, however, Geek Squad will need to continue to scan the environment and try new approaches to creating customer value.

One possible new approach is to find additional locations that are convenient to consumers. For example, Geek Squad locations are being tested in some FedEx stores and in some Office Depot stores. Another possible approach is to create new houses that are designed for the newest consumer electronics products. To test this idea

Questions

1 What are the key environmental factors that created an opportunity for Robert Stephens to start the Geek Squad?
2 What changes in the purchasing patterns of (*a*) all consumers, and (*b*) women made the acquisition of Geek Squad particularly important for Best Buy?
3 Based on the case information and what you know about consumer electronics, conduct an environmental scan for Geek Squad to identify key trends. For each of the five environmental forces (social, economic, technological, competitive, and regulatory), identify trends likely to influence Geek Squad in the near future.
4 What promotional activities would you recommend to encourage consumers who use independent installers to switch to Geek Squad?

4

Ethical and Social Responsibility in Marketing

LEARNING OBJECTIVES

After reading this chapter you should be able to:

LO1 Explain the differences between legal and ethical behavior in marketing.

LO2 Identify factors that influence ethical and unethical marketing decisions.

LO3 Describe the different concepts of social responsibility.

LO4 Recognize unethical and socially irresponsible consumer behavior.

RESPONSIBILITY MATTERS AT ANHEUSER-BUSCH

Why would a company spend more than $750 million since 1982 trying to persuade people not to abuse its products and millions of dollars more to decrease litter and solid waste? Ask Anheuser-Busch, the leading American brewer.

Anheuser-Busch has been an advocate for responsible drinking for nearly three decades. The company began an aggressive campaign to fight alcohol abuse and underage drinking with its landmark "Know When to Say When" campaign in 1982. In 1989, a Consumer Awareness and Education Department was established within the company. This department, now called the Corporate Social Responsibility (CSR) Department, is charged with developing and implementing programs, advertising, and partnerships that promote responsible drinking; helping prevent alcohol abuse; and helping curb underage drinking before it starts. For example, nearly 7 million copies of the company's *Family Talk about Drinking* guidebook have been distributed free to parents and educators.

In 2004, the brewer began a new chapter in its awareness and education efforts with the launch of its "Responsibility Matters" campaign. This effort emphasizes and implements effective education and awareness programs that promote responsibility and responsible behaviors, such as parents talking with their children about underage drinking, adults being designated drivers, retailers checking IDs to prevent sales to minors, and more. Anheuser-Busch believes these efforts are partly responsible for the sizable decline in drunk-driving accidents, underage drinking, and other forms of alcohol abuse since 1982.

Responsibility at Anheuser-Busch is broader than its successful alcohol awareness and education initiatives. The company is an advocate and sponsor of numerous efforts to preserve the natural environment. A notable example is its massive recycling effort through Anheuser-Busch Recycling Corporation (ABRC). ABRC is the world's largest recycler of aluminum cans. ABRC recycles over 27 billion cans annually, the equivalent of five cans for every four the company packages worldwide. The rationale for founding ABRC was simple: Voluntary recycling reduces litter and solid waste while conserving natural resources.

Anheuser-Busch acts on what it views as an ethical obligation to its customers and the general public with its alcohol awareness and education programs. At the same time, the company's efforts to protect the environment reflect its broader social responsibility. Not surprisingly, in 2010, the company ranked among the top companies for social responsibility in *Fortune* magazine's "World's Most-Admired Companies" list.[1]

NATURE AND SIGNIFICANCE OF MARKETING ETHICS

ethics
The moral principles and values that govern the actions and decisions of an individual or a group.

laws
Society's standards and values that are enforceable in the courts.

Ethics are the moral principles and values that govern the actions and decisions of an individual or group.[2] They serve as guidelines on how to act rightly and justly when faced with moral dilemmas.

Ethical/Legal Framework in Marketing

A good starting point for understanding the nature and significance of ethics is the distinction between legality and ethicality of marketing decisions.[3] Whereas ethics deal with personal moral principles and values, **laws** are society's values and standards that are enforceable in the courts. This distinction can sometimes lead to the rationalization that if a behavior is within reasonable ethical and legal limits, then it is not really illegal or unethical. When a recent survey asked the question, "Is it OK to get around the law if you don't actually break it?" about 61 percent of businesspeople who took part responded "yes."[4] How would you answer this question?

Judgment plays a large role in numerous situations in defining ethical and legal boundaries. Consider the following situations.[5]

1. More than 70 percent of the physicians in the Maricopa County (Arizona) Medical Society agreed to establish a maximum fee schedule for health services to curb rising medical costs. All physicians were required to adhere to this schedule as a condition for membership in the society. The U.S. Supreme Court ruled that this agreement to set prices violated the Sherman Act and represented price fixing, which is illegal. Was the society's action ethical?

2. A company in California sells a computer program to auto dealers showing that car buyers should finance their purchase rather than paying cash. The program omits the effect of income taxes and misstates the interest earned on savings over the loan period. The finance option always provides a net benefit over the cash option. Company employees agree that the program does mislead buyers, but they say the company will "provide what [car dealers] want as long as it is not against the law." Is this practice ethical?

3. China is the world's largest tobacco-producing country and has 300 million smokers. Approximately 700,000 Chinese die annually from smoking-related illnesses. This figure is expected to rise to more than 2 million by 2025. China legally restricts tobacco imports. U.S. trade negotiators advocate free trade, thus allowing U.S. tobacco companies to market their products in China. Is the Chinese trade position ethical?

4. Federal statutes state that the unauthorized reproduction, distribution, or exhibition of copyrighted motion pictures is illegal. A group of college students recorded movies at a local theater and then uploaded the movies to the Internet. The students then directed friends and family to a peer-to-peer Internet network that allowed them to download the movies for free, which they did. Are the students ethical? Are the students' friends and family ethical?

Current Perceptions of Ethical Behavior

There has been a public outcry about the ethical practices of businesspeople.[6] Public opinion surveys show that 58 percent of U.S. adults rate the ethical standards of business executives as only "fair" or "poor"; 90 percent think white-collar crime is "very common" or "somewhat common"; 76 percent say the lack of ethics in businesspeople contributes to tumbling societal moral standards; only the U.S. government is viewed as less trustworthy than corporations among institutions in the United States; and advertising practitioners, telemarketers, and car salespeople are thought to be among the least ethical occupations. Surveys of corporate employees generally confirm this public perception. When asked if they are aware of ethical problems in their companies, 49 percent say, "yes."

There are at least four possible reasons the state of perceived ethical business conduct is at its present level. First, there is increased pressure on businesspeople to make decisions in a society characterized by diverse value systems. Second, there is a growing tendency for business decisions to be judged publicly by groups with different values and interests. Third, the public's expectations of ethical business behavior have increased. Finally, and most disturbing, ethical business conduct may have declined.

1. What are ethics?

2. What are four possible reasons for the present state of ethical conduct in the United States?

UNDERSTANDING ETHICAL MARKETING BEHAVIOR

LO2

Researchers have identified numerous factors that influence ethical marketing behavior. Figure 4–1 presents a framework that shows these factors and their relationships.

Societal Culture and Norms

As described in Chapter 3, *culture* refers to the set of values, ideas, and attitudes that are learned and shared among the members of a group. Culture also serves as a socializing force that dictates what is morally right and just. This means that moral standards are relative to particular societies.[7] These standards often reflect the laws and regulations that affect social and economic behavior, which can create ethical dilemmas. Companies that compete in the global marketplace recognize this fact. Consider UPS, the world's largest package delivery company operating in more than 200 countries and territories worldwide.[8] According to the company's global compliance and ethics coordinator, "Although languages and cultures around the world may be different, we do not change our ethical standards at UPS. Our ethics program is global in nature." Not surprisingly, UPS is consistently ranked among the world's most ethical companies.

Societal values and attitudes also affect ethical and legal relationships among individuals, groups, and business institutions and organizations. Consider the copying of another's copyright, trademark, or patent. These are viewed as intellectual property. Unauthorized use, reproduction, or distribution of intellectual property is illegal in the United States and most countries, which can result in fines and prison terms for perpetrators. The owners of intellectual property also lose. For example, annual worldwide lost sales from the theft of intellectual property amount to $12.5 billion

FIGURE 4–1

A framework for understanding ethical behavior. Each of these influences will have an effect on ethical marketing behavior.

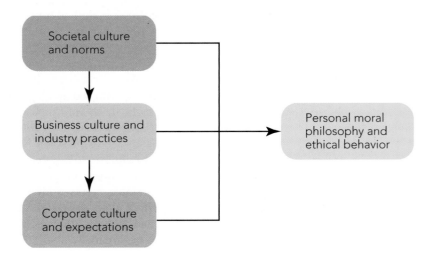

in the music industry, $18.2 billion in the movie industry, and $53.0 billion in the software industry.[9] Lost sales result in lost jobs, royalties, wages, and tax revenue. But what about a person downloading copyrighted music, movies, and software over the Internet or from peer-to-peer file-sharing programs, without paying the owner of this property? Is this an ethical or unethical act? It depends on who you ask. Surveys of the U.S. public show that the majority consider these acts unethical. But, only a third of U.S. college students say such practices are unethical.[10]

Business Culture and Industry Practices

Societal culture provides a foundation for understanding moral behavior in business activities. *Business cultures* "comprise the effective rules of the game, the boundaries between competitive and unethical behavior, [and] the codes of conduct in business dealings."[11] Consumers have witnessed numerous instances where business cultures in the brokerage (inside trading), insurance (deceptive sales practices), and defense (bribery) industries went awry. Business culture affects ethical conduct both in the exchange relationship between sellers and buyers and in the competitive behavior among sellers.

Ethics of Exchange The exchange process is central to the marketing concept. Ethical exchanges between sellers and buyers should result in both parties being better off after a transaction.

Before the 1960s, the legal concept of *caveat emptor*—let the buyer beware—was pervasive in the American business culture. In 1962, President John F. Kennedy outlined a **Consumer Bill of Rights** that codified the ethics of exchange between buyers and sellers. These were the right (1) to safety, (2) to be informed, (3) to choose, and (4) to be heard. Consumers expect and often demand that these rights be protected, as have American businesses.

The right to safety manifests itself in industry and federal safety standards for most products sold in the United States. In fact, the U.S. Consumer Product Safety Commission routinely monitors the safety of 15,000 consumer products. However, even the most vigilant efforts to ensure safe products cannot foresee every possibility. Personal claims and property damage from consumer product safety incidents cost companies more than $700 billion annually. Consider the case of batteries used in laptop and notebook computers. Dell Inc. learned that the lithium-ion batteries in its notebook computers, made by Sony Energy Devices Corporation of Japan, posed a fire hazard to consumers. The company recalled 2.7 million batteries and gave consumers a replacement before any personal injuries resulted.[12]

The right to be informed means that marketers have an obligation to give consumers complete and accurate information about products and services. This right also applies to the solicitation of personal information over the Internet and its subsequent use by marketers.[13] An FTC survey of Web sites indicated that 92 percent collect personal information such as consumer e-mail addresses, telephone numbers, shopping habits, and financial data. Yet, only two-thirds of Web sites inform consumers of what is done with this information once obtained. The FTC wants more than posted privacy notices that merely inform consumers of a company's data-use policy, which critics say are often vague, confusing, or too legalistic to be understood. This view is shared by two-thirds of consumers who worry about protecting their personal information online. The consumer right to be informed has spawned much federal legislation, such as the *Children's Online Privacy Protection Act* (1998) and self-regulation initiatives restricting disclosure of personal information.

Relating to the right to choose, today many supermarket chains demand "slotting allowances" from manufacturers, in the form of cash or free goods, to stock new products.[14] This practice could limit the number of new products available to consumers and interfere with their right to choose. One critic of this practice remarked, "If we had had slotting allowances a few years ago, we might not have had granola, herbal tea, or yogurt."

Consumer Bill of Rights

Codified the ethics of exchange between buyers and sellers, including rights to safety, to be informed, to choose, and to be heard.

The Federal Trade Commission (FTC) plays an active role in educating consumers and businesses about the importance of personal information privacy on the Internet. FTC initiatives are detailed on its Web site.

Finally, the right to be heard means that consumers should have access to public-policy makers regarding complaints about products and services. This right is illustrated in limitations put on telemarketing practices. The FTC established the Do Not Call Registry in 2003 for consumers who do not want to receive unsolicited telemarketing calls. Today, almost 167 million U.S. telephone numbers are listed in the registry, which is managed by the FTC. A telemarketer can be fined up to $16,000 for each call made to a telephone number posted on the registry.

Ethics of Competition Business culture also affects ethical behavior in competition. Two kinds of unethical behavior are most common: (1) economic espionage and (2) bribery.

Economic espionage is the clandestine collection of trade secrets or proprietary information about a company's competitors. This practice is illegal and unethical and carries serious criminal penalties for the offending individual or business. Espionage activities include illegal trespassing, theft, fraud, misrepresentation, wiretapping, the search of a competitor's trash, and violations of written and implicit employment agreements with noncompete clauses. More than half of the largest firms in the United States have uncovered espionage in some form, costing them $300 billion annually in lost sales.[15]

Economic espionage is most prevalent in high-technology industries, such as electronics, specialty chemicals, industrial equipment, aerospace, and pharmaceuticals, where technical know-how and trade secrets separate industry leaders from followers. But espionage can occur anywhere—even in the soft drink industry! Read the Making Responsible Decisions box on the next page to learn how Pepsi-Cola responded to an offer to obtain confidential information about its archrival's marketing plans.[16]

The second form of unethical competitive behavior is giving and receiving bribes and kickbacks. Bribes and kickbacks are often disguised as gifts, consultant fees, and favors. This practice is more common in business-to-business and government marketing than in consumer marketing.

In general, bribery is most evident in industries experiencing intense competition and in countries in the earlier stages of economic development. According to a United Nations study, 15 percent of all companies in industrialized countries have to pay bribes to win or retain business. In Asia, this figure is 40 percent. In Eastern Europe, 60 percent of all companies must pay bribes to do business. A recent poll of senior executives engaged in global marketing revealed that Afghanistan and Somalia were the most likely countries to evidence bribery to win or retain business. Denmark and New Zealand were the least likely.[17]

The prevalence of economic espionage and bribery in international marketing has prompted laws to curb these practices. Two significant laws, the *Economic Espionage Act* (1996) and the *Foreign Corrupt Practices Act* (1977), address these practices in the United States. Both are detailed in Chapter 7.

Corporate Culture and Expectations

A third influence on ethical practices is corporate culture. *Corporate culture* is the set of values, ideas, and attitudes that is learned and shared among the members of an organization. The culture of a company demonstrates itself in the dress ("We don't wear ties"), sayings ("The IBM Way"), and manner of work (team efforts) of

Corporate Conscience in the Cola War

Suppose you are a senior executive at Pepsi-Cola and a Coca-Cola employee offers to sell you the marketing plan and sample for a new Coke product at a modest price. Would you buy it knowing Pepsi-Cola could gain a significant competitive edge in the cola war?

When this question was posed in an online survey of marketing and advertising executives, 67 percent said they would buy the plan and product sample if there were no repercussions. What did Pepsi-Cola do when this offer actually occurred? The company immediately contacted Coca-Cola, which contacted the FBI. An undercover FBI agent paid the employee $30,000 in cash stuffed in a Girl Scout cookie box as a down payment and later arrested the employee and her accomplices. When asked about the

incident, a Pepsi-Cola spokesperson said: "We only did what any responsible company would do. Competition must be tough, but must always be fair and legal."

Why did the 33 percent of respondents in the online survey say they would decline the offer? Most said they would prefer competing ethically so they could sleep at night. According to a senior advertising agency executive who would decline the offer: "Repercussions go beyond potential espionage charges. As long as we have a conscience, there are repercussions."

So what happened to the Coca-Cola employee and her accomplices? She was sentenced to eight years in prison and ordered to pay $40,000 in restitution. Her accomplices were each sentenced to five years in prison.

---

employees. Culture is also apparent in the expectations for ethical behavior present in formal codes of ethics and the ethical actions of top management and co-workers.

code of ethics

A formal statement of ethical principles and rules of conduct.

Codes of Ethics A **code of ethics** is a formal statement of ethical principles and rules of conduct. It is estimated that 86 percent of U.S. companies have some sort of ethics code and one of every four large companies has corporate ethics officers. At United Technologies, for example, 160 corporate ethics officers distribute the company's ethics code, translated into 24 languages, to employees who work for this defense and engineering giant around the world.[18] Ethics codes and committees typically address contributions to government officials and political parties, relations with customers and suppliers, conflicts of interest, and accurate recordkeeping.

However, an ethics code is rarely enough to ensure ethical behavior. Coca-Cola has an ethics code and emphasizes that its employees must be ethical in their behavior. But that did not stop some Coca-Cola employees from rigging the results of a test market for a frozen soft drink to win Burger King's business. Coca-Cola subsequently agreed to pay Burger King and its operators more than $20 million to settle the matter.[19]

Lack of specificity is a major reason for the violation of ethics codes. Employees must often judge whether a specific behavior is unethical. The American Marketing Association has addressed this issue by providing a detailed statement of ethics, which all members agree to follow. This statement can be found at the American Marketing Association Web site (www.marketingpower.com).

Ethical Behavior of Top Management and Co-Workers A second reason for violating ethics codes rests in the perceived behavior of top management and co-workers.[20] Observing peers and top management and gauging responses to unethical behavior play an important role in individual actions. A study of business executives reported that 40 percent had been implicitly or explicitly rewarded for engaging in ethically troubling behavior. And, 31 percent of those who refused to engage in unethical behavior were penalized, either through outright punishment or a diminished status in the company.[21] Clearly, ethical dilemmas can bring personal and professional conflict. For this reason, numerous states have laws protecting *whistle-blowers*, employees who report an employer's unethical or illegal actions.

Your Personal Moral Philosophy and Ethical Behavior

Ultimately, ethical choices are based on the personal moral philosophy of the decision maker. Moral philosophy is learned through the process of socialization with friends and family and by formal education. It is also influenced by the societal, business, and corporate culture in which a person finds him- or herself. Two prominent personal moral philosophies have direct bearing on marketing practice: (1) moral idealism and (2) utilitarianism.

moral idealism
A personal moral philosophy that considers certain individual rights or duties as universal, regardless of the outcome.

Moral Idealism **Moral idealism** is a personal moral philosophy that considers certain individual rights or duties as universal, regardless of the outcome. This philosophy exists in the Consumer Bill of Rights and is favored by moral philosophers and consumer interest groups. For example, the right to know applies to probable defects in an automobile that relate to safety.

This philosophy also applies to ethical duties. A fundamental ethical duty is to do no harm. Adherence to this duty prompted the recent decision by 3M executives to phase out production of a chemical 3M had manufactured for nearly 40 years. The substance, used in far-ranging products from pet food bags, candy wrappers, carpeting, and 3M's popular Scotchgard fabric protector, had no known harmful health or environmental effect. However, the company discovered that the chemical appeared in minuscule amounts in humans and animals around the world and accumulated in tissue. Believing that the substance could be possibly harmful in large doses, 3M voluntarily stopped its production, resulting in a $200 million loss in annual sales.[22]

utilitarianism
A personal moral philosophy that focuses on the "greatest good for the greatest number."

What does 3M's Scotchgard have to do with ethics, social responsibility, and a $200 million loss in annual sales? Read the text to find out.

Utilitarianism An alternative perspective on moral philosophy is **utilitarianism**, which is a personal moral philosophy that focuses on "the greatest good for the greatest number" by assessing the costs and benefits of the consequences of ethical behavior. If the benefits exceed the costs, then the behavior is ethical. If not, then the behavior is unethical. This philosophy underlies the economic tenets of capitalism and, not surprisingly, is embraced by many business executives and students.[23]

Utilitarian reasoning was apparent in Nestlé Food Corporation's marketing of Good Start infant formula, sold by Nestlé's Carnation Company. The formula, promoted as hypoallergenic, was designed to prevent or reduce colic caused by an infant's allergic reaction to cow's milk, a condition suffered by 2 percent of babies. However, some severely milk-allergic infants experienced serious side effects after using Good Start, including convulsive vomiting. Physicians and parents charged that the hypoallergenic claim was misleading, and the Food and Drug Administration investigated the matter. A Nestlé vice president defended the claim and product, saying, "I don't understand why our product should work in 100 percent of cases. If we wanted to say it was foolproof, we would have called it allergy-free. We call it hypo-, or less, allergenic."[24] Nestlé officials seemingly believed that most allergic infants would benefit from Good Start—"the greatest good for the greatest number." But, other views prevailed. The claim was dropped from the product label.

An appreciation for the nature of ethics, coupled with a basic understanding of why unethical behavior arises, alerts a person to when and how ethical issues exist in marketing decisions. Ultimately, ethical behavior rests with the individual, but the consequences affect many.

UNDERSTANDING SOCIAL RESPONSIBILITY IN MARKETING

LO3

social responsibility
The idea that organizations are part of a larger society and are accountable to that society for their actions.

As we saw in Chapter 1, the societal marketing concept stresses marketing's social responsibility to not only satisfy the needs of consumers but also provide for society's welfare. **Social responsibility** means that organizations are part of a larger society and are accountable to that society for their actions. Like ethics, agreement on the nature and scope of social responsibility is often difficult to come by, given the diversity of values present in different societal, business, and corporate cultures.

Three Concepts of Social Responsibility

Figure 4–2 shows three concepts of social responsibility: (1) profit responsibility, (2) stakeholder responsibility, and (3) societal responsibility.

Profit Responsibility   *Profit responsibility* holds that companies have a simple duty: to maximize profits for their owners or stockholders. This view is expressed by Nobel Laureate Milton Friedman, who said, "There is one and only one social responsibility of business—to use its resources and engage in activities designed to increase its profits so long as it stays within the rules of the game, which is to say, engages in open and free competition without deception or fraud."[25] Genzyme, the maker of Cerezyme, a drug that treats a genetic illness called Gaucher's disease that affects 20,000 people worldwide, has been criticized for apparently adopting this view in its pricing practices. Genzyme charges up to $170,000 for a year's worth of Cerezyme. A Genzyme spokesperson responded saying the company spends about $150 million annually to manufacture Cerezyme and freely gives the drug to patients

FIGURE 4–2
Three concepts of social responsibility. Each concept of social responsibility relates to particular constituencies. There is often conflict in satisfying all constituencies at the same time.

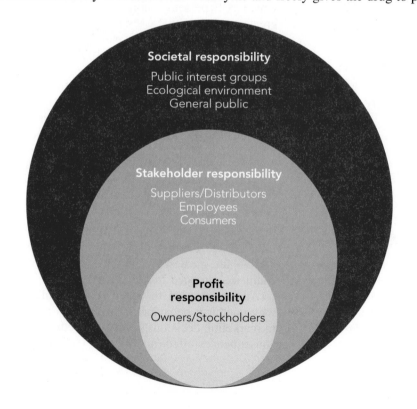

Societal responsibility
Public interest groups
Ecological environment
General public

Stakeholder responsibility
Suppliers/Distributors
Employees
Consumers

Profit
responsibility
Owners/Stockholders

without insurance. Also, the company has invested considerable dollars in research to develop Cerezyme, and the drug's profits are reinvested in ongoing R&D programs.[26]

Stakeholder Responsibility Criticism of the profit view has led to a broader concept of social responsibility. *Stakeholder responsibility* focuses on the obligations an organization has to those who can affect achievement of its objectives. These constituencies include consumers, employees, suppliers, and distributors. Source Perrier S.A., the supplier of Perrier bottled water, exercised this responsibility when it recalled 160 million bottles of water in 120 countries after traces of a toxic chemical were found in 13 bottles. The recall cost the company $35 million, and $40 million more in lost sales. Even though the chemical level was not harmful to humans, Source Perrier's president believed he acted in the best interests of the firm's constituencies by removing "the least doubt, as minimal as it might be, to weigh on the image of the quality and purity of our product"—which it did.[27]

Failure to consider a company's broader constituencies can have negative consequences. For example, Toyota Motor Corporation executives were widely criticized for how they responded to complaints about the safety of selected Toyota brands. These cars had been linked to sticky gas pedals, which can lead to sudden acceleration problems. The company recalled more than 9 million cars worldwide under pressure from the National Highway Traffic Safety Administration. After the recall, Toyota sales fell, which affected Toyota employees, suppliers, and distributors as well.[28]

Societal Responsibility An even broader concept of social responsibility has emerged in recent years. *Societal responsibility* refers to obligations that organizations have (1) to the preservation of the ecological environment and (2) to the general public. Today, emphasis is placed on what is termed the *triple-bottom line*—recognition of the need for organizations to improve the state of people, the planet, and profit simultaneously if they are to achieve sustainable, long-term growth.[29] Growing interest in green marketing, cause marketing, social audits, and sustainable development reflect this recognition.

Green marketing—marketing efforts to produce, promote, and reclaim environmentally sensitive products—takes many forms.[30] At 3M, product development opportunities emanate from both consumer research and its "Pollution Prevention Pays" program. This program solicits employee suggestions on how to reduce pollution and recycle materials. Since 1975, this program has generated over 8,000 3P projects that eliminated more than 3 billion pounds of air, water, and solid-waste pollutants from the environment. Xerox's "Design for the Environment" program focuses on ways to make its equipment recyclable and remanufacturable. Today, 100 percent of Xerox-designed products are remanufacturable. This effort has kept more than 2 billion pounds of equipment from being discarded in U.S. landfills since 1991. Walmart has instituted buying practices that encourage its suppliers to use containers and packaging made from corn, not oil-based resins. The company expects this initiative will save 800,000 barrels of oil annually. These voluntary responses to environmental issues have been implemented with little or no additional cost to consumers and have resulted in cost savings to companies.

Socially responsible efforts on behalf of the general public are becoming more common. A formal practice is **cause marketing**, which occurs when the charitable contributions of a firm are tied directly to the customer revenues produced through the promotion of one of its products.[31] This definition distinguishes cause marketing from a firm's standard charitable contributions, which are outright donations. For example, Procter & Gamble raises funds for the Special Olympics when consumers purchase selected company products, and MasterCard International links usage of its card with fund-raising for institutions that combat cancer, heart disease, child abuse, drug abuse, and muscular dystrophy. Barnes & Noble promotes literacy, and Coca-Cola sponsors local Boys and Girls Clubs. Avon Products, Inc., focuses on different issues

green marketing
Marketing efforts to produce, promote, and reclaim environmentally sensitive products.

cause marketing
Tying the charitable contributions of a firm directly to sales produced through the promotion of one of its products.

Avon Products, Inc., successfully employs cause marketing programs in the fight against breast cancer.

Marketing Matters > > > > > > customer value

Will Consumers Switch Brands for a Cause? Yes, If . . .

American Express Company pioneered cause marketing when it sponsored the renovation of the Statue of Liberty. This effort raised $1.7 million for the renovation, increased card usage among cardholders, and attracted new cardholders. In 2001, U.S. companies raised more than $5 billion for causes they champion. It is estimated that cause marketing raised over $10 billion in 2010.

Cause marketing benefits companies as well as causes. Research indicates that 85 percent of U.S. consumers say they have a more favorable opinion of companies that support causes they care about. Also, 79 percent of consumers say they will likely switch to a brand or retailer that supports a good cause if the price and quality of brands or retailers are equal. In short, cause marketing may be a valued point of difference for brands and companies, all other things being equal.

For more information, including news, links, and case studies, visit the Cause Marketing Forum Web site at www.causemarketingforum.com.

in different countries. These include breast cancer, domestic violence, and disaster relief, among many others.

Cause marketing programs incorporate all three concepts of social responsibility by addressing public concerns and satisfying customer needs. They can also enhance corporate sales and profits as described in the Marketing Matters box.[32]

The Social Audit and Sustainable Development: Doing Well by Doing Good

Converting socially responsible ideas into actions involves careful planning and monitoring of programs. Many companies develop, implement, and evaluate their social responsibility efforts by means of a **social audit**, which is a systematic assessment of a firm's objectives, strategies, and performance in terms of social responsibility. Frequently, marketing and social responsibility programs are integrated. Consider McDonald's. The company's concern for the needs of families with children who are chronically or terminally ill was converted into some 300 Ronald McDonald Houses around the world. These facilities, located near treatment centers, enable families to stay together during the child's care. In this case, McDonald's is contributing to the welfare of a portion of its target market.

A social audit consists of five steps:[33]

social audit
A systematic assessment of a firm's objectives, strategies, and performance in the domain of social responsibility.

1. Recognition of a firm's social expectations and the rationale for engaging in social responsibility endeavors.
2. Identification of social responsibility causes or programs consistent with the company's mission.
3. Determination of organizational objectives and priorities for programs and activities it will undertake.
4. Specification of the type and amount of resources necessary to achieve social responsibility objectives.
5. Evaluation of social responsibility programs and activities undertaken and assessment of future involvement.

Marketing and social responsibility programs are often integrated, as is the case with McDonald's. Its concern for ill children worldwide is apparent in the opening of another Ronald McDonald House for children and their families, this time in China.

Corporate attention to social audits will increase as companies seek to achieve sustainable development and improve the quality of life in a global economy. *Sustainable development* involves conducting business in a way that protects the natural environment while making economic progress. Ecologically responsible initiatives such as green marketing represent one such initiative. Recent initiatives related to working conditions at offshore manufacturing sites that produce goods for U.S. companies focus on quality-of-life issues. Public opinion surveys show that 90 percent of U.S. citizens are concerned about working conditions under which products are made in Asia and Latin America. Companies such as Reebok, Nike, Liz Claiborne, Levi Strauss, and Mattel have responded by imposing codes of conduct to reduce harsh or abusive working conditions at offshore manufacturing facilities.[34] Reebok, for example, now monitors production of its sporting apparel and equipment to ensure that no child labor is used in making its products.

Companies that evidence societal responsibility have been rewarded for their efforts. Research has shown that these companies (1) benefit from favorable word of mouth among consumers and (2) typically outperform less responsible companies financially.[35]

Turning the Table: Consumer Ethics and Social Responsibility

LO4

Consumers also have an obligation to act ethically and responsibly in the exchange process and in the use and disposition of products. Unfortunately, consumer behavior is spotty on both counts.

The unethical practices of consumers are a serious concern to marketers.[36] These practices include filing warranty claims after the claim period; misredeeming coupons; making fraudulent returns of merchandise; providing inaccurate information on credit applications; tampering with utility meters; tapping cable TV lines; pirating music, movies, and software from the Internet; and submitting phony insurance claims.

The cost to marketers of such behavior in lost sales and prevention expenses is huge. For example, consumers who redeem coupons for unpurchased products or use coupons for other products cost manufacturers $1 billion each year. Fraudulent automobile insurance claims cost insurance companies more than $10 billion annually. In addition, retailers lose about $30 billion yearly from shoplifting and $9.6 billion annually from fraudulent returns of merchandise. Consumers also act unethically toward each other. According to the FBI, consumer complaints about online auction fraud, in which consumers misrepresent their goods to others, outnumber all other reports of online crime.

Nike has been a leader in improving workplace conditions in Asian factories that produce its sporting apparel and equipment.

Research on unethical consumer behavior indicates that these acts are rarely motivated by economic need. This behavior appears to be influenced by (1) a belief that a consumer can get away with the act and it is worth doing and (2) the rationalization that the act is justified or driven by forces outside the individual—"everybody does it." These reasons were vividly expressed by a 24-year-old man who pirated a movie, was sentenced to six months of house arrest, three years of probation, and a $7,000 fine. He said, "I didn't like paying for movies," and added, "so many people do it, you never think you're going to get caught."[37]

Consumer purchase, use, and disposition of environmentally sensitive products relate to consumer social responsibility. Research indicates that consumers are sensitive to ecological issues.[38] For example, a recent survey of U.S. consumers indicated that 50 percent were personally willing to change their lifestyle to improve the environment. However, only 28 percent could identify their own shopping or living habits over the past five years that help protect the environment. Related research shows that consumers (1) may be unwilling to sacrifice convenience and pay higher prices to protect the environment and (2) lack the knowledge to make informed decisions dealing with the purchase, use, and disposition of products.

Consumer confusion over which products are environmentally safe also exists given marketers' rush to produce "green products." For example, few consumers realize that nonaerosol "pump" hair sprays are the second-largest cause of air pollution, after drying paint. In California alone, 27 tons of noxious hair spray fumes are expelled every day. And some environmentally safe claims made by marketers have been labeled *greenwashing*—the practice of making an unsubstantiated or misleading claim about the environmental benefits of a product, service, technology, or company practice.[39]

To address such claims the FTC has drafted guidelines that provide a framework for using environmental advertising and avoiding misleading claims. For example, an advertisement or product label touting a package as "50 percent more recycled content than before" could be misleading if the recycled content has increased from 2 percent to 3 percent.

Marketers and consumers are accountable for ethical and socially responsible behavior. The 21st century will prove to be a testing period for both.

---

learning review

6. What is meant by social responsibility?

7. Marketing efforts to produce, promote, and reclaim environmentally sensitive products are called _____.

8. What is a social audit?

LEARNING OBJECTIVES REVIEW

LO1 *Explain the differences between legal and ethical behavior in marketing.*
A good starting point for understanding the nature and significance of ethics is the distinction between the legality and the ethicality of marketing decisions. Whereas ethics deal with personal moral principles and values, laws are society's values and standards that are enforceable in the courts. This distinction can lead to the rationalization that if a behavior is within reasonable ethical and legal limits, then it is not really

illegal or unethical. Judgment plays a large role in defining ethical and legal boundaries in marketing. Ethical dilemmas arise when acts or situations are not clearly ethical and legal or unethical and illegal.

LO2 *Identify factors that influence ethical and unethical marketing decisions.*
Four factors influence ethical marketing behavior. First, societal culture and norms serve as socializing forces that dictate

what is morally right and just. Second, business culture and industry practices affect ethical conduct in both the exchange relationships between buyers and sellers and the competitive behavior among sellers. Third, corporate culture and expectations are often defined by corporate ethics codes and the ethical behavior of top management and co-workers. Finally, an individual's personal moral philosophy, such as moral idealism or utilitarianism, will dictate ethical choices. Ultimately, ethical behavior rests with the individual, but the consequences affect many.

LO3 *Describe the different concepts of social responsibility.*
Social responsibility means that organizations are part of a larger society and are accountable to that society for their actions. There are three concepts of social responsibility. First, profit responsibility holds that companies have a simple duty: to maximize profits for their owners or stockholders. Second, stakeholder responsibility focuses on the obligations an organization has to those who can affect achievement of its objectives. Those constituencies include consumers, employees, suppliers, and distributors. Finally, societal responsibility focuses on obligations that organizations have to the preservation of the ecological environment and the general public. Companies are placing greater emphasis on societal responsibility today and are reaping the rewards of positive

word of mouth from their consumers and favorable financial performance.

LO4 *Recognize unethical and socially irresponsible consumer behavior.*
Consumers, like marketers, have an obligation to act ethically and responsibly in the exchange process and in the use and disposition of products. Unfortunately, consumer behavior is spotty on both counts. Unethical consumer behavior includes filing warranty claims after the claim period; misredeeming coupons; pirating music, movies, and software from the Internet; and submitting phony insurance claims, among other behaviors. Unethical behavior is rarely motivated by economic need. Rather, research indicates that this behavior is influenced by (*a*) a belief that a consumer can get away with the act and it is worth doing and (*b*) the rationalization that such acts are justified or driven by forces outside the individual—"everybody does it." Consumer purchase, use, and disposition of environmentally sensitive products relate to consumer social responsibility. Even though consumers are sensitive to ecological issues they (*a*) may be unwilling to sacrifice convenience and pay potentially higher prices to protect the environment and (*b*) lack the knowledge to make informed decisions dealing with the purchase, use, and disposition of products.

FOCUSING ON KEY TERMS

cause marketing p. 87
code of ethics p. 84
Consumer Bill of Rights p. 82
ethics p. 80

green marketing p. 87
laws p. 80
moral idealism p. 85
social audit p. 88

social responsibility p. 86
utilitarianism p. 85

APPLYING MARKETING KNOWLEDGE

1 What concepts of moral philosophy and social responsibility are applicable to the practices of Anheuser-Busch described in the introduction to this chapter? Why?
2 Compare and contrast moral idealism and utilitarianism as alternative personal moral philosophies.

3 How would you evaluate Milton Friedman's view of the social responsibility of a firm?
4 Cause marketing programs have become popular. Describe two such programs with which you are familiar.

building your marketing plan

Consider these potential stakeholders that may be affected in some way by the marketing plan on which you are working: shareholders (if any), suppliers, employees, customers, and society in general. For each group of stakeholders:

1 Identify what, if any, ethical and social responsibility issues might arise.
2 Describe, in one or two sentences, how your marketing plan addresses each potential issue.

video case 4   Starbucks Corporation: Serving More than Coffee

Wake up and smell the coffee—Starbucks is everywhere! As the world's No. 1 specialty coffee retailer, Starbucks serves more than 25 million customers in its stores every week. The concept of Starbucks goes far beyond being a coffeehouse or coffee brand. It represents the dream of its founder, Howard Schultz, who wanted to take

the experience of an Italian—specifically, Milan—espresso bar to every corner of every city block in the world. So what is the *Starbucks experience*? According to the company,

> You get more than the finest coffee when you visit Starbucks. You get great people, first-rate music, a comfortable and upbeat meeting place, and sound advice on brewing excellent coffee at home. At home you're part of a family. At work

you're part of a company. And somewhere in between there's a place where you can sit back and be yourself. That's what a Starbucks store is to many of its customers—a kind of "third place" where they can escape, reflect, read, chat, or listen.

But there is more. Starbucks has embraced corporate social responsibility like few other companies. A recent Starbucks Corporate Social Responsibility Annual Report described the company's views on social responsibility:

> Starbucks defines corporate social responsibility as conducting our business in ways that produce social, environmental, and economic benefits to the communities in which we operate. In the end, it means being responsible to our stakeholders.
>
> There is a growing recognition of the need for corporate accountability. Consumers are demanding more than "product" from their favorite brands. Employees are choosing to work for companies with strong values. Shareholders are more inclined to invest in business with outstanding corporate reputations. Quite simply, being socially responsible is not only the right thing to do; it can distinguish a company from its industry peers.

Starbucks not only recognizes the central role that social responsibility plays in its business. It also takes constructive action to be socially responsible.

THE COMPANY

Starbucks is the leading retailer, roaster, and brand of specialty coffee in the world with more than 7,500 retail locations in North America, Latin America, Europe, the Middle East, and the Pacific Rim. Beginning in 1971 with a single retail location in Seattle, Washington, Starbucks became a *Fortune* 500 company in 2003 with annual sales exceeding $4 billion. In addition, Starbucks is ranked as one of the "Ten Most Admired Companies in America" and one of the "100 Best Companies to Work For" by *Fortune* magazine. It has been recognized as one of the "Most Trusted Brands" by *Ad Week* magazine. *Business Ethics* magazine placed Starbucks 21st in its list of the "100 Best Citizens" in 2003. Starbucks' performance can be attributed to a passionate pursuit of its mission and adherence to six guiding principles. Both appear in Figure 1.

COMMITMENT TO CORPORATE SOCIAL RESPONSIBILITY

Starbucks continually emphasizes its commitment to corporate social responsibility. Speaking at the annual shareholders meeting in March 2004, Howard Schultz said,

> From the beginning, Starbucks has built a company that balances profitability with a social conscience. Starbucks business practices are even more relevant today as consumers take a cultural audit of the goods and services they use. Starbucks is known not only for serving the highest quality coffee, but for enriching the daily lives of its people, customers, and coffee farmers. This is the key to Starbucks' ongoing success and we are pleased to report our positive results to shareholders and partners (employees).

Each year, Starbucks makes public a comprehensive report on its corporate social responsibility initiatives. A central feature of this annual report is the alignment of the company's social responsibility decisions and actions with Starbucks' Mission Statement and Guiding Principles. The Starbucks 2003 Corporate Social Responsibility Report, titled "Living Our Values," focused on six topical areas: (*a*) partners, (*b*) diversity, (*c*) coffee, (*d*) customers, (*e*) community and environment, and (*f*) profitability.

Partners

Starbucks employs some 74,000 people around the world. The company considers its employees as partners following the creation of Starbucks' stock option plan in 1991, called "Bean Stock." The company believes that giving eligible full- and part-time employees an ownership in the company and sharing the rewards of Starbucks' financial success has made the sense of partnership real. In addition, the company has one of the most competitive employee benefits and compensation packages in the retail industry. Ongoing training, career advancement opportunities, partner recognition programs, and diligent efforts to ensure a healthy and safe work environment have all contributed to the fact that Starbucks has one of the lowest employee turnover rates within the restaurant and fast-food industry.

FIGURE 1

Starbucks' Mission Statement and Guiding Principles

Establish Starbucks as the premier purveyor of the finest coffee in the world while maintaining our uncompromising principles as we grow.

The following six principles will help us measure the appropriateness of our decisions:

1. Provide a great work environment and treat each other with respect and dignity.
2. Embrace diversity as an essential component in the way we do business.
3. Apply the highest standards of excellence to the purchasing, roasting, and fresh delivery of our coffee.
4. Develop enthusiastically satisfied customers all the time.
5. Contribute positively to our communities and our environment.
6. Recognize that profitability is essential to our future success.

Diversity

Starbucks strives to mirror the customers and communities it serves. On a quarterly basis, the company monitors the demographics of its workforce to determine whether they reflect the communities in which Starbucks operates. In 2003, Starbucks' U.S. workforce was comprised of 63 percent women and 24 percent people of color. The company also is engaged in a joint venture called Urban Coffee Opportunities (UCO) created to bring Starbucks stores to diverse neighborhoods. There were 52 UCO locations employing almost 1,000 Starbucks partners at the end of 2003.

Supplier diversity is also emphasized. To do business with Starbucks as a diverse supplier, that company must be 51 percent owned, operated, and managed by women, minorities, or socially disadvantaged individuals and meet Starbucks requirements of quality, service, value, stability, and sound business practice. The company spent $80 million with diverse suppliers in 2003 and $95 million with diverse suppliers in 2004.

Coffee

Starbucks' attention to quality coffee extends to its coffee growers located in more than 20 countries. Sustainable development is emphasized. This means that Starbucks pays coffee farmers a fair price for the beans; that the coffee is grown in an ecologically sound manner; and that Starbucks invests in the farming communities where its coffees are produced.

One long-standing initiative is Starbucks' partnership with Conservation International, a nonprofit organization dedicated to protecting soil, water, energy, and biological diversity worldwide. Starbucks is particularly focused on environmental protection and helping local farmers earn more for their crops. In 2003, Starbucks invested more than $1 million in social programs, notably health and education projects, that benefited farming communities in nine countries, from Colombia to Indonesia.

Customers

Starbucks serves customers in 32 countries. The company and its partners are committed to providing each customer the optimal Starbucks experience every time they visit a store. For very loyal Starbucks customers, that translates into 18 visits per month on average.

Making a connection with customers at each store and building the relationship a customer has with Starbucks *baristas*, or coffee brewers, are important in creating the Starbucks experience. Each barista receives 24 hours of training in customer service and basic retail skills, as well as "Coffee Knowledge" and "Brewing the Perfect Cup" classes. Baristas are taught to anticipate the customers' needs and to make eye contact while carefully explaining the various coffee flavors and blends. Starbucks also enhances the customer relationship by soliciting feedback

and responding to patrons' experiences and concerns. Starbucks Customer Relations reviews and responds to every inquiry or comment, often within 24 hours for telephone calls and e-mails.

Community and Environment

Efforts to contribute positively to the communities it serves and the environments in which it operates are emphasized in Starbucks' guiding principles. "We aren't in the coffee business, serving people. We are in the people business, serving coffee," says Howard Schultz. Starbucks and its partners have been recognized for volunteer support and financial contributions to a wide variety of local, national, and international social, economic, and environmental initiatives. For example, the "Make Your Mark" program rewards partners' gifts of time for volunteer work with charitable donations from Starbucks. In addition, Starbucks is a supporter of CARE International, a nonprofit organization dedicated to fighting global poverty.

Starbucks is also committed to environmental responsibility. Starbucks has a long-time involvement with Earth Day activities. It has instituted companywide energy and water conservation programs and waste reduction, recycling, and reuse initiatives proposed by partner *Green Teams*.

Profitability

At Starbucks, profitability is viewed as essential to its future success. When Starbucks' guiding principles were conceived, profitability was included but intentionally placed last on the list. This was done not because profitability was the least important. Instead, it was believed that adherence to the five other principles would ultimately lead to good financial performance. In fact, it has.

Questions

1 How does Starbucks' approach to social responsibility relate to the three concepts of social responsibility described in the text?

2 What role does sustainable development play in Starbucks' approach to social responsibility?

Individuality is Beautiful

5 Understanding Consumer Behavior

LEARNING OBJECTIVES

After reading this chapter you should be able to:

LO1 Describe the stages in the consumer purchase decision process.

LO2 Distinguish among three variations of the consumer purchase decision process: routine, limited, and extended problem solving.

LO3 Identify major psychological influences on consumer behavior.

LO4 Identify the major sociocultural influences on consumer behavior.

ENLIGHTENED CARMAKERS KNOW WHAT CUSTOM(H)ERS VALUE

Who buys 68 percent of new cars? Who influences 83 percent of new-car buying decisions? Women. Yes, women.

Women are a driving force in the U.S. automobile industry. Enlightened carmakers have hired women designers, engineers, and marketing executives to better understand and satisfy this valuable car buyer and influencer. What have they learned? Women and men think and feel differently about key elements of the new-car buying decision process and experience.

- *The sense of styling.* Women and men care about styling. For men, styling is more about a car's exterior lines and accents. Women are more interested in interior design and finishes. Designs that fit their proportions, provide good visibility, offer ample storage space, and make for effortless parking are particularly important.

- *The need for speed.* Both sexes want speed, but for different reasons. Men think about how many seconds it takes to get from zero to 60 miles per hour. Women want to feel secure that the car has enough acceleration to outrun an 18-wheeler trying to pass them on a freeway entrance ramp.

- *The substance of safety.* Safety for men is about features that help avoid an accident, such as antilock brakes and responsive steering. For women, safety is about features that help to survive an accident, including passenger airbags and reinforced side panels.

- *The shopping experience.* The new-car buying experience differs between men and women. Generally, men decide upfront what car they want and set out alone to find it. By contrast, women approach it as an intelligence-gathering expedition. They actively seek information and postpone a purchase decision until all options have been evaluated. Women frequently visit auto-buying Web sites, read car-comparison articles, and scan car advertisements. Still, recommendations of friends and relatives matter most. Women typically shop three dealerships before making a purchase decision—one more than men. While only a third of women say that price is the most influential factor when they shop for a new car, 71 percent say price determines the final decision.

Carmakers have learned that women, more than men, dislike the car-buying experience. In particular, women dread the price negotiations that are often involved in buying a new car. Not surprisingly, 76 percent of women car buyers take a man with them to finalize the terms of sale.[1]

This chapter examines **consumer behavior**, the actions a person takes in purchasing and using products and services, including the mental and social processes that come before and after these actions. This chapter shows how the behavioral sciences help answer questions such as why people choose one product or brand over another, how they make these choices, and how companies use this knowledge to provide value to consumers.

CONSUMER PURCHASE DECISION PROCESS AND EXPERIENCE

LO1

Behind the visible act of making a purchase lies an important decision process and consumer experience that must be investigated. The stages a buyer passes through in making choices about which products or services to buy is the **purchase decision process**. This process has the five stages shown in Figure 5–1: (1) problem recognition, (2) information search, (3) alternative evaluation, (4) purchase decision, and (5) postpurchase behavior.

Problem Recognition: Perceiving a Need

Problem recognition, the initial step in the purchase decision, is perceiving a difference between a person's ideal and actual situations big enough to trigger a decision.[2] This can be as simple as finding an empty milk carton in the refrigerator; noting, as a first-year college student, that your high school clothes are not in the style that other students are wearing; or realizing that your notebook computer may not be working properly.

In marketing, advertisements or salespeople can activate a consumer's decision process by showing the shortcomings of competing (or currently owned) products. For instance, an advertisement for a new generation smart phone could stimulate problem recognition because it emphasizes "maximum use from one device."

Information Search: Seeking Value

After recognizing a problem, a consumer begins to search for information, the next stage in the purchase decision process. First, you may scan your memory for previous experiences with products or brands.[3] This action is called *internal search*. For frequently purchased products such as shampoo and conditioner, this may be enough.

In other cases, a consumer may undertake an *external search* for information.[4] This is needed when past experience or knowledge is insufficient, the risk of making a wrong purchase decision is high, and the cost of gathering information is low. The primary sources of external information are: (1) *personal sources*, such as relatives and friends whom the consumer trusts; (2) *public sources*, including various product-rating organizations such as *Consumer Reports*, government agencies, and TV "consumer programs"; and (3) *marketer-dominated sources*, such as information from sellers including advertising, company Web sites, salespeople, and point-of-purchase displays in stores.

Suppose you are considering buying a new smart phone. You will probably tap several of these information sources: friends and relatives, advertisements, brand and company Web sites, and stores carrying these phones (for demonstrations). You also might study the comparative evaluation of selected smart phones appearing in *Consumer Reports*, a portion of which appears in Figure 5–2.[5]

FIGURE 5–1
The purchase decision process consists of five stages.

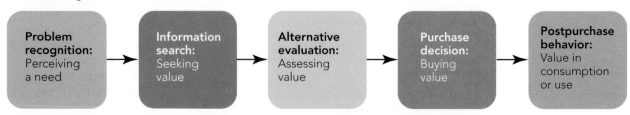

| Problem recognition: Perceiving a need | Information search: Seeking value | Alternative evaluation: Assessing value | Purchase decision: Buying value | Postpurchase behavior: Value in consumption or use |

BRAND	MODEL	CARRIER	RETAIL PRICE	DISPLAY	NAVIGATION	VOICE QUALITY	MULTIMEDIA	BATTERY LIFE
Apple	iPhone 3GS	AT&T	$150	Excellent	Excellent	Fair	Excellent	Excellent
BlackBerry	Bold	AT&T	200	Very Good	Very Good	Good	Excellent	Good
HTC	Evo 4G	Sprint	200	Excellent	Excellent	Fair	Excellent	Good
Google	Nexus One	T-Mobile	180	Excellent	Excellent	Very Good	Excellent	Very Good
T-Mobile	G1	T-Mobile	100	Very Good	Excellent	Very Good	Excellent	Very Good
Nokia	5230 Nuron	T-Mobile	70	Very Good	Good	Fair	Excellent	Very Good
Motorola	Droid	Verizon	200	Excellent	Excellent	Good	Excellent	Very Good
Samsung	Omnia	Verizon	50	Excellent	Very Good	Fair	Excellent	Very Good

Rating: Excellent · Very Good · Good · Fair · Poor

Source: "Smart Phone Ratings," *Consumer Reports*, July 2010.

FIGURE 5–2
Consumer Reports's evaluation of smart phones.

Alternative Evaluation: Assessing Value

The information search stage clarifies the problem for the consumer by (1) suggesting criteria to use for the purchase, (2) yielding brand names that might meet the criteria, and (3) developing consumer value perceptions. Given only the information shown in Figure 5–2, which selection criteria would you use in buying a smart phone? Would you use price, display quality, navigation or ease of use, battery life, camera resolution, or some other combination of these or other criteria?

For some of you, the information provided may be inadequate because it does not contain all the factors you might consider when evaluating smart phones. These factors are a consumer's *evaluative criteria*, which represent both the objective attributes of a brand (such as display) and the subjective ones (such as prestige) you use to compare different products and brands.[6] Firms try to identify and capitalize on both types of criteria to create the best value for the money paid by you and other consumers. These criteria are often displayed in advertisements.

Consumers often have several criteria for evaluating brands. Knowing this, companies seek to identify the most important evaluative criteria that consumers use when judging brands. For example, among the evaluative criteria shown in the columns of Figure 5–2, suppose you use three in considering smart phones: (1) a retail price of $200 or less, (2) very good or excellent display quality, and (3) excellent navigation, and (4) very good or excellent battery life. These criteria establish the brands in your *consideration set*—the group of brands that a consumer would consider acceptable from among all the brands of which he or she is aware in the product class.[7] Your evaluative criteria result in three brands and their respective models (Apple iPhone 3GS, Google Nexus One, and Motorola Droid) in your consideration set. If these alternatives are unsatisfactory, you can change your evaluative criteria to create a different consideration set of models and brands. For example, a phone's camera resolution (in megapixels—if you like taking pictures) or a carrier's network coverage, quality (dropped calls), and contract terms (length, buyout) may join your list of evaluative criteria and change the composition of your consideration set.

Purchase Decision: Buying Value

Having examined the alternatives in the consideration set, you are almost ready to make a purchase decision. Two choices remain: (1) from whom to buy and (2) when to buy. For a product like a smart phone, the information search process probably involved visiting retail stores, seeing different brands in catalogs, and viewing a smart phone on a seller's Web site. The choice of which seller to buy from will depend on such considerations as the terms of sale, your past experience buying from the seller, and the return policy. Often a purchase decision involves a simultaneous evaluation of both product attributes and seller characteristics. For example, you might choose the second-most preferred smart phone brand at a store or Web site with a liberal refund and return policy versus the most preferred brand with more conservative policies.

Deciding when to buy is determined by a number of factors. For instance, you might buy sooner if one of your preferred brands is on sale or its manufacturer offers a rebate. Other factors such as the store atmosphere, the pleasantness or ease of the shopping experience, salesperson assistance, time pressure, and financial circumstances could also affect whether a purchase decision is made or postponed.[8]

Use of the Internet to gather information, evaluate alternatives, and make buying decisions adds a technological dimension to the consumer purchase decision process and buying experience. Consumer benefits and costs associated with this technology and its marketing implications are detailed in Chapter 18.

Postpurchase Behavior: Value in Consumption or Use

After buying a product, the consumer compares it with his or her expectations and is either satisfied or dissatisfied. If the consumer is dissatisfied, marketers must determine whether the product was deficient or consumer expectations were too high. Product deficiency may require a design change. If expectations are too high, perhaps the company's advertising or the salesperson oversold the product's features and benefits.

Sensitivity to a customer's consumption or use experience is extremely important in a consumer's value perception. For example, research on telephone services provided by Sprint and AT&T indicates that satisfaction or dissatisfaction affects consumer value perceptions.[9] Studies show that satisfaction or dissatisfaction affects consumer communications and repeat-purchase behavior. Satisfied buyers tell three other people about their experience. Dissatisfied buyers complain to nine people.[10] Satisfied buyers also tend to buy from the same seller each time a purchase occasion arises. The financial impact of repeat-purchase behavior is signficant, as described in the Marketing Matters box.[11]

Firms such as General Electric (GE), Johnson & Johnson, Coca-Cola, and British Airways focus attention on postpurchase behavior to maximize customer satisfaction and retention. These firms, among many others, now provide toll-free telephone numbers, offer liberalized return and refund policies, and engage in extensive staff training to handle complaints, answer questions, record suggestions, and solve consumer problems. For example, GE, which handles 3 million calls annually, has a database that stores 750,000 answers to questions about 8,500 of its models in 120 product lines. Such efforts produce positive postpurchase communications among consumers and foster relationship building between sellers and buyers.

Often a consumer is faced with two or more highly attractive alternatives, such as a BlackBerry or Samsung smart phone. If you choose a BlackBerry, you might think, "Should I have purchased the Samsung?" This feeling of postpurchase psychological tension or anxiety is called *cognitive dissonance*. To alleviate it, consumers often attempt to applaud themselves for making the right choice. So after your purchase, you may seek information to confirm your choice by asking friends questions like, "Don't you like my new phone?" or by reading ads of the brand you chose. You might even look for negative features about

A satisfactory or unsatisfactory consumption or use experience is an important factor in postpurchase behavior. As described in the text, marketer attention to this stage can pay huge dividends.

Marketing Matters > > > > > customer value

The Value of a Satisfied Customer to the Company

Customer satisfaction and experience underlie the marketing concept. But how much is a satisfied customer worth?

This question has prompted firms to calculate the financial value of a satisfied customer over time. Frito-Lay, for example, estimates that the average loyal consumer in the southwestern United States eats 21 pounds of snack chips a year. At a price of $2.50 a pound, this customer spends $52.50 annually on the company's snacks such as Lays and Ruffles potato chips, Doritos and Tostitos tortilla chips, and Fritos corn chips. Exxon estimates that a loyal customer will spend $500 annually for its branded gasoline, not including candy, snacks, oil, or repair services purchased at its gasoline stations. Kimberly-Clark reports that a loyal customer will buy 6.7 boxes of its Kleenex tissues each year and will spend $994 on facial tissues over 60 years, in today's dollars.

These calculations have focused marketer attention on the buying experience, customer satisfaction, and retention. Ford Motor Company set a target of increasing customer retention—the percentage of Ford owners whose next car is also a Ford—from 60 percent to 80 percent. Why? Ford executives say that each additional percentage point is worth a staggering $100 million in profits.

This calculation is not unique to Ford. Research shows that a 5 percent improvement in customer retention can increase a company's profits by 70 to 80 percent.

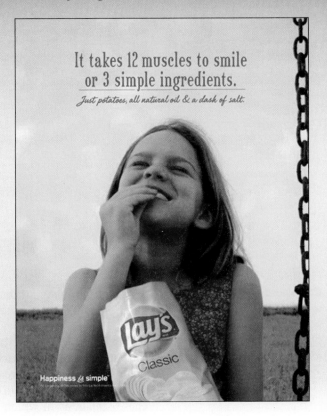

It takes 12 muscles to smile or 3 simple ingredients.

Just potatoes, all natural oil & a dash of salt.

Lay's Classic

Happiness *is* simple

---

the brand you didn't buy and decide that the Samsung headset didn't feel right. Firms often use ads or follow-up calls from salespeople in this postpurchase behavior stage to comfort buyers that they made the right decision. For many years, Buick ran an advertising campaign with the message, "Aren't you really glad you bought a Buick?"

Consumer Involvement and Problem-Solving Variations

involvement
The personal, social, and economic significance of a purchase to the consumer.

Sometimes consumers don't engage in the five-stage purchase decision process. Instead, they skip or minimize one or more stages depending on the level of **involvement**, the personal, social, and economic significance of the purchase to the consumer.[12] High-involvement purchase occasions typically have at least one of three characteristics: The item to be purchased (1) is expensive, (2) can have serious personal consequences, or (3) could reflect on one's social image. For these occasions, consumers engage in extensive information search, consider many product attributes and brands, form attitudes, and participate in word-of-mouth communication. Low-involvement purchases, such as toothpaste and soap, barely involve most of us, but audio and video systems and automobiles are very involving.

There are three general variations in the consumer purchase decision process based on consumer involvement and product knowledge. Figure 5–3 on the next page shows some of the important differences between the three problem-solving variations.

Extended Problem Solving   In extended problem solving, each of the five stages of the consumer purchase decision process is used, with considerable time and effort devoted to the external information search and the identification and evaluation of alternatives. Several brands are included in the consideration set, and these are

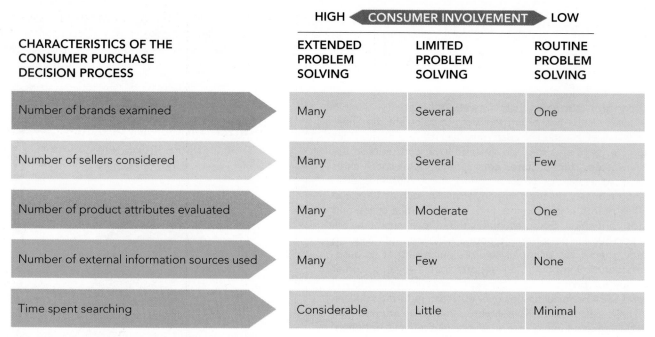

HIGH ◀ CONSUMER INVOLVEMENT ▶ LOW			
CHARACTERISTICS OF THE CONSUMER PURCHASE DECISION PROCESS	EXTENDED PROBLEM SOLVING	LIMITED PROBLEM SOLVING	ROUTINE PROBLEM SOLVING
Number of brands examined	Many	Several	One
Number of sellers considered	Many	Several	Few
Number of product attributes evaluated	Many	Moderate	One
Number of external information sources used	Many	Few	None
Time spent searching	Considerable	Little	Minimal

FIGURE 5–3

Comparison of problem-solving variations: extended problem solving, limited problem solving, and routine problem solving.

What does this ad for Campbell's V8 vegetable juice have to do with getting it into a consumer's consideration set? Read the text to find out.

evaluated on many attributes. Extended problem solving exists in high-involvement purchase situations for items such as automobiles and audio systems.

Limited Problem Solving In limited problem solving, consumers typically seek some information or rely on a friend to help them evaluate alternatives. Several brands might be evaluated using a moderate number of attributes. Limited problem solving might be used in choosing a toaster, a restaurant for lunch, and other purchase situations in which the consumer wants to spend little time or effort.

Routine Problem Solving For products such as table salt and milk, consumers recognize a problem, make a decision, and spend little effort seeking external information and evaluating alternatives. The purchase process for such items is virtually a habit and typifies low-involvement decision making. Routine problem solving is typically the case for low-priced, frequently purchased products.

Involvement and Marketing Strategy Low and high consumer involvement has important implications for marketing strategy. If a company markets a low-involvement product and its brand is a market leader, attention is placed on (1) maintaining product quality, (2) avoiding stockout situations so that buyers don't substitute a competing brand, and (3) using repetitive advertising messages to reinforce a consumer's knowledge or assure buyers they have made the right choice. Market challengers have a different task. They must break buying habits and use free samples, coupons, and rebates to encourage trial of their brand. Advertising messages will focus on getting their brand into a consumer's consideration set. For example, Campbell's V8 vegetable juice's advertising message—"I could have had a V8!"—is targeted at consumers who routinely purchase fruit juices and soft drinks. Marketers can also link their brand attributes with high-involvement issues. Hershey's does this by linking consumption of Hershey's Extra Dark™ Chocolate with improved blood pressure and blood vessel function in addition to a great taste.

Marketers of high-involvement products know that their consumers constantly seek and process information about objective and subjective brand attributes, form evaluative criteria, rate product attributes in various brands, and combine these ratings for an overall brand evaluation—like that described in the smart phone purchase decision. Market leaders ply consumers with product information through advertising and personal selling and create chat rooms and communities on their company or brand Web sites. Market challengers capitalize on this behavior through comparative advertising that focuses on existing product attributes and often introduce novel evaluative criteria for judging competing brands. Challengers also benefit from Internet search engines such as Microsoft Bing and Google that assist buyers of high-involvement products.

Situational Influences

Often the purchase situation will affect the purchase decision process. Five *situational influences* have an impact on the purchase decision process: (1) the purchase task, (2) social surroundings, (3) physical surroundings, (4) temporal effects, and (5) antecedent states.[13] The purchase task is the reason for engaging in the decision. Information searching and evaluating alternatives may differ depending on whether the purchase is a gift, which often involves social visibility, or for the buyer's own use. Social surroundings, including the other people present when a purchase decision is made, may also affect what is purchased. Consumers accompanied by children buy about 40 percent more items than consumers shopping by themselves. Physical surroundings such as decor, music, and crowding in retail stores may alter how purchase decisions are made. Temporal effects such as time of day or the amount of time available will influence where consumers have breakfast and lunch and what is ordered. Finally, antecedent states, which include the consumer's mood or the amount of cash on hand, can influence purchase behavior and choice. For example, consumers with credit cards purchase more than those with cash or debit cards.

Figure 5–4 shows the many influences that affect the consumer purchase decision process. The decision to buy a product also involves important psychological and sociocultural influences. These two influences are covered in the remainder of this chapter. Marketing mix influences are described later in Part 4 of the book.

FIGURE 5–4

Influences on the consumer purchase decision process come from both internal and external sources.

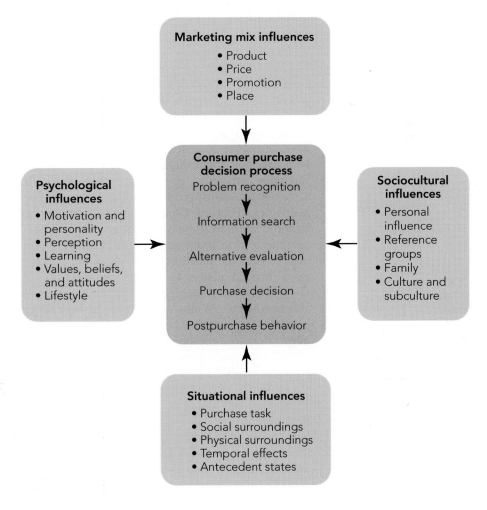

learning review

1. What is the first stage in the consumer purchase decision process?

2. The brands a consumer considers buying out of the set of brands in a product class of which the consumer is aware are called the _____.

3. What is the term for postpurchase anxiety?

PSYCHOLOGICAL INFLUENCES ON CONSUMER BEHAVIOR

Psychology helps marketers understand why and how consumers behave as they do. In particular, psychological concepts such as motivation and personality; perception; learning; values, beliefs, and attitudes; and lifestyle are useful for interpreting buying processes and directing marketing efforts.

Motivation and Personality

Motivation and personality are two familiar psychological concepts that have specific meanings and marketing implications. These concepts are closely related and are used to explain why people do some things and not others.

motivation
The energizing force that stimulates behavior to satisfy a need.

Motivation   **Motivation** is the energizing force that stimulates behavior to satisfy a need. Because consumer needs are the focus of the marketing concept, marketers try to arouse these needs.

An individual's needs are boundless. People possess physiological needs for basics such as water, shelter, and food. They also have learned needs, including self-esteem, achievement, and affection. Psychologists point out that these needs may be hierarchical; that is, once physiological needs are met, people seek to satisfy their learned needs.

Figure 5–5 shows one need hierarchy and classification scheme that contains five need classes.[14] *Physiological needs* are basic to survival and must be satisfied first. A Red Lobster advertisement featuring a seafood salad attempts to activate the need for food. *Safety needs* involve self-preservation as well as physical and financial well-being. Smoke detector and burglar alarm manufacturers focus on these needs, as do insurance companies and retirement plan advisors. *Social needs* are concerned with love and friendship. Dating services, such as Match.com and eHarmony, and fragrance companies try to arouse these needs. *Personal needs* include the need for achievement, status, prestige, and self-respect. The American Express Platinum Card and Brooks Brothers Clothiers appeal to these needs. Sometimes firms try to arouse multiple needs to stimulate problem recognition. Michelin has combined safety with parental love to promote tire replacement for automobiles. *Self-actualization needs* involve personal fulfillment. For example, a long-running U.S. Army recruiting program invited enlistees to "Be all you can be."

personality
A person's consistent behaviors or responses to recurring situations.

Personality   While motivation is the energizing force that makes consumer behavior purposeful, a consumer's personality guides and directs behavior. **Personality** refers to a person's consistent behaviors or responses to recurring situations.

Although many personality theories exist, most identify *key traits*—enduring characteristics within a person or in his or her relationship with others. Such traits include assertiveness, extroversion, compliance, dominance, and aggression, among others. These traits are inherited or formed at an early age and change little over the years. Research suggests that compliant people prefer known brand names and use more mouthwash and toilet soaps. Aggressive types use razors, not electric shavers, apply more cologne and aftershave lotions, and purchase signature goods such as Gucci, Yves St. Laurent, and Donna Karan as an indicator of status.[15]

FIGURE 5–5

The hierarchy of needs is based on the idea that motivation comes from a need. If a need is met, it's no longer a motivator, so a higher-level need becomes the motivator. Higher-level needs demand support of lower-level needs.

Self-actualization needs: Self-fulfillment

Personal needs: Status, respect, prestige

Social needs: Friendship, belonging, love

Safety needs: Freedom from harm, financial security

Physiological needs: Food, water, shelter, oxygen

These personality characteristics are often revealed in a person's *self-concept*, which is the way people see themselves and the way they believe others see them. Marketers recognize that people have an actual self-concept and an ideal self-concept. The actual self refers to how people actually see themselves. The ideal self describes how people would like to see themselves. These two self-images are reflected in the products and brands a person buys, including automobiles, home appliances and furnishings, magazines, consumer electronics, clothing, grooming and leisure products, and frequently, the stores a person shops. The importance of self-concept is summed up by a senior marketing executive at Lenovo, a global supplier of notebook computers: "The notebook market is getting more like cars. The car you drive reflects you, and notebooks are becoming a form of self-expression as well."[16]

Perception

One person sees a Cadillac as a mark of achievement; another sees it as ostentatious. This is the result of **perception**—the process by which an individual selects, organizes, and interprets information to create a meaningful picture of the world.

perception
The process by which a person selects, organizes, and interprets information to create a meaningful picture of the world.

Selective Perception Because the average consumer operates in a complex environment, the human brain attempts to organize and interpret information with a process called *selective perception*, a filtering of exposure, comprehension, and retention. *Selective exposure* occurs when people pay attention to messages that are consistent with their attitudes and beliefs and ignore messages that are inconsistent. Selective exposure often occurs in the postpurchase stage of the consumer decision process, when consumers read advertisements for the brand they just bought. It also occurs when a need exists—you are more likely to "see" a McDonald's advertisement when you are hungry rather than after you have eaten a pizza.

Selective comprehension involves interpreting information so that it is consistent with your attitudes and beliefs. A marketer's failure to understand this can have disastrous results. For example, Toro introduced a small, lightweight snowblower called the Snow Pup. Even though the product worked, sales failed to meet expectations. Why? Toro later found out that consumers perceived the name to mean that Snow Pup was a toy or too light to do any serious snow removal. When the product was renamed Snow Master, sales increased sharply.[17]

Selective retention means that consumers do not remember all the information they see, read, or hear, even minutes after exposure to it. This affects the internal and external information search stage of the purchase decision process. This is why furniture and automobile retailers often give consumers product brochures to take home when they leave the showroom.

Because perception plays an important role in consumer behavior, it is not surprising that the topic of subliminal perception is a popular item for discussion. *Subliminal perception* means that you see or hear messages without being aware of them. The presence and effect of subliminal perception on behavior is a hotly debated issue, with more popular appeal than scientific support. Indeed, evidence suggests that such messages have limited effects on behavior.[18] If these messages did influence behavior, would their use be an ethical practice? (See the Making Responsible Decisions box on the next page.)[19]

perceived risk
The anxiety felt when a consumer cannot anticipate possible negative outcomes of a purchase.

Perceived Risk Perception plays a major role in the perceived risk in purchasing a product or service. **Perceived risk** represents the anxiety felt because the consumer cannot anticipate the outcomes of a purchase but believes there may be

The Ethics of Subliminal Messages

For about 50 years, the topic of subliminal perception and the presence of subliminal messages and images embedded in commercial communications have sparked heated debate.

The Federal Communications Commission has denounced subliminal messages as deceptive. Still, consumers spend $50 million a year for subliminal messages designed to help them raise their self-esteem, quit smoking, or lose weight. Almost two-thirds of U.S. consumers think subliminal messages are present in commercial communications; about half are firmly convinced that this practice can cause them to buy things they don't want.

Subliminal messages are not illegal in the United States, however, and marketers are often criticized for pursuing opportunities to create these messages in both electronic and print media. A book by August Bullock, *The Secret Sales Pitch: An Overview of Subliminal Advertising,* is devoted to this topic. Bullock identifies images and advertisements that he claims contain subliminal messages and describes techniques that can be used for conveying these messages.

Do you believe that a marketer's attempts to implant subliminal messages in electronic and print media are a deceptive practice and unethical, regardless of their intent?

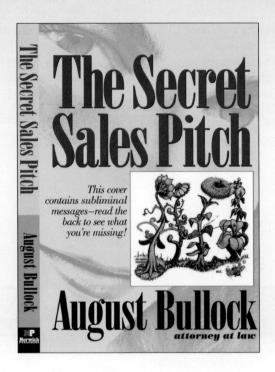

negative consequences. Examples of possible negative consequences are the size of the financial outlay required to buy the product (Can I afford $500 for those skis?), the risk of physical harm (Is bungee jumping safe?), and the performance of the product (Will the whitening toothpaste work?). A more abstract form is psychosocial (What will my friends say if I get a tattoo?). Perceived risk affects information search, because the greater the perceived risk, the more extensive the external search stage is likely to be.

Recognizing the importance of perceived risk, companies develop strategies to reduce the consumer's risk and encourage purchases. These strategies and examples of firms using them include the following:

- *Obtaining seals of approval:* The Good Housekeeping seal for Fresh Step cat litter.
- *Securing endorsements from influential people:* Unilever claims endorsements for its Promise buttery soft spread from 9 out of 10 cardiologists.
- *Providing free trials of the product:* Samples of Mary Kay's Velocity fragrance.
- *Giving extensive usage instructions:* Clairol hair coloring.
- *Providing warranties and guarantees:* Kia Motors's 10-year, 100,000-mile warranty.

Learning

Much consumer behavior is learned. Consumers learn which information sources to consult for information about products and services, which evaluative criteria to use when assessing alternatives, and, more generally, how to make purchase decisions. **Learning** refers to those behaviors that result from (1) repeated experience and (2) reasoning.

learning
Behaviors that result from repeated experience or reasoning.

Why does Clorox tout the Good Housekeeping seal for its Fresh Step cat litter? Why does Mary Kay, Inc., offer a free sample of its Velocity brand fragrance through its Web site? The answers appear in the text.

Behavioral Learning   *Behavioral learning* is the process of developing automatic responses to a situation built up through repeated exposure to it. Four variables are central to how consumers learn from repeated experience: drive, cue, response, and reinforcement. A *drive* is a need that moves an individual to action. Drives, such as hunger, might be represented by motives. A *cue* is a stimulus or symbol perceived by consumers. A *response* is the action taken by a consumer to satisfy the drive, whereas a *reinforcement* is the reward. Being hungry (drive), a consumer sees a cue (a billboard), takes action (buys a sandwich), and receives a reward (it tastes great!).

Marketers use two concepts from behavioral learning theory. *Stimulus generalization* occurs when a response elicited by one stimulus (cue) is generalized to another stimulus. Using the same brand name for different products is an application of this concept, such as Tylenol Cold & Flu and Tylenol P.M. *Stimulus discrimination* refers to a person's ability to perceive differences in stimuli. Consumers' tendency to perceive all light beers as being alike led to Budweiser Light commercials that distinguished between many types of "light beers" and Bud Light.

Cognitive Learning   Consumers also learn through thinking, reasoning, and mental problem solving without direct experience. This type of learning, called *cognitive learning*, involves making connections between two or more ideas or simply observing the outcomes of others' behaviors and adjusting your own accordingly. Firms also influence this type of learning. Through repetition in advertising, messages such as "Advil is a headache remedy" attempt to link a brand (Advil) and an idea (headache remedy) by showing someone using the brand and finding relief.

Brand Loyalty   Learning is also important to marketers because it relates to habit formation—the basis of routine problem solving. Furthermore, there is a close

brand loyalty
A favorable attitude toward and consistent purchase of a single brand over time.

link between habits and **brand loyalty**, which is a favorable attitude toward and consistent purchase of a single brand over time. Brand loyalty results from the positive reinforcement of previous actions. A consumer reduces risk and saves time by consistently purchasing the same brand of shampoo and has favorable results—healthy, shining hair. There is evidence of brand loyalty in many commonly purchased products in the United States and the global marketplace. However, the incidence of brand loyalty appears to be declining in North America, Western Europe, and Japan.[20]

Values, Beliefs, and Attitudes

Values, beliefs, and attitudes play a central role in consumer decision making and related marketing actions.

attitude
A tendency to respond to something in a consistently favorable or unfavorable way.

beliefs
A consumer's perceptions of how a product or brand performs.

Attitude Formation An **attitude** is a "learned predisposition to respond to an object or class of objects in a consistently favorable or unfavorable way."[21] Attitudes are shaped by our values and beliefs, which are learned. Values vary by level of specificity. We speak of American core values, including material well-being and humanitarianism. We also have personal values, such as thriftiness and ambition. Marketers are concerned with both but focus mostly on personal values. Personal values affect attitudes by influencing the importance assigned to specific product attributes. Suppose thriftiness is one of your personal values. When you evaluate cars, fuel economy (a product attribute) becomes important. If you believe a specific car brand has this attribute, you are likely to have a favorable attitude toward it.

Beliefs also play a part in attitude formation. **Beliefs** are a consumer's subjective perception of how a product or brand performs on different attributes. Beliefs are based on personal experience, advertising, and discussions with other people. Beliefs about product attributes are important because, along with personal values, they create the favorable or unfavorable attitude the consumer has toward certain products, services, and brands.

Attitudes toward Colgate Total toothpaste and Hellmann's Real Mayonnaise were successfully changed by these ads. How? Read the text to find out how marketers can change consumer attitudes toward products and brands.

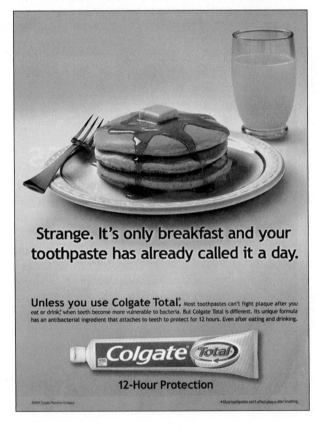

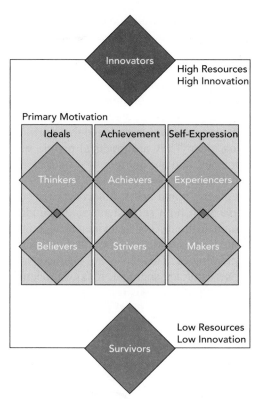

The VALS classification system places consumers with abundant resources—psychological, physical, and material means and capacities—near the top of the chart and those with minimal resources near the bottom. The chart segments consumers by their basis for decision making: ideals, achievement, or self-expression. The boxes intersect to indicate that some categories may be considered together. For instance, a marketer may categorize Thinkers and Believers together.

Attitude Change Marketers use three approaches to try to change consumer attitudes toward products and brands, as shown in the following examples.[22]

1. *Changing beliefs about the extent to which a brand has certain attributes.* To allay mothers' concerns about ingredients in its mayonnaise, Hellmann's successfully communicated the product's high Omega 3 content, which is essential to human health.
2. *Changing the perceived importance of attributes.* Pepsi-Cola made freshness an important product attribute when it stamped freshness dates on its cans. Before doing so, few consumers considered cola freshness an issue. After Pepsi spent about $25 million on advertising and promotion, a consumer survey found that 61 percent of cola drinkers believed freshness dating was an important attribute.
3. *Adding new attributes to the product.* Colgate-Palmolive included a new antibacterial ingredient, tricloson, in its Colgate Total toothpaste and spent $100 million marketing the brand. The result? Colgate replaced Crest as the market leader for the first time in 25 years.

Consumer Lifestyle

Lifestyle is a mode of living that is identified by how people spend their time and resources, what they consider important in their environment, and what they think of themselves and the world around them. The analysis of consumer lifestyles, called *psychographics*, provides insights into consumer needs and wants.

Psychographics, the practice of combining psychology, lifestyle, and demographics, is often used to uncover consumer motivations for buying and using products and services. A prominent psychographic system is VALS™ from Strategic Business Insights (SBI).[23] The VALS system identifies eight consumer segments based on (1) their primary motivation for buying and having certain products and services and (2) their resources.

According to SBI researchers, consumers are motivated to buy products and services and seek experiences that give shape, substance, and satisfaction to their lives. But not all consumers are alike. Consumers are inspired by one of three primary motivations—ideals, achievement, and self-expression—that give meaning to their self or the world and govern their activities. The different levels of resources enhance or constrain a person's expression of his or her primary motivation. A person's resources include psychological, physical, demographic, and material capacities such as income, self-confidence, and risk-taking.

The VALS system seeks to explain why and how consumers make purchase decisions.

- *Ideals-motivated groups.* Consumers motivated by ideals are guided by knowledge and principle. *Thinkers* are mature, reflective, and well-educated people who value order, knowledge, and responsibility. They are practical consumers and deliberate information-seekers, who value durability and functionality in products over styling and newness. *Believers*, with fewer resources, are conservative, conventional people with concrete beliefs based on traditional, established codes: family, religion, community, and the nation. They choose familiar products and brands, favor American-made products, and are generally brand loyal.
- *Achievement-motivated groups.* Consumers motivated by achievement look for products and services that demonstrate success to their peers or to a peer group they aspire to. *Achievers* have a busy, goal-directed lifestyle and a deep commitment to career and family. Image is important to them. They favor established, prestige products and services and are interested in time-saving devices given their hectic schedules. *Strivers* are trendy, fun-loving, and less self-confident than Achievers. They also have lower levels of education and household income. Money defines success for them. They favor stylish products and are as impulsive as their financial circumstances permit.

- *Self-expression-motivated groups.* Consumers motivated by self-expression desire social or physical activity, variety, and risk. *Experiencers* are young, enthusiastic, and impulsive consumers who become excited about new possibilities but are equally quick to cool. They savor the new, the offbeat, and the risky. Their energy finds an outlet in exercise, sports, outdoor recreation, and social activities. Much of their income is spent on fashion items, entertainment, and socializing and particularly on looking good and having the latest things. *Makers*, with fewer resources, express themselves and experience the world by working on it—raising children or fixing a car. They are practical people who have constructive skills, value self-sufficiency, and are unimpressed by material possessions except those with a practical or functional purpose.
- *High- and low-resource groups.* Two segments stand apart. *Innovators* are successful, sophisticated, take-charge people with high self-esteem and abundant resources of all kinds. Image is important to them, not as evidence of power or status, but as an expression of cultivated tastes, independence, and character. They are receptive to new ideas and technologies. Their lives are characterized by variety. *Survivors*, with the least resources of any segment, focus on meeting basic needs (safety and security) rather than fulfilling desires. They represent a modest market for most products and services and are loyal to favorite brands, especially if they can be purchased at a discount.

Each of these segments exhibits unique media preferences. Experiencers and Strivers are the most likely to visit Internet chat rooms. Innovators, Thinkers, and Achievers tend to read business and news magazines such as *Fortune* and *Time*. Makers read automotive magazines. Believers are the heaviest readers of *Reader's Digest*. GeoVALS™ estimates the percentage of each VALS group by zip code.

---

learning review

4. The problem with the Toro Snow Pup was an example of selective _____.

5. What three attitude-change approaches are most common?

6. What does *lifestyle* mean?

SOCIOCULTURAL INFLUENCES ON CONSUMER BEHAVIOR

LO4

Sociocultural influences, which evolve from a consumer's formal and informal relationships with other people, also exert a significant impact on consumer behavior. These involve personal influence, reference groups, family influence, culture, and subculture.

Personal Influence

A consumer's purchases are often influenced by the views, opinions, or behaviors of others. Two aspects of personal influence are very important to marketing: opinion leadership and word-of-mouth activity.

opinion leaders
Individuals who have social influence over others.

Opinion Leadership Individuals who exert direct or indirect social influence over others are called **opinion leaders**. Opinion leaders are considered to be knowledgeable about or users of particular products and services, so their opinions influences others' choices. Opinion leadership is widespread in the purchase of cars and trucks, entertainment, clothing and accessories, club membership, consumer electronics, vacation locations, food, and financial investments. A study by *Popular Mechanics* magazine identified 18 million opinion leaders who influence the purchases of some 85 million consumers for do-it-yourself products.

Have you recently heard about a new product, movie, Web site, book, or restaurant from someone you know . . . or a complete stranger? If so, you may have had a word-of-mouth experience.

Marketers recognize the power of word of mouth. The challenge has been to harness that power. BzzAgent Inc. does just that. Its worldwide volunteer army of over 600,000 natural-born talkers channel their chatter toward products and services they deem authentically worth talking about. "Our goal is to capture honest word of mouth," says David Balter, BzzAgent's founder, "and to build a network that turns passionate customers into brand evangelists."

BzzAgent's method is simple. Once a client signs on with Bzz-Agent, the company searches its "agent" database for those who match the demographic and psychographic profile of the target market for a client's offering. Agents then can sign up for a buzz campaign and receive a sample product and a training manual for buzz-creating strategies. Each time an agent completes an activity, he or she is expected to file an online report describing the nature of the buzz and its effectiveness. BzzAgent coaches respond with encouragement and feedback on additional techniques.

Agents keep the products they promote. They also earn points redeemable for books, CDs, and other items by filing detailed reports. Who are the agents? About 65 percent are older than 25, 70 percent are women, and two are *Fortune* 500 CEOs. All are gregarious and genuinely like the product or service, otherwise they wouldn't participate in the buzz campaign.

Estée Lauder, Monster.com, Anheuser-Busch, Penguin Books, VF Corporation (Lee jeans), Arby's, Nestlé, Hershey Foods, and Volkswagen have used BzzAgent. But BzzAgent's buzz isn't cheap, and not everything is buzz worthy. Deploying 1,000 agents on a 12-week campaign can cost a company $95,000, exclusive of product samples. BzzAgent researches a product or service before committing to a campaign and rejects about 80 percent of the companies that seek its service. It also refuses campaigns for politicians, religious groups, and certain products, such as firearms. Interested in BzzAgent? Visit its Web site at www.bzzagent.com.

About 10 percent of U.S. adults are opinion leaders.[24] Identifying, reaching, and influencing opinion leaders is a major challenge for companies. Some firms use sports figures or celebrities as spokespersons to represent their products, such as actress Cindy Crawford and swimmer Michael Phelps for OMEGA watches. Others promote their products in media believed to reach opinion leaders. Still others use more direct approaches. For example, a carmaker recently invited influential community leaders and business executives to test-drive its new models. Some 6,000 accepted the offer, and 98 percent said they would recommend their tested car. The company estimated that the number of favorable recommendations totaled 32,000.

word of mouth

People influencing each other in personal conversations.

Word of Mouth The influencing of people during conversations is called **word of mouth**. Word of mouth is the most powerful and authentic information source for consumers because it typically involves friends viewed as trustworthy. Research shows that 67 percent of U.S. consumer product sales are directly based on word-of-mouth activity among friends, family, and colleagues.[25]

The power of personal influence has prompted firms to promote positive and retard negative word of mouth. For instance, "teaser" advertising campaigns are run in advance of new-product introductions to stimulate conversations. Other techniques such as advertising slogans, music, and humor also heighten positive word of mouth. Many commercials shown during the Super Bowl are created expressly to initiate conversations about the advertisements and the featured product or service the next day. Increasingly, companies recruit and deploy people to produce *buzz*—popularity created by consumer word of mouth. Read the Marketing Matters box to learn how this is done by BzzAgent.[26]

Firms use actors or athletes as spokespersons to represent their products, such as Cindy Crawford and Michael Phelps for OMEGA watches.

On the other hand, rumors about Kmart (snake eggs in clothing), McDonald's (worms in hamburgers), Corona Extra beer (contaminated beer), and Snickers candy bars in Russia (a cause of diabetes) have resulted in negative word of mouth, none of which was based on fact. Overcoming or neutralizing negative word of mouth is difficult and costly. Supplying factual information, providing toll-free numbers for consumers to call the company, and giving appropriate product demonstrations have proven helpful to marketers facing negative word of mouth.

The power of word of mouth has been magnified by the Internet through online forums, chat rooms, blogs, bulletin boards, and Web sites. In fact, Ford uses special software to monitor online messages and find out what consumers are saying about its vehicles.

Reference Groups

Reference groups are people to whom an individual looks as a basis for self-appraisal or as a source of personal standards. Reference groups affect consumer purchases because they influence the information, attitudes, and aspiration levels that help set a consumer's standards. For example, one of the first questions one asks others when planning to attend a social occasion is, "What are you going to wear?" Reference groups influence the purchase of luxury products but not necessities—reference groups exert a strong influence on the brand chosen when its use or consumption is highly visible to others.

Consumers have many reference groups, but three groups have clear marketing implications. A *membership group* is one to which a person actually belongs, including fraternities and sororities, social clubs, and the family. Such groups are easily identifiable and are targeted by firms selling insurance, insignia products, and charter vacations. An *aspiration group* is one that a person wishes to be a member of or wishes to be identified with, such as a professional society. Firms frequently rely on spokespeople or settings associated with their target market's aspiration group in their advertising. A *dissociative group* is one that a person wishes to maintain a distance from because of differences in values or behaviors.

Family Influence

Family influences on consumer behavior result from three sources: consumer socialization, passage through the family life cycle, and decision making within the family or household.

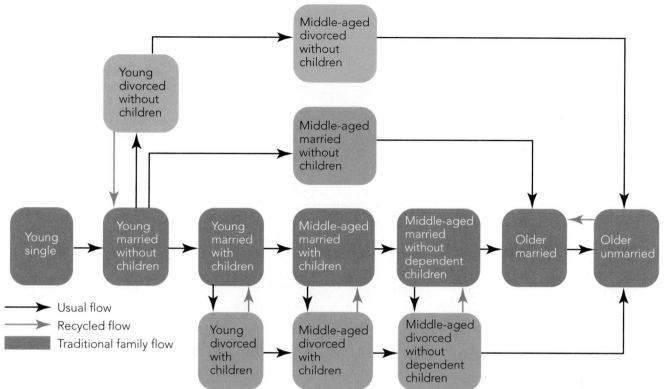

Usual flow

Recycled flow

Traditional family flow

FIGURE 5–6
Modern family life cycle stages and flows. Can you identify people you know in different stages? Do they follow the purchase patterns described in the text?

family life cycle

A family's progression from formation to retirement, each phase bringing with it distinct purchasing behaviors.

Consumer Socialization The process by which people acquire the skills, knowledge, and attitudes necessary to function as consumers is *consumer socialization*.[27] Children learn how to purchase (1) by interacting with adults in purchase situations and (2) through their own purchasing and product usage experiences. Research shows that children evidence brand preferences at age two, and these preferences often last a lifetime. This knowledge prompted the licensing of the well-known Craftsman brand name to MGA Entertainment for its children's line of My First Craftsman power tools. Other firms profiting from this research include Time, Inc., which launched *Sports Illustrated for Kids*, and Yahoo! and America Online, which offer special areas where young audiences can view their children's menu—Yahoo! Kids and Kids Only, respectively.

Family Life Cycle Consumers act and purchase differently as they go through life. The **family life cycle** concept describes the distinct phases that a family progresses through from formation to retirement, each phase bringing with it identifiable purchasing behaviors.[28] Figure 5–6 illustrates the traditional progression as well as contemporary variations of the family life cycle. Today, the *traditional family*—married couple with children younger than 18 years—constitutes just 22 percent of all U.S. households. The remaining 78 percent of U.S. households include single parents, unmarried couples, divorced, never-married, or widowed individuals, and older married couples whose children no longer live at home.

Young singles' buying preferences are for nondurable items, including prepared foods, clothing, personal care products, and entertainment. They represent a target market for recreational travel, automobile, and consumer electronics firms. Young married couples without children are typically more affluent than young singles because usually both spouses are employed. These couples exhibit preferences for furniture, housewares, and gift items for each other. Young marrieds with children are driven by the needs of their children. They make up a sizable market for life insurance, various children's products, and home furnishings. Single parents with children are the least financially secure of households with children. Their buying preferences are often affected by a limited economic status and tend toward convenience foods, child care services, and personal care items.

In the **female** the ability to match colors comes at an early age.

In the **male** it comes when he marries a female.

The City Casuals three-button, crepe jacket, 100% cotton, French-yarn shirt, Bedford cord pants, and a touch of color.

HAGGAR
Stuff you can work with.

Middle-aged married couples with children are typically better off financially than their younger counterparts. They are a significant market for leisure products and home improvement items. Middle-aged couples without children typically have a large amount of discretionary income. These couples buy better home furnishings, status automobiles, and financial services. Persons in the last two phases—older married and older unmarried—make up a sizable market for prescription drugs, medical services, vacation trips, and gifts for younger relatives.

The Haggar Clothing Co. recognizes the important role women play in the choice of men's clothing. The company directs a large portion of its advertising toward women because they influence and purchase men's clothing.

Family Decision Making A third influence in the decision-making process occurs within the family.[29] Two decision-making styles exist: spouse-dominant and joint decision making. With a joint decision-making style, most decisions are made by both husband and wife. Spouse-dominant decisions are those for which either the husband or the wife is mostly responsible. Research indicates that wives tend to have more say when purchasing groceries, children's toys, clothing, and medicines. Husbands tend to be more influential in home and car maintenance purchases. Joint decision making is common for cars, vacations, houses, home appliances and electronics, and medical care. As a rule, joint decision making increases with the education of the spouses.

Roles of individual family members in the purchase process are another element of family decision making. Five roles exist: (1) information gatherer, (2) influencer, (3) decision maker, (4) purchaser, and (5) user. Family members assume different roles for different products and services. This knowledge is important to firms. For example, 89 percent of wives either influence or make outright purchases of men's clothing. Knowing this, Haggar Clothing, a menswear marketer, advertises in women's magazines such as *Vanity Fair* and *Redbook*. Even though women are often the grocery decision maker, they are not necessarily the purchaser. More than 40 percent of all food-shopping dollars are spent by male customers.

Increasingly, preteens and teenagers are the information gatherers, influencers, decision makers, and purchasers of products and services for the family, given the prevalence of working parents and single-parent households. Children under age 12 directly influence more than $365 billion in annual family purchases. Teenagers influence another $650 billion and spend $208 million of their own money annually. These figures help explain why, for example, Nabisco, Johnson & Johnson, Hewlett-Packard, Apple, Kellogg, P&G, Sony, and Oscar Mayer, among countless other companies, spend more than $55 billion annually in electronic and print media that reach preteens and teens.

Culture and Subculture

As described in Chapter 3, *culture* refers to the set of values, ideas, and attitudes that is learned and shared among the members of a group. Thus, we often refer to the American culture, the Latin American culture, or the Japanese culture. Cultural underpinnings of American buying patterns were described in Chapter 3; Chapter 7 will explore the role of culture in global marketing.

Subgroups within the larger, or national, culture with unique values, ideas, and attitudes are referred to as **subcultures**. Various subcultures exist within the American culture. The three largest racial/ethnic subcultures in the United States are Hispanics, African Americans, and Asian Americans. Collectively, they are expected to account for one in four U.S. consumers and spend about $3.7 trillion for goods and services in 2014.[30] Each group exhibits sophisticated social and cultural behaviors that affect buying patterns, which provides the basis for multicultural marketing programs described in Chapter 3.

Hispanic Buying Patterns

Hispanics represent the largest racial/ethnic subculture in the United States in terms of population and spending power. About 50 percent of Hispanics in the United States are immigrants, and the majority are under the age of 25. One-third of Hispanics are younger than 18.

Research on Hispanic buying practices has uncovered several consistent patterns:[31]

1. Hispanics are quality and brand conscious. They are willing to pay a premium price for premium quality and are often brand loyal.
2. Hispanics prefer buying American-made products, especially those offered by firms that cater to Hispanic needs.
3. Hispanic buying preferences are strongly influenced by family and peers.
4. Hispanics consider advertising a credible product information source, and U.S. firms spend more than $4 billion annually on advertising to Hispanics.
5. Convenience is not an important product attribute to Hispanic homemakers with respect to food preparation or consumption, nor is low caffeine in coffee and soft drinks, low fat in dairy products, and low cholesterol in packaged foods.

Despite some consistent buying patterns, marketing to Hispanics has proven to be a challenge for two reasons. First, the Hispanic subculture is diverse and composed of Mexicans, Puerto Ricans, Cubans, and others of Central and South American ancestry. Cultural differences among these nationalities often affect product preferences. For example, Campbell Soup Company sells its Casera line of soups, beans, and sauces using different recipes to appeal to Puerto Ricans on the East Coast and Mexicans in the Southwest. Second, a language barrier exists, and commercial messages are frequently misinterpreted when translated into Spanish. Volkswagen learned this lesson when the Spanish translation of its "Drivers Wanted" slogan suggested "chauffeurs wanted." The Spanish slogan was changed to "*Agarra calle,*" a slang expression that can be loosely translated as "let's hit the road."

Sensitivity to the unique needs of Hispanics by firms has paid huge dividends. For example, Metropolitan Life Insurance is the largest insurer of Hispanics. Goya Foods dominates the market for ethnic food products sold to Hispanics. Best Foods' Mazola Corn Oil captures two-thirds of the Hispanic market for this product category. Time, Inc., has more than 4 million readers of its *People en Español*.

Why does Best Foods advertise its Mazola Corn Oil in Spanish? Read the text for the answer.

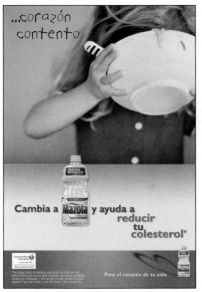

African American Buying Patterns

African Americans have the second-largest spending power of the three racial/ethnic subcultures in the United States. Consumer research on African American buying patterns has focused on similarities and differences with Caucasians. When socioeconomic status differences between African Americans and Caucasians are removed, there are more similarities than differences. Differences in buying patterns are greater within the African American subculture, due to levels of socioeconomic status, than between African Americans and Caucasians of similar status.

Even though similarities outweigh differences, there are consumption patterns that do differ between African Americans and Caucasians.[32] For example, African Americans spend far more than Caucasians on boy's clothing, rental goods, and audio equipment. Adult African Americans spend twice as much for online services, on a per capita basis, than Caucasians. African American women spend three times more on health and beauty products than Caucasian women. Furthermore, the typical African American family is

African American women represent a large market for health and beauty products. Cosmetic companies such as Bonne Bell Cosmetics, Inc., actively seek to serve this market.

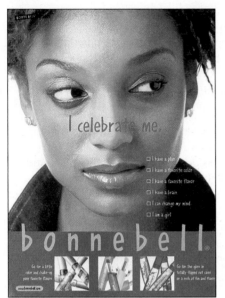

This advertisement featured NBA basketball star Yao Ming and ran in Asian-language print publications nationwide, focusing on Asian Americans.

five years younger than the typical Caucasian family. This factor alone accounts for some of the observed differences in preferences for clothing, music, shelter, cars, and many other products, services, and activities. Finally, it must be emphasized that, historically, African Americans have been deprived of higher-level employment and educational opportunities in the United States. Both factors have resulted in income disparities between African Americans and Caucasians, which influence purchase behavior.

Recent research indicates that while African Americans are price conscious, they are strongly motivated by quality and choice. They respond more to products such as apparel and cosmetics and advertising that appeal to their African American pride and heritage as well as address their ethnic features and needs regardless of socioeconomic status.

Asian American Buying Patterns Asian Americans represent the third largest racial/ethnic subculture in the United States in terms of population and spending power. About 70 percent of Asian Americans are immigrants. Most are under the age of 30.

The Asian subculture is composed of Chinese, Japanese, Filipinos, Koreans, Asian Indians, people from Southeast Asia, and Pacific Islanders. The diversity of the Asian subculture is so great that generalizations about buying patterns of this group are difficult to make.[33] Consumer research on Asian Americans suggests that individuals and families divide into two groups. *Assimilated* Asian Americans are conversant in English, highly educated, hold professional and managerial positions, and exhibit buying patterns very much like the typical American consumer. *Nonassimilated* Asian Americans are recent immigrants who still cling to their native languages and customs.

The diversity of Asian Americans evident in language, customs, and tastes requires marketers to be sensitive to different Asian nationalities. For example, Anheuser-Busch's agricultural products division sells eight varieties of California-grown rice, each with a different Asian label to cover a range of nationalities and tastes. The company's advertising also addresses the preferences of Chinese, Japanese, and Koreans for different kinds of rice bowls. McDonald's actively markets to Asian Americans. According to a company executive, "We recognize diversity in this market. We try to make our messages in the language they prefer to see them." Recently, McDonald's launched an advertising campaign that emphasized the company's Chicken Select product for Chinese, Vietnamese, and Korean consumers.

Studies show that the Asian American subculture as a whole is characterized by hard work, strong family ties, appreciation for education, and median family incomes exceeding those of any other ethnic group. This subculture is also the most entrepreneurial in the United States, as evidenced by the number of Asian-owned businesses. These qualities led Metropolitan Life Insurance to identify Asian Americans as a target for insurance following the company's success in marketing to Hispanics.

7. What are the two primary forms of personal influence?

8. Marketers are concerned with which types of reference groups?

9. What two challenges must marketers overcome when marketing to Hispanic consumers?

LEARNING OBJECTIVES REVIEW

LO1 *Describe the stages in the consumer purchase decision process.*

The consumer purchase decision process consists of five stages. They are problem recognition, information search, alternative evaluation, purchase decision, and postpurchase behavior. *Problem recognition* is perceiving a difference between a person's ideal and actual situation big enough to trigger a decision. *Information search* involves remembering previous purchase experiences (internal search) and engaging in external search behavior such as seeking information from other sources. *Alternative evaluation* clarifies the problem for the consumer by (*a*) suggesting the evaluative criteria to use for the purchase, (*b*) yielding brand names that might meet the criteria, and (*c*) developing consumer value perceptions. The *purchase decision* involves the choice of an alternative, including from whom to buy and when to buy. *Postpurchase behavior* involves the comparison of the chosen alternative with a consumer's expectations, which leads to satisfaction or dissatisfaction and subsequent purchase behavior.

LO2 *Distinguish among three variations of the consumer purchase decision process: routine, limited, and extended problem solving.*

Consumers don't always engage in the five-stage purchase decision process. Instead, they skip or minimize one or more stages depending on the level of involvement—the personal, social, and economic significance of the purchase. For low-involvement purchase occasions, consumers engage in routine problem solving. They recognize a problem, make a decision, and spend little effort seeking external information and evaluating alternatives. For high-involvement purchase occasions, each of the five stages of the consumer purchase decision process is used, with considerable time and effort devoted to the external information search and the identification and evaluation of alternatives. With limited problem solving, consumers typically seek some information or rely on a friend to help them evaluate alternatives.

LO3 *Identify major psychological influences on consumer behavior.*

Psychology helps marketers understand why and how consumers behave as they do. In particular, psychological concepts such as motivation and personality; perception; learning; values, beliefs, and attitudes; and lifestyle are useful for interpreting buying processes. Motivation is the energizing force that stimulates behavior to satisfy a need. Personality refers to a person's consistent behaviors or responses to recurring situations. Perception is the process by which an individual selects, organizes, and interprets information to create a meaningful picture of the world. Consumers filter information through selective exposure, comprehension, and retention.

Much consumer behavior is learned. Learning refers to those behaviors that result from (*a*) repeated experience and (*b*) reasoning. Brand loyalty results from learning. Values, beliefs, and attitudes are also learned and influence how consumers evaluate products, services, and brands. A more general concept is lifestyle. Lifestyle, also called psychographics, combines psychology and demographics and focuses on how people spend their time and resources, what they consider important in their environment, and what they think of themselves and the world around them.

LO4 *Identify the major sociocultural influences on consumer behavior.*

Sociocultural influences, which evolve from a consumer's formal and informal relationships with other people, also affect consumer behavior. These involve personal influence, reference groups, the family, culture, and subculture. Opinion leadership and word-of-mouth behavior are two major sources of personal influence on consumer behavior. Reference groups are people to whom an individual looks as a basis for self-approval or as a source of personal standards. Family influences on consumer behavior result from three sources: consumer socialization, passage through the family life cycle, and decision making within the family or household. Finally, a person's culture and subculture have been shown to influence product preferences and buying patterns.

FOCUSING ON KEY TERMS

attitude p. 106
beliefs p. 106
brand loyalty p. 106
consumer behavior p. 96
family life cycle p. 111
involvement p. 99

learning p. 104
motivation p. 102
opinion leaders p. 108
perceived risk p. 103
perception p. 103
personality p. 102

purchase decision process p. 96
reference groups p. 110
subcultures p. 113
word of mouth p. 109

APPLYING MARKETING KNOWLEDGE

1 Review Figure 5–2, which shows the smart phone attributes identified by *Consumer Reports*. Which attributes are important to you? What other attributes might you consider? Which brand would you prefer?

2 Suppose research at Panasonic reveals that prospective buyers are anxious about buying high-definition television sets. What strategies might you recommend to the company to reduce consumer anxiety?

3 Assign one or more levels of the hierarchy of needs and the motives described in Figure 5–5 to the following products: (*a*) life insurance, (*b*) cosmetics, (*c*) *The Wall Street Journal*, and (*d*) hamburgers.

4 Indicate the stage in the family life cycle with which the purchase of the following products and services would be most closely identified: (*a*) bedroom furniture, (*b*) life insurance, (*c*) a Caribbean cruise, (*d*) a house mortgage, and (*e*) children's toys.

building your marketing plan

To do a consumer analysis for the product—the good, service, or idea—in your marketing plan:
1 Identify the consumers who are most likely to buy your product—the primary target market—in terms of (*a*) their demographic characteristics and (*b*) any other kind of characteristics you believe are important.
2 Describe (*a*) the main points of difference of your product for this group and (*b*) what problem these characteristics help solve for the consumer, in terms of the first stage in the consumer purchase decision process in Figure 5–1.
3 Identify the one or two key influences for each of the four outside boxes in Figure 5–4: (*a*) marketing mix, (*b*) psychological, (*c*) sociocultural, and (*d*) situational influences.

This consumer analysis will provide the foundation for the marketing mix actions you develop later in your plan.

video case 5 Best Buy: Using Customer Centricity to Connect with Consumers

"So much of our business success comes down to understanding consumer behavior," explains Joe Brandt, a store service manager at one of Best Buy's newest stores. "What we do is we try to keep our ear to the railroad tracks. In essence, we listen to the customer to be able to change on a dime when a customer wants us to tailor that experience a certain way and provide certain shopping experiences and certain services.

"Consumers look at a lot of different things," Joe added. "They look at brands, shopability of the store, how easy it is to navigate the store, how pleasant the employees are, price, and how we take care of the customer." Overall there are many factors that "customers look at when they're making a purchase decision."

THE COMPANY

Best Buy is the world's largest consumer electronics retailer with 1,172 stores, 140,000 employees, and $35.9 billion in revenue. Its U.S. and Canadian market share is almost 20 percent, far ahead of rivals Walmart and Costco.

Best Buy operates superstores that provide a limited number of product categories with great depth within the categories. The retailer sells consumer electronics, home office products, appliances, entertainment software, and related services. In addition to its U.S. and Canadian stores, Best Buy has recently opened stores in China and has announced plans to open stores in Puerto Rico, Mexico, and Turkey. Best Buy also offers its products online through bestbuy.com and provides design and installation services through Geek Squad and Magnolia Audio and Video.

Best Buy began as The Sound of Music, a small specialty audio retailer, in 1966. A tornado severely damaged one of its stores in 1981. Instead of closing the store for repairs, Dick Schulze, the owner, had a tornado sale in which more goods were brought in from its other stores and prices were slashed. The sale was so successful that it was repeated the following two years. "When the tornado hit, we decided to market to the community as a whole, and get electronics out there to everybody. We geared ourselves up to win by understanding what consumers want in technology," said Joe Brandt. In 1983, The Sound of Music changed its name to Best Buy and opened its first superstore.

The company continued to grow as the consumer electronics category exploded in the 1980s and 1990s. Based on consumer feedback, Best Buy moved away from the traditional sales approach in 1989 by eliminating commissioned sales representatives. This move was embraced by customers but questioned by some suppliers and Wall Street analysts who thought it would reduce sales and profits. Best Buy's approach was successful at generating growth in stores and revenues. However, company expenses increased and profits declined. When growth of the consumer electronics market slowed and mass marketers such as Walmart, Target, Costco, and Sam's Club became competitors, Best Buy considered changes to its approach.

Best Buy began to differentiate itself from the mass marketers by offering more services, delivery, and installation. Instead of selling individual products, it concentrated on selling entire systems. The acquisition of Geek Squad to provide in-store, home, and office computer services and Magnolia Home Theater to provide complete audio and home theater systems reflects these changes. These additions significantly increased profit and insulated the company from discount store competition. Responding to customer needs and competitive changes was an important part of Best Buy's strategy.

ADOPTING "CUSTOMER CENTRICITY" AT BEST BUY

When Dick Schulze stepped down as CEO, his successor, Brad Anderson, began looking for new ideas to continue the company's growth. He invited Larry Seldon of Columbia University to present his theory of "customer centricity." Seldon's theory suggested that some customers account for a disproportionate amount of a firm's sales and profits. Anderson adapted the theory to try to understand the needs and behaviors of specific types of customers, or segments. Initial research identified five segments:

- **Barry:** The affluent professional who wants the best technology and entertainment, and who demands excellent service.
- **Jill:** The prototypical "soccer mom" who is a busy suburban mom who wants to enrich her children's lives with technology and entertainment.
- **Carrie and Buzz:** The "early adopter," active, younger customer who wants the latest technology and entertainment.
- **Ray:** The "practical adopter" who is a family man who wants technology that improves his life through technology and entertainment.
- **Small business:** The customer who runs his or her own business and has specific needs relating to growing sales and increasing the profitability of the business.

Best Buy used "lab" stores to test product offerings, store designs, and service offerings targeted at each segment. Successful offerings and designs were then expanded to a larger number of pilot stores that would undergo significant physical changes and require substantial new training of sales associates. The cost of applying customer centricity to a store was often as much as $600,000. Early results were impressive as customer centricity stores reported sales much higher than the chain average. As Best Buy began rapid conversion of hundreds of Best Buy stores to the centricity formats, however, expenses increased and profits declined.

THE ISSUES

The impact of Best Buy's new approach on profitability led the company to continue to adapt its ideas about customers. One consideration, for example, was that the "Jill" segment should be broadened to include all females. Research showed that women spend $68 billion on consumer electronics each year and influence 89 percent of all purchases. Unfortunately, females did not embrace the Best Buy experience, largely because its stores were male-oriented in merchandise, appearance, and staffing. "Men and women shop very differently," observes Brandt. Men "typically love the technology" and they like to "play with it" while women are "looking for a knowledgeable person who can answer their questions in a simple manner." To address this problem Best Buy began to implement many changes that would make Best Buy *the* place for women to shop (and work!).

Today, Best Buy is trying a variety of new approaches. Its stores, for example, are being changed to be more appealing to women. Store layout has been changed to include larger aisles, softer colors, less noise, and reduced visibility of boxes and extra stock. In addition, Best Buy now offers women, and all customers, a personal shopping assistant who will walk a customer through the store, demonstrate how the products function, and arrange for delivery and installation after the sale. Best Buy has also created rooms that resemble a home in the store to show customers exactly how the products will look when they are installed. According to Brandt, "We try to personalize the experience as much as possible, and we really try to build a relationship. Once we do that we have the opportunity to really listen and answer questions that customers have." Best Buy is undertaking other initiatives as well. It created the Women's Leadership Forum (WOLF) to develop female leaders within the company. Early results have yielded an increase in applications and a decline in turnover. Overall, these changes appear to be working. Best Buy has observed an increase in its female market share in consumer electronics!

In the future Best Buy's customer centricity efforts will continue to focus on understanding consumer behavior and improving the customer experience. Brandt explains: "Customer centricity, in simple terms, is listening to the customer, putting the customer at the forefront of everything we do. That is, whatever shopping experience that they are looking for, we gear our company and our structure to satisfy that need as much as possible."

Questions

1 How has an understanding of consumer behavior helped Best Buy grow from a small specialty audio retailer to the world's largest consumer electronics retailer?

2 What were the advantages and disadvantages of using "customer centricity" to create five segments of Best Buy customers?

3 How are men and women different in their consumer behavior when they are shopping in a Best Buy store?

4 What are two or three (*a*) objective evaluative criteria and (*b*) subjective evaluative criteria female consumers use when shopping for electronics at Best Buy?

5 What challenges does Best Buy face in the future?

findm▶re™ jcp.com | 1.800.222.6161

JCPenney

Every Day Matters

89⁹⁹
KISAREE TWIN
COMFORTER
SET, p. 3

STYLE SOURCE | ROOMS KIDS LOVE | SPRING 2010

6

Understanding Organizations as Customers

BUYING IS MARKETING, TOO! PURCHASING PUBLICATION PAPER AT JCPENNEY

Kim Nagele views paper differently than most people do. As the senior procurement agent at JCPMedia, he and a team of purchasing professionals buy more than 240,000 tons of publication paper annually at a cost of hundreds of millions of dollars.

JCPMedia is the print and paper purchasing arm for JCPenney, the fifth-largest retailer in the United States and the largest catalog merchant of general merchandise in the Western Hemisphere. Paper is serious business at JCPMedia, which buys publication paper for JCPenney catalogs, newspaper inserts, and direct-mail pieces. Some 10 companies from around the world, including Verso Paper in the United States, Catalyst Paper Inc. in Canada, Norske Skog in Norway, and UPM-Kymmene Inc. in Finland, supply paper to JCPMedia.

The choice of paper and suppliers is also a significant business decision given the sizable revenue and expense consequences. Therefore, JCPMedia paper buyers work closely with JCPenney marketing personnel and within budget constraints to ensure that the right quality and quantity of publication paper are purchased at the right price point for the millions of catalogs, newspaper inserts, and direct-mail pieces distributed every year.

In addition to paper quality and price, buyers formally evaluate supplier capabilities, often by extended visits to supplier facilities. These include a supplier's capacity to deliver on time selected grades of paper from specialty items to magazine papers, the availability of specific types of paper to meet printing deadlines, and ongoing environmental programs. For example, a supplier's forestry management and sustainability practices are considered in the JCPMedia buying process.

The next time you thumb through a JCPenney catalog, newspaper insert, or direct-mail piece, notice the paper. Considerable effort and attention were given to its selection and purchase by Kim Nagele and JCPMedia paper buyers.[1]

Purchasing paper for JCPMedia is one example of organizational buying. This chapter examines types of organizational buyers; key characteristics of organizational buying, including online buying; different buying situations; unique aspects of the organizational buying process; and typical buying procedures and decisions in today's organizational markets.

THE NATURE AND SIZE OF ORGANIZATIONAL MARKETS

business marketing
The marketing of products and services to firms, governments, or not-for-profit organizations.

organizational buyers
Manufacturers, wholesalers, retailers, and government agencies that buy goods and services for their own use or for resale.

Understanding organizational markets and buying behavior is a necessary prerequisite for effective business marketing. **Business marketing** is the marketing of products and services to companies, governments, or not-for-profit organizations for use in the creation of goods and services that they can produce and market to others. Because over half of all U.S. business school graduates take jobs in firms that engage in business marketing, it is important to understand the characteristics of organizational buyers and their buying behavior.

Organizational buyers are those manufacturers, wholesalers, retailers, and government agencies that buy goods and services for their own use or for resale. For example, these organizations buy computers and telephone services for their own use. However, manufacturers buy raw materials and parts that they reprocess into the finished goods they sell. Wholesalers and retailers resell the goods they buy without reprocessing them. Organizational buyers include all buyers in a nation except ultimate consumers. These organizational buyers purchase and lease large volumes of capital equipment, raw materials, manufactured parts, supplies, and business services. In fact, because they often buy raw materials and parts, process them, and sell the upgraded product several times before it is purchased by the final organizational buyer or ultimate consumer, the total annual purchases of organizational buyers are far greater than those of ultimate consumers. IBM alone buys nearly $40 billion in goods and services each year for its own use or resale.[2]

Organizational buyers are divided into three markets: (1) industrial, (2) reseller, and (3) government.[3] Each market is described next.

Industrial Markets

There are about 7.2 million firms in the industrial, or business, market. These *industrial firms* in some way reprocess a product or service they buy before selling it again to the next buyer. This is certainly true for Corning, Inc., which transforms an exotic blend of materials to create optical fiber capable of carrying much of the telephone traffic in the United States on a single strand. It is also true (if you stretch your imagination) for a firm selling services, such as a bank that takes money from its depositors, reprocesses it, and "sells" it as loans to borrowers.

The importance of services in the United States today is emphasized by the composition of industrial markets. Companies that primarily sell physical goods (manufacturers; mining; construction; and farms, timber, and fisheries) represent 25 percent of all the industrial firms. The services market sells diverse services such as legal advice,

The Orion lunar spacecraft to be designed, developed, tested, and evaluated by Lockheed Martin Corp. is an example of a purchase by a government unit, namely the National Aeronautics and Space Administration (NASA). Read the text to find out how much NASA will pay for the Orion lunar spacecraft.

auto repair, and dry cleaning. Comprised of finance, insurance, real estate, transportation, communication, and public utility firms as well as not-for-profit organizations (such as the American Red Cross), service companies represent 75 percent of all industrial firms.

Reseller Markets

Wholesalers and retailers that buy physical products and resell them again without any reprocessing are *resellers*. In the United States there are almost 2 million retailers and 430,000 wholesalers. In this chapter, we look at these resellers mainly as organizational buyers in terms of (1) how they make their own buying decisions and (2) which products they choose to carry.

Government Markets

Government units are the federal, state, and local agencies that buy goods and services for the constituents they serve. There are about 89,500 of these government units in the United States. These purchases include the $3.9 billion the National Aeronautics and Space Administration (NASA) intends to pay to Lockheed Martin to develop and produce the Orion lunar spacecraft scheduled for launch in 2015 as well as lesser amounts spent by local school and sanitation districts.[4]

MEASURING DOMESTIC AND GLOBAL INDUSTRIAL, RESELLER, AND GOVERNMENT MARKETS

North American Industry Classification System (NAICS)

Provides common industry definitions for Canada, Mexico, and the United States.

The measurement of industrial, reseller, and government markets is an important first step for a firm interested in gauging the size of one, two, or all three of these markets in the United States and around the world. This task has been made easier with the **North American Industry Classification System (NAICS)**.[5] The NAICS provides common industry definitions for Canada, Mexico, and the United States, which makes it easier to measure economic activity in the three member countries of the North American Free Trade Agreement (NAFTA). The NAICS replaced the Standard Industrial Classification (SIC) system, a version of which has been in place for more than 50 years in the three NAFTA member countries. The SIC neither permitted comparability across countries nor accurately measured new or emerging industries. Furthermore, the NAICS is consistent with the International Standard Industrial Classification of All Economic Activities, published by the United Nations, to facilitate measurement of global economic activity.

The NAICS groups economic activity to permit studies of market share, demand for goods and services, import competition in domestic markets, and similar studies. It designates industries with a numerical code in a defined structure. A six-digit coding system is used. The first two digits designate a sector of the economy, the third digit designates a subsector, and the fourth digit represents an industry group. The fifth digit designates a specific industry and it is the most detailed level at which comparable data are available for Canada, Mexico, and the United States. The sixth digit designates individual country-level national industries. Figure 6–1 on the next page shows a breakdown within the information industries sector (code 51) to illustrate the classification scheme.

The NAICS permits a firm to find the NAICS codes of its present customers and then obtain NAICS-coded lists for similar firms. Also, it is possible to monitor NAICS categories to determine the growth in various sectors and industries to identify promising marketing opportunities. However, the NAICS has an important limitation. Five-digit national industry codes are not available for all three countries because the respective governments will not reveal data when too few organizations exist in a category.

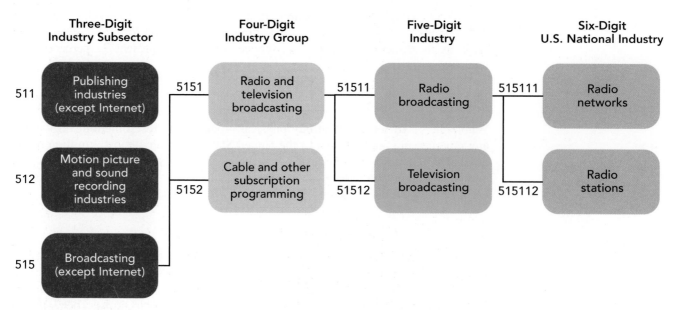

FIGURE 6–1
NAICS breakdown for information industries sector: NAICS code 51 (abbreviated).

| learning review | 1. What are the three main types of organizational buyers? |
| | 2. What is the North American Industry Classification System (NAICS)? |

CHARACTERISTICS OF ORGANIZATIONAL BUYING

LO2

Organizations are different from individuals, so buying for an organization is different from buying for yourself or your family. In both cases the objective in making the purchase is to solve the buyer's problem—to satisfy a need or want. But unique objectives and policies of an organization put special constraints on how it makes buying decisions. Understanding the characteristics of organizational buying is essential in designing effective marketing programs to reach these buyers. Key characteristics of organizational buying are listed in Figure 6–2 and discussed next.[6]

Demand Characteristics

derived demand
The demand for industrial products and services is driven by demand for consumer products and services.

Consumer demand for products and services is affected by their price and availability and by consumers' personal tastes and discretionary income. By comparison, industrial demand is derived. **Derived demand** means that the demand for industrial products and services is driven by, or derived from, demand for consumer products and services. For example, the demand for Weyerhaeuser's pulp and paper products is based on consumer demand for newspapers, FedEx packages, and disposable diapers. Derived demand is based on expectations of future consumer demand. For instance, Whirlpool buys parts for its washers and dryers in anticipation of consumer demand, which is affected by the replacement cycle for these products and by consumer income.

Size of the Order or Purchase

The size of the purchase involved in organizational buying is typically much larger than that in consumer buying. The dollar value of a single purchase made by an

CHARACTERISTICS	DIMENSIONS

Market characteristics
- Demand for industrial products and services is derived.
- Few customers typically exist, and their purchase orders are large.

Product or service characteristics
- Products or services are technical in nature and purchased on the basis of specifications.
- Many of the goods purchased are raw and semifinished.
- Heavy emphasis is placed on delivery time, technical assistance, and postsale service.

Buying process characteristics
- Technically qualified and professional buyers follow established purchasing policies and procedures.
- Buying objectives and criteria are typically spelled out, as are procedures for evaluating sellers and their products or services.
- There are multiple buying influences, and multiple parties participate in purchase decisions.
- There are reciprocal arrangements, and negotiation between buyers and sellers is commonplace.
- Online buying over the Internet is widespread.

Marketing mix characteristics
- Direct selling to organizational buyers is the rule, and distribution is very important.
- Advertising and other forms of promotion are technical in nature.
- Price is often negotiated, evaluated as part of broader seller and product or service qualities, and frequently affected by quantity discounts.

FIGURE 6–2

Key characteristics and dimensions of organizational buying behavior.

organization often runs into thousands or millions of dollars. For example, Siemens Energy & Automation's Airport Logistics Division was awarded a $28 million contract to build a baggage handling and security system for JetBlue Airways' terminal at John F. Kennedy International Airport.[7] With so much money at stake, most organizations place constraints on their buyers in the form of purchasing policies or procedures. Buyers must often get competitive bids from at least three prospective suppliers when the order is above a specific amount, such as $5,000. When the order is above an even higher amount, such as $50,000, it may require the review and approval of a vice president or even the president of the company. Knowing how order size affects buying practices is important in determining who participates in the purchase decision and makes the final decision and the length of time required to arrive at a purchase agreement.

Number of Potential Buyers

Firms selling consumer products or services often try to reach thousands or millions of individuals or households. For example, your local supermarket or bank probably serves thousands of people. Kellogg tries to reach 80 million North American households with its breakfast cereals and probably succeeds in selling to a third or half of these in any given year. Firms selling to organizations are often restricted to far fewer buyers. Gulfstream Aerospace Corporation can sell its business jets to a few thousand organizations throughout the world, and Goodyear sells its original equipment tires to fewer than 10 car manufacturers.

Organizational Buying Objectives

Organizations buy products and services for one main reason: to help them achieve their objectives. For business firms the buying objective is usually to increase profits through reducing costs or increasing revenues. For example, 7-Eleven buys automated inventory systems to increase the number of products that can be sold through its convenience stores and to keep them fresh. Nissan Motor Company switched its advertising agency because it expects the new agency to devise a more effective ad campaign to help it sell more cars and increase revenues. To improve executive decision making, many firms buy advanced computer systems to process data. Recognizing the high costs of energy, Sylvania promotes the cost savings and increased profits made possible by its fluorescent and halogen lights. The objectives of nonprofit firms and government agencies are usually to meet the needs of the groups they serve.

Many companies today have broadened their buying objectives to include an emphasis on buying from minority- and women-owned suppliers and vendors. Companies such as Pitney Bowes, PepsiCo, Coors, and JCPenney report that sales, profits, and customer satisfaction have increased because of their minority- and women-owned supplier and vendor initiatives.[8] Not surprisingly, "Supplier diversity is no longer an issue of social conscience," says A. G. Lafley, chairman of the board, president, and chief executive officer at Procter & Gamble. "It is a fundamental business strategy."[9]

Other companies include environmental initiatives. For example, Lowe's and Home Depot no longer purchase lumber from companies that harvest timber from the world's endangered forests.[10] Successful business marketers recognize that understanding buying objectives is a necessary first step in marketing to organizations.

Organizational Buying Criteria

In making a purchase, the buying organization must weigh key buying criteria that apply to the potential supplier and what it wants to sell. *Organizational buying criteria* are the objective attributes of the supplier's products and services and the capabilities of the supplier itself. These criteria serve the same purpose as the evaluative criteria used by consumers and described in Chapter 5. The most commonly used criteria are (1) price, (2) ability to meet the quality specifications required for the item, (3) ability to meet required delivery schedules, (4) technical capability, (5) warranties and claim policies in the event of poor performance, (6) past performance on previous contracts, and (7) production facilities and capacity. Suppliers that meet or exceed these criteria create customer value.

Many organizational buyers today are transforming their buying criteria into specific requirements that are communicated to prospective suppliers. This practice, called *supplier development*, involves the deliberate effort by organizational buyers to build relationships that shape suppliers' products, services, and capabilities to fit a buyer's needs and those of its customers. Consider Deere & Company, the maker of John Deere farm, construction, and lawn-care equipment. Deere employs supplier-development engineers who work full-time with the company's suppliers to improve their efficiency and quality and reduce their costs. According to a Deere senior executive, "Their quality, delivery, and costs are, after all, our quality, delivery, and costs."[11] Read the Marketing Matters box to learn how Harley-Davidson emphasizes supplier collaboration in its product design.[12]

Buyer–Seller Relationships and Supply Partnerships

Another distinction between organizational and consumer buying behavior lies in the nature of the relationship between organizational buyers and suppliers. Specifically, organizational buying is more likely to involve complex negotiations concerning delivery schedules, price, technical specifications, warranties, and claim policies. This was the case when the Lawrence Livermore National Laboratory acquired two IBM supercomputers—each with capacity to perform 360 trillion mathematical operations per second—at a cost of $290 million.[13]

Marketing Matters > > > > > > customer value

Harley-Davidson's Supplier Collaboration Creates Customer Value . . . and a Great Ride

It's nice to be admired. Harley-Davidson's well-deserved reputation for innovation, product quality, and talented management and employees has made it a perennial member of *Fortune* magazine's list of "America's Most Admired Companies."

Harley-Davidson is also respected by suppliers for the way it collaborates with them in product design. According to a Harley-Davidson executive, "We involve our suppliers as much as possible in future products, new-product development, and get them working with us." Emphasis is placed on quality benchmarks, cost control, delivery schedules, and technological innovation as well as building mutually beneficial, long-term relationships. Face-to-face communication is encouraged, and many suppliers have personnel stationed at Harley-Davidson's Product Development Center.

The relationship between Harley-Davidson and Milsco Manufacturing is a case in point. Milsco has been the sole source of original equipment motorcycle seats and a major supplier of after-market parts and accessories, such as saddlebags, for Harley-Davidson since 1934. Milsco engineers and designers work closely with their Harley counterparts in the design of each year's new products.

The notion of a mutually beneficial relationship is expressed by Milsco's manager of industrial design: "Harley-Davidson refers to us as stakeholders, someone who can win or lose from a successful or failed program. We all share responsibility toward one another." He also notes that Harley-Davidson is not Milsco's only customer. It is simply the customer that he most respects.

Reciprocal arrangements also exist in organizational buying. *Reciprocity* is an industrial buying practice in which two organizations agree to purchase each other's products and services. The U.S. Justice Department disapproves of reciprocal buying because it restricts the normal operation of the free market. However, the practice exists and can limit the flexibility of organizational buyers in choosing alternative suppliers.

Long-term contracts are also prevalent.[14] For instance, Kraft Foods, Inc., is spending $1.7 billion over seven years for global information technology services provided by Electronic Data Systems. Hewlett-Packard has a 10-year, $3 billion contract to manage Procter & Gamble's information technology in 160 countries.

In some cases, buyer–seller relationships evolve into supply partnerships.[15] A *supply partnership* exists when a buyer and its supplier adopt mutually beneficial objectives, policies, and procedures for the purpose of lowering the cost or increasing the value of products and services delivered to the ultimate consumer. Intel, a manufacturer of microprocessors and the "computer inside" of most personal computers, is an example. Intel supports its suppliers by offering them quality management programs and by investing in supplier equipment that produces fewer product defects and boosts supplier productivity. Suppliers, in turn, provide Intel with consistent high-quality products at a lower cost for its customers, the makers of personal computers, and finally you, the ultimate customer. Retailers, too, have forged partnerships with their suppliers. Walmart has such a relationship with Procter & Gamble for ordering and replenishing P&G's products in its stores. By using computerized cash register scanning equipment and direct electronic linkages to P&G, Walmart can tell P&G what merchandise is needed, along with how much, when, and at which store on a daily basis.

Supply partnerships often include provisions for what is called *sustainable procurement*. This buying practice is described in the Making Responsible Decisions box on the next page.[16]

Sustainable Procurement for Sustainable Growth

Manufacturers, retailers, wholesalers, and governmental agencies are increasingly sensitive to how their buying decisions affect the environment. Concerns about the depletion of natural resources; air, water, and soil pollution; and the social consequences of economic activity have given rise to the concept of sustainable procurement. Sustainable procurement aims to integrate environmental considerations into all stages of an organization's buying process with the goal of reducing the impact on human health and the physical environment.

Starbucks is a pioneer and worldwide leader in sustainable procurement. The company's attention to quality coffee extends to its coffee growers located in more than 20 countries. This means that Starbucks pays coffee farmers a fair price for the beans; that the coffee is grown in an

ecologically sound manner; and that Starbucks invests in the farming communities where its coffees are produced. In this way, Starbucks focuses on the sustainable growth of its suppliers.

THE ORGANIZATIONAL BUYING PROCESS AND THE BUYING CENTER

organizational buying behavior

The process by which organizations determine the need for goods and then choose among alternative suppliers.

Organizational buyers, like consumers, engage in a decision process when selecting products and services. **Organizational buying behavior** is the decision-making process that organizations use to establish the need for products and services and identify, evaluate, and choose among alternative brands and suppliers. There are important similarities and differences between the two decision-making processes. To better understand the nature of organizational buying behavior, we first compare it with consumer buying behavior. We then describe a unique feature of organizational buying—the buying center.

Stages in the Organizational Buying Process

As shown in Figure 6–3, the five stages a student might use in buying a smart phone also apply to organizational purchases. However, comparing the two smart phone columns in Figure 6–3 reveals some key differences. For example, when a manufacturer buys an earbud headset for its units from a supplier, more individuals are involved, supplier capability becomes more important, and the postpurchase evaluation behavior is more formal. The earbud headset buying decision process is typical of the steps made by organizational buyers.

The Buying Center: A Cross-Functional Group

LO3

buying center

The group of people in an organization who participates in the buying process.

For routine purchases with a small dollar value, a single buyer or purchasing manager often makes the purchase decision alone. In many instances, however, several people in the organization participate in the buying process. The individuals in this group, called a **buying center**, share common goals, risks, and knowledge important to purchase decisions. For most large multistore chain resellers, such as Sears, 7-Eleven convenience stores, Target, or Safeway, the buying center is highly formalized and is called a *buying committee*. However, most industrial firms or government units use informal groups of people or call meetings to arrive at buying decisions.

The importance of the buying center means that a firm marketing to many industrial firms and government units must understand the structure, technical, and business functions represented and the behavior of these groups.[17] Four questions provide guidance in

STAGE IN THE BUYING DECISION PROCESS	CONSUMER PURCHASE: SMART PHONE FOR A STUDENT	ORGANIZATIONAL PURCHASE: EARBUD HEADSET FOR A SMART PHONE
Problem recognition	Student doesn't like the features of the smart phone now owned and desires a new one.	Marketing research and sales departments observe that competitors are improving the earbud headsets for their smart phones. The firm decides to improve the earbud headsets on its own new models, which will be purchased from an outside supplier.
Information search	Student uses past experience, that of friends, ads, the Internet, and *Consumer Reports* to collect information and uncover alternatives.	Design and production engineers draft specifications for earbud headsets. The purchasing department identifies suppliers of earbud headsets.
Alternative evaluation	Alternative smart phones are evaluated on the basis of important attributes desired in a phone, and several stores are visited.	Purchasing and engineering personnel visit with suppliers and assess (1) facilities, (2) capacity, (3) quality control, and (4) financial status. They drop any suppliers not satisfactory on these factors.
Purchase decision	A specific brand of smart phone is selected, the price is paid, and the student leaves the store.	They use (1) quality, (2) price, (3) delivery, and (4) technical capability as key buying criteria to select a supplier. Then they negotiate terms and award a contract.
Postpurchase behavior	Student reevaluates the purchase decision, may return the phone to the store if it is unsatisfactory.	They evaluate suppliers using a formal vendor rating system and notify a supplier if the earbud headsets do not meet their quality standard. If the problem is not corrected, they drop the firm as a future supplier.

FIGURE 6–3

Comparing the stages in a consumer and organizational purchase decision process.

Effective marketing to organizations requires an understanding of buying centers and their role in purchase decisions.

understanding the buying center in these organizations: (1) Which individuals are in the buying center for the product or service? (2) What is the relative influence of each member of the group? (3) What are the buying criteria of each member? (4) How does each member of the group perceive our firm, our products and services, and our salespeople?

People in the Buying Center The composition of the buying center in a given organization depends on the specific item being bought. Although a buyer or purchasing manager is almost always a member of the buying center, individuals from other functional areas are included, depending on what is to be purchased. In buying a million-dollar machine tool, the president (because of the size of the purchase) and the production vice president or manager would probably be members. For key components to be included in a final manufactured product, a cross-functional group of individuals from research and development (R&D), engineering, and quality control are likely to be added. For new word-processing equipment, experienced secretaries who will use the equipment would be members. Still, a major question in penetrating the buying center is finding and reaching the people who will initiate, influence, and actually make the buying decision.

Roles in the Buying Center Researchers have identified five specific roles that an individual in a buying center can play.[18] In some purchases the same person may perform two or more of these roles.

- *Users* are the people in the organization who actually use the product or service, such as a secretary who will use a new word processor.
- *Influencers* affect the buying decision, usually by helping define the specifications for what is bought. The information systems manager would be a key influencer in the purchase of a new mainframe computer.
- *Buyers* have formal authority and responsibility to select the supplier and negotiate the terms of the contract. Kim Nagele performs this role as senior procurement agent at JCPMedia as described in the chapter opening example.
- *Deciders* have the formal or informal power to select or approve the supplier that receives the contract. Whereas in routine orders the decider is usually the buyer or purchasing manager, in important technical purchases it is more likely to be someone from R&D, engineering, or quality control. The decider for a key component being incorporated in a final manufactured product might be any of these three people.
- *Gatekeepers* control the flow of information in the buying center. Purchasing personnel, technical experts, and secretaries can all keep salespeople or information from reaching people performing the other four roles.

buy classes

Three types of organizational buying situations: new buy, straight rebuy, or modified rebuy.

FIGURE 6–4

The buying situation affects buying center behavior in different ways. Understanding these differences can pay huge dividends.

Buying Situations and the Buying Center The number of people in the buying center largely depends on the specific buying situation. Researchers who have studied organizational buying identify three types of buying situations, called **buy classes**. These buy classes vary from the routine reorder, or *straight rebuy,* to the completely new purchase, termed *new buy*. In between these extremes is the *modified rebuy.* Figure 6-4 summarizes how buy classes affect buying center tendencies in different ways.[19] Some examples will clarify the differences.[20]

- *Straight rebuy.* Here the buyer or purchasing manager reorders an existing product or service from the list of acceptable suppliers, probably without even checking with

	BUY-CLASS SITUATION		
BUYING CENTER DIMENSION	**NEW BUY**	**STRAIGHT REBUY**	**MODIFIED REBUY**
People involved	Many	One	Two to three
Decision time	Long	Short	Moderate
Problem definition	Uncertain	Well-defined	Minor modifications
Buying objective	Good solution	Low-priced supplier	Low-priced supplier
Suppliers considered	New/present	Present	Present
Buying influence	Technical/operating personnel	Purchasing agent	Purchasing agent and others

users or influencers from the engineering, production, or quality control departments. Office supplies and maintenance services are usually obtained as straight rebuys.

- *Modified rebuy.* In this buying situation the users, influencers, or deciders in the buying center want to change the product specifications, price, delivery schedule, or supplier. Although the item purchased is largely the same as with the straight rebuy, the changes usually necessitate enlarging the buying center to include people outside the purchasing department.
- *New buy.* Here the organization is a first-time buyer of the product or service. This involves greater potential risks in the purchase, so the buying center is enlarged to include all those who have a stake in the new buy. Procter & Gamble's purchase of a multimillion-dollar fiber-optic network from Corning Inc. for its corporate offices in Cincinnati represented a new buy.[21]

learning review

3. What one department is almost always represented by a person in the buying center?

4. What are the three types of buying situations or buy classes?

ONLINE BUYING IN ORGANIZATIONAL MARKETS

LO4

Organizational buying behavior and business marketing continues to evolve with the application of Internet technology. Organizations dwarf consumers in terms of online transactions made, average transaction size, and overall purchase volume. In fact, organizational buyers account for about 80 percent of the global dollar value of all online transactions.[22] Online organizational buyers around the world will purchase between $8 trillion and $10 trillion worth of products and services by 2010. Organizational buyers in the United States will account for about 60 percent of these purchases.

Prominence of Online Buying in Organizational Markets

Online buying in organizational markets is prominent for three major reasons.[23] First, organizational buyers depend heavily on timely supplier information that describes product availability, technical specifications, application uses, price, and delivery schedules. This information can be conveyed quickly via Internet technology. Second, this technology has been shown to substantially reduce buyer order processing costs. At General Electric, online buying has cut the cost of a transaction from $50 to $100 per purchase to about $5. Third, business marketers have found that Internet technology can reduce marketing costs, particularly sales and advertising expense, and broaden their potential customer base for many types of products and services.

For these reasons, online buying is popular in all three kinds of organizational markets. For example, airlines electronically order over $400 million in spare parts from the Boeing Company each year. Customers of W. W. Grainger, a large U.S. wholesaler of maintenance, repair, and operating supplies, buy more than $425 million worth of these products annually online. Supply and service purchases totaling $650 million each year are made online by the Los Angeles County government.

e-marketplaces
Online trading communities that bring together buyers and supplier organizations.

E-Marketplaces: Virtual Organizational Markets

A significant development in organizational buying has been the creation of online trading communities, called **e-marketplaces**, that bring together buyers and supplier

organizations. These online communities go by a variety of names, including business-to-business (B2B) exchanges and e-hubs, and make possible the real-time exchange of information, money, products, and services.

E-marketplaces can be independent trading communities or private exchanges.[24] Independent e-marketplaces act as a neutral third party and provide an Internet technology trading platform and a centralized market that enable exchanges between buyers and sellers. They charge a fee for their service and exist in settings that have one or more of the following features: (1) thousands of geographically dispersed buyers and sellers, (2) volatile prices caused by demand and supply fluctuations, (3) time sensitivity due to perishable offerings and changing technologies, and (4) easily comparable offerings between a variety of sellers.

Examples of independent e-marketplaces include PlasticsNet (plastics), Hospital Network.com (health care supplies and equipment), and Textile Web (garment and apparel products). Small business buyers and sellers, in particular, benefit from independent e-marketplaces. These e-marketplaces offer them an economical way to expand their customer base and reduce the cost of products and services. To serve entrepreneurs and the small business market in the United States, eBay launched eBayBusiness. Read the Marketing Matters box to learn more about this independent trading community.[25]

Large companies tend to favor private exchanges that link them with their network of qualified suppliers and customers. Private exchanges focus on streamlining a company's purchase transactions with its suppliers and customers. Like independent e-marketplaces, they provide a technology trading platform and central market for buyer–seller interactions. They are not a neutral third party, however, but represent the interests of their owners. For example, Agentrics is an international business-to-business exchange that serves the e-marketplace. It connects more than 250 retail customers with 80,000 suppliers. Its members include Best Buy, Campbell Soup, Costco, Radio Shack, Safeway, Target, Tesco, and Walgreens.[26] The Global Healthcare

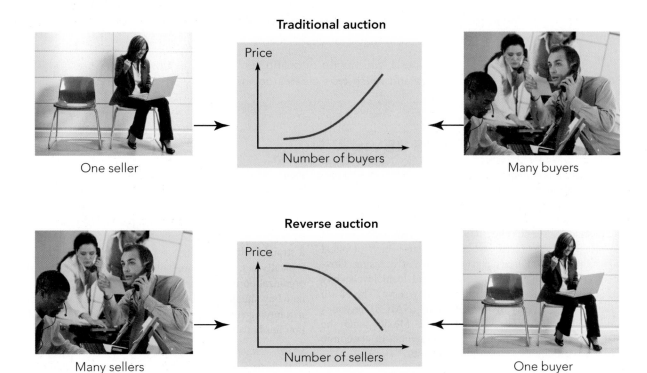

Traditional auction

One seller

Price

Number of buyers

Many buyers

Reverse auction

Many sellers

Price

Number of sellers

One buyer

FIGURE 6–5
Buyer and seller participants and price behavior differ by type of online auction. As an organizational buyer, would you prefer to participate in a traditional auction or a reverse auction?

Exchange engages in the buying and selling of health care products for some 1,400 hospitals and more than 100 health care suppliers, such as Abbott Laboratories, GE Medical Systems, Johnson & Johnson, Medtronic USA, and McKesson Corporation. These private exchanges have saved their members over $2 billion since 2000 due to efficiencies in purchase transactions.[27]

Online Auctions in Organizational Markets

Online auctions have grown in popularity among organizational buyers and business marketers. Many e-marketplaces offer this service. Two general types of auctions are common: (1) a traditional auction and (2) a reverse auction.[28] Figure 6–5 shows how buyer and seller participants and price behavior differ by type of auction. Let's look at each auction type more closely to understand the implications of each for buyers and sellers.

In a **traditional auction** a seller puts an item up for sale and would-be buyers are invited to bid in competition with each other. As more would-be buyers become involved, there is an upward pressure on bid prices. Why? Bidding is sequential. Prospective buyers observe the bids of others and decide whether or not to increase the bid price. The auction ends when a single bidder remains and "wins" the item with its highest price. Traditional auctions are often used to dispose of excess merchandise. For example, Dell Inc. sells surplus, refurbished, or closeout computer merchandise at its dellauction.com Web site.

A reverse auction works in the opposite direction from a traditional auction. In a **reverse auction**, a buyer communicates a need for a product or service and would-be suppliers are invited to bid in competition with each other. As more would-be suppliers become involved, there is a downward pressure on bid prices for the buyer's business. Why? Like traditional auctions, bidding is sequential and prospective suppliers observe the bids of others and decide whether or not to decrease the bid price. The auction ends when a single bidder remains and "wins" the business with its lowest price. Reverse auctions benefit organizational buyers by reducing the cost of their purchases. As an example, United Technologies Corp. estimates that it has saved $600 million on the purchase of $6 billion in supplies using online reverse auctions.[29]

traditional auction
Occurs when a seller puts an item up for sale and would-be buyers bid in competition with each other.

reverse auction
Occurs when a buyer communicates a need for something and would-be suppliers bid in competition with each other.

learning review

5. What are e-marketplaces?

6. In general, which type of online auction creates upward pressure on bid prices and which type creates downward pressure on bid prices?

LEARNING OBJECTIVES REVIEW

LO1 *Distinguish among industrial, reseller, and government organizational markets.*

There are three different organizational markets: industrial, reseller, and government. Industrial firms in some way reprocess a product or service they buy before selling it to the next buyer. Resellers—wholesalers and retailers—buy physical products and resell them again without any reprocessing. Government agencies, at the federal, state, and local levels, buy goods and services for the constituents they serve. The North American Industry Classification System (NAICS) provides common industry definitions for Canada, Mexico, and the United States, which facilitates the measurement of economic activity for these three organizational markets.

LO2 *Describe the key characteristics of organizational buying that make it different from consumer buying.*

Seven major characteristics of organizational buying make it different from consumer buying. These include demand characteristics, size of the order or purchase, number of potential buyers, buying objectives, buying criteria, buyer–seller relationships and supply partnerships, and multiple buying influences within organizations. The organizational buying process itself is more formalized, more individuals are involved, supplier capability is more important, and the postpurchase evaluation behavior often includes performance of the supplier and the item purchased. Figure 6–3 details how the consumer and organizational purchase of a smart phone differs.

LO3 *Explain how buying centers and buying situations influence organizational purchasing.*

Buying centers and buying situations have an important influence on organizational purchasing. A buying center consists of a group of individuals who share common goals, risks, and knowledge important to a purchase decision. A buyer or purchasing manager is almost always a member of a buying center. However, other individuals may affect organizational purchasing due to their unique roles in a purchase decision. Five specific roles that a person may play in a buying center include users, influencers, buyers, deciders, and gatekeepers. The specific buying situation will influence the number of people involved and the different roles played in a buying center. For a routine reorder of an item— a straight rebuy situation—a purchasing manager or buyer will typically act alone in making a purchasing decision. When an organization is a first-time purchaser of a product or service—a new buy situation—a buying center is enlarged and all five roles in a buying center often emerge. A modified rebuy buying situation lies between these two extremes.

LO4 *Recognize the importance and nature of online buying in industrial, reseller, and government organizational markets.*

Organizations dwarf consumers in terms of online transactions made and purchase volume. Online buying in organizational markets is popular for three reasons. First, organizational buyers depend on timely supplier information that describes product availability, technical specifications, application uses, price, and delivery schedules. This information can be conveyed quickly via Internet technology. Second, this technology substantially reduces buyer order processing costs. Third, business marketers have found that Internet technology can reduce marketing costs, particularly sales and advertising expense, and broaden their customer base. Two developments in online buying have been the creation of e-marketplaces and online auctions. E-marketplaces provide a technology trading platform and a centralized market for buyer–seller transactions and make possible the real-time exchange of information, money, products, and services. These e-marketplaces can be independent trading communities or private exchanges. Online traditional and reverse auctions represent a second major development. With traditional auctions, the highest-priced bidder "wins." Conversely, the lowest-priced bidder "wins" with reverse auctions.

FOCUSING ON KEY TERMS

business marketing p. 120
buy classes p. 128
buying center p. 126
derived demand p. 122

e-marketplaces p. 129
North American Industry Classification System (NAICS) p. 121
organizational buyers p. 120

organizational buying behavior p. 126
traditional auction p. 131
reverse auction p. 131

APPLYING MARKETING KNOWLEDGE

1 Describe the major differences among industrial firms, resellers, and government units in the United States.

2 List and discuss the key characteristics of organizational buying that make it different from consumer buying.

3 What is a buying center? Describe the roles assumed by people in a buying center and what useful questions should be raised to guide any analysis of the structure and behavior of a buying center.

4 A firm that is marketing multimillion-dollar wastewater treatment systems to cities has been unable to sell a new type of system. This setback has occurred even though the firm's systems are cheaper than competitive systems and meet U.S. Environmental Protection Agency (EPA) specifications. To date, the firm's marketing efforts have been directed to city purchasing departments and the various state EPAs to get on approved bidder's lists. Talks with city-employed personnel have indicated that the new system is very different from current systems and therefore city sanitary and sewer department engineers, directors of these two departments, and city council members are unfamiliar with the workings of the system. Consulting engineers, hired by cities to work on the engineering and design features of these systems and paid on a percentage of system cost, are also reluctant to favor the new system. (*a*) What roles do the various individuals play in the purchase process for a wastewater treatment system? (*b*) How could the firm improve the marketing effort behind the new system?

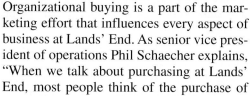

building your marketing plan

Your marketing plan may need an estimate of the size of the market potential or industry potential (see Chapter 8) for a particular product-market in which you compete. Use these steps:

1 Define the product-market precisely, such as ice cream.

2 Visit the NAICS Web site at www.census.gov.

3 Click "NAICS" and enter a keyword that describes your product-market (e.g., ice cream).

4 Follow the instructions to the specific NAICS code and economic census data that detail the dollar sales and provide the estimate of market or industry potential.

video case 6   Lands' End: Where Buyers Rule

Organizational buying is a part of the marketing effort that influences every aspect of business at Lands' End. As senior vice president of operations Phil Schaecher explains, "When we talk about purchasing at Lands' End, most people think of the purchase of merchandise for resale, but we buy many other things aside from merchandise, everything from the simplest office supply to the most sophisticated piece of material-handling equipment." As a result, Lands' End has developed a sophisticated approach to organizational buying, which is one of the keys to its success.

THE COMPANY

The company started by selling sailboat equipment, duffle bags, rainsuits, and sweaters from a basement location in Chicago's old tannery district. In its first catalog, the company name was printed with a typing error—the apostrophe in the wrong place—but the fledgling company couldn't afford to correct and reprint it. So ever since, the company name has been Lands' End—with the misplaced apostrophe.

When the company outgrew its Chicago location, founder Gary Comer relocated it to Dodgeville, Wisconsin, where he had fallen in love with the rolling hills and changing seasons. The original business ideas were simple: "Sell only things we believe in, ship every order the day it arrives, and unconditionally guarantee everything." Over time, the company developed eight principles of doing business:

- Never reduce the quality of a product to make it cheaper.
- Price products fairly and honestly.
- Accept any return for any reason.
- Ship items in stock the day after the order is received.
- What is best for the customer is best for Lands' End.
- Place contracts with manufacturers who are cost-conscious and efficient.
- Operate efficiently.
- Encourage customers to shop in whatever way they find most convenient.

These principles became the guidelines for the company's dedicated local employees and helped create extraordinary expectations from Lands' End customers.

Today, Lands' End is one of the world's largest direct merchants of traditionally styled clothing for the family, soft luggage, and products for the home. The products are offered through catalogs, on the Internet, and in retail stores. In one year, Lands' End distributes more than 200 million catalogs designed for specific segments, including *The Lands' End Catalog, Lands' End Men, Lands' End Plus Size Collection, Lands' End Kids, Lands' End for School Uniforms, Lands' End Home,* and *Lands' End Business Outfitters.* In a typical day, catalog shoppers place more than 40,000 telephone calls to the company. The Lands' End Web site (www.landsend .com) also offers every Lands' End product and a wide variety of Internet shopping innovations such as a 3-D model customized to each customer (called My Virtual Model™); individually tailored clothes (called Lands' End Custom™); and a feature that allows customers to "chat" online directly with a customer service representative (called Lands' End Live™). Lands' End also operates stores in the United States, the United Kingdom, Germany, and Japan. Selected Lands' End merchandise is also sold in Sears stores, following the purchase of Lands' End by Sears in 2002.

The company's goal is to please customers with the highest levels of quality and service in the industry. Lands' End maintains the high quality of its products through several important activities. For example, the company works directly with mills and manufacturers to retain control of quality and design. "The biggest difference between Lands' End and some other retailers or catalog businesses is that we actually design all the product here and we do all the specifications. Therefore, the manufacturer is building that product directly to our specs, we are not buying off of somebody else's line," explains Joan Mudget, vice president of quality assurance. In addition, Lands' End tests its products for comfort and fit by paying real people (local residents and children) to "wear-test" and "fit-test" all types of garments.

Service has also become an important part of the Lands' End reputation. Customers expect prompt, professional service at every step—initiating the order, making selections, shipping, and follow-up (if necessary). Some of the ways Lands' End meets these expectations include offering the simplest guarantee in the industry— "Guaranteed. Period."—toll-free telephone lines open 24 hours a day, 364 days a year, continuous product training for telephone representatives, and two-day shipping. Lands' End operators even send personal responses to all e-mail messages, approximately 230,000 per year.

ORGANIZATIONAL BUYING AT LANDS' END

The sixth Lands' End business principle (described earlier) is accomplished through the company's organizational buying process. First, its buyers specify fabric quality, construction, and sizing standards, which typically exceed industry standards, for current and potential Lands' End products. Then the buyers literally search around the world for the best possible source of fabrics and products. Once a potential supplier is identified, one of the company's 150 quality assurance personnel makes an information-gathering visit. The purpose of the visit is to understand the supplier's values, to assess four criteria (economic, quality, service, and vendor), and to determine if the Lands' End standards can be achieved.

Lands' End evaluations of potential suppliers lead to the selection of what the company hopes will become long-term partners. As Mudget explains, "When we're looking for new manufacturers we are looking for the long term. I think one of the most interesting things is we're not out there looking for new vendors every year to fill the same products." In fact, Lands' End believes that the term *supplier* does not adequately describe the importance the company places on the relationships. Lands' End suppliers are viewed as allies, supporters, associates, colleagues, and stakeholders in the future of the company. Once an alliance is formed the product specifications and the performance on those specifications are regularly evaluated.

Lands' End buyers face a variety of buying situations. Straight rebuys involve reordering an existing product— such as shipping boxes—without evaluating or changing specifications. Modified rebuys involve changing some aspect of a previously ordered product—such as the collar of a knit shirt—based on input from consumers, retailers, or other people involved in the purchase decision. Finally, new buys involve first-time purchases—such as Lands' End's addition of men's suits to its product line. The complexity of the process can vary with the type of purchase. Schaecher explains, "As you get more complicated in the purchase there are more things you look at to decide on a vendor."

FUTURE CHALLENGES FOR LANDS' END

Lands' End faces several challenges as it pursues improvements in its organizational buying process. First, new technologies offer opportunities for fast, efficient, and accurate communication with suppliers. Ed Smidebush, general inventory manager, describes a new system at Lands' End: "Our quick response system is a computerized system where we transmit electronically to our vendors each Sunday night, forecast information as well as stock positions and purchase order information so that on Monday morning this information will be incorporated directly into their manufacturing reports so that they can prioritize their production." Occasionally Lands' End must work with its suppliers to improve their technology and information system capabilities.

Another challenge for Lands' End is to anticipate changes in consumer interests. While it has many years of experience with retail consumers, preferences for colors, fabrics, and styles change frequently, requiring buyers to constantly monitor the marketplace. In addition, Lands' End's more recent offerings to corporate customers require constant attention "because business customers' wants and incentives, and the environment in which they're shopping, are very different from consumers at home," explains marketing manager Hilary Kleese.

Finally, Lands' End must anticipate the quantities of each of its products consumers are likely to order. To do this, historical information is used to develop forecasts. One of the best tests of their forecast accuracy is the holiday season, when Lands' End receives more than 100,000 calls each day. Having the right products available is important because, as every employee knows from Principle 4, every order must be shipped the day after it is received.

Questions

1 *(a)* Who is likely to comprise the buying center in the decision to select a new supplier for Lands' End? *(b)* Which of the buying center members are likely to play the roles of users, influencers, buyers, deciders, and gatekeepers?

2 *(a)* Which stages of the organizational buying decision process does Lands' End follow when it selects a new supplier? *(b)* What selection criteria does the company utilize in the process?

3 Describe the types of purchases Lands' End buyers typically face in each of the three buying situations: straight rebuy, modified rebuy, and new buy.

I CHOOSE TO
TAKE MY OWN PATH
I CHOOSE DELL

It was an unlikely pairing. By marrying tradition and technology, Anupam gave life to a whole new way for Indians to find love. Shaadi now caters to two million members and is a household name in matrimonial services. Shaadi relies on secure and highly scalable Dell PowerEdge™ 2900 Servers, powered by Intel® Xeon® Processors, to match its ever-growing data management needs.

Anupam Mittal
Creator of popular marriage website, Shaadi.com and Founder of People Group

What's your path?

SMS 'TYOP6' TO 56767
TAKEYOUROWNPATH.COM

(intel)
Xeon
inside
Powerful.
Efficient.

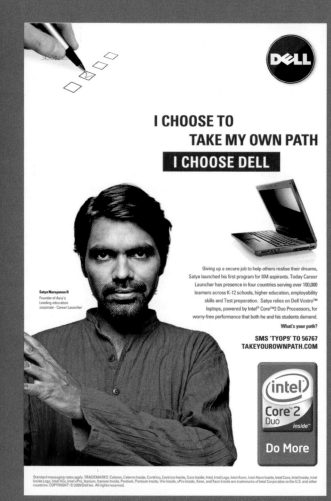

I CHOOSE TO
TAKE MY OWN PATH
I CHOOSE DELL

Giving up a secure job to help others realise their dreams, Satya launched his first program for IIM aspirants. Today Career Launcher has presence in four countries serving over 100,000 learners across K-12 schools, higher education, employability skills and Test preparation. Satya relies on Dell Vostro™ laptops, powered by Intel® Core™2 Duo Processors, for worry-free performance that both he and his students demand.

Satya Narayanan R
Founder of Asia's leading education corporate - Career Launcher

What's your path?

SMS 'TYOP9' TO 56767
TAKEYOUROWNPATH.COM

(intel)
Core™2
Duo
inside
Do More

I CHOOSE TO
TAKE MY OWN PATH
I CHOOSE DELL

Believing in empowering kids with computer skills, Kishore turned his vision into one of the largest education systems in the world. Today, he provides virtual and interactive learning classrooms to over 40,000 schools in India. Kishore uses reliable Dell Vostro™ 220 Desktops, powered by Intel® Core™2 Duo Processors, to keep his business at the top of its class.

P. Kishore
Founder of Everonn Systems, Pioneer in computerising school education

What's your path?

SMS 'TYOP8' TO 56767
TAKEYOUROWNPATH.COM

(intel)
Core™2
Duo
inside
Do More

I CHOOSE TO
TAKE MY OWN PATH
I CHOOSE DELL

With a relentless passion to bring enjoyment to people, Neeraj created India's most popular music, video, and gaming entertainment portals. Today, Hungama is the leading South Asian mobile and digital content publisher. Neeraj trusts Dell PowerEdge™ 2950 Servers, powered by Intel® Xeon® Processors, for their high-speed performance to keep up with his fast-paced business.

Neeraj Roy
CEO of Hungama, India's premier digital and mobile entertainment company

What's your path?

SMS 'TYOP7' TO 56767
TAKEYOUROWNPATH.COM

(intel)
Xeon
inside
Powerful.
Efficient.

7

Understanding and Reaching Global Consumers and Markets

LEARNING OBJECTIVES

After reading this chapter you should be able to:

LO1 Identify the major trends that have influenced world trade and global marketing.

LO2 Identify the environmental forces that shape global marketing efforts.

LO3 Name and describe the alternative approaches companies use to enter global markets.

LO4 Explain the distinction between standardization and customization when companies craft worldwide marketing programs.

DELL'S QUEST FOR GROWTH IN EMERGING ECONOMIES

Why has Dell, Inc., embarked on a bold global growth initiative? Simply put, "Our success is going to be largely dependent on our ability to expand globally," says Steve Felice, president of Dell Asia Pacific and Japan.

Dell's global initiative focuses on emerging economies in Asia, Africa, and Latin America. Compared with mature economies in North America and Western Europe, emerging economies offer significant growth potential, according to Michael Dell, Dell's founder and chief executive officer.

Dell's global initiative is bold in its departure from prior product development practices and in its change to its sales and distribution strategy. The company now designs low-cost notebook and desktop personal computers for customers in China, India, and other emerging economies. "We used to design products for global requirements and distribute the same product globally," says Felice. "In this situation, we started with talking to emerging country customers, designing a product for emerging countries, and initially launching the product in only emerging countries. That's a big departure in our strategy."

Dell's signature direct sales and distribution strategy has broadened as part of its global growth initiative. The company built its U.S. business with telephone- and Internet-based sales without retailers. In emerging economies, however, customers prefer to see, touch, and use a personal computer before they buy. Also, credit cards aren't widespread and customers are often leery of purchasing personal computers online or over the phone. In response, Dell has opened "experience centers" to help customers get comfortable with "buying direct." More boldly, the company decided to distribute its products through electronics retailers to reach more buyers quickly. Commenting on this move, Felice says: "These [emerging] economies are growing so fast that we didn't want to miss out on the opportunity. But if we just use the direct model, it might take us too long to get there." Dell's global growth initiative illustrates the importance of understanding global customers and reaching them by adapting to their needs.[1]

This chapter describes today's complex and dynamic global marketing environment. It begins with an overview of world trade and the emergence of a borderless economic world. Attention is then focused on prominent cultural, economic, and political-regulatory factors that present both an opportunity and a challenge for global marketers. Four major global market entry strategies are then detailed. Finally, the task of designing, implementing, and evaluating worldwide marketing programs for companies such as Dell, Inc., is described.

DYNAMICS OF WORLD TRADE

LO1

The dollar value of world trade has more than doubled in the past decade, despite the recent recession. Manufactured goods and commodities account for 75 percent of world trade. Service industries, including telecommunications, transportation, insurance, education, banking, and tourism, represent the other 25 percent of world trade. Four trends have significantly affected world trade and global marketing:

Trend 1: Gradual decline of economic protectionism by individual countries.

Trend 2: Formal economic integration and free trade among nations.

Trend 3: Global competition among global companies for global customers.

Trend 4: Development of networked global marketspace.

Decline of Economic Protectionism

protectionism

The practice of shielding one or more industries within a country's economy from foreign competition through the use of tariffs or quotas.

Protectionism is the practice of shielding one or more industries within a country's economy from foreign competition, usually through the use of tariffs or quotas. The economic argument for protectionism is that it preserves jobs, protects a nation's political security, discourages economic dependency on other countries, and encourages the development of domestic industries.

tariff

A government tax on goods or services entering a country, primarily serving to raise prices on imports.

A **tariff** is a tax on goods or services entering a country. Because a tariff raises the price of an imported product, tariffs give a price advantage to domestic products competing in the same market. The effect of tariffs on world trade and consumer prices is substantial.[2] Consider U.S. rice exports to Japan. The U.S. Rice Millers' Association claims that if the Japanese rice market were opened to imports by lowering tariffs, lower prices would save Japanese consumers $6 billion annually, and the United States would gain a large share of the Japanese rice market. Similarly, tariffs imposed on bananas by Western European countries cost consumers $2 billion a year, and U.S. consumers pay $5 billion annually for tariffs on imported shoes.

quota

A restriction placed on the amount of a product allowed to enter or leave a country.

A **quota** is a restriction placed on the amount of a product allowed to enter or leave a country. By limiting the supply of foreign products, an import quota helps domestic industries retain a certain percentage of the domestic market. For consumers, however, the limited supply may mean higher prices for domestic products. The best-known quota concerns the limits of foreign automobile sales in many countries. Less visible quotas apply to the importation of mushrooms, heavy motorcycles, textiles, color TVs, and sugar. For example, U.S. sugar import quotas have existed for over 50 years and preserve about half of the U.S. sugar market for domestic producers. American consumers pay almost $2 billion annually in extra food costs because of this quota.

World Trade Organization

Institution that sets rules governing trade between its members through a panel of trade experts.

Both tariffs and quotas discourage world trade (Figure 7–1). As a result, the major industrialized nations of the world formed the **World Trade Organization** (WTO) in 1995 to address a broad array of world trade issues. The 153 member countries of the WTO, which includes the United States, account for more than 97 percent of world trade.[3] The WTO sets rules governing trade between its members through panels of trade experts who decide on trade disputes between members and issue binding decisions. The WTO reviews more than 200 disputes each year.

Rise of Economic Integration

In recent years, a number of countries with similar economic goals have formed transnational trade groups or signed trade agreements for the purpose of promoting free trade among member nations and enhancing their individual economies. Two of the best-known examples are the European Union (or simply EU) and the North American Free Trade Agreement (NAFTA).

FIGURE 7–1
How does protectionism affect world trade? Protectionism hinders world trade through tariff and quota policies of individual countries. Tariffs increase prices and quotas limit supply.

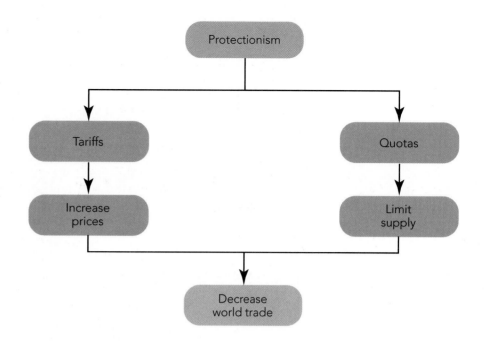

European Union The European Union consists of 27 member countries that have eliminated most barriers to the free flow of goods, services, capital, and labor across their borders (see Figure 7–2 on the next page).[4] This single market houses more than 500 million consumers with a combined gross domestic product larger than that of the United States. In addition, 16 countries have adopted a common currency called the *euro*. Adoption of the euro has been a boon to electronic commerce in the EU by eliminating the need to continually monitor currency exchange rates.

The EU creates abundant marketing opportunities because firms no longer find it necessary to market their products and services on a nation-by-nation basis. Rather, pan-European marketing strategies are possible due to greater uniformity in product and packaging standards; fewer regulatory restrictions on transportation, advertising, and promotion imposed by countries; and the removal of most tariffs that affect pricing practices. For example, Colgate-Palmolive Company now markets its Colgate toothpaste with one formula and package across EU countries at one price. Black & Decker—the maker of electrical hand tools, appliances, and other consumer products—now produces 8, not 20, motor sizes for the European market, resulting in production and marketing cost savings. These practices were previously impossible with different government and trade regulations. Europeanwide distribution from fewer locations is also feasible given open borders. French tire maker Michelin has closed 180 of its European distribution centers and now uses just 20 to serve all EU countries.

North American Free Trade Agreement The North American Free Trade Agreement (NAFTA) lifted many trade barriers between Canada, Mexico, and the United States and created a marketplace with more than 450 million consumers.[5] NAFTA has stimulated trade flows among member nations as well as cross-border retailing, manufacturing, and investment. For example, NAFTA paved the way for Walmart to move to Mexico and Mexican supermarket giant Gigante to move into the United States. Whirlpool Corporation's Canadian subsidiary stopped making washing machines in Canada and moved that operation to Ohio. Whirlpool then shifted the production of kitchen ranges and compact dryers to Canada. Ford invested $60 million in its Mexico City manufacturing plant to produce smaller cars and light trucks for global sales.

FIGURE 7–2
The European Union in late
2010 consists of 27 countries
with more than 500 million
consumers.

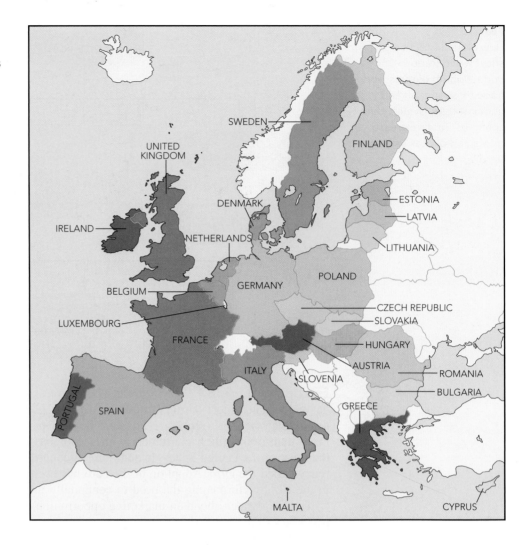

A recent comprehensive free trade agreement among Costa Rica, the Dominican Republic, El Salvador, Guatemala, Honduras, Nicaragua, and the United States extended many NAFTA benefits to Central American countries and the Dominican Republic. Called CAFTA-DR, this agreement is viewed as a step toward a 34-country Free Trade Area of the Americas for the Western Hemisphere.

A New Reality: Global Competition among Global Companies for Global Consumers

The emergence of a largely borderless economic world has created a new reality for marketers of all shapes and sizes. Today, world trade is driven by global competition among global companies for global consumers.

global competition

Exists when firms originate, produce, and market their products and services worldwide.

Global Competition **Global competition** exists when firms originate, produce, and market their products and services worldwide. The automobile, pharmaceutical, apparel, electronics, aerospace, and telecommunication fields represent well-known industries with sellers and buyers on every continent. Other industries that are increasingly global in scope include soft drinks, cosmetics, ready-to-eat cereals, snack chips, and retailing.

Global competition broadens the competitive landscape for marketers. The familiar "cola war" waged by Pepsi-Cola and Coca-Cola in the United States has

Pepsi-Cola, now available in more than 190 countries and territories, accounts for a quarter of all soft drinks sold internationally. This Brazilian ad—"How to make jeans last 10 years"—features the popular Diet Pepsi brand targeted at weight-conscious consumers.

been repeated around the world, including India, China, and Argentina. Procter & Gamble's Pampers and Kimberly-Clark's Huggies have taken their disposable diaper rivalry from the United States to Western Europe. Boeing and Europe's Airbus vie for lucrative commercial aircraft contracts on virtually every continent.

Global Companies Three types of companies populate and compete in the global marketplace: (1) international firms, (2) multinational firms, and (3) transnational firms.[6] All three employ people in different countries, and many have administrative, marketing, and manufacturing operations (often called *divisions* or *subsidiaries*) around the world. However, a firm's orientation toward and strategy for global markets and marketing defines the type of company it is.

An *international firm* engages in trade and marketing in different countries as an extension of the marketing strategy in its home country. Generally speaking, these firms market their existing products and services in other countries the same way they do in their home country. Avon, for example, successfully distributes its product line through direct selling in Asia, Europe, and South America, employing virtually the same marketing strategy used in the United States.

A *multinational firm* views the world as consisting of unique parts and markets to each part differently. Multinationals use a **multidomestic marketing strategy**, which means that they have as many different product variations, brand names, and advertising programs as countries in which they do business. For example, Lever Europe, a division of Unilever, markets its fabric softener known as Snuggle in the United States in 10 European countries under seven brand names, including Kuschelweich in Germany, Coccolino in Italy, and Mimosin in France. These products have different packages, different advertising programs, and occasionally different formulas. Procter & Gamble markets Mr. Clean, its popular multipurpose cleaner, in North America and Asia. But you won't necessarily find the Mr. Clean brand in other parts of the world. In many Latin American countries, Mr. Clean is Mastro Limpio. Mr. Clean is Mr. Proper in most parts of Europe, Africa, and the Middle East.

A *transnational firm* views the world as one market and emphasizes universal consumer needs and wants more than differences among cultures. Transnational marketers employ a **global marketing strategy**—the practice of standardizing marketing activities when there are cultural similarities and adapting them when cultures differ.

multidomestic marketing strategy

A multinational firm's strategy of offering as many different product variations, brand names, and advertising programs as countries in which it does business.

global marketing strategy

The practice of standardizing marketing activities when there are cultural similarities and adapting them when cultures differ.

Marketing Matters > > > > > > customer value

The Global Teenager—A Market of 2 Billion Voracious Consumers with $200 Billion to Spend

The "global teenager" market consists of 2 billion 13- to 19-year-olds in Europe, North and South America, and industrialized nations of Asia and the Pacific Rim who have experienced intense exposure to television (MTV broadcasts in 169 countries in 33 languages), movies, travel, the Internet, and global advertising by companies such as Apple, Sony, Nike, and Coca-Cola. The similarities among teens across these countries are greater than their differences. For example, a global study of middle-class teenagers' rooms in 25 industrialized countries indicated it was difficult, if not impossible, to tell whether the rooms were in Los Angeles, Mexico City, Tokyo, Rio de Janeiro, Sydney, or Paris. Why? Teens spend $200 billion annually for a common gallery of products: Nintendo video games, Tommy Hilfiger apparel, Levi's blue jeans, Nike and

Adidas athletic shoes, Swatch watches, Apple iPods, Benneton apparel (shown in the photo), and Procter & Gamble Clearasil facial medicine.

Teenagers around the world appreciate fashion and music and desire novelty and trendier designs and images. They also acknowledge an Americanization of fashion and culture based on another study of 6,500 teens in 26 countries. When asked what country had the most influence on their attitudes and purchase behavior, 54 percent of teens from the United States, 87 percent of those from Latin America, 80 percent of the Europeans, and 80 percent of those from Asia named the United States. This phenomenon has not gone unnoticed by parents. As one parent in India said, "Now the youngsters dress, talk, and eat like Americans."

Global marketing strategies are popular among many business-to-business marketers such as Caterpillar and Komatsu (heavy construction equipment) and Texas Instruments, Intel, Hitachi, and Motorola (semiconductors). Consumer goods marketers such as Timex, Seiko, and Swatch (watches), Coca-Cola and Pepsi-Cola (cola soft drinks), Mattel and Lego (children's toys), Gillette (personal care products), L'Oréal and Shiseido (cosmetics), and McDonald's (quick-service restaurants) successfully execute this strategy.

global brand

A brand marketed under the same name in multiple countries with similar and centrally coordinated marketing programs.

Each of these companies markets a **global brand**—a brand marketed under the same name in multiple countries with similar and centrally coordinated marketing programs.[7] Global brands have the same product formulation or service concept, deliver the same benefits to consumers, and use consistent advertising across multiple countries and cultures. This isn't to say that global brands are not sometimes tailored to specific cultures or countries. However, adaptation is only used when necessary to better connect the brand to consumers in different markets.

Consider McDonald's.[8] This global marketer has adapted its proven formula of "food, fun, and families" across 118 countries on six continents. Although the Golden Arches and Ronald McDonald appear worldwide, McDonald's tailors other aspects of its marketing program. It serves beer in Germany, wine in France, and coconut, mango, and tropical mint shakes in Hong Kong. Hamburgers are made with different meat and spices in Japan, Thailand, India, and the Philippines. But McDonald's

Sweden's IKEA is capitalizing on the home-improvement trend sweeping through China. The home-furnishings retailer is courting young Chinese consumers who are eagerly updating their housing with modern, colorful, but inexpensive furniture. IKEA entered China in 1998 and now has stores in all major Chinese cities.

global consumers

Consumer groups living around the world who have similar needs or seek similar benefits from products or services.

world-famous french fry is standardized. Its french fry in Beijing, China, tastes like the one in Paris, France, which tastes like the one in your neighborhood.

Global Consumers   Global competition among global companies often focuses on the identification and pursuit of global consumers, as described in the Marketing Matters box.[9] **Global consumers** consist of consumer groups living in many countries or regions of the world who have similar needs or seek similar features and benefits from products or services.

Evidence suggests the presence of a global middle-income class, a youth market, and an elite segment, each consuming or using a common assortment of products and services, regardless of geographic location. A variety of companies have capitalized on the global consumer. Whirlpool, Sony, and IKEA have benefited from the growing global middle-income class desire for kitchen appliances, consumer electronics, and home furnishings, respectively. Levi's, Nike, Coca-Cola, and Apple have tapped the global youth market. DeBeers, Chanel, Gucci, Rolls-Royce, and Sotheby's and Christie's, the world's largest fine art and antique auction houses, cater to the elite segment for luxury goods worldwide.

Emergence of a Networked Global Marketspace

The use of Internet technology as a tool for exchanging goods, services, and information on a global scale is the fourth trend affecting world trade. Over 1.7 billion businesses, educational institutions, government agencies, and households worldwide are expected to have Internet access by 2012. The broad reach of this technology suggests that its potential for promoting world trade is huge.

The promise of a networked global marketspace is that it enables the exchange of goods, services, and information from companies *anywhere* to customers *anywhere* at *any time* and at a lower cost. This promise has become a reality for buyers and sellers in industrialized countries that possess the telecommunications infrastructure necessary to support Internet technology.

Marketers recognize that the networked global marketspace offers unprecedented access to prospective buyers on every continent. Companies that have successfully capitalized on this access manage multiple country and language Web sites that customize content and communicate with consumers in their native tongue. Nestlé, the world's largest packaged food manufacturer, coffee roaster, and chocolate maker, is a case in point. The company operates 65 individual country Web sites in more than 20 languages that span five continents.

Nestlé is an innovator in customizing Web site content and communicating with consumers in their native languages. The Web site shown here is for Hungary.

learning review

1. What is protectionism?

2. The North American Free Trade Agreement was designed to promote free trade among which countries?

3. What is the difference between a multidomestic marketing strategy and a global marketing strategy?

A GLOBAL ENVIRONMENTAL SCAN

LO2

Global companies conduct continuing environmental scans of the five environmental forces described earlier in Figure 3–1 (social, economic, technological, competitive, and regulatory forces). This section focuses on three kinds of uncontrollable environmental variables—cultural, economic, and political-regulatory—that affect global marketing practices in strikingly different ways than those in domestic markets.

Cultural Diversity

cross-cultural analysis
The study of similarities and differences among consumers in two or more nations or societies.

Marketers must be sensitive to the cultural underpinnings of different societies if they are to initiate and consummate mutually beneficial exchange relationships with global consumers. A necessary step in this process is **cross-cultural analysis**, which involves the study of similarities and differences among consumers in two or more nations or societies.[10] A thorough cross-cultural analysis involves an understanding of and an appreciation for the values, customs, symbols, and languages of other societies.

values
A society's personally or socially preferable modes of conduct or states of existence that tend to persist over time.

Values A society's **values** represent personally or socially preferable modes of conduct or states of existence that tend to persist over time. Understanding and working with these aspects of a society are important factors in global marketing. For example,

- McDonald's does not sell beef hamburgers in its restaurants in India because the cow is considered sacred by almost 85 percent of the population. Instead,

McDonald's sells its popular Maharaja Mac in India. Read the text to discover its ingredients.

customs

Norms and expectations about the way people do things in a specific country.

Foreign Corrupt Practices Act (1977)

A law that makes it a crime for U.S. corporations to bribe an official of a foreign government or political party to obtain or retain business.

cultural symbols

Things that represent ideas or concepts in a specific culture.

Cultural symbols evoke deep feelings. What cultural lesson did Coca-Cola executives learn when they used the Eiffel Tower and the Parthenon in a global advertising campaign? Read the text to find the answer.

McDonald's sells the Maharaja Mac: two all-chicken patties, special sauce, lettuce, cheese, pickles, and onions on a sesame-seed bun.

- Germans have not been overly receptive to the use of credit cards such as Visa or MasterCard and installment debt to purchase goods and services. Indeed, the German word for debt, *Schuld,* is the same as the German word for guilt.

Customs **Customs** refer to the normal and expected ways of doing things in a specific country. Clearly customs can vary significantly from country to country. Some other customs may seem unusual to Americans. Consider, for example, that in France, men wear more than twice the number of cosmetics than women do and that Japanese women give Japanese men chocolates on Valentine's Day.

The custom of giving token business gifts is popular in many countries where they are expected and accepted. However, bribes, kickbacks, and payoffs offered to entice someone to commit an illegal or improper act on behalf of the giver for economic gain is considered corrupt in any culture. The prevalence of bribery in global marketing has led to an agreement among the world's major exporting nations to make bribery of foreign government officials a criminal offense. This agreement is patterned after the **Foreign Corrupt Practices Act (1977)**, as amended by the *International Anti-Dumping and Fair Competition Act* (1998). These acts make it a crime for U.S. corporations to bribe an official of a foreign government or political party to obtain or retain business in a foreign country. For example, the German engineering company Siemens AG paid an $800 million fine for $1 billion in alleged bribes of government officials around the globe.[11]

Cultural Symbols **Cultural symbols** are things that represent ideas and concepts in a specific culture. Symbols and symbolism play an important role in cross-cultural analysis because different cultures attach different meanings to things. By cleverly using cultural symbols, global marketers can tie positive symbolism to their products, services, and brands to enhance their attractiveness to consumers. However, improper use of symbols can spell disaster. A culturally sensitive global marketer will know that[12]

- North Americans are superstitious about the number 13, and Japanese feel the same way about the number 4. *Shi,* the Japanese word for four, is also the word for death. Knowing this, Tiffany & Company sells its fine glassware and china in sets of five, not four, in Japan.
- "Thumbs-up" is a positive sign in the United States. However, in Russia and Poland, this gesture has an offensive meaning when the palm of the hand is

What does the Nestlé Kit Kat bar have to do with academic achievement in Japan? Read the text to find out.

Microsoft operates in over 100 countries and more often than not speaks to its customers in their own language. Read the text to learn how langage affects global marketing.

shown, as AT&T learned. The company reversed the gesture depicted in ads, showing the back of the hand, not the palm.

Cultural symbols evoke deep feelings. Consider how executives at Coca-Cola Company's Italian office learned this lesson. In a series of advertisements directed at Italian vacationers, the Eiffel Tower, the Empire State Building, and the Tower of Pisa were turned into the familiar Coca-Cola bottle. However, when the white marble columns in the Parthenon that crowns the Acropolis in Athens were turned into Coca-Cola bottles, the Greeks were outraged. Greeks refer to the Acropolis as the "holy rock," and a government official said the Parthenon is an "international symbol of excellence" and that "whoever insults the Parthenon insults international culture." Coca-Cola apologized for the ad.[13]

Language   Global marketers should know not only the native tongues of countries in which they market their products and services but also the nuances and idioms of a language. Even though about 100 official languages exist in the world, anthropologists estimate that at least 3,000 different languages are spoken. There are 23 official languages spoken in the European Union, and Canada has two official languages (English and French). Seventeen major languages are spoken in India alone.

English, French, and Spanish are the principal languages used in global diplomacy and commerce. However, the best language to use to communicate with consumers is their own, as any seasoned global marketer will attest to. Unintended meanings of brand names and messages have ranged from the absurd to the obscene:

- When the advertising agency responsible for launching Procter & Gamble's successful Pert shampoo in Canada realized that the name means "lost" in French, it substituted the brand name Pret, which means "ready."
- The Vicks brand name common in the United States is German slang for sexual intimacy; therefore, Vicks is called Wicks in Germany.

The Coca-Cola Company has made a huge financial investment in bottling and distribution facilities in Russia. The company derives about 83 percent of its profits from outside North America.

back translation

Retranslating a word or phrase back into the original language using a different interpreter to catch errors.

Experienced global marketers use **back translation**, where a translated word or phrase is retranslated into the original language by a different interpreter to catch errors. For example, IBM's first Japanese translation of its "Solution for a small planet" advertising message yielded "Answers that make people smaller." The error was caught and corrected. Nevertheless, unintended translations can produce favorable results. Consider Kit Kat bars marketed by Nestlé worldwide. Kit Kat is pronounced "kitto katsu" in Japanese, which roughly translates to "I will win." Japanese teens eat Kit Kat bars for good luck, particularly when taking crucial school exams.[14]

Economic Considerations

Global marketing is also affected by economic considerations. Therefore, a scan of the global marketplace should include (1) an assessment of the economic infrastructure in different countries, (2) measurement of consumer income in different countries, and (3) recognition of a country's currency exchange rates.

Economic Infrastructure   The *economic infrastructure*—a country's communications, transportation, financial, and distribution systems—is a critical consideration in determining whether to try to market to a country's consumers and organizations. Parts of the infrastructure that North Americans or Western Europeans take for granted can present huge problems elsewhere—not only in developing nations but even in Eastern Europe, the Indian subcontinent, and China, where such an infrastructure is assumed to be in place. For example, PepsiCo intends to invest $1.5 billion beginning in 2010 for transportation, manufacturing, and distribution systems in China and India.[15]

The communication infrastructures in these countries also differ. This infrastructure includes telecommunication systems and networks in use, such as telephones, cable television, broadcast radio and television, computer, satellite, and wireless telephones. In general, the communication infrastructure in many developing countries is limited or antiquated compared with that of developed countries.

Even the financial and legal system can cause problems. Formal operating procedures among financial institutions and the notion of private property are still limited. As a consequence, for example, it is estimated that two-thirds of the commercial transactions in Russia involve nonmonetary forms of payment. The legal red tape involved in obtaining titles to buildings and land for manufacturing, wholesaling, and retailing operations also has been a huge problem. Nevertheless, at least three corporations have made the decision to invest in facilities located in Russia; the Coca-Cola Company has invested $750 million to build bottling and distribution facilities; Frito-Lay has spent $60 million to build a plant to make Lay's potato chips; and Mars has opened a $200 million candy factory outside Moscow.

Consumer Income and Purchasing Power A global marketer selling consumer goods must also consider what the average per capita or household income is among a country's consumers and how the income is distributed to determine a nation's purchasing power. Per capita income varies greatly between nations. Average yearly per capita income in EU countries is about $34,000 and is less than $500 in some developing countries such as Liberia. A country's income distribution is important because it gives a more reliable picture of a country's purchasing power. Generally, as the proportion of middle-income households in a country increases, the greater a nation's purchasing power tends to be.[16]

Seasoned global marketers recognize that people in developing countries often have government subsidies for food, housing, and health care that supplement their income. So people with seemingly low incomes are actually promising customers for a variety of products. For instance, a consumer in South Asia earning the equivalent of $250 per year can afford Gillette razors. When that consumer's income rises to $1,000, a Sony television becomes affordable, and a new Volkswagen or Nissan can be bought with an annual income of $10,000. In developing countries of Eastern Europe, a $1,000 annual income makes a refrigerator affordable, and $2,000 brings an automatic washer within reach—good news for Whirlpool, the world's leading manufacturer and marketer of major home appliances.

Currency Exchange Rates A **currency exchange rate** is the price of one country's currency expressed in terms of another country's currency. As economic conditions change, so can the exchange rate between countries. One day the U.S. dollar may be worth 121.7 Japanese yen or 1.5 Swiss francs. But the next day it may be worth 120.5 Japanese yen or 1.3 Swiss francs.

Fluctuations in exchange rates among the world's currencies can affect everyone from international tourists to global companies. For example, when the U.S. dollar is "strong" against the euro, it takes fewer dollars to purchase goods in the EU. As a result, more U.S. tourists will travel to Europe. This is great news for Europe's travel industry, but bad news for European consumers who want to buy U.S. goods, as they will have to pay more for them. And they may choose not to buy. Mattel learned this lesson the hard way. The company was recently unable to sell its popular Holiday Barbie doll and accessories in many international markets because they were too expensive. Why? Barbie prices, expressed in U.S. dollars, were set without regard for how they would translate into other currencies and were too high for many foreign buyers.[17]

Political-Regulatory Climate

The political and regulatory climate for marketing in a country or region of the world means not only identifying the current climate but determining how long a favorable or unfavorable climate will last. An assessment of a country or regional political-regulatory climate includes an analysis of its political stability and trade regulations.

Political Stability Trade among nations or regions depends on political stability. Billions of dollars have been lost in the Middle East and Africa as a result of internal political strife, terrorism, and war. Losses such as these encourage careful selection of politically stable countries and regions of the world for trade.

Political stability in a country is affected by numerous factors, including a government's orientation toward foreign companies and trade with other countries. These factors combine to create a political climate that is favorable or unfavorable for marketing and financial investment in a country or region of the world.

Trade Regulations   Countries have rules that govern business practices within their borders. These rules often serve as trade barriers.[18] For example, Japan has some 11,000 trade regulations. Japanese car safety rules effectively require all automobile replacement parts to be Japanese and not American or European; public health rules make it illegal to sell aspirin or cold medicine without a pharmacist present. The Malaysian government has regulations stating that "advertisements must not project or promote an excessively aspirational lifestyle," Greece bans toy advertising, Sweden outlaws all advertisements to children, and Saudi Arabia bans Mattel's Barbie dolls because they are a symbol of Western decadence.

learning review

4. Cross-cultural analysis involves the study of _____.

5. When foreign currencies can buy more U.S. dollars, are U.S. products more or less expensive for a foreign consumer?

COMPARING GLOBAL MARKET-ENTRY STRATEGIES

LO3

Once a company has decided to enter the global marketplace, it must select a means of market entry. Four general options exist: (1) exporting, (2) licensing, (3) joint venture, and (4) direct investment.[19] As Figure 7–3 demonstrates, the amount of financial commitment, risk, marketing control, and profit potential increases as the firm moves from exporting to direct investment.

FIGURE 7–3
A firm's profit potential and control over marketing activities increase as it moves from exporting to direct investment as a global market-entry strategy. But so does the firm's financial commitment and risk. Firms often engage in exporting, licensing, and joint ventures before pursuing a direct investment strategy.

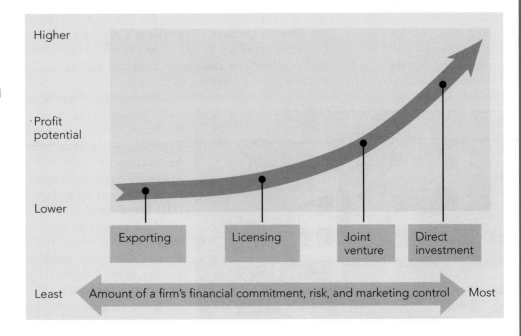

Marketing Matters > > > > entrepreneurship

Creative Cosmetics and Creative Export Marketing in Japan

How does a medium-sized U.S. cosmetics firm sell 1.5 million tubes of lipstick in Japan annually? Fran Wilson Creative Cosmetics can attribute its success to a top-quality product, effective advertising, and a novel export marketing program. The firm's Moodmatcher lip coloring comes in green, orange, silver, black, and six other hues that change to a shade of pink, coral, or red, depending on a woman's chemistry when it's applied.

The company does not sell to department stores. According to a company spokesperson, "Shiseido and Kanebo (two large Japanese cosmetics firms) keep all the other Japanese or import brands out of the major department stores." Rather, the company sells its Moodmatcher lipstick through a network of Japanese distributors that reach Japan's 40,000 beauty salons.

The result? The company, with its savvy Japanese distributors, accounts for 20 percent of the lipsticks exported annually to Japan by U.S. cosmetics companies.

夏くちびるにマッチする。水につよい自然派口紅。

McDonald's uses franchising as a market-entry strategy. Note that the golden arches appear prominently—one aspect of its global brand promise. Read the text to find out what percent of McDonald's sales come from non-U.S. operations.

Exporting

Exporting involves producing goods in one country and selling them in another country. This entry option allows a company to make the least number of changes in terms of its product, its organization, and even its corporate goals.

Indirect exporting is when a firm sells its domestically produced goods in a foreign country through an intermediary. This strategy has the least amount of commitment and risk but will probably return the least profit. Indirect exporting is ideal for a company that has no overseas contacts but wants to market abroad. The intermediary is often a distributer that has the marketing know-how and resources necessary for the effort to succeed. Fran Wilson Creative Cosmetics of New York uses an indirect exporting approach to sell its products in Japan. Read the Marketing Matters box to find out how this innovative marketer and its Japanese distributors sell 20 percent of the lipsticks exported to Japan by U.S. cosmetics companies.[20]

Direct exporting is when a firm sells its domestically produced goods in a foreign country without intermediaries. Most companies become involved in direct exporting when they believe their volume of sales will be sufficiently large and easy to obtain so that they do not require intermediaries. For example, the exporter may be approached by foreign buyers that are willing to contract for a large volume of purchases. Direct exporting involves more risk than indirect exporting for the company but also opens the door to increased profits. The Boeing Company applies a direct exporting approach. Boeing is the world's largest aerospace company and the largest U.S. exporter.

Even though exporting is commonly employed by large firms, it is the prominent global market-entry strat-

Strauss Group's joint venture with PepsiCo markets Frito-Lay's Cheetos, Ruffles, and Doritos and other snacks in Israel.

egy among small- and medium-sized companies. Sixty percent of U.S. firms exporting products have fewer than 100 employees. These firms account for about 20 percent of total U.S. merchandise exports.[21]

Licensing

Under *licensing*, a company offers the right to a trademark, patent, trade secret, or other similarly valued item of intellectual property in return for a royalty or fee. The advantages to the company granting the license are low risk and the chance to enter a foreign market at little cost. The licensee gains information that allows it to start with a competitive advantage. The foreign country gains employment by having the product manufactured locally. For instance, Yoplait yogurt is licensed from Sodima, a French cooperative, by General Mills for sales in the United States.

There are some serious drawbacks to this mode of entry, however. The licensor forgoes control of its product and reduces the potential profits gained from it. In addition, while the relationship lasts, the licensor may be creating its own competition. Some licensees are able to modify the product somehow and enter the market with product and marketing knowledge gained at the expense of the company that got them started. To offset this disadvantage, many companies strive to stay innovative so that the licensee remains dependent on them for improvements and successful operation. Finally, should the licensee prove to be a poor choice, the name or reputation of the company may be harmed.

A variation of licensing is *franchising*. Franchising is one of the fastest-growing market-entry strategies. More than 75,000 franchises of U.S. firms are located in countries throughout the world. Franchises include soft-drink, motel, retailing, fast-food, and car rental operations and a variety of business services. McDonald's is a premier global franchiser. About 66 percent of McDonald's sales come from non-U.S. operations.[22]

Joint Venture

joint venture
When a foreign company and a local firm invest together to create a local business, sharing ownership, control, and the profits of the new company.

When a foreign company and a local firm invest together to create a local business, it is called a **joint venture**. These two companies share ownership, control, and the profits of the new company. For example, Strauss Group has a joint venture with PepsiCo to market Frito-Lay's Cheetos, Ruffles, and Doritos and other snacks in Israel.

The advantages of this option are twofold. First, one company may not have the necessary financial, physical, or managerial resources to enter a foreign market alone. The joint venture between Ericsson, a Swedish telecommunications firm, and CGCT, a French switch maker, enabled them together to beat out AT&T for a $100 million French contract. Ericsson's money and technology combined with CGCT's knowledge of the French market helped them to win the contract that neither of them could have won alone. Similarly, Ford and Volkswagen formed a joint venture to make four-wheel-drive vehicles in Portugal. Second, a government may require or strongly encourage a joint venture before it allows a foreign company to enter its market. This is the case in China, where thousands of Chinese-foreign joint ventures exist.

The disadvantages arise when the two companies disagree about policies or courses of action for their joint venture or when governmental bureaucracy bogs down the effort. For example, U.S. firms often prefer to reinvest earnings gained, whereas some foreign companies may want to spend those earnings. Or a U.S. firm may want to return profits earned to the United States, while the local firm or its government may oppose this—the problem faced by many potential joint ventures in Eastern Europe, Russia, Latin America, and South Asia.

Nestlé has made a sizable direct investment in ice cream manufacturing in China to produce its global brands such as Drumstick. Nestlé operates 26 factories in China.

Direct Investment

The biggest commitment a company can make when entering the global market is **direct investment**, which entails a domestic firm actually investing in and owning a foreign subsidiary or division. Examples of direct investment are Nissan's Smyrna, Tennessee, plant that produces pickup trucks and the Mercedes-Benz factory in Vance, Alabama, that makes the M-class sport-utility vehicle. Many U.S.-based global companies also use this mode of entry. Reebok entered Russia by creating a subsidiary known as Reebok Russia.

For many companies, direct investment often follows one of the other three market-entry strategies. For example, both FedEx and UPS entered China through joint ventures with Chinese companies. Each subsequently purchased the interests of its partner and converted the Chinese operations into a division.[23]

The advantages to direct investment include cost savings, a better understanding of local market conditions, and fewer local restrictions. Firms entering foreign markets using direct investment believe that these advantages outweigh the financial commitments and risks involved, such as the possible nationalization of assets.

---

learning review

6. What mode of entry could a company follow if it has no previous experience in global marketing?

7. How does licensing differ from a joint venture?

CRAFTING A WORLDWIDE MARKETING PROGRAM

LO4

The choice of a market-entry strategy is a necessary first step for a marketer when joining the community of global companies. The next step involves the challenging task of designing, implementing, and evaluating marketing programs worldwide.

Successful global marketers standardize global marketing programs whenever possible and customize them wherever necessary. The extent of standardization and

FIGURE 7–4

Five product and promotion strategies for global marketing exist based on whether a company extends or adapts its product and promotion message for consumers in different countries and cultures.

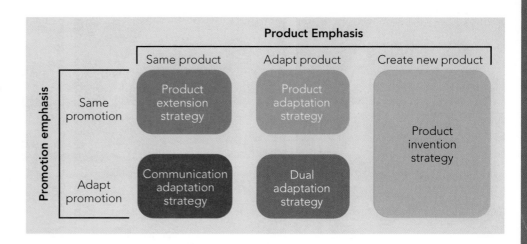

customization is often rooted in a careful global environment scan supplemented with judgment based on experience and marketing research.

Product and Promotion Strategies

Global companies have five strategies for matching products and their promotion efforts to global markets. As Figure 7–4 shows, the strategies focus on whether a company extends or adapts its product and promotion message for consumers in different countries and cultures.

A product may be sold globally in one of three ways: (1) in the same form as in its home market (product extension), (2) with some adaptations (product adaptation), or (3) as a totally new product (product invention):[24]

1. *Product extension.* Selling virtually the same product in other countries is a product extension strategy. It works well for products such as Coca-Cola, Gillette razors, Wrigley's gum, Levi's jeans, Sony consumer electronics, Harley-Davidson motorcycles, Nike apparel and shoes, and Apple iPhones. As a general rule, product extension seems to work best when the consumer market target for the product is alike across countries and cultures—that is, consumers share the same desires, needs, and uses for the product.

2. *Product adaptation.* Changing a product in some way to make it more appropriate for a country's climate or consumer preferences is a product adaptation strategy. Exxon sells different gasoline blends based on each country's climate. Frito-Lay produces and markets its potato chips in Russia, but don't expect them to taste like the chips eaten in North America. Russians prefer dairy, meat, and seafood-flavored potato chips. Likewise, Gerber baby food comes in different varieties in different countries. Vegetable and rabbit meat is a favorite blend in Poland. Freeze-dried sardines and rice is popular in Japan. Maybelline's makeup is formulaically adapted to local skin types and weather across the globe, including an Asia-specific mascara that doesn't run during the rainy season.

3. *Product invention.* Alternatively, companies can invent totally new products designed to satisfy common needs across countries. Black & Decker did this with its Snake Light Flexible Flashlight. Created to address a global need for portable lighting, the product became a best-seller in North America, Europe, Latin America, and Australia and is the most successful new product developed by Black & Decker. Similarly, Whirlpool developed a compact, automatic clothes washer specifically for households in developing countries with annual household incomes of $2,000. Called Ideale, the washer features bright colors because

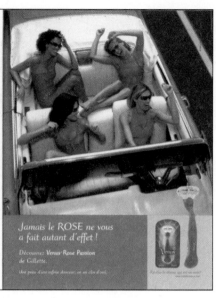

What is it about PINK that makes you feel so good?

Introducing Passion Pink Venus. From Gillette.

¿Qué tiene el ROSA que te hace sentir tan bien?

Presentamos Venus de Gillette en un escandaloso nuevo color, Rosa Pasión.

Jamais le ROSE ne vous a fait autant d'effet !

Découvrez Venus Rose Passion de Gillette.

Gillette delivers the same global message whenever possible, as shown in the Gillette for Women Venus ads from France, Mexico, and the United States.

washers are often placed in home living areas, not hid in laundry rooms (which don't exist in many homes in developing countries).

An identical promotion message is used for the product extension and product adaptation strategies around the world. Gillette uses the same global message for its men's toiletries: "Gillette, the Best a Man Can Get." Even though Exxon adapts its gasoline blends for different countries based on climate, the promotion message is unchanged: "Put a Tiger in Your Tank."

Global companies may also adapt their promotion message. For instance, the same product may be sold in many countries but advertised differently. As an example, L'Oréal, a French health and beauty products marketer, introduced its Golden Beauty brand of sun care products through its Helena Rubenstein subsidiary in Western Europe with a communication adaptation strategy. Recognizing that cultural and buying motive differences related to skin care and tanning exist, Golden Beauty advertising features dark tanning for northern Europeans, skin protection to avoid wrinkles among Latin Europeans, and beautiful skin for Europeans living along the Mediterranean Sea, even though the products are the same.

Other companies use a dual adaptation strategy by modifying both their products and promotion messages. Nestlé does this with Nescafé coffee. Nescafé is marketed using different coffee blends and promotional campaigns to match consumer preferences in different countries.

These examples illustrate the simple rule applied by global companies: Standardize product and promotion strategies whenever possible and customize them wherever necessary. This is the art of global marketing.[25]

Distribution Strategy

Distribution is of critical importance in global marketing. The availability and quality of retailers and wholesalers as well as transportation, communication, and warehousing facilities are often determined by a country's economic infrastructure. Figure 7–5 outlines the channel through which a product manufactured in one country must travel to reach its destination in another country. The first step involves the seller; its headquarters is the starting point and is responsible for the successful distribution to the ultimate consumer.

The next step is the channel between two nations, moving the product from one country to another. Intermediaries that can handle this responsibility include resident buyers in a foreign country, independent merchant wholesalers who buy and sell the product, or agents who bring buyers and sellers together.

FIGURE 7–5
Channels of distribution in global marketing are often long and complex.

Once the product is in the foreign nation, that country's distribution channels take over. These channels can be very long or surprisingly short, depending on the product line. In Japan, fresh fish go through three intermediaries before getting to a retail outlet. Conversely, shoes go through only one intermediary.

The sophistication of a country's distribution channels increases as its economic infrastructure develops. Supermarkets facilitate selling products in many nations, but they are not popular or available in many others where culture and lack of refrigeration dictate shopping on a daily rather than a weekly basis. When Coke and Pepsi entered China, both had to create direct-distribution channels, investing in refrigerator units for small retailers.

Pricing Strategy

Global companies also face many challenges in determining a pricing strategy as part of their worldwide marketing effort. Individual countries, even those with free trade agreements, may impose considerable competitive, political, and legal constraints on the pricing latitude of global companies. For example, antitrust authorities in Germany limited Walmart from selling some items too low to lure shoppers. Without the practice, Walmart was unable to compete against German discount stores. This, and other factors, led Walmart to leave Germany following eight years without a profit.[26]

Pricing too low or too high can have dire consequences. When prices appear too low in one country, companies can be charged with dumping, a practice subject to severe penalties and fines. **Dumping** is when a firm sells a product in a foreign country below its domestic price or below its actual cost. A recent trade dispute involving U.S. apple growers and Mexico is a case in point. Mexican trade officials claimed that U.S. growers were selling their red and golden delicious apples in Mexico below the actual cost of production. They imposed a 101 percent tariff on U.S. apples, and a severe drop in U.S. apple exports to Mexico resulted. Subsequent negotiations set a price floor on the price of U.S. apples sold to Mexico.[27]

When companies price their products very high in some countries but competitively in others, they face a gray market problem. A **gray market**, also called *parallel importing,* is a situation where products are sold through unauthorized channels of distribution.[28] A gray market comes about when individuals buy products in a lower-priced country from a manufacturer's authorized retailer, ship them to higher-priced countries, and then sell them below the manufacturer's suggested retail price through unauthorized retailers. Many well-known products have been sold through gray markets, including Olympus cameras, Seiko watches, Chanel perfume, and Mercedes-Benz cars. Parallel importing is legal in the United States. It is illegal in the European Union.

dumping
When a firm sells a product in a foreign country below its domestic price or below its actual cost.

gray market
A situation in which products are sold through unauthorized channels of distribution.

learning review

8. Products may be sold globally in three ways. What are they?
9. What is dumping?

LEARNING OBJECTIVES REVIEW

LO1 *Identify the major trends that have influenced world trade and global marketing.*

Four major trends have influenced the landscape of global marketing in the past decade. First, there has been a gradual decline of economic protectionism by individual countries, leading to a reduction in tariffs and quotas. Second, there is growing economic integration and free trade among nations, reflected in the creation of the European Union and the North American Free Trade Agreement. Third, there exists global competition among global companies for global consumers, resulting in firms adopting global marketing strategies and promoting global brands. And finally, a networked global marketspace has emerged using Internet technology as a tool for exchanging goods, services, and information on a global scale.

LO2 *Identify the environmental forces that shape global marketing efforts.*

Three major environmental forces shape global marketing efforts. First, there are cultural forces, including values, customs, cultural symbols, and language. Economic forces also shape global marketing efforts. These include a country's stage of economic development and economic infrastructure, consumer income and purchasing power, and currency exchange rates. Finally, political-regulatory forces in a country or region of the world create a favorable or unfavorable climate for global marketing efforts.

LO3 *Name and describe the alternative approaches companies use to enter global markets.*

Companies have four alternative approaches for entering global markets. These are exporting, licensing, joint venture, and direct investment. Exporting involves producing goods in one country and selling them in another country. Under licensing, a company offers the right to a trademark, patent, trade secret, or similarly valued item of intellectual property in return for a royalty or fee. In a joint venture, a foreign company and a local firm invest together to create a local business. Direct investment entails a domestic firm actually investing in and owning a foreign subsidiary or division.

LO4 *Explain the distinction between standardization and customization when companies craft worldwide marketing programs.*

Companies distinguish between standardization and customization when crafting worldwide marketing programs. Standardization means that all elements of the marketing program are the same across countries and cultures. Customization means that one or more elements of the marketing program are adapted to meet the needs or preferences of consumers in a particular country or culture. Global marketers apply a simple rule when crafting worldwide marketing programs: Standardize marketing programs whenever possible and customize them wherever necessary.

FOCUSING ON KEY TERMS

back translation p. 147
cross-cultural analysis p. 144
cultural symbols p. 145
currency exchange rate p. 148
customs p. 145
direct investment p. 152
dumping p. 155
exporting p. 150

Foreign Corrupt Practices Act (1977) p. 145
global brand p. 142
global competition p. 140
global consumers p. 143
global marketing strategy p. 141
gray market p. 155
joint venture p. 151

multidomestic marketing strategy p. 141
protectionism p. 138
quota p. 138
tariff p. 138
values p. 144
World Trade Organization p. 138

APPLYING MARKETING KNOWLEDGE

1 What is meant by this statement: "Quotas are a hidden tax on consumers, whereas tariffs are a more obvious one"?

2 How successful would a television commercial in Japan be if it featured a husband surprising his wife in her dressing area on Valentine's Day with a small box of chocolates containing four candies? Why?

3 As a novice in global marketing, which alternative for global market-entry strategy would you be likely to start

with? Why? What other alternatives are available for a global market entry?

4 Coca-Cola is sold worldwide. In some countries, Coca-Cola owns the bottling facilities; in others, it has signed contracts with licensees or it relies on joint ventures. When selecting a licensee in each country, what factors should Coca-Cola consider?

Does your marketing plan involve reaching global customers outside the United States? If the answer is no, read no further and do not include a global element in your plan. If the answer is yes, try to identify:

1   What features of your product are especially important to potential customers.

2   In which countries these potential customers live.

3   Special marketing issues that are involved in trying to reach them.

Answers to these questions will help in developing more detailed marketing mix strategies described in later chapters.

video case 7   CNS Breathe Right Strips: Going Global

"It's naive to treat 'international' as one big market—particularly within OTC," explains Marti Morfitt, president and CEO of CNS, the company that manufactures Breathe Right® nasal strips. "There are many discrete, unique markets, and local expertise is needed to understand the dynamics within each and address them effectively."

"OTC" refers to over-the-counter medical products such as aspirin or cough syrup that customers can buy without a doctor's prescription. Breathe Right nasal strips qualify as an OTC product. But that doesn't mean there isn't a lot of technology and medical science behind it.

Breathe Right nasal strips are innovative adhesive strips with patented dual flex bars inside. When attached to the nose, they gently lift and hold open nasal passages, making it easier to breathe. Breathe Right strips are used for a variety of reasons, all to help breathe better through the nose: athletes hoping to play their best (particularly when wearing mouth guards); snorers (and their spouses) hoping for a quiet night's sleep; and allergy, sinusitis, and cold sufferers looking for drug-free relief from nasal congestion.

HOW IT ALL BEGAN

Breathe Right strips were invented by Bruce Johnson, a chronic nasal congestion sufferer. At times Johnson put straws or paper clips in his nose at night to keep his nasal passages open. He eventually came up with a prototype for Breathe Right strips. He brought his invention to CNS, Inc., which recognized its market potential. CNS took the strips to the Food and Drug Administration for approval of claims for relief of snoring and nasal congestion.

CNS, a small company, had a limited marketing budget. However, it got a big public relations break when Jerry Rice, the legendary wide receiver for the San Francisco 49ers, wore a Breathe Right strip on national TV and scored two touchdowns during the 49ers' 1995 Super Bowl victory. Demand for the strips soared.

"What really helped sales of Breathe Right strips was that CNS had done a very effective job of getting press kits in the hands of news and sports media," says Morfitt. "When people on television asked, 'What is that funny looking thing on his nose?' the reporters could talk about how the strip was an effective consumer product for everyone. And a $1.4 million business turned into a $45 million business in just one year."

THE DECISION TO GO GLOBAL

As awareness and trial in the United States was building, CNS began to get inquiries from people in other countries asking where they could buy strips. In 1995 CNS decided to take advantage of global interest and introduce Breathe Right strips internationally.

What countries did CNS choose to enter with its Breathe Right strips? "Countries we focus on are those with a large OTC market, high per-capita spending in the OTC market, and future prospects for growth," says Kevin McKenna, vice president for international at CNS. All these factors relate to market size. "But the real key to success in a market is a local partner that is entrepreneurial and has an ability to execute in terms of achieving distribution and sales."

IMPORTANCE OF LOCAL PARTNERS

Dynamic world market changes in the past 30 years have influenced opportunities for global sales of Breathe Right strips. Key trends include increased availability of OTC products formerly available only by prescription; and a global push toward self-care, spurred by the increasing cost of health and medical care. Additionally, OTC products have extended beyond the traditional boundary of the pharmacy and into grocery and other channels; and the role of the pharmacist has expanded from that of medical professional to one that includes selling and marketing OTC products to consumers.

At the same time, changes were taking place within CNS. When Morfitt joined CNS in 1998, she began pulling together a new management group with extensive experience in marketing consumer packaged goods, both in the United States and abroad. CNS began seeking "hungry" international partners who would bring greater localized market expertise and direct-selling capabilities than past partners. Morfitt also wanted partners with demonstrated entrepreneurial spirit to match that of the new management team.

The company's partner in Italy, BluFarm Group, uses its local knowledge and direct-selling skills to partner with pharmacists to teach them how to increase sales of Breathe Right strips in their stores. In Italy, as throughout much of Europe, OTC products such as antacids, aspirin, and nasal strips are typically placed behind pharmacy counters and therefore are not visible to customers. The only way to sell a product is for a customer to ask for it by name. BluFarm Group recognized the importance of in-store advertising and sales execution to build awareness and created point-of-sale materials such as window and

Stage 1: Explore/Test

↓

Stage 1 to Stage 2 Criteria Screen
- Relevant market: Cough/cold category size, GDP and GDP growth
- Quality of partners
- Product acceptance
- Cost to launch/support
- Political stability

↓

Stage 2: Establish the Product

↓

Stage 2 to Stage 3 Criteria Screen
- Proven partner and distribution strength
- Effective consumer ad and education programs
- Met initial trial and repeat targets
- Clear path to profits

↓

Stage 3: Manage the Product

counter displays to let customers know that Breathe Right strips were available in the store. "BluFarm's ability to capture consumers' awareness of Breathe Right strips as they walk in the retailer's door has beneficial results for CNS, BluFarm, pharmacists, and consumers," says McKenna.

"Working with an experienced local partner helps overcome surprises in global markets," says Nick Naumann, senior marketing communications manager at CNS. One surprise: universal product codes (UPC) on packaging aren't "universal"— they are used only in the United States and Canada. "Different forms of those codes in other countries can take a few weeks to six months or more of government review to obtain," he says.

Even the same packaging colors don't work around the globe. Research with U.S. consumers revealed they wanted darker packaging to suggest the strips' use at night by snorers and those with stuffed noses. "'Too grim and negative' Asian and European consumers told us," says Naumann. Breathe Right strips in those countries have a lighter, airier look than in the United States to convey the open feeling one gets from the nasal strips.

MANAGING GLOBAL GROWTH

Today, Breathe Right strips are sold in more than 25 countries. To ensure the Breathe Right brand continues to meet growth expectations, CNS now uses a three-stage approach to penetrate and develop new markets:

- Stage 1: Explore/test the concept.
  —Use screening criteria to identify high-potential markets.
  —Identify potential partners.
  —Validate concept with research.
  —Develop strategy and launch test market.

- Stage 2: Establish the product.
  —Penetrate the marketplace.
  —Refine messages for local market.
  —Evaluate partnership and marketing strategies.

- Stage 3: Manage the product.
  —Achieve sustainability/profitability.
  —Exploit new product and new use opportunities.

Overall, this approach starts with what works in the United States and extends it into new markets, paying close attention to local needs and customs. Throughout the three stages CNS conducts market research and makes financial projections.

As shown in the figure, at each stage of the market development process, performance must be met for the product to enter the next stage. Once success with Breathe Right nasal strips is established in a country, the groundwork is laid and international partners have the ability to introduce other Breathe Right products.

LOOKING FORWARD

"We believe the Breathe Right brand has great potential, both domestically and around the world," says Morfitt. "Growth will come both from further expansion of Breathe Right nasal strips and from other drug-free, better-breathing line extensions."

Questions

1 What are the advantages and disadvantages for CNS taking Breathe Right strips into international markets?
2 What are the advantages to CNS of (*a*) using its three-stage process to enter new global markets and (*b*) having specific criteria to move through the stages?
3 Using the CNS criteria, with what you know, which countries should have highest priority for CNS?
4 Which single segment of potential Breathe Right strip users would you target to enter new markets?
5 Which marketing mix variables should CNS emphasize the most to succeed in a global arena? Why?

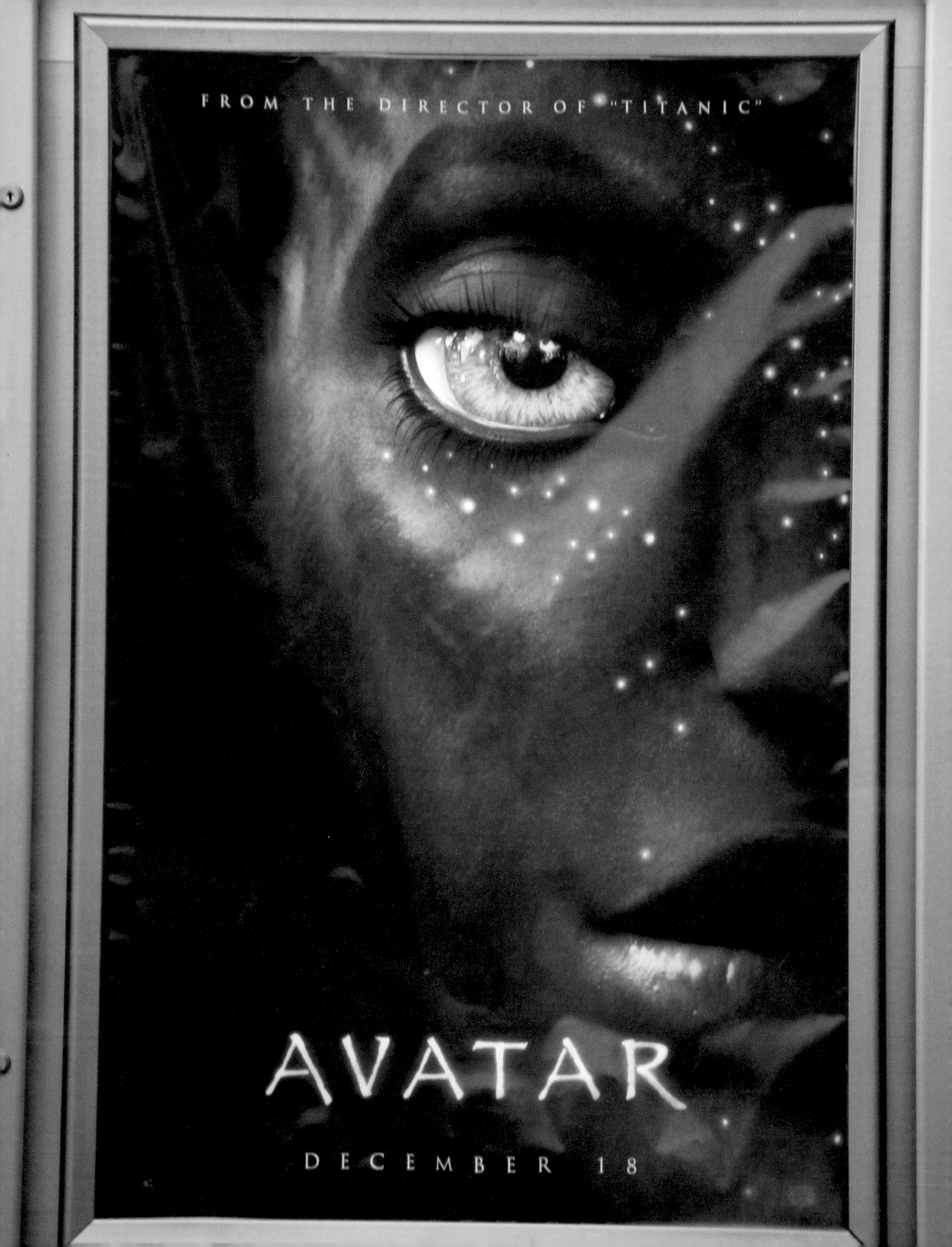
FROM THE DIRECTOR OF "TITANIC"
AVATAR
DECEMBER 18

8

Marketing Research: From Customer Insights to Actions

TEST SCREENINGS: HOW LISTENING TO CONSUMERS REDUCES MOVIE RISKS

Avatar, Iron Man 2, Harry Potter and the Deathly Hallows, and *Shrek Forever After* are movies that their studios count on for huge profits. But what can these studios do to try to reduce the costly risks of a movie's box-office failure?[1]

What's in a Movie Name?

Fixing bad names for movies—like *Shoeless Joe* and *Rope Burns*—can turn potential disasters into hugely successful blockbusters. Don't remember seeing these movies? Well, test screenings—a form of marketing research—found that moviegoers like you had problems with these titles. Here's what happened:

- Shown frequently on television now, *Shoeless Joe* became *Field of Dreams* because audiences thought Kevin Costner might be playing a homeless person.

- *Rope Burns* became *Million Dollar Baby* because audiences didn't like the original name. The movie won the 2005 Academy Award™ for Best Picture and starred Hilary Swank as a woman boxer and Clint Eastwood as her trainer.

Filmmakers want movie titles that are concise, grab attention, capture the essence of the film, and have no legal restrictions to reduce risk to both the studio and audiences—the same factors that make a good brand name.[2]

The Risks of Today's (and Tomorrow's) Blockbuster Movies

Bad titles, poor scripts, temperamental stars, costly special effects, and several blockbuster movies released at the same time are just a few of the nightmares studios face. With a typical film costing $107 million to produce and market,[3] studios try to reduce their risks by:

- *Conducting test screenings.* In test screenings, 300 to 400 prospective moviegoers are recruited to attend a "sneak preview" of a film before its release. After viewing the movie, the audience fills out an exhaustive survey to critique its title, plot, characters, music, and ending as well as the marketing program (posters, trailers, and so on) to identify improvements to make in the final edit.[4]

Test screenings resulted in *Fatal Attraction* having one of the most commercially successful "ending-switches" of all time. In sneak previews, audiences liked everything but the ending, which had Alex (Glenn Close) committing suicide and framing Dan (Michael Douglas) as her murderer. The studio shot $1.3 million of new scenes for the ending that audiences eventually saw. The new ending for *Fatal Attraction* undoubtedly contributed to the movie's box-office success.[5]

Director James Cameron even had to produce a short "mini" test screening of a 3D segment of *Avatar* to convince four Twentieth Century Fox executives to fund his movie. *Avatar*, of course, quickly became #1 in all-time worldwide gross ticket sales.[6]

- *Using tracking studies.* Immediately before an upcoming film's release, studios will ask prospective moviegoers in the target audience three key questions: (1) Are you aware of the film? (2) Are you interested in seeing the film? and (3) Will you see the film this weekend?[7] Studios then use the data collected to forecast the movie's opening weekend box office sales; if necessary, they will run last-minute ads to increase awareness and interest for the film.

Test screenings and tracking studies for movies like *Iron Man 2* can help avoid potential risks by improving movie titles, endings, and characters.

These examples show how marketing research is the link between marketing strategy and decisive marketing actions, the main topic of this chapter. Also, marketing research is often used to help a firm develop its sales forecasts, the final topic of this chapter.

THE ROLE OF MARKETING RESEARCH

Let's (1) look at what marketing research is, (2) identify some difficulties with it, and (3) describe the five steps marketers use to conduct it.

What Is Marketing Research?

marketing research
The process of collecting and analyzing information in order to recommend actions.

Marketing research is the process of defining a marketing problem and opportunity, systematically collecting and analyzing information, and recommending actions.[8] Although imperfect, marketers conduct marketing research to reduce the risk of and thereby improve marketing decisions.

The Challenges in Doing Good Marketing Research

Whatever the marketing issue involved—whether discovering consumer tastes or setting the right price—good marketing research is challenging. For example:

- Suppose your firm is developing a new product never before seen by consumers. Would consumers really know whether they are likely to buy a product that they have never thought about before?
- Imagine if you, as a consumer, were asked about your personal hygiene habits. Even though you know the answers, would you reveal them? When personal or status questions are involved, will people give honest answers?
- Will consumers' actual purchase behavior match their stated interest or intentions? Will they buy the same brand they say they will?

Marketing research must overcome these difficulties and obtain the information needed so that marketers can make reasonable estimates about what consumers want and will buy.

Five-Step Marketing Research Approach

A *decision* is a conscious choice from among two or more alternatives. All of us make many such decisions daily. At work we choose from alternative ways to accomplish an assigned task. At college we choose from alternative courses. As consumers we choose from alternative brands. No magic formula guarantees correct decisions.

Managers and researchers have tried to improve the outcomes of decisions by using more formal, structured approaches to *decision making,* the act of consciously choosing from alternatives. The systematic marketing research approach used to collect information to improve marketing decisions and actions described in this chapter uses five steps and is shown in Figure 8–1 on the next page. Although the five-step approach described here focuses on marketing decisions, it provides a systematic checklist for making both business and personal decisions.

STEP 1: DEFINE THE PROBLEM

For how Fisher-Price does marketing research on young children who can't read, see the text.

Every marketing problem faces its own research challenges. For example, toy designers at Fisher-Price conduct marketing research to discover how children play, how they learn, and what they like to play with.[9] As part of its marketing research, Fisher-Price invites children to play at its state-licensed nursery school in East Aurora, New York. From behind one-way mirrors, toy designers and marketing researchers watch the children use—and abuse—toys, which helps the firm develop better products.

The original model of a classic Fisher-Price toy, the Chatter Telephone™, was simply a wooden phone with a dial that rang a bell. However, observers noted that the children kept grabbing the receiver like a handle to pull the phone along behind them, so a designer added wheels, a noisemaker, and eyes that bobbed up and down.

A careful look at Fisher-Price's toy marketing research shows the two key elements of defining a problem: setting the research objectives and identifying possible marketing actions.

Set the Research Objectives

Research objectives are specific, measurable goals the decision maker—in this case, an executive at Fisher-Price—seeks to achieve in conducting the marketing research. For Fisher-Price, the immediate research objective was to decide whether to market the old or new telephone design. In setting these research objectives, marketers have to be clear on the purpose of the research that leads to marketing actions.

Identify Possible Marketing Actions

measures of success
Criteria or standards used in evaluating proposed solutions to a problem.

Effective decision makers develop specific **measures of success**, which are criteria or standards used in evaluating proposed solutions to the problem. Different research outcomes—based on the measure of success—lead to different marketing actions. For the Fisher-Price problem, if a measure of success were the total time children spent playing with each of the two telephone designs, the results of observing them would lead to clear-cut actions as follows:

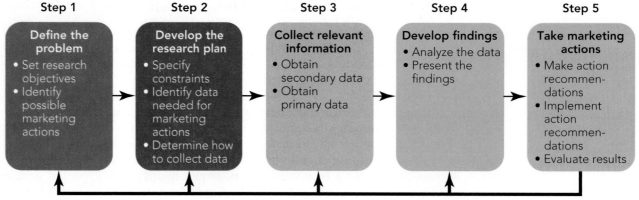

Step 1	Step 2	Step 3	Step 4	Step 5
Define the problem • Set research objectives • Identify possible marketing actions	**Develop the research plan** • Specify constraints • Identify data needed for marketing actions • Determine how to collect data	**Collect relevant information** • Obtain secondary data • Obtain primary data	**Develop findings** • Analyze the data • Present the findings	**Take marketing actions** • Make action recommendations • Implement action recommendations • Evaluate results

Feedback to learn lessons for future research

FIGURE 8–1

Five-step marketing research approach leading to marketing actions. Lessons learned from past research mistakes are fed back to improve each of the steps.

The wheels, noisemaker, and bobbing eyes on Fisher-Price's hugely successful Chatter Telephone resulted from careful marketing research on children.

Measure of Success: Playtime

- Children spent more time playing with old design.
- Children spent more time playing with new design.

Possible Marketing Action

- Continue with old design; don't introduce new design.
- Introduce new design; drop old design.

One test of whether marketing research should be done is if different outcomes will lead to different marketing actions. If all the research outcomes lead to the same action—such as top management sticking with the older design regardless of what the observed children liked—the research is useless and a waste of money. In this case, research results showed that kids liked the new design, so Fisher-Price introduced its noisemaking pull-toy Chatter Telephone, which became a toy classic and has sold millions.

Marketing researchers know that defining a problem is an incredibly difficult task. For example, if the objectives are too broad, the problem may not be researchable. If they are too narrow, the value of the research results may be seriously lessened. This is why marketing researchers spend so much time defining a marketing problem precisely and writing a formal proposal that describes the research to be done.[10]

STEP 2: DEVELOP THE RESEARCH PLAN

The second step in the marketing research process requires that the researcher (1) specify the constraints on the marketing research activity, (2) identify the data needed for marketing decisions, and (3) determine how to collect the data.

Specify Constraints

The **constraints** in a decision are the restrictions placed on potential solutions to a problem. Examples include the limitations on the time and money available to solve the problem. Thus, Fisher-Price might set two constraints on its decision to select either the old or new version of the Chatter Telephone: The decision must be made in 10 weeks and no research budget is available beyond that needed for collecting data in its nursery school.

Identify Data Needed for Marketing Actions

Often marketing research studies wind up collecting a lot of data that are interesting but irrelevant for marketing decisions that result in marketing actions. In the Fisher-Price Chatter Telephone case, it might be nice to know the children's favorite colors, whether they like wood or plastic toys better, and so on. In fact, knowing answers to these questions might result in later modifications of the toy, but right now the problem is to select one of two toy designs. So this study must focus on collecting data that will help managers make a clear choice between the two telephone designs.

Determine How to Collect Data

Determining how to collect useful marketing research data is often as important as actually collecting the data—step 3 in the process, which is discussed later. Two key elements in deciding how to collect the data are (1) concepts and (2) methods.

Concepts   In the world of marketing, *concepts* are ideas about products or services. To find out about consumer reaction to a potential new product, marketing researchers frequently develop a *new-product concept*, that is, a picture or verbal description of a product or service the firm might offer for sale. For example, Fisher-Price's addition of a noisemaker, wheels, and eyes to the basic design of its Chatter Telephone made the toy more fun for children and increased sales.

Methods   *Methods* are the approaches that can be used to collect data to solve all or part of a problem. For example, if you were the marketing researcher at Fisher-Price responsible for the Chatter Telephone, you would face a number of methods issues in developing your research plan, including the following:

- Can we actually ask three- or four-year-olds meaningful questions that they can answer about their liking or disliking of the two designs of toys?
- Are we better off not asking them questions but simply observing their behavior in playing with the two designs of toys?
- If we simply observe the children's playing behavior, how can we do this in a way to get the best information without biasing the results?

How can you find and use the methods that other marketing researchers have found successful? Information on useful methods is available in tradebooks, textbooks, and handbooks that relate to marketing and marketing research. Some periodicals and technical journals, such as the *Journal of Marketing* and the *Journal of Marketing Research*, both published by the American Marketing Association, summarize methods and techniques valuable in addressing marketing problems.

Special methods vital to marketing are (1) sampling and (2) statistical inference. For example, marketing researchers often use *sampling* by selecting a group of distributors, customers, or prospects, asking them questions, and treating their answers as typical of all those in whom they are interested. They may then use *statistical inference* to generalize the results from the sample to much larger groups of distributors, customers, or prospects to help decide on marketing actions.

learning review

1. What is marketing research?
2. What is the five-step marketing research approach?
3. What are constraints, as they apply to developing a research plan?

STEP 3: COLLECT RELEVANT INFORMATION

LO3

data
The facts and figures related to a problem.

secondary data
Facts and figures that have already been recorded before the project at hand.

primary data
Facts and figures that are newly collected for a project.

Collecting enough relevant information to make a rational, informed marketing decision sometimes simply means using your knowledge to decide immediately. At other times it entails collecting an enormous amount of information at great expense.

Figure 8–2 shows how the different kinds of marketing information fit together. **Data**, the facts and figures related to the problem, are divided into two main parts: secondary data and primary data. **Secondary data** are facts and figures that have already been recorded before the project at hand. As shown in Figure 8–2, secondary data divide into two parts—internal and external secondary data—depending on whether the data come from inside or outside the organization needing the research. **Primary data** are facts and figures that are newly collected for the project. Figure 8–2 shows that primary data can be divided into observational data, questionnaire data, and other sources of data.

Secondary Data: Internal

Examples of internal secondary data include detailed sales breakdowns by product line, by region, by customer, and by sales representative, as well as customer inquiries and complaints. So internal secondary data are often the starting point for a new marketing research study because using this information can result in huge time and cost savings.

Secondary Data: External

Published data from outside the organization are external secondary data. The U.S. Census Bureau publishes a variety of useful reports. Best known is the Census 2010, which is the most recent count of the U.S. population that occurs every 10 years. Recently, the Census Bureau began collecting data annually from a smaller number

FIGURE 8–2
Types of marketing information. Researchers must choose carefully among these to get the best results, considering time and cost constraints.

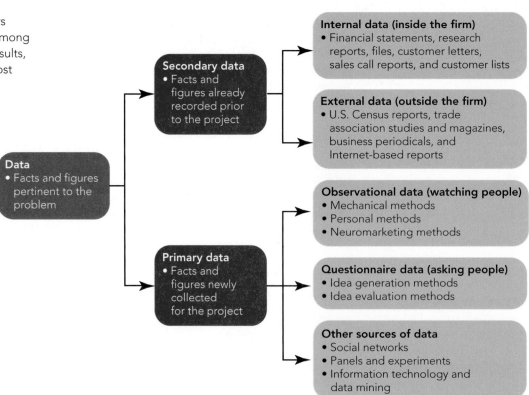

Scanner data at supermarket checkout counters provide valuable information for marketing decisions.

of people through the American Community Survey. Both surveys contain detailed information on American households, such as the number of people per household and their age, sex, race/ethnic background, income, occupation, and education. Marketers use these data to identify characteristics and trends of ultimate consumers.

The Census Bureau also publishes the Economic Census, which is conducted every five years. These reports are vital to business firms selling products and services to organizations. The 2007 Economic Census contains data on the number and sales of establishments in the United States that produce a good or service based on its geography (states, counties, ZIP codes, etc.), industry sector (manufacturing, retail trade, etc.), and North American Industry Classification System (NAICS) code.

Several market research companies pay households and businesses to record all their purchases using a paper or electronic diary. Such *syndicated panel* data economically answer questions that require consistent data collection over time, such as how many times did our customers buy our products this year compared to last year? Examples of syndicated panels that provide a standard set of data on a regular basis are the Nielsen Media Research's TV ratings and the J. D. Power's automotive quality and customer satisfaction surveys.

Some data services provide comprehensive information on household demographics and lifestyle, product purchases, TV viewing behavior, and responses to coupon and free-sample promotions. Their advantage is that a single firm can collect, analyze, interrelate, and present all this information. For consumer product firms such as Procter & Gamble, sales data from various channels are critical to allocate scarce marketing resources. As a result, they use services such as SymphonyIRIGroup's InfoScan and Nielsen's Scantrack to collect product sales and coupon/free-sample redemptions that have been scanned at the checkout counters of supermarket, drug, convenience, and mass merchandise retailers.

Finally, trade associations, universities, and business periodicals provide detailed data of value to market researchers and planners. These data are now available online via the Internet and can be identified and located using a search engine such as Google or Bing. The Marketing Matters box on the next page provides examples.

Advantages and Disadvantages of Secondary Data

A general rule among marketing people is to obtain secondary data first and then collect primary data. Two important advantages of secondary data are (1) the tremendous time savings because the data have already been collected and published or exist internally and (2) the low cost, such as free or inexpensive Census reports. Furthermore, a greater level of detail is often available through secondary data, especially U.S. Census Bureau data.

However, these advantages must be weighed against some significant disadvantages. First, the secondary data may be out of date, especially if they are U.S. Census data collected only every 5 or 10 years. Second, the definitions or categories might not be quite right for a researcher's project. For example, the age groupings or product categories might be wrong for the project. Also, because the data are collected for another purpose, they may not be specific enough for the project. In such cases it may be necessary to collect primary data.

learning review

4. What is the difference between secondary and primary data?

5. What are some advantages and disadvantages of secondary data?

Information contained in online databases available via the Internet consists of indexes to articles in periodicals and statistical or financial data on markets, products, and organizations that are accessed either directly or via Internet search engines or portals through keyword searches.

Statistical and financial data on markets, products, and organizations include:

- *The Wall Street Journal* (www.wsj.com), CNBC (www.cnbc.com), and *Fox Business News* (www.foxbusiness.com) provide up-to-the-minute business news and security prices plus research reports on companies, industries, and countries.
- STAT-USA (www.stat-usa.gov) and the Census Bureau (www.census.gov) of the U.S. Department of Commerce

provide information on U.S. business, economic, and trade activity collected by the federal government.

Portals and search engines include:

- USA.gov (www.usa.gov) is the portal to all U.S. government Web sites. Users click on links to browse by topic or enter keywords for specific searches.
- Google (www.google.com) is the most popular portal to the entire Internet. Users click on links to browse by topic or enter keywords for specific searches.

Some of these Web sites are accessible only if your educational institution has paid a subscription fee. Check with your institution's Web site.

Primary Data: Watching People

LO4

Observing people and asking them questions are the two principal ways to collect new or primary data for a marketing study. Facts and figures obtained by watching, either mechanically or in person, how people actually behave is the way marketing researchers collect **observational data**. Observational data can be collected by mechanical (including electronic), personal, or neuromarketing methods.

observational data
Facts and figures obtained by watching, either mechanically or in person, how people behave.

Mechanical Methods National TV ratings, such as those of Nielsen Media Research shown in Figure 8–3 are an example of mechanical observational data collected by a "people meter." The people meter is a box that (1) is attached to TV sets, VCRs, DVRs (digital video recorders), cable boxes, and satellite dishes in more than 9,000 households across the country; (2) has a remote that operates the meter when a viewer begins and finishes watching a TV program; and (3) stores and then transmits the viewing information each night to Nielsen Media Research. Data are also collected using less sophisticated meters or TV diaries (a paper-pencil measurement system).[11]

By 2011, Nielsen will implement a new measurement program dubbed the *Anytime Anywhere Media Measurement (A2/M2) Initiative.* The purpose of A2/M2 is to "follow the video" of 21st century viewers. New people meter technology will measure all types of TV viewing behavior from a variety of devices and sources: DVR (digital video recorders), VOD (video on demand), Internet-delivered TV shows on computers via iTunes, streaming media, and mobile media devices (cell phones, iPods, etc.), as well as outside the home in bars, fitness clubs, airports, and so on.

What determines if *American Idol* stays on the air? For the importance of the TV "ratings game," see the text.

On the basis of all these observational data, Nielsen Media Research then calculates the rating and share of each TV program. With 114.9 million TV households in the United States, a single ratings point equals 1 percent, or 1,149,000 TV households.[12] For TV viewing, a share point is the percentage of TV sets in use tuned to a particular program. Because TV and cable networks

FIGURE 8–3

Nielsen Television Index Ranking Report for network TV prime-time households, week of May 17–23, 2010. The difference of a few share points in Nielsen TV ratings affects the cost of a TV ad on a show and even whether the show remains on the air.

Rank	Program	Network	Rating	Share
1	Dancing with the Stars	ABC	12.1	19
2	American Idol—Wednesday	FOX	11.1	18
3	American Idol—Tuesday	FOX	10.5	17
4	NCIS	CBS	9.9	16
5	Grey's Anatomy	ABC	9.7	16
6	NCIS: Los Angeles	CBS	9.5	16
7	The Mentalist	CBS	9.4	16
8	The Big Bang Theory	CBS	8.9	14
9	Dancing with the Stars—Results	ABC	8.6	14
10	CSI	CBS	8.6	14

Source: Copyright 2010, The Nielsen Company. All times Eastern. Viewing estimates include live viewing and DVR playback on the same day, defined as 3 A.M. to 3 A.M. Rank is based on U.S. Household Rating % from Nielsen Media Research's National People Meter Sample.

sell over $60 billion annually in advertising and set advertising rates to advertisers on the basis of those data, precision in the Nielsen data is critical.[13] Thus, a change of 1 percentage point in a rating can mean gaining or losing millions of dollars in advertising revenues because advertisers pay rates on the basis of the size of the audience for a TV program. So as Figure 8–3 shows, we might expect to pay more for a 30-second TV ad on *NCIS* than one on *The Mentalist*. Broadcast and cable networks may change the time slot or even cancel a TV program if its ratings are consistently poor and advertisers are unwilling to pay a rate based on a higher guaranteed rating.

But TV advertisers today have a special problem: With about three out of four TV viewers skipping ads with TiVo or channel surfing during commercials, how many people are actually seeing their TV ad? Now services such as Nielsen Media Research and Media Check offer advertisers minute-by-minute measurement of how many viewers stay tuned during commercials. The viewership data in Figure 8–3 include not only live TV but also programs recorded on DVRs. With these more precise measures of who is likely to see a TV ad, buying TV ads is becoming more scientific.[14]

Nielsen NetRatings also uses an electronic meter to record Internet user behavior. These data are collected via a meter installed on computers that tracks the actual mouse clicks made by a large sample of panelists in the United States as they surf the Internet. In 2010, the five most popular U.S. Web site "brands" were Google, Yahoo!, Facebook, Microsoft Bing, and YouTube.

Personal Methods Observational data can take some strange twists. Jennifer Voitle, a laid-off investment bank employee with four advanced degrees, responded to an Internet ad and found a new career: *mystery shopper*. Companies pay mystery shoppers to check on the quality and pricing of their products and the integrity of and customer service provided by their employees. Jennifer gets paid to travel to exotic hotels, eat at restaurants, play golf, test-drive new cars, shop for clothes, and play arcade games. But her role posing as a customer gives her client unique marketing research information that can be obtained in no other way. Says Jennifer, "Can you believe they call this work?"[15]

Is this *really* marketing research? A *mystery shopper* at work.

Watching consumers in person or recording them are two other observational approaches. For example, Procter & Gamble watches women do their laundry, clean the floor, put on makeup, and so on because they comprise 80 percent of its customers! And Gillette records consumers brushing their teeth in their own bathrooms to see how they really brush—not just how they say they brush. The new-product result: Gillette's Oral-B CrossAction toothbrush.[16]

Ethnographic research is a specialized observational approach in which trained observers seek to discover subtle behavioral and emotional reactions as consumers encounter products in their "natural use environment," such as in their home or car.[17] Recently, Kraft launched Deli Creations, which are sandwiches made with its Oscar Mayer meats, Kraft cheeses, and Grey Poupon mustard, after spending several months with consumers in their kitchens. Kraft discovered that consumers wanted complete, ready-to-serve meals that are easy to prepare—and it had the products to create them.[18]

Personal observation is both useful and flexible, but it can be costly and unreliable when different observers report different conclusions when watching the same event. And while observation can reveal *what* people do, it cannot easily determine *why* they do it. This is the principal reason for using neuromarketing and questionnaires, our next topics.

Neuromarketing Methods As a global brand expert, Martin Lindstrom has consulted for clients that market everything from chocolate and TV remote controls to toothpaste and iPod speakers. Not being satisfied with the results obtained from traditional marketing research, Lindstrom used brain scanning to analyze the buying processes of more than 2,000 participants. Lindstrom merged neuroscience—the study of the brain—with marketing! His controversial findings using "neuromarketing" are summarized in his 2008 breakthrough book *Buy•ology*. Several of his findings appear in the Marketing Matters box.[19]

Based on the resuts of neuromarketing studies, Campbell Soup Company changed the labels of most of its soup cans in late 2009. Some of the changes: Steam now rises from more vibrant images of soup; the "unemotional spoons" have disappeared; and the script logo is smaller and has been moved to the bottom of the can.[20]

Primary Data: Asking People

How many dozens of times have you filled out some kind of a questionnaire? Maybe a short survey at school or a telephone or e-mail survey to see if you are pleased with the service you received. Asking consumers questions and recording their answers is the second principal way of gathering information.

We can divide this primary data collection task into (1) idea generation methods and (2) idea evaluation methods, although they sometimes overlap and each has a number of special techniques.[21] Each survey method results in valuable **questionnaire data**, which are facts and figures obtained by asking people about their attitudes, awareness, intentions, and behaviors.

Idea Generation Methods—Coming Up with Ideas In the past the most common way of collecting questionnaire data to generate ideas was through an *individual interview*, which involves a single researcher asking questions of one respondent. This approach has many advantages, such as being able to probe for additional ideas using follow-up questions to a respondent's initial answers, but it is very expensive. Later in the chapter we'll discuss some alternatives.

General Mills sought ideas about why Hamburger Helper didn't fare well when introduced. Initial instructions called for cooking a half-pound of hamburger separately from the noodles or potatoes, which were later mixed with the hamburger. So General Mills researchers used a special kind of individual interview called *depth interviews* in which researchers ask lengthy, free-flowing kinds of questions to probe

questionnaire data
Facts and figures obtained by asking people about their attitudes, awareness, intentions, and behaviors.

Marketing Matters >>>>>>>>>> technology

Buy•ology: How "Neuromarketing" Is Trying to Understand Consumers

Is much of the more than $12 *billion* spent on traditional market research (focus groups, surveys, and so on) wasted? Brand guru Martin Lindstrom believes so. Why? Because 85 percent of consumers' thoughts, feelings, or preferences toward products, brands, and advertisements reside deep within the subconscious part of the brain and can't be understood using traditional techniques.

Lindstrom is a believer in the relatively new field of "neuromarketing," which uses high-tech brain scanning instruments to record the brain's responses to various marketing stimuli (package designs, brand logos, fragrances, TV ads, and so on) via the five senses (sight, sound, smell, touch, and taste). Two instruments are typically used when stimuli are presented: (1) an expensive, doughnut-shaped functional magnetic resonance imaging (fMRI) scanner, where different areas of the brain "light up" and can be mapped, and (2) a less costly cap with dozens of sensors plugged into an electroencephalograph (EEG), where the real-time changes in brain wave patterns can be seen (see photo).

So why is neuromarketing important to marketers? Lindstrom draws these fascinating conclusions that could have a significant impact on current marketing actions:

- **Brand logos don't work.** Instead, brands should focus on indirect logo signals, such as shapes, sound, smell, color, and so on.
- **Ads with sex appeal don't sell.** Men in particular don't recall these types of ads nearly as much as nonsexually oriented ads.
- **Successful brands function like religion.** Participants' brains respond similarly to brand messages and religious icons.
- **Warning labels on cigarettes don't work.** Interestingly, the labels stimulate the area of the brain responsible for cravings.

So, what do you think about neuromarketing? Are you concerned that marketers will invade your privacy by influencing what you buy? Stay tuned!

Individual interviews have the advantage of enabling interviewers to ask probing follow-up questions about a respondent's answers.

for underlying ideas and feelings. These depth interviews showed that consumers (1) didn't think it contained enough meat and (2) didn't want the hassle of cooking in two different pots. So the Hamburger Helper product manager changed the recipe to call for a full pound of meat and to allow users to prepare it in one dish. This marketing action converted a potential failure into a success.

Focus groups are informal sessions of 6 to 10 past, present, or prospective customers in which a discussion leader, or moderator, asks their opinions about the firm's and its competitors' products, how they use these products, and special needs they have that these products don't address. Often recorded and conducted in special interviewing rooms with a one-way mirror, these groups enable marketing researchers and managers to hear and watch consumer reactions. The informality and peer support in an effective focus group help uncover ideas that are often difficult to obtain with individual interviews. For example, 3M ran eight focus groups around the United States and heard consumers complain that standard steel wool pads scratched their expensive cookware. These interviews led to 3M's internationally successful Scotch-Brite® Never Scratch soap pad.[22]

Finding "the next big thing" for consumers has become the obsession not only for consumer product firms but also for firms in many other industries. The result is that marketing researchers have come to rely on other—many would say bizarre—techniques than more traditional individual or focus group interviews. These "fuzzy front end" methods attempt early identification of elusive consumer tastes or trends. For example, Trend Hunter is

Listening carefully in focus groups to student and instructor suggestions benefits this text, such as providing answers to the Learning Review questions.

a firm that seeks to anticipate and track "the evolution of cool." Trend hunting (or watching) is the practice of identifying "emerging shifts in social behavior," which are driven by changes in pop culture that can lead to new products. Trend Hunter has identified over 73,000 "micro trends" through its global network of 39,000 members and features several of these trends on its daily Trend Hunter TV broadcast via its Web site (see www.trend-hunter.com/tv).[23]

Idea Evaluation Methods—Testing an Idea In idea evaluation, the marketing researcher tries to test ideas discovered earlier to help the marketing manager recommend marketing actions. Idea evaluation methods often involve conventional questionnaires using personal, mail, telephone, fax, and online (e-mail or Internet) surveys of a large sample of past, present, or prospective consumers. In choosing among them, the marketing researcher balances the cost of the particular method against the expected quality of the information and speed with which it is obtained.

Personal interview surveys enable the interviewer to be flexible in asking probing questions or getting reactions to visual materials but are very costly. Mail surveys are usually biased because those most likely to respond have had especially positive or negative experiences with the product or brand. While telephone interviews allow flexibility, unhappy respondents may hang up on the interviewer, even with the efficiency of computer-assisted telephone interviewing (CATI). Fax surveys, a method in decline, are restricted to respondents having the technology.

Increasingly, marketing researchers have begun to use online (e-mail and Internet) surveys to collect primary data. The reason: Most consumers have an Internet connection and an e-mail account. Marketers can embed a survey in an e-mail sent to targeted respondents. When they open the e-mail, consumers can either see the survey or click on a link to access it from a Web site. Marketers can also ask consumers to complete a "pop up" survey in a separate window when they access an organization's Web site. Many organizations use this method to have consumers assess their products and services or evaluate the design and usability of their Web sites.

The advantages of online surveys are that the cost is relatively minimal and the turnaround time from data collection to report presentation is much quicker than the traditional methods discussed earlier. However, online surveys have serious drawbacks: Some consumers may view e-mail surveys as "junk" or "spam" and may either choose to not receive them (if they have a "spam blocker") or purposely or inadvertently delete them, unopened. For Internet surveys, some consumers have a "pop-up blocker" that prohibits a browser from opening a separate window that contains the survey; thus, they may not be able to participate in the research. For both e-mail and Internet surveys, consumers can complete the survey multiple times, creating a significant bias in the results. This is especially true for online panels. Research firms, such as MarketTools that markets Zoomerang, have developed sampling technology to prohibit this practice.[24]

The high cost of reaching respondents in their homes using personal interviews has led to a dramatic increase in the use of *mall intercept interviews*, which are personal interviews of consumers visiting shopping centers. These face-to-face interviews reduce the cost of personal visits to consumers in their homes while providing the flexibility to show respondents visual cues such as ads or actual product samples. However, a critical disadvantage of mall intercept interviews is that the people selected for the interviews may not be representative of the consumers targeted, giving a biased result.

The foundation of all research using questionnaires is developing precise questions that get clear, unambiguous answers from respondents. Figure 8–4 shows a number of formats for questions taken from a Wendy's survey that assessed fast-food restaurant preferences among present and prospective consumers. Question 1 is an example of an *open-ended question*, which allows respondents to express opinions, ideas, or behaviors in their own words without being forced to choose among alternatives that have been predetermined by a marketing researcher. This information is invaluable to marketers because it captures the "voice" of respondents, which is useful in understanding consumer behavior, identifying product benefits, or developing advertising messages. In contrast, *closed-end* or *fixed alternative questions* require respondents to select one or more response options from a set of predetermined choices. Question 2 is an example of a *dichotomous question*, the simplest form of a fixed alternative question that allows only a "yes" or "no" response.

A fixed alternative question with three or more choices uses a *scale*. Question 5 is an example of a question that uses a *semantic differential scale*, a five-point scale in

FIGURE 8–4

To obtain the most valuable information from consumers, the Wendy's survey utilizes five different kinds of questions discussed in the text *(continued on the next page)*.

1. What things are most important to you when you decide to eat out and go to a fast-food restaurant?

_____

_____

_____

2. Have you eaten at a fast-food restaurant in the past month?

☐ Yes   ☐ No

3. If you answered yes to question 2, how often do you eat fast food?

☐ Once a week   ☐ 2 to 3 times a month   ☐ Once a month or less

4. How important is it to you that a fast-food restaurant satisfies you on the following characteristics? [Check the box that describes your feelings for each item listed.]

CHARACTERISTIC	VERY IMPORTANT	SOMEWHAT IMPORTANT	IMPORTANT	UNIMPORTANT	SOMEWHAT UNIMPORTANT	VERY UNIMPORTANT
• Taste of food	☐	☐	☐	☐	☐	☐
• Cleanliness	☐	☐	☐	☐	☐	☐
• Price	☐	☐	☐	☐	☐	☐
• Variety of menu	☐	☐	☐	☐	☐	☐

5. For each of the characteristics listed below, check the space on the scale that describes how you feel about Wendy's. Mark an X on only **one** of the five spaces for each item listed.

CHARACTERISTIC		CHECK THE SPACE THAT DESCRIBES THE DEGREE TO WHICH WENDY'S IS . . .					
• Taste of food	Tasty	____	____	____	____	____	Not tasty
• Cleanliness	Clean	____	____	____	____	____	Dirty
• Price	Inexpensive	____	____	____	____	____	Expensive
• Variety of menu	Broad	____	____	____	____	____	Narrow

6. Check one box that describes your agreement or disagreement with each statement listed below:

STATEMENT	STRONGLY AGREE	AGREE	DON'T KNOW	DISAGREE	STRONGLY DISAGREE
• Adults like to take their families to fast-food restaurants	☐	☐	☐	☐	☐
• Our children have a say in where the family chooses to eat	☐	☐	☐	☐	☐

7. How important are each of the following sources of information to you when selecting a fast-food restaurant at which to eat? [Check one box for each source listed.]

SOURCE OF INFORMATION	VERY IMPORTANT	SOMEWHAT IMPORTANT	NOT AT ALL IMPORTANT
• Television	☐	☐	☐
• Newspapers	☐	☐	☐
• Radio	☐	☐	☐
• Billboards	☐	☐	☐
• Flyers	☐	☐	☐

8. How often do you eat out at each of the following fast-food restaurants? [Check one box for each source listed.]

RESTAURANT	ONCE A WEEK OR MORE	2 TO 3 TIMES A MONTH	ONCE A MONTH OR LESS
• Burger King	☐	☐	☐
• McDonald's	☐	☐	☐
• Wendy's	☐	☐	☐

9. Please answer the following questions about you and your household. [Check only one for each item.]

a. What is your gender? ☐ Male ☐ Female

b. What is your marital status? ☐ Single ☐ Married ☐ Other (widowed, divorced, etc.)

c. How many children under age 18 live in your home? ☐ 0 ☐ 1 ☐ 2 ☐ 3 or more

d. What is your age? ☐ Under 25 ☐ 25–44 ☐ 45 or older

e. What is your total annual individual or household income?

☐ <$15,000 ☐ $15,000–49,000 ☐ $50,000 or more

FIGURE 8–4
(continued)

which the opposite ends have one- or two-word adjectives that have opposite meanings. For example, depending on how clean the respondent feels that Wendy's is, he or she would check the left-hand space on the scale, the right-hand space, or one of the five intervening points. Question 6 uses a *Likert scale*, in which the respondent indicates the extent to which he or she agrees or disagrees with a statement.

The questionnaire in Figure 8–4 provides valuable information to the marketing researcher at Wendy's. Questions 1 to 8 inform him or her about the likes and dislikes in eating out, frequency of eating out at fast-food restaurants generally and at Wendy's specifically, and sources of information used in making decisions about fast-food restaurants. Question 9 gives details about the respondent's personal or household characteristics, which can be used in trying to segment the fast-food market, a topic discussed in Chapter 9.

It is essential that marketing research questions be worded precisely so that all respondents interpret the same question similarly. For example, in a question asking whether you eat at fast-food restaurants regularly, the word *regularly* is ambiguous. Two people might answer "yes" to the question, but one might mean "once a day"

Wendy's does marketing research continuously to discover changing customer wants.

while the other means "once or twice a month." Both answers appear as "yes" to the researcher who tabulates them, but they suggest that dramatically different marketing actions be directed to each of these two prospective consumers.

Electronic technology has revolutionized traditional concepts of interviews or surveys. Today, respondents can walk up to a kiosk in a shopping center, read questions off a screen, and key their answers into a computer on a touch screen. Even fully automated telephone interviews exist: An automated voice questions respondents over the telephone, who then key their replies on a touch-tone telephone.

Primary Data: Other Sources

Three other methods of collecting primary data exist that overlap somewhat with the observational or questionnaire methods just discussed. These involve using (1) social networks, (2) panels and experiments, and (3) information technology and data mining.

Social Networks At this moment, someone—maybe even you!—is communicating with someone else online with your mobile phone using a social network. Many consumers use social networking Web sites such as Facebook, LinkedIn, and

How do marketers track information on social networks such as Facebook or Twitter? Why do they care? For the answers, see the text.

Twitter to communicate with and share opinions among friends, family, and other like-minded individuals around the world. Social networks allow for more intimate and frequent contact among people who share common interests—at a lower cost than other media.

Why is this important to marketers? Because consumers often share their opinions about the offerings they use or want on these social networking Web sites or in online blogs (a personal diary or commentary) and forums (a place to hold discussions that allows participants to post comments)—it's like an online version of word of mouth! As a result, marketing researchers increasingly want to glean information from these sites to "mine" their raw consumer-generated content in real time. This content may signal a trend in the marketplace that can lead to marketing actions. Some organizations have established their own brand-related social networks to obtain consumer insights about both the organization and its offerings, which can increase brand loyalty.

What's likely to happen in the future? For marketers such as Procter & Gamble (P&G) and Unilever, a much larger portion of their market research budgets will be allocated to online research such as social network data mining. They believe that social networks are more in touch with today's consumer lifestyles. However, when relying on consumer-generated content, the sample of individuals from whom this content was gleaned may not be statistically representative of the marketplace.[25]

Panels and Experiments Two special ways that observations and questionnaires are sometimes used are panels and experiments.

Marketing researchers often want to know if consumers change their behavior over time, so they take successive measurements of the same people. A *panel* is a sample of consumers or stores from which researchers take a series of measurements. For example, the NPD Group collects data about consumer purchases such as apparel, food, and electronics from its Online Panel, which consists of more than 2.5 million individuals worldwide. So a firm like General Mills can count the frequency of consumer purchases to measure switching behavior from one brand of its breakfast cereal (Wheaties) to another (Cheerios) or to a competitor's brand (Kellogg's Special K). A disadvantage of panels is that the marketing research firm needs to recruit new members continually to replace those who drop out. These new recruits

To discover how Walmart used test markets to help develop its internationally successful supercenters, see the text.

must match the characteristics of those they replace to keep the panel representative of the marketplace.

An *experiment* involves obtaining data by manipulating factors under tightly controlled conditions to test cause and effect. The interest is in whether changing one of the independent variables (a cause) will change the behavior of the dependent variable that is studied (the result). In marketing experiments, the independent variables of interest—sometimes called the marketing *drivers*—are often one or more of the marketing mix elements, such as a product's features, price, or promotion (like advertising messages or coupons). The ideal dependent variable usually is a change in the purchases (incremental unit or dollar sales) of individuals, households, or organizations. For example, food companies often use *test markets*, which offer a product for sale in a small geographic area to help evaluate potential marketing actions. In 1988, Walmart opened three experimental stand-alone supercenters to gauge consumer acceptance before deciding to open others. Today, Walmart operates over 2,700 supercenters around the world.

A potential difficulty with experiments is that outside factors (such as actions of competitors) can distort the results of an experiment and affect the dependent variable (such as sales). A researcher's task is to identify the effect of the marketing variable of interest on the dependent variable when the effects of outside factors in an experiment might hide it.

Information Technology and Data Mining *Information technology* involves operating computer networks that can store and process data. Today information technology can extract hidden information from large databases such as those containing retail sales collected through barcode scanners at checkout counters and households' product purchases and TV viewing behavior.

Figure 8–5 shows how marketers use information technology, data, models, and queries to obtain results that lead to marketing actions.

FIGURE 8–5

How marketing researchers and managers use information technology to turn information into action.

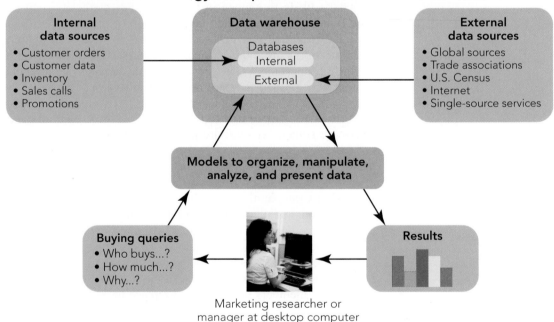

Marketing researcher or manager at desktop computer

At 10 P.M., what is this man likely to buy besides these diapers? For the curious answer that data mining gives, see the text.

Today's marketing managers can be drowned in an ocean of data; they need to adopt strategies for dealing with complex, changing views of the competition, the market, and the consumer. The Internet and PC power help make sense out of this data ocean. The marketer's task is to convert this data ocean into useful information that leads to marketing actions.[26]

At the top of Figure 8–5, marketers use information technology that consists of computers linked together through sophisticated communication networks to access and retrieve data from internal and external sources. These data sources are stored, organized, and managed in databases. Collectively, these databases form a *data warehouse*.

At the bottom of Figure 8–5, marketers query the databases in the data warehouse with marketing questions that need answers. These questions go through statistical models that organize and manipulate the data to analyze and identify the relationships that exist. The results are then presented using tables and graphics for easier interpretation. When querying a database, marketers can use *sensitivity analysis* to ask "what if" questions to determine how hypothetical changes in product or brand "drivers"—the factors that influence the buying decisions of a household or organization—can affect sales.

Traditional marketing research typically involves identifying possible drivers and then collecting data. For example, we might collect data to test the hypothesis that increasing couponing (the driver) during spring will increase trials by first-time buyers (the result).

In contrast, *data mining* is the extraction of hidden predictive information from large databases to find statistical links between consumer purchasing patterns and marketing actions. Some of these are common sense: Since many consumers buy peanut butter and grape jelly together, it may be a good idea to run a joint promotion between Skippy peanut butter and Welch's grape jelly. But would you have expected that men buying diapers in the evening sometimes buy a six-pack of beer as well? This is exactly what supermarkets discovered when they mined checkout data from scanners. So they placed diapers and beer near each other, then placed potato chips between them—and increased sales on all three items! On the near horizon is RFID (radio frequency identification) technology using a "smart tag" microchip on the diapers and beer to tell whether they wind up in the same shopping bag—at 10 in the evening.[27] Still, the success in data mining depends on the judgments of the marketing managers and researchers in how to select, analyze, and interpret the information.

Advantages and Disadvantages of Primary Data

Compared with secondary data, primary data have the advantages of being more flexible and more specific to the problem being studied. The main disadvantages are that primary data are usually far more costly and time consuming to collect than secondary data.

learning review

6. What is the difference between observational and questionnaire data?

7. Which type of survey provides the greatest flexibility for asking probing questions: mail, telephone, or personal interview?

8. What is the difference between a panel and an experiment?

STEP 4: DEVELOP FINDINGS

LO5

Mark Twain once observed, "Collecting data is like collecting garbage. You've got to know what you're going to do with the stuff before you collect it." Thus, marketing data and information have little more value than garbage unless they are analyzed carefully and translated into logical findings, which is step 4 in the marketing research approach.[28]

Analyze the Data

How are sales doing? To see how marketers at Tony's Pizza assessed this question and the results, read the text.

Let's consider the case in early 2010 of Tony's Pizza and Teré Carral, the marketing manager responsible for the Tony's brand. We will use hypothetical data to protect Tony's proprietary information.

Teré is concerned about the limited growth in the Tony's brand over the past four years. She hires a consultant to collect and analyze data to explain what's going on with her brand and to recommend ways to improve its growth. Teré asks the consultant to put together a proposal that includes the answers to two key questions:

1. How are Tony's sales doing on a household basis? For example, are fewer households buying Tony's pizzas, or is each household buying fewer Tony's? Or both?
2. What factors might be contributing to Tony's very flat sales over the past four years?

Facts uncovered by the consultant are vital. For example, is the average household consuming more or less Tony's pizza than in previous years? Is Tony's flat sales performance related to a specific factor? With answers to these questions Teré can identify actions in her marketing plan and implement them over the coming year.

Present the Findings

Findings should be clear and understandable from the way the data are presented. Managers are responsible for *actions*. Often it means delivering the results in clear pictures and, if possible, in a single page.

The consultant gives Teré the answers to her questions using the marketing dashboards in Figure 8–6, a creative way to present findings graphically. Let's look over the shoulders of Teré and the consultant while they interpret these findings:

- Figure 8–6A, Annual Sales—This shows the annual growth of the Tony's Pizza brand is stable but virtually flat from 2006 through 2009.
- Figure 8–6B, Average Annual Sales per Household—Look closely at this graph. At first glance, it may seem like sales in 2009 are *half* what they were in 2006, right? But be careful to read the numbers on the vertical axis. They show that household purchases of Tony's have been steadily declining over the past four years, from an average of 3.4 pizzas per household in 2006 to 3.1 pizzas per household in 2009. (Significant, but hardly a 50 percent drop.) Now the question is, if Tony's annual sales are stable, yet the average individual household is buying fewer Tony's pizzas, what's going on? The answer is, more households are buying pizzas—it's just that each household is buying fewer Tony's pizzas. That households aren't choosing Tony's is a genuine source of concern. But again, here's a classic example of a marketing problem represent-

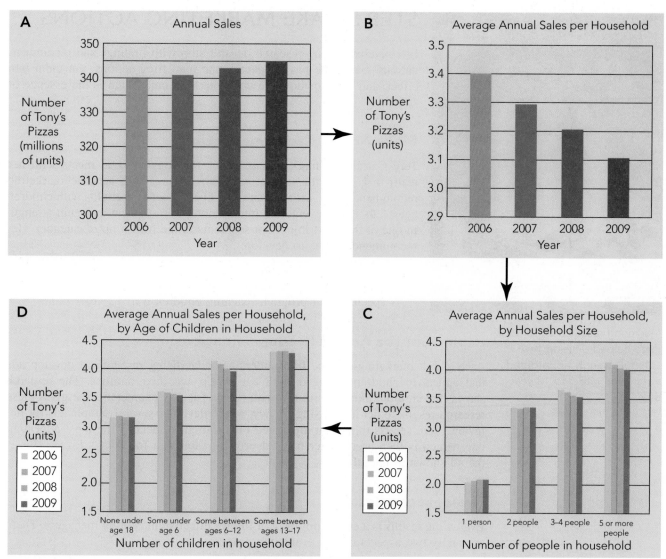

FIGURE 8–6

These marketing dashboards present findings to Tony's marketing manager that lead to recommendations and actions.

Source: Teré Carral, Tony's Pizza.

ing a marketing opportunity. The number of households buying pizza is *growing*, and that's good news for Tony's.

- Figure 8–6C, Average Annual Sales per Household, by Household Size—This chart starts to show a source of the problem: Even though average sales of pizza to households with only one or two people is stable, households with three or four people and those with five or more are declining in average annual pizza consumption. Which households tend to have more than two people? Answer: Households *with children*. Therefore, we should look more closely at the pizza-buying behavior of households with children.

- Figure 8–6D, Average Annual Sales per Household, by Age of Children in the Household—The picture is becoming very clear now: The real problem is in the serious decline in average consumption in the households with younger children, especially in households with children in the 6- to 12-year-old age group.

Identifying a sales problem in households with children 6 to 12 years old is an important discovery, as Tony's sales are declining in a market segment that is known to be one of the heaviest in buying pizzas.

Marketing research at Tony's Pizza helped develop this colorful, friendly ad targeted at families with 6 to 12 year olds.

STEP 5: TAKE MARKETING ACTIONS

Effective marketing research doesn't stop with findings and recommendations—someone has to identify the marketing actions, put them into effect, and monitor how the decisions turn out, which is the essence of step 5.

Make Action Recommendations

Teré Carral, the marketing manager for Tony's Pizza, meets with her team to convert the market research findings into specific marketing recommendations with a clear objective: Target households with children ages 6 to 12 to reverse the trend among this segment and gain strength in one of the most important segments in the frozen pizza category. Her recommendation is to develop:

- An advertising campaign that will target children 6 to 12 years old.
- A monthly promotion calendar with this age group target in mind.
- A special event program reaching children 6 to 12 years old.

Implement the Action Recommendations

As her first marketing action, Teré undertakes advertising research to develop ads that appeal to children in the 6-to-12 age group and their families. The research shows that children like colorful ads with funny, friendly characters. She gives these research results to her advertising agency, which develops several sample ads for her review. Teré selects three that are tested on children to identify the most appealing one, which is then used in her next advertising campaign for Tony's Pizza. This is the ad shown to the left.

Evaluate the Results

Evaluating results is a continuing way of life for effective marketing managers. There are really two aspects of this evaluation process:

- *Evaluating the decision itself.* This involves monitoring the marketplace to determine if action is necessary in the future. For Teré, is her new ad successful in appealing to 6 to 12 year olds and their families? Are sales increasing to this target segment? The success of this strategy suggests Teré add more follow-up ads with colorful, funny, friendly characters.
- *Evaluating the decision process used.* Was the marketing research and analysis used to develop the recommendations effective? Was it flawed? Could it be improved for similar situations in the future? Teré and her marketing team must be vigilant for ways to improve the analysis and results—to learn lessons that might apply to future marketing research efforts at Tony's.

Again, systematic analysis does not guarantee success. But, as in the case of Tony's Pizza, it can improve a firm's success rate for its marketing decisions.

learning review

9. How does data mining differ from traditional marketing research?
10. In the marketing research for Tony's Pizza, what is an example of (a) a finding and (b) a marketing action?

SALES FORECASTING TECHNIQUES

sales forecast
The total sales of a product that a firm expects to sell during a specified time period under specified conditions.

Forecasting or estimating potential sales is often a key goal in a marketing research study. Good sales forecasts are important for a firm as it schedules production. The term **sales forecast** refers to the total sales of a product that a firm expects to sell during a specified time period under specified environmental conditions and its own marketing efforts. For example, Betty Crocker might develop a sales forecast of 4 million cases of cake mix for U.S. consumers in 2012, assuming consumers' dessert preferences remain constant and competitors don't change prices.

Three main sales forecasting techniques are often used: (1) judgments of the decision maker, (2) surveys of knowledgeable groups, and (3) statistical methods.

Judgments of the Decision Maker

Probably 99 percent of all sales forecasts are simply the judgment of the person who must act on the results of the forecast—the individual decision maker. *A direct forecast* involves estimating the value to be forecast without any intervening steps. Examples appear daily: How many quarts of milk should I buy? How much money should I get out of the ATM?

A *lost-horse forecast* involves starting with the last known value of the item being forecast, listing the factors that could affect the forecast, assessing whether they have a positive or negative impact, and making the final forecast. The technique gets its name from how you'd find a lost horse: go to where it was last seen, put yourself in its shoes, consider those factors that could affect where you might go (to the pond if you're thirsty, the hayfield if you're hungry, and so on), and go there.

For example, in early 2009 Under Armour introduced its first line of running shoes. This required it to broaden its appeal from boys and young men who often used its knee pads and cleats in team sports to women, older consumers, and casual athletes. Suppose an Under Armour marketing manager in early 2010 needs to make a sales forecast through 2012. She would take the known value of 2009 sales and list positive factors (good acceptance of its high-tech designs, great publicity) and the negative factors (the economic recession, competition from established name brands) to arrive at the final series of sales forecasts.[29]

How might a marketing manager at Under Armour forecast running shoe sales through 2012? Use a lost-horse forecast, as described in the text.

Surveys of Knowledgeable Groups

If you wonder what your firm's sales will be next year, ask people who are likely to know something about future sales. Two common groups that are surveyed to develop sales forecasts are prospective buyers and the firm's salesforce.

A *survey of buyers' intentions forecast* involves asking prospective customers if they are likely to buy the product during some future time period. For industrial products with few prospective buyers, this can be effective. There are only a few hundred customers in the entire world for Boeing's large airplanes, so Boeing surveys them to develop its sales forecasts and production schedules.

A *salesforce survey forecast* involves asking the firm's salespeople to estimate sales during a coming period. Because these people are in contact with customers and are likely to know what customers like and dislike, there is logic to this approach. However, salespeople can be unreliable forecasters—painting too rosy a picture if they are enthusiastic about a new product and too grim a forecast if their sales quota and future compensation are based on it.

Statistical Methods

The best-known statistical method of forecasting is *trend extrapolation*, which involves extending a pattern observed in past data into the future. When the pattern

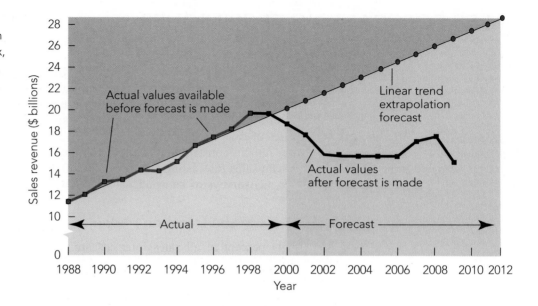

FIGURE 8–7
Linear trend extrapolation of sales revenues at Xerox, made at the start of 2000.

is described with a straight line, it is *linear trend extrapolation*. Suppose that in early 2000 you were a sales forecaster for the Xerox Corporation and had actual sales data running from 1988 to 1999 (see Figure 8–7). Using linear trend extrapolation, you draw a line to fit the past sales data and project it into the future to give the forecast values shown for 2000 to 2012.

If in 2010 you want to compare your forecasts with actual results, you are in for a surprise—illustrating the strength and weakness of trend extrapolation. Trend extrapolation assumes that the underlying relationships in the past will continue into the future, which is the basis of the method's key strength: simplicity. If this assumption proves correct, you have an accurate forecast. However, if this proves wrong, the forecast is likely to be wrong. In this case your forecasts from 2001 through 2009 were too high, as shown in Figure 8–7, largely because of fierce competition in the photocopying industry.

---

learning review

11. What are the three kinds of sales forecasting techniques?

12. How do you make a lost-horse forecast?

LEARNING OBJECTIVES REVIEW

LO1 *Identify the reason for conducting marketing research.*
To be successful, products must meet the wants and needs of potential customers. So marketing research reduces risk by providing the vital information to help marketing managers understand those wants and needs and translate them into marketing actions.

LO2 *Describe the five-step marketing research approach that leads to marketing actions.*
Marketing researchers engage in a five-step decision-making process to collect information that will improve marketing decisions. The first step is to define the problem, which requires setting the research objectives and identifying possible marketing actions. The second step is to develop the research plan, which involves specifying the constraints, identifying data needed for

marketing decisions, and determining how to collect the data. The third step is to collect the relevant information, which includes considering pertinent secondary data (both internal and external) and primary data (by observing and questioning consumers) as well as using information technology and data mining to trigger marketing actions. The fourth step is to develop findings from the marketing research data collected. This involves analyzing the data and presenting the findings of the research. The fifth and last step is to take marketing actions, which involves making and implementing the action recommendations.

LO3 *Explain how marketing uses secondary and primary data.*
Secondary data have already been recorded before the start of the project and consist of two parts: (*a*) internal secondary data, which originate from within the organization, such as sales

reports and customer comments, and (*b*) external secondary data, which are created by other organizations, such as the U.S. Census Bureau (which provides data on the country's population, manufacturers, retailers, and so on) or business and trade publications (which provide data on industry trends, market size, etc.). Primary data are collected specifically for the project and are obtained by either observing or questioning people.

LO4 *Discuss the uses of observations, questionnaires, panels, experiments, and newer data collection methods.*
Marketing researchers observe people in various ways, such as electronically using Nielsen people meters to measure TV viewing behavior or personally using mystery shoppers or ethnographic techniques. A recent electronic innovation is neuromarketing—using high-tech brain scanning to record the responses of a consumer's brain to marketing stimuli like packages or TV ads. Questionnaires involve asking people questions (*a*) in person using interviews or focus groups or (*b*) via a questionnaire using a telephone, fax, print, e-mail, or Internet survey. Panels involve a sample of consumers or stores that are repeatedly measured through time to see if their behaviors change. Experiments, such as test markets, involve measuring the effect of marketing variables such as price or advertising on sales. Collecting data from social networks like Facebook or Twitter is increasingly important because users can share their opinions about products and services with countless "friends" around the globe.

LO5 *Explain how information technology and data mining lead to marketing actions.*
Today's marketing managers are often overloaded with data—from internal sales and customer data to external data on TV viewing habits or grocery purchases from the scanner data at checkout counters. Information technology enables this massive amount of marketing data to be stored, accessed, and processed. The resulting databases can be queried using data mining to find statistical relationships useful for marketing decisions and actions.

LO6 *Describe three approaches to developing a company's sales forecast.*
One approach uses subjective judgments of the decision maker, such as direct or lost-horse forecasts. A direct forecast involves estimating the value to be forecast without any intervening steps. A lost-horse forecast starts with the last known value of the item being forecast, and then lists the factors that could affect the forecast, assesses whether they have a positive or negative impact, and makes the final forecast. Surveys of knowledgeable groups, a second method, involves obtaining information such as the intentions of potential buyers or estimates of the salesforce. Statistical methods involving extending a pattern observed in past data into the future are a third approach. The best-known statistical method is linear trend extrapolation.

FOCUSING ON KEY TERMS

constraints p. 164	**measures of success** p. 163	**questionnaire data** p. 170
data p. 166	**observational data** p. 168	**sales forecast** p. 181
marketing research p. 162	**primary data** p. 166	**secondary data** p. 166

APPLYING MARKETING KNOWLEDGE

1 Suppose your dean of admissions is considering surveying high school seniors about their perceptions of your school to design better informational brochures for them. What are the advantages and disadvantages of doing (*a*) telephone interviews and (*b*) an Internet survey of seniors requesting information about the school?

2 Wisk detergent decides to run a test market to see the effect of coupons and in-store advertising on sales. The index of sales is as follows:

Element in Test Market	Weeks before Coupon	Week of Coupon	Week after Coupon
Without in-store ads	100	144	108
With in-store ads	100	268	203

What are your conclusions and recommendations?

3 Suppose Fisher-Price wants to run a simple experiment to evaluate a proposed Chatter Telephone design. It has two different groups of children on which to run its experiment for one week each. The first group has the old toy telephone, whereas the second group is exposed to the newly designed pull toy with wheels, a noisemaker, and bobbing eyes. The dependent variable is the average number of minutes during the two-hour play period that one of the children is playing with the toy, and the results are as follows:

Element in Experiment	First Group	Second Group
Independent variable	Old design	New design
Dependent variable	13 minutes	62 minutes

Should Fisher-Price introduce the new design? Why?

4 Nielsen Media Research obtains ratings of local TV stations in small markets by having households fill out diary questionnaires. These give information on (*a*) who is watching TV and (*b*) what program. What are the limitations of this questionnaire method?

5 The format in which information is presented is often vital. (*a*) If you were a harried marketing manager and queried your information system, would you rather see the results in tables or charts and graphs?

(*b*) What are one or two strengths and weaknesses of each format?

6 (*a*) Why might a marketing researcher prefer to use secondary data rather than primary data in a study? (*b*) Why might the reverse be true?

7 Which of the following variables would linear trend extrapolation be more accurate for? (*a*) Annual population of the United States or (*b*) annual sales of cars produced in the United States by Ford. Why?

building your marketing plan

To help you collect the most useful data for your marketing plan, develop a three-column table:

1 In column 1, list the information you would ideally like to have to fill holes in your marketing plan.

2 In column 2, identify the source for each bit of information in column 1, such as an Internet search, talking to prospective customers, looking at internal data, and so forth.

3 In column 3, set a priority on information you will have time to spend collecting by ranking them: 1 = most important; 2 = next most important, and so forth.

video case 8   Ford Consulting Group, Inc.: From Data to Actions

"The fast pace of working as a marketing professional isn't getting any easier," agrees David Ford, as he talks with Mark Rehborg, Tony's Pizza brand manager. "The speed of communication, the availability of real-time market information, and the responsibility for a brand's profit make marketing one of the most challenging professional jobs today."

Mark responds, "Ten years ago, we could reach 80 percent of our target market with 3 television spots—but today, to reach the same 80 percent, we would have to buy 97 spots. We haven't the luxury to be complacent—our core consumer, the 6- to 12-year-old 'big kid,' is part of a savvy, wired culture that is changing rapidly."

DASHBOARDS: DATA INTO ACTIONS

David Ford, president of Ford Consulting Group (FCG), prepares business analysis, often in the form of a dashboard, to assist clients such as Tony's in translating the market and sales information into marketing actions. David works with Mark to grow Tony's sales and profit performance. Mark uses information to choose where to spend his funds to promote his products. Many times, the sales force requests additional promotion funds to help them hit their sales targets.

The information used most often for sales and promotion analysis comes from places like Scantrack and InfoScan that summarize sales data from grocery stores and other outlets that scan purchases at the checkout.

FCG helps clients make sense of their existing information, *not* collect more information. The project that fol-

lows is typical of the work Ford Consulting Group (www.fordconsultinggroup.com) undertakes for a client. The data are hypothetical, but the situation is a very typical one in the grocery products industry. Here's a snapshot of some of the terms in the case:

- "You" have just come on the job, as the new marketing person.
- "NE" is the Northeastern sales region of Tony's.
- "SE, NW, SW" are the other sales regions.
- "Mark" is a Tony's brand manager and your boss.

PART 1: A TYPICAL QUESTION, ON A TYPICAL DAY

Let's dive into a typical question you might face on a typical day. You are given two memos—one that provides background information and one from Mark to you.

You dig into data files and develop Table 1, which shows how Tony's is doing in the company's four sales regions and the entire United States on key marketing dimensions. Without reading further, take a deep breath and try to answer question 1.

PART 2: UNCOVERING THE TRUTH

Let's assume your analysis (question 1) shows the NE is a problem, so we need to understand what's going on in the NE. Further effort enables you to develop Table 2. It shows the situation for the four largest supermarket chains in the Northeast sales region that carry Tony's. Now answer question 2.

TO: Mark Rehborg, Tony's Brand Manager
FROM: Steve Quam, Tony's Field Sales
CC: Margaret Loiaza, NE Sales Region Manager
RE: Feedback on Sales Call at Food-Fast

Hi Mark—

Our sales call at Food-Fast wasn't so great. They don't see how our Tony's is going to sell well enough to justify the additional shelf space. I also talked to Margaret and she said that second quarter may be weaker than planned across all the NE, and I should give you a heads-up. She's on vacation this week. She's planning to schedule some time with you to talk about additional promotion money to do catch-up in the third quarter. She'll be there next week.

Steve

TO: You, the New Marketing Person
FROM: Mark Rehborg, Tony's Brand Manager (Your Boss)
RE: Small Project due Friday

Hi You,

Can you help out here? I've got a meeting with Margaret on Friday afternoon, and she's concerned that Food-Fast and the whole NE is going to need some additional promotion dollars.

Lauretta started the analysis and was hurt in a kick-boxing accident yesterday and won't be back to work for a week. Her files are attached. Can you look through her files and summarize what's going on in the NE and the rest of the U.S.? Does Margaret need more promotion money?

Let's discuss Friday A.M.

Mark

Questions

1 Study Table 1. (*a*) How does the situation in the Northeast compare with the other regions in the United States? (*b*) Why are sales soft? (*c*) Write a 150-word e-mail with attachments to Mark Rehborg, your boss, giving your answers to (*b*).

2 Study Table 2. (*a*) What do you conclude from this information? (*b*) Summarize your conclusions in a 150-word e-mail with attachments to Mark, who needs them for a meeting tomorrow with Margaret, the Northeast sales region manager. (*c*) What marketing actions might your memo suggest?

Region	Quarterly Change in Volume (%)	Distribution[a] (%)	Price ($)	Price Gap[b] ($)	Promotion Support[c] (%)	Promotion Volume[d] (%)
NE	3%	93%	$1.29	+8	7%	14%
SE	5	95	1.11	−1	9	16
NW	8	98	1.19	+1	8	15
SW	6	96	1.25	0	8	15
U.S.	6	97	1.19	0	8	15

TABLE 1. COMPARISON OF TONY'S PERFORMANCE, BY REGION

[a] % of outlets carrying Tony's.
[b] Price gap = (Our price) − (Competitor's price).
[c] Promotion support = % of the time brand was promoted.
[d] Promotion volume = % of the volume sold on promotion.

Super-Market Chain	Quarterly Change in Volume (%)	Distribution[a] (%)	Price ($)	Price Gap[b] ($)	Promotion Support[c] (%)	Promotion Volume[d] (%)
Save-a-lot	5%	95%	$1.39	+10	10%	19%
Food-Fast	0	90	1.28	−1	3	4
Get-Fresh	0	90	1.30	+1	3	4
Dollars-Off	7	97	1.34	+5	7	14

TABLE 2. COMPARISON OF MAJOR SUPERMARKET CHAINS IN THE NORTHEAST

 ZETA   **Free Shipping Both Ways!***   --Search--   Search   Go to Zappos.com Classic
POWERED by SERVICE™   365-Day Return Policy   Search by: Size • Narrow Shoes • Wide Shoes • Popular Searches   --Visit Our Other Sites--

View All Departments ▼ | Shoes | Clothing | Bags & Handbags | Watches | Sunglasses | New Arrivals | Brands | Women's | Men's | Kids'

Alphabetical Brand Index   # A B C D E F G H I J K L M N O P Q R S T U V W X Y Z

Women's Shoes	**Men's Shoes**	**Kids' Shoes**	**Women's Clothing**	**Men's Clothing**	**Kids' Clothing**	**Bags and Handbags**	**More Departments**
▸ What's New	▸ What's New	▸ What's New	▸ What's New	▸ What's New	▸ What's New	Backpacks	▸ What's New
Sandals	Boots	Sneakers	Tops	Shirts	Clothing Sets	Messenger Bags	Accessories
Heels	Sneakers	Flats	Shorts	Shorts	Shirts	Diaper Bags	Housewares
Boots	Oxfords	Sandals	Skirts	Pants	Shorts	Laptop Bags	Beauty
Sneakers	Sandals	Boots	Pants	Jackets & Coats	Pants	Tote Bags	Jewelry
Slippers	Loafers	First Walkers	Jackets & Coats	Suits	Jackets & Coats	Hobo Bags	Watches
Flats	Boat Shoes	**More Kids' Shoes**	Swimsuits	Swimsuits	Swimwear	Shoulder Bags	Sporting Goods
Clogs & Mules	Slippers		Sleepwear	Sleepwear	Baby One-Pieces	Clutch Bags	**More Departments**
More Women's Shoes	**More Men's Shoes**		**More Women's Clothing**	**More Men's Clothing**	**More Kids' Clothing**	**More Bags**	

FREE RETURNS · 365-DAY RETURN POLICY · 24/7 CUSTOMER SERVICE · 1.800.927.7671

Shopping Recommendations For You

Onitsuka Tiger by Asics Ultimate 81 **$66.95**	**Converse** All Star Core OX **$45.00**	**Converse** Chuck Taylor All Star Ox **$45.00**	**Sperry Top-Sider** Authentic Original **$64.95**	**Vans** Classic Slip-On Core Classics **$42.00**

What's New At Zappos!	**Zappos Top Sellers!**	**Find What You Need Quickly**	**The Zappos Culture**
Women's Shoes	**Women's** Sandals	**By Gender** Women Men Girls Boys	Learn about what inspires Zappos to provide the best service!
		Special Interest Wide Shoes Narrow Shoes Western Shoes Eco-Friendly Shoes Brands	**Zappos Core Values:** 10 Values We Live By
			Customer Testimonials: Our Customers Connect
			Enjoy Fun and A Little Weirdness: Check out Zappos Blogs
		Specialty Site Couture Bike shop Running Outdoor	**The Zappos Experience:** Share Your Zappos Videos
			Unique Customers: Zappos Furry Customers Zappos Customers In Training
			Become a Part of Our Culture: Careers at Zappos
			Get Inspired:

9

Market Segmentation, Targeting, and Positioning

LEARNING OBJECTIVES

After reading this chapter you should be able to:

LO1 Explain what market segmentation is and when to use it.

LO2 Identify the five steps involved in segmenting and targeting markets.

LO3 Recognize the bases used to segment consumer and organizational markets.

LO4 Develop a market-product grid to identify a target market and recommend resulting actions.

LO5 Explain how marketing managers position products in the marketplace.

ZAPPOS.COM: DELIVERING "WOW" THROUGH MARKET SEGMENTATION AND SERVICE

Tony Hsieh (opposite page) showed signs of being an entrepreneur early in life. He's now chief executive officer (CEO) of online retailer Zappos.com. The company name is derived from the Spanish word *zapatos*, which means shoes.

At age 12, Hsieh brought in several hundred dollars a month with his button-making business. In college, Hsieh sold pizzas out of his dorm room. Fellow entrepreneur Alfred Lin bought pizzas from Hsieh and then sold them by the slice to other students. Pizza-slice marketer Alfred Lin is the chief operating officer at Zappos.com today.[1]

A Clear Market Segmentation Strategy

Hsieh, Lin, and founder Nick Swinmurn have given Zappos.com a clear, specific market segmentation strategy: Offer a huge selection of shoes to people who will buy them online. Recently Zappos.com has added lines of clothes, accessories, beauty aids, and housewares. This focus on the segment of online buyers generates over $1 billion in sales annually.[2]

"With Zappos, the shoe store comes to you," says Pamela Leo, a New Jersey customer. "I can try the shoes in the comfort of my own home. . . . It's fabulous."[3] Besides the in-home convenience, Zappos.com offers free shipping both ways. The choices for its online customers are staggering. A recent Zappos.com home page describes how it offers more than 1,000 brands to customers.

Delivering WOW Customer Service

Asked about Zappos.com, Hsieh says, "We try to spend most of our time on stuff that will improve customer-service levels."[4] This customer-service obsession for its market segment of online customers means that all new Zappos.com employees—whether the chief financial officer or the children's footwear buyer—go through four weeks of customer-loyalty training. Hsieh offers $2,000 to anyone completing the training who wants to leave Zappos.com. The theory: If you take the money and run, you're not right for Zappos.com. Few take the money!

Ten "core values" are the foundation for the Zappos.com culture, brand, and business strategies. Some examples:[5]

#1. Deliver WOW through service. This focus on exemplary customer service encompasses all 10 core values.

#3. Create fun and a little weirdness. In a Zappos.com day, cowbells ring, parades appear, and modified-blaster gunfights arise.

#6. Build open and honest relationships with communications.
Employees are told to say what they think.

The other Zappos.com core values appear on its Web site: www.Zappos.com. Tony Hsieh's strategy on core values and customer service appears on Twitter, where he has more than 1.6 million followers.[6]

The Zappos.com strategy illustrates successful market segmentation and targeting, the first topics in Chapter 9. The chapter ends with the topic of positioning the organization, product, or brand.

WHY SEGMENT MARKETS?

A business firm segments its markets so it can respond more effectively to the wants of groups of potential buyers and thus increase its sales and profits. Not-for-profit organizations also segment the clients they serve to satisfy client needs more effectively while achieving the organization's goals. Let's describe (1) what market segmentation is and (2) when to segment markets, sometimes using the Zappos.com segmentation strategy as an example.

What Market Segmentation Means

market segmentation
Aggregates potential buyers into groups that have common needs and will respond similarly to a marketing action.

market segments
The relatively homogeneous groups of prospective buyers that result from the market segmentation process.

product differentiation
The strategy of using different marketing mix activities to help consumers perceive a product as being different and better than competing products.

People have different needs and wants, even though it would be easier for marketers if they didn't. **Market segmentation** involves aggregating prospective buyers into groups that (1) have common needs and (2) will respond similarly to a marketing action. **Market segments** are the relatively homogeneous groups of prospective buyers that result from the market segmentation process. Each market segment consists of people who are relatively similar to each other in terms of their consumption behavior.

The existence of different market segments has caused firms to use a marketing strategy of **product differentiation**. This strategy involves a firm using different marketing mix activities, such as product features and advertising, to help consumers perceive the product as being different and better than competing products. The perceived differences may involve physical features, such as size or color, or nonphysical ones, such as image or price.

Segmentation: Linking Needs to Actions The process of segmenting a market and selecting specific segments as targets is the link between the various buyers' needs and the organization's marketing program, as shown in Figure 9–1. Market segmentation is only a means to an end: It leads to tangible marketing actions that can increase sales and profitability.

Effective market segmentation does two key things: (1) It forms meaningful groupings and (2) it develops specific marketing mix actions. People or organizations should be grouped into a market segment according to the similarity of their needs and the benefits they look for in making a purchase. The market segments must relate to specific marketing actions that the organization can take. These actions may involve separate offerings or other aspects of the marketing mix, such as price, promotion, or distribution strategies.

FIGURE 9–1
Market segmentation links market needs to an organization's marketing program—specific marketing mix actions to satisfy those needs.

Identify market needs	Link needs to actions	Execute marketing program actions
Benefits in terms of: • Product features • Expense • Quality • Savings in time and convenience	Take steps to segment and target markets	A marketing mix in terms of: • Product • Price • Promotion • Place (distribution)

Core value #3—"create fun and a little weirdness"— helped in naming Zappos .com one of the 2008 "Marketers of the Year" by *Advertising Age* magazine.

The Successful Zappos.com Footwear Segmentation Strategy The Zappos.com target customer segment consists of people who want to (1) have a wide selection of shoes, (2) shop online in the convenience of their own homes, and (3) receive the guarantee of quick delivery and free returns. Zappos's actions include offering a huge inventory of shoes and other products, using an online selling strategy, and providing overnight delivery. This enables Zappos .com to create a positive customer experience and generate repeat purchases. On any given day, about 75 percent of Zappos.com shoppers are repeat customers.

With over 8 million customers and 5,000 calls daily to Zappos's service center, Zappos.com executives believe that the speed with which a customer receives an online purchase plays a big role in gaining repeat customers.[7] The company will continue to stress this point of difference, made possible by stocking in its warehouse every item it sells. And if customers continue to associate Zappos.com with the absolute best service among online sellers with its footwear, clothing, and other offerings, both Zappos.com's weirdness (its third core value) and its sales are on solid footing!

When and How to Segment Markets

The one-size-fits-all mass markets—like that for Tide laundry detergent of 40 years ago—no longer exist. The global marketing officer at Procter & Gamble, which markets Tide, says, "Every one of our brands is targeted." Welcome to today's customer relationship era that consists of market segmentation and target marketing.[8]

A business goes to the trouble and expense of segmenting its markets when it expects that this will increase its sales, profit, and return on investment. When expenses are greater than the potentially increased sales from segmentation, a firm should not attempt to segment its market. Three specific segmentation strategies that illustrate this point are (1) one product and multiple market segments, (2) multiple products and multiple market segments, and (3) segments of one, or mass customization.

One Product and Multiple Market Segments When an organization produces only a single product or service and attempts to sell it to two or more market segments, it avoids the extra costs of developing and producing additional versions of the product. In this case, the incremental costs of taking the product into new market segments are typically those of a separate promotional campaign or a new channel of distribution.

These *different* covers for the *same* magazine issue show a very effective market segmentation strategy. For which strategy it is and why it works, see the text.

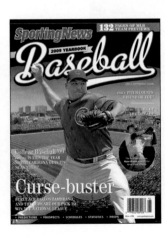

Does Harry Potter appeal only to the English-speaking kids' segment? See the text for more about this amazing publishing success story.

Magazines and books are single products frequently directed at two or more distinct market segments. The *Sporting News Baseball Yearbook* uses 16 different covers featuring a baseball star from each of its regions in the United States. Harry Potter's phenomenal seven-book success is based on both author J. K. Rowling's fiction-writing wizardry and her publisher's creativity in marketing to preteen, teen, and adult segments of readers around the world. By 2010, more than 400 million Harry Potter books had been sold in 64 languages.[9] In the United States, the books were often at the top of *The New York Times* fiction best-seller list—for adults. Although separate covers for magazines or separate advertisements for books are expensive, these expenses are minor compared with the costs of producing multiple versions of magazines or books for multiple age or geographic market segments.

Multiple Products and Multiple Market Segments Ford's different lines of cars, SUVs, and pickup trucks are each targeted at a different type of customer—examples of multiple products aimed at multiple market segments. Producing these different vehicles is clearly more expensive than producing only a single vehicle. But this strategy is very effective if it meets customers' needs better, doesn't reduce quality or increase price, and adds to Ford's sales revenues and profits.

Marketers increasingly emphasize a two-tier marketing strategy—what some call "Tiffany/Walmart strategies." Many firms now offer different variations of the same basic offering to high-end and low-end segments. Gap's Banana Republic chain sells blue jeans for $58, whereas its Old Navy stores sell a slightly different version for $22.

Segments of One: Mass Customization American marketers are rediscovering today what their ancestors running the corner general store knew a century ago: Each customer has unique needs and wants and desires special tender loving care. Economies of scale in manufacturing and marketing during the past century made mass-produced goods so affordable that most customers were willing to compromise their individual tastes and settle for standardized products. Today's Internet ordering and flexible manufacturing and marketing processes have made

Ann Taylor Stores Corporation's LOFT chain tries to reach value-conscious women with a casual lifestyle while its flagship Ann Taylor chain targets more sophisticated women. Do these store fronts convey this difference? For the potential dangers of this two-segment strategy, see the text.

mass customization possible, which means tailoring goods or services to the tastes of individual customers on a high-volume scale.

Mass customization is the next step beyond *build-to-order* (BTO), manufacturing a product only when there is an order from a customer. Apple uses BTO systems that trim work-in-progress inventories and shorten delivery times to customers. To do this, Apple restricts its computer manufacturing line to only a few basic models that can be assembled in four minutes. This gives customers a good choice with quick delivery. But even this system falls a bit short of total mass customization because customers do not have an unlimited number of features from which to choose.[10]

The Segmentation Trade-Off: Synergies versus Cannibalization

The key to successful product differentiation and market segmentation strategies is finding the ideal balance between satisfying a customer's individual wants and achieving *organizational synergy*, the increased customer value achieved through performing organizational functions such as marketing or manufacturing more efficiently. The "increased customer value" can take many forms: more products, improved quality on existing products, lower prices, easier access to products through improved distribution, and so on. So the ultimate criterion for an organization's marketing success is that customers should be better off as a result of the increased synergies.

The organization should also achieve increased revenues and profits from the product differentiation and market segmentation strategies it uses. When the increased customer value involves adding new products or a new chain of stores, the product differentiation–market segmentation trade-off raises a critical issue: Are the new products or new chain simply stealing customers and sales from the older, existing ones? This is known as *cannibalization*.

Unfortunately, the lines between customer segments can often blur and lead to problems, such as the Ann Taylor flagship store competing with its LOFT outlets. The flagship Ann Taylor chain targets polished, sophisticated women while its sister Ann Taylor LOFT chain targets women wanting moderately priced, trendy, casual clothes they can wear to the office. The nightmare: Annual sales of the LOFT stores recently passed those of the Ann Taylor chain, which has struggled to reach its target customers. The result: More than 100 stores from both chains were to be closed by 2010.[11]

---

learning review

1. Market segmentation involves aggregating prospective buyers into groups that have two key characteristics. What are they?

2. In terms of market segments and products, what are the three market segmentation strategies?

STEPS IN SEGMENTING AND TARGETING MARKETS

LO2

Figure 9–2 on the next page identifies the five-step process used to segment a market and select the target segments on which it wants to focus. Segmenting a market requires both detailed analysis and large doses of common sense and managerial judgment. So market segmentation is both science and art!

For the purposes of our discussion, assume that you have just purchased a Wendy's restaurant. Your Wendy's is located next to a large urban university, one that offers both day and evening classes. Your restaurant offers the basic Wendy's fare: hamburgers, chicken and deli sandwiches, salads, French fries, and Frosty desserts. Even though you are part of a chain that has some restrictions on menu and décor, you are free to set your hours of business and to develop local advertising. How can

FIGURE 9–2

The five key steps in segmenting and targeting markets link the market needs of customers to the organization's marketing program.

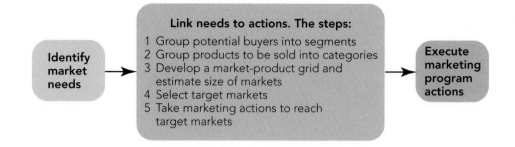

Identify market needs

Link needs to actions. The steps:
1 Group potential buyers into segments
2 Group products to be sold into categories
3 Develop a market-product grid and estimate size of markets
4 Select target markets
5 Take marketing actions to reach target markets

Execute marketing program actions

market segmentation help? In the sections that follow, you will apply the five-step process for segmenting and targeting markets to arrive at marketing actions for your restaurant.

Step 1: Group Potential Buyers into Segments

It's not always a good idea to segment a market. Grouping potential buyers into meaningful segments involves meeting some specific criteria that answer the questions, "Would segmentation be worth doing?" and "Is it possible?" If so, a marketer must find specific variables that can be used to create these various segments.

Criteria to Use in Forming the Segments   A marketing manager should develop market segments that meet five essential criteria:[12]

This appliance includes everything from a small refrigerator, freezer, and microwave oven to a charging station for laptops and cell phones. To which market segment might this appeal? The answer appears in the text.

MICROFRIDGE REVOLUTIONIZES THE REFRIGERATOR.

AGAIN.

The leader in combination appliances brings you a newly engineered design to deliver the ultimate in convenience for any small space environment.

The most popular combination appliance in America now offers new features. A fully integrated Dual Charging Station allows you to charge laptops, cell phones, digital cameras, MP3 players and more, all with the safety and energy conservation benefits of Safe Plug® technology.

This is no ordinary refrigerator. So if you haven't seen the new MicroFridge®, now's the time to see how the best just got better.

Dual Charging Station - A brand new feature that makes it easy and convenient to charge personal electronic devices.

Safe Plug® Technology - A patent-pending power management system that conserves energy and prevents circuit overloads.

10-Year Warranty - Our on-site service only adds to what is by far an industry best warranty.

To get the world's most revolutionary refrigerator, call 1-800-994-0165 or visit microfridge.com

- *Simplicity and cost-effectiveness of assigning potential buyers to segments.* A marketing manager must be able to put a market segmentation plan into effect. This means identifying the characteristics of potential buyers in a market and then cost-effectively assigning them to a segment.
- *Potential for increased profit.* The best segmentation approach is the one that maximizes the opportunity for future profit and return on investment (ROI). If this potential is maximized without segmentation, don't segment. For nonprofit organizations, the criterion is the potential for serving clients more effectively.
- *Similarity of needs of potential buyers within a segment.* Potential buyers within a segment should be similar in terms of common needs that, in turn, lead to a common marketing action, such as product features sought or advertising media used.
- *Difference of needs of buyers among segments.* If the needs of the various segments aren't very different, combine them into fewer segments. A different segment usually requires a different marketing action that, in turn, means greater costs. If increased sales don't offset extra costs, combine segments and reduce the number of marketing actions.
- *Potential of a marketing action to reach a segment.* Reaching a segment requires a simple but effective marketing action. If no such action exists, don't segment.

Ways to Segment Consumer Markets   Four general bases of segmentation can be used to segment U.S. consumer markets. These four segmentation bases are (1) *geographic segmentation*, which is based on where prospective customers live or work (region, city size); (2) *demographic segmentation*, which is based on some

LO3

Who are your target customers? What are they like? Where do they live? How can you reach them? These questions are answered by Nielsen Claritas, whose PRIZM classifies every household into one of 66 demographically and behaviorally distinct neighborhood segments to identify lifestyles and purchase behavior within a defined geographic market area, such as zip code.

Want to know what your neighborhood is like? Go to claritas.com/MyBest Segments/Default.jsp and click the "You Are Where You Live" image. Then, type in your zip code (and security code) to find out what the most common segments are in your neighborhood. For a description of these segments, click the "Segment Look-Up" tab. Is this your "flock"?

objective physical (gender, race), measurable (age, income), or other classification attribute (birth era, occupation) of prospective customers; (3) *psychographic segmentation*, which is based on some subjective mental or emotional attributes (personality), aspirations (lifestyle), or needs of prospective customers; and (4) *behavioral segmentation*, which is based on some observable actions or attitudes by prospective customers—such as where they buy, what benefits they seek, how frequently they buy, and why they buy. Some examples are:

- *Geographic segmentation: Region.* Campbell Soup Company found that its canned nacho cheese sauce, which could be heated and poured directly onto nacho chips, was too spicy for Americans in the East and not spicy enough for those in the West and Southwest. The result: Campbell's plants in Texas and California produced a hotter nacho cheese sauce than that produced in the other plants to serve their regions better.
- *Demographic segmentation: Household size.* More than half of all U.S. households are made up of only one or two persons, so Campbell packages meals with only one or two servings for this market segment.
- *Psychographic segmentation: Lifestyle.* Nielsen Claritas's lifestyle segmentation is based on the belief that "birds of a feather flock together." Thus, people of similar lifestyles tend to live near one another, have similar interests, and buy similar offerings. This is of great value to marketers. Claritas's PRIZM classifies every household in the United States into one of 66 unique market segments. See the Marketing Matters box for a profile of where you live.
- *Behavioral segmentation: Product features.* Understanding what features are important to different customers is a useful way to segment markets because it can lead directly to specific marketing actions, such as a new product, an ad campaign, or a distribution system. For example, college dorm residents frequently want to keep and prepare their own food to save money or have a late-night snack. However, their dorm rooms are often woefully short of space. MicroFridge understands this and markets a combination microwave, refrigerator, freezer, and charging station appliance targeted to these students.
- *Behavioral segmentation: Usage rate.* **Usage rate** is the quantity consumed or patronage—store visits—during a specific period. It varies significantly among different customer groups. Airlines have developed frequent-flier programs to

usage rate
The quantity consumed or the number of store visits during a specific period.

encourage passengers to use the same airline repeatedly to create loyal customers. This technique, sometimes called *frequency marketing*, focuses on usage rate. One key conclusion emerges about usage: In market segmentation studies, some measurement of usage by, or sales obtained from, various segments is central to the analysis.

The Aberdeen Group recently analyzed which segmentation bases were used by the 20 percent most profitable organizations of the 220 surveyed. From highest to lowest, these were the segmentation bases they used:

- Geographic bases—88 percent.
- Behavioral bases—65 percent.
- Demographic bases—53 percent.
- Psychographic bases—43 percent.

The top 20 percent often use more than one of these bases in their market segmentation studies, plus measures such as purchase histories and usage rates of customers.[13]

Experian Simmons continuously surveys over 25,000 adults each year to obtain quarterly, projectable usage rate data from the U.S. national population for more than 450 consumer product categories and 8,000+ brands. Its purpose is to discover how the products and services they buy and the media they use relate to their behavioral, psychographic, and demographic characteristics.[14]

Usage rate is sometimes referred to in terms of the **80/20 rule**, a concept that suggests 80 percent of a firm's sales are obtained from 20 percent of its customers. The percentages in the 80/20 rule are not really fixed at exactly 80 percent and 20 percent but suggest that a small fraction of customers provides a large fraction of a firm's sales.

As part of its survey, Experian Simmons asked adults which fast-food restaurant(s) was (1) the sole or only restaurant, (2) the primary one, or (3) one of several secondary ones they patronized. As a Wendy's restaurant owner, the information depicted in Figure 9–3 should give you some ideas in developing a marketing program for your local market. For example, the Wendy's bar graph in Figure 9–3 shows that your sole (0.5 percent) and primary (17.6 percent) user segments are somewhat behind Burger King and far behind McDonald's. Thus, your challenge is to look at these two competitors and devise a marketing program to win customers from them.

The nonusers part of the Wendy's bar graph in Figure 9–3 also provides ideas. It shows that 13.8 percent of adult Americans don't go to fast-food restaurants in a typical month and are really nonprospects—unlikely to ever patronize any fast-food

FIGURE 9–3

Comparison of various kinds of users and nonusers for Wendy's, Burger King, and McDonald's fast-food restaurants. This table gives a Wendy's restaurant a snapshot of its customers compared to those of its major competitors.

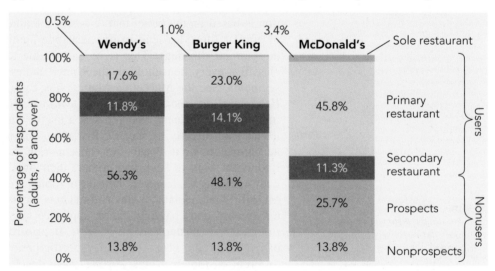

Source: Experian Simmons Winter 2010 Full-Year NCS/NHCS Choices 3 System Crosstabulation Report based on visits within the past 30 days.

restaurant. However, 56.3 percent of nonusers are prospects who may be worth a targeted marketing program. These adults use the product category (fast food) but do not yet patronize Wendy's. New menu items, such as the Bacon & Blue Hamburger, or promotional strategies, such as the "You Can't Fake Real" TV ad, may succeed in converting these prospects into users that patronize Wendy's.

Variables to Use in Forming Segments   To analyze your Wendy's customers, you need to identify which variables to use to segment them. Because the restaurant is located near a large urban university, the most logical starting point for segmentation is really behavioral: Are the prospective customers students or nonstudents?

To segment the students, you could try a variety of (1) geographic variables, such as city or zip code, (2) demographic variables, such as gender, age, year in school, or college major, or (3) psychographic variables, such as personality or needs. But none of these variables really meets the five criteria listed previously—particularly, the fifth criterion about leading to a doable marketing action to reach the various segments. The bases of segmentation for the "students" segment really combines two variables: (1) where students live and (2) when they are on campus. This results in four "student" segments:

* Students living in dormitories (university residence halls, sororities, fraternities).
* Students living near the university in apartments.
* Day commuter students living outside the area.
* Night commuter students living outside the area.

The three main segments of "nonstudents" include:

* Faculty and staff members who work at the university.
* People who live in the area but aren't connected with the university.
* People who work in the area but aren't connected with the university.

People in each of these nonstudent segments aren't quite as similar as those in the student segments, which makes them harder to reach with a marketing program or action. Think about (1) whether the needs of all these segments are different and (2) how various advertising media can be used to reach these groups effectively.

Ways to Segment Organizational Markets   A number of variables can be used to segment organizational markets: For example, a product manager at Xerox responsible for its new line of color printers might use these segmentation bases and corresponding variables:

* *Geographic segmentation: Statistical area.* Firms located in a metropolitan statistical area might receive a personal sales call, whereas those in a micropolitan statistical area might be contacted by telephone.
* *Demographic segmentation: NAICS code.* Firms categorized by the North American Industry Classification System code as manufacturers that deal with customers throughout the world might have different document printing needs than do retailers or lawyers serving local customers.
* *Demographic segmentation: Number of employees.* The size of the firm is related to the volume of digital documents produced, so firms with varying numbers of employees might be specific target markets for different Xerox copier systems.
* *Behavioral segmentation: Usage rate.* Similar to this segmentation variable for consumer markets, features are often of major importance in organizational markets. So Xerox can target organizations needing fast printing, copying, and scanning in color—the benefits and features emphasized in the ad for its Xerox WorkCentre 7655 Color MFP system.

What variables might Xerox use to segment organizational markets to respond to a firm's color-copying problems? For the possible answer and related marketing actions, see the text.

3. The process of segmenting and targeting markets is a bridge between which two marketing activities?

4. What is the difference between the demographic and behavioral bases of market segmentation?

Step 2: Group Products to Be Sold into Categories

What does your Wendy's restaurant sell? Of course you are selling individual products such as Frostys, hamburgers, and fries. But for marketing purposes you're really selling combinations of individual products that become a "meal." This distinction is critical, so let's discuss both (1) individual Wendy's products and (2) groupings of Wendy's products.

Individual Wendy's Products When Dave Thomas founded Wendy's in 1969, he offered only four basic items: "Hot 'n juicy" hamburgers, Frosty Dairy Desserts (Frostys), French fries, and soft drinks. Since then, Wendy's has introduced many new products and innovations to compete for customers' fast-food dollars. Some of these are shown in Figure 9–4. New products include salads, low trans fat chicken sandwiches, and Frescata deli sandwiches. But there are also nonproduct innovations to increase consumer convenience like drive-thru services and E-Pay to enable credit card purchases.

Figure 9–4 also shows that each product or innovation is not targeted equally to all market segments based on gender, needs, or university affiliation. The cells in Figure 9–4 labeled "P" represent Wendy's primary target market segments when it introduced each product or innovation. The boxes labeled "S" represent the secondary target market segments that also bought these products or used these innovations.

FIGURE 9–4
Wendy's new products and other innovations target specific market segments based on a customer's gender, needs, or university affiliation.

MARKET SEGMENT		HOT 'N JUICY HAMBURGER (1969)	DRIVE-THRU (1970)	99¢ SUPER VALUE MEALS (1989)	SALAD SENSATIONS (2002)	E-PAY (2003)	ADULT COMBO MEALS (2004)	LOW TRANS FAT CHICKEN SANDWICHES (2006)	FRESCATA DELI SANDWICHES (2006)	BREAKFAST SANDWICHES (2007)
GENERAL	GROUP WITH NEED									
GENDER	Male	P	P	P	S	P	P	S	P	P
	Female				P	P	S	S	P	P
NEEDS	Price/Value			P	S		P			
	Health-Conscious				P			P	P	
	Convenience	S	P		S	P	S			P
	Meat Lovers	P		S			P	S	S	S
UNIVERSITY AFFILIATION	Affiliated (Students, Faculty, Staff)	P	S	P	P	P	S	P	P	S
	Nonaffiliated (Residents, Workers)	S	P	S	S	S	P	S	S	P

Key: P = Primary market   S = Secondary market

In some cases, Wendy's discovered that large numbers of people in a segment not originally targeted for a particular product or innovation bought it anyway.

Groupings of Wendy's Products: Meals Finding a means of grouping the products a firm sells into meaningful categories is as important as grouping customers into segments. If the firm has only one product or service, this isn't a problem. But when it has dozens or hundreds, these must be grouped in some way so buyers can relate to them. This is why department stores and supermarkets are organized into product groups, with the departments or aisles containing related merchandise. Likewise, manufacturers have product lines that are the groupings they use in the catalogs sent to customers.

What are the product groupings for your Wendy's restaurant? It could be the item purchased, such as hamburgers, salads, a Frosty, and French fries. This is where judgment—the qualitative aspect of marketing—comes in. Customers really buy an eating experience—a meal occasion that satisfies a need at a particular time of day. So the product groupings that make the most marketing sense are the five "meals" based on the time of day consumers buy them: breakfast, lunch, between-meal snack, dinner, and after-dinner snack. These groupings are more closely related to the way purchases are actually made and permit you to market the entire meal, not just your individual items such as French fries or hamburgers.

Step 3: Develop a Market-Product Grid and Estimate the Size of Markets

LO4

A **market-product grid** is a framework to relate the market segments of potential buyers to products offered or potential marketing actions by an organization. In a complete market-product grid analysis, each cell in the grid can show the estimated market size of a given product sold to a specific market segment. Let's first look at forming a market-product grid for your Wendy's restaurant and then at estimating market sizes.

market-product grid
A framework relating the segments of a market to products or marketing actions of the firm.

Forming a Market-Product Grid Developing a market-product grid means identifying and labeling the markets (or horizontal rows) and product groupings (or vertical columns), as shown in Figure 9–5. From our earlier discussion we've chosen to divide the market segments into students versus nonstudents, with subdivisions

FIGURE 9–5
Selecting a target market for your Wendy's fast-food restaurant next to an urban university. The numbers in this market-product grid show the estimated size of the market in each cell, which leads to selecting the shaded target market.

MARKET SEGMENTS	PRODUCTS: MEALS				
	Break-fast	Lunch	Between-Meal Snack	Dinner	After-Dinner Snack
Student					
Dormitory	0	1	3	0	3
Apartment	1	3	3	1	1
Day commuter	0	3	2	1	0
Night commuter	0	0	1	3	2
Nonstudent					
Faculty or staff	0	3	1	1	0
Live in area	0	1	2	2	1
Work in area	1	3	0	1	0

Key: 3 = Large market; 2 = Medium market; 1 = Small market; 0 = No market.

A late night oasis on the highway of hunger.

Wendy's Late Night Pick-up Window is open 'til midnight or later. So, you can get a hot 'n juicy Classic Single, Classic Double with cheese or Classic Triple with cheese, and eat great, even late.

How can Wendy's target different market segments like late-night customers or commuting college students? For the answer, see the text and Figure 9–6.

of each. The columns—or "products"—are really the meals (or eating occasions) customers enjoy at the restaurant.

Estimating Market Sizes   Now the size of the market in each cell (the unique market-product combination) of the market-product grid must be estimated. For your Wendy's restaurant, this involves estimating the sales of each kind of meal expected to be sold to each student and nonstudent market segment.

The market size estimates in Figure 9-5 vary from a large market ("3") to no market at all ("0") for each cell in the market-product grid. These may be simple guesstimates if you don't have the time or money to conduct formal marketing research (as discussed in Chapter 8). But even such crude estimates of the size of specific markets using a market-product grid are helpful in determining which target market segments to select and which product groupings to offer.

Step 4: Select Target Markets

A firm must take care to choose its target market segments carefully. If it picks too narrow a set of segments, it may fail to reach the volume of sales and profits it needs. If it selects too broad a set of segments, it may spread its marketing efforts so thin that the extra expense exceeds the increased sales and profits.

Criteria to Use in Selecting the Target Segments   Two kinds of criteria in the market segmentation process are those used to (1) divide the market into segments (discussed earlier) and (2) actually pick the target segments. Even experienced marketing executives often confuse these two different sets of criteria. Five criteria can be used to select the target segments for your Wendy's restaurant:

- *Market size.* The estimated size of the market in the segment is an important factor in deciding whether it's worth going after. There is really no market for breakfasts among dormitory students with meal plans (Figure 9–5), so you should not devote any marketing effort toward reaching this tiny segment.
- *Expected growth.* Although the size of the market in the segment may be small now, perhaps it is growing significantly or is expected to grow in the future. Sales of fast-food meals eaten outside the restaurants are projected to exceed those eaten inside. And Wendy's is the fast-food leader in average time to serve a drive-thru order—it is 16.7 seconds faster than McDonald's. This speed and convenience is potentially very important to night commuters in adult education programs.[15]
- *Competitive position.* Is there a lot of competition in the segment now or is there likely to be in the future? The less the competition, the more attractive the segment is. For example, if the college dormitories announce a new policy of "no meals on weekends," this segment is suddenly more promising for your restaurant. Wendy's recently introduced E-Pay pay-by-credit-card service at its restaurants to keep up with a similar service at McDonald's.
- *Cost of reaching the segment.* A segment that is inaccessible to a firm's marketing actions should not be pursued. For example, the few nonstudents who live in the area may not be reachable with ads in newspapers or other media. As a result, do not waste money trying to advertise to them.
- *Compatibility with the organization's objectives and resources.* If your Wendy's restaurant doesn't yet have the cooking equipment to make breakfasts and has a policy against spending more money on restaurant equipment, then don't try

to reach the breakfast segment. As is often the case in marketing decisions, a particular segment may appear attractive according to some criteria and very unattractive according to others.

Choose the Segments Ultimately, a marketing executive has to use these criteria to choose the segments for special marketing efforts. As shown in Figure 9–5, let's assume you've written off the breakfast product grouping for two reasons: It's too small a market and it's incompatible with your objectives and resources. In terms of competitive position and cost of reaching the segment, you focus on the four student segments and *not* the three nonstudent segments (although you're certainly not going to turn their business away!). This combination of market-product segments—your target market—is shaded in Figure 9–5.

Step 5: Take Marketing Actions to Reach Target Markets

The purpose of developing a market-product grid is to trigger marketing actions to increase sales and profits. This means that someone must develop and execute an action plan in the form of a marketing program.

Your Immediate Wendy's Segmentation Strategy With your Wendy's restaurant you've already reached one significant decision: There is a limited market for breakfast, so you won't open for business until 10:30 A.M. In fact, Wendy's first attempt at a breakfast menu was a disaster and was discontinued in 1986. Wendy's evaluates possible new menu items continuously to compete not only with McDonald's and Burger King but also with a complex array of convenience stores and gas stations that sell reheatable packaged foods as well as new "easy-lunch" products.

Another essential decision is where and what meals to advertise to reach specific market segments. An ad in the student newspaper could reach all the student segments, but it might be too expensive. If you choose three segments for special attention (Figure 9–6), advertising actions to reach them might include:

FIGURE 9–6
Advertising actions to market various meals to a range of possible market segments of students.

MARKET SEGMENTS	PRODUCTS: MEALS			
	Lunch	Between-Meal Snack	Dinner	After-Dinner Snack
Dormitory students	1	3	0	3
Apartment students	3	3	1	1
Day commuter students	3	2	1	0
Night commuter students	0	1	3	2

Ads in buses; flyers under windshield wipers of cars in parking lots

Ad campaign: "Ten percent off all purchases between 2:00 and 4:30 P.M. during winter quarter"

Ad on flyer under windshield wipers of cars in night parking lots: "Free Frosty with this coupon when you buy a drive-thru meal between 5:00 P.M. and 8:00 P.M."

Key: 3 = Large market; 2 = Medium market; 1 = Small market; 0 = No market.

- *Day commuters* (an entire market segment). Run ads inside commuter buses and put flyers under the windshield wipers of cars in parking lots used by day commuters. These ads and flyers promote all the meals at your restaurant to a single segment of students, a horizontal cut through the market-product grid.
- *Between-meal snacks* (directed to all four student markets). To promote eating during this downtime for your restaurant, offer "Ten percent off all purchases between 2:00 and 4:30 P.M. during winter quarter." This ad promotes a single meal to all four student segments, a vertical cut through the market-product grid.
- *Dinners to night commuters.* The most focused of all three campaigns, this ad promotes a single meal to the single segment of night commuter students. The campaign might consist of a windshield flyer offering a free Frosty with the coupon when the person buys a meal between 5 P.M. and 8 P.M. using the drive-thru window.

Depending on how your advertising actions work, you can repeat, modify, or drop them and design new campaigns for other segments you deem are worth the effort. This advertising example is just a small piece of a complete marketing program for your Wendy's restaurant. Note that Wendy's focus on late-night customers (shown above) has been successful; customers like that the late-night pickup window is open until midnight or later.

Future Strategies for Your Wendy's Restaurant Changing customer tastes and competition mean you must alter your strategies when necessary. This involves looking at (1) what Wendy's headquarters is doing, (2) what competitors are doing, and (3) what might be changing in the area served by your restaurant.

Wendy's headquarters recently announced an aggressive new marketing program that includes:[16]

- Targeting 25-to-49-year-old customers, not just 18-to-24-year-old ones.
- Positioning Wendy's as a lower-cost fast-food chain.
- Responding to the 2009–2010 recession by aggressively marketing three 99-cent sandwiches.
- Introducing new menu items as the chain breaks into the breakfast market again.

The Wendy's strategy has been remarkably successful. In 2009, Wendy's was rated the best fast-food chain, with over 5,000 restaurants.[17]

But other competitors such as McDonald's and Burger King are not sitting still, and you must be aware of their strategies. For example, in 2010 McDonald's actively promoted its lower-priced items that customers perceive as having good value, such as its Dollar Menu. Also, McDonald's has broadened its menu to attract more mothers and kids and to offer pricey new drinks like Frappes and Smoothies.[18] And Burger King recently rolled out its BK® Buck Double Cheeseburger.

With these corporate Wendy's plans and new actions from competitors, maybe you'd better rethink your market segmentation decisions on hours of operation and breakfasts. Also, if new businesses have moved into your area, what about a new strategy to reach people that work in the area? Or a new promotion for the night owls and early birds—the 12 A.M. to 5 A.M. customers—that now generate one-sixth of revenues at some McDonald's restaurants?

How has Apple moved from its 1977 Apple II to today's iMac? The Marketing Matters box and text discussion provide insights into Apple's current market segmentation strategy.

Apple's Ever-Changing Segmentation Strategy Steve Jobs and Steve Wozniak didn't realize they were developing today's multibillion-dollar PC industry when they invented the Apple I in a garage on April Fool's Day in 1976. Hobbyists, the initial target market, were not interested in the product. However, when the Apple II was displayed at a computer trade show in 1977, consumers loved it and Apple Computer was born. Typical of young companies, Apple focused on its products and

Marketing Matters >>>>>>>>> technology

Apple's Segmentation Strategy—Camp Runamok No Longer

Camp Runamok was the nickname given to Apple in the early 1980s because the innovative company had no coherent series of product lines directed at identifiable market segments. Today, Apple has targeted its various lines of Macintosh computers at specific market segments, as shown in the accompanying market-product grid. Because the market-product grid shifts as a firm's strategy changes, the one here is based on Apple's product lines in mid-2010. The grid suggests the market segmentation strategy Steve Jobs is using to compete in the digital age.

MARKETS		COMPUTER PRODUCTS					
Sector	Segment	Mac Pro	MacBook Pro	iMac	MacBook	MacBook Air	Mac Mini
Consumer	Individuals	✓	✓	✓	✓	✓	✓
	Small/home office	✓	✓	✓	✓	✓	
	Students			✓	✓		✓
	Teachers		✓	✓			
Professional	Medium/large business	✓	✓	✓		✓	
	Creative	✓	✓	✓			
	College faculty	✓		✓		✓	
	College staff			✓	✓		✓

had little concern for its markets. Its creative, young engineers were often likened to "Boy Scouts without adult supervision."[19]

Steve Jobs left Apple in 1985, the company languished, and it constantly altered its market-product strategies. When Steve Jobs returned in 1997, he detailed his vision for a reincarnated Apple by describing a new market segmentation strategy that he called the "Apple Product Matrix." This strategy consisted of developing two general types of computers (desktops and portables) targeted at two general kinds of market segments—the consumer and professional sectors.

In most segmentation situations, a single product does not fit into an exclusive market niche. Rather, product lines and market segments overlap. So Apple's market segmentation strategy enables it to offer different products to meet the needs of different market segments, as shown in the Marketing Matters box.

Market-Product Synergies: A Balancing Act

Recognizing opportunities for key synergies—that is, efficiencies—is vital to success in selecting target market segments and making marketing decisions. Market-product grids illustrate where such synergies can be found. How? Let's consider Apple's market-product grid in the accompanying Marketing Matters box and examine the difference between marketing synergies and product synergies shown there.

- *Marketing synergies.* Running horizontally across the grid, each row represents an opportunity for efficiency in terms of a market segment. Were Apple to focus on just one group of consumers, such as the medium/large business segment, its marketing efforts could be streamlined. Apple would not have to spend time learning about the buying habits of students or college faculty. So it could probably create a single ad to reach the medium/large business target segment (the yellow row), highlighting the only products they'd need to worry about developing: the Mac Pro, the MacBook Pro, the iMac, and the MacBook Air. Although clearly not Apple's strategy today, new firms often focus only on a single customer segment.
- *Product synergies.* Running vertically down the market-product grid, each column represents an opportunity for efficiency in research and development (R&D) and production. If Apple wanted to simplify its product line, reduce R&D and production expenses, and manufacture only one computer, which might it choose? Based on the market-product grid, Apple might do well to focus on the iMac (the orange column), because every segment purchases it.

Marketing synergies often come at the expense of product synergies because a single customer segment will likely require a variety of products, each of which will have to be designed and manufactured. The company saves money on marketing but spends more on production. Conversely, if product synergies are emphasized, marketing will have to address the concerns of a wide variety of consumers, which costs more time and money. Marketing managers responsible for developing a company's product line must balance both product and marketing synergies as they try to increase the company's profits.

learning review

5. What factor is estimated or measured for each of the cells in a market-product grid?

6. What are some criteria used to decide which segments to choose for targets?

7. How are marketing and product synergies different in a market-product grid?

POSITIONING THE PRODUCT

LO5

product positioning
The place a product occupies in consumers' minds on important features relative to competitive products.

product repositioning
Changing the place a product occupies in consumers' minds relative to competitive products.

When a company introduces a new product, a decision critical to its long-term success is how prospective buyers view it in relation to those products offered by its competitors. **Product positioning** refers to the place a product occupies in consumers' minds on important attributes relative to competitive products. By understanding where consumers see a company's product or brand today, a marketing manager can seek to change its future position in their minds. This requires **product repositioning**, *changing* the place a product occupies in a consumer's mind relative to competitive products.

Two Approaches to Product Positioning

Marketers follow two main approaches to positioning a new product in the market. *Head-to-head positioning* involves competing directly with competitors on similar product attributes in the same target market. Using this strategy, Dollar rental car competes directly with Avis and Hertz.

Differentiation positioning involves seeking a less-competitive, smaller market niche in which to locate a brand. McDonald's tried to appeal to the health-conscious segment when it introduced the low-fat McLean Deluxe hamburger to avoid competing directly with Wendy's and Burger King. However, it was eventually dropped from the menu.

More "zip" for chocolate milk? The text and Figure 9–7 describe how American dairies have successfully repositioned chocolate milk to appeal to adults.

perceptual map
A means of displaying the position of products or brands in consumers' minds.

FIGURE 9–7
The strategy American dairies are using to reposition chocolate milk to reach adults: Have adults view chocolate milk as both more nutritional and more "adult."

Writing a Positioning Statement

Marketing managers often convert their positioning ideas for the offering into a succinct written positioning statement. The positioning statement not only is used internally within the marketing department, but also for others, outside it, such as research and development engineers or advertising agencies.[20] Here is the Volvo positioning statement for the North American market:

> For upscale American families who desire a carefree driving experience, Volvo is a premium-priced automobile that offers the utmost in safety and dependability.

This focuses Volvo's North American marketing strategy, so Volvo advertising almost always mentions safety and dependability.

Product Positioning Using Perceptual Maps

A key to positioning a product or brand effectively is discovering the perceptions in the minds of potential customers by taking four steps:

1. Identify the important attributes for a product or brand class.
2. Discover how target customers rate competing products or brands with respect to these attributes.
3. Discover where the company's product or brand is on these attributes in the minds of potential customers.
4. Reposition the company's product or brand in the minds of potential customers.

As shown in Figure 9-7, from these data it is possible to develop a **perceptual map**, a means of displaying or graphing in two dimensions the location of products or brands in the minds of consumers to enable a manager to see how consumers perceive competing products or brands, as well as the firm's own product or brand.

A Perceptual Map to Reposition Chocolate Milk for Adults

Recently U.S. dairies decided to reposition chocolate milk in the minds of American adults to increase its sales. This is how dairies repositioned chocolate milk for American adults using the four steps listed above:

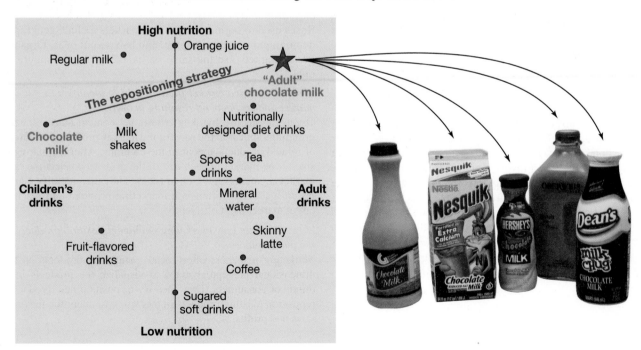

1. *Identify the important attributes (or scales) for adult drinks.* Research reveals the key attributes adults use to judge various drinks are (*a*) low versus high nutrition and (*b*) children's drinks versus adult drinks, as shown by the two axes in Figure 9–7.
2. *Discover how adults see various competing drinks.* Locate various adult drinks on these axes, as shown in Figure 9–7.
3. *Discover how adults see chocolate milk.* Figure 9–7 shows adults see chocolate milk as moderately nutritious (on the vertical axis) but as mainly a child's drink (on the horizontal axis).
4. *Reposition chocolate milk to make it more appealing to adults.* What actions did U.S. dairies take to increase sales? They repositioned chocolate milk to the location of the star shown in the perceptual map in Figure 9–7.

The dairies' arguments are nutritionally powerful. For women, chocolate milk provides calcium, critically important in female diets. And dieters get a more filling, nutritious beverage than with a soft drink for about the same calories.[21] The result: Chocolate milk sales increased dramatically, much of it because of adult consumption.[22] Part of this is due to giving chocolate milk "nutritional respectability" for adults, but another part is due to the innovative packaging that enables many new chocolate milk containers to fit in a car's cup holders.

learning review

8. What is the difference between product positioning and product repositioning?
9. Why do marketers use perceptual maps in product positioning decisions?

LEARNING OBJECTIVES REVIEW

LO1 *Explain what market segmentation is and when to use it.*
Market segmentation involves aggregating prospective buyers into groups that (*a*) have common needs and (*b*) will respond similarly to a marketing action. Organizations go to the expense of segmenting their markets when it increases their sales, profits, and ability to serve customers better.

LO2 *Identify the five steps involved in segmenting and targeting markets.*
Step 1 is to group potential buyers into segments. Buyers within a segment should have similar characteristics to each other and respond similarly to marketing actions like a new product or a lower price. Step 2 involves putting related products to be sold into meaningful groups. In step 3, organizations develop a market-product grid with estimated sizes of markets in each of the market-product cells of the resulting table. Step 4 involves selecting the target market segments on which the organization should focus. Step 5 involves taking marketing mix actions —often in the form of a marketing program—to reach the target market segments.

LO3 *Recognize the bases used to segment consumer and organizational markets.*
Bases used to segment consumer markets include geographic, demographic, psychographic, and behavioral ones. Organizational markets use the same bases except for psychographic ones.

LO4 *Develop a market-product grid to identify a target market and recommend resulting actions.*
Organizations use five key criteria to segment markets, whose groupings appear in the rows of the market-product grid. Groups of related products appear in the columns. After estimating the size of the market in each cell in the grid, they select the target market segments on which to focus. They then identify marketing mix actions—often in a marketing program—to reach the target market most efficiently.

LO5 *Explain how marketing managers position products in the marketplace.*
Marketing managers often locate competing products on two-dimensional perceptual maps to visualize the products in the minds of consumers. They then try to position new products or reposition existing products in this space to attain the maximum sales and profits.

FOCUSING ON KEY TERMS

80/20 rule p. 194
market-product grid p. 197
market segmentation p. 188

market segments p. 188
perceptual map p. 203
product differentiation p. 188

product positioning p. 202
product repositioning p. 202
usage rate p. 193

APPLYING MARKETING KNOWLEDGE

1 What variables might be used to segment these consumer markets? (*a*) lawn mowers, (*b*) frozen dinners, (*c*) dry breakfast cereals, and (*d*) soft drinks.

2 What variables might be used to segment these industrial markets? (*a*) industrial sweepers, (*b*) photocopiers, (*c*) computerized production control systems, and (*d*) car rental agencies.

3 In Figure 9–5, the dormitory market segment includes students living in college-owned residence halls, sororities, and fraternities. What market needs are common to these students that justify combining them into a single segment in studying the market for your Wendy's restaurant?

4 You may disagree with the estimates of market size given for the rows in the market-product grid in Figure 9–5. Estimate the market size, and give a brief justification for these market segments: (*a*) dormitory students, (*b*) day commuters, and (*c*) people who work in the area.

5 Suppose you want to increase revenues for your fast-food restaurant even further. Referring to Figure 9–6, what advertising actions might you take to increase revenues from (*a*) dormitory students, (*b*) dinners, and (*c*) after-dinner snacks from night commuters?

6 Locate these drinks on the perceptual map in Figure 9–7: (*a*) cappuccino, (*b*) beer, and (*c*) soy milk.

building your marketing plan

Your marketing plan (*a*) needs a market-product grid to focus your marketing efforts and also (*b*) leads to a forecast of sales for the company. Use these steps:

1 Define the market segments (the rows in your grid) using the bases of segmentation used to segment consumer and organizational markets.

2 Define the groupings of related products (the columns in your grid).

3 Form your grid and estimate the size of the market in each market-product cell.

4 Select the target market segments on which to focus your efforts with your marketing program.

5 Use the information and the lost-horse forecasting technique to make a sales forecast (company forecast).

video case 9   Prince Sports, Inc.: Tennis Racquets for Every Segment

"Over the last decade we've seen a dramatic change in the media to reach consumers," says Linda Glassel, vice president of sports marketing and brand image of Prince Sports, Inc.

PRINCE SPORTS IN TODAY'S CHANGING WORLD

"Today—particularly in reaching younger consumers—we're now focusing so much more on social marketing and social networks, be it Facebook, Twitter, MySpace, and internationally with Hi5, Bebo, and Orkut," she adds.

Linda Glassel's comments are a snapshot look at what Prince Sports faces in the changing world of tennis in the 21st century.

Prince Sports is a racquet sports company whose portfolio of brands includes Prince (tennis, squash, and badminton), Ektelon (racquetball), and Viking (platform/paddle tennis). Its complete line of tennis products alone is astounding: more than 150 racquet models; more than 50 tennis strings; over 50 footwear models; and countless types of bags, apparel, and other accessories.

Prince prides itself on its history of innovation in tennis—including inventing the first "oversize" and "longbody" racquets, the first "synthetic gut" tennis string, and the first "Natural Foot Shape" tennis shoe. Its challenge today is to continue to innovate to meet the needs of all levels of tennis players.

"One favorable thing for Prince these days is the dramatic growth in tennis participation—higher than it's been in many years," says Nick Skally (center in the photo below), senior marketing manager. A recent study by the Sporting Goods Manufacturers Association confirms this point: Tennis participation in the U.S. was up 43 percent from 2000 to 2008—the fastest growing traditional individual sport in the country.

TAMING TECHNOLOGY TO MEET PLAYERS' NEEDS

Every tennis player wants the same thing: to play better. But they don't all have the same skills, or the same ability to swing a racquet fast. So adult tennis players fall very broadly into three groups, each with special needs:

- *Those with shorter, slower strokes.* They want maximum power in a lightweight frame.
- *Those with moderate to full strokes.* They want the perfect blend of power and control.
- *Those with longer, faster strokes.* They want greater control with less power.

To satisfy all these needs in one racquet is a big order.

"When we design tennis racquets, it involves an extensive amount of market research on players at all levels," explains Tyler Herring, global business director for performance tennis racquets. In 2005, Prince's research led it to introduce its breakthrough O^3 technology. "Our O^3 technology solved an inherent contradiction between racquet speed and sweet spot," he says. Never before had a racquet been designed that simultaneously delivers faster racquet speed with a dramatically increased "sweet spot." The "sweet spot" in a racquet is the middle of the frame that gives the most power and consistency when hitting. In 2009, Prince introduced its latest evolution of the O^3 platform called EXO^3. Its newly patented design suspends the string bed from the racquet frame—thereby increasing the sweet spot by up to 83 percent while reducing frame vibration up to 50 percent.

SEGMENTING THE TENNIS MARKET

"The three primary market segments for our tennis racquets are our performance line, our recreational line, and our junior line," says Herring. He explains that within each of these segments Prince makes difficult design trade-offs to balance (1) the price a player is willing to pay, (2) what playing features (speed versus spin, sweet

spot versus control, and so on) they want, and (3) what technology can be built into the racquet for the price point.

Within each of these three primary market segments, there are at least two sub-segments—sometimes overlapping! Figure 1 gives an overview of Prince's market segmentation strategy and identifies sample racquet models. The three right-hand columns show the design variations of length, unstrung weight, and head size. The table shows the complexities Prince faces in converting its technology into a racquet with physical features that satisfy players' needs.

DISTRIBUTION AND PROMOTION STRATEGIES

"Prince has a number of different distribution channels— from mass merchants like Walmart and Target, to sporting goods chains, to smaller specialty tennis shops," says Nick Skally. For the large chains Prince contributes co-op advertising for its in-store circulars, point-of-purchase displays, in-store signage, consumer brochures, and even "space planograms" to help the retailer plan the layout of Prince products in its tennis area. Prince aids for small tennis specialty shops include a supply of demo racquets, detailed catalogs, posters, racquet and string guides, merchandising fixtures, and hardware, such as racquet hooks and footwear shelves, in addition to other items. Prince also provides these shops with "player standees," which are corregated life-size cutouts of professional tennis players.

Prince reaches tennis players directly through its Web site (www.princetennis.com), which gives product information, tennis tips, and the latest tennis news. Besides using social networks like Facebook and Twitter, Prince runs ads in regional and national tennis publications and develops advertising campaigns for online sites and broadcast outlets.

In addition to its in-store activities, advertising, and online marketing, Prince invests heavily in its Teaching Pro program. These sponsored teaching pros receive all the latest product information, demo racquets, and equipment from Prince, so they can truly be Prince ambassadors in their community. Aside from their regular lessons, instructors and teaching professionals hold local "Prince Demo events" around the country to give poten-

FIGURE 1
Prince Targets Racquets at Specific Market Segments

Market Segments			Product Features in Racquet			
Main Segments	**Sub-segments**	**Segment Characteristics (Skill level, age)**	**Brand Name**	**Length (Inches)**	**Unstrung Weight (Ounces)**	**Head Size (Sq. In.)**
Performance	Precision	For touring professional players wanting great feel, control, and spin	EXO³ Ignite 95	27.0	11.8	95
	Thunder	For competitive players wanting a bigger sweet spot and added power	EXO³ Red 95	27.25	9.9	105
Recreational	Small head size	Players looking for a forgiving racquet with added control	AirO Lightning MP	27.0	9.9	100
	Larger head size	Players looking for a larger sweet spot and added power	AirO Maria Lite OS	27.0	9.7	110
Junior	More experienced young players	Ages 8 to 15; somewhat shorter and lighter racquets than high school adult players	AirO Team Maria 23	23.0	8.1	100
	Beginner	Ages 5 to 11; much shorter and lighter racquets; tennis balls with 50% to 75% less speed for young beginners	Air Team Maria 19	19.0	7.1	82

tial customers a hands-on opportunity to see and try various Prince racquets, strings, and grips.

Prince also sponsors over 100 professional tennis players who appear in marquee events such as the four Grand Slam tournaments (Wimbledon and the Australian, French, and U.S. Opens). TV viewers can watch Russia's Maria Sharapova walk onto a tennis court carrying a Prince racquet bag or France's Gael Monfils hit a service ace using his Prince racquet.

Where is Prince headed in the 21st century? "As a marketer, one of the biggest challenges is staying ahead of the curve," says Glassel. And she stresses, "It's learning, it's studying, it's talking to people who understand where the market is going."

Questions

1 In the 21st century what trends in the environmental forces (social, economic, technological, competi-

tive, and regulatory) (*a*) work for and (*b*) work against success for Prince Sports in the tennis industry?

2 Because sales of Prince Sports in tennis-related products depends heavily on growth of the tennis industry, what marketing activities might it use in the U.S. to promote tennis playing?

3 What promotional activities might Prince use to reach (*a*) recreational players and (*b*) junior players?

4 What might Prince do to help it gain distribution and sales in (*a*) mass merchandisers like Target and Walmart and (*b*) specialty tennis shops?

5 In reaching global markets outside the U.S. (*a*) what are some criteria that Prince should use to select countries in which to market aggressively, (*b*) what three or four countries meet these criteria best, and (*c*) what are some marketing actions Prince might use to reach these markets?

iPad

Our most advanced technology in a magical
and revolutionary device at an unbelievable price.

Learn more ▶

10

Developing New Products and Services

LEARNING OBJECTIVES

After reading this chapter you should be able to:

LO1 Recognize the various terms that pertain to products and services.

LO2 Identify the ways in which consumer and business products and services can be classified.

LO3 Describe four unique elements of services.

LO4 Explain the significance of "newness" in new products and services as it relates to the degree of consumer learning involved.

LO5 Describe the factors contributing to the success or failure of a new product or service.

LO6 Explain the purposes of each step of the new-product process.

APPLE'S NEW-PRODUCT INNOVATION MACHINE

The stage in front of an auditorium is empty except for a chair, a table, and a huge screen with a large white logo. Then in walks a legend ready for his magic show in his black turtleneck, jeans, and gray New Balance sneakers.

Apple's Innovation Machine

The legend, of course, is Steve Jobs (opposite page), co-founder and CEO of Apple, Inc. *Fortune* rated Apple as the world's most admired company in 2010 and Steve Jobs as CEO of the decade, and *Bloomberg Businessweek* has perennially rated Apple as the world's most innovative company.[1] The magic shows Jobs has put on over the years have introduced many of Apple's market-changing innovations, such as the:

- Apple II—the first commercial personal computer.

- Macintosh—the first personal computer with a mouse and a graphical user interface.

- MacBook Air—the world's thinnest notebook that uses a solid state drive instead of a hard disk.

- iPod—the first commercially successful MP3 digital player. The iPod family (iPod shuffle, iPod nano, iPod classic, and iPod touch) has sold more than 250 million units since the iPod's 2001 launch.

- iPhone 4—the revolutionary multitouch mobile phone and media player. New for 2010: FaceTime, which "makes video calling a reality."

- iPad (opposite page)—the thin, tablet-shaped device with a color 10-inch screen that enables users to read books, newspapers, and magazines as well as access an array of "apps," such as video games and other software. The iPad's big virtual keyboard pops up when needed.

Where Is the Revolutionary iPad Headed?

In introducing the iPad in his January 27, 2010, magic show, Steve Jobs said, "Its so much more intimate than a laptop, and so much more capable than a smartphone."[2]

The *Economist* magazine predicts that the iPad, "a giant iPhone on steroids," will change the landscape of the computing world. This means transforming not just one industry but three—computing, telecommunications, and media. Apple intends to position the iPad to reach a market niche between smartphones and laptops. It then can provide on-the-go users with a combination e-reader, music and video player, Internet-access device, and video game consol.[3]

The life of an organization depends on how it conceives, produces, and markets *new* products (goods, services, and ideas), the topic of this chapter. Chapter 11 discusses the process of managing *existing* products, services, and brands.

WHAT ARE PRODUCTS AND SERVICES?

The essence of marketing is in developing products and services to meet buyer needs. A **product** is a good, service, or idea consisting of a bundle of tangible and intangible attributes that satisfies consumers' needs and is received in exchange for money or something else of value. Let's look more carefully at the meanings of goods, services, and ideas.

product
A good, service, or idea consisting of tangible and intangible features that satisfies consumer's needs and is received in exchange for money or something else of value.

A Look at Goods, Services, and Ideas

A *good* has tangible attributes that a consumer's five senses can perceive. For example, Apple's iPad can be touched and its features can be seen and heard. A good also may have intangible attributes consisting of its delivery or warranties and embody more abstract concepts, such as becoming healthier or wealthier. Goods also can be divided into nondurable goods and durable goods. A *nondurable* good is an item consumed in one or a few uses, such as food products and fuel. A *durable* good is one that usually lasts over many uses, such as appliances, cars, and mobile phones. This classification method also provides direction for marketing actions. For example, nondurable goods, such as Wrigley's gum, rely heavily on consumer advertising. In contrast, costly durable goods, such as cars, generally emphasize personal selling.

services
Intangible activities or benefits that an organization provides to satisfy consumers' needs in exchange for money or something else of value.

Services are intangible activities or benefits that an organization provides to satisfy consumers' needs in exchange for money or something else of value. Services have become a significant part of the U.S. economy, exceeding 40 percent of its gross domestic product. Hence, a good may be the breakfast cereal you eat, whereas a service may be a tax return an accountant fills out for you.

Finally, in marketing, an *idea* is a thought that leads to an action, such as a concept for a new invention or getting people out to vote.

Throughout this book *product* generally includes not only physical goods but services and ideas as well. When *product* is used in its narrower meaning of "goods," it should be clear from the example or sentence.

Classifying Products

Two broad categories of products widely used in marketing relate to the type of user. **Consumer products** are products purchased by the ultimate consumer, whereas **business products** (also called *B2B products* or *industrial products*) are products organizations buy that assist in providing other products for resale. But some products can be considered both consumer and business items. For example, an Apple iMac computer can be sold to consumers for personal use or to business firms for office use. Each classification results in different marketing actions. Viewed as a consumer product, the iMac would be sold through its retail stores or directly from its Web site. As a business product, an Apple salesperson might contact a firm's purchasing department directly and offer discounts for multiple purchases.

consumer products
Products purchased by the ultimate consumer.

business products
Products organizations buy that assist directly or indirectly in providing other products for resale.

Consumer Products The four types of consumer products shown in Figure 10–1 differ in terms of the (1) effort the consumer spends on the decision, (2) attributes used in making the purchase decision, and (3) frequency of purchase. *Convenience products* are items that the consumer purchases frequently, conveniently,

BASIS OF COMPARISON	CONVENIENCE PRODUCT	SHOPPING PRODUCT	SPECIALTY PRODUCT	UNSOUGHT PRODUCT
Product	Toothpaste, cake mix, hand soap, ATM cash withdrawal	Cameras, TVs, briefcases, airline tickets	Rolls-Royce cars, Rolex watches, heart surgery	Burial insurance, thesaurus
Price	Relatively inexpensive	Fairly expensive	Usually very expensive	Varies
Place (distribution)	Widespread; many outlets	Large number of selective outlets	Very limited	Often limited
Promotion	Price, availability, and awareness stressed	Differentiation from competitors stressed	Uniqueness of brand and status stressed	Awareness is essential
Brand loyalty of consumers	Aware of brand but will accept substitutes	Prefer specific brands but will accept substitutes	Very brand loyal; will not accept substitutes	Will accept substitutes
Purchase behavior of consumers	Frequent purchases; little time and effort spent shopping	Infrequent purchases; needs much comparison shopping time	Infrequent purchases; needs extensive search and decision time	Very infrequent purchases; some comparison shopping

FIGURE 10–1

How a consumer product is classified significantly affects which products consumers buy and the marketing strategies used.

The text describes how the broad Little Remedies product line benefits both consumers and retailers.

and with a minimum of shopping effort. *Shopping products* are items for which the consumer compares several alternatives on criteria such as price, quality, or style. *Specialty products* are items that the consumer makes a special effort to search out and buy. *Unsought products* are items that the consumer does not know about or knows about but does not initially want.

Figure 10–1 shows how each type of consumer product stresses different marketing mix actions, degrees of brand loyalty, and shopping effort. But how a consumer product is classified depends on the individual. One woman may view a camera as a shopping product and visit several stores before deciding on a brand, whereas her friend may view a camera as a specialty product and will make a special effort to buy only a Nikon.

Business Products A major characteristic of business products is that their sales are often the result of *derived demand*; that is, sales of business products frequently result (or are derived) from the sale of consumer products. For example, as consumer demand for Ford cars (a consumer product) increases, the company may increase its demand for paint spraying equipment (a business product).

Business products may be classified as components or support products. *Components* are items that become part of the final product. These include raw materials such as grain or lumber, as well as assemblies or parts, such as a Ford car engine or car door hinges. *Support products* are items used to assist in producing other goods and services. These include:

- *Installations*, such as buildings and fixed equipment.
- *Accessory equipment*, such as tools and office equipment.
- *Supplies*, such as stationery, paper clips, and brooms.
- *Industrial services*, such as maintenance, repair, and legal services.

Strategies to market business products reflect both the complexities of the product involved (paper clips versus computer-machine tools) and the buy-class situations discussed in Chapter 6.

Product Items, Product Lines, and Product Mixes

product item

A specific product that has a unique brand, size, or price.

Most organizations offer a range of products and services to consumers. A **product item** is a specific product that has a unique brand, size, or price. For example, Ultra Downy softener for clothes comes in several different sizes. Each size is a separate *stock keeping unit* (SKU), which is a unique identification number that defines an item for ordering or inventory purposes.

product line

A group of products that are closely related because they are similar in terms of consumer needs and uses, market segments, sales outlets, or prices.

A **product line** is a group of product or service items that are closely related because they satisfy a class of needs, are used together, are sold to the same customer group, are distributed through the same outlets, or fall within a given price range. Nike's product lines include shoes and clothing, whereas the Mayo Clinic's service lines consist of inpatient hospital care and outpatient physician services. Each product line has its own marketing strategy.

The Little Remedies® product line consists of more than a dozen nonprescription medicines for infants and young children sold in a family of creative packages. A broad product line enables both consumers and retailers to simplify their buying decisions. If a family has a good experience with one Little Remedies product, it might buy another one in the line. And an extensive line enables Little Remedies to obtain distribution chains such as Babies "Я" Us and Walmart, avoiding the need for retailers to deal with many different suppliers.

product mix

All the product lines offered by a company.

Many firms offer a **product mix** that consists of all of the product lines offered by an organization. For example, Cray Inc. has a small product mix of four supercomputer lines that are sold mostly to governments and large businesses. Fortune Brands, however, has a large product mix that includes product lines such as sporting equipment (Titleist golf balls) and plumbing supplies (Moen faucets).

Classifying Services

Services can be classified according to whether they are delivered by (1) people or equipment, (2) business firms or nonprofit organizations, or (3) government agencies. Organizations in each of these categories often use significantly different kinds of market-mix strategies to promote their services.

Delivery by People or Equipment Figure 10–2 shows the great diversity of organizations that offer services. People-based professional services include those

FIGURE 10–2

Services can be classified as equipment-based or people-based.

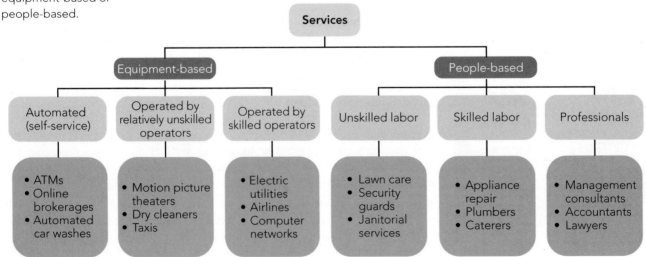

offered by advertising agencies or medical doctors. Sears utilizes skilled labor to offer appliance repair services. Broadview Security uses relatively unskilled labor to provide its security guard services. The quality of all these people-based services can vary significantly depending on the abilities of the person delivering the service.

Figure 10–2 also suggests that equipment-based services do not have the marketing concern of inconsistent quality because employees do not have direct contact when providing the service to consumers. Instead, consumers receive these automated services without interacting with any service employees, such as doing self check-in at Southwest Airlines, watching a movie at a local theater, or using Schwab's online stock trading.[4]

Delivery by Business Firms or Nonprofit Organizations As discussed in Chapter 2, privately owned firms must make profits to survive, while nonprofit organizations seek to satisfy clients and be efficient. The kinds of services each offers affect their marketing activities. Recently, many nonprofit organizations, such as The American Red Cross, have used marketing to improve their communications and better serve those in need.

Delivery by Government Agencies Governments at the federal, state, and local levels provide a broad range of services. These organizations also have adopted many marketing practices used by business firms. For example, the United States Postal Service's "Easy Come. Easy Go" marketing campaign is designed to allow it to compete better with UPS, FedEx, DHL, and foreign postal services for global package delivery business.

The Uniqueness of Services

LO3

Four unique elements distinguish services from goods. These are *intangibility, inconsistency, inseparability,* and *inventory*—referred to as the **four I's of services**.

four I's of services
The four unique elements that distinguish services from goods: intangibility, inconsistency, inseparability, and inventory.

Intangibility Being intangible, services can't be touched or seen before the purchase decision. Instead, services tend to be a performance rather than an object, which makes them much more difficult for consumers to evaluate. To help consumers assess and compare services, marketers try to make them tangible or show the benefits of using the service.

Inconsistency Services depend on the people who provide them. As a result, their quality varies with each person's capabilities and day-to-day job performance. Inconsistency is more of a problem in services than it is with tangible goods. Tangible products can be good or bad in terms of quality, but with modern production lines, their quality will at least be consistent. On the other hand, the Philadelphia Phillies baseball team may have great hitting and pitching one day and the next day lose by 10 runs. Organizations attempt to reduce inconsistency through standardization and training.[5]

Inseparability Inseparability means that the consumer cannot distinguish the service provider from the service itself. For example, if the quality of large lectures at your university or college is excellent, but if you don't get your questions answered, find the counseling services poor, or do not receive adequate library assistance, you may not be satisfied with the entire educational experience delivered. Therefore, you probably won't separate your perception of the "educational experience"—the service itself—from all the people delivering the educational services for that institution.

idle production capacity
When the service provider is available but there is no demand for the service.

Inventory Many goods have inventory handling costs that relate to their storage, perishability, and movement. With services, these costs are more subjective and are related to **idle production capacity**, which is when the service provider is available but there is no demand for the service. For a service, inventory cost involves paying the service provider along with any needed equipment. If a physician is paid to see patients but no one schedules an appointment, the idle physician's salary must be

FIGURE 10–3

The goods–services continuum shows how offerings can vary from goods-dominated (salt) to services-dominated (teaching) to many gradations in between.

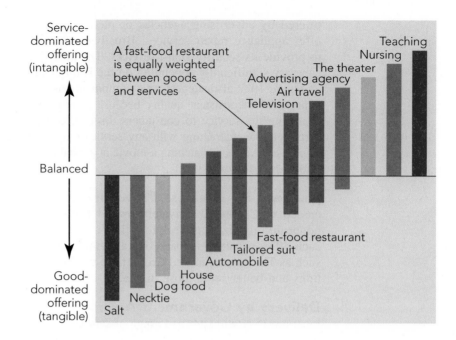

paid regardless of whether the service was performed. In service businesses that pay employees a commission, such as a part-time clerk at Sears, the sales clerk's work hours can be reduced to lower Sears's idle production capacity.

Today, many businesses find it useful to distinguish between their core product—either a good or a service—and supplementary services. U.S. Bank has both a core service (a checking account) and supplementary services, such as deposit assistance, parking, drive-throughs, and ATMs. Supplementary services often allow service providers to differentiate their offerings from competitors to add value for consumers.[6]

The Goods–Services Continuum

Figure 10–3 shows that many organizations are not strictly goods- or services-based. Is Hewlett-Packard a computer or service firm? Although it manufactures computers, printers, and other goods, many of the company's employees work in its services division providing systems integration, networking, consulting, and product support.[7] Organizations can offer a range of products from the tangible (goods-dominant) to the intangible (services-dominant), which is referred to as the *goods–services continuum.*

Salt, neckties, and dog food are tangible goods-dominant offerings, whereas teaching, nursing, and the theater are intangible, services-dominant activities. A fast-food restaurant is about half tangible goods (the food) and half intangible services (courtesy, cleanliness, speed, and convenience).

---

learning review

1. What are the four main types of consumer products?

2. What is the difference between a product line and a product mix?

3. What are the 4 I's of services?

Marketing Matters > > > > > > customer value

Feature Bloat: Geek Squad to the Rescue!

Adding more features to a product to satisfy more consumers seems like a no-brainer strategy.

Feature Bloat

In fact, most marketing research with potential buyers of a product done *before* they buy shows they say they *do want* more features in the product. It's when the new product gets home that the "feature bloat" problems occur—often overwhelming the consumer with mind-boggling complexity.

Computers pose a special problem for homeowners because there's no in-house technical assistance like that existing in large organizations. Also, to drive down prices of home computers, usually little customer support service is available. Ever call the manufacturer's toll-free "help" line? One survey showed that 29 percent of the help-line callers wound up swearing at the customer service representative and 21 percent just screamed.

The Geek Squad to the Rescue

Computer feature bloat has given rise to what TV's *60 Minutes* says is "the multibillion-dollar service industry populated by the very people who used to be shunned in the high-school cafeteria: Geeks like Robert Stephens!"

More than a decade ago he turned his geekiness into the Geek Squad—a group of technically savvy people who can fix almost any computer problem. "There's usually some frantic customer at the door pointing to some device in the corner that will not obey," Stephens explains.

"The biggest complaint about tech support people is rude, egotistical behavior," says Stephens. So he launched the Geek Squad to show some friendly humility by having team members work their wizardry while:

1. Showing genuine concern to customers.
2. Dressing in geeky white shirts, black clip-on ties, and white socks, a "uniform" borrowed from NASA engineers.
3. Driving to customer homes or offices in black-and-white VW "geekmobiles."

Do customers appreciate the 6,000-person Geek Squad, now owned by Best Buy? Robert Stephens answers by explaining, "People will say, 'They saved me . . . they saved my data.'" This includes countless college students working on their papers or theses with data lost somewhere in their computers—"data they promised themselves they'd back up next week."

NEW PRODUCTS AND WHY THEY SUCCEED OR FAIL

New products are the lifeblood of a company and keep it growing, but the financial risks can be large. Before discussing how new products reach the market, we'll begin by looking at *what* a new product is.

LO4

What Is a New Product?

The term *new* is difficult to define. Is Sony's PlayStation 3 *new* when there was a PlayStation 2? Is Nintendo's Wii *new* when its GameCube launch goes back to 2001? What does *new* mean for new-product marketing? Newness from several points of view are discussed next.

Newness Compared with Existing Products   If a product is functionally different from existing products, it can be defined as new. Sometimes this newness is revolutionary and creates a whole new industry, as in the case of the Apple II computer. At other times more features are added to an existing product to try to appeal to more customers. And as microprocessors now appear everywhere from computers to appliances, consumers' lives get far more complicated. This proliferation of extra features—sometimes called "feature bloat"—overwhelms many consumers. The Marketing Matters box describes how founder Robert Stephens and his Geek Squad work to address the rise of feature bloat.[8]

The text describes the potential benefits and dangers of an incremental innovation such as Purina's Elegant Medleys, its restaurant-inspired food for cats.

Newness in Legal Terms The U.S. Federal Trade Commission (FTC) advises that the term *new* be limited to use with a product up to six months after it enters regular distribution. The difficulty with this suggestion is in the interpretation of the term *regular distribution*.

Newness from the Organization's Perspective Successful organizations view newness and innovation in their products at three levels. The lowest level, which usually involves the least risk, is a product line extension. This is an incremental improvement of an existing product for the company. For example, Purina added its "new" line of Elegant Medleys®, a "restaurant-inspired food for cats," to its existing line of 50 varieties of its Fancy Feast® gourmet cat food. This has the potential benefit of adding new customers but the twin dangers of increasing expenses and cannibalizing its existing line.

At the next level is a significant jump in the innovation or technology, such as from a regular landline telephone to a cell phone. The third level is true innovation, a truly revolutionary new product, such as the first Apple computer in 1976. Effective new-product programs in large firms exist at all three levels.

Newness from the Consumer's Perspective A fourth way to define new products is in terms of their effects on consumption. This approach classifies new products according to the degree of learning required by the consumer, as shown in Figure 10–4.

With a *continuous innovation*, consumers don't need to learn new behaviors. Toothpaste manufacturers can add new attributes or features like "whitens teeth" or "removes plaque" when they introduce a new or improved product. But the extra features in the new toothpaste do not require buyers to learn new tooth-brushing behaviors, so it is a continuous innovation. The benefit of this simple innovation is that effective marketing mainly depends on generating awareness, so there is no need to reeducate customers.

With a *dynamically continuous innovation*, only minor changes in behavior are required. Heinz launched its EZ Squirt Ketchup in an array of unlikely hues—from green and orange to pink and teal—with kid-friendly squeeze bottles and nozzles.[9] Encouraging kids to write their names on hot dogs or draw dinosaurs on burgers as they use this new product requires only minor behavioral changes. So the marketing strategy here is to educate prospective buyers on the product's benefits, advantages, and proper use.

FIGURE 10–4
The degree of "newness" in a new product affects the amount of learning effort consumers must exert to use the product and the resulting marketing strategy.

	LOW ←	Degree of New Consumer Learning Needed	→ HIGH
BASIS OF COMPARISON	**CONTINUOUS INNOVATION**	**DYNAMICALLY CONTINUOUS INNOVATION**	**DISCONTINUOUS INNOVATION**
Definition	Requires no new learning by consumers	Disrupts consumer's normal routine but does not require totally new learning	Requires new learning and consumption patterns by consumers
Examples	New improved shaver, detergent, and toothpaste	Electric toothbrush, compact disc player, and automatic flash unit for cameras	Wireless router, digital video recorder, and electric car
Marketing strategy	Gain consumer awareness and wide distribution	Advertise points of difference and benefits to consumers	Educate consumers through product trial and personal selling

New-product success or failure? For the special problems these two products faced, see the text.

A *discontinuous innovation* involves making the consumer learn entirely new consumption patterns to use the product. Have you bought a wireless router for your computer? Congratulations if you installed it yourself! Recently, one-third of those bought at Best Buy were returned because they were too complicated to set up—the problem with a discontinuous innovation. So marketing efforts for discontinuous innovations usually involve not only gaining initial consumer awareness but also educating consumers on both the benefits and proper use of the innovative product, activities that can cost millions of dollars—and maybe rely on Geek Squad help.

Why Products and Services Succeed or Fail

We all know the giant product and service successes—such as Apple's iPhone, Google, and CNN. Yet the thousands of product failures every year that slide quietly into oblivion cost American businesses billions of dollars. Ideally, a new product or service needs a precise *protocol*, a statement that, before product development begins, identifies (1) a well-defined target market; (2) specific customers' needs, wants, and preferences; and (3) what the product will be and do.

Research suggests that it takes about 3,000 raw unwritten ideas to produce a single commercially successful new product.[10] To learn marketing lessons and convert potential failures to successes, we can analyze why new products fail and then study several failures in detail. As we go through the new-product process later in the chapter, we can identify ways such failures might have been avoided—admitting that hindsight is clearer than foresight.

Marketing Reasons for New-Product Failures Both marketing and nonmarketing factors contribute to new-product failures. Using the research results from several studies on new-product success and failure, we can identify critical marketing factors—which sometimes overlap—that often separate new-product winners and losers:[11]

LO5

1. *Insignificant point of difference.* Research shows that a distinctive point of difference is the single most important factor for a new product to defeat competitive ones—having superior characteristics that deliver unique benefits to the user. In the mid-1990s, General Mills introduced Fingos, a sweetened cereal flake about the size of a corn chip. Consumers were supposed to snack on them dry, but they didn't.[12] The point of difference was not important enough to get consumers to stop eating competing snacks such as popcorn and potato chips.

Lessons from new-product failures: Why might consumers not buy a tissue to kill cold and flu germs . . .

. . . or a spray to get rid of scary creatures from a child's bedroom? Answers appear in the text.

2. *No economical access to buyers.* Grocery products provide an example of this factor. Today's mega-supermarkets carry more than 30,000 different SKUs. With about 20,000 new packaged goods (food, beverage, health and beauty aids, household, and pet items) introduced globally each month, the cost to gain access to retailer shelf space is huge. Because shelf space is judged in terms of sales per square foot, Thirsty Dog! (a zesty beef-flavored, vitamin-enriched, mineral-loaded, lightly carbonated bottled water for your dog) must displace an existing product on the supermarket shelves, a difficult task with the high sales-per-square-foot demands of these stores. Thirsty Dog! failed to generate enough sales to meet these requirements.

3. *Incomplete market and product protocol before product development starts.* Without this protocol, firms try to design a vague product for a phantom market. Developed by Kimberly-Clark, Avert Virucidal tissues contained vitamin C derivatives scientifically designed to kill cold and flu germs when users sneezed, coughed, or blew their noses into them. It failed in test marketing. People didn't believe the claims and were frightened by the "cidal" in the brand name, which they connected to words like *suicidal*. A big part of Avert's failure was its lack of a product protocol that clearly defined how it would satisfy consumer wants and needs.[13]

4. *Not satisfying customer needs on critical factors.* Overlapping somewhat with point 1, this factor stresses that problems on one or two critical factors can kill the product, even though the general quality is high. For example, the Japanese, like the British, drive on the left side of the road. Until 1996, U.S. carmakers sent Japan few right-hand-drive cars—unlike German carmakers, which exported right-hand-drive models in several of their brands.

5. *Bad timing.* This results when a product is introduced too soon, too late, or when consumer tastes are shifting dramatically. Bad timing gives new-product managers nightmares. Microsoft, for example, introduced its Zune player a few years after Apple launched its iPod and other competitors offered their new MP3 players.

6. *Poor product quality.* This factor often results when a product is not thoroughly tested. The costs to an organization for poor quality can be staggering and include the labor, materials, and other expenses to fix the problem—not to mention the lost sales, profits, and market share that usually result. For example, after Microsoft launched its Xbox 360 video game console, millions began to experience the "red ring of death." The problem: The consoles' microprocessors ran too hot, causing them to "pop off" their motherboards. Microsoft had to set aside $1.1 billion to extend its warranty and fix any affected console for free—costing it future sales and reducing its market share lead in the multibillion dollar market over rivals Sony and Nintendo.[14]

7. *Too little market attractiveness.* The ideal is a large target market with high growth and real buyer need. But often the target market is too small or competitive to warrant the huge expenses necessary to reach it. OUT! International's Hey! There's A Monster In My Room spray was designed to rid scary creatures from a kid's bedroom and had a bubble-gum fragrance. While a creative and cute product, the brand name probably kept the kids awake at night more than their fear of the monsters because it implied the monster was still hiding in the bedroom. Also, was this a real market?

8. *Poor execution of the marketing mix: brand name, package, price, promotion, distribution.* Somewhere in the marketing mix there can be a showstopper that kills the product. Introduced by Gunderson & Rosario, Inc., Garlic Cake was supposed to be served as an hors d'oeuvre with sweet breads, spreads, and meats, but somehow the company forgot to tell this to potential consumers. Garlic Cake died because consumers were left to wonder just what a Garlic Cake is and when on earth a person would want to eat it.

Simple marketing research should have revealed the problems. Developing successful new products may sometimes involve luck, but more often it involves having a product that really meets a need and has significant points of difference over competitive products.

What Were They Thinking? Organizational Problems in New-Product Failure A number of other organizational problems can cause new-product disasters. Key ones—some that overlap—include:

1. *Not really listening to the "voice of the consumer."* Product managers may believe they "know better" than their customers or feel they "can't afford" the valuable marketing research that could uncover problems.

2. *Skipping stages in the new-product process.* Although details may vary, the seven-stage new-product process discussed in the next section is a sequence used in some form by most large organizations. Skipping a stage often leads to disaster. This is why many firms have a "gate" to ensure that one step is completed satisfactorily before going on to the next step.[15]

3. *Pushing a poorly conceived product into the market to generate quick revenue.* Today's marketing managers are under incredible pressure from top management to meet quarterly revenue targets. This focus on speed often results in overlooking the network of services needed to support the physical product.[16]

4. *Encountering "groupthink" in task force and committee meetings.* Someone in the new-product planning meeting knows or suspects the product concept is a dumb idea. But that person is afraid to speak up for fear of being cast as a "negative thinker" and "not a team player" and then being ostracized from real participation in the group. And a strong public commitment to a new product by its key advocate may make it difficult to kill the product even when new negative information comes to light.[17]

5. *Not learning critical takeaway lessons from past failures.* The easiest lessons are from "intelligent failures"—ones that happen early in the new-product process. At this point these failures are less expensive and immediately give better understanding of customers' wants and needs.

6. *Avoiding the "NIH problem."* A great idea is a great idea, regardless of its source. Yet in the bureaucracy that can occur in large organizations, ideas from outside often get rejected simply because they come from outside—what has been termed the "not-invented-here (NIH) problem."

Many of these organizational problems contribute to the eight marketing reasons for new-product failure listed above.

How Marketing Dashboards Can Reduce New-Product Failures

The Using Marketing Dashboards box on the next page shows how marketers measure actual market performance versus the goals set in new-product planning. In the scenario described, you have set a goal of 10 percent annual growth for the new snack you have developed. You choose a marketing metric of "annual % sales change" to measure the annual growth rate from 2009 to 2010 for each of the 50 states in which your snack is sold. Your special concerns in the marketing dashboard are the states shown in red, where sales have actually declined. As shown in the box, having identified the northeastern United States as a problem region, you conduct some in-depth marketing research to lead to corrective actions.

learning review

4. What kind of innovation would an improved electric toothbrush be?

5. Why can an "insignificant point of difference" lead to new-product failure?

6. What marketing metric might you use in a marketing dashboard to discover which states have weak sales?

In 2008, you started your own company to sell a nutritious, high-energy snack you developed. It is now January 2010. As a marketer, you ask yourself, "How well is my business growing?"

Your Challenge The snack is sold in all 50 states. Your goal is 10 percent annual growth. To begin 2010, you want to quickly solve any sales problems that occurred during 2009. You know that states whose sales are stagnant or in decline are offset by those with greater than 10 percent growth.

Studying a table of the sales and percent change versus a year ago in each of the 50 states would work, but it would be very time consuming. A good graphic is better. You choose the following marketing metric, where "sales" is measured in units:

Annual %
sales change

$$= \frac{(2009\ Sales - 2008\ Sales) \times 100}{2008\ Sales}$$

You want to act quickly to improve sales. In your map growth that is greater than 10 percent is GREEN, 0 to 10 percent growth is ORANGE, and decline is RED. Notice that you (1) picked a metric and (2) made your own rules that GREEN is good, ORANGE is bad, and RED is very bad.

Your Findings You see that sales growth in the northeastern states is weaker than the 10 percent target, and sales are actually declining in many of the states.

Your Action Marketing is often about grappling with sales shortfalls. You'll need to start by trying to identify and correct the problems in the largest volume states that are underperforming—in this case, in the northeastern United States.

You'll want to do marketing research to see if the problem starts with (1) an external factor, like changing consumer tastes, or (2) an internal factor, like a breakdown in your distribution system.

Annual Percentage Change in Unit Volume, by State

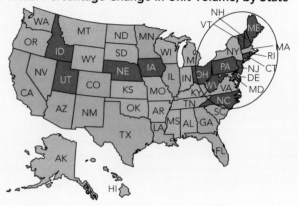

THE NEW-PRODUCT PROCESS

LO6

Finding ways to stimulate American innovation and provide jobs is a vital concern to federal and state governments, business firms, and citizens alike.[18] Organizations conduct global searches to find the scientists and engineers that can achieve the creative breakthroughs needed for new high-tech products. For example, Chinese, Indian, Russian, and other immigrant engineers represent half the total number of engineers in California's Silicon Valley.[19]

To develop new products efficiently, companies such as General Electric and 3M use a specific sequence of steps to make their products ready for market. Figure 10–5 shows the **new-product process**, the seven stages an organization goes through to identify business opportunities and convert them into salable products or services.

new-product process
The seven stages an organization goes through to identify business opportunities and convert them into salable products or services.

Stage 1: New-Product Strategy Development

For companies, *new-product strategy development* is the stage of the new-product process that defines the role for a new product in terms of the firm's overall objectives. During this stage, the firm uses both a SWOT analysis (Chapter 2) and environmental scanning (Chapter 3) to assess its strengths and weaknesses relative to the trends it identifies as opportunities or threats. The outcome not only defines the vital "protocol" for each new-product idea but also identifies the strategic role it might serve in the firm's business portfolio.

New-product development in services, such as buying a stock or airline ticket or watching a Major League Baseball game, is often difficult. Why? Because services

FIGURE 10–5
Carefully using the seven stages in the new-product process increases the chances of new-product success.

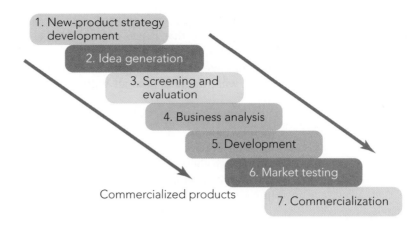

1. New-product strategy development
2. Idea generation
3. Screening and evaluation
4. Business analysis
5. Development
6. Market testing
7. Commercialization

Commercialized products

are intangible and performance-oriented. Nevertheless, service innovations can have a huge impact on our lives. For example, the online brokerage firm E*TRADE has revolutionized the financial services industry through its online trading.

A Major League Baseball park is a study in new-product innovation. If you visit Turner Field, home of the Atlanta Braves, you may be in for a shock about what's going on besides baseball on the field. There's the members-only 755 club—honoring Hank Aaron's home run total—and the Chophouse bar and grill for 20-somethings and a big playground sponsored by Cartoon Network. Each of these attractions become part of the customer experience that the team wants its fans to enjoy—and the attractions are almost as important as fielding a winning team.[20]

Stage 2: Idea Generation

Idea generation, the second stage of the new-product process, involves developing a pool of concepts to serve as candidates for new products, building upon the previous stage's results. Many forward-looking companies have discovered their own organization is not generating enough useful new-product ideas. This has led to *open innovation*, in which an organization finds and executes creative new-product ideas by developing strategic relationships with outside individuals and organizations. Open innovation helps organizations overcome the not-invented-here barriers discussed earlier. This section contains examples of open innovation relationships.[21]

Customer and Supplier Suggestions Firms ask their salespeople to talk to customers and ask their purchasing personnel to talk to suppliers to discover

A visit to watch an Atlanta Braves baseball game is often a lot more than the game itself. As described in the text, it may involve a meal at the Chophouse or many other services.

new-product ideas.[22] Whirlpool gets ideas from customers on ways to standardize components so that it can cut the number of different product platforms to reduce costs.[23] Business researchers emphasize that firms must actively involve customers and suppliers in the new-product development process. This means the focus should be on what the new product will actually *do* for them rather than simply *what they want*.[24]

A. G. Lafley, CEO of Procter & Gamble (P&G), gave his executives a *revolutionary* thought: "Look outside the company for solutions to problems rather than insisting P&G knows best." When he ran P&G's laundry detergent business, he had to redesign the laundry boxes so they were easier to open. Why? While consumers *said* P&G's laundry boxes were "easy to open," cameras they agreed to have installed in their laundry rooms showed they opened the boxes with *screwdrivers*![25]

"Crowdsourcing" might be an even better idea-generation method if an R&D-marketing team wants ideas from 10,000 or 20,000 customers or suppliers. *Crowdsourcing* involves generating insights leading to actions based on massive numbers of people's ideas. It requires a precise question to focus the idea-generation process. An example is when Netflix asked, "How do we achieve a 10 percent improvement in our online recommendations rating system that generates 30 billion recommendations each day?" Over 50,000 crowdsourcing participants later, Netflix awarded a $1 million prize to a team that developed a mathematical algorithm surpassing the 10 percent goal. Dell used crowdsourcing to develop an online site to generate 13,464 ideas for new products and Web site and marketing improvements, of which 402 of them were implemented.[26]

Employee and Co-Worker Suggestions
Employees should be encouraged to suggest new-product ideas through suggestion boxes. The idea for Nature Valley granola bars from General Mills came when one of its marketing managers observed co-workers bringing granola to work in plastic bags.

Auto industry studies show that women buy about two-thirds of all vehicles and influence about 85 percent of all sales. However, many automakers do marketing research on car-loving, "gear-head" guys to get ideas on new-car features. To bridge the gender gap, Volvo obtained ideas on new-car features from all-female focus groups from its Swedish workforce. It then named a five-woman team of Volvo managers to design a "concept car"—what the auto industry uses to test new designs, technical innovations, and consumer reactions. One innovative feature: when pressing an ignition key button, the car's gull-wing doors pop open and the steering wheel pulls in so the driver can enter the car more easily.[27]

Research and Development Laboratories
Another source of new products is a firm's own research and development laboratories. Apple is a world leader in new-product development in computers and smartphones. Apple is also world-class in *industrial design*, an applied art that improves the aesthetics and usefulness of mass-produced products for users. Apple's sleek iPad, iPhone, and iMac models came out of its Apple Industrial Design Group, which is driven by the obsessive concerns of Steve Jobs for cutting-edge industrial design in all the company's products.[28] But even Apple sometimes goes outside its own labs—for example, when it found its original "mouse" at IDEO.

Professional R&D laboratories that are outside the walls of large corporations are sources of open innovation and provide new-product ideas.[29] Labs at Arthur D. Little helped put the "crunch" in the Quaker Oats Company's Cap'n Crunch cereal and the flavor in Carnation's Instant Breakfast. As described in the Marketing Matters box, IDEO is a world-class new-product development firm, having designed more than 4,000 of them.[30]

Brainstorming sessions conducted at IDEO can generate 100 new ideas in an hour. IDEO's "shop-a-long" visits with client firms let a client's

Would women *really* help design this car? For how Volvo said "yes," see the text.

Marketing Matters > > > > > > technology

IDEO—the Innovation Lab Superstar in Designing New Products

The Apple mouse. The Palm V PDA. The Crest Neat Squeeze toothpaste dispenser. The Steelecase Leap adjustable office chair. These are just some of the thousands of new products designed by IDEO, an innovation lab you've probably never heard of but benefit from everyday.

For David Kelley, co-founder of IDEO, product design is really "industrial design" and includes both artistic and functional elements. And to foster this creativity, IDEO allows its designers and engineers much freedom—its offices look like schoolrooms; employees can hang their bicycles from the ceiling; there are rubber-band fights; and on Monday mornings, there are show-and-tell sessions.

Fresh Express asked IDEO to design an innovative single-serve package for salads. IDEO's solution (photo): A five-section package—one large section for the salad greens and four smaller ones for proteins, dressings, and so on—each section sealed in plastic.

Visit IDEO's Web site (www.ideo.com) to view its recent inventions and innovations for clients such as McDonald's self-ordering kiosk, the Zyliss' Mandolin fruit and vegetable slicer, LifePort's kidney transporter, Pepsi's High Visibility vending machine, and Nike's all-terrain sunglasses.

---

managers experience firsthand what their customers do. A sample recommendation from a shop-a-long visit with managers from a large U.S. health maintenance organization came from actually playing the part of a patient: Make examining rooms larger to enable the nervous patient to have a friend or relative in the room while waiting for the doctor.[31]

Competitive Products Analyzing the competition can lead to new-product ideas. For six months, the Marriott Corporation sent a six-person intelligence team to travel and stay at economy hotels around the country. The team assessed the competition's strengths and weaknesses on everything from the soundproof qualities of the rooms to the softness of the towels. Marriott then budgeted $500 million for a new economy hotel chain—Fairfield Inns.

Smaller Firms, Universities, and Inventors Many firms look for outside visionaries that have inventions or innovative ideas that can become products. Some sources of this open innovation strategy include:

Gary Schwartzberg partnered with Kraft Foods to get his cream cheese–filled bagels in stores across the United States.

- *Smaller, nontraditional firms.* Small technology firms and even small, nontraditional firms in adjacent industries provide creative advances. General Mills partnered with Weight Watchers to develop Progresso Light soups, the first consumer packaged product in any grocery category to carry the Weight Watchers endorsement with a 0 points value per serving.[32]

- *Universities.* Many universities have technology transfer centers that often partner with business firms to commercialize faculty inventions. The first-of-its-kind carbonated yogurt Go-Gurt Fizzix was launched in late 2007 as a result of General Mills partnering with Brigham Young University to license the university's patent to put the "fizz" into the yogurt.[33]

- *Inventors.* Many lone inventors and entrepreneurs develop brilliant new-product ideas—like Gary Schwartzberg's tube-shaped bagel filled with cream cheese. A portable breakfast for the on-the-go person, the innovative bagel couldn't get widespread distribution. So Schwartzberg sold his idea to Kraft Foods, Inc., which now markets its Bagel-Fuls filled with Kraft's best-selling Philadelphia cream cheese in supermarkets across the United States.[34]

Great ideas can come from almost anywhere—the challenge is recognizing and implementing them.

Stage 3: Screening and Evaluation

Screening and evaluation is the stage of the new-product process that internally and externally evaluates new-product ideas to eliminate those that warrant no further effort.

Internal Approach A firm's employees evaluate the technical feasibility of a proposed new-product idea to determine whether it meets the objectives defined in the new-product strategy development stage. For example, 3M scientists develop many world-class innovations in the company's labs. A recent innovation was its micro-replication technology—one that has 3,000 tiny gripping "fingers" per square inch. An internal assessment showed 3M that this technology could be used to improve the gripping of golf or work gloves.

Organizations that develop service-dominated offerings need to ensure that employees have the commitment and skills to meet customer expectations and sustain customer loyalty—an important criterion in screening a new-service idea. This is the essence of **customer experience management (CEM)**, which is the process of managing the entire customer experience within the company. Marketers must consider employees' interactions with customers so that the new services are consistently delivered and experienced, clearly differentiated from other service offerings, and relevant and valuable to the target market.

External Approach Firms use *concept tests*, external evaluations with consumers that consist of preliminary testing of a new-product idea rather than an actual product. Generally, these tests are more useful with minor modifications of existing products than with new, innovative products with which consumers are not familiar.[35] Concept tests rely on written descriptions of the product but may be augmented with sketches, mockups, or promotional literature. Key questions for concept testing include: How does the customer perceive the product? Who would use it? and How would it be used?

customer experience management (CEM)
The process of managing the entire customer experience within the company.

---

learning review

7. What is the new-product strategy development stage in the new-product process?

8. What are the main sources of new-product ideas?

9. How do internal and external screening and evaluation approaches differ?

Stage 4: Business Analysis

Business analysis specifies the features of the product and the marketing strategy needed to bring it to market and make financial projections. This is the last checkpoint before significant resources are invested to create a *prototype*—a full-scale operating model of the product. The business analysis stage assesses the total "business fit" of the proposed new product with the company's mission and objectives—from whether the product can be economically developed and manufactured to the marketing strategy needed to have it succeed in the marketplace.

This process requires not only detailed financial projections but also assessments of the marketing and product synergies related to the company's existing operations. Will the new product require a lot of new machinery to produce it or can it be produced using the unused capacity of existing machines? Will the new product cannibalize sales

How do you print ink-jet images on Pringles chips safely and inexpensively? The text describes how a global search found the critical technology.

of existing products or will it increase revenues by reaching new market segments? Can the new product be protected with a patent or copyright? Financial projections of expected profits require estimates of expected prices per unit and units sold, as well as detailed estimates of the costs of R&D, production, and marketing.

For services, business analysis must consider *capacity management*, integrating the service component of the marketing mix with efforts to influence consumer demand. Most services are perishable and have a limited capacity due to the inseparability of the service from its provider. Therefore, a service provider must manage the availability of the offering so that demand matches capacity over the duration of the demand cycle (one day, a week, and so on). For example, airlines and mobile phone service providers use *off-peak pricing* to charge different prices for different times of the day or week to reflect the variations in demand for their services. This enables them to maximize profit.[36]

Stage 5: Development

Development is the stage of the new-product process that turns the idea on paper into a prototype. This results in a demonstrable, producible product that involves not only manufacturing the product but also performing laboratory and consumer tests to ensure it meets the standards established for it in the protocol. Moreover, the new product must be able to be manufactured at reasonable cost with the required quality.

A brainstorming session at Procter & Gamble produced the idea of printing pop culture images on its Pringles chips. But how do you print sharp images—like those for *Spider-Man 3*—using edible dyes on millions of chips? Internal development would be too long and costly, so P&G circulated a description of its unusual printing need globally. A university professor in Bologna, Italy, had invented an ink-jet method for printing edible images on cakes and cookies. In less than a year, P&G adapted the process and launched its new "Pringle Prints"—at a fraction of the time and cost internal development would have taken.[37]

For services, developing customer service delivery expectations is critical. This involves analyzing the entire sequence of steps or "service encounters" that make up the service to study the points of interaction between consumers and the service provider.[38] High-contact services such as hotels, car rental agencies, and Web sites use this approach to enhance customer relationships. That white, plain-vanilla Google home page may look like it was designed by a child. But the Marketing Matters box on the next page describes how Google's Marissa Mayer has spent thousands of hours and done countless experiments to get exactly the right "feel" for Google's millions of users.[39]

Safety tests are also critical for when the product isn't used as planned. To make sure seven-year-olds can't bite Barbie's head off and choke, Mattel clamps her foot in steel jaws in a test stand and then pulls on her head with a wire. Similarly, car manufacturers have done extensive safety tests by crashing their cars into concrete walls.

During development, laboratory tests like this one on Barbie result in safer dolls and toys for children.

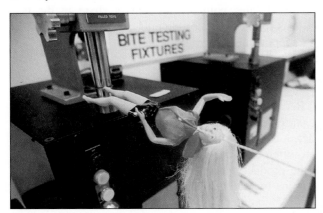

Stage 6: Market Testing

Market testing is the stage of the new-product process that involves exposing actual products to prospective consumers under realistic purchase conditions to see if they will buy. Often a product is developed, tested, refined, and then tested again to get consumer reactions through either test marketing or simulated test markets.

Marketing Matters > > > > > > customer value

Marissa Mayer: The Talent behind Google's Familiar *White* Home Page

Unknown to you, Google Employee No. 20, Marissa Mayer, probably impacts your life at least 5 or 10 times a week.

The New York Times calls her the "gatekeeper of Google's home page," the one person who "controls the look, feel, and functionality of the Internet's most heavily trafficked search engine." Virtually every new design or feature—from the color of the Google tool bar to the exact words on a Google page—needs her stamp of approval. The very clear, very plain, very white Google home page reflects Mayer's passion about obtaining a favorable user experience. Her job title: vice president of search products and user experience.

At Google, Mayer has introduced over 100 products and features, such as Google News, Gmail, and Image Search. Sounding like a combination English teacher and art instructor, Mayer sets the design standards for Google. Many of these are based on her internal Google experi-

ments to measure user preferences. Her precise design rules include:

- Avoid first- and second-person pronouns.
- Write "Google" instead of "we."
- Don't switch tenses.
- Avoid italics because they are hard to read on a computer screen.

And beyond the grammar lessons, there are also precise design and graphic arts guidelines: "If you want to make the design on the page simpler, take away one of these: A type of font, a color, or an image."

An engineer, Mayer has a Google life that goes far beyond the pronouns and colors of Google's Web pages. As *The New York Times* notes, "She oversees 200 product managers who in turn supervise 3,000 engineers, or more than 10 percent of Google's workforce." Comments one colleague, "She functions at the executive level but is just as comfortable at the engineer level."

Test Marketing *Test marketing* involves offering a product for sale on a limited basis in a defined area. This test is done to determine whether consumers will actually buy the product and to try different ways of marketing it. Only about a third of the products tested do well enough to go on to the next stage. These market tests are usually conducted in cities that are viewed as being representative of U.S. consumers. For example, Wichita Falls, Texas, most closely matched the U.S. average found in the 2000 Census.[40] Other criteria used in selecting test market cities include cable systems to deliver different ads to different homes and tracking systems to measure sales resulting from different advertising campaigns. The 2010 Census will probably reveal different U.S. cities that better represent the national average demographic characteristics. These cities will become the new preferred test market cities.

This information indicates potential sales volume and market share in the test area. Companies also use market tests to check other elements of the marketing mix, such as price, level of advertising support, and distribution. Because market tests are so time consuming and expensive and can alert competitors to a firm's plans, some firms skip test markets or use simulated test markets.

Simulated Test Markets Because of the time, cost, and confidentiality problems of test markets, consumer packaged goods companies often turn to *simulated* (or *laboratory*) *test markets (STM)*, a technique that simulates a full-scale test market but in a limited fashion. STMs are often run in shopping malls, where consumers are questioned to identify who uses the product class being tested. Next, willing participants are questioned on usage, reasons for purchase, and important product attributes. Qualified persons are then shown TV commercials or print ads for the test product along with competitors' advertising. Finally, they are given money and introduced to a real or simulated store environment in which they may choose to buy either the firm's product or competitors' products.

When Test Markets Don't Work   Not all products can use test marketing. Test marketing a service is very difficult because it is intangible and consumers can't see what they are buying. For example, how do you test market a new building for an art museum?

Similarly, test markets for expensive consumer products such as cars or costly industrial products such as jet engines are impractical. For these products, reactions of potential buyers to mockups or one-of-a-kind prototypes are all that is feasible.

Stage 7: Commercialization

Finally, the product is brought to the point of *commercialization*—the stage of the new-product process that positions and launches a new product in full-scale production and sales. Companies proceed very carefully at the commercialization stage because this is the most expensive stage for most new products. If competitors introduce a product that leapfrogs the firm's own new product or if cannibalization of its own existing products looks significant, the firm may halt the new-product launch permanently.

Countless other questions arise. Should we make an advance announcement of the new-product introduction to stimulate interest and potential sales?[41] Do we need to add new salespeople?[42] Do the salespeople need extra training?

Large companies use *regional rollouts*, introducing the product sequentially into geographical areas of the United States, to allow production levels and marketing activities to build up gradually to minimize the risk of new-product failure. Grocery product manufacturers and telephone service providers are examples of firms that use this strategy.

Burger King's French Fries: The Complexities of Commercialization
Burger King's "improved French fries" are an example of what can go wrong at the commercialization stage. In the fast-food industry, McDonald's French fries are the gold standard against which all other fries are measured. Burger King decided to take on McDonald's fries and spent millions of R&D dollars developing a starch-coated fry designed to retain heat longer and add crispiness. This crispiness was even defined: "An audible crunch that should be present for seven or more chews!"

A 100-person team set to work and developed the starch-coated fry that beat McDonald's fries in taste tests, 57 percent to 35 percent, with 8 percent having no opinion. After "certifrying" 300,000 managers and employees on the new frying procedures, the fries were launched with a $70 million marketing budget. The launch turned into disaster. The reason: The new fry proved too complicated to get right day after day in Burger King restaurants, except under ideal conditions, and was dropped.[43]

The Special Risks in Commercializing Grocery Products   New grocery products pose special commercialization problems. Because shelf space is so limited, many supermarkets require a *slotting fee* for new products, a payment a manufacturer makes to place a new item on a retailer's shelf. This can run to several million dollars for a single product. But there's even another potential expense. If a new grocery product does not achieve a predetermined sales target, some retailers require a *failure fee*, a penalty payment a manufacturer makes to compensate a retailer for devoting valuable shelf space to a product that failed to sell. These costly slotting fees and failure fees are further examples of why large grocery product manufacturers use regional rollouts.

Speed as a Factor in New-Product Success   Companies have discovered that speed or *time to market* (TtM) is often vital in introducing a new product. Recent studies have shown that high-tech products coming to market on time are far more profitable than those arriving late. So some companies—such as Sony, BMW,

Commercializing a new French fry: To learn whether Burger King's improved French fries succeeded at the commercialization stage, see the text.

3M, and Hewlett-Packard—have overlapped the sequence of stages described in this chapter.

With this approach, termed *parallel development*, cross-functional team members who conduct the simultaneous development of both the product and the production process stay with the product from conception to production. This has enabled Hewlett-Packard to reduce the development time for notebook computers from 12 to 7 months. In software development, *fast prototyping* uses a "do it, try it, fix it" approach—encouraging continuing improvement even after the initial design. To speed up time to market, many large companies are placing protective "fences" around their new product teams. These fences seek to insulate team members from routine administrative tasks to keep them from getting bogged down in bureaucratic red tape.[44]

learning review

10. How does the development stage of the new-product process involve testing the product inside and outside the firm?

11. What is a test market?

12. What is the commercialization of a new product?

LEARNING OBJECTIVES REVIEW

LO1 *Recognize the various terms that pertain to products and services.*

A product is a good, service, or idea consisting of a bundle of tangible and intangible attributes that satisfies consumers and is received in exchange for money or something else of value.

A good has tangible attributes that a consumer's five senses can perceive and intangible ones such as warranties; a laptop computer is an example. Goods also can be divided into nondurable goods, which are consumed in one or a few uses, and durable goods, which usually last over many uses. Services are intangible activities or benefits that an organization provides to satisfy consumer needs in exchange for money or something else of value, such as an airline trip. An idea is a thought that leads to a product or action, such as eating healthier foods.

LO2 *Identify the ways in which consumer and business products and services can be classified.*

By type of user, the major distinctions are consumer products, which are products purchased by the ultimate consumer, and business products, which are products that assist an organization in providing other products for resale.

Consumer products can be broken down based on the effort involved in the purchase decision process, marketing mix attributes used in the purchase, and the frequency of purchase: (*a*) convenience products are items that consumers purchase frequently and with a minimum of shopping effort; (*b*) shopping products are items for which consumers compare several alternatives on selected criteria; (*c*) specialty products are items that consumers make special efforts to seek out and buy; and (*d*) unsought products are items that consumers either do not know about or do not initially want.

Business products can be broken down into (*a*) components, which are items that become part of the final product, such as raw materials or parts, and (*b*) support products, which are items used to assist in producing other goods and services and include installations, accessory equipment, supplies, and industrial services.

Services can be classified in terms of whether they are delivered by (*a*) people or equipment, (*b*) business firms or nonprofit organizations, or (*c*) government agencies.

Firms can offer a range of products, which involve decisions regarding the product item, product line, and product mix.

LO3 *Describe four unique elements of services.*

The four unique elements of services—the four I's—are intangibility, inconsistency, inseparability, and inventory. Intangibility refers to the tendency of services to be a performance that cannot be held or touched, rather than an object. Inconsistency is a characteristic of services because they depend on people to deliver them, and people vary in their capabilities and in their day-to-day performance. Inseparability refers to the difficulty of separating the deliverer of the services (hair stylist) from the service itself (hair salon). Inventory refers to the need to have service production capability when there is service demand.

LO4 *Explain the significance of "newness" in new products and services as it relates to the degree of consumer learning involved.*

From the important perspective of the consumer, "newness" is often seen as the degree of learning that a consumer must engage in to use the product. With a continuous innovation, no new behaviors must be learned. With a dynamically continuous innovation, only minor behavioral changes are needed. With a discontinuous innovation, consumers must learn entirely new consumption patterns.

LO5 *Describe the factors contributing to the success or failure of a new product or service.*

A new product or service often fails for these marketing reasons: (*a*) insignificant points of difference, (*b*) incomplete market and product protocol before product development starts, (*c*) not satisfying customer needs on critical factors, (*d*) bad timing, (*e*) too little market attractiveness, (*f*) poor product quality, (*g*) poor execution of the marketing mix, and (*h*) no economical access to buyers.

LO6 *Explain the purposes of each step of the new-product process.*

The new-product process consists of seven stages a firm uses to develop salable products or services: (*a*) New-product strategy development involves defining the role for the new product within the firm's overall objectives. (*b*) Idea genera-
tion involves developing a pool of concepts from consumers, employees, basic R&D, and competitors to serve as candidates for new products. (*c*) Screening and evaluation involves evaluating new product ideas to eliminate those that are not feasible from a technical or consumer perspective. (*d*) Business analysis involves defining the features of the new product, developing the marketing strategy and marketing program to introduce it, and making a financial forecast. (*e*) Development involves not only producing a prototype product but also testing it in the lab and with consumers to see that it meets the standards set for it. (*f*) Market testing involves exposing actual products to prospective consumers under realistic purchasing conditions to see if they will buy the product. (*g*) Commercialization involves positioning and launching a product in full-scale production and sales with a specific marketing program.

FOCUSING ON KEY TERMS

business products p. 210	**four I's of services** p. 213	**product item** p. 212
consumer products p. 210	**idle production capacity** p. 213	**product line** p. 212
customer experience management (CEM) p. 224	**new-product process** p. 220	**product mix** p. 212
	product p. 210	**services** p. 210

APPLYING MARKETING KNOWLEDGE

1 Products can be classified as either consumer or business products. How would you classify the following products? (*a*) Johnson's baby shampoo, (*b*) a Black & Decker two-speed drill, and (*c*) an arc welder.

2 Are Nature Valley Granola bars and Eddie Bauer hiking boots convenience, shopping, specialty, or unsought products?

3 Based on your answer to question 2, how would the marketing actions differ for each product and the classification to which you assigned it?

4 Explain how the four I's of services would apply to a Marriott Hotel.

5 Idle production capacity may be related to inventory or capacity management. How would the pricing component of the marketing mix reduce idle production capacity for (*a*) a car wash, (*b*) a stage theater group, and (*c*) a university?

6 In terms of the behavioral effect on consumers, how would a PC, such as an Apple iMac, be classified? In light of this classification, what actions would you suggest to PC manufacturers to increase their sales in the market?

7 What methods would you suggest to assess the potential commercial success for the following new products? (*a*) a new, improved ketchup; (*b*) a three-dimensional television system that took the company 10 years to develop; and (*c*) a new children's toy on which the company holds a patent.

8 Concept testing is an important step in the new-product process. Outline the concept tests for (*a*) an electrically powered car and (*b*) a new loan payment system for automobiles that is based on a variable interest rate. What are the differences in developing concept tests for products as opposed to services?

building your marketing plan

In fine-tuning the product strategy for your marketing plan, do these two things:

1 Develop a simple three-column table in which (*a*) market segments of potential customers are in the first column and (*b*) the one or two key points of difference
of the product to satisfy the segment's needs are in the second column.

2 In the third column of your table, write ideas for specific new products for your business in each of the rows in your table.

If a company told you it was marketing a handheld, on-demand cleaning gadget that also sanitizes, eliminating greater than 99.9 percent of harmful bacteria—and uses simply the tap water from your faucet—what would you think?

You'd probably think it was just another overly hyped gadget involving false, exaggerated claims and featured on late-night infomercials!

That's exactly the problem that Activeion Cleaning Solutions, a small start-up company with a revolutionary technology, faced in late 2009. Let's have you give the company some *pro bono* (free!) marketing advice.

THE TECHNOLOGY: SAFE, SMART, SUSTAINABLE CLEANING

Activeion Cleaning Solutions is a privately held technology company created to revolutionize the cleaning industry through the manufacturing, marketing, and distribution of advanced technologies and products that address the ever-growing need for sustainable cleaning.

In 2008, Activeion licensed a new chemical-free cleaning technology from a mid-sized industrial company using the technology on the large scrubbing machines it sells to factories and warehouses. Other forms of the base chemical-free cleaning technology are used in hospitals for wound cleaning, in food-processing plants for sanitizing produce, and in pharmaceutical plants for maximizing cleanliness. Activeion decided to miniaturize these large, expensive versions of the technology, integrate the technology into a portable handheld sprayer, and market it to commercial cleaning professionals, as well as consumers, at a reasonable price.

The technology makes use of the energy stored in water molecules. First, tap water is passed through a membrane to create oxygen-rich micro-bubbles. Next, this water passes through an electrical charge to separate it into acidic and alkaline ionized or "activated" water. Because dirt and grime are naturally charged themselves, they are attracted to the activated water, which then breaks down the dirt and grime, lifts them from the surface, and enables the resulting dirt and grime particles to be wiped away easily.

Effective on a range of surfaces—from glass and stainless steel to wood and carpet—*R&D Magazine* named the technology as one of the most technologically significant developments of 2008. Through the innovation, cleaning

professionals can meet the demand for green cleaning without the negative environmental and health concerns associated with producing, packaging, transporting, using, and disposing of traditional cleaning chemicals.

PRODUCTS AND MARKETS

In 2009, Activeion Cleaning Solutions introduced the Ionator for professional commercial cleaners as well as a consumer version for homes.

"The benefits from the Ionator are dramatic," explains Scott Beine, custodial manager for the Target Center Arena in Minneapolis, Minnesota, and a believer in the technology. "With its activated water-cleaning process, we've been able to eliminate most general-purpose cleaning products, thereby providing health and safety benefits to our custodial staff and building occupants."

The most stunning benefit of the Ionator is in the environmental area. It avoids the problems associated with traditional chemical detergents and their related packaging, which must be produced, transported, and then disposed of into the waste stream. The Ionator also can replace the hundreds of millions of chemical-laden cleaning bottles used—and disposed of—every day, around the world. On April 22, 2009, Ellen DeGeneres featured the product on her "Earth Day" show—calling it one of the best green products available. The Ionator is now priced at $299.

Markets for the Ionator range from schools and hospitals to hotels and restaurants—virtually anywhere traditional, general-purpose cleaning chemicals are in use. There are millions of these locations in the United States that use general-purpose cleaning chemicals.

To reach consumers, the company has recently introduced a version for home use, selling at about half the price of the commercial Ionator. This product seeks to reach the 117 million single-family homes, especially those with families interested in creating a safer, healthier, more sustainable living space.

BENEFITS

"We believe we have a fantastic story to tell," says Amber Arnseth, product marketing manager for Activeion. She lists the key benefits Activeion technology offers both professional cleaners and consumers:

• *Safety.* By converting tap water into a powerful cleaner

and sanitizer, the Ionator eliminates cleaning chemicals. The technology is one of the only cleaning products in the world without a health-related warning label.

- *Simplicity*. Just fill with tap water and go! This is the ultimate form of "cleaning on the go" that so many households and cleaning professionals want and need. There's nothing to add, mix, or batch (it's portable)—just spray, clean, and wipe dry whenever and wherever there's a spill or a mess (it's on-demand).

- *Sustainability*. In a carbon footprint analysis, the University of Tennessee/Eco-Form compared cleaning with the Ionator to cleaning with traditional general-purpose chemicals. It found significant benefits to using the Ion-

ator. It not only reduces environmental problems but also significantly reduces energy consumption.

- *Savings*. With a technology that works as well as or better than existing general-purpose cleaning chemicals, the Ionator eliminates the purchasing, storing, refilling, and managing of toxic cleaning supplies most organizations face today when they clean. The Grand Haven (Michigan) Area Public School District reports savings of over $20,000 annually by converting to the Ionator. Many other testimonials just like this one exist.

- *Fun*. In a recent blogging event with the Silicon Valley Moms group (www.svmoms.com), virtually all bloggers reported the same results: The Ionator is cool, it helps make cleaning fun, and kids love using it because of the futuristic green glow and the buzzing sound.

CHALLENGES

Despite the numerous benefits, introducing a new, disruptive technology comes with some challenges. "Almost everyone who hears about our product and technology loves the promise of what it can do," says Arnseth. "Yet we know it won't be easy to get people to convert."

Among the obvious challenges:

- *Defining "clean."* Aside from the removal of visible dirt and grime, how can one tell if a surface is clean?

Or if harmful bacteria have been eliminated? Chemical companies mitigate this challenge by adding scents, bubbles, and colors—to "signal" clean.

- *Assessing new technology risk*. It's difficult enough to introduce any new technology to a fast-paced, short-attention-spanned world—much less a technology that is seemingly so unbelievable. Consumers are notoriously finicky in adopting new technologies.

- *Defining a new category*. The category of "high-tech cleaning gadgets for everyday, hard-surface, cleaning on-the-go throughout the home" does not exist today. Activeion is creating a new category in the marketplace—which has historically been one of the most difficult of marketing objectives.

Welcome to the challenges of bringing a new technology into the world!

Questions

1 What are the major points of difference for the Activeion portable handheld cleaning and sanitizing devices for (*a*) business users and (*b*) households?

2 From information in the case and a visit to the Activeion Web site (www.activeion.com), what are the characteristics of the main target markets for the Activeion cleaning tools among (*a*) business users and (*b*) households?

3 Look again at the eight key reasons for new-product success and failure in the chapter. Using a five-point scale (5 = very favorable, 3 = neutral, 1 = very unfavorable), evaluate (*a*) the Ionator for business users and (*b*) the consumer version for households on each of the eight reasons. Briefly justify your answers.

4 When introducing the consumer version for households, (*a*) identify three key target markets, (*b*) suggest media you might use to reach them, and (*c*) create one or two simple messages to communicate the product's points of difference.

5 What other handheld applications could Activeion pursue for its technology?

SERENA

SERENA

G2

LESS CALORIES
FOR MORE ATHLETES

11

Managing Successful Products, Services, and Brands

LEARNING OBJECTIVES

After reading this chapter you should be able to:

LO1 Explain the product life-cycle concept.

LO2 Identify ways that marketing executives manage a product's life cycle.

LO3 Recognize the importance of branding and alternative branding strategies.

LO4 Describe the role of packaging and labeling in the marketing of a product.

LO5 Recognize how the four Ps framework is expanded in the marketing of services.

GATORADE: QUENCHING THE ACTIVE THIRST WITHIN YOU

Why is the thirst for Gatorade unquenchable? Look no further than constant product improvement and masterful brand development.

Like Kleenex in the tissue market, Jell-O among gelatin desserts, and iPod for digital music players, Gatorade is synonymous with sports drinks. Concocted in 1965 at the University of Florida as a rehydration beverage for the school's football team, the drink was coined "Gatorade" by an opposing team's coach after watching his team lose to the Florida Gators in the Orange Bowl. The name stuck, and a new beverage product class was born. Stokely-Van Camp Inc. bought the Gatorade formula in 1967 and commercialized the product. The original Gatorade had one flavor—lemon-lime.

The Quaker Oats Company acquired Stokely-Van Camp in 1983 and quickly increased Gatorade sales through a variety of means. More flavors were added. Multiple package sizes were offered using different containers. Distribution expanded from convenience stores and supermarkets to mass merchandisers such as Walmart. Consistent advertising and promotion effectively conveyed the product's unique performance benefits and links to athletic competition. International opportunities were vigorously pursued. Today, Gatorade is sold in more than 80 countries in North America, Europe, Latin America, the Middle East, Africa, Asia, and Australia and is now a global brand.

Masterful brand management spurred Gatorade's success. Gatorade Frost® was introduced in 1997 and aimed at expanding the brand's reach beyond organized sports to other usage occasions. Gatorade Fierce® appeared in 1999. In the same year, Gatorade entered the bottled-water category with Propel Fitness Water, a lightly flavored water fortified with vitamins. The Gatorade Performance Series was introduced in 2001, featuring a Gatorade Energy Bar, Gatorade Energy Drink, and Gatorade Nutritional Shake.

Brand development accelerated after PepsiCo Inc. purchased Quaker Oats and the Gatorade brand in 2001. Gatorade All Stars, designed for teens, and Gatorade Xtremo, developed with a bilingual label for Latino consumers, were launched in 2002. Gatorade X-Factor followed in 2003. In 2005, Gatorade Endurance Formula was created for serious runners, construction workers, and other people doing long, sweaty workouts. Gatorade Rain, a lighter tasting version of regular Gatorade, arrived in 2006. In 2007, Gatorade AM, with no caffeine, debuted for the morning workout consumer. A low-calorie Gatorade called G2 was successfully marketed in 2008.

Gatorade's marketing performance is a direct result of continuous product improvement and masterful brand management.

In 2009, Gatorade executives unleashed a bevy of enhanced beverages in bold new packaging. "Just like any good athlete, Gatorade is taking it to the next level," said Gatorade's chief marketing officer. "Whether you're in it for the win, for the thrill or for better health, if your body is moving, Gatorade sees you as an athlete, and we're inviting you into the brand." According to a company announcement, "The new Gatorade attitude would be most visible through a total packaging redesign." For example, Gatorade Thirst Quencher now displays the letter G front and center along with the brand's iconic bolt. "For Gatorade, G represents the heart, hustle, and soul of athleticism and will become a badge of pride for anyone who sweats, no matter where they're active."

To differentiate the range of Gatorade offerings from the traditional Gatorade Thirst Quencher, newly enhanced beverages convey the attitude of a tough-love coach or personal trainer through in-your-face names on the label and nutrition benefits inside. Gatorade Fierce is now Bring It™, Gatorade X-Factor is now Be Tough™, Gatorade AM is now Shine On™, and Gatorade Rain is now No Excuses™. Continuing product development efforts guided two new products in 2010. Prime is formulated to be consumed before exercise, while Recover is designed to be used after exercise. Some 45 years after its creation, Gatorade remains a vibrant multibillion-dollar brand.[1]

The marketing of Gatorade illustrates continuous product development and masterful brand management in a dynamic marketplace. This chapter shows how the actions taken by Gatorade executives exemplify those made by successful marketers.

CHARTING THE PRODUCT LIFE CYCLE

product life cycle
The stages a new product goes through in the marketplace: introduction, growth, maturity, and decline.

Products, like people, are viewed as having a life cycle. The concept of the **product life cycle** describes the stages a new product goes through in the marketplace: introduction, growth, maturity, and decline (Figure 11–1).[2] The two curves shown in this figure, total industry revenue and total industry profit, represent the sum of sales revenue and profit of all firms producing the product. The reasons for the changes in each curve and the marketing decisions involved are detailed in the following pages.

Introduction Stage

The introduction stage of the product life cycle occurs when a product is introduced to its intended target market. During this period, sales grow slowly, and profit is minimal. The lack of profit is often the result of large investment costs in product development, such as the millions of dollars spent by Gillette to develop the Gillette Fusion razor shaving system. The marketing objective for the company at this stage is to create consumer awareness and stimulate *trial*—the initial purchase of a product by a consumer.

Companies often spend heavily on advertising and other promotion tools to build awareness and stimulate product trial among consumers in the introduction stage. For example, Gillette budgeted $200 million in advertising to introduce the Fusion shaving system to male shavers. The result? Over 60 percent of male shavers became aware of the new razor within six months and 26 percent tried the product.[3]

Advertising and promotion expenditures in the introduction stage are often made to stimulate *primary demand*, the desire for the product class rather than for a specific brand, since there are few competitors with the same product. As more competitors

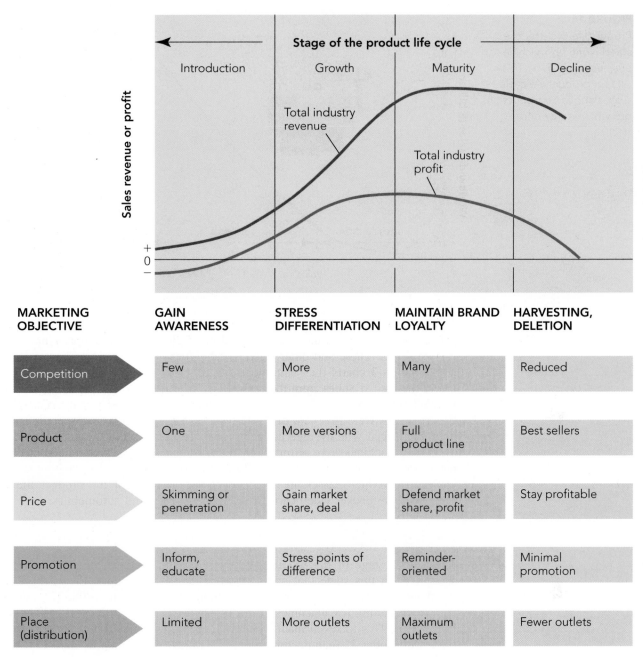

MARKETING OBJECTIVE	GAIN AWARENESS	STRESS DIFFERENTIATION	MAINTAIN BRAND LOYALTY	HARVESTING, DELETION
Competition	Few	More	Many	Reduced
Product	One	More versions	Full product line	Best sellers
Price	Skimming or penetration	Gain market share, deal	Defend market share, profit	Stay profitable
Promotion	Inform, educate	Stress points of difference	Reminder-oriented	Minimal promotion
Place (distribution)	Limited	More outlets	Maximum outlets	Fewer outlets

FIGURE 11–1

The stages of the product life cycle relate to a firm's marketing objectives and marketing mix actions.

launch their own products and the product progresses along its life cycle, company attention is focused on creating *selective demand*, the preference for a specific brand.

Other marketing mix variables also are important at this stage. Gaining distribution can be a challenge because channel intermediaries may be hesitant to carry a new product. Also, a company often restricts the number of variations of the product to ensure control of product quality. Remember that the original Gatorade came in only one flavor—lemon-lime.

During introduction, pricing can be either high or low. A high initial price may be used as part of a *skimming* strategy to help the company recover the costs of development as well as capitalize on the price insensitivity of early buyers. A master of this strategy is 3M. According to a 3M manager, "We hit fast, price high, and get the heck out when the me-too products pour in."[4] High prices tend to attract competitors eager to enter the market because they see the opportunity for profit.

FIGURE 11–2

Product life cycle for the stand-alone fax machine for business use: 1970–2012. All four product life-cycle stages appear: introduction, growth, maturity, and decline.

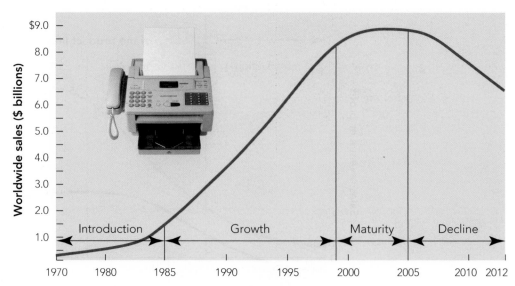

To discourage competitive entry, a company can price low, referred to as *penetration pricing*. This pricing strategy helps build unit volume, but a company must closely monitor costs. These and other pricing techniques are covered in Chapter 12.

Figure 11–2 charts the stand-alone fax machine product life cycle for business use in the United States from the early 1970s to 2012.[5] As shown, sales grew slowly in the 1970s and early 1980s after Xerox pioneered the first portable fax machine. Fax machines were first sold direct to businesses by company salespeople and were premium priced. The average price for a fax machine in 1980 was a hefty $12,700. Those fax machines were primitive by today's standards. They contained mechanical parts, not electronic circuitry, and offered few features seen in today's models.

Several product classes are in the introductory stage of the product life cycle. These include pocket video cameras and electric-powered automobiles.

Growth Stage

The growth stage of the product life cycle is characterized by rapid increases in sales. It is in this stage that competitors appear. For example, Figure 11–2 shows the dramatic increase in sales of fax machines from 1985 to 1998. The number of companies selling fax machines also increased, from one in the early 1970s to four in the late 1970s to seven manufacturers in 1983, which sold nine brands. By 1998 there were some 25 manufacturers and 60 brands from which to choose.

The result of more competitors and more aggressive pricing is that profit usually peaks during the growth stage. For instance, the average price for a fax machine plummeted from $3,300 in 1985 to $500 in 1995. At this stage, advertising shifts emphasis to stimulating selective demand; product benefits are compared with those of competitors' offerings for the purpose of gaining market share.

Product sales in the growth stage grow at an increasing rate because of new people trying or using the product and a growing proportion of *repeat purchasers*—people who tried the product, were satisfied, and bought again. For the Gillette Fusion razor, over 60 percent of men who tried the razor adopted the product permanently. For successful products, the ratio of repeat to trial purchases grows as the product moves through the life cycle. Durable fax machines meant that replacement purchases were rare. However, it became common for more than one machine to populate a business as the machine's use became more widespread.

Changes appear in the product in the growth stage. To help differentiate a company's brand from those of competitors, an improved version or new features are added

Electric automobiles made by General Motors are in the introductory stage of the product life cycle. Digital cameras produced by Olympus are in the growth stage. Each product and company faces unique challenges based on its product life-cycle stage.

to the original design, and product proliferation occurs. Changes in fax machines included (1) models with built-in telephones; (2) models that used plain, rather than thermal, paper for copies; and (3) models that integrated electronic mail.

In the growth stage, it is important to gain as much distribution for the product as possible. In the retail store, for example, this means that competing companies fight for display and shelf space. Expanded distribution in the fax industry is an example. Early in the growth stage, 11 percent of office machine dealers carried this equipment. By the mid-1990s, over 70 percent of these dealers sold fax equipment, and distribution was expanded to other stores selling electronic equipment.

Numerous product classes or industries are in the growth stage of the product life cycle. Examples include e-books, smart phones, and digital cameras.

Maturity Stage

The maturity stage is characterized by a slowing of total industry sales or product class revenue. Also, marginal competitors begin to leave the market. Most consumers who would buy the product are either repeat purchasers of the item or have tried and abandoned it. Sales increase at a decreasing rate in the maturity stage as fewer new buyers enter the market. Profit declines due to fierce price competition among many sellers, and the cost of gaining new buyers at this stage rises.

Marketing attention in the maturity stage is often directed toward holding market share through further product differentiation and finding new buyers. Fax machine manufacturers developed Internet-enabled multifunctional models with new features such as scanning, copying, and color reproduction. They also designed fax machines suitable for small and home businesses, which today represent a substantial portion of sales. Still, a major consideration in a company's strategy in this stage is to control overall marketing cost by improving promotional and distribution efficiency.

Technological substitution that creates value for customers often causes the decline stage in the product life cycle. Will e-mail replace fax machines?

This question has been debated for years. Even though e-mail continues to grow with broadening Internet access, millions of fax machines are still sold each year. Industry analysts estimate that the number of e-mail mailboxes worldwide will grow to 2.5 billion in 2012. However, the phenomenal popularity of e-mail has not brought fax machines to extinction. Why? The two technologies do not directly compete for the same messaging applications.

E-mail is used for text messages, and faxing is predominately used for communicating formatted documents by business users. Fax usage is expected to increase through 2010, even though unit sales of fax machines have declined on a worldwide basis. Internet technology and e-mail may eventually replace facsimile technology and paper and make fax machines extinct, but not in the immediate future.

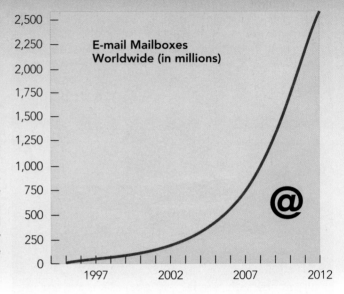

Fax machines entered the maturity stage in the late 1990s. At that time, about 90 percent of industry sales were captured by five producers (Hewlett-Packard, Brother, Sharp, Lexmark, and Samsung), reflecting the departure of marginal competitors. By 2004, 200 million stand-alone fax machines were installed throughout the world, sending more than 120 billion faxes annually.

Numerous product classes and industries are in the maturity stage of their product life cycle. These include soft drinks and DVD players.

Decline Stage

The decline stage occurs when sales drop. Fax machines for business use moved to this stage in early 2005. The average price for a fax machine by that time had sunk below $100. Frequently, a product enters this stage not because of any wrong strategy on the part of companies, but because of environmental changes. For example, digital music players pushed compact discs into decline in the recorded music industry. Will Internet technology and e-mail make fax machines extinct any time soon? The Marketing Matters box offers one perspective on this question.[6]

Products in the decline stage tend to consume a disproportionate share of management and financial resources relative to their future worth. A company will follow one of two strategies to handle a declining product: deletion or harvesting.

Deletion Product *deletion*, or dropping the product from the company's product line, is the most drastic strategy. Because a residual core of consumers still consume or use a product even in the decline stage, product elimination decisions are not taken lightly. For example, Sanford Corporation continues to sell its Liquid Paper correction fluid for use with typewriters in the era of word-processing equipment.

Harvesting A second strategy, *harvesting*, is when a company retains the product but reduces marketing costs. The product continues to be offered, but salespeople do not allocate time in selling nor are advertising dollars spent. The purpose of harvesting is to maintain the ability to meet customer requests. Coca-Cola, for instance, still sells Tab, its first diet cola, to a small group of die-hard fans. According to Coke's CEO, "It shows you care. We want to make sure those who want Tab, get Tab."[7]

Three Aspects of the Product Life Cycle

Three important aspects of product life cycles are (1) their length, (2) the shape of their sales curves, and (3) the rate at which consumers adopt products.

Length of the Product Life Cycle There is no set time that it takes a product to move through its life cycle. As a rule, consumer products have shorter life cycles than business products. For example, many new consumer food products such as Frito-Lay's Baked Lay's potato chips move from the introduction stage to maturity in 18 months. The availability of mass communication vehicles informs consumers quickly and shortens life cycles. Also, technological change tends to shorten product life cycles as new-product innovation replaces existing products.

Shape of the Product Life Cycle The product life-cycle sales curve shown in Figure 11–1 is the *generalized life cycle*, but not all products have the same shape to their curve. In fact, there are several life-cycle curves, each type suggesting different marketing strategies. Figure 11–3 shows the shape of life-cycle sales curves for four different types of products: high-learning, low-learning, fashion, and fad products.

A *high-learning product* is one for which significant customer education is required and there is an extended introductory period (Figure 11–3A). It may surprise you, but personal computers had this life-cycle curve. Consumers in the 1980s had to learn the benefits of owning the product or be educated in a new way of performing familiar tasks. Convection ovens for home use required consumers to learn a new way of cooking and alter familiar recipes used with conventional ovens. As a result, these ovens spent years in the introductory period.

In contrast, sales for a *low-learning product* begin immediately because little learning is required by the consumer, and the benefits of purchase are readily understood (Figure 11–3B). This product often can be easily imitated by competitors, so the marketing strategy is to broaden distribution quickly. In this way, as competitors rapidly enter, most retail outlets already have the innovator's product. It is also important to have the manufacturing capacity to meet demand. A successful low-learning product is Gillette's Fusion razor. This product achieved $1 billion in worldwide sales in less than three years.

FIGURE 11–3

Alternative product life-cycle curves based on product types. Note the long introduction stage for a high-learning product compared with a low-learning product. Read the text for an explanation of the different product life-cycle curves.

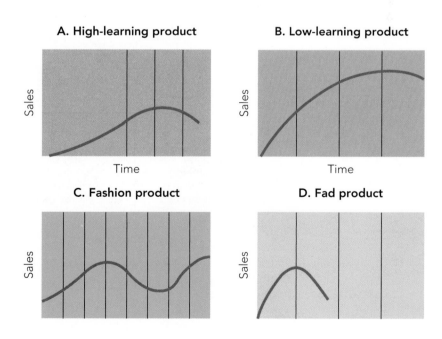

A. High-learning product

Sales / Time

B. Low-learning product

Sales / Time

C. Fashion product

Sales

D. Fad product

Sales

A *fashion product* (Figure 11–3C) is a style of the times. Life cycles for fashion products frequently appear in women's and men's apparel. Fashion products are introduced, decline, and then seem to return. The length of the cycles may be months, years, or decades. Consider women's hosiery. Product sales have been declining for years. Women consider it more fashionable to not wear hosiery—bad news for Hanes brands, the leading marketer of women's sheer hosiery. According to an authority on fashion, "Companies might as well let the fashion cycle take its course and wait for the inevitable return of pantyhose."[8]

A *fad product* experiences rapid sales on introduction and then an equally rapid decline (Figure 11–3D). These products are typically novelties and have a short life cycle. They include car tattoos sold in southern California and described as the first removable and reusable graphics for automobiles, and vinyl dresses and fleece bikinis made by a Minnesota clothing company.

The Life Cycle and Consumers The life cycle of a product depends on sales to consumers. Not all consumers rush to buy a product in the introductory stage, and the shapes of the life-cycle curves indicate that most sales occur after the product has been on the market for some time. In essence, a product diffuses, or spreads, through the population, a concept called the *diffusion of innovation*.[9]

Some people are attracted to a product early. Others buy it only after they see their friends or opinion leaders with the item. Figure 11–4 shows the consumer population divided into five categories of product adopters based on when they adopt a new product. Brief profiles accompany each category. For any product to be successful, it must be purchased by innovators and early adopters. This is why manufacturers of new pharmaceuticals try to gain adoption by respected hospitals, clinics, and physicians. Once accepted by innovators and early adopters, the adoption of new products moves on to the early majority, late majority, and laggard categories.

Several factors affect whether a consumer will adopt a new product or not. Common reasons for resisting a product in the introduction stage are usage barriers (the product is not compatible with existing habits), value barriers (the product provides no incentive to change), risk barriers (physical, economic, or social), and psychological barriers (cultural differences or image).[10]

FIGURE 11–4
Five categories and profiles of product adopters. For a product to be successful, it must be purchased by innovators and early adopters.

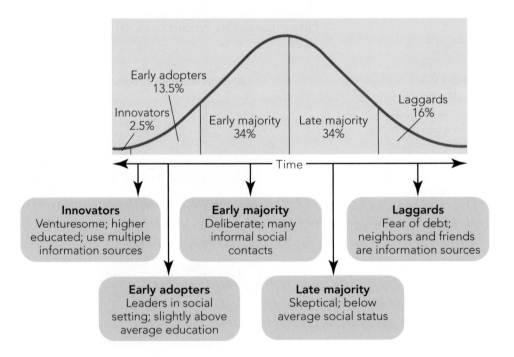

Companies attempt to overcome these barriers in numerous ways. They provide warranties, money-back guarantees, extensive usage instructions, demonstrations, and free samples to stimulate initial trial of new products. For example, software developers offer demonstrations downloaded from the Internet. Cosmetic consumers can browse through the Cover Girl ColorMatch system on its Web site to find out how certain makeup products will look. Free samples are one of the most popular means to gain consumer trial. In fact, 71 percent of consumers consider a sample to be the best way to evaluate a new product.[11]

---

learning review

1. Advertising plays a major role in the _____ stage of the product life cycle, and _____ plays a major role in the maturity stage.

2. How do high-learning and low-learning products differ?

MANAGING THE PRODUCT LIFE CYCLE

LO2

An important task for a firm is to manage its products through the successive stages of their life cycles. This section describes the role of the product manager, who is usually responsible for this, and presents three ways to manage a product through its life cycle: modifying the product, modifying the market, and repositioning the product.

Role of a Product Manager

The product manager, sometimes called a *brand manager*, manages the marketing efforts for a close-knit family of products or brands. Introduced by Procter & Gamble in 1928, the product manager style of marketing organization is used by consumer goods firms, including General Mills and PepsiCo, and by industrial firms such as Intel and Hewlett-Packard. The U.S. Postal Service also employs product managers.

All product managers are responsible for managing existing products through the stages of the life cycle. Some are also responsible for developing new products. Product managers' marketing responsibilities include developing and executing a marketing program for the product line described in an annual marketing plan and approving ad copy, media selection, and package design.

Product managers also engage in extensive data analysis related to their products and brands. Sales, market share, and profit trends are closely monitored. Managers often supplement these data with two measures: (1) a category development index (CDI) and (2) a brand development index (BDI). These indexes help to identify strong and weak market segments (usually demographic or geographic segments) for specific consumer products and brands and provide direction for marketing efforts. The calculation, visual display, and interpretation of these two indexes for Hawaiian Punch are described in the Using Marketing Dashboards box on the next page.

Modifying the Product

Product modification involves altering a product's characteristic, such as its quality, performance, or appearance, to increase the product's value to customers and increase sales. Wrinkle-free and stain-resistant clothing made possible by nanotechnology revolutionized the men's and women's apparel business and stimulated industry sales of casual pants, shirts, and blouses.

Using Marketing Dashboards
Knowing Your CDI and BDI

Where are sales for my product category and brand strongest and weakest? Data related to this question are displayed in a marketing dashboard using two indexes: (1) a category development index and (2) a brand development index.

Your Challenge You have joined the marketing team for Hawaiian Punch, the top fruit punch drink sold in the United States. The brand has been marketed to mothers with children under 13 years old. The majority of Hawaiian Punch sales are in gallon and 2-liter bottles. Your assignment is to examine the brand's performance and identify growth opportunities for the Hawaiian Punch brand among households that consume prepared fruit drinks (the product category).

Your marketing dashboard displays a category development index (CDI) and a brand development index (BDI) provided by a syndicated marketing research firm. Each index is based on the calculations below:

Category Development Index (CDI) =
$$\frac{\text{Percent of a product category's total U.S. sales in a market segment}}{\text{Percent of the total U.S. population in a market segment}} \times 100$$

Brand Development Index (BDI) =
$$\frac{\text{Percent of a brand's total U.S. sales in a market segment}}{\text{Percent of the total U.S. population in a market segment}} \times 100$$

A CDI over 100 indicates above-average product category purchases by a market segment. A number under 100 indicates below-average purchases. A BDI over 100 indicates a strong brand position in a segment; a number under 100 indicates a weak brand position.

You are interested in CDI and BDI displays for four household segments that consume prepared fruit drinks: (1) households without children; (2) households with children 6 years old or under; (3) households with children aged 7 to 12; and (4) households with children aged 13 to 18.

Your Findings The BDI and CDI measures displayed below show that Hawaiian Punch is consumed by households with children, and particularly households with children under age 12. The Hawaiian Punch BDI is over 100 for both segments—not surprising since the brand is marketed to these segments. Households with children 13 to 18 years old evidence high fruit drink consumption with a CDI over 100. But Hawaiian Punch is relatively weak in this segment with a BDI under 100.

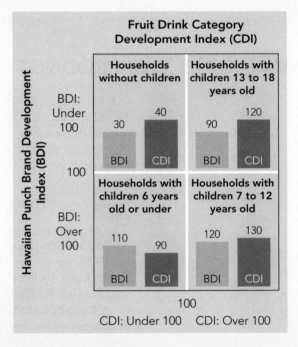

Your Action An opportunity for Hawaiian Punch exists among households with children 13 to 18 years old—teenagers. You might propose that Hawaiian Punch be repositioned for teens. In addition, you might recommend that Hawaiian Punch be packaged in single-serve cans or bottles to attract this segment, much like soft drinks. Teens might also be targeted for advertising and promotions.

New features, packages, or scents can be used to change a product's characteristics and give the sense of a revised product. Procter & Gamble revamped Pantene shampoo and conditioner with a new vitamin formula and relaunched the brand with a multimillion-dollar advertising and promotion campaign. The result? Pantene, a brand first introduced in the 1940s, is now the top-selling shampoo and conditioner in the United States in an industry with more than 1,000 competitors.

Harley-Davidson redesigned some of its motorcycle models to feature smaller hand grips, a lower seat, and an easier-to-pull clutch lever to create a more comfortable ride for women. According to Genevieve Schmitt, founding editor of WomenRidersNow. com, "They realize that women are an up-and-coming segment and that they need to accommodate them."

Modifying the Market

With *market modification* strategies, a company tries to find new customers, increase a product's use among existing customers, or create new use situations.

Finding New Customers Produce companies have begun marketing and packaging prunes as dried plums to attract younger buyers. Harley-Davidson has tailored a marketing program to encourage women to take up biking, thus doubling the number of potential customers for its motorcycles.[12]

Increasing a Product's Use Promoting more frequent usage has been a strategy of Campbell Soup Company. Because soup consumption rises in the winter and declines during the summer, the company now advertises more heavily in warm months to encourage consumers to think of soup as more than a cold-weather food. Similarly, the Florida Orange Growers Association advocates drinking orange juice throughout the day rather than for breakfast only.

Creating a New Use Situation Finding new uses for an existing product has been the strategy behind Dockers, the U.S. market leader in casual pants. Originally intended as a single pant for every situation, Dockers now promotes different looks for different usage situations: work, weekend, dress, and golf.[13]

Repositioning the Product

Often a company decides to reposition its product or product line in an attempt to bolster sales. *Product repositioning* changes the place a product occupies in a consumer's mind relative to competitive products. A firm can reposition a product by changing one or more of the four marketing mix elements. Four factors that trigger the need for a repositioning action are discussed next.

Reacting to a Competitor's Position One reason to reposition a product is because a competitor's entrenched position is adversely affecting sales and market share. New Balance, Inc., successfully repositioned its athletic shoes to focus on fit, durability, and comfort rather than competing head-on against Nike and Adidas on fashion and professional sports. The company offers an expansive range of shoes and it networks with podiatrists, not sport celebrities.[14]

Reaching a New Market When Unilever introduced iced tea in Britain, sales were disappointing. British consumers viewed it as leftover hot tea, not suitable for drinking. The company made its tea carbonated and repositioned it as a cold soft drink to compete as a carbonated beverage and sales improved. Johnson & Johnson effectively repositioned St. Joseph aspirin. Once regarded as a product for infants, it is now seen as an adult low-strength aspirin to reduce the risk of heart problems or strokes.[15]

Catching a Rising Trend Changing consumer trends also lead to product repositioning. Growing consumer interest in foods that offer health and dietary benefits is an example. Many products have been repositioned to capitalize on this trend. Quaker Oats makes the FDA-approved claim that oatmeal, as part of a low-saturated-fat, low-cholesterol diet, may reduce the risk of heart disease. Calcium-enriched products, such as Kraft American cheese and Uncle Ben's Calcium Plus rice, emphasize healthy bone structure for children and adults. Weight-conscious consumers have embraced low-fat and low-calorie diets in growing numbers. Today, most food and beverage companies offer reduced-fat and low-calorie versions of their products.

Changing the Value Offered   In repositioning a product, a company can decide to change the value it offers buyers and trade up or down. *Trading up* involves adding value to the product (or line) through additional features or higher-quality materials. Michelin, Bridgestone, and Goodyear have done this with a "run-flat" tire that can travel up to 50 miles at 55 miles per hour after suffering total air loss. Mass merchandisers, such as Target and JCPenney, can trade up by adding a designer clothes section to their stores.

Trading down involves reducing the number of features, quality, or price. For example, airlines have added more seats, thus reducing legroom, and limited snack service. Trading down exists when companies engage in *downsizing*—reducing the package content without changing package size and maintaining or increasing the package price. Firms are criticized for this practice, as described in the Making Responsible Decisions box.[16]

learning review

3. What does "creating a new use situation" mean in managing a product's life cycle?

4. Explain the difference between trading up and trading down in product repositioning.

BRANDING AND BRAND MANAGEMENT STRATEGY

LO3

A basic decision in marketing products is **branding**, in which an organization uses a name, phrase, design, symbols, or combination of these to identify its products and distinguish them from those of competitors. A **brand name** is any word, device (design, sound, shape, or color), or combination of these used to distinguish a seller's goods or services. Some brand names can be spoken, such as "Gatorade" or "Rollerblade." Other brand names cannot be spoken, such as the apple in the *logotype* or *logo* for Apple computers.

Making Responsible Decisions > > > > > > > ethics

Consumer Economics of Downsizing—Get Less, Pay More

For more than 30 years, Starkist put 6.5 ounces of tuna into its regular-sized can. Today, Starkist puts 6.125 ounces of tuna into its can but charges the same price. Frito-Lay (Doritos and Lay's snack chips), Procter & Gamble (Pampers and Luvs disposable diapers), and Nestlé (Poland Spring and Calistoga bottled waters) have whittled away at package contents 5 to 10 percent while maintaining their products' package size, dimensions, and prices. Kimberly-Clark cut its retail price on its jumbo pack of Huggies diapers from $13.50 to $12.50, but reduced the number of diapers per pack from 48 to 42. Georgia-Pacific reduced the content of its Brawny paper towel six-roll pack by 20 percent without lowering the price.

Consumer advocates charge that downsizing the content of packages while maintaining prices is a subtle and unannounced way of taking advantage of consumer buying habits. They also say downsizing is a price increase in disguise and deceptive, but legal. Manufacturers argue that this prac-

tice is a way of keeping prices from rising beyond psychological barriers for their products.

Is downsizing an unethical practice if manufacturers do not inform consumers that the package contents are less than they were previously?

---

branding

An organization's use of a name, phrase, design, symbol, or combination of these to identify and distinguish its products.

brand name

Any word, device (design, shape, sound, or color), or combination of these used to distinguish a seller's goods or services.

brand personality

A set of human characteristics associated with a brand name.

brand equity

The added value a brand name gives to a product beyond the functional benefits provided.

Consumers may benefit most from branding. Recognizing competing products by distinct trademarks allows them to be more efficient shoppers. Consumers can recognize and avoid products with which they are dissatisfied, while becoming loyal to other, more satisfying brands. As discussed in Chapter 5, brand loyalty often eases consumers' decision making by eliminating the need for an external search.

Brand Personality and Brand Equity

Product managers recognize that brands offer more than product identification and a means to distinguish their products from competitors.[17] Successful and established brands take on a **brand personality**, a set of human characteristics associated with a brand name. Research shows that consumers often assign personality traits to products—traditional, romantic, rugged, sophisticated, rebellious—and choose brands that are consistent with their own or desired self-image. Marketers can and do imbue a brand with a personality through advertising that depicts a certain user or usage situation and conveys certain emotions or feelings to be associated with the brand. The personality traits associated with Coca-Cola are all-American and real; with Pepsi, young and exciting; and with Dr Pepper, nonconforming and unique. The traits linked to Harley-Davidson are masculinity, defiance, and rugged individualism.

Brand name importance to a company has led to a concept called **brand equity**, the added value a brand name gives to a product beyond the functional benefits provided. This value has two distinct advantages. First, brand equity provides a competitive advantage. The Sunkist brand implies quality fruit. The Disney name defines children's entertainment. A second advantage is that consumers are often willing to pay a higher price for a product with brand equity. Brand equity, in this instance, is represented by the premium a consumer will pay for one brand over another when the functional benefits provided are identical. Gillette razors and blades, Bose audio systems, Duracell batteries, and Louis Vuitton luggage all enjoy a price premium arising from brand equity.

Can you describe the brand personality traits for these two fragrance brands?

FIGURE 11–5
The customer-based brand equity pyramid shows the four-step building process that forges strong, favorable, and unique customer associations with a brand.

Consumer-brand connection

Consumer judgments | Consumer feelings

Brand performance | Brand imagery

Brand awareness

Creating Brand Equity Brand equity doesn't just happen. It is carefully crafted and nurtured by marketing programs that forge strong, favorable, and unique customer associations and experiences with a brand. Brand equity resides in the minds of consumers and results from what they have learned, felt, seen, and heard about a brand over time. Marketers recognize that brand equity is not easily or quickly achieved. Rather, it arises from a sequential building process consisting of four steps (see Figure 11–5).[18]

• The first step is to develop positive brand awareness and an association of the brand in consumers' minds with a product class or need to give the brand an identity. Gatorade and Kleenex have achieved this in the sports drink and facial tissue product classes, respectively.

• Next, a marketer must establish a brand's meaning in the minds of consumers. Meaning arises from what a brand stands for and has two dimensions—a functional, performance-related dimension and an abstract, imagery-related dimension. Nike has done this through continuous product development and improvement and its links to peak athletic performance in its integrated marketing communications program.

• The third step is to elicit the proper consumer responses to a brand's identity and meaning. Here attention is placed on how consumers think and feel about a brand.

Thinking focuses on a brand's perceived quality, credibility, and superiority relative to other brands. Feeling relates to the consumer's emotional reaction to a brand. Michelin elicits both responses for its tires. Not only is

Ralph Lauren has a long-term licensing agreement with Luxottica Group, S.P.A. of Milan for the design, production, and worldwide distribution of prescription frames and sunglasses under the Ralph Lauren brand. The agreement is an ideal fit for both companies. Ralph Lauren is a leader in the design, marketing, and distribution of premium lifestyle products. Luxottica is the global leader in the premium and luxury eyewear sector.

Michelin thought of as a credible and superior-quality brand, but consumers also acknowledge a warm and secure feeling of safety, comfort, and self-assurance without worry or concern about the brand.

- The final, and most difficult, step is to create a consumer–brand connection evident in an intense, active loyalty relationship between consumers and the brand. A deep psychological bond characterizes a consumer–brand connection and the personal identification customers have with the brand. Brands that have achieved this status include Harley-Davidson, Apple, and eBay.

Valuing Brand Equity Brand equity also provides a financial advantage for the brand owner.[19] Successful, established brand names, such as Gillette, Nike, Gatorade, and Nokia, have an economic value in the sense that they are intangible assets. The recognition that brands are assets is apparent in the decision to buy and sell brands. For example, Triarc Companies bought the Snapple brand from Quaker Oats for $300 million and sold it three years later to Cadbury Schweppes for $900 million. This example illustrates that brands, unlike physical assets that depreciate with time and use, can appreciate in value when effectively marketed. However, brands can lose value when they are not managed properly. Consider the purchase and sale of Lender's Bagels. Kellogg bought the brand for $466 million only to sell it to Aurora Foods for $275 million three years later following deteriorating sales and profits.

Financially lucrative brand licensing opportunities arise from brand equity.[20] *Brand licensing* is a contractual agreement whereby one company (licensor) allows its brand name(s) or trademark(s) to be used with products or services offered by another company (licensee) for a royalty or fee. For example, Disney makes billions of dollars each year licensing its characters for children's toys, apparel, and games. Licensing fees for Winnie the Pooh alone exceed $3 billion annually.

Successful brand licensing requires careful marketing analysis to ensure a proper fit between the licensor's brand and the licensee's products. World-renowned designer Ralph Lauren earns over $140 million each year by licensing his Ralph Lauren, Polo, and Chaps brands for dozens of products, including paint by Glidden, furniture by Henredon, footwear by Rockport, eyewear by Luxottica, and fragrances by L'Oreal.[21] Mistakes, such as Kleenex diapers, Bic perfume, and Domino's fruit-favored bubble gum, are a few examples of poor matches and licensing failures.

Picking a Good Brand Name

We take brand names such as Red Bull, iPod, and Axe for granted, but it is often a difficult and expensive process to pick a good name. Companies will spend between $25,000 and $100,000 to identify and test a new brand name. Five criteria are mentioned most often when selecting a good brand name.[22]

- *The name should suggest the product benefits.* For example, Accutron (watches), Easy Off (oven cleaner), Glass Plus (glass cleaner), Cling-Free (antistatic cloth for drying clothes), Chevy Volt (electric car), and Tidy Bowl (toilet bowl cleaner) all clearly describe the benefits of purchasing the product.
- *The name should be memorable, distinctive, and positive.* In the auto industry, when a competitor has a memorable name, others quickly imitate. When Ford named a car the Mustang, Pintos, Colts, and Broncos soon followed. The Thunderbird name led to the Phoenix, Eagle, Sunbird, and Firebird.
- *The name should fit the company or product image.* Sharp is a name that can apply to audio and video equipment. Bufferin, Excedrin, Anacin, and Nuprin are scientific-sounding names, good for analgesics. Eveready, Duracell, and DieHard suggest reliability and longevity—two qualities consumers want in a battery.
- *The name should have no legal or regulatory restrictions.* Legal restrictions produce trademark infringement suits, and regulatory restrictions arise through improper use of words. For example, the U.S. Food and Drug Administration discourages the use of the word *heart* in food brand names. This restriction led to changing the name of Kellogg's Heartwise cereal to Fiberwise, and Clorox's Hidden Valley Ranch Take Heart Salad Dressing had to be modified to Hidden Valley Ranch Low-Fat Salad Dressing. Increasingly, brand names need a corresponding address on the Internet. This further complicates name selection because about 140 million domain names are already registered.
- *The name should be simple* (such as Bold laundry detergent, Axe deodorant and body spray, and Bic pens) *and should be emotional* (such as Joy and Obsession perfumes). In the development of names for international use, having a nonmeaningful brand name has been considered a benefit. A name such as Exxon does not have any prior impressions or undesirable images among a diverse world population of different languages and cultures. The 7Up name is another matter. In Shanghai, China, the phrase means "death through drinking" in the local dialect. Sales have suffered as a result.

Different Branding Strategies

Companies can employ several different branding strategies, including multiproduct branding, multibranding, private branding, or mixed branding (see Figure 11–6).

multiproduct branding
A branding strategy in which a company uses one name for all its products in a product class.

Multiproduct Branding Strategy With **multiproduct branding**, a company uses one name for all its products in a product class. This approach is sometimes called *family branding* or *corporate branding* when the company's trade name is used. For example, Microsoft, General Electric, Samsung, Gerber, and Sony engage in corporate branding—the company's trade name and brand name are identical. Church & Dwight uses the Arm & Hammer family brand name for all its products featuring baking soda as the primary ingredient.

There are several advantages to multiproduct branding. Capitalizing again on brand equity, consumers who have a good experience with the product will transfer this favorable attitude to other items in the product class with the same name. Therefore, this brand strategy makes possible *product line extensions*, the practice of using a current brand name to enter a new market segment in its product class.

Branding strategy			
Multiproduct branding strategy Toro makes: • Toro snowblowers • Toro lawn mowers • Toro garden hoses • Toro sprinkler systems	**Multibranding strategy** Procter & Gamble makes: • Tide • Cheer • Ivory Snow • Bold	**Private branding strategy** Sears has: • Kenmore appliances • Craftsman tools • DieHard batteries	**Mixed branding strategy** Michelin makes: • Michelin tires • Sears tires Epson makes: • Epson printers • IBM printers

FIGURE 11–6

Alternative branding strategies are available to marketers. Each has advantages and disadvantages, as described in the text.

Kimberly-Clark was able to leverage the strong Huggies brand equity among mothers when it introduced a full line of baby and toddler toiletries first in the United States and then globally. The success of this brand extension strategy is evident in the $500 million in annual sales generated globally.

multibranding

A branding strategy that involves giving each product a distinct name.

Campbell Soup Company employs a multiproduct branding strategy with soup line extensions. It offers regular Campbell soup, home-cooking style, and chunky varieties and more than 100 soup flavors. This strategy can result in lower advertising and promotion costs because the same name is used on all products, thus raising the level of brand awareness. A risk with line extension is that sales of an extension may come at the expense of other items in the company's product line. Line extensions work best when they provide incremental company revenue by taking sales away from competing brands or attracting new buyers.[23]

Some multiproduct branding companies employ *subbranding*, which combines a corporate or family brand with a new brand, to distinguish a part of its product line from others. Gatorade successfully used subbranding with the introduction of Gatorade G2. Similarly, Porsche successfully markets its higher-end Porsche Carrera and its lower-end Porsche Boxster.

A strong brand equity also allows for *brand extension*, the practice of using a current brand name to enter a different product class. For instance, equity in the Huggies family brand name has allowed Kimberly-Clark to successfully extend its name to a full line of baby and toddler toiletries. Honda's established name for motor vehicles has extended easily to snowblowers, lawn mowers, marine engines, and snowmobiles.

However, there is a risk with brand extensions. Too many uses for one brand name can dilute the meaning of a brand for consumers. Marketing experts claim this has happened to the Arm & Hammer brand given its use for toothpaste, laundry detergent, gum, cat litter, air freshener, carpet deodorizer, and antiperspirant.[24]

Multibranding Strategy Alternately, a company can engage in **multibranding**, which involves giving each product a distinct name. Multibranding is a useful strategy when each brand is intended for a different market segment. P&G makes Camay soap for those concerned with soft skin and Safeguard for those who want deodorant protection. Black & Decker markets its line of tools for the household do-it-yourselfer segment with the Black & Decker name but uses the DeWalt name for its professional tool line. Disney uses the Miramax and Touchstone Pictures names for films directed at adults and its Disney name for children's films.

Multibranding is applied in a variety of ways. Some companies array their brands on the basis of price-quality segments.[25] Marriott International offers 15 hotel and resort brands, each suited for a particular traveler experience and budget. To illustrate, The Ritz-Carlton offers luxury amenities at a premium price. Marriott and

Marriott International uses a multibranding strategy to suit different market segments based on traveler experience and budget.

Renaissance hotels offer medium- to high-priced accommodations. Courtyard hotels and TownPlace Suites appeal to economy-minded travelers, whereas the Fairfield Inn is for those on a very low travel budget.

Other multibrand companies introduce new product brands as defensive moves to counteract competition. Called *fighting brands*, their chief purpose is to confront competitor brands.[26] For instance, Ford launched its Fusion brand to halt the defection of Ford owners who were buying competitors' midsize cars. According to Ford's car group marketing manager, "Every year we're losing around 50,000 people from our products to competitors' midsize cars. We're losing Mustang, Focus, and Taurus owners. Fusion is our interceptor."[27]

Compared with the multiproduct strategy, advertising and promotion costs tend to be higher with multibranding. The company must generate awareness among consumers and retailers for each new brand name without the benefit of any previous impressions. The advantages of this strategy are that each brand is unique to each market segment and there is no risk that a product failure will affect other products in the line. Still, some large multibrand firms have found that the complexity and expense of implementing this strategy can outweigh the benefits. For example, Unilever recently pruned its brands from some 1,600 to 400 through product deletion and sales to other companies.[28]

Private Branding Strategy A company uses *private branding*, often called *private labeling* or *reseller branding*, when it manufactures products but sells them under the brand name of a wholesaler or retailer. Rayovac, Paragon Trade Brands, and Ralcorp Holdings are major suppliers of private-label alkaline batteries, diapers, and grocery products, respectively. Radio Shack, Costco, Sears, Walmart, and Kroger are large retailers that have their own brand names. Private branding is popular because it typically produces high profits for manufacturers and resellers. Consumers also buy them. It is estimated that one of every five items purchased at U.S. supermarkets, drugstores, and mass merchandisers bears a private brand.[29]

Mixed Branding Strategy A fourth branding strategy is *mixed branding*, where a firm markets products under its own name(s) and that of a reseller because the segment attracted to the reseller is different from its own market. Beauty and fragrance marketer Elizabeth Arden is an example. The company sells its Elizabeth Arden brand through department stores and a line of skin care products at Walmart with the "skinsimple" brand name. Companies such as Del Monte, Whirlpool, and Dial produce private brands of pet foods, home appliances, and soap, respectively, for resellers.

PACKAGING AND LABELING PRODUCTS PROPERLY

The *packaging* component of a product refers to any container in which it is offered for sale and on which label information is conveyed. A *label* is an integral part of the package and typically identifies the product or brand, who made it, where and when it was made, how it is to be used, and package contents and ingredients. To a great extent, the customer's first exposure to a product is the package and label and both are an expensive and important part of marketing strategy. For Pez Candy, Inc., the character head-on-a-stick plastic container that dispenses a miniature tablet candy is the central element of its marketing strategy, as described in the Marketing Matters box.[30]

Creating Customer Value through Packaging— Pez Heads Dispense More Than Candy

Customer value can assume numerous forms. For Pez Candy, Inc. (www.pez.com), customer value manifests itself in some 450 Pez character candy dispensers. Each refillable dispenser ejects tasty candy tablets in a variety of flavors that delight preteens and teens alike in more than 60 countries.

Pez was formulated in 1927 by Austrian food mogul Edward Haas III and successfully sold in Europe as an adult breath mint. Pez, which comes from the German word for peppermint, *pfefferminz*, was originally packaged in a hygienic, headless plastic dispenser. Pez first appeared in the United States in 1953 with a headless dispenser, marketed to adults. After conducting extensive marketing research, Pez was repositioned with fruit flavors, repackaged with licensed character heads on top of the dispenser, and remarketed as a children's product in the mid-1950s. Since then, most top-level licensed characters and hundreds of other characters have become Pez heads. Consumers eat more than 3 billion Pez tablets annually in the United States alone, and company sales growth exceeds that of the candy industry as a whole.

The unique Pez package dispenses a "use experience" for its customers beyond the candy itself, namely, fun. And fun translates into a 98 percent awareness level for Pez among teenagers and 89 percent among mothers with children. Pez has not advertised its product for years. With that kind of awareness, who needs advertising?

Creating Customer Value and Competitive Advantage through Packaging and Labeling

Packaging and labeling cost U.S. companies more than $120 billion annually and account for about 15 cents of every dollar spent by consumers for products.[31] Despite the cost, packaging and labeling are essential because both provide important benefits for the manufacturer, retailer, and ultimate consumer. Packaging and labeling also can provide a competitive advantage.

Can you name this soft-drink brand? If you can, then the package has fulfilled its purpose.

Communication Benefits A major benefit of packaging is the label information conveyed to the consumer, such as directions on how, where, and when to use the product and the source and composition of the product, which is needed to satisfy legal requirements of product disclosure. For example, the labeling system for packaged and processed foods in the United States provides a uniform format for nutritional and dietary information. Many packaged foods contain informative recipes to promote usage of the product. Campbell Soup estimates that the green bean casserole recipe on its cream of mushroom soup can accounts for $20 million in soup sales each year![32] Other information consists of seals and symbols, either government required or commercial seals of approval (such as the Good Housekeeping seal).

Lay's Stax potato crisps and Procter & Gamble's Pringles illustrate the functional role of packaging in product and brand management.

Functional Benefits Packaging often plays a functional role, such as storage, convenience, protection, or product quality. Storing food containers is one example, and beverage companies have developed lighter and easier ways to stack products on shelves and in refrigerators. Examples include Coca-Cola beverage packs designed to fit neatly onto refrigerator shelves and Ocean Spray Cranberries's rectangular juice bottles that allow 10 units per package versus 8 of its former round bottles.

The convenience dimension of packaging is increasingly important. Kraft Miracle Whip salad dressing, Heinz ketchup, and Skippy Squeez'It peanut butter are sold in squeeze bottles; microwave popcorn has been a major market success; and Chicken of the Sea tuna is packaged in single-serving portions. Nabisco offers portion-control package sizes for the convenience of weight-conscious consumers. It offers 100-calorie packs of Oreos, Cheese Nips, and other products in individual pouches.

Consumer protection is another important function of packaging, including the development of tamper-resistant containers. Today, companies commonly use safety seals or pop-tops that reveal previous opening. But, no package is truly tamper resistant. U.S. law now provides for maximum penalties of life imprisonment and $250,000 fines for package tampering. Consumer protection through labeling exists in "open dating," which states the expected shelf life of the product.

Functional features of packaging also can affect product quality. Procter & Gamble's Pringles and Lay's Stax potato crisps, with cylindrical packaging, offer uniform chips, minimal breakage, and for some consumers, better value for the money than flex-bag packages for chips. Consumers are the final judge of which chip packaging stacks up better.

Perceptual Benefits A third component of packaging and labeling is the perception created in the consumer's mind. Package and label shape, color, and graphics distinguish one brand from another, convey a brand's positioning, and build brand equity. According to the director of marketing for L'eggs hosiery, "Packaging is important to the positioning and equity of the L'eggs brand."[33] Why? Packaging and labeling have been shown to enhance brand recognition and facilitate the formation of strong, favorable, and unique brand associations.[34] This logic applies to Celestial Seasonings' packaging and labeling, which uses delicate illustrations, soft and warm colors, and quotations about life to reinforce the brand's positioning as a New Age, natural herbal tea.

Successful marketers recognize that changes in packages and labels can update and uphold a brand's image in the customer's mind. For example, Pepsi-Cola has embarked on a packaging change to uphold its image among teens and young adults. For a time, Pepsi-Cola debuted new graphics on its cans and bottles every three or four weeks to reflect the "fun, optimistic, and youthful spirit" of the brand to its customers.[35]

Because labels list a product's source, brands competing in the global marketplace can benefit from "country of origin or manufacture" perceptions as described in Chapter 7. Consumers tend to have stereotypes about country-product pairings that they judge "best"—English tea, French perfume, Italian leather, and Japanese electronics—which can affect a brand's image. Increasingly, Chinese firms are adopting the English language and Roman letters for their brand labels. This is being done because of a common perception in many Asian countries that "things Western are good."[36]

The distinctive design of Celestial Seasonings' tea boxes reinforces the brand's positioning as a New Age, natural herbal tea.

Packaging and Labeling Challenges and Responses

Package and label designers face four challenges. They are (1) the continuing need to connect with customers; (2) environmental concerns; (3) health, safety, and security issues; and (4) cost reduction.

Connecting with Customers Packages and labels must be continually updated to connect with customers. The challenge lies in creating aesthetic and functional design features that attract customer attention and deliver customer value in their use. If done right, the rewards can be huge.[37]

For example, the marketing team responsible for Kleenex tissues converted its standard rectangular box into an oval shape with colorful seasonal graphics. Sales soared with this aesthetic change in packaging. After months of in-home research, Kraft product managers discovered that consumers often transferred Chips Ahoy! cookies to jars for easy access and to avoid staleness. The company solved both problems by creating a patented resealable opening on the top of the bag. The result? Sales of the new package doubled that of the old package.

Environmental Concerns Because of widespread worldwide concern about the growth of solid waste and the shortage of viable landfill sites, the amount, composition, and disposal of packaging material continues to receive much attention.[38] For example, PepsiCo, Coca-Cola, and Nestlé have decreased the amount of plastic in their beverage bottles to reduce solid waste. Recycling packaging material is another major thrust. Procter & Gamble now uses recycled cardboard in over 70 percent of its paper packaging. Its Spic and Span liquid cleaner is packaged in 100 percent recycled material. Other firms, such as Walmart, are emphasizing the use of less packaging material. In 2008, the company began working with its 600,000 global suppliers to reduce overall packaging and shipping material by 5 percent by 2013.

Health, Safety, and Security Issues A third challenge involves the growing health, safety, and security concerns of packaging materials. Today, most U.S. and European consumers believe companies should make sure products and their packages are safe and secure, regardless of the cost, and companies are responding in numerous ways. Most butane lighters sold today, like those made by Scripto, contain a child-resistant safety latch to prevent misuse and accidental fire. Child-proof caps on pharmaceutical products and household cleaners and sealed lids on food packages are now common. New packaging technology and materials that extend a product's *shelf life* (the time a product can be stored) and prevent spoilage continue to be developed with special applications for developing countries.

Cost Reduction About 80 percent of packaging material used in the world consists of paper, plastics, and glass. As the cost of these materials rises, companies are constantly challenged to find innovative ways to cut packaging costs while delivering value to their customers. As an example, Hewlett-Packard reduced the size and weight of its Photosmart product package and shipping container. Through design and material changes, packaging material costs fell by more than 50 percent. Shipping costs per unit dropped 41 percent.[39]

MANAGING THE MARKETING OF SERVICES

LO5

In this section we conclude the chapter with a brief discussion of the marketing mix for services. As such, it is necessary to expand the four Ps framework to include

McDonald's familiar Golden Arches logo is an important part of the company's branding.

productivity, people, physical environment, and process, which is called the **eight Ps of services marketing**.[40]

Product (Service)

To a large extent, the concepts of the product component of the marketing mix apply equally well to Cheerios (a product) and to American Express (a service). Yet there are three aspects of the product/service element of the mix that warrant special attention when dealing with services: exclusivity, brand name, and capacity management.

Chapter 10 pointed out that one favorable dimension in a new product is its ability to be patented. Recall that a patent gives the manufacturer of a product exclusive rights to its production for 17 years. However, services cannot be patented. Hence the creator of a successful quick-service restaurant chain could quickly discover the concept being copied by others. Domino's Pizza, for example, has seen competitors, such as Pizza Hut, copy the quick delivery advantage that originally propelled the company to success.

An important aspect in marketing products is the branding strategy used. However, because services are intangible and, therefore, more difficult to describe, the brand name or identifying logo of the service organization is particularly important in consumer decisions. Brand names help make the abstract nature of services more concrete. Service marketers apply branding concepts in the same way as product marketers. Consider American Express. It has applied subbranding with its American Express Green, Gold, Platinum, Optima, Blue, and Centurian credit cards, with unique service offerings for each.

Productivity

Most services have a limited capacity due to the inseparability of the service from the service provider and the perishable nature of the service. For example, a patient must be in the hospital at the same time as the surgeon to "buy" an appendectomy, and only one patient can be helped at that time. Similarly, no additional surgery can be conducted tomorrow because of an unused operating room or an available surgeon today—the service capacity is lost if it is not used. So the service component of the mix must be integrated with efforts to influence consumer demand. This is referred to as **capacity management**.

Price

In the service industries, *price* is referred to in various ways. The terms used vary, depending upon whether the services are provided by hospitals (charges); consultants, lawyers, physicians, or accountants (fees); airlines (fares); and hotels (rates). Regardless of the term used, price plays two essential roles: (1) to affect consumer perceptions and (2) to be used in capacity management. Because of the intangible nature of services, price can indicate the quality of the service. Would you wonder about the quality of a $100 surgery? Studies show that when there are few cues by which to judge product or service quality, consumers use price.[41]

The capacity management role of price is also important to movie theaters, airlines, restaurants, and hotels. Many service businesses use **off-peak pricing**, which consists of charging different prices during different times of the day or days of the week to reflect variations in demand for the service. Airlines offer seasonal discounts and movie theaters offer matinee prices.

Place (Distribution)

Place or distribution is a major factor in developing a service marketing strategy because of the inseparability of services from the producer. Historically, little attention has been paid to distribution in services marketing. But as competition grows, the value of convenient distribution is being recognized. Hairstyling chains

Easy come. Easy go.

Order pre-paid, flat-rate Priority Mail® envelopes you can fill up and then just hand to your Letter Carrier.

These convenient Priority Mail® envelopes are as easy to order as they are to use. Simply call to order a pack of 10 to keep in your drawer. The next time you need a document sent 2-3 day delivery — just fill one up and hand it to your Letter Carrier. No meters. No hassles. Just pre-paid and easy!

Order a Priority Mail® 10-pack today — only $38.50!
Call 1-800-THE-USPS, ext. 000000 or return the attached form.

Order NOW and we'll send you a calculator!**

*Weight restrictions may apply. See envelope for details.
** One calculator per customer.

UNITED STATES POSTAL SERVICE

© 2004 United States Postal Service. Eagle symbol is a registered trademark of the United States Postal Service.   usps.com

The United States Postal Service uses advertising to stress the convenience of its service.

such as Cost Cutters Family Hair Care, tax preparation offices such as H&R Block, and accounting firms such as PricewaterhouseCoopers all use multiple locations for the distribution of services. In the banking industry, customers of participating banks using the Cirrus system can access any one of thousands of automatic teller systems throughout the United States. The availability of electronic distribution through the Internet now provides global coverage for travel services, banking, entertainment, and many other information-based services.

Promotion

The value of promotion, specifically advertising, for services is to show the benefits of using the service. It is valuable to stress availability, location, consistent quality, and efficient, courteous service. Also, services must be concerned with their image. Promotional efforts, such as Merrill Lynch's use of the bull in its ads, contribute to image and positioning strategies. In general, promotional concerns of services are similar to those of products.

Another form of promotion, publicity, has played a major role in the promotional strategy of nonprofit services and some professional organizations. Nonprofit organizations such as public school districts, the Chicago Symphony Orchestra, religious organizations, and hospitals have used publicity to disseminate their messages. Because of the heavy reliance on publicity, many services use public service announcements (PSAs), and because PSAs are free, nonprofit groups have tended to rely on them as the foundation of their media plan. However, the timing and location of a PSA are under the control of the medium, not the organization. Thus, the nonprofit service group cannot control who sees the message or when the message is given.

People

Many services depend on people for the creation and delivery of the customer service experience. The nature of the interaction between employees and customers strongly influences the customer's perceptions of the service experience. Customers will often judge the quality of the service experience based on the performance of the people providing the service. This aspect of services marketing has led to a concept called customer experience management.

Customer experience management (CEM) is the process of managing the entire customer experience with the company. CEM experts suggest that the process should be intentional and planned, consistent so that every experience is similar, differentiated from other service offerings, and relevant and valuable to the target market. Companies such as Disney, Southwest Airlines, Hilton, and Starbucks all manage the experience they offer customers. They integrate their activities to connect with customers at each contact point to move beyond customer relationships to customer loyalty. Zappos.com, an online retailer, requires that all employees complete a four-week customer loyalty training program to deliver one of the company's core concepts—"Deliver WOW through service."[42]

Physical Environment

The appearance of the environment in which the service is delivered and where the firm and customer interact can influence the customer's perception of the service. The physical evidence of the service includes all the tangibles surrounding the service: the buildings, landscaping, vehicles, furnishings, signage, brochures, and equipment. Service firms need to manage physical evidence carefully and systematically to convey the proper impression of the service to the customer. This is sometimes referred to as impression, or evidence, management.[43] For many services, the physical environment provides an opportunity for the firm to send consistent and strong messages about the nature of the service to be delivered.

Process

Process refers to the actual procedures, mechanisms, and flow of activities by which the service is created and delivered. The actual creation and delivery steps that the customer experiences provide customers with evidence on which to judge the service. These steps involve not only "what" gets created but also "how" it is created. Grease Monkey believes that it has the right process in the vehicle oil change and fluid exchange service business. Customers do not need appointments, stores are open six days per week, the service is completed in 15–20 minutes, and a waiting room allows customers to read or work while the service is being completed.

---

learning review

5. What is the difference between a line extension and a brand extension?

6. Explain the role of packaging in terms of perception.

7. How do service businesses use off-peak pricing?

LEARNING OBJECTIVES REVIEW

LO1 *Explain the product life-cycle concept.*
The product life cycle describes the stages a new product goes through in the marketplace: introduction, growth, maturity, and decline. Product sales growth and profitability differ at each stage, and marketing managers have marketing objectives and marketing mix strategies unique to each stage based on consumer behavior and competitive factors. In the introductory stage, the need is to establish primary demand, whereas the growth stage requires selective demand strategies. In the maturity stage, the need is to maintain market share; the decline stage necessitates a deletion or harvesting strategy. Some important aspects of product life cycles are (*a*) their length, (*b*) the shape of the sales curve, and (*c*) the rate at which consumers adopt products.

LO2 *Identify ways that marketing executives manage a product's life cycle.*
Marketing executives manage a product's life cycle in three ways. First, they can modify the product itself by altering its characteristics, such as product quality, performance, or appearance. Second, they can modify the market by finding new customers for the product, increasing a product's use among existing customers, or creating a new use situation for the product. Finally, they can reposition the product using any one or a combination of marketing mix elements. Four factors trigger a repositioning action. They include reacting to a competitor's position, reaching a new market, catching a rising trend, and changing the value offered to consumers.

LO3 *Recognize the importance of branding and alternative branding strategies.*
A basic decision in marketing products is branding, in which an organization uses a name, phrase, design, symbols, or a combination of these to identify its products and distinguish them from those of its competitors. Product managers recognize that brands offer more than product identification and a means to distinguish their products from competitors. Successful and established brands take on a brand personality and acquire brand equity—the added value a given brand name gives to a product beyond the functional benefits provided—that is crafted and nurtured by marketing programs that forge strong, favorable, and unique consumer associations with a brand. A good brand name should suggest the product benefits, be memorable, fit the company or product image, be free of legal restrictions, and be simple and emotional. Companies can and do employ several different branding strategies. With multiproduct branding, a company uses one name for all its products in a product class. A multibranding strategy involves giving each product a distinct name. A company uses private branding when it manufactures products but sells them under the brand name of a wholesaler or retailer. Finally, a company can employ mixed branding, where it markets products under its own name(s) and that of a reseller.

LO4 *Describe the role of packaging and labeling in the marketing of a product.*
Packaging and labeling play numerous roles in the marketing of a product. The packaging component of a product refers to any container in which it is offered for sale and on which label information is conveyed. Manufacturers, retailers, and consumers acknowledge that packaging and labeling provide communication, functional, and perceptual benefits. Contemporary packaging and labeling challenges include (*a*) the continuing need to connect with customers, (*b*) environmental concerns, (*c*) health, safety, and security issues, and (*d*) cost reduction.

LO5 *Recognize how the four Ps framework is expanded in the marketing of services.*

The four Ps framework also applies to services with some adaptations. Because services cannot be patented, unique offerings are difficult to protect. In addition, because services are intangible, brands and logos (which can be protected) are particularly important. The inseparability of production and consumption of services means that productivity, or capacity management, is important to services. The intangible nature of services makes price an important indication of service quality. Distribution has become an important marketing tool for services, and electronic distribution allows some services to provide global coverage. In recent years, service organizations have increased their promotional activities. Finally, the performance of people, the physical environment appearance, and process involved in delivering a service are recognized as central to the customer experience.

FOCUSING ON KEY TERMS

brand equity p. 245
brand name p. 244
brand personality p. 245
branding p. 244

capacity management p. 254
eight Ps of services marketing p. 254
multibranding p. 249
multiproduct branding p. 248

off-peak pricing p. 254
product life cycle p. 234

APPLYING MARKETING KNOWLEDGE

1 Listed below are three different products in various stages of the product life cycle. What marketing strategies would you suggest to these companies? (*a*) Canon digital cameras—growth stage, (*b*) Hewlett Packard tablet computers—introductory stage, and (*c*) handheld manual can openers—decline stage.

2 It has often been suggested that products are intentionally made to break down or wear out. Is this strategy a planned product modification approach?

3 The product manager of GE is reviewing the penetration of trash compactors in American homes. After more than two decades in existence, this product is in relatively few homes. What problems can account for this poor acceptance? What is the shape of the trash compactor life cycle?

4 For years, Ferrari has been known as the manufacturer of expensive luxury automobiles. The company plans to attract the major segment of the car-buying market that purchases medium-priced automobiles. As Ferrari considers this trading-down strategy, what branding strategy would you recommend? What are the trade-offs to consider with your strategy?

building your marketing plan

For the product offering in your marketing plan,

1 Identify (*a*) its stage in the product life cycle and (*b*) key marketing mix actions that might be appropriate, as shown in Figure 11–1.

2 Develop (*a*) branding and (*b*) packaging strategies, if appropriate for your offering.

video case 11 Philadelphia Phillies, Inc.: Sports Marketing 101

"Unfortunately we can't promise fans in the stands a win every game," laughs David Montgomery, president and chief executive officer of the Philadelphia Phillies, Inc. But in 2008 his Phillies came close enough to that: They beat the

Tampa Bay Rays to win the World Series (photo).

Montgomery goes on to explain key elements of the Phillies's marketing strategy, starting with moving into its new Citizens Bank Park baseball stadium in 2004. "Bring everyone in closer. Have fans feel 'I'm not alone here; lots of others are in the seats. This is a *happening*!'" he says. "Our new facility and the fact that it's a game played in summer out in the open air really takes you to a much broader audience," he says. "Our challenge is to appeal to all the segments in that audience." In the new baseball-only ballpark, every seat is angled toward home plate to give fans the best view of the action.

The new fan-friendly Phillies stadium is just one element in today's complex strategy to effectively market the Philadelphia Phillies to several different segments of fans—a far different challenge than in the past. A century ago Major League Baseball was pretty simple. You built a stadium. You hired the ballplayers. You printed tickets—hoping and praying a winning team would bring in fans and sell those tickets. And your advertising consisted of printing the team's home schedule in the local newspaper.

THE PHILLIES TODAY: APPEALS, SEGMENTS, AND ACTIVITIES

Baseball, like other sports, is a service whose primary benefit is entertainment. Marketing a Major League Baseball team is far different today.

"How do you market a product that is all over the board?" asks David Buck, the Phillies's vice president of marketing. He first gives a general answer to his question: "The ballpark experience is the key. As long as you project an image of a fun ballpark experience in everything you do, you're going to be in good shape. Our best advertising is word of mouth from happy fans." Next come the specifics. Marketing the appeal of a fun ballpark experience to all segments of fans is critical because the Phillies can't promise a winning baseball team.

Reaching the different segments of fans is a special challenge because each segment attends a game for different reasons and therefore will respond to different special promotions:

* *The diehards.* Intense baseball fans who are there to watch the strategy and see the Phillies win.

* *Kids 14 years and under.* At the game with their families, to get bat or bobble-head doll premiums, and have a "run-the-bases" day.
* *Women and men 15 years and older.* Special "days out," such as Mother's Day or Father's Day.
* *Seniors, 60 years and over.* A "stroll-the-bases" day.
* *The 20- and 30-somethings.* Meet friends at the ballpark and restaurants for a fun night out.
* *Corporate and community groups.* At the game to have fun but also to get to know members of their respective organizations better.

It's clear that not all fans are there for exactly the same "fun ballpark experience."

The "fun ballpark experience" today also goes beyond simply watching the Phillies play a baseball game. Fans at Citizens Bank Park can:

* Buy souvenirs at the Phanatic Attic, within the Majestic Clubhouse Store.
* Romp in the Phanatic Phun Zone, the largest soft-play area for kids in Major League Baseball.
* Test their skills in a pitching game.
* Stroll through Ashburn Alley (named for a famous Phillie), an outdoor food and entertainment area.
* Eat at McFadden's Restaurant and Saloon year round or Harry the K's Bar & Grill.

PROMOTIONAL ACTIVITIES

The range of the Phillies's promotional activities today is mind numbing. Before and during the season, the Phillies run a series of TV ads to generate and/or maintain fan interest. A recent ad campaign targeted kids by showing that the Phillies's players themselves are just like them. The tagline: "There's a little fan in all of us."

The Phillies also use "special promotion days," which typically increase fan attendance by 30 to 35 percent for a game, according to David Buck. These days often generate first-time visits by people who have never seen a Major League Baseball game. They generally fall into three categories: (1) theme nights, (2) event days, and (3) premium gift days.

Theme nights are devoted to special community groups or other fan segments. Examples include College

Sources of Revenue	Approx. %
1. Ticket sales (home and away games)	52%
2. National media (network TV and radio)	13
3. Local media (over-the-air TV, pay TV, radio)	13
4. Advertising (publications, co-sponsorship promotions)	12
5. Concessions (food, souvenirs, restaurants)	10
Total	100

Nights (fellow classmates, alumni, and faculty), dates for families of the military and law enforcement, and Rooftop Thursdays (having a luau with friends on the stadium rooftop), among others. Event days can involve camera days where fans can have their photo taken with a favorite Phillies player. Or they can involve fireworks, an old-timers' game, or running or strolling the bases. Five "Dollar Dog Nights" during the season let fans eat as many hot dogs as they can for $1.

The Phillies premiums or giveaways are also directed at specific market segments. These premiums range from baseball caps, beach towels, and T-shirts to a Phillies team photo or bobble-head dolls. To control expenses, the Phillies try to keep the cost of the premiums in the range of $1 to $3.

Other promotional activities fall in both the traditional and nontraditional categories. Personal appearances at public and charity events by Phillies players and their wives, radio and TV ads, and special events paid for by sponsors have been used by baseball teams for decades. The "Phillies Ballgirls" involve a clearly new, nontraditional promotional activity. These 20 women are all college softball players and are ambassadors for the Phillies. Besides taking on other softball teams on the diamond, they make four or five appearances a week at charity events, schools, or golf outings. They also help promote the Phillies sense of social responsibility and its focus on recycling and the environment.

The Internet and social networks have revolutionized the Phillies media strategies. "I remember the days we used to mail press releases that took four or five days to get to recipients," says the Phillies vice president of communications, Bonnie Clark. Fans not only can order tickets on the team's Web site (www.phillies.com), but also can buy Phillies jerseys and caps and get the inside scoop on players—like who's going on the disabled list and so on. The social networks now have huge importance. "Six months after launching a Phillies Twitter, we have 7,400 followers," she says. "And we now have more than 190,000 Facebook friends."

Probably the best-known mascot in professional sports, the Phillie Phanatic is a Philadelphia legend. This over-sized, green furry mascot has been around for over 25 years. It not only appears in the ballpark at all Phillies home games, but also makes appearances at charity and public events year round. Or rather the *three* Phanatics do so, because the demand is too great for a single Phanatic. "The Phanatic is a great character because he doesn't carry wins or losses," says David Montgomery. "Fans young and old can relate to him . . . he makes you smile, makes you laugh, and adds to the enjoyment of the game."

BOTTOM LINE: REVENUES AND EXPENSES

"We're a private business that serves the public," David Montgomery points out. "And we've got to make sure our revenues more than cover our expenses." He identifies five key sources of revenues and the approximate annual percentages for each:

Balanced against these revenues are some major expenses that include players' salaries (about $130 million) and the salaries of more than 150 full-time employees. Other expenses are those for scouting and drafting 40 to 60 new players per year, operating six minor-league farm clubs, and managing a labor force of 400 persons for each of the Phillies's 81 regular-season home games at Citizens Bank Park.

David Montgomery never gets bored. "When I finished business school, I had to choose between a marketing research job at a large paper products company or marketing the Philadelphia Phillies," explains Montgomery, who started with the Phillies by selling season and group tickets. "And it was no real decision because there never has been one day on this job that wasn't different and exciting."

Questions

1 (*a*) What is the "product" that the Phillies market? (*b*) What "products" are the Phillies careful not to market?

2 How does the "quality" dimension in marketing the Philadelphia Phillies as an entertainment service differ from that in marketing a consumer product such as a breakfast cereal?

3 In terms of a social network marketing strategy, (*a*) what are the likely characteristics of the Phillies fans and (*b*) what should the Phillies's Facebook fan page contain?

4 Considering all five elements of the promotional mix (advertising, personal selling, public relations, sales promotion, and direct marketing), what specific promotional activities should the Phillies use? Which should be used off-season? During the regular season?

5 What kinds of special promotion gift days (with premiums) and event days (no premiums) can the Phillies use to increase attendance by targeting these fan segments: (*a*) 14 and under, (*b*) 15 and over, (*c*) other special fan segments, and (*d*) all fans?

12

Pricing Products and Services

LEARNING OBJECTIVES

After reading this chapter you should be able to:

LO1 Describe the nature and importance of pricing and the approaches used to select an approximate price level.

LO2 Explain what a demand curve is and the role of revenues in pricing decisions.

LO3 Explain the role of costs in pricing decisions and describe how combinations of price, fixed cost, and unit variable cost affect a firm's break-even point.

LO4 Recognize the objectives a firm has in setting prices and the constraints that restrict the range of prices a firm can charge.

LO5 Describe the steps taken in setting a final price.

VIZIO, INC.—WHERE VISION MEETS VALUE™ IN HDTV

Can you name North America's fastest-growing HDTV and consumer electronics company? It's Vizio, Inc., an entrepreneurial Irvine, California–based company with a bold agenda. "Our goal is to be the next Sony in 20 to 30 years," says William Wang, Vizio's co-founder and chief executive officer.

In 2002, Wang was struck by an ad for a $10,000 flat-panel HDTV set and immediately saw an opportunity. Instead of marketing these sets as luxury items, Wang thought he could make and market a flat-panel HDTV that was affordable to the average consumer. Like many entrepreneurs, he borrowed money from friends and family and mortgaged his home. Within a year, he formed a company that is now known as Vizio, Inc., and delivered its first HDTV to Costco for distribution through that company's stores. Vizio HDTVs are now sold through Costco, Walmart, BJ's Wholesale, Sears, Sam's Club, and Target stores nationwide along with authorized online partners.

Vizio's ability to deliver affordable flat-panel HDTVs to the average consumer is based on a novel strategy. Instead of investing in expensive manufacturing facilities, Vizio relies on contract manufacturers in Taiwan to build its products. Product development and marketing specialists in the United States handle product design and marketing. That's "Where Vision Meets Value," the company's motto, comes into play. "The whole goal is to ensure that we have the right product at the right time and the right price and really drive a seamless end-to-end value chain," says John Morriss, Vizio's general manager vice president of Vizio's TV business unit. "Vizio HDTVs are more popular and in greater demand than ever," added Laynie Newsome, Vizio's co-founder and vice president of sales and marketing communications. "Consumers want to save money without sacrificing quality or technology, which is why we continue to be the fastest growing HDTV company in the United States."

Vizio's powerful and profitable price-value position has resonated with consumers and produced annual sales that approach $3 billion. Remember Sony? Vizio is now the largest seller of HDTVs in North America. Not bad for a company with about 160 employees that is less than 10 years old![1]

Welcome to the fascinating—and intense—world of pricing, where many forces come together to determine the price buyers will be asked to pay. This chapter covers important factors used in setting prices for products and services.

NATURE AND IMPORTANCE OF PRICE

LO1

The price paid for products and services goes by many names. You pay *tuition* for your education, *rent* for an apartment, *interest* on a bank credit card, and a *premium* for car insurance. Your dentist or physician charges you a *fee*, a professional or social organization charges *dues,* and airlines charge a *fare*. And what you pay for clothes or a haircut is termed a *price*.

What Is a Price?

price

The money or other considerations (including other products and services) exchanged for the ownership or use of a product or service.

These examples highlight the many varied ways that price plays a part in our daily lives. From a marketing viewpoint, **price** is the money or other considerations (including other products and services) exchanged for the ownership or use of a product or service. Recently, Wilkinson Sword exchanged some of its knives for advertising used to promote its razor blades. This practice of exchanging products and services for other products and services rather than for money is called *barter*. These transactions account for billions of dollars annually in domestic and international trade.

For most products and services, money is exchanged. However, the amount paid is not always the same as the list, or quoted, price because of discounts, allowances, and extra fees. While discounts, allowances, and rebates make the effective price lower, other marketing tactics raise the real price. One new 21st century pricing tactic is to use "special fees" and "surcharges." This practice is driven by consumers' zeal for low prices combined with the ease of making price comparisons on the Internet. Buyers are more willing to pay extra fees than a higher list price, so sellers use add-on charges as a way of having the consumer pay more without raising the list price.[2]

All the factors that increase or decrease the final price of an offering help construct a "price equation," which is shown for a few products in Figure 12–1. They are key considerations when you buy your next car. For example, suppose you want to get "plugged in" and buy a 2011 Tesla Roadster Sport, the world's leading all-electric, zero-emission car that has a 245-mile range and can be recharged in three hours. This exciting "green" vehicle can move you from 0 to 60 miles per hour in 3.7 seconds at a top speed of 125 miles per hour.

The Tesla Roadster Sport has a list price of $128,500, but you want several options (leather interior, carbon fiber hard top, electronics upgrade, metallic paint, performance wheels, and others) that will cost $20,000. An extended warranty will add an additional $5,000. However, if you put $50,000 down now and finance the balance over the next year, you will receive a rebate of $3,500 off the list price.

Using the *Kelley Blue Book* (www.kbb.com) trade-in value for your 2005 Honda Civic DX four-door sedan that has 75,000 miles and is in good condition, the dealer gives you a trade-in allowance of $5,000. In addition, you will have to pay a 7.5 percent sales tax of $10,200, an auto registration fee of $500 to the state, and a $500 destination charge to ship the car. But because the Tesla Roadster Sport is an alternative energy vehicle, you qualify for a $2,500 state rebate and a $7,500 federal tax credit! Finally, your total finance charge is $2,687 based on an annual interest rate of 5 percent.[3]

Applying the price equation shown in Figure 12–1 to your purchase, your final price is:

In deciding whether to buy a new Tesla Roadster Sport electric car, consider incentives, allowances, and extra fees—as well as the original list price!

$$\text{Final price} = [\text{List price}] - [(\text{Incentives}) + (\text{Allowances})] + [\text{Extra fees}]$$

$$= [\$128,500] - [(\$3,500 + \$2,500 + \$7,500) + (\$5,000)]$$

$$+ [\$20,000 + \$5,000 + \$500 + \$500 + \$10,200 + \$2,687]$$

$$= \$148,887$$

PRICE EQUATION

ITEM PURCHASED	PRICE	= LIST PRICE	INCENTIVES AND − ALLOWANCES	+ EXTRA FEES
New car bought by an individual	Final price	= List price	− Rebate Cash discount Old car trade-in	+ Financing charges Special accessories Destination charges
Term in college bought by a student	Tuition	= Published tuition	− Scholarship Other financial aid Discounts for number of credits taken	+ Special activity fees
Merchandise bought from a wholesaler by a retailer	Invoice price	= List price	− Quantity discount Cash discount Seasonal discount Functional or trade discount	+ Penalty for late payment

FIGURE 12–1
The "price" a buyer pays can take different names, depending on what is purchased, and can change depending on the price equation.

value
The ratio of perceived benefits to price.

Note that your final price is $20,387 more than the list price. Your monthly payment for the one-year loan of $96,200 (including the total finance charge) is $8,241. Are you still interested in the Tesla Roadster Sport? If so, put yourself on the waiting list!

Price as an Indicator of Value

From a consumer's standpoint, price is often used to indicate value when it is compared with the perceived benefits such as quality, durability, and so on of a product or service. Specifically, **value** is the ratio of perceived benefits to price, or

$$\text{Value} = \frac{\text{Perceived benefits}}{\text{Price}}$$

This relationship shows that for a given price, as perceived benefits increase, value increases. For example, if you're used to paying $9.99 for a medium pizza, wouldn't a large pizza at the same price be more valuable? Conversely, for a given price, value decreases when perceived benefits decrease.

For some products, price influences consumers' perception of overall quality and ultimately its value to consumers.[4] In a survey of home furnishing buyers, 84 percent agreed with the statement: "The higher the price, the higher the quality."[5] Kohler introduced a walk-in bathtub that is safer for children and the elderly. Although priced higher than conventional step-in bathtubs, it has proven very successful because buyers are willing to pay more for what they perceive as the benefit of the extra safety.

Here "value" involves the judgment by a consumer of the worth and desirability of a product or service relative to substitutes that satisfy the same need. In this instance a "reference value" emerges, which involves comparing the costs and benefits of substitute items.

Price in the Marketing Mix

profit equation
Profit equals total revenue minus total cost.

Pricing is a critical decision made by a marketing executive because price has a direct effect on a firm's profits. This is apparent from a firm's **profit equation**:

Profit = Total revenue − Total cost

= (Unit price × Quantity sold) − (Fixed cost + Variable cost)

What makes this relationship even more complicated is that price affects the quantity sold, as illustrated with demand curves later in this chapter. Furthermore, since the quantity sold usually affects a firm's costs because of efficiency of production, price also indirectly affects costs. Thus, pricing decisions influence both total revenue (sales) and total cost, which makes pricing one of the most important and most difficult decisions marketing executives face.

GENERAL PRICING APPROACHES

A key for a marketing manager setting a price for a product is to find an approximate price level to use as a reasonable starting point. Four common approaches used to find this approximate price level are (1) demand-oriented, (2) cost-oriented, (3) profit-oriented, and (4) competition-oriented approaches (Figure 12–2). Although these approaches are discussed separately below, some of them overlap, and an effective marketing manager will consider several in selecting an approximate price level.

Demand-Oriented Pricing Approaches

Demand-oriented approaches weigh factors underlying expected customer tastes and preferences more heavily than such factors as cost, profit, and competition when selecting a price level.

Skimming Pricing A firm introducing a new or innovative product can use *skimming pricing,* setting the highest initial price that customers really desiring the product are willing to pay. These customers are not very price sensitive because they weigh the new product's price, quality, and ability to satisfy their needs against the same characteristics of substitutes. As the demand of these customers is satisfied, the firm lowers the price to attract another, more price-sensitive segment. Thus, skimming pricing gets its name from skimming successive layers of "cream," or customer segments, as prices are lowered in a series of steps.

Skimming pricing is an effective strategy when (1) enough prospective customers are willing to buy the product immediately at the high initial price to make these sales profitable, (2) the high initial price will not attract competitors, (3) lowering the price has only a minor effect on increasing the sales volume and reducing the unit costs, and (4) customers interpret the high price as a signal of high quality.[6]

FIGURE 12–2
Four approaches for selecting an approximate price level.

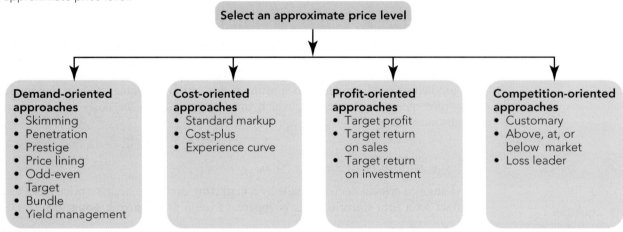

264

Energizer's Lesson in Price Perception—Value Lies in the Eye of the Beholder

Battery manufacturers are as tireless as a certain drum-thumping bunny in their efforts to create products that perform better, last longer, and, not incidentally, outsell the competition. The commercialization of new alkaline battery technology at a price that creates value for consumers is not always obvious or easy. Just ask the marketing executives at Energizer about their experience with pricing Energizer Advanced Formula and Energizer e^2 AA alkaline batteries.

When Duracell launched its high-performance Ultra brand AA alkaline battery with a 25 percent price premium over standard Duracell batteries, Energizer quickly countered with its own high-performance battery—Energizer Advanced Formula. Believing that consumers would not pay the

premium price, Energizer priced its Advanced Formula brand at the same price as its standard AA alkaline battery, expecting to gain market share from Duracell. It did not happen. Why? According to industry analysts, consumers associated Energizer's low price with inferior quality in the high-performance segment. Instead of gaining market share, Energizer lost market share to Duracell and Rayovac, the No. 3 battery manufacturer.

Having learned its lesson, Energizer subsequently released its e^2 high-performance battery, this time priced 4 percent higher than Duracell Ultra and about 50 percent higher than Advanced Formula. The result? Energizer recovered lost sales and market share. The lesson learned? Value lies in the eye of the beholder.

These four conditions are most likely to exist when the new product is protected by patents or copyrights or its uniqueness is understood and valued by consumers. Gillette, for example, adopted a skimming strategy for its five-blade Fusion brand shaving system since many of these conditions applied.

Penetration Pricing Setting a low initial price on a new product to appeal immediately to the mass market is *penetration pricing*, the exact opposite of skimming pricing. Nintendo consciously chose a penetration strategy when it introduced the Nintendo Wii, its popular videogame console.

The conditions favoring penetration pricing are the reverse of those supporting skimming pricing: (1) many segments of the market are price sensitive, (2) a low initial price discourages competitors from entering the market, and (3) unit production and marketing costs fall dramatically as production volumes increase. A firm using penetration pricing may (1) maintain the initial price for a time to gain profit lost from its low introductory level or (2) lower the price further, counting on the new volume to generate the necessary profit.

Prestige Pricing Although consumers tend to buy more of a product when the price is lower, sometimes the reverse is true. If consumers are using price as a measure of the quality of an item, a company runs the risk of appearing to offer a low-quality product if it sets the price below a certain point. *Prestige pricing* involves setting a high price so that quality- or status-conscious consumers will be attracted to the product and buy it. Rolls-Royce cars, Chanel perfume, and Cartier jewelry have an element of prestige pricing in them and may sell worse at lower prices than at higher ones.[7] As described in the Marketing Matters box, this is the pricing strategy Energizer used with its very successful e^2 high-performance AA batteries.[8]

Odd-Even Pricing Sears offers a Craftsman radial saw for $499.99, the suggested retail price for the Gillette Fusion shaving system is $11.99, and Kmart sells Windex glass cleaner on sale for 99 cents. Why not simply price these items at $500,

$12, and $1, respectively? These firms are using *odd-even pricing*, which involves setting prices a few dollars or cents under an even number. The presumption is that consumers see the Sears radial saw as priced at "something over $400" rather than "about $500." In theory, demand increases if the price drops from $500 to $499.99. There is some evidence to suggest this does happen. However, research suggests that overuse of odd-ending prices tends to mute their effect on demand.[9]

Target Pricing   Manufacturers will sometimes estimate the price that the ultimate consumer would be willing to pay for a product. They then work backward through markups taken by retailers and wholesalers to determine what price they can charge wholesalers for the product. This practice, called *target pricing*, results in the manufacturer deliberately adjusting the composition and features of a product to achieve the target price to consumers. Canon uses this practice for pricing its cameras.

Bundle Pricing   A frequently used demand-oriented pricing practice is *bundle pricing*—the marketing of two or more products in a single package price. For example, Delta Air Lines offers vacation packages that include airfare, car rental, and lodging. Bundle pricing is based on the idea that consumers value the package more than the individual items. This is due to benefits received from not having to make separate purchases and enhanced satisfaction from one item given the presence of another. Moreover, bundle pricing often provides a lower total cost to buyers and lower marketing costs to sellers.

Yield Management Pricing   Have you ever been on an airplane and discovered the person next to you paid a lower price for her ticket than you paid? Annoying, isn't it? But what you observed is *yield management pricing*—the charging of different prices to maximize revenue for a set amount of capacity at any given time. Airlines, hotels, and car rental firms engage in capacity management (described in Chapter 11) by varying prices based on time, day, week, or season to match demand and supply. American Airlines estimates that yield management pricing produces an annual revenue that exceeds $500 million.[10]

Cost-Oriented Pricing Approaches

With cost-oriented approaches, a price setter stresses the cost side of the pricing problem, not the demand side. Price is set by looking at the production and marketing costs and then adding enough to cover direct expenses, overhead, and profit.

How was the price of the Rock and Roll Hall of Fame and Museum determined? Read the text to find out.

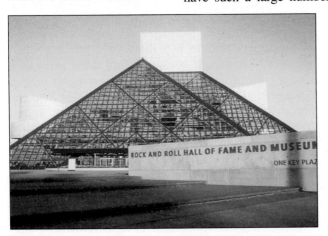

Standard Markup Pricing   Managers of supermarkets and other retail stores have such a large number of products that estimating the demand for each product as a means of setting price is impossible. Therefore, they use *standard markup pricing*, which entails adding a fixed percentage to the cost of all items in a specific product class. This percentage markup varies depending on the type of retail store (such as furniture, clothing, or grocery) and the product involved. High-volume products usually have smaller markups than do low-volume products. Supermarkets such as Kroger, Safeway, and Jewel have different markups for staple items and discretionary items. The markup on staple items like sugar, flour, and dairy products varies from 10 percent to 23 percent, whereas markups on discretionary items like snack foods and candy range from 27 percent to 47 percent. These markups must cover all expenses of the store, pay for overhead costs, and contribute something to

How many picture frames must the store owner of a picture frame store sell to make a $7,000 profit? Read the text to find out.

profits. For supermarkets these markups, which may appear very large, result in only a 1 percent profit on sales revenue.

Cost-Plus Pricing Many manufacturing, professional services, and construction firms use a variation of standard markup pricing. *Cost-plus pricing* involves summing the total unit cost of providing a product or service and adding a specific amount to the cost to arrive at a price. Cost-plus pricing is the most commonly used method to set prices for business products. For example, this pricing approach was used in setting the price for the $92 million Rock and Roll Hall of Fame and Museum in Cleveland, Ohio.

This method is finding favor among business-to-business marketers in the service sector. For example, the rising cost of legal fees has prompted some law firms to adopt a cost-plus pricing approach. Rather than billing business clients on an hourly basis, lawyers and their clients agree on a fixed fee based on expected costs plus a profit for the law firm. Many advertising agencies now use this approach. Here, the client agrees to pay the agency a fee based on the cost of its work plus some agreed-on profit.

Profit-Oriented Pricing Approaches

A price setter may choose to balance both revenues and costs to set price using profit-oriented approaches. These might either involve a target of a specific dollar volume of profit or express this target profit as a percentage of sales or investment.

Target Profit Pricing When a firm sets an annual target of a specific dollar volume of profit, this is called *target profit pricing.* For example, if you owned a picture frame store and wanted to achieve a target profit of $7,000, how much would you need to charge for each frame? Because profit depends on revenues and costs, you would have to know your costs and then estimate how many frames you would sell. Based on sales in previous years, let's assume that you expect to frame 1,000 pictures next year. The cost of your time and materials to frame an average picture is $22, while your overhead expenses (rent, manager salaries, etc.) are $26,000. Finally, your goal is to achieve a profit of $7,000. How do you calculate your price per picture?

Profit = Total revenue − Total costs

= (Pictures sold × Price/picture) −
[(Cost/picture × Pictures sold) + Overhead cost]

Solving for price per picture, the equation becomes,

$$\text{Price/picture} = \frac{\text{Profit} + [(\text{Cost/picture} \times \text{Pictures sold}) + \text{Overhead cost}]}{\text{Pictures sold}}$$

$$= \frac{\$7,000 + [(\$22 \times 1,000) + \$26,000]}{1,000}$$

$$= \frac{\$7,000 + \$48,000}{1,000}$$

$$= \$55 \text{ per picture}$$

Clearly, this pricing method depends on an accurate estimate of demand. Because demand is often difficult to predict, this method has the potential for disaster if the estimate is too high. Generally, a target profit pricing strategy is best for firms offering new or unique products, without a lot of competition. What if other frame stores in your area were charging $40 per framed picture? As a marketing manager, you'd have to offer improved customer value with your more expensive frames, lower your costs, or settle for less profit.

Target Return-on-Sales Pricing Firms such as supermarkets often use *target return-on-sales pricing* to set prices that will give them a profit that is a specified percentage—say, 1 percent—of the sales volume. This price method is often used because of the difficulty in establishing a benchmark of sales or investment to show how much of a firm's effort is needed to achieve the target.

Target Return-on-Investment Pricing Firms such as General Motors and many public utilities use *target return-on-investment pricing* to set prices to achieve a return-on-investment (ROI) target such as a percentage that is mandated by its board of directors or regulators. For example, an electric utility may decide to seek a 10 percent ROI. If its investment in plant and equipment is $50 billion, it would need to set the price of electricity to its customers at a level that results in $5 billion a year in profit.

Competition-Oriented Pricing Approaches

Rather than emphasize demand, cost, or profit factors, a price setter can stress what competitors or "the market" is doing.

Customary Pricing For some products where tradition, a standardized channel of distribution, or other competitive factors dictate the price, *customary pricing* is used. Candy bars offered through standard vending machines have a customary price of 75 cents, and a significant departure from this price may result in a loss of sales for the manufacturer. Hershey typically has changed the amount of chocolate in its candy bars depending on the price of raw chocolate rather than vary its customary retail price so that it can continue selling through vending machines.

Above-, At-, or Below-Market Pricing The "market price" of a product is what customers are generally willing to pay, not necessarily the price that the firm sets. For most products it is difficult to identify a specific market price for a product or product class. Still, marketing managers often have a subjective feel for the competitors' price or the market price. Using this benchmark, they then may deliberately choose a strategy of *above-, at-,* or *below-market pricing.*

Among watch manufacturers, Rolex takes pride in emphasizing that it makes one of the most expensive watches you can buy, a clear example of above-market pricing. Manufacturers of national brands of clothing such as Hart Schaffner & Marx and Christian Dior and retailers such as Bloomingdale's deliberately set premium prices for their products.

Large department store chains such as JCPenney generally use at-market pricing. These chains often establish the going market price in the minds of their competitors. Similarly, Revlon cosmetics and Arrow brand shirts are generally priced "at market." They also provide a reference price for competitors that use above- and below-market pricing.

In contrast, a number of firms use below-market pricing. Manufacturers of generic products and retailers that offer their own private brands of products ranging from peanut butter to shampoo deliberately set prices for these products about 8 percent to 10 percent below the prices of nationally branded competitive products such as Skippy peanut butter or Vidal Sassoon shampoo.

Companies use a "price premium" to assess whether their products and brands are above, at, or below the market. An illustration of how the price premium measure is calculated, displayed, and interpreted appears in the Using Marketing Dashboards box.

What competition-oriented pricing approach is used by Bloomingdale's? Read the text to find out.

268

Using Marketing Dashboards

Are Cracker Jack Prices Above, At, or Below the Market?

How would you determine whether a firm's retail prices are above, at, or below the market? You might visit retail stores and record what prices retailers are charging for products or brands. This laborious activity can be simplified by combining two consumer market share measures to create a "price premium" display on your marketing dashboard.

Your Challenge Frito-Lay is considering whether to buy the Cracker Jack brand of caramel popcorn from Borden Inc. Frito-Lay research shows that Cracker Jack has a strong brand equity. But, Cracker Jack's dollar sales market share and pound volume market share declined recently and trailed the Crunch 'n Munch brand as shown in the table.

Borden's management used an above-market, premium pricing strategy for Cracker Jack. Specifically, Cracker Jack's suggested retail price was set to yield an average price premium per pound of 28 percent relative to Crunch 'n Munch. As a Frito-Lay marketer studying Cracker Jack, your challenge is to calculate and display Cracker Jack's actual price premium relative to Crunch 'n Munch. A price premium is the percentage by which the actual price charged for a specific brand exceeds (or falls short of) a benchmark established for a similar product or basket of products. This premium can be calculated as follows:

$$\text{Price Premium (\%)} = \frac{\text{Dollar Sales Market Share for a Brand}}{\text{Unit Volume Market Share for a Brand}} - 1$$

Brand	Dollar Sales Market Share	Pound Volume Market Share
Crunch 'n Munch	32%	32%
Cracker Jack	26	19
Fiddle Faddle	7	8
Private Brands	4	8
Seasonal, Specialty, and Regional (S,S,R) Brands	31	33
	100%	100%

Your Findings Using caramel popcorn brand market share data, the Cracker Jack price premium is 1.368, or 36.8 percent, calculated as follows: (26 percent ÷ 19 percent) − 1 = 0.368. By comparison, Crunch 'n Munch enjoys no price premium. Its dollar sales market share and unit (pound) market share are equal: (32 percent ÷ 32 percent) − 1 = 0, or zero percent. The price premium, or lack thereof, of other brands can be displayed in a marketing dashboard as shown below.

Your Action Cracker Jack's price premium clearly exceeds the 28 percent Borden benchmark relative to Crunch 'n Munch. Cracker Jack's price premium may have overreached its brand equity. Consideration might be given to assessing Cracker Jack's price premium relative to its market position should Frito-Lay purchase the brand.

Price Premium Display

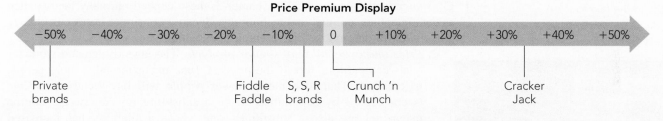

Loss-Leader Pricing For a special promotion retail stores deliberately sell a product below its customary price to attract attention to it. The purpose of this *loss-leader pricing* is not to increase sales but to attract customers in hopes they will buy other products as well, particularly the discretionary items with large markups. For example, Best Buy, Target, and Walmart sell CDs at about half of music companies' suggested retail price to attract customers to their stores.[11]

learning review

1. Value is _____.

2. What circumstances in pricing a new product might support skimming or penetration pricing?

ESTIMATING DEMAND AND REVENUE

LO2

Basic to setting a product's price is the extent of customer demand for it. Marketing executives must also translate this estimate of customer demand into estimates of revenues the firm expects to receive.

Fundamentals of Estimating Demand

How much money would you pay for your favorite magazine? If the price kept going up, at some point you would probably quit buying it. Conversely, if the price kept going down, you might eventually decide not only to keep buying your magazine but also to get your friend a subscription, too. The lower the price, the higher the demand. The publisher wants to sell more magazines, but will it sell enough additional copies to make up for the lower price per copy? That is an important question for marketing managers. Here's how one firm decided to find out.

Newsweek conducted a pricing experiment at newsstands in 11 cities throughout the United States. At that time, Houston newsstand buyers paid $2.25, while in Fort Worth, New York, Los Angeles, and Atlanta they paid the regular $2.00 price. In San Diego, the price was $1.50, while in Minneapolis–St. Paul, New Orleans, and Detroit it was only $1.00. By comparison, the regular newsstand price for *Time* and *U.S. News & World Report, Newsweek*'s competitors, was $1.95. Why did *Newsweek* conduct the experiment? According to a *Newsweek* executive, "We want to figure out what the demand curve for our magazine at the newsstand is."[12]

demand curve
A graph relating the quantity sold and the price, which shows how many units will be sold at a given price.

Read the text to learn about *Newsweek*'s price experiment.

The Demand Curve A **demand curve** is a graph relating the quantity sold and the price, which shows the maximum number of units that will be sold at a given price. Demand curve D_1 in Figure 12–3A shows the newsstand demand for *Newsweek* under the existing conditions. Note that as price falls, more people decide to buy and unit sales increase. But price is not the complete story in estimating demand. Economists emphasize three other key factors:

1. *Consumer tastes.* As we saw in Chapter 3, these depend on many factors such as demographics, culture, and technology. Because consumer tastes can change quickly, up-to-date marketing research is essential.

2. *Price and availability of similar products.* The laws of demand work for one's competitors, too. If the price of *Time* magazine falls, more people will buy it. That then means fewer people will buy *Newsweek. Time* is considered by economists to be a substitute for *Newsweek.* Online magazines are also a substitute—one whose availability has increased tremendously in recent years. The point to remember is, as the price of substitutes falls or their availability increases, the demand for a product (*Newsweek,* in this case) will fall.

3. *Consumer income.* In general, as real consumer income (allowing for inflation) increases, demand for a product also increases.

The first of these two factors influences what consumers *want* to buy, and the third affects what they *can* buy. Along with price, these are often called *demand factors,* or factors that determine consumers' willingness and ability to pay for products and services. As discussed earlier in Chapters 8 and 10, it is often very difficult to estimate demand for new products, especially because consumer likes and dislikes are often so difficult to read clearly.

Movement Along versus Shift of a Demand Curve Demand curve D_1 in Figure 12–3A shows that as the price is lowered from $2.00 to $1.50, the quantity demanded increases from 3 million (Q_1) to 4.5 million

A Demand curve under initial conditions

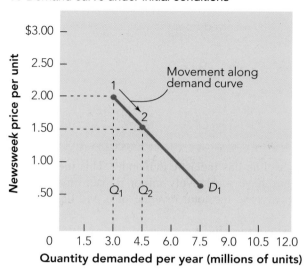

B Shift in the demand curve with more favorable conditions

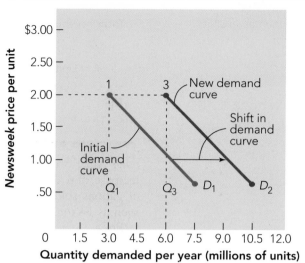

FIGURE 12–3

Demand curves for *Newsweek* showing the effect on annual sales (quantity demanded per year) by a change in price caused by (A) a movement along the demand curve and (B) a shift in the demand curve.

(Q_2) units per year. This is an example of a *movement along a demand curve* and assumes that other factors (consumer tastes, price and availability of substitutes, and consumer income) remain unchanged.

What if some of these factors change? For example, if advertising causes more people to want *Newsweek,* newsstand distribution is increased, or if consumer incomes rise, then the demand increases. Now the original curve, D_1 (the blue line in Figure 12–3B), no longer represents the demand; a new curve must be drawn (D_2). Economists call this a *shift in the demand curve*—in this case, a shift to the right, from D_1 to D_2. This increased demand means that more *Newsweek* magazines are wanted for a given price: At a price of $2, the demand is 6 million units per year (Q_3) on D_2 rather than 3 million units per year (Q_1) on D_1.

What price did *Newsweek* select after conducting its experiment? It kept the price at $2.00. However, through expanded newsstand distribution and more aggressive advertising, *Newsweek* was later able to shift its demand curve to the right and charge a price of $2.50 without affecting its newsstand volume.

price elasticity of demand

The percentage change in the quantity demanded relative to a percentage change in price.

Price Elasticity of Demand Marketing managers are especially interested in the **price elasticity of demand**—a key consideration related to the product's demand curve. Price elasticity of demand is the percentage change in quantity demanded relative to a percentage change in price. It measures how sensitive consumer demand and the firm's revenues are to changes in the product's price.

A product with *elastic demand* is one in which a slight decrease in price results in a relatively large increase in demand, or units sold. The reverse is also true: With elastic demand, a slight increase in price results in a relatively large decrease in demand. Marketing experiments on soft drinks and snack foods show them often to have elastic demand. So marketing managers may cut price to increase the demand, the units sold, and total revenue for one of these products, depending on what competitors' prices are. Recent research studies show that price elasticity for these products is increasing, probably because consumers are more often trying to take advantage of temporary price promotions and deals.[13]

In contrast, a product with *inelastic demand* means that slight increases or decreases in price will not significantly affect the demand, or units sold, for the product. Products and services considered as necessities usually have inelastic demand. What about gasoline for your car? Will an increase of a dollar per gallon cause you to drive fewer miles and buy less gasoline? No? Then you're like millions of

FIGURE 12–4

Fundamental revenue concept.

Total revenue (TR) is the total money received from the sale of a product. If

TR = Total revenue

P = Unit price of the product

Q = Quantity of the product sold

Then,

TR = P $\times$ Q

other Americans, which is why gasoline has inelastic demand.[14] This means that an increase of a dollar per gallon may have a relatively minor impact on the number of gallons sold and will actually increase the total revenue of a gasoline producer, such as ExxonMobil.

Price elasticity of demand is determined by a number of factors. First, the more substitutes a product or service has, the more likely it is to be price elastic. For example, a new sweater, shirt, or blouse has many possible substitutes and is price elastic, but gasoline has almost no substitutes and is price inelastic. Second, products and services considered to be nondiscretionary are price inelastic, so open-heart surgery is price inelastic, whereas airline tickets for a vacation are price elastic. Third, items that require a large cash outlay compared with a person's disposable income are price elastic. Accordingly, cars and yachts are price elastic; pulp fiction books tend to be price inelastic.

Fundamentals of Estimating Revenue

total revenue

The total money received from the sale of a product; the unit price of a product multiplied by the quantity sold.

While economists may talk about "demand curves," marketing executives are more likely to speak in terms of "revenues generated." Demand curves lead directly to an essential revenue concept critical to pricing decisions: **total revenue**. As summarized in Figure 12–4, total revenue (TR) equals the unit price (P) times the quantity sold (Q). Using this equation, let's recall our picture frame shop and assume our annual demand has improved so we can set a price of $100 per picture framed and sell 400 pictures per year. So,

TR = P $\times$ Q

= $100 $\times$ 400

= $40,000

This combination of price and quantity sold annually will give us a total revenue of $40,000 per year. Is that good? Are you making money, making a profit? Alas, total revenue is only part of the profit equation that we saw earlier:

Total profit = Total revenue − Total cost

The next section covers the other part of the profit equation: cost.

learning review

3. What three key factors are necessary when estimating consumer demand?

4. Price elasticity of demand is _____.

DETERMINING COST, VOLUME, AND PROFIT RELATIONSHIPS

LO3

While revenues are the moneys received by the firm from selling its products or services to customers, costs or expenses are the monies the firm pays out to its employees and suppliers. Marketing managers often use break-even analysis to relate revenues and costs, topics covered in this section.

Total cost (TC) is the total expense incurred by a firm in producing and marketing a product. Total cost is the sum of fixed cost and variable cost.

Fixed cost (FC) is the sum of the expenses of the firm that are stable and do not change with the quantity of a product that is produced and sold. Examples of fixed costs are rent on the building, executive salaries, and insurance.

Variable cost (VC) is the sum of the expenses of the firm that vary directly with the quantity of a product that is produced and sold. For example, as the quantity sold doubles, the variable cost doubles. Examples are the direct labor and direct materials used in producing the product and the sales commissions that are tied directly to the quantity sold. As mentioned above,

$$TC = FC + VC$$

Unit variable cost (UVC) is expressed on a per unit basis, or

$$UVC = \frac{VC}{Q}$$

The Importance of Controlling Costs

Understanding the role and behavior of costs is critical for all marketing decisions, particularly pricing decisions. Four cost concepts are important in pricing decisions: **total cost,** *fixed cost, variable cost,* and *unit variable cost* (Figure 12–5).

Many firms go bankrupt because their costs get out of control, causing their total costs—the sum of their fixed costs and variable costs—to exceed their total revenues over an extended period of time. So firms are increasingly trying to control their fixed costs, like insurance and executive salaries, and reduce the variable costs in their manufactured items by having production done outside the United States. This is why sophisticated marketing managers make pricing decisions that balance both revenues and costs.

Break-Even Analysis

Marketing managers often employ an approach that considers cost, volume, and profit relationships based on the profit equation. **Break-even analysis** is a technique that analyzes the relationship between total revenue and total cost to determine profitability at various levels of output. The *break-even point (BEP)* is the quantity at which total revenue and total cost are equal. Profit then comes from all units sold beyond the BEP. In terms of the definitions in Figure 12–5,

$$BEP_{Quantity} = \frac{Fixed\ cost}{Unit\ price - Unit\ variable\ cost} = \frac{FC}{P - UVC}$$

Calculating a Break-Even Point   Consider a picture frame store. Suppose you wish to identify how many pictures you must sell to cover your fixed cost at a given price. Let's assume demand for your framed pictures is strong so the average price customers are willing to pay for each picture is $120. Also, suppose your fixed cost (FC) is $32,000 (for real estate taxes, interest on a bank loan, and other fixed expenses) and unit variable cost (UVC) for a picture is now $40 (for labor, glass, frame, and matting). Your break-even quantity (BEP$_{Quantity}$) is 400 pictures, as follows:

$$BEP_{Quantity} = \frac{Fixed\ cost}{Unit\ price - Unit\ variable\ cost} = \frac{FC}{P - UVC}$$
$$= \frac{\$32,000}{\$120 - \$40}$$
$$= 400\ pictures$$

total cost
The total expenses incurred by a firm in producing and marketing a product; total cost is the sum of fixed costs and variable costs.

break-even analysis
A technique that examines the relationship between total revenue and total cost to determine profitability at different levels of output.

Quantity of Pictures Sold (Q)	Price per Picture (P)	Total Revenue (TR) = (P × Q)	Unit Variable Cost (UVC)	Total Variable Cost (VC) = (UVC × Q)	Fixed Cost (FC)	Total Cost (TC) = (FC + VC)	Profit = (TR − TC)
0	$120	$ 0	$40	$ 0	$32,000	$32,000	$−32,000
200	120	24,000	40	8,000	32,000	40,000	−16,000
400	120	48,000	40	16,000	32,000	48,000	0
600	120	72,000	40	24,000	32,000	56,000	16,000
800	120	96,000	40	32,000	32,000	64,000	32,000
1,000	120	120,000	40	40,000	32,000	72,000	48,000
1,200	120	144,000	40	48,000	32,000	80,000	64,000

FIGURE 12–6

Calculating a break-even point for the picture frame store in the text example shows its profit starts at 400 framed pictures per year.

The row shaded in orange in Figure 12–6 shows that your break-even quantity at a price of $120 per picture is 400 pictures. At less than 400 pictures, your picture frame store incurs a loss, and at more than 400 pictures, it makes a profit. Figure 12–6 also shows that if you could increase your annual picture sales to 1,000—the row shaded in green—your store would make a profit of $48,000.

Figure 12–7 shows a graphic presentation of the break-even analysis, called a *break-even chart*. It shows that total revenue and total cost intersect and are equal at a quantity of 400 pictures sold, which is the break-even point at which profit is exactly $0. You want to do better? If your frame store could increase the quantity sold annually to 1,000 pictures, the graph in Figure 12–7 shows you can earn an annual profit of $48,000, just as shown by the row shaded in green in Figure 12–6.

Applications of Break-Even Analysis   Because of its simplicity, break-even analysis is used extensively in marketing, most frequently to study the impact on profit of changes in price, fixed cost, and variable cost. The mechanics of break-even analysis are the basis of the widely used electronic spreadsheets offered by computer programs

FIGURE 12–7

A break-even analysis chart for the picture frame store example shows the break-even point at 400 pictures and $48,000 in revenue.

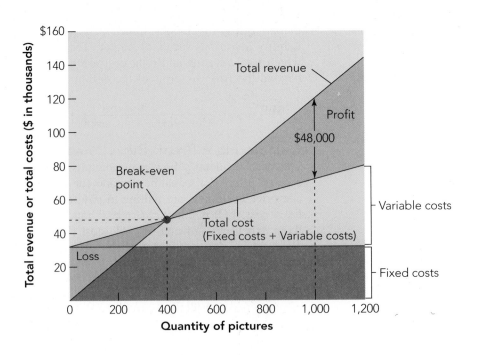

such as Microsoft Excel. These programs permit managers to answer hypothetical "what if" questions about the effect of changes in price and cost on their profit.

learning review

5. What is the difference between fixed costs and variable costs?

6. What is a break-even point?

PRICING OBJECTIVES AND CONSTRAINTS

LO4

With such a variety of alternative pricing strategies available, a marketing manager must consider the pricing objectives and constraints that will narrow the range of choices. While pricing objectives frequently reflect corporate goals, pricing constraints often relate to conditions existing in the marketplace.

Identifying Pricing Objectives

pricing objectives
Expectations that specify the role of price in an organization's marketing and strategic plans.

Pricing objectives specify the role of price in an organization's marketing and strategic plans. To the extent possible, these pricing objectives are carried to lower levels in the organization, such as in setting objectives for marketing managers responsible for an individual brand. These objectives may change depending on the financial position of the company as a whole, the success of its products, or the segments in which it is doing business. Apple, for example, has specific pricing objectives for its iPhone brand that vary by country.

Profit Three different objectives relate to a firm's profit, which is often measured in terms of return on investment. These objectives have different implications for pricing strategy. One objective is *managing for long-run profits,* in which a company—such as many Japanese car or TV set manufacturers—gives up immediate profit in exchange for achieving a higher market share. Products are priced relatively low compared to their cost to develop, but the firm expects to make greater profits later because of its high market share.

A *maximizing current profit* objective, such as for a quarter or year, is common in many firms because the targets can be set and performance measured quickly. American firms are sometimes criticized for this short-run orientation. As noted earlier, a *target return* objective occurs when a firm sets a profit goal (such as 20 percent for return on investment), usually determined by its board of directors. These three profit objectives have different implications for a firm's pricing objectives.

Another profit consideration for firms such as movie studios and manufacturers is to ensure that those firms in their channels of distribution make adequate profits. Without profits for these channel members, the movie studio or manufacturer is cut off from its customers. For example, Figure 12–8 on the next page shows where each dollar of your movie ticket goes. The 51 cents the movie studio gets must cover its profit plus the cost of making and marketing the movie. Although the studio would like more than 51 cents of your dollar, it settles for this amount to make sure theaters and distributors are satisfied and willing to handle its movies.[15]

Sales Given that a firm's profit is high enough for it to remain in business, an objective may be to increase sales revenue, which will in turn lead to increases in market share and profit. Objectives related to sales revenue or unit sales have the advantage of being translated easily into meaningful targets for marketing managers responsible for a product line or brand. However, while cutting the price on one product in a firm's line may increase its sales revenue, it may also reduce the sales revenue of related products.

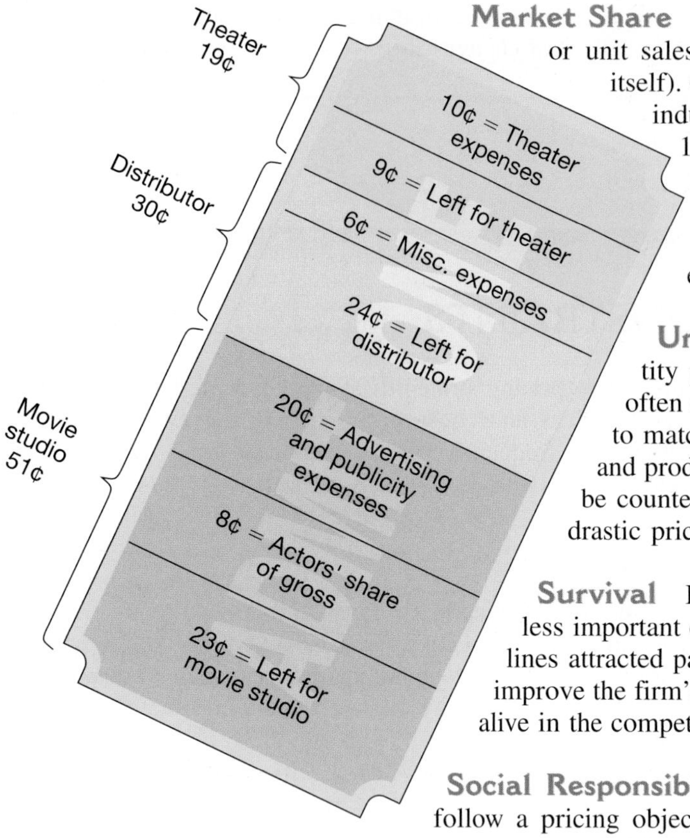

Figure 12-8

Theater
19¢

Distributor
30¢

Movie
studio
51¢

10¢ = Theater expenses

9¢ = Left for theater

6¢ = Misc. expenses

24¢ = Left for distributor

20¢ = Advertising and publicity expenses

8¢ = Actors' share of gross

23¢ = Left for movie studio

FIGURE 12–8
Where each dollar of your movie ticket goes.

pricing constraints
Factors that limit the range of prices a firm may set.

Market Share Market share is the ratio of the firm's sales revenues or unit sales to those of the industry (competitors plus the firm itself). Companies often pursue a market share objective when industry sales are relatively flat or declining. In the late 1990s, Boeing cut prices drastically to try to maintain its 60 percent market share and encountered huge losses. Although increased market share is a primary goal of some firms, others see it as a means to other ends: increasing sales and profits.

Unit Volume Many firms use unit volume, the quantity produced or sold, as a pricing objective. These firms often sell multiple products at very different prices and need to match the unit volume demanded by customers with price and production capacity. Using unit volume as an objective can be counterproductive if a volume objective is achieved, say, by drastic price cutting that drives down profit.

Survival In some instances, profits, sales, and market share are less important objectives of the firm than mere survival. Frontier Airlines attracted passengers with low fares and aggressive promotions to improve the firm's cash flow. This pricing objective helped Frontier stay alive in the competitive airline industry following its bankruptcy in 2008.

Social Responsibility A firm may forgo higher profit on sales and follow a pricing objective that recognizes its obligations to customers and society in general. Medtronics followed this pricing policy when it introduced the world's first heart pacemaker. Gerber supplies a specially formulated product free of charge to children who cannot tolerate foods based on cow's milk.

Identifying Pricing Constraints

Factors that limit the range of prices a firm may set are **pricing constraints**. Consumer demand for the product clearly affects the price that can be charged. Other constraints on price vary from factors within the organization to competitive factors outside it.

Demand for the Product Class, Product, and Brand The number of potential buyers for a product class (high-definition TVs), product (flat-panel display), and brand (Panasonic) clearly affects the price a seller can charge. So does whether the item is a luxury or a necessity, like bread and a roof over your head. Generally speaking, the higher the demand for a product class and product, the higher the price can be set. Demand for HDTVs and flat-panel displays is high given the switch from analog to digital television signals in 2009.[16]

Newness of the Product: Stage in the Product Life Cycle The newer the product and the earlier it is in its life cycle, the higher the price that can usually be charged. The high initial price is possible because of patents and limited competition in the early stage. HDTVs are in the growth stage of the product life cycle. However, competitors are entering the market, thus leading to greater price competition.

Cost of Producing and Marketing the Product In the long run, a firm's price must cover all the costs of producing and marketing a product. If the price doesn't cover these costs, the firm will fail; so in the long run, a firm's costs set a floor under its price. The cost to produce HDTVs and flat-panel displays is

What pricing constraints do high-definition television manufacturers face? Read the text to appreciate the pricing challenges in this market.

decreasing by 15 percent per year. However, newer manufacturers have entered the market with aggressive pricing tactics, thus decreasing profit margins.

Competitors' Prices   A firm must know what specific price its present competitors are charging while also anticipating what its potential competitors will charge in the future. Also, a firm must assess the possibility of dangerous, costly price wars. Some industry forecasters are predicting an HDTV price war by 2011, with many lesser-known companies and brands leaving the market.

Legal and Ethical Considerations   Setting a final price is clearly a complex process. The task is further complicated by legal and ethical issues. Four pricing practices that have received special scrutiny are described below:

- *Price fixing.* A conspiracy among firms to set prices for a product is termed price fixing. Price fixing is illegal under the Sherman Act. When two or more competitors collude to explicitly or implicitly set prices, this practice is called *horizontal price fixing.* For example, six foreign vitamin companies recently pled guilty to price fixing in the human and animal vitamin industry and paid the largest fine in U.S. history: $335 million.[17] *Vertical price fixing* involves controlling agreements between independent buyers and sellers (a manufacturer and a retailer) whereby sellers are required to not sell products below a minimum retail price. This practice, called *resale price maintenance,* was declared illegal in 1975 under provisions of the Consumer Goods Pricing Act.
- *Price discrimination.* The Clayton Act as amended by the Robinson-Patman Act prohibits price discrimination—the practice of charging different prices to different buyers for goods of like grade and quality. However, not all price differences are illegal; only those that substantially lessen competition or create a monopoly are deemed unlawful.
- *Deceptive pricing.* Price deals that mislead consumers fall into the category of deceptive pricing. Deceptive pricing is outlawed by the Federal Trade Commission. *Bait and switch* is an example of deceptive pricing. This occurs when

a firm offers a very low price on a product (the bait) to attract customers to a store. Once in the store, the customer is persuaded to purchase a higher-priced item (the switch) using a variety of tricks, including (1) degrading the promoted item and (2) not having the promised item in stock or refusing to take orders for it.

- *Predatory pricing.* Predatory pricing is the practice of charging a very low price for a product with the intent of driving competitors out of business. Once competitors have been driven out, the firm raises its prices. Proving the presence of this practice has been difficult and expensive because it must be shown that the predator explicitly attempted to destroy a competitor and the predatory price was below the defendant's average cost.

It should be clear that laws cannot be passed and enforced to protect consumers and competitors against all of these practices, so it is essential to rely on the ethical standards of those setting prices.

SETTING A FINAL PRICE

LO5

The final price set by the marketing manager serves many functions. It must be high enough to cover the cost of providing the product or service *and* meet the objectives of the company. Yet it must be low enough that customers are willing to pay it. But not too low, or customers may think they're purchasing an inferior product. Dizzy yet? Setting price is one of the most difficult tasks the marketing manager faces, but three generalized steps are useful to follow.

Step 1: Select an Approximate Price Level

Before setting a final price, the marketing manager must understand the market environment, the features and customer benefits of the particular product, and the goals of the firm. A balance must be struck between factors that might drive a price higher (such as a profit-oriented approach) and other forces (such as increased competition from substitutes) that may drive a price down.

Marketing managers consider pricing objectives and constraints first, then choose among the general pricing approaches—demand-, cost-, profit-, or competition-oriented—to arrive at an approximate price level. This price is then analyzed in terms of cost, volume, and profit relationships. Break-even analyses may be run at this point, and finally if this approximate price level "works," it is time to take the next step: setting a specific list or quoted price.

Step 2: Set the List or Quoted Price

A seller must decide whether to follow a one-price or flexible-price policy.

One-Price Policy A *one-price policy*, also called *fixed pricing*, is setting one price for all buyers of a product or service. CarMax uses this approach in its stores and features a "no haggle, one price" price for cars. Some retailers have married this policy with a below-market approach. Dollar Valley Stores and 99¢ Only Stores sell everything in their stores for $1 or less. Family Dollar Stores sell everything for $2.

Making Responsible Decisions > > > > > > > ethics

Flexible Pricing—Is There Race and Gender Discrimination in Bargaining for a New Car?

What do 60 percent of prospective buyers dread when looking for a new car? That's right! They dread negotiating the price. Price bargaining demonstrates a shortcoming of flexible pricing when purchasing a new car: the potential for minority price discrimination.

A National Bureau of Economic Research study of 750,000 car purchases indicated that African Americans, Hispanics, and women, on average, paid roughly $423, $483, and $105 more, respectively, for a new car in the $21,000 range than the typical purchaser. Smaller price premiums remained after adjusting for income, education, and other factors that may affect price negotiations.

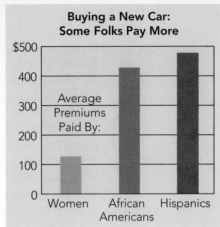

Buying a New Car: Some Folks Pay More

Average Premiums Paid By:

Women / African Americans / Hispanics

Flexible-Price Policy In contrast, a *flexible-price policy* involves setting different prices for products and services depending on individual buyers and purchase situations in light of demand, cost, and competitive factors. Dell Inc. uses flexible pricing as it continually adjusts prices in response to changes in its own costs, competitive pressures, and demand from its various personal computer segments (home, small business, corporate, etc.). "Our flexibility allows us to be [priced] different even within a day," says a Dell spokesperson.[18]

Chain apparel stores use the beginning of the week to discover what isn't selling well to make plans for the high-traffic weekends. So the best deals in their flexible-price policy come Wednesdays through Fridays, right before the weekend. Some apparel chains have specific days for nationwide price markdowns: Wednesdays for Gap and Thursdays for J. Crew and Eddie Bauer.[19]

Flexible pricing is not without its critics because of its discriminatory potential. For example, car dealers have traditionally used flexible pricing on the basis of buyer–seller negotiations to agree on a final sales price. However, flexible pricing may result in discriminatory practices in car buying as detailed in the Making Responsible Decisions box.[20]

What is the best day of the week to shop at Eddie Bauer, Gap, and J. Crew with their flexible-pricing approach? For the answers, see the text.

Step 3: Make Special Adjustments to the List or Quoted Price

When you pay 75 cents for a bag of M&Ms in a vending machine or receive a quoted price of $10,000 from a contractor to renovate a kitchen, the pricing sequence ends with the last step just described: setting the list or quoted price. But when you are a manufacturer of M&M candies and sell your product to dozens or hundreds of wholesalers and retailers in your channel of distribution, you may need to make a variety of special adjustments to the list or quoted price. Wholesalers also must adjust the list or quoted prices they set for retailers. Three special adjustments to the list or quoted price are (1) discounts, (2) allowances, and (3) geographical adjustments.

Discounts   *Discounts* are reductions from list price that a seller gives a buyer as a reward for some activity of the buyer that is favorable to the seller. Four kinds of discounts are especially important in marketing strategy: (1) quantity, (2) seasonal, (3) trade (functional), and (4) cash.

- *Quantity discounts.* To encourage customers to buy larger quantities of a product, firms at all levels in the channel of distribution offer quantity discounts, which are reductions in unit costs for a larger order. For example, an instant photocopying service might set a price of 10 cents a copy for 1 to 24 copies, 9 cents a copy for 25 to 99 copies, and 8 cents a copy for 100 copies or more. Because the photocopying service gets more of the buyer's business and has longer production runs that reduce its order-handling costs, it is willing to pass on some of the cost savings in the form of quantity discounts to the buyer.

- *Seasonal discounts.* To encourage buyers to stock inventory earlier than their normal demand would require, manufacturers often use seasonal discounts. A firm such as Toro that manufactures lawn mowers and snow throwers offers seasonal discounts to encourage wholesalers and retailers to stock up on lawn mowers in January and February and snow throwers in July and August—five or six months before the seasonal demand by ultimate consumers. This enables Toro to smooth out seasonal manufacturing peaks and troughs, thereby contributing to more efficient production. It also rewards wholesalers and retailers for the risk they accept in assuming increased inventory carrying costs and means they have supplies in stock at the time they are wanted by customers.

- *Trade (functional) discounts.* To reward wholesalers and retailers for marketing functions they will perform in the future, a manufacturer often gives trade, or functional, discounts. These reductions off the list or base price are offered to resellers in the channel of distribution on the basis of (1) where they are in the channel and (2) the marketing activities they are expected to perform in the future.

    Traditional trade discounts have been established in various product lines such as hardware, food, and pharmaceutical items. Although the manufacturer may suggest the trade discounts, the sellers are free to alter the discount schedule depending on their competitive situation.

- *Cash discounts.* To encourage retailers to pay their bills quickly, manufacturers offer them cash discounts. Suppose a retailer receives a bill quoted at $1,000, 2/10 net 30. This means that the bill for the product is $1,000, but the retailer can take a 2 percent discount ($1,000 × 0.02 = $20) if payment is made within 10 days and send a check for $980. If the payment cannot be made within 10 days, the total amount of $1,000 is due within 30 days. It is usually understood by the buyer that an interest charge will be added after the first 30 days of free credit.

A retailer like Payless that plans an early summer sale on sandals often tries to take advantage of several of these discounts to increase its revenues and profits.

Allowances   Allowances—like discounts—are reductions from list or quoted prices to buyers for performing some activity.

- *Trade-in allowances.* A new-car dealer can offer a substantial reduction in the list price of that new Toyota Camry by offering you a trade-in allowance of $500 for your Chevrolet. A trade-in allowance is a price reduction given when a used product is part of the payment on a new product. Trade-ins are an effective way to lower the price a buyer has to pay without formally reducing the list price.

Manufacturers provide a variety of discounts to assist channel members such as Payless, a shoe retailer promoting an early summer sandals sale.

- *Promotional allowances.* Sellers in the channel of distribution can qualify for promotional allowances for undertaking certain advertising or selling activities to promote a product. Various types of allowances include an actual cash payment or an extra amount of "free goods" (as with a free case of pizzas to a retailer for every dozen cases purchased). Frequently, a portion of these savings is passed on to the consumer by retailers.

Some companies, such as Procter & Gamble, have chosen to reduce promotional allowances for retailers by using everyday low pricing. *Everyday low pricing* (EDLP) is the practice of replacing promotional allowances with lower manufacturer list prices. EDLP promises to reduce the average price to consumers while minimizing promotional allowances that cost manufacturers billions of dollars every year.

Geographical Adjustments Geographical adjustments are made by manufacturers or even wholesalers to list or quoted prices to reflect the cost of transportation of the products from seller to buyer. The two general methods for quoting prices related to transportation costs are (1) FOB origin pricing and (2) uniform delivered pricing.

- *FOB origin pricing.* FOB means "free on board" some vehicle at some location, which means the seller pays the cost of loading the product onto the vehicle that is used (such as a barge, railroad car, or truck). FOB origin pricing usually involves the seller's naming the location of this loading as the seller's factory or warehouse (such as "FOB Detroit" or "FOB factory"). The title to the goods passes to the buyer at the point of loading, so the buyer becomes responsible for picking the specific mode of transportation, for all the transportation costs, and for subsequent handling of the product. Buyers farthest from the seller face the big disadvantage of paying the higher transportation costs.
- *Uniform delivered pricing.* When a uniform delivered pricing method is used, the price the seller quotes includes all transportation costs. It is quoted in a contract as "FOB buyer's location," and the seller selects the mode of transportation, pays the freight charges, and is responsible for any damage that may occur because the seller retains title to the goods until delivered to the buyer.

learning review

9. What are the three steps in setting a final price?

10. What is the purpose of (a) quantity discounts and (b) promotional allowances?

LEARNING OBJECTIVES REVIEW

LO1 *Describe the nature and importance of pricing and the approaches used to select an approximate price level.*
Price is the money or other considerations (such as barter) exchanged for the ownership or use of a product or service. Although price typically involves money, the amount exchanged is often different from the list or quoted price because of incentives (rebates, discounts, etc.), allowances (trade), and extra fees (finance charges, surcharges, etc.).

Demand, cost, profit, and competition influence the initial consideration of the approximate price level for a product or service. Demand-oriented pricing approaches stress consumer demand and revenue implications of pricing and include seven types: skimming, penetration, prestige, odd-even, target, bundle, and yield management. Cost-oriented pricing approaches emphasize the cost aspects of pricing and include two types: standard markup and cost-plus pricing. Profit-oriented pricing approaches focus on a balance between revenues and costs to set a price and include three types: target profit, target return-on-sales, and target return-on-investment pricing. And finally, competition-oriented pricing approaches stress what competitors or the marketplace are doing and include three types: customary; above-, at-, or below-market; and loss-leader pricing.

LO2 *Explain what a demand curve is and the role of revenues in pricing decisions.*
A demand curve is a graph relating the quantity sold and price, which shows the maximum number of units that will be sold at a given price. Three demand factors affect price: (*a*) consumer tastes, (*b*) price and availability of substitute products, and (*c*) consumer income. These demand factors determine consumers' willingness and ability to pay for products and services. Assuming these demand factors remain unchanged, if the price of a product is lowered or raised, then the quantity demanded for it will increase or decrease, respectively. The demand curve relates to a firm's total revenue, which is the total money received from sale of a product, or the price of one unit times the quantity of units sold.

LO3 *Explain the role of costs in pricing decisions and describe how combinations of price, fixed cost, and unit variable cost affect a firm's break-even point.*
Four important costs impact a firm's pricing decisions: (*a*) total cost, or total expenses, the sum of the fixed costs and variable costs incurred by a firm in producing and marketing a product; (*b*) fixed cost, the sum of the expenses of the firm that are stable and do not change with the quantity of a product that is produced and sold; (*c*) variable cost, the sum of the expenses of the firm that vary directly

with the quantity of a product that is produced and sold; and (*d*) unit variable cost, the variable cost expressed on a per unit basis.
Break-even analysis is a technique that analyzes the relationship between total revenue and total cost to determine profitability at various levels of output. The break-even point is the quantity at which total revenue and total cost are equal. Assuming no change in price, if the costs of a firm's product increase due to higher fixed costs (manufacturing or advertising) or variable costs (direct labor or materials), then its break-even point will be higher. And if total cost is unchanged, an increase in price will reduce the break-even point.

LO4 *Recognize the objectives a firm has in setting prices and the constraints that restrict the range of prices a firm can charge.*
Pricing objectives specify the role of price in a firm's marketing strategy and may include profit, sales revenue, market share, unit volume, survival, or some socially responsible price level. Pricing constraints that restrict a firm's pricing flexibility include demand, product newness, production and marketing costs, prices of competitive substitutes, and legal and ethical considerations.

LO5 *Describe the steps taken in setting a final price.*
Three common steps marketing managers often use in setting a final price are (1) select an approximate price level as a starting point; (2) set the list or quoted price, choosing between a one-price policy or a flexible-price policy; and (3) modify the list or quoted price by considering discounts, allowances, and geographical adjustments.

FOCUSING ON KEY TERMS

break-even analysis p. 273
demand curve p. 270
price p. 262
price elasticity of demand p. 271

pricing constraints p. 276
pricing objectives p. 275
profit equation p. 263
total cost p. 273

total revenue p. 272
value p. 263

APPLYING MARKETING KNOWLEDGE

1 How would the price equation apply to the purchase price of (*a*) gasoline, (*b*) an airline ticket, and (*c*) a checking account?
2 Under what conditions would a camera manufacturer adopt a skimming price approach for a new product? A penetration approach?
3 What are some similarities and differences between skimming pricing, prestige pricing, and above-market pricing?
4 Touché Toiletries Inc. has developed an addition to its Lizardman Cologne line tentatively branded Ode

d'Toade Cologne. Unit variable costs are 45 cents for a 3-ounce bottle, and heavy advertising expenditures in the first year would result in total fixed costs of $900,000. Ode d'Toade Cologne is priced at $7.50 for a 3-ounce bottle. How many bottles of Ode d'Toade must be sold to break even?
5 What would be your response to the statement, "Profit maximization is the only legitimate pricing objective for the firm"?

1. In starting to set a final price, think about your customers and competitors and set three possible prices.
2. Assume a fixed cost and unit variable cost and (*a*) calculate the break-even points and (*b*) plot a break-even chart for the three prices specified in step 1.
3. Using your best judgment, select one of these prices as your final price.

---

video case 12 Washburn Guitars: Using Break-Even Points to Make Pricing Decisions

"We offer a guitar at every price point for every skill level," explains Kevin Lello, vice president of marketing at Washburn Guitars. Washburn is one of the most prestigious guitar manufacturers in the world, offering instruments that range from one-of-a-kind, custom-made acoustic and electric guitars and basses to less-expensive, mass-produced guitars. Lello has responsibility for marketing Washburn's products and ensuring that the price of each product matches the company's objectives related to sales, profit, and market share. "We do pay attention to break-even points," adds Lello. "We need to know exactly how much a guitar costs us, and how much the overhead is for each guitar."

THE COMPANY

The modern Washburn Guitars company started in 1977 when a small Chicago firm bought the century-old Washburn brand name and a small inventory of guitars, parts, and promotional supplies. At that time, annual company sales of about 2,500 guitars generated revenues of $300,000. Washburn's first catalog, appearing in 1978, told a frightening truth:

> Our designs are translated by Japan's most experienced craftsmen, assuring the consistent quality and craftsmanship for which they are known.

At that time, the American guitar-making craft was at an all-time low. Guitars made by Japanese firms, such as Ibane and Yamaha, were in use by an increasing number of professionals.

Times have changed for Washburn. Today, the company sells about 50,000 guitars each year and annual revenues exceed $40 million. All this resulted from Washburn's aggressive marketing strategies to develop product lines with different price points targeted at musicians in distinctly different market segments.

THE PRODUCTS AND MARKET SEGMENTS

One of Washburn's early successes was the trendsetting Festival Series of cutaway, thin-bodied flattops, with built-in bridge pickups and controls. This guitar became the standard for live performances as its popularity with rock and country stars increased. Over the years several generations of musicians have used Washburn guitars. Early artists included Bob Dylan, Dolly Parton, Greg Allman, and the late George Harrison of the Beatles. In recent years, Mike Kennerty of the All American Rejects, Rick Savage of Def Leppard, and Hugh McDonald of Bon Jovi have been among the many musicians who use Washburn products.

Until 1991, all Washburn guitars were manufactured in Asia. That year Washburn started building its high-end guitars in the United States. Today, Washburn marketing executives divide its product line into four categories to appeal to different market segments. From high end to low end these are:

- One-of-a-kind, custom instruments.
- Batch-custom instruments.
- Mass-customized instruments.
- Mass-produced instruments.

The one-of-a-kind custom products appeal to the many stars who use Washburn instruments as well as collectors. The batch-custom products appeal to professional musicians. The mass-customized products appeal to musicians with intermediate skill levels who may not yet be professionals. Finally, the mass-produced units are targeted at first-time buyers and are still manufactured in Asian factories.

PRICING ISSUES

Setting prices for its various lines presents a continuing challenge for Washburn. Not only do the prices have to reflect the changing tastes of its various segments of musicians, but the prices must also be competitive with the prices of other guitars manufactured and marketed globally. The price elasticity of demand, or price sensitivity, for Washburn's products varies between its segments. To reduce the price sensitivity for some of its products, Washburn uses endorsements by internationally known musicians who play its instruments and lend their names to lines of Washburn signature guitars. Stars playing Washburn guitars such as Nuno Bettencourt of Extreme, Paul Stanley of KISS, Scott Ian of Anthrax, and Dan Donegan of Disturbed have their own lines of signature guitars—the "batch-custom" units mentioned earlier. These guitars receive excellent reviews. *Total Guitar* magazine, for example, recently said, "If you want a truly original axe that has been built with great attention to detail . . . then the Washburn Maya Pro DD75 could be the one."

Bill Abel, Washburn's vice president of sales, is responsible for reviewing and approving prices for the company's lines of guitars. Setting a sales target of 2,000 units for a new line of guitars, he is considering a suggested retail price of $349 per unit for customers at one of the hundreds of retail outlets carrying the Washburn line. For planning purposes, Abel estimates half of the final retail price will be the price Washburn nets when it sells its guitar to the wholesalers and dealers in its channel of distribution.

Looking at Washburn's financial data for its present plant, Abel estimates that this line of guitars must bear these fixed costs:

Rent and taxes	= $14,000
Depreciation of equipment	= $ 4,000
Management and quality control program	= $20,000

In addition, he estimates the variable costs for each unit to be:

Direct materials = $25/unit

Direct labor = 15 hours/unit @$8/hour

Carefully kept production records at Washburn's plant make Abel believe that these are reasonable estimates. He explains, "Before we begin a production run, we have a good feel for what our costs will be. The U.S.–built N-4, for example, simply costs more than one of our foreign-produced electrics."

Caught in the global competition for guitar sales, Washburn continually searches for ways to reduce and control costs. For example, Washburn recently purchased Parker Guitar, another guitar manufacturer that designed products for professionals and collectors, and will combine the two production facilities in a new location. Washburn expects the acquisition to lower its fixed and variable costs. Specifically, Washburn projects that its new factory location will reduce its rent and taxes expense by 40 percent, and the new skilled employees will reduce the hours of work needed for each unit by 15 percent.

By managing the prices of its products, Washburn also helps its dealers and retailers. In fact, Abel believes it is another reason for Washburn's success: "We have excellent relationships with the independent retailers. They're our lifeblood, and our outlet to sell our product. We sell through chains and online dealers, but it's the independent dealer that sells the guitars. So we take a smaller margin from them because they have to do more work. They appreciate it, and they go the extra mile for us."

Questions

1 What factors are most likely to affect the demand for the lines of Washburn guitars (*a*) bought by a first-time guitar buyer and (*b*) bought by a sophisticated musician who wants a signature model?

2 For Washburn, what are examples of (*a*) shifting the demand curve to the right to get a higher price for a guitar line (movement of the demand curve) and (*b*) pricing decisions involving moving along a demand curve?

3 In Washburn's factory, what is the break-even point for the new line of guitars if the retail price is (*a*) $349, (*b*) $389, and (*c*) $309? Also, (*d*) if Washburn achieves the sales target of 2,000 units at the $349 retail price, what will its profit be?

4 Assume that the merger with Parker leads to the cost reductions projected in the case. What will be the (*a*) new break-even point at a $349 retail price for this line of guitars and (*b*) new profit if it sells 2,000 units?

5 If, for competitive reasons, Washburn eventually has to move all its production back to Asia, (*a*) which specific fixed and variable costs might be lowered and (*b*) what additional fixed and variable costs might it expect to incur?

Callaway
PURE
SAP
Callaway GOLF
FT9
SAP
BOMB IT OR BEND IT.
The FT-9™ Driver is designed for both.
Golf Digest HOT LIST
Carbon composite construction, External Web Weighting and explosive titanium Hyperbolic Face Cup Technology™ combine to provide unbelievable distance and shot-shaping control. So go ahead. Hit a draw. Hit a fade. Hit it pure.
callawaygolf.com/pure
Callaway
© 2009 Callaway Golf Company. FT-9, Hyperbolic Face Cup Technology, the Chevron Device and Callaway Golf are trademarks and/or registered trademarks of Callaway Golf Company.

13

Managing Marketing Channels and Supply Chains

LEARNING OBJECTIVES

After reading this chapter you should be able to:

LO1 Explain what is meant by a marketing channel of distribution and why intermediaries are needed.

LO2 Distinguish among traditional marketing channels, electronic marketing channels, and different types of vertical marketing systems.

LO3 Describe factors that marketing executives consider when selecting and managing a marketing channel.

LO4 Explain what supply chain and logistics management are and how they relate to marketing strategy.

CALLAWAY GOLF: DESIGNING AND DELIVERING THE GOODS FOR GREAT GOLF

What do Ernie Els, a world-class golf professional, and Justin Timberlake, a pop icon and avid amateur golfer, have in common? Both use Callaway Golf equipment, accessories, and apparel when playing their favorite sport.

With annual sales about $1 billion, Callaway Golf is one of the most recognized and highly regarded companies in the golf industry. With its commitment to continuous product innovation and broad distribution in the United States and more than 100 countries worldwide, Callaway Golf has built a strong reputation for designing and delivering the goods for great golf for golfers of all skill levels, both amateur and professional.

Callaway Golf primarily markets its products through more than 15,000 on- and off-course golf retailers and sporting goods retailers, such as Golf Galaxy, Inc., Dick's Sporting Goods, Inc., and PGA Tour Superstores, which sell quality golf products and provide a level of customer service appropriate for the sale of such products. The company also has its own online store (Shop.Callawaygolf.com), which makes it a full-fledged multichannel marketer, and a successful one as well. The chief executive of PGA America called Callaway's online store "innovative in that it combines that old legacy relationship with the retail channel with the new innovation of the Web" soon after the online store was launched. Callaway's chief executive officer, George Fellows, says Callaway's online store is useful for consumers who are looking for accessories or apparel and for those who know their preferred golf club specifications: "There are always going to be certain people that will not feel comfortable buying online. But for those that do feel comfortable, we really represent the most seamless process."

Callaway Golf considers its marketing channel partners a valued marketing asset. For example, when the company opened its online store, careful attention was placed on how Callaway Golf "could satisfy the consumer but do so in a way that didn't violate our relationships with our loyal trade partners," Fellows said. The solution? Callaway Golf has one of its retailers get credit for the sale. This retailer then fulfills a buyer's order within 24 hours. Consumers, retailers, and Callaway Golf all benefit from this arrangement.[1]

This chapter focuses on managing marketing channels of distribution and supply chains. Each is an important element in the marketing mix.

NATURE AND IMPORTANCE OF MARKETING CHANNELS

Reaching prospective buyers, either directly or indirectly, is a prerequisite for successful marketing. At the same time, buyers benefit from distribution systems used by companies.

What Is a Marketing Channel of Distribution?

LO1

You see the results of distribution every day. You may have purchased Lay's Potato Chips at a 7-Eleven convenience store, a book online through Amazon.com, and Levi's jeans at a Kohl's department store. Each of these items was brought to you by a marketing channel of distribution, or simply a **marketing channel**, which consists of individuals and firms involved in the process of making a product or service available for use or consumption by consumers or industrial users.

marketing channel
Individuals and firms involved in the process of making a product or service available for use or consumption by consumers or industrial users.

Marketing channels can be compared with a pipeline through which water flows from a source to a terminus. Marketing channels make possible the flow of goods from a producer, through intermediaries, to a buyer. Intermediaries go by various names (see Figure 13–1) and perform various functions. Some intermediaries purchase items from the seller, store them, and resell them to buyers. For example, Celestial Seasonings produces specialty teas and sells them to food wholesalers. The wholesalers then sell these teas to supermarkets and grocery stores, which, in turn, sell them to consumers. Other intermediaries such as brokers and agents represent sellers but do not actually take title to products—their role is to bring a seller and buyer together. Century 21 real estate agents are examples of this type of intermediary.

Value Is Created by Intermediaries

FIGURE 13–1
Terms used for marketing intermediaries vary in specificity and use in consumer and business markets.

The importance of intermediaries is made even clearer when we consider the functions they perform and the value they create for buyers.

Important Functions Performed by Intermediaries Intermediaries make possible the flow of products from producers to ultimate consumers by performing three basic functions (see Figure 13–2). Intermediaries perform a

TERM	DESCRIPTION
Middleman	Any intermediary between manufacturer and end-user markets
Agent or broker	Any intermediary with legal authority to act on behalf of the manufacturer
Wholesaler	An intermediary who sells to other intermediaries, usually to retailers; term usually applies to consumer markets
Retailer	An intermediary who sells to consumers
Distributor	An imprecise term, usually used to describe intermediaries who perform a variety of distribution functions, including selling, maintaining inventories, extending credit, and so on; a more common term in business markets but may also be used to refer to wholesalers
Dealer	A more imprecise term than *distributor* that can mean the same as distributor, retailer, wholesaler, and so forth

Borders, a leading U.S. book retailer, works closely with book publishers. Read the text to learn how this is done.

transactional function when they buy and sell goods or services. But an intermediary such as a wholesaler also performs the function of sharing risk with the producer when it stocks merchandise in anticipation of sales. If the stock is unsold for any reason, the intermediary—not the producer—suffers the loss.

The logistics of a transaction (described at length later in this chapter) involve the details of preparing and getting a product to buyers. Gathering, sorting, and dispersing products are some of the *logistical functions* of the intermediary—imagine the several books required for a literature course sitting together on one shelf at your college bookstore! Finally, intermediaries perform *facilitating functions* that, by definition, make a transaction *easier* for buyers. For example, JCPenney issues credit cards to consumers so they can buy now and pay later.

All three functions must be performed in a marketing channel, even though each channel member may not participate in all three. Channel members often negotiate about which specific functions they will perform. Borders, a leading U.S. book retailer, is a case in point. It has negotiated agreements with major book publishers whereby they assume responsibility for choosing books for Borders to buy, displaying the assortment of books on its shelves, and providing information on new titles and consumer reading preferences in specific book categories. For example, HarperCollins has responsibility for cookbooks, Random House for children's books, and Pearson for computer books.[2]

Consumers Also Benefit from Intermediaries Consumers also benefit from intermediaries. Having the goods and services you want, when you want them, where you want them, and in the form you want them is the ideal result of marketing channels.

In more specific terms, marketing channels help create value for consumers through the four utilities described in Chapter 1: time, place, form, and possession. *Time utility* refers to having a product or service when you want it. For example, FedEx provides next-morning delivery. *Place utility* means having a product or service available where consumers want it, such as having a Texaco gas station located on a long stretch of lonely highway. *Form utility* involves enhancing a product or service to make it more appealing to buyers. Consider the importance of bottlers in the soft-drink industry. Coca-Cola and Pepsi-Cola manufacture the flavor concentrate (cola, lemon-lime) and sell it to bottlers—intermediaries—which then add sweetener and the concentrate to

FIGURE 13–2
Marketing channel intermediaries perform these fundamental functions, each of which consists of different activities.

TYPE OF FUNCTION	ACTIVITIES RELATED TO FUNCTION
Transactional function	• *Buying*: Purchasing products for resale or as an agent for supply of a product • *Selling*: Contacting potential customers, promoting products, and seeking orders • *Risk taking*: Assuming business risks in the ownership of inventory that can become obsolete or deteriorate
Logistical function	• *Assorting*: Creating product assortments from several sources to serve customers • *Storing*: Assembling and protecting products at a convenient location to offer better customer service • *Sorting*: Purchasing in large quantities and breaking into smaller amounts desired by customers • *Transporting*: Physically moving a product to customers
Facilitating function	• *Financing*: Extending credit to customers • *Grading*: Inspecting, testing, or judging products, and assigning them quality grades • *Marketing information and research*: Providing information to customers and suppliers, including competitive conditions and trends

carbonated water and package the beverage in bottles and cans, which are then sold to retailers. *Possession utility* entails efforts by intermediaries to help buyers take possession of a product or service, such as having airline tickets delivered by a travel agency.

learning review

1. What is meant by a marketing channel?

2. What are the three basic functions performed by intermediaries?

CHANNEL STRUCTURE AND ORGANIZATION

LO2

A product can take many routes on its journey from a producer to buyers. Marketers continually search for the most efficient route from the many alternatives available. As you'll see, there are some important differences between the marketing channels used for consumer products and those for business products.

Marketing Channels for Consumer Products and Services

Figure 13–3 shows the four most common marketing channels for consumer products and services. It also shows the number of levels in each marketing channel, as evidenced by the number of intermediaries between a producer and ultimate buyers. As the number of intermediaries between a producer and buyer increases, the channel is viewed as increasing in length. Thus, the producer → wholesaler → retailer → consumer channel is longer than the producer → consumer channel.

Direct Channel Channel A represents a *direct channel* because the producer and the ultimate consumers deal directly with each other. Many products and services are distributed this way. Many insurance companies sell their services using a direct channel and branch sales offices. The Schwan Food Company of Marshall, Minnesota, markets a full line of frozen foods in 50 countries, including the United States, using route salespeople who sell from refrigerated trucks. Because there are no intermediaries with a direct channel, the producer performs all channel functions.

FIGURE 13–3

Common marketing channels for consumer products and services differ by the kind and number of intermediaries involved.

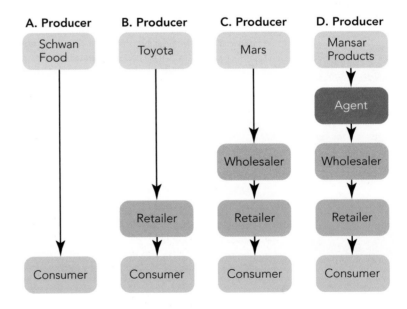

Indirect Channel The remaining three channel forms in Figure 13-3 are *indirect channels* because intermediaries are inserted between the producer and consumers and perform numerous channel functions. Channel B, with a retailer added, is most common when a retailer is large and can buy in large quantities from a producer or when the cost of inventory makes it too expensive to use a wholesaler. Automobile manufacturers such as Toyota use this channel, and a local car dealer acts as a retailer. Why is there no wholesaler? So many variations exist in the product that it would be impossible for a wholesaler to stock all the models required to satisfy buyers; in addition, the cost of maintaining an inventory would be too high. However, large retailers such as Sears, 7-Eleven, Staples, Safeway, and Home Depot buy in sufficient quantities to make it cost effective for a producer to deal with only a retail intermediary.

Adding a wholesaler in Channel C is most common for low-cost, low-unit value items that are frequently purchased by consumers, such as candy, confectionary items, and magazines. For example, Mars sells case quantities of its line of candies to wholesalers, who then break down (sort) the cases so that individual retailers can order in boxes or much smaller quantities.

Channel D, the most indirect channel, is employed when there are many small manufacturers and many small retailers; in this type of channel, an agent is used to help coordinate a large supply of the product. Mansar Products, Ltd., is a Belgian producer of specialty jewelry that uses agents to sell to wholesalers in the United States, who then sell to many small independent jewelry retailers.

Marketing Channels for Business Products and Services

The four most common channels for business products and services are shown in Figure 13–4. In contrast with channels for consumer products, business channels typically are shorter and rely on one intermediary or none at all because business users are fewer in number, tend to be more concentrated geographically, and buy in larger quantities.

Direct Channel Channel A in Figure 13-4, represented by IBM's large, mainframe computer business, is a direct channel. Firms using this channel maintain their own salesforce and perform all channel functions. This channel is employed when buyers are large and well defined, the sales effort requires extensive negotiations, and the products are of high unit value and require hands-on expertise in terms of installation or use.

FIGURE 13–4

Common marketing channels for business products and services differ by the kind and number of intermediaries involved.

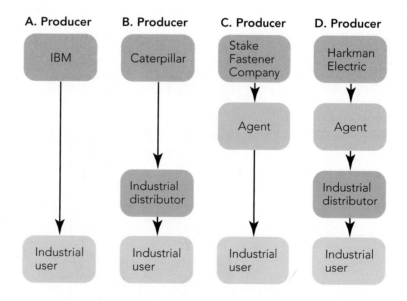

Indirect Channel   Channels B, C, and D in Figure 13–4 are indirect channels with one or more intermediaries to reach industrial users. In Channel B, an *industrial distributor* performs a variety of marketing channel functions, including selling, stocking, delivering a full product assortment, and financing. In many ways, industrial distributors are like wholesalers in consumer channels. Caterpillar uses industrial distributors to sell its construction and mining equipment in over 200 countries. In addition to selling, Caterpillar distributors stock 40,000 to 50,000 parts and service equipment using highly trained technicians.

Channel C introduces a second intermediary, an *agent*, who serves primarily as the independent selling arm of producers and represents a producer to industrial users. For example, Stake Fastener Company, a producer of industrial fasteners, has an agent call on industrial users rather than employing its own salesforce.

Channel D is the longest channel and includes both agents and industrial distributors. For instance, Harkman Electric, a producer of electric products, uses agents to call on electrical distributors who sell to industrial users.

Electronic Marketing Channels

These common marketing channels for consumer and business products and services are not the only routes to the marketplace. Advances in electronic commerce have opened new avenues for reaching buyers and creating customer value.

Interactive electronic technology has made possible *electronic marketing channels*, which employ the Internet to make products and services available for consumption or use by consumers or business buyers. A unique feature of these channels is that they combine electronic and traditional intermediaries to create time, place, form, and possession utility for buyers.

Figure 13–5 shows the electronic marketing channels for books (Amazon.com), automobiles (Autobytel.com), reservation services (Orbitz.com), and personal computers (Dell.com). Are you surprised that they look a lot like common consumer product marketing channels? An important reason for the similarity resides in the channel functions detailed in Figure 13–2. Electronic intermediaries can and do perform transactional and facilitating functions effectively and at a relatively lower cost than traditional intermediaries because of efficiencies made possible by information technology. However, electronic intermediaries are incapable of performing elements of the logistical function, particularly for products such as books and automobiles. This function remains with traditional intermediaries or with the producer, as evident with Dell, Inc., and its direct channel.

Many services can be distributed through electronic marketing channels, such as car rental reservations marketed by Alamo.com, financial securities by Schwab.com,

FIGURE 13–5

Consumer electronic marketing channels look much like those for consumer products and services. Read the text to learn why.

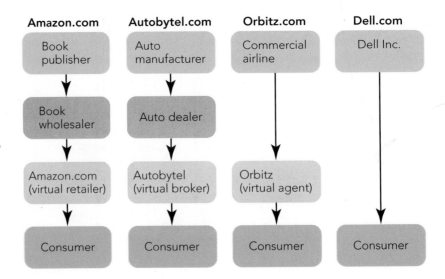

and insurance by MetLife.com. However, many other services, such as health care and auto repair, still involve traditional intermediaries.

Direct and Multichannel Marketing

Many firms also use direct and multichannel marketing to reach buyers. *Direct marketing channels* allow consumers to buy products by interacting with various advertising media without a face-to-face meeting with a salesperson. Direct marketing channels include mail-order selling, direct-mail sales, catalog sales, telemarketing, interactive media, and televised home shopping (the Home Shopping Network). Some firms sell products almost entirely through direct marketing. These firms include L.L. Bean (apparel) and Newegg.com (consumer electronics). Marketers such as Nestlé, in addition to using traditional channels composed of wholesalers and retailers, employ direct marketing through catalogs and telemarketing to reach more buyers.

multichannel marketing
The blending of different communication and delivery channels that are mutually reinforcing in attracting, retaining, and building relationships with consumers.

Multichannel marketing is the *blending* of different communication and delivery channels that are *mutually reinforcing* in attracting, retaining, and building relationships with consumers who shop and buy in traditional intermediaries and online. Multichannel marketing seeks to integrate a firm's electronic and delivery channels. At Eddie Bauer, for example, every effort is made to make the apparel shopping and purchase experience for its customers the same across its retail store, catalog, and Web site channels. According to an Eddie Bauer marketing manager, "We don't distinguish between channels because it's all Eddie Bauer to our customers."[3]

Multichannel marketing also can leverage the value-adding capabilities of different channels. For example, retail stores leverage their physical presence by allowing customers to pick up their online orders at a nearby store or return or exchange nonstore purchases if they wish. Catalogs can serve as shopping tools for online purchasing, as they do for store purchasing. Web sites can help consumers do their homework before visiting a store. Office Depot has leveraged its store, catalog, and Web site channels with impressive results. The company does more than $4 billion in online retail sales annually and is the fourth largest Internet retailer in the United States.[4]

Dual Distribution and Strategic Channel Alliances

dual distribution
An arrangement whereby a firm reaches different buyers by using two or more different types of channels for the same basic product.

In some situations, producers use **dual distribution**, an arrangement whereby a firm reaches different buyers by employing two or more different types of channels for the same basic product. For example, GE sells its large appliances directly to home and apartment builders but uses retail stores, including Lowe's home centers, to sell to consumers. In some instances, firms pair multiple channels with a multibrand strategy (see Chapter 11). This is done to minimize cannibalization of the firm's family brand and differentiate the channels. For example, Hallmark sells its Hallmark greeting cards through Hallmark stores and select department stores and its Ambassador brand of cards through discount and drugstore chains.

A recent innovation in marketing channels is the use of *strategic channel alliances*, whereby one firm's marketing channel is used to sell another firm's products. An alliance between Kraft Foods and Starbucks is a case in point. Kraft distributes Starbucks coffee in U.S. supermarkets and internationally. Strategic alliances are popular in global marketing, where the creation of marketing channel relationships is expensive and time consuming. For example, General Mills and Nestlé have an extensive alliance that spans 130 international markets from Mexico to China. Read the Marketing Matters box on the next page so you won't be surprised when you are served Nestlé (not General Mills) Cheerios when traveling outside North America.[5]

Vertical Marketing Systems

The traditional marketing channels described so far represent a loosely knit network of independent producers and intermediaries brought together to distribute goods and services. However, other channel arrangements exist for the purpose of improving

Can you say Nestlé Cheerios *miel amandes*? Millions of French start their day with this European equivalent of General Mills's Honey Nut Cheerios, made possible by Cereal Partners Worldwide (CPW). CPW is a strategic alliance designed from the start to be a global business. It joined the cereal manufacturing and marketing capability of U.S.–based General Mills with the worldwide distribution clout of Swiss-based Nestlé.

From its headquarters in Switzerland, CPW first launched General Mills cereals under the Nestlé label in France, the United Kingdom, Spain, and Portugal in 1991. Today, CPW competes in more than 130 international markets.

The General Mills–Nestlé strategic channel alliance also increased the ready-to-eat cereal worldwide market share of these companies, which are already rated as the two best-managed firms in the world. CPW currently accounts for more than 8 percent of global breakfast cereal sales, with about $1.4 billion in annual revenue.

---

vertical marketing systems
Professionally managed and centrally coordinated marketing channels designed to achieve channel economies and maximum marketing impact.

efficiency in performing channel functions and achieving greater marketing effectiveness. These arrangements are called vertical marketing systems. **Vertical marketing systems** are professionally managed and centrally coordinated marketing channels designed to achieve channel economies and maximum marketing impact.[6] Figure 13–6 depicts the major types of vertical marketing systems: corporate, contractual, and administered.

Corporate Systems The combination of successive stages of production and distribution under a single ownership is a *corporate vertical marketing system*. For example, a producer might own the intermediary at the next level down in the channel. This practice, called *forward integration*, is exemplified by Ralph Lauren, which

Tiffany & Co. and H&R Block represent two different types of vertical marketing systems. Read the text to find out how they differ.

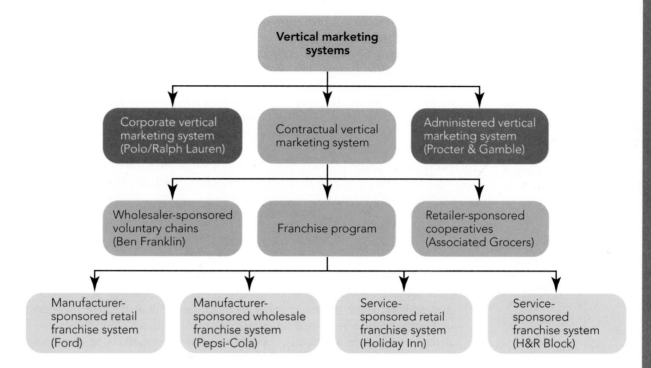

Vertical marketing systems

- Corporate vertical marketing system (Polo/Ralph Lauren)
- Contractual vertical marketing system
  - Wholesaler-sponsored voluntary chains (Ben Franklin)
  - Franchise program
    - Manufacturer-sponsored retail franchise system (Ford)
    - Manufacturer-sponsored wholesale franchise system (Pepsi-Cola)
    - Service-sponsored retail franchise system (Holiday Inn)
    - Service-sponsored franchise system (H&R Block)
  - Retailer-sponsored cooperatives (Associated Grocers)
- Administered vertical marketing system (Procter & Gamble)

FIGURE 13–6

There are three major types of vertical marketing systems—corporate, contractual, and administered. Contractual systems are the most popular for reasons described in the text.

manufactures clothing and also owns apparel shops. Other examples of forward integration include Goodyear, Apple, and Sherwin-Williams. Alternatively, a retailer might own a manufacturing operation, a practice called *backward integration*. For example, Kroger supermarkets operate manufacturing facilities that produce everything from aspirin to cottage cheese for sale under the Kroger label. Tiffany & Co., the exclusive jewelry retailer, manufactures about half of the fine jewelry items for sale through its 150 stores and boutiques worldwide.

Companies seeking to reduce distribution costs and gain greater control over supply sources or resale of their products pursue forward and backward integration. However, both types of integration increase a company's capital investment and fixed costs. For this reason, many companies favor contractual vertical marketing systems to achieve channel efficiencies and marketing effectiveness.

Contractual Systems Under a *contractual vertical marketing system*, independent production and distribution firms integrate their efforts on a contractual basis to obtain greater functional economies and marketing impact than they could achieve alone. Contractual systems are the most popular among the three types of vertical marketing systems.

Three variations of contractual systems exist. *Wholesaler-sponsored voluntary chains* involve a wholesaler that develops a contractual relationship with small, independent retailers to standardize and coordinate buying practices, merchandising programs, and inventory management efforts. With the organization of a large number of independent retailers, economies of scale and volume discounts can be achieved to compete with chain stores. IGA and Ben Franklin variety and craft stores represent wholesaler-sponsored voluntary chains. *Retailer-sponsored cooperatives* exist when small, independent retailers form an organization that operates a wholesale facility cooperatively. Member retailers then concentrate their buying power through the wholesaler and plan collaborative promotional and pricing activities. Examples of retailer-sponsored cooperatives include Associated Grocers and Ace Hardware.

The most visible variation of contractual systems is franchising. *Franchising* is a contractual arrangement between a parent company (a franchisor) and an individual or firm (a franchisee) that allows the franchisee to operate a certain type of business under an established name and according to specific rules.

Four types of franchise arrangements are most popular. *Manufacturer-sponsored retail franchise systems* are prominent in the automobile industry, where a manufacturer such as Ford licenses dealers to sell its cars subject to various sales and service conditions. *Manufacturer-sponsored wholesale franchise systems* exist in the soft-drink industry, where Pepsi-Cola licenses wholesalers (bottlers) that purchase concentrate from Pepsi-Cola and then carbonate, bottle, promote, and distribute its products to retailers and restaurants. *Service-sponsored retail franchise systems* are provided by firms that have designed a unique approach for performing a service and wish to profit by selling the franchise to others. Holiday Inn, Avis, and McDonald's represent this type of franchising approach. *Service-sponsored franchise systems* exist when franchisors license individuals or firms to dispense a service under a trade name and specific guidelines. Examples include Snelling and Snelling, Inc., employment services and H&R Block tax services.

Administered Systems In comparison, *administered vertical marketing systems* achieve coordination at successive stages of production and distribution by the size and influence of one channel member rather than through ownership. Procter & Gamble, given its broad product assortment ranging from disposable diapers to detergents, is able to obtain cooperation from supermarkets in displaying, promoting, and pricing its products. Walmart can obtain cooperation from manufacturers in terms of product specifications, price levels, and promotional support, given its position as the world's largest retailer.

---

learning review

3. What is the difference between a direct and an indirect channel?

4. Why are channels for business products typically shorter than channels for consumer products?

5. What is the principal distinction between a corporate vertical marketing system and an administered vertical marketing system?

MARKETING CHANNEL CHOICE AND MANAGEMENT

LO3

Marketing channels not only link a producer to its buyers but also provide the means through which a firm implements various elements of its marketing strategy. Therefore, choosing a marketing channel is a critical decision.

Factors Affecting Channel Choice and Management

Marketing executives consider three questions when choosing a marketing channel and intermediaries:

1. Which channel and intermediaries will provide the best coverage of the target market?
2. Which channel and intermediaries will best satisfy the buying requirements of the target market?
3. Which channel and intermediaries will be the most profitable?

Target Market Coverage Achieving the best coverage of the target market requires attention to the *density*—that is, the number of stores in a geographical area—and type of intermediaries to be used at the retail level of distribution. Three degrees of distribution density exist: intensive, exclusive, and selective.

Intensive distribution means that a firm tries to place its products and services in as many outlets as possible. Intensive distribution is usually chosen for convenience products or services such as candy, fast food, newspapers, and soft drinks. For example, Coca-Cola's retail distribution objective is to place its products "within an arm's reach of desire." Cash, yes cash, is distributed intensively by Visa. It operates over 1.4 million automatic teller machines in more than 200 countries.

Exclusive distribution is the extreme opposite of intensive distribution because only one retailer in a specified geographical area carries the firm's products. Exclusive distribution is typically chosen for specialty products or services, such as some women's fragrances and men's and women's apparel and accessories. Gucci, one of the world's leading luxury products companies, uses exclusive distribution in the marketing of its Yves Saint Laurent, Sergio Rossi, Boucheron, Opium, and Gucci brands.

Selective distribution lies between these two extremes and means that a firm selects a few retailers in a specific geographical area to carry its products. Selective distribution weds some of the market coverage benefits of intensive distribution to the control over resale evident with exclusive distribution. For example, Dell, Inc., chose selective distribution when it decided to sell its products through U.S. retailers along with its direct channel.[7] According to Michael Dell, the company's CEO, "There were plenty of retailers who said, 'sell through us,' but we didn't want to show up everywhere." The company now sells a limited range of its products through Walmart, Best Buy, and Staples, an office-products retailer. Dell's decision was consistent with current trends. Today, selective distribution is the most common form of distribution intensity.

Buyer Requirements A second consideration in channel choice is gaining access to channels and intermediaries that satisfy at least some of the interests buyers might want fulfilled when they purchase a firm's products or services. These interests fall into four broad categories: (1) information, (2) convenience, (3) variety, and (4) pre- or postsale services. Each relates to customer experience.

Information is an important requirement when buyers have limited knowledge or desire specific data about a product or service. Properly chosen intermediaries communicate with buyers through in-store displays, demonstrations, and personal selling. Consumer electronics manufacturers such as Apple have opened their own retail outlets staffed with highly trained personnel to communicate how their products can better satisfy each customer's needs.

Convenience has multiple meanings for buyers, such as proximity or driving time to a retail outlet. For example, 7-Eleven stores, with more than 36,000 outlets worldwide, many of which are open 24 hours a day, satisfy this interest for buyers. Candy and snack-food firms benefit by gaining display space in these stores. For other consumers, convenience means a minimum of time and hassle. Jiffy Lube, which promises to change engine oil and filters quickly, appeals to this aspect of convenience. For those who shop on the Internet, convenience means that Web sites must be easy to locate and navigate, and image downloads must be fast. A commonly held view among Web site developers is the "eight second rule": Consumers will abandon their efforts to enter or navigate a Web site if download time exceeds eight seconds.[8]

Variety reflects buyers' interest in having numerous competing and complementary items from which to choose. Variety is evident in the breadth and depth of products and brands carried by intermediaries, which enhances their attraction to buyers. Thus, manufacturers of pet food and supplies seek distribution through pet superstores such as PETCO and PetSmart, which offer a wide array of pet products.

Do you remember which buying requirements are satisfied by Jiffy Lube and PETCO?

Pre- or postsale services provided by intermediaries are an important buying requirement for products such as large household appliances that require delivery, installation, and credit. Therefore, Whirlpool seeks dealers that provide such services.

Steven Jobs's decision to distribute Apple products through company-owned stores was motivated by the failure of retailers to deliver on these four consumer interests for Apple. The success of Apple stores speaks for itself.

Profitability The third consideration in choosing a channel is profitability, which is determined by the margins earned (revenue minus cost) for each channel member and for the channel as a whole. Channel cost is the critical dimension of profitability. These costs include distribution, advertising, and selling expenses associated with different types of marketing channels. The extent to which channel members share these costs determines the margins received by each member and by the channel as a whole.

Companies routinely monitor the performance of their marketing channels. Read the Using Marketing Dashboards box to see how Charlesburg Furniture views the sales and profit performance of its marketing channels.

Managing Channel Relationships: Conflict and Cooperation

Unfortunately, because channels consist of independent individuals and firms, there is always the potential for disagreements concerning who performs which channel functions, how profits are allocated, which products and services will be provided by whom, and who makes critical channel-related decisions. These channel conflicts necessitate measures for dealing with them.

Sources of Conflict in Marketing Channels **Channel conflict** arises when one channel member believes another channel member is engaged in behavior that prevents it from achieving its goals. Two types of conflict occur in marketing channels: vertical conflict and horizontal conflict.

Vertical conflict occurs between different levels in a marketing channel—for example, between a manufacturer and a wholesaler or retailer or between a wholesaler and a retailer. Three sources of vertical conflict are most common.[9] First, conflict arises when a channel member bypasses another member and sells or buys products direct, a practice called **disintermediation**. This conflict emerged when Jenn-Air, a producer of kitchen appliances, decided to terminate its distributors and sell directly

channel conflict
Arises when one channel member believes another channel member is engaged in behavior that prevents it from achieving its goals.

disintermediation
A channel conflict that arises when a channel member bypasses another member and sells or buys products direct.

Using Marketing Dashboards
Channel Sales and Profit at Charlesburg Furniture

Charlesburg Furniture is one of 1,000 wood furniture manufacturers in the United States. The company sells its furniture through furniture store chains, independent furniture stores, and department store chains, mostly in the southern United States. The company has traditionally allocated its marketing funds for cooperative advertising, in-store displays, and retail sales support on the basis of dollar sales by channel.

Your Challenge As the vice president of sales & marketing at Charlesburg Furniture, you have been asked to review the company's sales and profit in its three channels and recommend a course of action. The question: Should Charlesburg Furniture continue to allocate its marketing funds on the basis of channel dollar sales or profit?

Your Findings Charlesburg Furniture tracks the sales and profit from each channel (and individual customer) and the three-year trend of sales by channel on its marketing dashboard. This information is displayed in the marketing dashboard below.

Several findings stand out. Furniture store chains and independent furniture stores account for 85.2 percent of Charlesburg Furniture sales and 93 percent of company profit. These two channels also evidence growth as measured by annual percentage change in sales. By comparison, department store chains annual percentage sales growth has declined and recorded negative growth in 2009. This channel accounts for 14.8 percent of company sales and 7 percent of company profit.

Your Action Charlesburg Furniture should consider abandoning the practice of allocating marketing funds solely on the basis of channel sales volume. The importance of independent furniture stores to Charlesburg's profitability warrants further spending, particularly given this channel's favorable sales trend. Doubling the percentage allocation for marketing funds for this channel may be too extreme, however. Rather, an objective-task promotional budgeting method should be adopted (see Chapter 18). Charlesburg Furniture might also consider the longer term role of department store chains as a marketing channel.

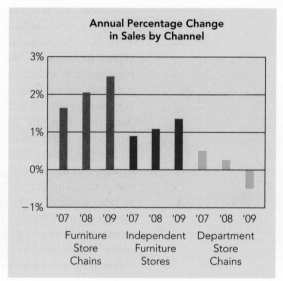

to retailers. Second, conflict occurs due to disagreements over how profit margins are distributed among channel members. This happened when the world's biggest music company, Universal Music Group, adopted a pricing policy for CDs that squeezed the profit margins for specialty music retailers. A third conflict situation arises when manufacturers believe wholesalers or retailers are not giving their products adequate attention. For example, Nike stopped shipping popular sneakers such as Nike Shox NZ to Foot Locker in retaliation for the retailer's decision to give more shelf space to shoes costing under $120.

Channel conflict is sometimes visible to consumers. Read the text to learn what antagonized independent Goodyear tire dealers.

Horizontal conflict occurs between intermediaries at the same level in a marketing channel, such as between two or more retailers (Target and Kmart) or two or more wholesalers that handle the same manufacturer's brands. Two sources of horizontal conflict are common.[10] First, horizontal conflict arises when a manufacturer increases its distribution coverage in a geographical area. For example, a franchised Buick dealer in Chicago might complain to General Motors that another franchised Buick dealer has located too close to its dealership. Second, dual distribution causes conflict when different types of retailers carry the same brands. For instance, independent Goodyear tire dealers became irate when Goodyear Tire Company decided to sell its brands through Sears, Walmart, and Sam's Clubs. Many switched to competing tire makers.

Securing Cooperation in Marketing Channels Conflict can have destructive effects on the workings of a marketing channel so it is necessary to secure cooperation among channel members. One means is through a *channel captain,* a channel member that coordinates, directs, and supports other channel members. Channel captains can be producers, wholesalers, or retailers. P&G assumes this role because it has a strong consumer following in brands such as Crest, Tide, and Pampers. Therefore, it can set policies or terms that supermarkets will follow. McKesson, a pharmaceutical drug wholesaler, is a channel captain because it coordinates and supports the product flow from numerous small drug manufacturers to drugstores and hospitals nationwide. Walmart is a retail channel captain because of its strong consumer image, number of outlets, and purchasing volume.

A firm becomes a channel captain because it is the channel member with the ability to influence the behavior of other members. Influence can take four forms. First, economic influence arises from the ability of a firm to reward other members given its strong financial position or customer franchise. Microsoft Corporation and Walmart have such influence. Expertise is a second source of influence. For example, American Hospital Supply helps its customers (hospitals) manage inventory and streamline order processing for hundreds of medical supplies. Third, identification with a particular channel member can create influence for that channel member. For instance, retailers may compete to carry the Ralph Lauren line, or clothing manufacturers may compete to be carried by Neiman Marcus, Nordstrom, or Bloomingdale's. In both instances, the desire to be identified with a channel member gives that firm influence over others. Finally, influence can arise from the legitimate right of one channel member to direct the behavior of other members. This situation would occur under contractual vertical marketing systems where a franchisor can legitimately direct how a franchisee behaves.

learning review

6. What are the three questions marketing executives consider when choosing a marketing channel and intermediaries?

7. What are the three degrees of distribution density?

LOGISTICS AND SUPPLY CHAIN MANAGEMENT

LO4

logistics
Those activities that focus on getting the right amount of the right products to the right place at the right time at the lowest possible cost.

A marketing channel relies on logistics to make products available to consumers and industrial users. **Logistics** involves those activities that focus on getting the right amount of the right products to the right place at the right time at the lowest possible cost. The performance of these activities is *logistics management,* the practice of organizing the cost-effective flow of raw materials, in-process inventory, finished goods, and related information from point of origin to point of consumption to satisfy *customer requirements.*

Three elements of this definition deserve emphasis. First, logistics deals with decisions needed to move a product from the source of raw materials to consumption—that is, the *flow* of the product. Second, those decisions have to be *cost effective.* Third, while it is important to drive down logistics costs, there is a limit: A firm needs to drive down logistics costs as long as it can deliver expected *customer service,* which means satisfying customer requirements. The role of management is to see that customer needs are satisfied in the most cost-effective manner. When properly done, the results can be spectacular. Consider Procter & Gamble. Beginning in the 1990s, the company set out to meet consumer needs more effectively by collaborating and partnering with its suppliers and retailers to ensure that the right products reached store shelves at the right time and at a lower cost. The effort was judged a success when, during an 18-month period, P&G's retail customers posted a $65 million savings in logistics costs and customer service increased.[11]

The Procter & Gamble experience is not an isolated incident. Companies now recognize that getting the right items needed for consumption or production to the right place at the right time in the right condition at the right cost is often beyond their individual capabilities and control. Instead, collaboration, coordination, and information sharing among manufacturers, suppliers, and distributors are necessary to create a seamless flow of goods and services to customers. This perspective is represented in the concept of a supply chain and the practice of supply chain management.

Supply Chains versus Marketing Channels

supply chain
The various firms involved in performing the activities required to create and deliver a product or service to consumers or industrial users.

A **supply chain** refers to the various firms involved in performing the activities required to create and deliver a product or service to consumers or industrial users. It differs from a marketing channel in terms of the firms involved. A supply chain includes suppliers that provide raw material inputs to a manufacturer as well as the wholesalers and retailers that deliver finished products to consumers. The management process is also different. *Supply chain management* is the integration and organization of information and logistics activities *across firms* in a supply chain for the purpose of creating and delivering products and services that provide value to consumers. The relation among marketing channels, logistics management, and supply chain management is shown in Figure 13–7 on the next page. An important feature of supply chain management is its application of sophisticated information technology that allows companies to share and operate systems for order processing, transportation scheduling, and inventory and facility management.

Sourcing, Assembling, and Delivering a New Car: The Automotive Supply Chain

All companies are members of one or more supply chains. A supply chain is essentially a series of linked suppliers and customers in which every customer is, in turn, a supplier to another customer until a finished product reaches the ultimate consumer. Even the simplified supply chain diagram for carmakers shown in Figure 13–8 on the next page illustrates how complex a supply chain can be.[12] A carmaker's supplier network includes

FIGURE 13–7

Relating logistics
management and supply
chain management to
supplier networks and
marketing channels.

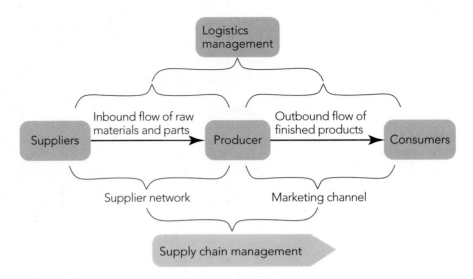

thousands of firms that provide the 5,000 or so parts in a typical automobile. They provide items ranging from raw materials, such as steel and rubber, to components, including transmissions, tires, brakes, and seats, to complex subassemblies and assemblies such as in chassis and suspension systems that make for a smooth, stable ride. Coordinating and scheduling material and component flows for their assembly into actual automobiles by carmakers are heavily dependent on logistical activities, including transportation, order processing, inventory control, materials handling, and information technology. A central link is the carmaker supply chain manager, who is responsible for translating customer requirements into actual orders and arranging for delivery dates and financial arrangements for automobile dealers.

Logistical aspects of the automobile marketing channel are also an important part of the supply chain. Major responsibilities include transportation (which involves the selection and oversight of external carriers—trucking, airline, railroad, and shipping companies—for cars and parts to dealers), the operation of distribution centers, the management of finished goods inventories, and order processing for sales. Supply chain managers also play an important role in the marketing channel. They work with car dealer networks to ensure that the right mix of automobiles is delivered to each location. In addition, they make sure that spare and service parts are available so that dealers can meet the car maintenance and repair needs of consumers. All of this is done with the help of information technology that links the entire automotive supply chain. What does all of this cost? It is estimated that logistics costs represent 25 to 30 percent of the retail price of a typical new car.

Supply Chain Management and Marketing Strategy

The automotive supply chain illustration shows how information and logistics activities are integrated and organized across firms to create and deliver a car for you.

FIGURE 13–8

The automotive supply chain includes thousands of firms that provide the 5,000 or so electronic components and parts in a typical car.

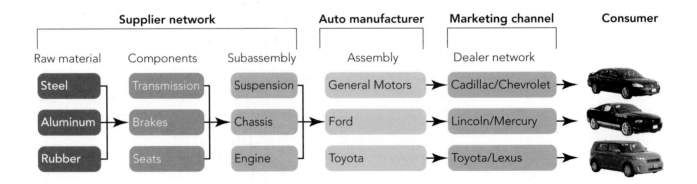

What's missing from this illustration is the linkage between a specific company's supply chain and its marketing strategy. Just as companies have different marketing strategies, they also design and manage supply chains differently. The goals to be achieved by a firm's marketing strategy determine whether its supply chain needs to be more responsive or efficient in meeting customer requirements.

Aligning a Supply Chain with Marketing Strategy   There are a variety of supply chain configurations, each of which is designated to perform different tasks well. Marketers today recognize that the choice of a supply chain follows from a clearly defined marketing strategy and involves three steps:[13]

1. *Understand the customer.* To understand the customer, a company must identify the needs of the customer segment being served. These needs, such as a desire for a low price or convenience of purchase, help a company define the relative importance of efficiency and responsiveness in meeting customer requirements.
2. *Understand the supply chain.* Second, a company must understand what a supply chain is designed to do well. Supply chains range from those that emphasize being responsive to customer requirements and demand to those that emphasize efficiency with a goal of supplying products at the lowest possible delivered cost.
3. *Harmonize the supply chain with the marketing strategy.* Finally, a company needs to ensure that what the supply chain is capable of doing well is consistent with the targeted customer's needs and its marketing strategy. If a mismatch exists between what the supply chain does particularly well and a company's marketing strategy, the company will either need to redesign the supply chain to support the marketing strategy or change the marketing strategy. Read the Marketing Matters box to learn how IBM overhauled its complete supply chain to support its marketing strategy.[14]

How are these steps applied and how are efficiency and responsive considerations built into a supply chain? Let's look at how two well-known companies—Dell and Walmart—have harmonized their supply chain and marketing strategy.[15]

Dell: A Responsive Supply Chain The Dell marketing strategy primarily targets customers who desire having the most up-to-date computer systems customized to their needs. These customers are also willing to (1) wait to have their customized computer system delivered in a few days, rather than picking out a model at a retail store, and (2) pay a reasonable, though not the lowest, price in the marketplace. Given Dell's customer segment, the company has the option of adopting an efficient or responsive supply chain.

An efficient supply chain may use inexpensive, but slower, modes of transportation, emphasize economies of scale in its production process by reducing the variety of system configurations offered, and limit its assembly and inventory storage facilities to a single location, say Austin, Texas, where the company is headquartered. If Dell opted only for efficiency in its supply chain, it would be difficult to satisfy its target customers' desire for rapid delivery and a wide variety of customizable products. Dell instead opted for a responsive supply chain. It relies on more expensive express transportation for receipt of components from suppliers and delivery of finished products to customers. The company achieves product variety and manufacturing efficiency by designing common platforms across several products and using common components. Also, Dell has invested heavily in information technology to link itself with suppliers and customers.

Walmart: An Efficient Supply Chain Now let's consider Walmart. Walmart's marketing strategy is to be a reliable, lower-price retailer for a wide variety of mass consumption consumer goods. This strategy favors an efficient supply chain designed to deliver products to consumers at the lowest possible cost. Efficiency is achieved in a variety of ways. For instance, Walmart keeps relatively low inventory levels, and most is stocked in stores available for sale, not in warehouses gathering dust. The low inventory arises from Walmart's use of *cross-docking*—a practice that involves unloading products from suppliers, sorting products for individual stores, and quickly reloading products onto its trucks for a particular store. No warehousing

or storing of products occurs, except for a few hours or, at most, a day. Cross-docking allows Walmart to operate only a small number of distribution centers to service its vast network of Walmart stores, Supercenters, Neighborhood Markets, Marketside stores, and Sam's Clubs, which contributes to efficiency. On the other hand, the company runs its own fleet of trucks to service its stores. This does increase cost and investment, but the benefits in terms of responsiveness justify the cost in Walmart's case.

Walmart has invested much more than its competitors in information technology to operate its supply chain. The company feeds information about customer requirements and demand from its stores back to its suppliers, which manufacture only what is being demanded. This large investment has improved the efficiency of Walmart's supply chain and made it responsive to customer needs.

Three lessons can be learned from these two examples. First, there is no one best supply chain for every company. Second, the best supply chain is the one that is consistent with the needs of the customer segment being served and complements a company's marketing strategy. And finally, supply chain managers are often called upon to make trade-offs between efficiency and responsiveness on various elements of a company's supply chain.

TWO CONCEPTS OF LOGISTICS MANAGEMENT IN A SUPPLY CHAIN

The objective of logistics management in a supply chain is to minimize total logistics costs while delivering the appropriate level of customer service.

Total Logistics Cost Concept

total logistics cost
Expenses associated with transportation, materials handling and warehousing, inventory, stockouts, order processing, and return products handling.

For our purposes **total logistics cost** includes expenses associated with transportation, materials handling and warehousing, inventory, stockouts (being out of inventory), order processing, and return products handling. Note that many of these costs are interrelated so that changes in one will impact the others. For example, if a firm attempts to reduce its transportation costs by shipping in larger quantities, it will increase its inventory levels. While larger inventory levels will increase inventory costs, they should also reduce stockouts. It is important, therefore, to study the impact on all of the logistics decision areas when considering a change.

Customer Service Concept

customer service
The ability of logistics management to satisfy users in terms of time, dependability, communication, and convenience.

Because a supply chain is a *flow,* the end of it—or *output*—is the service delivered to customers. Within the context of a supply chain, **customer service** is the ability of logistics management to satisfy users in terms of time, dependability, communication, and convenience. As suggested by Figure 13–9, a supply chain manager's key task is to balance these four customer service factors against total logistics cost factors.[16]

Time In a supply chain setting, time refers to *order cycle* or *replenishment* time for an item, which means the time between the ordering of an item and when it is received and ready for use or sale. The various elements that make up the typical order cycle include recognition of the need to order, order transmittal, order processing, documentation, and transportation. A current emphasis in supply chain management is to reduce order cycle time so that the inventory levels of customers may be minimized. Another emphasis is to make the process of reordering and receiving products as simple as possible, often through inventory systems called *quick response* and *efficient consumer response* delivery systems. For example, at Saks Fifth Avenue, point-of-sale scanner technology records each day's sales. When stock falls below a minimum level, a replenishment order is automatically produced. Vendors such as Donna Karan (DKNY) receive the order, which is processed and delivered within 48 hours.[17]

Dependability Dependability is the consistency of replenishment. This is important to all firms in a supply chain—and to consumers. How often do you return to a store if it fails to have in stock the item you want to purchase? Dependability can be broken into three elements: consistent lead time, safe delivery, and complete delivery. Consistent service allows planning (such as appropriate inventory levels), whereas inconsistencies create surprises. Intermediaries may be willing to accept longer lead times if they know about them in advance and can thus make plans.

FIGURE 13–9
Supply chain managers balance total logistics cost factors against customer service factors.

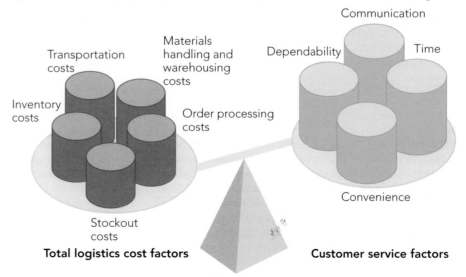

Communication Communication is a two-way link between buyer and seller that helps in monitoring service and anticipating future needs. Status reports on orders are a typical example of communication between buyer and seller.

Convenience The concept of convenience for a supply chain manager means that there should be a minimum of effort on the part of the buyer in doing business with the seller. Is it easy for the customer to order? Are the products available from many outlets? Will the seller arrange all necessary details, such as transportation? This customer service factor has promoted the use of **vendor-managed inventory** (VMI), whereby the *supplier* determines the product amount and assortment a customer (such as a retailer) needs and automatically delivers the appropriate items.

Campbell Soup's system illustrates how VMI works.[18] Every morning, retailers electronically inform the company of their demand for all Campbell products and the inventory levels in their distribution centers. Campbell uses that information to forecast future demand and determine which products need replenishment based on upper and lower inventory limits established with each retailer. Trucks leave the Campbell shipping plant that afternoon and arrive at the retailer's distribution centers with the required replenishments the same day.

vendor-managed inventory

An inventory management system whereby the supplier determines the product amount and assortment a customer (such as a retailer) needs and automatically delivers the appropriate items.

learning review

8. What is the principal difference between a marketing channel and a supply chain?

9. The choice of a supply chain involves what three steps?

10. A manager's key task is to balance which four customer service factors against which five logistics cost factors?

LEARNING OBJECTIVES REVIEW

LO1 *Explain what is meant by a marketing channel of distribution and why intermediaries are needed.*
A marketing channel of distribution, or simply a marketing channel, consists of individuals and firms involved in the process of making a product or service available for use or consumption by consumers or industrial users. Intermediaries make possible the flow of products from producers to buyers by performing three basic functions. The transactional function involves buying, selling, and risk taking because intermediaries stock merchandise in anticipation of sales. The logistical function involves the gathering, storing, and dispensing of products. The facilitating function assists producers in making products and services more attractive to buyers. The performance of these functions by intermediaries creates time, place, form, and possession utility for consumers.

LO2 *Distinguish among traditional marketing channels, electronic marketing channels, and different types of vertical marketing systems.*
Traditional marketing channels describe the route taken by products and services from producers to buyers. This route can range from a direct channel with no intermediaries, because a producer and ultimate consumers deal directly with each other, to indirect channels where intermediaries (agents, wholesalers, distributors, or retailers) are inserted between a producer and consumer and perform numerous channel functions. Electronic market-

ing channels employ the Internet to make products and services available for consumption or use by consumer or business buyers. Vertical marketing systems are professionally managed and centrally coordinated marketing channels designed to achieve channel economies and maximum marketing impact. There are three major types of vertical marketing systems (VMSs). A corporate VMS combines successive stages of production and distribution under a single ownership. A contractual VMS exists when independent production and distribution firms integrate their efforts on a contractual basis to obtain greater functional economies and marketing impact than they could achieve alone. An administered VMS achieves coordination at successive stages of production and distribution by the size and influence of one channel member rather than through ownership.

LO3 *Describe factors that marketing executives consider when selecting and managing a marketing channel.*
Marketing executives consider three questions when selecting and managing a marketing channel and intermediaries. (1) Which channel and intermediaries will provide the best coverage of the target market? Marketers typically choose one of three levels of market coverage: intensive, selective, or exclusive distribution. (2) Which channel and intermediaries will best satisfy the buying requirements of the target market? These buying requirements fall into four categories: information, convenience, variety, and attendant services. (3) Which channel and

intermediaries will be the most profitable? Here marketers look at the margins earned (revenues minus cost) for each channel member and for the channel as a whole.

LO4 *Explain what supply chain and logistics management are and how they relate to marketing strategy.*
A supply chain refers to the various firms involved in performing the various activities required to create and deliver a product or service to consumers or industrial users. Supply chain management is the integration and organization of information and logistics across firms for the purpose of creating value for consumers. Logistics involves those activities that focus on getting the right amount of the right products to the right place at the right time at the lowest possible cost. Logistics management includes the coordination of the flows of both inbound and outbound prod-

ucts, an emphasis on making these flows cost effective, and customer service. A company's supply chain follows from a clearly defined marketing strategy. The alignment of a company's supply chain with its marketing strategy involves three steps. First, a supply chain must reflect the needs of the customer segment being served. Second, a company must understand what a supply chain is designed to do well. Supply chains range from those that emphasize being responsive to customer requirements and demands to those that emphasize efficiency with the goal of supplying products at the lowest possible delivered cost. Finally, a supply chain must be consistent with the targeted customer's needs and the company's marketing strategy. The Dell and Walmart examples in the chapter illustrate how this alignment is achieved by two market leaders.

FOCUSING ON KEY TERMS

channel conflict p. 298
customer service p. 305
disintermediation p. 298
dual distribution p. 293
exclusive distribution p. 297

intensive distribution p. 297
logistics p. 301
marketing channel p. 288
multichannel marketing p. 293
selective distribution p. 297

supply chain p. 301
total logistics cost p. 305
vendor-managed inventory p. 306
vertical marketing systems p. 294

APPLYING MARKETING KNOWLEDGE

1 A distributor for Celanese Chemical Company stores large quantities of chemicals, blends these chemicals to satisfy the requests of customers, and delivers the blends to a customer's warehouse within 24 hours of receiving an order. What utilities does this distributor provide?

2 Suppose the president of a carpet manufacturing firm has asked you to look into the possibility of bypassing the firm's wholesalers (who sell to carpet, department, and furniture stores) and selling direct to these stores. What caution would you voice on this matter, and what type of information would you gather before making this decision?

3 What type of channel conflict is likely to be caused by dual distribution, and what type of conflict can be reduced by direct distribution? Why?

4 How does the channel captain idea differ among corporate, administered, and contractual vertical marketing systems with particular reference to the use of the different forms of influence available to firms?

5 List the customer service factors that would be vital to buyers in the following types of companies: (*a*) manufacturing, (*b*) retailing, (*c*) hospitals, and (*d*) construction.

building your marketing plan

Does your marketing plan involve selecting channels and intermediaries? If the answer is no, read no further and do not include this element in your plan. If the answer is yes,

1 Identify which channel and intermediaries will provide the best coverage of the target market for your product or service.

2 Specify which channel and intermediaries will best satisfy the important buying requirements of the target market.

3 Determine which channel and intermediaries will be the most profitable.

4 Select your channel(s) and intermediary(ies).

video case 13 Act II Microwave Popcorn: The Surprising Channel

"We developed the technology that launched the microwave popcorn business and helped make ACT II the number one brand in the world," says Jack McKeon, president of Golden Valley Microwave Foods, a division of ConAgra Foods, Inc. "But we were also

lucky along the way, as we backed into what has become one of the biggest distribution channels in the industry today, one that no one ever saw coming." Founded in 1978, ACT II is a global leader in producing and marketing microwave popcorn. But it hasn't always been easy.

THE LAUNCH: THE IDEA AND THE TECHNOLOGY

In the mid-1980s, only about 15 percent of U.S. households had microwave ovens, so launching a microwave foods business was risky. ACT II's initial marketing research turned up two key points of difference or benefits that people wanted in their microwave popcorn: (1) fewer unpopped kernels and (2) good popping results in all types of microwave ovens, even low-powered ovens—the kind that many households with microwaves had at the time. ACT II's research and development (R&D) staff successfully addressed these wants by developing a microwave popcorn bag utilizing a thin strip of material laminated between layers of paper, which focused the microwave energy to produce high-quality popped corn, regardless of an oven's power. This breakthrough significantly increased the size of the microwave popcorn market (and is still used in all microwave popcorn bags today). Using its revolutionary package, ACT II was introduced in 1984.

THE LUCKY DAY: BOTH CAPITAL AND MASS MERCHANDISERS

From 1978 until it became public in September 1986, ACT II was privately owned. Like most start-ups, ACT II was severely undercapitalized due to the cost of developing and introducing the brand. As a result, ACT II needed a partner to help develop the business. Its solution was to enter into a licensing agreement to share its technology for packaging microwave popcorn with one of the largest food manufacturers in the industry. The licensing partner would sell the popcorn under its own brand name in grocery stores and supermarkets. In turn, ACT II agreed it would not distribute its ACT II brand in U.S. grocery stores or supermarkets for 10 years. This meant that ACT II had to find other channels of distribution in which to sell its microwave popcorn.

For the next 10 years, the company developed many new channels. ACT II products were sold through vending machines, video stores (Blockbuster), institutions (movie theaters, colleges, military bases), drugstores (Walgreen's, Rite-Aid, CVS/Pharmacy), warehouse club stores (e.g., Sam's Club, Costco, BJ's), and convenience stores (7-Eleven, Circle K). "But the huge opportunity we discovered and developed was the mass merchandiser channel through chains like Walmart and Target," says McKeon. "ACT II microwave popcorn was the first item of any kind to sell a million units in a week for Target, and that happened in 1987. Walmart, too, was on the front end of this market and today is the top seller of microwave popcorn in any channel, selling far more popcorn than the leading grocery chains. Mass merchandisers now account for over a third of all the microwave popcorn sold in the United States. They created the ACT II business as we know it today, and it was accomplished without a dime of conventional consumer promotions. That's one of the really unique parts of the ACT II story."

THE SITUATION TODAY

In the United States, more than 90 percent of households own microwave ovens. In addition, more than 60 percent of households are microwave popcorn consumers who

spent more than $665 million on the product category in 2008. Orville Redenbacher's popcorn, also owned by ConAgra Foods, is now the market share leader with $142 million in sales while ACT II is No. 5 with $59 million in sales. "Our marketing research shows ACT II is especially strong in young families with kids," says Frank Lynch, vice president of marketing at Golden Valley. This conjures up an image of Mom and Dad watching a movie on TV with the kids and eating ACT II popcorn, a picture close to reality. "ACT II has good market penetration in almost all age, income, urban versus rural, and ethnic segments," he continues.

"From the beginning, ACT II has been a leader in the microwave popcorn industry," says McKeon, "and we plan to continue that record." As evidence, he cites a number of ACT II "firsts":

- First mass-marketed microwave popcorn.
- First flavored microwave popcorn.
- First microwave popcorn tub.
- First fat-free microwave popcorn.
- First extra-butter microwave popcorn.
- First one-step sweetened microwave popcorn.

This list highlights a curious market segmentation phenomenon that has emerged in the last five years—the no-butter versus plenty-of-butter consumers. Originally, popcorn was seen as junk food. Later studies by nutritionists pointed out its health benefits: low calories and high fiber. This caused ACT II to introduce its low-fat popcorn to appeal to the health-conscious segment of consumers. However, when it comes to eating popcorn while watching a movie at home on TV, the more butter on their popcorn, the better. Recently, much of the growth in popcorn sales has been in the spoil-yourself-with-a lot-of-butter-on-your-popcorn segment.

Because of these diverse consumer tastes in popcorn, ACT II has developed a variety of popcorn products around its brand. Besides the low-fat and extra butter versions, these include the original flavors (natural, butter, and Kettle Corn), sweet glazed products (Caramel Corn and Buttery Cinnamon), and popcorn in tubs, mini-bags, and balls.

ACT II is positioned as unpretentious, fun, and youthful—a great product at a reasonable price. By stressing value, ACT II is responding to today's growing value consciousness of consumers seeking quality products at reasonable prices. These strategies have enabled ACT II to remain a leader in the microwave popcorn market.

OPPORTUNITIES FOR FUTURE GROWTH

For many years, the growth of the microwave popcorn industry closely followed the growth of household ownership of microwave ovens—from under 20 percent to more than 90 percent. But now, with a microwave oven in virtually every U.S. home, ACT II is trying to identify new market segments, new products, and innovative ways to appeal to all the major marketing channels.

In the United States, ACT II's strategy must include finding creative ways to continue to work with existing channels where it has special strength, such as the mass merchandiser channel. It also needs to further develop opportunities in the grocery store and supermarket channel. Now that the 10-year restriction on sales in grocery stores and supermarkets has expired, distribution through wholesalers that reach grocery stores and supermarkets is possible.

Global markets also present opportunities. ACT II has followed the penetration of microwave ovens in countries around the world and used brokers to help gain distribution in those markets. However, foreign markets represent foreign tastes, something that does not always lend itself to standardized products. United Kingdom consumers, for example, think of popcorn as a candy or child's food rather than the salty snack it is in the United States. Even in DisneylandParis, France, American-style popcorn is absent, as French consumers sprinkle sugar on their popcorn. On the other hand, Swedes like theirs very buttery while many Mexicans like jalapeno-flavored popcorn.

Questions

1 Visit ACT II's Web site at www.ACTII.com and examine the assortment of products offered today. How are the assortment and packaging of ACT II products related to the firm's channels of distribution or the segments they serve?
2 Use Figure 13–3 to create a description of the channels of distribution used for ACT II popcorn today.
3 Compared to selling through the nongrocery channels, what kind of product, price, and promotion strategies might ConAgra Foods use to reach the grocery channel more effectively?
4 What special marketing issues does ConAgra Foods face as it pursues growth in global markets?

GLOBAL
globalcomputer.com
CYBER MONDAY
MADNESS
1 DAY
CLICK HERE
SALE!
Search over 100,000 Products in Stock...
Deal Alerts via RSS
We are open 24 hours a day, 7 days a week. Call us at 888-845-6225
WHEN CALLING USE PRIORITY CODE: GLOEM609

14

Retailing and Wholesaling

LEARNING OBJECTIVES

After reading this chapter you should be able to:

(LO1) Identify retailers in terms of the utilities they provide.

(LO2) Explain the alternative ways to classify retail outlets.

(LO3) Describe the many methods of nonstore retailing.

(LO4) Specify the retailing mix actions used to implement a retailing strategy.

(LO5) Explain changes in retailing with the wheel of retailing and the retail life cycle concepts.

(LO6) Describe the types of firms that perform wholesaling activities and their functions.

84 MILLION CONSUMERS WERE SHOPPING ONLINE ON CYBER MONDAY. WERE YOU ONE OF THEM?

Two of the biggest days of the retailing year are the Friday after Thanksgiving—Black Friday—and the Monday after Thanksgiving—Cyber Monday. The days are so popular for shoppers that retailers report more than $20 billion in sales on Black Friday and almost $1 billion in sales on Cyber Monday. The names have interesting histories. Black Friday was an accounting term used to suggest when retailers finally became profitable, and Cyber Monday was the result of consumers shopping from their broadband connections at work on their first day back after the holiday. The number of Cyber Monday shoppers has been growing dramatically. Are you one of them?

Several factors account for the growth in Cyber Monday shopping and online shopping in general. First, the number of fast Internet connections in homes and businesses has grown to about 100 million. Second, large retailers such as Amazon, Home Depot, and Walmart have given online shopping a lot of visibility. Many retailers now move their Friday in-store sales and promotions to their Web sites on Monday to attract the shoppers who didn't want to park, stand in line, or deal with crowds in the stores.

While retailers may encourage online shopping with promotions as simple as e-mail notifications, cyber shopping is also the result of many new, interesting, and exciting online approaches. OfficeMax, for example, drives traffic to its Web site with an online application called "Elf Yourself" that allows visitors to e-mail an animated elf to friends. New Web sites such as Mpire.com track the price of products like TVs, clothing, and books to let consumers know if prices are increasing or decreasing. Like.com provides a visual search engine that finds products that are similar in appearance—just draw a box around the product or part of the product that you like and the site shows other products that are similar! For many consumers, buying new products leads to selling old products, and sites such as gazelle.com now calculate the value of used products, offer users a price for the product, and even send a box in which to mail it. There is even an official Cyber Monday Web site where more than 500 retailers have special online offers![1]

Cyber Monday and online shopping are just a few examples of the many exciting changes occurring in retailing today. This chapter examines the critical role of retailing in the marketplace and the challenging decisions retailers face as they strive to create value for customers.

What types of products will consumers buy through catalogs, television, the Internet, or by telephone? In what type of store will consumers look for products they don't buy directly? How important is the location of the store? Will customers expect services such as alterations, delivery, installation, or repair? What price should be charged for each product? These are difficult and important questions that are an integral part of retailing. In the channel of distribution, retailing is where the customer meets the product. It is through retailing that exchange (a central aspect of marketing) occurs. **Retailing** includes all activities involved in selling, renting, and providing products and services to ultimate consumers for personal, family, or household use.

THE VALUE OF RETAILING

Retailing is an important marketing activity. Not only do producers and consumers meet through retailing actions, but retailing also creates customer value and has a significant impact on the economy. To consumers, the value of retailing is in the form of utilities provided (Figure 14–1). Retailing's economic value is represented by the people employed in retailing as well as by the total amount of money exchanged in retail sales.

Consumer Utilities Offered by Retailing

The utilities provided by retailers create value for consumers. Time, place, form, and possession utilities are offered by most retailers in varying degrees, but one utility is often emphasized more than others. Look at Figure 14–1 to see how well you can match the retailer with the utility being emphasized in the description.

FIGURE 14–1
Which retailer best provides which utilities?

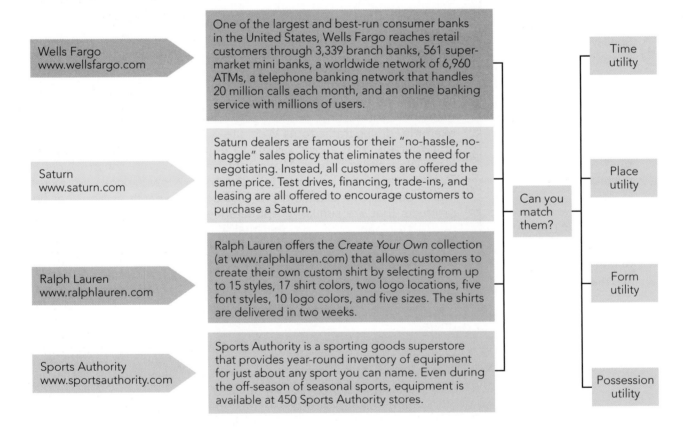

Tesco is one of the largest retailers outside the United States.

Providing mini banks in supermarkets, as Wells Fargo does, puts the bank's products and services close to the consumer, providing place utility. By providing financing or leasing and taking used cars as trade-ins, Saturn makes the purchase easier and provides possession utility. Form utility—production or alteration of a product—is offered by Ralph Lauren through its online *Create Your Own* program, which offers shirts that meet each customer's specifications. Finding the right sporting equipment during the off-season is the time utility provided by Sports Authority. Many retailers offer a combination of the four basic utilities. Some supermarkets, for example, offer convenient locations (place utility); are open 24 hours a day (time utility); customize purchases in the bakery, deli, and florist (form utility); and allow several payment and credit options (possession utility).

The Global Economic Impact of Retailing

Retailing is important to the U.S. and global economies. Four of the 30 largest businesses in the United States are retailers (Walmart, Costco, Home Depot, and Target). Walmart's $408 billion in annual sales in 2009 surpassed the gross domestic product of all but 27 countries for that same year. Walmart, Costco, Home Depot, and Target together have more than 2.8 million employees—more than the combined populations of Jacksonville, Florida; El Paso, Texas; and Stockton, California.[2] Many retailers, including food stores, automobile dealers, and general merchandise outlets, are also significant contributors to the U.S. economy.[3]

Outside the United States, large retailers include Daiei in Japan, Carrefour in France, Metro Group in Germany, and Tesco in Britain.[4] In emerging economies such as China and Mexico, a combination of local and global retailers is evolving. Walmart, for example, has more than 3,600 stores outside the United States, including stores in Brazil, China, Japan, Mexico, and the United Kingdom.[5]

learning review

1. When Ralph Lauren makes shirts to a customer's exact preferences, what utility is provided?

2. Two measures of the impact of retailing in the global economy are _____ and _____.

CLASSIFYING RETAIL OUTLETS

LO2

For manufacturers, consumers, and the economy, retailing is an important component of marketing that has several variations. Because of the large number of alternative forms of retailing, it is easier to understand the differences among retail institutions by recognizing that outlets can be classified in several ways. First, *form of ownership* distinguishes retail outlets based on whether individuals, corporate chains, or contractual systems own the outlet. Second, *level of service* is used to describe the degree of service provided to the customer. Three levels of service are provided by self-, limited-, and full-service retailers. Finally, the type of *merchandise line* describes how many different types of products a store carries and in what assortment. The alternative types of outlets are discussed in greater detail in the following pages. For many consumers today, each of the types of outlets discussed are viewed in terms of their environmentally friendly, or green, activities. The Making Responsible Decisions box on the next page gives examples of the green activities of several retailers.[6]

Environmentally Friendly Retailing Takes Off!

Sustainability has been a topic of interest for some retailers for many years. Recently, however, it has become a movement for the entire industry. What happened? A combination of factors contributed to the change: environmental consciousness among consumers has reached an all-time high, publicity related to global warming has increased, "green" has become an important element of company image and reputation, and most environmental initiatives save retailers money!

When consumers learned that food packaging creates 50 percent of all household waste, they added packaging to their purchase decision criteria. Walmart responded by requiring its suppliers to trim one square inch of packaging from its toy lines and

reduced packaging by 3,500 tons. Electronics retailer Best Buy recently began using solar energy in some of its stores with the goal of reducing CO_2 emissions by 8 percent by 2012. Mountain Equipment company is building on its green image by collecting rainwater to water grass at the store and to use in its toilets. When Home Depot switched its in-store light fixture displays to compact fluorescent light bulbs it saved $16 million per year. Other companies are using motion detectors to turn lights on and off, improving the fuel economy of delivery vehicles, and designing "zero waste" stores.

Are your favorite retailers "green"? Do sustainability efforts influence your purchase decisions?

Form of Ownership

There are three general forms of retail ownership—independent retailer, corporate chain, and contractual system.

Independent Retailer   One of the most common forms of retail ownership is the independent business owned by an individual. Independent retailers account for most of the 1.1 million retail establishments in the United States and include hardware stores, convenience stores, clothing stores, and computer and software stores. In addition, there are 29,600 jewelry stores, 21,100 florists, and 43,100 sporting goods and hobby stores. The advantage of this form of ownership for the owner is that he or she can be his or her own boss. More than 50 percent of all retail establishments have four or fewer employees.[7] For customers, the independent store can offer convenience, personal service, and lifestyle compatibility.

Corporate Chain   A second form of ownership, the corporate chain, involves multiple outlets under common ownership. Many of the department store names you may know—Bon Marche, Lazurus, Burdines, Famous Barr, Filenes, Foleys, and Marshall Field's—are now one of 810 Macy's stores nationwide. Macy's Inc. also owns 40 Bloomingdale's, which compete with other chain stores such as Saks Fifth Avenue and Neiman Marcus. In a chain operation, centralization in decision making and purchasing is common. Chain stores have advantages in dealing with manufacturers, particularly as the size of the chain grows. A large chain can bargain with a manufacturer to obtain good service or volume discounts on orders. Consumers also benefit in dealing with chains because there are multiple outlets with similar merchandise and consistent management policies.

Retailing has become a high-tech business for many large chains. Walmart, for example, has developed a sophisticated inventory management and cost control system that allows rapid price changes for each product in every store. In addition, stores such as Walmart and Target are implementing pioneering new technologies such as radio frequency identification (RFID) tags to improve the quality of information available about products.

Contractual Systems Contractual systems involve independently owned stores that band together to act like a chain. The three kinds described in Chapter 13 are retailer-sponsored cooperatives, wholesaler-sponsored voluntary chains, and franchises. One retailer-sponsored cooperative is Associated Grocers, which consists of neighborhood grocers that all agree with several other independent grocers to buy their goods directly from food manufacturers. In this way, members can take advantage of volume discounts commonly available to chains and also give the impression of being a large chain, which may be viewed more favorably by some consumers. Wholesaler-sponsored voluntary chains such as Independent Grocers' Alliance (IGA) try to achieve similar benefits.

Subway is a popular business-format franchisor.

As noted in Chapter 13, in a franchise system an individual or firm (the franchisee) contracts with a parent company (the franchisor) to set up a business or retail outlet. The franchisor usually assists in selecting the location, setting up the store or facility, advertising, and training personnel. The franchisee usually pays a one-time franchise fee and an annual royalty, usually tied to the franchise's sales. There are two general types of franchises: *business-format franchises*, such as McDonald's, Radio Shack, and Subway, and *product-distribution franchises*, such as a Ford dealership or a Coca-Cola distributor. In business-format franchising, the franchisor provides step-by-step procedures for most aspects of the business and guidelines for the most likely decisions a franchisee will face.

Franchise fees paid to the franchisor can range from $15,000 for a Subway franchise to $45,000 for a McDonald's restaurant franchise. When the fees are combined with other costs such as real estate and equipment, however, the total investment can be much higher. Franchisees also pay an ongoing royalty fee that ranges from 2 percent for a Sonic Drive In to 12.5 percent for a McDonald's. By selling franchises, an organization reduces the cost of expansion but loses some control. A good franchisor, however, will maintain strong control of the outlets in terms of delivery and presentation of merchandise and try to enhance recognition of the franchise name.[8]

Level of Service

Even though most customers perceive little variation in retail outlets by form of ownership, differences among retailers are more obvious in terms of level of service. In some department stores, such as Loehmann's, very few services are provided. Some grocery stores, such as the Cub Foods chain, encourage customers to bag the food themselves and recycle their plastic bags. Other outlets, such as Neiman Marcus, provide a wide range of customer services from gift wrapping to wardrobe consultation.

Self-Service Self-service outlets require customers to perform many functions themselves. Warehouse clubs such as Costco, for example, are usually self-service, with all nonessential customer services eliminated. Similarly, most gas stations today are self-service. New forms of self-service are being developed at airlines, hotels, and even libraries! Hilton Hotels, for example, now includes self-service kiosks in the lobby of each of its hotels. The kiosks allow guests to check in, print keys, check for messages, check out, print hotel receipts, and print airline boarding passes. The Palm Beach County library system is moving in the same direction; it is adding self-service checkout machines to each of its branches. In general, the trend is toward retailing experiences that make customers co-creators of the value they receive.[9]

Limited Service Limited-service outlets provide some services, such as credit and merchandise return, but not others, such as clothing alterations. General merchandise stores such as Walmart, Kmart, and Target are usually considered limited service outlets. Customers are responsible for most shopping activities, although salespeople are available in departments such as consumer electronics, jewelry, and lawn and garden.

Full Service Full-service retailers, which include most specialty stores and department stores, provide many services to their customers. Neiman Marcus, Nordstrom, and Saks Fifth Avenue, for example, all rely on better service to sell more distinctive, higher-margin goods and to retain their customers. Nordstrom offers a wide variety of services, including free exchanges, easy returns, credit cards through Nordstrom bank, a live help line, an online gift finder, catalogs, a four-level loyalty program called Nordstrom Fashion Rewards, and an online beauty specialist. Some Nordstrom stores also offer a "Personal Touch" department, which provides shopping assistants for consumers who need help with style, color, and size selection, and a concierge service for assistance with anything else. Nordstrom stores typically have 50 percent more salespeople on the floor than similarly sized stores, and the salespeople are renowned for their professional and personalized attention to customers. Nordstrom also offers e-mail and RSS (Really Simple Syndication) feeds to notify customers with online updates when new merchandise is available.[10]

Type of Merchandise Line

Retail outlets also vary by their merchandise lines, the key distinction being the breadth and depth of the items offered to customers (see Figure 14–2). *Depth of product line* means the store carries a large assortment of each item, such as a shoe store that offers running shoes, dress shoes, and children's shoes. *Breadth of product line* refers to the variety of different items a store carries, such as appliances and CDs.

Depth of Line Stores that carry a considerable assortment (depth) of a related line of items are limited-line stores. Sports Authority sporting goods stores carry considerable depth in sports equipment ranging from weight-lifting accessories to running shoes. Stores that carry tremendous depth in one primary line of merchandise are single-line stores. Victoria's Secret, a nationwide chain, carries great depth in women's lingerie. Both limited- and single-line stores are often referred to as *specialty outlets*.

Specialty discount outlets focus on one type of product, such as electronics (Best Buy), office supplies (Staples), or books (Barnes and Noble) at very competitive prices. These outlets are referred to in the trade as *category killers* because they often dominate the market. Best Buy, for example, is the largest consumer electronics retailer with more than 1,000 stores, and Staples is the leader in office supplies.[11]

Staples is the category killer in office supplies.

FIGURE 14–2

Stores vary in terms of the breadth and depth of their merchandise lines.

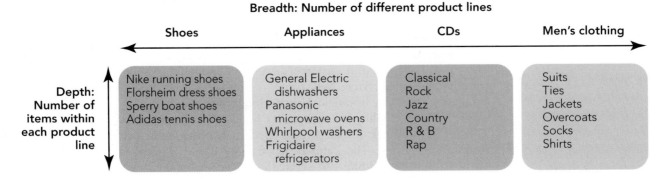

Breadth: Number of different product lines

	Shoes	Appliances	CDs	Men's clothing
Depth: Number of items within each product line	Nike running shoes Florsheim dress shoes Sperry boat shoes Adidas tennis shoes	General Electric dishwashers Panasonic microwave ovens Whirlpool washers Frigidaire refrigerators	Classical Rock Jazz Country R & B Rap	Suits Ties Jackets Overcoats Socks Shirts

Breadth of Line Stores that carry a broad product line, with limited depth, are referred to as *general merchandise stores*. For example, large department stores such as Dillard's, Macy's, and Neiman Marcus carry a wide range of different types of products but not unusual sizes. The breadth and depth of merchandise lines are important decisions for a retailer. Traditionally, outlets carried related lines of goods. Today, however, **scrambled merchandising**, offering several unrelated product lines in a single store, is common. The modern drugstore carries food, camera equipment, magazines, paper products, toys, small hardware items, and pharmaceuticals. Supermarkets rent videos, print photos, and sell flowers.

scrambled merchandising
Offering several unrelated product lines in a single retail store.

---

learning review

3. Centralized decision making and purchasing are an advantage of _____ ownership.

4. What are some examples of new forms of self-service retailers?

5. Would a shop for big men's clothes carrying pants in sizes 40 to 60 be classified as having a broad or deep product line?

NONSTORE RETAILING

LO3

Most of the retailing examples discussed earlier in the chapter, such as corporate chains, department stores, and limited- and single-line specialty stores, involve store retailing. Many retailing activities today, however, are not limited to sales in a store. Nonstore retailing occurs outside a retail outlet through activities that involve varying levels of customer and retailer involvement. The six forms of nonstore retailing are automatic vending, direct mail and catalogs, television home shopping, online retailing, telemarketing, and direct selling.

Automatic Vending

Vending machines offer many products found in convenience stores.

Nonstore retailing includes vending machines, which make it possible to serve customers when and where stores cannot. Machine maintenance, operating costs, and location leases can add to the cost of the products, so prices in vending machines tend to be higher than those in stores. About 48 percent of the products sold from vending machines are cold beverages, another 19 percent are candy and snacks, and 10 percent is food. Many new types of products are quickly becoming available in vending machines. Best Buy now uses vending machines to sell cell phone and computer accessories, digital cameras, flash drives, and other consumer electronics products in airports. Similarly, YoNaturals uses vending machines to distribute healthy and organic snacks in schools, health clubs, and hospitals in 135 U.S. cities. The 11.5 million vending machines currently in use in the United States generate more than $46 billion in annual sales.[12]

Improved technology is making vending machines easier to use by reducing the need for cash. In the United States, about 17,500 machines currently accept credit cards or PayPass cards and many more will be equipped with card readers soon. In Japan, Korea, and the Philippines, consumers use cell phones that transmit payments to vending machines via an infrared beam or a radio wave. Another improvement in vending machines is the trend toward "green" machines that consume less energy by using more efficient compressors, more efficient lighting, and better insulation. Vending machines are popular with consumers; recent consumer

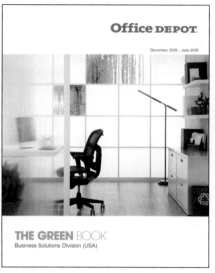

Catalogs improve efficiency through segmentation and targeting.

satisfaction research indicates that 82 percent of consumers believe purchasing from a vending machine is equal to or superior to a store purchase.[13]

Direct Mail and Catalogs

Direct-mail and catalog retailing is attractive because it eliminates the cost of a store and clerks. For example, it costs a traditional retail store $34 to acquire a new customer, whereas catalog customers are acquired for approximately $14. In addition, direct mail and catalogs improve marketing efficiency through segmentation and targeting, and they create customer value by providing a fast and convenient means of making a purchase. The average U.S. household now receives 18 direct-mail items or catalogs each week. The Direct Marketing Association estimates that direct-mail and catalog retailing creates 1.7 million jobs and $1.9 trillion in sales. Direct-mail and catalog retailing is popular outside of the United States also. Furniture retailer IKEA delivered 198 million copies of its catalog in 27 languages to 35 countries last year.[14]

Several factors have had an impact on direct-mail and catalog retailing in recent years. The influence of large retailers such as IKEA, Crate and Barrel, JCPenney, and others has been positive as their marketing activities have increased the number and variety of products consumers purchase through direct mail and catalogs. Higher paper costs and increases in postage rates, the growing interest in do-not-mail legislation, the concern for "green" mailings and catalogs, and the possibility of the U.S. Postal Service reducing delivery to five days, however, have caused direct-mail and catalog retailers to search for ways to improve their efficiency and provide additional customer value. One approach has been to focus on proven customers rather than prospective customers. Williams-Sonoma, for example, reduces mailings to zip codes that have not been profitable.[15]

Television home shopping programs serve millions of customers each year.

Television Home Shopping

Television home shopping is possible when consumers watch a shopping channel on which products are displayed; orders are then placed over the telephone or the Internet. Currently, the three largest programs are QVC, HSN, and ShopNBC. QVC ("quality, value, convenience") broadcasts live 24 hours each day, 364 days a year, and reaches 166 million cable and satellite homes in the United States, United Kingdom, Germany, Japan, and Italy. The company generates sales of $7 billion from its 50 million customers by offering more than 1,150 products each week, answering 181 million telephone calls, and shipping more than 166 million packages each year.[16]

In the past, television home shopping programs have attracted mostly 40- to 60-year-old women. To begin to attract a younger audience, QVC has invited celebrities onto the show. For example, Ellen DeGeneres has been on the show promoting her collection of holistic pet care products and supermodel Heidi Klum has been a host selling her line of jewelry. The shopping programs are also using other forms of retailing. QVC now has three types of retail stores: a studio store at its headquarters, QVC@THE MALL in Minnesota's Mall of America, and four outlet stores. Similarly, the Home Shopping Network now offers retail experiences on TV, online, in catalogs, and in stores. Finally, several television shopping programs are developing online video platforms and interactive technology that allows viewers to place orders with their remote control rather than the telephone.[17]

Online Retailing

Online retailing allows consumers to search for, evaluate, and order products through the Internet. For many consumers the advantages of this form of retailing are the 24-hour access, the ability to comparison shop, in-home privacy, and variety. Studies of online shoppers have indicated that men were initially more likely than women to buy something online. As the number of online households has increased, however, the profile of online shoppers has changed to include all shoppers. In addition, while the number of online retailers grew rapidly for several years, this figure has declined as many stand-alone, Internet-only businesses have failed or consolidated. Today, traditional and online retailers—"bricks and clicks"—are melding, using experiences from both approaches to create better value and experiences for customers. Walmart (www.walmart.com) recently introduced "site-to-store" service that allows customers to order online and pick up the order without a shipping fee at the store of their choice. Experts predict that online sales will reach $335 billion by 2012.[18]

Online retail purchases can be the result of several very different approaches. First, consumers can pay dues to become a member of an online discount service such as www.netMarket.com. The service offers tens of thousands of products and more than 1,200 brand names at very low prices to its 25 million subscribers. Another approach to online retailing is to use a shopping "bot" such as www.mysimon.com. This site searches the Internet for a product specified by the consumer and provides a report on the locations of the best prices available. Consumers can also use the Internet to go directly to online malls (www.fashionmall.com), apparel retailers (www.gap.com), bookstores (www.amazon.com), computer manufacturers (www.dell.com), grocery stores (www.peapod.com), music and video stores (www.tower.com), and travel agencies (www.travelocity.com). A final approach to online retailing is the online auction, such as www.ebay.com, where consumers bid on more than 50,000 categories of products.[19]

One of the biggest problems online retailers face is that nearly two-thirds of online shoppers make it to "checkout" and then leave the Web site to compare shipping costs and prices on other sites. Of the shoppers who leave, 70 percent do not return. One way online retailers are addressing this issue is to offer consumers a comparison of competitors' offerings. At Allbookstores.com, for example, consumers can use a "comparison engine" to compare prices with Amazon.com, Barnesandnoble.com, and as many as 25 other bookstores. Experts suggest that online retailers should think of their Web sites as dynamic billboards and be visible to search engines if they are to attract and retain customers.[20]

Shopping "bots" like mysimon.com find the best prices for products consumers specify.

Online retailers are also trying to improve the online retailing experience by adding experiential or interactive activities to their Web sites. Similarly, car manufacturers such as BMW, Mercedes, and Jaguar encourage Web site visitors to "build" a vehicle by selecting interior and exterior colors, packages, and options and then view the customized virtual car. In addition, the merger of television home shopping and online retailing will be possible through TV-based Internet platforms such as Microsoft's MSN TV2, which uses an Internet appliance attached to a television to connect to the Internet.

Telemarketing

Another form of nonstore retailing, called **telemarketing**, involves using the telephone to interact with and sell directly to consumers. Compared with direct mail, telemarketing is often viewed as a more efficient means of targeting consumers. Insurance companies, brokerage firms, and newspapers have often used this form of retailing as a way to cut costs but still maintain access to their customers. According to the Direct Marketing Association, annual telemarketing sales exceed $330 billion.[21]

The telemarketing industry has recently gone through dramatic changes as a result of new legislation related to telephone solicitations. Issues such as consumer privacy, industry standards, and ethical guidelines have encouraged discussion among consumers, Congress, the Federal Trade Commission, and businesses. The result was legislation that created the National Do-Not-Call registry (www.donotcall.gov) for consumers who do not want to receive telephone calls related to company sales efforts. Currently, there are more than 157 million phone numbers on the registry. Companies that use telemarketing have already adapted by adding compliance software to ensure that numbers on the list are not called. In addition, some firms are considering shifting their telemarketing budgets to direct-mail and door-to-door techniques.[22]

Direct Selling

Direct selling, sometimes called door-to-door retailing, involves the direct sale of products and services to consumers through personal interactions and demonstrations in their home or office. A variety of companies, including familiar names such as Avon, Fuller Brush, Mary Kay Cosmetics, and World Book, have created an industry with more than $110 billion in worldwide sales by providing consumers with personalized service and convenience. In the United States, there are more than 15 million direct salespeople working full-time and part-time in 70 product categories.[23]

Growth in the direct-selling industry is the result of two trends. First, many direct selling retailers are expanding into markets outside of the United States. Avon, for example, has 5.8 million sales representatives in 100 countries. More than 77 percent of Amway's $10.7 billion in sales now comes from outside the United States.[24] The second trend is the growing number of companies that are using direct selling to reach consumers who prefer one-on-one customer service and a social shopping experience rather than online shopping or big discount stores. The Direct Selling Association reports that the number of companies using direct selling has increased by 30 percent in the past five years. Interest among potential sales representatives has grown during the recent economic downturn as people seek independence and control of their work activities.[25]

learning review

6. To improve their efficiency and provide additional customer value, catalog retailers often focus on _____ rather than _____.

7. How are retailers increasing consumer interest and involvement in online retailing?

8. Where are direct selling retail sales growing? Why?

RETAILING STRATEGY

retailing mix
The activities related to managing the store and the merchandise in the store, which includes retail pricing, store location, retail communication, and merchandise.

LO4

This section describes how a retailer develops and implements a retailing strategy. In developing a retailing strategy, managers work with the **retailing mix**, which includes activities related to managing the store and the merchandise in the store. The retailing mix is shown in Figure 14-3. It is similar to the marketing mix and includes retail pricing, store location, retail communication, and merchandise.

Retail Pricing

In setting prices for merchandise, retailers must decide on the markup, markdown, and timing for markdowns. The *markup* refers to how much should be added to the cost the retailer paid for a product to reach the final selling price. Retailers decide on the *original markup*, but by the time the product is sold, they end up with a *maintained markup*. The original markup is the difference between retailer cost and initial selling price. When products do not sell as quickly as anticipated, their price is reduced. The difference between the final selling price and retailer cost is the maintained markup, which is also called the *gross margin*.

Discounting a product, or taking a *markdown*, occurs when the product does not sell at the original price and an adjustment is necessary. Often new models or styles force the price of existing models to be marked down. Discounts may also be used to increase demand for complementary products.[26] For example, retailers might take a markdown on CD players to increase sales of CDs or reduce the price of cake mix to generate frosting purchases. The *timing* of a markdown can be important. Many retailers take a markdown as soon as sales fall off to free up valuable selling space and cash. However, other stores delay markdowns to discourage bargain hunters and maintain an image of quality. There is no clear answer, but retailers must consider how the timing might affect future sales. Research indicates that frequent promotions increase consumers' ability to remember regular prices.[27]

Although most retailers plan markdowns, many retailers use price discounts as a part of their regular merchandising policy. Walmart and Home Depot, for example, emphasize consistently low prices and eliminate most markdowns with a strategy often called *everyday low pricing*.[28] Because consumers often use price as an indicator of product quality, however, the brand name of the product and the image of the store become important decision factors in these situations.[29] Another strategy, *everyday fair pricing*, is advocated by retailers that may not offer the lowest price but try to create value for customers through service and the total buying experience.[30]

FIGURE 14–3
Elements of a retailing strategy.

T.J. Maxx is a popular off-price retailer.

Consumers often use the prices of *benchmark* or *signpost* items, such as a can of Coke, to form an overall impression of the store's prices.[31] In addition, price is the most likely to influence consumers' assessment of merchandise value.[32] When store prices are based on rebates, retailers must be careful to avoid negative consumer perceptions if the rebate processing time is long (e.g., six weeks).[33]

Off-price retailing is a retail pricing practice that is used by retailers such as T.J. Maxx, Burlington Coat Factory, and Ross Stores. *Off-price retailing* involves selling brand-name merchandise at lower than regular prices. The difference between the off-price retailer and a discount store is that off-price merchandise is bought by the retailer from manufacturers with excess inventory at prices below wholesale prices. The discounter, however, buys at full wholesale price but takes less of a markup than do traditional department stores. Because of this difference in the way merchandise is purchased by the retailer, selection at an off-price retailer is unpredictable, and searching for bargains has become a popular activity for many consumers. "It's more like a sport than it is like ordinary shopping," says Christopher Boring of Columbus, Ohio's Retail Planning Associates.[34] Savings to the consumer at off-price retailers are reported as high as 70 percent off the prices of a traditional department store. A variation of off-price retailing includes outlet stores such as Nordstrom Rack and Off 5th (Saks Fifth Avenue outlet), which allow retailers to sell excess merchandise and still maintain an image of offering merchandise at full price in their primary store.

Store Location

A second aspect of the retailing mix involves deciding where to locate the store and how many stores to have. Department stores, which started downtown in most cities, have followed customers to the suburbs, and in recent years more stores have been opened in large regional malls. Most stores today are near several others in one of four settings: the central business district, the regional center, the strip mall, or the power center.

The *central business district* is the oldest retail setting, the community's downtown area. Until the regional outflow to suburbs, it was the major shopping area, but the suburban population has grown at the expense of the downtown shopping area. Consumers often view central business district shopping as less convenient because of lack of parking, higher crime rates, and exposure to the weather. Many cities such as Louisville, Denver, and San Antonio have implemented plans to revitalize shopping in central business districts by attracting new offices, entertainment, and residents to downtown locations.

Regional shopping centers consist of 50 to 150 stores that typically attract customers who live or work within a 5- to 10-mile range. These large shopping areas often contain two or three *anchor stores*, which are well-known national or regional stores such as Sears, Saks Fifth Avenue, and Bloomingdale's. The largest variation of a regional center is the West Edmonton Mall in Alberta, Canada. The shopping center is a conglomerate of more than 800 stores, 21 movie theaters, the world's largest indoor amusement park, 110 restaurants, and a 354-room Fantasyland hotel.[35]

Off 5th provides an outlet for excess merchandise from Saks Fifth Avenue.

Not every suburban store is located in a shopping mall. Many neighborhoods have clusters of stores, referred to as a *strip mall*, to serve people who are within a 5- to 10-minute drive. Gas station, hardware, laundry, grocery, and pharmacy outlets are commonly found in a strip mall. Unlike the larger shopping centers, the composition of these stores is usually unplanned. A variation of the strip mall is called the *power center*, which is a huge shopping strip with multiple anchor (or national) stores such as Home Depot, Best Buy, or JCPenney. Power centers are seen as having the convenient location found in many strip malls and the additional power of national stores. These large strip malls often have two to five anchor stores and often contain a supermarket, which brings the shopper to the power center on a weekly basis.[36]

The many forms of retail distribution described previously represent an exciting menu of choices for creating customer value in the marketplace. Each format allows retailers to offer unique benefits and meet particular needs of various customer groups. While each format has many successful applications, retailers in the future are likely to combine many of the formats to offer a broader spectrum of benefits and experiences and to appeal to different segments of consumers.[37] These **multichannel retailers** will utilize and integrate a combination of traditional store formats and nonstore formats such as catalogs, television, home shopping, and online retailing.[38] Barnes & Noble, for example, created Barnesandnoble.com to compete with Amazon.com. Similarly, Office Depot has integrated its store, catalog, and Internet operations to make shopping simpler and more convenient.

Retail Communication

A retailer's communication activities can play an important role in positioning a store and creating its image. While the traditional elements of communication and promotion are discussed in Chapter 16 on advertising and Chapter 17 on personal selling, the message communicated by the many other elements of the retailing mix are also important.

Deciding on the image of a retail outlet is an important retailing mix factor that has been widely recognized and studied since the late 1950s. Pierre Martineau described image as "the way in which the store is defined in the shopper's mind," partly by its functional qualities and partly by an aura of psychological attributes.[39] In this definition, *functional* refers to mix elements such as price ranges, store layouts, and breadth and depth of merchandise lines. The psychological attributes are the intangibles such as a sense of belonging, excitement, style, or warmth. Image has been found to include impressions of the corporation that operates the store, the category or type of store, the product categories in the store, the brands in each category, merchandise and service quality, and the marketing activities of the store.[40]

Closely related to the concept of image is the store's atmosphere or ambience. Many retailers believe that sales are affected by layout, color, lighting, and music in the store as well as by how crowded it is. In addition, the physical surroundings that influence customers may affect the store's employees.[41] In creating the right image and atmosphere, a retail store tries to attract its target audience with what those consumers seek from the buying experience, so the store will fortify the beliefs and the emotional reactions buyers are seeking.[42] While store image perceptions can exist independently of shopping experiences, consumers' shopping experiences can also influence store perceptions.[43]

Merchandise

A final element of the retailing mix is the merchandise offering. Managing the breadth and depth of the product line requires retail buyers who are familiar with the needs of the target market and the alternative products available from the many manufacturers that might be interested in having a product available in the store. A popular approach to managing the assortment of merchandise today is called **category management**. This approach assigns a manager the responsibility for selecting all products that consumers in a market segment might view as substitutes for each other, with the objective of maximizing sales and profits in the category. For example, a category manager might be responsible for shoes in a department store or paper products in a grocery store.

---

multichannel retailers
Retailers that use a combination of traditional store formats and nonstore formats, such as catalogs, television, and online retailing.

category management
An approach to managing the assortment of merchandise that maximizes sales and profits.

Using Marketing Dashboards

Why Apple Stores May Be the Best in the United States!

How effective is my retail format compared to other stores? How are my stores performing this year compared to last year? Information related to these questions is often displayed in a marketing dashboard using two measures: (1) sales per square foot, and (2) same store sales growth.

Your Challenge You have been assigned to evaluate the Apple store retail format. The store's simple, inviting, and open atmosphere has been the topic of discussion among many retailers. Apple, however, is relatively new to the retailing business and many experts have been skeptical of the format. To allow an assessment of Apple stores, use *sales per square foot* as an indicator of how effectively retail space is used to generate revenue and *same store sales growth* to compare the increase in sales of stores that have been open for the same period of time. The calculations for these two indicators are:

$$\text{Sales per square foot} = \frac{\text{Total sales}}{\text{Selling area in square feet}}$$

Same store sales growth

$$= \frac{\text{Store sales in year 2} - \text{Store sales in year 1}}{\text{Store sales in year 1}}$$

Your Findings You decide to collect sales information for Saks, Neiman Marcus, Best Buy, Tiffany, and Apple stores to allow comparisons with other successful retailers. The information you collect allows the calculation of *sales per square foot* and *same store growth* for each store. The results are then easy to compare in the graphs below.

Your Action The results of your investigation indicate that Apple stores' sales per square foot are higher than any of the comparison stores at $4,000. In addition, Apple's same store growth rate of 45 percent is higher than all of the other retailers. You conclude that the elements of Apple's format are very effective and even indicate that Apple may currently be the best retailer in the United States.

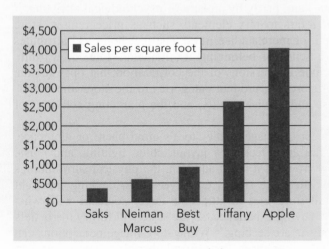

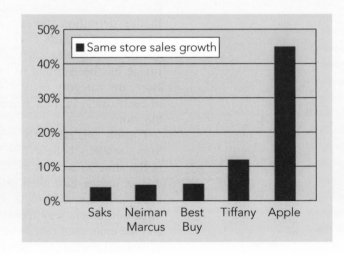

Many retailers are developing an advanced form of category management called *consumer marketing at retail* (CMAR). Recent surveys show that, as part of their CMAR programs, retailers are conducting research, analyzing the data to identify shopper problems, translating the data into retailing mix actions, executing shopper-friendly in-store programs, and monitoring the performance of the merchandise. Walmart, for example, has used the approach to test baby-product and dollar-product categories. Grocery stores such as Safeway and Kroger use the approach to determine the appropriate mix of brand name and private-label products. Specialty retailer Barnes & Noble recently won a best practice award for its application of the approach to the selection, presentation, and promotion of magazines.[44]

Retailers have a variety of marketing metrics that can be used to assess the effectiveness of a store or retail format. First, there are measures related to customers such as the number of transactions per customer, the average transaction size per customer, the number of customers per day or per hour, and the average length of a store visit. Second, there are measures related to products such as number of returns, inventory turnover, inventory carrying cost, and average number of items per transaction. Finally, there are financial measures, such as gross margin, sales per employee, return on sales, and markdown percentage.[45] The two most popular measures for retailers are *sales per square foot* and *same store sales growth*. The Using Marketing Dashboards box describes the calculation of these measures for Apple stores.[46]

learning review

9. How does original markup differ from maintained markup?

10. A huge shopping strip mall with multiple anchor stores is a _____ center.

11. What is a popular approach to managing the assortment of merchandise in a store?

THE CHANGING NATURE OF RETAILING

LO5

Retailing is the most dynamic aspect of a channel of distribution. New types of retailers are always entering the market, searching for a new position that will attract customers. The reason for this continual change is explained by two concepts: the wheel of retailing and the retail life cycle.

The Wheel of Retailing

wheel of retailing
A concept that describes how new forms of retail outlets enter the market.

The **wheel of retailing** describes how new forms of retail outlets enter the market.[47] Usually they enter as low-status, low-margin stores such as a drive-in hamburger stand with no indoor seating and a limited menu (Figure 14–4, box 1). Gradually

FIGURE 14–4
The wheel of retailing describes how retail outlets change.

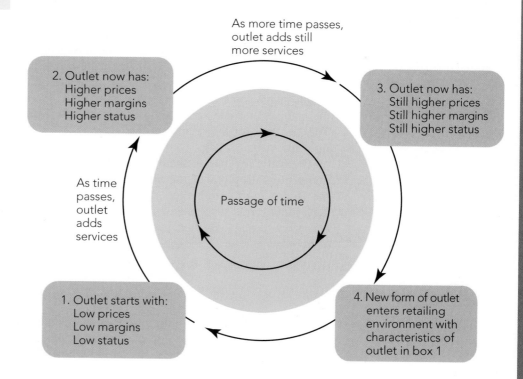

Outlets such as Checkers enter the wheel of retailing as low-status, low-margin stores.

these outlets add fixtures and more embellishments to their stores (in-store seating, plants, and chicken sandwiches as well as hamburgers) to increase the attractiveness for customers. With these additions, prices and status rise (box 2). As time passes, these outlets add still more services and their prices and status increase even further (box 3). These retail outlets now face some new form of retail outlet that again appears as a low-status, low-margin operator (box 4), and the wheel of retailing turns as the cycle starts to repeat itself.

When Ray Kroc started McDonald's in 1955, it opened shortly before lunch and closed just after dinner, offering a limited menu for the two meals without any inside seating for customers. Over time, the wheel of retailing has led to new products and services. In 1975, McDonald's introduced the Egg McMuffin and turned breakfast into a fast-food meal. Today, McDonald's has an extensive menu, seating, and services such as wireless Internet connections and McCafé premium coffee. For the future, McDonald's is testing new products such as fried chicken biscuits, frying oil without trans fats, and fruit smoothies; new formats such as seating "zones" for different types of customers; and 24/7 "always open" hours.

The changes are leaving room for new forms of outlets such as Checkers Drive-In Restaurants. The chain opened fast-food stores that offered only basics—burgers, fries, and cola, a drive-through window, and no inside seating—and now has more than 800 stores. The wheel is turning for other outlets too—Boston Market has added pick-up, delivery, and full-service catering to its original restaurant format, and it also provides Boston Market meal solutions through supermarket delis and Boston Market frozen meals in the frozen food sections. For still others, the wheel has come full circle. Taco Bell is now opening small, limited-offering outlets in gas stations, discount stores, or "wherever a burrito and a mouth might possibly intersect."[48]

The Retail Life Cycle

retail life cycle
The process of growth and decline that retail outlets experience over time.

Similar to the life cycle experienced by products, the **retail life cycle** describes the process of growth and decline that retail outlets experience over time.[49] Figure 14–5 shows the retail life cycle and the position of various current forms of retail outlets on it. Early growth is the stage of emergence of a retail outlet, with a sharp departure from existing competition. Market share rises gradually, although profits may be low because of start-up costs. In the next stage, accelerated development, both market share and profit achieve their greatest growth rates. Usually multiple outlets are established as companies focus on the distribution element of the retailing mix. In this stage, some later competitors may enter. Wendy's, for example, appeared on the hamburger chain scene almost 20 years after McDonald's had begun operation. The key goal for the retailer in this stage is to establish a dominant position in the fight for market share.

The battle for market share is usually fought before the maturity stage, and some competitors drop out of the market. In the wars among hamburger chains, Jack in the Box, Gino's Hamburgers, and Burger Chef used to be more dominant outlets. New retail forms such as Fatburger and In-N-Out Burger enter in the maturity stage, stores try to maintain their market share, and price discounting occurs.

WHOLESALING

LO6

Many retailers depend on intermediaries that engage in wholesaling activities—selling products and services for the purposes of resale or business use. There are several types of intermediaries, including wholesalers and agents (described briefly

FIGURE 14–5
The retail life cycle describes
the stages of growth and
decline for retail outlets.

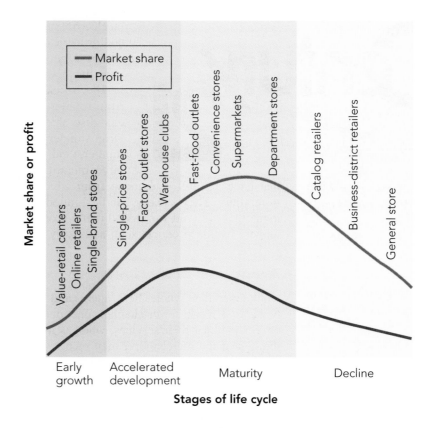

in Chapter 13), as well as manufacturers' sales offices, which are important to understand as part of the retailing process.

Merchant Wholesalers

merchant wholesalers
*Independently owned
firms that take title to the
merchandise they handle.*

Merchant wholesalers are independently owned firms that take title to the merchandise they handle. They go by various names, including industrial distributor (described earlier). Most firms engaged in wholesaling activities are merchant wholesalers.

Merchant wholesalers are classified as either full-service or limited-service wholesalers, depending on the number of functions performed. Two major types of full-service wholesalers exist. *General merchandise* (or *full-line*) *wholesalers* carry a broad assortment of merchandise and perform all channel functions. This type of wholesaler is most prevalent in the hardware, drug, and clothing industries. However, these wholesalers do not maintain much depth of assortment within specific product lines. *Specialty merchandise* (or *limited-line*) *wholesalers* offer a relatively narrow range of products but have an extensive assortment within the product lines carried. They perform all channel functions and are found in the health foods, automotive parts, and seafood industries.

Four major types of limited-service wholesalers exist. *Rack jobbers* furnish the racks or shelves that display merchandise in retail stores, perform all channel functions, and sell on consignment to retailers, which means they retain the title to the products displayed and bill retailers only for the merchandise sold. Familiar products such as hosiery, toys, housewares, and health and beauty items are sold by rack jobbers. *Cash and carry wholesalers* take title to merchandise but sell only to buyers who call on them, pay cash for merchandise, and furnish their own transportation for merchandise. They carry a limited product assortment and do not make deliveries, extend credit, or supply market information. This wholesaler is common in electric supplies, office supplies, hardware products, and groceries.

Drop shippers, or *desk jobbers*, are wholesalers that own the merchandise they sell but do not physically handle, stock, or deliver it. They simply solicit orders from retailers and other wholesalers and have the merchandise shipped directly from a producer to a buyer. Drop shippers are used for bulky products such as coal, lumber, and chemicals, which are sold in extremely large quantities. *Truck jobbers* are small wholesalers that have a small warehouse from which they stock their trucks for distribution to retailers. They usually handle limited assortments of fast-moving or perishable items that are sold for cash directly from trucks in their original packages. Truck jobbers handle products such as bakery items, dairy products, and meat.

Agents and Brokers

Unlike merchant wholesalers, agents and brokers do not take title to merchandise and typically perform fewer channel functions. They make their profit from commissions or fees paid for their services, whereas merchant wholesalers make their profit from the sale of the merchandise they own.

Manufacturer's agents and selling agents are the two major types of agents used by producers. **Manufacturer's agents**, or *manufacturer's representatives*, work for several producers and carry noncompetitive, complementary merchandise in an exclusive territory. Manufacturer's agents act as a producer's sales arm in a territory and are principally responsible for the transactional channel functions, primarily selling. They are used extensively in the automotive supply, footwear, and fabricated steel industries.

By comparison, *selling agents* represent a single producer and are responsible for the entire marketing function of that producer. They design promotional plans, set prices, determine distribution policies, and make recommendations on product strategy. Selling agents are used by small producers in the textile, apparel, food, and home furnishing industries.

Brokers are independent firms or individuals whose principal function is to bring buyers and sellers together to make sales. Brokers, unlike agents, usually have no continuous relationship with the buyer or seller but negotiate a contract between two parties and then move on to another task. Brokers are used extensively by producers of seasonal products (such as fruits and vegetables) and in the real estate industry.

A unique broker that acts in many ways like a manufacturer's agent is a food broker, representing buyers and sellers in the grocery industry. Food brokers differ from conventional brokers because they act on behalf of producers on a permanent basis and receive a commission for their services. For example, Nabisco uses food brokers to sell its candies, margarine, and Planters peanuts, but it sells its line of cookies and crackers directly to retail stores.

manufacturer's agents
Agents who work for several producers and carry noncompetitive, complementary merchandise in an exclusive territory.

brokers
Independent firms or individuals whose main function is to bring buyers and sellers together to make sales.

Manufacturer's Branches and Offices

Unlike merchant wholesalers, agents, and brokers, manufacturer's branches and sales offices are wholly owned extensions of the producer that perform wholesaling activities. Producers assume wholesaling functions when there are no intermediaries to perform these activities, customers are few in number and geographically concentrated, or orders are large or require significant attention. A *manufacturer's branch office* carries a producer's inventory and performs the functions of a full-service wholesaler. A *manufacturer's sales office* does not carry inventory, typically performs only a sales function, and serves as an alternative to agents and brokers.

12. According to the wheel of retailing, when a new retail form appears, how would you characterize its image?

13. Market share is usually fought out before the _____ stage of the retail life cycle.

14. What is the difference between merchant wholesalers and agents?

LEARNING OBJECTIVES REVIEW

LO 1 *Identify retailers in terms of the utilities they provide.*
Retailers provide time, place, form, and possession utilities. Time utility is provided by stores with convenient time-of-day (e.g., open 24 hours) or time-of-year (e.g., seasonal sports equipment available all year) availability. Place utility is provided by the number and location of the stores. Possession utility is provided by making a purchase possible (e.g., financing) or easier (e.g., delivery). Form utility is provided by producing or altering a product to meet the customer's specifications (e.g., custom-made shirts).

LO 2 *Explain the alternative ways to classify retail outlets.*
Retail outlets can be classified by their form of ownership, level of service, and type of merchandise line. The forms of ownership include independent retailers, corporate chains, and contractual systems that include retailer-sponsored cooperatives, wholesaler-sponsored voluntary chains, and franchises. The levels of service include self-service, limited-service, and full-service outlets. Stores classified by their merchandise line include stores with depth, such as sporting goods specialty stores, and stores with breadth, such as large department stores.

LO 3 *Describe the many methods of nonstore retailing.*
Nonstore retailing includes automatic vending, direct mail and catalogs, television home shopping, online retailing, telemarketing, and direct selling. The methods of nonstore retailing vary by the level of involvement of the retailer and the level of involvement of the customer. Vending, for example, has low involvement, whereas both the consumer and the retailer have high involvement in direct selling.

LO 4 *Specify the retailing mix actions used to implement a retailing strategy.*
Retailing mix actions are used to manage a retail store and the merchandise in a store. The mix variables include pricing, store location, communication activities, and merchandise. Two common forms of assessment for retailers are "sales per square foot" and "same store growth."

LO 5 *Explain changes in retailing with the wheel of retailing and the retail life-cycle concepts.*
The wheel of retailing concept explains how retail outlets typically enter the market as low-status, low-margin stores. Over time, stores gradually add new products and services, increasing their prices, status, and margins, and leaving an opening for new low-status, low-margin stores. The retail life cycle describes the process of growth and decline for retail outlets through four stages: early growth, accelerated development, maturity, and decline.

LO 6 *Describe the types of firms that perform wholesaling activities and their functions.*
There are three types of firms that perform wholesaling functions. First, merchant wholesalers are independently owned and take title to merchandise. They include general merchandise wholesalers, specialty merchandise wholesalers, rack jobbers, cash and carry wholesalers, drop shippers, and truck jobbers and can perform a variety of channel functions. Second, agents and brokers do not take title to merchandise and primarily perform marketing functions. Finally, manufacturer's branches, which may carry inventory, and sales offices, which perform sales functions, are wholly owned by the producer.

FOCUSING ON KEY TERMS

brokers p. 328
category management p. 323
manufacturer's agents p. 328
merchant wholesalers p. 327
multichannel retailers p. 323
retail life cycle p. 326
retailing p. 312
retailing mix p. 321
scrambled merchandising p. 317
telemarketing p. 320
wheel of retailing p. 325

APPLYING MARKETING KNOWLEDGE

1 Discuss the impact of the growing number of dual-income households on (*a*) nonstore retailing and (*b*) the retailing mix.

2 In retail pricing, retailers often have a maintained markup. Explain how this maintained markup differs from original markup and why it is so important.

3 What are the similarities and differences between the product and retail life cycles?

4 How would you classify Walmart in terms of its position on the wheel of retailing versus that of an off-price retailer?

5 Develop a chart to highlight the role of each of the four main elements of the retailing mix across the four stages of the retail life cycle.

6 Breadth and depth are two important components in distinguishing among types of retailers. Discuss the breadth and depth implications of the following retailers discussed in this chapter: (*a*) Nordstrom, (*b*) Walmart, (*c*) IKEA, and (*d*) Best Buy.

7 According to the wheel of retailing and the retail life cycle, what will happen to factory outlet stores?

8 The text discusses the development of online retailing in the United States. How does the development of this retailing form agree with the implications of the retail life cycle?

9 Comment on this statement: The only distinction among merchant wholesalers and agents and brokers is that merchant wholesalers take title to the products they sell.

building your marketing plan

Does your marketing plan involve using retailers? If the answer is no, read no further and do not include a retailing element in your plan. If the answer is yes:

1 Use Figure 14–3 to develop your retailing strategy by specifying the details of the retailing mix.

2 Develop a statement describing the breadth and the depth of the product line.

3 Describe an appropriate combination of retail pricing, store location, retail communication, and merchandise assortment.

video case 14 Mall of America: Shopping and a Whole Lot More

"If you build it, they will come" not only worked in the movie *Field of Dreams* but also applies—big time—to Mall of America.

Located in a suburb of Minneapolis, Mall of America (www.mallofamerica.com) is the largest completely enclosed retail and family-entertainment complex in the United States. "We're more than a mall, we're a destination," explains Maureen Cahill, an executive at Mall of America. More than 100,000 people each day—40 million visitors each year—visit the one-stop complex offering retail shopping, guest services, convenience, a huge variety of entertainment, and fun for all. "Guest services" include everything from high school and college classrooms to a doctor's office and a wedding chapel.

THE CONCEPT AND CHALLENGE

The idea for Mall of America came from the West Edmonton Mall in Alberta, Canada. The Ghermezian Brothers, who developed that mall, sought to create a unique mall that would attract not only local families but also tourists from the Upper Midwest, the nation, and even from abroad.

The two challenges for Mall of America: How can it (1) attract and keep the large number of retail establishments needed to (2) continue to attract even more millions of visitors than today? A big part of the answer is in Mall of America's positioning—"There is a place for fun in your life!"

THE STAGGERING SIZE AND OFFERINGS

Opened August 1992 amid tremendous worldwide publicity, Mall of America faced skeptics who had their doubts because of its size, its unique retail-entertainment mix, and the nationwide recession. Despite these concerns, it

opened with more than 80 percent of its space leased and attracted more than 1 million visitors its first week.

Mall of America is 4.2 million square feet, the equivalent of 88 football fields. This makes it three to four times the size of most other regional malls. It includes four anchor department stores: Nordstrom, Macy's, Bloomingdale's, and Sears. It also includes more than 520 specialty stores, from Brooks Brothers to DSW Shoe Warehouse. Approximately 36 percent of Mall of America's space is devoted to anchors and 64 percent to specialty stores. This makes the space allocation the reverse of most regional malls.

The retail-entertainment mix of Mall of America is incredibly diverse. For example, there are more than 100 apparel and accessory stores, 18 jewelry stores, and 33 shoe stores. Two food courts with 27 restaurants plus more than 30 other restaurants scattered throughout the building meet most food preferences of visitors. Another surprise: Mall of America is home to many "concept stores," where retailers introduce a new type of store or design. Because of its incredible size, the mall has 194 stores not found at competing regional malls. In addition, it has an entrepreneurial program for people with an innovative retail idea and limited resources. They can open a kiosk, wall unit, or small store for a specified time period or as a temporary seasonal tenant.

Unique features of Mall of America include:

* A seven-acre theme park with more than 50 attractions and rides, including a roller coaster, Ferris wheel, and games in a glass-enclosed, skylighted area with more than 400 trees.
* Underwater Adventures, where visitors are surrounded by sharks, stingrays, and sea turtles; can venture among fish native to the north woods; and can discover what lurks at the bottom of the Mississippi River.

- Entertainment choices that include a 14-screen theater, A.C.E.S. Flight Simulation, NASCAR Silicon Motor Speedway, and Dinosaur Walk Museum.
- The LEGO Land Imagination Center, a 6,000-square-foot showplace with more than 30 full-sized models.

As a host to corporate events and private parties, Mall of America has a rotunda that opens to all four floors that facilitates presentations, demonstrations, and exhibits. Organizations such as PepsiCo, Visa-USA, and Chevrolet have used the facilities to gain shopper awareness. Mall of America is a rectangle with the anchor department stores at the corners and amusement park in the skylighted central area, making it easy for shoppers to understand and navigate. It has 12,550 free parking ramp spaces on site and another 7,000 spaces nearby during peak times.

THE MARKET

The Minneapolis–St. Paul metropolitan area is a market with more than 3 million people. A total of 30 million people live within a day's drive of Mall of America. A survey of its shoppers showed that 32 percent of the shoppers travel 150 miles or more and account for more than 50 percent of the sales revenues. Located three miles from the Minneapolis/St. Paul International Airport, Mall of America provides a shuttle bus from the airport every half hour. Light-rail service from the airport and downtown Minneapolis is also available.

Tourism accounts for 4 out of 10 visits to Mall of America. About 6 percent of visitors come from outside the United States. Some come just to see and experience Mall of America, while others take advantage of the cost savings available on products (Japan) or taxes (Canada and states with sales taxes on clothing).

THE FUTURE: FACING THE CHALLENGES

Where does Mall of America head in the future?

"We just did a brand study and found that Mall of America is one of the most recognized brands in the world," Cahill says. "They might not know where we are

sometimes, but they've heard of Mall of America and they know they want to come.

"What we've learned since 1992 is to keep the Mall of America fresh and exciting," she explains. "We're constantly looking at what attracts people and adding to that. We're adding new stores, new attractions, and new events. We hold more than 350 events a year and with everyone from Garth Brooks to Sarah Ferguson to N Sync."

Mall of America announced a plan for a 5.6 million-square-foot expansion, the area of another 117 football fields, connected by pedestrian skyway to the present building. "The second phase will not be a duplicate of what we have," Cahill says. "We have plans for at least three hotels, a performing arts center, a business office complex, an art or history museum, and possibly even a television broadcast facility." The expansion is expected to attract an additional 20 million visitors annually. In addition, the development is designed to exceed environmental certification standards.

One of the first elements of the expansion includes a now open 306,000-square-foot IKEA store. Other new elements will include a 13,000-square-foot restaurant called Cantina Corona, a 6,000-seat performing arts auditorium created by AEG, a 300,000-square-foot Bass Pro store, a 500-room hotel, and a Mayo Clinic facility. All of these new additions and the many offerings of the current mall reinforce that Mall of America is a shopping destination and a whole lot more!

Questions

1 Why has Mall of America been such a marketing success so far?

2 What (*a*) retail and (*b*) consumer trends have occurred since Mall of America was opened in 1992 that it should consider when making future plans?

3 (*a*) What criteria should Mall of America use in adding new facilities to its complex? (*b*) Evaluate (*i*) retail stores, (*ii*) entertainment offerings, and (*iii*) hotels on these criteria.

4 What specific marketing actions would you propose that Mall of America managers take to ensure its continuing success in attracting visitors (*a*) from the local metropolitan area and (*b*) from outside of it?

Social Viewing Room Lounge

Join A Social Viewing Room

Browse viewing rooms and connect with others to share

Join family, friends and fellow fans and watch your favorite episodes of your favorite shows together. Boo the latest villains on CSI: Miami and CSI: NY at the same time, LOL in unison at the same crazy antics on Worst Week and Gary UnMarried and toss tomatoes at your least favorite Survivor. Hop right into one of the rooms below, invite your friends and start socializing!

◀ 2 / 2

Gary Unmarried Gary And His Half Brother
Season 1: Episode 19
Full Episode (21:36)

4 Fans in Room

Join Now ▶

View by myself 🖥

Other Rooms for This Show

Room 1   [3]   12 min. in
Room 2   [10]   2 min. in
Room 3   [2]   29 min. in
Room 4   [2]   25 min. in

➕ Invite your friends

⭐ Feedback

Quick Quiz

00:12

How many days do Jeff say the game last?

33

39

55

Want your own avatar picture? Register, it's free! | No, thanks

Laugh

Type here to comment

Survivor: Samoa - Episode 1
Air Date: 09/17/09
Full Episode 42:37

Twenty castaways are left to fend for themselves among Samoa's white sand beaches, lush green valleys and towering waterfalls.

15

Integrated Marketing Communications and Direct Marketing

LEARNING OBJECTIVES

After reading this chapter you should be able to:

LO1 Discuss integrated marketing communication and the communication process.

LO2 Describe the promotional mix and the uniqueness of each component.

LO3 Select the promotional approach appropriate to a product's target audience, life-cycle stage, and channel strategy.

LO4 Describe the elements of the promotion decision process.

LO5 Explain the value of direct marketing for consumers and sellers.

INTEGRATED MARKETING COMMUNICATIONS USHERS IN THE 'AGE OF ENGAGE'

How would you characterize today's marketplace? For most consumers the answer is interactive and connected—through cell phones, computers, the Web, and social networks such as Facebook, MySpace, Twitter, LinkedIn, and Flickr. In this marketplace the key to communicating with consumers is to engage them—a perfect job for integrated marketing communications campaigns!

How can media engage consumers? The options are endless for traditional and new forms of media. TV networks, for example, now offer online video streams of many series. CBS recently created social viewing rooms at CBS.com for programs such as *CSI* and *Survivor*. The rooms allow viewers to chat about what they are watching and to offer critical reactions to the program. Senior Vice President Anthony Soohoo explains, "When people are online they want to engage in a different way, they want to share the experience." The audience for online viewing is now 162 million viewers, compared to the 282 million who watch on their television.

New forms of communicating with customers, such as social media, also offer opportunities to engage consumers. Recent research shows that 85 percent of consumers believe that companies should be interacting through social channels. Many companies create a branded presence such as a fan page within virtual communities such as Facebook or MySpace to generate word-of-mouth advertising. Some companies, such as Saturn, have even created their own online communities as showcases for their brands and products. One advantage of this medium is that it is less expensive than other forms of marketing, even though it may require constant monitoring by someone at the company or its advertising agency.

Many other media can also engage consumers today. When Disney created a contest for the chance to play a fantasy role at Disneyland, more than 10,000 people submitted videos! eBay Motors worked with the makers of a car racing game called "Grid" for Xbox 360, Playstation 3, and Nintendo so that the auction platform would be integrated into the game and seen by a potential audience of 40 million game enthusiasts. Procter & Gamble used product placement to include its Crest Whitestrips in the movie *He's Just Not That into You* and then passed out free samples at the exits of the movie theaters. E-mail, blogs, gift cards, magazines, and sweepstakes are also potential forms of media that can engage today's consumers.[1]

The many types of promotion in these examples demonstrate the opportunity for engaging potential customers and the importance of integrating the various elements of a communication program.

promotional mix
The combination of one or more of the communication tools used to inform, persuade, or remind prospective buyers.

Promotion represents the fourth element in the marketing mix. The promotional element consists of communication tools, including advertising, personal selling, sales promotion, public relations, and direct marketing. The combination of one or more of these communication tools is called the **promotional mix**. All of these tools can be used to (1) inform prospective buyers about the benefits of the product, (2) persuade them to try it, and (3) remind them later about the benefits they enjoyed by using the product. In the past, marketers often viewed these communication tools as separate and independent. The advertising department, for example, often designed and managed its activities without consulting departments or agencies that had responsibility for sales promotion or public relations. The result was often an overall communication effort that was uncoordinated and, in some cases, inconsistent. Today, the concept of designing marketing communications programs that coordinate all promotional activities—advertising, personal selling, sales promotion, public relations, and direct marketing—to provide a consistent message across all audiences is referred to as **integrated marketing communications (IMC)**. In addition, by taking consumer expectations into consideration, IMC is a key element in a company's customer experience management strategy.[2]

integrated marketing communications
The concept of designing marketing communications programs that coordinate all promotional activities to provide a consistent message across all audiences.

This chapter provides an overview of the communication process, a description of the promotional mix elements, several tools for integrating the promotional mix, and a process for developing a comprehensive promotion program. One of the promotional mix elements, direct marketing, is also discussed in this chapter. Chapter 16 covers advertising, sales promotion, and public relations; and Chapter 17 discusses personal selling.

THE COMMUNICATION PROCESS

Communication is the process of conveying a message to others and requires six elements: a source, a message, a channel of communication, a receiver, and the processes of encoding and decoding[3] (see Figure 15–1). The *source* may be a company or person who has information to convey. The information sent by a source, such as a description of a new cellular telephone, forms the *message*. The message is conveyed by means of a *channel of communication* such as a salesperson, advertising media, or public relations tools. Consumers who read, hear, or see the message are the *receivers*.

communication
The process of conveying a message to others; it requires six elements: a source, a message, a channel of communication, a receiver, and the processes of encoding and decoding.

FIGURE 15–1
The communication process consists of six key elements.

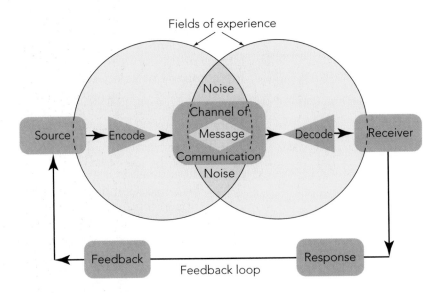

PECKINPAH ROAD, CA – *48 miles northeast of Fresno.*
To get to some of the most spectacular trails on Earth, you'll need one of the most capable off-road vehicles on Earth.
You'll also need available front and rear locking differentials, a 45.0:1 crawl ratio, and full underbody protection.
All engineered to take you anywhere in the midsize HUMMER H3. Find out more at HUMMER.com.

© General Motors Corporation 2005

N 37.23 W -119.46

HUMMER
LIKE NOTHING ELSE

How would you decode this ad?

Encoding and Decoding

Encoding and decoding are essential to communication. *Encoding* is the process of having the sender transform an idea into a set of symbols. *Decoding* is the reverse, or the process of having the receiver take a set of symbols, the message, and transform the symbols back to an idea. Look at the accompanying automobile advertisement: Who is the source, and what is the message?

Decoding is performed by the receivers according to their own frame of reference: their attitudes, values, and beliefs.[4] HUMMER is the source and the advertisement is the message, which appeared in *BusinessWeek* magazine (the channel). How would you interpret (decode) this advertisement? The picture and text in the advertisement show that the source's intention is to generate interest in its product with the headline "Welcome to the open"—a statement the source believes will appeal to the readers of the magazine.

The process of communication is not always a successful one. Errors in communication can happen in several ways. The source may not adequately transform the abstract idea into an effective set of symbols, a properly encoded message may be sent through the wrong channel and never make it to the receiver, the receiver may not properly transform the set of symbols into the correct abstract idea, or finally, feedback may be so delayed or distorted that it is of no use to the sender. Although communication appears easy to perform, truly effective communication can be very difficult.

For the message to be communicated effectively, the sender and receiver must have a mutually shared *field of experience*—a similar understanding and knowledge they apply to the message. Figure 15–1 shows two circles representing the fields of experience of the sender and receiver, which overlap in the message. Some of the better-known message problems have occurred when U.S. companies have taken their messages to cultures with different fields of experience. Many misinterpretations are merely the result of bad translations. For example, KFC made a mistake when its "finger-lickin' good" slogan was translated into Mandarin Chinese as "eat your fingers off!"[5]

Feedback

Figure 15–1 shows a line labeled *feedback loop*, which consists of a response and feedback. A *response* is the impact the message had on the receiver's knowledge, attitudes, or behaviors. *Feedback* is the sender's interpretation of the response and indicates whether the message was decoded and understood as intended. Chapter 16 reviews approaches called *pretesting*, which ensure that messages are decoded properly.

Noise

Noise includes extraneous factors that can work against effective communication by distorting a message or the feedback received (Figure 15–1). Noise can be a simple error, such as a printing mistake that affects the meaning of a newspaper advertisement or using words or pictures that fail to communicate the message clearly. Noise can also occur when a salesperson's message is misunderstood by a prospective buyer, such as when a salesperson's accent, use of slang terms, or communication style make hearing and understanding the message difficult.

learning review

1. What are the six elements required for communication to occur?

2. A difficulty for U.S. companies advertising in international markets is that the audience does not share the same _____.

3. A misprint in a newspaper ad is an example of _____.

THE PROMOTIONAL ELEMENTS

LO2

To communicate with consumers, a company can use one or more of five promotional alternatives: advertising, personal selling, public relations, sales promotion, and direct marketing. Figure 15–2 summarizes the distinctions among these five elements. Three of these elements—advertising, sales promotion, and public relations—are often said to use *mass selling* because they are used with groups of prospective buyers. In contrast, personal selling uses *customized interaction* between a seller and a prospective buyer. Personal selling activities include face-to-face, telephone, and interactive electronic communication. Direct marketing also uses messages customized for specific customers.

Advertising

advertising

Any paid form of nonpersonal communication about an organization, product, service, or idea by an identified sponsor.

Advertising is any paid form of nonpersonal communication about an organization, product, service, or idea by an identified sponsor. The *paid* aspect of this definition is important because the space for the advertising message normally must be bought. An occasional exception is the public service announcement, where the advertising time or space is donated. A full-page, four-color ad in *Time* magazine, for example, costs $287,440. The *nonpersonal* component of advertising is also important. Advertising involves mass media (such as TV, radio, and magazines), which are nonpersonal and do not have an immediate feedback loop as does personal selling.

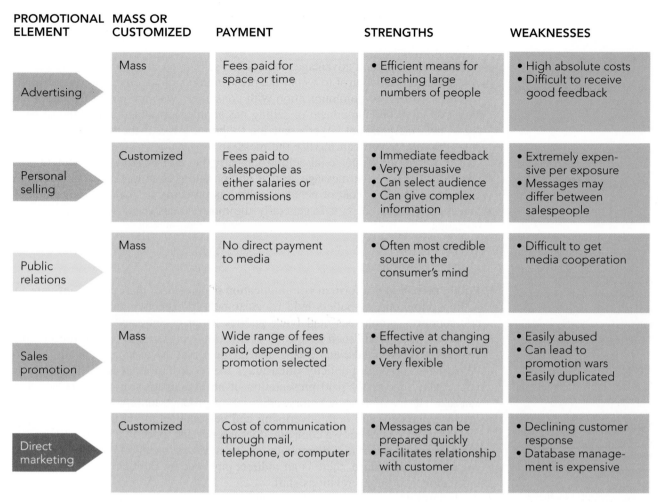

PROMOTIONAL ELEMENT	MASS OR CUSTOMIZED	PAYMENT	STRENGTHS	WEAKNESSES
Advertising	Mass	Fees paid for space or time	• Efficient means for reaching large numbers of people	• High absolute costs • Difficult to receive good feedback
Personal selling	Customized	Fees paid to salespeople as either salaries or commissions	• Immediate feedback • Very persuasive • Can select audience • Can give complex information	• Extremely expensive per exposure • Messages may differ between salespeople
Public relations	Mass	No direct payment to media	• Often most credible source in the consumer's mind	• Difficult to get media cooperation
Sales promotion	Mass	Wide range of fees paid, depending on promotion selected	• Effective at changing behavior in short run • Very flexible	• Easily abused • Can lead to promotion wars • Easily duplicated
Direct marketing	Customized	Cost of communication through mail, telephone, or computer	• Messages can be prepared quickly • Facilitates relationship with customer	• Declining customer response • Database management is expensive

FIGURE 15–2

The five elements of the promotional mix.

So before the message is sent, marketing research plays a valuable role; for example, it determines that the target market will actually see the medium chosen and that the message will be understood.

There are several advantages to a firm using advertising in its promotional mix. It can be attention-getting—as with the Havaianas ad shown on the next page—and also can communicate specific product benefits to prospective buyers. By paying for the advertising space, a company can control *what* it wants to say and, to some extent, to *whom* the message is sent. Advertising also allows the company to decide *when* to send its message (which includes how often). The nonpersonal aspect of advertising also has its advantages. Once the message is created, the same message is sent to all receivers in a market segment. If the pictorial, text, and brand elements of an advertisement are properly pretested, an advertiser can ensure the ad's ability to capture consumers' attention and trust that the same message will be decoded by all receivers in the market segment.[6]

Advertising has some disadvantages. As shown in Figure 15–2 and discussed in depth in Chapter 16, the costs to produce and place a message are significant, and the lack of direct feedback makes it difficult to know how well the message has been received.

Personal Selling

personal selling

The two-way flow of communication between a buyer and seller, often in a face-to-face encounter, designed to influence a person's or group's purchase decision.

The second major promotional alternative is **personal selling**, which is the two-way flow of communication between a buyer and seller designed to influence a person's or group's purchase decision. Unlike advertising, personal selling is usually face-to-face communication between the sender and receiver. Why do companies use personal selling?

There are important advantages to personal selling, as summarized in Figure 15–2. A salesperson can control to *whom* the presentation is made, reducing the amount of *wasted coverage*, or communication with consumers who are not in the target audience. The personal component of selling has another advantage in that the seller can see or hear the potential buyer's reaction to the message. If the feedback is unfavorable, the salesperson can modify the message.

The flexibility of personal selling can also be a disadvantage. Different salespeople can change the message so that no consistent communication is given to all customers. The high cost of personal selling is probably its major disadvantage. On a cost-per-contact basis, it is generally the most expensive of the five promotional elements.

Public Relations

Public relations is a form of communication management that seeks to influence the feelings, opinions, or beliefs held by customers, prospective customers, stockholders, suppliers, employees, and other publics about a company and its products or services.[7] Many tools such as special events, lobbying efforts, annual reports, press conferences, RSS feeds, and image management may be used by a public relations department, although publicity often plays the most important role.[8] **Publicity** is a nonpersonal, indirectly paid presentation of an organization, product, or service. It can take the form of a news story, editorial, or product announcement. A difference between publicity and both advertising and personal selling is the "indirectly paid" dimension. With publicity a company does not pay for space in a mass medium (such as television or radio) but attempts to get the medium to run a favorable story on the company. In this sense, there is an indirect payment for publicity in that a company must support a public relations staff.

An advantage of publicity is credibility. When you read a favorable story about a company's product (such as a glowing restaurant review), there is a tendency to believe it. Travelers throughout the world have relied on Frommer's guides such as *Australia from $60 a Day*. These books outline out-of-the-way, inexpensive restau-

Advertising, public relations, and sales promotion are three elements of the promotional mix.

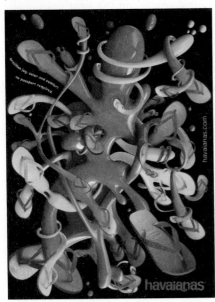

rants and hotels, giving invaluable publicity to these establishments. Such businesses do not (nor can they) buy a mention in the guide.

The disadvantage of publicity relates to the lack of the user's control over it. A company can invite media to cover an interesting event such as a store opening or a new product release, but there is no guarantee that a story will result, if it will be positive, or who will be in the audience. Social media, such as blogs, have grown dramatically and allow uncontrollable public discussions of almost any company activity. Many public relations departments now focus on facilitating and responding to online discussions. McDonald's, for example, responds to comments about McDonald's products and promotions on its corporate social responsibility blog, *Open for Discussion*.[9] Generally, publicity is an important element of most promotional campaigns, although the lack of control means that it is rarely the primary element. Research related to the sequence of IMC elements, however, indicates that publicity followed by advertising with the same message increases the positive response to the message.[10]

Sales Promotion

sales promotion
A short-term offer designed to arouse interest in buying a product or service.

A fourth promotional element is **sales promotion**, a short-term inducement of value offered to arouse interest in buying a product or service. Used in conjunction with advertising or personal selling, sales promotions are offered to intermediaries as well as to ultimate consumers. Coupons, rebates, samples, and sweepstakes are just a few examples of sales promotions.

The advantage of sales promotion is that the short-term nature of these programs (such as a coupon or sweepstakes with an expiration date) often stimulates sales for their duration. Offering value to the consumer in terms of a cents-off coupon or rebate may increase store traffic from consumers who are not store-loyal.[11]

Sales promotions cannot be the sole basis for a campaign because gains are often temporary and sales drop off when the deal ends. Advertising support is needed to convert the customer who tried the product because of a sales promotion into a long-term buyer. If sales promotions are conducted continuously, they lose their effectiveness. Customers begin to delay purchase until a coupon is offered, or they question the product's value. Some aspects of sales promotions also are regulated by the federal government.[12] These issues are reviewed in detail in Chapter 16.

Direct Marketing

direct marketing
Promotional element that uses direct communication with consumers to generate a response in the form of an order, a request for further information, or a visit to a retail outlet.

Another promotional alternative, **direct marketing**, uses direct communication with consumers to generate a response in the form of an order, a request for further information, or a visit to a retail outlet. The communication can take many forms including face-to-face selling, direct mail, catalogs, telephone solicitations, direct response advertising (on television and radio and in print), and online marketing.[13] Like personal selling, direct marketing often consists of interactive communication. It also has the advantage of being customized to match the needs of specific target markets. Messages can be developed and adapted quickly to facilitate one-to-one relationships with customers.

While direct marketing has been one of the fastest-growing forms of promotion, it has several disadvantages. First, most forms of direct marketing require a comprehensive and up-to-date database with information about the target market. Developing and maintaining the database can be expensive and time consuming. In addition, growing concern about privacy has led to a decline in response rates among some customer groups. Companies with successful direct marketing programs are sensitive to these issues and often use a combination of direct marketing alternatives together, or direct marketing combined with other promotional tools, to increase value for customers.

INTEGRATED MARKETING COMMUNICATIONS— DEVELOPING THE PROMOTIONAL MIX

LO3

A firm's promotional mix is the combination of one or more of the promotional tools it chooses to use. In putting together the promotional mix, a marketer must consider two issues. First, the balance of the elements must be determined. Should advertising be emphasized more than personal selling? Should a promotional rebate be offered? Would public relations activities be effective? Several factors that affect such decisions are the target audience for the promotion, the stage of the product's life cycle, and the channel of distribution. Second, because the various promotional elements are often the responsibility of different departments, coordinating a consistent promotional effort is necessary. A promotional planning process designed to ensure integrated marketing communications can facilitate this goal.

The Target Audience

Promotional programs are directed to the ultimate consumer, to an intermediary (retailer, wholesaler, or industrial distributor), or to both. Promotional programs directed to buyers of consumer products often use mass media because the number of potential buyers is large. Personal selling is used at the place of purchase, generally the retail store. Direct marketing may be used to encourage first-time or repeat purchases. Combinations of many media alternatives are a necessity for some target audiences today. The Marketing Matters box describes how Generation Y consumers can be reached through mobile marketing programs.[14]

Advertising directed to business buyers is used selectively in trade publications, such as *Restaurant News* magazine for buyers of restaurant equipment and supplies. Because business buyers often have specialized needs or technical questions, personal selling is particularly important. The salesperson can provide information and the necessary support after sales.

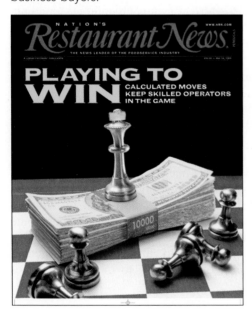

Publications such as *Restaurant News* reach business buyers.

Intermediaries are often the focus of promotional efforts. As with business buyers, personal selling is the major promotional ingredient. The salespeople assist intermediaries in making a profit by coordinating promotional campaigns sponsored by the manufacturer and by providing marketing advice and expertise. Intermediaries' questions often pertain to the allowed markup, merchandising support, and return policies.

The Product Life Cycle

All products have a life cycle (see Chapter 11), and the composition of the promotional mix changes over the four life-cycle stages (as shown for Purina Dog Chow in Figure 15-3):

- *Introduction stage.* Informing consumers in an effort to increase their level of awareness is the primary promotional objective in the introduction stage of the product life cycle. In general, all the promotional mix elements are used at this time.

Mobile Marketing Reaches Generation Y, 32/7!

The marketplace is flooded with new forms of media. In addition to traditional media such as television, radio, magazines, and newspapers, marketers can now use cell phones, social networks, RSS feeds, blogs, and a variety of other means to deliver messages. To cope with the volume of messages, consumers have applied multitasking to media use. A recent study of television viewers, for example, found that 58 percent were instant messaging, e-mailing, texting, or talking on the phone while they watched TV. This simultaneous media use is so common it has created 32-hour "media days" for consumers.

Generation Y is particularly adept, as up to 72 percent of that group is "connected" while watching television. Since using a single medium alone is a thing of the past for young consumers, advertising agencies, broadcasters, cable and satellite providers, and retailers must change their views of consumers' ability to absorb and remember advertising messages. Marketers can still communicate with Generation Y, however, by inte-

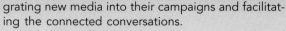

grating new media into their campaigns and facilitating the connected conversations.

With 259 million wireless phones in the United States, many experts believe that marketing through cell phones, or mobile marketing, is a logical addition to integrated campaigns. The Gap, for example, created a free iPhone application that allows consumers to put together an outfit and then generate a list of the items. According to Executive Vice President Ivy Ross, "We want to engage our customers where they're playing and really be where they are." Similarly, Kraft created the iFood Assistant to create recipes made with Kraft products. The application is now one of the iPhone's 100 most popular applications. Phones are also offering access to the Internet and social networks—an essential element as Generation Y members keep in touch with an average of 47 "friends."

Watch for other brands to try similar mobile programs, particularly for consumers who are connected multitaskers.

- *Growth stage.* The primary promotional objective of the growth stage is to persuade the consumer to buy the product. Advertising is used to communicate brand differences, and personal selling is used to solidify the channel of distribution.
- *Maturity stage.* In the maturity stage the need is to maintain existing buyers. Advertising's role is to remind buyers of the product's existence. Sales promotion, in the form of discounts, coupons, and events, is important in maintaining loyal buyers.

FIGURE 15–3

Promotional tools used over the product life cycle of Purina Dog Chow.

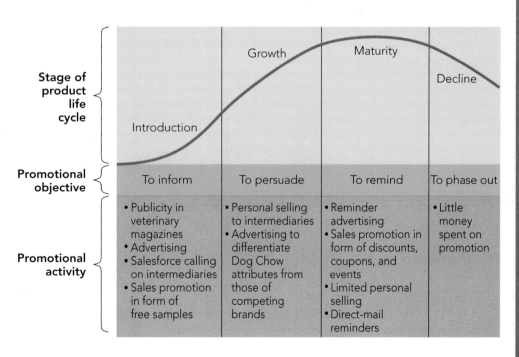

Why does this ad suggest readers should "Ask Your Doctor"? For the answer, see the text.

push strategy

Directing the promotional mix to channel members to encourage them to order and stock a product.

- *Decline stage.* The decline stage of the product life cycle is usually a period of phase-out for the product, and little money is spent in the promotional mix.

Channel Strategies

Chapter 13 discussed the channel flow from a producer to intermediaries to consumers. Achieving control of the channel is often difficult for the manufacturer, and promotional strategies can assist in moving a product through the channel of distribution. This is where a manufacturer has to make an important decision about whether to use a push strategy, pull strategy, or both in its channel of distribution.[15]

Push Strategy Figure 15–4A shows how a manufacturer uses a **push strategy**, directing the promotional mix to channel members to gain their cooperation in ordering and stocking the product. In this approach, personal selling and sales promotions play major roles. Salespeople call on wholesalers to encourage orders and provide sales assistance. Sales promotions, such as case discount allowances (20 percent off the regular case price), are offered to stimulate demand. By pushing the product through the channel, the goal is to get channel members to push it to their customers.

Ford Motor Company, for example, provides support and incentives for its 3,700 Ford and Lincoln-Mercury dealers. Through a multi-level program, Ford provides incentives to reward dealers for meeting sales goals. Dealers receive incentives when they are near a goal, and when they reach a goal, and they receive an even larger incentive if they exceed sales projections. Ford also offers some dealers special incentives for maintaining superior facilities or improving customer service. All of these actions are intended to encourage Ford dealers to "push" the Ford products through the channel to consumers.[16]

Pull Strategy In some instances, manufacturers face resistance from channel members who do not want to order a new product or increase inventory levels of an existing brand. As shown in Figure 15–4B, a manufacturer may then elect to

FIGURE 15–4
A comparison of push and pull promotional strategies.

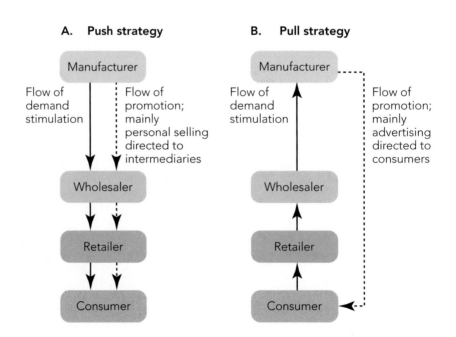

pull strategy
Directing the promotional mix at ultimate consumers to encourage them to ask the retailer for the product.

implement a **pull strategy** by directing its promotional mix at ultimate consumers to encourage them to ask the retailer for a product. Seeing demand from ultimate consumers, retailers order the product from wholesalers and thus the item is pulled through the intermediaries. Pharmaceutical companies, for example, now spend more than $5 billion annually on *direct-to-consumer* prescription drug advertising, to complement traditional personal selling and free samples directed only at doctors.[17] The strategy is designed to encourage consumers to ask their doctor for a specific drug by name—pulling it through the channel. Successful campaigns such as the print ad which says, "Ask your doctor if Zetia is right for you," can have dramatic effects on the sales of a product.

---

learning review

7. Promotional programs can be directed to _____, _____, or both.

8. Describe the promotional objective for each stage of the product life cycle.

9. Explain the differences between a push strategy and a pull strategy.

DEVELOPING AN IMC PROGRAM

LO4

Because media costs are high, promotion decisions must be made carefully, using a systematic approach. Paralleling the planning, implementation, and evaluation steps described in the strategic marketing process (Chapter 2), the promotion decision process is divided into (1) developing, (2) executing, and (3) assessing the promotion program (Figure 15–5).

Identifying the Target Audience

The first decision in developing the promotion program involves identifying the *target audience*, the group of prospective buyers toward which a promotion program is directed. To the extent that time and money permit, the target audience for the promotion program is the target market for the firm's product, which is identified from marketing research and market segmentation studies. The more a firm knows about its target audiences—including their lifestyle, attitudes, and values—the easier it is to develop a promotion program. If a firm wanted to reach you with television and magazine ads, for example, it would need to know what TV shows you watch and what magazines you read.

FIGURE 15–5
The promotion decision process includes planning, implementation, and evaluation.

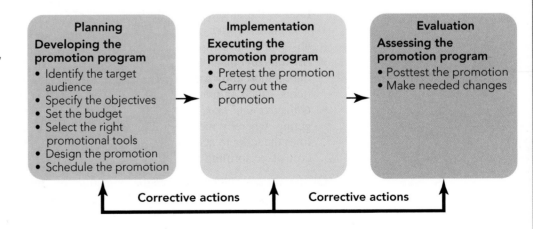

Planning	Implementation	Evaluation
Developing the promotion program	**Executing the promotion program**	**Assessing the promotion program**
• Identify the target audience • Specify the objectives • Set the budget • Select the right promotional tools • Design the promotion • Schedule the promotion	• Pretest the promotion • Carry out the promotion	• Posttest the promotion • Make needed changes

Corrective actions   Corrective actions

Specifying Promotion Objectives

After the target audience is identified, a decision must be reached on what the promotion should accomplish. Consumers can be said to respond in terms of a **hierarchy of effects**, which is the sequence of stages a prospective buyer goes through from initial awareness of a product to eventual action (either trial or adoption of the product).[18] The five stages are:

- *Awareness*—the consumer's ability to recognize and remember the product or brand name.
- *Interest*—an increase in the consumer's desire to learn about some of the features of the product or brand.
- *Evaluation*—the consumer's appraisal of the product or brand on important attributes.
- *Trial*—the consumer's actual first purchase and use of the product or brand.
- *Adoption*—through a favorable experience on the first trial, the consumer's repeated purchase and use of the product or brand.

For a totally new product, the sequence applies to the entire product category, but for a new brand competing in an established product category it applies to the brand itself. These steps can serve as guidelines for developing promotion objectives.

Although sometimes an objective for a promotion program involves several steps in the hierarchy of effects, it often focuses on a single stage. Regardless of what the specific objective might be, from building awareness to increasing repeat purchases, promotion objectives should possess three important qualities. They should (1) be designed for a well-defined target audience, (2) be measurable, and (3) cover a specified time period.

Setting the Promotion Budget

After setting the promotion objectives, a company must decide how much to spend. The promotion expenditures needed to reach U.S. households are enormous. Four companies—Procter & Gamble, AT&T, General Motors, and Time Warner—each spend a total of more than $3 billion annually on promotion.[19] Determining the ideal amount for the budget is difficult because there is no precise way to measure the exact results of spending promotion dollars. However, several methods can be used to set the promotion budget:[20]

- *Percentage of sales.* In the percentage of sales budgeting approach, the amount of money spent on promotion is a percentage of past or anticipated sales. A common budgeting method,[21] this approach is often stated in terms such as "our promotion budget for this year is 3 percent of last year's gross sales." See the Using Marketing Dashboards box for an application of the promotion-to-sales ratio to the automotive industry.
- *Competitive parity.* Competitive parity budgeting matches the competitor's absolute level of spending or the proportion per point of market share.[22]
- *All you can afford.* Common to many businesses, the all-you-can-afford budgeting method allows money to be spent on promotion only after all other budget items—such as manufacturing costs—are covered.
- *Objective and task.* The best approach to budgeting is objective and task budgeting, whereby the company (1) determines its promotion objectives, (2) outlines the tasks to accomplish those objectives, and (3) determines the promotion cost of performing those tasks.[23]

Of the various methods, only the objective and task method takes into account what the company wants to accomplish and requires that the objectives be specified.[24]

Using Marketing Dashboards
How Much Should You Spend on IMC?

Integrated marketing communications (IMC) programs coordinate a variety of promotion alternatives to provide a consistent message across audiences. The amount spent on the various promotional elements, or on the total campaign, may vary depending on the target audience, the type of product, where the product is in the product life cycle, and the channel strategy selected. Managers often use the promotion-to-sales ratio on their marketing dashboard to assess how effective the IMC program expenditures are at generating sales.

Your Challenge As a manager at General Motors you've been asked to assess the effectiveness of all promotion expenditures during the past year. The promotion-to-sales ratio can be used by managers to make year-to-year comparisons of their programs, to compare the effectiveness of their program with competitors' programs, or to make comparisons with industry averages. You decide to calculate the promotion-to-sales ratio for General Motors. In addition, to allow a comparison, you decide to make the same calculation for one of your competitors, Ford, and for the entire automobile industry. The ratio is calculated as follows:

Promotion-to-sales ratio =
Total promotion expenditures/Total sales

Your Findings The information needed for these calculations is readily available from trade publications and annual reports. The following graph shows the promotion-to-sales ratio for General Motors and Ford and the automotive industry. General Motors spent $3.01 billion on its IMC program to generate $182 billion in U.S. sales for a ratio of 1.65 (percent). Ford's ratio was 1.47, and the industry average was 1.56.

Your Action General Motors's promotion-to-sales ratio is higher than Ford's and higher than the industry average. This suggests that the current mix of promotional activities and the level of expenditures may not be creating an effective IMC program. In the future you will want to monitor the factors that may influence the ratio. The average ratio for the beverage industry has risen to 9 while the average for grocery stores is about 1.

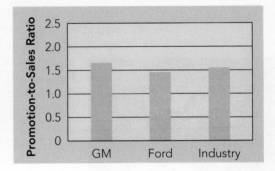

Selecting the Right Promotional Tools

Once a budget has been determined, the combination of the five basic IMC tools—advertising, personal selling, sales promotion, public relations, and direct marketing—can be specified. While many factors provide direction for selection of the appropriate mix, the large number of possible combinations of the promotional tools means that many combinations can achieve the same objective. Therefore, an analytical approach and experience are particularly important in this step of the promotion decision process. The specific mix can vary from a simple program using a single tool to a comprehensive program using all forms of promotion. The Olympics has become a very visible example of a comprehensive integrated communication program. Because the Games are repeated every two years, the promotion is continuous during "on" and "off" years. Included in the program are advertising campaigns, personal selling efforts by the Olympic committee and organizers, sales promotion activities such as product tie-ins and sponsorships, public relations programs managed by the host cities, online and digital communication, and direct marketing efforts targeted at a variety of audiences including governments, organizations, firms, athletes, and individuals.[25] At this stage, it is also important to assess the relative importance of the various tools. While it may be desirable to utilize and integrate several forms of promotion, one may deserve emphasis. The Olympics, for example, places primary importance on public relations and publicity.

The Olympics uses a comprehensive IMC program.

Designing the Promotion

The central element of a promotion program is the promotion itself. Advertising consists of advertising copy and the artwork that the target audience is intended to see or hear. Personal selling efforts depend on the characteristics and skills of the salesperson. Sales promotion activities consist of the specific details of inducements such as coupons, samples, and sweepstakes. Public relations efforts are readily seen in tangible elements such as news releases, and direct marketing actions depend on written, verbal, and electronic forms of delivery. The design of the promotion will play a primary role in determining the message that is communicated to the audience. This design activity is frequently viewed as the step requiring the most creativity. In addition, successful designs are often the result of insight regarding consumers' interests and purchasing behavior. All of the promotion tools have many design alternatives. Advertising, for example, can utilize fear, humor, attractiveness, or other themes in its appeal. Similarly, direct marketing can be designed for varying levels of personal or customized appeals. One of the challenges of IMC is to design each promotional activity to communicate the same message.[26]

Scheduling the Promotion

Once the design of each of the promotional program elements is complete, it is important to determine the most effective timing of their use. The promotion schedule describes the order in which each promotional tool is introduced and the frequency of its use during the campaign. Movie studio Columbia Pictures, for example, uses a schedule of several promotional tools for its movies. To generate interest in a movie such as *Angels and Demons*, a commercial was aired during the Super Bowl. The commercial generated more than 700,000 visits to the *Angels and Demons* Web site, which provided movie previews and clips, a Facebook link, and a contest with prizes related to movie scenes. In addition, Columbia held a press conference for science, religion, and entertainment journalists to initiate a public dialogue that would appear in periodicals, blogs, and social networks. It also released a movie "trailer" that was shown on television and in theaters. Then movie-related partnerships such as Mastercard's promotion offering an opportunity to win tickets to a prescreening of the film were announced. After the movie was released another contest and VIP parties encouraged fans to consider purchasing the DVD.[27]

Overall, the scheduling of the various promotions was designed to generate interest, bring consumers into theaters, and then encourage additional purchases after seeing the movie. Several factors such as seasonality and competitive promotion activity can also influence the promotion schedule. Businesses such as ski resorts, airlines, and professional sports teams are likely to reduce their promotional activity during the "off" season. Similarly, restaurants, retail stores, and health clubs are likely to increase their promotional activity when new competitors enter the market.

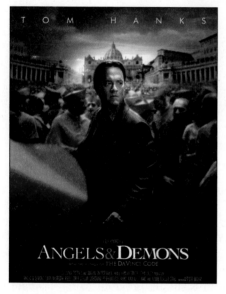

What promotional tools did Columbia Pictures use to support the release of this movie?

EXECUTING AND ASSESSING THE PROMOTION PROGRAM

As shown earlier in Figure 15–5, the ideal execution of a promotion program involves pretesting each design before it is actually used to allow for changes and modifications that improve its effectiveness. Similarly, posttests are recommended to evaluate the impact of each promotion and the contribution of the promotion toward achieving the program objectives. The most sophisticated pretest and posttest procedures have been developed for advertising and are discussed in Chapter 16. Testing procedures for sales promotion and direct marketing efforts currently focus on comparisons of different designs or responses of different segments. To fully benefit from IMC programs, companies must create and maintain a test-result database that allows comparisons of the relative impact of the promotional tools and their execution options in varying situations. Information from the database will allow informed design and execution decisions and provide support for IMC activities during internal reviews by financial or administrative personnel. The San Diego Padres baseball team, for example, developed a database of information relating attendance to its integrated campaign using a new logo, special events, merchandise sales, and a loyalty program.

Carrying out the promotion program can be expensive and time consuming. One researcher estimates that "an organization with sales less than $10 million can successfully implement an IMC program in one year, one with sales between $200 million and $500 million will need about three years, and one with sales between $2 billion and $5 billion will need five years." In addition, firms with a market orientation are more likely to implement an IMC program.[28] To facilitate the transition, approximately 200 integrated marketing communications agencies are in operation. In addition, some of the largest agencies are adopting approaches that embrace "total communications solutions."

Media agency Initiative, which recently won *Advertising Age* magazine's Media Agency of the Year award, for example, is part of an integrated network of 2,500 marketing professionals with 91 offices in 70 countries. The agency's services include planning, media buying, digital solutions, consumer research, ROI assessment, and sports and entertainment marketing. One of its integrated campaigns for Carl's Jr. restaurants included a partnership with the cable program *Family Guy*, a rap song for radio, bus bench advertising, video gaming, sports tie-ins, and free ring tones. The campaign resulted in a 47 percent increase in sales. Initiative has used this approach with other clients including Hyundai, MillerCoors, Dr Pepper, and Bayer. CEO Tim Spengler explains that one of the keys to the agency's success is an operations committee that encourages integration by including representatives that represent all forms of promotion. While many agencies may still be specialists, the trend today is clearly toward a long-term perspective in which all forms of promotion are integrated.[29]

An important factor in developing successful IMC programs is to create a process that facilitates their design and use. A tool used to evaluate a company's current process is the IMC audit. The audit analyzes the internal communication network of the company; identifies key audiences; evaluates customer databases; assesses messages in recent advertising, public relations releases, packaging, Web sites, and e-mail communication, signage, sales promotions, and direct mail; and determines the IMC expertise of company and agency personnel.[30] This process is becoming increasingly important as consumer-generated media such as blogs, RSS, podcasts, and social networks become more popular and as the use of search engines increases. Now, in addition to ensuring that traditional forms of communication are integrated, companies must be able to monitor consumer content, respond to inconsistent messages, and even answer questions from individual customers.[31]

learning review

10. What are the stages of the hierarchy of effects?

11. What are four approaches to setting the promotion budget?

12. How have advertising agencies changed to facilitate the use of IMC programs?

DIRECT MARKETING

Direct marketing has many forms and utilizes a variety of media. Several forms of direct marketing—direct mail and catalogs, television home shopping, telemarketing, and direct selling—were discussed as methods of nonstore retailing in Chapter 14. In addition, although advertising is discussed in Chapter 16, a form of advertising—direct response advertising—is an important form of direct marketing. Finally, interactive marketing is discussed in detail in Chapter 18. In this section, the growth of direct marketing, its value for consumers and sellers, and key global, technological, and ethical issues are discussed.

The Growth of Direct Marketing

The increasing interest in customer relationship management is reflected in the dramatic growth of direct marketing. The ability to customize communication efforts and create one-to-one interactions is appealing to most marketers, particularly those with IMC programs. While many direct marketing methods are not new, the ability to design and use them has increased with the availability of customer information databases and new printing technologies. In recent years, direct marketing growth has outpaced total economic growth. Direct marketing expenditures of $183 billion are expected to grow at a rate of 4 percent. Similarly, 2009 revenues of $2.1 trillion are expected to grow to $2.66 trillion by 2013. Direct marketing currently accounts for 10 percent of the total U.S. gross domestic product. E-mail, the most popular form of direct marketing, is used by 72 percent of marketers and generates less than a 1 percent response rate.[32] While e-mail is the most common form of direct marketing, most campaigns use several methods. Another component of the growth in direct marketing is the increasing popularity of the Internet. Total online sales have risen from close to nothing in 1996 to projections of $903 billion in 2013. Continued growth in the number of consumers with Internet access and the number of businesses with Web sites and electronic commerce offerings is likely to contribute to the future growth of direct marketing.

The Value of Direct Marketing

One of the most visible indicators of the value of direct marketing for consumers is the level of use of various forms of direct marketing. For example, 45 percent of the U.S. population has ordered merchandise or services by mail, phone, or Internet; 68 percent of households with Internet access shop online; consumers spent more than $156 billion on products available through television offers; and more than 21 percent of all adults make three to five purchases from a catalog each year. Consumers report many benefits, including the following: They don't have to go to a store; they can usually shop 24 hours a day; buying direct saves time; they avoid hassles with salespeople; they can save money; it's fun and entertaining; and direct marketing offers more privacy than in-store shopping. Many consumers also believe that direct marketing provides excellent customer service. Toll-free telephone numbers, customer service representatives with access to information regarding purchasing preferences, overnight delivery services, and unconditional guarantees all help create value for direct marketing customers. At Landsend.com, when customers need assistance they can click the Live Help icon to receive help from a sales representative on the phone or online until the correct product is found. "It's like we were walking down the aisle in a store," says one Lands' End customer.[33]

The value of direct marketing for sellers can be described in terms of the responses it generates. **Direct orders** are the result of offers that contain all the

Four Seasons uses direct mail to generate leads for its private residences.

information necessary for a prospective buyer to make a decision to purchase and complete the transaction. Priceline.com, for example, will send *PriceBreaker* RSS alerts to people in its database. The messages offer discounted fares and rates to customers who can travel on very short notice. **Lead generation** is the result of an offer designed to generate interest in a product or service and a request for additional information. Four Seasons Hotels now sells private residences in several of its properties and sends direct mail to prospective residents asking them to request additional information on the telephone or through a Web site. Finally, **traffic generation** is the outcome of an offer designed to motivate people to visit a business. Home Depot, for example, uses an opt-in e-mail alert to announce special sales that attract consumers to the store. Similarly, The Gap uses e-mails with coupons to increase store traffic.[34]

Technological, Global, and Ethical Issues in Direct Marketing

The information technology and databases described in Chapter 8 are key elements in any direct marketing program. Databases are the result of organizations' efforts to create profiles of customers so that direct marketing tools, such as e-mail and catalogs, can be directed at specific customers. While most companies try to keep records of their customers' past purchases, many other types of data are needed to use direct marketing to develop one-to-one relationships with customers. Some data, such as lifestyles, media use, and demographics, are best collected from the consumer. Other types of data, such as price, quantity, and brand, are best collected from the businesses where purchases are made. Increases in postage rates and the decline in the economy have also increased the importance of information related to the cost of direct marketing activities. Brookstone, for example, uses its database to mail more than 70 million catalogs to a specific profile of target customer each year. In addition, when the number of catalogs being sent to individual carrier routes is small, the database can add names to qualify for U.S. Postal Service discounts. This approach saves Brookstone $5,000 to $15,000 in postage each time it mails a catalog.[35]

Direct marketing faces several challenges and opportunities in global markets today. Several countries such as Italy and Denmark, for example, have requirements for mandatory "opt-in"—that is, potential customers must give permission to include their name on a list for direct marketing solicitations. In addition, the mail, telephone, and Internet systems in many countries are not as well developed as they are in the United States. The need for improved reliability and security in these countries has slowed the growth of direct mail, while the dramatic growth of mobile phone penetration has created an opportunity for direct mobile marketing campaigns. Another issue for global direct marketers is payment. The availability of credit and credit cards varies throughout the world, creating the need for alternatives such as C.O.D. (cash on delivery), bank deposits, and online payment accounts.[36]

Global and domestic direct marketers both face challenging ethical and sustainability issues today. Concerns about privacy, for example, have led to various attempts to provide guidelines that balance consumer and business interests. The European Union passed a consumer privacy law, called the *Data Protection Directive*, after several years of discussion with the Federation of European Direct Marketing and the U.K.'s Direct Marketing Association. In the United States, the Federal Trade Commission and many state legislatures have also been concerned about privacy. Several bills that call for a do-not-mail registry similar to the Do Not Call Registry are being discussed. Similarly, the proliferation of e-mail advertising, or "spam," has received increasing attention from consumers and marketers. Finally, in response to concerns raised by environmentalists, the industry is developing "green" best-

Making Responsible Decisions > > > > sustainability

Can Direct Marketing "Go Green"?

Each year consumers receive more than 100 billion pieces of direct mail. While this accounts for only 2.4 percent of the waste that ends up in landfills, it represents a huge opportunity for the direct marketing industry to adopt "green" business practices. A group of direct marketing companies and some of their corporate clients, called the Green Marketing Coalition, are developing best-practices guidelines. In addition, the United States Postal Service offers "green ideas for mailers" on its Web site. Some of the guidelines and ideas include:

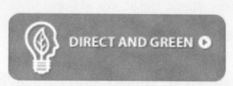

- Use chlorine-free recycled paper.
- Create an "environMAIList" by removing names of people who are unlikely to respond.
- Let people easily opt out of mailings.
- Use paper from forests certified by The Sustainable Forest Initiative or the Forest Stewardship Council.

- Use printers with green certification.
- Encourage customers to recycle the mailing once they've read it.

These guidelines will have increasing importance as the direct marketing industry continues to grow. Experts have observed that there has been a 35 percent shift in spending from telemarketing to direct marketing since the Do Not Call Registry came into effect in the United States. To evaluate the environmental impact of a company, you can use the Direct Marketing Association's checklist called the Environmental Planning Tool (www.the-dma.org/envgen/envgen1.php). Can you think of other ideas that would help the direct marketing industry minimize its impact on the environment?

practices guidelines for direct marketing companies.[37] The Making Responsible Decisions box offers examples of some of these guidelines.[38]

---

learning review

13. The ability to design and use direct marketing programs has increased with the availability of _____ and _____.

14. What are the three types of responses generated by direct marketing activities?

LEARNING OBJECTIVES REVIEW

LO1 *Discuss integrated marketing communication and the communication process.*

Integrated marketing communication is the concept of designing marketing communications programs that coordinate all promotional activities—advertising, personal selling, sales promotion, public relations, and direct marketing—to provide a consistent message across all audiences. The communication process conveys messages with six elements: a source, a message, a channel of communication, a receiver, and encoding and decoding. The communication process also includes a feedback loop and can be distorted by noise.

LO2 *Describe the promotional mix and the uniqueness of each component.*

There are five promotional alternatives. Advertising, sales promotion, and public relations are mass selling approaches, whereas personal selling and direct marketing use customized messages. Advertising can have high absolute costs but reaches large numbers of people. Personal selling has a high cost per contact but provides immediate feedback. Public relations is often difficult to obtain but is very credible. Sales promotion influences short-term consumer behavior. Direct marketing can help develop customer relationships although maintaining a database can be very expensive.

LO3 *Select the promotional approach appropriate to a product's target audience, life-cycle stage, and channel strategy.*
The promotional mix depends on the target audience. Programs for consumers, business buyers, and intermediaries might emphasize advertising, personal selling, and sales promotion, respectively. The promotional mix also changes over the product life-cycle stages. During the introduction stage, all promotional mix elements are used. During the growth stage advertising is emphasized, while the maturity stage utilizes sales promotion and direct marketing. Little promotion is used during the decline stage. Finally, the promotional mix can depend on the channel strategy. Push strategies require personal selling and sales promotions directed at channel members, while pull strategies depend on advertising and sales promotions directed at consumers.

LO4 *Describe the elements of the promotion decision process.*
The promotional decision process consists of three steps: planning, implementation, and evaluation. The planning step consists of six elements: identify the target audience, specify the objectives, set the budget, select the right promotional elements, design the promotion, and schedule the promotion. The implementation step includes pretesting. The evaluation step includes posttesting.

LO5 *Explain the value of direct marketing for consumers and sellers.*
The value of direct marketing for consumers is indicated by its level of use. For example, 68 percent of consumers have made a purchase by phone or mail, and 12 million people have purchased items from a television offer. The value of direct marketing for sellers can be measured in terms of three types of responses: direct orders, lead generation, and traffic generation.

FOCUSING ON KEY TERMS

advertising p. 336
communication p. 334
direct marketing p. 339
direct orders p. 348
hierarchy of effects p. 344

integrated marketing communications (IMC) p. 334
lead generation p. 349
personal selling p. 337
promotional mix p. 334
public relations p. 338

publicity p. 338
pull strategy p. 343
push strategy p. 342
sales promotion p. 339
traffic generation p. 349

APPLYING MARKETING KNOWLEDGE

1 After listening to a recent sales presentation, Mary Smith signed up for membership at the local health club. On arriving at the facility, she learned there was an additional fee for racquetball court rentals. "I don't remember that in the sales talk; I thought they said all facilities were included with the membership fee," complained Mary. Describe the problem in terms of the communication process.

2 Develop a matrix to compare the five elements of the promotional mix on three criteria—to *whom* you deliver the message, *what* you say, and *when* you say it.

3 Explain how the promotional tools used by an airline would differ if the target audience were (*a*) consumers who travel for pleasure and (*b*) corporate travel departments that select the airlines to be used by company employees.

4 Suppose you introduced a new consumer food product and invested heavily both in national advertising (pull strategy) and in training and motivating your field salesforce to sell the product to food stores (push strategy). What kinds of feedback would you receive from both the advertising and your salesforce? How could you increase both the quality and quantity of each?

5 Fisher-Price Company, long known as a manufacturer of children's toys, has introduced a line of clothing for children. Outline a promotional plan to get this product introduced in the marketplace.

6 Many insurance companies sell health insurance plans to companies. In these companies the employees pick the plan, but the set of offered plans is determined by the company. Recently Blue Cross–Blue Shield, a health insurance company, ran a television ad stating, "If your employer doesn't offer you Blue Cross–Blue Shield coverage, ask why." Explain the promotional strategy behind the advertisement.

7 Identify the sales promotion tools that might be useful for (*a*) Tastee Yogurt, a new brand introduction, (*b*) 3M self-sticking Post-it® Notes, and (*c*) Wrigley's Spearmint Gum.

8 Design an integrated marketing communications program—using each of the five promotional elements—for Rhapsody, the online music service.

9 BMW recently introduced its first sport activity vehicle, the X6, to compete with other popular crossover vehicles such as the Mercedes-Benz R-class and Buick's Enclave. Design a direct marketing program to generate (*a*) leads, (*b*) traffic in dealerships, and (*c*) direct orders.

10 Develop a privacy policy for database managers that provides a balance of consumer and seller perspectives. How would you encourage voluntary compliance with your policy? What methods of enforcement would you recommend?

To develop the promotion strategy for your marketing plan, follow the steps suggested in the planning phase of the promotion decision process described in Figure 15–5.

1 You should (*a*) identify the target audience, (*b*) specify the promotion objectives, (*c*) set the promotion budget, (*d*) select the right promotion tools, (*e*) design the promotion, and (*f*) schedule the promotion.

2 Also specify the pretesting and posttesting procedures needed in the implementation and evaluation phases.

3 Finally, describe how each of your promotion tools are integrated to provide a consistent message.

video case 15 Under Armour: Using IMC to Create a Brand for This Generation's Athletes

"Under Armour sees itself as the athletic brand of this generation. Everything that we create, every message that we put out, that's what we want to be," observes Marcus Stevens, senior creative director for Under Armour. Stevens is responsible for the complete brand aesthetic across all media, including broadcast, print, Web, and point-of-sale. His responsibility is to attract new customers and increase sales of the brand. When the company introduced its first product, a form-fitting moisture-wicking t-shirt to be worn under sportswear, the branding efforts were limited by a very small budget. Today, Under Armour is undertaking the challenge of creating an integrated marketing campaign that utilizes a much larger pool of resources and still delivers a consistent message. As a result of Under Armour's communication activities, "We are poised for growth in the future," explains Stevens.

THE COMPANY

Under Armour was founded by Kevin Plank, a University of Maryland football player who didn't like changing out of the sweat-soaked t-shirts he wore under his jersey during practices and games. In 1996 he developed a moisture-wicking fabric and modeled his first product after a typical cotton t-shirt. After several trips to the patent office, and some input from his brother, Kevin decided on the name Under Armour and set up the business in his grandmother's basement. Early sales depended entirely on word-of-mouth advertising that was generated by events such as a *USA Today* photo of an Oakland Raider football player wearing an Under Armour shirt, and Georgia Tech ordering more than 300 shirts for its entire football team. The turning point for the company came when Under Armour products were used in the movie *Any Given Sunday*. Plank decided to build on the exposure provided by the movie and purchased a full-page ad in *ESPN The Magazine*. That ad generated $750,000 in sales and began the incredible growth of the company.

As the company grew, Plank developed four "Keys of Greatness" to guide him and the Under Armour employees. The keys are:

- Build a great product
- Tell a great story about the product
- Provide great service
- Build a great team

The success of Under Armour's first product soon led to a complete line of performance sports apparel including shirts, pants, shorts, outerwear, gloves, footwear, and accessories. Telling the story was the responsibility of the marketing department and emphasized the need for integrated marketing communications. Great service required support from sales and service representatives. Finally, building a great team meant that Plank always hired the best and brightest people possible. The focus on athletes led to many applications of sports concepts to the business—meetings are called "huddles," the huddle doesn't end until a "play is called," and rapid response to changes in the environment may require "calling an audible." The approach creates a team atmosphere where everyone works together to act on the play.

Today, Under Armour's mission is to make all athletes better through passion, science, and the relentless pursuit of innovation. It offers its product assortment to men, women, and youth online and through more than 15,000 retail locations including Dick's Sporting Goods, the Sports Authority, Hibbett Sporting Goods, and Modell's Sporting Goods. International distribution includes outlets in the United Kingdom, France, Germany, Italy, New Zealand, and Japan. Headquarters has moved from Plank's grandmother's basement to Baltimore, Maryland, and the number of employees has increased to 2,200. Under Armour sales now exceed $700 million!

THE IMC PROGRAM

Stevens first met Plank at an advertising agency where Stevens worked. Plank's idea for an athletic brand for this generation's athlete was very exciting and Stevens soon left the agency to work with Plank. With a limited budget, the challenge was getting the message out to consumers. According to Stevens, "We didn't come in with a polished business plan—and a calendar to execute against; we came in with an idea and a lot of passion." To compete with much larger apparel manufacturers Stevens knew that Under Armour's marketing activities would need to provide a consistent message through advertising, public relations, personal selling, and all promotional efforts. Kevin Haley, senior vice president of sports marketing, agrees, "everything has to be integrated." Integrating all promotion activities allows Under Armour to increase the effectiveness of its budget as it strives to create and maintain its brand.

Advertising

Following the release of *Any Given Sunday* and its first print ad in *ESPN the Magazine,* Under Armour began work on a new television advertising campaign. The ad, featuring Eric Ogbogu as "Big E," introduced the tagline, "We must protect this house," and was released at the same time as ESPN's new series *Playmakers,* which featured football players wearing Under Armour apparel. According to Steven Battista, senior vice president of brand, the two coinciding events "propelled the brand into the national spotlight, and then soon after that you would see fans at games holding up signs saying, 'Protect this house.'" The phrase was used by sports fans, David Letterman, Oprah Winfrey, and many others and

soon became part of American lexicon. Other campaigns also helped develop the Under Armour brand and image. For example, "Click, Clack" featured the familiar sound made by cleated shoes, and appealed to athletes in many sports such as golf, lacrosse, and baseball, in addition to football.

Under Armour decided to advertise on the Super Bowl to introduce a new performance training shoe. The message in the ad focused on the athlete of tomorrow and included the tagline, "The future is ours." The athletes in the ad included Carl Weathers, a NASCAR driver; Ray Lewis, a football linebacker; Kimmie Meissner, a figure skater; and many others. The ad made a statement that Under Armour could help all athletes train like champions. "The future is ours" was a huge success ranking in the top-five ads according to *USA Today*'s Ad Meter. In addition, Web site traffic tripled following the ad and orders for the product began pouring in! The Super Bowl ad also helped make a statement about the Under Armour brand—that the company, the CEO, the product, and the consumers all represented a new prototype for the future.

Public Relations and Promotion

According to Battista, "Half the benefit of a 60-second ad in the Super Bowl is the PR leading up to it and the attention you get" from producing and running the advertisement. Marketing benefits also result from promotion activities such as athlete endorsements, sponsorships, and product placements. These activities play an important role

in Under Armour's integrated marketing communications strategy. Each potential athlete endorsement, for example, is evaluated in terms of the products they will be supporting, the media that would be used, and the potential for in-store and on-field visibility. Under Armour signed Alfonso Soriano, a Chicago Cubs baseball player, to support its baseball cleats and baseball apparel, the outdoor advertising at Wrigley Field, and the retail store in the Chicago market. Under Armour looks for athletes that are "all about performance," explains Haley. They "need to be a team player, who is doing everything they can to win on every single play."

Under Armour has also developed many sponsorship relationships with teams and organizations. For example, Under Armour is the official outfitter for the football programs at Auburn University, the University of Delaware, the University of Hawaii, the University of North Texas, the University of South Carolina, and many other schools. The company recently signed a 5-year agreement with the University of Maryland to outfit all of its 27 varsity sports. Similarly, Under Armour is the supplier for all 17 varsity athletic teams at Texas Tech University. Under Armour has also sponsored high school athletes, professional soccer teams, and the NFL.

Product placements in movies, television shows, and video games have reinforced Under Armour's branding efforts and provided exposure to new audiences. In addition to *Any Given Sunday* you may remember seeing Under Armour products in the movies *Gridiron Gang* and *The Replacements*. Television programs with Under Armour product placements include *Friday Night Lights*, *The Sopranos*, and *MTV Road Rules*. Under Armour even appears in video games such as *Tiger Woods Golf* and *Fight Night 3*!

Retail and Online

When Plank first started Under Armour, its Web site (www.underarmour.com) was its only means of sales and distribution. As the company grew it gained distribution in many retailers. The point-of-sale displays in the retailers, however, offered a unique opportunity to integrate Under Armour's branding. When Under Armour moved into large retailers it noticed that the mannequins in the stores didn't look like the athletes in the advertising because the mannequins did not have muscles. To create a consistent message Under Armour made its own mannequins for the stores so that the displays would look like the athletes in the commercials. Eventually, Under Armour also began opening its own stores. The first Under Armour store opened in Annapolis, Maryland, in 2008 and many others soon followed.

The Under Armour Web site remains an important part of the integrated marketing program. Approximately 15 percent of all sales come through the Web site, and many Under Armour consumers use the Web site to learn about new products, study technical details, or view print or television ads. Consumers who register on the site can receive e-mail messages about new or seasonal products

and new campaigns. Currently, the Under Armour Web site attracts an average of 35,000 visitors each day. The online program also includes several social networking elements. Under Armour, for example, is building a presence on Facebook and on Xbox Live marketplace. All of these activities help ensure that consumers will be exposed to a consistent message regardless of the medium they utilize.

FUTURE STRATEGY

How can Under Armour continue its incredible record of growth? Experts observe that future growth will require the company to broaden its appeal without alienating the original segment of athletes interested in performance. There are opportunities to expand exposure in many sports such as the fast-growing lacrosse segment, to attract more men, women, and youth, and to introduce new products to the current line. Under Armour, for example, recently introduced a line of running shoes—a large category with broad appeal to many consumers. Integrating the growth activities will be critical to the company's success. As Battista observes, everything has to "look right and have the same message points and the same type of branding and look and feel!"

The future is likely to be very exciting for Under Armour as it continues to introduce new products and enter new markets. For example, the company recently introduced mouth guards and a body suit that helps athletes recover from a workout faster. To expand in international markets Under Armour is creating distribution networks in Europe and Asia and signing endorsement deals with rugby players, Olympians, and other international athletes. In addition, to change perceptions that Under Armour products are used primarily by football players, the company now sponsors 27 boys' and girls' high school basketball teams. Under Armour's branding and communication strategies have been extraordinarily successful as the company now is the fastest growing performance sports brand. In fact, the company has grown so quickly that it plans to add an additional 135,000 square feet of new space across the street from its headquarters to provide showrooms and new offices. According to one newspaper headline, the company is a "runaway success"!

Questions

1 What promotional opportunities gave Under Armour its initial success?

2 Which of the promotional elements described in Figure 15-2 are used by Under Armour in its IMC campaigns?

3 What are several new strategies Under Armour might pursue as it attempts to continue its extraordinary record of growth?

DREAMWORKS
HOW TO TRAIN YOUR
DRAGON
3D
In Theatres, real D 3D and IMAX 3D March 26

16

Advertising, Sales Promotion, and Public Relations

LEARNING OBJECTIVES

After reading this chapter you should be able to:

LO1 Explain the differences between product advertising and institutional advertising and the variations within each type.

LO2 Describe the steps used to develop, execute, and evaluate an advertising program.

LO3 Explain the advantages and disadvantages of alternative advertising media.

LO4 Discuss the strengths and weaknesses of consumer-oriented and trade-oriented sales promotions.

LO5 Recognize public relations as an important form of communication.

ADVERTISING MOVES TO A NEW DIMENSION: THE THIRD DIMENSION

If Jeffery Katzenberg, James Cameron, and Steven Spielberg have their way, most visual media, including advertising, could be presented in digital 3-D in the near future. Their movie studio, DreamWorks, is developing a technology to bring a true third dimension to movie theaters and television screens!

DreamWorks's first 3-D movie, *Monsters vs. Aliens*, was a huge step for the company. "This is really a revolution," explains CEO Katzenberg. In fact, he believes the change is so important that in the future all DreamWorks's movies, such as the recent *How to Train Your Dragon*, will be made in 3-D. The technology is not just for movies and theaters, however; it will also change broadcasting, TV displays, gaming, videos, and all forms of advertising.

The first 3-D advertisements were 30-second spots during the Super Bowl for *Monsters vs. Aliens* and Sobe Life Water energy drinks. More than 125 million pairs of free 3-D glasses, using a new technology, were distributed in the United States for use during the Super Bowl. Other forms of 3-D are being developed also. For example, a Japanese company is developing a laser system that will project 3-D outdoor advertisements. Other applications will include digital billboards and signs. The combination of the two has the potential to allow consumers to experience advertising in a virtual 3-D environment.

Unlike traditional advertising, 3-D advertising is an opportunity to immerse consumers in an experience. Today's consumers are not passive; they want to be involved and engaged. The third dimension allows viewers to participate in the ad rather than just observe it. Advertisers can use 3-D to pull the audience into an ad to feel the message being communicated. Some observers believe that 3-D viewing is so close to a real experience that it will improve retention of the message. This new generation of 3-D technology is for both animation and live action. Comcast mixed animation and live action to create its recent 3-D ad campaign called "Comcast Town." The six TV spots create an imaginary 3-D world that illustrates connectivity and entertainment for live characters. Another ad, created by NBC, encoded a clip of its TV program *Chuck* in 3-D using only the live characters and setting.

Watch for a general trend toward 3-D. Katzenberg predicts that soon everyone will own a pair of 3-D glasses![1]

The 3-D explosion is just one of the many exciting changes occurring in the field of advertising today. They illustrate the importance of advertising as one of the five promotional mix elements in marketing communications programs. This chapter describes three of the promotional mix elements—advertising, sales promotion, and public relations. Direct marketing was covered in Chapter 15, and personal selling is covered in Chapter 17.

TYPES OF ADVERTISEMENTS

Chapter 15 described **advertising** as any paid form of nonpersonal communication about an organization, a product, a service, or an idea by an identified sponsor. As you look through any magazine, watch television, listen to the radio, or browse the Internet, the variety of advertisements you see or hear may give you the impression that they have few similarities. Advertisements are prepared for different purposes, but they basically consist of two types: product advertisements and institutional advertisements.

Product Advertisements

LO1

Focused on selling a product or service, **product advertisements** take three forms: (1) pioneering (or informational), (2) competitive (or persuasive), and (3) reminder. Look at the ads for Visa, Cadillac, and M&Ms to determine the type and objective of each ad.

Used in the introductory stage of the product life cycle, *pioneering* advertisements tell people what a product is, what it can do, and where it can be found. The key objective of a pioneering advertisement (such as the ad for Visa's new Black card) is to inform the target market. Informational ads, particularly those with specific information, have been found to be interesting, convincing, and effective.[2]

Advertising that promotes a specific brand's features and benefits is *competitive*. The objective of these messages is to persuade the target market to select the firm's brand rather than that of a competitor. An increasingly common form of competitive advertising is *comparative* advertising, which shows one brand's strengths relative to those of competitors.[3] The Cadillac ad, for example, highlights the competitive advantage of the Cadillac Escalade hybrid compared to other vehicles such as the BMW X3 and the Volvo XC90. Studies indicate that comparative ads attract more attention and increase the perceived quality of the advertiser's brand although their impact may vary by product type, message content, and audience gender.[4] Firms that use comparative advertising need market research to provide legal support for their claims.[5]

Reminder advertising is used to reinforce previous knowledge of a product. The M&Ms ad shown reminds consumers about a special event, in this case, Valentine's Day. Reminder advertising is good for products that have achieved a well-recognized position and are in the mature phase of their product life cycle. Another type of

Product advertisements serve varying purposes. Of the three ads featured, which one would be considered a pioneering ad? A competitive ad? A reminder ad?

reminder ad, *reinforcement*, is used to assure current users they made the right choice. One example is used in Dial soap advertisements: "Aren't you glad you use Dial. Don't you wish everybody did?"

Institutional Advertisements

institutional advertisements

Advertisements designed to build goodwill or an image for an organization, rather than promote a specific product or service.

The objective of **institutional advertisements** is to build goodwill or an image for an organization rather than promote a specific product or service. Institutional advertising has been used by companies such as Texaco, Pfizer, and IBM to build confidence in the company name.[6] Often this form of advertising is used to support the public relations plan or counter adverse publicity. Four alternative forms of institutional advertisements are often used:

A competitive institutional ad by dairy farmers tries to increase demand for milk.

1. *Advocacy* advertisements state the position of a company on an issue. Chevron places ads encouraging consumers to use less energy. Another form of advocacy advertisement is used when organizations make a request related to a particular action or behavior, such as a request by American Red Cross for blood donations.
2. *Pioneering institutional* advertisements, like the pioneering ads for products discussed earlier, are used for announcements about what a company is, what it can do, or where it is located. Recent Bayer ads stating, "We cure more headaches than you think," are intended to inform consumers that the company produces many products in addition to aspirin. Amway uses pioneering institutional ads in its "Now You Know" campaign to inform people about the company and its products.
3. *Competitive institutional* advertisements promote the advantages of one product class over another and are used in markets where different product classes compete for the same buyers. America's milk processors and dairy farmers use their "Got Milk?" campaign to increase demand for milk as it competes against other beverages.
4. *Reminder institutional* advertisements, like the product form, simply bring the company's name to the attention of the target market again. The Army branch of the U.S. military sponsors a campaign to remind potential recruits of the opportunities in the army.

> **learning review**
> 1. What is the difference between pioneering and competitive ads?
> 2. What is the purpose of an institutional advertisement?

DEVELOPING THE ADVERTISING PROGRAM

LO2

The promotion decision process described in Chapter 15 can be applied to each of the promotional elements. Advertising, for example, can be managed by following the three steps of the process (developing, executing, and assessing the advertising program).

Identifying the Target Audience

To develop an effective advertising program, advertisers must identify the target audience. All aspects of an advertising program are likely to be influenced by the characteristics of the prospective consumer. Understanding the lifestyles, attitudes, and demographics of the target market is essential. NBC, for example, promoted its medical/nurse drama "Mercy" to 18- to 34-year-old women with program trailers.[7] Similarly, the placement of ads depends on the audience. When Porsche began its 18-month-long "Can you afford a Porsche?" campaign, it used mobile phone ads to reach its target market—young, tech-savvy, connected men.[8] Even scheduling can depend on the audience. Nike schedules advertising, sponsorships, deals, and endorsements to correspond with the Olympics to appeal to "hard-core" athletes.[9] To eliminate possible bias that might result from subjective judgments about some population segments, the Federal Communications Commission suggests that advertising program decisions be based on market research about the target audience.[10]

Specifying Advertising Objectives

The guidelines for setting promotion objectives described in Chapter 15 also apply to setting advertising objectives. This step helps advertisers with other choices in the promotion decision process such as selecting media and evaluating a campaign. Advertising with an objective of creating awareness, for example, would be better matched with a magazine than a directory such as the Yellow Pages. The Magazine Publishers of America believe objectives are so important that they offer a $100,000 prize each year to the campaign that best meets its objectives. Recently, Pedigree food for dogs won with its "Adoption" campaign, which increased sales by 11 percent and raised $2.7 million for shelter dogs.[11] Similarly, the Advertising Research Foundation sponsors an Advertising Effectiveness Council to investigate new techniques for measuring the impact of all forms of advertising.[12]

Setting the Advertising Budget

During the 1990 Super Bowl, it cost companies $700,000 to place a 30-second ad. By 2010, the cost of placing a 30-second ad during Super Bowl XLIV was $3 mil-

lion. The reason for the escalating cost is the growing number of viewers: 100 million people, or about 50 percent of the viewing public, watch the game. In addition, the audience is attractive to advertisers because research indicates it is equally split between men and women and many viewers look forward to watching the 65 "spots." The ads are effective too: Movies promoted on the Super Bowl achieve 40 percent more revenue than movies not promoted during the Super Bowl; E*TRADE increased the number of new accounts by 32 percent in the week after the game; and Go Daddy estimates that it received $11.7 million in publicity as a result of its ads. As a result, the Super Bowl attracts relatively new advertisers, such as Hulu and Denny's, as well as regular advertisers, such as Anheuser-Busch, Doritos, and Coca-Cola.[13]

Do you remember this Doritos ad from the Super Bowl?

Designing the Advertisement

An advertising message usually focuses on the key benefits of the product that are important to a prospective buyer in making trial and adoption decisions. The message depends on the general form or appeal used in the ad and the actual words included in the ad.

Message Content Most advertising messages are made up of both informational and persuasional elements. Information and persuasive content can be combined in the form of an appeal to provide a basic reason for the consumer to act. Although the marketer can use many different types of appeals, common advertising appeals include fear, sex, and humor.

Fear appeals suggest to the consumer that he or she can avoid some negative experience through the purchase and use of a product or service, a change in behav-

It's the money you could be saving with GEICO.

GEICO.

See how much you could save, visit geico.com
or call 1-800-947-AUTO.

This Geico ad is an example
of a humor appeal.

ior, or a reduction in the use of a product. Examples with which you may be familiar include: automobile safety ads that depict an accident or injury; political candidate endorsements that warn against the rise of other, unpopular ideologies; or social cause ads warning of the serious consequences of drug and alcohol use. When using fear appeals, the advertiser must be sure that the appeal is strong enough to get the audience's attention and concern but not so strong that it will lead them to tune out the message. In fact, research on antismoking ads indicates that stressing the severity of long-term health risks may actually enhance smoking's allure among youth.[14]

In contrast, *sex appeals* suggest to the audience that the product will increase the attractiveness of the user. Sex appeals can be found in almost any product category, from automobiles to toothpaste. The contemporary women's clothing store Bebe, for example, designs its advertising to "attract customers who are intrigued by the playfully sensual and evocative imagery of the Bebe lifestyle." Studies indicate that sex appeals increase attention by helping advertising stand out in today's cluttered media environment. Unfortunately, sexual content does not always lead to changes in recall, recognition, or purchase intent. Experts suggest that sexual content is most effective when there is a strong fit between the use of a sex appeal in the ad and the image and positioning of the brand.[15]

Humor appeals imply either directly or subtly that the product is more fun or exciting than competitors' offerings. As with fear and sex appeals, the use of humor is widespread in advertising and can be found in many product categories. You may have smiled at the popular Geico ads that use cavemen, a gecko, and a stack of money with eyes named Kash to use humor to differentiate the company from its competitors. The ads have been so popular that Geico has created viral videos featuring the gecko and posted them on video-sharing Web sites such as YouTube, Metacafe, and Slide, where millions of viewers watch them within days.[16] You may have a favorite humorous ad character, such as the Energizer battery bunny, the AFLAC duck, or Travelocity's gnome. Advertisers believe that humor improves the effectiveness of their ads, although some studies suggest that humor wears out quickly, losing the interest of consumers. Another problem with humor appeals is that their effectiveness may vary across cultures if used in a global campaign.[17]

Creating the Actual Message Copywriters are responsible for creating the text portion of the messages in advertisements. Translating the copywriter's ideas into an actual advertisement is a complex process.

Designing quality artwork, layout, and production for an advertisement is costly and time consuming. High-quality TV commercials typically cost about $361,000 to produce a 30-second ad, a task done by about 2,000 small commercial production companies across the United States. One reason for the high costs is that as companies have developed global campaigns, the need to shoot commercials in exotic locations has increased. Audi recently filmed commercials in Germany, Australia, and Morocco. Actors are also expensive: Compensation for typical TV ad is $17,000.[18]

Advertising agency Crispin Porter & Bogusky was recently designated *Advertising Age* magazine's U.S. Agency of the Year for its unique ability to take "a simple proposition" and "somehow make it entertainment." Examples of the agency's approach include the "I'm a PC" campaign for Microsoft, the "Whopper Virgin" campaign for Burger King, and the "It's What the People Want" campaign for Volkswagen. Crispin was also recognized for adding product design to the services it offers clients. Some of its design ideas include a public bike-rental program, a pen version of WD-40, and an eco-friendly sponge![19]

learning review

3. The Federal Communications Commission suggests that advertising program decisions be based on _____

4. Describe three common forms of advertising appeals.

FIGURE 16–1

Television, direct mail, and newspapers account for 60 percent of all advertising expenditures (in millions).

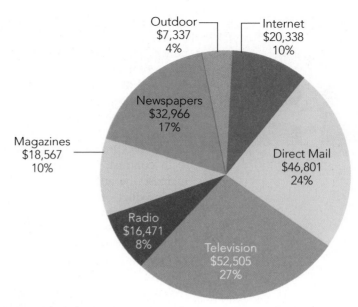

Selecting the Right Media

Every advertiser must decide where to place its advertisements. The alternatives are the *advertising media*, the means by which the message is communicated to the target audience. Newspapers, magazines, radio, and TV are examples of advertising media. This decision on media selection is related to the target audience, type of product, nature of the message, campaign objectives, available budget, and the costs of the alternative media. Figure 16–1 shows the distribution of the $195 billion spent on advertising among the many media alternatives.[20]

In deciding where to place advertisements, a company has several media to choose from and a number of alternatives, or vehicles, within each medium. Often advertisers use a mix of media forms and vehicles to maximize the exposure of the message to the target audience while at the same time minimizing costs. These two conflicting goals of (1) maximizing exposure and (2) minimizing costs are of central importance to media planning.

Because advertisers try to maximize the number of individuals in the target market exposed to the message, they must be concerned with reach. *Reach* is the number of different people or households exposed to an advertisement. The exact definition of reach sometimes varies among alternative media. Newspapers often use reach to describe their total circulation or the number of different households that buy the paper. Television and radio stations, in contrast, describe their reach using the term *rating*—the percentage of households in a market that are tuned to a particular TV show or radio station. In general, advertisers try to maximize reach in their target market at the lowest cost.

Although reach is important, advertisers are also interested in exposing their target audience to a message more than once. This is because consumers often do not pay close attention to advertising messages, some of which contain large amounts of relatively complex information. When advertisers want to reach the same audience more than once, they are concerned with *frequency*, the average number of times a person in the target audience is exposed to a message or advertisement. Like reach, greater frequency is generally viewed as desirable. Studies indicate that with repeated exposure to advertisements consumers respond more favorably to brand extensions.[21]

When reach (expressed as a percentage of the total market) is multiplied by frequency, an advertiser will obtain a commonly used reference number called *gross rating points* (GRPs). To obtain the appropriate number of GRPs to achieve an advertising campaign's objectives, the media planner must balance reach and frequency. The balance will also be influenced by cost. *Cost per thousand* (CPM) refers to the cost of reaching 1,000 individuals or households with the advertising message in a given medium (*M* is the Roman numeral for 1,000). See the Using Marketing Dashboards box for an example of the use of CPM in media selection.

Using Marketing Dashboards
What Is the Best Way to Reach 1,000 Customers?

Marketing managers must choose from many advertising options as they design a campaign to reach potential customers. Because there are so many media alternatives (television, radio, magazines, etc.) and multiple options within each of the media, it is important to monitor the efficiency of advertising expenditures on your marketing dashboard.

Your Challenge As the marketing manager for a company about to introduce a new soft drink into the U.S. market, you are preparing a presentation in which you must make recommendations for the advertising campaign. You have observed that competitors use magazine ads, newspaper ads, and even Super Bowl ads! To compare the cost of some of the alternatives you decide to use one of the most common measures in advertising: cost per thousand impressions (CPM). The CPM is calculated as follows:

Cost per thousand impressions =
Advertising cost ($)/Impressions generated (in 1,000s)

Your challenge is to determine the most efficient use of your advertising budget.

Your Findings Your research department helps you collect cost and audience size information for three options: full-page color ads in *Sports Illustrated* magazine and the

Media Alternative	Cost of Ad	Audience Size	Cost per Thousand Impressions
Sports Illustrated (magazine)	$336,000	3,150,000	$107
USA Today (newspaper)	$197,720	2,109,628	$94
Super Bowl (television)	$3,000,000	100,000,000	$30

USA Today newspaper, and a 30-second television ad during the Super Bowl. With this information you are able to calculate the cost per thousand impressions for each alternative.

Your Action Based on the calculations for these options, you see that there is a large variation in the cost of reaching 1,000 potential customers (CPM) and also in the absolute cost of the advertising. Although advertising during the Super Bowl has the lowest CPM, $30 for each 1,000 impressions, it also has the largest absolute cost! Your next step will be to consider other factors such as your total available budget, the profiles of the audiences each alternative reaches, and whether the type of message you want to deliver is better communicated in print or on television.

Different Media Alternatives

Figure 16–2 on the next page summarizes the advantages and disadvantages of the major advertising media, which are described in more detail below. The advantages and disadvantages of direct mail are discussed in Chapter 15.

Television Television is a valuable medium because it communicates with sight, sound, and motion. Print advertisements alone could never give you the sense of a sports car accelerating from a stop or cornering at high speed. In addition, network television reaches 98.9 percent of all households—114.9 million—more than any other advertising option. Unfortunately, the percentage of households watching network television has declined from 56 percent in 1973 to approximately 18 percent today. Out-of-home TV viewing, however, has been increasing as millions of viewers can now see televisions in bars, hotels, offices, airports, and college campuses.[22]

Television's major disadvantage is cost: The price of a prime-time, 30-second ad run during *Sunday Night Football* is $339,700, and the average price for all prime-time programs is $125,283. Because of these high charges, many advertisers choose less expensive "spot" ads, which run between programs in 10-, 15-, 30-, or 60-second lengths. Shorter ads reduce costs but severely restrict the amount of information and emotion that can be conveyed. Miller, however, increased sales by 8 percent in the week after it ran one-second ads during the Super Bowl. In addition, there is some indication that advertisers are shifting their interest to live events rather than programs that might be watched on a DVR days later.[23]

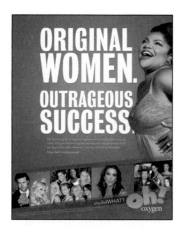

Specialized channels such as *Oxygen* help reduce wasted coverage.

MEDIUM	ADVANTAGES	DISADVANTAGES
Television	Reaches extremely large audience; uses picture, print, sound, and motion for effect; can target specific audiences	High cost to prepare and run ads; short exposure time and perishable message; difficult to convey complex information
Radio	Low cost; can target specific local audiences; ads can be placed quickly; can use sound, humor, and intimacy effectively	No visual element; short exposure time and perishable message; difficult to convey complex information
Magazines	Can target specific audiences; high-quality color; long life of ad; ads can be clipped and saved; can convey complex information	Long time needed to place ad; relatively high cost; competes for attention with other magazine features
Newspapers	Excellent coverage of local markets; ads can be placed and changed quickly; ads can be saved; quick consumer response; low cost	Ads compete for attention with other newspaper features; short life span; poor color
Yellow pages	Excellent coverage of geographic segments; long use period; available 24 hours/day 365 days/year	Proliferation of competitive directories in many markets; difficult to keep up-to-date
Internet	Video and audio capabilities; animation can capture attention; ads can be interactive and link to advertiser	Animation and interactivity require large files and more time to load; effectiveness is still uncertain
Outdoor	Low cost; local market focus; high visibility; opportunity for repeat exposures	Message must be short and simple; low selectivity of audience; criticized as a traffic hazard
Direct mail	High selectivity of audience; can contain complex information and personalized messages; high-quality graphics	High cost per contact; poor image (junk mail)

FIGURE 16–2
Advertisers must consider the advantages and disadvantages of the many media alternatives.

infomercials
Program-length (30-minute) advertisements that take an educational approach to communication with potential customers.

Another problem with television advertising is the likelihood of *wasted coverage*—having people outside the market for the product see the advertisement. The cost and wasted coverage problems of TV advertising can be reduced through the specialized cable and satellite channels. Advertising time is often less expensive on cable and satellite channels than on the broadcast networks. There are currently about 150 options, such as ESPN, MTV, Lifetime, Oxygen, the Speed Channel, the History Channel, the Science Channel, and the Food Network, that reach very narrowly defined audiences. Other forms of television viewing are changing advertising also. Many cable and satellite TV services offer DVRs and remotes with "skip" buttons for ad-zapping. Pay-per-view options and "download" services such as iTunes offer commercial-free viewing. In addition, Web sites such as Fancast, Hulu, Joost, and YouTube now provide access to cable and broadcast programming with limited advertising.[24]

Another popular form of television advertising is the infomercial. **Infomercials** are program-length (30-minute) advertisements that take an educational approach to communication with potential customers. What was one of the most successful infomercials? During his presidential campaign, Barack Obama ran an infomercial that attracted 33.5 million viewers—more than the final game of the World Series![25]

Radio The United States has more than 14,000 radio stations—eight times as many as there are television stations. The major advantage of radio is that it is a segmented medium. For example, the Farm Radio Network, the Family Life Network, Business Talk Radio, and the Performance Racing Network are all listened to by different market segments. The large number of media options today has reduced the amount of time spent listening to radio also. The average 18- to 24-year-old, however, still listens to radio an average of 2.5 hours each day, making radio an important medium for businesses with college students as a target market.[26]

A disadvantage of radio is that it has limited use for products that must be seen. Another problem is the ease with which consumers can tune out a commercial by switching stations. Satellite radio service Sirius XM offers more than 130 digital-quality, coast-to-coast channels to consumers for an annual subscription fee. Many of the channels are 100 percent commercial-free. Radio is also a medium that competes for people's attention as they do other activities such as driving, working, or relaxing. Radio listening time reaches its peak during the morning drive time (7 to 9 A.M.), remains high during the day, and then begins to decline in the afternoon (4 P.M.) as people return home and start evening activities.[27]

Magazines Magazines have become a very specialized medium, primarily because there are currently more than 19,532 magazines. Some 200 new magazines are introduced each year, such as *Disney Twenty-Three*, a quarterly magazine for Disney fans; *Bicycle Times*, a magazine about everyday bicycling experiences; and *Best You*, a magazine about health, diet, and exercise. A new form of existing magazines—issues containing reader-generated content—has also been introduced recently. *This Old House* and *BusinessWeek*, for example, have asked readers to create substantial portions of special issues of the magazines.[28]

The marketing advantage of this medium is the great number of special-interest publications that appeal to narrowly defined segments. Runners read *Runner's World*, sailors buy *Yachting*, gardeners subscribe to *Garden Design*, and children peruse *Sports Illustrated for Kids*. More than 645 publications focus on travel, 195 are dedicated to interior design and decoration, and 139 are related to golf. Each magazine's readers often represent a unique profile. Take the *Rolling Stone* reader, who tends to listen to music more than most people; Sirius XM satellite radio knows an ad in *Rolling Stone* is reaching the desired target audience. In addition, recent studies comparing advertising in different media suggest that magazine advertising is perceived to be more "trustworthy," "inspirational," and engaging than other media.[29]

The cost of advertising in national magazines is a disadvantage, but many national publications publish regional and even metro editions, which reduces the absolute cost and wasted coverage. *Time* publishes well over 400 editions, including Latin American, Canadian, Asian, South Pacific, European, and U.S. editions. The U.S. editions include geographic and demographic options.

Newspapers Newspapers are an important local medium with excellent reach potential. Daily publication allows advertisements to focus on specific current events, such as a 24-hour sale. Local retailers often use newspapers as their sole advertising medium. Newspapers are rarely saved by the purchaser, however, so companies are generally limited to ads that call for an immediate customer response (although customers can clip and save ads they select). Companies also cannot depend on newspapers for color reproduction as good as that in most magazines.

National advertising campaigns rarely include this medium except in conjunction with local distributors of their products. In these instances, both parties often share the advertising costs using a cooperative advertising program, which is described later in this chapter. Another exception is the use of newspapers such as *The Wall Street Journal* and *USA Today*, both of which have national distribution of more than 2 million readers.

Magazines such as *Sports Illustrated for Kids* appeal to narrowly defined segments.

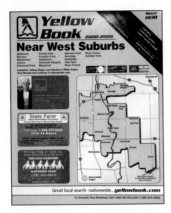

Yellow pages have many advantages, including a long life span.

DoubleClick's Dart Search service can provide an assessment of the effectiveness of a Web site.

Yellow Pages Yellow pages represent an advertising media alternative comparable to radio and magazines in terms of expenditures—about $15 billion in the United States and $25 billion globally. According to the Yellow Pages Association, consumers turn to print yellow pages more than 13 billion times annually and online yellow pages an additional 3.8 billion times per year. One reason for this high level of use is that the 6,500 yellow pages directories reach almost all households with telephones. Yellow pages are a directional medium because they help consumers know where purchases can be made after other media have created awareness and demand. A disadvantage is the proliferation of directories. AT&T (Real Yellow Pages), Idearc (Verizon Superpages), and R.H. Donnelley (DEX) now produce competing directories for many cities, neighborhoods, and ethnic groups.[30]

Internet The Internet represents a relatively new medium for advertisers although it has already attracted a wide variety of industries. Online advertising is similar to print advertising in that it offers a visual message. It has additional advantages, however, because it can also use the audio and video capabilities of the Internet. Sound and movement may simply attract more attention from viewers, or they may provide an element of entertainment to the message. Online advertising also has the unique feature of being interactive. Called *rich media*, these interactive ads have drop-down menus, built-in games, or search engines to engage viewers. Although online advertising is relatively small compared to other traditional media, it offers an opportunity to reach younger consumers who have developed a preference for online communication.

A disadvantage to online advertising is the difficulty of measuring impact. Several companies are testing methods of tracking where viewers go on their computer in the days and weeks after seeing an ad. Nielsen's online rating service, for example, measures actual Internet use through meters installed on the computers of 200,000 individuals in 10 countries. Measuring the relationship between online and offline behavior is also important. Recent research by ComScore, which studied 139 online ad campaigns, revealed that online ads didn't always result in a "click," but they increased the likelihood of a purchase by 17 percent and they increased visits to the advertiser's Web site by 40 percent.[31] The Making Responsible Decisions box describes how click fraud is increasing the necessity of assessing online advertising effectiveness.[32]

Outdoor advertising can be an effective medium for reminding consumers about a product.

Outdoor A very effective medium for reminding consumers about your product is outdoor advertising, such as the scoreboard at San Diego's Qualcomm Stadium. The most common form of outdoor advertising, called *billboards*, often results in good reach and frequency and has been shown to increase purchase rates.[33] The visibility of this medium is good supplemental reinforcement for well-known products, and it is a relatively low-cost, flexible alternative. A company can buy space just in the desired geographical market. A disadvantage to billboards, however, is that no opportunity exists for lengthy advertising copy. Also, a good billboard site depends on traffic patterns and sight lines.

If you have ever lived in a metropolitan area, chances are you might have seen another form of outdoor advertising, *transit advertising*. This medium includes messages on the interior and exterior of buses, subway and light-rail cars, and taxis. As the use of mass transit grows, transit advertising may become increasingly important. Selectivity is available to advertisers, who can buy space by neighborhood or bus route. One disadvantage to this medium is that the

Who Is Responsible for Click Fraud?

Spending on Internet advertising is expected to reach $36 billion in 2011 as many advertisers shift their budgets from print and TV to the Internet. For most advertisers one advantage of online advertising is that they pay only when someone clicks on their ad. Unfortunately, the growth of the medium has led to "click fraud," which is the deceptive clicking of ads solely to increase the amount advertisers must pay. There are several forms of click fraud. One method is the result of Paid-to-Read (PTR) Web sites that recruit and pay members to simply click on ads. Another method is the result of "clickbots," which are software programs that produce automatic clicks on ads. While the activity is difficult to detect and stop, experts estimate that up to 17 percent of clicks may be the result of fraud, and may be costing advertisers as much as $500 million each year!

Two of the largest portals for Internet advertising are Google and Yahoo! Both firms try to filter out illegitimate clicks, although some advertisers claim that they are still being charged for PTR and clickbot traffic. Although the laws that may govern click fraud are not very clear, Google and Yahoo! have each settled class action lawsuits and agreed to provide rebates or credits to advertisers who were charged for fraudulent clicks.

Investigations of the online advertising industry have discovered a related form of click fraud that occurs when legitimate Web site visitors click on ads without any intention of looking at the site. As one consumer explains, "I always try and remember to click on the ad banners once in a while to try and keep the sites free." Stephen Dubner calls this "webtipping"!

As the Internet advertising industry grows it will become increasingly important to resolve the issue of click fraud. Consumers, advertisers, Web sites that carry paid advertising, and the large Web portals are all involved in a complicated technical, legal, and social situation. Who do you think is responsible for click fraud? Who should lead the way in the effort to find a solution?

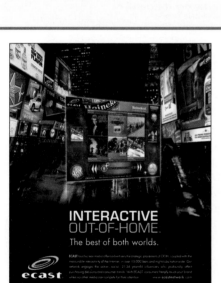

Out-of-home advertising is also becoming interactive.

heavy travel times, when the audiences are the largest, are not conducive to reading advertising copy. People are standing shoulder to shoulder on the subway, hoping not to miss their stop, and little attention is paid to the advertising.

Other Media As traditional media have become more expensive and cluttered, advertisers have been attracted to a variety of nontraditional advertising options called out-of-home advertising, or *place-based media*. Messages are placed in locations that attract a specific target audience such as airports, doctors' offices, health clubs, theaters (where ads are played on the screen before the movies are shown), grocery stores, and even the bathrooms of bars, restaurants, and nightclubs. Soon there will be advertising on video screens on gas pumps, ATMs, and in elevators, and increasingly it will be interactive. The $2.5 billion industry has attracted advertisers such as AT&T and JCPenney, which use in-store campaigns, and Geico, Sprint, and FedEx, which use out-of-home advertising to reach mobile professionals in health clubs, airports, and hotels. Research suggests that creative use of out-of-home advertising, such as preshow theater ads, enhances consumer recall of the ads.[34]

Scheduling the Advertising

There is no correct schedule to advertise a product, but three factors must be considered. First is the issue of *buyer turnover*, which is how often new buyers enter the market to buy the product. The higher the buyer turnover, the greater is the amount of advertising required. A second issue in scheduling is the *purchase frequency*; the more frequently the product is purchased, the less repetition is required. Finally, companies must consider the *forgetting rate*, the speed with which buyers forget the brand if advertising is not seen.

Setting schedules requires an understanding of how the market behaves. Most companies tend to follow one of three basic approaches:

1. *Continuous (steady) schedule.* When seasonal factors are unimportant, advertising is run at a continuous or steady schedule throughout the year.
2. *Flighting (intermittent) schedule.* Periods of advertising are scheduled between periods of no advertising to reflect seasonal demand.
3. *Pulse (burst) schedule.* A flighting schedule is combined with a continuous schedule because of increases in demand, heavy periods of promotion, or introduction of a new product.

For example, products such as breakfast cereals have a stable demand throughout the year and would typically use a continuous schedule of advertising. In contrast, products such as snow skis and suntan lotions have seasonal demands and receive flighting-schedule advertising during the seasonal demand period. Some products such as toys or automobiles require pulse-schedule advertising to facilitate sales throughout the year and during special periods of increased demand (such as holidays or new car introductions). Some evidence suggests that pulsing schedules are superior to other advertising strategies.[35] In addition, research indicates the effectiveness of a particular ad wears out quickly and, therefore, many alternative forms of a commercial may be more effective.[36]

learning review

5. You see the same ad in *Time* and *Fortune* magazines and on billboards and TV. Is this an example of reach or frequency?

6. Why has the Internet become a popular advertising medium?

7. Describe three approaches to scheduling advertising.

EXECUTING THE ADVERTISING PROGRAM

Executing the advertising program involves pretesting the advertising copy and actually carrying out the advertising program. John Wanamaker, the founder of Wanamaker's Department Store in Philadelphia, remarked, "I know half my advertising is wasted, but I don't know what half." By evaluating advertising efforts, marketers can try to ensure that their advertising expenditures are not wasted.[37] Evaluation is done usually at two separate times: before and after the advertisements are run in the actual campaign. Several methods used in the evaluation process at the stages of idea formulation and copy development are discussed below.

Pretesting the Advertising

pretests
Tests conducted before an advertisement is placed in any medium to determine whether it communicates the intended message or to select among alternative versions of the advertisement.

To determine whether the advertisement communicates the intended message or to select among alternative versions of the advertisement, **pretests** are conducted before the advertisements are placed in any medium.

Portfolio Tests Portfolio tests are used to test copy alternatives. The test ad is placed in a portfolio with several other ads and stories, and consumers are asked to read through the portfolio. Afterward, subjects are asked for their impressions of the ads on several evaluative scales, such as from "very informative" to "not very informative."

Jury Tests Jury tests involve showing the ad copy to a panel of consumers and having them rate how they liked it, how much it drew their attention, and how attractive they thought it was. This approach is similar to the portfolio test in that consumer reactions are obtained. However, unlike the portfolio test, a test advertisement is not hidden within other ads.

Theater Tests Theater testing is the most sophisticated form of pretesting. Consumers are invited to view new television shows or movies in which test commercials are also shown. Viewers register their feelings about the advertisements either on handheld electronic recording devices used during the viewing or on questionnaires afterward.

Carrying Out the Advertising Program

The responsibility for actually carrying out the advertising program can be handled by one of three types of agencies. The *full-service agency* provides the most complete range of services, including market research, media selection, copy development, artwork, and production. In the past, agencies that assisted a client by both developing and placing advertisements often charged a commission of 15 percent of the media costs. As corporations introduced integrated marketing approaches, however, many advertisers switched from paying commissions to incentive plans based on performance. These plans typically pay for agency costs and a 5 to 10 percent profit, plus bonuses if specific performance goals are met. In the future, many clients may move to a value-based approach where compensation is dependent on sales of the advertised product or brand.[38]

Limited-service agencies specialize in one aspect of the advertising process, such as providing creative services to develop the advertising copy, buying previously unpurchased media (media agencies), or providing Internet services (Internet agencies). Limited-service agencies that deal in creative work are compensated by a contractual agreement for the services performed. Finally, *in-house agencies* made up of the company's own advertising staff may provide full services or a limited range of services.

ASSESSING THE ADVERTISING PROGRAM

The advertising decision process does not stop with executing the advertising program. The advertisements must be evaluated to determine whether they are achieving their intended objectives, and results may indicate that changes must be made in the advertising program.

Posttesting the Advertising

An advertisement may go through **posttests** after it has been shown to the target audience to determine whether it accomplished its intended purpose. Five approaches common in posttesting are discussed here.[39]

Aided Recall After being shown an ad, respondents are asked whether their previous exposure to it was through reading, viewing, or listening. The Starch test shown in the accompanying photo uses aided recall to determine the percentage of those (1) who remember seeing a specific magazine ad (*noted*), (2) who saw or read any part of the ad identifying the product or brand (*seen-associated*), (3) who read any part of the ad's copy (read some), and (4) who read at least half of the ad (*read most*). Elements of the ad are then tagged with the results, as shown in the picture.[40]

Unaided Recall A question such as, "What ads do you remember seeing yesterday?" is asked of respondents without any prompting to determine whether they saw or heard advertising messages.

Starch scores for advertisement using aided recall.

GfK Custom Research, ® Starch Advertising Research
Cosmopolitan Magazine-November 2007
eStarch Readership Report
Garnier Fructis Advertisement

Noted	85%	Read Most	30%
Associated	84%	Brand Disposition	85% (top three score)
Read Some	69%		

Attitude Tests Respondents are asked questions to measure changes in their attitudes after an advertising campaign, such as whether they have a more favorable attitude toward the product advertised.[41]

Inquiry Tests Additional product information, product samples, or premiums are offered to an ad's readers or viewers. Ads generating the most inquiries are presumed to be the most effective.

Sales Tests Sales tests involve studies such as controlled experiments (e.g., using radio ads in one market and newspaper ads in another and comparing the results) and consumer purchase tests (measuring retail sales that result from a given advertising campaign). The most sophisticated experimental methods today allow a manufacturer, a distributor, or an advertising agency to manipulate an advertising variable (such as schedule or copy) through cable systems and observe subsequent sales effects by monitoring data collected from checkout scanners in supermarkets.[42]

---

learning review

8. Explain the difference between pretesting and posttesting advertising copy.

9. What is the difference between aided and unaided recall posttests?

SALES PROMOTION

LO4

Sales promotion has become a key element of the promotional mix, which now accounts for more than $45.8 billion in annual expenditures. In a recent survey by *Promo* magazine, marketing professionals reported that approximately 32 percent of their budgets were allocated to advertising, 37 percent to consumer promotion, 24 percent to trade promotion, and 7 percent to other marketing activities.[43] The allocation of marketing expenditures reflects the trend toward integrated promotion programs, which include a variety of promotion elements. Selection and integration of the many promotion techniques require a good understanding of the advantages and disadvantages of each kind of promotion.[44]

Consumer-Oriented Sales Promotions

consumer-oriented sales promotions
Sales tools, such as coupons, sweepstakes, and samples, used to support a company's advertising and personal selling efforts directed to ultimate consumers.

Directed to ultimate consumers, **consumer-oriented sales promotions**, or simply *consumer promotions*, are sales tools used to support a company's advertising and personal selling. The alternative consumer-oriented sales promotion tools include coupons, deals, premiums, contests, sweepstakes, samples, loyalty programs, point-of-purchase displays, rebates, and product placements.

Coupons Coupons are sales promotions that usually offer a discounted price to the consumer, which encourages trial. Approximately 302 billion coupons worth $386 billion are distributed in the United States each year. Most coupons are distributed as freestanding inserts in newspapers and reach 60 million households each week. Research indicates that 89 percent of consumers use coupons. For the first time in 16 years, coupon redemptions did not decline in 2008, as the weak economy increased the attractiveness of coupons. Consumers redeemed $2.8 billion of the coupons, which was approximately $8.57 per person. Companies that have increased

Coupons encourage trial by offering a discounted price.

their use of coupons include Procter & Gamble, Nestlé, and Kraft, while the top retailers for coupon redemption were Walmart and Kroger. The number of coupons generated at Internet sites (e.g., www.valpak.com and www.coupon.com) and cell phones has been increasing although they account for only 0.4 percent of all coupons. Coupons are often viewed as a key element of an integrated marketing program. Cream of Wheat recently ran banner ads on women's, parenting, food, and home and garden Web sites with the message "Free Cream of Wheat Is Just a Click Away." The link took people to a free sample order form. When the sample arrived in the mail, the package also contained a $1 coupon.[45]

Coupons are often far more expensive than the face value of the coupon; a 25-cent coupon can cost three times that after paying for the advertisement to deliver it, dealer handling, clearinghouse costs, and redemption. In addition, misredemption, or attempts to redeem a counterfeit coupon or a valid coupon when the product has not been purchased, should be added to the cost of the coupon. The Coupon Information Corporation estimates that companies pay out refunds of more than $300 million each year as a result of coupon fraud. Recent growth in coupon fraud has marketers considering adding holograms and visual aids to coupons to help cashiers identify those that are valid.[46]

Deals   Deals are short-term price reductions, commonly used to increase trial among potential customers or to retaliate against a competitor's actions. For example, if a rival manufacturer introduces a new cake mix, the company may respond with a "two packages for the price of one" deal. This short-term price reduction builds up the stock on the kitchen shelves of cake mix buyers and makes the competitor's introduction more difficult.

Premiums   A promotional tool often used with consumers is the premium, which consists of merchandise offered free or at a significant savings over its retail price. This latter type of premium is called self-liquidating because the cost charged to the consumer covers the cost of the item. McDonald's, for example, used a free premium in a promotional partnership with DreamWorks during the release of the movie *Monsters vs. Aliens*. Collectible toys that portrayed movie characters were given away free with the purchase of a Happy Meal. What are the most popular premiums? According to the Promotional Products Association International, the top premiums are apparel, writing instruments, shopping bags, cups and mugs, and desk accessories. By offering a premium, companies encourage customers to return frequently or to use more of the product. Research suggests that deal-prone consumers and value seekers are attracted to premiums.[47]

The American Idol sweepstakes attracts prospective customers.

Contests   A fourth type of sales promotion is the contest where consumers apply their skill or analytical or creative thinking to try to win a prize. This form of promotion has been growing as requests for videos, photos, and essays are a good match with the trend toward consumer-generated content. For example, Doritos sponsored the "Crash the Super Bowl" contest, asking people to create their own 30-second ad about Doritos. A panel of judges selected five finalists from the 2,000 entries, and the public voted online for its favorite. The winner aired on the Super Bowl, and when the ad hit No. 1 on *USA Today*'s Super Bowl Ad Meter, it was awarded a $1 million bonus! If you like contests, you can enter online now at Web sites such as www.contests.about.com.[48]

Sweepstakes   Sweepstakes are sales promotions that require participants to submit some kind of entry but are purely games of chance requiring no analytical or creative effort by the consumer. Popular sweepstakes include the HGTV "Dream Home Giveaway," which receives more than 40 million entries each year, and McDonald's Monopoly, which offers a grand prize of $1 million.[49]

Two variations of sweepstakes are popular now. First is the sweepstakes that offers products that consumers value as prizes. Mars Snackfood, for example, created a sweepstakes where consumers enter a UPC code from Mars products such as M&Ms, Milky Way, Snickers, Skittles, and 3 Musketeers for a chance to win a $1,000 Visa gift card. Coca-Cola has a similar sweepstakes called "My Coke Rewards" that allows consumers to use codes from bottle caps to enter to win prizes or to collect points to be redeemed for rewards. The second type of sweepstakes offers an "experience" as the prize. For example, one of television's most popular series, *American Idol*, and AT&T sponsor a sweepstakes for a chance to win a trip for two to the season finale of *American Idol* in Los Angeles. Similarly, KFC created a sweepstakes where consumers enter for a chance to win a trip to the Super Bowl. Federal laws, the Federal Trade Commission, and state legislatures have issued rules covering sweepstakes, contests, and games to regulate fairness, ensure that the chance for winning is represented honestly, and guarantee that the prizes are actually awarded.[50]

Samples   Another common consumer sales promotion is sampling, which involves offering the product free or at a greatly reduced price. Often used for new products, sampling puts the product in the consumer's hands. A trial size is generally offered that is smaller than the regular package size. If consumers like the sample, it is hoped they will remember and buy the product. When Mars changed its Milky Way Dark to Milky Way Midnight, it gave away more than 1 million samples to college students at nightclubs, several hundred campuses, and popular spring break locations. Awareness of the candy bar rose to 60 percent, trial rose 166 percent, and sales rose 25 percent. Recent research indicates that 63 percent of college students who receive a sample will also purchase the product. Overall, companies invest more than $2.3 billion in sampling programs each year.[51]

Loyalty Programs   Loyalty programs are a sales promotion tool used to encourage and reward repeat purchases by acknowledging each purchase made by a consumer and offering a premium as purchases accumulate. The most popular loyalty programs today are credit card reward programs. More than 75 percent of all cards offer incentives for use of their card. Citibank, for example, offers "Thank You" points for using Citi credit or debit cards. The points can be redeemed for books, music, gift cards, cash, travel, and special limited time rewards. Airlines, retailers, hotels, and grocery stores also offer popular loyalty programs. Some of the newest programs recently introduced have been by car rental and cruise line companies. There are now more than 1.8 billion loyalty program memberships, for an average of 14 for each household in the United States.[52]

Point-of-purchase displays help increase consumers' attention in a store.

Point-of-Purchase Displays   In a store aisle, you often encounter a sales promotion called a point-of-purchase display. These product displays take the form of advertising signs, which sometimes actually hold or display the product, and are often located in high-traffic areas near the cash register or the end of an aisle. The point-of-purchase display for Nabisco's annual back-to-school program is designed to maximize the consumer's attention to lunch box and after-school snacks and to provide storage for the products. Annual expenditures on point-of-purchase promotions now exceed $20.3 billion and are expected to grow as point-of-purchase becomes integrated with all forms of promotion.

Can you identify these product placements?

Rebates Another consumer sales promotion, the cash rebate, offers the return of money based on proof of purchase. For example, Apple recently offered a $100 rebate to consumers who purchased an Apple computer and a printer during a three-month promotion period. When a rebate is offered on lower-priced items, the time and trouble of mailing in a proof of purchase to get the rebate check often means that many buyers never take advantage of it. However, this "slippage" is less likely to occur with frequent users of rebate promotions.[53] In addition, online consumers are more likely to take advantage of rebates.

Product Placements A final type of consumer promotion, **product placement**, involves the use of a brand-name product in a movie, television show, video game, or commercial for another product. It was Steven Spielberg's placement of Hershey's Reese's Pieces in *E.T.* that first brought a lot of interest to the candy. Similarly, when Tom Cruise wore Bausch and Lomb's Ray-Ban sunglasses in *Risky Business* and its Aviator glasses in *Top Gun*, sales skyrocketed from 100,000 pairs to 7,000,000 pairs in five years. After *Toy Story*, Etch-A-Sketch sales increased 4,500 percent and Mr. Potato Head sales increased 800 percent. Product placement has also grown in television programs. *The Biggest Loser* ranks No. 1 in product placements with Zip-Lock baggies, Extra gum, Macy's department store, *Prevention* magazine, and many other products making appearances.[54] A variation of this form of promotion, called *reverse product placement*, brings fictional products to the marketplace. Bertie Bott's Every Flavor Beans, for example, began as an imaginary brand in Harry Potter books. Similarly, the movie *Forrest Gump* led to the Bubba Gump Shrimp Company restaurant chain. Finally, 7-Eleven converted 12 of its stores into Kwik-E-Marts, the imaginary convenience stores in the television cartoon series, *The Simpsons*, to coincide with the release of *The Simpsons Movie*.[55]

Trade-Oriented Sales Promotions

Trade-oriented sales promotions, or simply *trade promotions*, are sales tools used to support a company's advertising and personal selling directed to wholesalers, retailers, or distributors. Some of the sales promotions just reviewed are used for this purpose, but three other common approaches are targeted uniquely to these intermediaries: (1) allowances and discounts, (2) cooperative advertising, and (3) training of distributors' salesforces.

Allowances and Discounts Trade promotions often focus on maintaining or increasing inventory levels in the channel of distribution. An effective method for encouraging such increased purchases by intermediaries is the use of allowances and discounts. However, overuse of these price reductions can lead to retailers changing their ordering patterns in the expectation of such offerings. Although there are many variations that manufacturers can use with discounts and allowances, three common approaches are the merchandise allowance, the case allowance, and the finance allowance.[56]

Reimbursing a retailer for extra in-store support or special featuring of the brand is a *merchandise allowance*. Performance contracts between the manufacturer and trade member usually specify the activity to be performed, such as a picture of the product in a newspaper with a coupon good at only one store. The merchandise allowance then consists of a percentage deduction from the list case price ordered during the promotional period. Allowances are not paid by the manufacturer until it sees proof of performance (such as a copy of the ad placed by the retailer in the local newspaper).

A second common trade promotion, a *case allowance*, is a discount on each case ordered during a specific time period. These allowances are usually deducted from the invoice. A variation of the case allowance is the "free goods" approach, whereby retailers receive some amount of the product free based on the amount ordered, such as 1 case free for every 10 cases ordered.[57]

A final trade promotion, the *finance allowance*, involves paying retailers for financing costs or financial losses associated with consumer sales promotions. This trade promotion is regularly used and has several variations. One type is the floor stock protection program—manufacturers give retailers a case allowance price for products in their warehouse, which prevents shelf stock from running down during the promotional period. Also common are freight allowances, which compensate retailers that transport orders from the manufacturer's warehouse.

Cooperative Advertising   Resellers often perform the important function of promoting the manufacturer's products at the local level. One common sales promotional activity is to encourage both better quality and greater quantity in the local advertising efforts of resellers through **cooperative advertising**. These are programs by which a manufacturer pays a percentage of the retailer's local advertising expense for advertising the manufacturer's products.

Usually, the manufacturer pays a percentage, often 50 percent, of the cost of advertising up to a certain dollar limit, which is based on the amount of the manufacturer's products purchased by the retailer. In addition to paying for the advertising, the manufacturer often furnishes the retailer with a selection of different ad executions, sometimes suited for several different media. A manufacturer may provide, for example, several different print layouts as well as a few broadcast ads for the retailer to adapt and use.[58]

Training of Distributors' Salesforces   One of the many functions the intermediaries perform is customer contact and selling for the producers they represent. Both retailers and wholesalers employ and manage their own sales personnel. A manufacturer's success often rests on the ability of the reseller's salesforce to represent its products.

Thus, it is in the best interest of the manufacturer to help train the reseller's salesforce. Because the reseller's salesforce is often less sophisticated and knowledgeable about the products than the manufacturer might like, training can increase their sales performance. Training activities include producing manuals and brochures to educate the reseller's salesforce. The salesforce then uses these aids in selling situations. Other activities include national sales meetings sponsored by the manufacturer and field visits to the reseller's location to inform and motivate the salesperson to sell the products. The manufacturer also may develop incentive and recognition programs to motivate the reseller's salespeople to sell its products.

cooperative advertising
Advertising programs by which a manufacturer pays a percentage of the retailer's local advertising expense for advertising the manufacturer's products.

PUBLIC RELATIONS

LO5

publicity tools
Methods of obtaining nonpersonal presentation of an organization, product, or service without direct cost.

As noted in Chapter 15, public relations is a form of communication management that seeks to influence the image of an organization and its products and services. In developing a public relations campaign, several methods of obtaining nonpersonal presentation of an organization, product, or service without direct cost—**publicity tools**—are available to the public relations director. Many companies frequently use the *news release*, consisting of an announcement regarding changes in the company or the product line. The objective of a news release is to inform a newspaper, radio station, or other medium of an idea for a story.

A second common publicity tool is the *news conference*. Representatives of the media are all invited to an informational meeting, and advance materials regarding the content are sent. This tool is often used when new products are introduced or significant changes in corporate structure and leadership are being made.

Nonprofit organizations rely heavily on *public service announcements* (PSAs), which are free space or time donated by the media. For example, the charter of the American Red Cross prohibits any local chapter from advertising, so to solicit blood donations local chapters often depend on PSAs on radio or television to announce their needs.

| learning review | 12. What is a news release? |
| | 13. What type of publicity tool is used most often by nonprofit organizations? |

LEARNING OBJECTIVES REVIEW

LO1 *Explain the differences between product advertising and institutional advertising and the variations within each type.*
Product advertisements focus on selling a product or service and take three forms: (1) Pioneering advertisements tell people what a product is, what it can do, and where it can be found; (2) competitive advertisements persuade the target market to select the firm's brand rather than a competitor's; and (3) reminder advertisements reinforce previous knowledge of a product. Institutional advertisements are used to build goodwill or an image for an organization. They include advocacy advertisements, which state the position of a company on an issue, and pioneering, competitive, and reminder advertisements, which are similar to the product ads but focused on the institution.

LO2 *Describe the steps used to develop, execute, and evaluate an advertising program.*
The promotion decision process can be applied to each of the promotional elements. The steps to develop an advertising pro-

gram include identify the target audience, specify the advertising objectives, set the advertising budget, design the advertisement, create the message, select the media, and schedule the advertising. Executing the program requires pretesting, and evaluating the program requires posttesting.

LO3 *Explain the advantages and disadvantages of alternative advertising media.*
Television advertising reaches large audiences and uses picture, print, sound, and motion; its disadvantages, however, are that it is expensive and perishable. Radio advertising is inexpensive and can be placed quickly, but it has no visual element and is perishable. Magazine advertising can target specific audiences and can convey complex information, but it takes a long time to place the ad and is relatively expensive. Newspapers provide excellent coverage of local markets and can be changed quickly, but they have a short life span and poor color. Yellow pages advertising has a long use period and is available 24 hours per

day; its disadvantage, however, is that there is a proliferation of directories. Internet advertising can be interactive, but its effectiveness is difficult to measure. Outdoor advertising provides repeat exposures, but its message must be very short and simple. Direct mail, discussed in Chapter 15, can be targeted at very selective audiences, but its cost per contact is high.

LO4 *Discuss the strengths and weaknesses of consumer-oriented and trade-oriented sales promotions.*
Coupons encourage retailer support but may delay consumer purchases. Deals reduce consumer risk but also reduce perceived value. Premiums offer consumers additional merchandise they want, but they may be purchasing only for the premium. Contests create involvement but require creative thinking. Sweepstakes encourage repeat purchases, but sales drop after the sweepstakes. Samples encourage product trial but are expensive. Loyalty programs help create loyalty but are

expensive to run. Displays provide visibility but are difficult to place in retail space. Rebates stimulate demand but are easily copied. Product placements provide a positive message in a noncommercial setting but are difficult to control. Trade-oriented sales promotions include (*a*) allowances and discounts, which increase purchases but may change retailer ordering patterns, (*b*) cooperative advertising, which encourages local advertising, and (*c*) salesforce training, which helps increase sales by providing the salespeople with product information and selling skills.

LO5 *Recognize public relations as an important form of communication.*
Public relations activities usually focus on communicating positive aspects of the business. A frequently used public relations tool is publicity. Publicity tools include new releases and news conferences. Nonprofit organization often use public service announcements.

FOCUSING ON KEY TERMS

advertising p. 358
consumer-oriented sales
    promotions p. 370
cooperative advertising p. 374

infomercials p. 364
institutional advertisements p. 359
posttests p. 369
pretests p. 368

product advertisements p. 358
product placement p. 373
publicity tools p. 375
trade-oriented sales promotions p. 373

APPLYING MARKETING KNOWLEDGE

1 How does competitive product advertising differ from competitive institutional advertising?

2 Suppose you are the advertising manager for a new line of children's fragrances. Which form of media would you use for this new product?

3 You have recently been promoted to be director of advertising for the Timkin Tool Company. In your first meeting with Mr. Timkin, he says, "Advertising is a waste! We've been advertising for six months now and sales haven't increased. Tell me why we should continue." Give your answer to Mr. Timkin.

4 A large life insurance company has decided to switch from using a strong fear appeal to a humorous approach. What are the strengths and weaknesses of such a change in message strategy?

5 In the table that follows, which medium has the lowest cost per thousand?

Medium	Cost	Audience
TV show	$5,000	25,000
Magazine	2,200	6,000
Newspaper	4,800	7,200
FM radio	420	1,600

6 Some national advertisers have found that they can have more impact with their advertising by running a large number of ads for a period and then running no ads at all for a period. Why might such a flighting schedule be more effective than a continuous schedule?

7 Each year managers at Bausch and Lomb evaluate the many advertising media alternatives available to them as they develop their advertising program for contact lenses. What advantages and disadvantages of each alternative should they consider? Which media would you recommend to them?

8 What are two advantages and two disadvantages of the advertising posttests described in the chapter?

9 Federated Banks is interested in consumer-oriented sales promotions that would encourage senior citizens to direct deposit their Social Security checks with the bank. Evaluate the sales promotion options, and recommend two of them to the bank.

10 How can public relations be used by Firestone and Ford following investigations into complaints about tire failures?

building your marketing plan

To augment your promotion strategy from Chapter 15:

1 Use Figure 16–2 to select the advertising media you will include in your plan by analyzing how combinations of media (e.g., television and Internet advertising, radio and yellow pages advertising) can complement each other.
2 Select your consumer-oriented sales promotion activities (coupons, deals, premiums, contests, sweepstakes,

samples, loyalty programs, point-of-purchase displays, rebates, and/or product placements).
3 Specify which trade-oriented sales promotions and public relations tools you will use.

video case 16   Google, Inc.: The Right Ads at the Right Time

"So what we did, in essence, is we said advertising should be useful to a consumer just as much as the organic search results, and we don't want people just to buy advertising and be able to show an ad if it's irrelevant to the consumer's need," says Richard Holden, director of product management at Google. To accomplish this, Google developed a "Quality Score" model to predict how effective an ad will be. The model uses many factors such as click-through rates, advertiser history, and keyword performance to develop a score for each advertisement. "Essentially, what we're trying to do is predict ahead, before we actually show an ad, how a consumer will react to that ad, and our interest is in showing fewer ads, not more ads; just the right ads at the right time," Holden continues. The Google advertising model has revolutionized the advertising industry, and it continues to improve every day!

THE COMPANY

Google began in 1996 as a research project for Stanford computer science students Larry Page and Sergey Brin. They started with a simple idea—that a search engine based on the relationships between Web sites would provide a better ranking than a search engine based only on the number of times a key term appeared on a Web site. The success of their model led to rapid growth and the founders moved the company from their dorm room, to a friend's garage, to offices in Palo Alto, California, and eventually to its current location, known as the Google-plex, in Mountain View, California. In 2000, Google began selling advertising as a means of generating revenue. Its advertising model allowed advertisers to bid on

search words and pay for each "click" by a search-engine user. The ads were required to be simple and text-based so that the search result pages remained uncluttered and the search time was as fast as possible.

Page and Brin's first search engine was called "Back-Rub" because their technique was based on relationships, or backlinks, between Web sites. The name quickly changed, however. The name "Google" is a misspelling of the word "googol," which is a mathematical term for a 1 followed by 100 zeros. Page and Brin used the name in the original domain, www.google.stanford.edu, to reflect their interest in organizing the immense amount of information available on the Web. The domain name, of course, became www.google.com and eventually Webster's dictionary added the verb "google" with the definition "to use the Google search engine to obtain information on the Internet." The name has become so familiar that *Advertising Age* recently reported that Google is "the world's most powerful brand"!

Today Google receives several hundred million inquiries each day as it pursues its mission: to organize the world's information and make it universally accessible and useful. The company generates more than $21 billion in annual revenue and has more than 20,000 employees. As Google has grown it has developed 10 guidelines that represent the corporate philosophy. They are:

1. Focus on the user and all else will follow.
2. It's best to do one thing really, really well.
3. Fast is better than slow.
4. Democracy on the Web works.
5. You don't need to be at your desk to need an answer.
6. You can make money without doing evil.
7. There's always more information out there.

8. The need for information crosses all borders.
9. You can be serious without a suit.
10. Great just isn't good enough.

Using these guidelines Google strives to continually improve its search engine. "The perfect search engine," explains Google co-founder Larry Page, "would understand exactly what you mean and give back exactly what you want."

ONLINE ADVERTISING

Google generates revenue by offering online advertising opportunities—next to search results or on specific Web pages. The company always distinguishes ads from the search results or the content of a Web page and it never sells placement in the search results. This approach ensures that Google Web site visitors always know when someone has paid to put a message in front of them. The advantage of online advertising is that it is measurable and allows immediate assessment of its effectiveness. As Gopi Kallayil, product marketing manager, explains: "There is a very high degree of measurability and trackability that you get through online advertising." In addition, he says, "With online advertising you can actually track the value of every single dollar that you spend, understand which particular customers the ad reached, and what they did after they received the advertising message."

The online advertising market has grown from its initial focus on simple text ads to a much larger set of options. There are five key categories of online advertising. They are:

- Search: 47%
- Display: 35%
- Classified: 10%
- Referral: 7%
- E-mail: 1%

Google is the dominant provider of online search requests and receives more than 60 percent of the search advertising revenue. The fastest-growing advertising category, however, is display advertising where Yahoo! and Microsoft are established providers. Google believes that there is an opportunity to grow its display advertising sales by making the ads useful information instead of visual clutter. According to Google co-founder Sergey Brin, "It's like search—matching people with information they want. It just happens to be promotional."

Several improvements in technology and business practice tools contributed to Google's success. First, Google developed its patented PageRank™ algorithm which evaluates the entire link structure of the Web and uses the link structure to determine which pages are most important. Then the process uses hypertext-matching analysis to determine which pages are relevant to a spe-

cific search. A combination of the importance and the relevance of Web pages provides the search results—in just a fraction of a second. Second, Google developed two business practice tools—AdWords and AdSense—to help (1) advertisers create ads, and (2) content providers generate advertising revenue. Both tools have become essential elements of Google's advertising model.

AdWords

To help advertisers place ads on their search-engine results, Google developed an online tool called AdWords. Advertisers can use AdWords to create ad text, select target keywords, and manage their account. The process allows advertisers to reach targeted audiences. Frederick Vallaeys, an Adwords evangelist, explains: "One of my favorite things about AdWords is the fact that it really helps you find the right customer at the right time and show them the right message. With AdWords you can very specifically target your market because you're targeting them at a time when they do a search on Google. At that time they've told you a keyword, you know exactly what they're looking for, and here is your opportunity as a marketer to give them the exact answer to what they've just told you they wanted to find." Google has found that text ads that are relevant to the person reading them have much higher response ("clickthrough") rates than ads that are not targeted.

AdWords is also easy for any advertiser to use. Large or small businesses can simply open an account with a credit card and have ads appear within minutes. "When AdWords rolled out their self-service product, it really was one of the first times when it was very easy for a small business to put their ad up on the Internet on a search engine and compete on a level playing field alongside *Fortune* 1000 companies," says Vallaeys. Google has an experienced sales and service team available to help any advertiser select appropriate keywords, generate ad copy, and monitor campaign performance. The team is dedicated to helping its advertisers improve clickthrough rates because high clickthrough rates are an indication that ads are relevant to a user's interests. Methods of improving advertising performance include changing the keywords and rewriting copy. Because there is no limit to the number of keywords that an advertiser can select and each keyword can be matched with different ad copy, the potential for many very customer-specific options is high.

Another advantage of Google's AdWords program is that it allows advertisers to easily control costs. The ads appear as a "Sponsored Link" next to search results each time the Google search engine matches the search request with the ad's keywords and Quality Score, although the advertiser is not charged unless someone "clicks" on the link. In a traditional advertising model, advertisers were charged using a CPM (cost-per-thousand) approach, which charged for the impressions made by an ad. According to Holden, the Google model "transformed that to what we call a CPC, or a cost-per-click model, and this is a model that an advertiser, instead of paying for an impression, only pays when somebody actually clicks on that ad and is delivered to their Web site. So, in effect, they may be getting the benefit from impressions being shown, but we're not actually charging them anything unless there's a definite lead being delivered to their Web site." Google also offers advertisers real-time analytical services to allow assessment of and changes to any component of an advertising campaign.

AdSense

The AdSense program was designed for Web site owners as a tool for placing ads next to their Web page content rather than next to search results. Currently, thousands of Web site managers use AdSense to place ads on their sites and generate revenue. Google applies the same general philosophy to matching ads with Web sites as it does to matching ads to search requests. By delivering ads that precisely target the content on the site's pages, Google believes the advertising enhances the experience for visitors to the Web site. In this way advertisers, Web site publishers, and information seekers all benefit.

AdSense is one of the tools Google is using to pursue its goal of increasing its display advertising business. Yahoo! and Microsoft's MSN are leaders in display advertising because they can put ads on their own Web sites such as Yahoo! Finance and MSN Money. To provide additional outlets for display ads Google recently purchased YouTube. In addition, Google purchased DoubleClick, an advertising exchange where Web sites put space up for auction and ad agencies bid to place ads for their clients. Google is also trying to make it easy for anyone to create a display ad by introducing a new tool called Display Ad Builder. Some experts observe that because Google is so dominant at search advertising, its future growth will depend on success in display advertising.

GOOGLE'S FUTURE STRATEGY

How will Google continue its success? One possibility is that it will begin to try to win advertising away from the U.S. TV industry. While this is a new type of advertising requiring creative capabilities and relationships with large advertising agencies, Google has dedicated many of its resources to becoming competitive for television advertising expenditures. For example, Google recently helped Volvo develop a campaign that included a YouTube ad and Twitter updates. Google is also likely to develop new Web sites, establish blogs, and build relationships with existing sites.

Another opportunity for Google will be mobile telephone advertising. There are currently more than 3 billion mobile phones in use, and 600 million of those are Internet-capable. Just as Google's search engine provides a means to match relevant information with consumers, phones offer a chance to provide real-time and location-specific information. Some of the challenges in mobile advertising will be that the networks are not fast and that the ad formats are not standardized. Google believes its new phone and its Android operating system will also help.

Finally, as Google pursues its mission it will continue to expand throughout the world. Search results are already available in 35 languages and volunteers are helping with many others. It is obvious that Google is determined to "organize the world's information" and make it "accessible and useful."

Questions

1 Describe several unique characteristics about Google and its business practices.

2 What is Google's philosophy about advertising? How can less advertising be preferred to more advertising?

3 Describe the types of online advertising available today. Which type of advertising does Google currently dominate? Why?

4 How can Google be successful in the display advertising business? What other areas of growth are likely to be pursued by Google in the future?

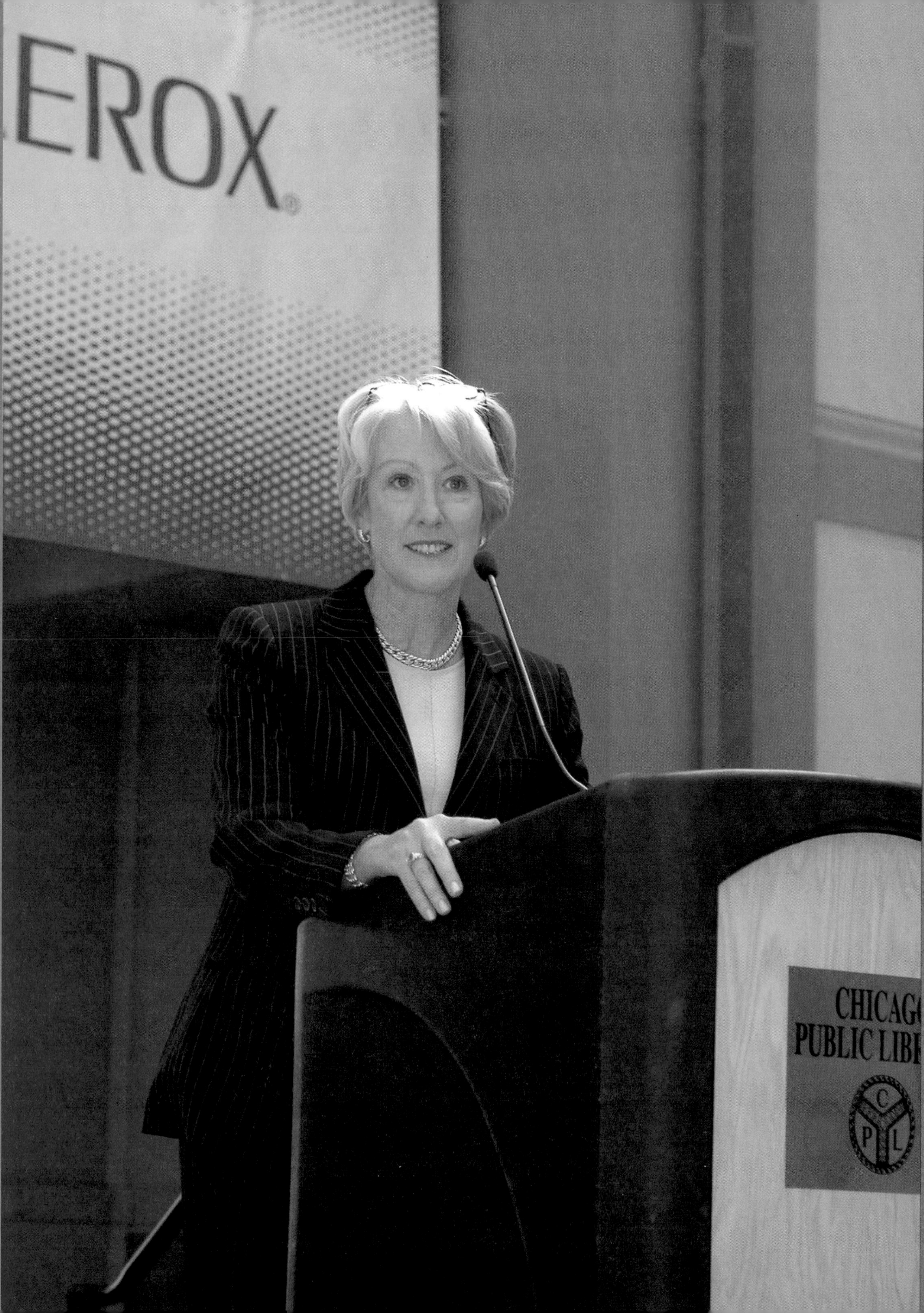

EROX
CHICAGO
PUBLIC LIBR
C
P L

17

Personal Selling and Sales Management

LEARNING OBJECTIVES

After reading this chapter you should be able to:

LO1 Discuss the nature and scope of personal selling and sales management in marketing.

LO2 Identify the different types of personal selling.

LO3 Explain the stages in the personal selling process.

LO4 Describe the major functions of sales management.

XEROX SUCCEEDS BY DOING WHAT'S RIGHT FOR THE CUSTOMER

Anne Mulcahy has a challenging assignment. As the chairman of the board at Xerox Corporation, she is successfully managing one of the greatest feats in the annals of business history: restoring Xerox's legendary marketing and financial vitality.

Her success can be attributed to staying in sync with Xerox customers and employees. "I believe strongly that my success as a leader is driven by my commitment to understanding and meeting customers' requirements, as well as developing and nurturing a motivated and proud workforce," says Mulcahy.

Mulcahy is ideally suited to the task. She began her 35-year Xerox career as a field sales representative and assumed increasingly responsible management and executive positions. These included chief staff officer, president of Xerox's General Markets Operations, and president and chief executive officer of Xerox. As chairman, Mulcahy had to muster the knowledge and experience gained from this varied background. Not surprisingly, her field sales background played a pivotal role.

"We started winning when we listened to customers," Mulcahy says. "We did that by providing greater value than our competitors—and that meant selling the way customers want to buy." She adds, "Doing what's right for the customer—that's our guiding principle." And attention to the customer buying experience has paid huge dividends. Xerox's sales revenue and net income have soared during Mulcahy's tenure as chairman and CEO. Her dedicated customer focus and field sales experience bode well for the continued success of Xerox.[1]

This chapter describes the scope and significance of personal selling and sales management in marketing and creating value for customers. It first highlights the different forms of personal selling. Next, the major steps in the selling process are outlined with an emphasis on building buyer–seller relationships. Attention is then focused on salesforce management and its critical role in achieving a company's broader marketing objectives. Three major salesforce management functions are then detailed. They are sales plan formulation, sales plan implementation, and salesforce evaluation. Finally, technology's persuasive influence on how selling is done and how salespeople are managed is described.

SCOPE AND SIGNIFICANCE OF PERSONAL SELLING AND SALES MANAGEMENT

Chapter 15 described personal selling and management of the sales effort as being part of the firm's promotional mix. Although it is important to recognize that personal selling is a useful vehicle for communicating with present and potential buyers, it is much more.

Nature of Personal Selling and Sales Management

LO1

personal selling
The two-way flow of communication between a buyer and seller, often in a face-to-face encounter, designed to influence a person's or group's purchase decision.

sales management
Planning the selling program and implementing and evaluating the personal selling effort of the firm.

Personal selling involves the two-way flow of communication between a buyer and seller, often in a face-to-face encounter, designed to influence a person's or group's purchase decision. However, with advances in telecommunications, personal selling also takes place over the telephone, and through video teleconferencing and Internet-enabled links between buyers and sellers.

Personal selling remains a highly human-intensive activity despite the use of technology. Accordingly, the people involved must be managed. **Sales management** involves planning the selling program and implementing and evaluating the personal selling effort of the firm. The tasks involved in managing personal selling include setting objectives; organizing the salesforce; recruiting, selecting, training, and compensating salespeople; and evaluating the performance of individual salespeople.

Selling Happens Almost Everywhere

"Everyone lives by selling something," wrote author Robert Louis Stevenson a century ago. His observation still holds true today. The Bureau of Labor Statistics reports that about 15 million people are employed in sales positions in the United States. Included in this number are manufacturing sales personnel, real estate brokers, stockbrokers, and salesclerks who work in retail stores. In reality, however, virtually every occupation that involves customer contact has an element of personal selling. For example, attorneys, accountants, bankers, and company personnel recruiters perform sales-related activities, whether or not they acknowledge it.

Personal Selling in Marketing

Personal selling serves three major roles in a firm's overall marketing effort. First, salespeople are the critical link between the firm and its customers. This role requires that salespeople match company interests with customer needs to satisfy both parties in the exchange process. Second, salespeople *are* the company in a consumer's eyes. They represent what a company is or attempts to be and are often the only personal contact a customer has with the company. For example, Sam Palmisano, IBM's chief executive officer, calls the company's 40,000-strong salesforce "our face to the client."[2] Third, personal selling may play a dominant role in a firm's marketing program. This situation typically arises when a firm uses a push marketing strategy, described in Chapter 15. Avon, for example, pays almost 40 percent of its total sales dollars for selling expenses.

Creating Customer Solutions and Value through Salespeople: Relationship Selling

As the critical link between the firm and its customers, salespeople can create customer value in many ways. For instance, by being close to the customer, salespeople can identify creative solutions to customer problems. Salespeople at Medtronic, Inc., the world leader in the heart pacemaker market, are in the operating room for more than 90 percent of the procedures performed with their product and are on call, wearing pagers, 24 hours a day. "It reflects the willingness to be there in every situation,

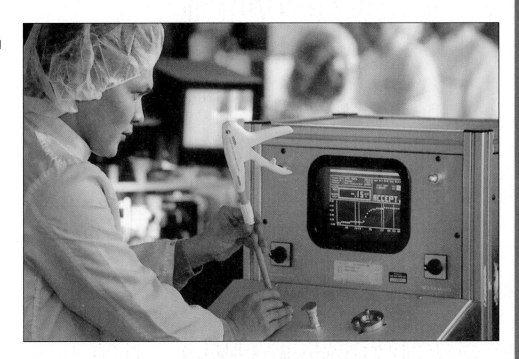

Could this be a salesperson in the operating room? Read the text to find out why Medtronic salespeople visit hospital operating rooms.

just in case a problem arises—even though nine times out of ten the procedure goes just fine," notes a satisfied customer.[3]

Salespeople can create value by easing the customer buying process. This happened at AMP, Inc., a producer of electrical products. Salespeople and customers had a difficult time getting product specifications and performance data on AMP's 70,000 products quickly and accurately. The company now records all information on CD-ROM disks that can be scanned thoroughly and instantly by salespeople and customers.

Customer value is also created by salespeople who follow through after the sale. At Jefferson Smurfit Corporation, a multibillion-dollar supplier of packaging products, one of its salespeople juggled production from three of the company's plants to satisfy an unexpected demand for boxes from General Electric. This person's action led to the company being given GE's Distinguished Supplier Award.

Customer value creation is made possible by **relationship selling**, the practice of building ties to customers based on a salesperson's attention and commitment to customer needs over time. Relationship selling involves mutual respect and trust among buyers and sellers. It focuses on creating long-term customers, not a one-time sale. A survey of 300 senior sales executives revealed that 96 percent consider "building long-term relationships with customers" to be the most important activity affecting sales performance. Companies such as Xerox, American Express, Motorola, Apple, and Owens-Corning have made relationship building a core focus of their sales effort.[4]

Relationship selling represents another dimension of customer relationship management. It emphasizes the importance of learning about customer needs and wants and tailoring solutions to customer problems as a means to customer value creation.

relationship selling
The practice of building ties to customers based on a salesperson's attention and commitment to customer needs over time.

learning review

1. What is personal selling?
2. What is involved in sales management?

THE MANY FORMS OF PERSONAL SELLING

Personal selling assumes many forms based on the amount of selling done and the amount of creativity required to perform the sales task. Broadly speaking, two types of personal selling exist: order taking and order getting. While some firms use only one of these types of personal selling, others use a combination of the two.

Order-Taking Salespeople

order taker
A salesperson who processes routine orders or reorders for products that were already sold by the company.

Typically, an **order taker** processes routine orders or reorders for products that were already sold by the company. The primary responsibility of order takers is to preserve an ongoing relationship with existing customers and maintain sales.

Two types of order takers exist. *Outside order takers* visit customers and replenish inventory stocks of resellers, such as retailers or wholesalers. For example, Frito-Lay salespeople call on supermarkets, convenience stores, and other establishments to ensure that the company's line of snack products (such as Doritos and Tostitos tortilla chips) is in adequate supply. In addition, outside order takers often provide assistance in arranging displays.

Inside order takers, also called *order clerks* or *salesclerks*, typically answer simple questions, take orders, and complete transactions with customers. Many retail clerks are inside order takers. Inside order takers are often employed by companies that use *inbound telemarketing*, the use of toll-free telephone numbers that customers can call to obtain information about products or services and make purchases. In business-to-business settings, order taking arises in straight rebuy situations as described in Chapter 6.

Order takers generally do little selling in a conventional sense. They engage in modest problem solving with customers. They often represent products that have few options, such as magazine subscriptions and highly standardized industrial products. Inbound telemarketing is also an essential selling activity for more "customer service" driven firms, such as Dell, Inc. At these companies, order takers undergo extensive training so that they can better assist callers with their purchase decisions.

A Frito-Lay salesperson takes inventory of snacks for the store manager to sign. In this situation, the manager will make a straight rebuy decision.

FIGURE 17–1

How do outside order-getting salespeople spend their time each week? You might be surprised after reading the text.

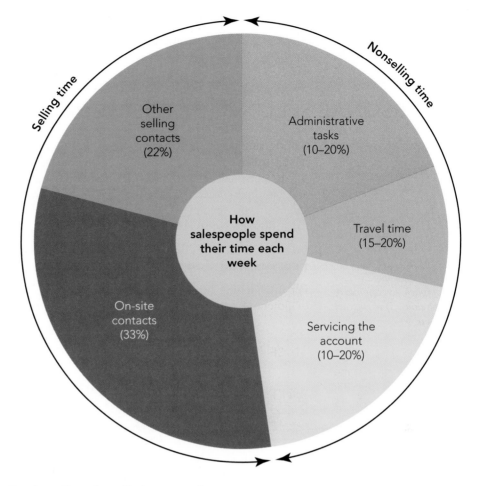

Order-Getting Salespeople

An **order getter** sells in a conventional sense and identifies prospective customers, provides customers with information, persuades customers to buy, closes sales, and follows up on customers' use of a product or service. Like order takers, order getters can be inside (an automobile salesperson) or outside (a Xerox salesperson).

Order getting involves a high degree of creativity and customer empathy and is typically required for selling complex or technical products with many options, so considerable product knowledge and sales training are necessary. In modified rebuy or new-buy purchase situations in business-to-business selling, an order getter acts as a problem solver who identifies how a particular product may satisfy a customer's need. Similarly, in the purchase of a service, such as insurance, a Metropolitan Life insurance agent can provide a mix of plans to satisfy a buyer's needs depending on income, stage of the family's life cycle, and investment objectives.

Order getting is not a 40-hour-per-week job. Industry research shows that outside order getters, or field service representatives, often work over 50 hours per week. As shown in Figure 17–1, 55 percent of their time is spent selling. Another 10 to 20 percent is devoted to customer service calls. The remainder of their workweek is occupied by getting to customers and performing administrative tasks.[5]

Order getting by outside salespeople is also expensive. It is estimated that the average cost of a single field sales call on a business customer is about $350, factoring in salespeople compensation, benefits, and travel-and-entertainment expenses. This cost illustrates why outbound telemarketing is popular. *Outbound telemarketing* is the practice of using the telephone rather than personal visits to contact current and prospective customers. A lower cost per sales call (from $20 to $25) and little or no field expense accounts for its widespread appeal.

learning review

3. What is the principal difference between an order taker and an order getter?

4. What percentage of an order-getting salesperson's time is spent selling?

THE PERSONAL SELLING PROCESS: BUILDING RELATIONSHIPS

LO3

Selling, and particularly order getting, is a complicated activity that involves building buyer–seller relationships. Although the salesperson–customer interaction is essential to personal selling, much of a salesperson's work occurs before this meeting and continues after the sale itself. The **personal selling process** consists of six stages: (1) prospecting, (2) preapproach, (3) approach, (4) presentation, (5) close, and (6) follow-up (see Figure 17–2).

personal selling process
Sales activities occurring before and after the sale itself, consisting of six stages: (1) prospecting, (2) preapproach, (3) approach, (4) presentation, (5) close, and (6) follow-up.

Prospecting: Identifying and Qualifying Prospective Customers

Personal selling begins with the *prospecting* stage—the search for and qualification of potential customers. There are three types of prospects. A *lead* is the name of

FIGURE 17–2
Stages and objectives of the personal selling process. Each stage is critical for successful selling and building a customer relationship.

STAGE	OBJECTIVE	COMMENTS
1. Prospecting	Search for and qualify prospects	Start of the selling process; prospects produced through advertising, referrals, and cold canvassing
2. Preapproach	Gather information and decide how to approach the prospect	Information sources include personal observation, other customers, and own salespeople
3. Approach	Gain a prospect's attention, stimulate interest, and make transition to the presentation	First impression is critical; gain attention and interest through reference to common acquaintances, a referral, or product demonstration
4. Presentation	Begin converting a prospect into a customer by creating a desire for the product or service	Different presentation formats are possible; however, involving the customer in the product or service through attention to particular needs is critical; important to deal professionally and ethically with prospect skepticism, indifference, or objections
5. Close	Obtain a purchase commitment from the prospect and create a customer	Salesperson asks for the purchase; different approaches include the trial close and assumptive close
6. Follow-up	Ensure that the customer is satisfied with the product or service	Resolve any problems faced by the customer to ensure customer satisfaction and future sales possibilities

Trade shows are a popular source for leads and prospects. Companies like TSCentral provide comprehensive trade show information.

a person who may be a possible customer. A *prospect* is a customer who wants or needs the product. If an individual wants the product, can afford to buy it, and is the decision maker, this individual is a *qualified prospect*.

Leads and prospects are generated using several sources. For example, advertising may contain a coupon or a toll-free number to generate leads. Some companies use exhibits at trade shows, professional meetings, and conferences to generate leads or prospects. Staffed by salespeople, these exhibits are used to attract the attention of prospective buyers and disseminate information. Others utilize the Internet for generating leads and prospects. Today, salespeople are using Web sites, e-mail, and social networks to connect to individuals and companies that may be interested in their products or services.

Another approach for generating leads is through *cold canvassing* or *cold calling*, either in person or by telephone. This approach simply means that a salesperson may open a directory, pick a name, and contact that individual or business. Despite a high refusal rate, cold canvassing can be successful.[6]

Cold canvassing is often criticized by U.S. consumers and is now regulated. A recent survey reported that 75 percent of U.S. consumers consider this practice an intrusion on their privacy, and 72 percent find it distasteful.[7] *The Telephone Consumer Protection Act* (1991) contains provisions to curb abuses such as early morning or late night calling. Additional federal regulations require more complete disclosure regarding solicitations, include provisions that allow consumers to avoid being called at any time through the Do Not Call Registry, and impose fines for violations. For example, satellite television provider DirecTV was fined $5.3 million for making thousands of calls to consumers who had put their telephone numbers on the Do Not Call Registry.[8]

Preapproach: Preparing for the Sales Call

Once a salesperson has identified a qualified prospect, preparation for the sale begins with the preapproach. The *preapproach* stage involves obtaining further information on the prospect and deciding on the best method of approach. Knowing how the prospect prefers to be approached and what the prospect is looking for in a product or service is essential.

For instance, a Merrill Lynch stockbroker will need information on a prospect's discretionary income, investment objectives, and preference for discussing brokerage services over the telephone or in person. For business product companies such as Texas Instruments, the preapproach involves identifying the buying role of a prospect (for example, influencer or decision maker), important buying criteria, and the prospect's receptivity to a formal or informal presentation. Identifying the best time to contact a prospect is also important. Northwestern Mutual Life Insurance Company suggests the best times to call on people in different occupations: dentists before 9:30 A.M., lawyers between 11:00 A.M. and 2:00 P.M., and college professors between 7:00 and 8:00 P.M.

Successful salespeople recognize that the preapproach stage should never be short-changed. Their experience, coupled with research on customer complaints, indicates that failure to learn as much as possible about the prospect is unprofessional and the ruin of a sales call.

Approach: Making the First Impression

The *approach* stage involves the initial meeting between the salesperson and the prospect, where the objectives are to gain the prospect's attention, stimulate interest, and build the foundation for the sales presentation itself and the basis for a working relationship. The first impression is critical at this stage, and it is common for salespeople to begin the conversation with a reference to common acquaintances, a referral, or even the product or service itself. Which tactic is taken will depend on the information obtained in the prospecting and preapproach stages.

How business cards are exchanged with Asian customers is very important. Read the text to learn the appropriate protocol in the approach stage of the personal selling process.

The approach stage is very important in different cultural settings. In many societies outside the United States, considerable time is devoted to nonbusiness talk designed to establish a rapport between buyers and sellers. For instance, it is common for two or three meetings to occur before business matters are discussed in the Middle East and Asia. Gestures are also very important. The initial meeting between a salesperson and a prospect in the United States customarily begins with a firm handshake. Handshakes also apply in France, but they are gentle, not firm. Forget the handshake in Japan. An appropriate bow is expected. What about business cards? Business cards should be printed in English on one side and the language of the prospective customer on the other. Knowledgeable U.S. salespeople know that their business cards should be handed to Asian customers using both hands, with the name facing the receiver. In Asia, anything involving a person's name demands respect.

Presentation: Tailoring a Solution for a Customer's Needs

The *presentation* stage is at the core of the order-getting selling process, and its objective is to convert a prospect into a customer by creating a desire for the product or service. Three major presentation formats exist: (1) stimulus-response format, (2) formula selling format, and (3) need-satisfaction format.

Stimulus-Response Format The *stimulus-response presentation* format assumes that given the appropriate stimulus by a salesperson, the prospect will buy. With this format the salesperson tries one appeal after another, hoping to hit the right button. A counter clerk at McDonald's is using this approach when he or she asks whether you'd like an order of French fries or a dessert with your meal. The counter clerk is engaging in what is called *suggestive selling*. Although useful in this setting, the stimulus-response format is not always appropriate, and for many products a more formalized format is necessary.

Rockport sales representatives are adept at adaptive selling to retail buyers.

Formula Selling Format The *formula selling presentation* format is based on the view that a presentation consists of information that must be provided in an accurate, thorough, and step-by-step manner to inform the prospect. A popular version of this format is the *canned sales presentation*, which is a memorized, standardized message conveyed to every prospect. Used frequently by firms in telephone and door-to-door selling of consumer products (for example, Kirby vacuum cleaners), this approach treats every prospect the same, regardless of differences in needs or preference for certain kinds of information.

Canned sales presentations can be advantageous when the differences between prospects are unknown or with novice salespeople who are less knowledgeable about the product and selling process than experienced salespeople. Although it guarantees a thorough presentation, it often lacks flexibility and spontaneity and, more important, does not provide for feedback from the prospective buyer—a critical component in the communication process and the start of a relationship.

Need-Satisfaction Format The stimulus-response and formula selling formats share a common characteristic: The salesperson dominates the conversation. By comparison, the *need-satisfaction presentation* format emphasizes probing and listening by the salesperson to identify needs and interests of prospective buyers. Once these are identified, the salesperson tailors the presentation to the prospect and highlights product benefits that may be valued by the prospect. The need-satisfaction format, which emphasizes problem solving and customer solutions, is the most consistent with the marketing concept and relationship building.

Two selling styles are common with this format.[9] **Adaptive selling** involves adjusting the presentation to fit the selling situation, such as knowing when to offer solutions and when to ask for more information. Sales research and practice show that knowledge of the customer and sales situation are key ingredients for adaptive selling. Many consumer service firms such as brokerage and insurance firms and consumer product firms like Rockport, AT&T, and Gillette effectively apply this selling style.

Consultative selling focuses on problem identification, where the salesperson serves as an expert on problem recognition and resolution. With consultative selling, problem solution options are not simply a matter of choosing from an array of existing products or services. Rather, novel solutions often arise, thereby creating unique value for the customer.

Consultative selling is prominent in business-to-business marketing. Johnson Controls's Automotive Systems Group, IBM's Global Services, and DHL Worldwide Express offer customer solutions through their consultative selling style, as does Xerox. According to a senior Xerox sales executive, "Our business is no longer about selling boxes. It's about selling digital, networked-based information management solutions, and this requires a highly customized and consultative selling process." But what does a customer solution really mean? The Marketing Matters box on the next page offers a unique answer.[10]

Handling Objections A critical concern in the presentation stage is handling objections. *Objections* are excuses for not making a purchase commitment or decision. Some objections are valid and are based on the characteristics of the product or service or price. However, many objections reflect prospect skepticism or indifference. Whether valid or not, experienced salespeople know that objections do not put an end to the presentation. Rather, techniques can be used to deal with objections

adaptive selling
A need-satisfaction sales presentation style that involves adjusting the presentation to fit the selling situation.

consultative selling
A need-satisfaction sales presentation style that focuses on problem identification, where the salesperson serves as an expert on problem recognition and resolution.

Solutions for problems are what companies are looking for from suppliers. At the same time, suppliers focus on customer solutions to differentiate themselves from competitors. So what is a customer solution and what does it have to do with selling?

Sellers view a solution as a customized and integrated combination of products and services for meeting a customer's business needs. But what do buyers think? From a buyer's perspective, a solution is one that (1) meets their requirements, (2) is designed to uniquely solve their problem, (3) can be implemented, and (4) ensures follow-up. This insight arose from a field study conducted by three researchers at Emory University. Their in-depth study also yielded insight into what

an effective customer solution offers. According to one buyer interviewed in their study:

> They (the supplier) make sure that their sales and marketing guys know what's going on. The sales and technical folks know what's going on, and the technical and support guys know what's going on with me. All these guys are in the loop, and it's not a puzzle for them.

So what does putting the customer into customer solutions have to do with selling? Three things stand out. First, considerable time and effort is necessary to fully understand a specific customer's requirements. Second, effective customer solutions are based on relationships among sellers and buyers. And finally, consultative selling is central to providing novel solutions for customers, thereby creating value for them.

---

in a courteous, ethical, and professional manner. The following six techniques are the most common:[11]

1. *Acknowledge and convert the objection.* This technique involves using the objection as a reason for buying. For example, a prospect might say, "The price is too high." The reply: "Yes, the price is high because we use the finest materials. Let me show you. . . ."
2. *Postpone.* The postpone technique is used when the objection will be dealt with later in the presentation: "I'm going to address that point shortly. I think my answer would make better sense then."
3. *Agree and neutralize.* Here a salesperson agrees with the objection, then shows that it is unimportant. A salesperson would say, "That's true. Others have said the same. But, they thought that issue was outweighed by other benefits."
4. *Accept the objection.* Sometimes the objection is valid. Let the prospect express such views, probe for the reason behind it, and attempt to stimulate further discussion on the objection.
5. *Denial.* When a prospect's objection is based on misinformation and clearly untrue, it is wise to meet the objection head on with a firm denial.
6. *Ignore the objection.* This technique is used when it appears that the objection is a stalling mechanism or is clearly not important to the prospect.

Each of these techniques requires a calm, professional interaction with the prospect and is most effective when objections are anticipated in the preapproach stage. Handling objections is a skill requiring a sense of timing, appreciation for the prospect's state of mind, and adeptness in communication. Objections also should be handled ethically. Lying or misrepresenting product or service features are grossly unethical practices.

Close: Asking for the Customer's Order or Business

The *closing* stage in the selling process involves obtaining a purchase commitment from the prospect. This stage is the most important and the most difficult because the

The closing stage involves obtaining a purchase commitment from the prospect. Read the text to learn how the close itself can take several forms.

salesperson must determine when the prospect is ready to buy. Telltale signals indicating a readiness to buy include body language (prospect reexamines the product or contract closely), statements ("This equipment should reduce our maintenance costs"), and questions ("When could we expect delivery?").

The close itself can take several forms. Three closing techniques are used when a salesperson believes a buyer is about ready to make a purchase: (1) trial close, (2) assumptive close, and (3) urgency close. A *trial close* involves asking the prospect to make a decision on some aspect of the purchase: "Would you prefer the blue or gray model?" An *assumptive close* entails asking the prospect to consider choices concerning delivery, warranty, or financing terms under the assumption that a sale has been finalized. An *urgency close* is used to commit the prospect quickly by making reference to the timeliness of the purchase: "The low interest financing ends next week," or "That is the last model we have in stock." Of course, these statements should be used only if they accurately reflect the situation; otherwise, such claims would be unethical. When a prospect is clearly ready to buy, the final close is used, and a salesperson asks for the order.

Follow-Up: Solidifying the Relationship

The selling process does not end with the closing of a sale; rather, professional selling requires customer follow-up. One marketing authority equated the follow-up with courtship and marriage, by observing, "The sale merely consummates the courtship. Then the marriage begins. How good the marriage is depends on how well the relationship is managed."[12] The *follow-up* stage includes making certain the customer's purchase has been properly delivered and installed and difficulties experienced with the use of the item are addressed. Attention to this stage of the selling process solidifies the buyer–seller relationship. Research shows that the cost and effort to obtain repeat sales from a satisfied customer is roughly half of that necessary to gain a sale from a new customer.[13] In short, today's satisfied customers become tomorrow's qualified prospects or referrals.

learning review

5. What are the six stages in the personal selling process?

6. Which presentation format is most consistent with the marketing concept? Why?

THE SALES MANAGEMENT PROCESS

LO4

Selling must be managed if it is going to contribute to a firm's marketing objectives. Although firms differ in the specifics of how salespeople and the selling effort are managed, the sales management process is similar across firms. Sales management consists of three interrelated functions: (1) sales plan formulation, (2) sales plan implementation, and (3) salesforce evaluation (see Figure 17–3 on the next page).

Sales Plan Formulation: Setting Direction

Formulating the sales plan is the most basic of the three sales management functions. According to the vice president of the Harris Corporation, a global communications company, "If a company hopes to implement its marketing strategy, it really needs a

FIGURE 17–3

The sales management
process involves sales
plan formulation, sales
plan implementation, and
salesforce evaluation.

**Sales plan
formulation**

- Setting objectives
- Organizing the
  salesforce
- Developing account
  management policies

**Sales plan
implementation**

- Salesforce recruit-
  ment and selection
- Salesforce training
- Salesforce motivation
  and compensation

**Salesforce
evaluation**

- Quantitative
  assessment
- Behavioral evaluation

sales plan

*A statement describing what
is to be achieved and where
and how the selling effort of
salespeople is to be deployed.*

detailed sales planning process."[14] The **sales plan** is a statement describing what is to be achieved and where and how the selling effort of salespeople is to be deployed. Sales plan formulation involves three tasks: (1) setting objectives, (2) organizing the salesforce, and (3) developing account management policies.

Setting Objectives Setting objectives is central to sales management because this task specifies what is to be achieved. In practice, objectives are set for the total salesforce and for each salesperson. Selling objectives can be output related and focus on dollar or unit sales volume, number of new customers added, and profit. Alternatively, they can be input related and emphasize the number of sales calls and selling expenses. Output- and input-related objectives are used for the salesforce as a whole and for each salesperson. A third type of objective that is behaviorally related is typically specific for each salesperson and includes his or her product knowledge, customer service satisfaction ratings, and selling and communication skills.

Whatever objectives are set, they should be precise and measurable and specify the time period over which they are to be achieved. Once established, these objectives serve as performance standards for the evaluation of the salesforce, the third function of sales management.

Organizing the Salesforce Establishing a selling organization is the second task in formulating the sales plan. Companies organize their salesforce on the basis of (1) geography, (2) customer, or (3) product or service. A geographical structure is the simplest organization, where the United States, or indeed the globe, is first divided into regions and each region is divided into districts or territories. Salespeople are assigned to each district with defined geographical boundaries and call on all customers and represent all products sold by the company. The main advantage of this structure is that it can minimize travel time, expenses, and duplication of selling effort. However, if a firm's products or customers require specialized knowledge, then a geographical structure is not suitable.

A customer sales organizational structure is used when different types of buyers have different needs. In practice this means that a different salesforce calls on each separate type of buyer or marketing channel. For example, Kodak recently switched from a geographical to a marketing channel structure with different sales teams serving specific retail channels: mass merchandisers, photo specialty outlets, and food and drug stores. The rationale for this approach is that more effective, specialized customer support and knowledge are provided to buyers. However, this structure often leads to higher administrative costs and some duplication of selling effort, because two separate salesforces are used to represent the same products.

A variation of the customer organizational structure is **major account management**, or *key account management*, the practice of using team selling to focus on important customers so as to build mutually beneficial, long-term, cooperative relationships. Major account management involves teams of sales, service, and often technical personnel who work with purchasing, manufacturing, engineering, logistics, and financial executives in customer organizations.[15] This approach, which often assigns company personnel to a customer account, results in "customer specialists" who can

**major account
management**

*The practice of using team
selling to focus on important
customers so as to build
mutually beneficial, long-
term, cooperative relationships; also called key account
management.*

Marketing Matters > > > > > > customer value

Creating and Sustaining Customer Value through Cross-Functional Team Selling

The day of the lone salesperson calling on a customer is rapidly becoming history. Today, 75 percent of companies employ cross-functional teams of professionals to work with customers to improve relationships, find better ways of doing things, and, of course, create and sustain value for their customers.

Xerox and IBM pioneered cross-functional team selling, but other firms were quick to follow as they spotted the potential to create and sustain value for their customers. Recognizing that corn growers needed a herbicide they could apply less often, a DuPont team of chemists, sales and marketing executives, and regulatory specialists created just the right product that recorded sales of $57 million in its first year. Procter & Gamble uses teams of marketing, sales, advertising, computer systems, and supply chain personnel to work with its major retailers, such as Walmart, to identify ways to develop, promote, and deliver products. Pitney Bowes, Inc., which produces sophisticated computer systems that weigh, rate, and track packages for firms such as UPS and FedEx, also uses sales teams to meet customer needs. These teams consist of sales personnel, "carrier management specialists," and engineering and administrative executives who continually find ways to improve the technology of shipping goods across town and around the world.

Efforts to create and sustain customer value through cross-functional team selling have become a necessity as customers seek greater value for their money. According to the vice president for procurement of a *Fortune* 500 company, "Today, it's not just getting the best price but getting the best value—and there are a lot of pieces to value."

provide exceptional service. Procter & Gamble uses this approach with Walmart as does Black & Decker with Home Depot. Other companies also have embraced this practice, as described in the Marketing Matters box.[16]

A product sales organizational structure is used when specific knowledge is required to sell a product. For example, Maxim Steel has a salesforce that sells drilling pipe to oil companies and another that sells specialty steel products to manufacturers. The primary advantage of this structure is that salespeople can develop expertise with technical characteristics, applications, and selling methods associated with a particular product or family of products. However, this structure also produces high administrative costs and duplication of selling effort because two company salespeople may call on the same customer.

In short, there is no one best sales organization for all companies in all situations. The organization of the salesforce should reflect the marketing strategy of the firm.

Developing Account Management Policies   The third task in formulating a sales plan involves developing **account management policies** specifying whom salespeople should contact, what kinds of selling and customer service activities should be engaged in, and how these activities should be carried out. These policies might state which individuals in a buying organization should be contacted, the amount of sales and service effort that different customers should receive, and the kinds of information salespeople should collect before or during a sales call.

An example of an account management policy in Figure 17–4 on the next page shows how different accounts or customers can be grouped according to level of opportunity and the firm's competitive sales position.[17] When specific account names

account management policies

Policies that specify whom salespeople should contact, what kinds of selling and customer service activities should be engaged in, and how these activities should be carried out.

	High	Low
High Account opportunity level	**1** *Attractiveness:* Accounts offer a good opportunity because they have high potential and the sales organization has a strong position. *Account management policy:* Accounts should receive high level of sales calls and service to retain and possibly build accounts.	**3** *Attractiveness:* Accounts may offer a good opportunity if the sales organization can overcome its weak position. *Account management policy:* Emphasize a heavy sales organization position or shift resources to other accounts if a stronger sales organization position is impossible.
Low	**2** *Attractiveness:* Accounts are somewhat attractive because the sales organization has a strong position, but future opportunity is limited. *Account management policy:* Accounts should receive moderate level of sales and service to maintain current position of sales organization.	**4** *Attractiveness:* Accounts offer little opportunity, and the sales organization position is weak. *Account management policy:* Consider replacing personal calls with telephone sales or direct mail to service accounts. Consider dropping account if unprofitable.

FIGURE 17–4

An account management policy grid grouping customers according to the level of opportunity and the firm's competitive sales position.

are placed in each cell, salespeople clearly see which accounts should be contacted, with what level of selling and service activity, and how to deal with them. Accounts in cells 1 and 2 might have high frequencies of personal sales calls and increased time spent on a call. Cell 3 accounts will have lower call frequencies, and cell 4 accounts might be contacted through telemarketing or direct mail rather than in person. For example, Union Pacific Railroad put its 20,000 smallest accounts on a telemarketing program. A subsequent survey of these accounts indicated that 84 percent rated Union Pacific's sales effort "very effective" compared with 67 percent before the switch.

Sales Plan Implementation: Putting the Plan into Action

The sales plan is put into practice through the tasks associated with sales plan implementation. Whereas sales plan formulation focuses on "doing the right things," implementation emphasizes "doing things right." The three major tasks involved in implementing a sales plan are (1) salesforce recruitment and selection, (2) salesforce training, and (3) salesforce motivation and compensation.

Salesforce Recruitment and Selection

Effective recruitment and selection of salespeople is one of the most crucial tasks of sales management. It entails finding people who match the type of sales position required by a firm. Recruitment and selection practices would differ greatly between order-taking and order-getting sales positions, given the differences in the demands of these two jobs. Therefore, recruitment and selection begin with a carefully crafted job analysis and job description followed by a statement of job qualifications.

A *job analysis* is a study of a particular sales position, including how the job is to be performed and the tasks that make up the job. Information from a job analysis is used to write a *job description*, a written document that describes job relationships and requirements that characterize each sales position. It explains (1) to whom a salesperson reports, (2) how a salesperson interacts with other company personnel, (3) the customers to be called on, (4) the specific activities to be carried out, (5) the physical and mental demands of the job, and (6) the types of products and services to be sold.

The job description is then translated into a statement of job qualifications, including the aptitudes, knowledge, skills, and a variety of behavioral characteristics considered necessary to perform the job successfully. Qualifications for order-getting sales positions often mirror the expectations of buyers: (1) imagination and problem-solving ability, (2) strong work ethic, (3) honesty, (4) intimate product knowledge, (5) effective communication and listening skills, and (6) attentiveness reflected in responsiveness to buyer needs and customer loyalty and follow-up. Firms use a variety of methods for evaluating prospective salespeople. Personal interviews, reference checks, and background information provided on application forms are the most frequently used methods.[18]

Salesforce training is an ongoing process. Read the text to learn how training is conducted.

Salesforce Training Whereas recruitment and selection of salespeople is a one-time event, salesforce training is an ongoing process that affects both new and seasoned salespeople.[19] Sales training covers much more than selling practices. For example, IBM Global Services salespeople, who sell consulting and various information technology services, take at least two weeks of in-class and Internet-based training on both consultative selling and the technical aspects of business.

On-the-job training is the most popular type of training, followed by individual instruction taught by experienced salespeople. Formal classes, seminars taught by sales trainers, and computer-based training are also popular.

Salesforce Motivation and Compensation A sales plan cannot be successfully implemented without motivated salespeople. Research on salesperson motivation suggests that (1) a clear job description, (2) effective sales management practices, (3) a personal need for achievement, and (4) proper compensation, incentives, or rewards will produce a motivated salesperson.[20]

The importance of compensation as a motivating factor means that close attention must be given to how salespeople are financially rewarded for their efforts. Salespeople are paid using one of three plans: (1) straight salary, (2) straight commission, or (3) a combination of salary and commission. Under a *straight salary compensation plan*, a salesperson is paid a fixed fee per week, month, or year. With a *straight commission compensation plan*, a salesperson's earnings are directly tied to the sales or profit generated. For example, an insurance agent might receive a 2 percent commission of $2,000 for selling a $100,000 life insurance policy. A *combination compensation plan* contains a specified salary plus a commission on sales or profit generated.

Each compensation plan has its advantages and disadvantages.[21] A straight salary plan is easy to administer and gives management a large measure of control over how salespeople allocate their efforts. However, it provides little incentive to expand sales volume. This plan is used when salespeople engage in many nonselling activities, such as account or customer servicing. A straight commission plan provides the maximum amount of selling incentive but can detract salespeople from providing customer service. This plan is common when nonselling activities are minimal. Combination plans are most preferred by salespeople and attempt to build on the advantages of salary and commission plans while reducing the potential shortcomings of each.

Nonmonetary rewards are also given to salespeople for meeting or exceeding objectives. These rewards include trips, honor societies, distinguished salesperson awards, and letters of commendation. Some unconventional rewards include the new pink Cadillacs and Buicks and jewelry given by Mary Kay Cosmetics to outstanding salespeople. Mary Kay, with 12,000 cars, has the largest fleet of General Motors cars in the world.[22]

Effective recruitment, selection, training, motivation, and compensation programs combine to create a productive salesforce. Ineffective practices often lead to costly salesforce turnover. The expense of replacing and training a new salesperson, including the cost of lost sales, can be high. Also, new recruits are often less productive than seasoned salespeople.[23]

Salesforce Evaluation: Measuring Results

The final function in the sales management process involves evaluating the salesforce. It is at this point that salespeople are assessed as to whether sales objectives were met and account management policies were followed. Both quantitative and behavioral measures are used to tap different selling dimensions.

Quantitative Assessments Quantitative assessments are based on input- and output-related objectives set forth in the sales plan. Input-related measures focus on the actual activities performed by salespeople such as those involving sales calls, selling expenses, and account management policies. The number of sales calls made, selling expense related to sales made, and the number of reports submitted to superiors are frequently used input measures.

Output measures often appear in a sales quota. A **sales quota** contains specific goals assigned to a salesperson, sales team, branch sales office, or sales district for a stated time period. Dollar or unit sales volume, last year/current sales ratio, sales of specific products, new accounts generated, and profit achieved are typical goals. The time period can range from one month to one year.

Behavioral Evaluation Behavioral measures are also used to evaluate salespeople. These include assessments of a salesperson's attitude, attention to customers, product knowledge, selling and communication skills, appearance, and professional demeanor. Even though these assessments are sometimes subjective, they are frequently considered and, in fact, inevitable, in salesperson evaluation. Why? These factors are often important determinants of quantitative outcomes.

About 60 percent of U.S. companies now include customer satisfaction as a behavioral measure of salesperson performance. For example, at Microsoft, half of a salesperson's commission is dependent on customer satisfaction ratings.[24]

Increasingly, companies are using marketing dashboards to track salesperson performance for evaluation purposes. An illustration appears in the Using Marketing Dashboards box.

Salesforce Automation and Customer Relationship Management

Personal selling and sales management have undergone a technological revolution with the integration of salesforce automation into customer relationship management processes. In fact, the convergence of computer, information, communication, and Internet technologies has transformed the sales function in many companies and made the promise of customer relationship management a reality. **Salesforce automation** (SFA) is the use of these technologies to make the sales function more effective and efficient. SFA applies to a wide range of activities, including each stage in the personal selling process and management of the salesforce itself.[25]

Salesforce automation exists in many forms. Examples of SFA applications include computer hardware and software for account analysis, time management, order processing and follow-up, sales presentations, proposal generation, and product and sales training. Each application is designed to ease administrative tasks and free time for salespeople to be with customers building relationships, designing solutions, and providing service. In fact, research shows that buyers believe that SFA increases

Using Marketing Dashboards
Tracking Salesperson Performance at Moore Chemical & Sanitation Supply, Inc.

Moore Chemical & Sanitation Supply, Inc. (MooreChem) is a large Midwestern supplier of cleaning chemicals and sanitary products. MooreChem sells to janitorial companies that clean corporate and professional office buildings.

MooreChem recently installed a sales and account management planning software package that included a dashboard for each of its sales representatives. Salespeople had access to their dashboards as well. These dashboards included seven metrics—sales revenue, gross margin, selling expense, profit, average order size, new customers, and customer satisfaction. Each metric was gauged to show actual salesperson performance relative to target goals.

Your Challenge As a newly promoted district sales manager at MooreChem, your responsibilities include tracking each salesperson's performance in your district. You are also responsible for directing the sales activities and practices of district salespeople.

In anticipation of a performance review with one of your salespeople, Brady Boyle, you review his dashboard for the previous quarter. Provide a constructive review of his performance.

Your Findings Brady Boyle's quarterly performance is displayed below. Boyle has exceeded targeted goals for sales revenue, selling expenses, and customer satisfaction. All of these metrics show an upward trend. He has met his target for gaining new customers and average order size. However, Boyle's gross margin and profit are below targeted goals. These metrics evidence a downward trend as well. Brady Boyle's mixed performance requires a constructive and positive correction.

Your Action Brady Boyle should already know how his performance compares with targeted goals. Remember, Boyle has access to his dashboard. Recall that he has exceeded his sales target, but is considerably under his profit target. Boyle's sales trend is up, but his profit trend is down.

You will need to focus attention on Boyle's gross margin and selling expense results and trend. Boyle, it seems, is spending time and money selling lower margin products that produce a targeted average order size. It may very well be that Boyle is actually expending effort selling more products to his customers. Unfortunately, the product mix yields lower gross margins, resulting in a lower profit.

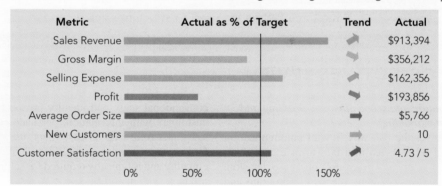

Metric	Actual as % of Target	Trend	Actual
Sales Revenue		↗	$913,394
Gross Margin		↘	$356,212
Selling Expense		↗	$162,356
Profit		↘	$193,856
Average Order Size		→	$5,766
New Customers		→	10
Customer Satisfaction		↗	4.73 / 5

a salesperson's professionalism, customer interaction frequency, responsiveness, and customer relationship quality.[26]

Salesforce Technology Technology has become an integral part of field selling. For example, salespeople for Godiva Chocolates use their laptop computers to process orders, plan time allocations, forecast sales, and communicate with Godiva personnel and customers. While in a department store candy buyer's office, such as Neiman Marcus, a salesperson can calculate the order cost (and discount), transmit the order, and obtain a delivery date within minutes from Godiva's order processing department.

Toshiba America Medical System salespeople use laptop computers with built-in CD-ROM capabilities to provide interactive presentations for their computerized tomography (CT) and magnetic resonance imaging (MRI) scanners. The customer can see elaborate three-dimensional animations, high-resolution scans, and video clips of the company's products in operation as well as narrated testimonials from

satisfied customers. Toshiba has found this application to be effective both for sales presentations and for training its salespeople.[27]

Salesforce Communication   Technology has changed the way salespeople communicate with customers, other salespeople, and sales and management. Facsimile, electronic mail, and voice mail are common communication technologies used by salespeople today. Cellular (phone) technology, which allows salespeople to exchange data, text, and voice transmissions, is also popular. Whether traveling or in a customer's office, these technologies provide information at the salesperson's fingertips to answer customer questions and solve problems.

Perhaps the greatest impact on salesforce communication is the application of Internet technology.[28] Today, salespeople are using their company's intranet for a variety of purposes. At HP Enterprise Services, a professional services firm, salespeople access its intranet to download client material, marketing content, account information, technical papers, and competitive profiles. In addition, HP Enterprise Services offers 7,000 training classes that salespeople can take anytime and anywhere.

Salesforce automation is clearly changing how selling is done and how salespeople are managed. Its numerous applications promise to boost selling productivity, improve customer relationships, and decrease selling cost.

Salespeople rely upon multiple communication technologies to perform their selling and nonselling tasks today.

learning review

7. What are the three types of selling objectives?

8. What three factors are used to structure sales organizations?

LEARNING OBJECTIVES REVIEW

LO1   *Discuss the nature and scope of personal selling and sales management in marketing.*

Personal selling involves the two-way flow of communication between a buyer and seller, often in a face-to-face encounter, designed to influence a person's or group's purchase decision. Sales management involves planning the selling program and implementing and controlling the personal selling effort of the firm. The scope of selling and sales management is apparent in three ways. First, virtually every occupation that involves customer contact has an element of personal selling. Second, selling plays a significant role in a company's overall marketing effort. Salespeople occupy a boundary position between buyers and sellers; they *are* the company to many buyers and account for a major cost of marketing in a variety of industries; and they can create value for customers. Finally, through relationship selling, salespeople play a central role in tailoring solutions to customer problems as a means to customer value creation.

LO2   *Identify the different types of personal selling.*

Two types of personal selling exist: (*a*) order taking and (*b*) order getting. Each type differs from the others in terms of actual selling done and the amount of creativity required to perform the sales task. Order takers process routine orders or reorders for products that were already sold by the company. They generally do little selling in a conventional sense and engage in only modest problem solving with customers. Order getters sell in a

conventional sense and identify prospective customers, provide customers with information, persuade customers to buy, close sales, and follow up on customers' use of a product or service. Order getting involves a high degree of creativity and customer empathy and is typically required for selling complex or technical products with many options.

LO3   *Explain the stages in the personal selling process.*

The personal selling process consists of six stages: (*a*) prospecting, (*b*) preapproach, (*c*) approach, (*d*) presentation, (*e*) close, and (*f*) follow-up. Prospecting involves the search for and qualification of potential customers. The preapproach stage involves obtaining further information on the prospect and deciding on the best method of approach. The approach stage involves the initial meeting between the salesperson and prospect. The presentation stage involves converting a prospect into a customer by creating a desire for the product or service. The close involves obtaining a purchase commitment from the prospect. The follow-up stage involves making certain that the customer's purchase has been properly delivered and installed and difficulties experienced with the use of the item are addressed.

LO4   *Describe the major functions of sales management.*

Sales management consists of three interrelated functions: (*a*) sales plan formulation, (*b*) sales plan implementation, and (*c*) evaluation of the salesforce. Sales plan formulation involves setting objectives, organizing the salesforce, and developing account management policies. Sales plan implementation involves salesforce recruitment, selection, training, motivation, and compensation. Finally, salesforce evaluation focuses on quantitative assessments of sales performance and behavioral measures such as customer satisfaction that are linked to selling objectives and account management policies.

FOCUSING ON KEY TERMS

account management policies p. 393
adaptive selling p. 389
consultative selling p. 389
major account management p. 392
order getter p. 385

order taker p. 384
personal selling p. 382
personal selling process p. 386
relationship selling p. 383
salesforce automation (SFA) p. 396

sales management p. 382
sales plan p. 392
sales quota p. 396

APPLYING MARKETING KNOWLEDGE

1 Jane Dawson is a new sales representative for the Charles Schwab brokerage firm. In searching for clients, Jane purchased a mailing list of subscribers to *The Wall Street Journal* and called them all regarding their interest in discount brokerage services. She asked if they have any stocks and if they have a regular broker. Those people without a regular broker were asked their investment needs. Two days later Jane called back with investment advice and asked if they would like to open an account. Identify each of Jane Dawson's actions in terms of the steps of selling.

2 Where would you place each of the following sales jobs on the order-taker/order-getter continuum shown at the end of this question? (*a*) Burger King counter clerk, (*b*) automobile insurance salesperson, (*c*) IBM computer salesperson, (*d*) life insurance salesperson, and (*e*) shoe salesperson.

Order taker — Order getter

3 Of the two firms described below, which compensation plan would you recommend for each firm and what reasons would you give for your recommendations? (*a*) A newly formed company that sells lawn care equipment on a door-to-door basis directly to consumers; and (*b*) the Nabisco Company, which sells heavily advertised products in supermarkets by having the salesforce call on these stores and arrange shelves, set up displays, and make presentations to store buying committees.

4 Suppose someone said to you, "The only real measure of a salesperson is the amount of sales produced." How might you respond?

building your marketing plan

Does your marketing plan involve a personal selling activity? If the answer is no, read no further and do not include a personal selling element in your plan. If the answer is yes:

1 Identify the likely prospects for your product or service.
2 Determine what information you should obtain about the prospect.

3 Describe how you would approach the prospect.
4 Outline the presentation you would make to the prospect for your product or service.
5 Develop a sales plan, focusing on the organizational structure you would use for your salesforce (geography, product, or customer).

video case 17 Xerox: Building Customer Relationships through Personal Selling

"I'm like the quarterback of the team. I manage 250 accounts, and anything from billing issues, to service issues, to selling the products. I'm really the face to the customer," says Alison Capossela, a Washington, D.C.–based Xerox sales representative.

As the primary company contact for Xerox customers, Alison is responsible for developing and maintaining customer relationships. To accomplish this she uses a sophisticated selling process that requires many activities from making presentations, to attending training sessions, to managing a team of Xerox personnel, to monitoring competitors' activities. The face-to-face interactions with customers, however, are the most rewarding for Capossela. "It's an amazing feeling; the more they challenge me the more I fight back. It's fun!" she explains.

THE COMPANY

Xerox Corporation's mission is to "help people find better ways to do great work by constantly leading in document technologies, products, and services that improve customers' work processes and business results." To accomplish this mission Xerox employs 53,700 people in 160 countries. With annual sales topping $15 billion, Xerox is the world's leading document management enterprise and a *Fortune* 500 company. Xerox offers a wide range of products and services. These include printers, copiers and fax machines, multifunction and network devices, high-speed color presses, digital imaging and archiving products and services, and supplies such as toner, paper, and ink. The entire company is guided by customer-focused and employee-centered core values (e.g., "We succeed through satisfied customers") and a passion for innovation, speed, and adaptability.

Xerox was founded in 1906 as a manufacturer of photographic paper called The Haloid Company. In 1947, the company purchased the license to basic xerographic patents. The following year it received a trademark for the word "Xerox." By 1973 Xerox had introduced the automatic, plain-paper copier, opened offices in Japan, and its Palo Alto Research Center (PARC) had invented the world's first personal computer (the Alto), the "mouse," and graphical user interface software. In 1994, Xerox adopted "The Document Company" as its signature and the partially digitized red "X" as its corporate symbol. Despite this extraordinary history of success, Xerox was $19 billion in debt by 2000 and was losing business rapidly. Many experts predicted that the company would fail.

The Xerox board of directors knew a change was needed and it asked Anne M. Mulcahy to serve as the company's CEO. Mulcahy had begun her career as a sales representative at Xerox and observed that "we had lost our way in terms of delivering value to customers." Mulcahy reduced the size of the workforce by one-third and invested in new technologies, while keeping the Xerox culture and values. The changes, coupled with Mulcahy's commitment to a sales organization that focused on customer relationships, reversed Xerox's decline. As Kevin Warren, vice president of sales, explains: "One of the reasons she has been so successful is that she absolutely resonates with all the people. I think [because of] the fact that she started out as a sales rep, people feel like she is one of them." The turnaround has been such an extraordinary success that Mulcahy was recognized by *Forbes* magazine as the 10th most powerful woman in the world!

THE SELLING PROCESS AT XEROX

When Mulcahy became CEO, Xerox began a shift to a consultative selling model that focused on helping customers solve their business problems rather than just placing more equipment in their office. The shift meant that sales reps needed to be less product-oriented and more relationship- and value-oriented. Xerox wanted to be a provider of total solutions. Today, Xerox has more than 8,000 sales professionals throughout the world who spend a large amount of their day developing customer relationships. Capossela explains: "Fifty percent of my day is spent with my customers, 25 percent is following up with

phone calls or emails, and another 25 percent involves preparing proposals." The approach has helped Xerox attract new customers and keep existing customers.

The sales process at Xerox typically follows the six stages of the personal selling process identified in Figure 17–2: (1) Xerox identifies potential clients through responses to advertising, referrals, and telephone calls; (2) the salesforce prepares for a presentation by familiarizing themselves with the potential client and its document needs; (3) a Xerox sales representative approaches the prospect and suggests a meeting and presentation; (4) as the presentation begins, the salesperson summarizes relevant information about potential solutions Xerox can offer, states what he or she hopes to get out of the meeting, explains how the products and services work, and reinforces the benefits of working with Xerox; (5) the salesperson engages in an action close (gets a signed document or a firm confirmation of the sale); and then (6) continues to meet and communicate with the client to provide assistance and monitor the effectiveness of the installed solution.

Xerox sales representatives also use the selling process to maintain relationships with existing customers. In today's competitive environment it is not unusual to have customers who have been approached by competitors or who are required to obtain more than one bid before renewing a contract. Xerox has teams of people who collect and analyze information about competitors and their products. The information is sent out to sales reps or offered to them through workshops and seminars. The most difficult competitors are the ones that have also invested in customer relationships. The selling process allows Xerox to continually react and respond to new information and take advantage of opportunities in the marketplace.

THE SALES MANAGEMENT PROCESS AT XEROX

The Xerox salesforce is divided into four geographic organizations: North America, which includes the United States and Canada; Europe, which includes 17 countries; Global Accounts, which manages large accounts that operate in multiple locations; and Developing Markets, which includes all other geographic territories that may require Xerox products and services. Within each geographic area, the majority of Xerox products and services are typically sold through its direct salesforce. Xerox also utilizes a variety of other channels, including value-added resellers, independent agents, dealers, systems integrators and telephone and Internet sales channels.

Motivation and compensation are an important aspect of any salesforce. At Xerox there is a passion for winning that provides a key incentive for sales reps. In addition, the compensation plan plays an important role. As Warren explains, "Our compensation plans are a combination of salary as well as an opportunity to leverage earnings through sales commissions and bonuses." Xerox also has a recognition program called the President's Club where the top performers are awarded a five-day trip to one of the top resorts in the world. The program has been a huge success and has now been offered for more than 30 years.

Perhaps the most well-known component of Xerox's sales management process is its sales representative training program. For example, Xerox developed the "Create and Win" program to help sales reps learn the new consultative selling approach. The components of the program consisted of interactive training sessions and distance-learning Webinars. Every new sales representative at Xerox receives eight weeks of training development in the field and at the Xerox Corporate University in Virginia. "The training program is phenomenal!" according to Capossela. The training and its focus on the customer is part of the Xerox culture outside of the sales organization also. Every senior executive at Xerox is responsible for working with at least one customer. They also spend a full day every month responding to incoming customer calls and inquiries.

tatives. For example, Xerox is accelerating the development of its top salespeople. Mentors are used to provide advice for day-to-day issues and long-term career planning. In addition, globalization has become such an important initiative at Xerox that experienced and successful sales representatives are quickly given opportunities to manage large global accounts. Xerox is also moving toward an approach that empowers sales representatives to make decisions about how to handle accounts. The large number of Xerox customers means there are a variety of different corporate styles, and the sales reps are increasingly the best qualified to manage the relationship. This approach is just one more example of Xerox's commitment to customers and creating customer value.

WHAT IS IN THE FUTURE FOR THE XEROX SALESFORCE?

The recent growth and success at Xerox is creating many opportunities for the company and for its sales represen-

Questions

1 Why was Anne Mulcahy's experience as a sales representative an important part of Xerox's growth in recent years?

2 How did the sales approach change after Mulcahy became the CEO of Xerox?

3 *(a)* How does Xerox create customer value through its personal selling process? *(b)* How does Alison Capossela provide solutions for Xerox customers?

4 Why is the Xerox training program so important to the company's success?

18

Implementing Interactive and Multichannel Marketing

LEARNING OBJECTIVES

After reading this chapter you should be able to:

LO1 Describe what interactive marketing is and how it creates customer value, customer relationships, and customer experiences.

LO2 Explain why certain types of products and services are particularly suited for interactive marketing.

LO3 Describe why consumers shop and buy online and how marketers influence online purchasing behavior.

LO4 Define cross-channel shoppers and the role of transactional and promotional Web sites in reaching these shoppers.

SEVEN CYCLES. ONE BIKE. YOURS.

"One bike: Yours" is the company motto for Seven Cycles, Inc., located in Watertown, Massachusetts. And for good reason.

Seven Cycles is the largest custom bicycle frame builder. The company produces a broad range of road, mountain, cyclo-cross, tandem, touring, single-speed, and commuter bikes annually, and no two bikes are exactly alike. At Seven Cycles, attention is focused on each customer's unique cycling experience through the optimum fit, function, performance, and comfort of his or her very own bike. According to one satisfied customer, "Getting a Seven is more of a creation than a purchase."

The marketing success of Seven Cycles is due to its state-of-the-art bicycle frames. But as Rob Vandermark, company founder and president, says, "Part of our success is that we are tied to a business model that includes the Internet."

Seven Cycles uses its multilanguage (English, German, Chinese, Japanese, Korean, and Flemish) Web site (www.sevencycles.com) to let customers get deeply involved in the frame building process and the selection of components to outfit their bikes. It enables customers to collaborate on the bike design using the company's Custom Kit fitting system that considers the rider's size, aspirations, and riding habits. Then customers can monitor their bike's progress through the development and production process by clicking "Where's My Frame?" on the Seven Cycles Web site.

This customization process and continuous feedback makes for a collaborative relationship between Seven Cycles, its 233 authorized dealers and distributors, and customers in 40 countries. "Each bike we build is unique, so each customer's experience deserves to be unique as well," explains Mattison Crowe, marketing manager at Seven Cycles.

In addition to the order process, Web site visitors can peruse weekly news stories, learn about new-product introductions, or link to the company president's blog to get a unique perspective on the business. They can read employee biographies online to learn more about the people who build the bikes. The Web site also offers a retailer-specific section as a 24/7 repository of updated information for channel partners.

Beyond the Web site, owners of a Seven Cycles bike receive a monthly e-mail newsletter, called Communiqué, that allows them to remain in touch and be the first to learn about the company's activities, strategic partnerships, and new offerings. Seven Cycles is also experimenting with other social media tools such as Facebook and Twitter, as a means to build a stronger sense of community around the brand.[1]

This chapter describes how companies design and implement interactive marketing programs. It begins by explaining how Internet technology can create customer value, build customer relationships, and produce customer experiences in novel ways. Next, it describes how Internet technology affects and is affected by consumer behavior and marketing practice. Finally, the chapter shows how marketers integrate and leverage their communication and delivery channels using Internet technology to implement multichannel marketing programs.

CREATING CUSTOMER VALUE, RELATIONSHIPS, AND EXPERIENCES IN MARKETSPACE

LO1

Consumers and companies populate two market environments today. One is the traditional *marketplace*. Here buyers and sellers engage in face-to-face exchange relationships in a material environment characterized by physical facilities (stores and offices) and mostly tangible objects. The other is the *marketspace*, an Internet-enabled digital environment characterized by face-to-screen exchange relationships and electronic images and offerings.

The existence of two market environments has been a boon for consumers. Today, consumers can shop for and purchase a wide variety of products and services in either market environment. Actually, many consumers now browse and buy in both market environments, and more are expected to do so in the future. Figure 18–1 shows the growth in online shoppers and estimated retail sales in the United States since 2003. About 94 percent of Internet users ages 15 and older shop online in the United States. They are expected to buy $335 billion worth of products and services in 2012.[2]

Customer Value Creation in Marketspace

Why has the marketspace captured the eye and imagination of marketers worldwide? Recall from Chapter 1 that marketing creates time, place, form, and possession utilities, thereby providing value. Marketers believe that the possibilities for customer value creation are greater in the digital marketspace than in the physical marketplace.

Consider place and time utility. In marketspace, the provision of direct, on-demand information is possible from marketers *anywhere* to customers *anywhere at any time.* Why? Operating hours and geographical constraints do not exist in marketspace. For example, Recreational Equipment (www.rei.com), an outdoor gear marketer, reports

FIGURE 18–1

Trends in online shoppers and online retail sales revenue in the United States.

Online shoppers in the United States

Millions of online shoppers

Percentage of online population

57% 59% 60% 61% 62% 64% 65% 66% 67% 68%

97 111 124 133 138 144 193 199 205 216

2003 '04 '05 '06 '07 '08 '09 '10 '11 '12

Online retail sales revenue in the United States

($ in billions)

$114 $142 $172 $202 $233 $266 $260 $298 $320 $335

2003 '04 '05 '06 '07 '08 '09 '10 '11 '12

that 35 percent of its orders are placed between 10:00 P.M. and 7:00 A.M., long after and before retail stores are open for business. Similarly, a U.S. consumer from Chicago can access Marks & Spencer (www.marks-and-spencer.co.uk), the well-known British department store, to shop for clothing as easily as a person living near London's Piccadilly Square.

Possession utility—getting a product or service to consumers so they can own or use it—is accelerated. Airline, car rental, and lodging electronic reservation systems such as Orbitz (www.orbitz.com) allow comparison shopping for the lowest fares, rents, and rates and almost immediate access to and confirmation of travel arrangements and accommodations. Internet usage among people who travel on a regular basis is 20 percent higher than it is among those who travel infrequently.[3]

The greatest marketspace opportunity for marketers, however, lies in its potential for creating form utility. Interactive two-way Internet-enabled communication capabilities in marketspace invite consumers to tell marketers specifically what their requirements are, making customization of a product or service to fit their exact needs possible.[4] For instance, Capital One lets its customers build their own mix of interest rates, fees, rewards, and cash back through its Card Lab Web site (www.capitalone.com/cardlab).

Interactivity, Individuality, and Customer Relationships in Marketspace

Seven Cycles creates form utility in its creation of customized bikes for its customers in 40 countries.

Marketers also benefit from two unique capabilities of Internet technology that promote and sustain customer relationships. One is *interactivity*; the other is *individuality*.[5] Both capabilities are important building blocks for buyer–seller relationships. For these relationships to occur, companies need to interact with their

Pavement. Dirt. **Whatever.**

No matter what form your two-wheeled passion takes. Whatever road, trail, or entirely improvised route you follow. There is a Seven for you. Expertly designed and handcrafted for who you are and the way you ride.

seven cycles

www.sevencycles.com　　telephone 617.923.7774　　email info@sevencycles.com　　One Bike. Yours.

Mars, Inc., uses choiceboard technology to decorate M&Ms with personal photos and messages. Other applications for choiceboards are described in the text.

customers by listening and responding to their needs. Marketers must also treat customers as individuals and empower them to (1) influence the timing and extent of the buyer–seller interaction and (2) have a say in the kind of products and services they buy, the information they receive, and in some cases, the prices they pay.

Internet technology allows for interaction, individualization, and customer relationship building to be carried out on a scale never before available and makes interactive marketing possible. **Interactive marketing** involves two-way buyer–seller electronic communication in a computer-mediated environment in which the buyer controls the kind and amount of information received from the seller. Interactive marketing is characterized by sophisticated choiceboard and personalization systems that transform information supplied by customers into customized responses to their individual needs.

Choiceboards A **choiceboard** is an interactive, Internet-enabled system that allows individual customers to design their own products and services by answering a few questions and choosing from a menu of product or service attributes (or components), prices, and delivery options.[6] Customers today can design their own computers with Dell's online configurator, style their own athletic shoe at Reebok.com, assemble their own investment portfolios with Schwab's mutual fund evaluator, build their own bicycle at SevenCycles.com, create a diet and fitness program at www.ediet.com that fits their lifestyle, and decorate M&Ms with photos of themselves and unique messages at www.mymms.com. Because choiceboards collect precise information about preferences and behavior of individual buyers, a company becomes more knowledgeable about a customer and better able to anticipate and fulfill that customer's needs.

Most choiceboards are essentially transaction devices. However, companies such as Dell have expanded the functionality of choiceboards using collaborative filtering technology. **Collaborative filtering** is a process that automatically groups people with similar buying intentions, preferences, and behaviors and predicts future purchases.[7] For example, say two people who have never met buy a few of the same CDs over time. Collaborative filtering software is programmed to reason that these two buyers might have similar musical tastes: If one buyer likes a particular CD, then the other will like it as well. The outcome? Collaborative filtering gives marketers the ability to make a dead-on sales recommendation to a buyer in *real time*. You see collaborative filtering applied each time you view a selection at Amazon.com and see "Customers who bought this (item) also bought. . . ."

Choiceboards and collaborative filtering represent two important capabilities of Internet technology and have changed the way companies operate today. According to an electronic commerce manager at IBM, "The business model of the past was make and sell. Now instead of make and sell, it's sense and respond."[8]

Personalization Choiceboards and collaborative filtering are marketer-initiated efforts to provide customized responses to the needs of individual buyers. Personalization systems are typically buyer-initiated efforts. **Personalization** is the consumer-initiated practice of generating content on a marketer's Web site that is custom tailored to an individual's specific needs and preferences. For example, Yahoo! (www.yahoo.com) allows users to create personalized MyYahoo! pages. Users can add or delete a variety of types of information from their personal pages, including specific stock quotes, weather conditions in any city in the world, and local television schedules. In turn, Yahoo! can use the buyer profile data entered when users register

Reebok has effectively used choiceboard technology for customizing athletic shoes.

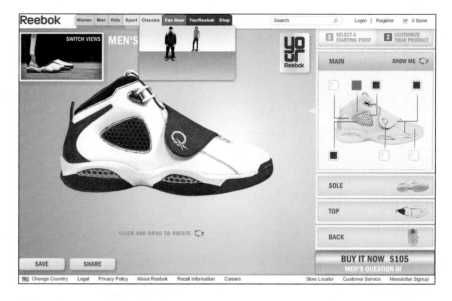

permission marketing
Asking for a consumer's consent (called opt-in*) to receive e-mail and advertising based on personal data supplied by the consumer.*

at the site to tailor e-mail messages, advertising, and content to the individual—and even post a happy birthday greeting on the user's special day.

An aspect of personalization is a buyer's willingness to have tailored communications brought to his or her attention. Obtaining this approval is called **permission marketing**—the solicitation of a consumer's consent (called *opt-in*) to receive e-mail and advertising based on personal data supplied by the consumer. Permission marketing is a proven vehicle for building and maintaining customer relationships, provided it is properly used.

Companies that successfully employ permission marketing adhere to three rules.[9] First, they make sure opt-in customers receive only information that is relevant and meaningful to them. Second, their customers are given the option to *opt-out*, or change the kind, amount, or timing of information sent to them. Finally, their customers are assured that their name or buyer profile data will not be sold or shared with others. This assurance is important because 75 percent of adult Internet users express concern about the privacy of their personal information.[10]

Creating an Online Customer Experience

A continuing challenge for companies is the design and execution of marketing programs that capitalize on the unique customer value-creation capabilities of Internet technology. Companies realize that applying Internet technology to create time, place, form, and possession utility is just a starting point for creating a meaningful marketspace presence. Today, the quality of the customer experience produced by a company is the standard by which a meaningful marketspace presence is measured.

From an interactive marketing perspective, *customer experience* is defined as the sum total of the interactions that a customer has with a company's Web site, from the initial look at a home page through the entire purchase decision process.[11] Companies produce a customer experience through seven Web site design elements. These elements are context, content, community, customization, communication, connection, and commerce. Each is summarized in Figure 18–2 on the next page. A closer look at these elements illustrates how each contributes to customer experience.

Context refers to a Web site's aesthetic appeal and functional look and feel reflected in site layout and visual design. A functionally oriented Web site focuses largely on the company's offering, be it products, services, or information. Travel Web sites, such as Travelocity.com, tend to be functionally oriented with an emphasis on destinations, scheduling, and prices. In contrast, beauty Web sites, such as

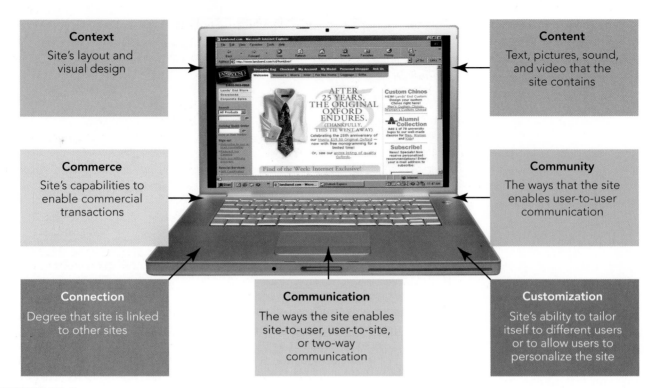

Context
Site's layout and visual design

Content
Text, pictures, sound, and video that the site contains

Commerce
Site's capabilities to enable commercial transactions

Community
The ways that the site enables user-to-user communication

Connection
Degree that site is linked to other sites

Communication
The ways the site enables site-to-user, user-to-site, or two-way communication

Customization
Site's ability to tailor itself to different users or to allow users to personalize the site

FIGURE 18–2
Seven Web site design elements that contribute to a customer's online experience.

Revlon.com, are more aesthetically oriented. As these examples suggest, context attempts to convey the core consumer benefit provided by the company's offerings. *Content* applies to all digital information on a Web site, including the presentation form—text, video, audio, and graphics. Content quality and presentation along with context dimensions combine to engage a Web site visitor and provide a platform for the five remaining design elements.

Web site *customization* is the ability of a site to modify itself to, or be modified by, each individual user. This design element is prominent in Web sites that offer personalized content, such as My eBay and MyYahoo! The *connection* element is the network of linkages between a company's site and other sites. These links are embedded in the Web site; appear as highlighted words, a picture, or graphic; and allow a user to effortlessly visit other sites with a mouse click. Connection is a major design element for informational Web sites such as *The New York Times*. Users of NYTimes.com can access the book review section and link to Barnes & Noble to order a book or browse related titles without ever visiting a store.

Communication refers to the dialogue that unfolds between the Web site and its users. Consumers—particularly those who have registered at a site—now expect that communication be interactive and individualized in real time much like a personal conversation. In fact, some Web sites now enable a user to talk directly with a customer representative while shopping the site. For example, two-thirds of the sales through Dell.com involve human sales representatives. In addition, an increasing number of company Web sites encourage user-to-user communications hosted by the company to create virtual communities, or simply, *community*. This design element is popular because it has been shown to enhance customer experience and build favorable buyer–seller relationships. Examples of communities range from the Huggies Baby Network hosted by Kimberly-Clark (www.huggies.com) to the Harley Owners Group (HOG) sponsored by Harley-Davidson (www.harley-davidson.com).

The seventh design element is *commerce*—the Web site's ability to conduct sales transactions for products and services. Online transactions are quick and simple in well-designed Web sites. Amazon.com has mastered this design element with "one-click shopping," a patented feature that allows users to order products with a single mouse click.

Most Web sites do not include every design element. Although every Web site has context and content, they differ in the use of the remaining five elements. Why? Web sites have different purposes. For example, only Web sites that emphasize the actual sale of products and services include the commerce element. Web sites that are used primarily for advertising and promotion purposes emphasize the communication element. The difference between these two types of Web sites is discussed later in the chapter in the description of multichannel marketing.

Companies use a broad array of measures to assess Web site performance. The amount of time per month visitors spend on their Web site, or "stickiness," is one measure used to gauge customer experience.[12] Read the Using Marketing Dashboards box on the next page to learn how stickiness is calculated, measured, and interpreted at Sewell Automotive Companies.

ONLINE CONSUMER BEHAVIOR AND MARKETING PRACTICE IN MARKETSPACE

LO2

Who are online consumers, and what do they buy? Why do they choose to shop and purchase products and services in the digital marketspace rather than or in addition to the traditional marketplace? Answers to these questions have a direct bearing on marketspace marketing practices.

Who Is the Online Consumer?

Online consumers are the subsegment of all Internet users who employ this technology to research products and services and make purchases. As a group, online consumers, like Internet users, are more likely to be women than men and tend to be better educated, younger, and more affluent than the general U.S. population, which makes them an attractive market.[13] Even though online shopping and buying are popular, a small percentage of online consumers still account for a disproportionate share of online retail sales in the United States. It is estimated that online consumers with household incomes of $75,000 or more account for about one-half of total consumer online sales. Also, women tend to purchase more products and services online than men.[14]

Numerous marketing research firms have studied the lifestyles and shopping habits of online consumers. A recurrent insight is that online consumers are diverse and represent different kinds of people seeking different kinds of online experiences. As

Using Marketing Dashboards
Sizing Up Site Stickiness at Sewell Automotive Companies

Automobile dealerships have invested significant time, effort, and money in their Web sites. Why? Car browsing and shopping on the Internet are now commonplace.

Dealerships commonly measure Web site performance by tracking visit, visitor traffic, and "stickiness"—the amount of time per month visitors spend on their Web site. Web site design, easy navigation, involving content, and visual appeal combine to enhance the interactive customer experience and Web site stickiness.

To gauge stickiness, companies monitor the average time spent per unique monthly visitor (in minutes) on their Web sites. This is done by tracking and displaying the average visits per unique monthly visitor and the average time spent per visit, in minutes, in their marketing dashboards. The relationship is as follows:

Average time spent per unique monthly visitor (minutes) =

$$\left(\begin{array}{c} \text{Average visits per} \\ \text{unique monthly visitor} \end{array}\right) \times \left(\begin{array}{c} \text{Average time spent} \\ \text{per visit (minutes)} \end{array}\right)$$

Your Challenge As the manager responsible for Sewell.com, the Sewell Automotive Companies Web site, you have been asked to report on the effect recent improvements in the company's Web site have had on the amount of time per month visitors spend on the Web site. Sewell ranks among the largest U.S. automotive dealerships and is a recognized customer service leader in the automotive industry. Its Web site reflects the company's commitment to an unparalleled customer experience at its family of dealerships.

Your Findings Examples of monthly marketing dashboard traffic and time measures are displayed below for June 2006, three months before the Web site improvements were made (green arrow), and June 2007, three months after the improvements were made (red arrow).

The average time spent per unique monthly visitor increased from 8.5 minutes in June 2006 to 11.9 minutes in June 2007—a sizable jump. The increase is due primarily to the upturn in the average time spent per visit from 7.1 minutes to 8.5 minutes. The average number of visits also increased, but the percentage change was much less.

Your Action Improvements in the Web site have noticeably "moved the needle" on average time spent per unique monthly visitor. Still, additional action may be required to increase average visits per unique monthly visitor. These actions might include an analysis of Sewell's Web advertising program, search engine initiatives with Google, links to automobile manufacturer corporate Web sites, and broader print and electronic media advertising.

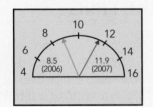 = 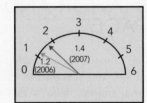 ×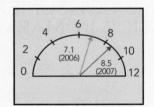

| Average Time Spent per Unique Monthly Visitor (minutes) | Average Visits per Unique Monthly Visitor | Average Time Spent per Visit (minutes) |

an illustration, the Marketing Matters box provides an in-depth look at the lifestyle and shopping habits of today's "Internet mom."[15]

What Online Consumers Buy

Much still needs to be learned about online consumer purchase behavior. Although research has documented the most frequently purchased products and services bought online, marketers also need to know why these items are popular in the digital marketspace.

Six general product and service categories dominate online consumer buying today and for the foreseeable future, as shown in Figure 18–3.[16] One category consists of items for which product information is an important part of the purchase decision, but prepurchase trial is not necessarily critical. Items such as computers, computer accessories, and consumer electronics sold by Dell.com fall into this category. So

Meet Today's Internet Mom—All 38 Million!

Do you have fond childhood memories of surfing the Internet with your mother? Today's children probably will.

By 2013, 38 million mothers will be online regularly. Typically, they will be 38 years old, and married, college educated, and working outside the home. A study conducted by C&R Research on behalf of Disney Online has identified four segments of mothers based on their Internet usage.

The *Yes Mom* segment represents 14 percent of online moms. They work outside the home, go online eight hours per week, and value the convenience of obtaining information about products and services. The *Mrs. Net Skeptic* segment accounts for 31 percent of online moms. They tend to be stay-at-home moms, are extremely family-oriented, and go online six hours per week for parenting and children's education information and food and cooking tips. The *Tech Nester* mom (32 percent of online moms) believes the Internet brings her family closer together. These moms average 10 hours per week online and prefer online shopping to in-store shopping. The fourth segment—*Passive Under Pressure* moms—tend to be Internet newbies and go online, but infrequently.

The first three segments, which account for 77 percent of online moms, agree that the Internet has simplified their lives. They also say that the Internet has been an invaluable information source for vacation travel, financial products, and automobiles and for useful ideas and suggestions on family-related topics. Online moms ranked weather, food and cooking, entertainment, news, health, and parenting as the most popular Web sites to visit.

do books, which accounts for the sales growth of Amazon.com and Barnes & Noble (www.barnesandnoble.com). Both booksellers publish short reviews of new books that visitors to their Web sites can read before making a purchase decision.

A second category includes items for which audio or video demonstration is important. This category consists of CDs and DVDs sold by Columbia House.com. The third category contains items that can be delivered digitally, including computer software, travel and lodging reservations and confirmations, financial brokerage services, and electronic ticketing. Popular Web sites for these items include Travelocity.com, Ticketmaster.com, and Schwab.com.

Unique items, such as collectibles, specialty goods, and foods and gifts, represent a fourth category. Collectible auction houses (www.sothebys.com), food merchants (www.harryanddavid.com), and flower marketers (www.1800flowers.com) sell these products. A fifth category includes items that are regularly purchased and where convenience is very important. Many consumer-packaged goods, such as grocery products, fall into this category. A final category of items consists of highly standardized products and services for which information about price is important. Certain kinds of insurance (auto and homeowners), home improvement products, casual apparel, and toys make up this category.

Why Consumers Shop and Buy Online

LO3

Marketers emphasize the customer value-creation possibilities, the importance of interactivity, individuality and relationship building, and producing customer experience in the new marketspace. However, consumers typically refer to six reasons they

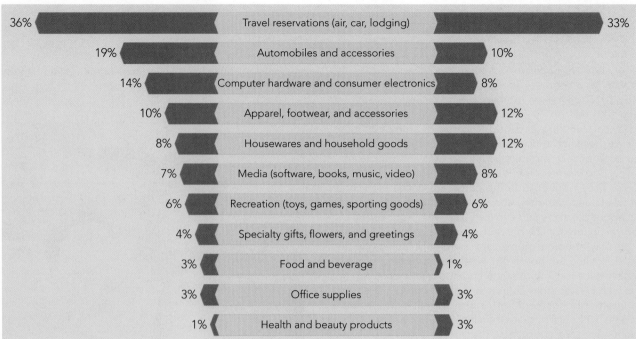

2007: Percent of Online Retail Sales	Product/service category	2012: Percent of Online Retail Sales
36%	Travel reservations (air, car, lodging)	33%
19%	Automobiles and accessories	10%
14%	Computer hardware and consumer electronics	8%
10%	Apparel, footwear, and accessories	12%
8%	Housewares and household goods	12%
7%	Media (software, books, music, video)	8%
6%	Recreation (toys, games, sporting goods)	6%
4%	Specialty gifts, flowers, and greetings	4%
3%	Food and beverage	1%
3%	Office supplies	3%
1%	Health and beauty products	3%

FIGURE 18–3
Estimated percentage of online retail sales by product/service category: 2007 and 2012.

bots
Electronic shopping agents or robots that comb Web sites to compare prices and product or service features.

shop and buy online: convenience, choice, customization, communication, cost, and control (Figure 18–4).

Convenience Online shopping and buying is *convenient*. Consumers can visit Walmart at www.walmart.com to scan and order from among thousands of displayed products without fighting traffic, finding a parking space, walking through long aisles, and standing in store checkout lines. Alternatively, online consumers can use **bots**, electronic shopping agents or robots that comb Web sites to compare prices and product or service features. In either instance, an online consumer has never ventured into a store. However, for convenience to remain a source of customer value creation, Web sites must be easy to locate and navigate, and image downloads must be fast.

Choice *Choice*, the second reason consumers shop and buy online, has two dimensions. First, choice exists in the product or service selection offered to consumers. Buyers desiring selection can avail themselves of numerous Web sites for almost anything they

FIGURE 18–4
Why do consumers shop and buy online? Read the text to learn how convenience, choice, customization, communication, cost, and control result in a favorable customer experience.

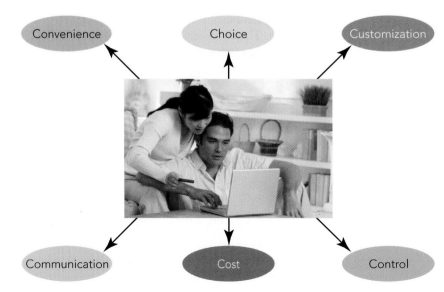

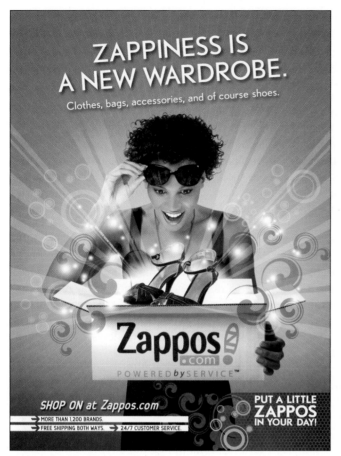

Zappos.com is successful because it meets all the requirements necessary for consumers to shop and buy online. In less than 10 years, the company has posted $1 billion in annual sales of shoes, apparel, bags, accessories, housewares, and jewelry.

Web communities
Web sites that allow people to meet online and exchange views on topics of common interest.

blog
A Web page that serves as a publicly accessible personal journal for an individual or organization.

spam
Electronic junk mail or unsolicited e-mail.

want. For instance, online buyers of consumer electronics can shop individual manufacturers such as Bose (www. bose.com) and QVC.com, a general merchant that offers more than 100,000 products.

Choice assistance is the second dimension. Here, the interactive capabilities of Internet-enabled technologies invite customers to engage in an electronic dialogue with marketers for the purpose of making informed choices. Choice assistance is one of the reasons for the continued success of Zappos.com. The company offers an online chat room that enables prospective buyers to ask questions and receive answers in real time. In addition, carefully designed search capabilities permit consumers to review products by brand and particular items.

Customization Even with a broad selection and choice assistance, some customers prefer one-of-a-kind items that fit their specific needs. *Customization* arises from Internet-enabled capabilities that make possible a highly interactive and individualized information and exchange environment for shoppers and buyers. Remember the earlier Reebok, Schwab, Dell, and Seven Cycles examples? To varying degrees, online consumers also benefit from *customerization*—the practice of not only customizing a product or service but also personalizing the marketing and overall shopping and buying interaction for each customer.[17] Customerization does more than offer consumers the right product, at the right time, and at the right price. It combines choiceboard and personalization systems to expand the exchange environment beyond a transaction and makes shopping and buying an enjoyable, personal experience.

Communication Online consumers particularly welcome the *communication* capabilities of Internet-enabled technologies. This communication can take three forms: (1) marketer-to-consumer e-mail notification, (2) consumer-to-marketer buying and service requests, and (3) consumer-to-consumer chat rooms and instant messaging, plus social networking Web sites such as Twitter, MySpace, and Facebook.

Communication has proven to be a double-edged sword for online consumers. On the one hand, the interactive communication capabilities of Internet-enabled technologies increase consumer convenience, reduce information search costs, and make choice assistance and customization possible. Communication also promotes the development of company-hosted and independent **Web communities**—Web sites that allow people to congregate online and exchange views on topics of common interest. For instance, Coca-Cola hosts MyCoke.com, and iVillage.com is an independent Web community for women and includes topics such as career management, personal finances, parenting, relationships, beauty, and health.

Web logs, or blogs, are another form of communication. A **blog** is a Web page that serves as a publicly accessible personal journal for an individual or organization. Blogs are popular because they provide online forums on a wide variety of subjects ranging from politics to car repair. Companies such as Hewlett-Packard, Frito-Lay, and Harley-Davidson routinely monitor blogs to gather customer insights.[18]

On the other hand, communications can take the form of electronic junk mail or unsolicited e-mail, called **spam**. The prevalence of spam has prompted many online services to institute policies and procedures to prevent spammers from spamming their subscribers, and several states have antispamming laws. In 2004, the *CAN-SPAM (Controlling the Assault of Non-Solicited Pornography and Marketing) Act*

About 75 percent of e-mail consists of spam. The United States is the largest source of spam, followed by China, Russia, and Brazil. These four countries produce about 40 percent of unsolicited e-mail worldwide.

viral marketing

An Internet-enabled promotional strategy that encourages users to forward marketer-initiated messages to others via e-mail.

dynamic pricing

The practice of changing prices for products and services in real time in response to supply and demand conditions.

cookies

Computer files that a marketer can download onto the computer of an online shopper who visits the marketer's Web site.

became effective and restricts information collection and unsolicited e-mail promotions on the Internet.

Internet-enabled communication capabilities also make possible *buzz*, a popular term for word-of-mouth behavior in marketspace. Chapter 5 described the importance of word of mouth in consumer behavior. Internet technology has magnified its significance. According to Jeff Bezos, president of Amazon.com, "If you have an unhappy customer on the Internet, he doesn't tell his six friends, he tells his 6,000 friends!"[19] Buzz is particularly influential for toys, cars, sporting goods, motion pictures, apparel, consumer electronics, pharmaceuticals, health and beauty products, and health care services. Some marketers have capitalized on this phenomenon by creating buzz through viral marketing.

Viral marketing is an Internet-enabled promotional strategy that encourages individuals to forward marketer-initiated messages to others via e-mail, social networking Web sites, and blogs. There are three approaches to viral marketing. Marketers can embed a message in the product or service so that customers hardly realize they are passing it along. The classic example is Hotmail, which was one of the first companies to provide free, Internet-based e-mail. Each outgoing e-mail message has the tagline: "Get Your Private, Free Email from MSN Hotmail." Today, Windows Live Hotmail has more than 100 million users.

Marketers can also make the Web site content so compelling that viewers want to share it with others. EBay has done this. The company reports that more than half its visitors are referred by other visitors. Finally, marketers can offer incentives (discounts, sweepstakes, or free merchandise) for referrals.

Cost Consumer *cost* is a fifth reason for online shopping and buying. Many popular items bought online can be purchased at the same price or cheaper than in retail stores. Lower prices also result from Internet-enabled software that permits **dynamic pricing**, the practice of changing prices for products and services in real time in response to supply and demand conditions. As described in Chapter 12, dynamic pricing is a form of flexible pricing and can often result in lower prices. It is typically used for pricing time-sensitive items such as airline seats, scarce items found at art or collectible auctions, and out-of-date items such as last year's models of computer equipment and accessories.

A consumer's cost of external information search, including time spent and often the hassle of shopping, is also reduced. Greater shopping convenience and lower external search costs are two major reasons for the popularity of online shopping and buying among women—particularly those who work outside the home.

Control The sixth reason consumers prefer to buy online is the *control* it gives them over their shopping and purchase decision process. Online shoppers and buyers are empowered consumers. They deftly use Internet technology to seek information, evaluate alternatives, and make purchase decisions on their own time, terms, and conditions. For example, studies show that shoppers spend an average of five hours researching cars online before setting foot in a showroom.[20] The result of these activities is a more informed consumer and a more discerning shopper. In the words of one marketing consultant, "In the marketspace, the customer is in charge."[21]

Even though consumers have many reasons for shopping and buying online, a segment of Internet users refrains from making purchases for privacy and security reasons. These consumers are concerned about a rarely mentioned seventh C—cookies.

Cookies are computer files that a marketer can download onto the computer and mobile phone of an online shopper who visits the marketer's Web site. Cookies allow the marketer's Web site to record a user's visit, track visits to other Web sites,

Travelocity.com has been a pioneer of dynamic pricing. It provides Internet and wireless reservations information for more than 700 airlines, 50,000 hotels, and 50 car rental companies for its more than 30 million registered members.

and store and retrieve this information in the future. Cookies also contain visitor information such as expressed product preferences, personal data, passwords, and financial information, including credit card numbers. Clearly, cookies make possible customized and personalized content for online shoppers. The controversy surrounding cookies is summed up by an authority on the technology: "At best a cookie makes for a user-friendly Web world: like a doorman or salesclerk who knows who you are. At worst, cookies represent a potential loss of privacy."[22] Read the Making Responsible Decisions box on the next page to learn more about privacy and security issues in the digital marketplace.[23]

When and Where Online Consumers Shop and Buy

Shopping and buying happen at different times in marketspace than in the traditional marketplace.[24] About 80 percent of online retail sales occur Monday through Friday. The busiest shopping day is Wednesday. By comparison, 35 percent of retail store sales are registered on the weekend. Saturday is the most popular shopping day. Monday through Friday online shopping and buying often occur during normal work hours—some 30 percent of online consumers say they visit Web sites from their place of work, which partially accounts for the sales level during the workweek. Favorite Web sites for workday shopping and buying include those featuring event tickets, auctions, online periodical subscriptions, flowers and gifts, consumer electronics, and travel. Web sites offering health and beauty items, apparel and accessories, and music and video tend to be browsed and bought from a consumer's home.

---

learning review

3. What is viral marketing?

4. What are the six reasons consumers prefer to shop and buy online?

CROSS-CHANNEL SHOPPERS AND MULTICHANNEL MARKETING

LO4

Consumers are more likely to browse than buy online. Consumer marketspace browsing and buying in the traditional marketplace has given rise to the cross-channel shopper and the importance of multichannel marketing.

cross-channel shopper
An online consumer who researches products online and then purchases them at a retail store.

Who Is the Cross-Channel Shopper?

A **cross-channel shopper** is an online consumer who researches products online and then purchases them at a retail store.[25] Recent research shows that 51 percent of U.S. online consumers are cross-channel shoppers. These shoppers represent both genders

Let the E-Buyer Beware

Privacy and security are two key reasons consumers are leery of online shopping and buying. A recent Pew Internet and American Life Project poll reported that 75 percent of online consumers have privacy and security concerns about the Internet. Even more telling, many have stopped shopping a Web site or forgone an online purchase because of these concerns. Industry analysts estimate that about $24.5 million in e-commerce sales are lost annually because of privacy and security concerns among online shoppers.

Consumer concerns are not without merit. According to the Federal Trade Commission, 46 percent of fraud complaints are Internet related, costing consumers $560 million. In addition, consumers lose millions of dollars each year due to identity theft resulting from breaches in company security systems. A percolating issue is whether the U.S. government should pass more stringent Internet privacy and security laws. About 70 percent of online consumers favor such action.

Companies, however, favor self-regulation. For example, TRUSTe (www.truste.com) awards its trademark to company Web sites that comply with standards of privacy protection and disclosure. Still, consumers are ultimately responsible for using care and caution when engaging in online behavior, including e-commerce. Consumers have a choice of whether or not to divulge personal information and monitor how their information is being used.

What role should the U.S. government, company self-regulation, and consumer vigilance play in dealing with privacy and security issues in the digital marketspace?

equally and are only slightly younger than online consumers. They have a higher education, earn significantly more money, and are more likely to embrace technology in their lives than online consumers who don't cross-channel shop.

Cross-channel shoppers want the right product at the best price, and they don't want to wait several days for delivery. The top reasons these shoppers research items online before buying in stores include (1) the desire to compare products among different retailers; (2) the need for more information than is available in stores; and (3) the ease of comparing their options without having to trek to multiple retail locations.

Implementing Multichannel Marketing

The prominence of cross-channel shoppers has focused increased attention on multichannel marketing. Recall from Chapter 13 that *multichannel marketing* is the blending of different communication and delivery channels that are mutually reinforcing in attracting, retaining, and building relationships with consumers who shop and buy in the traditional marketplace and online—the cross-channel shopper.

The most common cross-channel shopping and buying path is to browse one or more Web sites and then purchase an item at a retail store. This shopping path might suggest that company Web sites for cross-channel shoppers should be similar. But they are not. Web sites play a multifaceted role in multichannel marketing because they can serve as either a communication or delivery channel. Two general applications of Web sites exist based on their intended purpose: (1) transactional Web sites and (2) promotional Web sites.

Multichannel Marketing with Transactional Web Sites *Transactional Web sites* are essentially electronic storefronts. They focus principally on converting an online browser into an online, catalog, or in-store buyer using the Web site design elements described earlier. Transactional Web sites are most common among store and catalog retailers and direct selling companies, such as Tupperware. Retailers and direct selling firms have found that their Web sites, while cannibalizing sales volume from stores, catalogs, and sales representatives, attract new customers and influence sales. Consider Victoria's Secret, the well-known specialty retailer of intimate apparel for women ages 18 to 45. It reports that almost 60 percent of its Web site customers are men, most of whom generate new sales volume for the company.[26]

Transactional Web sites are used less frequently by manufacturers of consumer products. A recurring issue for manufacturers is the threat of *channel conflict*, described in Chapter 13, and the potential harm to trade relationships with their retailing intermediaries. Still, manufacturers do use transactional Web sites, often cooperating with retailers. For example, Callaway Golf Company markets its golf merchandise at www.callawaygolf.com but relies on a retailer close to the buyer to fill the order. The retailer ships the order to the buyer within 24 hours and is credited with the sale. The majority of retailers that sell Callaway merchandise participate in this relationship, including retail chains Golf Galaxy and Dick's Sporting Goods. According to Callaway's chief executive officer, "This arrangement allows us to satisfy the consumer but to do so in a way that doesn't violate our relationship with our loyal trade partners—those 15,000 outlets that sell Callaway products."[27]

Nestlé maintains promotional Web sites for many of its leading brands, such as its Baby Ruth snack bar. The company has found that these Web sites engage consumers. Read the text to learn the difference between transactional and promotional Web sites.

Multichannel Marketing with Promotional Web Sites   *Promotional Web sites* have a very different purpose than transactional sites. They advertise and promote a company's products and services and provide information on how items can be used and where they can be purchased. They often engage the visitor in an interactive experience involving games, contests, and quizzes with electronic coupons and other gifts as prizes. Procter & Gamble maintains separate Web sites for many of its leading brands, including Pringles potato chips (www.pringles.com), Scope mouthwash (www.getclose.com), and Pampers diapers (www.pampers.com). Promotional sites are effective in generating interest in and trial of a company's products (see Figure 18–5).[28] Hyundai Motor America reports that 80 percent of the people visiting a Hyundai store first visited the brand's Web site (www.hyundaiusa .com) and 70 percent of Hyundai leads come from its Web site.

Promotional Web sites also support a company's traditional marketing channel and build customer relationships. This is the objective of the Clinique Division of Estée Lauder, Inc., which markets cosmetics through department stores. Clinique reports that 80 percent of current customers who visit its Web site (www .clinique.com) later purchase a Clinique product at a department store, while 37 percent of non-Clinique buyers make a Clinique purchase after visiting the company's Web site.

The popularity of multichannel marketing is apparent in its growing impact on online retail sales.[29] Fully 70 percent of U.S. online retail sales in 2007 were made by companies that practiced multichannel marketing. Multichannel marketers are expected to register about 90 percent of U.S. online retail sales in 2012.

FIGURE 18–5

Implementing multichannel marketing with promotional Web sites is common today. Two successes are found at Hyundai Motor America and the Clinique Division of Estée Lauder, Inc.

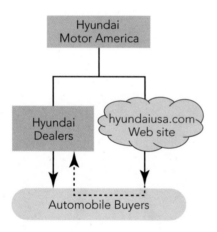

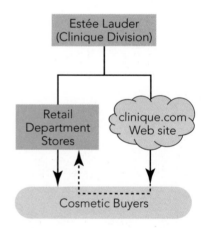

- 70% of Hyundai leads come from its Web site.
- 80% of people visiting a Hyundai dealer first visited its Web site.

- 80% of current Clinique buyers who visit its Web site later purchase a Clinique product at a store.
- 37% of non-Clinique buyers make a Clinique purchase after visiting its Web site.

learning review

5. A cross-channel shopper is _____.

6. Channel conflict between manufacturers and retailers is likely to arise when manufacturers use _____ Web sites.

LEARNING OBJECTIVES REVIEW

LO1 *Describe what interactive marketing is and how it creates customer value, customer relationships, and customer experiences.*

Interactive marketing involves two-way buyer–seller electronic communication in a computer-mediated environment in which the buyer controls the kind and amount of information received from the seller. It creates customer value by providing time, place, form, and possession utility for consumers. Customer relationships are created and sustained through two unique capabilities of Internet technology: interactivity and individuality. From an interactive marketing perspective, customer experience represents the sum total of the interactions that a customer has with a company's Web site, from the initial look at a home page through the entire purchase decision process. Companies produce a customer experience through seven Web site design elements. These elements are context, content, community, customization, communication, connection, and commerce.

LO2 *Explain why certain types of products and services are particularly suited for interactive marketing.*

Certain types of products and services seem to be particularly suited for interactive marketing. One category consists of items for which product information is an important part of the purchase decision, but prepurchase trial is not necessarily critical. A second category involves items for which audio or video demonstration is important. A third category contains items that can be digitally delivered. Unique items represent a fourth category. A fifth category includes items that are regularly purchased and where convenience is very important. A final category consists of highly standardized items for which information about price is important.

LO3 *Describe why consumers shop and buy online, and how marketers influence online purchasing behavior.*

There are six reasons consumers shop and buy online. They are convenience, choice, customization, communication, cost, and control. Marketers have capitalized on these reasons through a variety of means. For example, they provide choice assistance using choiceboard and collaborative filtering technology, which also provides opportunities for customization. Company-hosted Web communities and viral marketing practices capitalize on the communications dimensions of Internet-enabled technologies. Dynamic pricing provides real-time responses to supply and demand conditions, often resulting in lower prices to consumers. Permission marketing is popular given consumer interest in control.

LO4 *Define cross-channel shoppers and the role of transactional and promotional Web sites in reaching these shoppers.*

A cross-channel shopper is an online consumer who researches products online and then purchases them at a retail store. These shoppers are reached through multichannel marketing. Web sites play a multifaceted role in multichannel marketing because they can serve as either a delivery or communication channel. In this regard, transactional Web sites are essentially electronic storefronts. They focus principally on converting an online browser into an online, catalog, or in-store buyer using the Web site design elements described earlier. On the other hand, promotional Web sites serve to advertise and promote a company's products and services and provide information on how items can be used and where they can be purchased.

FOCUSING ON KEY TERMS

blog p. 413
bots p. 412
choiceboard p. 406
collaborative filtering p. 406
cookies p. 414

cross-channel shopper p. 415
dynamic pricing p. 414
interactive marketing p. 406
permission marketing p. 407
personalization p. 406

spam p. 413
viral marketing p. 414
Web communities p. 413

APPLYING MARKETING KNOWLEDGE

1 About 70 percent of Internet users have actually purchased something online. Have you made an online purchase? If so, why do you think so many people who have access to the Internet are not also online buyers? If not, why are you reluctant to do so? Do you think that electronic commerce benefits consumers even if they don't make a purchase?

2 Like the traditional marketplace, marketspace offers marketers opportunities to create greater time, place, form, and possession utility. How do you think Internet-enabled technology rates in terms of creating these values? Take a shopping trip at a virtual retailer of your choice (don't buy anything unless you really want to). Then compare the time, place, form, and possession utility provided by the virtual retailer that you enjoyed during a nonelectronic experience shopping for the same product category.

3 Visit Amazon.com (www.amazon.com) or Barnes & Noble (www.barnesandnoble.com). As you tour the company's Web site, think about how shopping for books online compares with a trip to your university bookstore to buy books. Specifically, compare and contrast your shopping experiences with respect to convenience, choice, customization, communication, cost, and control.

4 Visit the Web site for your university or college. Based on your visit, would you conclude that the site is a transactional site or a promotional site? Why? How would you rate the site in terms of the seven Web site design elements that affect customer experience?

Does your marketing plan involve a marketspace presence for your product or service? If the answer is no, read no further and do not include this element in your plan. If the answer is yes, then attention must be given to developing a Web site in your marketing plan. A useful starting point is to:

1 Describe how each Web site element—context, content, community, customization, communication, connection, and commerce—will be used to create a customer experience.

2 Identify a company's Web site that best reflects your Web site conceptualization.

video case 18   Pizza Hut and imc²: Becoming a Multichannel Marketer

It's no surprise that Pizza Hut is the world's largest pizza chain with more than 10,000 restaurants in 100 countries. But did you know that Pizza Hut is on track to becoming one of the top 35 U.S. Internet retailers in 2009?

According to Brian Niccol, Pizza Hut's chief marketing officer (CMO), "We've done what many would say is impossible. We successfully built an online business in three years that produces hundreds of millions of dollars in annual revenue. Today, Pizza Hut is a category leader in the interactive and emerging marketplace." So how did they do it? Pizza Hut simply revolutionized the quick serve restaurant (QSR) world through a multichannel marketing approach that created a customer experience and a customer engagement platform that was second to none.

THE RETAIL PIZZA BUSINESS

With three national competitors dominating the marketplace, the pizza business is very competitive. Even customers who could be considered heavy users of a particular brand regularly purchase from competitors on the basis of timing, pricing, and convenience.

In general, Pizza Hut's most frequent customers (and likely those of the other two major competitors) divide into two categories: (1) families, primarily time-starved mothers, looking for a quick and simple mealtime solution; and (2) young adult males who fuel their active lifestyle with one of the world's most versatile and convenient foods (no cooking, no utensils, no cleanup, and leftovers are perfect for breakfast). While these two groups could not be more dissimilar on the surface, value and convenience are important for both groups. Cost-conscious mothers look for a good quality product and a hassle-free eating experience.

Deal-seeking young adult males seek more of the food they love with less time and cash invested in the process.

The importance of the take-home and delivery segment of the U.S. pizza market is illustrated by the fact that Pizza Hut's principal national competitors focus exclusively on this aspect of the business. Most take-home and delivery sales are ordered before a customer enters the restaurant. By 2006, a growing number of retail pizza customers had become comfortable ordering pizza online. Pizza ordering, as it turned out, was an ideal product for the digital world. People understood the basic menu, generally knew that they could customize their order in a variety of ways, and were accustomed to not being in the store when ordering. Brand retail presence and established customer delivery networks also made the shift to online ordering easier for national pizza chains than other national quick serve restaurants. But as Pizza Hut understood, there is still an incredible level of complexity in making something truly sophisticated, simple, and easy for the customer.

CREATING A PLAN OF ACTION

For the most part, the intent of online ordering for the pizza business was to make transactions with the customer easier and cheaper for the brand. Pizza Hut recognized the opportunity to engage people with its brand and other people directly and do something special; namely, build sustainable relationships with its customers and enable Pizza Hut to engage people in a more meaningful and profitable way. In short, Pizza Hut set about to reinvent the retail pizza business by breaking away from a transactional platform to an efficient and powerful customer engagement platform by reaching out to customers' kitchens and couches to offer a better mealtime ordering, delivery, and dining experience.

Pizza Hut selected imc^2 (www.imc2.com) as one of its lead agencies to plan a comprehensive interactive strategy that focused first on the redesign of the Pizza Hut corporate Web site (including redefining the customer experience online and across all of the brand's touchpoints) and then on a series of progressively sophisticated and industry-leading customer engagement strategies. imc^2 brought 15 years of experience in interactive marketing and brand engagement to the assignment. Its clients included Coca-Cola, Johnson & Johnson, Pfizer, Omni Hotels, Hasbro, Procter & Gamble, and Samsung, among a host of other companies, large and small.

PIZZAHUT.COM, CUSTOMER EXPERIENCE, AND BRAND ENGAGEMENT

Pizza Hut and imc^2 executives agreed that the strategy for reinventing the retail pizza business would involve developing opportunities for customers to engage with the brand by using the right technologies to enable and encourage interaction. A new Web site was necessary to better address all major design elements. How Pizza Hut and imc^2 executed these design elements not only created value for its customers, but also served as a basis for differentiation in the retail pizza business. Let's look at these design elements and PizzaHut.com's performance.

The Pizza Hut Web site was completely redesigned to support nationwide online ordering in 2007 (including all franchise locations for the first time), and is updated frequently to keep up with the company's fast-paced marketing strategy and ambitious product innovation rollout schedule. Since promotions are an important expectation in pizza purchasing and speak to the brand's consumers in a language that clearly connects with their desire for value, the Web site *context* and *content* balances the ability to shop for a deal with quick and easy ordering access for people who arrive at PizzaHut.com ready to purchase. The site presents a number of Pizza Hut's current offers in the central viewing window as well as through the rolling navigation directly underneath the main content. Primary navigation for information, such as the menu, locations, and nutrition facts, are displayed horizontally across the top of the rotating content.

Web site *customization* is achieved in several ways, but the primary utility is to simplify ordering. For customers who have already registered, there are several personalization options, including rapid ordering called *Express Checkout*—a feature that's based on saved preferences similar to a "playlist." For example, if you have a group of friends that like to watch movies together, you might create an order named *Movie Night* that has your group's favorite pizzas. Using the *Express Checkout* option accessible directly on the home page, you can select *Movie Night*, quickly review the order, click the "submit" button, and the pizzas are on their way, relying on saved delivery and payment options through a stored *cookie* (a piece of digital code that is used to identify previous visitors) to speed the transaction. With this type of functionality, you can think of convenience as an investment that creates loyalty and somewhat insulates the brand against switching down the line when customers would have to register with and learn

a competitor's system, and where access to their favorite features might not be available.

Web site *content* and *communications* are integrated with the company's overall communications programs—including traditional media—with product innovations, promotions, and special events shared across platforms. True to the brand, communications are fun and energetic, matching bold images and vibrant color with a smart, clever, and lighthearted voice. One noteworthy example includes the 2008 April Fools' Day rebranding of the company as "Pasta Hut" to coincide with the launch of the brand's innovative line of Tuscani Pastas. This campaign included online support in the form of display media (banner ads) and the temporary rebranding of PizzaHut.com as PastaHut.com with special imagery and copy supporting the name change. The brand not only got plenty of coverage in the press, it deepened the connection with customers by showing their willingness to be spontaneous and fun, inviting people to play along with the joke.

Pizza Hut's integrated marketing communications approach enables the company to easily test and incorporate other items and brands under the larger corporate umbrella, such as the WingStreet operation and the pasta extension. This demonstrates the brand's ability to stretch the QSR concept beyond its pizza roots and suggests the direction the company may pursue in the future.

PizzaHut.com and the brand's other online assets are all about getting the world's favorite pizza and signature products into the hands and stomachs of customers. Since *commerce* is a huge consideration on the site, there are multiple pathways for ordering, including several onsite methods, a Facebook app (the first national pizza chain to produce an ordering application for the world's leading social networking site), a branded desktop widget, mobile ordering (aka Total Mobile Access, added in 2008, that includes both a WAP site and text ordering), and a sophisticated and simple iPhone app released in 2009 that lets customers build and submit their order visually. Additional revenue streams can also be quickly built online, as demonstrated by the eGift Card program conceived and implemented by imc^2 over a weekend during the 2008 holiday season.

Realizing that it did not make sense for the company or its customers to create a *community* on the site, Pizza Hut tapped into Facebook to achieve results in a very cost-effective manner. With approximately one million fans and the first-of-its-kind Facebook ordering application,

GET THE KILLER APP FOR YOUR APPETITE!

the brand can efficiently engage a huge group of people in a very natural way without disrupting their daily routine. Again, the brand understands that if you make something convenient, you can increase trust while securing greater transactional loyalty. Pizza Hut's 2009 program to identify a summer intern, or *Twintern*, responsible for monitoring and encouraging dialogue on Twitter and other social media networks, is another example of how the brand is building on existing platforms and making effective use of the massive social marketing infrastructure.

PizzaHut.com connects mobile, desktop, social networks, and other digital gateways to complement traditional media and its retail presence. So when Pizza Hut thinks about the *connection* design element, it includes more than just linking to other Web sites online. Rather, it provides a comprehensive approach to creating a seamless customer experience wherever and whenever people want to engage the brand.

PERFORMANCE MEASUREMENT AND OUTCOMES

Pizza Hut diligently measures the performance of Pizza Hut.com. The company created a customized marketing dashboard that allows the Pizza Hut management team to monitor various aspects of the brand's marketing program and provides an almost constant stream of fresh information that it can use to optimize engagement with people or tweak various aspects of performance.

The results have been remarkable, but understand that due to the highly competitive nature of the industry, they are fluid and only represent a moment in time. Consider, for example:

1. PizzaHut.com dominates the pizza category with number one rankings in Web site traffic and search volume. According to comScore, a global leader in digital analytics and measurement, the Pizza Hut site achieves the most traffic per online dollars spent in the pizza category.
2. PizzaHut.com is on track to become one of the top 35 Internet retailers in the United States in 2009, up from 45th in 2008.
3. Pizza Hut's iPhone app had more than 100,000 downloads in the first two weeks after release (http://www.techcrunch.com/2009/08/01/pizza-huts-delicious-iphone-app-tops-100000-downloads-in-two-weeks/).

WHAT'S NEXT

So what's next for PizzaHut.com? While the brand has made huge gains in a very short time period, staying on top in the rapidly evolving digital marketplace requires constant attention. Pizza Hut envisions that its online business will surpass the $1 billion mark within the next five years, with digital transactions leading all revenue within a decade.

While understandably protective of future strategy, Pizza Hut CMO Niccol has ambitious goals and he's not joking when he deadpans, "I want Pizza Hut to become the Amazon of foodservice and be pioneers for the digital space. I do not want us to be a brick and mortar company that just dabbles in the space." The transition to something along the lines of the Amazon model suggests that the brand might further evolve its identity as a pizza business and stretch or completely redefine the QSR model.

Most brands that want to grow in the evolving economy will have to think and plan long-term and be able to act swiftly as marketplace conditions change. imc² chief marketing officer Ian Wolfman, when assessing the future of the marketing, sums up the opportunity neatly. "Our agency believes that marketing's current transformation will result in a complete reorientation of how brands and companies engage with their consumers and other stakeholders. Brands that thrive will be those, like Pizza Hut, that can efficiently build sustainable relationships with people—relationships that have both high trust and high transactions" (see Figure 1). He goes on to explain that,

"(B)rands taking a longer view have an unexpected advantage over traditional models that often focus too tightly on hitting near-term quarterly targets." Referring to research his agency has done on the subject, Wolfman points out that the most successful brands in the future will likely be those that resonate with people on a deeply emotional level and operate with a clearly defined sense of purpose.

Pizza Hut, with its focus on digitally enabled customer convenience and category innovation, is ideally positioned to connect with people on a level that builds trust and increases transactions. Referring to the initial time investment, however modest, that customers have to make in registering with the system and enabling various devices, Niccol sees the landscape as very promising for brands that put their customers' interests and preferences first. "If we do our job right—creating authentic engagement and making it convenient and valuable for people to interact with the brand—the numbers follow."

Questions

1 What kind of Web site is PizzaHut.com?

2 How does PizzaHut.com incorporate the seven Web site design elements?

3 How are choiceboard and personalization systems used in the PizzaHut.com Web site?

FIGURE 1

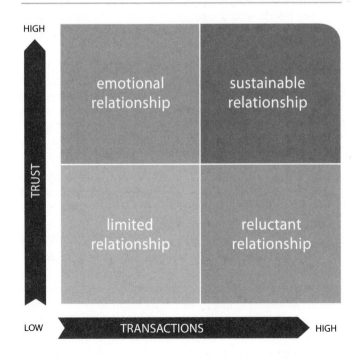

imc² Brand Sustainability Map™

PLANNING A CAREER IN MARKETING

GETTING A JOB: THE PROCESS OF MARKETING YOURSELF

Getting a job is usually a lengthy process, and it is exactly that—a *process* that involves careful planning, implementation, and evaluation. You may have everything going for you: a respectable grade point average (GPA), relevant work experience, several extracurricular activities, superior communication skills, and demonstrated leadership qualities. Despite these, you still need to market yourself systematically and aggressively; after all, even the best products lie dormant on the retailer's shelves unless marketed effectively.

The process of getting a job involves the same activities marketing managers use to develop and introduce products and brands into the marketplace.[1] The only difference is that you are marketing yourself, not a product. You need to conduct marketing research by analyzing your personal qualities (performing a self-audit) and by identifying job opportunities. Based on your research results, select a target market—those job opportunities that are compatible with your interests, goals, skills, and abilities—and design a marketing mix around that target market. *You* are the "product";[2] you must decide how to "position" yourself in the job market. The price component of the marketing mix is the salary range and job benefits (such as health and life insurance, vacation time, and retirement benefits) that you hope to receive. Promotion involves communicating with prospective employers through written and electronic correspondence (advertising) and job interviews (personal selling). The place element focuses on how to reach prospective employers—at the career services office or job fairs, for example.

This appendix will assist you in career planning by (1) providing information about careers in marketing and (2) outlining a job search process.

CAREERS IN MARKETING

The diversity of marketing opportunities is reflected in the many types of marketing jobs, including product management, marketing research, and public relations. While many of these jobs are found at traditional employers such as manufacturers, retailers, and advertising agencies, there are also many opportunities in a variety of other types of organizations. Professional services such as law, accounting, and consulting firms, for example, have a growing need for marketing expertise. Similarly, non-profit organizations such as universities, the performing arts, museums, and government agencies are developing marketing functions. Event organizations such as athletic teams, golf and tennis tournaments, and the Olympics are also new and visible sources of marketing jobs.

Recent studies of career paths and salaries suggest that marketing careers can also provide excellent opportunities for advancement and substantial pay. For example, one of every eight chief executive officers (CEOs) of the nation's 500 most valuable publicly held companies held positions in marketing before becoming CEO.[3] Similarly, reports of average starting salaries of college graduates indicate that salaries in marketing compare favorably with those in many other fields. The average starting salary of new marketing undergraduates in 2010 was $42,499, compared with $32,193 for communications majors and $39,800 for advertising majors.[4] The future is likely to be even better. The U.S. Department of Labor reports that employment of advertising, marketing, promotions, public relations, and sales managers is expected to grow at a rate of 12 percent through 2016, spurred by intense domestic and global competition in products and services offered to consumers.[5]

Figure B–1 describes marketing occupations in seven major categories: product management and physical distribution, advertising and promotion, retailing, sales, marketing research, global marketing, and nonprofit marketing. One of these may be right for you. Additional sources of marketing career information are provided at the end of this appendix.

Product Management and Physical Distribution

Many organizations assign one manager the responsibility for a particular product. For example, Procter & Gamble (P&G) has separate managers for Tide, Cheer, Gain, and Bold. Product or brand managers are involved in all aspects of a product's marketing program, such as marketing research, sales, sales promotion, advertising, and pricing, as well as manufacturing. Managers of similar products typically report to a category manager, or marketing director, and may be part of a *product management team*.[6]

Product or brand managers are involved in all aspects of a product's marketing program.

Several other jobs related to product management (Figure B–1) deal with physical distribution issues such as storing the manufactured product (inventory), moving the product from the firm to the customers (transportation), and engaging in many other aspects of the manufacture and sale of goods. Prospects for these jobs are likely to increase as wholesalers try to differentiate themselves from competitors by increasing their involvement with selling activities and by offering more services such as installation, maintenance, assembly, and even repair.[7]

Advertising and Promotion

Advertising positions are available in three kinds of organizations: advertisers, media companies, and agencies. Advertisers include manufacturers, retail stores, service firms, and many other types of companies. Often they have an advertising department responsible for preparing and placing their own ads. Advertising careers are also possible with the media: television, radio stations, magazines, and newspapers. Finally, advertising agencies offer job opportunities through their use of account management, research, media, and creative services.

Starting positions with advertisers and advertising agencies are often as assistants to employees with several years of experience. An assistant copywriter facilitates the development of the message, or copy, in an advertisement. An assistant art director participates in the design of visual components of advertisements. Entry-level media positions involve buying the media that will carry the ad or selling airtime on radio or television or page space in print media. Advancement to supervisory positions requires planning skills, a broad vision, and an affinity for spotting an effective advertising idea. Students interested in advertising should develop good communication skills and try to gain advertising experience through summer employment opportunities or internships.[8]

Retailing offers careers in merchandise management and store management.

Retailing

There are two separate career paths in retailing: merchandise management and store management. The key position in merchandising is that of a buyer, who is responsible for selecting merchandise, guiding the promotion of the merchandise, setting prices, bargaining with wholesalers, training the salesforce, and monitoring the competitive environment. The buyer must also be able to organize and coordinate many critical activities under severe time constraints. In contrast, store management involves the supervision of personnel in all departments and the general management of all facilities, equipment, and merchandise displays. In addition, store managers are responsible for the financial performance of each department and for the store as a whole. Typical positions beyond the store manager level include district manager, regional manager, and divisional vice president.[9]

Product Management and Physical Distribution

Product development manager creates a road map for new products by working with customers to determine their needs and with designers to create the product.

Product manager is responsible for integrating all aspects of a product's marketing program including research, sales, sales promotion, advertising, and pricing.

Supply chain manager oversees the part of a company that transports products to consumers and handles customer service.

Operations manager supervises warehousing and other physical distribution functions and often is directly involved in moving goods on the warehouse floor.

Inventory control manager forecasts demand for goods, coordinates production with plant managers, and tracks shipments to keep customers supplied.

Physical distribution specialist is an expert in the transportation and distribution of goods and also evaluates the costs and benefits of different types of transportation.

Sales

Direct or retail salesperson sells directly to consumers in the salesperson's office, the consumer's home, or a retailer's store.

Trade salesperson calls on retailers or wholesalers to sell products for manufacturers.

Industrial or semitechnical salesperson sells supplies and services to businesses.

Complex or professional salesperson sells complicated or custom-designed products to businesses. This requires understanding of the product technology.

Customer service manager maintains good relations with customers by coordinating the sales staff, marketing management, and physical distribution management.

Nonprofit Marketing

Marketing manager develops and directs marketing campaigns, fund-raising, and public relations.

Global Marketing

Global marketing manager is an expert in world-trade agreements, international competition, cross-cultural analysis, and global market-entry strategies.

Advertising and Promotion

Account executive maintains contact with clients while coordinating the creative work among artists and copywriters. Account executives work as partners with the client to develop marketing strategy.

Media buyer deals with media sales representatives in selecting advertising media and analyzes the value of media being purchased.

Copywriter works with art director in conceptualizing advertisements and writes the text of print or radio ads or the storyboards of television ads.

Art director handles the visual component of advertisements.

Sales promotion manager designs promotions for consumer products and works at an ad agency or a sales promotion agency.

Public relations manager develops written or video messages for the public and handles contacts with the press.

Internet marketing manager develops and executes the e-business marketing plan and manages all aspects of the advertising, promotion, and content for the online business.

Retailing

Buyer selects products a store sells, surveys consumer trends, and evaluates the past performance of products and suppliers.

Store manager oversees the staff and services at a store.

Marketing Research

Project manager for the supplier coordinates and oversees the market studies for a client.

Account executive for the supplier serves as a liaison between client and market research firm, like an advertising agency account executive.

In-house project director acts as project manager (see above) for the market studies conducted by the firm for which he or she works.

Competitive intelligence researcher uses new information technologies to monitor the competitive environment.

Data miner compiles and analyzes consumer data to identify behavior patterns, preferences, and user profiles for personalized marketing programs.

Source: Adapted from Lila B. Stair and Leslie Stair, *Careers in Marketing* (New York: McGraw-Hill, 2008); and David W. Rosenthal and Michael A. Powell, *Careers in Marketing*, ©1984, pp. 352–54.

FIGURE B–1
Seven major categories of marketing occupations.

Most starting jobs in retailing are trainee positions. A trainee is usually placed in a management training program and then given a position as an assistant buyer or assistant department manager. Advancement and responsibility can be achieved quickly because there is a shortage of qualified personnel in retailing and because superior performance of an individual is quickly reflected in sales and profits—two visible measures of success. In addition, the growth of multichannel retailing has created new opportunities such as Web site management and online merchandise procurement. The Bureau of Labor Statistics reports that retailing has a large number of openings and will be one of the fastest-growing employment opportunities in the future.[10]

Sales

College graduates from many disciplines are attracted to sales positions because of the increasingly professional nature of selling jobs and the many opportunities they can provide. A selling career offers benefits that are hard to match in any other field: (1) the opportunity for rapid advancement (into management or to new territories and accounts); (2) the potential for extremely attractive compensation; (3) the development of personal satisfaction, feelings of accomplishment, and increased self-confidence; and (4) independence—salespeople often have almost complete control over their time and activities.

Employment opportunities in sales occupations are found in a wide variety of organizations, including insurance agencies, retailers, and financial service firms. In addition, many salespeople work as manufacturer's representatives for organizations that have selling responsibilities for several manufacturers.[11] Activities in sales jobs include *selling duties*, such as prospecting for customers, demonstrating the product, or quoting prices; *sales-support duties*, such as handling complaints and helping solve technical problems; and *nonselling duties*, such as preparing reports, attending sales meetings, and monitoring competitive activities. Salespeople who can deal with these varying activities and have empathy for customers are critical to a company's success. According to *BusinessWeek*, "Great salespeople feel for their customers. They understand their needs and pressures; they get the challenges of their business. They see every deal through the customer's eyes."[12]

Xerox is well-known for its sales career opportunities.

Marketing Research

Marketing researchers play important roles in many organizations today. They are responsible for obtaining, analyzing, and interpreting data to facilitate making marketing decisions. This means marketing researchers are basically problem solvers. Success in the area requires not only an understanding of statistical analysis, research methods, and programming, but also a broad base of marketing knowledge, writing and verbal presentation skills, and an ability to communicate with colleagues and clients.[13] Individuals who are inquisitive, methodical, analytical, and solution oriented find the field particularly rewarding.

The responsibilities of the men and women currently working in the market research industry include defining the marketing problem, designing the questions, selecting the sample, collecting and analyzing the data, and, finally, reporting the results of the research. These jobs are available in three kinds of organizations. *Marketing research consulting firms* contract with large companies to provide research about their products or services.[14] *Advertising agencies* may provide research services to help clients with questions related to advertising and promotional problems. Finally, some companies have an *in-house research staff* to design and execute their research projects. Online marketing research, which is likely to become the most common form of marketing research in the near future, requires an understanding of new tools such as dynamic scripting, response validation, intercept sampling, instant messaging surveys, and online consumer panels.[15]

Buckle is an example of a company that encourages students to think about a job and a career.

International Careers

Many of the careers just described can be found in international settings—in large multinational U.S. corporations, small- to medium-size firms with export business, and franchises. The international consulting firm, Accenture, for example, has thousands of consultants around the world. Similarly, many franchises such as Blockbuster Entertainment, which has 8,000 locations, are rapidly expanding outside of the United States.[16] The changes in the European Union, Brazil, Russia, India, China, and other growing markets are likely to provide many opportunities for international careers. Several methods of gaining international experience are possible. For example, some companies may alternate periods of work at domestic locations with assignments outside of the United States. In addition, working for a firm with headquarters outside of the United States at one of its local offices may be appealing. In many organizations, international experience has become a necessity for promotion and career advancement. "If you are going to succeed, an expatriate assignment is essential," says Eric Kraus of Gillette Co. in Boston.[17]

THE JOB SEARCH PROCESS

Activities you should consider during your job search process include assessing yourself, identifying job opportunities, preparing your résumé and related correspondence, and going on job interviews.

Assessing Yourself

You must know your product—you—so that you can market yourself effectively to prospective employers. Consequently, a critical first step in your job search is conducting a self-inquiry or self-assessment. This activity involves understanding your interests, abilities, personality, preferences, and individual style. You must be confident that you know what work environment is best for you, what makes you happy, the balance you seek between personal and professional activities, and how you can be most effective at reaching your goals. This process helps ensure that you are matching your profile to the right job, or as business consultant and author Jim Collins explains, "Finding the right seat on the bus."[18]

A self-analysis, in part, entails identifying your strengths and weaknesses. To do so, draw a vertical line down the middle of a sheet of paper and label one side of the paper "strengths" and the other side "weaknesses." Record your strong and weak points in their respective column. Ideally, this cataloging should be done over a few days to give you adequate time to reflect on your attributes. In addition, you might seek input from others who know you well (such as parents, close relatives, friends, professors, or employers) and can offer more objective views. A hypothetical list of strengths and weaknesses is shown in Figure B–2.

Personality and vocational interest tests, provided by many colleges and universities, can give you other ideas about yourself. After tests have been administered and scored, test takers meet with testing service counselors to discuss the results. Test results generally suggest jobs for which students have an inclination. The most common tests at the college level are the Strong Interest Inventory and the Campbell Interest and Skill Survey. Some counseling centers and career coaches also use the Myers-Briggs® Type Indicator personality inventory and the Peoplemap™ assessments to help identify professions you may enjoy.[19] If you have not already done so, you may wish to see whether your school offers such testing services.

FIGURE B–2
Hypothetical list of a job candidate's strengths and weaknesses.

Strengths	Weaknesses
I have good communication skills.	I have minimal work experience.
I work well independently.	I have a mediocre GPA.
I am honest and dependable.	I will not relocate.
I am willing to travel in the job.	I lack a customer orientation.
I am a good problem solver.	I have poor technical skills.

Identifying Job Opportunities

To identify and analyze the job market, you must conduct some marketing research to determine what industries *and* companies offer promising job opportunities that relate to the results of your self-analysis. Several sources that can help in your search are discussed next.

Campus career centers and online databases such as Monster.com are excellent sources for job information.

Career Services Office   Your career services office is an excellent source of job information. Personnel in that office can (1) inform you about which companies will be recruiting on campus; (2) alert you to unexpected job openings; (3) advise you about short-term and long-term career prospects; (4) offer advice on résumé construction; (5) assess your interviewing strengths and weaknesses; and (6) help you evaluate a job offer. In addition, the office usually contains a variety of written materials focusing on different industries and companies and tips on job hunting.

Online Career and Employment Services   Many companies no longer make frequent on-campus visits. Instead, they may use the many online services available to advertise an employment opportunity or to search for candidate information. The National Association of Colleges and Employers, for example, maintains a site on the Internet called JobWeb (www.jobweb.org). Similarly, Monster.com and Careerbuilder.com are online databases of employment ads, candidate résumés, and other career-related information. Some of the information resources include career guidance, a cover letter library, occupational profiles, résumé templates, and networking services.[20] Employers may contact students directly when the candidate's qualifications meet their specific job requirements.

Library   The public or college library can provide you with reference materials that, among other things, describe successful firms and their operations, define the content of various jobs, and forecast job opportunities. For example, *Fortune* publishes a list of the 1,000 largest U.S. and global companies and their respective sales and profits, and Dun & Bradstreet publishes directories of more than 26 million companies in the United States. A librarian can indicate reference materials that will be most pertinent to *your* job search.

Advertisements   Help-wanted advertisements provide an overview of what is happening in the job market. Local (particularly Sunday editions) and college newspapers, trade publications (such as *Marketing News* or *Advertising Age*), and business magazines (such as *Sales & Marketing Management*) contain classified advertisement sections that generally have job opening announcements, often for entry-level positions. Reviewing the want ads can help you identify what kinds of positions are available and their requirements and job titles, which firms offer certain kinds of jobs, and levels of compensation.

Employment Agencies   An employment agency can make you aware of several job opportunities very quickly because of its large number of job listings available through computer databases. Many agencies specialize in a particular field (such as sales and marketing). The advantages of using an agency include that it (1) reduces the cost of a job search by bringing applicants and employers together, (2) often has exclusive job listings available only by working through the agency, (3) performs much of the job search for you, and (4) tries to find a job that is compatible with your qualifications and interests.[21]

Personal Contacts and Networking   An important source of job information that students often overlook is their personal contacts. People you know often may know of job opportunities, so you should advise them that you're looking for a job. Relatives and friends might aid your job search. Instructors you know well and business contacts can provide a wealth of information about potential jobs and even help arrange an interview with a prospective employer. They may also help arrange *informational interviews* with employers that do not have immediate openings. These interviews allow you to collect information about an industry or an employer and give you an advantage if a position does become available. It is a good idea to leave your résumé with all your personal contacts so they can pass it along to those who might be in need of your services.

State Employment Office   State employment offices have listings of job opportunities in their state and counselors to help arrange a job interview for you. Although state employment offices perform functions similar to employment agencies, they differ in that they list only job opportunities in their state and provide their services free.

Direct Contact   Another means of obtaining job information is direct contact—personally communicating to prospective employers (either by mail, e-mail, or in person) that you would be interested in pursuing job opportunities with them. Often you may not even know whether jobs are available in these firms. If you correspond with the companies in writing, a letter of introduction and an attached résumé should serve as your initial form of communication. Your goals in direct contact are to create a positive impression and, ultimately, to arrange a job interview.

Writing Your Résumé

A résumé is a document that communicates to prospective employers who you are. An employer reading a résumé is looking for a snapshot of your qualifications to decide if you should be invited to a job interview. It is imperative that you design a résumé that presents you in a favorable light and allows you to get to that next important step.[22] Personnel in your career services office can provide assistance in designing résumés.

The Résumé Itself   A well-constructed résumé generally contains up to nine major sections: (1) identification (name, address, telephone number, and e-mail address); (2) job or career objective; (3) educational background; (4) honors and awards; (5) work experience or history; (6) skills or capabilities (that pertain to a particular kind of job for which you may be interviewing); (7) extracurricular activities; (8) personal interests; and (9) personal references.[23] If possible, you should include quantitative information about your accomplishments and experience, such as "increased sales revenue by 20 percent" for the year you managed a retail clothing store.

Technology has created a need for a new type of résumé—the digital résumé. Although traditional versions of résumés may be visually appealing, today most career experts suggest that résumés accommodate delivery through mail, e-mail, and fax machines. In addition, résumés must accommodate employers who use scanning technology to enter résumés into their own databases or who search commercial online databases. To fully utilize online opportunities, an electronic résumé with a popular font (e.g., New Times Roman) and relatively large font size (e.g., 10–14 pt.)—and without italic text, graphics, shading, underlining, or vertical lines—must be available. In addition, because online recruiting starts with a keyword search, it is important to include keywords, focus on nouns rather than verbs, and avoid abbreviations. Related to this use of technology, don't forget that many employers may visit social networking sites such as Facebook and MySpace, or may simply "Google" your name, to see what comes up. Review your online profiles before you start your job search to provide a positive image![24]

The Cover Letter   The letter accompanying a résumé, or cover letter, serves as the job candidate's introduction. As a result, it must gain the attention and interest of the reader or it will fail to give the incentive to examine the résumé carefully. In designing a letter to accompany your résumé, address the following issues:

- Address the letter to a specific person.
- Identify the position for which you are applying and how you heard of it.

- Indicate why you are applying for the position.
- Summarize your most significant credentials and qualifications.
- Refer the reader to the enclosed résumé.
- Request a personal interview, and advise the reader when and where you can be reached.

As a general rule, nothing works better than an impressive cover letter and good academic credentials.[25]

Interviewing for Your Job

The job interview is a conversation between a prospective employer and a job candidate that focuses on determining whether the employer's needs can be satisfied by the candidate's qualifications. The interview is a "make or break" situation: If the interview goes well, you have increased your chances of receiving a job offer; if it goes poorly, you probably will be eliminated from further consideration.

Preparing for a Job Interview To be successful in a job interview, you must prepare for it so you can exhibit professionalism and indicate to a prospective employer that you are serious about the job. When preparing for the interview, several critical activities need to be performed.

Before the interview, gather facts about the industry, the prospective employer, and the job. Relevant information might include the general description for the occupation; the firm's products or services; the firm's size, number of employees, and financial and competitive position; the requirements of the position; and the name and personality of the interviewer. Obtaining this information will provide you with additional insight into the firm and help you formulate questions to ask the interviewer. This information might be gleaned, for example, from corporate annual reports, *The Wall Street Journal*, Moody's manuals, Standard & Poor's *Register of Corporations, Directors, and Executives, The Directory of Corporate Affiliations*, selected issues of *BusinessWeek*, or trade publications. If information is not readily available, you could call the company and indicate that you wish to obtain some information about the firm before your interview.[26]

Preparation for the job interview should also involve role playing, or pretending that you are in the "hot seat" being interviewed. Before role playing, anticipate questions interviewers may pose and how you might address them (see Figure B–3). Do not memorize your answers, though, because you want to appear spontaneous, yet logical and intelligent. Nonetheless, it is helpful to practice how you might respond to the questions. In addition, develop questions you might ask the interviewer that are important and of concern to you (see Figure B–4 on the next page). "It's an opportunity to show the recruiter how smart you are," comments one recruiter.[27]

Before the job interview you should attend to several details. Know the exact time and place of the interview; write them down—do not rely on your memory. Get the full company name straight. Find out what the interviewer's name is and how to pronounce it. Bring a notepad and pen along to the interview, in case you need to record anything. Make certain that your appearance is clean, neat, professional, and conservative. Finally, be punctual; arriving tardy to a job interview makes you appear unreliable.

FIGURE B–3
Anticipate questions frequently asked by interviewers to practice how you might respond.

Interviewer Questions
1. What do you consider to be your greatest strengths and weaknesses?
2. What do you see yourself doing in 5 years? In 10 years?
3. What are three important leadership qualities that you have demonstrated?
4. What jobs have you enjoyed the most? The least? Why?
5. Why do you want to work for our company?

FIGURE B–4

Interviewees should develop questions about topics that are important to them.

Interviewee Questions
1. What is the company's promotion policy?
2. Describe a typical first-year assignment for this job.
3. How is an employee evaluated?
4. Why do you enjoy working for this firm?
5. How much responsibility would I have in this job?

View the interview as a conversation between the prospective employer and you.

Succeeding in Your Job Interview   You have done your homework, and at last the moment arrives and it is time for the interview. Although you may experience some apprehension, view the interview as a conversation between the prospective employer and you. Both of you are in the interview to look over the other party, to see whether there might be a good match. When you meet the interviewer, greet him or her by name, be cheerful, smile, and maintain good eye contact. Take your lead from the interviewer at the outset. Sit down after the interviewer has offered you a seat. Sit up straight in your chair, and look alert and interested at all times. Appear relaxed, not tense. Be enthusiastic.

During the interview, be yourself. If you try to behave in a manner that is different from the real you, your attempt may be transparent to the interviewer or you may ultimately get the job but discover that you aren't suited for it. In addition to assessing how well your skills match those of the job, the interviewer will probably try to assess your long-term interest in the firm.

As the interview comes to a close, leave it on a positive note. Thank the interviewer for his or her time and the opportunity to discuss employment opportunities. If you are still interested in the job, express this to the interviewer. The interviewer will normally tell you what the employer's next step is—probably a visit to the company.[28] Rarely will a job offer be made at the end of the initial interview. If it is and you want the job, accept the offer; if there is any doubt in your mind about the job, however, ask for time to consider the offer.

Following Up on Your Job Interview   After your interview, send a thank-you note to the interviewer and indicate whether you are still interested in the job. If you want to continue pursuing the job, polite persistence may help you get it. While e-mail is a common form of communication today, it is often viewed as less personal than a letter or telephone call, so be confident that e-mail is preferred before using it to correspond with the interviewer.[29]

As you conduct your follow-up, be persistent but polite. If you are too eager, one of two things could happen to prevent you from getting the job: The employer might feel that you are a nuisance and would exhibit such behavior on the job, or the employer may perceive that you are desperate for the job and thus are not a viable candidate.

Handling Rejection You have put your best efforts into your job search. You developed a well-designed résumé and prepared carefully for the job interview. Even the interview appears to have gone well. Nevertheless, a prospective employer may send you a rejection letter. ("We are sorry that our needs and your superb qualification don't match.") Although you will probably be disappointed, not all interviews lead to a job offer because there normally are more candidates than there are positions available.

If you receive a rejection letter, you should think back through the interview. What appeared to go right? What went wrong? Perhaps personnel from your career services office can shed light on the problem, particularly if they are in the custom of having interviewers rate each interviewee. Try to learn lessons to apply in future interviews. Keep interviewing and gaining interview experience; your persistence will eventually pay off.

SELECTED SOURCES OF MARKETING CAREER INFORMATION

The following is a selected list of marketing information sources that you should find useful during your academic studies and professional career.

Business and Marketing Publications

Scott Dacko, *The Advanced Dictionary of Marketing: Putting Theory to Use* (Oxford: Oxford University Press, 2008). This dictionary focuses on leading-edge terminology for individuals who are serious about the theory and practice of marketing. Each term includes six elements: description, key insights, key words, implications, applications, and a bibliography.

Linda D. Hall, *Encyclopedia of Business Information Sources*, 25th ed. (Detroit: Gale Group, 2009). A bibliographic guide to over 35,000 citations covering more than 1,100 primary subjects of interest to business personnel.

Hoover's Handbook of World Business (Austin, TX: Hoover's Business Press, 2009). This source provides detailed information about companies outside of the United States, including firms from Canada, Europe, Japan, China, India, and Taiwan.

Barbara Lewis and Dale Littler, eds., *The Blackwell Encyclopedic Dictionary of Marketing* (Cambridge, MA: Blackwell Publishers, 2008). Part of the 10-volume *Blackwell Encyclopedia of Management*, this book provides clear, concise, up-to-the-minute, and highly informative definitions and explanations of the key concepts and terms in marketing management, consumer behavior, segmentation, organizational marketing, pricing, communications, retailing and distribution, product management, market research, and international marketing.

Cynthia L. Shamel, *Introduction to Online Market & Industry Research* (Mason, OH: Thomson Learning, 2004). This comprehensive reference provides search strategies and valuable data source information, including rankings of data sources, for industry researchers.

Career Planning Publications

Richard N. Bolles, *What Color Is Your Parachute? 2010: A Practical Manual for Job-Hunters and Career-Changers* (Berkeley, CA: Ten Speed Press, 2009). A companion workbook is also available. See www.jobhuntersbible.com.

Dennis V. Damp, Robert A. Juran, and Salvatori Concialdi, *The Book of U.S. Government Jobs: Where They Are, What's Available & How to Get One*, 10th ed., (McKees Rocks, PA: Bookhaven Press, 2008).

Margaret Riley Dikel and Frances E. Roehm, *Guide to Internet Job Searching* (New York : McGraw-Hill, 2008).

The National Job Bank (Avon, MA: Adams Media Corporation, 2009). See www.admasmedia.com.

Princeton Review: Best Entry-Level Jobs, 2009 Edition (New York: Random House Information Group, 2008).

Selected Periodicals

Advertising Age, Crain Communications, Inc. (weekly). See www.adage.com. Annual subscription: $99 per year.

BusinessWeek, McGraw-Hill Companies (weekly). See www.businessweek.com. Annual subscription: $46.

Journal of Marketing, American Marketing Association (quarterly). See www.marketingpower.com. Annual subscription rates: $90 nonmembers; $53 members.

Marketing Management, American Marketing Association (six times per year). See www.marketingpower.com. Annual subscription: $95.

Marketing News, American Marketing Association (biweekly). See www.marketingpower.com. Annual subscription: $85 nonmembers; $53 members.

Marketing Research, American Marketing Association (quarterly). See www.marketingpower.com. Annual subscription: $90.

The Wall Street Journal Interactive, Dow Jones & Company, Inc. (weekly). See www.wsj.com. Annual subscription: $103 online; $119 print; $140 online and print.

Professional and Trade Associations

American Advertising Federation
1101 Vermont Ave. N.W., Suite 500
Washington, DC 20005-6306
(202) 898-0089
www.aaf.org

American e-Commerce Association
2346 Camp St.
New Orleans, LA 70130
(504) 495-1748
www.aeaus.com

American Marketing Association
311 S. Wacker Dr., Suite 5800
Chicago, IL 60606
(800) AMA-1150
www.marketingpower.com

Direct Marketing Association
1120 Avenue of the Americas
New York, NY 10036-6700
(212) 768-7277
www.the-dma.org

Marketing Science Institute
1000 Massachusetts Ave.
Cambridge, MA 02138-5396
(617) 491-2060
www.msi.org

Sales and Marketing Executive
    International
P.O. Box 1390
Suma, WA 98295-1390
(312) 893-0751
www.smei.org

GLOSSARY

80/20 rule A concept that suggests 80 percent of a firm's sales are obtained from 20 percent of its customers. p. 194

account management policies Policies that specify whom salespeople should contact, what kinds of selling and customer service activities should be engaged in, and how these activities should be carried out. p. 393

adaptive selling A need-satisfaction sales presentation style that involves adjusting the presentation to fit the selling situation, such as knowing when to offer solutions and when to ask for more information. p. 389

advertising Any paid form of nonpersonal communication about an organization, product, service, or idea by an identified sponsor. pp. 336, 358

attitude A tendency to respond to an object or class of objects in a consistently favorable or unfavorable way. p. 106

baby boomers The generation of children born between 1946 and 1964. p. 62

back translation The practice where a translated word or phrase is retranslated into the original language by a different interpreter to catch errors. p. 147

beliefs A consumer's subjective perception of how a product or brand performs on different attributes based on personal experience, advertising, and discussions with other people. p. 106

blog A Web page that serves as a publicly accessible personal journal for an individual or organization. p. 413

bots Electronic shopping agents or robots that comb Web sites to compare prices and product or service features. p. 412

brand equity The added value a brand name gives to a product beyond the functional benefits provided. p. 245

brand loyalty A favorable attitude toward and consistent purchase of a single brand over time. p. 106

brand name Any word, device (design, shape, sound, or color), or combination of these used to distinguish a seller's goods or services. p. 244

brand personality A set of human characteristics associated with a brand name. p. 245

branding A marketing decision by an organization to use a name, phrase, design, or symbols, or combination of these to identify its products and distinguish them from those of competitors. p. 244

break-even analysis A technique that analyzes the relationship between total revenue and total cost to determine profitability at various levels of output. p. 273

brokers Independent firms or individuals whose principal function is to bring buyers and sellers together to make sales. p. 328

business The clear, broad underlying industry or market sector of an organization's offering. p. 26

business marketing The marketing of goods and services to companies, governments, or not-for-profit organizations for use in the creation of goods and services that they can produce and market to others. p. 120

business portfolio analysis A technique that managers use to quantify performance measures and growth targets of their firms' strategic business units. p. 31

business products Products that organizations buy that assist directly or indirectly in providing other products for resale. Also called *B2B products*, or *industrial products*. p. 210

buy classes Three types of organizational buying situations: straight rebuy, new buy, and modified rebuy. p. 128

buying center The group of people in an organization who participate in the buying process and share common goals, risks, and knowledge important to purchase decisions. p. 126

capacity management Integrating the service component of the marketing mix with efforts to influence consumer demand. p. 254

category management An approach to managing the assortment of merchandise in which a manager is assigned the responsibility for selecting all products that consumers in a market segment might view as substitutes for each other, with the objective of maximizing sales and profits in the category. p. 323

cause marketing Occurs when the charitable contributions of a firm are tied directly to the customer revenues produced through the promotion of one of its products. p. 87

channel conflict Arises when one channel member believes another channel member is engaged in behavior that prevents it from achieving its goals. p. 298

choiceboard An interactive, Internet-enabled system that allows individual customers to design their own products and services by answering a few questions and choosing from a menu of product or service attributes (or components), prices, and delivery options. p. 406

code of ethics A formal statement of ethical principles and rules of conduct. p. 84

collaborative filtering A process that automatically groups people with similar buying intentions, preferences, and behaviors and predicts future purchases. p. 406

communication The process of conveying a message to others; it requires six elements: a source, a message, a channel of communication, a receiver, and the processes of encoding and decoding. p. 334

competition The alternative firms that could provide a product to satisfy a specific market's needs. p. 69

constraints In a decision, the restrictions placed on potential solutions to a problem. p. 164

consultative selling A need-satisfaction sales presentation style that focuses on problem identification, where the salesperson serves as an expert on problem recognition and resolution. p. 389

consumer behavior The actions a person takes in purchasing and using products and services, including the mental and social processes that come before and after these actions. p. 96

Consumer Bill of Rights (1962) Codified the ethics of exchange between buyers and sellers, including rights to safety, to be informed, to choose, and to be heard. p. 82

consumer products Products purchased by the ultimate consumer. p. 210

consumerism A grassroots movement started in the 1960s to increase the influence, power, and rights of consumers in dealing with institutions. p. 71

consumer-oriented sales promotions Sales tools used to support a company's advertising and personal selling efforts directed to ultimate consumers. p. 370

cookies Computer files that a marketer can download onto the computer or mobile phone of an online shopper who visits the marketer's Web site. p. 414

cooperative advertising Advertising programs by which a manufacturer pays a percentage of the retailer's local advertising expense for advertising the manufacturer's products. p. 374

core values The fundamental, passionate, and enduring principles of an organization that guide its conduct over time. p. 25

cross-channel shopper An online consumer who researches offerings online and then purchases them at retail stores. p. 416

cross-cultural analysis The study of similarities and differences among consumers in two or more nations or societies. p. 144

cultural symbols Things that represent ideas or concepts in a specific culture. p. 145

culture The set of values, ideas, and attitudes that is learned and shared among the members of a group. p. 64

currency exchange rate The price of one country's currency expressed in terms of another country's currency. p. 148

customer experience management (CEM) The process of managing the entire customer experience within the firm. p. 255

customer service The ability of logistics management to satisfy users in terms of time, dependability, communication, and convenience. p. 305

customer value The unique combination of benefits received by targeted buyers that includes quality, convenience, on-time delivery, and both before- and after-sale service at a specific price. p. 9

customs What is considered normal and expected about the way people do things in a specific country. p. 145

data The facts and figures related to the problem, divided into two main parts: secondary data and primary data. p. 166

demand curve A graph relating the quantity sold and the price, which shows the maximum number of units that will be sold at a given price. p. 270

demographics Describing a population according to selected characteristics such as age, gender, ethnicity, income, and occupation. p. 60

derived demand The demand for industrial products and services is driven by, or derived from, demand for consumer products and services. p. 122

direct investment A global market-entry strategy that entails a domestic firm actually investing in and owning a foreign subsidiary or division. p. 152

direct marketing A promotion alternative that uses direct communication with consumers to generate a response in the form of an order, a request for further information, or a visit to a retail outlet. p. 339

direct orders The result of direct marketing offers that contain all the information necessary for a prospective buyer to make a decision to purchase and complete the transaction. p. 349

disintermediation A channel conflict that arises when a channel member bypasses another member and sells or buys products direct. p. 298

diversification analysis A technique a firm uses to search for growth opportunities from among current and new products and markets. p. 33

dual distribution An arrangement whereby a firm reaches different buyers by using two or more different types of channels for the same basic product. p. 294

dumping When a firm sells a product in a foreign country below its domestic price or below its actual cost. p. 155

dynamic pricing The practice of changing prices for products and services in real time in response to supply and demand conditions. p. 414

economy Pertains to the income, expenditures, and resources that affect the cost of running a business or household. p. 65

eight Ps of services marketing Expanding the four Ps framework to include productivity, people, physical environment, and process. p. 253

e-marketplaces Online trading communities that bring together buyers and supplier organizations to make possible the real-time exchange of information, money, products, and services. Also called *B2B exchanges* or *e-hubs*. p. 130

environmental forces The uncontrollable social, economic, technological, competitive, and regulatory forces that affect the results of a marketing decision. p. 9

environmental scanning The process of continually acquiring information on events occurring outside the organization to identify and interpret potential trends. p. 60

ethics The moral principles and values that govern the actions and decisions of an individual or a group. p. 80

exchange The trade of things of value between buyer and seller so that each is better off after the trade. p. 5

exclusive distribution A level of distribution density whereby only one retail outlet in a specific geographical area carries the firm's products. p. 297

exporting A global market-entry strategy in which a company produces goods in one country and sells them in another country. p. 150

family life cycle The distinct phases that a family progresses through from formation to retirement, each phase bringing with it identifiable purchasing behaviors. p. 111

Foreign Corrupt Practices Act (1977) A law, amended by the *International Anti-Dumping and Fair Competition Act* (1998), that makes it a crime for U.S. corporations to bribe an official of a foreign government or political party to obtain or retain business in a foreign country. p. 145

four I's of services The four unique elements that distinguish services from goods: intangibility, inconsistency, inseparability, and inventory. p. 213

Generation X Includes the 15 percent of the population born between 1965 and 1976. Also called *baby bust*. p. 62

Generation Y Includes the 72 million Americans born between 1977 and 1994. Also called *echo-boom* or *baby boomlet*. p. 63

global brand A brand marketed under the same name in multiple countries with similar and centrally coordinated marketing programs. p. 142

global competition Exists when firms originate, produce, and market their products and services worldwide. p. 140

global consumers Consumer groups living in many countries or regions of the world who have similar needs or seek similar features and benefits from products or services. p. 143

global marketing strategy The practice of standardizing marketing activities when there are cultural similarities and adapting them when cultures differ. p. 141

goals Targets of performance to be achieved, often by a specific time. Also called *objectives*. p. 26

gray market A situation in which products are sold through unauthorized channels of distribution. Also called *parallel importing*. p. 155

green marketing Marketing efforts to produce, promote, and reclaim environmentally sensitive products. p. 87

hierarchy of effects The sequence of stages a prospective buyer goes through from initial awareness of a product to eventual action (either trial or adoption of the product). The stages include awareness, interest, evaluation, trial, and adoption. p. 344

idle production capacity Occurs when the service provider is available but there is no demand for the service. p. 213

infomercials Program-length (30-minute) advertisements that take an educational approach to communication with potential customers. p. 364

institutional advertisements Advertisements designed to build goodwill or an image for an organization, rather than promote a specific product or service. p. 359

integrated marketing communications (IMC) The concept of designing marketing communications programs that coordinate all promotional activities—advertising, personal selling, sales promotion, public relations, and direct marketing—to provide a consistent message across all audiences. p. 334

intensive distribution A level of distribution density whereby a firm tries to place its products and services in as many outlets as possible. p. 297

interactive marketing Two-way buyer–seller electronic communication in a computer-mediated environment in which the buyer controls the kind and amount of information received from the seller. p. 406

involvement The personal, social, and economic significance of a purchase to the consumer. p. 99

joint venture A global market-entry strategy in which a foreign company and a local firm invest together to create a local business in order to share ownership, control, and the profits of the new company. p. 151

laws Society's values and standards that are enforceable in the courts. p. 80

lead generation The result of a direct marketing offer designed to generate interest in a product or service and a request for additional information. p. 349

learning Those behaviors that result from (1) repeated experience and (2) reasoning. p. 104

logistics Those activities that focus on getting the right amount of the right products to the right place at the right time at the lowest possible cost. p. 301

major account management The practice of using team selling to focus on important customers so as to build mutually beneficial, long-term, cooperative relationships; also called *key account management*. p. 392

manufacturer's agents Agents who work for several producers and carry noncompetitive, complementary merchandise in an exclusive territory. Also called manufacturer's representatives. p. 328

market People with both the desire and the ability to buy a specific offering. p. 8

market orientation Occurs when an organization focuses its efforts on (1) continuously collecting information about customers' needs, (2) sharing this information across departments, and (3) using it to create customer value. p. 13

market segmentation Involves aggregating prospective buyers into groups, or segments, that (1) have common needs and (2) will respond similarly to a marketing action. pp. 35, 188

market segments The relatively homogeneous groups of prospective buyers that result from the market segmentation process. p. 188

market share The ratio of a firm's sales revenue to the total sales revenue of all firms in the industry, including the firm itself. p. 27, 188

marketing The activity for creating, communicating, delivering, and exchanging offerings that benefit the organization, its stakeholders, and society at large. p. 4

marketing channel Individuals and firms involved in the process of making a product or service available for use or consumption by consumers or industrial users. p. 288

marketing concept The idea that an organization should strive to satisfy the needs of consumers while also trying to achieve the organization's goals. p. 13

marketing dashboard The visual display of the essential information related to achieving a marketing objective. p. 27

marketing metric A measure of the quantitative value or trend of a marketing activity or result. p. 28

marketing mix The controllable factors—product, price, promotion, and place—that can be used by the marketing manager to solve a marketing problem. p. 9

marketing plan A road map for the marketing activities of an organization for a specified future time period such as one year or five years. p. 28

marketing program A plan that integrates the marketing mix to provide a good, service, or idea to prospective buyers. p. 11

marketing research The process of defining a marketing problem and opportunity, systematically collecting and analyzing information, and recommending actions. p. 162

marketing strategy The means by which a marketing goal is to be achieved, usually characterized by a specified target market and a marketing program to reach it. p. 38

marketing tactics Detailed day-to-day operational decisions essential to the overall success of marketing strategies. p. 38

market-product grid A framework to relate the market segments of potential buyers to products offered or potential marketing actions by an organization. p. 197

marketspace An information- and communication-based electronic exchange environment occupied by sophisticated computer and telecommunications technologies and digitized offerings. p. 69

measures of success Criteria or standards used in evaluating proposed solutions to a problem. p. 163

merchant wholesalers Independently owned firms that take title to the merchandise they handle. p. 327

mission A statement or vision of an organization's function in society, often identifying its customers, markets, products, and technologies. Often used interchangeably with *vision*. p. 25

moral idealism A personal moral philosophy that considers certain individual rights or duties as universal, regardless of the outcome. p. 85

motivation The energizing force that stimulates behavior to satisfy a need. p. 102

multibranding A branding strategy that involves giving each product a distinct name when each brand is intended for a different market segment. p. 249

multichannel marketing The blending of different communication and delivery channels that are mutually reinforcing in attracting, retaining, and building relationships with consumers who shop and buy in traditional intermediaries and online. p. 293

multichannel retailers Retailers that utilize and integrate a combination of traditional store formats and nonstore formats, such as catalogs, television, and online retailing. p. 323

multicultural marketing Combinations of the marketing mix that reflect the unique attitudes, ancestry, communication preferences, and lifestyles of different races. p. 64

multidomestic marketing strategy A multinational firm's strategy of offering as many different product variations, brand names, and advertising programs as countries in which it does business. p. 141

multiproduct branding A branding strategy in which a company uses one name for all its products in a product class. p. 248

new-product process The seven stages an organization goes through to identify business opportunities and convert them to a salable good or service. p. 220

North American Industry Classification System (NAICS) Provides common industry definitions for Canada, Mexico, and the United States, which makes it easier to measure economic activity in the three member countries of the North American Free Trade Agreement (NAFTA). p. 121

objectives Targets of performance to be achieved, often by a specific time. Also called *goals*. p. 26

observational data Facts and figures obtained by watching, either mechanically or in person, how people actually behave. p. 168

off-peak pricing Charging different prices during different times of the day or days of the week to reflect variations in demand for the service. p. 254

opinion leaders Individuals who exert direct or indirect social influence over others. p. 108

order getter A salesperson who sells in a conventional sense and identifies prospective customers, provides customers with information, persuades customers to buy, closes sales, and follows up on customers' use of a product or service. p. 384

order taker A salesperson who processes routine orders or reorders for products that were already sold by the company. p. 384

organizational buyers Manufacturers, wholesalers, retailers, and government agencies that buy goods and services for their own use or for resale. p. 15, 120

organizational buying behavior The decision-making process that organizations use to establish the need for products and services and identify, evaluate, and choose among alternative brands and suppliers. p. 126

organizational culture The set of values, ideas, attitudes, and behavioral norms that is learned and shared among the members of an organization. p. 26

perceived risk The anxieties felt because the consumer cannot anticipate the outcomes of a purchase but believes that there may be negative consequences. p. 103

perception The process by which an individual selects, organizes, and interprets information to create a meaningful picture of the world. p. 103

perceptual map A means of displaying or graphing in two dimensions the location of products or brands in the minds of consumers to enable a manager to see how consumers perceive competing products or brands and then take marketing actions. p. 203

permission marketing The solicitation of a consumer's consent (called *opt-in*) to receive e-mail and advertising based on personal data supplied by the consumer. p. 407

personal selling The two-way flow of communication between a buyer and seller, often in a face-to-face encounter, designed to influence a person's or group's purchase decision. p. 337

personal selling process Sales activities occurring before and after the sale itself, consisting of six stages: (1) prospecting, (2) preapproach, (3) approach, (4) presentation, (5) close, and (6) follow-up. p. 386

personality A person's consistent behaviors or responses to recurring situations. p. 102

personalization The consumer-initiated practice of generating content on a marketer's Web site that is custom tailored to an individual's specific needs and preferences. p. 406

points of difference Those characteristics of a product that make it superior to competitive substitutes. p. 36

posttests Tests conducted after an advertisement has been shown to the target audience to determine whether it has accomplished its intended purpose. p. 369

pretests Tests conducted before an advertisement is placed in any medium to determine whether it communicates the intended message or to select among alternative versions of the advertisement. p. 368

price The money or other considerations (including other products and services) exchanged for the ownership or use of a product or service. p. 262

price elasticity of demand The percentage change in the quantity demanded relative to a percentage change in price. p. 271

pricing constraints Factors that limit the range of prices a firm may set. p. 276

pricing objectives Expectations that specify the role of price in an organization's marketing and strategic plans. p. 275

primary data Facts and figures that are newly collected for a project. p. 166

product A good, service, or idea consisting of a bundle of tangible and intangible attributes that satisfies consumers' needs and is received in exchange for money or something else of value. p. 210

product advertisements Advertisements that focus on selling a product or service and that take three forms: (1) pioneering (or informational), (2) competitive (or persuasive), and (3) reminder. p. 358

product differentiation A marketing strategy that involves a firm using different marketing mix activities, such as product features and advertising, to help consumers perceive a product as being different and better than competing products. p. 188

product item A specific product that has a unique brand, size, or price. p. 214

product life cycle The stages a new product goes through in the marketplace: introduction, growth, maturity, and decline. p. 234

product line A group of products or service items that are closely related because they satisfy a class of needs, are used together, are sold to the same customer group, are distributed through the same outlets, or fall within a given price range. p. 214

product mix All of the product lines offered by an organization. p. 214

product placement A consumer sales promotion that uses a brand-name product in a movie, television show, video, or commercial for another product. p. 373

product positioning The place a product occupies in consumers' minds on important features relative to competitive products. p. 202

product repositioning Changing the place an offering occupies in consumers' minds relative to competitive products. p. 202

profit The money left after a business firm's total expenses are subtracted from its total revenues or sales—the reward for the risk it undertakes in marketing its offerings. p. 22

profit equation Profit = Total revenue — Total cost; or Profit = (Unit price × Quantity sold) — (Fixed cost + Variable cost). p. 263

promotional mix The combination of one or more communication tools used to: (1) inform prospective buyers about the benefits of the product, (2) persuade them to try it, and (3) remind them later about the benefits they enjoyed by using the product. p. 334

protectionism The practice of shielding one or more industries within a country's economy from foreign competition through the use of tariffs or quotas. p. 138

public relations A form of communication management that seeks to influence the feelings, opinions, or beliefs held by customers, prospective customers, stockholders, suppliers, employees, and other publics about a company and its products or services. p. 338

publicity A nonpersonal, indirectly paid presentation of an organization, product, or service. p. 338

publicity tools Methods of obtaining nonpersonal presentation of an organization, product, or service without direct cost. Examples include news releases, news conferences, and public service announcements. p. 374

pull strategy Directing the promotional mix at ultimate consumers to encourage them to ask the retailer for a product. p. 343

purchase decision process The five stages a buyer passes through in making choices about which products and services to buy: (1) problem recognition, (2) information search, (3) alternative evaluation, (4) purchase decision, and (5) postpurchase behavior. p. 96

push strategy Directing the promotional mix to channel members to gain their cooperation in ordering and stocking the product. p. 342

questionnaire data Facts and figures obtained by asking people about their attitudes, awareness, intentions, and behaviors. p. 170

quota A restriction placed on the amount of a product allowed to enter or leave a country. p. 138

reference groups People to whom an individual looks as a basis for self-appraisal or as a source of personal standards. p. 110

regulation Restrictions that state and federal laws place on business with regard to the conduct of its activities. p. 70

relationship marketing Linking the organization to its individual customers, employees, suppliers, and other partners for their mutual long-term benefit. p. 10

relationship selling The practice of building ties to customers based on a salesperson's attention and commitment to customer needs over time. p. 383

retail life cycle The process of growth and decline that retail outlets, like products, experience over time. The retail life cycle consists of the early growth, accelerated development, maturity, and decline stages. p. 326

retailing All activities involved in selling, renting, and providing products and services to ultimate consumers for personal, family, or household use. p. 312

retailing mix The activities related to managing the store and the merchandise in the store, which includes retail pricing, store location, retail communication, and merchandise. p. 321

reverse auction In an e-marketplace, it is an online auction in which a buyer communicates a need for a product or service and would-be suppliers are invited to bid in competition with each other. p. 131

sales forecast The total sales of a product that a firm expects to sell during a specified time period under specified environmental conditions and its own marketing efforts. p. 181

sales management Planning the selling program and implementing and evaluating the personal selling effort of the firm. p. 382

sales plan A statement describing what is to be achieved and where and how the selling effort of salespeople is to be deployed. p. 392

sales promotion A short-term inducement of value offered to arouse interest in buying a product or service. p. 339

sales quota Specific goals assigned to a salesperson, sales team, branch sales office, or sales district for a stated time period. p. 396

salesforce automation (SFA) The use of computer, information, communication, and Internet technologies to make the sales function more effective and efficient. p. 396

scrambled merchandising Offering several unrelated product lines in a single retail store. p. 317

secondary data Facts and figures that have already been recorded before the project at hand. p. 166

selective distribution A level of distribution density whereby a firm selects a few retail outlets in a specific geographical area to carry its products. p. 297

self-regulation An alternative to government control, whereby an industry attempts to police itself. p. 73

services Intangible activities or benefits that an organization provides to satisfy consumers' needs in exchange for money or something else of value. p. 210

situation analysis Taking stock of where the firm or product has been recently, where it is now, and where it is headed in terms of the organization's plans and the external factors and trends affecting it. p. 34

social audit A systematic assessment of a firm's objectives, strategies, and performance in terms of social responsibility. p. 88

social forces The demographic characteristics of the population and its values. p. 60

social responsibility The idea that organizations are part of a larger society and are accountable to that society for their actions. p. 86

societal marketing concept The view that an organization should discover and satisfy the needs of its consumers in a way that also provides for society's well-being. p. 14

spam Communications that take the form of electronic junk mail or unsolicited e-mail. p. 413

strategic marketing process The approach whereby an organization allocates its marketing mix resources to reach its target markets. p. 34

strategy An organization's long-term course of action designed to deliver a unique customer experience while achieving its goals. p. 22

subcultures Subgroups within the larger, or national, culture with unique values, ideas, and attitudes. p. 113

supply chain The various firms involved in performing the activities required to create and deliver a product or service to consumers or industrial users. p. 301

SWOT analysis An acronym describing an organization's appraisal of its internal **S**trengths and **W**eaknesses and its external **O**pportunities and **T**hreats. p. 35

target market One or more specific groups of potential consumers toward which an organization directs its marketing program. p. 8

tariff A government tax on goods or services entering a country, primarily serving to raise prices on imports. p. 138

technology Inventions or innovations from applied science or engineering research. p. 67

telemarketing Using the telephone to interact with and sell directly to consumers. p. 320

total cost (TC) The total expenses incurred by a firm in producing and marketing a product; total cost is the sum of fixed costs and variable costs. p. 273

total logistics cost Expenses associated with transportation, materials handling and warehousing, inventory, stockouts (being out of inventory), order processing, and return products handling. p. 305

total revenue (TR) The total money received from the sale of a product; the unit price of a product multiplied by the quantity sold. p. 272

trade-oriented sales promotions Sales tools used to support a company's advertising and personal selling directed to wholesalers, distributors, or retailers. Also called *trade promotions*. p. 373

traditional auction In an e-marketplace, it is an online auction in which a seller puts an item up for sale and would-be buyers are invited to bid in competition with each other. p. 131

traffic generation The outcome of a direct marketing offer designed to motivate people to visit a business. p. 349

ultimate consumers The people who use the goods and services purchased for a household. Also called *consumers, buyers*, or *customers*. p. 15

usage rate The quantity consumed or patronage (store visits) during a specific period. p. 193

utilitarianism A personal moral philosophy that focuses on the "greatest good for the greatest number," by assessing the costs and benefits of the consequences of ethical behavior. p. 85

utility The benefits or customer value received by users of the product. p. 15

value The ratio of perceived benefits to price; Value = Perceived benefits ÷ Price. p. 263

values A society's personally or socially preferable modes of conduct or states of existence that tend to persist over time. p. 144

vendor-managed inventory An inventory management system whereby the supplier determines the product amount and assortment a customer (such as a retailer) needs and automatically delivers the appropriate items. p. 306

vertical marketing systems Professionally managed and centrally coordinated marketing channels designed to achieve channel economies and maximum marketing impact. p. 294

viral marketing An Internet-enabled promotional strategy that encourages individuals to forward marketer-initiated messages to others via e-mail, social networking Web sites, and blogs. p. 414

Web communities Web sites that allow people to congregate online and exchange views on topics of common interest. p. 413

wheel of retailing A concept that describes how new forms of retail outlets enter the market. p. 325

word of mouth People influencing each other in personal conversations. p. 109

World Trade Organization (WTO) A permanent institution that sets rules governing trade between its members through panels of trade experts who decide on trade disputes between members and issue binding decisions. p. 138

LEARNING REVIEW ANSWERS

CHAPTER 1

1. What is marketing?

Answer: Marketing is the activity for creating, communicating, delivering, and exchanging offerings that benefit the organization, its stakeholders, and society at large.

2. Marketing focuses on _____ and _____ consumer needs.

Answer: discovering; satisfying

3. An organization can't satisfy the needs of all consumers, so it must focus on one or more subgroups, which are its _____.

Answer: target market

4. What are the four marketing mix elements that make up the organization's marketing program?

Answer: product, price, promotion, place

5. What are environmental forces?

Answer: Environmental forces are those that the organization's marketing department can't control. These include social, economic, technological, competitive, and regulatory forces.

6. What are the two key characteristics of the marketing concept?

Answer: An organization should (1) strive to satisfy the needs of consumers (2) while also trying to achieve the organization's goals.

7. What is the difference between ultimate consumers and organizational buyers?

Answer: Ultimate consumers are the people who use the products and services purchased for a household. Organizational buyers are those manufacturers, wholesalers, retailers, and government agencies that buy products and services for their own use or for resale.

CHAPTER 2

1. What is the difference between a business firm and a nonprofit organization?

Answer: A business firm is a privately owned organization that serves its customers to earn a profit so that it can survive. A nonprofit organization is a nongovernmental organization that serves its customers but does not have profit as an organizational goal. Instead, its goals may be operational efficiency or client satisfaction.

2. What are examples of a functional level in an organization?

Answer: The functional level in an organization is where groups of specialists from the marketing, finance, manufacturing/operations, accounting, information systems, research and development, and/or human resources departments focus on a specific strategic direction to create value for the organization.

3. What is the meaning of an organization's mission?

Answer: A mission is a statement of the organization's function in society, often identifying its customers, markets, products, and technologies. It is often used interchangeably with *vision*.

4. What is the difference between an organization's business and its goals?

Answer: An organization's business describes the clear, broad, underlying industry or market sector of an organization's offering. An organization's goals (or objectives) are statements of an accomplishment of a task to be achieved, often by a specific time. Goals convert an organization's mission and business into long- and short-term performance targets to measure how well it is doing.

5. What is the difference between a marketing dashboard and a marketing metric?

Answer: A marketing dashboard is the visual computer display of the essential information related to achieving a marketing objective. Each variable in a marketing dashboard is a marketing metric, which is a measure of the quantitative value or trend of a marketing activity or result.

6. What is business portfolio analysis?

Answer: Business portfolio analysis is a technique that managers use to quantify performance measures and growth targets to analyze its clients' strategic business units (SBUs) as though they were a collection of separate investments.

7. Explain the four market–product strategies in diversification analysis.

Answer: The four market–product strategies in diversification analysis are: (1) Market penetration, which is a marketing strategy to increase sales of current products in current markets. There is no change in either the basic product line or the markets served. Rather, selling more of the product or selling the product at a higher price generates increased sales. (2) Market development, which is a marketing strategy to sell current products to new markets. (3) Product development, which is a marketing strategy of selling new products to current markets. (4) Diversification, which is a potentially high-risk marketing strategy of developing new products and selling them in new markets.

8. What are the three steps of the planning phase of the strategic marketing process?

Answer: The three steps of the planning phase of the strategic marketing process are: (1) Situation (SWOT) analysis, which involves taking stock of where the firm or product has been recently, where it is now, and where it is headed in terms of the organization's marketing plans and the external forces and trends affecting it. To do this, an organization uses a SWOT analysis, an acronym that describes an organization's appraisal of its internal **S**trengths and **W**eaknesses and its external **O**pportunities and **T**hreats. (2) Market–product focus and goal setting, which determines what products an organization will offer to which customers. This is often based on market segmentation—aggregating prospective buyers into groups or segments that have common needs and will respond similarly to a marketing action. (3) Marketing program, in which an organization develops the marketing mix elements and budget for each offering.

9. What are points of difference and why are they important?

Answer: Points of difference are those characteristics of a product that make it superior to competitive substitutes—offerings it faces in the marketplace. They are important factors in the success or failure of a new product.

10. What is the implementation phase of the strategic marketing process?

Answer: The implementation phase carries out the marketing plan that emerges from the planning phase and consists of: (1) obtaining resources; (2) designing the marketing organization; (3) developing schedules; and (4) executing the marketing program designed in the planning phase.

11. How do the goals set for a marketing program in the planning phase relate to the evaluation phase of the strategic marketing process?

Answer: The planning phase objectives are used as the benchmarks with which the actual performance results are compared in the evaluation phase to identify deviations from the written marketing plans and then correct negative ones or exploit positive ones.

CHAPTER 3

1. Describe three generational cohorts.

Answer: (1) Baby boomers are those among the U.S. population born between 1946 and 1964. These Americans are growing older and are the wealthiest generation in U.S. history. (2) Generation X are those among the 15 percent of the U.S. population born between 1965 and 1976. These well-educated Americans, also known as the baby bust cohort because of declining birthrates, have a collective net worth that is less than the baby boomer generation. (3) Generation Y are the 72 million Americans among the U.S. population born between 1977 and 1994. The rising birthrate of this "baby boomlet" cohort is the result of baby boomers having children. A subset of this generational cohort are millennials, which are younger Americans born since 1994. Because each generational cohort has its distinct attitudes and behaviors, marketers have developed generational marketing programs for each of them.

2. Why are many companies developing multicultural marketing programs?

Answer: Multicultural marketing programs consist of combinations of the marketing mix that reflect the unique attitudes, ancestry, communication preferences, and lifestyles of different races. The reasons for developing these programs are: (1) The racial and ethnic diversity of the United States is changing rapidly due to the increases in the African American, Asian, and Hispanic populations, which increases their economic impact. (2) An accurate understanding of the culture of each group is essential if marketing efforts are to be successful. (3) Based on an analysis of population demographic data, racial and ethnic groups tend to be concentrated in specific geographic regions.

3. How are important values such as sustainability reflected in the marketplace today?

Answer: An increasingly important value for consumers is sustainability. For example, these consumers buy hybrid cars and energy-efficient light bulbs. Consumers also prefer brands that have a strong link to social action (like Ben & Jerry's—see Chapter 2). Companies are responding to this consumer trend by using renewable energy in producing and reducing the packaging of their products.

4. What is the difference between a consumer's disposable and discretionary income?

Answer: Disposable income is the money a consumer has left after paying taxes to use for necessities such as food, housing, clothing, and transportation. Discretionary income is the money that remains after paying for taxes and necessities and is used for luxury items.

5. How does technology impact customer value?

Answer: (1) Consumers can now assess value on the basis of other dimensions, such as quality, service, and relationships, due to the decline in the cost of technology. (2) Technology provides value through the development of new products.

6. In pure competition there are _____ sellers.

Answer: a large number of

7. The _____ Act was punitive toward monopolies, whereas the _____ Act was preventive.

Answer: Sherman Antitrust; Clayton

8. Describe some of the recent changes in trademark law.

Answer: The *Trademark Law Revision Act* (1988) allows companies to secure rights to a name before its actual use by declaring an intent to use the name. In 2003, the United States agreed to participate in the *Madrid Protocol*, which is a treaty that facilitates the protection of U.S. trademark rights. Also, the U.S. Supreme Court recently ruled that a company may obtain trademarks for colors associated with their products. Finally, the *Federal Dilution Act* of 1995 prevents someone from using a trademark on a noncompeting product (such as the "Cadillac" of brushes).

9. How does the Better Business Bureau encourage companies to follow its standards for commerce?

Answer: The Better Business Bureau (BBB) uses moral suasion to get members to comply with its standards. Companies, which join the BBB voluntarily, must agree to follow these standards before they are allowed to display the BBB logo.

CHAPTER 4

1. What are ethics?

Answer: Ethics are the moral principles and values that govern the actions and decisions of an individual or group. They serve as guidelines on how to act rightly and justly when faced with moral dilemmas.

2. What are four possible reasons for the present state of ethical conduct in the United States?

Answer: (1) Pressure on businesspeople to make decisions in a society with diverse value systems. (2) Business decisions being judged publicly by groups with different values and interests. (3) The public's expectations of ethical business behavior have increased. (4) Ethical business conduct may have declined.

3. What rights are included in the Consumer Bill of Rights?

Answer: The rights to safety, to be informed, to choose, and to be heard.

4. Economic espionage includes what kinds of activities?

Answer: Economic espionage is the clandestine collection of trade secrets or proprietary information about a company's competitors. This practice includes trespassing, theft, fraud, misrepresentation, wiretapping, searching competitors' trash, and violations of written and implicit employment agreements with noncompete clauses.

5. What is meant by moral idealism?

Answer: Moral idealism is a personal moral philosophy that considers certain individual rights or duties as universal, regardless of the outcome.

6. What is meant by social responsibility?

Answer: Social responsibility means that organizations are part of a larger society and are accountable to that society for their actions. It comprises three concepts: (1) profit responsibility—maximizing profits for the organization's shareholders; (2) stakeholder responsibility—the obligations an organization has to those who can affect the achievement of its objectives; and (3) societal responsibility—the obligations an organization has to preserve the ecological environment and to the general public.

7. Marketing efforts to produce, promote, and reclaim environmentally sensitive products are called _____.

Answer: green marketing

8. What is a social audit?

Answer: A social audit is a systematic assessment of a firm's objectives, strategies, and performance in terms of social responsibility.

CHAPTER 5

1. What is the first stage in the consumer purchase decision process?

Answer: problem recognition

2. The brands a consumer considers buying out of the set of brands in a product class of which the consumer is aware is called the _____.

Answer: consideration set

3. What is the term for postpurchase anxiety?

Answer: cognitive dissonance

4. The problem with the Toro Snow Pup was an example of selective _____.

Answer: comprehension

5. What three attitude-change approaches are most common?

Answer: (1) Change beliefs about the extent to which a brand has certain attributes. (2) Change the perceived importance of the attributes. (3) Add new attributes to the product.

6. What does *lifestyle* mean?

Answer: Lifestyle is a mode of living that is identified by how people spend their time and resources, what they consider important in their environment, and what they think of themselves and the world around them.

7. What are the two primary forms of personal influence?

Answer: opinion leadership; word of mouth activity

8. Marketers are concerned with which types of reference groups?

Answer: membership groups; aspiration groups; dissociative groups

9. **What two challenges must marketers overcome when marketing to Hispanic consumers?**

Answer: (1) The diversity of nationalities among this subculture. (2) The language barrier that can lead to misinterpretation or mistranslation of commercial messages.

CHAPTER 6

1. **What are the three main types of organizational buyers?**

Answer: industrial firms; resellers; government units

2. **What is the North American Industry Classification System (NAICS)?**

Answer: The NAICS provides common industry definitions for Canada, Mexico, and the United States, which makes it easier to measure economic activity in the three member countries of NAFTA.

3. **What one department is almost always represented by a person in the buying center?**

Answer: purchasing department

4. **What are the three types of buying situations or buy classes?**

Answer: new buy; straight rebuy; modified rebuy

5. **What are e-marketplaces?**

Answer: E-marketplaces are online trading communities that bring together buyers and supplier organizations to make possible the real-time exchange of information, money, products, and services.

6. **In general, which type of online auction creates upward pressure on bid prices and which type creates downward pressure on bid prices?**

Answer: traditional auction; reverse auction

CHAPTER 7

1. **What is protectionism?**

Answer: Protectionism is the practice of shielding one or more industries within a country's economy from foreign competition through the use of tariffs or quotas.

2. **The North American Free Trade Agreement was designed to promote free trade among which countries?**

Answer: United States, Canada, and Mexico

3. **What is the difference between a multidomestic marketing strategy and a global marketing strategy?**

Answer: Multinational firms view the world as consisting of unique markets. As a result, they use a multidomestic marketing strategy because they have as many different product variations, brand names, and advertising programs as countries in which they do business. Transnational firms view the world as one market. As a result, they use a global marketing strategy to standardize marketing activities when there are cultural similarities and adapt it when cultures differ.

4. **Cross-cultural analysis involves the study of _____.**

Answer: similarities and difference among consumers in two or more nations or societies

5. **When foreign currencies can buy more U.S. dollars, are U.S. products more or less expensive for a foreign consumer?**

Answer: less expensive

6. **What mode of entry could a company follow if it has no previous experience in global marketing?**

Answer: indirect exporting through intermediaries

7. **How does licensing differ from a joint venture?**

Answer: Under licensing, a company offers the right to a trademark, patent, trade secret, or other similarly valued items of intellectual property in return for a fee or royalty. In a joint venture, a foreign company and a local firm invest together to create a local business to produce some product or service. The two companies share ownership, control, and profits of the new entity.

8. **Products may be sold globally in three ways. What are they?**

Answer: Products can be sold: (1) in the same form as in their home market (product extension); (2) with some adaptations (product adaptation); and (3) as a totally new product (product invention).

9. **What is dumping?**

Answer: Dumping is when a firm sells a product in a foreign country below its domestic price or below its actual cost to produce.

CHAPTER 8

1. **What is marketing research?**

Answer: Marketing research is the process of defining a marketing problem and opportunity, systematically collecting and analyzing information, and recommending actions.

2. **What is the five-step marketing research approach?**

Answer: The five-step marketing research approach provides a systematic checklist for making marketing decisions and actions. The five steps are: (1) define the problem; (2) develop the research plan; (3) collect relevant information (data); (4) develop findings; and (5) take marketing actions.

3. **What are constraints, as they apply to developing a research plan?**

Answer: Constraints in a decision are the restrictions placed on potential solutions to a problem, such as time and money.

4. **What is the difference between secondary and primary data?**

Answer: Secondary data are facts and figures that have already been recorded before the project at hand, whereas primary data are facts and figures that are newly collected for the project.

5. **What are some advantages and disadvantages of secondary data?**

Answer: Advantages of secondary data are the time savings, the low cost, and the greater level of detail that may be available. Disadvantages of secondary data are that the data may be out of date, unspecific, or have definitions, categories, or age groupings that are wrong for the project at hand.

6. **What is the difference between observational and questionnaire data?**

Answer: Observational data are facts and figures obtained by watching, either mechanically or in person, how people actually behave. Questionnaire data are facts and figures obtained by asking people about their attitudes, awareness, intentions, and behaviors.

7. **Which type of survey provides the greatest flexibility for asking probing questions: mail, telephone, or personal interview?**

Answer: personal interview (or individual or depth interview, which is a special kind of individual interview)

8. **What is the difference between a panel and an experiment?**

Answer: A panel is a sample of consumers or stores from which researchers take a series of measurements. An experiment involves obtaining data by manipulating factors under tightly controlled conditions to test cause and effect, such as changing a variable in a customer purchase decision (marketing drivers) and seeing what happens (increase/decrease in unit or dollar sales).

9. **How does data mining differ from traditional marketing research?**

Answer: Data mining is the extraction of hidden predictive information from large databases to find statistical links between consumer purchasing patterns and marketing actions. Marketing research identifies possible drivers and then collects data.

10. **In the marketing research for Tony's Pizza, what is an example of (a) a finding and (b) a marketing action?**

Answer: (a) Figure 8–6A depicts annual sales from 2006 to 2009; the finding is that annual sales are relatively flat, rising only 5 million units over the four-year period. (b) Figure 8–6D shows a finding (the decline in pizza consumption) that leads to a recommendation to develop an ad targeting children 6 to 12 years old.

11. **What are the three kinds of sales forecasting techniques?**

Answer: They are: (1) judgments of the decision maker; (2) surveys of knowledgeable groups; and (3) statistical methods.

12. How do you make a lost-horse forecast?

Answer: To make a lost-horse forecast, begin with the last known value of the item being forecast, list the factors that could affect the forecast, assess whether they have a positive or negative impact, and then make the final forecast.

CHAPTER 9

1. Market segmentation involves aggregating prospective buyers into groups that have two key characteristics. What are they?

Answer: The groups (1) should have common needs and (2) will respond similarly to a marketing action.

2. In terms of market segments and products, what are the three market segmentation strategies?

Answer: The three market segmentation strategies are: (1) one product and multiple market segments; (2) multiple products and multiple market segments; and (3) "segments of one," or mass customization.

3. The process of segmenting and targeting markets is a bridge between which two marketing activities?

Answer: identifying market needs and executing the marketing program

4. What is the difference between the demographic and behavioral bases of market segmentation?

Answer: Demographic segmentation is based on some objective physical (gender, race), measurable (age, income), or other classification attribute (birth era, occupation) of prospective customers. Behavioral segmentation is based on some observable actions or attitudes by prospective customers—such as where they buy, what benefits they seek, how frequently they buy, and why they buy.

5. What factor is estimated or measured for each of the cells in a market-product grid?

Answer: Each cell in the grid can show the estimated market size of a given product sold to a specific market segment.

6. What are some criteria used to decide which segments to choose for targets?

Answer: These criteria include market size, expected growth, competitive position, cost of reaching the segment, and compatibility with the organization's objectives and resources.

7. How are marketing and product synergies different in a market-product grid?

Answer: Marketing synergies run horizontally across a market-product grid. Each row represents an opportunity for efficiency in the marketing efforts to a market segment. Product synergies run vertically down the market-product grid. Each column represents an opportunity for efficiency in research and development (R&D) and production.

8. What is the difference between product positioning and product repositioning?

Answer: Product positioning refers to the place a product occupies in consumers' minds on important attributes relative to competitive products. Product repositioning involves changing the place a product occupies in a consumer's mind relative to competitive products.

9. Why do marketers use perceptual maps in product positioning decisions?

Answer: Perceptual maps are a means of displaying or graphing in two dimensions the location of products or brands in the minds of consumers. Managers use perceptual maps to see how consumers perceive competing products or brands as well as their own product or brand. Then, they can develop marketing actions to move their product or brand to an ideal position.

CHAPTER 10

1. What are the four main types of consumer products?

Answer: They are convenience products, shopping products, specialty products, and unsought products.

2. What is the difference between a product line and a product mix?

Answer: A product line is a group of product or service items that are closely related because they satisfy a class of needs, are used together, are sold to the same customer group, are distributed through the same outlets, or fall within a given price range. The product mix consists of all the product lines offered by an organization.

3. What are the 4 I's of services?

Answer: The 4 I's of services—intangibility, inconsistency, inseparability and inventory—are unique elements that distinguish services from goods. Intangibility refers to the tendency of services to be a performance rather than an object. Inconsistency refers to the variability of the quality of the performance of the people who deliver services. Inseparability means that the consumer cannot distinguish the service provider from the service itself. Inventory refers to the need to have serviced production capability when there is service demand.

4. What kind of innovation would an improved electric toothbrush be?

Answer: continuous innovation—no new learning is required

5. Why can an "insignificant point of difference" lead to new-product failure?

Answer: The product must have superior characteristics that deliver unique benefits to the user compared to those of competitors. Without these, the product will probably fail.

6. What marketing metric might you use in a marketing dashboard to discover which states have weak sales?

Answer: Annual percentage (%) sales change is a marketing metric that can measure the annual growth rate over a specified time period for each state of the United States.

7. What is the new-product strategy development stage in the new-product process?

Answer: New-product strategy development is the stage of the new-product process that defines the role for a new product in terms of the firm's overall objectives.

8. What are the main sources of new-product ideas?

Answer: Customer and supplier suggestions, employee and co-worker suggestions, R&D laboratories, competitive products, and universities, inventors, and smaller firms.

9. How do internal and external screening and evaluation approaches differ?

Answer: In internal screening, company employees evaluate the technical feasibility of new-product ideas to determine whether it meets the objectives defined in the new-product strategy development step. For services, employees are assessed to determine that they have the commitment and skills to meet customer expectations and sustain customer loyalty. In external screening, evaluation consists of preliminary testing of the new-product idea (not the actual product) with consumers.

10. How does the development stage of the new-product process involve testing the product inside and outside the firm?

Answer: The development stage results in a demonstrable, producible product that involves not only manufacturing the product but also performing laboratory and consumer tests to ensure it meets the standards established for it in the protocol.

11. What is a test market?

Answer: A test market is a city that is viewed as being representative of U.S. consumers. Test market cities also include cable TV systems to deliver different ads to different homes, and has tracking systems to measure sales from the different advertising campaigns.

12. What is commercialization of a new product?

Answer: Commercialization, the last stage of the new-product process, involves positioning and launching a new product in full-scale production and sales and is the most expensive stage for most new products.

CHAPTER 11

1. **Advertising plays a major role in the _____ stage of the product life cycle, and _____ plays a major role in maturity.**

   Answer: introductory; product differentiation

2. **How do high-learning and low-learning products differ?**

   Answer: A high-learning product requires significant customer education and there is an extended introductory period. A low-learning product requires little customer education because the benefits of purchase are readily understood, resulting in immediate sales.

3. **What does "creating a new use situation" mean in managing a product's life cycle?**

   Answer: Finding new uses or applications for an existing product.

4. **Explain the difference between trading up and trading down in repositioning.**

   Answer: Trading up involves adding value to the product (or line) through additional features or higher-quality materials. Trading down involves reducing the number of features, quality, price, or downsizing—reducing the content of packages without changing package size and maintaining or increasing the package price.

5. **What is the difference between a line extension and a brand extension?**

   Answer: A line extension uses a current brand name to enter a new market segment in its product class, whereas a brand extension involves using a current brand name to enter a completely different product class.

6. **Explain the role of packaging in terms of perception.**

   Answer: A package's shape, color, and graphics conveys a brand's positioning and builds brand equity.

7. **How do service businesses use off-peak pricing?**

   Answer: They charge different prices during different times of day or days of the week to reflect variations in demand for the service.

CHAPTER 12

1. **Value is _____.**

   Answer: the ratio of perceived benefits to price.

2. **What are the circumstances in pricing a new product that might support skimming or penetration pricing?**

   Answer: Skimming pricing is an effective strategy when (1) enough prospective customers are willing to buy the product immediately at the high initial price to make these sales profitable, (2) the high initial price will not attract competitors, (3) lowering price has only a minor effect on increasing the sales volume and reducing the unit costs, and (4) customers interpret the high price as signifying high quality. These four conditions are most likely to exist when the new product is protected by patents or copyrights or its uniqueness is understood and valued by consumers. The conditions favoring penetration pricing are the reverse of those supporting skimming pricing: (1) many segments of the market are price sensitive, (2) a low initial price discourages competitors from entering the market, and (3) unit production and marketing costs fall dramatically as production volumes increase.

3. **What are the three key factors when estimating consumer demand?**

   Answer: consumer tastes, price and availability of similar products, and consumer income

4. **Price elasticity of demand is _____.**

   Answer: the percentage change in the quantity demanded relative to a percentage change in price

5. **What is the difference between fixed costs and variable costs?**

   Answer: Fixed cost is the sum of the expenses of the firm that are stable and do not change with the quantity of the product that is produced and sold. Variable cost is the sum of the expenses of the firm that vary directly with the quantity of the product that is produced and sold.

6. **What is a break-even point?**

   Answer: A break-even point (BEP) is the quantity at which total revenue and total cost are equal.

7. **What is the difference between pricing objectives and pricing constraints?**

   Answer: Pricing objectives specify the role of price in an organization's marketing and strategic plans. Pricing constraints are factors that limit the range of prices a firm may set.

8. **Explain what bait and switch is and why it is an example of deceptive pricing.**

   Answer: Bait and switch is the practice of offering a very low price on a product (the bait) to attract customers to a store. Once in the store, the customer is persuaded to purchase a higher-priced item (the switch) using a variety of tricks, including (1) degrading the promoted item and (2) not having the promised item in stock or refusing to take orders for the item.

9. **What are the three steps in setting a final price?**

   Answer: (1) Select an approximate price level, (2) Set the list or quoted price, (3) Make special adjustments to the list or quoted price.

10. **What is the purpose of (a) quantity discounts and (b) promotional allowances?**

    Answer: Quantity discounts are used to encourage customers to buy larger quantities of a product. Promotional allowances are used to encourage sellers in the channel of distribution to undertake advertising or selling activities to promote a product.

CHAPTER 13

1. **What is meant by a marketing channel?**

   Answer: A marketing channel consists of individuals and firms involved in the process of making a product or service available for use or consumption by consumers or industrial users.

2. **What are the three basic functions performed by intermediaries?**

   Answer: Intermediaries perform transactional, logistical, and facilitating functions.

3. **What is the difference between a direct and an indirect channel?**

   Answer: A direct channel is one in which a producer of consumer or business products and services and ultimate consumers or industrial users deal directly with each other. An indirect channel has intermediaries that are inserted between the producer and ultimate consumers or industrial users and perform numerous channel functions.

4. **Why are channels for business products typically shorter than channels for consumer products?**

   Answer: Business channels are typically shorter than consumer channels because business users are fewer in number, tend to be more concentrated geographically, and buy in larger quantities.

5. **What is the principal distinction between a corporate vertical marketing system and an administered vertical marketing system?**

   Answer: A corporate vertical marketing system combines successive stages of production and distribution under a single ownership. An administered vertical marketing system achieves coordination by the size and influence of one channel member rather than through ownership.

6. **What are the three questions marketing executives consider when choosing a marketing channel and intermediaries?**

   Answer: The three questions to consider when choosing a marketing channel and intermediaries are: (1) Which will provide the best coverage of the target market? (2) Which will best satisfy the buying requirements of the target market? (3) Which will be the most profitable?

7. **What are the three degrees of distribution density?**

   Answer: intensive; exclusive; selective.

8. **What is the principal difference between a marketing channel and a supply chain?**

   Answer: A supply chain differs from a marketing channel in terms of membership. It includes suppliers who provide raw materials to a manufacturer as well as the wholesalers and retailers—the marketing channel—that deliver the finished goods to ultimate consumers.

9. **The choice of a supply chain involves what three steps?**

Answer: (1) Understand the customer. (2) Understand the supply chain. (3) Harmonize the supply chain with the marketing strategy.

10. **A manager's key task is to balance which four customer service factors against which five logistics cost factors?**

Answer: A supply chain manager's key task is to balance four customer service factors—time, dependability, communication, and convenience—against the five total logistics cost factors—transportation, materials handling and warehousing, inventory, stockouts, and order processing.

CHAPTER 14

1. **When Ralph Lauren makes shirts to a customer's exact preferences, what utility is provided?**

Answer: form utility

2. **Two measures of the impact of retailing in the global economy are _____ and _____.**

Answer: the total annual sales; the number of employees working at large retailers

3. **Centralized decision making and purchasing are an advantage of _____ ownership.**

Answer: corporate chain

4. **What are some examples of new forms of self-service retailers?**

Answer: Hotels (Hilton Hotels—self-serve kiosks in lobbies to allow patrons to check-in, etc.) and libraries (Palm Beach County Library—self-serve machines to check out books).

5. **Would a shop for big men's clothes carrying pants in sizes 40 to 60 have a broad or deep product line?**

Answer: deep product line; the range of sizes relates to the assortment of a product item (pants) rather than the variety of product lines (pants, shirts, shoes, etc.).

6. **To improve their efficiency and provide additional customer value catalog retailers often focus on _____ rather than _____.**

Answer: proven customers; prospective customers

7. **How are retailers increasing consumer interest and involvement in online retailing?**

Answer: Retailers have improved the online retailing experience by adding experiential or interactive activities to their Web sites, allowing customers to "build" virtual products by customizing their purchases.

8. **Where are direct selling retail sales growing? Why?**

Answer: Direct-selling retailers are (1) expanding into other global markets outside the U.S. due to a specific country's lack of effective distribution channels and/or a lack of consumer knowledge about certain products and brands and (2) reaching consumers who prefer one-on-one customer service and a social shopping experience rather than shopping online or at big discount stores.

9. **How does original markup differ from maintained markup?**

Answer: The original markup is the difference between retailer cost and initial selling price whereas maintained markup is the difference between the final selling price and retailer cost, which is also called the gross margin.

10. **A huge shopping mall with multiple anchor stores is a _____ center.**

Answer: power

11. **What is a popular approach to managing the assortment of merchandise in a store?**

Answer: Category management. This approach assigns a manager with the responsibility for selecting all products in a category with the objective of maximizing sales and profits.

12. **According to the wheel of retailing, when a new retail form appears, how would you characterize its image?**

Answer: A low-status, low-margin, low-price outlet.

13. **Market share is usually fought out before the _____ stage of the retail life cycle.**

Answer: maturity

14. **What is the difference between merchant wholesalers and agents?**

Answer: Merchant wholesalers are independently owned firms that take title to the merchandise they handle. Agents do not take title to merchandise and typically perform fewer channel functions.

CHAPTER 15

1. **What are the six elements required for communication to occur?**

Answer: The six elements required for communication to occur are: a source, a message, a channel of communication, a receiver, and the processes of encoding and decoding.

2. **A difficulty for U.S. companies advertising in international markets is that the audience does not share the same _____.**

Answer: field of experience

3. **A misprint in a newspaper ad is an example of _____.**

Answer: noise

4. **Explain the difference between advertising and publicity when both appear on television.**

Answer: Since advertising space on TV is paid for, a firm can control what it wants to say and to whom and how often the message is sent over a broadcast, cable, satellite, or local TV network. Since publicity is an indirectly paid presentation of a message about a firm or its products or services, the firm has little control over what is said to whom or when. Instead, it can only suggest to the TV medium that it run a favorable story on the firm or its offerings.

5. **Cost per contact is high with the _____ element of the promotional mix.**

Answer: personal selling

6. **Which promotional element should be offered only on a short-term basis?**

Answer: sales promotion

7. **Promotional programs can be directed to _____, to _____, or both.**

Answer: the ultimate consumer; an intermediary (retailer, wholesaler, or industrial distributor)

8. **Describe the promotional objective for each stage of the product life cycle.**

Answer: Introduction—to inform; growth—to persuade; maturity—to remind; and decline—to phase out.

9. **Explain the differences between a push strategy and a pull strategy.**

Answer: In a push strategy, a firm directs the promotional mix to channel members to gain their cooperation in ordering and stocking the product. In a pull strategy, a firm directs the promotional mix at ultimate consumers to encourage them to ask retailers for the product, who then orders it from wholesalers or the firm itself.

10. **What are the stages of the hierarchy of effects?**

Answer: The five stages of the hierarchy of effects are awareness, interest, evaluation, trial, and adoption.

11. **What are the four approaches to setting the promotion budget?**

Answer: The four approaches are percentage of sales, competitive parity, all you can afford, and objective and task.

12. **How have advertising agencies changed to facilitate the use of IMC programs?**

Answer: Some agencies have adopted: (1) a total communications solutions approach, (2) a long-term perspective in which all forms of promotion are integrated, and (3) an IMC audit to analyze the internal communication network of their clients.

13. **The ability to design and use direct marketing programs has increased with the availability of _____ and _____.**

Answer: customer information databases; new printing technologies

14. **What are the three types of responses generated by direct marketing activities?**

Answer: They are direct orders, lead generation, and traffic generation.

CHAPTER 16

1. **What is the difference between pioneering and competitive ads?**

   Answer: Pioneering ads, used in the introductory stage of the product life cycle, tell people what a product is, what it can do, and where it can be found. Competitive ads promote a specific brand's features and benefits to persuade the target market to select the firm's brand rather than that of a competitor.

2. **What is the purpose of an institutional advertisement?**

   Answer: The purpose of an institutional advertisement is to build goodwill or an image for an organization.

3. **The Federal Communications Commission suggests that advertising program decisions be based on _____.**

   Answer: marketing research about the target audience.

4. **Describe three common forms of advertising appeals.**

   Answer: Fear appeals suggest that a consumer avoid a negative experience; sex appeals suggest a way to increase attractiveness; humorous appeals imply fun and excitement.

5. **You see the same ad in *Time* and *Fortune* magazines and on billboards and TV. Is this an example of reach or frequency?**

   Answer: Reach—using more of the same media type (magazines) as well as using more of different types of media (magazines, billboards, and TV)—is an attempt to maximize the number of individuals in a target market to be exposed to the advertisement. Frequency uses the same medium/media more than once to present the advertising message.

6. **Why has the Internet become a popular advertising medium?**

   Answer: The Internet offers a visual message, can use both audio and video, is interactive through rich media, and tends to reach younger consumers.

7. **Describe three approaches to scheduling advertising.**

   Answer: continuous (steady) schedule; flighting (intermittent) schedule); pulse (burst) schedule

8. **Explain the difference between pretesting and posttesting advertising copy.**

   Answer: Pretests are conducted before ads are placed in any medium to determine whether they communicate the intended message or select among alternative versions of the ad. Posttests are conducted after an advertisement has been shown to the target audience to determine whether it accomplished its intended purpose.

9. **What is the difference between aided and unaided recall posttests?**

   Answer: Aided recall involves showing an ad to respondents who then are asked if their previous exposure to it was through reading, viewing, or listening. Unaided recall involves specifically asking respondents if they remember an ad without any prompting to determine if they saw or heard its message.

10. **Which sales promotional tool is most common for new products?**

    Answer: samples

11. **Which trade promotion is used to encourage local advertising efforts of resellers?**

    Answer: cooperative advertising

12. **What is a news release?**

    Answer: A news release is an announcement regarding changes in the company or the product line.

13. **What type of publicity tool is used most often by nonprofit organizations?**

    Answer: public service announcements (PSAs)

CHAPTER 17

1. **What is personal selling?**

   Answer: Personal selling involves the two-way flow of communication between a buyer and seller, often in a face-to-face encounter, designed to influence a person's or group's purchase decision.

2. **What is involved in sales management?**

   Answer: Sales management involves planning the selling program and implementing and evaluating the personal selling effort of the firm.

3. **What is the principal difference between an order taker and an order getter?**

   Answer: An order taker processes routine orders or reorders for products that were already sold by the company. An order getter sells in a conventional sense and identifies prospective customers, provides customers with information, persuades customers to buy, closes sales, and follows up on customers' use of a product or service.

4. **What percentage of an order-getting salesperson's time is spent selling?**

   Answer: 55 percent

5. **What are the six stages in the personal selling process?**

   Answer: The six stages in the personal selling process are: (1) prospecting, (2) preapproach, (3) approach, (4) presentation, (5) close, and (6) follow-up.

6. **Which presentation format is most consistent with the marketing concept? Why?**

   Answer: The need-satisfaction presentation format emphasizes probing and listening by the salesperson to identify needs and interests of prospective buyers and then tailors the presentation to the prospect and highlights product benefits, which is consistent with the marketing concept and its focus on relationship building.

7. **What are the three types of selling objectives?**

   Answer: The three types of selling objectives are: (1) output-related (dollars or unit sales, new customers, profit); (2) input-related (sales calls, selling expenses); and (3) behavioral-related (product knowledge, customer service, selling and communication skills).

8. **What three factors are used to structure sales organizations?**

   Answer: geography; customer; product/service

CHAPTER 18

1. **The consumer-initiated practice of generating content on a marketer's Web site that is custom tailored to an individual's specific needs and preferences is called _____.**

   Answer: personalization

2. **Companies produce a customer experience through what seven Web site design elements?**

   Answer: These design elements are: context, content, community, customization, communication, connection, and commerce.

3. **What is viral marketing?**

   Answer: An Internet-enabled promotional strategy that encourages individuals to forward marketer-initiated messages to others via e-mail, social networking Web sites, and blogs.

4. **What are the six reasons consumers prefer to shop and buy online?**

   Answer: convenience, choice, customization, communication, cost, and control

5. **A cross-channel shopper is _____.**

   Answer: an online consumer who researches products online and then purchases them at a retail store

6. **Channel conflict between manufacturers and retailers is likely to arise when manufacturers use _____ Web sites.**

   Answer: transactional

CHAPTER NOTES

Chapter 1

1. The 3M Post-it® Flag Highlighter and Post-it® Flag Pen examples are based on a series of interviews and meetings with David Windorski, 3M, from 2004 to 2010.

2. The *Oprah Winfrey Show,* January 15, 2008.

3. John Reinan, "Millionaire Whiz Kid," *Star Tribune,* October 13, 2006, pp. A1, A18; John Cloud, "The YouTube Gurus," *Time,* December 25, 2006–January 1, 2007, pp. 66–74; Lev Grossman, "Invention of the Year 2006," *Time,* November 13, 2006, pp. 64–65; "Two Kings Get Together," *The Economist,* October 14, 2006, pp. 67–68; and The Official YouTube Blog, "At Five Years, Two Billion Views per Day and Counting," May 16, 2010.

4. To compare the 2004 and 2007 American Marketing Association definitions of "marketing," see Lisa M. Keefe, "Marketing Defined," *Marketing News,* January 15, 2008, pp. 28–29.

5. Richard P. Bagozzi, "Marketing as Exchange," *Journal of Marketing,* October 1975, pp. 32–39; and Gregory T. Gundlach and Patrick E. Murphy, "Ethical and Legal Foundations of Relational Marketing Exchanges," *Journal of Marketing,* October 1993, pp. 35–46.

6. "The Rise of the Creative Consumer," *The Economist,* March 12, 2005, pp. 54–60.

7. Productscan® Online database of new products, from *Marketing Intelligence Service,* December 17, 2003, www.productscan.com.

8. Robert M. McMath and Thom Forbes, "What *Were* They Thinking?" (New York: Times Business, 1998), pp. 3–22.

9. From the New Product Works Web site, "Favorite Failures," www.newproductworks.com.

10. From the Hot Pockets Web site, www.EatFreely.org and www.hotpockets.com.

11. "AT&T CruiseCast℠ Will Deliver 22 Satellite TV and 20 Satellite Radio Channels into the Car for the First Time with Breakthrough Antenna and Receiver Technologies," AT&T CruiseCast press release. November 3, 2008. See www.cruisecast.com/press.html#press1. See also "Live TV in Your Car," *Fox Business News,* January 9, 2009.

12. Natalie Zmuda, "PepsiCo Still Finalizing Ad Lineup for Super Bowl," *Advertising Age,* January 27, 2009. See http://adage.com/mediaworks/article?article_id=134132 and "Pepsi Max: I'm Good (Full Version)" from Hulu.com.

13. Kara McGuire, "New Credit Rules Are No Reason to Let Guard Down," *Star Tribune,* January 31, 2010, pp. D1, D2; and Sandra Block, "How the Credit Card Reforms Will Affect You," *USA Today,* February 22, 2010, p. 38.

14. E. Jerome McCarthy, *Basic Marketing: A Managerial Approach* (Homewood, IL: Richard D. Irwin, 1960); and Walter van Waterschool and Christophe Van den Bulte, "The 4P Classification of the Marketing Mix Revisited," *Journal of Marketing,* October 1992, pp. 83–93.

15. Ashish Kothari and Joseph Lackner, "A Value Based Approach to Management," *Journal of Business and Industrial Marketing,* 21, no. 4, pp. 243–49; and James C. Anderson, James A. Narius, and Wouter van Rossum, "Customer Value Propositions in Business Markets," *Harvard Business Review,* March 2006, pp. 91–99.

16. For an examination of both the drivers and outcomes of consumer satisfaction programs, see Leslie M. Fine, "Spotlight on Marketing," *Business Horizons,* 49 (2006), pp. 179–83.

17. V. Kumar, *Managing Customers for Profit* (Upper Saddle River, NJ: Pearson Education, 2008); and "What's a Loyal Customer Worth?" *Fortune,* December 11, 1995, p. 182.

18. Michael Treacy and Fred D. Wiersema, *The Discipline of Market Leaders* (Reading, MA: Addison-Wesley, 1995); Michael Treacy and Fred Wiersema, "How Market Leaders Keep Their Edge," *Fortune* (February 6, 1995), pp. 88–89; and Michael Treacy, "You Need a Value Discipline—But Which One?" *Fortune* (April 17, 1995), p. 195.

19. Robert W. Palmatier, Rajiv P. Dant, Dhruv Grewal, and Kenneth R. Evans, "Factors Influencing the Effectiveness of Relationship Marketing: A Meta-Analysis," *Journal of Relationship Marketing,* October 2006, pp. 136–53; and William Boulding, Richard Staelin, Michael Ehret, and Wesley J. Johnson, "A Customer Relationship Management Roadmap: What Is Known, Potential Pitfalls, and Where to Go," *Journal of Marketing,* October 2005, pp. 155–66.

20. Susan Foumier, Susan Dobscha, and David Glen Mick, "Preventing the Premature Death of Relationship Marketing," *Harvard Business Review,* January–February 1998, pp. 42–51.

21. See www.oprah.com for January 15, 2008; and "Post-it® Flags Co-Sponsors Oprah's Live Web Event," *3M Stemwinder,* March 4–17, 2008, p. 3.

22. Reservations about and elaborations of these simplified stages appear in D.G. Brian Jones and Eric H. Shaw, "A History of Marketing Thought," Chapter 2 in *Handbook of Marketing,* edited by Barton Weitz and Robin Wensley (London: Sage Publications, 2006), pp. 39–65; Frederic E. Webster, Jr., "The Role of Marketing and the Firm," Chapter 3 in *Handbook of Marketing,* ed. Barton Weitz and Robin Wensley (London: Sage Publications, 2006), pp. 66–82; and Frederick E. Webster, Jr., "Back to the Future: Integrating Marketing as Tactics, Strategy and Organizational Culture," *Journal of Marketing,* October 2005, pp. 4–8.

23. Robert F. Keith, "The Marketing Revolution," *Journal of Marketing,* January 1960, pp. 35–38.

24. *Annual Report* (New York: General Electric Company, 1952), p. 21.

25. John C. Narver, Stanley F. Slater, and Brian Tietje, "Creating a Market Orientation," *Journal of Market Focused Management,* no. 2 (1998), pp. 241–55; Stanley F. Slater and John C. Narver, "Market Orientation and the Learning Organization," *Journal of Marketing,* July 1995, pp. 63–74; and George S. Day, "The Capabilities of Market-Driven Organizations," *Journal of Marketing,* October 1994, pp. 37–52.

26. The definition of customer relationship management is adapted from Rajendra K. Srivastava, Tasadduq A. Shervani, and Liam Fahey, "Marketing, Business Processes, and Shareholder Value: An Embedded View of Marketing Activities and the Discipline of Marketing," *Journal of Marketing,* special issue (1999), pp. 168–79; Gary F. Gebhardt, Gregory S. Carpenter, and John F. Sherry Jr., "Creating a Market Orientation: A Longitudinal, Multifirm, Grounded Analysis of Cultural Transformation," *Journal of Marketing,* October 2006, pp. 37–55; and Christopher Meyer and Andre Schwager, "Understanding Customer Experience," *Harvard Business Review,* February 2007, pp. 117–26.

27. Gary F. Gebhardt, Gregory S. Carpenter, and John F. Sherry Jr., "Creating a Market Orientation: A Longitudinal, Multifirm, Grounded Analysis of Cultural Transformation," *Journal of Marketing,* October 2006, pp. 37–55.

28. Christopher Meyer and Andre Schwager, "Understanding Customer Experience," *Harvard Business Review,* February 2007, pp. 117–26.

29. Michael E. Porter and Claas van der Linde, "Green and Competitive Ending the Stalemate," *Harvard Business Review,* September–October 1995, pp. 120–34; Jacquelyn Ottman, "Edison Winners Show Smart Environmental Marketing," *Marketing News,* July 17, 1995,

pp. 16, 19; and Jacquelyn Ottman, "Mandate for the '90s: Green Corporate Image," *Marketing News,* September 11, 1995, p. 8.

30. Jeff Strickler, "Fran's Story," *Star Tribune,* January 17, 2009, pp. E1, E10; "What Is a Social Entrepreneur?" Schwab Foundation for Social Entrepreneurship; www.schwabfound.org/sf/Social Entrepreneurs/index.htm; Roger L. Martin and Sally Osberg, "Social Entrepreneurship: The Case for Definition," *Stanford Social Innovation Review,* Spring 2007, pp. 34–35, www.ssireview.org/ images/articles/2007SP_feature_martinosberg.pdf; Geoff Colvin, "A CEO Masters Micro-Credit," *Fortune,* January 19, 2009, p. 22; and the Hand in Hand International Web site at www.hihseed .org.

31. Philip Kotler and Sidney J. Levy, "Broadening the Concept of Marketing," *Journal of Marketing,* January 1969, pp. 10–15; and Jim Rendon, "When Nations Need a Little Marketing," *The New York Times,* November 23, 2003, p. BU6.

32. Bernard Stamler, "Temples of Culture Are Needy, Too. Tai Chi, Anyone?" *The New York Times,* April 23, 2003, p. 2.

33. Peter Gumbel, "Louvre, Inc.," *Time,* August 11, 2008, pp. 51–52.

34. William L. Wilkie and Elizabeth S. Moore, "Marketing's Relationship to Society," Chapter 1 in *Handbook of Marketing,* ed. Barton Weitz and Robin Wensley (London: Sage Publications, 2006), pp. 9–38.

3M's Post-it® Flag Highlighters: This case was written by Michael J. Vessey and William Rudelius and is based on a series of personal interviews with David Windorski and 3M from 2004 to 2010.

Chapter 2

1. Information obtained from selected Web pages and press releases from the Ben & Jerry's Web site. See www.benjerry.com.

2. "Ice Cream: Global Industry Guide," *Datamonitor,* April 27, 2010, press release posted at MarketResearch.com.

3. Roger Kerin and Robert Peterson, *Strategic Marketing Problems: Cases and Comments,* 11th ed. (Upper Saddle River, NJ: Prentice Hall, 2007), p. 141.

4. Michael E. Porter, "What Is Strategy?" *Harvard Business Review* OnPoint Article, November–December 1996, p. 2.

5. Katherine Ellison, "The Bottom Line Redefined," *Nature Conservancy,* Winter 2002, pp. 45–54.

6. For a discussion on how industries are defined and offerings are classified, see the following resources: the American Marketing Association Web site, which provides one definition of an industry (www.marketingpower.com/mg-dictionary-view1509.php); and the Census Bureau's Economic Classification Policy Committee Issues Paper #1 (www.census.gov/epcd/naics/issues1), which aggregates industries in the NAICS (www.census.gov/epcd/www/ naicsdev.htm) from a "production-oriented" view (see Chapter 6).

7. W. Chan Kim and Reneé Mauborgne, "Blue Ocean Strategy: From Theory to Practice," *California Management Review* 47, no. 3 (Spring 2005), p. 105; Porter, "What Is Strategy?" p. 2.

8. Costas Markides, "What Is Strategy and How Do You Know If You Have One?" *Business Strategy Review* 15, no. 2 (Summer 2004), p. 5.

9. The definition of *strategy* reflects thoughts appearing in Porter, "What Is Strategy?" pp. 4, 8; a condensed definition of strategy is found on the American Marketing Association Web site www .marketingpower.com; and Gerry Johnson, Kevan Scholes, and Richard Wittington, *Exploring Corporate Strategy* (Upper Saddle River, NJ: Prentice Hall, 2005), p. 10.

10. Roger A. Kerin, "Strategic Marketing and the CMO," *Journal of Marketing,* October 2005, pp. 12–13; and The CMO Council: Biographies of Selected Advisory Board Members. See www.cmocouncil .org/advisoryboard.html.

11. Roger A. Kerin, Vijay Mahajan, and P. Rajan Varadarajan, *Contemporary Perspectives on Strategic Marketing Planning* (Boston: Allyn

& Bacon, 1990), ch. 1; and Orville C. Walker, Jr., Harper W. Boyd, Jr., and Jean-Claude Larreche, *Marketing Strategy* (Burr Ridge, IL: Richard D. Irwin, 1992), chs. 1 and 2.

12. Taken in part from Jim Collins and Jerry I. Porras, *Built to Last: Successful Habits of Visionary Companies* (New York: HarperCollins Publishers, 2002), p. 54.

13. Ibid., p. 73; Patrick M. Lencioni, "Make Your Values Mean Something," *Harvard Business Review,* July 2002, p. 6; and Aubrey Malphurs, *Values-Driven Leadership: Discovering and Developing Your Core Values for Ministry,* 2nd ed. (Grand Rapids, MI: BakerBooks, 2004), p. 31.

14. Collins and Porras, *Built to Last,* p. 73; and Lencioni, "Make Your Values Mean Something," p. 6.

15. Catherine M. Dalton, "When Organizational Values Are Mere Rhetoric," *Business Horizons* 49 (September–October 2006), p. 345.

16. Collins and Porras, *Built to Last,* pp. 94–95; and Tom Krattenmaker, "Write a Mission Statement That Your Company Is Willing to Live," *Harvard Management Communication Letter,* March 2002, pp. 3–4.

17. Janet Moore, "Change of Pace," *Star Tribune,* May 23, 2010, pp. D1, D7.

18. Sheila M. J. Bonini, Lenny T. Mendonca, and Jeremy M. Oppenheim, "When Social Issues Become Strategic," *The McKinsey Quarterly,* 2006, no. 2, pp. 23, 25, 30–31.

19. Kenneth E. Goodpaster and Thomas E. Holloran, "Anatomy of Spiritual and Social Awareness: The Case of Medtronic, Inc.," *Third International Symposium on Catholic Social Thought and Management Education,* Goa, India, 1999, pp. 9–11.

20. Theodore Levitt, "Marketing Myopia," *Harvard Business Review,* July–August 1960, pp. 45–56.

21. David Phelps, "Debt Threat," *Star Tribune,* January 26, 2009, pp. D1, D6.

22. Jeffrey A. Trachtenberg, "E-Books Rewrite Bookselling," *The Wall Street Journal,* May 21, 2010, pp. A1, A12.

23. Alyssa Abkowitz, "The Movie Man," *Fortune,* February 2, 2009, p. 24; David Pogue, "Any Movie, Any Time," *Star Tribune,* February 4, 2009, p. D6; and Nick Wingfield, "Netflix Boss Plots Life after the DVD," *The Wall Street Journal,* June 23, 2009, pp. A1, A12.

24. The definition is adapted from Stephen Few, *Information Dashboard Design: The Effective Visual Communication of Data* (Sebastopol, CA: O'Reilly Media, Inc., 2006), pp. 2–46.

25. Koen Pauwels et al., *Dashboards & Marketing: Why, What, How and What Research Is Needed?* (Hanover, NH: Tuck School, Dartmouth, May 2008).

26. Few, *Information Dashboard Design;* Bruce H. Clark, Andrew V. Abela, and Tim Ambler, "Behind the Wheel," *Marketing Management,* May–June 2006, pp. 19–23; Spencer E. Ante, "Giving the Boss the Big Picture," *BusinessWeek,* February 13, 2006, pp. 48-49; *Dashboard Tutorial* (Cupertino, CA: Apple Computer, Inc., 2006).

27. Few, *Information Dashboard Design,* p. 13.

28. Michael Krauss, "Balance Attention to Metrics with Intuition," *Marketing News,* June 1, 2007, pp. 6–8; John Davis, *Measuring Marketing: 103 Key Metrics Every Marketer Needs* (Singapore: John Wiley & Sons (Asia) Pte Ltd., 2007); Paul W. Farris, Neil T. Bendle, Phillip E. Pfeifer, and David J. Reibstein, *Marketing Metrics* (Upper Saddle River, NJ: Wharton School Publishing, 2006); and Marcel Corstjens and Jeffrey Merrihue, "Optimal Marketing," *Harvard Business Review,* October 2003, pp. 114–121.

29. Jacques Bughin, Amy Guggenheim Shenkan, and Mark Singer, "How Poor Metrics Undermine Digital Marketing," *The McKinsey Quarterly,* October 2008.

30. The now-classic reference on effective graphic presentation is Edward R. Tufte, *The Visual Display of Quantitative Information,* 2nd Edition (Cheshire, CN: Graphic Press, 2001); also see Few, *Information Dashboard Design,* Chaps. 3–5.

31. George Stalk, Phillip Evans, and Lawrence E. Shulman, "Competing on Capabilities: The New Rules of Corporate Strategy," *Harvard Business Review,* March–April 1992, pp. 57–69; and Darrell K. Rigby, *Management Tools 2007: An Executive's Guide* (Boston: Bain & Company, 2007), p. 22.

32. Michael Arndt, "High-Tech and Handcrafted," *BusinessWeek,* July 5, 2004, pp. 86–87.

33. Kerin and Peterson, *Strategic Marketing Problems,* pp. 2–3; and Derek F. Abell, *Defining the Business* (Englewood Cliffs, NJ: Prentice Hall, 1980), p. 18.

34. Robert D. Hof, "How to Hit a Moving Target," *BusinessWeek,* August 21, 2006, p. 3; and Peter Kim, *Reinventing the Marketing Organization* (Cambridge, MA: Forrester, July 13, 2006), pp. 7, 9, and 17.

35. Adapted from *The Experience Curve Reviewed, IV. The Growth Share Matrix of the Product Portfolio* (Boston: The Boston Consulting Group, 1973).

36. Kerin, Mahajan, and Vardarajan, *Contemporary Perspectives,* p. 52.

37. Jim Collins, "How Great Companies Turn Crisis into Opportunity," *Fortune,* February 2, 2009, pp. 49–52.

38. Mike Pasini, "Samsung Up, Kodak Holds On in Digicams," *Imaging Resource,* April 7, 2008; Nick Passmore, "Refocusing on Digital Cameras," *BusinessWeek,* June 4, 2008; Mike Pasini, "CIPA Releases 2009–2011 Camera Shipment Forecast," *Imaging Resource,* January 27, 2009; "Kodak Institutional Investor Meeting," February 4, 2009, pp. 9, 15, 21–22, 64, 74.

39. "Digital Photo Frames Market Driven by Gift-Giving Status," *In-Stat,* August 17, 2009; see http://www.instat.com/press .asp?ID=2593&sku=IN0904506ID.

40. Karen M. Cheung, "InfoTrends: Online Printing to Double by 2011," *DigitalCameraInfo.com,* August 13, 2007; Jefferson Graham, "Kodak Plans to Sell Inkjet Printers with Cheaper Ink," *USA Today,* February 6, 2007, p. 51; Simon Burns, "Printer Market Shows Steady Growth," VNUNET.com, September 19, 2007; Matthew Daneman, "Home Inkjet Printer Bright Spot for Kodak," *Democrat and Chronicle,* January 31, 2009; Ben Furfie, "Sector Guide: Inkjet/MFD Printers," *PC Retail,* January 8, 2009; Jennifer Nelson, "InfoTrends: Online Photo Printing Market Needs Innovation," *DigitalCameraInfo.com,* February 1, 2008; "Kodak Institutional Investor Meeting," February 4, 2009, pp. 10, 15, 22, 38, 40–41, 64, 74; and Dana Mattioli, "Kodak Chief Perez Plans to Curtail Patent Lawsuits," *The Wall Street Journal,* June 25, 2010, p. B1.

41. Melissa Korn, "Kodak Posts Profits as Settlement Helps Offset Consumer Weakness," *The Wall Street Journal,* April 30, 2010, p. B4; Matthew Daneman, "Kodak Clings to Film," *Democrat and Chronicle,* January 4, 2009; "Kodak Institutional Investor Meeting," February 4, 2009, pp. 9, 21, 64, 74; and Robert Tomsho, "Kodak to Take Kodachrome Away," *The Wall Street Journal,* June 23, 2009, pp. B1, B6.

42. Strengths and weaknesses of the BCG technique are based on Derek F. Abell and John S. Hammond, *Strategic Market Planning: Problem and Analytic Approaches* (Englewood Cliffs, NJ: Prentice Hall, 1979); Yoram Wind, Vijay Mahajan, and Donald Swire, "An Empirical Comparison of Standardized Portfolio Models," *Journal of Marketing,* Spring 1983, pp. 89–99; and J. Scott Armstrong and Roderick J. Brodie, "Effects of Portfolio Planning Methods on Decision Making: Experimental Results," *International Journal of Research in Marketing,* Winter 1994, pp. 73–84.

43. H. Igor Ansoff, "Strategies for Diversification," *Harvard Business Review,* September–October 1957, pp. 113–24.

44. Joanna Peot, "Sweet Success," *Dairy Foods,* November 1, 2008.

45. Linda Swenson and Kenneth E. Goodpaster, *Medtronic in China (A)* (Minneapolis, MN: University of St. Thomas, 1999), pp. 4–5.

46. Ben Dobbin, "Recession-Hit Kodak Outlines New Strategy," *BusinessWeek,* February 4, 2009; Meg Tirrell, "Kodak to Cut up to 4,500 Jobs, Restructure, Has Loss (Update 5)," *Bloomberg.com,* February 16, 2009; "Kodak Institutional Investor Meeting," February 4, 2009, pp. 6–8, 17–18, 21, 63; Josh Quittner, "Meet the Bitty Viddies," *Time,* December 15, 2008, p. 56; "Kodak Explodes onto the Pocket Video Camera Scene," Kodak press release, July 10, 2008; and "Rugged New Kodak Digital Video Camera Enables On-the-Go HD Video Capture," January 8, 2009, Kodak press release.

47. "Kodak Institutional Investor Meeting," February 4, 2009, pp. 56, 61.

General Mills Warm Delights: This case was prepared by David Ford based on interviews with Vivian Milroy Callaway.

Appendix A

1. Personal interview with Arthur R. Kydd, St. Croix Management Group.

2. Examples of guides to writing marketing plans include William A. Cohen, *The Marketing Plan,* 5th ed. (New York: Wiley and Sons, 2006); and Roman G. Hiebing, Jr., and Scott W. Cooper, *The Successful Marketing Plan: A Disciplined and Comprehensive Approach* (New York: McGraw-Hill, 2008).

3. Examples of guides to writing business plans include Rhonda Abrams, *Business Plan in a Day* (Palo Alto, CA: The Planning Shop, a Division of Rhonda, Inc., 2009); Rhonda Abrams, *The Successful Business Plan: Secrets & Strategies,* 4th ed. (Grants Pass, OR: Oasis Press/PSI Research, 2003); Joseph A. Covello and Brian J. Hazelgren, *The Complete Book of Business Plans,* 2nd ed. (Naperville, IL: Sourcebooks, 2006); Joseph A. Covello and Brian J. Hazelgren, *Your First Business Plan,* 5th ed. (Naperville IL: Sourcebooks, 2005); and Mike McKeever, *How to Write a Business Plan,* 8th ed. (Berkeley, CA: Nolo, 2007).

4. Abrams, *The Successful Business Plan,* p. 35.

5. Some of these points are adapted from Abrams, *The Successful Business Plan,* pp. 35–43; others are adapted from William Rudelius, *Guidelines for Technical Report Writing* (Minneapolis: University of Minnesota, undated). See also William Strunk, Jr., and E. B. White, *The Elements of Style,* 4th ed. (Needham Heights, MA: Allyn & Bacon, 2000).

6. Rebecca Zimoch, "The Dawn of the Frozen Age," *Grocery Headquarters,* December 2002; see www.groceryheadquarters.com.

7. ACNielsen Strategic Planner as reported to the National Frozen & Refrigerated Foods Association for the week ending February 24, 2007; see www.nfraweb.org.

8. Chuck Van Hyning, *NPD's National Eating Trends;* see www.npd foodworld.com

9. Jeffrey M. Humphreys, "The Multicultural Economy 2009," *Georgia Business and Economic Conditions* vol. 69, no. 3 (Third Quarter, 2009), pp. 1–13.

Chapter 3

1. Erin Biba, "The GPS Revolution," *Wired,* February 2009, pp. 64–69; Mathew Honan, "I Am Here," *Wired,* February 2009, pp. 70–75; Arundhati Parmar, "On the Map," *Marketing News,* February 15, 2008, p. 12; and Graham Kelly, "The GPS Revolution," ezinearticles.com, February 7, 2009.

2. "Breakthrough Ideas for 2009," *Harvard Business Review,* February 2009, pp. 19–40; Elisabeth A. Sullivan, "We Were Right!" *Marketing News,* December 15, 2008, p. 16; Gordon A. Wyner, "Out of Control: Beware of the Forces of Economic, Technological, and Population Change," *Marketing Management,* p. 8; Elisabeth A. Sullivan, "2008 Is the Year That Social Marketing Will Reach Critical Mass," *Marketing News,* January 15, 2008, p. 12; Nikki Hopewell, "The

Rules of Engagement," *Marketing News*, June 1, 2008, p. 6; "A Quarter-Century of Changes," *USA Today*, March 26, 2007, p. 8B; and "Social Networking, User-Generated Content and Green Technology Are Top Trends for 2007," *Wireless News*, January 21, 2007.

3. *2009 World Population Data Sheet* (Washington, DC: Population Reference Bureau, 2009), pp. 2, 8.

4. "Gross National Income per Capita 2008," *World Development Indicators Database* (Washington, DC: World Bank, October 17, 2008); and *World Population Prospects: The 2006 Revision* (Geneva: United Nations, Department of Economic and Social Affairs, 2007), Table I.1, p. 1.

5. "Projections of the Population and Components of Change for the United States," U.S. Census Bureau, Table 1, August 14, 2008; "Projections of the Population by Selected Age Groups and Sex for the United States," U.S. Census Bureau, Table 2, August 14, 2008; Lawrence A. Crosby, Sheree L. Johnson, and John Carroll III, "When We're 64," *Marketing Management*, December 2006, p. 14; and Bradley J. Fikes, "Jitterbug Phone Maker Dials into $38M," *North County Times*, June 25, 2008.

6. Emily Brandon, "10 Things You Didn't Know About Baby Boomers," USNews.com, January 15, 2009; Harry Maurer and Cristina Linblad, "Not-So-Golden Years," *BusinessWeek*, July 14, 2008, p. 8; and Christopher Musico, "The Boomer Boom," *CRM Magazine*, November 1, 2008, p. 34.

7. "New Hyatt Place Will Have No Front Desk," *Grand Rapids Press*, June 25, 2008, p. C1; Kimberly Palmer, "Gen X-ers: Stingy or Strapped?" USNews.com, February 14, 2007; Paul J. Lim, "Baby Boomers Outpace Gen X-ers," USNews.com, March 12, 2007; and Megan Rowe, "Marketing to Gen X," Financial & Insurance Meetings, July 1, 2006, p. 19.

8. Geoff Gloeckler, "Here Come the Millennials," *BusinessWeek*, November 24, 2008, p. 47; Sarah Littman, "Welcome to the New Millennials," *Response*, May 1, 2008, p. 74; "The Echo Boom Gets Louder," *Multi-Housing News*, December 4, 2008; Eileen P. Gunn, "Is Your Company Really Eco-Conscious?" USNews.com, October 9, 2008; "Welcome Generation Y," *Management Today*, July 10, 2008; Eileen P. Gunn, "10 Hot Green Careers for You," USNews.com, February 15, 2009; Sharon Jayson, "The Goal: Wealth and Fame, but 'the Good Life' Could Elude Gen Y," *USA Today*, January 10, 2007, p. 1D; Sharon Jayson, "Gen Y Makes a Mark: Their Imprint Is Entrepreneurship," *USA Today*, December 7, 2006, p. 1D; "Millennial Moral," *BusinessWeek*, November 6, 2006, p. 13; and Richard H. Levey, "Gen Y Phones It In," *Direct*, September 1, 2006, p. 18.

9. Robert Bernstein, "Utah Is Fastest-Growing State" (*U.S. Census Bureau News*, December 22, 2008); and Robert Bernstein, "Census Bureau Announces Most Populous Cities," *U.S. Census Bureau News*, June 28, 2007.

10. "Update of Statistical Area Definitions and Guidance on Their Use," Office Management and Budget, *OMB Bulletin* No. 08–01, November 20, 2007; Joshua Bolten, "Update of Statistical Area Definitions and Additional Guidance on Their Use," Office of Management and Budget, *OMB Bulletin* No. 04–03, February 18, 2004; and "About Metropolitan and Micropolitan Statistical Areas," U.S. Census Bureau, www.census.gov/population/www/estimates/aboutmetro.html.

11. Table 3: Annual Estimates of the Population by Sex, Race, and Hispanic Origin, (NC-EST2007-03), Population Division, U.S. Census Bureau, May 1, 2008; and "Mapping Census 2000: The Geography of U.S. Diversity," Population Division, U.S. Census Bureau.

12. Andrew Pierce, "Multiculti Markets Demand Multilayered Marketing," *Marketing News*, May 1, 2008, p. 21; "Buying Power," *Catalyst*, May 14, 2008; and Robert Bernstein, "Census Bureau Releases Population Estimates by Race," *U.S. Census Bureau News*, August 4, 2006.

13. "Despite Economic Crisis, Consumers Value Brands' Commitment to Social Purpose," PR Newswire, November 17, 2008; John Carey and

Michael Arndt, "Hugging the Tree-Huggers: Why So Many Companies Are Suddenly Linking Up with Eco Groups," *BusinessWeek*, March 12, 2007, p. 66; and David Kiley, "Toyota: How the Hybrid Race Went to the Swift," *BusinessWeek*, January 29, 2007, p. 58.

14. "College Cost in U.S. Hitting High Note," *UPI*, December 3, 2008; and "Losing Ground: A National Status Report on the Affordability of American Higher Education," The National Center for Public Policy and Higher Education, p. 2.

15. James C. Cooper, "This Recession Could Be Mild but Long," *BusinessWeek*, October 20, 2008, p. 12; and "The 2008 Economy in Recession," USNews.com, February 5, 2009.

16. Carmen Donavan-Walt, Bernadette D. Proctor, and Jessica C. Smith, "Income, Poverty and Health Insurance Coverage in the United States: 2008," *Current Population Reports* (Washington, DC: U.S. Census Bureau, September 2009), p. 29.

17. Mark Trumbull, "In Tough Times, U.S. Consumers Forging New Behaviors," *Christian Science Monitor*, February 3, 2009, p. 25.

18. "Consumer Expenditure Survey: 2007," U.S. Department of Labor, Bureau of Labor Statistics, November 28, 2008, Table 3; Kara McGuire, "Saving Back in Vogue," *Chattanooga Times Free Press*, February 4, 2009, p. C3; and Peter Coy, "Investment Outlook 2009," *BusinessWeek*, December 29, 2008, p. 34.

19. "SMEs Going Global: Eight Technology Trends," *The Edge Malaysia*, September 22, 2008; Steve Hamm, "Cheap Tech for Hard Times," *BusinessWeek*, November 24, 2008, p. 36; David Largesse, "5 Ways to Recharge Gadgets without Plugging In," USNews.com, February 5, 2009; Stephen Doyle and Zack Zavala, "The Future of Food," *Wired*, March 2007, p. 188; "10 Emerging Technologies in 2008," *MIT Technology Review*, www.technologyreview.com/specialreports, accessed February 13, 2009; "Business Futures," Institute for Global Futures, www.globalfuturist.com/future-trends, accessed February 13, 2009; and The Project on Emerging Nanotechnologies, www.nanotechproject.org/inventories/consumer, accessed February 14, 2009.

20. Eric Griffith, "The Best Free Software of 2008," *PC Magazine*, January 13, 2009; and Koen Pauwels and Allen Weiss, "Moving from Free to Fee: How Online Firms Market to Change Their Business Model Successfully," *Journal of Marketing*, May 2008, pp. 14–31.

21. Steven Levy, "The New Reality," *Wired*, November 2008, p. 114; Bruce Nussbaum, "The Best Global Design of 2008," *BusinessWeek*, July 28, 2008, p. 44; and Urea Khan, "Kindle 2 Aims to Be iPod for Readers," *The Daily Telegraph*, February 10, 2009, p .10.

22. "AT&T Tries to Catch Up to Verizon," *Americas Telecommunications Insights*, December 1, 2008; Jon Fine, "Is It Better to Be a Fox or a Mouse?" *BusinessWeek*, October 27, 2008, p. 85; James M. Cypher, "Economic Consequences of Armaments Production: Institutional Perspectives of J.K. Galbraith and T.B. Veblen," *Journal of Economic Issues*, March 1, 2008, p. 37.

23. Tim Hughes, "Way out of This Crisis—Solution Lies in Deregulation, Not Renewed Regulation," *The Courier Mail*, February 7, 2009, p. 69; Adam Aston, "Sempra Energy: All Charged Up in California," *BusinessWeek*, June 11, 2007, p. 62; Aaron Pressman, "New Spark in Utility Stocks," *BusinessWeek*, June 4, 2007, p 102; Harry Maurer and Cristina Linblad, "Tackling Microsoft Again," *BusinessWeek*, January 28, 2008, p. 8.

24. "Frequently Asked Questions," Small Business Administration, Office of Advocacy, www.sba.gov/advo, September 2008.

25. "Legal Roundup," *Billboard*, January 31, 2009; and "A New Copyright Law?" *BusinessWeek*, August 3, 1998, p. 45.

26. "Highlights of Food Labeling," *Marketing News*, March 15, 2004, p. 14.

27. Dorothy Cohen, "Trademark Strategy Revisited," *Journal of Marketing*, July 1991, pp. 46–59.

28. Maxine L. Retsky, "Review Int'l Filing Process for Marks," *Marketing News*, September 29, 2003, p. 8.

29. Ben Walters, "The Guide: Cut, Copy and Paste," *The Guardian*, January 17, 2009, p. 4; Kevin Higgins, "Jeben Berg, YouTube's Creative Innovationist and an MPlanet Presenter, Explains How YouTube Inspires Consumers to Empower Themselves," *Marketing News*, November 15, 2008, p. 14; Michael Fielding, "Doppelgangers: Monitor Parodies to Measure Brand Value," *Marketing News*, October 15, 2006, pp. 13–15; and Craig J. Thompson, Aric Rindfleisch, and Zeynep Arsel, "Emotional Branding and the Strategic Value of the Doppelganger Brand Image," *Journal of Marketing*, January 2006, pp. 50–64.

30. Paul Barrett, "High Court Sees Color as Basis for Trademarks," *The Wall Street Journal*, March 29, 1995, p. A6; Paul Barrett, "Color in the Court," *The Wall Street Journal*, January 5, 1995, p. A1; and David Kelly, "Rainbow of Ideas to Trademark Color," *Advertising Age*, April 24, 1995, pp. 20, 22.

31. Maxine L. Retsky, "Dilution of Trademarks Hard to Prove," *Marketing News*, May 12, 2003, p. 6.

32. "FTC Refines CAN-SPAM Act," *Marketing News*, August 15, 2008, p. 4; "Time's Up," *Marketing News*, December 15, 2007, p. 14; D'Arcy Doran, "Internet Marketer Sues over Unwanted Spam," *Marketing News*, April 1, 2007, p .20; Allison Enright, "Cingular Moves to Protect Its Turf," *Marketing News*, November 15, 2006, p. 4; Maxine L. Retsky, "Stakes Are High for Direct Mail Sweepstakes Promotions," *Marketing News*, July 3, 2000, p. 8; Catherine Arnold, "Picky, Picky, Picky," *Marketing News*, February 15, 2004, p. 17; and Catherine Arnold, "No Can Spam," *Marketing News*, January 15, 2004, p. 3.

33. BBB Online Program Standards, http://us.bbb.org, accessed February 15, 2009.

Geek Squad: This case was written by Steven Hartley. Sources: Mary Ellen Lloyd, "Camp Teaches Power of Geekdom," *The Wall Street Journal*, July 11, 2007; Dean Foust, Michael Mandel, Frederick F. Jespersen, and David Henry, "The Business Week 50—The Best Performers," *Business-Week*, March 26, 2007, p. 58; Jessica E. Vascellaro, "What's a Cellphone For? Businesses Are Finding All Sorts of New Uses for Mobile Devices," *The Wall Street Journal*, March 26, 2007, p. R5; Cade Metz, "Just How Stupid Are You? Geek Squad War Stories," *PC Magazine*, February 1, 2006; Brad Stone, "Lore of the Geek Squad," *Newsweek*, February 20, 2006, p. 44; Michelle Conlin, "Smashing the Clock," *BusinessWeek*, December 11, 2006, p. 60; "Best Buy: How to Break Out of Commodity Hell," *BusinessWeek*, March 27, 2006, p. 76; Pallavi Gogoi, "Meet Jane Geek," *BusinessWeek*, November 28, 2005, p. 94; Desiree J. Hanford, "Geek Squad Is Popular at Best Buy," *The Wall Street Journal*, December 14, 2005, p. 1; Michelle Higgins, "Getting Your Own IT Department," *The Wall Street Journal*, May 20, 2004, p. D1; and information contained on the Geek Squad Web site (www.geeksquad.com).

Chapter 4

1. www.beeresponsible.com, accessed February 10, 2010; "America's Most Admired Companies," *Fortune*, March 22, 2010.

2. For a discussion of the definition of ethics, see Patrick E. Murphy, Gene R. Laezniak, Norman E. Bowie, and Thomas A. Klein, *Ethical Marketing: Basic Ethics in Action* (Upper Saddle River, NJ: Prentice Hall, 2005).

3. Verne E. Henderson, "The Ethical Side of Enterprise," *Sloan Management Review*, Spring 1982, pp. 37–47. See also, Joseph L. Badaracco, Jr., *Defining Moments: When Managers Must Choose between Right and Right* (Boston: Harvard Business School Press, 1997).

4. "Honorable?" *Business 2.0*, February 2000, p. 92.

5. Roger O. Crockett, "Hauling In the Hollywood Hackers," *Business-Week*, May 15, 2006, pp. 80–82; "Exporting Death," *Time*, April 13, 1998, p. 63; Ray O. Werner, "Marketing and the Supreme Court in Transition, 1982–1984," *Journal of Marketing*, Summer 1985, pp. 97–105; and Jane Bryant Quinn, "Computer Program Deceives Consumers," *Dallas Morning News*, March 2, 1998, p. B3.

6. *The 2009 National Business Ethics Survey* (Washington, DC: Ethics Resource Center, 2009); "Poll: Ad Execs Are Icky," *Advertising Age*, January 16, 2006, p. 26; and Ronald W. Clement, "Just How Ethical Is American Business?" *Business Horizons*, July–August 2006, pp. 313–27.

7. See, for example, Linda K. Trevino and Katherine A. Nelson, *Managing Business Ethics: Straight Talk about How to Get It Right* (New York: Wiley and Sons, 2007).

8. Ethisphere Institute, "2008 World's Most Ethical Companies," ethisphere.com, March 2008.

9. These statistics were obtained from the Recording Industry Association of America (riaa.com), Motion Picture Association of America (mpaa.org), and the Business Software Alliance (bsa.org).

10. "A Poor Example for Their Elders," *AdweekMedia*, February 23, 2009, p. 15.

11. Vern Terpstra and Kenneth David, *The Cultural Environment of International Business*, 3rd ed. (Cincinnati: South-Western Publishing, 1991), p. 12.

12. Hukari Kane, "Recall Shows Battery Limits," *The Wall Street Journal*, August 18, 2006, p. A13; and "Dell Announces Recall of Notebook Computer Batteries Due to Fire Hazard," U.S. Consumer Product Safety Commission Press Release, August 15, 2006.

13. Timothy Muris, "Protecting Consumers' Privacy," FTC.gov, accessed January 3, 2005.

14. For an extensive examination on slotting fees, see Paul N. Bloom, Gregory T. Gundlach, and Joseph P. Cannon, "Slotting Allowances and Fees: Schools of Thought and Views of Practicing Managers," *Journal of Marketing*, April 2000, pp. 92–109. Also see, K. Sudhir and Vithala R. Rao, "Do Slotting Allowances Enhance Efficiency or Hinder Competition?" *Journal of Marketing Research*, May 2006, pp. 137–55.

15. Hedich Nasheri, *Economic Espionage and Industrial Spying* (Cambridge, England: Cambridge University Press, 2005).

16. "Coke Employee Faces Charges in Plot to Sell Secrets," *The Wall Street Journal*, July 6, 2006, p. B6; "Do the Right Thing? Not with a Rival's Inside Info," *Advertising Age*, July 17, 2006, p. 4; and "You Can't Beat the Real Thing," *Time*, July 17, 2006, pp. 10–11.

17. www.transparency.org, accessed February 9, 2010.

18. "U.S. Firms Raise Ethics Focus," *The Wall Street Journal*, November 28, 2005, p. B4.

19. "Coca-Cola Unit Head Resigns after Rigged Test," Forbes.com, accessed August 25, 2003.

20. *The 2009 National Business Ethics Survey*.

21. "Whistleblowers: Tales from the Back Office," *The Economist*, March 25, 2006, p. 67; and C. Fred Alford, *Whistleblowers: Broken Lives and Organizational Power* (Ithaca, NY: Cornell University Press, 2002).

22. "Scotchgard Working Out Recent Stain on Its Business," Mercurynews.com, accessed June 22, 2008; "Most Minnesota Fish Sampled Don't Carry Scotchguard Chemical," Duluthnewstribune .com., May 11, 2010.

23. James O. Wilson, "Adam Smith on Business Ethics," *California Management Review*, Fall 1989, pp. 57–72.

24. Alix M. Freedman, "Bad Reaction: Nestlé's Bid to Crash Baby-Formula Market in U.S. Stirs a Row," *The Wall Street Journal*, February 16, 1989, pp. Al, A6; and Alix Freedman, "Nestlé to Drop Claim on Label of Its Formula," *The Wall Street Journal*, March 13, 1989, p. B5.

25. Harvey S. James and Farhad Rassekh, "Smith, Friedman, and Self-Interest in Ethical Society," *Business Ethics Quarterly*, July 2000, pp. 659–74.

26. "Cost of Living," *The Economist*, March 1, 2003, p. 60.

27. "Perrier—Overresponding to a Crisis," in Robert F. Hartley, *Marketing Mistakes and Successes*, 10th ed. (New York: Wiley and Sons, 2006), pp. 119–30.

28. Michael Connor, "Toyota Recall: Five Critical Lessons," business-ethics.com, January 31, 2010.

29. Andrew W. Savitz with Karl Weber, *The Triple Bottom Line: How Today's Best Run Companies Are Achieving Economic, Social and Environmental Success* (San Francisco, CA: Jossey-Bass, 2006).

30. "3M Marks 35 Years of Pollution Prevention Pays," 3M Press Release, April 22, 2010; www.xerox.com/environment, accessed January 15, 2009; Elizabeth Royte, "Corn Plastic to the Rescue?" *Smithsonian*, August 2006, pp. 84–88; and "Hugging the Tree Huggers," *BusinessWeek*, March 12, 2007, pp. 66–68.

31. For a seminal discussion on this topic, see P. Rajan Varadarajan and Anil Menon, "Cause-Related Marketing: A Coalignment of Marketing Strategy and Corporate Philanthropy," *Journal of Marketing*, July 1988, pp. 58–74.

32. "CSR Seeps into Brand DNA," *Advertising Age*, October 26, 2009, Special Section. *Past.Present.Future.: The 25th Anniversary of Cause Marketing* (Boston, MA: Cone LLC, 2008); and Larry Chiagouris and Ipshita Ray, "Saving the World with Cause-Related Marketing," *Marketing Management*, July–August 2007, pp. 48–51.

33. These steps are adapted from J. J. Carson and G. A. Steiner, *Measuring Business Social Performance: The Corporate Social Audit* (New York: Committee for Economic Development, 1974). See also Risako Morinoto, John Ash, and Chris Hope, "Corporate Social Responsibility Audit: From Theory to Practice," *Journal of Business Ethics* (December 2005), pp. 315–25; and William B. Werther, Jr., and David Chandler, *Strategic Corporate Social Responsibility* (Thousand Oaks, CA: Sage Publications, Inc., 2006).

34. "Marketers Become Own Watchdogs," *Advertising Age*, June 12, 2006, p. 57; and "Sweatshops: Finally, Airing the Dirty Linen," *BusinessWeek*, June 23, 2003, pp. 100–01.

35. Unmesh Kher, "Getting Smart at Being Good . . . Are Companies Better Off for It?" *Time*, January 2006, pp. A1–A37; and Pete Engardio, "Beyond the Green Corporation," *BusinessWeek*, January 29, 2007, pp. 50–64.

36. This discussion is based on Wayne D. Hoyer and Deborah J. MacInnis, *Consumer Behavior*, 4th ed. (New York: Houghton Mifflin Company, 2008), pp. 535–37; "Factoids," *Research Alert*, December 8, 2005, p. 5; Elizabeth Woyke, "Attention Shoplifters," *BusinessWeek*, September 11, 2006, pp. 46–50; and "Putting Return Policies to the Test," *The Wall Street Journal*, February 22, 2007, p. D3.

37. "A Pirate and his Penance," *Time*, January 26, 2004, p. 60; and Crockett, "Hauling In the Hollywood Hackers."

38. Mark Dolliver, "Deflating a Myth," *Brandweek*, May 12, 2008, pp. 30–32.

39. Kenneth Hein, "'Green' Light Bulbs Symbolize a Bad Idea," *Brandweek*, January 12, 2009, p. 38.

Starbucks Corporation: This case is based on information on the company Web site (www.starbucks.com) and the following sources: "Living Our Values," *2003 Corporate Social Responsibility Annual Report*; "Starbucks Annual Shareholder Meeting," Starbucks press release, March 30, 2004; Ranjay Gulati, Sarah Haffman, and Gary Neilson, "The Barista Principle: Starbucks and the Rise of Relational Capital," *Strategy and Business*, 3rd Quarter 2002, pp. 58–69; and Andy Serwer, "Hot Starbucks to Go," *Fortune*, January 12, 2004, pp. 52ff.

Chapter 5

1. Sheryll Alexander, "What Women Want . . . in a Car," CNN.com, March 14, 2008; Sheryll Alexander, "Women and Cars: How Women Influence Car Design and Buying Power," aol.com, March 5, 2008; and "Buying a Car Is a Hassle for Women," *BusinessWire*, September 28, 2009.

2. Roger D. Blackwell, Paul W. Miniard, and James F. Engel, *Consumer Behavior*, 10th ed. (Florence, KY: South-Western Publishing, 2006).

3. For thorough descriptions of consumer expertise, see Joseph W. Alba and J. Wesley Hutchinson, "Knowledge Calibration: What Consumers Know and What They Think They Know," *Journal of Consumer Research*, September 2000, pp. 123–57.

4. For in-depth studies on external information search patterns, see Brian T. Ratchford, Debabrata Talukdar, and Myung-Soo Lee, "The Impact of the Internet on Consumers' Use of Information Sources for Automobiles: A Re-Inquiry," *Journal of Consumer Research*, June 2007, pp. 111–19; Joel E. Urbany, Peter R. Dickson, and William L. Wilkie, "Buyer Uncertainty and Information Search," *Journal of Consumer Research*, March 1992, pp. 452–63; and Sharon E. Beatty and Scott M. Smith, "External Search Effort: An Investigation across Several Product Categories," *Journal of Consumer Research*, June 1987, pp. 83–95.

5. "Smart Phone Ratings, Ratings Overview," accessed on July 1, 2010. See http://www.consumerreports.com.

6. For an extended discussion on evaluative criteria, see Del J. Hawkins and David L. Mothersbaugh, *Consumer Behavior*, 11th ed. (New York: McGraw-Hill/Irwin, 2010).

7. John A. Howard, *Buyer Behavior in Marketing Strategy*, 2nd ed. (Englewood Cliffs, NJ: Prentice Hall, 1994). For an extended discussion on consumer choice sets, see Allan D. Shocker, Moshe Ben-Akiva, Brun Boccara, and Prakesh Nedungadi, "Consideration Set Influences on Consumer Decision Making and Choice: Issues, Models, and Suggestions," *Marketing Letters*, August 1991, pp. 181–99.

8. Robert J. Donovan, John R. Rossiter, Gillian Marcoolyn, and Andrew Nesdale, "Store Atmosphere and Purchasing Behavior," *Journal of Retailing*, Fall 1994, pp. 283–94; and Eric A. Greenleaf and Donald R. Lehman, "Reasons for Substantial Delay in Consumer Decision Making," *Journal of Consumer Research*, September 1995, pp. 186–99.

9. Sunil Gupta and Valarie Zeithaml, "Customer Metrics and Their Impact on Financial Performance," *Marketing Science*, November–December 2006, pp. 718–39.

10. These estimates given in Jagdish N. Sheth and Banwari Mitral, *Consumer Behavior*, 2nd ed. (Florence, KY: South-Western Publishing, 2003), p. 32.

11. Frederick F. Reichheld and Thomas Teal, *The Loyalty Effect* (Boston: Harvard Business School Press, 1996); "What's a Loyal Customer Worth?" *Fortune*, December 11, 1995, p. 182; and Patricia Sellers, "Keeping the Buyers You Already Have," *Fortune*, Autumn–Winter 1993, p. 57. For an in-depth examination of this topic, see Sunil Gupta and Donald R. Lehmann, *Managing Customers as Investments* (Upper Saddle River, NJ: Pearson Education, Inc., 2005).

12. For an overview of research on involvement, see John C. Mowen and Michael Minor, *Consumer Behavior: A Framework*, 5th ed. (Upper Saddle River, NJ: Prentice Hall, 2001); and Wayne D. Hoyer and Deborah J. MacInnis, *Consumer Behavior*, 5th ed. (Florence, KY: South-Western Education Publishing, 2009).

13. Russell Belk, "Situational Variables and Consumer Behavior," *Journal of Consumer Research*, December 1975, pp. 157–63. The examples are found in Martin Lindstrom, *Buy.ology: Truth and Lies about Why We Buy* (New York: Doubleday Publishing, 2008).

14. A. H. Maslow, *Motivation and Personality* (New York: Harper & Row, 1970). Also see Richard Yalch and Frederic Brunel, "Need Hierarchies in Consumer Judgments of Product Design: Is It Time to Reconsider Maslow's Hierarchy?" in Kim Corfman and John Lynch

eds., *Advances in Consumer Research* (Provo, UT: Association for Consumer Research, 1996), pp. 405–10.

15. Joel B. Cohen, "An Interpersonal Orientation to the Study of Consumer Behavior," *Journal of Marketing Research*, August 1967, pp. 270–78; and Rena Bartos, *Marketing to Women around the World* (Cambridge, MA: Harvard Business School, 1989).

16. Jane Spencer, "Lenovo Puts Style in New Laptop," *The Wall Street Journal*, January 3, 2008, p. B5.

17. This example provided in Michael R. Solomon, *Consumer Behavior*, 4th ed. (Upper Saddle River, NJ: Prentice Hall, 1999), p. 59.

18. For further reading on subliminal perception, see Lindstrom, *Buy .ology*; B. Bahrami, N. Lavie, and G. Rees, "Attentional Load Modulates Responses of Human Primary Visual Cortex to Invisible Stimuli," *Current Biology*, March 2007, pp. 39–47; J. Karremans, W. Stroebe, and J. Claus, "Beyond Vicary's Fantasies: The Impact of Subliminal Priming and Brand Choice," *Journal of Experimental Social Psychology* 42 (2006), pp. 792–98; Dennis L. Rosen and Surendra N. Singh, "An Investigation of Subliminal Embedded Effect on Multiple Measures of Advertising Effectiveness," *Psychology & Marketing*, March–April 1992, pp. 157–73; and Kathryn T. Theus, "Subliminal Advertising and the Psychology of Processing Unconscious Stimuli: A Review of the Research," *Psychology & Marketing*, May–June 1994, pp. 271–90.

19. August Bullock, *The Secret Sales Pitch* (San Jose, CA: Norwich Publishers, 2004); E. Parpis, "Sex, Crackers and Subliminal Ads," *Adweek*, March 31, 2003, p. 18; "GOP Commercial Resurrects Debate on Subliminal Ads," *The Wall Street Journal*, September 13, 2000, p. B10; and "I Will Love This Story," *U.S. News & World Report*, May 12, 1997, p. 12.

20. Sholnn Freeman, "Brand Breakdown," *The Washington Post*, March 26, 2006, p. F1ff.

21. Martin Fishbein and I. Aizen, *Belief, Attitude, Intention and Behavior: An Introduction to Theory and Research* (Reading, MA: Addison-Wesley 1975), p. 6.

22. Richard J. Lutz, "Changing Brand Attitudes through Modification of Cognitive Structure," *Journal of Consumer Research*, March 1975, pp. 49–59.

23. "About VALS," www.strategicbusinessinsights.com, accessed March 1, 2010.

24. This discussion is based on Ed Keller and Jon Berry, *The Influentials* (New York: Simon and Schuster, 2003).

25. "Word of Mouth Is Where It's At," *Brandweek*, June 2, 2003, p. 26. Also, "Conversation Starter," *Brandweek*, April 12, 2010, p. 16.

26. BzzAgent.com, accessed February 25, 2010; and Matthew Creamer, "BzzAgent Seeks to Turn Word of Mouth into a Saleable Medium," *Advertising Age*, February13, 2006, p. 12.

27. For an extensive review on consumer socialization of children, see Deborah Roedder John, "Consumer Socialization of Children: A Retrospective Look at Twenty-Five Years of Research," *Journal of Consumer Research*, December 1999, pp. 183–213. Also see, Gwen Bachmann Achenreiner and Deborah Roedder John, "The Meaning of Brand Names to Children: A Developmental Investigation," *Journal of Consumer Psychology* 13, no. 3 (2003), pp. 205–19; and Elizabeth S. Moore, William L. Wilkie, and Richard J. Lutz, "Passing the Torch: Intergenerational Influences as a Source of Brand Equity," *Journal of Marketing*, April 2002, pp. 17–37.

28. J. Paul Peter and Jerry C. Olson, *Consumer Behavior and Marketing Strategy*, 8th ed. (New York: McGraw-Hill/Irwin, 2008). Also see, Rex Y. Du and Wagner A. Kamakura, "Household Life Cycles and Lifestyles in the United States," *Journal of Marketing Research*, February 2006, pp. 121–32.

29. This discussion is based on Hawkins and Mothersbaugh, *Consumer Behavior: Building Marketing Strategy*; Marissa Miley and Ann Mack, "The Rise of the Real Mom," *Advertising Age*, Novemeber 16, 2009, Special Section; "Dad Also Is Pulling the Purse Strings," *Brandweek* September 15, 2008, p. 19; *The Kids and Tweens Market*

in the U.S., 9th ed. (Rockville, MD: Packaged Facts, August 1, 2008); and "Teens Rule," MediaBuyer.com, accessed April 7, 2007.

30. Jeffrey M. Humphreys, "The Multicultural Economy in 2009," Selig Center for Economic Growth, Terry College of Business, The University of Georgia, accessed February 14, 2010.

31. The remainder of this discussion is based on Hoyer and MacInnis, *Consumer Behavior*; Richard Westerlund, "Marketing to Hispanics," *Brandweek*, November 30, 2009, Special Section; "Special Report: Hispanic Media," *Advertising Age*, January 30, 2008, p. S–6; and "Hispanics Wanted," *Brandweek*, April 12, 2004, p. 22.

32. The remainder of this discussion is based on Peter and Olson, *Consumer Behavior and Marketing Strategy*; Todd Wasserman, "Report Shows a Shifting African-American Population," *Brandweek*, January 11, 2010, p. 6; and Marissa Miley, "Don't Bypass African-Americans," *Advertising Age*, February 2, 2009, pp. 2, 3.

33. The remainder of this discussion is based on Hawkins and Mothersbaugh, *Consumer Behavior: Building Marketing Strategy*; and "Marketing to Asian-Americans," *Brandweek*, May 26, 2008, Special Section.

Best Buy: This case was written by David P. Brennan of the University of St. Thomas and is based on interviews with Joe Brandt, Best Buy employees and customers, and materials supplied by Best Buy.

Chapter 6

1. Interview with Kim Nagele, JCP Media, February 10, 2010.

2. John Paterson, "Evolution, Innovation Are Constants," *Purchasing*, September 7, 2006, p. 55.

3. Figures reported in this discussion are found in *Statistical Abstract of the United States: 2010*, 129th ed. (Washington, DC: U.S. Census Bureau, 2010).

4. "Lockheed Wins Major Spacecraft Job," *The Wall Street Journal*, September 1, 2006, p. A3; and "Lockheed Martin Readies Historic Operations & Checkout Facility for New Orion Spacecraft Integration Work," Lockheed Martin press release, January 27, 2009.

5. *2002 NAICS United States Manual* (Washington, DC: Office of Management and Budget, 2002).

6. This listing and portions of the following discussion are based on F. Robert Dwyer and John F. Tanner, Jr., *Business Marketing*, 4th ed. (New York: McGraw-Hill/Irwin, 2009); Michael D. Hutt and Thomas W. Speh, *Business Marketing Management*, international edition (Mason, OH: South-Western, 2009); and Frank G. Bingham, Jr., Roger Gomes, and Patricia A. Knowles, *Business Marketing*, 3rd ed. (New York: McGraw-Hill/Irwin, 2006).

7. "Siemens Awarded $28 Million Contract for JetBlue Airways' Baggage Handling System with Integrated Security," Siemens USA press release, July 12, 2006.

8. Adrienne Sieko, "The Business Case for Diversity," www.industryweek.com, accessed September 1, 2008.

9. www.pg.com, accessed May 10, 2010.

10. "Boise Cascade Turns Green," *The Wall Street Journal*, September 3, 2003, p. B6. Also see Minette E. Drumwright, "Socially Responsible Organizational Buying: Environmental Concern as a Noneconomic Buying Criterion," *Journal of Marketing*, July 1994, pp. 1–18.

11. This example is found in Sandy D. Jap and Jakki J. Mohr, "Leveraging Internet Technologies in B2B Relationships," *California Management Review*, Summer 2002, pp. 24–38.

12. "America's Most Admired Companies," *Fortune*, March 8, 2008, pp. 80ff; Traci Parum, "Harley-Davidson: Earning Accolades, Posting Profits," www.industryweek.com, November 17, 2005; Brian Milligan, "Medal of Excellence: Harley-Davidson Wins by Getting Suppliers on Board," *Purchasing*, September 2000, pp. 52–65; and "Harley-Davidson Company," *Purchasing Magazine Online*, September 4, 2003.

13. "The Smartest Machines on Earth," *Fortune*, September 28, 2006, pp. 129–36.

14. "The Kraft/EDS Outsourcing Deal: One Year After," EDS news release, June 12, 2007; and "HP Finalizes $3 Billion Outsourcing Agreement to Manage Procter & Gamble's IT Infrastructure," Hewlett-Packard news release, May 6, 2003.

15. This discussion is based on James C. Anderson, James A. Narus, and Das Narayandas, *Business Market Management*, 3rd ed. (Upper Saddle River, NJ: Prentice Hall, 2009); and Jeffrey K. Liker and Thomas Y. Choi, "Building Deep Supplier Relationships," *Harvard Business Review*, December 2004, pp. 104–13.

16. Helen Walker and Wendy Phillips, "Sustainable Procurement: Emerging Issues," *International Journal of Procurement Management* 2, no. 1 (2009), pp. 41–61.

17. Thomas V. Bonoma, "Major Sales: Who Really Does the Buying?" *Harvard Business Review,* May–June 1982, pp. 11–19. For recent research on buying centers, see Morry Ghingold and David T. Wilson, "Buying Center Research and Business Marketing Practices: Meeting the Challenge of Dynamic Marketing," *Journal of Business & Industrial Marketing* 13, no. 2 (1998), pp. 96–108; Philip L. Dawes, Don Y. Lee, and Grahame R. Dowling, "Information Control and Influence in Emerging Buying Centers," *Journal of Marketing,* July 1998, pp. 55–68; and Thomas Tellefsen, "Antecedents and Consequences of Buying Center Leadership: An Emergent Perspective," *Journal of Business-to-Business Marketing,* 13, no. 1 (2006), pp. 53–59.

18. Allison Enright, "It Takes a Committee to Buy into B-to-B," *Marketing News,* February 15, 2006, pp. 11–13. For academic research on roles in buying centers, see R. Vekatesh, Ajay Kohli, and Gerald Zaltman, "Influence Strategies in Buying Centers," *Journal of Marketing,* October 1995, pp. 61–72; Gary L. Lilien and Anthony Wong, "An Exploratory Investigation of the Structure of the Buying Center in the Metal Working Industry," *Journal of Marketing Research,* February 1984, pp. 1–11; and Wesley J. Johnston and Thomas V. Bonoma, "The Buying Center: Structure and Interaction Patterns," *Journal of Marketing,* Summer 1981, pp. 143–56. Also see Christopher P. Puto, Wesley E. Patton III, and Ronald H. King, "Risk Handling Strategies in Industrial Vendor Selection Decisions," *Journal of Marketing,* Winter 1985, pp. 89–98.

19. These definitions are adapted from Frederick E. Webster, Jr., and Yoram Wind, *Organizational Buying Behavior* (Englewood Cliffs, NJ: Prentice Hall, 1972), p. 6.

20. Representative studies on the buy-class framework that document its usefulness include Erin Anderson, Wujin Chu, and Barton Weitz, "Industrial Purchasing: An Empirical Exploration of the Buy-Class Framework," *Journal of Marketing*, July 1987, pp. 71–86; P. Matthyssens and W. Faes, "OEM Buying Process for New Components: Purchasing and Marketing Implications," *Industry Marketing Management*, August 1985, pp. 145–57; and Thomas W. Leigh and Arno J. Ethans, "A Script-Theoretic Analysis of Industrial Purchasing Behavior," *Journal of Marketing*, Fall 1984, pp. 22–32. Studies not supporting the buy-class framework include Joseph A. Bellizi and Philip McVey, "How Valid is the Buy-Grid Model?" *Industrial Marketing Management*, February 1983, pp. 57–62; Donald W. Jackson, Janet E. Keith, and Richard K. Burdick, "Purchasing Agents' Perceptions of Industrial Buying Center Influences: A Situational Approach," *Journal of Marketing*, Fall 1984, pp. 75–83; R. Vekatesh, Ajay Kohli, and Gerald Zaltman, "Influence Strategies in Buying Centers," *Journal of Marketing*, October 1995, pp. 61–72; Gary L. Lilien and Anthony Wong, "An Exploratory Investigation of the Structure of the Buying Center in the Metal Working Industry," *Journal of Marketing Research*, February 1984, pp. 1–11; and Wesley J. Johnston and Thomas V. Bonoma, "The Buying Center: Structure and Interaction Patterns," *Journal of Marketing*, Summer 1981, pp. 143–56.

21. "Can Corning Find Its Optic Nerve?" *Fortune*, March 19, 2001, pp. 148–50.

22. "B2B E-Commerrce Headed for Trillions," www.clickz.com, downloaded January 5, 2009.

23. This discussion is based on "B2B, Take 2," *BusinessWeek Online*, November 25, 2005; Jennifer Reinhold, "What We Learned in the New Economy," *Fast Company*, March 4, 2004, pp. 56ff; Mark Roberti, "General Electric's Spin Machine," *The Industry Standard*, January 22–29, 2001, pp. 74–83; "Grainger Lightens Its Digital Load," *Industrial Distribution*, March 2001, pp .77–79; and www.boeing.com/procurement, accessed March 10, 2007.

24. "B2B, Take 2," *BusinessWeek Online*, November 25, 2005.

25. "Former Ebay CEO Urges Action on Small Business," Washingtonpost.com, June 11, 2008; "New Study Reveals 724,000 Americans Rely on eBay Sales for Income," eBay press release, July 21, 2005; Robyn Greenspan, "Net Drives Profits to Small Biz," www.clickz.com, accessed March 25, 2006; Michael Krauss, "EBay 'Bids' on Small-Biz Firms to Sustain Growth," *Marketing News*, December 8, 2003, pp. 6, 7; "Ebay Realizes Success in Small-Biz Arena," *Marketing News*, May 1, 2004, p. 11; and www.ebaybusiness.com.

26. www.agentrics.com, accessed March 15, 2010.

27. www.ghx.com, accessed March 15, 2010.

28. This discussion is based on Robert J. Dolan and Youngme Moon, "Pricing and Market Making on the Internet," *Journal of Interactive Marketing*, Spring 2000, pp. 56–73; and Ajit Kambil and Eric van Heck, *Making Markets: How Firms Can Benefit from Online Auctions and Exchanges* (Boston: Harvard Business School Press, 2002).

29. Susan Avery, "Supply Management Is Core of Success at UTF," *Purchasing*, September 7, 2006, pp. 36–39.

Lands' End: This case is based on information available at www.landsend.com and the following sources: Robert Berner, "A Hard Bargain at Lands' End?" *BusinessWeek*, May 28, 2001, p. 14; Rebecca Quick, "Getting the Right Fit—Hips and All—Can a Machine Measure You Better Than Your Tailor?" *The Wall Street Journal*, October 18, 2000, p. B1; Stephanie Miles, "Apparel E-tailers Spruce Up for Holidays," *The Wall Street Journal*, November 6, 2001, p. B6; and Dana James, "Custom Goods Nice Means for Lands' End," *Marketing News*, August 14, 2000, p. 5.

Chapter 7

1. "Dell Unveils New Computers Targeting Emerging Markets," *Marketing News*, September 15, 2008, p. 32; "Dell Wants to Sell Emerging Consumers Their First PC," Reuters.com, September 23, 2008; "Dell Plans to Up Focus on India Biz," AdAge.com, October 24, 2008; and "Dell Upbeat about India, Sees Faster Growth Here Than China," economicstimes.indiatimes.com, March 24, 2010.

2. Dennis R. Appleyard and Alfred J. Field, Jr. and Steven Cobb, *International Economics,* 6th ed. (New York: McGraw-Hill/Irwin, 2008), chapter 15; Tansa Mesa, "Africa and Caribbean Fear EU Latam Banana Tariff Cuts," *International Herald Tribune*, August 26, 2008, p. 8; Yuri Kngeyama, "Selling Rice to Japan? U.S. Plans to Try," msnbc.com, March 7, 2004; "Shot in the Foot," *The Wall Street Journal.* September 6–7, 2008, p. A10; and *Economic Report of the President* (Washington, DC: U.S. Government Printing Office, 2009).

3. This discussion is based on information provided by the World Trade Organization, www.wto.org, downloaded March 10, 2010.

4. This discussion on the European Union is based on information provided at www.europa.eu, downloaded March 12, 2010.

5. This discussion is based on *Probable Effect of Certain Modifications to the North American Free Trade Agreement Rules of Origin* (Washington, DC: U.S. International Trade Commission, 2006); and Michael Fielding, "CAFTA-DR to Build Options Over Time," *Marketing News,* February 1, 2006, pp. 13–14.

6. For an overview of different types of global companies and marketing strategies, see, for example, Massaki Kotabe and Kristiaan Helsen,

Global Marketing Management, 4th ed. (New York: Wiley and Sons, 2008), p. 221; Warren J. Keegan and Mark C. Green, *Global Marketing*, 4th ed. (Upper Saddle River, NJ: Prentice Hall, 2005); and Michael Czinkota and Ilka A. Ronkainen, *International Marketing*, 8th ed. (Mason, OH: South-Western Publishing, 2007).

7. Johnny K. Johansson and Ilkka A. Ronkainen, "The Brand Challenge," *Marketing Management*, March–April 2004, pp. 54–55.

8. Michael Fielding, "Global Brands Need Balance of Identity, Cultural Respect," *Marketing News*, September 1, 2006, pp. 8–10; and Kevin Lane Keller, *Strategic Brand Management*, 3rd ed. (Upper Saddle River, NJ: Prentice Hall, 2008), pp. 602–603.

9. "Burgeoning Bourgeoise," *The Economist*, February 14, 2009, Special Section; "Coca-Cola, Nike and Adidas Top Brands for Teens Globally," www.teenresearch.com, March 2, 2009; D. Kjeldgaard and S. Askegaard, "The Globalization of Youth Culture: The Global Youth Segment as Structures of Common Difference," *Journal of Consumer Research*, September 2006, pp. 231–47; www.mtv.com/company, downloaded January 10, 2010; Elissa Moses, *The $100 Billion Allowance: Accessing the Global Teen Market* (New York: Wiley, 2000); and Bay Fong, "Spending Spree," *U.S. News & World Report*, May 1, 2006, pp. 42–50.

10. For comprehensive references on cross-cultural aspects of marketing, see Paul A. Herbig, *Handbook of Cross-Cultural Marketing* (New York: Halworth Press, 1998); Jean-Claude Usunier, *Marketing Across Cultures*, 4th ed. (London: Prentice Hall Europe, 2005); and Philip R. Cateora, Mary C. Gilly, and John L. Graham, *International Marketing*, 14th ed. (Burr Ridge, IL: McGraw-Hill/Irwin, 2008). Unless otherwise indicated, examples found in this section appear in these excellent sources.

11. Michael Esterl and David Crawford, "Siemens Pays Record Fine in Probe," *The Wall Street Journal*, December 16, 2008, p. B2.

12. These examples appear in Del I. Hawkins, David L. Mothersbaugh, and Roger J. Best, *Consumer Behavior*, 11th ed. (Burr Ridge, IL: McGraw-Hill/Irwin, 2009), chapter 2.

13. "Greeks Protest Coke's Use of Parthenon," *Dallas Morning News*, August 17, 1992, p. D4.

14. "If Only Krispy Kreme Meant 'Makes You Smarter,'" *Business 2.0*, August 2005, p. 108.

15. Valerie Bauerlein, "Pepsi, Bottler Put $1 Billion into Russia as U.S. Sags," *The Wall Street Journal*, July 7, 2009, pp. B1, B3.

16. Vijay Mahajan and Kamini Banga, *The 86 Percent Solution: How to Succeed in the Biggest Market Opportunity of the Next 50 Years* (Upper Saddle River, NJ: Pearson Education, 2006).

17. "Mattel Plans to Double Sales Abroad," *The Wall Street Journal*, February 11, 1998, pp. A3, A11.

18. Eric Clark, *The Real Toy Story* (New York: The Free Press, 2007); and Cateora, Gilly, and Graham, *International Marketing*.

19. For an extensive and recent examination of these market-entry options, see for example, Johnny K. Johansson, *Global Marketing: Foreign Entry, Local Marketing, and Global Management*, 3rd ed. (Burr Ridge, IL: McGraw-Hill/Irwin, 2003); A. Coskun Samli, *Entering & Succeeding in Emerging Countries: Marketing to the Forgotten Majority* (Mason, OH: South-Western, 2004); Keegan, *Global Marketing*; and Cateora, Gilly and Graham, *International Marketing*.

20. Based on an interview with Pamela Viglielmo, director of international marketing, Fran Wilson Creative Cosmetics; and "Foreign Firms Think Their Way into Japan," www.successstories.com/nikkei, downloaded March 24, 2003.

21. *Small and Medium Sized Exporting Companies: A Statistical Handbook* (Washington, DC: International Trade Administration, June 2007).

22. "Overseas Is McDonald's Kind of Place," www.forbes.com, February 8, 2008.

23. "FedEx Expands Reach in China with Buyout of Joint Venture," *The Wall Street Journal*, January 25, 2006.

24. This discussion is based on Todd J. Gillman, "Chip Off the Old Block," *Dallas Morning News*, July 30, 2006, pp. 1A, 22A; "Machines for the Masses," *The Wall Street Journal*, December 9, 2003, pp. A19–A20; "The Color of Beauty," *Forbes*, November 22, 2000, pp. 170–76; "It's Goo, Goo, Goo, Goo Vibrations at the Gerber Lab," *The Wall Street Journal*, December 4, 1996, pp. A1, A6; Donald R. Graber, "How to Manage a Global Product Development Process," *Industrial Marketing Management*, November 1996, pp. 483–98; and Herbig, *Handbook of Cross-Cultural Marketing*.

25. Jagdish N. Sheth and Atul Parvatiyar, "The Antecedents and Consequences of Integrated Global Marketing," *International Marketing Review* 18, no. 1 (2001), pp. 16–29. Also see D. Szymanski, S. Bharadwaj, and R. Varadarajan, "Standardization versus Adaptation of International Marketing Strategy: An Empirical Investigation," *Journal of Marketing*, October 1993, pp. 1–17.

26. "With Profits Elusive, Walmart to Exit Germany," *The Wall Street Journal*, July 29, 2006, pp. A1, A6.

27. "Rotten Apples," *Dallas Morning News*, April 7, 1998, p. 14A.

28. For an in-depth discussion on gray markets, see Kersi D. Antia, Mark Bergen, and Shantanu Dutta, "Competing with Gray Markets," *Sloan Management Review*, Fall 2004, pp. 63–69; and Kersi D. Antia, Mark E. Bergen, Shantanu Dutta, and Robert J. Fisher, "How Does Enforcement Deter Gray Market Incidence?" *Journal of Marketing*, January 2006, pp. 92–106.

CNS Breathe Right Strips: This case was prepared by Mary L. Brown based on interviews with Kevin McKenna, vice president, international, and Nick Naumann, senior marketing services manager of CNS Inc., September 2004.

Chapter 8

1. See www.boxofficemojo.com for the release schedule of movies for 2010, 2011, and beyond.

2. John Horn, "Studios Play Name Games," *Star Tribune*, August 10, 1997, p. F11; and "Flunking Chemistry," *Star Tribune*, April 11, 2003, p. E13.

3. Tad Friend, "The Cobra," *The New Yorker*, January 19, 2009, pp. 41–49.

4. Willow Bay, "Test Audiences Have Profound Effect on Movies," *CNN Newsstand & Entertainment Weekly*, September 28, 1998. See www.cnn.com/SHOWBIZ/Movies/9809/28/screen.test.

5. Helene Diamond, "Lights, Camera . . . Research!" *Marketing News*, September 11, 1989, pp. 10–11; and "Killer!" *Time*, November 16, 1987, pp. 72–79.

6. Carl Diorio, "Tracking Projectings: Box Office Calculations an Inexact Science," *Variety*, May 24, 2001.

7. Ronald Grover, Tom Lowry, and Michael White, "King of the World (Again)," *BusinessWeek*, February 1 & 8, 2010, pp. 48–56; and Richard Corliss, "Avatar Ascendant," *Time*, February 8, 2010, pp. 50–51.

8. A lengthier, expanded definition from 2004 is found on the American Marketing Association's Web site at www.marketingpower.com. For a researcher's comments on this and other definitions of marketing research, see Lawrence D. Gibson, "Quo Vadis, Marketing Research?" *Marketing Research*, Spring 2000, pp. 36–41.

9. Etienne Benson, "Toy Stories," *Observer* 19, no. 12 (December 2006).

10. Lawrence D. Gibson, "Defining Marketing Problems," *Marketing Research*, Spring 1998, pp. 4–12.

11. "Inside TV Ratings" and "National Audience Sample" from the Nielsen Media Research Web site, www.nielsenmedia.com; and Richard Siklos, "Made to Measure," *Fortune*, March 3, 2008, p. 72.

12. "Top TV Ratings" from Nielsen Media Research. See www.nielsen media.com.

13. "U.S. Advertising Spending Totals by Medium for 2009," *Advertising Age*, June 21, 2010, p. 22.

14. David Kiley, "Counting the Eyeballs," *BusinessWeek*, January 16, 2006, pp. 84–85; and "The Ultimate Marketing Machine," *The Economist*, July 8, 2006, pp. 61–64.

15. Colleen Moore-Mezler, "Mystery Shoppers Are an Important Resource," *Alert! Magazine*, Marketing Research Association 46, no. 4 (April 2008), pp. 10, 12; and Robert Frank, "How to Live Large and Largely for Free, Jennifer Voitle's Way," *The Wall Street Journal*, June 9, 2003, pp. A1, A8.

16. Sarah Ellison, "P&G Chief's Turnaround Recipe: Find Out What Women Want," *The Wall Street Journal*, June 1, 2005, p. A1; Mark Maremont, "New Toothbrush Is Big-Ticket Item," *The Wall Street Journal*, October 27, 1998, pp. B1, B6; and Emily Nelson, "P&G Checks Out Real Life," *The Wall Street Journal*, May 17, 2001, pp. B1, B4.

17. Gavin Johnson and Melinda Rea-Holloway, "Ethnography: How to Know If It's Right for Your Study," *Alert! Magazine*, Marketing Research Association 47, no. 2 (February 2009), pp. 1–4. See www.mra-net.org/alert.

18. Kenneth Chang, "Enlisting Science's Lessons to Entice More Shoppers to Spend More," *The New York Times*, September 19, 2006, p. D3; and Janet Adamy, "Cooking Up Changes at Kraft Foods," *The Wall Street Journal*, February 20, 2007, p. B1.

19. Martin Lindstrom, *Buy*ology: Truth and Lies about Why We Buy* (New York: Doubleday, 2008), pp. 8–36; C. B. Whittemore, "Martin Lindstrom's Buy*ology," *Flooring the Consumer blogspot*, March 1, 2009; Seth Brown, "Buyology Offers a Peek Inside Buyers Heads," *USA Today*, October 29, 2008; and Andrea Sachs, "Business Books," *Time*, October 23, 2008.

20. Ilan Brat, "The Emotional Quotient of Soup Shopping," *The Wall Street Journal*, February 17, 2010, p. B6.

21. For a more complete discussion of questionnaire methods, see Joseph F. Hair, Jr., Robert P. Bush, and David J. Ortinau, *Marketing Research*, 4th ed. (New York: McGraw-Hill/Irwin, 2009), Chaps. 6 and 13.

22. Constance Gustke, "Built to Last," *Sales & Marketing Management*, August 1997, pp. 78–83.

23. See www.trendhunter.com/about-trend-hunter.

24. "What Is Online Research?" Marketing Research Association, see http://www.mra-net.org/press/online.cfm; and see also www.markettools.com/pdfs/press_releases/release_20081204.pdf.

25. Douglas D. Bates, "The Future of Qualitative Research Is Online," *Alert! Magazine*, Marketing Research Association 47, no. 2 (February 2009); Jack Neff, "The End of Consumer Surveys?" *Advertising Age*, September 15, 2008; Jack Neff, "Marketing Execs: Researchers Could Use a Softer Touch," *Advertising Age*, January 27, 2009; Bruce Mendelsohn, "Social Networking: Interactive Marketing Lets Researchers Reach Consumers Where They Are," *Alert! Magazine*, Marketing Research Association 46, no. 4 (April 2008); Toby, "Social Media Research: Interview with Joel Rubinson of ARF: Part 1," *Diva Marketing Blog*, February 16, 2009; and Toby, "Social Media Research: Interview with Joel Rubinson of ARF: Part 2," *Diva Marketing Blog*, February 23, 2009.

26. "Data, Data Everywhere—A Special Report on Managing Information: A Different Game," *The Economist*, February 27, 2010, pp. 6–8.

27. Dale Buss, "The Race to RFID," *CEO Magazine*, November 2004, pp. 32–36.

28. The step 4 discussion was written by David Ford and Don Rylander of Ford Consulting Group Inc.; the Tony's Pizza example was provided by Teré Carral of Tony's Pizza.

29. Stephanie N. Mehta, "Under Armour Reboots," *Fortune*, February 2, 2009, pp. 29–33; and Michael McCarthy, "Under Armour Is Making a Run at Nike," *USA Today*, December 9, 2008, p. 1C.

Ford Consulting Group, Inc.: This case was written by David Ford of Ford Consulting Group, Inc.

Chapter 9

1. Kimberly Weisal, "A Shine in Their Shoes," *BusinessWeek*, December 5, 2005, p. 84; and information from the "Executive Biographies" section of the Zappos.com Web site.

2. Jeffrey M. O'Brien, "Zappos Knows How to Kick It," *Fortune*, February 2, 2009, pp. 55–60; and Max Chafkin, "Get Happy," *Inc.*, May 2009, pp. 66–71.

3. Weisal, "A Shine in Their Shoes," p. 84.

4. Duff McDonald, "Zappos.com: Success through Simplicity," *CIO-Insight*, November 10, 2006.

5. Jena McGregor, "Zappos' Secret: It's an Open Book," *BusinessWeek*, March 23 and 30, 2009, p. 62; Jeffrey M. O'Brien, "The 10 Commandments of Zappos," *Fortune*, January 22, 2009; http://money.cnn.com/2009/01/21/news/companies/obrien_zappos10.fortune/; and Zappos.com.

6. Christopher Palmeri, "Now for Sale, the Zappos Culture," *Bloomberg BusinessWeek*, January 11, 2010, p. 57.

7. Natalie Zmuda, "Marketer of the Year: Zappos," *Advertising Age*, October 20, 2008, p. 36.

8. Devin Leonard, "Nightmare on Madison Avenue," *Fortune*, June 28, 2004, pp. 93–108; Anthony Bianco, "The Vanishing Mass Market," *BusinessWeek*, July 12, 2004, pp. 61–65; and Geoff Colvin, "Selling P&G," *Fortune*, September 17, 2007, pp. 163–69.

9. Larry Neumeister, "Rowling to Testify against Fan in Bid to Block Publication of 'Harry Potter' Encyclopedia," StarTribune.com from an Associated Press article, April 13, 2008; www.startribune.com/entertainment/17761909.html.

10. "Special Report on Mass Communication: A Long March," *The Economist*, July 14, 2001, pp. 63–65.

11. Amy Merrick, "Once a Bellwether, Ann Taylor Fights Its Stodgy Image," *The Wall Street Journal*, July 12, 2005, pp. A1, A8; and "Ann Taylor Launches Strategic Restructuring Program to Enhance Profitability," press release dated January 30, 2008, http://investor.anntaylor.com.

12. The relation of these criteria to implementation is discussed in Jacqueline Dawley, "Making Connections: Enhance the Implementation of Value of Attitude-Based Segmentation," *Marketing Research*, Summer 2006, pp. 16–22.

13. Ian Michiels, "Customer Analytics: Segmentation beyond Demographics," *The Aberdeen Group*, August 2008, p. 11.

14. The discussion of fast-food trends and market share is based on Experian Simmons Winter 2010 Full-Year NCS/NHCS Choices 3 System Crosstabulation Report based on visits within the past 30 days.

15. Jennifer Ordonez, "Taco Bell Chief Has New Tactic: Be Like Wendy's," *The Wall Street Journal*, February 23, 2001, pp. B1, B4; and Jennifer Ordonez, "An Efficiency Drive: Fast-Food Lanes Are Getting Even Faster," *The Wall Street Journal*, May 18, 2000, pp. A1, A10.

16. Paul Ziobro, "Arby's Brand Eats into Wendy's Results," *The Wall Street Journal*, March 3, 2009, p. B7; and Janet Adamy, "Wendy's Comes Up with a New Strategic Recipe," *The Wall Street Journal*, September 30, 2008, p. 83.

17. "The 2009 Zagat Fast-Food Survey," June 8, 2009; www.zagat.com/fastfood.

18. Paul Ziobro, "Fast-Food Joints Push Chicken as Beef Prices Hit New Highs," *The Wall Street Journal*, May 20, 2010, p. B1; and Richard Gibson, "Have It *Whose* Way?" *The Wall Street Journal*, May 17, 2010, pp. R6, R7.

19. The discussion of Apple's segmentation strategies through the years is based on information from its Web site, www.apple.com; and www.apple-history.com/history.html.

20. Much of the discussion about positioning and perceptual maps is based on Roger A. Kerin and Robert A. Peterson, *Strategic Marketing Problems: Cases and Comments*, 11th ed. (Upper Saddle River, NJ: Prentice Hall, 2007), pp. 147–49; John M. Mullins, Orville C. Walker, Jr., Harper W. Boyd, Jr., and Jean-Claude Larreche, *Marketing Management: A Strategic Decision-Marketing Approach*, 5th ed. (New York: McGraw-Hill/Irwin, 2005), p. 216.

21. Nicholas Zamiska, "How Milk Got a Major Boost by Food Panel," *The Wall Street Journal*, August 30, 2004, pp. B1, B5.

22. Rebecca Winter, "Chocolate Milk," *Time*, April 30, 2001, p. 20.

Prince Sports: This case was written by William Rudelius and is based on personal interviews with Linda Glassel, Tyler Herring, and Nick Skally in 2009.

Chapter 10

1. Anna Bernasek, "The World's Most Admired Companies: 2010," *Fortune*, March 22, 2010, pp.121–126; Adam Lashinsky, "The Decade of Steve," *Fortune*, November 23, 2009, pp. 92–100; and Michael Arndt and Bruce Einhorn, "The 50 Most Innovative Companies," *Bloomberg Businessweek*, April 25, 2010, pp. 34–40.

2. "Steve Jobs and the Tablet of Hope," *The Economist*, January 30, 2010, p. 72.

3. Apple Unveils iPod touch. Apple, Inc. press release, September 5, 2007. See www.apple.com/pr/library/2007/09/05touch.html. "The Book of Jobs," *The Economist*, January 30, 2010, p. 11; Josh Quittner, "Apple's Vision of the Future," *Time*, February 8, 2010, pp. 34–35; and Steve Lohr, "The Apple of His Eye," *The New York Times*, January 31, 2010, pp. WK1, WK4.

4. Peter C. Honebein and Roy F. Cammarano, "Customers at Work: Self-Service Customers Can Reduce Costs and Become Co-creators of Value," *Marketing Management*, January–February 2006, pp. 26–31; and Matthew L. Meuter, Amy L. Ostrom, Robert I. Roundtree, and Mary Jo Bittner, "Self-Service Technologies: Understanding Customer Satisfaction with Technology-Based Service Encounters," *Journal of Marketing*, July 2000, pp. 50–64.

5. Janet R. McColl-Kennedy and Tina White, "Service Provider Training Programs at Odds with Customer Requirements in Five Star Hotels," *Journal of Services Marketing* 11, no. 4 (1997), pp. 249–64; Ellyn A. McColgan, "How Fidelity Invests in Service Professionals," *Harvard Business Review*, January–February 1997, pp. 137–43; and Frederick F. Reichheld and W. Earl Sasser, Jr., "Zero Defections: Quality Comes to Services," *Harvard Business Review*, September–October 1990, pp. 105–11.

6. Christopher Lovelock and Evert Gummesson, "Whither Services Marketing?" *Journal of Services Research* 7 (August 2004), pp. 20–41; and Christopher H. Lovelock and George S. Yip, "Developing Global Strategies for Service Businesses," *California Management Review*, Winter 1996, pp. 64–86.

7. "HP Positioned to Lead in New Era of Business Technology; New Solutions and Services to Help Enterprises Optimize Business Outcomes," *Business Wire*, April 24, 2007.

8. Interview with Geek Squad founder Robert Stephens on *60 Minutes*, January 28, 2007, www.geeksquad.com; Debora Viana Thompson, Rebecca W. Hamilton, and Roland Rust, "Feature Fatigue: When Product Capabilities Become Too Much of a Good Thing," *Journal of Marketing Research*, November 2005, pp. 431–42; and Ronald T. Rust, Debora Viana Thompson, Rebecca W. Hamilton, "Defeating Feature Fatigue," *Harvard Business Review*, February 2006, pp. 98–107.

9. Youngme Moon, "Break Free from the Product Life Cycle," *Harvard Business Review*, May 2005, pp. 86–94.

10. Greg A. Stevens and James Burley, "3,000 Raw Ideas = 1 Commercial Success!" *Research-Technology Management*, May–June 1997, pp. 16–27.

11. Robert G. Cooper, "New Products: What Separates the Winners from the Losers?" in *The PDMA Handbook of New Product Development*, eds. M. D. Rosenau, A. Griffin, G. Castellion, and N. Anscheutz (New York: Wiley and Sons, 1996), pp. 3–18; Robert G. Cooper, "The Impact of Product Innovativeness on Performance," *Journal of Product Innovation Management*, April 1999, pp. 115–33; Thomas D. Kuczmarski, "Measuring Your Return on Innovation," *Marketing Management*, Spring 2000, pp. 25–32; and Merle Crawford and Anthony D. Benedetto, *New Products Management*, 9th ed. (New York: McGraw-Hill/Irwin, 2008), pp. 61–71.

12. Julie Fortser, "The Lucky Charm of Steve Sanger," *BusinessWeek*, March 26, 2001, pp. 75–76.

13. The Avert Virucidal tissues, Hey! There's A Monster In My Room spray, and Garlic Cake examples are adapted from Robert M. McMath and Thom Forbes, *What Were They Thinking?* (New York: Random House, 1998); and Global New Products Database. See www.gnpd.com.

14. "Cost of Poor Quality," *SixSigma Dictionary*, www.isixsigma.com/dictionary/Cost_of_Poor_Quality - COPQ-63.htm; Ben Patterson, "Microsoft Fesses Up to Xbox 360 Glitches," Yahoo! Tech Blog, July 6, 2007, http://tech.yahoo.com; and Matt Richtel, "Xbox 360 Out of Order? For Loyalists, No Worries," *The New York Times*, August 13, 2007, www.nytimes.com/2007/08/13/technology/13halo.html.

15. Robert G. Cooper, "What Leading Companies Are Doing to Reinvent Their NPD Process," *PDMA Visions Magazine*, September 2008, pp. 6–10; Robert G. Cooper, "The Stage-Gate Idea-to-Launch Process—Update: What's New and NexGen Systems," *Journal of Product Innovation Management*, May 2008, pp. 213–32; Leland D. Shaeffer and Michael Zirkle, "Beyond 'Phase Gate'—Why Not a Tailored Solution?" *PDMA Visions Magazine*, June 2008, pp. 21–25; and Gloria Barczak, Abbie Griffin, and Kenneth B. Kahn, "Perspective: Trends and Drivers of Success in NPD Practices: Results of the 2003 PDMA Best Practices Study," *Journal of Product Innovation Management*, January 2009, pp. 3–23.

16. Dan P. Lovallo and Olivier Sibony, "Distortions and Deceptions in Strategic Decisions," *The McKinsey Quarterly* 1 (2006), pp. 19–29; and Byron G. Augusto, Eric P. Harmon, and Vivek Pandit, "The Right Service Strategies for Product Companies," *The McKinsey Quarterly* 1 (2006), pp. 41–51.

17. Isabelle Royer, "Why Bad Projects Are So Hard to Kill," *Harvard Business Review*, February 2003, pp. 48–56; John T. Morn, Dan P. Lovallo, and S. Patrick Viguerie, "Beating the Odds in Market Entry," *The McKinsey Quarterly* 4 (2005), pp. 35–45; Leslie Perlow and Stephanie Williams, "Is Silence Killing Your Company?" *Harvard Business Review*, May 2003, pp. 52–58; Beverly K. Brockman and Robert M. Morgan, "The Moderating Effect of Organizational Cohesiveness in Knowledge Use and New Product Development," *Journal of Marketing Science* 3 (Summer 2006), pp. 295–306; Eyal Biyalogorsky, William Boulding, and Richard Staelin, "Stuck in the Past: Why Managers Persist with New Product Failures," *Journal of Marketing*, April 2006, pp. 108–21; and Irwin L. Janis, *Groupthink* (New York: Free Press, 1988).

18. For a report on measuring and stimulating American innovation, see *Innovation Measurement: Tracking the State of Innovation in the American Economy* (Washington, DC: A Report to the Secretary of Commerce by The Advisory Committee on Measuring Innovation in the 21st Century Economy, January 2008), pp. 17–20.

19. Matt Richtel, "A Google Whiz Searches for His Place on Earth," *The New York Times*, April 12, 2009, pp. 1, 18, 19.

20. Ken Belson, "Oh, Yeah, There's a Ballgame, Too," *The New York Times*, October 22, 2006, pp. 3–1, 3–7.

21. Peter Erickson, "One Food Company's Foray into Open Innovation," *PDMA Visions Magazine*, June 2008, pp. 12–14; Benn Lawson, Kenneth J. Petersen, Paul D. Cousins, and Robert B. Handfield, "Knowledge Sharing in Interorganizational Product Development Teams: The Effect of Formal and Informal Socialization Mechanisms," *Journal of Product Innovation Management*, March 2009, pp. 156–72; and James I. Cash, Jr., Michael J. Earl, and Robert Morison, "Teaming Up to Crack Innovation and Enterprise Integration," *Harvard Business Review*, November 2008, pp. 90–100.

22. Kimberly Judson, Denise D. Schoenabachler, Geoffrey L. Gordon, Rick E. Ridnour, and Dan C. Weilbaker, "The New Product Development Process: Let the Voice of the Salesperson Be Heard," *Journal of Product & Brand Management* 15, no. 3 (2006), pp. 194–202.

23. Morgan L. Swink and Vincent A. Mabert, "Product Development Partnerships: Balancing Needs of OEMs and Suppliers," *Business Horizons*, May–June 2000, pp. 59–68.

24. C. K. Prahalad and Venkat Ramswamy, *The Future of Competition* (Boston: Harvard Business School Press, 2004); Steve Hamm, "Adding Customers to the Design Team," *BusinessWeek*, March 1, 2004, pp. 22–23; and Anthony W. Ulwick, "Turn Customer Input into Innovation" *Harvard Business Review*, January 2002, pp. 91–97.

25. Sarah Ellison, "P & G Chief's Turnaround Recipe: Find Out What Women Want," *The Wall Street Journal*, June 1, 2005, pp. A1, A16.

26. Elisabeth A. Sullivan, "A Group Effort," *Marketing News*, February 28, 2010, pp. 22–29.

27. Adam Aston and Gail Edmonson, "This Volvo Is Not a Guy Thing," *BusinessWeek*, March 15, 2004, pp. 84–86.

28. Daniel Turner, "The Secret of Apple Design," *MIT Technology Review*, May/June 2007; Leander Kahney, "Silicon Valley Loves Transparency and Cooperation. Not Steve Jobs. How Apple Got Everything Right by Doing Everything Wrong," *Wired Business Trends*, April 2008, pp. 137–43; and Karl T. Ulrich and Stephen D. Eppinger, *Product Design and Development* 4th ed. (New York: McGraw-Hill/Irwin, 2008), Chap 10.

29. Joseph Weber, Stanley Holmes, and Christopher Palmeri, "Mosh Pits' of Creativity," *BusinessWeek*, November 7, 2005, pp. 98–100.

30. Bruce Nussbaum, "The Best Global Design of 2008," *BusinessWeek*, July 28, 2008, pp. 44–46.

31. Bruce Nussbaum, "The Power of Design," *BusinessWeek*, May 17, 2004, pp. 86–94; the article gives many techniques for idea and concept generation, as do Appendixes A, B, and C in Merle Crawford and Anthony Di Benedetto, *New Products Management*, 9th ed. (New York: McGraw-Hill/Irwin, 2008).

32. Erickson, "One Food Company's Foray into Open Innovation," p. 12.

33. Erickson, "One Food Company's Foray into Open Innovation," p. 13.

34. Simona Covel, "My Brain, Your Brawn," *The Wall Street Journal,* October 13, 2008, p. R12.

35. Steve Hoeffler, "Measuring Preferences for Really New Products," *Journal of Marketing Research*, November 2003, pp. 406–20.

36. Christopher Lovelock and Jochen Wirtz, *Services Marketing* (Englewood Cliffs, NJ: Prentice Hall, 2007), pp. 260–84.

37. Larry Huston and Nobil Sakkab, "Connect and Develop," *Harvard Business Review*, March 2006, pp. 58–66; and "Pringles Announces First-of-Its-Kind Technology That Prints Directly on Individual Crisps," www.pg.com, accessed April 6, 2004.

38. Vicki Clift, "Everyone Needs Service Flow Charting," *Marketing News*, October 23, 1995, pp. 41, 43; Mary Jo Bitner, Bernard H. Booms, and Mary Stanfield Tetreault, "The Service Encounter: Diagnosing Favorable and Unfavorable Incidents," *Journal of Marketing*, January 1990, pp. 71–84; Eberhard Scheuing, "Conducting Customer Service Audits," *Journal of Consumer Marketing*, Summer 1989, pp. 35–41; and W. Earl Susser, R. Paul Olsen, and D. Daryl Wyckoff, *Management of Service Operations* (Boston: Allyn & Bacon, 1978).

39. Helen Walters, "Google Did," *Bloomberg Businessweek*, May 10–16, 2010; Laura M. Holson, "Putting a Bolder Face on Google," *The New York Times*, March 1, 2009, pp. BU1, BU8; and Julian Gutherie, "The Adventures of Marissa," *San Francisco*, March 2008.

40. Jack Neff, "White Bread, USA," *Advertising Age*, July 9, 2001, pp. 1, 12, 13.

41. Mark Leslie and Charles J. Holloway "The Sales Learning Curve," *Harvard Business Review*, July–August 2006, pp. 115–23.

42. Kim Schatzel and Roger Calantone, "Creating Market Anticipation: An Exploratory Evaluation of the Effect of Preannouncement Behavior on a New Product Launch," *Journal of the Academy of Marketing Sciences*, Summer 2006, pp. 357–66.

43. Jennifer Ordonez, "How Burger King Got Burned in Quest to Make the Perfect Fry," *The Wall Street Journal*, January 16, 2001, pp. A1, A8.

44. Kerry A. Dolan, "Speed: The New X Factor," *Forbes*, December 26, 2005, pp. 74–77.

Activeion Cleaning Solutions: This case was written by Chris Deets of Activeion Cleaning Solutions and William Rudelius.

Chapter 11

1. "Gatorade: Before and After," *The Wall Street Journal*, April 23, 2010, p. B8; "G2, Zyrtec Top New Product Sales in '08," *BrandWeek*, March 23, 2009; "Gatorade Refreshes Look," *BrandWeek*, January 15, 2009, p. 4; "Gatorade Unleashes New Attitude, Enhanced Beverages," PepsiCo press release, December 28, 2008, pp. D1, 5; and Darren Rovell, *First in Thirst: How Gatorade Turned the Science of Sweat into a Cultural Phenomenon* (New York: AMACOM, 2005).

2. For an extended discussion of the generalized product life cycle, see Donald R. Lehmann and Russell S. Winer, *Product Management*, 5th ed (New York: McGraw-Hill, 2008).

3. *Gillette Fusion Case Study* (New York: Datamonitor, June 6, 2008). All subsequent references to Gillette Fusion are based on this case study.

4. John W. Mullins, Orville C. Walker, Jr., Harper W. Boyd, Jr., and Jean-Claude Larréché, *Marketing Management: A Strategic Decision-Making Approach*, 5th ed. (New York: McGraw-Hill/Irwin, 2005), p. 396.

5. Portions of this discussion on the fax machine product life cycle are based on Karen Prema, "Faxes are Evolving," *Purchasing Magazine Online*, March 16, 2006; and "Atlas Electronics Corporation," in Roger A. Kerin and Robert A. Peterson, *Strategic Marketing Problems: Cases and Comments*, 8th ed. (Upper Saddle River, NJ: Prentice Hall, 1998), pp. 494–506.

6. "How Many Active E-mail Mailboxes Are There in the World Today?" The Radicate Group, Inc., January 25, 2007; and "Why Are Faxes Still Around?" *Wired*, January 2009, p. 47.

7. Kate MacArthur, "Coke Energizes Tab, Neville Isdell's Fave," *Advertising Age*, August 29, 2005, pp. 3, 21.

8. "Hosiery Sales Hit Major Snag," *Dallas Morning News*, December 18, 2006 p. 50.

9. Everett M. Rogers, *Diffusion of Innovations*, 5th ed. (New York: Free Press, 2003).

10. Jagdish N. Sheth and Banwasi Mitral, *Consumer Behavior: A Managerial Perspective*, 2nd ed. (Mason, OH: South-Western College Publishing, 2003).

11. "When Free Samples Become Saviors," *The Wall Street Journal*, August 14, 2001, pp. B1, B4.

12. "Hop on the Back, Jack," *Marketing News*, March 15, 2009, p. 5.

13. "Dockers Adds Diversity to Message," *BrandWeek*, September 11, 2006, p. 18.

14. "New Balance Steps Up Marketing Drive," *The Wall Street Journal*, March 21, 2008, p. B3.

15. Sheth and Mitral, *Consumer Behavior*; and Marsha Cohen, *Marketing to the 50+ Population* (New York: EPM Communications, Inc., 2007).

16. "The Lowdown on Downsizing," *Consumer Reports*, October 2008, pp. 10-11; Bruce Horovitz, "Shoppers Beware: Products Shrink

but Prices Stay the Same," www.usatoday, June 11, 2008; John Gourville, "How to Avoid a Price Increase," *Working Knowledge for Business Leaders* (Boston: Harvard Business School, June 28, 2004); and "More for Less," *Consumer Reports*, August 2004, p. 63.

17. This discussion is based on Kevin Lane Keller, *Strategic Brand Management*, 3rd ed. (Upper Saddle River, NJ: Prentice Hall, 2008). Also see Susan Fornier, "Building Brand Community on the Harley-Davidson Posse Ride," *Harvard Business School Note #5-501-502* (Boston: Harvard Business School, 2001); and Tulin Erdem, Joffre Swait, and Ana Valenzuela, "Brands as Signals: A Cross-Country Validation Study," *Journal of Marketing*, January 2006, pp. 34–49.

18. Keller, *Strategic Brand Management*.

19. This discussion is based on John Deighton, "How Snapple Got Its Juice Back," *Harvard Business Review*, January 2002, pp. 47–53; and "Breakfast King Agrees to Sell Bagel Business," *The Wall Street Journal*, September 28, 1999, pp. B1, B6. Also see Vithala R. Rao, Manj K. Agarwal, and Denise Dahlhoff, "How Is Manifest Branding Strategy Related to the Value of a Corporation?" *Journal of Marketing*, October 2004, pp. 125–41.

20. "Judge Pooh-Poohs Lawsuit over Disney Licensing Fees," *USAToday.com*, March 30, 2004; and Keller, *Strategic Brand Management*.

21. John Brodie, "The Many Faces of Ralph Lauren," *Fortune.com*, August 29, 2007; and "Polo Ralph Lauren Enters into Licensing Agreement with Luxottica Group, S.P.A.," www.thebusiness edition.com, February 28, 2006.

22. Beth Snyder Bulik, "What's in a (Good) Product Name? Sales," *Advertising Age*, February 2, 2009, p. 10; and Keller, *Strategic Brand Management*. Also see Chiranjeev Kohli and Douglas W. LaBahn, "Creating Effective Brand Names: A Study of the Naming Process," *Journal of Advertising Research*, January–February 1997, pp. 67–75.

23. Jack Neff, "The End of the Line for Line Extensions?" *Advertising Age*, July 7, 2008, pp. 3, 28.

24. "When Brand Extension Becomes Brand Abuse," *BrandWeek*, October 26, 1998, pp. 20, 22.

25. David Aaker, *Brand Portfolio Strategy* (New York: Free Press, 2004).

26. Mark Ritson, "Should You Launch a Fighter Brand?" *Harvard Business Review*, October 2009, pp. 87–94.

27. "Ribbons Roll Out on Rides," *Dallas Morning News*, September 30, 2005, p. 8D.

28. Nikhil Bahadur, "How to Slim Down a Brand Portfolio," *Strategy & Business*, Winter 2006, pp. 15–16.

29. "Consumers Flock to Private Labels," *Advertising Age*, February 2, 2009, p. 27; and Lien Lamey, Barbara Deleersnyder, Marnik G. Dekimpe, and Jan-Benedict E. M. Steenkamp, "How Business Cycles Contribute to Private-Label Success: Evidence from the United States and Europe," *Journal of Marketing*, January 2007, pp. 1–15.

30. www.pez.com, accessed February 1, 2010; David Welch, *Collecting Pez* (Murphysboro, IL: Bubba Scrubba Publications, 1995); and "Elements Design Adds Dimension to Perennial Favorite Pez Brand," *Package Design Magazine*, May 2006, pp. 37–38.

31. Fred Richards, "Memo to CMOs: It's the Packaging, Stupid," *BrandWeek*, August 17, 2009, p. 22; and "Market Statistics," Packaging-Gateway.com, accessed March 25, 2009.

32. "Green Bean Casserole Turns 50," *Dallas Morning News*, November 19, 2005, p. 10D.

33. "L'eggs Hatches a New Hosiery Package," *BrandWeek*, January 1, 2001, p. 6.

34. Representative scholarly research on packaging and labeling perceptions include Priya Rgahubir and Eric A. Greenleaf, "Ratios in Proportion: What Should the Shape of the Package Be?" *Journal of Marketing*, April 2006, pp. 95–107; Peter H. Bloch, Frederic F. Brunel, and Todd Arnold, "Individual Differences in the Centrality of Visual Product Aesthetics: Concept and Measurement," *Journal of Consumer Research*, March 2003, pp. 551–65; and Pamela Anderson,

Joan Giese, and Joseph A. Cote, "Impression Management Using Typeface Design," *Journal of Marketing*, October 2004, pp. 60–72.

35. Betsy McKay, "Pepsi's New Marketing Dance: Can Can," *The Wall Street Journal*, January 12, 2007, p. B3.

36. "Asian Brands Are Sprouting English Logos in Pursuit of Status, International Image," *The Wall Street Journal*, August 7, 2001, p. B7C.

37. Ellen Byron, "Consumer Products Getting a Makeover," *The Wall Street Journal*, June 2, 2008, p. B9; and Susanna Hammer, "Packaging That Pays," *Business 2.0*, July 26, 2006, pp. 68–69.

38. Betsy McKay, "Pepsi to Cut Plastic Used in Bottles," *The Wall Street Journal*, May 6, 2008, p. B2; "Walmart: Use Less Packaging," *Dallas Morning News*, September 23, 2006, p. 2D. For an overview of Procter & Gamble's environmental efforts, see *Sustainability Report 2008* (Cincinnati, OH: Procter & Gamble Company, 2009).

39. "Packaging," hp.com, accessed January 17, 2007.

40. This discussion is based on Valerie A. Zeithaml, Mary Jo Bitner, and Dwayne D. Gremler, *Services Marketing: Integrating Customer Focus across the Firm*, 5th ed. (Burr Ridge, IL: McGraw-Hill/Irwin, 2009).

41. Kent B. Monroe, *Pricing: Making Profitable Decisions*, 3rd ed. (Burr Ridge, IL: McGraw-Hill/Irwin, 2003).

42. Paula Andruss, "Delivering WOW through Service," *Marketing News*, October 15, 2008, p. 10.

43. Leonard L. Berry and Neeli Bedapudi, "Clueing in Customers," *Harvard Business Review*, February 2003, pp. 100–6.

Philadelphia Phillies: This case was prepared by William Rudelius based on interviews with David Montgomery, David Buck, Marisol Lezcano, and Scott Brandreth; internal company materials; http://asp.usatoday.com/sports/baseball/salaries/totalpayroll.aspx?year=2007; and the Phillies Web site (www.phillies.com).

Chapter 12

1. "Vizio Tops in U.S. LCD TV Market for 2009," PCMAG.com, February 22, 2010; "U.S. Upstart Takes on TV Giants in Price War," *The Wall Street Journal*, April 15, 2008, pp. B1, B6; Vizio press release, February 4, 2009; and "The Vizio Story," www.vizio.com, accessed March 10, 2010.

2. Lisa Gubernick, "The Little Extras That Count (Up)," *The Wall Street Journal*, July 12, 2001, pp. B1, B4; and Donald V. Potter, "Discovering Hidden Pricing Power," *Business Horizons,* November–December 2000, pp. 41–48..

3. Aaron Robinson, "2009 Tesla Roadster Road Test," *Car and Driver*, May 2009; for a list of cost of options, see www.edmunds.com/new/2009/tesla/roadster/101147356/options.html?action-1 and the Tesla Motors Web site for press releases and other information.

4. Numerous studies have examined the price-quality-value relationship. See, for example, Jacob Jacoby and Jerry C. Olsen, eds., *Perceived Quality* (Lexington, MA: Lexington Books, 1985); William D. Dodds, Kent B. Monroe, and Dhruv Grewal, "Effects of Price, Brand, and Store Information on Buyers' Product Evaluations," *Journal of Marketing Research*, August 1991, pp. 307–19; and Roger A. Kerin, Ambuj Jain, and Daniel Howard, "Store Shopping Experience and Consumer Price-Quality-Value Perceptions," *Journal of Retailing*, Winter 1992, pp. 235–45. For a thorough review of the price-quality-value relationship, see Valerie A. Zeithaml, "Consumer Perceptions of Price, Quality, and Value," *Journal of Marketing*, July 1988, pp. 2–22.

5. Roger A. Kerin and Robert A. Peterson, "Bates Manor Furniture, Inc. (A)," *Strategic Marketing Problems: Cases and Comments*, 12th ed. (Upper Saddle River, NJ: Prentice Hall, 2010), pp. 301–312.

6. The conditions favoring skimming versus penetration pricing are described in Kent B. Monroe, *Pricing: Making Profitable Decisions*, 3rd ed. (New York: McGraw-Hill/Irwin, 2003).

7. Jean-Noel Kapferer, *The New Strategic Brand Management: Creating and Sustaining Brand Equity*, 4th ed. (London: Kogan Page Ltd, 2008).

8. "Premium AA Alkaline Batteries," *Consumer Reports*, March 21, 2002, p. 54; Kemp Powers, "Assault and Batteries," *Forbes*, September 4, 2000, pp. 54, 56; and "Razor Burn at Gillette," *BusinessWeek*, June 18, 2001, p. 37.

9. "Bet Your Bottom Dollar on 99 Cents," NYtimes.com, February 8, 2009. For further reading on odd-even pricing, see Mark Stiving and Russell S. Winer, "An Empirical Analysis of Price Endings with Scanner Data," *Journal of Consumer Research*, June 1997, pp. 57–67; and Robert M. Schindler, "Patterns of Rightmost Digits Used in Advertised Prices: Implications for Nine-Ending Effects," *Journal of Consumer Research*, September 1997, pp. 192–201.

10. Robert J. Dolan and Hermann Simon, *Power Pricing: How Managing Price Transforms the Bottom Line* (New York: Free Press, 1996), p. 249.

11. "Is the Music Store Over?" *Business 2.0*, March 2004, pp. 115–19.

12. Frank Bruni, "Price of Newsweek: It Depends," *Dallas Times Herald*, August 14, 1986, pp. S1, S20. See also, Stephanie Clifford, "A Stress Test for Magazines: Raising Prices without Losing Readers," *The Wall Street Journal*, April 13, 2009, pp. B1, B5.

13. Thomas T. Nagle and Reed K. Holden, *The Strategy and Tactics of Pricing*, 4th ed. (Englewood Cliffs, NJ: Prentice Hall, 2009).

14. Peter Coy, "Can't Stop Guzzling," *BusinessWeek*, July 31, 2006, pp. 26–29.

15. For an overview on motion picture economics, see Charles C. Moul, ed., *A Concise Handbook of Movie Industry Economics* (Cambridge: Cambridge University Press, 2005).

16. Information pertaining to HDTV is based on Pete Engardio, "Flat Panels, Thin Margins," *BusinessWeek*, February 26, 2007, pp. 50–51; "Get Ready for Flatscreen TV Price Wars," CNNMoney.com, November 13, 2009; and "Samsung Edges Out TV Rivals," *The Wall Street Journal*, February 17, 2010, p. B4.

17. "Six Vitamin Firms Agree to Settle Price-Fixing Suit," *The Wall Street Journal*, October 11, 2000, p. B10.

18. "How Dell Fine-Tunes Its PC Pricing to Gain Edge in a Slow Market," *The Wall Street Journal*, June 8, 2001, pp. A1, A8.

19. Michael Levy and Barton A. Weitz, *Retailing Management*, 7th ed. (Burr Ridge, IL: McGraw-Hill/Irwin, 2009).

20. "Are Minority Shoppers Treated Unfairly? An Expensive Reason to Care," www.diversity.com, accessed May 18, 2003; Florian Zettelmeyer, Fiona Scott Morton, and Jorge Silva-Risso, "How the Internet Lowers Prices: Evidence from Matched Survey and Automobile Transaction Data," *Journal of Marketing Research*, May 2006, pp. 168–81; and Fiona Scott Morton, Florian Zettelmeyer, and Jorge Silva-Risso, "Consumer Information and Discrimination: Does the Internet Affect the Pricing of New Cars to Women and Minorities?" *Quantitative Marketing and Economics* 1 (2003), pp. 65–92.

Washburn Guitars: This case was edited by Steven Hartley. Sources: Burkhard Bilger, "String Theory, Building a Better Guitar," *The New Yorker*, May 14, 2007, p. 79; and the Washburn Guitars Web site (www.washburn.com).

Chapter 13

1. www.callawaygolf.com, accessed April 15, 2010; Stephanie Kang, "Callaway Will Use Retailers to Sell Goods Directly to Consumers Online," *The Wall Street Journal*, November 6, 2006, p. B5; and "Justin Timberlake Putting the 'Sexy' Back in Callaway Golf," sportinggoodsnewswire.com, November 19, 2008.

2. Andrew Raskin, "Who's Minding the Store?" *Business 2.0*, February 2003, pp. 70–74.

3. "Eddie Bauer's Banner Time of Year," *Advertising Age*, October 1, 2001, p. 55.

4. "Office Depot," InternetRetailer.com, February 24, 2010.

5. www.generalmills.com, accessed March 15, 2010; www.nestle.com, accessed March 15, 2010; Emily Woon, "Cereal Partners Worldwide Exploits Developing Markets," www.euromonitor.com, November 1, 2007.

6. For an overview of vertical marketing systems, see Lou Pelton, Martha Cooper, David Strutton, and James R. Lumpkin, *Marketing Channels*, 3rd ed. (New York: McGraw-Hill/Irwin, 2005); and Anne T. Coughlan, Erin Anderson, Louis W. Stern, and Adel I. El-Ansary, *Marketing Channels*, 7th ed. (Upper Saddle River, NJ: Prentice Hall, 2006).

7. "Dell Treads Carefully into Selling PCs in Stores," *The Wall Street Journal*, January 3, 2008, p. B1.

8. Rafi A. Mohammed, Robert J. Fisher, Bernard J. Jaworski, and Gordon J. Paddison, *Internet Marketing: Building Advantage in a Networked Economy*, 2nd ed. (New York: McGraw-Hill/Irwin, 2004).

9. Ethan Smith, "Why a Grand Plan to Cut CD Prices Went off the Track," *The Wall Street Journal*, June 4, 2004, pp. A1, A6; and "Feud with Seller Hurts Nike Sales, Shares," *Dallas Morning News*, June 28, 2003, p. 30.

10. "Dealer Surplus," *Forbes*, October 16, 2006, pp. 50–52; and Kevin Kelleher, "Giving Dealers a Raw Deal," *Business 2.0*, December 2004, pp. 82–83.

11. David Simchi-Levi, Philip Kaminsky, and Edith Simchi-Levi, *Designing and Managing the Supply Chain*, 4th ed. (Burr Ridge, IL: McGraw-Hill/Irwin, 2011).

12. *The Smarter Supply Chain of the Future: Automotive Industry Edition* (Somers, NY: IBM Corporation, 2009); Jeffrey McCracken, "Ford Seeks Big Savings by Overhauling Supply System," *The Wall Street Journal*, September 29, 2005, p. all; April Terreri, "Driving Efficiencies in Automotive Logistics," www.inboundlogistics.com, January 2004.

13. Major portions of this discussion are based on Sunil Chopra and Peter Meindl, *Supply Chain Management: Strategy, Planning, and Operations*, 4th ed. (Upper Saddle River, NJ: Prentice Hall, 2010), Chapters 1–3; and Hau L. Lee, "The Triple-A Supply Chain," *Harvard Business Review*, October 2004, pp. 102–12.

14. "AMR Research Supply Chain Top 25," www.amrresearch.com, accessed March 18, 2010; "IBM Leans Out Its Suppply Chain," *Modern Materials Handling*, November 9, 2005, p. 35; and Thomas A. Foster, "World's Best-Run Supply Chains Stay on Top Regardless of the Competition," *Global Logistics & Supply Chain Strategies*, February 2006, pp. 27–41.

15. This discussion is based on Kathryn Jones, "The Dell Way," *Business 2.0*, February 2003, pp. 61–66; Charles Fishman, "The Wal-Mart You Don't Know," *Fast Company*, December 2003, pp. 68–80; "Michael Dell: Still Betting on the Future of Online Commerce and Supply Chain Efficiencies," Knowledge@Wharton, September 7, 2006; and Chopra and Meindl, *Supply Chain Management*.

16. "Beyond Buying," *The Wall Street Journal*, March 10, 2008, p. R8.

17. "Logistics Are in Vogue with Designers," *The Wall Street Journal*, June 27, 2008, p. B1.

18. Chopra and Meindl, *Supply Chain Management*.

Golden Valley Microwave Foods: This case was written by Thomas J. Belich, Mark T. Spriggs, and Steven W. Hartley based on personal interviews with Jack McKeon and Frank Lynch, company data they provided, and the following sources: "Snagging a Pop Fly," *Snack Food and Wholesale Bakery* (May 2004), p. 48; "Choosing the Right Growth Strategy," *PR Newswire* (November 13, 2003); and "Company Information," from the Web site (see www.actii.com/company).

Chapter 14

1. "Technology: Front & Forward," *The Wall Street Journal*, February 17, 2009, p. R2; Jon Fine, "Bargain-Rate Buzz," *BusinessWeek*, February 9, 2009, p. 65; Anne D'Innocenzio, "E-Retailers Push E-Mail Discounts to Lure Shoppers," *Marketing News*, November 15, 2008, p. 30; Anne D'Innocenzio, "Online Retailers See Surge on 'Cyber Monday,'" *Associated Press Financial Wire*, December 3, 2008; Pete Barlas, "Online Retailers Get Sprinkling of Yule Cheer, 'Cyber Monday' Sales Up 15%," *Investor's Business Daily*, December 4, 2008, p. A4; and "Plunkett's Retail Industry," Plunkett Research, Ltd., www.plunkettresearch.com/Industries/Retailing/Trends, accessed February 21, 2009.

2. "The Fortune 500," *Fortune*, May 3, 2010, p. F-1; *The 2009 World Factbook* (Washington, DC: Central Intelligence Agency, 2010); *Statistical Abstract of the United States: 2010*, 129th ed. (Washington, DC: U.S. Department of Commerce, Bureau of the Census, 2010), Table 20, Large Metropolitan Statistical Areas.

3. *Statistical Abstract of the United States: 2009*, Table 1009, Retail Trade and Food Services.

4. "The Global 2000," *Forbes*, April 9, 2009, www.forbes.com/lists.

5. "Corporate Facts: Wal-Mart by the Numbers," Wal-Mart Stores, Inc., Facts & News, www.walmartstores.com, accessed February 22, 2009.

6. "Research and Markets: Learn about Sustainability & Retailing, 2008," *Business Wire*, February 23, 2009; "Research and Markets: Going Green Isn't Just Good for the Environment—It's Good for Business Too," *Business Wire*, February 20, 2009; Jason Kirby, "Going Green for Selfish Reasons," *MacLean's*, December 8, 2008, p. 39; and Adam Aston, "Wal-Mart," *BusinessWeek*, December 22, 2008, p. 48.

7. "Retail Trade—Establishments, Employees, and Payroll," *Statistical Abstract of the United States: 2009*, 128th ed. (Washington, DC: U.S. Department of Commerce, Bureau of the Census, 2008), Table 1008; "County Business Patterns," Bureau of the Census, www.censtats .census.gov/cgi-bin/cbpnaic/cbpdetl.pl, accessed February 22, 2009.

8. "Top 10 Franchises for 2009," 2009 Franchise 500, Entrepreneur .com, www.entrepreneur.com/franchise500/index.html, accessed February 22, 2009; and Scott Shane and Chester Spell, "Factors for New Franchise Success," *Sloan Management Review*, Spring 1998, pp. 43–50.

9. "Lufthansa to Replace Check-In Terminals," *Airline Industry Information*, February 13, 2009; "Hilton Hotels Corporation Place #2 in Information Week 500," *Business Wire*, September 30, 2008; "Check This Out: Palm Beach County Library System Adds Self-Service Checkouts," *South Florida Sun-Sentinel*, February 17, 2009; "Research Shows Consumers Seek More Self-Service Options Due to Pressures of Price and Time," *Business Wire*, January 12, 2009; and Peter C. Honebein and Roy F. Cammarano, "Customers at Work," *Marketing Management*, January/February 2006, pp. 26–31.

10. Michael A. Wiles, "The Effect of Customer Service on Retailers' Shareholder Wealth: The Role of Availability and Reputation Cues," *Journal of Retailing*, 2007, pp. 19–31; Cate T. Corcoran, "Nordstrom 'Simplifies' Customer Satisfaction," *Women's Wear Daily*, March 22, 2007, p. 8; and Vanessa O'Connell, "Posh Retailers Pile on Perks for Top Customers," *The Wall Street Journal*, April 26, 2007, p. D1.

11. Donna Goodison, "Circuit City Closing to Boost Big-Box Stores," *The Boston Herald*, February 1, 2009, p. 23; and "Staples Get Investment Grade Ratings on Senior Unsecured Debt from Fitch," Moody's," *Midnight Trader*, January 13, 2009.

12. Andy Johns, "Healthy Vending," *Chattanooga Times Free Press*, January 12, 2009, p. B2; Alan Wolf, "Best Buy Testing Airport Vending Machines," *Video Business*, August 11, 2008, p. 6; and Gene G. Marcial, "Vending Machines Are Learning to Love Plastic," *BusinessWeek*, August 13, 2007, p. 86.

13. Leslie Berlin, "Phones as Credit Cards? Americans Must Wait," *The New York Times*, January 25, 2009, p. 4; Edward West, "Dialing In Yet More Impulse Buyers," *Business Day*, January 31, 2009; Elliot Maras, "The Case for Vending," *Automatic Merchandiser*, January 2009, p. 28; and Joe Astrouski, "Eastern Illinois U. Vending Machines Go Green," *University Wire*, November 21, 2008.

14. "DMA Encourages Catalog and Direct Mail Recycling," *PR Newswire*, May 23, 2007; and Blake Gopnik, "The IKEA Idea: What to Make of These Modern Times," *The Washington Post*, August 17, 2008, p. M08.

15. Ira Teinowitz and Nat Ives, "No Day Is a Good Day for No Mail," *Advertising Age*, February 9, 2009, p. 8; "A Zip-Code Screen for Catalog Customers," *The Wall Street Journal*, June 24, 2008, p. B1; and Richard H. Levey, "It's All about Me," *Direct*, November 1, 2008.

16. "QVC Extends Global Reach to Italy," *PR Newswire*, September 26, 2008; and "Fact Sheet" from the QVC Web site, www.qvc.com/qic, accessed March 2, 2009.

17. Christine H. O'Toole, "Attention, QVC Shoppers. . ." *The Washington Post*, January 28, 2009, p. C2; "Ellen DeGeneres Says 'HALO' to QVC," *PR Newswire*, January 14, 2009; "QVC Mulls Further Channel Developments," *Retail Week*, October 17, 2008; Richard Mullins and Michael Messano, "HSN's New Deal," *Tampa Tribune*, August 20, 2008, p. 1; Laura Petrecca, "QVC Shops for Ideas for Future Sales," *USA TODAY*, May 5, 2008, p. 1B; and Jon Fine, "Lights, Camera, Shop!" *BusinessWeek*, January 12, 2009, p. 62.

18. "Walmart.com Kicks Off 'Cyber Monday' with Unbelievable Prices on Over 150 Top Online Gifts, and Extends Event for Five Straight Days," www.walmart.com; Online Specials Feature Savings of Up to 30 Percent, with Many Items Available for Free Shipping with Site to Store and 97-cent Shipping to Home," *PR Newswire*, December 1, 2008; "Over 875 Million Consumers Have Shopped Online," *The Nielsen Company News Release*, January 28, 2008; and "eMarketer Revises E-Commerce Forecast," emarketer.com, March 5, 2009.

19. "EBay Marketplaces Fact Sheet," eBay Web site, http://news.ebay .com/fastfacts.cfm, accessed March 6, 2009.

20. Nicole Paitsel, "Use Web to Help Shop and Ship," *Richmond Times Dispatch*, December 7, 2008, p. J5; and Stephen Thompson, "Is Your Snazzy New Site Cloaked in Invisibility?" *Advertising Age*, October 13, 2008, p. 24.

21. "Power of Direct Marketing Report," Direct Marketing Association, 2009, p. 108.

22. "Do Not Call Registrations Permanent and Fees Telemarketers Pay to Access Registry Set," *States News Service*, April 10, 2008; and Deborah L. Vence, "Majority Rules," *Marketing News*, February 15, 2006, p. 4.

23. "Direct Selling by the Numbers," Direct Selling Association, http:// www.dsa.org/pubs/numbers/, accessed March 6, 2009.

24. Betsy Verckey, "Avon Products Boosts Restructuring, Freezes Hiring," *The Associated Press*, February 19, 2009; "Avon Reports Fourth-Quarter and 2008 Results," *PR Newswire*, February 3, 2009; and "Herbalife Receives Approval for Five Provincial Direct-Selling Licenses In China," *Drug Week*, August 8, 2008.

25. Morris Kaplan, "Direct Selling Grows on the Net," *Weekend Australian*, March 7, 2009, p. 32; and "Mary Kay Inc. Offers Women Compelling Solution to Economic Downturn through Direct Selling," *Business Wire*, March 3, 2009.

26. Francis J. Mulhern and Robert P. Leon, "Implicit Price Bundling of Retail Products: A Multiproduct Approach to Maximizing Store Profitability," *Journal of Marketing*, October 1991, pp. 63–76.

27. Marc Vanhuele and Xavier Dreze, "Measuring the Price Knowledge Shoppers Bring to the Store," *Journal of Marketing*, October 2002, pp. 72–85.

28. "No Frills Store Go Above and Beyond to Bring Great Savings to Customers Everyday," *Canada News Wire*, February 2, 2009; Gwen Ortmeyer, John A. Quelch, and Walter Salmon, "Restoring Credibility to Retail Pricing," *Sloan Management Review*, Fall 1991, pp. 55–66.

29. William B. Dodds, "In Search of Value: How Price and Store Name Information Influence Buyers' Product Perceptions," *Journal of Consumer Marketing*, Spring 1991, pp. 15–24.

30. "Pier 1 Imports, Inc. Reports Third Quarter Financial Results," *Business Wire*, December 18, 2008; Leonard L. Berry, "Old Pillars of New Retailing," *Harvard Business Review*, April 2001, pp. 131–37.

31. Eric Anderson and Duncan Simester, "Mind Your Pricing Cues," *Harvard Business Review*, September 2003, pp. 96–103.

32. Julie Baker, A. Parasuraman, Dhruv Grewal, and Glenn B. Voss, "The Influence of Multiple Store Environment Cues on Perceived Merchandise Value and Patronage Intentions," *Journal of Marketing*, April 2002, pp. 120–41.

33. Hyeong Min Kim, "Consumer Responses to Price Presentation Formats in Rebate Advertisements," *Journal of Retailing*, no. 4 (2006), pp. 309–17.

34. Rita Koselka, "The Schottenstein Factor," *Forbes*, September 28, 1992, pp. 104, 106.

35. "WEM Trivia," West Edmonton Mall Web site, www.westedmall.com, accessed March 9, 2009.

36. Ernesto Portillo, "Home Depot Part of Center Plan," *McClatchy-Tribune Business News*, November 20, 2008; and Lisa A. Bernard, "Anchor ID'd for 'Big Box' Power Center," *Dayton Daily News*, July 19, 2007.

37. Umut Konus, Peter C. Verhoef, and Scott A. Neslin, "Multichannel Shopper Segments and Their Covariates," *Journal of Retailing*, December 2008, p. 398; Robert A. Peterson and Sridhar Balasubramanian, "Retailing in the 21st Century: Reflections and Prologue to Research," *Journal of Retailing*, Spring 2002, pp. 9–16.

38. Jim Carter and Norman Sheehan, "From Competition to Cooperation: E-Tailing's Integration with Retailing," *Business Horizons*, March–April 2004, pp. 71–8.

39. Pierre Martineau, "The Personality of the Retail Store," *Harvard Business Review*, January–February 1958, p. 47.

40. Julie Baker, Dhruv Grewal, and A. Parasuraman, "The Influence of Store Environment on Quality Inferences and Store Image," *Journal of the Academy of Marketing Science*, Fall 1994, pp. 328–39; Howard Barich and Philip Kotler, "A Framework for Marketing Image Management," *Sloan Management Review*, Winter 1991, pp. 94–104; Susan M. Keaveney and Kenneth A. Hunt, "Conceptualization and Operationalization of Retail Store Image: A Case of Rival Middle-Level Theories," *Journal of the Academy of Marketing Science*, Spring 1992, pp. 165–75; James C. Ward, Mary Jo Bitner, and John Barnes, "Measuring the Prototypicality and Meaning of Retail Environments," *Journal of Retailing*, Summer 1992, p. 194; and Dhruv Grewal, R. Krishnan, Julie Baker, and Norm Burin, "The Effect of Store Name, Brand Name and Price Discounts on Consumers' Evaluations and Purchase Intentions," *Journal of Retailing*, Fall 1998, pp. 331–52. For a review of the store image literature, see Mary R. Zimmer and Linda L. Golden, "Impressions of Retail Stores: A Content Analysis of Consumer Images," *Journal of Retailing*, Fall 1988, pp. 265–93.

41. Mary Jo Bitner, "Servicescapes: The Impact of Physical Surroundings on Customers and Employees," *Journal of Marketing*, April 1992, pp. 57–71.

42. Jans-Benedict Steenkamp and Michel Wedel, "Segmenting Retail Markets on Store Image Using a Consumer-Based Methodology," *Journal of Retailing*, Fall 1991, p. 300; and Philip Kotler, "Atmospherics as a Marketing Tool," *Journal of Retailing* 49 (Winter 1973–74), p. 61.

43. Roger A. Kerin, Ambuj Jain, and Daniel L. Howard, "Store Shopping Experience and Consumer Price-Quality-Value Perceptions," *Journal of Retailing*, Winter 1992, pp. 376–97.

44. "Cannondale's 2008 PoweRanking Study," *Progressive Grocer*, November 3, 2008; "Category Management Takes a Step Forward,

Becomes CMAR," *MMR*, April 16, 2007, p. 26; Kusam L. Ailwadi and Bari Harlam, "An Empirical Analysis of the Determinants of Retail Margins: The Role of Store-Brand Share," *Journal of Marketing*, January 2004, pp. 147–65; Joseph Tarnowski, "And the Awards Went to . . ." *Progressive Grocer*, April 15, 2004; Betsy Spethmann, "Shelf Sets," *Promo*, May 1, 2004, p. 6; and "Study Shows Continued Support for Category Management," *CSNews Online*, March 17, 2004.

45. John Davis, *Measuring Marketing* (Singapore: Wiley and Sons, 2007), p. 46.

46. Paul W. Farris, Neil T. Bendle, Phillip E. Pfeifer, and David J. Reibstein, *Marketing Metrics* (Philadelphia: Wharton School Publishing, 2006), p. 106; Jerry Useem, "Simply Irresistible," *Fortune*, March 19, 2007, pp. 107–12; "Apple 2.0," www.blogs.business2.com; Steve Lohr, "Apple, a Success at Stores, Bets Big on Fifth Avenue," *The New York Times*, May 19, 2006; Jim Dalrymple, "Inside the Apple Stores," *MacWorld*, June 2007, pp. 16–17; and Davis, *Measuring Marketing*, pp. 280–81.

47. The wheel of retailing theory was originally proposed by Malcolm P. McNair, "Significant Trends and Development in the Postwar Period," in *Competitive Distribution in a Free, High-Level Economy and Its Implications for the University*, ed. A. B. Smith (Pittsburgh: University of Pittsburgh Press, 1958), pp. 1–25; also see Stephen Brown, "The Wheel of Retailing—Past and Future," *Journal of Retailing*, Summer 1990, pp. 143–49; and Malcolm P. McNair and Eleanor May, "The Next Revolution of the Retailing Wheel," *Harvard Business Review*, September–October 1978, pp. 81–91.

48. Emily Bryson York and Natalie Zmuda, "McDonald's Sends McCafe onto Fashion Week Catwalks," *Advertising Age*, February 9, 2009, p. 2; Lauren Sheperd, "McDonald's Posts Profit," *The Associated Press*, January 26, 2009; Michael Arndt, "McDonald's 24/7," *BusinessWeek*, February 5, 2007, p. 64; and "Resolved: No Trans Fats in 2007," *BusinessWeek*, January 15, 2007, p. 27.

49. William R. Davidson, Albert D. Bates, and Stephen J. Bass, "Retail Life Cycle," *Harvard Business Review*, November–December 1976, pp. 89–96.

Mall of America: This case was written by David P. Brennan and is based on an interview with Maureen Cahill and materials provided by Mall of America.

Chapter 15

1. Joseph Fullman, "Collective Communication," *Promo*, January 1, 2009, p. 18; Amy Johannes, "Sampling by Surprise," *Promo*, March 1, 2009, p. 10; Brian Quinton, "Game On!" *Promo*, February 1, 2009, p. 28; Richard Tedesco, "Big Dreams," *Promo*, November 1, 2008, p. 14; Richard Tedesco, "Alternative Viewing," *Promo*, December 1, 2008, p. 8; "Email Marketing: Time to Can Spam and Get Personal," *Precision Marketing*, December 15, 2008, p. 25; and Alyssa S. Groom, "Integrated Marketing Communication Anticipating the 'Age of Engage,'" *Communication Research Trends*, December 1, 2008, p. 3.

2. Philip J. Kitchen, Ilchul Kim, and Don E. Schultz, "Integrated Marketing Communications: Practice Leads Theory," *Journal of Advertising Research*, December 2008, pp. 531–46; Bob Liodice, "Essentials for Integrated Marketing," *Advertising Age*, June 9, 2008, p. 26; Shu-pei Tsai, *Journal of Advertising* 34 (Winter 2005), pp. 11–23.

3. Wilbur Schramm, "How Communication Works," in *The Process and Effects of Mass Communication*, Wilbur Schramm, ed., (Urbana, IL: University of Illinois Press, 1955), pp. 3–26.

4. E. Cooper and M. Jahoda, "The Evasion of Propaganda," *Journal of Psychology* 22 (1947), pp. 15–25; H. Hyman and P. Sheatsley, "Some Reasons Why Information Campaigns Fail," *Public Opinion*

Quarterly 11 (1947), pp. 412–23; and J. T. Klapper, *The Effects of Mass Communication* (New York: Free Press, 1960), chap. VII.

5. "Translation Bloopers," Miami News, www.miamibeach411.com, April 5, 2005; and Cynthia L. Kemper, "Biting Wax Tadpole, Other Faux Pas," *Denver Post*, August 3, 1997, p. G4.

6. Rik Pieters and Michel Wedel, "Attention Capture and Transfer in Advertising: Brand Pictorial, and Text-Size Effects," *Journal of Marketing*, April 2004, pp. 36–50.

7. Adapted from American Marketing Association, Resource Library, Dictionary, www.marketingpower.com/_layouts/Dictionary.aspx?dLetter=P, accessed March 14, 2009.

8. David Robinson, "Public Relations Comes of Age," *Business Horizons* 49 (2006), pp. 247–56; and Dick Martin, "Gilded and Gelded: Hard-Won Lessons from the PR Wars," *Harvard Business Review*, October 2003, pp. 44–54.

9. "McDonald's All-Digital Corporate Responsibility Report," *U.S. Newswire*, October 29, 2008; "RSS, Blogs, Podcast and Social Media Experts to Share Knowledge at PR Online Convergence Conference," *Business Wire*, April 11, 2007; "Business and the Media Forum Focuses on Social Media," *Business Wire*, July 9, 2007; Sarah Murray, "Public Relations: The Ease of Online Communication Is Undermining Companies' Control of Their Image and Reputation," *Financial Times*, November 8, 2006, p. 14; and Matthew Creamer, "Slowly, Marketers Learn How to Let Go and Let Blog," *Advertising Age*, October 31, 2005, p. 1.

10. Marsha D. Loda and Barbara Carrick Coleman, "Sequence Matters: A More Effective Way to Use Advertising and Publicity," *Journal of Advertising Research* 45 (December 2005), pp. 362–71.

11. Kusum L. Ailawadi, Scott A. Neslin, and Karen Gedenk, "Pursuing the Value-Conscious Consumer: Store Brands versus National Brand Promotions," *Journal of Marketing*, January 2001, pp. 71–8.

12. Nikki Hopewell, "The Rules of Engagement: A Bevy of Rules and Best Practices Govern Promotions and Contests," *Marketing News*, June 1, 2008, p. 6; and Gerard Predergast, Yi-Zheng Shi, and Ka-Man Cheung, "Behavioural Response to Sales Promotion Tools," *International Journal of Advertising* (2005), pp. 467–486.

13. Adapted from American Marketing Association, Resource Library, Dictionary, http://www.marketingpower.com/_layouts/Dictionary.aspx?dLetter=D, accessed March 15, 2009.

14. "New Media vs. Traditional: When Progress Meets Tradition," *Marketing Week*, January 22, 2009, p. 23; Richard H. Levey, "It's All about Me," *Direct*, November 1, 2008, p. 15; "Kraft Provides Recipe for Mobile-Marketing Success," *Advertising Age*, January 26, 2009, p. 12; Natalie Zmuda, "Marketers Push for Mobile Tuesday as the New Black Friday," *Advertising Age*, December 1, 2008, p. 21; "Multitasking Sports Viewers Engaged with Advertising," *PR Newswire U.S.*, June 28, 2007; "How Is Multitasking Affecting TV Networks and Online Video Sites?" *Business Wire*, February 6, 2007; and Greg Lindsay, "Demanding Boomers, MultiTasking Gen Yers Decide What, How, When," *Advertising Age*, January 2, 2006, p. 22.

15. "McDonald's CMO: Erase Borders and Create Bonds," *Marketing News*, October 15, 2008, p. 20; Lauren McKay, "Holiday Humbug: Will Grinch Steal Retail's Favorite Season?" *CRM Magazine*, December 1, 2008, p. 19.

16. Terry Box, "Pressure's Rising for Ford Dealers," *Dallas Morning News*, February 10, 2007; and Richard Truett, "Ford to Dealers: We'll Support Sales," *Automotive News*, June 18, 2007, p. 3.

17. Hollie Shaw, "A Case of Much Ado?" *National Post*, October 10, 2008, p. 12; Sheng Yuan, "Public Response to Direct-to-Consumer Advertising of Prescription Drugs," *Journal of Advertising Research*, March 2008, pp. 30–41; and Fusun F. Gonul, Franklin Carter, Elina Petrova, and Kannan Srinivasan, "Promotion of Prescription Drugs and Its Impact on Physicians' Choice Behavior," *Journal of Marketing*, July 2001, pp. 79–90.

18. Robert J. Lavidge and Gary A. Steiner, "A Model for Predictive Measurement of Advertising Effectiveness," *Journal of Marketing*, October 1961, p. 61.

19. "100 Leading National Advertisers 2008," *Advertising Age*, June 23, 2008, p. S6.

20. George S. Low and Jakki J. Mohr, "Setting Advertising and Promotion Budgets in Multi-Brand Companies," *Journal of Advertising Research*, January/February 1999, pp. 67–78; Don E. Schultz and Anders Gronstedt, "Making Marcom an Investment," *Marketing Management*, Fall 1997, pp. 41–49; and J. Enrique Bigne, "Advertising Budget Practices: A Review," *Journal of Current Issues and Research in Advertising*, Fall 1995, pp. 17–31.

21. Brenda Marlin, "Adding It Up: You Can Save Time by Trying One of Three Short-Cut Approaches to an Annual Budget," *ABA Banking*, October 1, 2007, p. 36; James A. Shroer, "Ad Spending: Growing Market Share," *Harvard Business Review*, January–February 1990, pp. 44–48; and Jeffrey A. Lowenhar and John L. Stanton, "Forecasting Competitive Advertising Expenditures," *Journal of Advertising Research* 16, no. 2 (April 1976), pp. 37–44.

22. Daniel Seligman, "How Much for Advertising?" *Fortune,* December 1956, p. 123.

23. James E. Lynch and Graham J. Hooley, "Increasing Sophistication in Advertising Budget Setting," *Journal of Advertising Research* 30 (February–March 1990), pp. 67–75.

24. Jimmy D. Barnes, Brenda J. Muscove, and Javad Rassouli, "An Objective and Task Media Selection Decision Model and Advertising Cost Formula to Determine International Advertising Budgets," *Journal of Advertising* 11, no. 4 (1982), pp. 68–75.

25. "The Olympics Come But Once Every Two Years," *Marketing News*, November 1, 2008, p. 12; "Olympics Will Bring Online Opportunities for Many Brands," *Revolution*, July 14, 2008, p. 13; and Don E. Schultz, "Olympics Get the Gold Medal in Integrating Marketing Event," *Marketing News*, April 27, 1998, pp. 5, 10.

26. "Integrated Marketing: One Message, Many Media," *Marketing Week*, September 18, 2008, p. 31; Cornelia Pechman, Guangzhi Zhao, Marvin E. Goldberg, and Ellen Thomas Reibling, "What to Convey in Antismoking Advertisements for Adolescents: The Use of Protection Motivation Theory to Identify Effective Message Themes," *Journal of Marketing*, April 2003, pp. 1–18.

27. James Quilter, "MasterCard Ties Up Sony Pictures to Promote Da Vinci Code Prequel," Brand *Republic* news release, February 6, 2009, p. 1; Steffie Nelson, "Spinners Wary of Wild Web," *Daily Variety*, February 19, 2009, p. A5–7; "Super Bowl Ads Viewed More Than 28 Million Times Online Since Sunday," *Business Wire*, February 4, 2009.

28. Mike Reid, "Performance Auditing of Integrated Marketing Communication (IMC) Actions and Outcomes," *Journal of Advertising* 34 (Winter 2005), p. 41.

29. Michael Bush, "Media Agency of the Year: Initiative," *Advertising Age*, March 2, 2009, pp. 14–15; Initiative Web site, www.initiative.com, accessed March 18, 2009; and James Quilter, "The Integrated Riddle," *Promotions and Incentive*, September 1, 2008, p. 1.

30. "Integrated Marketing: The Benefits of Integrated Marketing," *Marketing Week*, September 18, 2008, p. 33; and Tom Duncan, "Is Your Marketing Communications Integrated?" *Advertising Age*, January 24, 1994, p. 26.

31. "Integrated Marketing: Digital Fuels Integration Boom," *Marketing Week*, December 11, 2008, p. 27; Don E. Schultz, "IMC Is Do or Die in New Pull Marketplace," *Marketing News*, August 15, 2006, p. 7; and Don E. Schultz, "Integration's New Role Focuses on Customers," *Marketing News*, September 15, 2006, p. 8.

32. *Statistical Factbook 2009* (New York: Direct Marketing Association), pp. 142, 143; *Direct Marketing Key Statistics at a Glance* (New York: Direct Marketing Association, 2006), pp. 1, 5.

33. *Statistical Factbook 2009,* "Six Ways Lands' End Makes Online Shopping a Joy," *PR Newswire,* November 21, 2007; and Robert Berner, "Going That Extra Inch," *BusinessWeek,* September 18, 2000, p. 84.

34. Theresa Howard, "E-Mail Grows as Direct-Marketing Tool: They're Quicker to Make, Cheap to Send," *USA Today,* November 28, 2008, p. 5B.

35. Tim Parry, "Fill-Mail Savings," *Catalog Age,* August 1, 2008, p. 35; and Christopher Hosford, "Database Face-to-Face," *B to B,* February 9, 2009, p. 21.

36. "China: New Media Blossoming as Business Models Revamp," BBC Monitoring World Media, December 9, 2008; "The Data Dilemma," *Marketing Direct,* February 6, 2007, p. 37; and Marc Nohr, "South Africa—A Worthy Contender," *Marketing Direct,* March 5, 2007, p. 20.

37. Jeffrey Bernstein, "Ensuring Data Protection within Singapore Non-profits," *The Business Times Singapore,* March 2, 2009; Allison Enright, "Direct Mail Challenged," *Marketing News,* April 1, 2007, p. 3; and "Spam Is Now 77% of All E-Mail," *The Calgary Herald,* February 1, 2007, p. E1.

38. Claudia H. Deutsch, "Direct Mail Tries to Go Green. No, Really," *The New York Times,* July 23, 2008, p. 7; and Jennifer Wells, "Pushing the Envelope," *The Globe and Mail,* March 22, 2008, p. B3.

Under Armour: This case was prepared by Steven Hartley. Sources: Jeremy Mullman, "Protecting This Brand While Running Ahead," *Advertising Age,* January 12, 2009, p. 16; Jeremy Mullman, "Under Armour Hopes to Outrun Nike," *Advertising Age,* April 28, 2008, p. 6; Jeremy Mullman, "No Sugar and Spice Here," *Advertising Age,* June 18, 2007, p. 3; Stanley Holmes, "Under Armour May Be Overstretched," *BusinessWeek,* April 30, 2007, p. 65; interviews with Marcus Stevens, Nathan Shriver, Steven Battista, and Kevin Haley; and information contained on the Under Armour Web site (www.underarmour.com).

Chapter 16

1. Mark Hachman, "What's Behind the First 3D Super Bowl Ads," *PC Magazine.com,* January 28, 2009; "Is 3D About to Boom in 2009?" *Audio Visual Magazine,* February 1, 2009, p. 6; David Hambling, "Laser Light Show Displays Adverts in Thin Air," *New Scientist,* April 25, 2009, p. 19; Burt Helm, "Blowing Up Pepsi," *Business Week,* April 27, 2009, p. 32; "Commercials: Comcast Ad Campaign," *Creative Review,* April 1, 2009, p 20; Jonathan Paul, "Commercial Convo Goes 3D," *Strategy,* May 1, 2009, p. 21; "Beam Your Ads Directly into Their Brains—Well Almost," *Revolution,* May 1, 2009, p. 42; and Josh Quittner, "The Next Dimension," *Time,* March 30, 2009, p. 54.

2. Karen V. Fernandez and Dennis L. Rosen, "The Effectiveness of Information and Color in Yellow Pages Advertising," *Journal of Advertising,* Summer 2000, p. 61; David A. Aaker and Donald Norris, "Characteristics of TV Commercials Perceived as Informative," *Journal of Advertising Research* 22, no. 2 (April–May 1982), pp. 61–70.

3. Larry D. Compeau and Dhruv Grewal, "Comparative Price Advertising: An Integrative Review," *Journal of Public Policy & Marketing,* Fall 1998, pp. 257–73; and William Wilkie and Paul W. Farris, "Comparison Advertising: Problems and Potentials," *Journal of Marketing,* October 1975, pp. 7–15.

4. Chingching Chang, "The Relative Effectiveness of Comparative and Noncomparative Advertising: Evidence for Gender Differences in Information-Processing Strategies," *Journal of Advertising,* Spring 2007, p. 21; Jerry Gotlieb and Dan Sorel, "The Influence of Type of Advertisement, Price, and Source Credibility on Perceived Quality," *Journal of the Academy of Marketing Science,* Summer 1992, pp. 253–60; and Cornelia Pechman and David Stewart, "The Effects of Comparative Advertising on Attention, Memory, and Purchase Intentions," *Journal of Consumer Research,* September 1990, pp. 180–92.

5. Kathy L. O'Malley, Jeffrey J. Bailey, Chong Leng Tan, and Carl S. Bozman, "Effects of Varying Web-Based Advertising-Substantiation Information on Attribute Beliefs and Perceived Product Quality," *Academy of Marketing Studies Journal,* 2007, p. 19; Bruce Buchanan and Doron Goldman, "Us vs. Them: The Minefield of Comparative Ads," *Harvard Business Review,* May–June 1989, pp. 38–50; Dorothy Cohen, "The FTC's Advertising Substantiation Program," *Journal of Marketing,* Winter 1980, pp. 26–35; and Michael Etger and Stephen A. Goodwin, "Planning for Comparative Advertising Requires Special Attention," *Journal of Advertising* 8, no. 1 (Winter 1979), pp. 26–32.

6. David W. Schumann, Jan M. Hathcote, and Susan West, "Corporate Advertising in America: A Review of Published Studies on Use, Measurement, and Effectiveness," *Journal of Advertising,* September 1991, p. 35; Lewis C. Winters, "Does It Pay to Advertise in Hostile Audiences with Corporate Advertising?" *Journal of Advertising Research,* June–July 1988, pp. 11–18; and Robert Selwitz, "The Selling of an Image," *Madison Avenue,* February 1985, pp. 61–69.

7. "Pandora Launches Innovative Video Platform for Entertainment Industry Advertisers," *Marketwire,* September 16, 2009.

8. Rita Chang, "Mobile Effort Gets More to Say 'I Can' Purchase a Porsche," *Advertising Age,* February 9, 2009, p. 18.

9. Jeremy Mullman, "Nike: What Slowdown?" *Advertising Age,* October 20, 2008, p. 34.

10. Ira Teinowitz, "Self-Regulation Urged to Prevent Bias in Ad Buying," *Advertising Age,* January 18, 1999, p. 4.

11. "$100,000 Grand Prize Will Literally Go to Dogs," *States News Service,* June 4, 2008; and Magazine Publishers of America Web site, www.magazine.org/advertising/kelly_awards, accessed April 2, 2009.

12. See the Advertising Research Foundation Web site, www.thearf.org/assets/ad-effectiveness-council accessed April 2, 2009.

13. Emily Fredrix, "This Year's Super Bowl Ads Go Goofy and Frugal," *The Associated Press,* February 5, 2010; Jeremy Mullman, "Yes, the Super Bowl Is Well Worth $3M a Spot," *Advertising Age,* January 26, 2009, p. 1; Bob Garfield, "Ed McMahon's Bad Ad Steals the Super Bowl," *Advertising Age,* February 2, 2009, p. 1; "NBC Sells Out Super Bowl Ads for Record $206M," *The Associated Press,* January 31, 2009; and Rama Ylkur, Chuck Tomkovick, and Patty Traczyk, "Super Bowl Effectiveness: Hollywood Finds the Games Golden," *Journal of Advertising Research,* March 2004, pp. 143–59.

14. Ioni Lewis, Barry Watson, Richard Tay, and Katherine M. White, "The Role of Fear Appeals in Improving Driver Safety," *The International Journal of Behavioral Consultation and Therapy,* June 22, 2007, p. 203; Lenore Skenazy, "Take the Fat Out of Your Food," *Advertising Age,* January 14, 2008, p. 12; Cornelia Pechmann, Guangzhi Zhao, Marvin E. Goldberg, and Ellen Thomas Reibling, "What to Convey in Antismoking Advertisements for Adolescents: The Use of Protection Motivation Theory to Identify Effective Message Themes," *Journal of Marketing,* April 2003, pp. 1–18; Jeffrey D. Zbar, "Fear!" *Advertising Age,* November 14, 1994, pp. 18–19; and John F. Tanner, Jr., James B. Hunt, and David R. Eppright, "The Protection Motivation Model: A Normative Model of Fear Appeals," *Journal of Marketing,* July 1991, pp. 36–45.

15. "About Bebe," Bebe Web site, www.bebe.com, accessed April 9, 2009; and Sanjay Putrevu, "Consumer Responses toward Sexual and Nonsexual Appeals: The Influence of Involvement, Need for Cognition (NFC), and Gender," *Journal of Advertising,* Summer 2008, p. 57.

16. Rupal Parekh, "With Strong Work for Walmart and Geico, Martin Agency Is Creating a New Specialty: Making Marketers Recession-Proof," *Advertising Age,* January 19, 2009, p. 30; and Louis Llovio, "Geico Gecko's Viral Videos," *Richmond Times Dispatch,* March 28, 2009, p. B-9.

17. Thomas W. Cline and James J. Kellaris, "The Influence of Humor Strength and Humor-Message Relatedness on Ad Memorability: A

Dual Process Model," *Journal of Advertising*, Spring 2007, p. 55; Yong Zhang and George M. Zinkham, "Responses to Humorous Ads," *Journal of Advertising*, Winter 2006, p. 113; and Yih Hwai Lee and Elison Ai Ching Lim, "What's Funny and What's Not: The Moderating Role of Cultural Orientation in Ad Humor," *Journal of Advertising*, Summer 2008, p. 71.

18. Kipp Cheng, *2007 Television Production Cost Survey* (New York: American Association of Advertising Agencies, 2008), p. 5; and Jean Halliday, "Exotic Ads Get Noticed," *Advertising Age*, April 9, 2001, p. S4.

19. "With a Growing Design Operation, Two Thriving Offices, and Successful Relationships with Massive Brands Like Coke, Crispin Is Once Again the Best Agency in the Land," *Advertising Age*, January 19, 2009, p. 22; and the Crispin Porter & Bogusky Web site, www.cpbgroup.com, accessed April 9, 2009.

20. "U.S. Ad-Spending Totals by Medium," *Advertising Age*, June 21, 2010, p. S-15.

21. Vicki R. Lane, "The Impact of Ad Repetition and Ad Content on Consumer Perceptions of Incongruent Extensions," *Journal of Marketing*, April 2000, pp. 80–91.

22. David Bauder, "Prime-Time Games Big in Nielsen Ratings," *The Associated Press*, March 31, 2009; James Poniewozik, "Here's to the Death of Broadcast," *Time*, April 6, 2009, p. 63; "Research and Markets: The Marketer's Guide to Digital Out-of-Home Media," *Business Wire*, March 10, 2009; "Nielsen and Integrated Media Measurement Launch Out-of-Home Television Ratings Measurement Service," *PR Newswire*, April 12, 2007; and "Media Trends Track" based on Nielsen Media Research data, www.tvb.org/rcentral/MediaTrendsTrack, accessed April 15, 2009.

23. Brian Steinberg, "Sunday Night Football Remains Costliest TV Show," *Advertising Age*, October 26, 2009, p. 8; and Jeremy Mullman, "High Life's One-Second Spots Yield 8.6% Boost after Super Bowl," *Advertising Age*, February 23, 2009, p. 3.

24. "Top 15 Cable Networks," *Advertising Age*, April 14, 2008, p. S-8; and "'TV Everywhere' May Shine Light on Cable's Weak Spot," *Advertising Age*, March 9, 2009, p. 10.

25. "The IMS Top 50 Infomercials and Short-Form Spots of 2008," *Response*, December 1, 2008, p. 42; Jacqueline Renfrow, "Dodge Debuts First Infomercial for Ram Trucks," *Response*, October 1, 2008, p. 12; and Bill Carter, "Infomercial for Obama Is Big Success in Ratings," *The New York Times*, October 31, 2008, p. 19.

26. "Broadcast Station Totals As of December 31, 2008," Federal Communications Commission, February 27, 2009; "Time Spent Listening," in *Radio Today*, 2008 edition, Arbitron, www.arbitron.com, accessed April 15, 2009.

27. "Corporate Overview," Sirius Satellite Radio Web site, www.sirius.com/aboutus, accessed April 15, 2009; and "Hour-by-Hour Listening," in *Radio Today*, 2008 edition, Arbitron, www.arbitron.com, accessed April 15, 2009.

28. "A Magazine for Everyone," *The Magazine Handbook 2008–2009*, New York: Magazine Publishers of America, 2008, p. 5; "What Recession? New Magazine Launches, Up, Up, Up," MRMagazine.com, March 29, 2009, www.mrmagazine.wordpress.com; Sarah Treleaven, "The Magic Kingdom's VIP Room," *National Post*, March 14, 2009, p. WP12; and Larry Dobrow, "Idea of the Year: Reader-Generated Content," *Advertising Age*, October 6, 2008, p. S-6.

29. "Growth of Magazines by Category," *Editorial Trends and Magazine Handbook 2008–2009* (New York: Magazine Publishers of America, 2008); "Magazines Are #1 Medium of Engagement across All Dimensions Measured," *The Magazine Handbook 2008–2009* (New York: Magazine Publishers of America, 2008), p. 28.

30. Carol Krol, "Yellow Pages Bleeding Red Ink," *B to B*, August 11, 2008, p. 1; and "Extinction Threatens Yellow-Pages Publishers," *The Wall Street Journal*, November 17, 2008.

31. See "Examine Web Audiences by Site, Size, Demographic Profile and Behavior," at Nielsen Online Web site, www.nielsen-online.com/solutions, accessed April 23, 2009; and Abbey Klaassen, "Why the Click Is the Wrong Metric for Online Ads," *Advertising Age*, February 23, 2009, p. 4.

32. Gareth Jones, "Briefing-Paid Search-Advertisers Stung by Rising Click Fraud," *Revolution*, May 1, 2009, p. 18; "30 Seconds on Click Fraud," *Marketing Direct*, December 1, 2008, p. 42; Brian Grow and Ben Elgin, "Click Fraud," *BusinessWeek*, October 2, 2006, pp. 46–57; Rob Hof, "Is Google Too Powerful?" *BusinessWeek*, April 9, 2007, p. 48; Eric J. Hansen, "Apply Online Market Data for Offline Insights," *Marketing News*, April 1, 2007, p. 30; "Out of Site at AdAge.com," *Advertising Age*, November 6, 2006, p. 12; Michael Fielding, "Click Fraud Settles Down," *Marketing News*, September 1, 2006, p. 4; and Brian Grow, "This Mouse for Hire," *BusinessWeek*, October 23, 2006, p. 104.

33. Arch G. Woodside, "Outdoor Advertising as Experiments," *Journal of the Academy of Marketing Science* 18 (Summer 1990), pp. 229–37.

34. "The Year Ahead for . . . Outdoor," *Campaign*, January 9, 2009, p. 28; Andrew Hampp, "Digital Out of Home. That's Those Pixilated Billboards, Right?" *Advertising Age*, March 30, 2009; Andrew Hampp, "Out of Home That Stood Out," *Advertising Age*, December 15, 2008, p. 22; and Daniel W. Baack, Rick T. Wilson, and Brian D. Till, "Creativity and Memory Effects," *Journal of Advertising*, Winter 2008, p. 85.

35. Schoon Park and Minhi Hahn, "Pulsing in a Discrete Model of Advertising Competition," *Journal of Marketing Research*, November 1991, pp. 297–405.

36. Peggy Masterson, "The Wearout Phenomenon," *Marketing Research*, Fall 1999, pp. 27–31; and Lawrence D. Gibson, "What Can One TV Exposure Do?" *Journal of Advertising Research*, March–April 1996, pp. 9–18.

37. Rob Norton, "How Uninformative Advertising Tells Consumers Quite a Bit," *Fortune*, December 26, 1994, p. 37; and "Professor Claims Corporations Waste Billions on Advertising," *Marketing News*, July 6, 1992, p. 5.

38. Stephen Fajen, "The Agency Model Is Bent but Not Broken," *Advertising Age*, July 7, 2008, p. 17; Jeremy Mullman, "Anheuser-Busch Whacks Retainers for Its Agencies," *Advertising Age*, February 16, 2009, p. 1; Jack Neff, "No One-Size-Fits-All Snuggie Model Exists for DRTV Shops," *Advertising Age*, March 23, 2009; and Ivan Pollard, "Agency Model of the Future? Keep an Eye on Media Guys," *Advertising Age*, April 2, 2007, p. 29.

39. The discussion of posttesting is based on William F. Arens, Michael F. Weigold, and Christian Arens, *Contemporary Advertising*, 12th ed. (New York: McGraw-Hill Irwin, 2009), pp. 228–30.

40. "ROI Metric Available in MRI Starch Syndicated," Mediamark Research & Intelligence, www.mediamark.com, accessed April 23, 2009.

41. David A. Aaker and Douglas M. Stayman, "Measuring Audience Perceptions of Commercials and Relating Them to Ad Impact," *Journal of Advertising Research* 30 (August–September 1990), pp. 7–17; and Ernest Dichter, "A Psychological View of Advertising Effectiveness," *Marketing Management* 1, no. 3 (1992), pp. 60–62.

42. David Krugel, "Television Advertising Effectiveness and Research Innovation," *Journal of Consumer Marketing*, Summer 1988, pp. 43–51; and Laurence N. Gold, "The Evolution of Television Advertising Sales Measurement: Past, Present, and Future, " *Journal of Advertising Research*, June–July 1988, pp. 19–24.

43. Patricia E. Odell, "Promo Lite," *Promo*, October 2008, p. 14.

44. Tom Hansen, "Media Mash," *Promo*, February 1, 2007, p. 66; Magid M. Abraham and Leonard M. Lodish, "Getting the Most Out of Advertising and Promotion," *Harvard Business Review*, May–June 1990, pp. 50–60; Steven W. Hartley and James Cross, "How Sales Promotion Can Work for and against You," *Journal of Consumer Marketing*, Summer 1988, pp. 35–42; Robert D. Buzzell, John A. Quelch, and Walter J. Salmon, "The Costly Bargain of Trade Promotion," *Harvard Business Review*, March–April 1990, pp. 141–49;

and Mary L. Nicastro, "Break-Even Analysis Determines Success of Sales Promotions," *Marketing News*, March 5, 1990, p. 11.

45. Patricia Odell, "Dishing Out Discounts," *Promo*, October 2008, p. 23; "Coupon Facts," *Promo*, March 1, 2009, p. 42; and Patricia Odell, "No Lumps," *Promo*, March 1, 2009, p. 8.

46. Amy Johannes, "Flying the Coup," *Promo*, July 1, 2008, p. 28; and "What Is Coupon Misredemption?" The Coupon Information Corporation, www.cents-off.com, accessed April 23, 2009.

47. Amy Johannes, "Premium Connections," *Promo*, October 2008, p. 34; and Gerard P. Prendergast, Alex S. L. Tsang, and Derek T. Y. Poon, *Journal of Advertising Research*, June 2008, p. 287.

48. "User Content Offers a New Perspective," *PR Week*, February 23, 2009, p. 21; and Randy A. Salas, "Seriously, Who Watches the Big NFL Game Just for Football? The Cool Commercials Are Really Where It's At," *StarTribune*, January 29, 2009, p. 1E.

49. "Florida Woman Wins $2Million Grand Prize Package in HGTV Dream Home Giveaway 2009," *PR Newswire*, March 16, 2009; and "How I Won $1 Million by Eating Breakfast," *PR Newswire*, October 7, 2008.

50. "Mars Snackfood US Will 'Treat' Consumers to Halloween Million Dollar Contest," *Entertainment Business Newsweekly*, November 16, 2008, p. 124; "AT&T Announces Fox's 'American Idol' Seventh Season Breaks All-Time Record for Text Messaging," *PR Newswire*, May 22, 2008; and Richard Tedesco, "KFC Takes Wing Title," *Promo*, December 1, 2008, p. 14.

51. Brian Quinton, "The Hands-On Experience," *Promo*, October 2008, p. 37; Larry Jaffee, "Try It," *Promo*, September 1, 2007, p. AR25; Lorin Cipolla, "Instant Gratification," *Promo*, April 1, 2004, p. 4; "Best Activity Generating Brand Awareness/Trial," *Promo*, September 2001, p. 51; and "Brand Handing," *Promo's 9th Annual Sourcebook* (2002), p. 32.

52. "Loyalty Rewards Membership on the Rise," *Brandweek.com*, April 17, 2009; "Financial Services Surpasses Airlines as Largest Single U.S. Market for Reward Programs," Colloquy Web site, www.colloquy.com, accessed April 20, 2009; and Richard Tedesco, "Winning the Customer Comeback," *Promo*, October 2008, p. 30.

53. Marvin A. Jolson, Joshua L. Wiener, and Richard B. Rosecky, "Correlates of Rebate Proneness," *Journal of Advertising Research*, February–March 1987, pp. 33–43.

54. Richard Tedesco, "Video Placements Proliferate," *Promo*, October 2008, p. 35; and Brandchannel.com Web site, www.brandchannel.com/brandcameo-films.asp, accessed April 30, 2009.

55. Amy Johannes, "Simpson Mania," *Promo*, November 1, 2008, p. 8; and Allison Enright, "Apu Buzz, Krusty—Oh My!" *Marketing News*, August 15, 2007, p. 3.

56. This discussion is drawn particularly from John A. Quelch, *Trade Promotions by Grocery Manufacturers: A Management Perspective* (Cambridge, MA: Marketing Science Institute, August 1982).

57. Michael Chevalier and Ronald C. Curhan, "Retail Promotions as a Function of Trade Promotions: A Descriptive Analysis," *Sloan Management Review* 18 (Fall 1976), pp. 19–32.

58. G. A. Marken, "Firms Can Maintain Control over Creative Co-op Programs," *Marketing News*, September 28, 1992, pp. 7, 9.

Google, Inc.: This case was written by Steven Hartley. Sources: Jessica E. Vascellaro, "Google Decides to Find Its Creative Side," *The Wall Street Journal*, October 7, 2009; Robert D. Hof, "Google's New Ad Weapon," *BusinessWeek*, June 22, 2009, p. 52; Maria Bartiromo, "Eric Schmidt on Where Google Is Headed," *BusinessWeek*, August 17, 2009, p. 11; "Why Microsoft-Yahoo Deal Could Be Good for Google," *Advertising Age*, August 10, 2009, p. 10; Peter Burrow, "Apple and Google: Another Step Apart," *BusinessWeek*, August 17, 2009, p. 24; Jeff Jarvis, "How the Google Model Could Help," *BusinessWeek*, February 9, 2009, p. 32; Abbey Klaasen, "Google Says Print Ads Isn't the Answer for Newspapers," *Advertising Age*, January 26, 2009, p. 17; Matthew Creamer, "Recession

Doesn't Dent Total Value of Top 100 Brands," *Advertising Age*, April 27, 2009; "The 500 Largest U.S. Corporations," *Fortune*, May 4, 2009, F-1; "ComScore Releases August 2009 U.S. Search Engine Rankings," www.comscore.com, October 10, 2009; interviews with Google personnel; and information contained on the Google Web site (www.google.com).

Chapter 17

1. Alexandra Levit, "Lessons from Xerox," www.wsj.com, February 7, 2010; Adam Bryant, "The Keeper of That Tapping Pen," *The New York Times*, March 22, 2009, pp. C1, 20; "Executive Biographies—Anne Mulcahy," www.xerox.com, accessed May 1, 2010; Henry Canaday, "Anne Mulcahy and the Xerox Revolution," www.selling-power.com, accessed April 15, 2009; and "Xerox—Dedicated to Customer Success," www.sspa.com, accessed February 20, 2007.

2. Jessi Hempel, "IBM's All-Star Salesman," www.cnnmoney.com, accessed September 26, 2008.

3. "Surgical Visits," *Business 2.0*, April 2006, p. 94.

4. Mark W. Johnson and Greg W. Marshall, *Relationship Selling*, 2nd ed. (New York: McGraw-Hill/Irwin, 2008).

5. Barton A. Weitz, Stephen B. Castleberry, and John F. Tanner, Jr., *Selling: Building Partnerships*, 6th ed. (New York: McGraw-Hill/Irwin, 2010).

6. Scott Sterns, "Cold Calls Have Yet to Breathe Their Last Gasp," *The Wall Street Journal*, December 14, 2006, p. D2.

7. Jim Edwards, "Dinner, Interrupted," *BrandWeek*, May 26, 2003, pp. 28–32.

8. Christopher Conkey, "Record Fine Levied for Telemarketing," *The Wall Street Journal*, December 14, 2005, pp. D1, D4.

9. This discussion is based on Weitz, Castleberry, and Tanner, *Selling*; and Johnston and Marshall, *Relationship Selling*.

10. Kapil R. Tuli, Ajay K. Kohli, and Sundar G. Bharadwaj, "Rethinking Customer Solutions: From Product Bundles to Relational Processes," *Journal of Marketing*, July 2007, pp. 1–17.

11. For an extensive discussion of objections, see Charles M. Futrell, *Fundamentals of Selling*, 10th ed. (New York: McGraw-Hill/Irwin, 2010), chap. 12.

12. Theodore Levitt, *The Marketing Imagination* (New York: Free Press, 1983), p. 111.

13. Weitz, Castleberry, and Tanner, *Selling*.

14. *Management Briefing: Sales and Marketing* (New York: Conference Board, October 1996), pp. 3–4.

15. Keith A Richards and Eli Jones, "Key Account Management: Elements of Account Fit to an Integrative Theoretical Framework," *Journal of Personal Selling & Sales Management*, Fall 2009, pp. 305–320; and Eli Jones, Andrea Dickson, Lawrence B. Chonko, and Joseph P. Cannon, "Key Accounts and Team Selling: A Review, Framework, and Research Agenda," *Journal of Personal Selling & Sales Management*, Spring 2005, pp. 181–98.

16. "Group Dynamics," *Sales & Marketing Management*, January/February 2007, p. 8; and Steve Atlas and Elise Atlas, "Team Approach," *Selling Power*, May 2000, pp. 126–28.

17. This discussion is based on William L. Cron and Thomas E. DeCarlo, *Dalrymple's Sales Management*, 10th ed. (Hoboken, NJ: Wiley and Sons, 2009).

18. René Y. Darmon, *Leading the Sales Force* (New York: Cambridge University Press, 2007).

19. Rosann L. Spiro, Gregory A. Rich, and William J. Stanton, *Management of the Sales Force*, 12th ed. (New York: McGraw-Hill/Irwin, 2008), chap. 7.

20. Ibid., chap. 8. Also see, Julia Chang, "Wholly Motivated," *Sales & Marketing Management*, March 2007, pp. 24ff.

21. This discussion is based on Mark W. Johnston and Greg Marshall, *Sales Force Management*, 9th ed. (New York: McGraw-Hill/Irwin, 2009), Chapter 11; and Andris Zoltner, Prabhakant Sinha, and Sally E. Lorimer, *The Complete Guide to Sales Force Incentive Compensation* (New York: AMACOM, 2006).

22. www.MaryKay.com, accessed March 23, 2010; Terry Box, "Mary Kay, GM in the Pink with Cadillacs," *Dallas Morning News*, August 6, 2006, p. D2.

23. René Y. Darmon, "The Concept of Salesperson Replacement Value: A Sales Force Turnover Management Tool," *Journal of Personal Selling & Sales Management*, Summer 2008, pp. 211–32.

24. Dina Bass, "Microsoft Turns Attention to Customer Satisfaction," www.seattlepi.com, accessed January 5, 2005.

25. Mark Cotteleer, Edward Inderrieden, and Felissa Lee, "Selling the Sales Force on Automation," *Harvard Business Review*, July–August 2006, pp. 18–22.

26. Othman Boujena, Wesley J. Johnston, and Dwight R. Merunka, "The Benefits of Sales Force Automation: A Customer's Perspective," *Journal of Personal Selling & Sales Management*, Spring 2009, pp. 137–150.

27. www.toshiba.com/technology, accessed May 15, 2007.

28. Darmon, *Leading the Sales Force*.

Xerox: This case was written by Steven Hartley and Roger Kerin. Sources: Joseph Kornik, "Table Talk: A Sales Leaders Roundtable," *Sales & Marketing Management*, February 2007; Philip Chadwick, "Xerox Global Service," *Printweek*, October 11, 2007, p. 32; Kevin Maney, "Mulcahy Traces Steps of Xerox's Comeback," *USA Today*, September 11, 2006, p. 48; Sarah Campbell, "What It's Like Working for Xerox," *The Times*, September 14, 2006, p. 9; "Anne Mulcahy: How I Compete," *BusinessWeek* August 21, 2006, p. 55; Simon Avery, "CEO's HR Skills Turn Xerox Fortunes," *The Globe and Mail*, June 2, 2006, p. B3; Julia Chang, "Ultimate Motivation Guide: Happy Sales Force, Happy Returns," *Sales & Marketing Management*, March 2006; "The World's Most Powerful Women," www.forbes.com, August 27, 2008; and resources available on the Xerox Web site, www.xerox.com, including About Xerox, Executive Biographies, the Xerox 2007 Fact Sheet, the Online Fact Book: Historical Highlights, and the Online Fact Book: How Xerox Sells.

Chapter 18

1. Interview with Mattison Crowe, director of marketing at Seven Cycles, Inc., May 1, 2009; and www.sevencycles.com, accessed January 15, 2010.

2. "Over 875 Million Consumers Have Shopped Online," The Nielsen Company news release, January 28, 2008; and "Retail E-Commerce Sales Flat for 2009," www.emarketer.com, accessed January 15, 2010.

3. "The Sky Will Now Have Some Limits," *BrandWeek*, June 18, 2007, pp. S62–63.

4. Kimberly Palmer, "The Store of You," *U.S. News & World Report*, November 10, 2008, pp. 54–56.

5. Rafi A. Mohammed, Robert J. Fisher, Bernard J. Jaworski, and Gordon J. Paddison, *Internet Marketing: Building Advantage in a Networked Economy*, 2nd ed. (New York: McGraw-Hill/Irwin, 2004).

6. Ward A. Hanson and Kirthi Kalyanam, *Internet Marketing & Electronic Commerce* (Mason, OH: Thompson Higher Education, 2007).

7. Ibid.

8. Michael Grebb, "Behavioral Science," *Business 2.0*, March 2000, p. 112.

9. Judy Strauss, Adel El-Ansary, and Raymond Frost, *E-Marketing*, 5th ed. (Upper Saddle River, NJ: Prentice Hall, 2009).

10. John B. Horrigan, "Online Shopping," www.pewinternet.org, accessed February 13, 2008.

11. This discussion is drawn from Jeffrey F. Rayport and Bernard J. Jaworski, *e-Commerce*, 2nd ed. (New York: McGraw-Hill/Irwin, 2004; and *The Essential Guide to Best Practices in eCommerce* (Portland, OR: Webtrends, Inc., 2006).

12. Mylene Mangalindan, "Web Sites Want You To Stick Around," *The Wall Street Journal*, April 15, 2008, p. B5.

13. "Internet User Profiles Reloaded," www.pewinternet.org, accessed March 1, 2010.

14. Patti Freeman Evans, "US Online Retail Forecast, 2008 To 2013," www.forresterresearch.com, March 4, 2009.

15. Beth Bulik, "Technology No Longer Just Kid Stuff," *Advertising Age*, February 2, 2009, p. 12; "Moms Online: More Influential Than Ever," eMarketer Special Report, May 2009; and "New Study Reveals Internet Is the Medium Moms Rely on Most," Disney Online news release, March 2004.

16. Category online retail sales estimates are based on *Statistical Abstract of the United States: 2009* (Washington, DC: Government Printing Office, 2009); Lisa Phillips, "Health and Beauty Online," www.eMarketer.com, accessed September 25, 2008; and "How Much Will Online Travel Slow?" www.eMarketer.com, accessed November 13, 2008.

17. Jerry Wind and Arvind Ranaswamy, "Customerization: The Next Wave in Mass Customization," *Journal of Interactive Marketing*, Winter 2001, pp. 13–32.

18. Tom Hayes and Michael S. Malone, "Marketing in the World of the Web," *The Wall Street Journal*, November 29–30, 2008, p. A13. Also see, Kate Fitzgerald, "Blogs Fascinate, Frighten Marketers," *Advertising Age*, March 5, 2007, p. S-4.

19. Strauss, et al., *E-Marketing*, p. 357.

20. Stephen Baker, "The Online Ad Surge," *BusinessWeek*, November 22, 2004, pp. 76–81.

21. "Branding on the Net," *BusinessWeek*, November 2, 1998, pp. 78–86.

22. David Kesmodel, "Marketers Seek to Make Cookies More Palatable," *The Wall Street Journal*, June 17, 2005, pp. B1, B2.

23. "Many Users Still Wary of Web Safety," www.eMarketer.com, March 25, 2010; Mary Lou Roberts, *Internet Marketing: Integrating Online and Offline Strategies*, 2nd ed. (Mason, OH: Thomson, 2008), chap. 12; *2009 Internet Crime Report*, www.ic3.gov; "Consumers Are Concerned about Online Privacy, But Few Understand It," www.internetretailer.com, accessed May 1, 2009; and "The Cookie That Won't Crumble," *Forbes*, January 18, 2010, p. 32.

24. "Survey: Many Admit to Online Shopping at Work," www.moneycentral.msn.com, accessed December 2, 2008; and Susan Adams, et al. "This Time It Is Personal: Employee Online Shopping at Work," *Interactive Marketing*, April 2005, pp. 326–336.

25. This discussion is based on "Online Research Drives Offline Sales," www.eMarketer.com, accessed February 26, 2008; "Study: More Consumers Do Research Online, Shop Offline," *BrandWeek*, November 3, 2008, p. 8; "Shop Online, Spend Offline," www.eMarketer.com, accessed July 11, 2007; and Tamera Mendelsohn, "The State of Multichannel Consumers in the U.S. and Europe," www.forresterresearch.com, accessed June 25, 2007.

26. "Retailers' Panty Raid on Victoria's Secret," *The Wall Street Journal*, June 20, 2007, pp. B1, B12.

27. Stephanie Kang, "Callaway Will Use Retailers to Sell Goods Directly to Consumers Online," *The Wall Street Journal*, November 6, 2006, p. B5.

28. Erik Hauser and Max Lenderman, "Experiential Marketing," *Brandweek*, September 20, 2008, Special Section.

29. "Overcoming Multichannel Hurdles," www.emarketer.com, December 24, 2009; and "Online Research Drives Offline Sales."

Pizza Hut: This case was prepared by Pizza Hut and imc² executives for exclusive use in this text.

Appendix B

1. Diane Brady, "Creating Brand You," *BusinessWeek*, August 22, 2007, pp. 72–73; and Denny E. McCorkle, Joe F. Alexander, and Memo F. Diriker, "Developing Self-Marketing Skills for Student Career Success," *Journal of Marketing Education*, Spring 1992, pp. 57–67.

2. Marianne E. Green, "Marketing Yourself: From Student to Professional," *Job Choices for Business & Liberal Arts Students*, 50th ed., 2007, pp. 30–31; and Joanne Cleaver, "Find a Job through Self-Promotion," *Marketing News*, January 31, 2000, pp. 12, 16.

3. "Leading CEO's: A Statistical Snapshot of S&P 500 Leaders," *Research & Insight, Spencer Stuart*, December 2008, www .spencerstuart.com/research/ceo/975/, accessed June 14, 2009.

4. "Average Yearly Salary Offers," NACE *Salary Survey* (Bethlehem, PA: National Association of Colleges and Employers, Winter 2010), p. 4.

5. "Advertising, Marketing, Promotions, Public Relations, and Sales Managers," *Occupational Outlook Handbook*, 2008–09 Edition (Washington, DC: U.S. Department of Labor, 2008), www.bls.gov/ oco/ocos020.htm, accessed June 12, 2009.

6. Matthew Creamer, "P&G Primes Its Pinpoint Marketing," *Advertising Age*, May 7, 2007.

7. "Wholesale Trade," *Occupational Handbook*, 2008–09 Edition (Washington, DC: U.S. Department of Labor, 2008), www.bls.gov/ oco/cg/cgs026.htm, accessed June 14, 2009.

8. S. William Pattis, *Careers in Advertising* (New York: McGraw-Hill, 2004).

9. Roslyn Dolber, *Opportunities in Retailing Careers* (New York: McGraw-Hill, 2008).

10. Peter Coy, "Help Wanted," *BusinessWeek*, May 11, 2009, pp. 40–46; and "The Way We'll Work," *Time*, May 25, 2009, pp. 39–50.

11. Rebecca Aronaur, "Shaping the Profession of Sales," *Sales & Marketing Management*, July 1, 2006.

12. Jack and Suzy Welch, "Dear Graduate . . . To Stand Out Among Your Peers, You Have to Overdeliver," *BusinessWeek*, June 19, 2006, p. 100.

13. Edmund Hershberger and Madhav N. Segal, "Ads for MR Positions Reveal Desired Skills," *Marketing News*, February 1, 2007, p. 28.

14. "Market Research Analyst," in Les Krantz, ed., *Jobs Rated Almanac*, 6th ed. (New York: St. Martin's Press, 2002).

15. Deborah L. Vence, "In an Instant, More Researchers Use IM for Fast, Reliable Results," *Marketing News*, March 1, 2006, p. 53; and Joshua Grossnickle and Oliver Raskin, "What's Ahead on the Internet," *Marketing Research*, Summer 2001, pp. 9–13.

16. International Franchise Association, http//franchise.org/ Blockbuster Inc franchise.aspx.

17. Lisa Bertagnoli, "Marketing Overseas Excellent for Career," *Marketing News*, June 4, 2001, p. 4.

18. Barbara Flood, "Turbo Charge Your Job Search, Job Searching and Career Development Tips," *Information Outlook*, May 1, 2007, p. 40.

19. Barbara Flood, "Turbo Charge Your Job Search, Job Searching and Career Development Tips," *Information Outlook*, May 1, 2007, p. 40.

20. Barbara Kiviat, "The New Rules of Web Hiring," *Time*, November 24, 2003, p. 57; Karen Epper Hoffman, "Recruitment Sites Changing Their Focus," *Internet World*, March 15, 1999; Pamela Mendels, "Now That's Casting a Wide Net," *BusinessWeek*, May 25, 1998: and James C. Gonyea, *The Online Job Search Companion* (New York: McGraw-Hill, 1995).

21. Ronald B. Marks, *Personal Selling: A Relationship Approach*, 6th ed. (New York: Pearson, 1996).

22. Marianne E. Green, "Marketing Yourself: From Student to Professional," *Job Choices for Business & Liberal Arts Students: 2009* (Bethlehem, PA: National Association of Colleges and Employers, 2008), pp. 28–29.

23. Marianne E. Green, "Resume Writing: Sell Your Skills to Get the Interview!" *Job Choices for Business & Liberal Arts Students*, 50th ed., 2007, pp. 39–47.

24. "Post with Caution: Your Online Profile and Our Job Search," *Job Choices for Business & Liberal Arts Students: 20009* (Bethlehem, PA: National Association of Colleges and Employers, 2008), p. 30; "If I 'Google' You, What Will I Find?" *Job Choices for Business and Liberal Arts Students*, 50th ed., 2007, p. 16; Joyce Lain Kennedy, "Computer-Friendly Résumé Tips," *Planning Job Choices: 1999*, 42nd ed. (Bethlehem, PA: National Association of Colleges and Employers, 1998), p. 49; and Joyce Lain Kennedy and Thomas J. Morrow, *Electronic Résumé Revolution* (New York: Wiley and Sons, 1994).

25. William J. Banis, "The Art of Writing Job-Search Letters," *Job Choices for Business and Liberal Arts Students*, 50th ed., 2007, pp. 32–38; and Arthur G. Sharp, "The Art of the Cover Letter," *Career Futures* 4, no. 1 (1992), pp. 50–51.

26. Alison Damast, "Recruiters' Top 10 Complaints," *BusinessWeek*, April 26, 2007; and Marilyn Moats Kennedy, "'Don't List' Offers Important Tips for Job Interviews," *Marketing News*, March 15, 2007, p. 26.

27. Dana James, "A Day in the Life of a Corporate Recruiter," *Marketing News*, April 10, 2000, pp. 1, 11.

28. Robert M. Greenberg, "The Company Visit—Revisited," *NACE Journal*, Winter 2003, pp. 21–27.

29. Mary E. Scott, "High-Touch vs. High-Tech Recruitment," *NACE Journal*, Fall 2002, pp. 33–39.

CREDITS

CHAPTER 1

P. 2, ©Tolken Media. P. 4, ©M. Hruby. P. 4, ©M. Hruby. P. 4, Courtesy YouTube LLC. P. 5, ©Michael Grecco Photography. P. 5, ©Douglas Adesko. P. 7, Courtesy New Product Works. P. 7, This photo made available as a courtesy by Nestlé USA. P. 7, Courtesy RaySat Broadcast Corp. P. 7, Courtesy Pepsi-Cola North America Beverages. P. 11, Courtesy Southwest Airlines. P. 11, Courtesy Starbucks Corporation. P. 11, Courtesy The Home Depot, Inc. P. 12, Courtesy 3M. P. 13, Courtesy 3M. P. 15, Réunion des Musées Nationaux/Art Resource, NY. P. 15, Annebicque Bernard/Corbis Sygma. P. 15, *No credit.* P. 19, Courtesy 3M.

CHAPTER 2

P. 20, *All* Courtesy Ben & Jerry's Homemade, Inc. P. 22, ©2009 Google. P. 25, Courtesy Medtronic. P. 26 , Photography by Sean Lamb, 2004. P. 28, Courtesy Oracle Corporation. P. 30, ©Rick Armstrong. P. 30, *All* Courtesy Eastman Kodak Company; Agency Ketchum Communications. P. 32, All Courtesy Eastman Kodak Company; Agency Ketchum Communications. P. 33, ©M. Hruby. P. 36, Courtesy Medtronic. P. 37, Courtesy Eastman Kodak Company. P. 39, Courtesy Eastman Kodak Company. P. 42, Courtesy General Mills; Photo: Bowen Marketing.

APPENDIX A

P. 48, ©1996 Paradise Kitchens, Inc. All photos & ads reprinted with permission.

CHAPTER 3

P. 58, Courtesy Defense Industry Daily, LLC in association with Watershed Publishing. P. 62, ©The Procter & Gamble Company. Used by permission. P. 62, Courtesy Global Hyatt Corporation. P. 62, Courtesy Samsung Telecommunications America, LLP. P. 63, Copyright© NetImapact. P. 67, Courtesy Regent Seven Seas Cruises. P. 68, Courtesy Samsung Telecommunications America, LLP. P. 68, Citrix, Citrix Online and GoToMeeting are registered trademarks of Citrix Systems, Inc. P. 68, Courtesy MySpace.com. P. 71, ©M. Hruby. P. 73, Courtesy American Marketing Association/ Marketing News Magazine. P. 73, Courtesy of Better Business Bureau, Inc. P. 76, Photo by Tim Boyle/Getty Images. P. 77, Photo by Tim Boyle/Getty Images.

CHAPTER 4

P. 78, Courtesy Anheuser-Busch Companies. P. 83, Martin Poole/Stockbyte/Getty Images. P. 84, ©5 Creative, L.P. Illustration C. Tew & J. Robinson. P. 85, ©M. Hruby. P. 87, Courtesy Susan G. Komen Breast Cancer Foundation. P. 88, PhotoDisc Blue. P. 89, AP Photo/Elizabeth Dalziel. P. 90, AP Photo/Richard Vogel. P. 93, ©Michael Newman/PhotoEdit.

CHAPTER 5

P. 94, Courtesy TBWA Chiat Day/New York. P. 98, Karin Dreyer/Blend Images/Getty Images. P. 99, Courtesy PepsiCo, Inc./Frito-Lay, Inc. P. 100, Courtesy Campbell Soup Company. P. 104 , The Secret Sales Pitch: An Overview of Subliminal Advertising. Copyright ©2004 by August Bullock. All Rights Reserved. Used with permission. SubliminalSex.com. P. 105, FRESH STEPS® is a registered trademark of The Clorox Pet Products Company. Used with permission. ©2009 The Clorox Pet Products Company. Reprinted with permission. P. 105, ©2001 Mary Kay, Inc. Photos by: Grace Huang for Sarah Laird. P. 106, Courtesy Cogate-Palmolive Company. P. 106, Courtesy Unilever U.S. Inc.; Photographer: Martin Thompson; Photography: Smoke & Mirrors. P. 107, Courtesy SRI Consulting Business Intelligence (SRIC-BI), Menlo Park, CA. VALS™ is a trademark of SRI Consulting Business Intelligence. Reprinted with permission. P. 109, Courtesy BzzAgent, LLC. P. 110, *Both ads:* Courtesy Omega SA. P. 112, Courtesy of Haggar Clothing Co. P. 113, Courtesy ACH Food Companies, Inc. P. 114, Courtesy Bonne Bell, Inc. P. 114, Used with permission from McDonald's Corporation. P. 117, ©Gary Conner/PhotoEdit.

Figure 5-2, Copyright 2010 by Consumers Union of U.S., Inc. Yonkers, NY 10703-1057, a nonprofit organization. Adapted with permission from the January 2010 issue of *Consumer Reports®* for educational purposes only. No commercial use or reproduction permitted. www.ConsumerReports.org.

CHAPTER 6

P. 118, Courtesy J.C. Penney Company, Inc. P. 120, Courtesy Lockheed Martin Company. P. 121, Courtesy U.S. Department of Commerce/ Bureau of the Census. P. 125, Lluis Gene/ AFP/Getty Images. P. 126, Jewel Samad/AFP/ Getty Images. P. 127, VEER Mark Adams/ Photonica/Getty Images. P. 130, Courtesy Slack Barshinger/Chicago. P. 131, Jim Esposito/blend Images/Getty Images. P. 131, Comstock Images/ Getty Images. P. 131, Comstock Images/Getty Images. P. 131, Jim Esposito/blend Images/ Getty Images. P. 134, ©M. Hruby.

CHAPTER 7

P. 136, *All Courtesy* Enfatico Agency/New York. P. 141, Courtesy ALMA/BBDO São Paulo. P. 142, ©Benetton Group SPA; Photo by: Oliviero Toscani. P. 143, Courtesy Saatchi & Saatchi/ Beijing. P. 143, Courtesy of Nestlé S.A. P. 145, Used with permission from McDonald's Corporation. P. 145, ©Robert Holmes. P. 145, Antonio M. Rosario/The Image Bank/Getty Images. P. 146, Courtesy of Nestlé S.A. P. 146, *Both ads:* Courtesy Microsoft Corporation. P. 147, Courtesy The Coca-Cola Company. P. 150, Courtesy Fran Wilson Creative Cosmetics, Inc. P. 150, Courtesy McDonald's Corporation. P. 151, Courtesy Elite Industries, Ltd. P. 152, Courtesy Nestlé S.A. P. 154, *All* Courtesy The Gillette Company/Procter & Gamble. P. 157, Courtesy CNS, Inc.

CHAPTER 8

P. 160, Andy Kropa/Redux. P. 162, ©Shooting Star. P. 163, Fisher-Price, Inc. a subsidiary of Mattel, Inc. East Aurora, NY 14052 U.S.A. ©2006 Mattel, Inc. All Rights Reserved. P. 164, Fisher-Price, Inc. a subsidiary of Mattel, Inc. East Aurora, NY 14052 U.S.A. ©2006 Mattel, Inc. All Rights Reserved. P. 167, Copyright © David Young-Wolff/PhotoEdit. P. 168, Photo by M. Caulfield/American Idol 2008/Getty Images. P. 169, Macduff Everton/The Image Bank/Getty Images. P. 171, ©Louie Psihoyos/Science Faction/Corbis. P. 171, Comstock Images/Getty Images. P. 172, ©Spencer Grant/PhotoEdit. P. 175, Courtesy Wendy's International, Inc. P. 175, Dan Kitwood/Getty Images. P. 176, Photo by Cancan Chu/Getty Images Asiapac. P. 176, Todd Warnock/Lifesize/Getty Images. P. 177, ©Brent Jones. P. 178, Courtesy Schwan's Consumer Brands North America, Inc. P. 180, Courtesy Schwan's Consumer Brands North America, Inc. P. 181, ©M. Hruby.

Figure 8-3, Copyrighted information of The Nielsen Company, licensed for use herein.

CHAPTER 9

P. 186, ©2008 Zappos.com., Inc. P. 186, ©2008 Zappos.com., Inc. P. 189, ©2008 Zappos.com., Inc. P. 189, *All* Courtesy of Sporting News Yearbooks. P. 190, ©Shooting Star. P. 190, *Both:* Jill Braaten/The McGraw-Hill Digital Library. P. 192, Microfridge® Courtesy Mac-Gray. P. 193, Courtesy Claritas. P. 195, Courtesy Xerox Corporation. P. 196, *All* ©2007 Oldemark, LLC. Reprinted with permission. The Wendy's name, design and logo, Mandarin Chicken and Frosty are trademarks of Oldemark, LLC and are licensed to Wendy's International, Inc. P. 198, Courtesy Wendy's International, Inc. P. 200, *All* Courtesy Apple Computer. P. 203, ©M. Hruby. P. 203, ©M. Hruby. P. 206, Courtesy Prince Sports. P. 207, Courtesy Prince Sports.

CHAPTER 10

P. 208, Courtesy of Apple. P. 211, Courtesy Vetco, Inc. Consumer Health Care. P. 215, AP Photo/Dino Vournas. P. 216, Courtesy Nestle Purina Pet Care Company. P. 217, Courtesy The New Product Works. P. 217, Courtesy of the Original Pet Drink. P. 218, Courtesy The New Product Works. P. 218, Courtesy The New Product Works. P. 221, ©Erik S. Lesser/The New York Times/Redux. P. 222, Courtesy Volvo of North America. P. 223, Courtesy of IDEO. P. 223, Courtesy Gary Schwarzberg. P. 225, ©M. Hruby. P. 225, Jose Azel/Aurora. P. 226, Jim Wilson/The New York Times/Redux. P. 227, ©M. Hruby. P. 230, Courtesy Activeion Cleaning Solutions, LLC. P. 231, Courtesy Activeion Cleaning Solutions, LLC.

CHAPTER 11

P. 232, Photo by Chris Weeks/WireImage/Getty Images. P. 234, Photo by J. Meric/Getty Images. P. 236, Getty Images. P. 237, AP Photo/Mary Altaffer. P. 237, Courtesy Mullen. P. 243, ©2009 Blue Moon. P. 244, Courtesy Lowe Worldwide; Photo: Brian Kuhlman; Talent: Cameo Amato. P. 245, *No credit.* P. 246, Courtesy Oracle Beauty Brands LLC. P. 246, Courtesy Unilever U.S., Inc. P. 247, *No credit.* P. 249, ©M. Hruby. P. 250, Courtesy Marriott International, Inc. P. 251, Courtesy of Pez Candy, Inc. P. 251, Photo by: Arthur Meyerson. "Coca-Cola, the Contour Bottle design and the Coca-Cola Fridge Pack are trademarks of The Coca-Cola Company. Copyright 1994. All rights reserved. P. 252, ©M. Hruby. P. 252, ©M. Hruby. P. 254, Used with permission from McDonald's Corporation. P. 255, Trademarks and copyrights used herein are properties of the United States Postal Service and are used under license to McGraw-Hill. All Rights Reserved. P. 257, Photo by Rob Tringali/Sportschrome/Getty Images. P. 258, Courtesy Philadelphia Phillies.

CHAPTER 12

P. 260, Courtesy Vizio, Inc. P. 262, ©Robert Yager. P. 265, ©Terry McElroy. P. 266, Courtesy of Rock & Roll Hall of Fame. P. 267, Courtesy of The Caplow Company. P. 268, ©Najlah Feanny/Corbis. P. 270, ©M. Hruby P. 277, Courtesy Panasonic Consumer Electronics Company. P. 279, Photo by James Leynse/Corbis. P. 281, Courtesy Mardi Larsen Communications. P. 284, Photo by Neil Lupin/Redferns.

CHAPTER 13

P. 286, Courtesy Callaway Golf; Photo by Sam Greenwood/Getty Images. P. 289, Courtesy Border's Group, Inc. P. 294, Courtesy Nestle SA. P. 294, AP Photo/Nick Ut. P. 298, Courtesy Jiffy Lube International, Inc. P. 298, ©Amy Etra. P. 300, ©Joe & Kathy Heiner. P. 302, ©M. Hruby. P. 302, ©M. Hruby. P. 302, ©M. Hruby. P. 303, Courtesy IBM Corporation. P. 303, Courtesy Dell, Inc. P. 304, Courtesy Wal-Mart Stores, Inc., P. 308, ©M. Hruby. P. 308, Mark Wilson/Getty Images. P. 308, Justin Sullivan/Getty Images. P. 308, Justin Sullivan/Getty Images.

CHAPTER 14

P. 310, Robyn Beck/AFP/Getty Images. P. 313, ©Daniel Hambury/Corbis. P. 314, *No credit.* P. 315, Courtesy Doctor's Associates, Inc. P. 316, Courtesy Staples, Inc. P. 317, Courtesy Yo-Naturals Inc. P. 318, ©M. Hruby. P. 318, Courtesy Office Depot, Inc. P. 318, Courtesy L.L. Bean, Inc. P. 318, Photo by Matthew Peyton/Getty Images for QVC. P. 319, Courtesy MySimon, Inc. P. 322, Photo by Tim Boyle/Getty Images. P. 322, AP Photo/Paul Sakuma. P. 326, ©Brent Jones. P. 328, Courtesy Century 21 Real Estate LLC. P. 331, *Both* Courtesy Mall of America.

CHAPTER 15

P. 333, *Both* Courtesy CBS Interactive, Inc. P. 335, Courtesy Modernista! Ltd. P. 338, Courtesy ALMAP/BBDO – São Paulo. P. 338, ©2007 Llewellyn/Frommer's Australia From $60 a Day. Reprinted with permission of John Wiley & Sons, Inc. P. 338, Courtesy PepsiCo, Inc./Frito-Lay, Inc. P. 340, Courtesy Nation's Restaurant News. P. 341, Courtesy Nokia North America. P. 342, Artwork supplied by Merck-Schering/Plough Pharmaceuticals. P. 345, Press Association via AP Images. P. 346, ©Shooting Star. P. 348, Courtesy 4 Seasons Hotels & Resorts. P. 350, *No credit.* P. 353, Courtesy Under Armour, Inc. P. 354, Photo by Joe Robbins/Getty Images.

CHAPTER 16

P. 356, Photo by Leigh Vogel/Getty Images. P. 358, BLACKCARD is a registered trademark. BLACK and BLACK CARD family of marks are trademarks of Black Card LLC. Copyright ©2007-2009. P. 358, Courtesy GM Archives. P. 358, Courtesy Mars, Inc. P. 359, Courtesy National Fluid Milk Processor Promotion Board; Agency: Lowe Worldwide/New York. P. 360, Courtesy PepsiCo, Inc./Frito-Lay, Inc. P. 361, Courtesy GEICO. P. 363, Courtesy Lifetime Television. P. 365, Photo by Heinz Kluetmeier/Sports Illustrated/Getty Images. P. 366, ©M. Hruby. P. 366, Courtesy Double Click, Inc. P. 366, Courtesy Nationwide Insurance. P. 367,

BananaStock/PictureQuest. P. 367, Courtesy ecast. P. 369, Courtesy GfK Custom Research North America. P. 371, Courtesy of Valpak Direct Marketing Systems, Inc. P. 371, *No credit.* P. 372, *No credit.* P. 373, Photo by: NBC Universal Photo Bank. P. 373, Photo by David McNew/Getty Images. P. 377, ©2009 Google.

CHAPTER 17

P. 381, Courtesy of Xerox Corporation. P. 383, Courtesy Medtronic. P. 384, ©Mitch Kezar/Windigo Images. P. 387, ©Einzig Photography. P. 388, ©Image Source/Corbis. P. 389, ©Richard Pasley/Stock Boston, LLC. P. 390, Frank Herholdt/Stone/Getty Images. P. 391, Purestock/GettyImages. P. 393, Courtesy Xerox Corporation. P. 395, Comstock Images/Getty Images. P. 398, Royalty-Free/Corbis. P. 401, Courtesy Xerox Corporation.

CHAPTER 18

P. 403, *Both* Courtesy Seven Cycles, Inc. P. 406, ©Kainaz Amaria. P. 407, Courtesy Reebok International Ltd. P. 408, *No credit.* P. 411, ©Paul Barton/Corbis. P. 412, ©Tom Grill/Corbis. P. 413, ©2008 Zappos.com., Inc. P. 414, *No credit.* P. 415, Courtesy Travelocity. P. 416, ©Ray Bartkus. P. 417, Courtesy Nestle USA/Nestle Confections. P. 420, Courtesy Pizza Hut, Inc. P. 421, Courtesy Pizza Hut, Inc. P. 422, Courtesy Pizza Hut, Inc.

APPENDIX B

P. 424, ©Brad Trent. P. 425, ©Paul Elledge. P. 425, Courtesy Macy's Inc. P. 427, Courtesy Xerox Corporation. P. 427, Courtesy The Buckle, Inc. P. 429, Reprinted from Job Choices 2002, with permission of the National Association of Colleges & Employers. P. 429, Courtesy Monster. P. 432, White Packert/The Image Bank/Getty Images. P. 432, Thatch cartoon by Jeff Shesol; Reprinted with permission of Vintage Books.

Cartoon: Reprinted by permission of Jeff Shesol.

NAME INDEX

A

Aaker, David A., 459, 464, 465
Aaron, Hank, 221
Abel, Bill, 284
Abela, Andrew V., 448
Abell, Derek A., 449
Abkowitz, Alyssa, 448
Abraham, Magid M., 466
Abrams, Rhonda, 45, 449
Adams, Susan, 467
Adamy, Janet, 456
Agarwal, Manj K., 459
Ailawadi, Kusum L., 462, 463
Aizen, I., 453
Alba, Joseph W., 452
Alexander, Joe F., 468
Alexander, Sheryll, 452
Alford, C. Fred, 451
Allman, Greg, 283
Ambler, Tim, 448
Anderson, Brad, 117
Anderson, Eric, 462
Anderson, Erin, 454, 460
Anderson, James C., 447, 454
Anderson, Pamela, 459
Andruss, Paula, 459
Anscheutz, N., 457
Ansoff, H. Igor., 449
Ante, Spencer E., 448
Antia, Kersi D., 455
Appleyard, Dennis R., 454
Arens, Christian, 465
Arens, William F., 465
Armstrong, J. Scott, 449
Arndt, Michael, 449, 450, 457, 462
Arnold, Catherine, 451
Arnold, Todd, 459
Arnseth, Amber, 230
Aronaur, Rebecca, 468
Arsel, Zeynep, 451
Aschenreinver, Gwen Bachmann, 453
Ash, John, 452
Askegaard, S., 455
Aston, Adam, 450, 458, 461
Astrouski, Joe, 461
Atlas, Elise, 466
Atlas, Steve, 466
Augusto, Byron G., 457
Avery, Simon, 467
Avery, Susan, 454

B

Baack, Daniel W., 465
Badaracco, Joseph L., Jr., 451
Bagozzi, Richard P., 447
Bahadur, Nikhil, 459

Bahrami, B., 453
Bailey, Jeffrey J., 464
Baker, Julie, 462
Baker, Stephen, 467
Bakken, Earl, 25
Balasubramanian, Sridhar, 462
Balter, David, 109
Banga, Kamini, 455
Banis, William J., 468
Barczak, Gloria, 457
Barich, Howard, 462
Barlas, Pete, 461
Barnes, Jimmy D., 463
Barnes, John, 462
Barrett, Paul, 451
Bartiromo, Maria, 466
Bartos, Rena, 453
Bass, Dina, 467
Bass, Stephen J., 462
Bates, Albert D., 462
Bates, Douglas D., 456
Battista, Steven, 353, 464
Bauder, David, 465
Bauerlein, Valerie, 455
Bay, Willow, 455
Beatty, Sharon E., 452
Bedapudi, Neeli, 459
Beine, Scott, 230
Belich, Thoma J., 460
Belk, Russell, 452
Bellizi, Joseph A., 454
Belson, Ken, 458
Ben-Akiva, Moshe, 452
Bendle, Neil T., 448, 462
Benedetto, Anthony D., 457
Benson, Etienne, 455
Berg, Jeben, 73
Bergen, Mark, 455
Berlin, Leslie, 461
Bernard, Lisa A., 462
Bernasek, Anna, 457
Berner, Robert, 454, 464
Bernstein, Jeffrey, 464
Bernstein, Robert, 450
Berry, Jon, 453
Berry, Leonard L., 459, 462
Bertagnoli, Lisa, 468
Best, Roger J., 455
Bettencourt, Nuno, 284
Bezos. Jeff, 414
Bharadwaj, Sundar G., 455, 466
Bianco, Anthony, 456
Biba, Erin, 449
Bigne, J. Enrique, 463
Bilger, Burkhard, 460
Bingham, Frank G., Jr., 453
Bittner, Mary Jo, 457, 458, 459, 462
Biyalogorsky, Eyal, 457
Blackwell, Roger D., 452

Bloch, Peter H., 459
Block, Sandra, 447
Bloom, Paul N., 451
Boccara, Brun, 452
Bolles, Richard N., 433
Bolten, Joshua, 450
Bon Jovi, Jon, 283
Bonini, Sheila M. J., 448
Bonoma, Thomas V., 454
Booms, Bernard H., 458
Boring, Christopher, 322
Boujena, Othman, 467
Boulding, William, 447, 457
Bowie, Norman E., 451
Box, Terry, 463, 467
Boyd, Harper W., Jr., 448, 457, 458
Bozman, Carl S., 464
Brady, Diane, 468
Brandon, Emily, 450
Brandreth, Scott, 459
Brandt, Joe, 116, 117, 453
Brat, Ilan, 456
Brennan, David P., 453, 462
Brin, Sergey, 377, 378
Brockman, Beverly K., 457
Brodie, John, 459
Brodie, Roderick J., 449
Brooks, Garth, 331
Brown, Mary L., 455
Brown, Seth, 456
Brown, Stephen, 462
Brunel, Frederic F., 453, 459
Bruni, Frank, 460
Bryant, Adam, 466
Buchanan, Bruce, 464
Buck, David, 258, 459
Bughin, Jacques, 448
Bulik, Beth, 467
Bulik, Beth Synder, 459
Bullock, August, 104, 453
Burdick, Richard K., 454
Burin, Norm, 462
Burley, James, 457
Burns, Simon, 449
Burrow, Peter, 466
Bush, Michael, 463
Bush, Robert P., 456
Buss, Dale, 456
Buzzell, Robert D., 466
Byron, Ellen, 459

C

Cahill, Maureen, 330, 331, 462
Calantone, Roger, 458
Callaway, Vivian Milroy, 42–43, 449
Cameron, James, 162, 357
Cammarano, Roy F., 457, 461
Campbell, Sarah, 467

Canaday, Henry, 466
Cannon, Joseph P., 451, 466
Capossela, Alison, 399, 400, 401
Carey, John, 450
Carpenter, Gregory S., 447
Carral, Teré, 178, 179, 180
Carroll, John, III, 450
Carson, J. J., 452
Carter, Bill, 465
Carter, Franklin, 463
Carter, Jim, 462
Cash, James I., Jr., 458
Castellion, G., 457
Castleberry, Stephen B., 466
Cateora, Philip R., 455
Chadwick, Philip, 467
Chafkin, Max, 456
Chandler, David, 452
Chang, Chingching, 464
Chang, Julia, 467
Chang, Kenneth, 456
Chang, Rita, 464
Chen, Steve, 5
Cheng, Kipp, 465
Cheung Ka-Man, 463
Cheung, Karen M., 449
Chevalier, Michael, 466
Chiagouris, Larry, 452
Choi, Thomas Y., 454
Chonko, Lawrence B., 466
Chopra, Sunil, 460
Cipolla, Lorin, 466
Clark, Bonnie, 259
Clark, Bruce H., 448
Clark, Eric, 455
Claus, J., 453
Cleaver, Joanne, 468
Clement, Ronald W, 451
Clifford, Stephanie, 460
Clift, Vicki, 458
Cline, Thomas W., 465
Close, Glenn, 162
Cloud, John, 447
Cobb, Steven, 454
Cohen, Ben, 21
Cohen, Dorothy, 451, 464
Cohen, Joel B., 453
Cohen, William A., 449
Coleman, Barbara Carrick, 463
Collins, Jim, 428, 448, 449
Colvin, Geoff, 448, 456
Comer, Gary, 133
Compeau, Larry D., 464
Concialdi, Salvatori, 433
Conkey, Christopher, 466
Conlin, Michelle, 451
Connor, Michael, 452
Cooper, E., 463
Cooper, James C., 450

Cooper, Martha, 460
Cooper, Robert G., 457
Cooper, Scott W., 449
Corcoran, Cate T., 461
Corfman, Kim, 453
Corliss, Richard, 455
Costjens, Marcel, 448
Costner, Kevin, 161
Cote, Joseph A., 459
Cotteleer, Mark, 467
Coughlan, Anne T., 460
Cousins, Paul D., 458
Covel, Simona, 458
Covello, Joseph A., 449
Coy, Peter, 450, 460, 468
Crawford, Cindy, 109, 110
Crawford, David, 455
Crawford, Merle, 457, 458
Creamer, Matthew, 453, 463, 466, 468
Crockett, Roger O., 451
Cron, William L., 467
Crosby, Lawrence A., 450
Cross, James, 466
Crowe, Mattison, 403, 467
Cruise, Tom, 373
Curhan, Ronald C., 466
Cypher, James M., 450
Czinkota, Michael, 455

D

D'Innocenzio, Anne D., 461
Dacko, Scott, 433
Dahlhoff, Denise, 459
Dalrymple, Jim, 462
Dalton, Catherine M., 448
Damast, Alison, 468
Damp, Dennis V., 433
Daneman, Matthew, 449
Dant, Rajiv P., 447
Darmon, René Y., 467
David, Kenneth, 451
Davidson, William R., 462
Davis, John, 448, 462
Dawes, Philip L., 454
Dawley, Josephine, 456
Day, George S., 447
DeCarlo, Thomas E., 467
Deets, Chris, 458
DeGeneres, Ellen, 230, 319
Deighton, John, 459
Dekimpe, Marnik G., 459
Deleersnyder, Barbara, 459
Dell, Michael, 137, 297
Deutsch, Claudia H., 464
Di Benedetto, Anthony, 458
Diamond, Helene, 455
Dichter, Ernest, 465
Dickson, Andrea, 466
Dickson, Peter R., 452

Dikel, Margaret Riley, 433
Diorio, Carl, 455
Diriker, Memo F., 468
Dobbin, Ben, 449
Dobrow, Larry, 465
Dobscha, Susan, 447
Dodds, William B., 459, 462
Dolan, Kerry A., 458
Dolan, Robert J., 454, 460
Dolber, Roslyn, 468
Dolliver, Mark, 452
Donavan-Walt, Carmen, 450
Donegan, Dan, 284
Donovan, Robert J., 452
Doran, D'Arcy, 451
Douglas, Michael, 162
Dowling, Grahame R., 454
Doyle, Stephen, 450
Dreze, Xavier, 462
Drumright, Minette E., 453
Du, Rex Y., 453
Dubner, Stephen, 367
Duncan, Tom, 463
Dutta, Shantanu, 455
Dwyer, F. Robert, 453
Dylan, Bob, 283

E

Earl, Michael J., 458
Eastwood, Clint, 161
Edmondson, Gail, 458
Edwards, Jim, 466
Ehret, Michael, 447
Einhorn, Bruce, 457
El-Ansary, Adel I., 460, 467
Elgin, Ben, 465
Ellison, Katherine, 448
Ellison, Sarah, 456, 458
Els, Ernie, 287
Engardio, Pete, 452, 460
Engel, James F., 452
Enright, Allison, 451, 454, 464, 466
Eppinger, Stephen D., 458
Eppright, David R., 464
Erdem, Tulin, 459
Erickson, Peter, 458
Esterl, Michael, 455
Etger, Michael, 464
Ethans, Arno J., 454
Evans, Kenneth R., 447
Evans, Phillip, 449

F

Faes, W., 454
Fahey, Liam, 447
Fajen, Stephen, 465
Farris, Paul W., 448, 462, 464
Felice, Steve, 137
Fellows, George, 287

Ferguson, Sarah, 331
Fernandez, Karen V., 464
Few, Stephen, 448
Field, Alfred J., Jr., 454
Fielding, Michael, 451, 455, 465
Fikes, Bradley J., 450
Fine, Jon, 450, 461
Fine, Leslie M., 447
Fishbein, Martin, 453
Fisher, Robert J., 455, 460, 467
Fishman, Charles, 460
Fitzgerald, Kate, 467
Flood, Barbara, 468
Fong, Bay, 455
Forbes, Thom, 447, 457
Ford, David, 184, 449, 456
Fornier, Susan, 459
Forster, Julie, 457
Foster, Thomas A., 460
Foumier, Susan, 447
Foust, Dean, 451
Frank, Robert, 456
Fredrix, Emily, 464
Freedman, Alix M., 451
Freeman, Sholnn, 453
Friedman, Milton, 86
Friend, Tad, 455
Frost, Raymond, 467
Fullman, Joseph, 462
Furfie, Ben, 449
Futrell, Charles M., 466

G

Galbraith, John Kenneth, 450
Garfield, Bob, 464
Gebhardt, Gary F., 447
Gedenk, Karen, 463
Ghermezian Brothers, 330
Ghingold, Morry, 454
Gibson, Lawrence D., 455, 456, 465
Gibson, Richard, 457
Giese, John, 459
Gillman, Todd J., 455
Gilly, Mary C., 455
Glassel, Linda, 205, 207, 457
Gloeckler, Geoff, 450
Gogoi, Pallavi, 451
Gold, Laurence N., 466
Goldberg, Marvin D., 463, 464
Golden, Linda L., 462
Goldman, Doron, 464
Gomes, Roger, 453
Gonul, Fusum T., 463
Gonyea, James C., 468
Goodison, Donna, 461
Goodpaster, Kenneth E., 448, 449
Goodwin, Stephen A., 464
Gopnik, Blake, 461
Gordon, Geoffrey L., 458
Gotlieb, Jerry, 464

Gourville, John, 459
Graber, Donald R., 455
Graham, Jefferson, 449
Graham, John L., 455
Grebb, Michael, 467
Green, Marianne E., 468
Green, Mark C., 455
Greenberg, Robert M., 468
Greenfield, Jerry, 21
Greenleaf, Eric A., 452, 459
Greenspan, Robyn, 454
Gremler, Dwayne D., 459
Grewal, Dhruv, 447, 459, 462, 464
Griffin, Abbie, 457
Griffith, Eric, 450
Gronstedt, Anders, 463
Groom, Alyssa S., 462
Grossman, Lev, 447
Grossnickle, Joshua, 468
Grover, Ronald, 455
Grow, Brian, 465
Gubernick, Lisa, 459
Gulati, Ranjay, 452
Gumbel, Peter, 448
Gummeson, Evert, 457
Gundlach, Gregory T., 447, 451
Gunn, Eileen P., 450
Gupta, Sunil, 452
Gustke, Constance, 456
Gutherie, Julian, 458

H

Haas, Edward, III, 251
Hachman, Mark, 464
Haffman, Sarah, 452
Hahn, Minhi, 465
Hair, Joseph F., Jr., 456
Haley, Kevin, 353, 354, 464
Hall, Linda D., 433
Halliday, Jean, 465
Hambling, David, 464
Hamilton, Rebecca W., 457
Hamm, Steve, 450, 458
Hammer, Susanna, 459
Hammond, John S., 449
Hampp, Andrew, 465
Handfield, Robert B., 458
Hanford, Desiree J., 451
Hansen, Eric J., 465
Hansen, Tom, 466
Hanson, Ward A., 467
Harlam, Bari, 462
Harmon, Eric P., 457
Harrison, George, 283
Hartley, Robert F., 452
Hartley, Steven W., 451, 460, 464, 466, 467
Hastings, Reed, 26
Hathcote, Jan M., 464
Hauser, Erik, 468

Hawkins, Del I., 452, 453, 455
Hayes, Tom, 467
Hazelgren, Brian J., 449
Hein, Kenneth, 452
Helm, Burt, 464
Helsen, Khristiaan, 455
Hempel, Jessi, 466
Henderson, Verne E., 451
Henry, David, 451
Herbig, Paul A., 455
Hering, Tyler, 206
Hershberger, Edmund, 468
Hiebing, Roman G., Jr., 449
Higgins, Kevin, 451
Higgins, Michelle, 451
Hochman, Sara, 63
Hoeffler, Steve, 458
Hof, Robert D., 449, 465, 466
Hoffman, Karen Epper, 468
Holden, Reed K., 460
Holden, Richard, 377, 379
Holloran, Thomas E., 448
Holloway, Charles J., 458
Holmes, Stanley, 458, 464
Holson, Laura M., 458
Honan, Mathew, 449
Honebein, Peter C., 457, 461
Hooley, Graham J., 463
Hope, Chris, 452
Hopewell, Nikki, 450, 463
Horn, John, 455
Horovitz, Bruce, 459
Horrigan, John B., 467
Hosford, Christopher, 464
Howard, Daniel L., 459, 462
Howard, John A., 452
Howard, Theresa, 464
Hoyer, Wayne D., 452, 453
Hsieh, Tony, 186, 187, 188
Hughes, Tim, 450
Humphreys, Jeffrey M., 449, 453
Hunt, James B., 464
Hunt, Kenneth A., 462
Hurley, Chad, 5
Huston, Larry, 458
Hutchinson, J. Wesley, 452
Hutt, Michael D., 453
Hyman, H., 463

I

Inderrieden, Edward, 467
Ives, Nat, 461

J

Jackson, Donald W., 454
Jacoby, Jacob, 459
Jaffee, Larry, 466
Jahoda, M., 463
Jain, Ambuj, 459, 462

James, Dana, 468
James, Diana, 454
James, Harvey S., 452
Janis, Irwin L., 457
Jap, Sandy D., 453
Jarvis, Jeff, 466
Jaworski, Bernard J., 460, 467
Jayson, Sharon, 450
Jespersen, Frederick F., 451
Jobs, Steven, 200–201, 208–209, 222, 298
Johannes, Amy, 462, 466
Johansson, Johnny K., 455
John, Deborah Roedder, 453
John, Elton, 21
Johns, Andy, 461
Johnson, Bruce, 157
Johnson, Gavin, 456
Johnson, Gerry, 448
Johnson, Sheree L., 450
Johnston, Mark W., 466, 467
Johnston, Wesley J., 447, 454, 467
Jolson, Marvin A., 466
Jones, D. G. Brian, 447
Jones, Eli, 466
Jones, Gareth, 465
Jones, Kathryn, 460
Judson, Kimberly, 458
Juran, Robert A., 433

K

Kahn, Kenneth B., 457
Kahney, Leander, 458
Kallayil, Gopi, 378
Kalyanam, Kirthi, 467
Kamakura, Wagner A., 453
Kambil, Ajit, 454
Kaminsky, Philip, 460
Kane, Hukari, 451
Kang, Stephanie, 460, 468
Kapferer, Jean-Noel, 460
Kaplan, Morris, 461
Karim, Jawed, 5
Karremans, J., 453
Katzenberg, Jeffrey, 357
Keaveney, Susan M., 462
Keefe, Lisa M., 447
Keegan, Warren J., 455
Keith, Janet E., 454
Keith, Robert F., 447
Kellaris, James J., 465
Kelleher, Kevin, 460
Keller, Ed, 453
Keller, Kevin Lane, 455, 459
Kelly, David, 223, 451
Kemper, Cynthia L., 463
Kennedy, John F., 82
Kennedy, Joyce Lain, 468
Kennedy, Marilyn Moats, 468

Kerin, Roger A., 448, 449, 457, 458, 459, 460, 462, 467
Kesmodel, David, 467
Khan, Urea, 450
Kher, Unmesh, 452
Kiley, David, 450, 456
Kim, Hyeong Min, 462
Kim, Ilchul, 462
Kim, Peter, 449
Kim, W. Chan, 448
King, Ronald H., 454
Kirby, Jason, 461
Kitchen, Philip J., 462
Kiviat, Barbara, 468
Kjeldgaard, D., 455
Klaassen, Abbey, 465, 466
Klapper, J. T., 463
Kleese, Hilary, 135
Klein, Thomas A., 451
Klum, Heidi, 319
Kngeyama, Yuri, 454
Knowles, Patricia A., 453
Kohli, Ajay K., 454, 466
Konus, Umut, 462
Korn, Melissa, 449
Kornik, Joseph, 467
Koselka, Rita, 462
Kotabe, Massaki, 455
Kothari, Ashish, 447
Kotler, Philip, 448, 462
Krattenmaker, Tom, 448
Kraus, Eric, 428
Krauss, Michael, 448, 454
Krishnan, R., 462
Kroc, Ray, 326
Krol, Carol, 465
Krugel, David, 465
Kuczmarski, Thomas D., 457
Kumar, V., 447
Kydd, Arthur R., 44, 449

L

LaBahn, Douglas W., 459
Lackner, Joseph, 447
Laezniak, Gene R., 451
Lafley, A. G., 124, 222
Lamey, Lien, 459
Lane, Vicki R., 465
Largesse, David, 450
Larréché, Jean-Claude, 448, 457, 458
Lashinsky, Adam, 457
Lavidge, Robert J., 463
Lavie, N., 453
Lawson, Benn, 458
Lee, Don Y., 454
Lee, Felissa, 467
Lee, Hau L., 460
Lee, Myung-Soo, 452
Lee, Yih Hwai, 465
Lehmann, Donald R., 452, 458

Leigh, Thomas W., 454
Lello, Kevin, 283
Lencioni, Patrick M., 448
Lenderman, Max, 468
Leo, Pamela, 187
Leon, Robert P., 461
Leonard Devin, 456
Leporini, Christopher, 455
Leslie, Mark, 458
Letterman, David, 353
Levey, Richard H., 450, 461, 463
Levit, Alexandra, 466
Levitt, Theodore, 26, 448, 466
Levy, Michael, 460
Levy, Sidney J., 448
Levy, Steven, 450
Lewis, Barbara, 433
Lewis, Ioni, 464
Lewis, Ray, 353
Leyden, Peter, 63
Lezcano, Michael, 459
Liker, Jeffrey K., 454
Lilien, Gary L., 454
Lim, Paul J., 450
Lin, Alfred, 187
Linblad, Cristina, 450
Lindsay, Greg, 463
Lindstrom, Martin, 170, 171, 452, 453, 456
Liodice, Bob, 462
Littler, Dale, 433
Littman, Sarah, 450
Llovio, Louis, 465
Lloyd, Mary Ellen, 451
Loda, Marsha D., 463
Lodish, Leonard M., 466
Lohr, Steve, 457, 462
Loiaza, Margaret, 185
Lorimer, Sally E., 467
Lovallo, Dan P., 457
Lovelock, Christopher H., 457, 458
Low, George S., 463
Lowenhar, Jeffrey A., 463
Lowry, Tom, 455
Lumpkin, James R., 460
Lutz, Richard J., 453
Lynch, Frank, 309, 460
Lynch, James E., 463
Lynch, John, 453

M

Mabert, Vincent A., 458
MacArthur, Kate, 458
MacInnis, Deborah J., 452, 453
Mack, Ann, 453
Mahajan, Vijay, 448, 449, 455
Malone, Michael S., 467
Malphurs, Aubrey, 448
Mandel, Michael, 451
Maney, Kevin, 467

Mangalindan, Mylene, 467
Maras, Elliot, 461
Marcial, Gene G., 461
Marcoolyn, Gillian, 452
Maremont, Mark, 456
Marken, G. A., 466
Markides, Costas, 448
Marks, Barbara B., 468
Marlin, Brenda, 463
Marshall, Greg W., 466, 467
Martin, Dick, 463
Martin, Roger L., 448
Martineau, Pierre, 323, 462
Maslow, Abraham H., 453
Masterson, Peggy, 465
Matthyssens, P., 454
Mauborgne, Renée, 448
Maurer, Harry, 450
May, Eleanor, 462
Mayer, Marissa, 225, 226
McCarthy, E. Jerome, 10, 447
McCarthy, Michael, 456
McColgan, Ellyn A., 457
McColl-Kennedy, Janet R., 457
McCorkle, Denny E., 468
McCracken, Jeffrey, 460
McDonald, Duff, 456
McDonald, Hugh, 283
McGregor, Jena, 456
McGuire, Kara, 447, 450
McKay, Betsy, 459
McKay, Lauren, 463
McKeever, Mike, 449
McKenna, Kevin, 158, 455
McKeon, Jack, 307, 308, 309, 460
McMath, Robert M., 8, 447, 457
McNair, Malcolm P., 462
McVey, Philip, 454
Mehta, Stephanie N., 456
Meindl, Peter, 460
Meissner, Kimmie, 353
Mendels, Pamela, 468
Mendelsohn, Bruce, 456
Mendelsohn, Tamera, 467
Mendonca, Lenny T., 448
Menon, Anil, 452
Merrick, Amy, 456
Merunka, Dwight R., 467
Mesa, Tansa, 454
Messano, Michael, 461
Metz, Cade, 451
Meuter, Matthew L., 457
Meyer, Christopher, 447
Michaels, Ian, 456
Mick, David Glen, 447
Miles, Stephanie, 454
Miley, Marissa, 453
Milligan, Brian, 453
Miniard, Paul W., 452
Minor, Michael, 452
Mitral, Banwasi, 452, 458, 459
Mohammed, Rafi A., 460, 467

Mohr, Jakki J., 453, 463
Monfils, Gael, 207
Monroe, Kent B., 459, 460
Montgomery, David, 257, 259, 459
Moon, Youngme, 454, 457
Moore, Elizabeth S., 448, 453
Moore, Janet, 448
Moore-Mezler, Colleen, 456
Morfitt, Marti, 157, 158, 159
Morgan, Robert M., 457
Morinoto, Risako, 452
Morn, John T., 457
Morrison, Robert, 458
Morriss, John, 261
Morrow, Thomas J., 468
Morton, Fiona Scott, 460
Moses, Elissa, 455
Mothersbaugh, David L., 452, 453, 455
Moul, Charles C., 460
Mowen, John C., 452
Mudget, Joan, 134
Mulcahy, Anne M., 380, 381, 400, 401, 466
Mulhern, Francis J., 461
Mullins, John M., 457, 458
Mullins, Richard, 461
Mullman, Jeremy, 464, 465
Muris, Timothy, 451
Murphy, Patrick E., 447, 451
Murray, Sarah, 463
Muscove, Brenda J., 463
Musico, Christopher, 450

N

N Sync, 331
Nagele, Kim, 119, 128, 453
Nagle, Thomas T., 460
Narus, James A., 447, 454
Narver, John C., 447
Nasheri, Hedich, 451
Naumann, Nick, 158, 455
Nedungadi, Prakesh, 452
Neff, Jack, 456, 458, 459, 465
Neilson, Gary, 452
Neimeister, Larry, 456
Nelson, Emily, 456
Nelson, Jennifer, 449
Nelson, Katherine A., 451
Nelson, Steffie, 463
Nesdale, Andrew, 452
Neslin, Scott A., 462, 463
Newsome, Laynie, 261
Nicastro, Mary L., 466
Niccol, Brian, 420, 423
Nohr, Marc, 464
Norris, Donald, 464
Norton, Rob, 465
Nussbaum, Bruce, 458

O

Obama, Barack, 364
O'Brien, Jeffrey M., 456
O'Connell, Vanessa, 461
Odell, Patricia F., 466
Ogbogu, Eric, 353
Olsen, R. Paul, 458
Olson, Jerry C., 453, 459
O'Malley, Kathy L., 464
Openheim, Jeremy M., 448
Ordonez, Jennifer, 456, 458
Ortinau, David J., 456
Ortmeyer, Gwen, 462
Osberg, Sally, 448
Ostrom, Amy L., 457
O'Toole, Christine H., 461
Ottman, Jacquelyn, 447, 448

P

Paddison, Gordon J., 467
Page, Larry, 377, 378
Paitsel, Nicole, 461
Palmatier, Robert W., 447
Palmer, Kimberly, 450, 467
Palmeri, Christopher, 456, 458
Palmisano, Samuel J., 303, 382
Pandit, Vivek, 457
Parasuraman, A., 462
Parekh, Rupal, 465
Park, Schoon, 465
Parmar, Arundhati, 449
Parpis, E., 453
Parry, Tim, 464
Parton, Dolly, 283
Parum, Traci, 453
Parvatiyar, Atul, 455
Pasini, Mike, 449
Passmore, Nick, 449
Paterson, John, 453
Patterson, Ben, 457
Pattis, S. William, 468
Patton, Welsey E., III, 454
Paul, Jonathan, 464
Pauwels, Koen, 448, 450
Pechman, Cornelia, 463, 464
Pelow, Leslie, 457
Pelton, Lou, 460
Peot, Joanna, 449
Peter, J. Paul, 453
Peters, Leah E., 46, 47
Peters, Randall F., 46, 47
Petersen, Kenneth J., 458
Peterson, Robert A., 448, 449, 457, 458, 460, 462
Petrecca, Laura, 461
Petrova, Elina, 463
Pfeiffer, Phillip E., 448, 462
Phelps, David, 448
Phelps, Michael, 109, 110

Phillips, Lisa, 467
Phillips, Wendy, 454
Pierce, Andrew, 450
Pieters, Rik, 463
Plank, Kevin, 352, 354
Pogue, David, 448
Pollard, Ivan, 465
Poniewozik, James, 465
Poon, Derek T. Y., 466
Porras, Jerry I., 448
Porter, Michael E., 447, 448
Portillo, Ernesto, 462
Potter, Donald V., 459
Powell, Michael A., 426
Powers, Keemp, 460
Prahalad, C. K., 458
Prema, Karen, 458
Prendergast, Gerard P., 463, 466
Pressman, Aaron, 450
Proctor, Bernadette D., 450
Puto, Christopher P., 454
Putrevu, Sanjay, 465

Q

Quam, Steve, 185
Quelch, John A., 462, 466
Quick, Rebecca, 454
Quilter, James, 463
Quinn, Jane Bryant, 451
Quinton, Brian, 462, 466
Quittner, Josh, 449, 457, 464

R

Ramaswamy, Arvind, 467
Ramaswamy, Venkat, 458
Rao, Vithala R., 451, 459
Raskin, Andrew, 460
Raskin, Oliver, 468
Rassekh, Farhad, 452
Rassouli, Javad, 463
Ratchford, Brian T., 452
Ray, Ipshita, 452
Rayport, Jeffrey F., 467
Rea-Holloway, Melinda, 456
Rees, G., 453
Rehbord, Mark, 184, 185
Reibling, Ellen Thomas, 463, 464
Reibstein, David J., 448, 462
Reichheld, Frederick F., 452, 457
Reid, Mike, 463
Reinan, John, 447
Reinhold, Jennifer, 454
Rendon, Jim, 468
Renfrow, Jacqueline, 465
Retsky, Maxine L., 451
Rgahubir, Priya, 459
Rice, Jerry, 157
Rich, Gregory A., 467
Richards, Fred, 459

Richards, Keith A., 466
Richtel, Matt, 457, 458
Ridnour, Rick E., 458
Rigby, Darrell K., 449
Rindfleisch, Aric, 451
Ritson, Mark, 459
Roberti, Mark, 454
Roberts, Mary Lou, 467
Robinson, Aaron, 459
Robinson, David, 463
Roehm, Frances W., 433
Rogers, Everett M., 458
Ronkainen, IlkaA., 455
Rosecky, Richard B., 466
Rosen, Dennis L., 453, 464
Rosenau, M. D., 457
Rosenthal, David W., 426
Ross, Ivy, 341
Rossiter, John R., 452
Roundtree, Robert I., 457
Rovell, Darren, 458
Rowe, Megan, 450
Rowling, J. K., 190
Royer, Isabelle, 457
Royte, Elizabeth, 452
Rubinson, Joel, 456
Rudelius, William, 448, 449, 457, 458, 459
Rust, Ronald T., 457
Rylander, Don, 456

S

Sachs, Andrea, 456
Salas, Randy A., 466
Salmon, Walter J., 462, 466
Samli, A. Coskin, 455
Sasser, W. Earl, Jr., 457, 458
Savitz, Andrew W., 452
Schaecher, Phil, 133, 134
Schaeffer, Leland D., 457
Schatzel, Kim, 458
Scheuing, Eberhard, 458
Schindler, Robert M., 460
Schmitt, Genevieve, 243
Schoenbachler, Denise D., 458
Scholes, Kevan, 448
Schramm, Wilbur, 463
Schultz, Don E., 462, 463, 464
Schultz, Howard, 91–93
Schulze, Dick, 116, 117
Schumann, David W., 464
Schwager, Andre, 447
Schwartzenberg, Gary, 223
Scott, Mary E., 468
Segal, Madhav N., 468
Seldon, Larry, 117
Seligman, Daniel, 463
Sellers, Patricia, 452
Selwitz, Robert, 464
Serwer, Andy, 452

Shamel, Cynthia, 433
Shane, Scott, 461
Sharapova, Maria, 207
Sharp, Arthur G., 468
Shaw, Eric H., 447
Shaw, Hollie, 463
Sheatsley, P., 463
Sheehan, Norman, 462
Shenkan, Amy Guggenheim, 448
Sheperd, Lauren, 462
Sherry, John F., Jr., 447
Shervani, Tasadduq A., 447
Sheth, Jagdish N., 452, 455, 458, 459
Shi Yi-Zheng, 463
Shocker, Allan D., 452
Shriver, Nathan, 464
Shroer, James A., 463
Shulman, Lawrence E., 449
Sibony, Olivier, 457
Sieko, Adrienne, 453
Siklos, Richard, 456
Silva-Risso, Jorge, 460
Simchi-Levi, David, 460
Simchi-Levi, Edith, 460
Simester, Duncan, 462
Simon, Hermann, 460
Singer, Mark, 448
Singh, Surendra N., 453
Sinha, Prabhakant, 467
Skally, Nick, 205–206, 457
Skenazy, Lenore, 464
Slater, Stanley F., 447
Smidebush, Ed, 135
Smith, A. B., 462
Smith, Ethan, 460
Smith, Jessica C., 450
Smith, Scott M., 452
Solomon, Michael R., 453
Soohoo, Anthony, 333
Sorel, Dan, 464
Soriano, Alfonso, 354
Speh, Thomas W., 453
Spell, Chester, 461
Spencer, Jane, 453
Spengler, Tim, 347
Spielberg, Steven, 357
Spiro, Rosann L., 467
Spriggs, Mark T., 460
Srinivasan, Kannan, 463
Srivastava, Rajendra K., 447
Staelin, Richard, 447, 457
Stair, Leslie, 426
Stair, Lila B., 426
Stalk, George, 449
Stamler, Bernard, 448
Stanley, Paul, 284
Stanton, John L., 463
Stanton, William J., 467
Stayman, Douglas M., 465
Steenkamp, Jan-Benedict E. M., 459, 462
Steinberg, Brian, 465

Steiner, Gary A., 452, 463
Stephens, Robert, 75–77, 215, 216, 457
Stern, Louis W., 460
Sterns, Scott, 466
Stevens, Greg A., 457
Stevens, Marcus, 352, 353, 464
Stevenson, Robert Louis, 382
Stewart, David, 464
Stiving, Mark, 460
Stone, Brad, 451
Strauss, Judy, 467
Strickler, Jeff, 448
Stroebe, W., 453
Strunk, William, Jr., 449
Strutton, David, 460
Sudhir, K., 451
Sullivan, Elizabeth A., 449, 458
Swait, Joffre, 459
Swank, Hilary, 161
Swenson, Linda, 449
Swimmurn, Nick, 187
Swink Morgan L., 458
Swire, Donald, 449
Szymanski, D., 455

T

Talukdar, Debabrata, 452
Tan, Chong Leng, 464
Tanner, John F., Jr., 453, 464, 466
Tarnowski, Joseph, 462
Tay, Richard, 464
Teal, Thomas, 452
Tedesco, Richard, 462, 466
Teinowitz, Ira, 461, 464
Teixeira, Ruy, 63
Tellefsen, Thomas, 454
Terpstra, Vern, 451
Terreri, April, 460
Tetreault, Mary Stanfield, 458
Theus, Kathryn T., 453
Thomas, Dave, 196
Thompson, Craig J., 451
Thompson, Debora Viana, 457
Thompson, Stephen, 461
Tietje, Brian, 447
Till, Brian D., 465
Timberlake, Justin, 287
Tomkovick, Chuck, 464
Tomsho, Robert, 449
Trachtenberg, Jeffrey A., 448
Traczyk, Patty, 464
Treacy, Michael, 447
Treleaven, Sarah, 465
Trevino, Linda K., 451
Truett, Richard, 463
Trumbull, Mark, 450
Tsang, Alex S. L., 466
Tufte, Edward R., 448
Tuli, Kapil R., 466
Turner, Daniel, 458
Twain, Mark, 178

U

Ulrich, Karl T., 458
Ulwick, Anthony W., 458
Urbany, Joel E., 452
Useem, Jerry, 462
Usunier, Jean-Claude, 455

V

Valenzuela, Ana, 459
Vallaeys, Frederick, 378
Van den Bulte, Christophe, 447
Van der Linde, Claas, 447
Van Heck, Eric, 454
Van Hyning, Chuck, 449
Van Rossum, Wouter, 447
Van Waterschool, Walter, 447
Vandermark, Rob, 403
Vanhuele, Marc, 462
Varadarajan, P. Rajan, 448, 449, 452, 455
Vascellaro, Jessica E., 451, 466
Veblen, Thorstein B., 450
Vekatesh, R., 454
Vence, Deborah L., 461, 468
Verckey, Betsy, 461
Verhoef, Peter C., 462
Vessey, Michael J., 448
Viglielmo, Pamela, 455
Viguerie, S. Patrick, 457
Voight, Joan, 452
Voitle, Jennifer, 169
Voss, Glenn B., 462

W

Walker, Helen, 454, 458
Walker, Orville C., Jr., 448, 457, 458
Walters, Ben, 451
Wanamaker, John, 368
Wang, William, 261
Ward, James C., 462
Warren, Kevin, 400
Wasserman, Todd, 453
Watson, Barry, 464
Weathers, Carl, 353
Weber, Joseph, 458
Weber, Karl, 452
Webster, Frederick E., Jr., 447, 454
Wedel, Michel, 462, 463
Weigold, Michael F., 465
Weilbaker, Dan C., 458
Weisal, Kimberly, 456
Weiss, Allen, 450
Weitz, Barton A., 447, 448, 454, 460, 466
Welch, David, 459
Welch, Jack, 468
Welch, Suzy, 468

Wells, Jennifer, 464
Wensley, Robin, 447, 448
Werner, Ray O., 451
Werther, William B., Jr., 452
West, Edward, 461
West, Susan, 464
Westerlund, Richard, 453
White, E. B., 449
White, Katherine M., 464
White, Michael, 455
White, Tina, 457
Whittemore, C. B., 456
Wiener, Joshua L., 466
Wiersema, Fred D., 447
Wiles, Michael A., 461
Wilkie, William L., 448, 452, 453, 464
Williams, Serena, 232
Williams, Stephanie, 457
Wilson, David T., 454
Wilson, James O., 451

Wilson, Rick T., 465
Wind, Jerry, 467
Wind, Yoram, 449, 454
Windorski, David, 3, 12, 13, 18–19, 447, 448
Winer, Russell S., 458, 460
Winfrey, Oprah, 3, 13, 353
Wingfield, Nick, 448
Winter, Rebecca, 457
Winters, Lewis C., 464
Wirtz, Jochen, 458
Wittington, Richard, 448
Wolf, Alan, 461
Wolfman, Ian, 423
Wong, Anthony, 454
Woodside, Arch G., 465
Woon, Emily, 460
Woyke, Elizabeth, 452
Wozniak, Steve, 200
Wujin Chu, 454

Wyckoff, D. Daryl, 458
Wyner, Gordon A., 449

Y

Yalch, Richard, 453
Yao Ming, 114
Yip, Gorge S., 457
Ylkur, Rama, 464
York, Emily Bryson, 462
Yuan, Sheng, 463

Z

Zaltman, Gerald, 454
Zamiska, Nicholas, 457
Zavala, Zack, 450
Zbar, Jeffrey D., 464
Zeithaml, Valerie A., 452, 459

Zettelmeyer, Florian, 460
Zhang, Yong, 465
Zhao, Guangzhi, 463, 464
Zimmer, Mary R., 462
Zimoch, Rebecca, 449
Zinkham, George M., 465
Ziobro, Paul, 456, 457
Zirkle, Michael, 457
Zmuda, Natalie, 447, 456, 462, 463
Zoltner, Andris, 467

COMPANY/PRODUCT INDEX

A

Abbott Laboratories, 131
Accenture, 427
Ace Hardware, 295
ACNielsen, 130
Act II Microwave Popcorn, case, 307–309
Activeion Clearing Solutions, case, 230–231
Activision, 68
Adidas, 17, 142, 243, 316
Advil, 105
AFLAC, 361
Agentrics, 130
Airbus Industrie, 141
Alamo.com, 292
Allbookstores.com, 319
Amazon.com, 26, 68, 292, 311, 319, 323, 406, 409, 411, 414, 419, 423
American Airlines, 75, 266
American Express Company, 254, 383
 cause marketing, 88
American Express Platinum Card, 102
American Hospital Supply, 300
American Idol, 168, 169
American Red Cross, 27, 121, 213, 359, 375
 mission statement, 25
America Online, 111
AMP, Inc., 383
Amway, 320, 359
Anacin, 248
Angels and Demons, 346
Anheuser-Busch Companies, 75, 109, 114, 360
 social responsibility initiatives, 79
Anheuser-Busch Recycling Corporation, 79
Ann Taylor Corporation LOFT chain, 190, 191
Any Given Sunday, 352, 353, 354
Anytime Anywhere Media Measurement Initiative, 168
Apple, Inc., 4, 11, 59, 112, 142, 143, 191, 216, 222, 247, 295, 297, 298, 373, 383
 new-product innovation, 209–210
 segmentation strategy, 200–202
Apple II computer, 7, 209, 215
Apple iMac, 211, 222, 228
Apple Industrial Design Group, 222
Apple iPad, 208–210, 222
Apple iPhone, 68, 97, 153, 209, 217, 222, 275, 341
Apple iPod, 26, 68, 142, 169, 170, 209, 210, 218, 233, 248

Apple Stores, 324, 325
Arby's, 109
Arm & Hammer, 248, 249
Arrow shirts, 268
Arthur D. Little, 222
Ashburn Alley, 258
Associated Grocers, 295, 315
AT&T, 8, 69, 98, 146, 151, 344, 367, 389
AT&TCruiseCast, 8
Atlanta Braves, 221
Audi, 361
Autobytel.com, 292
Avatar, 160, 161, 162
Avert Virucidal, 218
Aviator glasses, 373
Avis, 202, 296
Avon Products, Inc., 16, 87, 141, 320, 381
Axe deodorant, 248

B

Babies "R" Us, 212
Baby Ruth, 417
Bagel-Fuls, 223
Banana Republic, 190
Barbie doll, 148, 149, 225
Barnes & Noble, 26, 87, 316, 323, 408, 411, 419
Baseball magazine, 189
Bass Pro, 331
Bausch and Lomb, 373, 376
Bayer, 347, 359
Bebe clothing store, 361
Bell bicycle helmets, 7
Ben & Jerry's Homemade Holdings, 24, 25, 28, 30, 41
 company history, 21
 diversification analysis, 33
 marketing dashboard for, 29
 SWOT analysis, 35
Ben Franklin stores, 295
Benneton, 142
Bertie Bott's Every Flavor Beans, 373
Best Buy, 77, 130, 217, 269, 297, 314, 316, 317, 322, 324, 329
 case, 116–117
 purchase of Geek Squad, 76
Best Foods, 113
Best You, 365
Be Tough, 234
Betty Crocker, 181
Betty Crocker Dessert Bowls, 42–43
Betty Crocker Warm Delights, 42–43
Bic perfume, 247
Bicycle Times, 365
Big Bang Theory, 169

Biggest Loser, 373
BJ's Wholesale, 261, 308
Black & Decker, 139, 153, 228, 249, 393
Blackberry, 98
Blackberry Storm 9530, 97
Blockbuster Entertainment, 308, 428
Bloomberg Businessweek, 30
Bloomingdale's, 268, 314, 322, 330
Blue Cross Blue Shield, 351
BlueFarm Group, 158
BMW, 227, 320, 351, 358
Boeing Company, 69, 129, 141, 150, 181, 276
Bold detergent, 248, 425
Bon Marche, 314
Bonnie Bell Cosmetics, Inc., 114
Bose audio systems, 245
Boston Consulting Group, 31, 32, 41
Boston Market, 326
Boucheron, 297
Boys and Girls Clubs, 87
Brawny, 245
Breathe Right Strips, case, 157–159
Bridgestone, 244
Bridging, 15
Brillo, 15
Bring It, 234
Brita's Filter for Good campaign, 65
British Airways, 98
Broadview Security, 213
Bronco, 248
Brooks Brothers Clothiers, 102, 330
Brookstone, 349
Brother, 238
Bubba Gump Shrimp Company, 373
Budweiser Light, 105
Bufferin, 248
Buick, 99, 395
Buick Enclave, 351
Burdines, 314
Burger Chef, 326
Burger King, 84, 199, 200, 202, 227, 361, 399
 market segments, 194
Burlington Coat Factory, 322
Business Talk Radio, 365
BusinessWeek, 365
BzzAgent, Inc., 109

C

Cadbury Schweppes, 247
Cadillac, 103, 302, 395
Cadillac Escalade, 358
Callaway Golf Company, 286, 417
 marketing channels, 287
Camay, 249

Campbell Soup Company, 113, 130, 170, 193, 243, 249, 251, 306
C&R Research, 411
Canon, 32, 266
Cantina Corona, 331
Capital One, 405
Cap'n Crunch, 222
Careerbuilder.com, 429
CARE International, 93
Carl's Jr., 347
CarMax, 278
Carnation Corporation, 85
Carnation Instant Breakfast, 17, 222
Carrefour, 313
Cartier, 265
Cartoon Network, 221
Casera soups, 113
Catalyst Paper, Inc., 119
Caterpillar, Inc., 142, 291, 292
CBS, 333
Celanese Chemical Company, 307
Celestial Seasonings, 252, 288
Century 21, 328
Cerazyme, 86, 87
Cereal Partners Worldwide, 294
CGCT, 151
Champion pacemaker, 36
Chanel, 143, 155, 265
Chaps brand, 247
Charlesburg Furniture, 298, 299
Charles Schwab, 399, 413
Checkers Drive-In Restaurants, 326
Cheer, 425
Cheerios, 175, 293
Cheese Nips, 252
Cheetos, 151
Chevrolet, 280, 302, 331
Chevron, 359
Chevy Tahoe, 73
Chevy Volt, 248
Chicago Cubs, 354
Chicago Symphony Orchestra, 255
Chicken of the Sea, 252
Chips Ahoy!, 253
Chophouse Bar and Grill, 221
Christian Dior, 268
Christie's, 143
Church & Dwight, 248
Circle K., 308
Cirrus systems, 255
Citibank, 372
Clairol, 104
Claritas, 193
Clearasil, 142
Cling-free, 248
Clinique, 418
Clorox, 105, 248
CNBC, 8
CNN, 217
CNS, case, 157–159

Coca-Cola Company, 72, 87, 98, 140, 142, 143, 145, 146, 147, 148, 153, 155, 156, 238–239, 245, 252, 253, 289, 297, 315, 360, 372, 413, 421
cola war, 84
Coccolino, 141
Colgate-Palmolive Company, 107, 139
Colgate toothpaste, 139
Colgate Total, 106, 107
Colt, 248
Columbia House, 411
Columbia Pictures, 346
Comcast, 357
ComScore, 366
ConAgra Foods, Inc., 307, 309
Cones 2 Career, 21
Conservation International, 93
Consumer Electronics Association, 76
Coors Brewing, 124
Corning, Inc., 121, 129
Corona Extra, 110
Cosmopolitan Magazine, 369
Costco, 11, 50, 116, 130, 250, 261, 308, 313
Cost Cutters Family Hair Care, 254
Coupon Information Corporation, 371
Cover Girl ColorMatch, 241
Cracker Jack, 269
Craftsman tools, 111, 265
Craigslist Inc., 26
Crate and Barrel, 318
Cray Inc., 212
Cream of Wheat, 371
Crest toothpaste, 107, 300
Crest Whitestrips, 333
Crispin Porter & Bogusky, 361
Crunch 'n Munch, 269
CSI, 169
Cub Foods, 315
CVS/Pharmacy, 308

D

Daiei, 313
Dallas Museum of Art, 15
Dancing with the Stars, 169
Dean's milk, 203
DeBeers Diamond Corporation, 143
Deere & Company, 124
Deli Creations, 170
Dell, Inc., 82, 131, 136, 222, 279, 292, 297, 303, 384, 406
in emerging economies, 137
Dell.com, 292, 408, 410
Dell Japan, 137
Dell On-Call, 77
Dell Pacific, 137
Del Monte, 250

Delta Air Lines, 266
DeWalt tools, 249
DEX, 366
DHL Worldwide Express, 213, 389
Dial soap, 250, 359
Dick's Sporting Goods, Inc., 287, 352, 417
DieHard, 248
Diet Pepsi, 8
Diet Pepsi Max, 8
Dillard's, 317
DirecTV, 387
Disney Channel, 8
Disney Online, 411
Disney Twenty-Three, 365
DKNY, 305
Dockers, 243
Dollar Rent-A-Car, 202
Dollar Valley Stores, 278
Domino's bubble gum, 247
Domino's Pizza, 254
Don Miguel, 52
Donna Karan, 102, 305
Doritos, 151, 245, 338, 360, 371, 384
DoubleClick, 366, 379
Dr. Care Toothpaste, 7, 8
Dream Works, 3-D movie, 357
Dr Pepper, 245, 347
Drumstick, 152
DSW Shoe Warehouse, 330
Dun & Bradstreet, 429
Duracell, 245, 248, 265
Duracell Ultra, 265

E

E. T., 373
Eagle, 248
Eastman Kodak; *see* Kodak
Easy Off, 248
eBay, 130, 247, 414
eBayBusiness, 130
eBay.com, 319
eBay Motors, 333
Eddie Bauer, 279, 293
Ediet.com, 406
eHarmony, 102
Ekelon, 205
Electronic Data Systems, 125
Elizabeth Arden, 250
Energizer Advanced, 265
Energizer batteries, 265, 361
Energizer e2 alkaline batteries, 265
Energy Smart bulbs, 65
Ericsson, 151
ESPN, 364
ESPN The Magazine, 352, 353
Estée Lauder, Inc., 109, 418
Etch-A-Sketch, 373
eToys, 16
E*Trade, 221, 360
Eveready, 248

Excedrin, 248
Experian Simmons, 194
Extra Gum, 373
Exxon, 153, 154, 248
ExxonMobil, 272
EZ Squirt Ketchup, 216

F

Facebook, 169, 175, 205, 333, 346, 355, 403, 413, 422, 430
Family Dollar Stores, 278
Family Guy, 347
Family Life Network, 365
Famous Barr, 314
Fancy Feast, 216
Fantasyland hotel, 322
Farm Radio Network, 365
Fashionmall.com, 319
Fatal Attraction, 162
Fatburger, 326
Federal Express, 77, 122, 152, 213, 289, 367, 393
Festival Series guitars, 283
Fiberwise, 248
Field of Dreams, 161
Filene's, 314
Fingos, 217–218
Firebird, 248
Fisher Price Chatter Telephone, 183
marketing research for, 163–165
Fisher-Price Company, 351
Flickr, 59, 333
Florida Orange Growers Association, 243
Florsheim, 316
Foley's, 314
Food Network, 364
Foot Locker, 299
Ford Consulting Group, Inc., case, 184–185
Ford Focus, 250
Ford Fusion, 250
Ford Motor Company, 99, 110, 151, 190, 211, 248, 250, 295, 302, 315, 343
Forrest Gump, 373
Fortune Brands, 212
Four Seasons Hotels, 348, 349
Fox Business News, 168
Fran Wilson Creative Cosmetics, 150
Fresh Step cat litter, 104, 105
Friday Night Lights, 354
Friday Night 3, 354
Frigidaire, 316
Frito-Lay Company, 99, 148, 151, 153, 239, 245, 269, 384, 413
Fritos corn chips, 99
Frommer's Australia from $60 a Day, 338
Frontier Airlines, 276
Fuller Brush, 320

G

Gain detergent, 425
GameCube, 215
Gap.com, 319
Gap Inc., 190, 279, 349
Garden Design, 365
Garlic Cake, 218
Garmin, 59
Gatorade, 244, 246, 247, 255
product extensions, 233–234
Gatorade All Stars, 233
Gatorade AM, 233, 234
Gatorade Endurance Formula, 233
Gatorade Energy Bar, 233
Gatorade Energy Drink, 233
Gatorade Fierce, 233, 234
Gatorade Frost, 233
Gatorade G2, 232, 233, 249
Gatorade Nutritional Shake, 233
Gatorade Performance Series, 233
Gatorade Rain, 233, 234
Gatorade Thirst Quencher, 234
Gatorade X-Factor, 233, 234
Gatorade Xtreme, 233
Geek Squad, 116, 215, 216, 217
case, 75–77
Geico, 361, 367
General Electric, 4, 14, 24, 65, 98, 129, 248, 293, 316
Distinguished Supplier Award, 383
General Electric Medical Systems, 131
General Mills, 151, 170, 175, 217–218, 222, 223, 241, 293
case, 42–43
joint venture, 294
General Motors, 237, 268, 300, 344, 345, 395
Genzyme, 86
Georgia-Pacific, 245
Gerber, 75, 153, 248, 276
GfK Custom Research, 369
Ghostbusters, 76
Gigante, 139
Gillette Company, 142, 148, 153, 154, 170, 247, 389, 428
Gillette for Women, 154
Gillette Fusion, 234, 236, 239, 265
Gino's Hamburgers, 326
Glass Plus, 248
Glidden, 247
Global Healthcare Exchange, 130–131
Go Daddy, 360
Godiva Chocolates, 397
GoGurt Pizzas, 223
Golden Beauty, 154
Golden Valley Microwave Foods, case, 307–309
Golf Galaxy, 287, 417
Good Start, 85

Goodyear Tire & Rubber, 123, 244, 295, 300
Google, Inc., 5, 22, 59, 101, 167, 168, 169, 217, 225, 367, 410, 430
    case, 377–379
Google Apps, 68
Google Gmail, 226
Google Image Search, 226
Google News, 226
GoTo Meeting, 68
Goya Foods, 113
Grease Monkey, 256
Great Atlantic & Pacific Tea Company, 70
Green Marketing Coalition, 350
Green Teams, 93
Grey Poupon, 170
Grey's Anatomy, 169
Gridiron Gang, 354
Gucci, 102, 143, 297
Guitar Hero, 68
Gulfstream Aerospace Corporation, 123
Gunderson & Rosario, Inc., 218

H

H. J. Heinz Company, 15, 216
Haggar Clothing Company, 112
Hallmark Cards, 293
Haloid Company, 400
Hamburger Helper, 170–171
H&R Block, 254, 294, 295, 296
Hanes, 240
Harkman Electric, 291, 292
Harley-Davidson, 124, 153, 243, 245, 247, 408, 413
    supplier partnership, 125
Harley Owners Group, 408
HarperCollins, 289
Harris Corporation, 391–392
Harryanddavid.com, 411
Harry Potter and the Deathly Hollows, 161
Harry Potter books, 190
Harry the K's Bar & Grill, 258
Hart Schaffner & Marx, 268
Hasbro, 421
Havianas, 337, 338
Hawaiian Punch, 242
Heinz ketchup, 252
Helena Rubinstein, 154
Hellmann's Real Mayonnaise, 106
Henredon, 247
Hermitage Museum, 15
Hershey Foods, 100, 109, 268, 373
Hershey's chocolate milk, 203
Hershey's Extra Dark, 100
Hertz Rent-A-Car, 17, 202
He's Just Not That into You, 333
Hewlett-Packard, 32, 112, 125, 214, 228, 238, 241, 253, 413

Hey! There's A Monster In My Room, 218
HGTV, 372
Hibbett Sporting Goods, 352
Hidden Valley Low-Fat Salad Dressing, 248
Hidden Valley Ranch Take Heart Salad Dressing, 248
Hilton Hotels, 255, 315
History Channel, 364
Hitachi, 142
Holiday Barbie doll, 148
Holiday Inn, 295, 296
Home Depot, 11, 124, 311, 313, 314, 321, 322, 349, 393
Home Shopping Network, 293, 319
Honda Civic, 262
Honda Motor Company, 249
Honey Nut Cheerios, 294
Hospital Network.com, 130
Hotmail, 414
Hot Pockets Pizza Snacks, 8
Hot Pockets Sideshots, 7, 8
Hot Pockets Subs, 8
Howlin' Coyote Chili, 29, 46–57
HP Enterprise Services, 398
HTC Touch Diamond, 97
Huggies, 141, 245, 249
Huggies Baby Network, 408
Hulu, 364
Hummer, 335
Hyatt Corporation, 63
Hyatt Place all-suite hotels, 63
Hyundai Motor America, 418
Hyundai Motor Corporation, 347

I

Ibane, 283
IBM, 15, 16, 83, 121, 124, 147, 291, 303, 359, 382, 393, 399, 406
    integrated supply chain, 303
IBM Global Services, 389, 395
Ideale washing machine, 153
Idearc, 366
IDEO, 222
    innovation at, 223
IGA, 295
IKEA, 143, 318, 329, 331
imc2, case, 420–423
Independent Grocers' Alliance, 315
Information Resources, Inc., 29
InfoScan, 167
Initiative, 347
In-N-Out Burger, 326
Intel Corporation, 125, 136, 142
Ionator, 230–231
Iron Man 2, 161, 162
iVillage.com, 413

J

J. Crew, 279
J. D. Power, 167
Jack in the Box, 326
Jaguar, 320
JCPenney, 118, 124, 244, 268, 289, 318, 322, 367
    paper purchasing, 119
JCPMedia, 119, 128
Jefferson Smurfit Corporation, 383
Jell-O, 71, 233
Jenn-Air, 298
JetBlue Airways, 123
Jewel Supermarkets, 266
Jiffy Lube, 297
Jitterbug, 62
JobWeb, 429
John Deere equipment, 124
Johnson & Johnson, 11, 24, 98, 112, 131, 243, 421
Johnson Controls Automotive Systems Group, 389
Johnson's baby shampoo, 228
Jose Ole, 52
Joust, 364
Joy, 248
JOYity, 59

K

Kanebo, 150
Kellogg, 112, 123, 247
Kellogg's Heartwise cereal, 248
Kellogg's Special K, 175
Kentucky Fried Chicken, 356, 372
Kia Motors, 104
Kimberly-Clark, 99, 141, 218, 245, 249, 408
Kindle, 26, 68
Kirby vacuum cleaners, 389
Kit Kat, 146, 147
Kleenex, 4, 11, 99, 233, 246, 253
Kleenex diapers, 247
Kmart, 265, 300, 316
Kodak, 21, 31, 38, 75, 392
    product line, 30
    strategic business units, 32–33
Kodak digital camera, 30, 32
Kodak digital picture frames, 30, 32
Kodak film, 30, 32, 33
Kodak inkjet printers, 30, 32
Kodak Zio pocket video camera, 37
Kohler, 263
Kohl's, 288
Komatsu, 142
Kraft American cheese, 243

Kraft Foods, Inc., 125, 170, 223, 253, 293, 341, 371
Kraft Miracle Whip, 252
Kroger, 250, 266, 295, 324, 371
Kuschelweich, 141
Kwik-E-Marts, 373

L

Lands' End, 11, 30
    case, 133–135
Landsend.com, 349
Lands' End Custom, 134
Lay's potato chips, 99, 148, 239, 288
Lay's snack chips, 245
Lay's Stax, 252
Lazarus, 314
Lee jeans, 109
L'eggs, 252
Lego, 142
LEGO Land Imagination Center, 331
Lender's Bagels, 247
Lenovo, 103
Lever Europe, 141
Levi's, 142, 143, 153, 288
Levi Straus, 89
Lexmark, 238
Lexus, 302
LG Incite, 97
Lifetime channel, 364
Like.com, 311
Lincoln, 302
Lincoln-Mercury dealers, 343
LinkedIn, 175, 333
Liquid Paper, 238
Little Remedies, 211, 212
Liz Claiborne, 30
L.L.Bean, 293, 318
Lockheed Martin Corporation, 69, 120, 121
Loehmann's, 315
L'Oréal, 142, 154, 247
Louis Vuitton, 245
Louvre Museum, 15
Lowe's, 124, 293
Luvs, 245
Luxottica, 247

M

MacBook Air, 209
Macintosh computer, 201, 209
Macy's, Inc., 314, 317, 330, 373, 425
Magnolia Audio and Video, 116
Magnolia Home Theater, 116
Majestic Clubhouse Store, 258
Major League Baseball, 220–221, 257–259
Mall of America, 319
    case, 330–331
M&Ms, 9, 279, 358, 372, 406

Mansar Products, Ltd., 290, 291
MapQuest, 59
Maricopa County Medical Society, Arizona, 80
Market Tools, 172
Marks & Spencer, 405
Marriott Corporation, 223
Marriott International, 11, 14, 15, 249–250
Mars, Inc., 148, 290, 406
Marshall Field's, 314
Mars Snackfood, 372
Mary Kay Cosmetics, 104, 105, 320, 395
MasterCard International, 87, 145, 346
Mastro Limpio, 141
Match.com, 102
Mattel, 89, 142, 148, 149, 225
Maxim Steel, 393
Maybelline, 153
Mayo Clinic, 212, 331
Mazola Corn Oil, 113
McDonald's, 88, 89, 103, 110, 114, 142–143, 144–145, 150, 151, 198, 199, 200, 202, 227, 254, 296, 315, 326, 339, 371, 388
  market segments, 194
McDonald's Monopoly, 372
McFadden's Restaurant and Saloon, 258
McKesson Corporation, 131
Medtronic, Inc., 21, 26, 30, 41, 44, 131, 276, 381, 383
  marketing plan, 36
  mission statement, 25
Men in Black, 76
Mentalist, The, 169
Mercedes, 320
Mercedes-Benz, 152, 155, 351
Mercury, 302
Merrill Lynch, 255, 387–388
Metacafe, 361
MetLife.com, 293
Metro Group, 313
Metropolitan Life Insurance, 113, 114, 385
Metropolitan Museum of Art, 75
MGA Entertainment, 111
Michelin, 102, 139, 244, 246–247
MicroFridge, 192, 193
Microsoft Bing, 101, 167, 169
Microsoft Corporation, 69, 146, 248, 300, 320, 361, 378, 379, 396
Microsoft Excel, 275
Microsoft Xbox 360, 218, 333
Microsoft Zune, 218
Milk Processor Education Program, 244
Milky Way, 372
Milky Way Dark, 372
Milky Way Midnight, 372
Miller Brewing, 75, 363

MillerCoors, 347
Million Dollar Baby, 161
Mimosin, 141
Miramax, 249
Mission Foods, 52
Modell's Sporting Goods, 352
Moen faucets, 212
Mona Lisa, 15
Monster.com, 109, 429
Monsters vs. Aliens, 357, 371
Moodmatcher, 150
Moore Chemical & Sanitation Supply, Inc., 397
Motorola, 142, 383
Mountain Equipment Company, 314
Mpire.com, 311
Mr. Clean, 141
Mr. Potato Head, 373
Mr. Proper, 141
MSN Money, 379
MTV, 364
MTV Road Rules, 354
Mustang, 248, 250
MyCoke.com, 413
My eBay, 408
My First Craftsman, 111
Mysimms.com, 406
MySimon.com, 319
MySpace, 205, 333, 413, 430
MyYahoo!, 406, 408

N

Nabisco Company, 112, 252, 328, 372, 399
National Center for Public Policy and Higher Education, 66
National Geographic, 17
Nature Conservancy, 16, 22
Nature Valley Granola bars, 222, 228
NBC, 357, 360
NCIS, 169
NCIS Los Angeles, 169
Neiman Marcus, 300, 315, 316, 317, 324, 397
Nescafé, 154
Nesquik, 203
Nestlé Food Corporation, 85, 109, 143, 144, 146, 147, 152, 154, 245, 253, 293, 371, 417
  joint venture, 294
Netflix, 26, 222
Net Impact, 63
NetMarket.com, 319
New Age herbal tea, 252
New Balance, Inc., 243
Newegg.com, 293
Newsweek, price experiment, 270–271
New York Giants, 17
Nickelodeon, 8
Nielsen Claritas, 193

Nielsen Media Check, 169
Nielsen Media Research, 167, 168, 169
Nielsen's online rating service, 366
Nike, Inc., 22, 89, 90, 142, 143, 212, 243, 247, 299, 316, 360
Nikon, 211
99-cents Only Stores, 278
Nintendo, 333
Nintendo Wii, 68, 215, 265
Nissan Motor Company, 124, 148
Nissan Smyrna, 152
Nissan USA.com, 94
No Excuses, 234
Nokia, 59, 247
Nordstrom, 316, 329
Nordstrom bank, 316
Nordstrom Fashion Rewards, 316
Nordstrom Rack, 322
Norske Skog, 119
Northrup Grumman, 69
Northwestern Mutual Life Insurance Company, 388
NPD Group, 50, 175
Nuprin, 248
NutraSweet, 72
NYTimes.com, 408

O

Obsession, 248
Ocean Spray Cranberries, 252
Off 5th, 322
Office Depot, 19, 77, 293, 318, 323
Office Max, 19, 311
Olay, 62
Old Navy, 190
Olympics, 345, 360
Olympus cameras, 155, 237
OMEGA watches, 109, 110
Omni Hotels, 421
1800flowers.com, 411
Opium, 297
Oracle Corporation, 28
Oral-B CrossAction toothbrush, 170
Orbitz.com, 292, 405
Oreos, 252
Orion lunar spacecraft, 120, 121
Orville Redenbacher, 309
Oscar Mayer, 112, 170
OUT! International, 218
Owens-Corning Fiberglass Corporation, 72, 383
Oxygen channel, 363, 364

P

Paid-to-Read Web site, 367
Palm Pre, 97
Palo Alto Research Center, 400
Pampers, 141, 245, 300, 418
Panasonic, 115, 276, 277, 316

Panasonic Viera, 4
Pancast, 364
Pantene, 242
Paradise Kitchens, Inc., 28
  company background, 46
  marketing plan, 46–57
Paragon Trade Brands, 250
Parker Guitar, 284
PartnerShop, 21
Payless Shoe Stores, 280, 281
PayPal, 5
PayPass, 317
PC Magazine, 68
Peapod.com, 319
Pearson, 289
Pedigree dog food, 360
Penguin Books, 109
PepsiCo, 8, 83, 107, 124, 140, 142, 147, 151, 155, 233, 245, 252, 253, 289, 295, 296, 331
  cola war, 84
PepsiMax, 7, 8
Perrier bottled water, 87
Pert shampoo, 146
PETCO, 297, 298
PetSmart, 297, 298
Pew Internet and American Life Project, 416
Pez Candy, Inc., 250, 251
Pfizer, Inc., 359, 421
PGA America, 287
PGA Tour Superstores, 287
Phanatic Attic, 258
Philadelphia cream cheese, 223
Philadelphia Phillies, Inc., 213
  case, 257–259
Phoenix, 248
Photomart, 253
Pillsbury Company, 51
Pinto, 248
Pitney Bowes, Inc., 124, 393
Pizza Hut, 254
  case, 420–423
PizzaHut.com, 421, 423
Planters Peanuts, 328
PlasticsNet, 130
Playmakers, 353
Playstation2, 215
Playstation3, 215, 333
Polo brand, 247
Popular Mechanics, 108
Population Reference Bureau, 60
Porsche, 360
Porsche Boxter, 249
Porsche Carrara, 249
Post-it brand products, 3, 10
Post-it Flag, 3, 4, 12
Post-it Flag Highlighter, 12
  case, 18–19
Post-it Flag Pen, 12, 13
Post-it Note, 3, 4, 12, 351
Powercast, 68
Pret shampoo, 146

Prevention magazine, 373
Priceline.com, 349
Price Sports, Inc., case, 205–207
PricewaterhouseCoopers, 255
Pringles, 225, 252
Prius, 36, 65
Procter & Gamble, 87, 112, 124, 125,
    129, 141, 142, 146, 167, 170,
    175, 189, 222, 225, 241, 242,
    245, 249, 252, 253, 281, 295,
    296, 301, 333, 344, 371, 393,
    418, 421, 425
Progresso Light soups, 223
Promise spread, 104
Promo magazine, 370
Promotional Products Association
    International, 371
Propel Fitness Water, 233
Purina Dog Chow, 340, 341
Purina's Elegant Medleys, 216

Q

Qtips, 71
Quaker Oats Company, 222, 233,
    243, 247, 425
QVC, 318–319
QVC@THEMALL, 319

R

R. H. Donnelley, 366
Race for the Cure, 15
Radio Shack, 130, 250, 315
Random House, 289
Ralcorp Holdings, 250
Ralph Lauren, 247, 294–295, 300,
    312, 313
Ray Ban, 373
Rayovac, 250, 265
RaySat Broadcasting, 8
Reader's Digest, 108
Real Yellow Pages, 366
Recreational Equipment, 404–405
Redbook, 112
Red Bull, 248
Red Lobster, 102
Reebok International, 89, 152, 406,
    407, 413
Reebok Russia, 152
Reese's Pieces, 373
Regent cruise, 66–67
Renaissance hotels, 249
Replacements, The, 354
Restaurant News, 340
Revlon, 268
Revlon.com, 408
Rhapsody, 351
Risky Business, 373
Rite Aid, 308
Ritz-Carlton, 249

Rock and Roll Hall of Fame and
    Museum, 266, 267
Rockport, 247, 389
Rolex, 268
Rollerblade, 244
Rolling Stone, 365
Rolls-Royce, 143, 265
Ronald McDonald Houses, 88, 89
Rope Burns, 161
Ross Stores, 322
Ruffles, 99, 151
Ruiz Foods, 52
Runner's World, 365

S

Safeguard, 249
Safeway, 126, 130, 266, 291, 324
St. Croix Venture Partners, 44
St. Joseph aspirin, 243
Saks Fifth Avenue, 305, 314, 316,
    322, 324
Sam's Club, 116, 261, 300,
    304, 308
Samsung Blackjack II, 97
Samsung Electronics, 62, 68, 98, 238,
    248, 421
San Diego Padres, 347
Sanford Corporation, 238
Saturn Corporation, 312, 313, 333
Scantrack, 167
Schwab.com, 292, 411
Schwan Food Company, 290
Science Channel, 364
Scoopers Making Change, 21
Scope, 418
Scotch-Brite Never Rust, 4, 15
Scotch-Brite Never Scratch soap
    pad, 171
Scotchgard, 85
Scripto, 253
Sears, 126, 213, 214, 250, 261, 265,
    266, 291, 300, 322
Seiko, 142, 155
Sergio Rossi, 297
Seven Cycles, Inc., 402, 405, 413
    interactive marketing, 403
SevenCycles.com, 406
7-Eleven Stores, 123–124, 126, 288,
    291, 297, 308, 373
7-Up, 248
Sewell Automotive Companies, 409,
    410
Sharp, 238
Sherwin-Williams, 295
Shine On, 234
Shiseido, 142, 150
Shoeless Joe, 161
ShopCallawaygolf.com, 287
ShopNBC, 318
Shrek Forever After, 161
Siemens AG, 145

Siemens Energy & Automation,
    Airport Logistics Division, 123
Simpsons, The, 373
Simpsons Movie, The, 373
Sirius XM, 365
Skippy peanut butter, 177, 268
Skippy Squeez'It, 252
Skittles, 372
Slide, 361
Snake Light Flexible Flashlight, 153
Snapple, 247
Snelling and Snelling Inc., 296
Snickers, 110, 372
Snow Master, 103
Snow Pup, 103
Snuggle, 141
Sobe Life Water, 357
Sodima, 151
Sonic Drive In, 315
Sony Corporation, 32, 112, 142, 143,
    148, 227, 248, 261
Sony Energy Devices
    Corporation, 82
Sopranos, The, 354
SOS pads, 15
Sotheby's, 143
Sothebys.com, 411
Sound of Music, 116; *see also* Best
    Buy
Source Perrier S. A., 87
Southwest Airlines, 11, 27, 213, 255
    mission statement, 25
Speed Channel, 364
Sperry boat shoes, 316
Spic and Span, 253
Spider-Man 3, 225
Sports Authority, 312, 313, 316, 352
Sports Illustrated, 363
Sports Illustrated for Kids, 111, 365
Sprint, 69, 98, 367
Stake Fastener Company, 291, 292
Staples, 291, 297, 316
Starbucks Corporation, 11, 73, 126,
    255, 293
    case, 91–93
Starch Advertising Research, 369
Starkist, 245
STAT-USA, 168
Stokely-Van Camp, Inc., 233
Strategic Business Insights, 107
Strauss Group, 151
Subway, 315
Sunbird, 248
Sunday Night Football, 363
Sunkist, 245
Swatch watches, 142
SymphonyIRIGroup, 167

T

Taco Bell, 326
Tampa Bay Rays, 257

Target Stores, 4, 15, 16, 19, 50, 126,
    130, 244, 261, 300, 308, 313,
    316
Tastee Yogurt, 351
Taurus, 250
Tesco, 130, 313
Tesla Roadster Sport, 262–263
Texaco, 289, 359
Texas Instruments, 142
Textile Web, 130
Thirsty Cat, 217
Thirsty Dog, 217, 218
This Old House, 365
T.J. Maxx, 322
3M Corporation, 10, 15, 85, 87, 171,
    224, 228, 235
    case, 18–19
    marketing program, 12–13
    marketing research by, 3
    Pollution Prevention Pays, 23
Three Musketeers, 372
Thunderbird, 248
Ticketmaster.com, 411
Tide detergent, 189, 300, 425
Tidy Bowl, 248
Tiffany & Company, 145, 294, 295,
    324
Tiger Woods Golf, 354
Time, 5, 270–271, 356, 365
Time, Inc., 111, 113
Time Warner, 69, 344
Timex, 142
Titleist, 212
TiVo, 169
T-Mobile, 69
T-Mobile G1, 97
Tommy Hilfiger, 142
TomTom, 59
Tony's Pizza
    and Ford Consulting Group, Inc.,
    184–185
    marketing research, 178–180
Top Gun, 373
Toro, 103, 280
Toshiba America Medical System,
    397
Tostitos, 384
Touchstone Pictures, 249
Tower.com, 319
Toyota Camry, 280
Toyota Motor Corporation, 36, 65,
    87, 290, 291, 302
Toy Story, 373
Travelocity.com, 319, 361, 407, 411,
    415
Trend Hunter, 172
Triarc Companies, 247
TRUSTe, 416
TSCentral, 387
Tumblr, 59
Tupperware, 417
Twitter, 59, 175, 205, 333, 379, 403,
    413, 422

U

Tylenol Cold & Flu, 105
Tylenol P.M., 105

Ultra Downy, 212
Uncle Ben's Calcium Plus rice, 243
Under Armour, 181
  case, 352–355
Unilever, 35, 141, 175, 243, 250
  purchase of Ben & Jerry's, 21
Union Pacific Railroad, 394
United Parcel Service, 81, 152, 213, 393
United States Postal Service, 213, 241, 255, 318, 349, 350
United States Rice Miller's Association, 138
United Technologies Corporation, 84, 131
Universal Music Group, 299
UPM-Kymmene Inc., 119
Urban Coffee Opportunities, 93
U.S. Bank, 214
U.S. News & World Report, 270
U.S. Open tennis tournament, 17
USA Today, 363, 365, 371

V

Valpak, 371
Vanity Fair, 112
Vaseline, 71

V8 vegetable juice, 100
Velocity fragrance, 105
Verizon Superpages, 366
Verizon Wireless, 69
Verso Paper, 119
VF Corporation, 109
Viacom, 69
Vicks, 146
Victoria's Secret, 316, 417
Vidal Sassoon, 268
Viking, 205
Visa USA, 145, 297, 331, 358, 372
Vizio, Inc., 260
  pricing policy, 261
Volkswagen, 109, 113, 148, 151, 361
Volkswagen Beetles, 76
Volvo, 203, 222, 358, 379

W

W. W. Grainger, 129
Walgreens, 130, 308
Wall Street Journal, 365
Walmart, 11, 19, 50, 65, 76, 87, 116, 125, 139, 155, 176, 212, 250, 253, 261, 269, 296, 297, 300, 303, 304, 308, 311, 313, 314, 316, 319, 321, 324, 329, 371, 393
Walmart Marketside Stores, 304
Walmart Neighborhood Markets, 304
Walmart Supercenters, 304
Walt Disney Company, 69, 245, 247, 249, 255, 333

Wanamaker's Department Store, 368
Washburn Guitars, case, 283–285
Washburn Maya Pro DD75, 284
Weight Watchers, 223
Welch's grape jelly, 177
Wells Fargo, 312, 313
Wendy's, 191, 202, 326
  marketing research, 173–175
  market segments, 194–195
  product groups, 196–198
  segmentation strategy, 199–200
West Edmonton Mall, 322, 330
Weyerhaeuser, 122
Wheaties, 175
Whirlpool Corporation, 122, 139, 143, 148, 153, 222, 250, 298, 316
Whopper, 72
Wicks, 146
Wilkinson Sword, 262
Williams-Sonoma, 318
Windex, 265
Windows Live Hotmail, 414
Winged Victory of Samothrace, 15
Wired, 17
World Book, 320
Wrigley's, 153, 210
Wrigley's Spearmint, 351

X

Xbox Live, 355
Xerox Corporate University, 401

Xerox Corporation, 9, 72, 75, 87, 182, 236, 380, 383, 385, 389, 393, 427
  case, 399–401
  Palo Alto Research Center, 400
  personal selling, 381
  sales management, 381
Xerox WorkCentre 7655 Color MFP system, 195

Y

Yachting magazine, 365
Yahoo!, 111, 169, 367, 378, 406
Yahoo! Finance, 379
Yahoo! Kids, 111
Yamaha, 283
Yellow Pages Association, 366
YoNaturals, 317
Yoplait, 151
YouTube, 4, 37, 39, 40, 73, 169, 361, 364, 379
  founding of, 5
Yves Saint Laurent, 102, 297

Z

Zappos.com, 186, 189, 255, 413
  customer service, 187–188
  market segmentation, 187–188
Zetia, 342, 343
Zip-Lock Baggies, 373
Zoomerang, 172

SUBJECT INDEX

Note: Glossary terms and the page numbers where they are defined are **boldface**.

A

Above-, at-, or below-market pricing
  marketing dashboard for, 269
  uses, 268
Accepting objections, 390
Accessory equipment, 211
Account executive, 426
Account management policies, 393
  policy grid, 394
Achievement-motivated groups, 107
Achievers, 107
Actual self-concept, 103
Adaptation, dual, 153
Adaptive selling, 389
Administered vertical marketing
    systems, 296
Adoption, 344
AdSense, 379
Advertisements
  message content
    fear appeals, 360–361
    humor appeals, 361
    sex appeals, 361
  message creation, 361
Advertising, 336, 358
  activities involved in, 346
  advantages for firms, 337
  and brand equity, 245
  to business buyers, 340
  careers in, 425–426
  case, 377–379
  celebrity endorsements, 104, 109
  competitive, 358, 359
  cooperative, 374
  corrective, 73
  costs with multibranding, 250
  environmental, 90
  and Federal Trade Commission,
    73
  in growth stage, 341
  institutional, 359
  in introduction stage, 234–235
  in maturity stage, 341
  misuse of cultural symbols,
    145–146
  nonpersonal component,
    336–337
  paid aspect of, 336
  payment method, 337
  by pharmaceutical companies,
    343
  pioneering, 358, 359
  posttesting
    aided recall, 369
    attitude tests, 370
    inquiry tests, 370
    sales tests, 370
    unaided recall, 369
  pretesting
    jury tests, 368
    portfolio tests, 368
    theater tests, 369
  for products, 358–359
  to promote responsible drinking,
    79

of promotional Web sites, 418
reinforcement, 359
reminder, 358–359
sex-appeal ads, 171
strengths and weaknesses, 337
subliminal messages, 104
Super Bowl commercials, 109
teaser campaign, 109
with 3-D technology, 357
by Under Armour, 353
unintended language errors, 146
Advertising Age, 347, 361, 429
Advertising agencies
  careers in, 425
  full-service, 369
  in-house, 369
  limited-service, 369
  operation of, 361
  research services, 427
Advertising budget, 360
Advertising careers
  account executive, 426
  art director, 426
  copywriter, 426
  Internet marketing manager, 426
  media buyer, 426
  public relations manager, 426
  sales promotion manager, 426
Advertising department, 334
Advertising Effectiveness Council,
  360
Advertising expenditures
  breakdown by media, 362
  cost per thousand, 362
  for coupons, 370
  for message creation, 361
  on promotions, 372
  sales promotion, 370
  Super Bowl commercials, 360
  TV cost disadvantage, 363
  Yellow Pages, 366
Advertising media
  billboards, 366
  criteria
    cost per thousand, 362–363
    frequency, 362
    ratings, 362
    reach, 362
  Internet, 366
  magazines, 365
  newspapers, 365
  outdoor, 366–367
  place-based, 367
  radio, 365
  selection
    maximizing exposure, 362
    minimizing costs, 362
    target audience, 362
  television, 363–364
  transit advertising, 366–367
  Yellow Pages, 366
Advertising program
  designing ads
    message content, 360–361
    message creation, 361
  execution of
    carrying out, 369
    pretesting, 368
  media alternatives, 363–367
  media selection, 362
  posttesting, 369–370

scheduling, 367–368
setting budget, 360
specifying objectives, 360
target audience, 359–360
Advertising-related legislation, 73
Advertising Research Foundation,
  360
Advocacy advertisements, 359
AdWords, 378–379
Ad-zapping, 364
African Americans
  consumer spending, 64
  discrimination in car sales, 279
Agents, 292
  commissions and fees, 328
  description, 288
  of manufacturers, 328
  selling agents, 328
Aggressive people, 102
Agree and neutralize technique, 390
Aided recall, 369
Airline frequent-flyer programs,
  193–194
Air pollution, from hair spray, 90
Alcohol awareness and education
    initiative, 79
Allowances, 262
  case, 373–374
  finance, 374
  freight, 374
  merchandise, 374
  promotional, 281
  trade-in, 280
All-you-can-afford budgeting, 344
Alternative evaluation
  in consumer behavior
    consideration set, 97
    evaluative criteria, 97
  in organizational buying, 127
Ambience, 323
American Advertising Federation,
  433
American Community Services, 167
American e-Commerce Association,
  433
American Enterprise Institute, 130
American Marketing Association,
  5, 433
  code of ethics, 84
Anchor stores, 322–323
Antecedent states, 101
Antitrust law
  Clayton Act, 70, 72
  and monopoly, 70
  per se illegal concept, 72
  Robinson-Patman Act, 70
  Sherman Antitrust Act, 70, 72, 80
Approach stage
  cultural settings, 388
  first impressions, 388
  objectives, 386
Art director, 426
Artwork, 361
Asian Americans
  assimilated, 114
  buying patterns, 114
  consumer spending, 64
  diversity of, 114
  nonassimilated, 114
Aspiration group, 110
Assimilated Asian Americans, 114

Assorting, logistical function, 2̲0̲2̲
Assumptive close, 391
Attitudes, 106
  and beliefs, 106
  change in, 107
  formation of, 106
  and selective comprehension,
    103
  and selective exposure, 103
  and values, 106
Attitude tests, 370
Auctions
  reverse, 131
  traditional, 131
Automatic vending, 317–318
Automobile industry
  idea generation, 222
  indirect marketing channels, 291
  logistics management, 302
  marketing channels, 302
  multiple products for multiple
    segments, 190
  promotion budget, 345
  right-hand drive, 218
  supply chain management,
    301–302
  women as customers, 95
  women employees, 95
Awareness, 235, 344
  of brands, 246

B

Baby boomers, 62
Baby boomlet, 63
Baby bust, 62
Back translation, 147
Backward integration, 295
Bait and switch pricing, 277–278
Baristas (coffee brewers), 93
Barter, 262
Behavioral learning, 105
Behaviorally related objectives, 392
Behavioral salesforce evaluation, 396
Behavioral segmentation
  consumer markets
    by product, 193
    by usage rate, 193–195
  percentage of firms using, 194
Beliefs, 106
  and selective comprehension,
    103
Believers, 107
Below-market pricing, 268
Benchmark items, 322
Better Business Bureau, 73–74
Bicycle manufacturing, 403
Billboards, 366
  digital, 358
Biotechnology, 68
Black Friday, 310
Blogs, 175, 413
Bloomberg Businessweek, 209
Bots, 319, 412
Brainstorming, 222, 225
Brand awareness, 246
Brand development index, 241–242
Brand equity, 245
  competitive advantage, 245
  creating, 246–247

Brand equity—*Cont.*
    brand awareness, 246
    brand meaning, 246
    consumer response, 246
    financial advantage, 247
    and price, 245
Brand extensions, 249
Brand identity, 246
Branding, 245
Branding strategy for services, 254
Brand logos, 171
Brand loyalty, 106
    and consumer learning, 105–106
    decline of, 106
    maintaining, 235
    and types of consumer behavior, 211
Brand management
    brand equity, 245–247
    brand extensions, 249
    branding, 244–245
    brand names, 244–245
    brand personality, 245–247
    and fighting brands, 250
    at Gatorade, 233
    mixed branding, 250
    multibranding, 249–250
    multiproduct branding, 248–249
    picking brand names, 248
    private branding and labeling, 250
    product line extensions, 248–249
    subbranding, 249
Brand names, 245
    and brand equity, 245
    criteria for choosing, 248
    of services, 254
    unintended meanings, 146
Brand personality, 245
Brands
    attribute change, 107
    and cause marketing, 88
    children's preferences, 111
    consideration set, 97
    evaluative criteria, 97
    fighting, 250
    forgetting rate, 367
    global, 142–143
    high or low involvement, 99–101
    licensing, 247
    perceptual maps for, 203–204
    stimulus discrimination, 105
    stimulus generalization, 105
    successful, 171
Brand switching, 65, 88
Breadth of product line, 316, 317
Break-even analysis, 273
    applications, 274–275
    break-even chart, 274
    calculating break-even point, 273–274
    for price level, 278
Break-even chart, 274
Break-even point
    calculating, 273–274
    definition, 273
Break-even quantity, 274
Bribery, 83, 145
Brigham Young University, 223
Brokers, 328
    description, 288
    food brokers, 328
Build-to-order, 191
Bundle pricing, 266

Bureau of Labor Statistics, 67
    on retail openings, 426
Burst schedule, 368
Business, 26
Business analysis
    capacity management, 225
    for new consumer products, 224–225
    off-peak pricing, 225
    for services, 225
Business culture, 82–83
Business Ethics, 92
Business firm, 22
Business fit, 224
Business-format franchises, 315
Business marketing, 120
Business model, *26*
Business myopia focus, 26
Businesspeople, ethics of, 80–81
Business plan, 44
    versus marketing plan, 44–45
    questions from outside audiences, 45
Business portfolio analysis, 31
    at Kodak, 31–33
    market growth rate, 31, 32
    primary strength of, 33
    quadrants, 31–32
    relative market share, 31, 32
    weakness of, 33
Business products, cost-plus pricing, 267
Business products/services, **210**; *see also* Organizational buying
    components, 211
    derived demand for, 211
    electronic marketing channels, 292–293
    marketing channels
        direct, 291
        indirect, 292
    marketing strategies, 212
    support products, 211
Business publications, 167, 433
Business-to-business e-commerce
    dollar volume of, 131
    e-marketplaces, 129–131
    low transaction costs, 129
    marketing cost reduction, 129
    online auctions, 131
    prominence of, 129
    supplier information, 129
Business-to-business marketers
    cost-plus pricing, 267
    electronic marketing channels, 292–293
Business-to-business products, 210
Business-to-business selling
    order getter, 385
    order taker, 384
    preapproach stage, 388
BusinessWeek, 335, 424, 427, 431
Buy classes, 128
    modified rebuy
        buying situation, 128
        definition, 129
    new buy
        buying situation, 128
        definition, 129
    straight rebuy
        buying situation, 128
        definition, 128–129
Buyers
    in buying centers, 128

    careers as, 425, 426
    goals of marketing for, 6
    grouped into segments
        differences in needs, 192
        similarity of needs, 192
    kinds of, 16
    no access to, 218
    requirements in channel choice
        convenience, 297
        information, 297
        pre- or post-sale service, 298
        variety, 297
Buyer–seller relationships, 124–125
Buyer turnover, 367
Buying, transactional function, 289
Buying center, 126
    buy classes
        modified rebuy, 129
        new buy, 129
        straight rebuy, 128–129
    as buying committee, 126
    composition of, 127–128
    questions for guidance, 127
    roles in
        buyers, 128
        deciders, 128
        gatekeepers, 128
        influencers, 128
        users, 128
Buying committee, 126
Buying patterns
    African Americans, 113–114
    Asian Americans, 114
    Hispanics, 113
Buying process, organizational buying behavior, 123
Buying situations
    buy classes, 128–129
    and buying centers, 128–129
Buying stations, at Lands' End, 134
Buy•ology (Lindstrom), 171
Buzz, 414

C

Cable TV, 364
CAFTA-DR trade agreement, 140
Campbell Interest and Skill Survey, 428
Canada
    and North American Free Trade Agreement, 139–140
    number of languages, 146
Canned sales presentation, 389
Cannibalization, 191
CAN-SPAM Act of 2004, 73, 413–414
Capacity management, 225, 254
    role of price, 254
Career services office, 429
Careers in marketing, 4–5
    advancement potential, 424
    categories of occupations, 426
    diversity of opportunities, 424
    getting a job, 424
    information sources, 433
    international careers, 427–428
    job search process
        handling rejection, 433
        identifying opportunities, 429–430
        job interview, 431

        résumé, 430–431
        self-assessment, 428
    marketing research, 427
    physical distribution, 425
    product management, 425
    projected growth, 424
    retailing, 425–426
    sales, 427
    starting salaries, 424
Careers in small business, 5
Car sales
    discrimination in, 279
    trade-in allowances, 280
Case allowance, 374
Cases
    Act II Microwave Popcorn, 307–309
    Activeion Cleaning Solutions, 230–231
    Best Buy, 116–117
    Breathe Right Strips, 157–159
    Ford Consulting Group, 184–185
    Geek Squad, 75–77
    General Mills, 42–43
    Google, Inc., 377–379
    Lands' End, 133–135
    Mall of America, 330–331
    Philadelphia Phillies, Inc., 257–259
    Pizza Hut, 420–423
    Starbucks Corporation, 91–93
    3M Corporation, 18–19
    Under Armour, 352–355
    Washburn Guitars, 283–285
    Xerox Corporation, 399–401
Cash and carry wholesalers, 327–328
Cash cows
    definition, 31
    for Kodak, 32
Cash discounts, 280
Catalog retailing, 318
Catalog sales, 293
    Lands' End, 134
Category development index, 241–242
Category killers, 316
Category management, 323
Cause marketing, 87
    at American Express, 88
    and brand switching, 88
    examples, 87–88
Caveat emptor concept, 82
Cease and desist orders, 73
Celebrity endorsements, 104, 109, 110
Cellular phone technology, 398
Census 2000, 226
Census 2010, 166, 226
Census Bureau, 64, 66, 168
    publications, 166–167
Central business district, 322
Cents-off coupons, 55
Channel captain, 300
Channel conflict, 298
    and disintermediation, 289–299
    from dual distribution, 300
    horizontal, 300
    over profit margins, 299
    transactional Web sites, 417
    vertical, 299–300
Channel cost, 298
Channel of communication, 334
Channels of distribution
    assuring profit for, 175

in global marketing, 154–155
unauthorized, 155
Channel strategies
pull strategy, 342–343
push strategy, 342
Charitable contributions vs. cause
marketing, 87
Charities, marketing by, 16
Chief executive officers, 23
prior marketing careers, 424
Chief marketing officer, 23, 28
Child Protection Act, 71
Children, early brand preferences,
111
Children's Online Privacy Protection
Act, 73, 82
China
Medtronic in, 36
population of, 61
trade restrictions, 80
Choice, 16
in online shopping, 412–413
Choice assistance, 413
Choiceboard, 406
Cities, for test markets, 226
Claim policies, organizational buying
criterion, 124
Clayton Act, 70, 72
Closed-end questions, 173
Closing stage
assumptive close, 391
difficulty, 390–391
objectives, 386
trial close, 391
urgency close, 391
Cloud computing, 67, 68
Code of ethics, 84
Cognitive learning, 105
Cola war, 84, 140–141
Cold calling, 387
Cold canvassing, 387
Collaborative filtering, 406
College students
research on study habits, 3
tuition increases, 66
Combination compensation plan, 395
Combined statistical areas, 64
Commerce element, in Web sites, 409
Commercialization
complexities of, 227
definition, 227
fast prototyping, 228
parallel development, 228
regional rollouts, 227
risks in grocery products, 227
speed factor, 227–228
time to market, 227–228
Communication, 334
benefits of packaging
labeling, 251
errors in, 335
forms in promotional mix, 337
by intermediaries, 297
in logistics management, 306
message, 334
in online shopping
blogs, 413
buzz, 414
spam, 413–414
viral marketing, 414
Web communities, 413
receivers, 334
salesforce, 398
source, 334

tools of, 334
wasted coverage, 338
in Web sites, 408
Communication infrastructure, 147
Communication process
decoding, 335–336
encoding, 335–336
feedback, 336
field of experience, 335–336
key elements, 334
noise, 336
Community, virtual, 408
Companies, 22
Company analysis, Paradise
Kitchens, 51
Comparative advertising, 358
Comparison shopping in car
buying, 95
Compensation plans
combination plans, 395
and nonmonetary rewards, 395
starting salaries in marketing,
424
straight commission, 395
straight salary, 395
at Xerox, 400–401
Competencies, 30
Competition, 16, 69
cola war, 84
ethics of
bribery and kickbacks, 83
economic espionage, 83
forms of, 69
and Geek Squad, 76–77
global, 140–141
laws to protect, 70
in product life cycle, 235
and restructuring, 10
from small businesses, 70
and strategic directions, 30
Competition-oriented pricing
approaches; see Pricing
approaches
Competitive advantage
of brand equity, 245
from core competencies, 30
Paradise Kitchens, 48
Competitive advertising
institutional, 359
for products, 358
Competitive bidding
in auctions, 131
in organizational buying, 123
Competitive forces
summary of, 60
trends identified in, 61
Competitive intelligence
researcher, 426
Competitive parity
budgeting, 344
Competitive position, target
market, 98
Competitive products, 223
Competitor analysis,
Paradise Kitchens, 50–51
Competitors
in growth stage, 236
and low-learning products, 239
and predatory pricing, 278
price fixing by, 277
pricing of, and pricing
constraints, 277
reacting to, 243
Complete delivery, 305

Complex or professional
salesperson, 426
Compliant people, 102
Components, 211
Computer-assisted telephone
interviewing, 172
Computers, and Geek Squad, 215
Concepts, 165
Concept tests, 224
Connection, in Web sites, 408
Consideration set, 97
Consistent lead time, 305
Constraints, 164
Consultative selling, 389
Consulting firms, 427
Consumer Awareness and Education
Department, 79
Consumer behavior, 96; *see also*
Online consumer behavior
and Best Buy, 116–117
cognitive dissonance, 98–99
hierarchy of effects, 344
observing, 170
postpurchase behavior, 98–99
psychological influences,
102–108
purchase decision process,
96–101
sociocultural influences, 108–114
women as car buyers, 95
Consumer Bill of Rights, 82, 85
Consumer ethics, 89–90
Consumer Expenditure Survey, 67
Consumer Goods Pricing Act, 277
Consumer income, 66–67, 148
and demand estimates, 270
Consumer involvement
extended problem
solving, 99–100
high-involvement purchases, 99
limited problem solving, 100
low-involvement purchases, 99
and marketing strategy, 100–101
routine problem solving, 100
Consumerism, 71
Consumer lifestyle
definition, 107
and psychographics, 107–108
Consumer marketing at retail, 324
Consumer markets
behavioral segmentation
by product features, 193
by usage rate, 193–195
demographic segmentation, 192,
193
geographic segmentation, 192,
193
psychographic segmentation, 193
variables for forming segments,
195
Consumer needs
discovering, 7
and four Ps of marketing, 10
met with new products, 7–8
satisfying, 9–10
and wants, 8–9
**Consumer-oriented sales
promotion, 370**
contests, 371
coupons, 370–371
deals, 371
loyalty programs, 372
point-of-purchase displays, 372
premiums, 371

product placements, 373
rebates, 373
samples, 372
sweepstakes, 371–372
Consumer Product Safety Act, 71, 82
Consumer Product Safety
Commission, 71
Consumer products/services, **210**
basis of comparison, 211
kinds of, 210–211
marketing channels
direct, 290
indirect, 291
Consumer protection
desired extent of, 9
from packaging, 252
Consumer Reports, 51, 96–97
Consumers; *see also* Customers
benefits from intermediaries
form utility, 289–290
place utility, 289
possession utility, 290
time utility, 289
benefits of marketing for, 16
and brand equity, 246–247
and brands
consideration set, 97
evaluative criteria, 97
cross-channel shoppers, 415–416
ecological issues, 90
education of, 7
environmental issues, 65
forms of communicating with,
333
geo-enthusiastic, 59
global, 142
and high-learning products, 239
learning process, 104–106
and low-learning products, 239
media preferences, 108
motivation
achievement-motivated
groups, 107
high-resource groups, 108
ideals-motivated group, 107
innovators, 108
low-resource groups, 108
self-expression-motivated
groups, 108
survivors, 108
not listening to, 219
organizational, 16
perspective on innovation,
216–217
price and demand factors, 270
price as indicator of quality, 263
product downsizing, 244, 245
and product life cycle, 240–241
profiles of product adopters, 240
resistance to products, 240
in social networks, 175
status-conscious, 265
stereotypes of country-product
pairings, 252
target market, 9
two market environments, 404
ultimate, 16
unethical behavior, 89–90
utilities from retailing, 312–313
value as judgment, 263
value of direct marketing, 348
value perception, 98
view of cause marketing, 88
zeal for low prices, 262

Consumers—*Cont.*
Consumer socialization, 111
Consumer spending
  by African Americans, 64
  by Asian Americans, 64
  government monitoring of, 67
  by Hispanics, 64
  necessary adjustments, 66
  by subcultures, 113–114
Consumer tastes, 270
  in popcorn, 309
Content, in Web sites, 407–408
Contests, 371
Context, in Web site design, 407–408
Continuous innovation, 216
Continuous (steady) schedule, 368
Contracts, long-term, 125
Contractual systems
  franchises systems, 315
  retailer-sponsored cooperatives,
    315
  wholesaler-sponsored voluntary
    chains, 315
Contractual vertical marketing
    systems
  franchising, 295–296
  retailer sponsored, 295
  wholesaler-sponsored, 295
Control in online shopping, 414–415
Controllable environmental forces, 10
Controlling the Assault of Non-
    Solicited Pornography
    and Marketing Act, 73,
    413–414
Convenience
  buyer requirement, 297
  in logistics management, 306
  in online shopping, 412
  of packaging, 252
Convenience products, 210–211
Convert the objection, 390
Cookies, 414–415
Cooperative advertising, 374
Copyright infringement, 81–82
Copyright law, 71
Copyrights, 265
Copywriters, 361, 425, 426
Core competencies, 30
  Paradise Kitchens, 48
Core products/services, 214
Core values, 25, 106
  at Zappos.com, 187–188
Corporate branding, 248
Corporate conscience, 84
Corporate culture; *see also*
    Organizational culture
  behavior of co-workers, 84–85
  behavior of top management,
    84–85
  codes of ethics, 84
  definition, 83
  ethical practices, 83–84
Corporate level, 23
Corporate retail chains, 314
Corporate social responsibility, at
    Starbucks, 92–93
Corporate Social Responsibility
    department, 79
Corporate vertical marketing systems
  backward integration, 295
  forward integration, 294–295
Corporations, 22
Corrective advertising, 73
Cost(s)
  of advertising message, 361

and break-even analysis,
    273–275
  of direct mail and catalogs, 318
  of field sales, 385
  to firms for packaging, 251
  importance of controlling, 273
  of inventory for services,
    213–214
  of marketing channels, 298
  in online shopping, 414
  of promotion program, 347
  of reaching target market, 198
  of Super Bowl commercials, 360
  of television advertising, 363
  total logistics costs, 305
  types of, 273
Cost-effective logistics management,
    301
Cost-oriented pricing approaches; *see*
    Pricing approaches
Cost per thousand, 362
Cost-plus pricing, 267
Cost reduction, in packaging, 253
Costs of production, as pricing
    constraint, 276–277
Country-product pairings, 252
Coupon fraud, 371
Coupons
  cents-off, 55
  companies using, 370–371
  costs of, 371
  fraud in use of, 371
  in integrated marketing program,
    371
  misredemption, 371
  number and value per year, 370
Cover letter, 430–431
Co-workers
  ethical behavior, 84–85
  new product ideas from, 222
Credit card reward programs, 372
Crime, bribery, and kickbacks, 145
Critical strategy-related factors, 35
Cross-channel shoppers, 415–416
  and multichannel marketing,
    416–418
  objectives, 416
Cross-cultural analysis, 64, 144
Cross-docking, 304
Cross-functional teams, 24, 228
Cross-functional team selling, 393
Crowdsourcing, 222
Cues, 105
Cultural diversity
  and approach stage, 388
  and back translation, 147
  cross-cultural analysis, 144
  customs, 145
  language, 146–147
  symbols, 145–146
  values, 144–145
Cultural symbols, 145
  misused in advertising, 145–146
Culture, 64
  characteristics, 112
  components, 64–65
  and Geek Squad, 76–77
  as socializing force, 81
Currency exchange rate, 148
Customary pricing, 268
Customer analysis, Paradise Kitchens
  consumer characteristics, 51
  health/nutrition concerns, 52
Customer buying experience, 381
Customer buying process, easing, 383

Customer continuity, 117
Customer dissatisfaction, 98
Customer experience, 14; *see
    also* Online customer
    experience
  definition, 407
  with 3-D technology, 357
**Customer experience management,
    224, 255**
Customerization, 413
Customer needs
  discovering, 3, 6
  satisfying, 3, 6
  unsatisfied by new product, 218
Customer problems, relating to,
    382–383
Customer relations, effective, 390
Customer relationship era, 14
Customer relationship management,
    14
  case, 399–401
  in marketspace
    choiceboards, 406
    collaborative filtering, 406
    interactive marketing,
      406–407
    permission marketing, 407
    personalization, 406–407
  salesforce automation, 396–398
Customer relationships
  long-term, 11
  and marketing program, 10–11
  in relationship marketing, 11
Customer requirements, 301
Customers; *see also* Consumers
  direct contact with, 14
  80/20 rule, 194
  finding new, 243
  indirect contact with, 14
  listening to, 381
  long-term, 383
  marketer's understanding of, 303
  new product ideas from, 221–222
  online shoppers, 319
  packaging and labeling to
      connect with, 253
  of Starbucks, 93
  and strategic directions, 30
Customer sales organizational
      structure, 392
Customer satisfaction, 98
  organizational goal, 27
  value to companies, 99
Customer service, 305
  Lands' End, 134
  in logistics management, 301
    communication, 306
    convenience, 306
    dependability, 305
    order cycle time, 305
    quick response, 305
    replenishment, 305
    time, 305
  at Zappos.com, 187–188
Customer service manager, 426
Customer specialists, 392–393
Customer value, 10, 14
  created in marketspace, 404–405
  creating, 3
  from cross-functional team
      selling, 393
  and customer relations, 390
  and customer satisfaction, 99
  and fax machines, 238
  and feature bloat, 215

at Google, Inc., 226
  impact of technology on, 68
  many forms of, 191
  from packaging and labeling,
      251–252
  from personal selling, 382–383
  price perception, 265
  from supplier collaboration, 125
Customization, 403
  in online shopping, 413
  of Web sites, 408
Customized interaction, 336
Customs, 145
Cyber Monday, 310, 311

D

Data, 166
  from supermarket scanners, 167
  syndicated panel, 167
  on usage rate, 194
Data analysis
  findings from, 178–179
  process, 178
Databases
  to analyze promotional
      tools, 347
  in direct marketing, 339, 349
Data collection, determining
      means of concepts, 165
  methods, 165
Data collection methods
  data mining, 177
  experiments, 176
  idea evaluation, 172–175
  idea generation, 170–172
  by information technology,
      176–177
  observational data, 168–171
  online databases, 168
  panels, 175–176
  primary data, 168–176
  questionnaire data, 170–172
  sampling, 165
  secondary data, 166–167
  social networks, 175
  statistical inference, 165
  summary of, 166
Data miner, 426
Data mining, 176–177
Data Protection Directive (EU), 349
Data services, 167
Data warehouse, 177
Dealers, 288
Deals, 371
Deceptive Mail Prevention and
      Enforcement Act, 73
Deceptive pricing, 277–278
Deciders, in buying centers, 128
Decision making, 163
  evaluation of process, 180
Decisions, 163
  evaluation of, 180
Decline stage; *see* Product life cycle
Decoding, 335–336
Deletion strategy, 235, 238
Delivery
  complete, 305
  efficient customer response, 305
  organizational buying
      criterion, 124
  safe, 305
Delivery of services
  by firms or nonprofits, 213

by government agencies, 213
by people or equipment, 212–213
Demand; see also Price elasticity of
demand
in organizational markets, 122
as pricing constraint, 276
primary, 234–235
selective, 235
Demand curve, 270
movement along vs. shift in,
270–271
and price elasticity of demand,
271–272
Demand estimation
fundamentals
demand curve, 270
movement along a demand
curve, 270–271
price elasticity of demand,
271–272
shift in demand curve, 271
and target profit pricing, 267
Demand factors, 270
Demand-oriented pricing approaches;
see Pricing approaches
Demographics, 60–61
Census Bureau data, 166–167
of employees, 93
and Geek Squad, 76
information sources, 60–61
and multicultural marketing, 64
population
generational cohorts, 62–63
shifts in, 63–64
of United States, 61–62
of world, 61
racial and ethnic diversity, 64
Demographic segmentation
consumer markets, 192, 193
organizational markets, 195
percentage of firms using, 194
Denial of objections, 390
Density of target market, 296–297
Department of Commerce, 168
Department of Justice
Microsoft case, 69
on reciprocity, 125
Department of Labor
Consumer Expenditure Survey,
67
marketing job projections, 424
Departments, 24
Department stores, 314
at-market pricing, 268
full-service, 316
general merchandise retailers,
317
locations, 322
Dependability in logistics
management, 305
Depth interviews, 170–171
Depth of product line, 316
Derived demand, 122
for business products, 211
Desk jobbers, 328
Developing countries, poverty level,
23
Development
brainstorming, 225
parallel, 228
safety tests, 225
for services, 225
Deviations, acting on, 39–40
Differentiation positioning, 202
Diffusion of innovation, 240

Digital billboards, 358
Digital Millennium Copyright Act, 71
Digital résumé, 430
Digital technology
and copyright law, 71
use and misuse of trademarks, 73
Direct channel
business products, 291
consumer products, 290
Direct exporting, 150
Direct forecast, 181
Direct investment, 152
Direct job search contact, 430
Direct mail
advantages and disadvantages,
364
expenditures, 362
Direct-mail retailing, 318
Direct-mail sales, 293
Direct marketing
activities involved in, 346
challenges in global economy,
349
and customer relationship
management, 348
databases, 349
databases needed for, 339
direct orders, 348–349
by e-mail, 348
expenditures, 348
and Federal Trade Commission,
349
forms of, 348
green best practices guidelines,
349–350
growth of, 348
information technology for, 349
lead generation, 349
online sales, 348
payment method, 337
percent of GDP, 348
privacy issues, 349
strengths and weaknesses, 337
target audience, 340
traffic generation, 349
value for consumers, 348
value for sellers, 348–349
Direct marketing, 339
Direct Marketing Association, 318,
320, 433
Environmental Planning Tool,
350
Direct Marketing Association (UK),
349
Direct marketing channels, 293
Direct orders, 348–349
Director of Corporate Affiliation, 431
Direct sales, by Dell Inc., 137
Direct salesperson, 426
Direct selling, 320
Direct Selling Association, 320
Direct-to-consumer advertising, 343
Discontinuous innovation, 217
Discounting, 72
Discounts, 262, 321
cash discounts, 280
definition, 280
quantity discounts, 280
seasonal discounts, 280
trade discounts, 280
in trade promotion, 373–374
Discretionary income, 66–67
Discrimination in car sales, 279
Disintermediation, 298–299
Disposable income, 66

Dissociative group, 110
Distribution; see also Channels of
distribution; Place
by Dell Inc., 137
in European Union, 139
in growth stage, 237
in introduction stage, 235
pre-launch issues, 19
of services, 254–255
and types of consumer behavior,
211
Distribution-related legislation
exclusive dealing, 72
exclusive territorial distributorships,
72
requirement contracts, 72
tying arrangements, 72
Distribution strategy
in global marketing, 154–155
in marketing program, 13
for Medtronic, 36–37
Paradise Kitchens, 55
in product life cycle, 235
in sports marketing, 206–207
Distributors
description, 288
industrial, 292
salesforce training, 374
Diversification, market-product strategy,
33
Diversification analysis, 33
diversification strategy, 33
market development, 33
market penetration, 33
product development, 33
Diversity
of Asian American population,
114
of Hispanic population, 113
at Starbucks, 93
Diversity index map, 65
Divisions, 141
Dogs
definition, 31
for Kodak, 33
Door-to-door retailing, 320
Downsizing of products, 244–245
Drivers, 176
Drives, 105
Drop shippers, 328
Dual adaptation, 153
Dual distribution, 293
source of channel conflict, 300
strategy, 154
Dues, 262
Dumping, 155
Durable goods, 210
Dynamically continuous innovation,
216–217
Dynamic pricing, 414

E

Early adopters, 240
Early majority, 240
Echo-boom, 63
Economic Census, 167
Economic considerations
exchange rates, 148
income and purchasing power,
148
infrastructure, 147–148
Economic Espionage Act, 83
Economic forces

consumer income, 66–67
and Geek Squad, 76–77
macroeconomic factors, 65–66
summary of, 60
trends identified in, 61
Economic growth vs. environmental
issues, 23
Economic influences, 300
Economic infrastructure
communication, 147
financial and legal systems,
147–148
transportation, 147
Economic integration, 138–140
CAFTA-DR, 140
European Union, 139, 140
North American Free Trade
Agreement, 139–140
Economist, 209
Economy, 65
Efficient customer response, 305
Eight Ps of services marketing, 253
Eight-second rule, 297
80/20 rule, 194
Elastic demand, 271
Electronic business technologies, 69
Electronic commerce, 69
Electronic junk mail, 413–414
Electronic marketing channels
for books, 292
for services, 292–293
utilities created by, 292
Electronics industry, 77
Electronic technology, for surveys
and interviews, 175
E-mail surveys, 172
E-marketplaces, 129–130
independent trading
communities, 130
private exchanges, 130–131
Emerging economies, Dell Inc. in,
137
Emory University, 390
Employees
new product ideas from, 222
Employee welfare, organizational
goal, 27
Employment agencies, 429
Encoding, 335–336
Endorsements, 104
Entrepreneurship
Ben & Jerry's, 21
Creative Cosmetics, 150
at eBay, 130
social, 15
YouTube startup, 5
Environmental advertising, 90
Environmental forces, 10
competitive, 69–70
controllable, 10
economic, 65–67
and Geek Squad, 76–77
influence on marketing, 6
kinds of, 60
regulatory, 70–74
social, 61–65
technological, 67–69
types of, 6
uncontrollable, 10
Environmental issues
and consumer ethics, 90
consumer interest, 65
versus economic growth, 23
and Generation Y, 62
green marketing, 87

Environmental issues—*Cont.*
  issue in packaging, 253
  in organizational buying, 124
  and societal responsibility, 89
  at Starbucks, 93
Environmentally friendly retailing, 314
Environmental scanning, 60; *see also* Global environmental scan
  competitive forces, 69–70
  economic forces, 65–67
  in new-product process, 220
  regulatory forces, 70–74
  social forces, 60–65
  SWOT analysis, 34–35
  technological forces, 67–69
  of today's marketing plan, 60
  trends identified by, 61
Equipment-based services, 213
Espionage, 83
Ethical behavior
  current perceptions, 80–81
  framework for understanding, 81
Ethical duties, 85
Ethicality compared to legality, 80
Ethical/legal framework, 80
Ethical marketing behavior, factors in
  business culture, 82–83
  corporate culture and expectations, 83–85
  industry practices, 82–83
  personal moral philosophy, 85
  societal culture and norms, 81–82
Ethics, 14, 80
  of businesspeople, 80–82
  of competition, 83
  of consumers, 89–90
  corporate conscience, 84
  of downsizing, 245
  of flexible pricing, 279
  in online shopping, 416
Ethics of exchange
  caveat emptor concept, 82
  Consumer Bill of Rights, 82
  right to be heard, 83
  right to be informed, 82
  right to choose, 82
  right to privacy, 82
  right to safety, 82
Ethnic diversity
  and multicultural marketing, 64
  trend in United States, 64
Ethnographic research, 170
European Union
  Data Protection Act, 73
  Data Protection Directive, 349
  description, 139
  membership map, 140
  Microsoft case, 69
  number of languages, 146
  per capita income, 148
Evaluation, 344
Evaluative criteria, 97
Everyday fair pricing, 321–322
Everyday low pricing, 281, 321
Evidence management, 256
Exchange, 6
  by barter, 262
  by money, 262
Exchange rate fluctuations, 148
Exclusive dealing, 72
Exclusive distribution, 297
Exclusive territorial distributorships, 72

Experiencers, 108
Experiments, 176
Expertise, 300
Exporting, 150
  direct, 150
  indirect, 150
  by small businesses, 150–151
Extended problem solving, 99–100
External information search
  market-dominated sources, 96
  personal sources, 96
  public sources, 96–97
External screening and evaluation, 224
Extra fees, 263
Extranets, 69

F

Facilitating function
  activities related to, 289
  of electronic marketing channels, 292
Fad products, life cycle, 239
Failure fees, 227
Fair Packaging and Labeling Act, 71
Family branding, 248
Family decision making
  role of family members, 112
  styles, 112
Family influences, 110–112
  consumer socialization, 111
  decision making styles, 112
  family life cycle, 111–112
  role of family members, 112
Family life cycle, 111
  middle-age married couples, 112
  older married or unmarried, 112
  single parents, 111
  traditional family, 111
  young married couples, 111
  young singles, 111
Family Talks about Drinking, 79
Fares, 262
Fashion products, life cycle, 239
Fast-food restaurants, usage rate, 194–195
Fast prototyping, 228
Fax machine life cycle, 236–238
Fear appeals, 360–361
Feature bloat, 215
Federal Bureau of Investigation
  and cola war, 84
  and online auction fraud, 89–90
Federal Communications Commission
  on advertising, 360
  on subliminal messages, 104
Federal Dilution Act, 72
Federal safety standards, 82
Federal Trade Commission
  cease and desist orders, 73
  consumer privacy right, 82
  on contests and sweepstakes, 372
  corrective advertising, 73
  on deceptive pricing, 277–278
  on environmental advertising, 90
  monitoring advertising, 73
  National Do Not Call Register, 83
  on online fraud, 416
  role in educating consumers, 83
  and telemarketing, 320
Federation of European Direct Marketing, 349
Fee, 262

Feedback
  in communication process, 336
  continuous, 403
  from marketing research, 164
Feedback loop, 336
  lacking in advertising, 337
Field of experience, 335–336
Field service representative, 385
Fighting brands, 250
Finance allowance, 374
Financial data, Paradise Kitchens, 55–56
Financial system, in global marketing, 147–148
Financing, facilitating function, 289
Firms, 22
  costs of packaging, 251
  divisions of, 141
  global, 141–143
  number of franchises, 151
  and opinion leaders, 109
  services delivered by, 213
  subsidiaries, 141
  types of goals, 26–27
  value of customer satisfaction, 99
Fixed alternative questions, 173
Fixed cost, 273
Fixed pricing, 279
Flexible-pricing policy, 279
Flighting (intermittent) schedule, 368
Floor stock protection program, 374
Flow of products, 301
FOB buyer's location, 281
FOB origin pricing, 281
Focus groups, 171
Follow-up on job interview, 432
Follow-up stage
  characteristics, 391
  objectives, 386
Food and Drug Administration, 85, 243
Food and drug laws, 71
Food brokers, 328
Foreign Corrupt Practices Act, 83, 145
Foreign direct investment, 152
Forgetting rate, 367
Forms of ownership, in retailing
  contractual systems, 314
  corporate chains, 314
  definition, 313
  independent retailers, 314
Formula selling format, 389
Form utility, 16, 289–290, 292
  from marketspace, 405
  from retailing, 312–313
Fortune, 26, 79, 92, 108, 125, 209, 429
Forums, 175
Forward integration, 294–295
Four I's of services, 213
Four Ps of marketing, 10
Franchise fees, 315
Franchising, 295–296
  business-format, 315
  definition, 151
  manufacturer-sponsored retail, 296
  manufacturer-sponsored wholesale, 296
  by McDonalds, 150
  product distribution, 315
  service-sponsored franchise systems, 296
  service-sponsored retail, 296
Fraud
  in coupon use, 371
  in online advertising, 366–367
  in online auctions, 89–90

Free samples, 241, 372
Free trials, 104
Freight allowance, 374
Frequency marketing, 193–194
Frequency of ads, 362
Frequent-flyer programs, 193–194
Frozen food trends, 50
Full-line wholesalers, 327
Full-service advertising agencies, 369
Full-service retailers, 316
Functional benefits of packaging and labeling, 251
Functional discounts, 280
Functional level, 24

G

Gatekeepers, in buying centers, 128
Gender discrimination, in car sales, 279
Generalized life cycle, 239
General merchandise stores, 316, 317
General merchandise wholesalers, 327
Generational cohorts, 62–63
Generational marketing program, 63
Generation X, 62
Generation Y, 63
  mobile marketing media, 341
Generic trademark, 72
Geographical price adjustments
  FOB origin pricing, 281
  uniform delivered pricing, 281
Geographical salesforce, 392
Geographic segmentation
  consumer markets, 192, 193
  organizational markets, 195
  percentage of firms using, 194
GeoVals, 108
Global brand, 142
Global companies, 141–143
  environmental scan by, 144–149
  global brands, 142
  global consumers, 143
  global marketing strategy, 141–142
  international firms, 141
  multinational firms, 141
  transnational firms, 141–142
Global competition, 10, 140
  and strategic directions, 30
  Washburn Guitars in, 284
Global consumers, 143
Global economy
  direct selling in, 320
  impact of retailing, 313
Global environment, 23
Global environmental scan
  cultural diversity, 144–147
  economic considerations
    consumer income, 148
    exchange rates, 148
    infrastructure, 147–148
    purchasing power, 148
    political-regulatory climate, 148–149
Global growth stage, 158–159
Global initiative, 137
Global market-entry strategies; *see* Market-entry strategies
Global marketing
  Act II Microwave Popcorn, 309
  bribes and kickbacks, 145
  case, 157–159

competition, 140–141
by Dell Inc., 137
environmental scan
cultural diversity, 144–147
economic infrastructure,
147–148
political-regulatory climate,
148–149
global brands, 142
global companies, 141–143
global consumers, 143
local partners in, 158
market-entry strategies, 149–152
marketing program, 152–155
and moral standards, 81
networked marketspaces,
143–144
strategies, 141–142
and world trade, 138–144
Global marketing careers, 426
Global marketing managers, 426
Global marketing strategy, 141–142
Global positioning system, 59
Goals, 26; *see also* Objectives
organizational, 26–27
Paradise Kitchens, 48
Goal setting, 35–36
by Medtronic, 36
Good Housekeeping seal, 251
Goods and services, 210
marketing of, 15–16
sales in online shopping,
410–411, 412
Goods-services continuum, 214
Government, services delivered by,
213
Government markets
measurement of, 121–122
sustainable procurement, 126
Government regulation of spam,
413–414
Government subsidies, 148
Government units, 121
Grading, facilitating function, 289
Gray market, 155
Green direct marketing, 349–350
Green jobs, 63
Green marketing, 87
Green products, 90
Green retailers, 314
Green vehicle, 262–263
Greenwashing, 90
Grocery products
failure fees, 227
slotting fees, 227
Gross domestic product
direct marketing percentage of,
348
size of service sector, 210
small business percentage of, 70
Gross income, 66
Gross margin, 321
Gross rating points, 362
Groupthink, 219
Growth estimates, target market, 98
Growth share matrix, 31–32
Growth stage; *see* Product life cycle
Growth strategies
business portfolio analysis,
31–33
diversification analysis, 33
Guarantees, 104

H

Hair spray pollution, 90
Handling objections, 389–390
Harvesting strategy, 235, 238–239
Head-to-head positioning, 202
Health, issue in packaging, 253
Help-wanted ads, 429
Hierarchy of effects, 344
Hierarchy of needs, 102, 103
High-involvement purchases, 100
High-learning products, 239
High-resource groups, 108
High-tech industries, economic
espionage, 83
Hispanics
buying patterns, 113
composition of, 113
consumer spending, 64
discrimination in car sales, 279
purchasing power, 50
Horizontal conflict, 300
Horizontal price fixing, 277
Households
demographic segmentation, 193
income of, 66
PRIZM classification, 193
Humor appeals, 362

I

Ice cream making, 21
Idea, in marketing, 210
Idea evaluation, from questionnaire
data, 172–175
Idea generation
new-product process, 221–224
from competitive products,
223
consumer suggestions,
221–222
crowdsourcing, 222
by employees/co-workers,
222
by inventors, 223
for new services, 224
open innovation, 221
research and development
labs, 222–223
from smaller firms, 223
supplier suggestions,
221–222
by universities, 223
from questionnaire data, 170–172
Ideal self-concept, 103
Ideals-motivated groups, 107
Ideas, marketing of, 15–16
Identification with a channel, 300
Idle production capacity, 213
Ignoring objections, 390
Image, 107
Impression management, 256
Inbound telemarketing, 384
Income
adjusted for inflation, 66
of consumers
discretionary, 66–67
disposable, 66
gross, 66
from eBay, 130
global levels, 61
Inconsistency of services, 213
Independent retailers, number of, 314

Independent trading communities, 130
India
Medtronic in, 36
number of languages, 146
population of, 61
Indirect channel
business products, 292
consumer products, 291
Indirect exporting, 150
Individual interviews, 170–171
Individuality, 405–406
Industrial design, 222–223
Industrial distributors, 292
Industrial markets
definition, 120–121
measurement of, 121–122
Industrial products, 210; *see also*
Business products:
Organizational buying
Industrial salesperson, 426
Industrial services, 211
Industry, 22
analysis by Paradise Kitchens, 50
in marketing plan preparation, 44
Industry codes, 121–122
Industry practices
bribes and kickbacks, 83
economic espionage, 83
ethics of competition, 83
ethics of exchange, 82–83
Industry safety standards, 82
Inelastic demand, 271–272
Infant Formula Act, 71
Inflation
impact on consumer spending,
65–66
income adjusted for, 66
Influencers, in buying centers, 128
Infomercials, 364
Information
buyer requirement, 297
consumer right to, 82
learning process, 104–106
selective perception, 103
selective retention, 103
Information search
external, 96–97
internal, 96
in online shopping, 414
in organizational buying, 127
and perceived risk, 103–104
as problem identification, 97
Information technology
components, 176
definition, 177
in direct marketing, 349
for marketing research, 176–177
in relationship marketing, 11
in supply chain
management, 301
In-house ad agencies, 369
In-house product director, 426
In-house research, 427
Innovation
at Apple Inc., 209–210
consumer perspective, 216–217
continuous, 216
diffusion of, 240
discontinuous, 217
dynamically continuous,
216–217
open, 221
organizational perspective, 216
stimulating, 220

Innovators, 108, 240
Input-related objectives, 392
Inquiry tests, 370
Inseparability of services, 213
Inside order takers, 384
Installations, 211
Institutional advertisements, 359
In-store demonstrations, 55
Intangibility of services, 213
**Integrated marketing
communications, 334**
case, 352–355
costs of implementing, 347
engaging consumers, 333
promotional mix
channel strategies, 342–343
product life cycle, 340–342
target audience, 340
types of promotion, 333
Integrated marketing communications
audit, 347
Integrated marketing communications
program
designing promotion, 346
identifying target audience, 343
scheduling, 346
selecting promotional tools, 345
setting budget, 344–345
specifying objectives, 344
Integrated marketing program,
coupons in, 371
Integrated supply chain, 303
Intellectual property
licensing of, 151
theft of, 81–82
Intelligent failures, 219
Intensive distribution, 297
Interactive marketing, 406
choiceboards, 406
collaborative filtering, 406
permission marketing, 407
personalization, 406–407
real-time buying, 406
Seven Cycles, Inc., 403
Interactive media, 293
Interactivity, 405–406
of promotional Web sites, 418
Interest, 262, 344
Intermediaries; *see also* Channel
entries; Marketing
channels
communication by, 297
consumer benefits from,
289–290
facilitating functions, 289
focus of promotional efforts, 340
logistics function, 289
negotiating over functions, 289
terminology for, 277
transactional functions, 277–289
Intermittent schedule, 368
Internal information search, 96
Internal screening and evaluation,
224
International Anti-Dumping and Fair
Competition Act, 145
International firms, 141
International marketing careers, 427
International Standard Industrial
Classification of All
Economic Activity (UN),
121
International trade; *see* World trade
Internet; *see also* Online *entries*

Internet—*Cont.*
consumer privacy rights, 82
electronic distribution by, 255
electronic marketing channels,
292–293
for e-mail surveys, 172
extent of access to, 143
and marketspace, 404
networked global marketspace,
143–144
for organizational buying,
129–131
power of word of mouth, 110
spam, 172
user behavior, 169
Internet advertising; *see* Online
advertising
Internet-based sales, 137
Internet-based technology, 69
Internet-based training, 395
Internet connections, 311
Internet marketing manager, 426
Internet purchases, 11
Internet Tax Freedom Act, 73
Internet technology, 398
individuality, 405–406
interactivity, 405–406
Intranet, 69
Introduction stage; *see* Product life
cycle
Inventors, ideas from, 223
Inventory
holding costs for services,
213–214
order cycle time, 305
vendor-managed, 306
Inventory control manager, 426
Investors, in Paradise Kitchens, 45
Invoice price, 263
Involvement, 99

J

Japan
Fran Wilson Creative Cosmetics
in, 150
rice imports, 138
Job analysis, 394
Job description, 394–395
Job interview
follow-up, 432
handling rejection, 433
interviewee questions, 432
interviewer questions, 431
preparing for
attention to details, 431
information gathering, 431
role playing, 431
succeeding in, 432
Job qualification statement, 395
Jobs
in direct-mail retailing, 318
process of getting, 424
Job search process
identifying opportunities
career services office, 429
direct contact, 430
employment agencies, 429
help-wanted ads, 429
libraries, 429
networking, 429–430
online employment services,
429
personal contacts, 429–430
state employment office, 430

job interview, 431–433
résumé, 430–431
self-assessment
personality tests, 428
vocational interest tests, 428
Joint decision making, 112
Joint ventures, 151
Journal of Marketing, 165
Journal of Marketing Research, 165
Junk mail, electronic, 413–414
Jury tests, 368

K

Kelly Blue Book, 262
Key account management, 392–393
Key personality traits, 102
Kickbacks, 83, 145
Kiosks, 315
Know When to Say When campaign,
79

L

Label, 250
Labeling
challenges and responses
connecting to customer, 253
cost reduction, 253
environmental concerns, 253
health and safety, 253
customer value
communication, 251
functional benefits, 252
perceptual benefits, 252
open dating on, 252
Laboratory test markets, 226–227
Laggards, 240
Language(s)
back translation, 147
in global marketing, 146–147
number of, 146
Lanham Act, 71–72
Late majority, 240
Lawrence Livermore National
Laboratory, 124
Laws, 80
Leadership in Energy and
Environmental Design, 63
Lead generation, 349, 386–387
Learning, 104
behavioral, 105
and brand loyalty, 105–106
cognitive, 105
from repeated experiences, 105
by socialization, 111
Legal and ethical issues in pricing
bait and switch, 277–278
deceptive pricing, 277–278
predatory pricing, 278
price discrimination, 277
price fixing, 277
Legality of marketing
decisions, 80
Legal system in global marketing,
147–148
Lenders to Paradise Kitchens, 45
Level of service
definition, 313
full service, 316
limited service, 316
self-service, 315
Library research, for job
opportunities, 429

Licensing
of brands, 247
drawbacks, 151
market-entry strategy, 151
Licensing agreements, 308
Lifestyle
definition, 107
market segmentation by, 193
and psychographics, 107–108
Likert scale, 174
Limited-line stores, 316
Limited-line wholesalers
cash and carry wholesalers,
327–328
definition, 327
drop shippers, 328
rack jobbers, 327
truck jobbers, 328
Limited problem solving, 100
Limited-service advertising
agencies, 369
Limited-service outlets, 316
Linear trend extrapolation, 182
List or quoted price, 263
flexible-pricing policy, 279
one-price policy, 278
special adjustments to, 279–281
allowances, 280–281
discounts, 280
geographical, 281
Litigation, product safety, 82
Location-based marketing, 59
Location of online shopping, 415
Logistics, 301
activities related to, 289
cross-docking, 304
and electronic marketing
channels, 292–293
Logistics management
in auto industry, 302
cost effective, 301
for customer requirements, 301
customer service, 301
flow of products, 301
by Procter & Gamble, 301
in supply chain
customer service, 305–306
objectives, 304
total costs, 305
transportation, 302
Logo/Logotype, 244, 254
Long-term contracts, 125
Long-term customer relationships, 11
Long-term customers, 383
Losses from theft of intellectual
property, 81–82
Loss-leader pricing, 269
Lost-horse forecast, 181
low-involvement purchases, 100
Low-learning products, 239
Low-resource groups, 108
Loyalty programs, 372

M

Macroeconomic conditions, 65–66
Madrid Protocol, 72
Magazine advertising
advantages and disadvantages,
364
cost problem, 365
expenditures, 362
number of magazines, 365
special interest publications, 365
Magazine Publishers of America, 360

Mail-order selling, 293
Mail surveys, 172
Maintained markup, 321
**Major account management,
392–393**
Makers, 108
Mall intercept interviews, 172
Mall of America, 319
case, 330–331
Managing for long-run profits, 175
Manufacturers
below-market pricing, 268
case allowances, 374
channel strategies, 342–343
cooperative advertising, 374
evolution of market orientation,
14
exclusive dealing by, 72
exclusive territorial
distributorships, 72
failure fees, 227
marketing plan, 44–45
organizational chart, 38
pre-launch issues, 18
premium prices, 268
and relationship marketing, 11
and retail chains, 314
slotting allowances, 83
slotting fees, 227
target pricing, 266
training distributors' salesforces,
374
transactional Web sites, 417
Manufacturer's agents, 328
Manufacturer's branch offices, 328
Manufacturer-sponsored retail
franchise system, 296
Manufacturer-sponsored wholesale
franchise systems, 296
Manufacturer's representative, 328
Manufacturer's sales offices, 328
Markdown
definition, 321
timing of, 321
Market(s), 9
kinds of, 15
for Mall of America, 331
new, 243
organizational buying behavior,
123
Market attractiveness, 218
Market development, market-product
strategy, 33
Market-dominated information sources,
96
Market-entry strategies, 149–152
direct investment, 152
exporting, 150–151
franchising, 151
joint ventures, 151
licensing, 151
profit potential, 149
Marketers, 15
Market growth rate, 31–32
Marketing, 5; *see also* Careers
in marketing; Ethical
marketing behavior;
Services marketing
breadth and depth of, 15–16
business market, 120
careers, 4–5
challenges for General Mills, 42
controllable factors, 10
costs as pricing constraint,
276–277
to create customer value, 3

customer value and utility, 16
discovering consumer needs, 7–9
effects of technology, 68
ethical/legal framework, 80
ethics and, 14
everyday consumer decisions, 4
evolution of market orientation
  customer experience, 14
  customer relationship era, 14
  marketing concept era, 14
  production era, 14
  sales era, 14
to global consumers, 143
and global positioning system, 59
goals of, 35
of goods and services, 15–16
groups benefited by, 16
implications of reference groups,
  110
kinds of customers, 16
kinds of markets, 15
location-based, 59
opportunities in European Union,
  139
personal selling roles, 382
satisfying consumer needs, 9–10
social responsibility, 15
trends affecting future, 60
uncontrollable factors, 10
Marketing actions
based on data analysis, 178–179
  evaluation of results, 180
  implementation, 180
  recommendations, 180
conclusions from
  neuromarketing, 171
factors influencing, 6
identifying, 164
identifying needed data,
  164–165
linking needs to, 188
potential for reaching
  segments, 192
to reach target market, 199–201
Marketing channels, 288; *see also*
  Logistics management;
  Supply chain management
auto industry, 302
business products/services
  direct channel, 291
  indirect channel, 292
Callaway Golf, 287
case, 307–309
consumer products and services
  direct channel, 290
  indirect channel, 291
cost of, 298
direct, 293
dual distribution, 293
electronic, 292–293
factors affecting choice
  buyer requirements, 297–298
  profitability, 298
  target market coverage,
    296–297
intermediaries
  functions, 288
  terminology for, 288
  value created by, 288–290
marketing dashboard for, 299
multichannel marketing, 293
relation to logistics and supply
  chain, 302
securing cooperation, 300
sources of channel conflict,
  298–299

strategic alliances, 293
as valued marketing asset, 287
vertical systems
  administered, 296
  contractual, 295–296
  corporate, 294–295
  definition, 294
Marketing communication
  programs, 334
Marketing communications
  agencies, 347
Marketing concept, 14
Marketing concept era, 14
Marketing dashboards, 27–28
  above-, at-, or below-market
    pricing, 269
  for Ben and Jerry's, 28
  brand development index, 242
  category development
    index, 242
  channel sales and profit, 299
  for cost per thousand, 363
  marketing metrics, 28
  and marketing plan, 28–29
  for marketing research, 184
  at Oracle Corporation, 28
  origin of, 28
  for promotion budget, 345
  to reduce new-product
    failure, 219–220
  retail format, 324
  salesperson performance, 397
  Web site performance, 410
Marketing department, 6
  focus on consumer needs, 9
  key role of, 24
  organization of, 9
Marketing drivers, 176
Marketing environment
  competitive forces
    forms of competition, 69
    small businesses, 70
  economic forces
    consumer income, 66–67
    macroeconomic conditions,
      65–66
  environmental scanning of, 60
  regulatory forces
    advertising-related
      legislation, 73
    distribution-related
      legislation, 72
    pricing-related legislation,
      72
    product-related
      legislation, 70–72
    promotion-related legislation,
      73
    protecting competition, 70
    self-regulation, 73–74
  social forces
    culture, 64–65
    demographics, 60–64
  technological forces
    electronic business
      technologies, 69
    impact on customer value,
      68
    technology of tomorrow,
      67–68
Marketing information research, 289
Marketing managers, 426
  key for price setting, 264
Marketing metric, 28
Marketing mix, 10
  controllable factors in, 10

drivers in, 176
four Ps of, 10
in introduction stage, 235
and marketing program, 13
in marketing program, 37
organizational buying behavior,
  123
poor execution, 218
price in., 263–264
product differentiation, 188
promotion in, 334
for services, 253–256
uncontrollable factors in, 10
"Marketing Myopia" (Levitt), 26
Marketing News, 429
Marketing organization, designing,
  37–38
Marketing plan, 28
  versus business plan, 44–45
  elements of, 45
  kind and complexity of
    organization, 44
  Kydd on, 44
  nature of industry, 44
  Paradise Kitchens, Inc.
    company analysis, 51
    company background, 46
    competitive advantage, 48
    competitor analysis, 50–51
    core competencies, 48
    customer analysis, 51–52
    evaluation, 57
    financial data and
      projections,
        55–56
    goals, 48
    implementation, 57
    industry analysis, 50
    interpreting, 46–47
    marketing and promotion
      objectives, 52–53
    mission, 47
    organizational chart, 56–57
    points of difference, 53
    positioning, 53
    situation analysis, 49–52
    strategic focus, 47–48
    SWOT analysis, 49–50
    target markets, 53
  questions from outside
    audiences, 45
  target audience and purpose, 44
  writing and style suggestions,
    45–46
Marketing program, 12
  customer relationships, 10–11
  customer value, 10–11
  development of, 10
  elements and rationale, 13
  execution of, 38
  generational, 63
  global, 152–155
    distribution strategy, 153–154
    price strategy, 155
    product strategies, 153–154
    promotion strategies, 153–154
  marketing mix activities, 37
  Paradise Kitchens, Inc.
    distribution strategy, 55
    price strategy, 54
    product strategy, 54
    promotion strategy, 54–55
  relationship marketing, 11
  social responsibility program,
    88, 89
  target market, 9

at 3M Corporation, 18
  execution of, 12–13
  moving from idea to
    product, 12
  product line extension, 12
Marketing publications, 433
Marketing research, 162
  careers in, 427
  case, 184–185
  challenges of, 162
  on college students, 3
  cross-cultural analysis, 144
  on customer satisfaction, 99
  data analysis, 178–179
  data collection
    with online databases, 168
    primary data, 166, 168–177
    secondary data, 166–167
  feedback from, 164
  by Fisher-Price, 163–165
  five-step approach, 163
  identifying marketing actions,
    163–164
  marketing actions taken, 180
  measures of success, 162–164
  by movie industry, 161–162
  plan development, 164–165
  problem definition, 163–164
  sales forecasting techniques,
    181–182
  sensitivity analysis, 177
  setting objectives, 163
  by 3M Corporation, 18
Marketing research careers
  account executive, 426
  competitive intelligence
    researcher, 426
  data miner, 426
  in-house project director, 426
  project manager, 426
Marketing research consulting firms,
  427
Marketing research plan
  identifying needed data, 164–165
  specifying constraints, 164
Marketing Science Institute, 433
Marketing strategy, 38
  Act II Microwave Popcorn, 309
  aligned with supply chain,
    303–304
  and consumer involvement,
    100–101
  at Dell Inc., 304
  in European Union, 139
  global, 141–142
  international firms, 141
  multidomestic, 141
  product differentiation, 188
  and supply chain management,
    302–304
  two-tier, 190
  Under Armour, 352–355
  at Walmart, 304
Marketing synergies, 202
Marketing tactics, 38
Market modification
  creating new use, 243
  finding new customers, 243
  increasing product use, 243
Market orientation, 14
Market penetration, 33
Marketplace, traditional, 404
Market price, 268
Market-product grid, 197
  Apple, Inc., 201–202
  estimating market size, 198

Market-product strategy—*Cont.*
forming, 197–198
Prince Sports, Inc., 207
Wendy's, 199
Market-product strategy, 35–36
diversification, 33
market development, 33
market penetration, 33
Paradise Kitchens
objectives, 52–53
points of difference, 53
positioning, 53
target markets, 53
product development, 33
Market-product synergies, 201–202
Market segmentation, 35, 188
Act II Microwave Popcorn, 309
case, 205–207
consumer markets
behavioral, 193
demographic, 193
geographic, 193
psychographic, 193
by usage rate, 193–195
linking needs to actions, 188
marketing mix action, 188
and mass customization,
190–191
meaningful group formation, 188
meaning of, 188
with multiple product and
multiple segments,
190
with one product and multiple
segments, 189–190
organizational markets
behavioral, 195
demographic, 195
geographic, 195
product differentiation strategy,
188
strategy at Apple Inc., 201
synergies vs. cannibalization,
191
timing of, 189
at Zappos.com, 187–188, 189
Market segmentation steps, 191–202
buyer groupings
bases of segmentation,
192–195
criteria, 192
for organizational markets,
195
variables to use, 195
market-product grid, 197–198
market size estimation, 198
product category groups
industrial products, 196–197
multiple products, 197
reaching target markets
at Apple Inc., 200–201
market-product synergies,
201–202
at Wendy's, 199–200
target market selection
choosing segments, 199
criteria, 198–199
Market segments, 188
at Best Buy, 117
choosing, 199
criteria for forming
buyer needs, 192
cost-effectiveness, 192
marketing action potential,
192

profit potential, 192
grouping potential buyers into,
192–196
and mass customization,
190–191
multibranding strategies, 250
multiple
with multiple products, 190
with one product, 189–190
problems with, 191
Washburn Guitars, 283
Market share, 27, 276
holding, 237
versus immediate profit, 275
organizational goal, 27
profit objective, 276
relative, 31–32
in retail life cycle, 321
Market size
estimating, 198
target market, 198
Marketspace, 69
case, 420–423
consumer behavior
characteristics of consumers,
409–410
product/service categories,
410–411
reasons for shopping,
411–415
time and location of
shopping, 415
creating customer experience
commerce, 409
communication, 408
community, 408
connection, 408
content, 408
context, 407–408
customization, 408
cross-channel shoppers, 415–416
customer relationship
management
choiceboards, 406
interactive marketing, 406
permission marketing, 407
personalization, 406–407
customer value creation,
404–405
definition, 404
individuality, 405–407
interactivity, 405–407
networked global, 143–144
privacy and security issues, 416
utilities offered, 404–405
Web site performance, 410
Market testing
definition, 225
versus prototypes, 227
simulated test markets, 226–227
test marketing, 226
Markup, 266–267
maintained, 321
original, 321
Massachusetts Institute of Technology,
68
Mass customization, 190–191
Mass markets, disappearing, 189
Mass merchandisers, 308
Mass selling, 336
Maturity stage; *see* Product life cycle
Maximizing current profit, 175
Measures of success, 163
Media; *see also* Advertising media
consumer preferences, 108

new and old forms, 341
Media buyer, 426
Membership group, 110
Merchandise allowance, 374
Merchandise line
breadth of, 317
category killers, 316
definition, 313
depth of, 316
scrambled merchandising, 317
Merchandise management, 425
category management, 323
consumer marketing at retail, 324
marketing dashboard for, 324
marketing metrics, 325
sales per square foot, 325
Merchant wholesalers, 327
cash and carry wholesalers,
327–328
desk jobbers, 328
drop shippers, 328
full-line wholesalers, 327
general merchandise wholesalers,
327
profits for, 328
rack jobbers, 327
specialty merchandise retailers,
327
truck jobbers, 328
Mergers and acquisitions, Unilever/
Ben & Jerry's, 21
Message, 334
Messages
selective perception, 103
subliminal perception, 103, 104
Methods; *see* Data collection methods
Metropolitan divisions, 64
Metropolitan statistical areas, 64
Mexican food trends, 50
Mexico
dumping accusation from, 155
and North American Free Trade
Agreement, 139–140
Micropolitan statistical areas, 64
Middle-aged couples, 112
Middlemen, 288
Millennials; *see* Generation Y
Minorities, 62
African Americans, 64, 279
Asian Americans, 64, 114
Hispanics, 50, 64, 115, 279
organizational buying from, 124
Mission, 25
Paradise Kitchens, 48
Mission statement
examples, 25
Lands' End, 133
social element, 25
Starbucks, 91–93
Mixed branding, 250
Modified rebuy, 128, 129
Money-back guarantees, 241
Money vs. barter, 262
Monopolistic competition, 69
Monopoly
antitrust laws, 70
definition, 69
Moody's manuals, 431
Moral idealism, 85
Moral philosophy
acquisition of, 85
moral idealism, 85
utilitarianism, 85
Moral standards, 81
Motivation, 102

achievement-motivated groups,
107
ideals-motivated groups, 107
and individual needs, 102, 103
and lifestyle, 107–108
of salesforce, 395–396
self-expression motivated
groups, 108
at Xerox, 400–401
Movement along a demand curve,
270–271
Movie industry
product positioning, 373
profit objectives, 275, 276
promotion scheduling, 346
risk in blockbusters, 161
sneak previews, 161
test screenings, 161–162
theft of intellectual property, 81–82
3-D films, 357
title changes, 161
tracking studies, 162
Multibranding, 249
Multichannel marketing, 293
case, 420–423
cross-channel shopping, 416
with promotional Web sites, 418
Seven Cycles, Inc., 403
with transactional Web sites, 417
Multichannel retailers, 323
Multicultural marketing, 64
**Multidomestic marketing strategy,
141**
Multilanguage Web site, 403
Multinational firms, 141
Multiproduct branding, 248
brand extensions, 249
product line extensions, 248–249
subbranding, 249
Museums, 15–16
Music industry, theft of intellectual
property, 81–82
Myers-Briggs Type Indicator, 429
Mystery shoppers, 169

N

Nanotechnology, 67, 68
National Association of Colleges and
Employers, 429
National Bureau of Economic
Research, 279
National Do Not Call Registry, 73,
83, 320, 349, 350, 387
National Highway Traffic Safety
Commission, 87
National television ratios, 168–169
Needs, 8–9
hierarchy of, 103
market, 188
perceiving, 96
similar or different, 192
Need-satisfaction presentation
adaptive selling, 389
consultative selling, 389
Negative deviation, 40
Negative word of mouth, 110
Networked global marketspace,
143–144
Networking, job search, 429–430
Network technologies, 69
Neuromarketing, 170, 171
New buy, 128, 129
New car buying, 95

New-product concept, 165
New-product failures, 4
  examples, 8
  marketing dashboards to reduce,
    219–220
  organizational problems, 219
  preventing, 8
  reasons for, 217–219
    bad timing, 218
    incomplete protocol, 218
    insignificant points of
      difference,
      217–218
    little market attractiveness,
      218
    no access to buyers, 218
    poor execution of marketing
      mix, 218
    poor quality, 218
    unsatisfied customer needs,
      218
New-product launch
  Act II Microwave Popcorn, 308
  key suggestions for, 8
  penetration pricing, 265
  research for, 3
  skimming pricing, 264–265
  by 3M Corporation, 18–19
New-product process, 220
  at Apple Inc., 209–210
  business analysis, 224–225
  case, 230–231
  commercialization
    complexities, 227
    regional rollouts, 227
    time to market, 227–228
  cross-functional teams, 228
  development stage
    brainstorming, 225
    safety tests, 225
    for services, 225
  fast prototyping, 228
  groupthink drawback, 219
  idea generation, 221–224
    brainstorming, 222–223
    from competitive products,
      223
    by consumers and suppliers,
      221–222
    from employees/co-workers,
      222
    at IDEO, 223
    by inventors, 222
    research and development
      labs, 222–223
    from smaller firms, 223
    by universities, 222
  market testing
    versus prototyping, 227
    simulated test marketing,
      226–227
    test marketing, 226
  parallel development, 228
  screening and evaluation, 224
  skipping stages in, 219
  strategy development, 220–221
New products
  compared to existing products,
    215–216
  from consumer perspective,
    216–217
  defining, 215–217
  design at 3M, 3
  from ideas to, 12
  lack of long-run success, 7–8

in legal terms, 216
to meet consumer needs, 7
number of ideas needed for, 217
from organizational
    perspective, 216
pre-launch issues, 18–19
protocol, 217
from technological change,
    67–68
New-product strategy development,
    220–221
News conference, 375
Newspaper advertising
  advantages and disadvantages,
    364
  expenditures, 362
  local medium, 365
  national distribution, 365
Newspaper circulation, 362
News release, 375
New York Times, 190, 226
Noise, 336
Nonassimilated Asian Americans,
    114
Nondiscretionary products or
    services, 272
Nondurable goods, 210
Nonmonetary rewards, 395
  at Xerox, 401
Nonpersonal component of
    advertising, 337–338
Nonprofit marketing careers, 426
Nonprofit organizations, 22
  service marketing by, 255
  services delivered by, 213
Nonselling duties, 427
Nonstore retailing
  automatic vending, 317–318
  catalog retailing, 318
  direct-mail retailing, 318
  direct selling, 320
  online retailing, 319–320
  telemarketing, 320
  television home shopping,
    318–319
Norms, 81–82
North American Free Trade
    Agreement, 121
  description, 139–140
**North American Industry
    Classification System,
    121,** 167
  and demographic segmentation,
    195
Not-invented-here problem, 219
Nutritional Labeling and Education
    Act, 71

Objections
  definition, 389
  techniques for handling, 390
Objective and task budgeting, 344
Objectives, 26
  of advertising program, 360
  of logistics management in
    supply chain, 304
  of organizational buying,
    123–124
  in personal selling process, 386
  of pricing, 275–276
  of promotion program, 344
  of salesforce, 392

Observational data, 168
Observational data collection
  mechanical methods
    Internet ratings, 169
    TV ratings, 168–169
    neuromarketing, 170, 171
  personal methods
    ethnographic research, 170
    mystery shoppers, 169
    watching consumer behavior,
      170
Odd-even pricing, 265–266
Offerings, 22
Off-peak pricing, 225, 254
Off-price retailing, 322
Ohio Retail Planning Associates, 322
Older married or unmarried, 112
Oligopoly, 6
One-price policy, 278
One-size-fits-all mass markets, 189
Online advertising
  advantages, 366
  categories, 378
  click fraud, 366–367
  expenditures, 362
  interactivity, 366
  measuring impact, 366
  rating, 366
  as rich media, 366
  technology improvements,
    378–379
Online auctions, 131
  fraud in, 89–90
Online career and employment
    services, 429
Online communities, 333
Online consumer behavior
  consumer characteristics,
    409–410
  cross-channel shoppers, 415–416
  purchases, 410–411
  reasons for shopping, 411–415
    choice, 412–413
    communication, 413–414
    control, 414–415
    convenience, 412
    costs, 414
    customization, 413
  time and place of shopping, 415
Online consumer experience
  commerce, 409
  communication, 408
  community, 408
  connection, 408
  content, 408
  context, 407–408
  customization, 408
  opt-in consent, 407
  opt-out option, 407
  Pizza Hut, 421–422
Online consumers
  privacy and security, 416
  Web site performance, 409–410
Online databases, 168
Online fraud, 416
Online malls, 319
Online marketing research, 427
Online retailing
  advantage for
    consumers, 319
  approaches, 319
  bricks and clicks approach, 319
  Create Your Own program, 313
  on Cyber Monday, 311
  failure to check out, 319

interactive, 320
new approaches, 311
Online sales
  from direct marketing, 348
  in multichannel marketing, 418
  by product/service categories, 412
  by Under Armour, 354–355
Online shopping
  consumer preferences, 414
  and cookies, 414–415
  in direct marketing, 348–349
  eight-second rule, 297
  Lands' End, 134
  number of shoppers in U.S., 404
  in organizational markets
    auctions, 131
    dollar volume, 131
    e-marketplaces, 129–131
    low transaction costs, 129
    marketing cost reductions,
      129
    prominence of, 129
    supplier information, 129
  at Pizza Hut, 420
  sales projections, 404
  sales revenue in U.S., 404
  Web site performance, 410
  at Zappos.com, 187–188, 189
Online surveys, 172
On-the-job training, 395
Open dating, 252
Open-ended questions, 173
Open innovation, 221
Operations manager, 426
Opinion leaders, 108
Opportunities; *see* SWOT analysis
Opt-in, 407
Opt-in e-mail alert, 349
Opt-out, 407
Orange Bowl, 233
Order clerks, 384
Order cycle time, 305
Order getter, 385
Order size in organizational buying,
    122–123
Order taker, 384
Organizational buyers, 16, 120
  advertising to, 340
  and business markets, 120
  competitive bidding, 123
  government units, 121
  industrial markets, 120–121
  JCPMedia, 119
  kinds of purchases, 120
  measuring markets, 121–122
  online buying
    auctions, 131
    marketing cost reductions,
      129
    supplier information for, 129
    transaction costs, 129
  reseller markets, 121
  trade promotions for, 373–374
Organizational buying
  buyer–seller relationships,
    124–125
  case, 133–135
  complex negotiations, 124
  cost-plus pricing, 267
  criteria, 124–125
  demand characteristics, 122
  long-term contracts, 125
  number of potential buyers, 123
  objectives, 123–124
  reciprocity in, 125

size of order or purchase, 122–123
supplier partnerships, 124–125
sustainable procurement, 125–126
Organizational buying behavior, 126
buying centers, 126–129
characteristics, 123
dimensions, 123
purchases from minorities and women, 124
stages, 126, 127
Organizational chart, 6, 23
manufacturing firm, 38
marketing department, 9
Paradise Kitchens, 56–57
Organizational culture, 26
at Google, Inc., 377–378
Organizational direction, 24
business model, 26
goals and objectives, 26–27
Organizational foundation, 24–27
core values, 26
mission, 26
organizational culture, 27
Organizational goals, 198–199
Organizational markets
behavioral segmentation, 195
demographic segmentation
by NAICS, 195
by number of employees, 195
derived demand in, 122
geographic segmentation, 195
government units, 121
industrial, 120–121
measuring, 121–122
online buying, 129–131
reseller, 121
Organizational strategies, 24
variation by level, 27
variation by offering, 27
Organizational structure
corporate level, 23
functional level, 24
and organizational strategies, 26
strategic business unit level, 24
Organizational synergy, 191
Organizational triple bottom line, 87
Organizations
benefits of marketing for, 5–6, 16
business firms, 22
codes of ethics, 84
core competencies, 30
definition, 22
departments, 24
evolution of market orientation, 14
focus on customer value, 10–11
and industry, 22
influence on marketing, 6
in marketing plan preparation, 44
nonprofit, 22
open innovation, 221
perspective on innovation, 216
profit, 22
restructuring, 10
social responsibility, 86–90
societal marketing concept, 15
strategy, 22
sustainable development, 22–23
top management, 23
visionary, 24–26
Original markup, 321

Outbound telemarketing, 385
Outdoor advertising
advantages and disadvantages, 364
billboards, 366
expenditures, 362
place-based media, 367
transit advertising, 366–367
Output-related objectives, 392
Outside order takers, 384

P

Package tampering, 252
Packaging
annual company costs, 251
challenges and responses
connecting to customers, 253
cost reduction, 253
environmental concerns, 253
health and safety issues, 253
consumer protection, 252
convenience, 252
customer value
in communication, 251
functional benefits, 252
perceptual benefits, 252
definition, 250
downsizing, 244, 245
Paradise Kitchens, 54
Pez Candy, Inc., 251
and product quality, 252
storage function, 252
PageRank algorithm, 378
Paid aspect of advertising, 337
Palm Beach County library system, 315
Panels, 175–176
Paper companies, 119
Parallel development, 228
Parallel importing, 155
Patent infringement, 81–82
Patent law, 71
Patent protection, 265
Patents, licensing of, 151
Peer groups, 107
Penetration pricing, 236, 265
People-based services, 212–213
Peoplemap, 428
Per capita income, 148
Per capita income ranges, 61
Perceived risk, 103–104
Percentage of sales budgeting, 344
Perception, 103
created by packaging/labeling, 252
perceived risk, 103–104
selective, 103
selective comprehension, 103
selective exposure, 103
selective retention, 103
subliminal, 103, 104
Perceptual maps, 203
uses of, 203–204
Permission marketing, 407
Per se illegal concept, 72
Personal contacts in job search, 429–430
Personal influence
buzz, 414
opinion leaders, 108–109
word of mouth, 109–110
Personal information sources, 96
Personal interviews, 172

Personality, 102
key traits, 102
self-concept, 103
Personality tests, 428
Personalization, 406–407
Personal methods of data collection, 169–170
Personal moral philosophy; *see* Moral philosophy
Personal needs, 102, 103
Personal selling, 337–338, 382
activities involved in, 346
advantages, 338
case, 399–401
creating customer relations, 382–383
creating value, 383
in growth stage, 341
human-intensive activity, 382
inbound telemarketing, 384
lack of flexibility, 338
order getters, 385
order takers, 384
outbound telemarketing, 385
payment method, 337
pervasiveness of, 382
push strategy, 342
relationship selling, 382–383
roles in marketing, 382
strengths and weaknesses, 337
target audience, 340
tasks involved, 382
and telecommunications, 382
at Xerox, 381
Personal selling process, 386
approach, 388
closing stage, 390–391
follow-up, 391
handling objections, 389–390
preapproach, 387–388
presentation, 388–390
prospecting, 386–387
stages, 386
Personal values, 106
Pharmaceutical companies, direct-to-consumer advertising, 343
Physical distribution careers, 425, 426
Physical distribution specialist, 426
Physical surroundings, 101
Physiological needs, 102, 103
Pioneering advertising
institutional, 359
for products, 358
Pirated movies, 80
Place, 19; *see also* Distribution
Place-based media, 367
Place utility, 16, 289, 292
from marketspace, 404–405
from retailing, 312–313
Planning gap, 39
Planning schedule, 38
Point-of-purchase displays, 372
Points of difference, 36
insignificant, 217–218
Paradise Kitchens, 53
Political-regulatory climate
political stability, 148–149
trade regulations, 149
Pollution Prevention Pays program, 23
Pollution prevention program, 87
Population
age structure, 61
census data, 166–167

growth expected in United States, 62
statistical areas, 64
of United States, 61–62
world, 61
Population explosion, 61
Population Reference Bureau, 60–61
Population shifts, 63–64
Pop-up blockers, 172
Pop-up surveys, 172
Portfolio tests, 368
Positioning, 36
Positioning statement, 203
Positive deviation, 49
Possession utility, 16, 290, 292
from marketspace, 405
from retailing, 312–313
Postpone technique, 390
Postpurchase behavior
cognitive dissonance, 98–99
customer satisfaction, 98
in organizational buying, 127
Posttests, 369
aided recall, 369
attitude tests, 370
inquiry tests, 370
of promotion program, 347
sales tests, 370
unaided recall, 369
Poverty in developing countries, 23
Power centers, 322–323
Preapproach stage, 387–388
objectives, 386
Predatory pricing, 278
Preferences, anticipating change in, 135
Premium, 262
Premiums, 371
Pre- or postsale service, 298
Presentation stage
adaptive selling, 389
canned sales presentation, 389
consultative selling, 389
formula selling format, 389
handling objections, 389–390
need-satisfaction format, 389
objectives, 386
stimulus-response format, 388
suggestive selling, 388
Prestige pricing, 265
Preteens, in family decision making, 112
Pretesting, 336
Pretests, 368
jury tests, 368
portfolio tests, 368
of promotion program, 346–347
theater tests, 369
Price(s), 262
and availability of similar products, 270
and brand equity, 245
capacity management role, 254
common terms for, 262
definition, 19
and demand factors, 270
factors the increase or decrease, 262–263
importance of, 262–264
indicator of value, 263
in marketing mix, 263–264
means of lowering, 262
organizational buying criterion, 124
and perception of quality, 263

pre-launch issues, 19
in reverse auctions, 131
of services, 254
with special fees or surcharges, 262
in traditional auctions, 131
and types of consumer behavior, 211
Price competition, 69
Price discrimination
flexible pricing, 279
legal and illegal, 277
off-peak pricing, 225, 254
yield management pricing, 266
Price elasticity of demand, 271
determining factors, 272
elastic demand, 271
inelastic demand, 271–272
Price fixing, 72
court ruling on, 80
horizontal, 277
illegality, 277
resale price maintenance, 277
vertical, 277
Price level, setting, 278
Price perception, 265
Price premium, 268
Price setting
adjustments to list price, 279–281
allowances, 280–281
discounts, 280
geographical adjustments, 281
approximate price level, 278
case, 283–285
final price, 278–281
list or quoted price
flexible-pricing policy, 279
one-price policy, 278
Price strategy
in global marketing, 155
and gray market, 155
in marketing program, 13
for Medtronic, 36–37
Paradise Kitchens, 54
in product life cycle, 235
Price-value position, 261
Pricing; *see also* Retail pricing
deceptive
bait and switch, 277–278
predatory pricing, 278
dynamic, 414
in growth stage, 236
off-peak, 225
in online shopping, 414
penetration pricing, 236
skimming strategy, 235
Pricing approaches
competition-oriented
above-, at-, or below-market pricing, 268–269
customary pricing, 268
loss leader pricing, 269
market pricing, 269
cost-oriented
cost-plus, 267
standard markup, 266–267
and demand estimation, 270–272
demand-oriented
bundle pricing, 266
off-even pricing, 265–266
penetration pricing, 265
prestige pricing, 265
skimming pricing, 264–265

target pricing, 266
yield management pricing, 266
everyday low pricing, 281
by *Newsweek,* 270–271
profit-oriented
target profit pricing, 267
target return-on-investment pricing, 268
target return-on-sales pricing, 268
and revenue estimation, 272
Vizio, Inc., 261
Pricing constraints, 276
costs of production, 276–277
demand, 276
legal and ethical issues
deceptive pricing, 277–278
predatory pricing, 278
price discrimination, 277
price fixing, 277
marketing costs, 276–277
newness of product, 276
Pricing objectives, 275
Primary data, 166
advantages and disadvantages, 177
data mining, 177
experiments, 176
and information technology, 176–177
observational, 168–171
panels, 175–176
from questionnaires, 170–175
social networks, 175
from test markets, 176
Primary demand, 234–235
Privacy issues
in direct marketing, 349
in online shopping, 416
Privacy rights, 82
Private branding, 250
Private exchange, 130–131
Private labeling, 250
PRIZM household classification, 193
Problem definition/recognition
consumer behavior, 96
for marketing research, 163–164
in organizational buying, 127
Procurement
buying centers, 126–129
case, 133–135
by JCPMedia, 119
online auctions, 131
online organizational buying, 129–131
organizational buying criteria, 124
organizational buying objectives, 123–124
supplier partnerships, 124–125
sustainable, 125–126
Product(s), 210; *see also* New product *entries*
attribute change, 107
beliefs about, 106
benchmark items, 322
build-to-order, 191
business products, 211–212
competitive, 223
consumer products, 210–211
core, 214
creating new use, 243
defining, 19
degree of innovation, 216–217

downsizing, 244, 245
durable or nondurable, 210
elastic demand, 271
element of services, 254
feature bloat, 215
free trials, 104
in gray market, 155
green, 90
grouped for segmentation, 196–197
guarantees, 104
high-learning, 239
high or low involvement, 99–101
increase use of, 243
inelastic demand, 271–272
items, lines, and mixes, 212
low-learning, 239
mass customization, 190–191
in multiple market segments, 189–190
newness vs. existing products, 215–216
nondiscretionary, 272
organizational buying behavior, 123
and organizational strategies, 26
packaging and labeling, 250–253
points of difference, 35
poorly conceived, 219
pre-launch issues, 19
reasons for resistance to, 240
and self-image, 103
shelf life, 252, 253
stock keeping units, 212
supplementary, 214
usage instructions, 104
variety in, 297
in vending machines, 317
warranties, 104
Product adaptation in global marketing, 153
Product adopter profiles, 240
Product advertisements, 358
Product development;
see also New-product process
manager, 426
market-product strategy, 33
Product differentiation, 188
at Gatorade, 234
strategy, 235
synergies versus cannibalization, 191
Product-distribution franchises, 315
Product features, segmentation by, 193
Product goals, 35
Product invention, in global marketing, 153–154
Production capacity, organizational buying criterion, 124
Production era, 14
Product item, 212
Productivity in services, 254
Product life cycle, 234
and consumers, 240–241
decline stage
deletion strategy, 238
for fax machines, 238
harvesting strategy, 238–239
for fax machines, 236–238
for Gatorade, 233–234
growth stage
competitors in, 236
gaining distribution, 237

product proliferation, 236–237
repeat purchasers, 236
introduction stage
gaining distribution, 235
penetration pricing, 236, 265
primary demand, 234–235
selective demand, 235
skimming pricing, 264–265
skimming strategy, 235
trial, 234
length, 239
maturity stage
characteristics, 237
fax machines, 238
holding market share, 237
as pricing constraint, 276
promotional mix changes
decline stage, 342
growth stage, 341
introduction stage, 340
maturity stage, 341
shape
fad products, 240
fashion products, 240
generalized, 239
high-learning products, 239
low-learning products, 239
Product life cycle management
brand development index, 241–242
category development index, 241–242
market modification
creating new use, 243
finding new customers, 243
increasing product use, 243
product manager role, 241
product modification, 241–242
product repositioning
catching rising trend, 243
change in value offered, 244
reaching new markets, 243
reacting to competitors, 243
Product life cycle sales curve
fad products, 239
fashion products, 239
high-learning products, 239
low-learning products, 239
Product line, 212
at Gatorade, 233–234
Paradise Kitchens, 54
Product line extension, 12
in global marketing, 153
with multiproduct branding, 248–249
Product management careers, 425
inventory control manager, 426
operations manager, 426
physical distribution specialist, 426
product development manager, 426
product managers, 426
supply chain manager, 426
Product management team, 425
Product manager, 426
Product mix, 212
Product modification, 241–242
Product newness, as pricing constraint, 276
Product phase-out, 342
Product placement, 373
Product positioning, 36, 202
Act II Microwave Popcorn, 309

differentiation, 202
head-to-head, 202
key steps, 203
using perceptual maps, 203–204
Product proliferation, 236–237
Product-related legislation, 70–72
    Child Protection Act, 71
    Consumer Product Safety Act, 71
    copyright law, 71
    Digital Millennium Copyright
        Act, 71
    Fair Packaging and Labeling
        Act, 71
    Federal Dilution Act, 72
    Infant Formula Act, 71
    Lanham Act, 71–72
    and Madrid Protocol, 72
    Nutritional Labeling and
        Education Act, 71
    patent law, 71
    Trademark Law Revision Act, 72
Product repositioning, 202
    catching rising trend, 243
    change in value offered, 244
    reaching new markets, 243
    reacting to competitors, 243
Product sales organizational
    structure, 393
Product strategy
    in global marketing
        adaptation, 153
        extension, 153
        invention, 153–154
    in marketing program, 13
    for Medtronic, 36–37
    Paradise Kitchens, 54
    in product life cycle, 235
Product synergies, 202
Professional associations, 433
Profit, 22
    identifying objectives
        current and long-run profit,
            275
        market share, 276
        sales, 275
        social responsibility, 276
        survival, 276
        unit volume, 276
        at Vizio, Inc., 261
    in maturity stage, 236, 237
    for movie studios, 275, 276
    objective of organizational
        buying, 123–124
    objectives of pricing
        channels of distribution, 275
        current profit, 275
        long-run, 275
        organizational goal, 26
    from segmentation, 191
Profitability
    and channel selection, 298
    at Starbucks, 93
Profit equation, 263–264
Profit margins, conflict over, 299
Profit-oriented pricing approaches;
    see Pricing approaches
Profit potential, 192
    in market-entry strategy, 149
Profit responsibility, 86–87
Project manager, 426
Promotion
    careers in, 425
    case, 352–355
    costs with multibranding, 250
    definition, 19

designing, 346
new types of, 333
objectives, 344
pre-launch issues, 19
in services marketing, 255
in sports marketing, 258–259
and types of consumer
    behavior, 211
viral marketing, 414
Promotional allowances, 72, 281
Promotional mix, 334
    advertising, 336–337
    for customized interaction, 336
    direct marketing, 339
    integrated marketing
        communications
        channel strategies, 342–343
        product life cycle, 340–342
        target audience, 340
    mass selling, 336
    personal selling, 337–338
    publicity, 338–339
    public relations, 338–339
    sales promotion, 339
    selecting tools from, 345
    summary of, 337
Promotional tools, 345
Promotional Web sites, 418
Promotion budget
    all-you-can-afford approach, 344
    competitive parity approach, 344
    examples, 344
    marketing dashboard for, 345
    objective and task approach, 344
    percentage of sales approach,
        344
Promotion careers; see Advertising
    careers
Promotion program
    costs of implementing, 347
    developing
        design of promotion, 346
        identifying target audience,
            343
        scheduling, 346
        setting budget, 344–345
        specifying objectives, 344
    executing and assessing,
        346–347
    posttests, 346–347
    pretests, 346
    scheduling, 346
Promotion-related legislation, 73
Promotion strategy
    in global marketing, 153–154
    in marketing program, 13
    for Medtronic, 36–37
    Paradise Kitchens, 54–55
        cents-off coupons, 55
        in-store demonstrations, 55
        recipes, 55
    in product life cycle, 235
    in sports marketing, 206–207
Prospecting stage
    cold calling, 387
    cold canvassing, 387
    lead generation, 386–387
    objectives, 386
    prospect, 387
    qualified prospect, 387
    and Telephone Consumer
        Protection Act, 387
Prospects, 387
Protectionism, 138
    decline of, 138

effect on world trade, 139
by quotas, 138–139
by tariffs, 138–139
and World Trade
    Organization, 138
Protocol, 217
    defining, 220
    incomplete, 218
Prototype, 224, 227
Psychographics, 107–108
Psychographic segmentation
    consumer markets, 193
    percentage of firms using, 194
Psychological barriers, 240
Psychological influences on
    consumer behavior
    attitudes, values, and beliefs,
        106–107
    learning, 104–106
    lifestyle, 107–108
    motivation, 102
    perception, 103–104
    personality, 102–103
Public information sources, 96–97
Publicity, 338
    compared to advertising/personal
        selling, 338
    credibility advantage, 338–339
    disadvantage in lack of control,
        339
    forms of, 338
    for services, 255
    social media for, 339
Publicity tools, 375
Public relations, 338
    activities involved in, 346
    compared to advertising/personal
        selling, 338
    news conferences, 375
    news releases, 375
    payment method, 337
    public service announcements,
        375
    social media, 339
    strengths and weaknesses, 337
    tools of, 338
    by Under Armour, 353–354
Public relations manager, 426
Public service announcements, 255,
    337, 375
Pull strategy, 342–343
Pulse (burst) schedule, 368
Purchase decision
    choice in, 97–98
    determining factors, 98
    in families
        decision making styles, 112
        preteens and teens, 112
        role of individual
            members, 112
    in organizational
        buying, 127
    and types of consumer
        behavior, 211
    in VALS system, 107–108
Purchase decision process, 96; *see
    also* Organizational buying
    entries
    alternative evaluation, 97
    information search, 96–97
    need perception, 96
    postpurchase behavior, 98–99
    problem recognition, 96
    problem-solving variables,
        99–101

purchase decision, 97–98
repeat purchases, 98
situational influences, 101
women as car buyers, 95
Purchase frequency, 367
Purchase size in organizational
    buying, 122–123
Purchase task, 101
Purchasing power, 148
    of Hispanics, 50
    of minorities, 64
Pure competition, 69
Pure monopoly, 69
Purpose in marketing plan
    preparation, 44
Push strategy, 342

Q

Qualified prospect, 387
Quality
    Lands' End, 134
    organizational buying
        criterion, 124
    organizational goal, 27
    and packaging, 252
    Paradise Kitchens, 54
    poor in new products, 218
    price as indicator of, 263
Quantitative salesforce assessments
    input-related measures, 396
    sales quotas, 396
Quantity discounts, 72, 280
Question marks
    definition, 31
    for Kodak, 32–33
Questionnaire data, 170
    closed-end questions, 173
    conventional questionnaire, 172
    differential scale, 173–174
    and electronic technology, 175
    e-mail surveys, 172
    fixed alternative questions, 173
    focus groups, 171
    idea evaluation, 172–175
    idea generation, 170–172
    Likert scale, 174
    mail surveys, 172
    mall intercept interviews, 172
    open-ended questions, 173
    precise questions, 173–175
    telephone surveys, 172
    trend identification, 171–172
Quick response, 305
Quotas, 138
Quoted price; *see* List or quoted price

R

Racial discrimination in car sales,
    279
Racial diversity
    and multicultural marketing, 64
    trend in United States, 64
Rack jobbers, 327
Radio advertising
    advantages and disadvantages,
        364
    expenditures, 362
    number of stations, 365
    peak listening time, 365
    segmented medium, 365

Radio frequency identification technology, 177, 314
Railroads, business myopia at, 26
Rating, 362
Reach, 362
Real time, 406
Rebates, 262, 263, 322, 373
Receivers, 334
Recession, impact on consumer spending, 65–66
Recipes, 55
Reciprocity, 125
Recruitment of salesforce, 394–395
Recycling, 79
Reference groups, 110
Regional rollouts, 227
Regional shopping centers, 322
Registered trademark, 72
Regulation, 70
Regulatory forces
    advertising-related legislation, 73
    distribution-related legislation, 72
    and Geek Squad, 76–77
    pricing-related legislation, 72
    product-related legislation, 70–72
    promotion-related legislation, 73
    protecting competition, 70
    self-regulation, 73–74
    summary of, 60
    trends identified in, 61
Reinforcement, 105
Relationship marketing, 11
    and marketing managers, 12
Relationship selling, 383
    creating customer value, 382–383
Relative market share, 31–32
Reminder advertising
    institutional, 359
    for products, 358–359
Rent, 262
Repeat purchase behavior, 98
Repeat purchasers, 236
Replenishment time, 305
Requirement contracts, 72
Resale price maintenance, 277
Research and development laboratories, 222–223
Reseller branding, 250
Reseller markets, 121
    measurement of, 121–122
Resources, obtaining, 37
Response, 105
Responsibility Matters campaign, 79
Restaurant News, 340
Restructuring, 10
Résumé
    cover letter, 431
    digital, 430
    sections of, 430
Retail communication
    atmosphere and ambience, 323
    store image, 323
Retailers; *see also* Intermediaries
    category killers, 316
    cooperative advertising, 374
    description, 288
    flexible-pricing policy, 279
    in global marketing, 154
    indirect marketing channels, 291
    loss-leader pricing, 269
    mass merchandisers, 308
    multichannel, 323

number of, 121
    as organizational buyers, 120
    outside United States, 313
    standard markup pricing, 266–267
    supply partnerships, 125
    sustainable procurement, 126
    as valued marketing asset, 287
Retailer-sponsored cooperatives, 315
Retail format, 324–325
Retailing, 312
    on Black Friday, 310
    careers in, 425–426
    case, 330–331
    changing nature of, 325–326
    on Cyber Monday, 310
    environmentally friendly, 314
    global economic impact, 313
    high-tech, 314
    nonstore
        automatic vending, 317–318
        catalogs, 318
        direct mail, 318
        direct selling, 320
        online retailing, 319–320
        telemarketing, 320
        television home shopping, 318–319
    by Pizza Hut, 420
    retail life cycle, 326, 327
    by Under Armour, 354–355
    utilities offered by, 312–313
    wheel of, 325–326
Retailing careers
    buyers, 426
    store managers, 426
Retailing mix, 321
    store image, 323
Retailing strategy
    category management, 323–324
    communication, 323
    elements of, 321
    merchandise management, 323–325
    pricing, 321–322
    and retailing mix, 321
    store locations, 322–323
Retail life cycle, 326
Retail outlets, 313–317
    classification, 313
    forms of ownership, 313
        contractual systems, 315
        corporate chains, 314
        independent retailers, 314
    functional qualities, 323
    level of service
        full service, 316
        limited service, 315
        self-service, 315
    at Mall of America, 330
    store locations, 322–323
    types of merchandise line
        breadth of line, 317
        depth of line, 316
        scrambled merchandising, 317
Retail pricing
    benchmark items, 322
    discounts, 321
    everyday fair pricing, 321–322
    everyday low pricing, 321
    gross margin, 321
    maintained markup, 321
    markdowns, 321
    off-price retailing, 322

original markup, 321
    timing of markdown, 321
Retail salesperson, 426
Retail-sponsored cooperatives, 295
Return on investment, 192
    pricing to achieve, 268
Return on investments, 26
Revenue
    desire for quick, 219
    from direct marketing, 348
    from segmentation, 191
Revenue estimation, 272
Reverse auction, 131
Reverse product positioning, 373
Right to be heard, 83
Right to be informed, 82
Right to choose, 82
Right to safety, 82
Risk
    perceived, 103–104
    strategies to reduce, 104
Risk barriers, 240
Risk-taking, 289
Robinson-Patman Act, 70, 74, 277
Role playing, 431
Routine problem solving, 100
Rumors, 110
Russia, financial/legal climate, 147–148

S

Safe delivery, 305
Safety
    in automobiles, 95
    in packaging, 253
Safety needs, 102, 103
Safety standards, 82
Safety tests, 225
Sales
    careers in, 427
    from catalog sales, 318
    in decline stage, 238
    from direct mail retailing, 318
    from direct selling, 320
    on eBayBusiness, 130
    80/20 rule, 194
    in growth stage, 236
    Internet-based, 137
    in maturity stage, 236
    in multichannel marketing, 418
    from online retailing, 319
    organizational goal, 26
    Paradise Kitchens, 55–56
    profit objective, 275
    in television home shopping, 319
    by vending machines, 317
Sales and Marketing Executives International, 433
Sales and Marketing Management, 429
Sales careers
    complex or professional salesperson, 426
    customer service manager, 426
    direct of retail salesperson, 426
    industrial or semitechnical salesperson, 426
    trade salesperson, 426
Sales clerks, 384
Sales era, 14
Salesforce
    compensation plans, 395–396

cross-functional team selling, 393
    evaluation
        behavioral measures, 396
        input-related measures, 396
        quantitative assessments, 396
        sales quotas, 396
    as marketing channel, 291
    motivation of, 395–396
    organizing
        customer sales basis, 392
        geographic basis, 392
        major account management, 392–393
        product sales basis, 393
    recruitment and selection
        job analysis, 394
        job description, 394–395
        job qualification statement, 395
    training of, 395
    training of distributors', 374
    at Xerox, 400–401
Salesforce automation, 396
    forms of, 396–397
    salesforce communication, 398
    salesforce technology, 397–398
Salesforce communication, 398
Salesforce survey forecast, 181
Salesforce technology, 397–398
Sales forecast, 181
    of buyers' intentions, 181
    direct, 181
    lost-horse forecast, 181
    by salesforce, 181
Sales forecasting techniques
    judgments of decision makers, 181
    salesforce survey, 181
    statistical methods
        linear trend extrapolation, 181–182
        trend extrapolation, 181–182
    survey of buyers' intentions, 181
Sales management, 382
    case, 400–401
    at Xerox, 381
Sales management process
    customer relationship management, 396–398
    marketing dashboard for, 397
    salesforce automation, 396–398
    salesforce communication, 398
    salesforce evaluation
        behavioral assessments, 396
        quantitative assessments, 396
    sales force technology, 397–398
    sales plan formulation, 391–394
        account management policies, 393–394
        organizing salesforce, 392–393
        setting objectives, 392
    sales plan implementation
        compensation plans, 395–396
        motivation, 395–396
        recruitment and selection, 394–395
        training, 395
Salespeople
    creating customer value, 382–383
    number in direct selling, 320

Sales plan—*Cont.*
   number of, in United States, 382
   order getters, 385
   order takers, 384
   personal selling roles, 382
   relationship selling, 382–383
Sales per square foot, 325
Sales plan, 392
   formulation, 391–394
      account management
         policies, 393–394
      organizing salesforce,
         392–393
      setting objectives, 392
   implementation
      compensation plans,
         395–396
      motivation, 395–396
      recruitment and selection,
         394–395
      training, 395
Sales promotion, 339
   activities involved in, 346
   advertising support for, 339
   annual expenditures, 370
   budget allocation, 370
   consumer-oriented, 370–373
   in maturity stage, 341
   payment method, 337
   push strategy, 342
   short-term nature of, 339
   strengths and weaknesses, 337
   trade-oriented, 373–374
Sales promotion manager, 426
Sales quota, 396
Sales tests, 370
Samples, 372
Sampling, 165
Satellite radio, 365
Satellite TV, 364
Savings rate decline, 67
Scanner data, 167
Scheduling
   of advertising
      basic approaches, 368
      criteria, 367
   of promotion, 346
Scrambled merchandising, 317
Screening and evaluation
   concept tests, 224
   external approach, 224
   internal approach, 224
   for service-dominated offerings,
      224
Seals of approval, 104
Seasonal discounts, 280
Secondary data, 166
   advantages and disadvantages,
      167
   external sources, 166–167
   internal sources, 166
Secret Sales Pitch (Bullock), 104
Security
   in online shopping, 416
   in packaging, 253
Selection of salesforce, 394–395
Selective comprehension, 103
Selective demand, 235
Selective distribution, 297
Selective exposure, 103
Selective perception, 103
Selective retention, 103
Self-actualization needs, 102, 103
Self-analysis, 428

Self-concept, 103
Self-expression motivated groups,
   108
Self-regulation, 73–74
   and Better Business Bureau, 74
   in online shopping, 416
   problems with, 73–74
Self-service outlets, 315
Sellers
   goals of marketing for, 6
   value of direct marketing,
      348–349
Selling, transactional function, 289
Selling agents, 328
Selling duties, 427
Semantic differential scale, 173–174
Semitechnical salesperson, 426
Sensitivity analysis, 177
Services, 210
   capacity management, 225
   classification by delivery,
      213–215
   core, 213–214
   delivery development, 225
   distributed by electronic
         marketing channels,
      292–293
   high-contact, 225
   inconsistency, 213
   and industrial market, 120–121
   inseparability, 213
   intangibility, 213
   inventory holding costs, 213–214
   marketing of, 15–16
   new product ideas for, 224
   new-product strategy
         development, 220–221
   nondiscretionary, 272
   supplementary, 214
Service sector, 120–121
   size of, 210
Services marketing
   branding strategy, 254
   capacity management, 254
   case, 257–259
   customer experience
         management, 255
   distribution, 254–255
   eight Ps of, 253–256
   impression management, 256
   by nonprofits, 255
   off-peak pricing, 254
   physical environment, 255–256
   price, 254
   process, 256
   product element, 254
   productivity, 254
   promotion, 255
Service-sponsored franchise systems,
   296
Service-sponsored retail franchise
   systems, 296
Sex-appeal ads, 171, 362
Shelf life, 252, 253
Sherman Antitrust Act, 70, 72, 80,
   277
Shift in the demand curve, 271
Shopping bots, 319
Shopping experience, 95
Shopping products, 211
Signpost items, 322
Simulated test markets, 226–227
Single-line stores, 316
Single parents, 111

Situational influences on purchase
   process, 101
Situation analysis, 34
   Paradise Kitchens, 49–52
Skimming pricing, 235, 264–265
SKU; *see* Stock keeping units
Slotting allowances/fees, 82, 227
Small businesses
   as competitors, 70
   exporting by, 150–151
   ideas from, 223
   marketing careers in, 5
   marketing plan, 44–45
Sneak previews, 161
Social audit, 88
Social element of mission statement,
   25
Social entrepreneurship, 15
Social forces, 60
   culture, 64–65
   demographics, 60–64
   and Geek Squad, 76
   trends identified in, 61
Social needs, 102, 103
Social networks, 175
Social responsibility, 15, 86
   at Anheuser-Busch, 79
   case, 91–93
   concepts
        profit responsibility, 86–87
        societal responsibility, 87–88
        stakeholder responsibility, 87
   and consumer ethics, 89–90
   organizational goal, 27
   profit objective, 276
   social audit, 88
   sustainable development, 89
Social surroundings, 101
Societal culture and norms, 81–82
Societal marketing concept, 15
Societal responsibility
   cause marketing, 87–88
   definition, 87
   green marketing, 87
   at Starbucks, 93
   triple bottom line, 87
Society
   benefits of marketing for, 5–6, 16
   influence on marketing, 6
Sociocultural influences on consumer
   behavior
   culture, 112
   family influence, 110–112
   personal influence, 108–110
   reference groups, 110
   subcultures, 113–114
Software industry, theft of intellectual
   property, 81–82
Sorting, logistical function, 289
Source, 334
Spam, 172, 413–414
Special fees, 262
Specialty merchandise wholesalers,
   327
Specialty outlets, 316
Specialty products, 211
   exclusive distribution, 297
Speed
   factor in commercialization,
      227–228
   need for, 95
Sports marketing
   Philadelphia Phillies, Inc.,
      258–259

   Prince Sports, Inc., 205–207
   Under Armour, 354–355
Spouse-determinant decisions, 112
Stakeholder responsibility, 87
Stakeholders
   benefits of marketing for, 5–6
   kinds of, 25
Standard and Poor's *Register of
   Corporations,* 431
Standard Industrial Classification
   system, 121
Standard markup pricing, 266–267
Starch tests, 369
Stars
   definition, 31
   for Kodak, 32
State employment office, 430
Statistical areas, 64
Statistical inference, 165
Statistical sales forecasting
   linear trend extrapolation,
      181–182
   trend extrapolation, 181–182
Statistics, and data mining, 177
Statue of Liberty renovation, 88
Status-conscious consumers, 265
Steady schedule, 368
Stimulus discrimination, 105
Stimulus generalization, 105
Stimulus-response presentation, 388
Stockholders, responsibility to, 86–87
Stock keeping units, 212
   number in supermarkets, 218
Storage, packaging function, 252
Store image, 323
Store location
   central business district, 322
   multichannel retailers, 323
   power centers, 322–323
   regional shopping centers, 322
   strip malls, 322–323
Store management, 425
Store manager, 426
Storing, logistical function, 289
Straight commission compensation
   plan, 395
Straight rebuy, 128–129
Straight salary compensation plan,
   395
Strategic business unit level, 24
Strategic business units
   business portfolio analysis,
      31–33
   cash cows, 31, 32
   definition, 24
   dogs, 31, 32
   growth share matrix, 31–32
   at Kodak, 32–33
   question marks, 31, 32
   stars, 31, 32
Strategic channel alliances, 293
Strategic directions
   competencies, 30
   competitors, 30
   current status, 29–30
   customers, 30
   growth strategies
      business portfolio analysis,
         31–33
      diversification analysis, 33
Strategic focus, Paradise Kitchens, 47
Strategic marketing process, 34
   based on market segmentation,
      35

evaluation phase
acting on deviations, 39–40
comparing results with
plans, 39
goals of, 38–39
at General Mills
evaluation phase, 43
implementation phase,
42–43
planning phase, 42
implementation phase
designing marketing
organization,
37–38
developing planning
schedules, 38
obtaining resources, 37
planning phase
goal setting, 35–36
marketing program, 36–37
market-product focus, 35–36
SWOT analysis, 34–35
Strategic performance, marketing
dashboards for, 27–29
Strategy, 22
Strengths; *see* SWOT analysis
Strip malls, 322–323
Strivers, 107
Strong Interest Inventory, 429
Style in automobiles, 95
Subbranding, 249
Subcultures, 113
African Americans, 113–114
Asian Americans, 114
Hispanics, 113
Subliminal perception, 103, 104
Subsidiaries, 141
Substitutes
and demand estimates, 270
and price elasticity of demand,
272
Successful Business Plan (Abrams),
45
Sugar import quotas, 138
Suggestive selling, 388
Super Bowl Ad Meter, 371
Super Bowl commercials, 109, 346
cost per thousand, 363
costs of, 360
effectiveness, 360
Supermarkets
failure fees, 227
for global distribution, 155
number of stock keeping units, 218
slotting allowances, 82, 227
standard markup pricing,
266–267
target return-on-sales pricing, 268
Supermarket scanners, 177
Supplementary products, 214
Supplier collaboration, 125
Supplier development, 124
Supplier diversity, 124
Suppliers
competitive bidding from, 123
inventory management, 306
to JCPMedia, 119
to Lands' End, 134
new product ideas from, 221–222
organizational buying criteria,
124
Supplies, 211
Supply, limited by tariffs and quotas,
138

Supply chain, 301
integrated, 303
logistics management in
customer service, 305–306
objectives, 304
total costs, 305
marketer's understanding of, 303
Supply chain management
auto industry, 301–302
convenience in, 306
definition, 301
at Dell Inc., 304
information technology in, 301
and marketing strategy, 302–304
relation to logistics and
marketing channels,
302
at Walmart, 304
Supply chain manager, 426
Supply partnerships, 124–125
Support products, 211
Surcharge, 262
Survey of buyers' intentions forecast,
181
Survival, profit objective, 276
Survivors, 108
Sustainability
environmental, 63
environmentally friendly
retailing, 314
Sustainable competitive advantage, 48
Sustainable development, 22
in global environment, 23
origin of term, 23
and societal responsibility, 89
at Starbucks, 93
Sustainable procurement, 125–126
Sweepstakes, 371–372
SWOT analysis, 34–35, 35
actions derived from, 35
basis of, 35
in new-product process, 220
Paradise Kitchens, 49–50
Syndicated panel data, 167
Synergies vs. cannibalization, 191

T

Tangible products, 213
Target audience
of advertising media, 362
for advertising program, 359–360
for direct marketing, 340
in marketing plan preparation, 44
for personal selling, 340
for promotion, 343
Target market, 9
choosing segments, 199
density, 296–297
in introduction stage, 234
marketing actions to reach,
199–201
marketing program elements and
rationale, 13
market synergies, 201–202
PRIZM classification, 193
product synergies, 202
selection criteria
compatibility with goals,
198–199
competitive position, 198
cost of reaching, 198
growth estimates, 198

market size, 198
selection of, 35
Target market coverage
density of market, 296–297
exclusive distribution, 297
intensive distribution, 297
selective distribution, 297
Target market segments, 35
Target pricing, 266
Target profit pricing, 267
Target return-on-investment
pricing, 268
Target return on profit, 175
Target return-on-sales pricing, 268
Tariffs, 138
Teaser advertising campaign, 109
Technical capability, 124
Technical pre-launch issues, 18
Technological change/innovation
and business model change, 26
and length of product
life cycle, 239
Technological forces
case, 75–77
electronic business technologies,
69
impact on consumer value, 68
summary of, 60
technology of tomorrow, 67–68
trends identified in, 61
Technology, 68
at Google, Inc., 378–379
at IDEO, 223
Internet-based, 69
mobile marketing media, 341
online data bases, 168
online mothers, 411
for salesforce, 397–398
segmentation strategies, 201
in sports marketing, 206
for 3-D films, 357
of tomorrow
biotechnology, 68
cloud computing, 67–68
nanotechnology, 67–68
wireless power process,
67–68
use and misuse of trademarks, 73
Technology transfer centers, 223
Teenagers, in family decision
making, 112
Telemarketing, 293, 320
inbound, 384
legislation affecting, 320
National Do Not Call Register,
73, 83
outbound, 385
Telephone Consumer Protection Act,
73, 387
Telephone surveys, 172
Television
decline in watching, 363
number of households, 363
out-of-home viewing, 363
product positioning in, 373
ratings, 362
Television advertising
advantages, 364
ad-zapping, 364
cost disadvantage, 363
expenditures, 362
infomercials, 364
on Super Bowl, 109
viewer avoidance, 168–169

wasted coverage, 364
Television home shopping, 293
with other kinds of retailing, 319
sales in, 319
size of audience, 318–319
Television rating organizations,
168–169
Temporal effects, 101
Test marketing, 226
Test markets, 176
Test screenings, 161–162
Textbooks, student use of, 3
Theater tests, 369
Thinkers, 107
Threat; *see* SWOT analysis
Tiffany-Walmart strategies, 190
Time
of online shopping, 415
in supply chain setting, 305
Time, 108
Time to market, 227–228
Time utility, 16, 289, 292
from marketspace, 404–405
from retailing, 312–313
Timing
bad for new products, 218
of markdowns, 321
of promotion, 346
Top management, 23
ethical behavior, 84–85
Total cost, 273
Total logistics cost, 305
Total revenue, 272
Tracking studies, 162
Trade associations, 167, 433
Trade barriers/restrictions, 149
by China, 80
Trade discounts, 280
Trade-in allowances, 280
Trademark infringement, 81–82
Trademark Law Revision Act, 72
Trademarks
court ruling, 72
generic vs. registered, 72
Internet use and misuse, 73
Lanham Act, 71–72
licensing of, 151
Madrid Protocol, 72
**Trade-oriented sales promotions,
373**
allowances, 373–374
cooperative advertising, 374
discounts, 373–374
purpose, 373
training of salesforces, 374
Trade regulations, 149
Trade salesperson, 426
Trading down, 243
Trading up, 244
Traditional auctions, 131
Traditional family, 111
Traffic generation, 349
Trainees, in retailing, 426
Training
of distributors' sales forces, 374
of salesforce, 395
at Xerox, 401
Transactional function
activities related to, 288–289
of electronic marketing channels,
292
Transactional Web sites, 417
Transit advertising, 366–367
Transnational firms, 141–142

Transportation, 302
Transportation infrastructure, 147
Transporting, 289
Trend extrapolation, 39, 181–182
Trends
    catching, 243
    identifying, 171–172
Trial, 234, 344
Trial close, 391
Trial size, 372
Triple bottom line, 87
Truck jobbers, 328
Tuition, 262, 263
Two-tier marketing strategy, 190
Tying arrangements, 72

U

Ultimate consumers, 16
Unaided recall, 369
Uncontrollable environmental forces,
    10
Unethical behavior
    bribes and kickbacks, 83
    in cola war, 84
    by consumers, 89–90
    economic espionage, 83
    theft of intellectual property, 81–82
    whistle-blowers, 85
Uniform delivered pricing, 281
United Kingdom, Direct Marketing
    Association, 349
United Nations, 23, 60–61
    International Standard Industrial
        Classification of All
        Economic Activity,
        121
    study on bribery, 83
United States
    aging population, 61
    diversity index map, 65
    exports of rice to Japan, 138
    generational cohorts
        baby boomers, 62
        baby bust, 62–63
        Generation X, 62–63
        Generation Y, 63
    and North American Free Trade
        Agreement, 139–140
    number of industrial forms, 120
    number of online shoppers, 404
    number of retailers, 121
    number of salespeople, 382
    number of small businesses, 70
    number of wholesalers, 121
    number of wireless phones, 341
    online sales revenue, 404
    population of, 61–62
    population shifts, 63–64
    racial and ethnic diversity, 64

recessions 1973–2008, 66
size of service sector, 210
subcultures, 113–114
sugar import quotas, 138
United States Supreme Court
    on price-setting agreements, 80
    ruling on trademarks, 72
Unit variable cost, 273
Unit volume, profit objective, 276
Universities, ideas from, 223
University of Chicago, 63
University of Florida, 233
Unmarried individuals, 112
Unsought products, 211
Urgency close, 391
Usage barriers, 240
Usage instructions, 104
Usage rate, 193, 193–195
    behavioral segmentation by, 194
    data, 194
    80/20 rule, 194
    fast-food restaurants, 194–195
    frequency marketing, 194
    organizational markets, 195
Users, in buying centers, 128
Utilitarianism, 85
Utilities/Utility, 16
    benefits of intermediaries,
        289–290
    from electronic marketing
        channels, 292
    offered by marketspace, 404–405
    offered by retailing, 312–313
    types of, 16

V

VALS system
    consumer segments, 107–108
    GeoVALS, 108
    media preferences, 108
Value, 263
    assessing, 97
    of brand equity, 247
    buying, 97–98
    consumer perception, 98
    seeking, 96
    trading down, 244
    trading up, 244
Value barriers, 240
Values, 144
    and attitudes, 106
    core, 106
    examples, 144–145
    personal, 106
    societal, 81–82
Variable cost, 273
Variety, buyer requirement, 297
Vending machines
    annual sales, 317

payment options, 317
popularity of, 317–318
Vendor-managed inventory, 306
Vertical conflict, 299–300
Vertical marketing systems, 294
    administered, 296
    contractual, 295–296
    corporate, 294–295
    definition, 294
Vertical price fixing, 277
Viral marketing, 414
Virtual communication, 333
Virtual communities, 408
Virtual organizational markets,
    129–131
Vision, 25
Visionary organizations, 24–26
Vocational interest tests, 428

W

Wall Street Journal, 168, 431
Wants, 8–9
Warning labels unheeded, 171
Warranties, 104, 241
    organizational buying criterion,
        124
Wasted coverage
    in communication, 338
    in television advertising, 363
Weaknesses; *see also* SWOT analysis
Web communities, 413
Web site(s); *see also* Marketspace
    design of
        commerce element, 409
        communication element, 408
        connection element, 408
        content, 408
        context, 407–408
        creation of communities, 408
        customization, 408
    multilanguage, 403
    performance of, 410
    Pizza Hut, 421–422
    promotional, 418
    transactional, 417
West Edmonton Mall, 322
Wheel of retailing, 325
    new forms of outlets, 321
    retail outlet changes, 325–326
Whistle-blowers, 85
Wholesalers, 326–328; *see also*
    Intermediaries
    adjustments to list price, 279
    agents and brokers, 328
    allowances by, 280–281
    description, 288
    discounts by, 280
    geographical price adjustments,
        281

in global marketing, 154
manufacturers branch offices,
    328
merchant wholesalers, 317–328
number of, 121
as Organizational buyers, 120
sustainable procurement, 126
Wholesaler-sponsored voluntary
    chains, 295, 315
Wichita Falls, Texas, 226
Wireless phones, number of, 341
Wireless power process, 67, 68
Women
    and Best Buy, 117
    discrimination in car sales, 279
    employed in auto industry, 95
    idea generation, 222
    as new car buyers, 95
Women's Leadership Forum, Best
    Buy, 117
Word of mouth, 109
    buzz, 414
    and BzzAgent, Inc., 109
    on Internet, 110
    negative, 110
Working conditions, offshore, 89
World population, 61
World trade
    barriers to, 149
    decline of protectionism, 138
    dumping, 155
    dynamics of, 138–144
    economic integration, 138–140
    exchange rates, 148
    global brands, 142–143
    global companies, 141–143
    global competition, 140–141
    global consumers, 143
    global marketing strategy,
        141–142
    networked global marketspace,
        143–144
    parallel importing, 155
World Trade Organization, 138

Y

Yellow Pages, 360
    advantages and disadvantages,
        364
    expenditures on, 366
    proliferation of directories, 366
    wide reach of, 366
Yield management pricing, 266
Young married couples, 111
Young singles, 111

Want an online, **searchable version** of your textbook?

Wish your textbook could be **available online** while you're doing your assignments?

Connect™ Plus Marketing eBook

If you choose to use *Connect™ Plus Marketing*, you have an affordable and searchable online version of your book integrated with your other online tools.

Connect™ Plus Marketing eBook offers features like:

- Topic search
- Direct links from assignments
- Adjustable text size
- Jump to page number
- Print by section

Want to get more **value** from your textbook purchase?

Think learning marketing should be a bit more **interesting**?

Check out the STUDENT RESOURCES section under the *Connect™* Library tab.

Here you'll find a wealth of resources designed to help you achieve your goals in the course. You'll find things like **quizzes, PowerPoints, and Internet activities** to help you study. Every student has different needs, so explore the STUDENT RESOURCES to find the materials best suited to you.

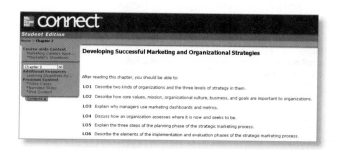

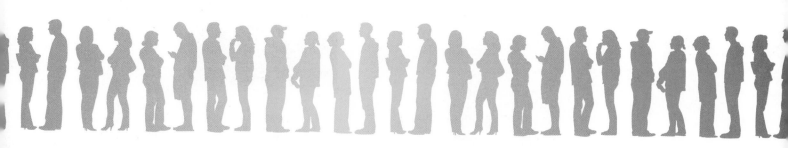

STUDENTS...

Want to get **better grades?** *(Who doesn't?)*

Ready to do **online interactive assignments** that help you apply what you've learned? *(You need to know how to use this stuff in the real world...)*

Need **new ways** to study before the big test? *(A little peace of mind is a good thing...)*

With **McGraw-Hill's** *Connect™ Plus Marketing,*

STUDENTS GET:

- **Interactive, engaging** content.

- Interactive Applications – chapter assignments that help you **APPLY** what you've learned in the course.

- **Immediate feedback** on how you're doing. (No more wishing you could call your instructor at 1 a.m.)

- **Quick access** to lectures, practice materials, eBook, and more. (All the material you need to be successful is right at your fingertips.)

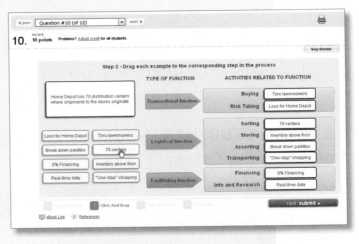